DYSLEXIA

CONTEMPORARY PROBLEMS OF CHILDHOOD: A Bibliographic Series
Series Editor: Carol Ann Winchell

THE GIFTED STUDENT: An Annotated Bibliography
Jean Laubenfels

CHILD ABUSE AND NEGLECT: An Annotated Bibliography
Beatrice J. Kalisch

BEHAVIOR MODIFICATION AND THE CHILD: An Annotated Bibliography
Hazel B. Benson

THE HYPERKINETIC CHILD: An Annotated Bibliogaphy, 1974-1979
Carol Ann Winchell

DYSLEXIA

AN ANNOTATED BIBLIOGRAPHY

Martha M. Evans

Contemporary Problems of Childhood, Number 5

GREENWOOD PRESS
Westport, Connecticut • London, England

Library of Congress Cataloging in Publication Data

Evans, Martha M.
  Dyslexia.

  (Contemporary problems of childhood, ISSN 0147-1082 ;
no. 5)
  Includes indexes.
  1. Dyslexia—Bibliogaphy. 2. Dyslexic children—
Bibliography. I. Title. II. Series.
Z6671.52.D97E9 [RJ496.A5] 016.61892'8553   81-20319
ISBN 0-313-21344-5 (lib. bdg.)   AACR2

Library of Congress Catalog Card Number: 81-20319
ISBN: 0-313-21344-5
ISSN: 0147-1082

First published in 1982

Greenwood Press
A division of Congressional Information Service, Inc.
88 Post Road West, Westport, Connecticut 06881

Printed in the United States of America

10 9 8 7 6 5 4 3 2 1

For Bertel Milas Sparks

THE NORMAL READER'S PRAYER

For the joy of ear and eye,
For the heart and brain's delight,
For the mystic harmony
Linking sense to sound and sight,
    Lord of all, to Thee we raise
    This our hymn of grateful praise.

            Folliott S. Pierpoint (1864)

CONTENTS

SERIES FOREWORD

The attention focused on children's problems has become increasingly pronounced in the United States during the last two decades. Particular interest and involvement have been directed toward certain problems: pathological conditions, the handicapped child, the educationally and culturally deprived child, and various behavior disorders. This interest has produced a voluminous body of knowledge. One needs only a cursory perusal through the literature to realize that it has now proliferated into an extensive, but unorganized, number of publications. Through modern technology, masses of material have been flowing from the presses; given this plethora of publication, it is frequently difficult to locate specific materials. A Tower of Babel situation has developed in that some of this valuable information is unknown to the researcher who might wish to be aware of its existence.

The purpose of *Contemporary Problems of Childhood* is to identify, collect, classify, abstract, and index relevant material on the following topics in need of systematic control: the gifted child, child abuse, behavior modification techniques with children, the autistic child, the child with dyslexia, and the hyperkinetic syndrome. Not only have these topics been the subject of academe, but the mass media—magazines, newspapers, and commercial and educational television specials—have recently devoted considerable attention to these problems. To bring some order to this discipline, it was decided to issue a series of volumes, each considering one of these topics and following the format of an earlier volume by this editor, *The Hyperkinetic Child: A Bibliography of Medical, Educational, and Psychological Studies* (Greenwood Press, 1975). These volumes are intended to aid the retrieval of information for educators, psychologists, physicians, researchers, parents, and others interested in etiology, diagnosis, and management.

The volumes in the series are broad in scope, interdisciplinary, comprehensive in coverage, and contain retrospective and current citations. The titles cited mainly reflect developments over the last decade, but some earlier titles of relevance are included. Selection of citations is based on the quality and direct applicability to the topic under consideration. For these publications only English-language sources are selected.

The entries are culled from extensive searches of manual and computerized information sources. Basic indexing and abstracting services, as well as many diverse and widely scattered sources, have been searched. Books, chapters in books, journal articles, conference reports, pamphlets, government documents, dissertations, and proceedings of symposiums are included. Since a bewildering variety of terminology exists for each subject, compilers have attempted to weed out unexplicitly defined topics.

Front matter contains appropriate introductory material: preface, contents, and a "state-of-the-art" message by a specialist in the area. Entries are classified and arranged alphabetically by author under the correct subject heading and appear only once in the bibliography.

Citations include complete and verified bibliographic information: author, title, source, volume, issue number, publisher, place, date, number of pages, and references. An attempt is made to annotate all citations that can be located, giving context, scope, and possible findings and results of the book or article.

Appendixes, author and key-word subject indexes, and journal abbreviations complete each volume.

It is hoped that the documentation provided by *Contemporary Problems of Childhood* will facilitate access to retrospective and current sources of information and help bring bibliogaphic control to this rapidly expanding body of literature.

Carol A. Winchell
General Editor

PREFACE

The literature concerned with reading and learning disorders and dyslexia is extensive and continues to expand. Estimates on the volume of publication range from more than twenty thousand papers[1] to "tens of thousands of articles"[2] already in print on this subject. More than one researcher has written that we urgently need collection, organization, and dissemination of existing knowledge on dyslexia. This book is offered as a step in that direction. As there are some difficulties with the terminology and many differing opinions in the literature, this book is published with a plea for tolerance of divergent views.

Dyslexia is an annotated bibliography listing more than twenty-four hundred English-language items. Books, journal articles, conference reports, proceedings of symposia, government documents, dissertations, collections of papers, relevant chapters or parts of books, and articles from the popular press are all given full bibliographic listing. Author, title, publisher, date, edition, number of pages, and place of publication are given. In the case of articles, journal name, volume, issue number, month and year of publication, inclusive pages, and the number of references cited in the article are listed. Material from the fields of medicine, education, and psychology furnish most of the material, but other sources are included as necessary to cover the subject.

Relevancy, not recentness, was the primary consideration in selecting materials for inclusion in the bibliography. Computerized and manual searches were done from the sources listed in Appendix A. Many problems that beset early workers in the field of reading disabilities are still unresolved and being actively discussed, so a search was made in each source starting with the most recent edition available at the date of search and going back to the beginning of that particular index. In some cases this meant searches that reached back into the nineteenth century and almost always into the early twentieth century. Each item in the bibliography has been individually inspected, either in hard copy or in photographic reproduction of the original. Exceptions are those entries carrying an ED number from the Educational Resources Information Center (ERIC) and the occasional entry where no abstract appears. Copies of items that list an ED number can be ordered from ERIC. Libraries can provide information on how to place an order.

The works of many writers with diverse viewpoints have been gathered, organized by subject, and abstracted. Comprehensive coverage of the entire span has been attempted, creating a bibliographic record of the evolution of thought in the field of reading disabilities that spans almost a hundred years.

Abstracts are nonevaluative. A consistent effort has been made to translate technical terms into equivalent everyday English if it could be done without losing the accuracy of the author's meaning. No judgment is offered as to the relative importance of an entry's place within the literature of dyslexia. Every effort has been made to reflect faithfully the import and spirit of each author's contribution. It has been left to the good judgment of the user to determine the usefulness to him or her of the literature abstracted.

The usual practice in this book has been to define dyslexia as referring to children of normal intelligence who are normally motivated, are of adequate cultural background, have adequate educational opportunity, and who have no obvious emotional problems, but who still have extreme difficulty in learning to read. However, in order to aid as many researchers in the field as possible and because of the divergence of opinion as to definition, these guidelines have been given a broad interpretation. The wide range of viewpoints expressed in the literature on dyslexia is reflected.

The terminology used in connection with reading disabilities is imprecise. Little agreement exists among persons working in the area as to what terms should be used to describe the causes, diagnosis, or treatment. No effort has been made to resolve any of these debates. In most cases the attempt was made to exclude material if it concerned: (1) books intended for the dyslexic himself; (2) difficulties caused by vision or hearing problems alone; (3) reading disability in persons suffering from general mental defectiveness or from unequivocal brain damage; (4) materials dealing primarily with general aphasia (the lack or loss of speech); and (5) materials concerned with acquired dyslexia in the adult or child who was once able to read, but through disease or injury has lost that power. Exceptions to this last rule are found in the section on historical materials. Many of these nineteenth-century studies are often cited in modern articles about dyslexia, and it was believed valuable to provide readers with accurate citations and abstracts. Many of these early writings concern adults who lost the power to read through brain damage from disease or accident. Also excluded was most of the material concerning high school, college age, or adult retarded readers.

Because the literature of dyslexia springs from many fields of learning and much of it discusses more than one kind of problem, some exclusions may appear to have imprecise boundaries. Less emphasis has been given to materials concerning learning disabilities in general as opposed to reading disabilities in particular. Materials dealing primarily with reading failure as a result of or a concomitant of cultural deprivation, delinquency, bilingualism, lack of motivation, or the primary use of a nonstandard English dialect are less comprehensively represented in the bibliography than are writings falling within the more centrally accepted definitions of dyslexia. Because of the differing definitions of dyslexia, it seemed appropriate to include as Appendix B a selection of some of the better-known viewponts on definition.

Section V is titled "Causes and Frequently Observed Accompanying Factors." No allegation is intended that all the materials included here concern causes and/or symptoms of dyslexia. References are grouped under this general heading for convenience and ease of use only. Some researchers have been careful to point out that their findings were not necessarily causes of dyslexia but were associated with it. For convenience, these papers have been classified under the associated finding as if it were a cause. There is no intention to distort research conclusions; the intention is to make such associated findings easy to locate.

Items are listed under causes and accompanying factors whether findings of the study were negative or positive. For classification purposes an article was placed according to the topic studied, not whether the findings confirmed the factor as a cause or underlying factor. On rare occasions materials were included only because they were thought to contain contiguous information of use to persons working with dyslexics.

Book reviews are not included, with one exception: a review of O. Wernicke's *Congenital Word Blindness* published in 1904. Collections of reprints are included with an abstract of the book. The contents of reprint collections are cited and abstracted separately under their original place of publication. In the case of volumes of original articles, the book is abstracted as a whole; individual articles are not separately abstracted. The best example of this is the *Bulletin of the Orton Society*, where the entire set is entered with an abstract, but the separate papers comprising the various issues of the *Bulletin* are not included. Volumes of papers, whether proceedings or other types of publication, are entered under the editor's name. The exception is the case of conferences where there is a date, name of conference, and place of meeting. When the same article appeared in more than one journal, the practice has been to cite only one source. A particular item appears only once in the bibliography.

The monumental bibliographies on the general subject of reading, such as the series published by Wiliam S. Gray and others, are not included in this bibliography. Outstanding as these summaries and bibliographies are, they include much material concerning the reading problems of adults as well as children, and they also contain material concerned with reading difficulties stemming from many causes not related to dyslexia. These are incorporated in the listings with items about normal readers. Bibliographies more exclusively concerned with the developmental reading problems of children are included.

Because of the breadth of the terminology in dyslexia, a glossary of terms is offered as an aid to the reader (see Appendix C). An Author Index and a Selective Key Word Subject Index made from words appearing in titles also are included.

NOTES

1. Critchley, Macdonald. *The dyslexic child.* 2d edition. London: Heinemann Medical, 1970. 137 p. (At page 122. See Item No. 426.)

2. Rourke, Byron P. "Brain-behavior relationships in children with learning disabilities; a research program." *Am Psychol* 30(9): 911-20, September 1975. (At page 917.)

ACKNOWLEDGMENTS

Gratitude is expressed to all of the many persons who aided this project. Special thanks are due to Miss Florence Blakely, Assistant University Librarian—Collection Development, William R. Perkins Library, Duke University, through whose good offices the initial opportunity for this work came. To Dr. Macdonald Critchley, eminent neurologist, author, and befriender of the dyslexic, who found time in the midst of pressing writing commitments to prepare the introduction for this book, my sincere gratitude is expressed. Innumerable members of the staffs of the Duke University libraries and the libraries of the University of North Carolina at Chapel Hill have cheerfully contributed their time and expertise. Especially I would like to express my appreciation to the reference staffs of Duke's Perkins Library, East Campus Library, and the Duke Medical Center Library. Thanks are in order also to the reference departments of the University of North Carolina Louis Round Wilson Library and UNC's Health Sciences Library. In these five places a major part of the work was done. Mr. Emerson Ford, Jr., and his staff in the Interlibrary Loan Department of Perkins Library were more than generous with time and effort in obtaining much otherwise unavailable material, a service for which I am most appreciative. Substantial use was also made of the D. H. Hill Library of the North Carolina State University, Raleigh. Generous help from the Hill Library reference department is also acknowledged. Other libraries whose facilities were used include the Regenstein Library of the University of Chicago; the John Crerar Library, Chicago; and the Library of Health Sciences of the University of Illinois Chicago Medical Center. Special thanks are due to Ila H. Gehman, Associate Professor Emeritus of Medical Psychology, Department of Psychiatry, and Chief Psychologist in the Division of Child Psychiatry, Duke University, for her generous gift of time and willingness to share her great knowledge of the field of dyslexia. I would also like to acknowledge Beverly I. McDonald, Head, Authority Files Section, Cataloguing Services, The Ohio State University Libraries, for her assistance with the finer points of filing and alphabetizing; Noelle Van Pulis, Information Specialist, Mechanized Information Center, The Ohio State University Libraries, who helped develop the Key Word Index; Linda

Schamber, Lecturer, The Ohio State University School of Journalism, for copyediting; and Jean Stouder, for painstakingly typing the final manuscript. Carol Ann Winchell, Series Editor, The Ohio State University Libraries, provided irreplaceable assistance and experienced good judgment. Finally, heartfelt and honest thanks go to my husband, who furthered this undertaking in more ways than I can count.

PERMISSIONS AND COPYRIGHT ACKNOWLEDGMENTS

A special word of appreciation is expressed to the authors and publishers who have given permission to reprint portions of their copyrighted works, which are found in Appendix B. The quotation from *Collier's Encyclopedia* was reprinted with permission from *Collier's Encyclopedia*, copyright 1975, Macmillan Educational Corporation. The table, "A Hierarchial Classification of the Causes and Types of Dyslexia," from Alexander Bannatyne, *Language, Reading and Learning Disabilities: Psychology, Neuropsychology, Diagnosis and Remediation*, 1971, is reprinted courtesy of Charles C. Thomas, Publisher, Springfield, Illinois. The quotation from Dr. Macdonald Critchley's book, *The Dyslexic Child*, is reprinted with the permission of William Heinemann Medical Books, Ltd., and the portion of his article that appeared in *Deficits in Cognition*, Jerome Hellmuth, editor, is quoted with the consent of Brunner/Mazel, Inc. Material by Richard B. Adams from the *Journal of Learning Disabilities* 2(12): 618, December 1969; and by E. Y. Zedler from the *Journal of Learning Disabilities* 2(12): 631-32, December 1969, is reprinted by special permission of The Professional Press, Inc., holder of the copyright. The lines from Alan S. Cohen's article are reprinted with permission of *The Encyclopedia Americana*, copyright 1969, The Americana Corporation. The quotation from the *American Journal of Ophthalmology* is reprinted with the permission of the editor of that journal and of the author, John V. V. Nicholls. The publisher and the authors have given permission for use of material from the following books: Knud Hermann, *Reading Disability: A Medical Study of Word-Blindness and Related Handicaps*, copyright 1959, Munksgaard International Publishers, Ltd., Copenhagen, Denmark; Bertil Hallgren, "Specific Dyslexia ('Congenital Word-Blindess'):A Clinical and Genetic Study." *Acta Psychiatrica et Neurologica. Supplement 65*, copyright 1950, Munksgaard International Publishers, Ltd., Copenhagen, Denmark. The *University of Michigan Medical Center Journal* and the author, Dr. Arthur L. Drew, have granted permission for the use of the quotation from Dr. Drew's article which appeared in the *University of Michigan Medical Bulletin*. The Association for Research in Nervous and Mental Disease, holder of the copyright, has granted permission for reprinting of the quotations by Ralph D. Rabinovitch, Arthur L. Drew, Russel N. DeJong, et al. from Volume 34 of the Association's *Research Publications*.

Gratitude is expressed to H. K. Lewis and Co., Ltd., London, for use of the quotation from James Hinshelwood. The quotation from Folliott S. Pierpoint that appears at the front of this book under the heading "The Normal Reader's Prayer," is now in the public domain. Nevertheless, the author is sincerely appreciative to Oxford University Press for its use. *American Education* does not require permission to reproduce contents. However, thanks are in order for use of the quotation from Eloise Calkins. The author is grateful for the permission given in each instance, and in all cases all rights are reserved by the respective copyright owners of the publications concerned.

INTRODUCTION

I have been graciously invited to write an introduction to a volume which, alas, I have not yet seen. The general scope has been explained to me, and I can appreciate the potential value of such a compilation to the serious writer, who, in his effort to be encyclopaedic, does not dare omit referring to every contribution, however ephemeral. This practice, although the vogue, is far from ideal. What is needed is not a catalog of names but insight into the relative merits of Tweedledum and Tweedledee. Perhaps this annotated bibliography will afford us the opportunity to track down each contribution and then to judge for ourselves.

Dr. Samuel Johnson certainly knew what he was talking about when he spoke of a lexicographer as a "harmless drudge." A drudge he most certainly is, for he is at the mercy of anyone who has been rash enough to put black upon white. Harmless, I am not so sure about. Certainly he is not harmful, and sometimes he is actually helpful.

Such I believe to be the case in this present volume. The literature upon the subject of dyslexia has virtually got out of hand, overgrown as it has been by the imprecise notion of "learning disabilities." The monstrous agglomeration of writings upon the topic cannot all be of equal merit. Some are masterly; some mischievous; while others are futile, like weeds choking a trim garden. And yet the conscientious student does not dare overlook a paper which, stripped of its verbiage, may harbor one tiny pearl of value or merely one of utility. This deluge of print, like the wartime leaflet raids, may offend or irritate, but cannot safely be swept aside. This contemporary trend is the product of today's pernicious academic "publish or perish" doctrine.

It is also the product of the importuner of which there are two classes. There is the wily publisher who inveigles clinicians to interrupt their useful work so that they may behold their names in print. Then there is the all-too-eager individual, often still *in statu pupillari*, who prevails upon a publisher to accept his inconsiderable handiwork.

Here is a work of reference that is a worthy addition to the library of the "neuroeducator," as Cruickshank would say, who is seriously engrossed in the problems of the dyslexic child. Of course no volume like this, however ambitious, can possibly be comprehensive, for not more than one in twenty articles or talks is listed. Notwithstanding, the items are clearly set out, and the reader is given a thumbnail sketch of what the paper aspires to expound.

Unfortunately, no system of marking was possible that would afford the researcher some idea as to the intrinsic merit of each entry. This would have imposed upon the editor an intolerable and invidious burden; no, the reader must himself find the paper, study it with care, and make up his own mind. At least he has been given a clue. Nonetheless, we would appreciate one day a Guide Michelin to dyslexia, complete with stars and rosettes.

Osler classified authors into three categories: the creators, the transmuters, and the transmitters. The first of these is rare, some are inspiring, others dangerous. The transmuters outnumber the creators by one hundred to one, but at least they are discriminating and have it within their power to differentiate the good from the bad, handing on and amplifying only that which is worthwhile within the pages of the creators. Transmuters are not to be despised. On the contrary, they play a valuable role in the communication of ideas. It is to be hoped that this annotated bibliography will help the research worker identify the more important of the transmuters. Then come the transmitters who probably swamp the transmuters by one thousand to one at the very least. Let us hope that these do not clutter up this reference book to an inordinate degree, like Shakespeare's intolerable deal of sack to one half-pennyworth of bread. To quote Osler once again: "Books follow a law of nature. Thousands of germs are needed for the transmission of an individual of any species. In the case of the salmon only one in a thousand is fertilized and of these not one in a thousand reaches maturity. So it is with books—a thousand or more are needed to secure the transmission of a single one of our very limited stock of ideas."

If this compilation provides such a service it will indeed have been worthwhile.

Perhaps I have appeared over-critical of those who have hurried into print too precipitously. After all, William Harvey pondered for twelve years after his discovery before he published "The Circulation of the Blood." Let us remember that readers as well as writers have their duties if they are to derive any benefit at all. Very many years ago it was laid down that there are four sorts of readers: "Sponges which attract all things without distinguishing them; Howre-glasses which receive and poure out as fast; Bagges which only retain the dregges of the spices and let the wine escape; and Sives which retain the best onely."

I really believe that the work of Martha Evans, drudgery though it must often have been, will assist us to attain the "Sive" stage of our reading.

Macdonald Critchley

ABBREVIATIONS

EEG   electroencephalogram
ERIC   Educational Resources Information Center
ITA   Initial Teaching Alphabet, sometimes written i.t.a.
ITPA   Illinois Test of Psycholinguistic Abilities
LD   Learning Disabled; Learning Disabilities
MBD   Minimal Brain Dysfunction
VAKT   Visual, auditory, kinesthetic, tactile (used to refer to methods of treatment of dyslexia)
WAIS   Wechsler Adult Intelligence Scale
WISC   Wechsler Intelligence Scale for Children
WPPSI   Wechsler Pre-school and Primary Scale of Intelligence
WRAT   Wide Range Achievement Test

SAMPLE BOOK ENTRY

SAMPLE BOOK ENTRY

①   ②   ③   ④   ⑤

17 Hartstein, Jack, ed. *Current concepts in dyslexia.* St. Louis, Missouri: Mosby, 1971. 212p. (Bibliography).

       ⑥   ⑦   ⑧

⑨The purpose of this book is to provide a rounded view of the terms, people, and areas of study necessary for evaluating dyslexics. A collection of original articles written especially for this volume, the book introduces the reader to the roles of the ophthalmologist, reading teacher, orthoptist, and neurologist in the diagnosis and treatment of the dyslexic child. Educational remediation, the use of drugs in their treatment, and auditory problems are among areas covered.

1. Item number
2. Author(s)
3. Title of book
4. Place of publication
5. Publisher
6. Date of publication
7. Number of pages
8. Presence of bibliography
9. Annotation

SAMPLE JOURNAL ENTRY

①   ②   ③

573 Keller, James F.; Croake, James W.; Riesenman, Carolyn. "Relationships among handedness, intelligence, sex and reading achievement of school age children." *Percept Mot Skills* 37(1): 159-62, August, 1973. (14 References).

                 ④   ⑤   ⑥   ⑦   ⑧

⑨A sample of 277 boys and girls in grades three through twelve in Tallahassee, Florida, was tested for IQ, reading achievement, and handedness. Those of mixed laterality were deleted from the sample. When IQ, grade level, handedness, and sex were controlled, no significant differences were found in mean reading achievement. When sex, handedness, and grade level were controlled, no significant differences in mean IQs were found. Significant correlation was found between IQ and reading achievement. The correlation between IQ and reading achievement was significantly lower among left-handers than among right-handed children.

1. Item number
2. Author(s)
3. Title of article
4. Name of journal (abbreviation)
5. Volume and issue number
6. Inclusive pagination
7. Month and year of publication
8. Number of bibliogaphical references
9. Annotation

DYSLEXIA

I

Comprehensive Works

1 Applebee, Arthur N. "Research in reading retardation: two critical
       problems." J Child Psychol Psychiatry 12(2): 91-113, August,
       1971. (37 References).
Reviews the research in reading retardation and points out the many definitions of the condition and their confused use in practice. This
confusion has led to an unjustified assumption of homogeneity in the
samples. Six different approaches to the causes of reading disability
which appear in the literature are explained. Primarily American investigations are considered.

2 Bannatyne, Alexander. Language, reading and learning disabilities:
       psychology, neuropsychology, diagnosis, and remediation. Spring-
       field, Illinois: Thomas, 1971. 787p. (Bibliography).
All phases of language learning and reading disabilities are considered
in this book. The principal conclusions of a number of researchers in
the field of language development are summarized. The discussion of dyslexia is developed from four major classifications of causes: (1) primary
communicative dyslexia, caused by the circumstances of the very young
child's life (e.g., a disinterested mother who does not talk to her
child); (2) minimal neurological dysfunction dyslexia; (3) genetic dyslexia; and (4) dyslexia of social, cultural, and educational deprivation
origins. Results of research in each area are presented. Material on
aphasia, on emotional and motivational problems, and on diagnosis, testing, and remediation is included. Education is viewed critically.
Schools and colleges do not inspire interest in reading as they should.

3 Bateman, Barbara. "Learning disorders." Rev Educ Res 36(1): 93-
       119, February, 1966. (96 References).
Provides an overview of research findings in the general field of learning disorders. Characteristics of children with learning disorders are
reported. A wide range of diagnostic tests and methods of remediation
are explored. While the discussion concerns the entire range of learning
disabilities, much of it concerns reading disabilities in particular.

4 Benton, Arthur L. "Developmental dyslexia: neurological aspects."
      In: Friedlander, Walter J., ed. Current reviews of higher nervous
      system dysfunction. New York: Raven Press, 1975. 1-47. (189
      References). (Advances in Neurology, Vol. 7).
This state-of-the-art paper presents the status of research findings in
the field of developmental dyslexia. Features of the condition are described, including a list of widely reported errors typical of dyslexic
children, and a listing of perceptual, neurological, and other characteristics of dyslexics. The influence of heredity is discussed. Some of
the literature dealing with a large number of the specific deficits encountered in dyslexia is reviewed. These include visuoperceptive deficits; impaired directional sense; defects in intersensory integration,
sequential perception, and finger recognition; incomplete cerebral
dominance; and neurological abnormalities. It is concluded that a neurological basis for dyslexia has not been established, but such an explanation is as tenable as others. Present studies reveal a morass of contradictory and inconsistent findings. Other approaches are recommended.
The lack of adequate description of the condition in much of the research
is pointed out. Classification of dyslexics on the basis of their performance is necessary. It should not be assumed that all dyslexics suffer from the same basic deficiency. Little support is found in the
research reports for either of the neurological theories commonly set
forth: parietal maldevelopment or deficiencies in interhemispheric
integration. Studies of ocular factors appear not to have produced useful results.

5 Betts, Emmett Albert. The prevention and correction of reading dis-
      abilities. Evanston, Illinois: Row, Peterson, 1936. 402p.
      (Bibliography).
Summarizes and gives an interpretation of research findings in prevention and correction of reading disabilities. Topics include incidence
of the condition, reversals, intelligence, parent education, and causes
of reading disability. Symptoms of reading disability that teachers
should watch for are listed. Also included are directions for the use
of Betts' reading tests, and a glossary. Bibliographic references are
in each chapter.

6 ————. "Reading disabilities and their correction: a critical
      summary of selective research." Elem Engl Rev 12(3): 69-73,
      March, 1935; 12(4): 106-10, April, 1935; 12(5): 131-41, May,
      1935; 12(6): 157-65, June, 1935. (0 References).
Summarizes selected research in the field of reading disabilities. Leaders
in the field were canvassed: from 125 abstracts of scientific studies
relating to reading disabilities which were submitted to them, forty-
three were selected for publication. In each case brief statements of
the problem, procedures, and conclusions are given. A prefatory note
explains the selection procedure. Within the limits of the material
abstracted, twenty-five implications and conclusions are drawn. These
findings include: (1) From 8 to 15 percent of pupils in intermediate
grades present specific reading disabilities. (2) The reading readiness
concept includes both psychological and physiological readiness to read.
(3) Large type, good lighting, and the best classroom seats are helpful
to disabled readers. (4) Eye dominance is probably unrelated to sex,
intelligence, and visual acuity. (5) Reversal errors and mixed hand-eye
dominance are probably unrelated. (6) Left-handed persons do not make
more reversal errors than right-handed persons, and these errors tend

to disappear with maturity. It is also concluded that poor readers have inadequate motor and perceptual reading habits. Kinesthetic training is probably essential in helping disabled readers. School administrative policies may be a factor in school failures. Good readers exceed poor ones in "purposefulness, technique, discrimination, and association."

7 ————. "Retardation in reading." Elem Engl Rev 14(4): 141-46, April, 1937. (0 References).
States conclusions reached in a survey of some 2,000 publications related to reading problems. It appears that there will be "much fruitful research in the near future." Cooperative research effort by students and other researchers is needed. Teachers of beginning readers need to be better prepared for their tasks. Interpretation of research findings is limited by variations in definitions of retardation in reading, variations in terminology, increasing areas under investigation, and inadequacy of researchers and techniques. More emphasis on adequate beginning teaching and maintenance procedures should reduce the importance of remedial reading in the future.

8 ————. "Retardation in reading." J Except Child 3(5): 150-52, June, 1937. (0 References).
Presents conclusions reached in the study of some 2,000 publications related to reading problems. Findings are discussed, including recent developments in remedial reading. It is observed that there are so many variables in the areas of investigation covered in these studies that the findings are difficult to interpret. Five chief limitations of these research projects are mentioned and discussed: (1) confusions in the definition of retardation in reading; (2) variation of concepts underlying terminology; (3) the increasing number of areas under investigation; (4) the uncertain preparation for the task on the part of some investigators resulting in "dabbling" research; and (5) inadequacy of research techniques.

9 Blom, Edward C. "Mirror-writing." Psychol Bull 25(10): 582-94, October, 1928. (81 References).
This review of English, French, and German literature on mirror writing and handedness published between 1878 and 1927 includes material representing the pathological, psychological, physiological, and educational points of view. It is concluded that: (1) mirror writing is as normal for left-handed persons as conventional writing is for the right-handed; (2) the child who mirror-writes is likely to have trouble reading and spelling; and (3) a left-handed child can be taught to write with his right hand without any serious consequences in most cases. Should a change be necessary, the left-handed child could soon learn to write as well with his right hand as he did with his left hand. Mirror writing is not an indication of inferior intelligence.

10 Bond, Guy L., and Tinker, Miles A. Reading difficulties: their diagnosis and correction. 3rd ed. New York: Appleton-Century-Crofts, 1973. 604p. (Bibliography).
Written for the classroom teacher, the remedial teacher, and the clinician, the six parts of this book include material dealing with the nature and causes of reading difficulties and their diagnoses. Treatment of word-recognition difficulties and comprehension difficulties is discussed separately. In a section titled "Special Problems," teachers are admonished to find out what the child is interested in, and provide reading material of the correct level of difficulty. Since most reading-disabled

children dislike reading, books for them should be especially attractive.
Teaching methods for the extremely reading-disabled child are outlined.
These include the kinesthetic-auditory-visual emphasis, sometimes called
Fernald-Keller, method; auditory (sound-blending)-emphasis, or Monroe,
method; and the visual-structural emphasis method favored by Gates.

11 de Ajuriaguerra, J.; Antonini, P.; Besson, A.; et al. "Problems posed
      by dyslexia." J Learn Disabil 1(3): 158-70, March, 1968. (0
      References).
Surveys literature and current research and theories on dyslexia that
European researchers consider to be in need of major research, particularly: (1) study of the mechanisms that intervene in the integration
process of word acquisition; and (2) study of how the "catching-up"
process works. Understanding in these areas may enable researchers to
differentiate teaching methods in relation to various dyslexics. Results
of a survey of ninety dyslexic children five years after initial examination revealed that half the cases had been effectively reeducated. No
bibliography is attached to the article, but what are identified as
"extensive references" may be obtained from the journal.

12 Dyslexia Symposium, Melbourne, 1968. Dyslexia symposium; proceedings.
      Edited and compiled by R. N. Harrison, and Freda Hooper. Melbourne,
      Australia: Australian College of Speech Therapists, [1968?], 232p.
The papers read at a five-day meeting and collected in this volume cover
the range of professional interest in dyslexia. Speakers included educators, a pediatrician, an ophthalmologist, psychologists, speech therapists, and social workers, among others. Marianne Frostig contributed
four lectures. She explains the rationale behind her "educational
therapy" approach to the child with learning problems. Both quantity and
quality of material taught is different in her program. Her remedial
program takes into account the child's developmental lags and inadequacies.
Teaching method for academic subjects is modified according to test findings for each child. The Frostig sensory-motor skills training for preschool and primary-grade children is explained. This program includes
training in movement in space, manipulation, awareness of the body, and
awareness of the environment. Visual perceptual disturbances and remedial
reading methods were topics of other lectures by Frostig. The neurological and ophthalmological assessment of dyslexics; educational problems
encountered by the schools in working with dyslexic pupils; and the reaction of parents to reading failure are among other areas covered.

13 Franklin, Alfred White, ed. Word-blindness or specific developmental
      dyslexia; proceedings of a conference called by the Invalid Chil-
      dren's Aid Association, 12 April 1962, and held in The Medical
      College of St. Bartholomew's Hospital, London. London: Pitman
      Medical, 1962. 148p.
This collection reproduces papers read and the group discussions at a
one-day conference. It progresses from a general statement about the
syndrome of developmental dyslexia to presentations of the programs for
treating dyslexics at various institutions. Theories about causes,
methods for diagnosis, and treatment are given. Among those present were
J. Roswell Gallagher, Patrick Meredith, Macdonald Critchley, L. Maisie
Holt, and T. R. Miles.

Gallagher reviews the early work of researchers on word blindness, and
attempts to distinguish it from "poor reading." Persons who may read
slowly, but without the strange errors of dyslexia are distinguished from

those who make the inaccurate and bizarre mistakes of specific reading
disability. Preschool screening is urged to prevent trouble. Also urged
is an alphabetic-phonetic method of teaching reading and spelling for use
with children whose symptoms or family histories make it appear that dyslexia will be likely to appear.

A paper by Patrick Meredith, a "psycho-physical mathematician," suggests
that we need an atlas of the brain "showing the taxonomy of psycho-
physical events produced by the distribution of excitations in the brain,"
no matter how incomplete a first attempt at making such an atlas might
be. We need a systematic approach for determining the probability that
a given pattern of excitation will occur at any point within the brain.
The words we learn may not be stored in one point in the brain, but may
involve the whole storage volume of the brain. This "redundancy" helps
the brain insure itself against damage to one part. The recall of a
word from the brain is influenced by the circumstances under which it
was learned. This theory is implicit in the word-association test, an
old technique. It is pointed out that the literature does not reflect
any comprehensive pattern in existing studies of the field.

Critchley's paper is a review of some of the more common neurological
deficits which appear to be a part of the fundamental makeup of dyslexics,
including general clumsiness, and minor sensory disorders which may make
it difficult for the child to comprehend such words as "up," "down," "in
front of," and so on. Also present may be a difficulty in moving the
eyes from the end of one line to the beginning of the next. Defects in
the child's image of his own body, confusion of right and left, faulty
estimations of time, difficulty in interpreting the meaning of facial
expressions, and arithmetical difficulties are among other problems.

After reviewing some of the work with dyslexics at Saint Bartholomew's
Hospital, and describing some of the difficulties of these children, L.
Maisie Holt explains the phonetic approach used there. The method is to
say the letter, sound, or word to provide an auditory image; write it at
the same time to make a motor image; and look at it as one writes to link
the two.

T. R. Miles describes another approach. Finding that two children referred to him were using phonetic cues to spell, that is, they were being
guided in their spelling by the tongue, lip, and throat movements the
word elicited when spoken, he reports having the children concentrate on
the careful production of the various vowels. Word lists were developed
with words using the various vowel sounds. Miles emphasizes that the
method has not been tested scientifically, but that it may have promise.

14 Gates, Arthur Irving. The psychology of reading and spelling; with
    special reference to disability. New York: Teachers College,
    Columbia University, 1922. 108p. (Bibliography). (Contributions
    to Education, No. 129).
A group of 109 pupils in grades three through eight was given batteries
of group and individual tests. Median IQ was about 116. Only a few fell
below 100, and but two were less than ninety. Tests of general mental
ability, achievement in school subjects, tests of various reactions to
visual stimuli, reactions to spoken words, and tests of sensory and motor
mechanisms and reactions made up the batteries. About 25 percent of these
children appeared to have really serious difficulties in learning. Reading and spelling were found to be substantially correlated with scores
representing a composite of verbal abilities. Difficulties in spelling
were found to be closely associated with those in reading, although they

were not always identical. The necessity of considering carefully the significance of general mental ability in diagnostic and remedial work is expressed. There is a difference in the way good and poor spellers and readers perceive words, although these differences do not appear in perception of other materials. Word perception was found to be an important determinant of success in pronunciation of words and in oral reading. Characteristic errors in pronunciation stemmed from vague perception of words as wholes, the perception of parts of words only, or other inappropriate perceptual habits. Word perception was also found to be an important factor in success in spelling. The most common cause of misspelling was found in inadequate acquaintance with the visual form of the word. Inability to make an analytical attack on an unfamiliar word characterized poor spellers.

The causes of poor reading and spelling are summarized as: (1) unfavorable training or environment, e.g., being taught by the "word" method rather than trained in visual perception or analysis, which frequently results in wrong methods of observing words; (2) generally unfavorable behavior, i.e., emotional or nervous instability; (3) defects of vision or hearing; (4) defects in motor mechanisms, including lack of general motor coordination and inappropriate eye movements or eye-voice span; and (5) defects or deficiencies in "connecting mechanisms" which include factors such as general mental ability, congenital defects in special cortical areas, defects in visual or auditory memory, or in "visual imagery," or the idea that a child may have a "special disability." This last idea is not favored. Lack of training in methods of perceiving words and inappropriate eye movements and eye-voice span were found to be the most commom and most marked deficiencies in the poorest readers and spellers in this group of children. Reading and spelling are enormously complex mental functions, it is concluded. The task of educational diagnosis and treatment is serious business. A case of inability to read may be a tangle of difficulties too extreme ever to be disentangled.

15 ————. "Viewpoints underlying the study of reading disabilities." Elem Engl Rev 12(4): 85-90, 105, April, 1935. (0 References). Early work on the causes of reading disability established the viewpoint that it resulted from some single organic deficiency. Such terms as "word blindness" were used. An organic etiology might lead persons to wait and hope for discovery of a single cause of reading disability. The better viewpoint reflected in more recent literature is that many different factors produce reading disability. Various constitutional factors such as eye defects, visual and auditory perception, hand and eye dominance, associative learning, and others are merely predisposing factors to reading disability. Many researchers in the field are named and their viewpoints and work discussed. It is noted that few studies have yet employed partial or multiple correlation statistical techniques. Many investigations of classroom conditions, materials, and methods have been made. The problems of reading readiness and maturity will be investigated in the future. It is being discovered that the reading deficiencies of some children are highly specialized. Various fallacies in remedial programs are noted. Those that are too narrow, e.g., teaching only by kinesthetic means, or only phonetics, are mistaken because all nonreaders are not the same. It is a fallacy to assume that remedial methods must be very different from regular classroom methods. Remedial instruction is first of all individual instruction.

16 Hallahan, Daniel P., and Cruickshank, William M. Psychoeducational foundations of learning disabilities. Englewood Cliffs, New

Jersey: Prentice-Hall, 1973. 317p. (Bibliography p. 273-310).
(Prentice-Hall Series in Special Education).
Traces the history of learning disabilities, including language disorders,
by focusing on leaders in the field and the issues that gave impetus to
the genesis and development of the field of learning disabilities. Between 1935 and 1970 there has been a vast increase in published articles
concerning learning disabilities in children. Perceptual-motor training
and behavior modification have been the two prevailing methods, with the
former more popular. Brief biographical summaries of many leaders in
learning disabilities are given, including De Hirsch, Kirk, Orton, Kephart,
Frostig, and others. Summaries of their work serve to set the literature
within an historical and systematic framework. Major educational and
psychological issues are discussed. The relationship between perceptual-
motor and cognitive development and the effectiveness of perceptual-motor
training is discussed. Implications for the future of the field are
included.

17 Hartstein, Jack, ed. <u>Current concepts in dyslexia</u>. St. Louis,
       Missouri: Mosby, 1971. 212p. (Bibliography).
The purpose of this book is to provide a rounded view of the terms,
people, and areas of study necessary for evaluating dyslexics. A collection of original articles written especially for this volume, the book
introduces the reader to the roles of the ophthalmologist, reading teacher,
orthoptist, and neurologist in the diagnosis and treatment of the dyslexic child. Educational remediation, the use of drugs in their treatment, and auditory problems are among areas covered.

18 International Reading Association. <u>Conference proceedings: reading</u>
       <u>disability and perception</u>. Vol. 13(Part 3). Edited by George D.
       Spache. Newark, Delaware: International Reading Association,
       1969. 151p.
The papers included in this book were drawn from symposia on these topics:
(1) interpretations of dyslexia, which include medical, educational, and
psychiatric viewpoints; (2) how to identify the dyslexic; (3) the role
of visual perception in dyslexia; (4) various methods of treating dyslexia, including the suggestion that such children should remain in the
regular classroom with supplementary training; and (5) methods for improving perception. The collection closes with George D. Spache's
satirical discussion of what he regards as the excesses and follies that
have appeared in the treatment of reading disability.

19 Irwin, John V., and Marge, Michael, eds. <u>Principles of childhood</u>
       <u>language disabilities</u>. New York: Appleton-Century-Crofts, 1972.
       406p. (Bibliography).
This collection of sixteen original articles brings together findings
from basic research and from clinical management of language disabilities
in children. Linguistic approaches to the problem are discussed in
articles concerning the structure of language and its onset in young children. Six articles discuss various causes of language disabilities,
including neurological aspects, and the problems of the emotionally disturbed child, the deaf child, disadvantaged children, and retarded children. Diagnosis is viewed from both medical and nonmedical standpoints.
Educational, medical, and social management of language-impaired children
is discussed.

20 Jastak, Joseph. "Interferences in reading." <u>Psychol Bull</u> 31(4):
       244-72, April, 1934. (171 References).

Reviews 171 books and journal articles concerned with reading disabilities. They are classified under the general headings of "symptoms,"
"etiological explanations," and "remedial treatment." French, German,
and English works, works of Morgan, Nettleship, and Thomas, and more
recent titles by Gates, Orton, Fernald, and Critchley are included. Bibliographies by Gray, and reviews of the literature by Illing and Hoffmann
are cited as works representing the educators, the medical viewpoint, and
the experimental laboratories, respectively. Pointing out the gigantic
proportions the literature on reading has attained, this review emphasizes what is considered to be the most important studies of specific
reading disability.

21 Johnson, Doris J., and Myklebust, Helmer R. Learning disabilities;
    educational principles and practices. New York: Grune & Stratton,
    1967. 336p. (Bibliography).
Does not use "dyslexia" as a general term. The book concerns much besides dyslexia, and its focus includes a full description of learning
disabilities in general. Special education and remediation programs are
discussed. Disorders of auditory language, written language, reading,
arithmetic, and nonverbal disorders are presented. Nonverbal disorders
of learning covered include such conditions as inability of the child to
pretend or to understand gestures. Disorders of reading are divided into
visual dyslexia and auditory dyslexia. Various impairments in memory,
left-right orientation, time, and body image are discussed. The outlook
for remedial programs and the implications for school programs are considered. The emphasis of the book is psychoneurological, that is, the
study of disorders in behavior in which the cause is neurological.

22 Malmquist, Eve. "A decade of reading research in Europe, 1959-1969:
    a review." J Educ Res 63(7): 309-29, March, 1970. (181 Refer-
    ences).
Reviews reading research studies done in the decade 1959-1969 in Europe
and the United States. Findings are summarized. The report is selective.
It is organized under four headings: the sociology of reading, the psychology of reading, the physiology of reading, and the teaching of reading. Concerns of the normal reader are considered, but emphasis is on
the problems of the poor reader, and much material is included on reading
disabilities considered from the four standpoints indicated. Studies
focusing on environment, personality, components of the reading task,
genetic and constitutional causes of dyslexia, a wide range of teaching
problems encountered in reading instruction, and many other topics are
described. Investigations are reported with sufficient concrete description of experimental method to place the results in context. Studies in
a number of languages, many in English, are included in the bibliography.

23 ————. "What's happening in reading in Sweden? Part II." Read
    Teach 12(2): 98-102, December, 1958. (3 References).
Research in reading disabilities has followed two main directions: medical
and educational-psychological. The medical interest has leaned toward
the idea that a congenital defect or disease of the cerebral cortex is
involved in "congenital word blindness." The medical point of view was
dominant in Sweden until the 1950s. The psychological point of view is
now being stressed. Some cases of reading disability are no doubt
"congenital word blindness," but many other causes cover most of the
cases. "Children with reading disabilities" and "poor readers" are vague
terms, admittedly. It would be helpful if agreement could be reached on
the scope of these terms. What are seen as Sweden's unique contributions

to the knowledge of reading disabilities are summarized. Studies have
been made from normal populations of children, not from reading clinics
or other special groups. Several variables have been studied, not only
in isolation, but also in interaction with other variables. Nationally
constructed and standardized reading tests have made it possible to determine clearly the frequency of reading disability in Sweden. Investigations have been extensive. Factors most closely related to reading disability are found to be intelligence, ability to concentrate, persistence,
spelling ability, social status and educational level of parents, and
experience of the teacher, among others. Reading disabilities appear
never to be isolated defects. No types of oral reading errors were found
to be characteristic of poor readers. More adequate group tests are
needed at all levels. Research procedure and areas where research is
needed are discussed.

24 Pollack, Myron Frank W., and Piekarz, Josephine A. <u>Reading problems</u>
    <u>and problem readers</u>. New York: McKay, 1963. 242p.
Based on the belief that most retarded readers can be helped, this book
was written to give parents and teachers insights to help them in understanding their problem readers and the difficulties faced by these children. No specific directions for diagnosis and treatment of reading disability are given. Material on the physical, psychological, and educational factors that cause reading disability is presented. Most of the
book is devoted to case studies.

25 Sampson, Olive C. "Fifty years of dyslexia: a review of the litera-
        ture, 1925-75. II practice." <u>Res Educ</u> No. 15: 39-53, May, 1976.
        (96 References).
Reviews the literature from 1925 to 1975 concerned with the practical
management of dyslexia. Emphasis is on educational concepts, diagnosis,
and treatment rather than on causes. The literature is divided into
three sections: the behavioral picture; the most important remedial techniques; and the degree of understanding of the child's problem by the
person attempting to treat him. Writers on the behavior of dyslexics
report some harshness and misunderstanding of the plight of such children,
but on the whole the literature reflects sympathy. Dyslexics constitute
a "hard core" among all kinds of poor readers. No speedy recovery should
be expected. Brief, vivid descriptions of the dyslexic's behavior are
found in the literature. Case histories are common, but often imprecise
and disappointing. Characteristics of dyslexic children are detailed;
however, they frequently reflect the writer's own bias.

The methods for treating dyslexia are summarized. These include: (1)
Orton's individual approach; (2) the basic retraining of prerequisite
skills used by Delacato, Kephart, and others; (3) the Gillingham and
Stillman phonic, multisensory approach; (4) Gattegno's use of color in
teaching reading; (5) the whole-word approaches, resting on a different
philosophy of the teaching of reading; and (6) a mixed group of other
methods. The method of treatment reflects the way the user views the
nature of the disability. The success or failure of that method may reflect the truth or fallacy of the basic principles assumed by the user.
The literature is in fair agreement that no one method is best, and that
any method must be applied with flexibility. Research evidence has not
been very helpful as a guide for choosing a method of treatment.
Bannatyne's list of "ideal techniques" is given, along with the names of
other workers in the field who have published similar lists. Those
treating dyslexia affirm, almost universally, that the child is more

important than the symptom. The teacher's understanding of the actual
demands of the pupil provide a better guide for the teacher than theoretical findings. Emphasis now is turning more to techniques of prevention.

26 Spache, George D. <u>Investigating the issues of reading disabilities</u>.
    Boston, Massachusetts: Allyn and Bacon, 1976. 482p. (Bibliogra-
    phy).
Provides background knowledge for practice in the field of remedial reading. It is noted that this is not a how-to-do-it book: it explores the
answers to questions about "why" or "what good are" various aspects of
diagnosis and remediation rather than offering detailed suggestions for
testing and treatment. It is suggested that this book be used in conjunction with the author's <u>Diagnosing and Correcting Reading Disabilities</u>
which offers more practical suggestions. This book is planned to prepare
the reader to understand the practical suggestions of <u>Diagnosing</u>. The
book is divided into four parts: etiological areas, diagnosis, remediation, and organizational aspects. The last topic is concerned with implementing diagnostic findings, a comparison of methods of teaching reading,
and how to evaluate research in reading instruction. Etiological considerations include visual and auditory perception, eye movements, the
integration of perception from the various senses, reading problems
created by the teacher, estimating the child's intellectual potential,
neurological factors (including a discussion of the definitions, signs,
and symptoms of dyslexia), sociocultural factors in reading problems, and
personality problems. Ways to select and interpret diagnostic tools are
discussed. Various remedial approaches are outlined, including the outcome of visual perception training programs and experiments. A bibliography completes each chapter.

27 Stock, Claudette, compiler. <u>Minimal brain dysfunction child: some</u>
    <u>clinical manifestations, definitions, descriptions and remediation</u>
    <u>approaches</u>. Boulder, Colorado: Pruett Press, 1969. 64p. (Bib-
    liography).
Discusses remediation of learning disabilities and provides a table of
teaching materials related to psychological and motor functions. Dyslexia,
agraphia, and acalculia (inability to read, write, or do arithmetic,
respectively) are the specific disabilities covered. Information is
presented throughout this book in tabular form. Under a column headed
"clinical manifestation," eleven symptoms of minimal brain dysfunction
are listed. The other two columns in the book are headed "definition
and description," and "techniques-training management." Among the behavioral manifestations of MBD analyzed are disorganization, distractibility,
figure-ground confusion, hyperactivity, concrete behavior, and attention-
span problems. The three specific learning disabilities--dyslexia,
agraphia, and acalculia--are explained in the same tabular form.
Bannatyne's chart of hierarchical classification of causes and types of
dyslexia is reproduced. From the bibliography are drawn many definitions
of dyslexia and the other conditions as well as the teaching and training
techniques applicable to the various manifestations of MBD. Dyslexia is
given fuller coverage than the other problems included in the book.

28 Strang, Ruth May. <u>Reading diagnosis and remediation</u>. Newark,
    Delaware: International Reading Association, 1968. 190p. (Bib-
    liography p. 160-85).
Detailed discussion of the causes of reading achievement and disability
and of factors that may be related to it is followed by separate consideration of what is termed "severe reading disabilities" (dyslexia).

Consideration is given to its causes, identification, and treatment.
Diagnostic technique and remedial methods are covered, and material is
included on the diagnosis of reading disability in special groups of
children, including the mentally retarded, emotionally disturbed, disadvantaged, and the gifted. In addition to the bibliography, a list of
reading tests is included. A companion volume to this book is Reading
Diagnosis and Remediation, an annotated bibliography. (See Item No.
2386).

29 Strother, C. R. "Minimal cerebral dysfunction: a historical over-
        view." In: De La Cruze, Felix; Fox, Bernard H.; Roberts, Richard
        H., eds. Minimal brain dysfunction. Ann NY Acad Sci 205: 6-17,
        February 28, 1973. (138 References).
Reviews some of the literature, both early twentieth century and contemporary, on the description and treatment of dyslexia. Considered also
is some of the literature on developmental defects in oral language,
cerebral palsy, and brain damage. The occurrence of MBD has been established, and a plausible relationship established between this dysfunction
and a wide range of behavioral and learning problems. The work of several
conferences is discussed. Children now included under the category of
MBD are a heterogeneous group. The next important step is to refine the
concept by finding common causes and responses to treatment.

30 Tarver, Sara, and Hallahan, Daniel P. "Children with learning dis-
        abilities: an overview." In: Kauffman, James M., and Hallahan,
        Daniel P., eds. Teaching children with learning disabilities:
        personal perspectives. Columbus, Ohio: Charles E. Merrill, 1976.
        2-57. (169 References).
Discusses the terminology, causes, and characteristics of the condition
affecting children known variously as "learning disabled," "dyslexic,"
"educationally handicapped," and "slow learner," among other terms. It
is pointed out that much confusion of terms exists in the field. The
terms "learning disabled" and "dyslexic" are used almost interchangeably.
Perceptual-motor characteristics and theories are given, and the professional positions of some leaders in the field are explained, including
those of Samuel Orton, Lauretta Bender, Katrina De Hirsch, and Helmer
Myklebust. The need for early identification is explained. Some of the
diagnostic instruments are covered, including the ITPA, and the Frostig
Development Test of Visual Perception. Educational methods and techniques
for working with learning-disabled children are described, including
structured classrooms, behavior modification, perceptual-motor training
programs, and linguistic approaches.

31 Tinker, Miles A. "Trends in diagnostic and remedial reading as shown
        by recent publications in this field." J Educ Res 32: 293-303,
        December, 1938. (54 References).
Research and clinical practice in the field of reading disability have
expanded rapidly since 1920. In most cases of reading disability prognosis is good. Recent developments are reviewed.

32 Traxler, Arthur E. "Research in reading in the United States." J
        Educ Res 42: 481-99, March, 1949. (22 References).
Presents summaries of all areas of reading research, including that pertaining to reading disability with emphasis on the period from 1930 to
1948.

33 Wallin, J. E. W. "An historical conspectus on the existence of con-
        genital wordblindness." <u>J Spec Educ</u> 2(2): 203-7, Winter, 1968.
        (46 References).
Surveys opinion on the concept of word blindness, especially earlier
studies and articles which emphasize the hereditary or familial basis of
the condition. The writings of those holding other opinions are also
reviewed. It is concluded that the issues then, as now, are unclear,
with much disagreement among later writers on the subject.

34 Working Party on the Needs of the Dyslexic Adult. <u>People with dys-
        lexia; report of a working party commissioned by the British Council
        for Rehabilitation of the Disabled under the chairmanship of John
        Kershaw</u>. London: British Council for the Rehabilitation of the
        Disabled, 1974. 161p. (Bibliography p. 149-60).
This book is intended to assist dyslexics and those seeking to help them
by treatment and teaching. The focus is especially on adults who are
developmental dyslexics rather than on adults who have become dyslexic
by disease or injury. These persons must find help with their reading
problems if they are to advance in almost any sort of employment. The
report was written after evidence was heard from a long list of witnesses
holding divergent views.

The problem of definition of dyslexia is dealt with. The impact of dyslexia in childhood and on the young adult is discussed. Causes, prevention, prevalence, and the identification of dyslexia, both in children
and in adults, are covered. Individual assessment is needed for childhood dyslexics. Adult dyslexics have the advantage of strong motivation.
It is pointed out that many thousands of dyslexic adults could benefit
from remedial training, but they have not come forward to get it.

The vocational implications of dyslexia are considered. A greater awareness among employers of the nature of dyslexia is recommended. The
remedial services available to both adult and childhood dyslexics in
England are described, and the dyslexic's place in the community is
discussed.

Recommendations include increased efforts to identify dyslexic children
early in life, the expansion of remedial provisions for the dyslexic
adult, and an effort to train more remedial teachers. Suggestions are
made for more adequate employment of dyslexics. Case histories and a
list of organizations dealing with dyslexic persons are included. Research developments are reviewed.

35 World Congress on Dyslexia, Mayo Clinic, 1974. <u>Reading, perception,
        and language: papers from the World Congress on Dyslexia</u>. Drake
        D. Duane, and Margaret B. Rawson, eds.; sponsored by the Orton
        Society in cooperation with the Mayo Clinic. Baltimore, Maryland:
        York Press, 1975. 272p.
These contributions represent the state-of-the-art papers presented as
part of the twenty-fifth annual meeting of the Orton Society and the
commemoration of that group's twenty-fifth anniversary held in connection
with a World Congress on Dyslexia. It was held in Rochester, Minnesota,
in cooperation with the Mayo Clinic. Each paper is a state-of-the-art
summary of a different area of language disability. Macdonald Critchley
presents an historical overview of the field. Other papers examine an
understanding of the language as a prerequisite for learning to read;
the neuroanatomy underlying language function; and the roles of memory,
cognitive skills, auditory perception, and vision. The development of

cross-modal skills necessary for learning about an object through sight, touch, and hearing, for example, as it relates to reading is explored. Some research in this area is discussed. Papers on the phychiatric aspects of language disability and the educational treatment of developmental dyslexia and its results are included.

II
Collected Works

36 Bateman, Barbara D., ed. <u>Learning disorders: reading</u>. Vol. 4.
      Seattle,Washington: Special Child Publications, 1971. 544p.
      (Bibliography).
This collection of original articles on reading and its disorders presents material on beginning reading instruction, and on the diagnosis and
remediation of reading disabilities. Issues current at the time of publication and the trends of future research in reading disabilities are
included. Articles touch on the controversies surrounding the question
of how reading should be taught; whether the term "dyslexia" is useful or
should be abandoned; and whether reading failure is caused by faulty
teaching or is inherent in the child. Material is included on inner-city
reading programs.

37 ————. <u>Reading performance and how to achieve it</u>. Seattle, Wash-
      ington: Bernie Straub and Special Child Publications, 1973. 384p.
      (Bibliography).
This collection of articles reprinted from various journals includes
material on the causes of reading disability and its characteristics. Two
approaches to teaching dyslexic children are discussed: (1) teaching to
the disabled reader's weaknesses; and (2) teaching to neither strengths
nor weaknesses, but determining teaching method from the nature of the
task to be learned. One of the editor's own articles describes reading
as a "rote, non-meaningful, auditory process." Other authors refer to
reading as learning a set of skills, or as a learning problem. Viewpoints
on the causes of dyslexia include, among others, that dyslexia is a basic
defect in neurological functioning, and that reading disability can best
be predicted by measuring skills involving integrative or automatic-
sequential level activities. The general view of the collection is that
reading is not a visual, meaningful process, but only decoding, and that
it should be taught by conditioning programs. Responsibility for reading
failure rests with the teaching methods used, not with the child.

38 Calkins, Eloise, ed. <u>Reading forum: a collection of reference papers</u>
      <u>concerned with reading disability</u>. Bethesda, Maryland: National

Institute of Neurological Diseases and Stroke; for sale by the
Superintendent of Documents, U. S. Government Printing Office,
1971. 256p. (NINDS Monograph No. 11. DHEW Publication No. (NIH)
73-44).
A selection of eighteen of the background papers which were contributed
by leaders in the field of reading disorders to the Secretary's (HEW)
National Advisory Committee on Dyslexia and Related Reading Disorders.
The papers published in Reading Forum are not included in the committee's
report. Reading Forum includes, among others, the work of Corrine E.
Kass, Katrina De Hirsch, Barbara Bateman, Jeanne Chall, Margaret B. Rawson,
Albert J. Harris, Jerome Kagan, and two by Gaston E. Blom. Bases for
classification of reading disorders; a review of some methods of treating dyslexia; and preschool treatment for potential dyslexics are considered. Other articles present material on the causes of dyslexia and
various phases of its diagnosis and treatment. Two articles consider
new trends in the general teaching of reading, and general understanding
of learning disabilities. (For the committee's report see Item No. 216).

39 Denburg, Marvin L., ed. Readings for the psychology of the excep-
      tional child: emphasis on learning disabilities. New York: MSS
      Information Corp., 1972. 300p. Rev. ed., 1974. 201p.
This collection of articles reprinted from various journals contains
material on learning disabilities, including reading disability and the
problems of the brain-injured child. Some material on reading disability
concerns a neurological appraisal of inherited word blindness; methods
for diagnosis and treatment of dyslexia; and the possible importance of
such factors as lateral dominance and directional confusion in dyslexia.
Sections also cover mental retardation and the intellectually gifted
child. The smaller revised edition does not contain any material about
the gifted child. Otherwise it retains essentially the same range of
topics as the original edition.

40 Durr, W. K., ed. Reading difficulties: diagnosis, correction, and
      remediation. Newark, Delaware: International Reading Association,
      1970. 276p. (Bibliography).
This selection of papers presented at the International Reading Association's 1969 annual meeting concerns the diagnosis, correction, and treatment of reading difficulties. Among the topics are: (1) the causes of
dyslexia, including a discussion of the confusion of terms used to apply
to dyslexia or specific reading difficulty; (2) the cognitive skills of
kindergartners; (3) how the teacher can diagnose the disabled reader;
(4) the specific reading disabilities of disadvantaged children; and (5)
the use of reading tests. Various considerations basic to correction of
reading difficulties, including sex differences in reading skill and
remedial programs in both the regular classroom and under a special
teacher are covered.

41 Dyslexia. Acta Paedopsychiatr 38(4): 101-32, April, 1971. (Ref-
      erences).
This entire number of the journal is devoted to dyslexia. Articles include a description of the more common symptoms of dyslexia by Leon Tec.
Suggestions on dealing with the dyslexic child in the home are included.
The opinion is expressed that it is of congenital origin. A. T.
Ravenette's article expresses doubt that a genetic explanation is adequate. These two articles are in English. Other articles not in English
have English summaries. Editorial comment in English suggests that the
"illimitable confusion" over reading disabilities exists because such

disorders belong to neuropsychology, somewhere between psychology and
psychiatry. The differing views stated in these articles are presented
in the hope of stimulating better understanding and help for dyslexic
children. Abstracts of other literature are also included.

42 Flower, Richard M.; Gofman, Helen F.; Lawson, Lucie I., eds. Reading
    disorders; a multidisciplinary symposium. Philadelphia, Pennsylvania:
    F. A. Davis, 1965. 146p. (Bibliography).
This collection of papers, originally presented at a symposium held under
the auspices of the University of California San Francisco Medical Center,
includes material on how to identify and evaluate children with reading
disorders, on remediation, and on teaching slum-area boys. Reading disorders are seen from the viewpoints of the pediatrician, the psychologist,
the educator, the ophthalmologist, the speech therapist, the audiologist,
the educational therapist, and the neurologist.

43 Frierson, Edward C., and Barbe, Walter B., eds. Educating children
    with learning disabilities; selected readings. New York: Appleton-
    Century-Crofts, 1967. 502p. (Bibliography).
Forty-two articles reprinted from many sources include material on learning disabilities in general. Diagnostic and teaching methods used with
children suffering from various learning disorders; the problems of brain-
injured children and their parents; remedial teaching of dyslexics;
spelling problems; and neurological considerations in reading problems
are all covered. A glossary of terms used in connection with learning
disabilities is given.

44 Frostig, Marianne, et al. Individual learning disabilities. 1968.
    43p. (ED 029 418).
Includes articles on learning and reading disabilities by Marianne Frostig,
Gilbert Schiffman, Katrina De Hirsch, and John Irwin.

45 Gunderson, Doris V., compiler. Language and reading: an interdis-
    ciplinary approach. 1970. 278p. (ED 037 722).
This collection of articles is divided into three parts: (1) reading
and language which deals with theories of reading; (2) reading research,
which discusses the direction reading research should take; and (3) reading problems. The last section contains material on factors contributing
to reading disability, confusion in the use of the term "dyslexia," and
reading disability in Japan. A paper on the state of reading instruction
is also included.

46 Johns Hopkins Conference on Research Needs and Prospects in Dyslexia
    and Related Aphasic Disorders, Johns Hopkins Medical Institutions,
    1961. Reading disability; progress and research needs in dyslexia.
    John Money, ed. Baltimore, Maryland: Johns Hopkins Press, 1962.
    222p. (Bibliography).
Thirteen papers read at a conference, plus one more chapter which is a
synoptic postconference review incorporating the main themes of the
conference discussion, comprise this book. Topics include psychiatric
considerations; the relationship of dyslexia to form perception, directional sense, and cerebral dominance; and dyslexia as a neurological
problem in childhood. The recognition and treatment of dyslexia in the
schools is also considered. Investigative experimental studies and detailed clinical studies are thought to be of more value than large testing
surveys. The general viewpoint of the papers is that ocular and optical
defects are of little significance in dyslexia. There is no foolproof

method for diagnosing dyslexia, but in general, children with defective
vision, general mental deficiency, improper or insufficient schooling,
or a lack of sufficient motivation to learn to read would not be included
among those termed "dyslexic." Attention is given to acquired adult disorders of reading as an aid to understanding why childhood dyslexia occurs
and what it is. Differentiating the slow bloomers from the dyslexic
handicapped is a major problem for future research. Characteristics of
specific dyslexia were discussed, but the conference viewpoint does not
question the existence of the syndrome of developmental dyslexia. It is
simple to identify reading retardation, but difficult to make the differential diagnosis of specific dyslexia. No unique identifying sign exists.
The dyslexic's problem is not just one of right-left orientation, but a
three-dimensional space-movement perception problem, as when a normal
person closes his eyes and attempts to write on his own forehead. At
least twice as many boys as girls have dyslexia. No explanation is
offered for this. Dyslexia usually appears without any sign of brain
injury, and positive EEG findings are not usual in developmental dyslexia.
A glossary of terms is included.

47 Karnes, Lucia Rooney. Dyslexia in special education. Pomfret,
        Connecticut: Orton Society, 1965. 95p. (Orton Society Monograph
        No. 1).
This collection of papers presented at the forty-second annual convention
of the Council for Exceptional Children includes: (1) an overview of
what is meant by "specific dyslexia"; (2) material on how to teach dyslexic children; (3) how to identify and help prevent specific dyslexia
in young children; and (4) neurological and psychological aspects of the
disorder. June Lyday Orton, Katrina De Hirsch, and Herman Goldberg are
among the authors represented.

48 Kirk, Samuel A., and McCarthy, Jeanne McRae, eds. Learning disabil-
        ities: selected ACLD papers. Boston, Massachusetts: Houghton
        Mifflin, 1975. 395p. (Bibliography).
Consists of an anthology of articles selected from the proceedings of the
annual meetings of the Association for Children with Learning Disabilities
which began in 1963. Organized into ten sections, the book includes
selections dealing with the beginning of ACLD, an overview of what is
meant by learning disabilities, diagnosis, medical practices, and parents'
problems, among other topics. Section Seven is the only one dealing
directly with dyslexia. Called "Reading and Dyslexia," it has one selection each from Macdonald Critchley, Janet W. Lerner, and John McLeod.

49 Natchez, Gladys, ed. Children with reading problems: classic and
        contemporary issues in reading disability: selected readings.
        New York: Basic Books, 1968. 445p. (Bibliography).
This book is divided into three parts: causes of learning disorders,
diagnostic considerations, and treatment. Articles are reprinted from
many sources, and most have at least a short bibliography. Part One
includes articles by writers who view reading problems as primarily
emotional, neurophysiological, or social in origin. Writers from each
school of thought are grouped separately. Diagnosis is also presented
from a variety of viewpoints. The section on treatment is divided into
two parts: (1) material concerning schoolchildren from grades one through
eight who read below expectations; and (2) discussions of the treatment
of children of varying ages who suffer from reading difficulty of a more
severe nature. Selections from Samuel Orton, Arthur I. Gates, Katrina
De Hirsch, and Marianne Frostig, among many others, are included.

50   National Conference on Dyslexia, Philadelphia, 1966. Dyslexia; diag-
        nosis and treatment of reading disorders. Arthur H. Keeney, and
        Virginia T. Keeney, eds. St. Louis, Missouri: Mosby, 1968. 182p.
This collection of papers includes a discussion of the historical development of neurological knowledge of the brain with the conclusion that there
is as yet no objective test to determine the presence of brain lesion in
dyslexia. Other papers concern diagnosis and prediction of reading
failure; the relation of dyslexia to vision and perception; acquired dyslexia; and some advice on therapy. The viewpoint in general distinguishes
constitutional, or primary, dyslexia of no known origin, from secondary
dyslexias caused by birth injury, brain damage by disease or accident,
developmental delay, or emotional disturbances. Keeney's classification
system for the dyslexias is given. Critchley, De Hirsch, Bender, Goldberg,
June L. Orton, and Rabinovitch are among authors represented.

51   Newman, Harold, ed. Reading disabilities; selections on identifica-
        tion and treatment. n.p.: Odyssey Press, 1969. 652p. (Bibliog-
        raphy).
Fifty selections reprinted from many sources are included in this collection on the causes and diagnoses of reading problems. All phases and
methods of remedial teaching are covered: improving word recognition,
comprehension, and motivation. Detailed, specific teaching techniques
are spelled out in a series of articles reprinted from publications of
the Board of Education of New York City.

52   Orton, June Lyday, ed. Specific language disabilities; a compilation
        of selected papers presented chiefly at annual meetings of The
        Orton Society, Inc. and published in volumes VII - XII bulletins
        of The Orton Society, 1957-1962. Pomfret, Connecticut: Orton
        Society, 1963. 186p. (Bulletin of The Orton Society, Vol. 13).
        (Bibliography).
In addition to material reprinted from the Society's bulletins, this book
contains articles reprinted from other sources, and some material prepared for this volume. Samuel T. Orton's 1928 article on strephosymbolia
in which he sets forth his basic teachings concerning the role of indefinite cerebral dominance as a cause of reading disability is reprinted
from JAMA. He views the condition as a physiologic variant rather than
as a general mental defect. Background articles on the concept of dyslexia, and articles describing diagnostic methods and treatment are included. Problems in preparing teachers for the field, and existing public
school projects for dealing with dyslexic children are reported. A bibliography of Dr. Samuel T. Orton's writings may be found in the volume.

53   Orton, Samuel Torrey. "Word-blindness" in school children and other
        papers on strephosymbolia (specific language disability - dyslexia)
        1925-1946. June Lyday Orton, compiler. Pomfret, Connecticut:
        Orton Society, 1966. 280p. (Bibliography). (Orton Society
        Monograph, No. 2).
This collection of twenty of Dr. Orton's papers on what are termed "developmental language disabilities," compiled by his wife, contains all
but one of the journal articles by Dr. Orton on various problems of
language acquisition. They are reprinted from many journals. Stuttering
and spelling problems are considered as well as reading disability.
Familial occurrences of reading disabilities and neurological bases for
it are among topics covered. A complete bibliography of all of Samuel
Orton's writing is included.

54 Paine, Richmond S.; Myklebust, Helmer; Weiss, Deso; <u>et al</u>. <u>Dyslexia</u>
     <u>and reading disabilities; papers</u>. New York: MSS Information Corp.,
     1972. 224p.
Seventeen papers are reprinted from various journals. Three are of a
general nature and concern etiologic factors in children's learning disorders, and the psychotherapeutic approach to reading retardation. Others
describe various neurological characteristics frequently observed in dyslexics: "minimal cerebral damage"; problems with right-left discrimination; cerebral dominance; and cluttering as a manifestation of a central
language imbalance. There is also a section on perceptual integration
and its relation to reading disabilities. Case studies are presented in
various areas of reading achievement; the effect of auditory training on
the reading skills of retarded readers; and the comparative frequency of
reading disability in German- and English-speaking countries.

55 Schell, Leo M., and Burns, Paul C., eds. <u>Remedial reading; an anthol-</u>
     <u>ogy of sources</u>. Boston, Massachusetts: Allyn and Bacon, 1968.
     468p. (Bibliography p. 421-50).
Material on the causes, identification, diagnoses, and prognoses of reading disability comprises this collection of reprinted articles from many
sources. Covered are: (1) principles and procedures for instruction of
disabled readers; (2) dealing with the emotionally disturbed poor reader;
(3) suggested instructional materials; and (4) how to organize a remedial
reading program. An effort is made to give a variety of viewpoints, and
to make it clear that controversy exists in the field of reading disability. Reading skills as such are not stressed. Sixty authors are
represented.

56 Solan, Harold A., ed. <u>The psychology of learning and reading diffi-</u>
     <u>culties</u>. New York: Simon & Schuster, 1973. 476p. (Bibliography).
Presents a collection of forty-seven journal articles representing various
viewpoints. Factors causing reading and learning difficulties are considered in five sections: reading readiness; visual, auditory, and
speech correlates; physiological and neurological correlates; perceptual
and psychological correlates; and disadvantaged children. Dyslexia is
dealt with in its relationship to cerebral dominance, maturation of
visual function, physiological aspects, and the role of brain damage in
congenital dyslexia. Articles on the diagnosis and treatment of specific
reading disability, classifications of reading disorders, and more general
treatments of language disorders in children are presented. The full
citation for the original place of publication is not always given. A
glossary is found in the volume.

57 ————. <u>Psychology of reading difficulties</u>. New York: Selected
     Academic Readings, a Division of Associated Educational Service
     Corp., 1968. 332p.
The thirty-six articles in this collection were selected to represent the
different viewpoints in current literature on reading difficulties. Reprinted from various journals, each article concerns the relationship of
one factor to reading difficulty. Factors include: (1) reading readiness; (2) visual, auditory, and speech considerations; (3) perceptual;
(4) psychological; (5) physiological; and (6) neurological factors as
they relate to reading difficulty.

58 Tarnopol, Lester, and Tarnopol, Muriel, eds. <u>Reading disabilities;</u>
     <u>an international perspective</u>. Baltimore, Maryland: University
     Park Press, 1976. 341p. (Bibliography).

Presents twenty articles summarizing the problem of reading and/or learning disabilities in nineteen countries. Authors are persons working in
some phase of special education in the country concerned. An introductory
chapter by the Tarnopols presents a survey of the field of reading and
learning problems. Based in part on information received in reply to a
survey questionnaire, this chapter discusses: (1) the confusion in terminology among and within countries; (2) the causes of reading disability;
(3) factors related to reading problems; (4) methods of remediation; and
(5) teacher training. In general, reading disorders are seen as related
to genetic and neurological dysfunctions with secondary emotional problems. It is recognized that this still leaves many reading-disabled
children unaccounted for. In many places there is no official recognition
of the problem. Or, if it is recognized, in countries where many children receive little education at best, those with problems drop out un-
observed. It is found, however, that around the world there is an awareness of the problems of children with specific reading and learning disorders. Most industralized nations now have special programs for such
children. There is reason for optimism for the future. In general, each
chapter includes material on the frequency of occurrence of reading disorders in the country concerned. Programs and facilities for such children, and methods of remedial training and diagnosis are discussed. In
some cases, government policy toward remedial reading training, ongoing
research, and available tests for diagnosis are among topics considered.
An occasional case study is presented. The chapter on reading problems
of Chinese children describes how writing is taught in China. Countries
included are Argentina, Australia, Austria, Belgium, Canada, China,
Czechoslovakia, Denmark, Finland, Germany, Great Britain, Hungary, Ireland,
the Netherlands, Norway, Rhodesia, the Republic of South Africa, the
United States, and the Virgin Islands.

III
Surveys of the Field

59 Adams, Richard B. "Dyslexia: a discussion of its definition." J
    Learn Disabil 2(12): 616-33, December, 1969. (23 References).
Numerous definitions of dyslexia are presented, both from various diction-
aries and published sources, and from personal communications with persons
working in the fields of neurology and ophthalmology. It is concluded
that "dyslexia" is a word of obscure meaning that has divided the efforts
of professionals, when collaboration would have been better. The word
is likened to Frankenstein's monster, "wreaking havoc in the discourse
of sensible men." Likening some of the arguments over definition to
Alice in Wonderland's problems in conversing with the Walrus, and to
Humpty Dumpty, it is concluded that it would be more useful to determine
what to do about the disability than to continue to dissipate time and
energy over naming it.

60 "Aid for the word-blind: treatment essential." Times Educ Suppl
    2495: 524, March 15, 1963. (0 References).
This description of the contents of a bulletin issued by the Association
for Word-Blind Children presents the symptoms of dyslexia; cites briefly
two case histories; and notes that although the cause may be an anatomical
abnormality, no one is really sure of the origin of the condition.

61 Anapolle, Louis. "Profile of a visual dyslexic." Am J Optom 48(5):
    385, May, 1971. (8 References).
Outlines and summarizes the typical personality characteristics, scholastic
achievement, and vision problems of the developmental dyslexic. Because
of his short attention span, he may be a classroom disturber, or he may
be drowsy and daydream. He may at first achieve a visual acuity of only
20/200 on the Snellen chart, but with coaxing may do much better, even
20/20. He is of normal intelligence, but behind his peers in scholastic
attainment, a condition which leads to emotional problems. He may be
immature in his visual perception. His visual fusion may be unstable.
It is estimated that developmental dyslexia affects 10 to 15 percent of
the school population.

62 Anderson, Ellen. "Some problems in training word-blind adults at the
     Kofoed Training School and the Amager School for the Word-Blind."
     J Learn Disabil 1(3): 201-6, March, 1968. (0 References).
Among the word-blind students at the Kofoed and Amager Schools in Denmark
many are delinquents, the majority are of low intelligence, and 90 percent
are from broken homes. They have multiple problems. Most of the students
have difficulty in obtaining jobs because they cannot read. Often they
live in fear of having their handicap discovered. A plea is made for
public understanding of the problems of word-blind persons. Details of
their everyday struggles are described.

63 Arkell, Helen. Dyslexia: introduction; a dyslexic's eye view.
     London: The Helen Arkell Dyslexia Centre, 1974. 23p.
Explains in unscientific terms what it is like to be dyslexic, and what
sort of problems it brings. Written by a remedial teacher who was herself dyslexic as a child, and who is a member of a family where dyslexia
is common, the book defines and explains for the layman a number of the
common factors associated with dyslexia. Material is included on poor
visual perception; poor auditory perception; the kinesthetic approach to
writing; sequencing of letters or sounds; orientation of letters; motor
control; and the effect of dyslexia on use of other symbols, e.g., figures
and punctuation. The problems are explained in practical terms with
examples from the author's own experience. The emotional effect of dyslexia is considered. Some myths about dyslexia are discussed and dismissed. Diagnostic suggestions are given, and suggestions for teachers
for coping with dyslexic children are offered.

64 Bakwin, Ruth Morris. "Reading disabilities in children." J Am Med
     Wom Assoc 2(3): 89-91, March, 1947. (0 References).
Describes the common symptoms of dyslexia. Many factors cause reading
disability: lack of reading readiness; physical handicaps; developmental
defects which are sometimes referred to as "congenital word-blindness";
emotional handicaps; and improper training. Suggestions for remediation
are given.

65 Bakwin, Ruth Morris, and Bakwin, Harry. "Specific reading disability."
     J Pediatr 32(4): 465-72, April, 1948. (10 References).
Describes the symptoms of specific reading disability, and explains the
causes largely in terms of Orton's theories of lack of cerebral dominance.
Other factors causing reading disability are given, such as the sight
method of teaching reading, emotional factors, and encouraging ambidextrous children to use both hands as they please. Suggestions for differential diagnosis and management of the condition are given. Most poor
readers eventually learn to read as well as other children.

66 Barker, Philip; Fee, Rosemary; Sturrock, George W. "A note on re-
     tarded readers in Dundee." J Child Psychol Psychiatry 8(3-4):
     227-32, December, 1967. (17 References).
All nine-year-olds of normal intelligence (IQ 90 or more on the Terman-
Merrill scale) attending schools for normal children in Dundee, Scotland,
were surveyed. About 1 percent were severely retarded readers with reading ages of six and one-half years or less. Poor school attendance was
much more common among reading-disabled children than among normal readers,
but it did not seem to be a factor in the majority of cases. A group of
good readers was used as controls. Many more boys than girls were found
to be disabled readers, in agreement with other studies. No social class
differences appeared between the normal control group and the group of
disabled readers.

67 Barnes, Donald L. "Reading disability and remediation in the United
    States." Int Rev Educ 10(1): 35-50, 1964. (31 Bibliographic
    Footnotes).
There was a great burst of research activity in reading in the 1950s, but
such research goes well back into the nineteenth century. Reading disability appears to be caused by many factors, including poor mental ability, unfortunate teaching methods, emotional disturbances, impairments of
vision and hearing, inconsistent cerebral dominance, and speech defects.
Environmental rather than hereditary influences appear to account for the
larger proportion of boys than girls who have reading disabilities. Diagnosis and remediation are discussed.

68 Bateman, Barbara. "Learning disabilities--yesterday, today, and
    tomorrow." Except Child 31(3): 167-77, December, 1964. (51
    References).
Three major subcategories of learning disabilities are identified: (1)
dyslexia, or reading disability; (2) verbal communication disorders,
which include both speaking and the comprehension of spoken language; and
(3) visual-motor integration problems. The last often, but not always,
occurs with reading problems, and includes difficulties with spatial
orientation, body image, perception, and coordination. Some of the literature on the causes, diagnosis, and treatment of learning disabilities
is reviewed. Trends in special education are assessed.

69 Bender, James F. "Backward child may be word blind." Sci Dig 17(1):
    25-28, January, 1945. (0 References).
Word blindness, or reading disability, is common; estimates of its incidence range from 8 to 25 percent of all schoolchildren. Males outnumber
females four to one. Two main classifications of reading disability
exist: acquired alexia and developmental alexia. Acquired alexia includes cases where inability to read follows a brain injury in a person
who formerly could read. Such a case is described. War injuries account
for many of these cases. Far more numerous are cases of developmental
alexia in children. An illustrative case of a twelve-year-old boy is
presented. Efficient readers' eyes move forward in spurts and they are
able to remember the thought as they read. Children who have trouble
reading may have thyroid problems or be clumsy. These children should
be tested for eye dominance. Emotional maladjustments may be present.

70 ————. "Do you know a dyslexiac?" Sci Mon 63(4, Whole No. 373):
    299-304, October, 1946. (6 References).
Describes the main symptoms of developmental dyslexia. Children of normal
intelligence who confuse letters and words and have difficulty in learning to read often have short auditory memory spans, speech defects, and
may be clumsy. They reverse or transpose letters or syllables. Each
case should be studied individually since it involves a whole personality.
Dyslexics should be checked for hand and eye preference, for visual acuity
and coordination, and for hearing acuity. If the child is not ready to
read at age six, it may be advisable to delay reading instruction until
second or third grade. Dyslexics may display emotional problems arising
from their reading problems. Acquired dyslexia may develop from injury
or brain tumor or other brain lesion.

71 Blom, Gaston E., and Jones, Arlene Whiteman. "Bases of classifica-
    tion of reading disorders." J Learn Disabil 3(12): 606-17,
    December, 1970. (25 References).

Reading disorders are grouped into four categories: (1) functional, or
how the child behaves; (2) etiological, i.e., by cause; (3) theoretical
models, which include classification from the psychoanalytic viewpoint;
and (4) classification as a nosological system, i.e., the classification
of reading disorders as a disease. It is concluded that a "descriptive
behavioral method of classification" would serve best for use by teachers.

72 Blumberg, Harris M. "Dyslexic problems and behavioral consequences."
     Am Orthopt J 18: 103-6, 1968. (13 References).
All dyslexic problems are caused by some kind of neurological difficulty.
Dyslexic children show some characteristics similar to brain-injured
children. Perceptual problems in dyslexia, including reversals, problems
of figure-ground relationships, and spatial relations are described.
The child's deep feelings of inadequacy will usually require psychotherapy.
Special educational teaching techniques should be used, including the
visual-auditory-kinesthetic approach. Early diagnosis is most important.

73 Boykin, Eleanor. "Maybe he can't read." Parents Mag 23(3): 36,
     100-104, March, 1948. (0 References).
Parents and even teachers may be unaware that a child's school failure
is caused by a reading disability. Defective sight or vision, mixed
dominance, poor instructional methods, and emotional factors are among
the causes. Individual instruction may be needed, including training in
vocabulary building, phonics, and spelling.

74 Bradbury, Will. "An agony of learning." Life 73(14): 57-58, 60-
     62, 64, 67-68, October 6, 1972. (0 References).
Describes the educational program for learning-disabled children at the
Center School, Bound Brook, New Jersey. Symptoms of the syndrome (variously called "learning disabled," "dyslexia," "word-blind," and "minimal
brain damage") are illustrated by the case histories of two children.
Causes, the clues to look for in diagnosing perceptual difficulties, ways
to get help for the child, and methods of treatment are discussed.

75 Bronner, Augusta Fox. "Special defects of language ability." In:
     The psychology of special abilities and disabilities. Chap. 6.
     Boston, Massachusetts: Little, Brown, 1917. 75-117. (Biblio-
     graphic Footnotes).
The reading process involves perception of form and sound; association
of sounds with visually perceived letters; motor, visual, and auditory
memory; and the motor processes used in inner speech and reading aloud.
Much work has been done on the physical aspects of the process, e.g., the
role of the eye. So far as is known, analysis of the mental processes
involved in reading has never been applied to individual cases of inability to learn to read. Some case histories concerning congenital word
blindness from Morgan, Nettleship, and other writers are reviewed. The
standpoint of virtually all the neurologists is that word blindness
follows cerebral lesions in persons who formerly could read: this is a
loss of function rather than absence of function. Other writers suggest
heredity as a cause. Some of this literature is reviewed. It is suggested that the term "congenital word blindness" has no particular value;
that it may be nothing more than a blanket term, easy to apply but offering little help. What is needed is careful study of individual cases,
with thoughtful analysis of results. Some of the problems of spoken
language, including congenital word deafness, are considered. A number
of case histories illustrating defects in language ability are given.

The full bibliographic citations of nineteenth- and early twentieth-
century work in the field cover works in English, German, and French.

76 Brown, Joe R.; Darley, Frederic L.; Gomez, Manuel R. "Disorders of
    communication." Pediatr Clin North Am 14(4): 725-48, November,
    1967. (50 References).
Traces the developmental milestones in the acquisition of speech and
language by the child. Various clinical syndromes comprising normal development or lack of it are discussed. Included are hearing; anatomic
problems delaying the acquisition of speech; motor problems; dysfluency
(repetition and hisitations in speech); aphasia; dyslexia; autism; mental
retardation; and environmental deprivation. Each is described, and suggestions are offered for differential diagnosis and treatment. Among
the disorders of communication, dyslexia is the most common problem in
schoolchildren. Inability to distinguish letters or words, short attention span, and disordered behavior characterize the dyslexic. Most dyslexic children can be taught to read. Remedial methods are suggested.

77 Brown, Virginia L., and Botel, Morton. Dyslexia: definition or
    treatment? 1972. 75p. (ED 058 014).
Reviews research literature on dyslexia since 1955, with emphasis on the
late 1960s. An ERIC/CRIER state-of-the-art paper, the monograph has as
its aim the construction of a framework for use by future researchers.
Chapters cover the problems related to definition of dyslexia, problems
of diagnosis, and various approaches for treatment of dyslexia. It is
admitted at the outset that no precise definition of dyslexia is possible.

78 Bryant, N. Dale. "Characteristics of dyslexia and their remedial
    implications." Except Child 31: 195-99, December, 1964. (7
    References).
Dyslexics consistently display at least three characteristics: (1) Difficulty in associating letter symbols and letter sounds. This is related
to abstracting common elements from varying experiences. (2) Insufficient use of recognition cues within a word. The child's attention
usually is centered primarily on initial letter and general shape of the
word. Details are ignored. (3) Confusions and reversals of letters.
Clues for successful remediation are to be found in the nature of the
difficulties. Discrimination training, e.g., filling in missing letters
in new words, and kinesthetic practice are recommended.

79 Burt, C. "Counterblast to dyslexia." AEP Newsl No. 5: 2-6, March,
    1966.

80 "Can't read, can't spell; curing word blindness." Times Educ Suppl
    2448: 793, April 20, 1962. (0 References).
In this report on a conference held in London by the Invalid Children's
Aid Association, Dr. J. Roswell Gallagher of Boston is quoted as saying
that there is disagreement as to the causes of dyslexia. Dr. Gallagher
lists the symptoms of the disorder. He believes that the alphabetic-
phonic method of teaching brings great improvement, and that the whole-
word method is very unsuitable for dyslexics. Work with dyslexics in
Denmark and France is described. Discussion at the conference ranged
from disbelief in the concept of word blindness to the possibility of
setting up a center for treatment of such children.

81 Carrow, Elizabeth. "Dyslexia." Arch Otolaryngol 98(1): 1, July,
    1973. (6 References).

Misconceptions about the nature of reading are discussed. Reading requires an integration of visual and auditory abilities, and it is a mistake to ascribe reading failure to a lack of visual perception alone.
Prevention of reading failure is easier and less costly than remedial
training. Therefore early identification is important. The use of a
team of professionals to diagnose and follow the child medically and
educationally is the best approach.

82   Charlton, M. H. "Minimal brain dysfunction: clinical aspects."
     Electroencephalogr Clin Neurophysiol 29(4):   412-13, October,
     1970. (0 References).
Dyslexia in children is usually the result of minimal cerebral dysfunction which includes both cases of familial origin and cases resulting
from birth trauma. Symptoms of the latter are listed. The best tool for
diagnosis is psychometric testing, especially the WISC. Treatment of
remediable disease, control of hyperactivity by drugs, and adequate educational measures all are included in treatment.

83   "Child reads backward? Suspect dyslexia." Sci News Lett 87(4):
     61, January 23, 1965. (0 References).
If a child reads "was" for "saw," suspect him of a language disability
called dyslexia. Dyslexia is not the only reason children do not read
well, but 5 to 20 percent of children of normal or above-normal intelligence have it. It has symptoms, but should not be considered a disease.
Dyslexic children can be rehabilitated if the condition is recognized
early. There is disagreement as to why it occurs. Heredity may play a
role. Speech problems may also be blamed on dyslexia.

84   Clarke, Jane L. "Verbal and non-verbal learning disabilities." In:
     Burkowsky, Mitchell R., ed. Orientation to language and learning
     disorders. St. Louis, Missouri: Warren H. Green, 1973. 54-100.
     (57 References).
Two broad categories of learning disabilities--verbal and nonverbal--
occur in children of normal intelligence. Verbal disabilities include
reading, spelling, writing, and auditory language problems. A child who
cannot recognize words visually cannot read. If he can recognize words,
but cannot recall them (revisualize), he cannot write. If the child can
understand what is spoken to him, but cannot use these same words to
express understanding (reauditorize), he cannot communicate any knowledge.
These conditions can be helped by the use of specific teaching techniques
to provide training in associating visual and auditory symbols (associating what is seen with what is heard); training in sequencing; and training in visual-motor coordination. Nonverbal disabilities, i.e., weakness
in comprehension, stem from the child's lack of understanding of the
social environment. He does not understand life as it goes on around
him and draw correct inferences. This condition can be helped with teaching techniques using analysis of forms and shapes, and the use of series
of photographs describing cause-and-effect situations.

85   "Congenital word blindness." Lancet 2(7453): 36, July 2, 1966.
     (9 References).
Reviews briefly the history of the term "congenital word blindness," a
term still used in place of "dyslexia." The condition has been recognized
as one of educational importance in England, Denmark, and the United
States. Various causes are listed.

86   Cook, J. W. "Dyslexia: a critical comment." <u>AEP J Newsl</u> 3(3):
     51-60, Winter, 1973. (42 References).

87   Crabtree, Tom. "Dyslexia, goodbye." <u>New Soc</u> 35(691): 10-11,
     January 1, 1976. (10 References).
Dismisses the concept of dyslexia as neurological myth. The concept has
been of very little use from a practical standpoint, and its theoretical
base is highly dubious. Before labeling a child with the impressive-
sounding, neurologically phony term "dyslexic," parents should make certain that the poor reading is not caused by factors such as environment,
emotional stress, developmental immaturity, neurological problems (vision,
hearing, clumsiness, handedness), poor intellectual ability, and lack of
regular, systematic teaching. Dyslexia is no answer to anything, but
daily phonics in the first school is an answer. Daily, systematic reading is needed. The term is not useful for educational purposes and has
no scientific meaning.

88   ————. "Hitting a myth; does dyslexia really exist?" <u>Times Educ</u>
     <u>Suppl</u> 3147: 36, September 26, 1975. (0 References).
Dyslexia is a myth. Like all effective myths, it contains the right blend
of vague concepts and scientific jargon. The dyslexic world is presided
over by gods--a small international group of neurologists. Symptoms of
the condition are listed. Many persons presenting these symptoms learn
to read. Great semantic confusion exists about dyslexia. There are
genuine reasons that children do not learn to read: emotional problems,
poor teaching, lack of motivation, ill health, personal antipathies, and
changes of school. Dyslexia, however, is a high-status reason; it ab-
solves everybody of blame if the child fails in reading. Children exposed
to early and systematic teaching of reading learn to read. Japanese,
French, and German children are taught phonetically, and the number of
children with reading problems is much lower than in England. An example
is given of one method used successfully to teach a so-called dyslexic
child to read.

89   Critchley, Macdonald. <u>Developmental dyslexia</u>. London: Heinemann
     Medical, 1964. 104p. (Bibliography p. 90-102).
Expressing unhappiness with the "muddled ideas" of multiple causes for
dyslexia, this neurologist makes the case for a "constitutional" or
specific inborn cause of dyslexia. Early reports of "word blindness"
beginning in the late nineteenth century are reviewed. Causes linked to
maternal and natal factors, ophthalmological aspects, cerebral dominance,
minor neurological signs, and genetic considerations are all discussed.
A protest is lodged against having those who are victims of "a constitutional specific type of dyslexia" placed indiscriminately with "the
miscellany of cases of poor readers." Neurotic reactions to the difficulty of being unable to learn to read are to be expected. The number of
persons involved and what to expect of the dyslexic as he grows up are
other aspects considered. The bibliography covers a wide range of literature in several languages.

90   ————. "Developmental dyslexia." <u>Pediatr Clin North Am</u> 15(3):
     669-76, August, 1968. (5 References).
Defines developmental dyslexia as specific difficulty in learning to read,
often of genetic origin, which exists in spite of good general intelligence, and without emotional disturbance, brain damage, impairment of
vision or hearing, and without deficiency in conventional instruction.
A brief history of the interest in word blindness in medical circles is

given. Psychological and opthalmological problems are discussed. The
notion of minimal brain damage, and of dyslexia viewed as a specific
maturational lag, are discussed.

91 ————. "Dyslexia." Br Med J 1(6003): 217, January 24, 1976.
        (0 References).
Letter to editor. The concept of "developmental dyslexia" is not substantially different from the condition referred to by some as "specific reading retardation." Dyslexia is to be preferred as the "crisper and
gramatically more flexible term." It indicates a syndrome, not an isolated defect in reading. The condition is constitutional, not environmental. The first member of a team for treatment should be the family
doctor; diagnosis is essentially a medical responsibility. The teacher's
cooperation is needed. The child benefits from having a firm diagnostic
label of "developmental dyslexia." His morale is lifted when he is no
longer labeled "lazy," "stupid," or "brain-damaged."

92 ————. "Some defects of reading and writing in children: their
        association with word-blindness and mirror-writing." J State Med
        35(4): 217-23, April, 1927. (0 References).
Many cases of gross reading problems in children of normal intelligence
are really cases of congenital word blindness. Such children tend to be
overlooked by teachers and considered dull. Possibly the anatomical
basis for the defect is an abnormal development of the angular gyri. An
analogous acquired condition is produced by lesions of the angular gyrus
on the left side of the brain. Many of these children are left-handed
or ambidextrous, which tends to produce mirror writing. When the child
mirror-writes, he appears oblivious to his mistake. He confuses palin-
dromic words, and although alert at figures, music, and other intellectual
attainments, he is very backward in grasping the meaning of graphic
symbols. The child probably has very little visual memory in the early
days of learning to write. Kinesthetic memories are developed in the
child by copying. The congenitally word-blind child, having learned to
read late and with great difficulty, finds correcting his writing errors
very difficult.

93 ————. "Some observations upon developmental dyslexia." In:
        Williams, Denis, ed. Modern trends in neurology. Series 4. New
        York: Appleton-Century-Crofts, 1967. 135-44. (10 References).
The dyslexic's difficulty involves both the process of interpretation
and the problem of dealing with two properties of the written word: its
meaning and its acoustic properties. From these problems arises the dyslexic's difficulty with spelling. Boys are more often affected than
girls, and the condition has genetic properties. Neurotic problems are
secondary reactions arising from frustration and mishandling. At the
center of the continuum of reading disability cases exists a hard core
of cases which are organically and genetically determined. These are
highly specific in nature, and are the true dyslexics. No evidence that
subtypes exist has yet been presented. Poor readers with demonstrable
brain damage--perinatal or postnatal--should be excluded from this group.
Few dyslexics appear to have well-established hemispheric dominance. A
difference of two years or more between a child's chronological and his
reading age is usually necessary to diagnose dyslexia. The child's problem relates to verbal symbols and not to other graphic or pictorial
representations. It is often suggested that dyslexia results from cerebral immaturity and maturational lag. This contention cannot be confirmed
or denied with certainty. Penmanship and spelling are usually very poor
in dyslexics. Characteristics of the dyslexic's writing are listed.

94 Critchley, Macdonald, and Critchley, Eileen A. <u>Dyslexia defined</u>.
     Springfield, Illinois: Thomas, 1978. 161p. (Bibliography).
Addressed to parents and teachers of dyslexic children, this book is so
written that chapters may be read individually, not necessarily sequentially. The terminology of reading retardation is explored. The reasoning behind the adoption of such terms as "dyslexia," "word blindness,"
"congenital word blindness," and "developmental dyslexia" is set forth.
The point of view of the book is that "developmental," or "primary" dyslexia is a genetically determined and constitutional disorder which affects children of every intellectual level. "Specific developmental"
dyslexia is inherent, innate, and genetically determined. It is far more
common in boys than in girls. "Secondary," or "symptomatic," dyslexia,
on the other hand, is not constitutional, and is not genetically determined. One of the most common causes of the secondary type is minimal
brain damage. It is pointed out that in the literature the two types of
dyslexia have been confused, or sometimes regarded as identical. Some
writers have referred to primary dyslexia as a cognitive disorder, meaning it results from an anomaly of mentation, and is not the result of
physical or structural defect in the brain.

The kinds of mistakes the dyslexic makes in reading and writing are described. Examples of dyslexics' writing are reproduced. Dyslexics are
not necessarily clumsy, but it is the exception if they are able to write
neatly. Instruction in how to hold a pen better is more helpful than
physical exercises aimed at overcoming alleged clumsiness or incoordination. The basic problem, however, is a cognitive one, and will not be
overcome by more adequate teaching in penmanship.

The subtle signs of dyslexia which may appear in very young children are
discussed as well as cerebral dominance in dyslexics. The anomaly of
cerebral dominance called crossed laterality is explained. Crossed laterality, i.e., using the right hand to write or throw a ball, but the left
foot for kicking and the left eye for one-eyed sighting, or some other
combination of these, is described as the result of a lack of firm superiority of one half of the brain over the other. The underlying physiological cause is obscure. That crossed laterality is a detriment to the
learning process is a myth. Results of studies of cerebral dominance in
children with reading problems are presented.

Dyslexia may be either mild or severe. How well the child will respond
to treatment depends on many factors. Favorable circumstances for improvement are: (1) a good native intellectual level; (2) early diagnosis;
(3) a sympathetic attitude on the part of teachers and parents; (4) availability of good remedial teaching; and (5) a powerful drive to suceed.

Many factors complicate treatment. Most common are: (1) a bilingual
background; (2) changes in schools so that education is inconsistent; and
(3) inadequate teaching techniques. Problems commonly faced by the adult
dyslexic are discussed. Variants of dyslexia, including such problems
as poor spelling or arithmetical ability, are discussed. It is concluded
that the isolation of subtypes of dyslexia is a project for further study.
The clinical symptoms referred to as "soft" neurological signs, often
mentioned but rarely explained, are discussed and explained. It is concluded that developmental dyslexia is treatable and that its most likely
cause is delay in maturation of the parts of the brain concerned with
reading skills.

95 Crosby, Robert MacGonigle Nelson. "Reading: the dyslexic child."
     <u>Todays Educ</u> 60(7): 46-48, October, 1971. (0 References).

Defines dyslexia as inability to read because of neurological "misfunc-
tion." The term should be used only to indicate reading disability caused
by specific, demonstrable neurological abnormalities. Unfortunately, it
has been used in other contexts, resulting in great confusion. Dyslexia
is not a disease but a complex state, or dysfunction, of multiple types.
All dyslexic children do not appear to be the same. The teacher is the
basic unit of the team that also includes the psychologist and the neurologist. Preventing emotional trauma is the most important aspect in treating the dyslexic child. Parents, school administrators, school boards,
and the community all have special responsibilities to dyslexics. These
are discussed.

96 Crosby, Robert MacGonigle Nelson with Liston, Robert A. "Dyslexia:
    what you can--and can't--do about it." Grade Teach 86(6): 74-88,
    February, 1969. (0 References).
Considers dyslexia as a neurological impairment which makes it difficult
for the child to perceive shapes and sounds. The dysfunctions are minor,
but highly debilitating because they make learning to read and write
difficult. Dyslexics can almost always read to some extent. Dyslexia
occurs much more often in boys than in girls. It may be genetic in origin, and may have some relationship to left-handedness. The condition
may improve as maturation progresses. Symptoms of the condition and diagnostic procedures are described. It is the teacher's responsibility to
treat the condition.

97 Davidson, C. "Dyslexia, an educational problem." Mod Teach 4:
    48-51, April, 1969.

98 Dearborn, Walter F. "The nature of special abilities and disabili-
    ties." Sch Soc 31(802): 632-36, May 10, 1930. (0 References).
Disabilities in reading and learning may develop when the naturally left-
handed child must learn the right-handed movements of hand and eye required by our reading and writing. Disabilities may also occur when
lateral dominance is not established and the word images stored in the
mind are faulty. When faced with these problems, the intelligent child
frequently compensates by developing special mechanical, artistic, or
mathematical skill.

99 De Hirsch, Katrina. "Are hyperlexics dyslexics?" J Spec Educ 5(3):
    243-45, Fall, 1971. (18 References).
Contends that hyperlexic children (those who have a skill at word-calling
with little comprehension) are in fact dyslexic. Reading is much more
than word-calling. Hyperlexics and dyslexics are not at opposite poles
of the reading continuum. Hyperlexics do poorly on many aspects of
language and abstract behavior including the verbal section of the WISC,
where their scores tend to be lower than on the performance section.
Hyperlexics are a special instance within the larger category of reading
disability. The term "hyperlexic" is unfortunate because it diverts
attention from the problem of poor reading comprehension and its implication for later school failure.

100 ————. "Specific dyslexia or strephosymbolia." Folia Phoniatr
    4: 231-48, 1952. (54 References).
Specific dyslexia is an associative disorder. Learning to read requires
forming new associations between the printed letter and the sound it
represents. Inability to form letter-sound associations is at the root
of every reading difficulty. It should not be confused with learning

disability which may have a number of causes. Dyslexia and learning disabilities are different conditions. There is a familial element in specific dyslexia. Dyslexic children show immaturities in their nervous systems. They may be hyperkinetic. Treatment should be aimed at reinforcing associations. For children who have trouble with organization of visual patterns, the whole-word, or look-and-say teaching method is harmful. Phonetic techniques are better. Early diagnosis is important.

101 Dinkmeyer, Don, et al. Personalization--individualization for learning: a conference report. Conference on Personalization-Individualization for Learning, Cheyenne, Wyoming, October 10-11, 1968. 1969. 46p. (ED 035 017).
Presents papers by Don Dinkmeyer and Alex Bannatyne. Among topics discussed are children considered as individuals in the school; the role of the teacher in developing self-concept in his pupils; and the school administrator's role in guidance of pupils. Dyslexia and neurological dysfunction are explained by Bannatyne, as are diagnosis, testing procedures, and teaching techniques.

102 "Dyslexia." Br Med J 4(5999): 724-25, December 27, 1975. (2 References).
Two main types of reading disorder exist: general reading backwardness and specific reading retardation. The former affects both boys and girls, and occurs most often in children with other learning problems who come from large families and lower social classes. Abnormal neurological findings are common. Specific reading retardation affects three times more boys than girls; is rarely associated with neurological abnormality; and occurs in children who are average or good in other school skills. Such children do not have all the characteristics listed in the World Federation of Neurology definition of dyslexia. Indeed, doubt has arisen that specific dyslexia actually exists. There may be a constitutional reason for specific reading retardation, but it appears likely that it involves multiple causes. Educational and remedial implications for the two groups are uncertain but important. Treatment should probably be different.

103 Ellingson, Careth. The shadow children: a book about children's learning disorders. Chicago, Illinois: Topaz Books, 1967. 254p. (Bibliography).
"Shadow children" are those who are unable to learn in the regular classroom environment. They are in the gray area between normal and abnormal. They are unable to function comfortably in the world of the normal, and they cannot expect the special treatment accorded the abnormal. Shadow children include those suffering from dyslexia and minimal brain dysfunction. Causes and symptoms of these conditions are described. Testing, diagnosis, and techniques for teaching these children are discussed. More than half the book consists of a directory of public and private agencies that provide testing, diagnostic, and educational services to children with learning disorders. Agencies are listed by state.

104 "The eye and learning disabilities." Sight Sav Rev 41(4): 183-84, Winter, 1971. (15 References).
Presents a joint organizational statement prepared by several pediatric and ophthalmological professional groups stating five conclusions reached after review of the eye and visual training in the treatment of dyslexia and associated learning disabilities. A multidisciplinary approach is necessary. Eye care should not be carried out in isolation when the

patient has a reading problem. No peripheral eye defect produces dyslexia and associated learning disabilities; eye defects do not produce
reversals of letters, words, or numbers. No known scientific evidence
supports claims for improving reading ability of dyslexic children by use
of visual training or neurologic organizational training. Glasses do not
help dyslexics in the absence of true correctable ocular defects. Teaching dyslexic children is a problem for educational science.

105 "Eyes trick poor reader." Sci Dig 21(2): 65-66, February, 1947.
     (0 References).
Children who have dyslexia (inability to learn to read by usual methods)
may confuse similarly shaped letters, and read "pot" for "top," etc.
Children may become rebellious and delinquent because of it. A very
common condition, reading difficulty is estimated to exist in 8 to 25
percent of all children. Stuttering and other speech defects may be
present. About four times as many males are affected as females.

106 Faigel, Harris C. "Dyslexia (continued)." Pediatrics 45(2): 344-
     45, February, 1970. (6 References).
Letter to the editor with reply, commenting on Snyder and Mortimer (Item
No. 202). Dyslexia is not a single well-defined entity. Examples are
cited of dyslexics who have achieved in the academic, business, and professional worlds. Early diagnosis is emphasized. Physicians who care
for children should be thoroughly familiar with the syndrome. A reply
is included from Snyder and Mortimer in which it is agreed that many dyslexics do achieve, and study of these persons might provide clues to
proper management of the problem. Dyslexia is frequently seen as part of
a broader language problem. The benefits of attempts at identification
before school age are questioned. Young children want very much to be
normal, and any process that singles a child out as abnormal should be
used with caution. The reply contains one reference.

107 Fazekas, Joseph F., and Haugan, Gertrude M. "Developmental dyslexia."
     Med Ann DC 38(6): 313-16, June, 1969. (9 References).
Presents six case histories with general discussion of the causes of dyslexia. The condition remains confusing to those attempting to treat it.
Early and precise diagnosis is important. Treatment should be governed
by the diagnosis, not aimed at merely relieving symptoms. The family of
a dyslexic should be acquainted with the true nature of dyslexia to avoid
confusing it with mental retardation. No generally accepted remedial
method is yet available, but the outlook is good for those diagnosed and
treated at early ages.

108 Ford, Frank R. "Developmental word blindness and mirror writing."
     In: Diseases of the nervous system in infancy, childhood and
     adolescence. 6th ed. Springfield, Illinois: Thomas, 1973. 130-
     34. (14 References).
Defines congenital word blindness as the inability of the child to learn
the meaning of graphic symbols. He is thus unable to make proper progress
in learning to read and write even though application, vision, and intelligence are normal. The condition is common, especially in schools where
modern teaching methods are employed. It is not known whether there is
a defect in the cerebral cortex. The dysfunction has been attributed to
genetic factors. Clinical features include confusion of letters with
similar form but differing orientation, as "p" and "q," reversals of
letters and words, and grossly defective spelling. Dyslexic children
appear normal until they enter school. They usually have no difficulty

in understanding what is said to them. Characteristic features of their
writing are described. Dominance of the left hand is not so important as
left-eye dominance in these cases. Factors that must be considered in
diagnosis are discussed. Treatment depends on a skilled teacher. There
is usually slow improvement even in severe cases. Old-fashioned teaching
methods of learning the alphabet, then words and sentences, are generally
best.

109 Freeman, J. D. J. "Reading difficulties in childhood." Trans
     Ophthalmol Soc UK 77: 611-13, 1957. (5 References).
Typical word blindness may involve the inability to appreciate the significance of visual symbols. Words may be perceived as wholes, as if
they were pictures or objects, and small differences overlooked. The
cause of dyslexia is unknown. Treatment is difficult. Phonetic teaching methods are applicable. The child should copy from written text
rather than from dictation. These children should accompany normal children in the classroom. The difficulties will be gradually overcome.

110 Freshour, Frank W. "Dyslexia: a sure cure." Elem Engl 51(6):
     864-65, 893, September, 1974. (0 References).
Believes the term "dyslexia" should be abandoned: it has been misused
for years. Assorted self-proclaimed experts misuse the term and other
similar ones. It is an umbrella term currently in vogue. "Dyslexia"
lets everyone off the hook: surely no one is responsible if the child
is dyslexic. Perceptual materials like templates and tracing, balance
boards, drugs, creeping and crawling, eye-hand dominance, and other
methods which have little or no relation to reading are suggested as
treatment. Many methods are perpetuated by those who stand to profit
from continued use of the term "dyslexia." The child's reading probably
does improve, not because of the treatment, but because of the individual
attention. the child received. The sure-fire cure for "dyslexia" is to
cease using the term. Educators should find out the child's needs and
plan a program to meet them.

111 Friedenberg, Harold L. "Dyslexia! How come you do me like you do?"
     J Am Optom Assoc 41(2): 158-61, February, 1970. (5 References).
Cites and explains the concepts advanced by various authors who approach
the subject of dyslexia from several points of view. Also expressed is
concern for the child labeled "dyslexic." Dyslexia is seen as a descriptive entity that has produced anxiety, trepidation, challenges, hand-
wringing, and confusion among parents, teachers, and others working with
children.

112 Gallagher, J. Roswell. "Can't spell, can't read." Atl Mon 181:
     35-39, June, 1948. (0 References).
Poor reading and writing skill is not the same as disability. The term
"specific language disability" should be applied only to children who
read and write below their general level of intelligence, and who come
from families where this tendency is manifested. One boy in ten is handicapped by language disability. The causes are not proved. The condition
appears to be increasing, probably because many more persons go beyond
fourth grade than formerly. To prevent the development of language disability, diagnosis should be made in the first year of school. Immature
children should not be forced to learn to read until more mature, and
should be taught to read by the phonetic method.

113 ————. "Specific language disability (dyslexia)." Clin Proc
     Child Hosp DC 16(1): 3-15, January, 1960. (33 References).
Defines specific language disability as a condition in which it is very
difficult for the child to learn to read and spell, although he is intelligent otherwise and usually does better in arithmetic. He tends to
reproduce language in an unusual fashion. The cause is unknown, but
probably it is some disturbance of neurological function. The condition
is described and some of the published studies are reviewed. Diagnostic
procedures are outlined. Early detection is advised to avoid school
problems.

114 Godfrey, C. M. "Cerebral dysfunction in children." Appl Ther
     11(11): 573-74, November, 1969. (5 References).
Dyslexia has been called an area of "neuropsychiatric darkness." Diagnosis of cerebral dysfunction is difficult, but it can be made by known
clinical procedures if the physician is prepared to believe such a condition may be present. Frequently, reading retardation is the chief complaint. Other symptoms and suggestions for remedial programs are described.

115 Gofman, Helen P., and Allmond, Bayard W., Jr. "Learning and language
     disorders in children. I. The preschool child." Curr Probl
     Pediatr 1(10): 3-45, August, 1971. (45 References).
In an entire journal issue devoted to the topic, some general concepts—
both theoretical and practical—of the language disorders of children
are considered. They are intended primarily for the physician who works
with children presenting learning and language development difficulties.
Terminology and definitions are set forth; the normal child's language
development is outlined; and tests for screening for deviant language
development are listed and explained. Deviations in language development
which may cause difficulties for the child, the child's own temperamental
differences, and the central nervous system development necessary to learn
to read, write, and spell are all discussed.

116 Goldstein, Raphael. "The problem of reading disabilities." Clin
     Pediatr 3(2): 105-7, February, 1964. (15 References).
Defines dyslexia as exaggerated difficulty in learning to read in a person of otherwise normal intellectual, emotional, and neurologic constitu-
tion. This definition eliminates reading disabilities stemming from
environmental causes, mental retardation, or physical problems. The disagreement on definitions probably is the reason for the frequent wide
variation (1 to 15 percent) in the estimates of the occurrence of reading
disability. Primary congenital dyslexia can often lead to secondary psychological difficulties. Conditions to expect upon clinical examination
of children with dyslexia are discussed. Children who suffer brain
lesions in the dominant hemisphere, and lose the ability to speak, usually
make good recoveries if the nondominant hemisphere has not been affected.
This being the case, the outlook for victims of dyslexia appears favorable. Rehabilitation should be similar to that for an aphasic patient.
The aim of treatment should be to transfer function to the nondominant
side. No single method for teaching reading to dyslexics can be used.
A diversity of methods is always employed.

117 Gomez, Manuel R. "Specific learning disorders in childhood."
     Psychiatr Ann 2(5): 49-65, May, 1972.
Discusses specific learning disorders in terms of: (1) definition; (2)
etiology; and (3) educational remediation. The symptoms and treatment

of developmental dyslexia, writing disability, dyscalculia, drawing disability, and dyspraxia are also considered.

118 Gow, David. "The measure of success--how confidence grows through improved skills: 'dear mon and dab'." Indep Sch Bull 32(2): 36-38, December, 1972. (0 References).
Defines "dyslexia" as a Greek-derived term indicating an abnormal difficulty in handling words, especially in learning to read. Symptoms are listed and explained through the use of the case of Michael, a fourteen-year-old dyslexic. Teaching methods for teen-age dyslexics, most of them boys now embarrassed and unhappy after years of school failure, are described. Tremendous effort is required in two areas: conquest of the boy's academic handicaps, and overcoming negative attitudes. Oral instruction and enormous amounts of practice, drill, and repetition are stressed. Teachers need great patience and a thorough grasp of the problem. Special techniques of instruction are necessary. The dyslexic does best in a highly structured environment with little free time to worry and indulge in self-pity. Athletics are important as an outlet for frustration and as a means for building confidence and self-respect.

119 Graff, Mary; Scott, William E.; Stehbens, James A. "The physician and reading problems." Am J Dis Child 128(4): 516-20, October, 1974. (50 References).
Acquaints the practicing physician with current concepts on the causes and treatment of dyslexia. The manifestations and causes remain ambiguous. The dyslexic child may never completely overcome his problem. Special teaching techniques are available, and are described. The physician can play an important role in the treatment of the dyslexic child, and as a counselor to the child and his family.

120 Gutelius, Margaret F., and Layman, Emma M. "Reading disability, or developmental dyslexia." Clin Proc Child Hosp DC 16(1): 15-27, January, 1960. (26 References).
Defines developmental dyslexia as the inability of a child to read at a level commensurate with his general intelligence and educational opportunity. The history of recognition of the problem and typical characteristics of the condition are presented. Causes are numerous and may be "nonspecific," including factors such as poor health, poor teaching, or emotional problems. "Specific" causes include factors such as faulty cerebral dominance, cerebral defects, or developmental lags. Suggestions are made for diagnosis, prevention, and treatment of dyslexia. The physician's duty is to provide advice and reassurance to both parents and child. Private tutoring for several years is recommended.

121 Hagger, T. D. "Congenital word blindness or specific developmental dyslexia: a review." Med J Aust 1(19): 783-89, May 11, 1968. (26 References).
In classifying reading disabilities, specific developmental dyslexia is a condition for which a cause has not been established. It is defined as excluding cases of reading disability caused by mental retardation, sensory deprivation, inadequate schooling, and emotional or social problems: these are more easily dealt with because the cause is known. Few facts about the cause of specific developmental dyslexia are known, but the influence of sex and heredity, and disturbances of cerebral dominance are clearest. Early diagnosis, before secondary emotional disturbance occurs, is of urgent importance. The treatment of dyslexics in the regular classroom is discussed. Phonetics is preferred to the whole-word

recognition method. More information on remedial techniques for these
children is needed.

122   Hallahan, Daniel Patrick, and Kauffman, James. Introduction to
      learning disabilities: a psycho-behavioral approach. Englewood
      Cliffs, New Jersey: Prentice-Hall, 1976. 310p. (Bibliography
      p. 267-99). (Prentice-Hall Special Education Series).
This book is a general discussion of learning disabilities, including the
historical background of the concept. Distinction is made among learning disabilities, emotional disturbance, and educable mental retardation.
Although dyslexia as such is not the book's primary focus, much material
is included on visual perceptual disabilities, and on visual-motor, motor,
tactual, and kinesthetic disabilities (problems concerned with the coordination of the eyes and the hands). Language disabilities are also
considered. Discussion of distractibility, hyperactivity, and learning
problems arising from social-emotional disorders is also included. A
bibliography of thirty-three pages covers items in a wide area of relevant literature.

123   "Helping the youngster with a reading disorder. Exploring one prob-
      lem common to education, psychology, and mental health: summary of
      a conference." Clin Pediatr 10(4): 13A-14A, April, 1971. (0
      References).
From 10 to 20 percent of United States schoolchildren suffer from reading problems that can be helped with better instruction. Another 5 percent of all United States schoolchildren suffer from specific types of
reading problems which cannot be helped by presently known methods. Children born prematurely and those who are slow to learn to talk are more
likely to have reading difficulties. Reading performance as a function
of cerebral activity, the relationship of sex to reading problems, and
teaching approaches are discussed.

124   Holt, L. Emmett. "Reading disability in children." Good House-
      keeping 141: 122-23, July, 1955. (0 References).
Describes the symptoms of specific reading disability including frequent
left-handedness, stuttering, reversing letters and syllables, confused
spelling, immature handwriting, and seeking friends among younger children. A reading-disabled child is not stupid. With proper remedial
reading instruction he can compete with his peers. The general principle
employed in remedial reading emphasizes phonetics, the exact relation
between the sound and the written word.

125   Hood, Joyce. "Poor readers." Todays Educ 63(3): 37-39, September-
      October, 1974. (0 References).
Children with reading disability are those whose reading power is less
than their general learning power, in spite of the fact that they have
had adequate instruction and home environment and no physical or emotional
problems. Reversals of letters and words, left-right confusion, poor
handwriting and spelling, problems with time and space relationships, and
short attention span characterize such children. "Dyslexia" appears to
be a better term than "minimal brain dysfunction" (MBD) to describe these
children in the presence of diagnosable brain damage or dysfunction. The
term "reading disability" is applicable in the case of severe reading
difficulties with no identifiable cause. Instructional procedures should
be the same whether or not brain damage is diagnosed. No simple cure
exists for dyslexic or disabled readers. Schools can help these children
by gearing the rate of instruction to their rate of learning. Dyslexics
and disabled readers should weigh carefully the decision to go to college.

126 Houghton, V. P. "Why dyslexia?" In: <u>International Reading Sympo-</u>
    <u>sium, 2d, College of St. Mark and St. John, 1965.</u> Edited by John
    Downing, and Amy L. Brown. London: Cassell, 1967. 261-73. (19
    References).
The definitions of "dyslexia" appear to be such that diagnosis is made
largely by elimination. The term is often criticized as being merely
descriptive, and the description has been confused with explanation.
Personality and environment play a part in reading failure. It is a mistake to regard a child's intelligence as absolutely fixed and incapable
of being improved with instruction. Some children of very low intelligence (IQs from 25 to 50) can read some, a condition termed "eulexic."
It is reported that an overwhelming majority of educational psychologists
working in remedial reading clinics who were asked if they found the
concept of dyslexia helpful in working with the children replied that
they did not. It is concluded that if there were more knowledge of the
condition, it would be possible to help the children more.

127 Hughes, John Malcolm. <u>Reading and reading failures</u>. London: Evans
    Bros., 1975. 248p. (Bibliography p. 232-41).

128 "Inability to read." <u>Sci News Lett</u> 62(16): 255, October 18, 1952.
    (0 References).
If a child shows an obvious dread and hate of school accompanied sometimes by indigestion or other physical symptoms, parents should look
carefully into his reading ability. "Dyslexia" is defined as the medical
term for inability to read. Some of the factors interfering with ability
to read include low intelligence, bad hearing, poor vision, and strephosymbolia, or mixed symbols. Much more strephosymbolic dyslexia exists
in schools where the flash method is used to teach reading than in schools
where instruction is individualized. The approach to the problem should
be a correct diagnosis; giving the child plenty of love and attention;
and less emphasis on school and reading with concentration in another
field where the child has skills.

129 Ingram, T. T. S. "The dyslexic child." <u>Practitioner</u> 192(1150):
    503-16, April, 1964. (19 References).
Discusses the diagnosis, causes, and management of children with specific
dyslexia. Specific dyslexia is defined as difficulty in learning to read
and write in children who are not backward in other school subjects. It
affects only a minority of those having trouble learning to read and
write. Teachers should refer children for help early. The causes of
specific dyslexia are usually multiple, and act cumulatively to produce
the educational handicap. Diagnosis is simplified if there is a standard
procedure of study. Family background, neurological study, and the exact
nature of the difficulties the child is having should all be investigated.
Classifications of specific kinds of errors and difficulties are given.
Management depends on the nature of the difficulties, their severity,
and the extent of anxiety.

130 ————. "Specific dyslexia." <u>Nurs Times</u> 60(43): 1386-88,
    October, 1964. (6 References).
Describes the causes, symptoms, and management of cases of specific dyslexia. The types of errors made by such children in reading and writing
are described. It is emphasized that children suffering from specific
dyslexia are a minority of all children who have difficulty in learning
to read and write. Although some dyslexics have suffered brain damage
at birth or in early childhood, this is not true in most cases. Familial

tendencies to reading and spelling difficulties are common. Proper assessment requires both medical and psychological examination. Dyslexics often
develop unhealthy attitudes toward school and teachers. The first step
in treatment should be to explain the nature of his learning disabilities
to the child, his parents, and his teachers.

131 ————. "Specific learning difficulties in childhood." Public
      Health 79(2): 70-80, January, 1965. (19 References).
Considers factors involved in the processes of reading and writing. The
observations and conclusions about dyslexia given in early literature on
the topic (late nineteenth and early twentieth centuries) are considered,
as well as those of more recent studies. Reading and writing errors made
by dyslexic children are listed and described. Normal children make reversal errors or have difficulty associating spoken and written sounds
at age five or six. Dyslexic children continue to make these types of
mistakes much longer, sometimes into adult life. Reading errors may also
be classified as visuo-spatial, correlating, or speech-sound difficulties.
These terms are explained. Dyslexia patients can be grouped by cause as
those having brain malformation or damage, and those whose dyslexia is
genetically determined. Dyslexics can also be divided between those whose
speech development was normal, and those in whom it was not. Suggestions
are made for treating dyslexic children.

132 Ingram, T. T. S., and Mason, Mrs. A. W. "Reading and writing diffi-
      culties in childhood." Br Med J 2(5459): 463-65, August 21, 1965.
      (8 References).
Discusses the recognition and diagnosis of reading problems by teachers
or physicians. Medical and psychological information which should be
obtained for assessment of the child is discussed. Causes include mental
retardation, brain damage, specific dyslexia and dysgraphia, and environmental conditions. Suggestions for in-depth management are beyond the
scope of the article, but remedial approaches are covered briefly.

133 Jampolsky, Arthur; Grow, Kenneth A.; Shirley, Hale F.; et al. "Read-
      ing disabilities in children; a symposium." Calif Med 83(2): 79-
      88, August, 1955. (11 References).
Includes presentations on ophthalmological factors in reading disabilities; the implications of pressure to read before the child is ready to
do so; the problems of slow learners; confused cerebral dominance; poor
visual memory; emotional factors; and incorrect teaching methods. Corrective measures are outlined.

134 Jani, Subhash N. "Dyslexia: a summary of representative views."
      J Assoc Study Percept 8(2): 30-37, Fall, 1973. (11 References).
Presents a summary of the definitions of dyslexia given by nine authorities in the field, and the definition of the World Federation of Neurology
given in 1968. Included is Bannatyne's hierarchial classification of
the causes and types of dyslexia. The article also presents the definitions of Critchley, Rabinovitch, Goldberg, McGlannon, Johnson and
Myklebust, Hartstein, Kephart, and Keeney and Keeney.

135 Jastak, Joseph. "Understanding the non-reader." Ment Hyg 23(2):
      228-40, April, 1939. (0 References).
Intelligence and reading ability are somewhat independent of each other.
Lack of opportunity to learn to read does not account entirely for failure
of some persons to do so. Reading disability is not the only characteristic of nonreaders. A cluster of symptoms usually is found in persons

who have difficulty in learning to read. Reversal tendencies, speech
defects, poor directional orientation, and limited vocabulary characterize them. The nonreader is not verbal, but a "born" mechanic. Mixed
laterality may be the cause. Nonreaders can be taught to read. Phonetic
methods are advised; many reading problems are caused by using the "look-
and-guess" method of teaching reading.

136 Jervey, J. W. "Reading difficulty in children." J SC Med Assoc
     47(10): 363-65, October, 1951. (40 References).
Outlines the causes, diagnosis, and treatment of dyslexia. All children
want to learn, and all children of average intelligence with reading
difficulties can be taught to read. Phonetic methods of teaching are
better for dyslexic children than flash methods. The best educated and
highest paid teachers should be in the primary grades. The child will
probably improve under special tutoring by any method because of the very
fact that something is being done for him.

137 Kemp, Elizabeth A. "Reading disorders in childhood." Med J Aust
     2(19): 678-79, November 9, 1957. (0 References).
Distinguishes three types of reading disability among well-motivated
children with adequate opportunity for education: the immature child
slightly slower than his peers; the child with a generalized language
disability; and the child whose difficulty is so severe that it appears
to be some sort of mental crippling. It is suggested that the child is
better served if parental criticism and nagging could be eased, and less
emphasis placed on book learning while more emphasis is given to training in other skills.

138 Kephart, Newell C. "Let's not misunderstand dyslexia." Instructor
     78(1): 62-63, August-September, 1968. (0 References).
Considers five areas of misunderstanding about dyslexia: (1)"Dyslexia"
and "learning disability" are not synonymous terms. (2) Dyslexics can
be helped by parents and teachers. (3) Perception and language are both
involved in reading. (4) All dyslexics do not have the same problem.
(5) Treatment cannot be limited to a single approach.

139 Keys, Marshall P. "Dyslexia and reading disorders." In: Kelley,
     Vincent C., ed. Practice of pediatrics. Vol. 4(Part 2), Chap. 57A.
     Hagerstown, Maryland: Harper & Row, 1977. 10p. (11 References).
The physician should not withdraw from the patient with reading disability.
If he does, the silence is taken as approval for the many spurious cure-
alls being put forward. Secondary reading disabilities may be caused by
delayed maturation, emotional problems, seizures states, limited intelligence, environmental deprivation, or physical handicaps. Primary reading
disability, or dyslexia, excludes all the secondary causes, and assumes
normal motivation. Dyslexia involves an acquired neurologic deficit involving the dominant hemisphere. Learning disability is discussed in
terms of four basic functions: input, integration (i.e., sequencing and
interpreting of information), memory, and output. Suggestions for diagnosis are made. General physical and neurologic examination; questioning
about school performance; and a general ophthalmologic examination may
be included. Special education, medication, and psychotherapy are acceptable treatments. Warnings are given against controversial therapies
including such methods as "visual training" and reorganization of neurologic development. Areas of concern emphasized are that there is no
single best approach to the treatment of reading disorders; and that dyslexia is not produced by a peripheral eye defect. Treatment directed

only toward visual training deprives the child of proper multidisciplinary
treatment, wastes money, and delays proper instruction.

140 Kirk, Winifred D. "The relationship of reading disabilities to learn-
        ing disabilities." J Spec Educ 9(2): 133-37, Summer, 1975. (8
        References).
Argues that categorization of the problem of disabled readers into two
fields of study--reading and learning disabilities--may have created a
spurious dichotomy and mistaken presentation of both fields. Not all
reading problems are of concern to the learning disabilities field. Poor
teaching, emotional disturbance, poor school attendance, and other extrinsic problems produce reading problems, but they are not the primary
concern of the learning disabilities specialist. The specialist is concerned with intrinsic bases of the problem such as central processing
difficulties. The distinction between corrective and remedial reading
programs, definitions of dyslexia, and the effects of a "learning-disabled"
label are discussed. Task analysis as a diagnostic procedure required
by both fields is discussed. It is suggested that terminology is a
stumbling block to understanding possible differences between the two
fields. Such differences may arise mainly from a difference in emphasis,
and the two fields may be closer together than they appear.

141 Klasen, Edith. The syndrome of specific dyslexia; with special
        consideration of its physiological, psychological, testpsychological,
        and social correlates. Baltimore, Maryland: University Park Press,
        1972. 235p. (Bibliography of 153 entries).
Translated from the German, where it was published under the title Das
Syndrom der Legasthenie, this book reviews an extensive literature on the
observable characteristics and causes of dyslexia. Included are such
aspects as the relationship of dyslexia to speech disorders, laterality,
sensory perception, and psychological factors. Psychoanalytical theories
as to cause, and the value of psychotherapy in the treatment of dyslexia
are considered. Findings on the WISC and other intelligence measures
are given. The viewpoint is that dyslexia occurs at all levels of intelligence. Conclusions are based on the study and statistical analysis
of the records of 500 dyslexics at the Ellen K. Rascob Learning Institute,
Oakland, California. There is a warning against oversimplification. At
present, dyslexia must be regarded as a syndrome having multiple causes.
There is no such thing as the dyslexic: "We only find an individual
with all his uniqueness who suffers from dyslexia."

It was found that failing readers were weak in three test areas on the
WISC: arithmetic, digit span, and digit symbol. Since such weakness
characterizes the brain-injured, it strengthens the hypothesis that neurological disorders play a frequent role in dyslexia. Anxiety was the most
frequently observed psychopathological symptom. Environmental factors
seemed to contribute least to the learning problems in the sample studied.
No significant correlations were observed between socioeconomic family
situation, working mothers, birth order, or other environmental considerations. The bibliography includes German and English works.

142 Kolson, Clifford J., and Kaluger, George. Clinical aspects of
        remedial reading. Springfield, Illinois: Thomas, 1963. 146p.
        (Bibliography).
Remedial readers are defined as those who cannot be helped in the regular
classroom. They are divided into two groups: primary and secondary
reading disability. The primary group includes children who have dyslexia

(difficulty in reading); dysgraphia (difficulty in writing); dyscalculia
(difficulty in arithmetic); trouble with right-left orientation; and
agnosia (inability to recognize configurations). The defect is constitutional (part of the child's fundamental makeup), and may be familial in
origin. These children fail in reading unless a method using visual,
auditory, kinesthetic, and tactile reinforcement is used. Secondary
reading disability is acquired, and may arise from physiological, intellectual, sociological, or emotional factors. Reading-disabled children
respond to remedial treatment, and can be returned to the regular classroom. Causes and methods of diagnosis and treatment for both primary
and secondary disabilities are set forth in detail. The advantages of
early identification and prevention of reading problems are discussed.
Descriptions of the various kinds of reading clinics are given.

143 Krise, Morley. "The child who is deficient in reading." Northwest
     Med 59(11): 1391-92, November, 1960. (0 References).
Deficient reading problem cases are children who read better on lower
levels, but who do not read well on any level. Such a child is not just
behind in reading; he is sick or confused in his reading. A healthy
teacher-pupil relationship is necessary before the child's reading can
be improved. One teaching technique is as good as another if it rests on
a base of acquaintance with children and focuses on helping the child to
school success as soon as possible. Many causes are proposed, but it is
suggested that the real one is a deficiency in a "basic innate language
capacity." If this is true, the outlook is not bright. However, they
warrant all the help we can give them. They can become, and remain,
adequate readers.

144 Lerner, Janet W. "Dyslexia or reading disability: a theme by any
     name." Paper presented at Association for Children with Learning
     Disabilities Conference, Fort Worth, Texas, March 6-8, 1969. 1969.
     12p. (ED 028 911).
Reviews the literature and presents the historical development of the term
"dyslexia." Medical and educational viewpoints are outlined. The medical
studies have sought a clear-cut cause. Educators have emphasized many
causes and have explored the developmental sequence of reading skills in
looking for the break in the child's developmental reading pattern.
Medical personnel are likely to emphasize individual treatment. Educators
are more often seeking preventive measures in a reading program for the
entire school. A need is seen for the pooling of thought and research in
the two professions.

145 ————. "Reading and learning disabilities." Elem Engl 50(2):
     265-69, February, 1973. (12 References).
Considers the impact of developments in learning disabilities on the
field of reading. Learning disabilities has emerged as a category within
special education; the field of reading has not. Major areas of interest
in learning disabilities which have an effect on reading include the
process of diagnosis and teaching; motor development; perception; memory;
language; cognitive skills; and maturational, social, and psychological
factors.

146 ————. "Reading disability as a language disorder." Acta Symb
     3(1): 39-45, 1972. (25 References).
Reading disability should be viewed as more than a language disorder.
To gain proper perspective, it should be placed within a global system
of reading. This system contains four dimensions: prerequisites, skills,

the read-learning process, and the teaching of reading. These four concepts are explained.

147 ————. "A thorn by any other name: dyslexia or reading dis-
    ability." Elem Engl 48(1): 75-80, January, 1971. (25 References).
Two bodies of literature, medical and educational, are available concerning dyslexia. Medical studies have concluded, to date, that there is
still no means of clearly identifying the dyslexic child. Educators, in
their attempts to find the causes of reading disability, have seen the
problem in terms of how the child perceives the world and how he learns
to read. It is hoped that authorities will lay aside the various terms
and begin to work together.

148 ————. "Two perspectives: reading and learning disabilities."
    In: Kirk, Samuel A., and McCarthy, Jeanne McRae, eds. Learning
    disabilities: selected ACLD papers. Boston, Massachusetts:
    Houghton Mifflin, 1975. 271-85. (38 References). (Paper pre-
    sented at Association for Children with Learning Disabilities,
    Eleventh International Conference, February 27-March 2, 1974).
Two fields, that of reading and of learning disabilities, present two
perspectives concerning children who are disabled readers. They overlap
in an area called reading problems. Reading problems, for the reading
specialist, are called remedial reading, reading disability, and reading
retardation. Reading problems may be caused by a variety of factors,
including emotional disturbance, mental retardation, sensory handicaps,
and educational deprivation. For the learning disabilities (LD) specialist, reading problems may be referred to as reading disabilities, dyslexia,
or receptive written language disorders. The LD specialist attempts to
rule out the pluralistic causes which concern the reading specialist, and
looks for the cause in brain injury or a central nervous system dysfunction. Some points of difference in approach: the reading specialist
analyzes reading problems in terms of the child's level of reading skills
development or lack of it; the LD specialist is concerned with underlying
mental processing abilities. The reading specialist tends to see remedial
reading programs as similar to those used in good developmental reading
programs; the LD specialist sees the need for highly specialized, specific,
and differentiated approaches to children failing in reading. Some of
the "new" approaches turn out not to be new, e.g., cookies baked in the
shape of letters was a teaching device used in both colonial America and
in 54 B.C.

One group of specialists says there is no such entity as dyslexia. The
LD people are busy at the same time doing research, publishing books,
and holding conferences on it. So great has been the interest by both
the lay public and professionals in dyslexia that the play Forty Carats
includes as part of the American dream getting married, buying a suburban
home, and having a son treated for dyslexia.

With regard to definition, the reading specialist view originated largely
in the United States. It has an educational perspective found in the
writings of educators, psychologists, and reading specialists. The LD
view originated largely in Europe in a medical framework in the writings
of medicine, psychiatry, neurology, ophthalmology, and speech pathology.
The historic development and the nature of the differences in these two
views of dyslexia are reviewed. In eighty years some 20,000 items have
been published on the medical viewpoint. Those writing from the educational viewpoint are unwilling to attribute the cause of the problem to
a single factor--neurological damage. They perceive a multiplicity of

factors in the causes of severe reading disability. The educational view
--that of the reading specialist--sees the label of "dyslexia" as confusing, adding little of diagnostic or therapeutic value.

Task-analysis is another contrasting area. The reading specialist uses
it to evaluate the task: how difficult a book can this child read? The
LD specialist uses task-analysis to evaluate and analyze the processing
abilities required of a child to understand and perform tasks: how does
this child process information?

149 Levin, S. "Compensated dys-perception." S Afr Med J 43(23): 715-
     19, June 7, 1969. (37 References).
"Dys-perception" is one of many labels, including "dyslexia" and "specific
reading disability," applied to the problem affecting children who have
school difficulties. These children have difficulty with spelling, cannot readily distinguish similar objects (e.g., makes of cars), and are
easily disoriented. They get lost easily. They are clumsy and have
poor visual imagery, i.e., they cannot visualize how a rearrangement of
objects would look. It is pointed out that intellectual faculties do
not necessarily depend on perceptual faculties. Conditions such as left-
right confusion, finger agnosia, and visual perceptual disturbances are
all consequences of a deeper disorder. They are associations of dyslexia,
not causes of it. When intelligence level is carefully controlled, no
important relationship exists between right-left discrimination and reading ability. There is a tendency toward spontaneous improvement. Management is difficult. There is no substitute for a good teacher.

150 Levine, Jane B. "Anticipated developments in research on dyslexia."
     Read Teach 23(3): 273, 275, December, 1969. (4 References).
Important progress is expected soon in research on dyslexia, but there
are general obstacles. One is lack of agreement on a definition of the
term "dyslexia." Another is the confusion in terminology used to describe
the condition. Public interest in dyslexia is great. The Secretary of
Health, Education, and Welfare appointed a committee in 1968 to examine
research in the field. It is hoped that a better integrated effort to
coordinate research and publish findings will be forthcoming.

151 ————. "The University of Pennsylvania dyslexia center." In:
     International Reading Association. Conference proceedings: read-
     ing disability and perception. Vol. 13(Part 3). Edited by George
     D. Spache. Newark, Delaware: International Reading Association,
     1969. 46-51. (0 References).
Realizing the great need to create a complete bibliography on dyslexia,
the author took on the responsibility for collecting citations at the
Reading Clinic of the University of Pennsylvania. Among problems encountered were: (1) the rate at which material is being published; (2)
the many different disciplines where material is found, notably medicine,
education, and psychology; and (3) the wide variety of headings in indexes
where relevant material might be located. The need for systematic information-gathering on dyslexia is urgent. It is noted that as of July
1967 there were 331 programs in progress on dyslexia funded by more than
$32 million from the United States Department of Health, Education, and
Welfare.

152 Lightfoot, Dorothy Ingram. "Remedial reading." Hygeia 25(9):
     696-97, 715, September, 1947. (0 References).

Explains Orton's theory of mixed dominance as a cause of reading failure.
No more children who will have difficulty learning to read are being born
now than in previous years. In previous generations children who did not
learn to read adequately dropped out of school. Since such children no
longer drop out, the number of reading-disabled children appears to be
increasing. Actually it is not; circumstances have changed. There is no
foolproof way to prevent reading problems. If a child has not learned
to read adequately by the end of second grade, expert help should be
sought.

153 Lubkin, Virginia. "The ophthalmologist and the reading problem."
     Bull NY Acad Med 44(4): 459-69, April, 1968. (36 References).
Discusses the symptoms of reading disability and analyzes laterality, or
cerebral dominance, and visual perception from the standpoint of the
ophthalmologist's need for awareness of the reading disability problem.
Few cases of reading disability are caused by ophthalmological problems,
but the ophthalmologist must examine them all, and channel dyslexic children to the neurologist, psychologist, educator, or other appropriate
professional for treatment. Secondary emotional problems arising from
reading disabilities are also discussed.

154 McCarthy, James Jerome, and McCarthy, Joan F. Learning disabilities.
     Boston, Massachusetts: Allyn and Bacon, 1969. 138p. (Bibliography
     p. 125-31).
Learning disabilities as used here include dyslexia, dysgraphia, perceptual and neurological handicaps, and autism, among other conditions.
Identification and diagnosis of the causes of retardation, disorder, or
delay in a child's speech, reading, writing, or other language development are covered. Educational procedures are discussed by way of a brief
presentation of the opinions and work of leaders in the field. Various
programs for helping reading-disabled and learning-disabled children are
described. Information on parent groups and on the legislation aimed at
helping such children is included.

155 McCready, E. Bosworth. "Defects in the zone of language (word-
     deafness and word-blindness) and their influence in education and
     behavior." Am J Psychiatry 6(2): 267-77, October, 1926. (19
     References).
Reviews some of the work on aphasic conditions in children including word
blindness. The work of Broadbent, Wallin, and Orton is cited. It is
suggested that word blindness, if uncorrected, may lead to retardation
in school and behavior, and to social difficulties.

156 MacDougall, Ursula Cooke. If your child has reading difficulties...
     New York: Dalton School, 1952. 63p.
Written for parents or others concerned about a problem reader, this book
lists many causes of reading disability including the physical problems
of vision, speech, hearing, and confusion of lateral dominance. Educational and emotional problems and combinations of educational, emotional,
and physical problems are explained as causes. Ways parents and schools
can help the nonreader are discussed. The role of remedial reading
specialists is explained.

157 MacTaggart, M. M. "Reading and writing difficulties." New Era
     19: 194-96, July, 1938.

158 Merritt, John E. "Recent developments in Great Britain." J Read
     17(5): 367-72, February, 1974. (10 References).

Discusses the implications for the teaching of reading in two reports published by the Department of Education and Science in Great Britain in 1972. One concerns special reading difficulties and the other standards of reading. The second probably will have more far-reaching effects as educators try to account for the fact that for ten years there has apparently been no improvement in standards of reading, and possibly even a slight decline. The limitations of the testing are discussed as possible sources of error in the conclusions. What happens in schools where the pupil is given some responsibility for his own learning is discussed. That the teaching of reading has not been more emphasized in English colleges of education is deplored.

The other, the so-called Tizard report, recognizes that there is probably a syndrome of developmental dyslexia with specific underlying cause and symptoms. It recommends using the term "specific reading difficulties" rather than "dyslexia." Many children with such problems have been getting no treatment at all, it is reported, and efficient screening procedures are recommended as routine procedure. The problems of the validity of such screening procedures are considered.

159 Miles, Thomas Richard. The dyslexic child. Hove, Sussex, England: Priory Press, 1974. 140p. (Bibliography).
Beginning with four case studies, this book progresses into sections that attempt to describe what dyslexia is, how it can be recognized, and what can be done about the condition. Causes of dyslexia and the problems encountered in diagnosing it are discussed. Teaching methods are not emphasized, but suggestions on finding a suitable teacher and suitable times and places for remedial work are offered. The outlook for the dyslexic child as he grows up is considered. The viewpoint on dyslexia in general is that it is a constitutional factor, i.e., built into the person's basic makeup either through inheritance or developmental problems very early in life.

160 Millar, Thomas P. "Reading retardation." Northwest Med 59(11): 1385-90, November, 1960. (7 References).
Reading retardation is a very common symptom. Incidence varies from estimates of 10 to 20 percent in American classrooms to as high as 85 percent among delinquents. Educators need help from pediatricians, neurologists, ophthalmologists, psychologists, and psychiatrists in understanding individual cases of reading difficulty. It is called by many names, and there are many theories as to the causes. These include an organic, neurological defect akin to aphasia; developmental lag; or emotional involvements. Rabinovitch's three major groups for purposes of diagnosing reading difficulty are listed and defined: organic causes, and primary and secondary reading retardation. Psychiatric considerations are emphasized, notably the guilts and frustrations of these children. Treatment requires good teaching; love alone will not teach them to read.

161 Moore, Colin E. "Developmental dyslexia." Med J Aust 1(20): 717-20, May 15, 1965. (2 References).
Describes developmental dyslexia as an inborn defect of reading and writing. The specific fault is in the visual interpretation of symbols. The exact cause is not known. Lack of firm left cerebral dominance is suggested. Neurologists are more aware of the condition than are ophthalmologists, although dyslexics may be brought to the latter first. It is important that dyslexics be recognized because of the emotional and

social consequences of the condition. The case history of an eleven-year-old boy is given.

162 Moorehead, Caroline. "Dispelling illusions about dyslexia." Times
     Educ Suppl 2970: 11, April 21, 1972. (0 References).
Reports the attempt of Sandhya Naidoo to dispel two widely held beliefs
in her book, Specific Dyslexia: that everyone naturally learns to read,
and that children who do not are dull. The book is a report of research
done at the Word Blind Centre in London. Most dyslexic children show
unevenness in development. No clear definition of dyslexia can be given.
Victims need specialized teaching.

163 Myklebust, Helmer R., and Johnson, Doris. "Dyslexia in children."
     Except Child 29(1): 14-25, September, 1962. (34 References).
Without doubt dyslexia occurs in children. It is a language disorder in
which the victim cannot relate the printed word to the object or concept
for which the written symbols stand. It has three primary causes: disease, accidents, or heredity. Symptoms of the syndrome include: (1)
lack of orientation as to left and right and the points of the compass;
(2) inability to read maps, blueprints, and similar material; (3) difficulties in appreciating the significance of sequence and time; and (4)
problems in learning to read, write, and spell. Dyslexic children have
difficulty in physical coordination and neurological disturbances. Three
case histories are given. When a precise diagnosis is made, the outlook
for successful treatment of dyslexic children should be good.

164 Newcomb, Daniel L., ed. Proceedings, 1967 International Convocation
     on Children and Young Adults with Learning Disabilities (Pittsburgh,
     Pennsylvania, February 24-26, 1967). 1967. (ED 020 603).
Considers three areas related to learning disabilities: (1) causes and
identification; (2) education and remediation; and (3) rehabilitation
and innovation. Language, reading, and communication disabilities are
among topics discussed. The roles of teachers, pediatricians, and other
concerned specialists are considered.

165 Nicholls, John V. V. "Reading disabilities in the young." J Sch
     Health 39(6): 357-63, June, 1969. (13 References).
Defines and distinguishes the terms "dyslexia" and "slow reader." The
former occurs in children of average or superior intelligence and appears
to be a disturbance in brain function. The slow reader is a child who
has difficulty learning to read because of low intelligence, faulty
vision, or hearing. The slow reader's condition may also be called
"secondary dyslexia." The first condition may be referred to as "congenital or specific dyslexia." Symptoms of both conditions are listed.
Cross dominance appears to have little relation to dyslexia. Treatment
is an educational matter, to a great extent an art. An increasing volume
of literature concerning reading disabilities has appeared in recent
years. Many of the studies have been poorly done and the terminology has
become increasingly confused.

166 Novak, Josephine. Dyslexia: what is it? 1971. 16p. (ED 068 901).
This series of nine articles which appeared in The Baltimore Evening Sun
details methods of identifying and teaching dyslexic children. The
failure of the schools in dealing with dyslexics is discussed. One
article calls attention to the differing views about dyslexia and other
language disabilities. Case histories are presented, and an overview is
given of current methods of research and education.

167 Oettinger, Leon, Jr. "Dyssymbolia: the inability to recognize and
     utilize symbols." <u>Claremont Coll Read Conf Yearb</u> 34: 136-40,
     1970. (0 References).
Each concerned professional looks at reading and its problems and defines
it in his own terms, like the blind men describing the elephant. The
polemics have become such that the real problem is obscured. It is quite
a different thing to tell a story and to write it. The view is expressed
that "dyssymbolia" is the most serious disease of childhood because symbols are the basic tools of our lives. Cultures and their symbols are
intertwined and cannot be separated.

168 Oettinger, Leon, Jr., and Majovski, Lawrence. "Research in learning
     disabilities." <u>Claremont Coll Read Conf Yearb</u> 37: 173-80, 1973.
     (33 References).
This report on the highlights of research in learning disabilities points
out that findings in regard to the specialization of the cerebral hemispheres puts in doubt the usefulness of such treatments for reading disability as Frostig and Kephart have advocated. Dyslexic children do not
make special mistakes, but simply more of every kind of mistake than
normal readers. Attempts to assess immaturity in dyslexic children have
been carried out by assessing bone age. Drugs have also been used in
attempts to improve learning ability. Reading and reading aloud should
be distinguished since the latter may be done with little understanding.
The same distinction may be made between writing and drawing. More research is needed in early education methods before they can be of real
help in relieving dyslexia and other problems.

169 Otto, Wayne; Peters, Nathaniel A.; Peters, Charles W. <u>Reading prob-</u>
     <u>lems: a multidisciplinary perspective</u>. Reading, Massachusetts:
     Addison-Wesley, 1977. 457p. (Bibliography).

170 Paul, Samuel E. "Specific language disabilities." <u>J Sch Health</u>
     34(5): 240-41, May, 1964. (0 References).
Describes the symptoms of reading disability or "strephosymbolia." First-
grade teachers should be alert to the disorder. Delay in treatment
causes frustration and behavior problems. Phonics methods of instruction
appear to achieve good results with reading-disabled children.

171 Pearse, Benjamin H. "Dyslexia: what is it? What's being done
     about it?" <u>Am Educ</u> 5(4): 9-13, April, 1969. (0 References).
Describes dyslexia and some methods for helping reading-disabled children.
Early diagnosis is a most important factor. A diagnosis of dyslexia does
not mean that the child is retarded. There is disagreement on a definition for the term, but the disorder in ability to learn is widespread.
Some authorities believe as many as 20 percent of schoolchildren are
affected to some degree. The United States Department of Health, Education, and Welfare now supports more than 300 programs dealing with the
problem, most of them at colleges and universities. Two forms of dyslexia are now generally recognized: primary, or developmental dyslexia
reflecting a neurological malfunction; and secondary, or reactive dyslexia, caused by external factors in the environment or emotional climate.
Causes usually overlap so that no single cause can be isolated. Methods
for improving a child's sense of direction and motor coordination, and
some diagnostic methods are described.

172 Pinkerton, Florence. "Dyslexia." <u>Br Med J</u> 1(6009): 587, March 6,
     1976. (0 References).

Letter to editor. Doubt no longer exists that the syndrome of dyslexia exists. Doctors should reassure parents of dyslexic children that the children do not have some terrible brain disease, and, with patience and suitable management, can be expected to learn to read. At the first school medical examination it would be helpful in identifying children who are at high risk of having difficulty in learning to read if the level of speech development, motor coordination, and laterality could be noted. Diagnosis of dyslexia may be medical, but treatment is educational.

173   "Poor readers' problems highlighted." Times Educ Suppl 3177:   10,
        April 23, 1976. (0 References).
Based on findings derived from the Schonell Silent Reading Test A, a report by the Association of Remedial Teachers of Ireland estimates that some 22 percent of children entering post-primary schools in Ireland have reading difficulties. The report stands to be criticized by the Irish National Teachers Organization. The survey finds that more boys than girls are affected, and that more children from lower socioeconomic groups are likely to have reading problems. Children with reading difficulties tend to be older than the normal age of about twelve when entering post-primary school. Recommendations include better remedial programs; changes in the system for transferring pupils from primary to post-primary schools; and changes in the system of governmental examination for assessing students.

174   Porter, N. M. "Nonreader." Sch Community 47(9):   12, 14, May,
        1961. (0 References).
Briefly discusses the nonreader in terms of: (1) definition; (2) potential; and (3) classroom remediation.

175   Preston, Ralph C. "An appraisal of medical research on dyslexia."
        In: World Congress on Reading, 2d, Copenhagen, 1968. Proceedings:
        reading: a human right and a human problem. Vol. 2. Edited by
        Ralph C. Staiger, and Oliver Andresen. Newark, Delaware: Inter-
        national Reading Association, 1969. 172-79. (25 References).
Briefly reviews the literature on the causes, diagnosis, incidence, and treatment of dyslexia, pointing out the differences in viewpoint between educators and medical professionals. Failure to agree on characteristics of dyslexia has been a chief block to advancement of knowledge about it. As more interdisciplinary team research by persons in education and medicine is launched, the gulf between them concerning dyslexia will begin to disappear.

176   Rabkin, Jerome. "Reading disability in children." S Afr Med J
        30(27):   678-81, July 21, 1956. (7 References).
Dyslexia occurs more commonly than believed, but it is frequently not recognized. It is specific; often children suffering from reading disability appear very bright until they start school. Abnormalities in lateral dominance and speech disturbances are common in such children. A familial tendency seems to exist. Emotional problems arising from the reading difficulty are often the complaint which brings these children and their parents to the doctor. Better understanding and more skilled management might save much unnecessary trouble for teachers and children. Suggestions concerning causes and treatment are given.

177   "Reading difficulties in children." Drug Ther Bull 7(16):   63-64,
        August 1, 1969. (3 References).

Defines dyslexia and differentiates specific dyslexia from general intellectual backwardness or retardation because of defective hearing, vision,
or brain damage. Reading failure may also be caused by emotional problems. The difficulty is usually noted before the child is seven years
old. Specialized techniques are available for teaching such children.
Difficulty in reading is apt to impair the child's relationships with his
parents, teachers, and peers. As he gets older it becomes an increasing
handicap.

178 "Reading disabilities in children." <u>J Sch Health</u> 20(7): 207-8,
        September, 1950. (4 Bibliographic Footnotes).
About 12 percent of all children in the United States fail to learn to
read as well as the average child. Brain abnormality is probably not the
cause. Emotional factors play a role, and the flash method of teaching
reading is believed by some persons active in the field to be an important contributing cause. Some children need to be taught by the phonetic
method. Early recognition and treatment, sympathetic handling, remedial
reading, and restoring the child's confidence are important measures in
treatment. Dyslexia is best treated by special institutions staffed with
specialists.

179 "Reading disability." <u>Can Med Assoc J</u> 100(2): 81-82, January 11,
        1969. (12 References).
Describes the process of normal reading, pointing out that the age at
which a child can learn to read varies considerably. About 10 percent
of all children appear to have some degree of reading disability, with
boys outnumbering girls three to one. The definitions of dyslexia given
by Critchley, Rabinovitch, and Orton are discussed. Early recognition
of dyslexia is very important, with diagnosis giving a basis for understanding and acceptance. Reading difficulties can be anticipated. Treatment is a confused area because of the emotion generated, and because of
the conflicting claims of various groups.

180 <u>Reading: issues and actions; current trends in school politics and
        programs</u>. 1974. 64p. (ED 098 518).
Designed for school practitioners and others concerned with educational
problems, this special report describes trends in school policies and
programs. Information is given on reading programs throughout the country.
Samples of successful programs are included. Areas discussed cover
methods of teaching reading; teacher training; the use of volunteers in
reading programs; the use of standardized tests; the dyslexic child; and
the public relations aspects of reading instruction, among other topics.

181 Reid, Jessie F., ed. <u>Reading: problems and practices: a selection
        of papers</u>. London: Ward Lock, 1972. 415p.

182 Reinhold, M. "Congenital dyslexia." <u>AEP Newsl</u> No. 4: 13-17,
        Autumn, 1965.

183 Reinmuth, O. M. "Dyslexia: some thoughts of an interested physi-
        cian." <u>J Fla Med Assoc</u> 56(3): 200-204, August, 1969. (9 Refer-
        ences).
Most children are eager to learn to read for their own practical reasons.
When they fail, their self-image suffers. The earlier dyslexic tendencies
are found and treated, the better. Physicians owe it to children who are
having trouble learning to read to help teachers and parents steer a
sensible course between unrestrained optimism and too ready rejection of

all effort. Helen Keller, although not a dyslexic, is an example of a
case where much would have been lost if she and her teacher had given up
too easily. Psychological aspects of dyslexia are discussed in terms of
the child's desire to learn, the teacher's more frequent frowns when he
does not do so, and the child's use of misbehavior to gain attention.
Eye-movement training programs, measures designed to alter hand and/or
eye dominance, and use of drugs for treatment of dyslexia are discussed.
It is pointed out that it is easier in theory than in practice to distinguish the dyslexic child from the child who is not quite so bright,
and whose total intellectual capacity is first challenged by attempting
to learn to read.

184 Richardson, Sylvia O. "Learning disabilities: an introduction."
       In: Kirk, Samuel A., and McCarthy, Jeanne McRae, eds. Learning
       disabilities: selected ACLD papers. Boston, Massachusetts:
       Houghton Mifflin, 1975. 30-38. (0 References).
The probability is great that a child's "specific disability" will be
demonstrated in inability to learn to read. Those concerned with such
children continue to note many characteristics. It is suggested that
perhaps we have gone as far as we can in search for cause at this time;
we must begin a search for more suitable teaching techniques. It is
highly doubtful that we are describing one condition. These children
respond to many different techniques. Some children respond to one technique, some to another. The technique that succeeds may reveal the cause
of the disability.

185 Ritchie, H. M. "Dyslexia." Lancet 1(7702): 755-56, April 10,
       1971. (0 References).
Letter to editor. Describes two syndromes found in dyslexic children.
The first is termed "classic dyslexia," and involves mixed cerebral dom-
iance. These children have left-right confusion, cannot remember how a
word looks, and have difficulty in the sequences of letters or numbers.
The second syndrome includes children with perceptual motor incoordination resulting in clumsiness, poor handwriting, and inability to do
precision work. Verbal IQ is likely to be much higher than performance.
The child is usually intelligent enough to appreciate his problems, and
frustration and personality problems result.

186 Robinson, Helen M. "The poor reader, why?" Libr J 78(10): 875-
       77, May 15, 1953. (0 References).
Defines the poor reader as a pupil of any academic level whose intelligence, as measured by tests that do not require reading, arithmetic
skill, and comprehension from listening, surpasses his reading achievement. His interests are usually much in advance of his reading ability.
He usually dislikes reading, is unhappy and baffled by his failure, and
is often emotionally disturbed. Poor readers may be handicapped by physical, emotional, and language difficulties, but the same difficulties
appear among good readers, making the causes of reading failure hard to
identify. Environmental factors, especially the home and parents, contribute to the success or failure of the reader. The majority of poor
readers can be rehabilitated educationally.

187 Rome, Paula D. "Toward a new understanding of youngsters with read-
       ing problems." Parents Mag 44(11): 72-73, 135-36, November,
       1969. (0 References).
If a child has normal intelligence and is seriously retarded in reading,
almost certainly he has a specific language disability or dyslexia.

Causes are obscure, but many experts believe it is inherited. The whole-word method of teaching reading is unsuited for these children. Phonics instruction alone cannot solve the problem, but the dyslexic child has a better start at reading if that method of teaching is used. Dyslexia exists in varying degrees and may go undetected for years. More good remedial programs are needed. Two illustrative composite case histories are given.

188 Rosner, Stanley L. "Word games in reading diagnosis." Read Teach
     24(4): 331-35, January, 1971. (0 References).
Attempts to define the terms "dyslexia," "minimal brain damage," "specific learning disability," "developmental lag," and "reading disability" (reading retardation). Practice and research should be aimed at prescribing help for students, not simply describing their problem. The term "dyslexia" was formerly used in a very specific way. It is now so broadly applied as to be almost useless. In diagnosing reading disabilities, many teachers use terms so loosely and inaccurately that the jargon of the profession has tended to slide toward meaninglessness. Steps should be taken to arrive at some standard terminology in reading.

189 Rossi, Albert O. "Child with reading disability." NY State J Med
     68(16): 2145-50, August 15, 1968. (18 References).
At least one child in ten who has the intelligence to read does not have the ability to read at a level proportionate to his intelligence. Symptoms of reading disability are described. Some of the literature presenting various causes for it is discussed. It is suggested that concept formation, language acquisition, and reading are all interrelated facets of the cognitive process. Various factors are involved in the maturation of the cognitive processes. Testing at kindergarten or prekindergarten levels to screen for the presence of dyslexia and perceptual-motor deficiencies at an early stage should be done. Some limitations of research being done in the search for a common syndrome are pointed out.

190 Roswell, Florence G., and Natchez, Gladys. Reading disability;
     diagnosis and treatment. 2nd ed. New York: Basic Books, 1971.
     277p. (Bibliography).
Considers the causes of reading disability and how to evaluate the reading-disabled child's situation in the light of test results. Specific tests are discussed. Factors considered by the psychologist in arriving at a diagnosis of the causes of reading disability, and psychotherapeutic principles that should be followed in remedial reading instructions, are both included in the book. The importance of the attention and understanding given the child and the relationship of such factors to improvement in reading are stressed. Techniques of instruction are not so important as the attention and understanding given the child in his struggle to learn to read. The pupil should be involved in the search for the best remedial method. Methods of teaching word recognition to dyslexic children are included. Remedial methods for older children and ways to help the underachiever in high school are given. Also covered are: (1) case histories; (2) an evaluation of approximately fifty reading tests; (3) lists of books suitable for use with reading-disabled children at various levels of proficiency; and (4) lists of games, devices, and workbooks. Each chapter includes a short bibliography.

191 Sampson, Olive C. "The uses of dyslexia." AEP J 3(8): 33-35,
     Winter, 1975. (14 References).

The vast literature on dyslexia is a "wilderness of confusion." It has been claimed that 160 viewpoints can be assembled. At least fifteen different "aliases" for describing the condition are listed. No consensus exists on other aspects, notably the congenital/constitutional element. Many experts in the field realize that the theoretical situation is unsatisfactory. Nevertheless, dyslexia has established itself. Although it is being used as a diagnosis, and grants are made for research in the field, the nature of dyslexia remains unclear. How often it occurs and its causes are not known. The fear is expressed that just at a time when acceptance of a neurological base and really profitable research seems near, some of the discussion about dyslexia is becoming meaningless. Opinions about dyslexia are taking on the coloration of a belief system, not open to discussion or modification. Yet the study of dyslexia is worthwhile. The work of pioneers in the field like Hinshelwood and Orton is worth exploring.

192 Sauer, Louis W. "Learning disabilities." PTA Mag 64(1): 24, September, 1969. (0 References).
Describes the symptoms of dyslexia and lists some of the possible causes. Dyslexia is discussed in terms of its relationship to minimal cerebral dysfunction. Drugs help the high-strung child only temporarily. Parents should follow the advice of the school psychologist. Tutoring by specially trained teachers usually gives best results. Spontaneous improvement in dyslexics is sometimes observed at about age eighteen. Dyslexia is probably an inherited handicap.

193 Saunders, Roger E. "Dyslexia: more than reading retardation." Slow Learn Child 11(3): 137-44, 1965. (10 References).
"Dyslexia" is a diagnostic label for severe reading retardation. It is a serious national problem in the United States and many other countries. Dyslexia is discussed from the viewpoint that it is a deficiency dependent upon constitutional factors (heredity), and exists in spite of good intelligence, adequate instruction, normal motivation, and intact vision and hearing. The ramifications of such a diagnosis are explored. To cope with dyslexia, one must understand the "language function," and the manner in which it "spreads" to affect both reception and expression of language; and recognize that this disability may be much more severe in some persons than in others. The effect of dyslexia on the child's speech development, his ability to learn to read, spell, and write, and his handwriting are all discussed. Teaching methods are considered. The effects of dyslexia extend beyond the classroom into the areas of personality, family relationships, job skills, and nonconforming behavior. Emotional symptoms may be prevented if the dyslexia is diagnosed and treated early.

194 Schatz, Albert. "The reading problem in school: how it began and how it ended." J Read 18(8): 602-5, May, 1975. (0 References).
Most children used to learn to read in school. The reading problem began when an enterprising professor discovered that he could use the few children with reading problems to get money out of Washington. As more and more reading projects developed, fewer children learned to read. After $1,940,000 was spent on 143,897 projects during a fifteen-year period, a national survey revealed that 92 percent of the schools below college level were teaching nothing but reading. Illiteracy was increasing rapidly at the same time. Then it was discovered that the way to end reading problems was to encourage students to drop out of school. Those who dropped out of school learned to read better than those who remained

in school. This dried up the federal funds. Schools reintroduced subjects other than reading, children got interested again, and learned to read because they wanted to learn to read.

195 Schechter, Marshall D. "Dyslexia." Aust Paediatr J 7(3): 123-34,
     September, 1971. (11 References).
Reviews some of the literature giving definitions of dyslexia, its symptoms, and causes. Dyslexia is considered as a "corollary syndrome" of minimal cerebral dysfunction. Treatment recommended includes sensorimotor training; exercises for sequencing of thoughts and motor performance; and ungraded classes from kindergarten through grade three. The educational system should be modified so vocational training begins early, perhaps by grade three. Dyslexia continues to be a problem into adult life. Two case histories are documented.

196 Scheidemann, Norma Valentine. "The congenitally word-blind child."
     In: Psychology of exceptional children. Vol. 1. (Chap. 14).
     Boston, Massachusetts: Houghton Mifflin, 1931. 403-29. (15 References).
Presents a general description of word blindness with some review of the literature and some case studies. The relationship of dyslexia to sex, visual perception, left-handedness, and possible neurological bases are discussed. The chapter offers suggestions for treatment.

197 Shipman, Madeleine. "Children who cannot read." Hygeia 26(4):
     274-75, 287, April, 1948. (0 References).
Lists reasons for reading disability: confused dominance, physical problems, insufficient mental age, and lack of motivation. Some of the resulting maladjustments are described, including various forms of antisocial behavior and daydreams. Corrective teaching must aim first at getting the child's interest.

198 Shultz, Gladys Denny. "Does reading throw your child for a loss?"
     Better Homes Gard 20(3): 78-80, 82, November, 1941. (0 References).
Explains Orton's theory of mixed cerebral dominance and the symptoms of reading disability attributed to it. Diagnostic and treatment techniques are described. Early treatment with the use of phonics is recommended.

199 Silberberg, Norman E., and Silberberg, Margaret C. "If the over-
     emphasis on reading was called a fetish 70 years ago, does that
     make it a perversion now?" J Spec Educ 5(3): 265-67, Fall, 1971.
     (2 References).
Written as a rebuttal to criticisms of the authors' earlier article on hyperlexia, this article points out that educational researchers and theoreticians continue to avoid questions that remain, such as: Why does remedial reading fail to work? Why does the government continue to push "Right to Read" programs which have failed in the past and continue to do so? Does equal educational opportunity mean that all children must be the same? Is it appropriate to use IQ to arrive at a level of reading expectation? Do we need to worry about such a level at all? People continue to define dyslexia and hyperlexia however they like. Dyslexia is an amorphous concept. It is difficult to quantify. The schools, not the children, should be evaluated and changed.

200 Sims, Barbara. "The dyslexic college student." Paper presented at
     Conference on College Composition and Communication, Anaheim,
     California, April 4-6, 1974. 1974. 7p. (ED 092 991).

Since an estimated 10 percent of elementary pupils are dyslexic, it is logical to assume that there would be fewer dyslexic college students. However, with more awareness of reading problems and more programs for special education in public schools, colleges should be prepared for increasing numbers of dyslexic students in college. College teachers, especially freshman English instructors, should learn to recognize and help the dyslexic college student. Composition teachers should be prepared with concrete methods to improve reading and composition skills.

201 Snyder, Russell D. "How much reading?" <u>Pediatrics</u> 55(3): 306-8, March, 1975. (14 References).
Reading is a complex neural function. Neurological abnormalities occurring in association with reading disability are of questionable significance. Reading disability is probably caused by a developmental delay; few disabled readers are total nonreaders as adults. We should realize that television, movies, recordings, and public gatherings are among many substitutes for the teacher and the book as sources of education. This should lead us to adopt a more flexible and realistic approach to the reading-disabled child.

202 Snyder, Russell D., and Mortimer, Joan. "Diagnosis and treatment: dyslexia." <u>Pediatrics</u> 44(4): 601-5, October, 1969. (23 References).
Dyslexia is an important problem in pediatrics. Symptoms are discussed. Although typical characteristics are clear, the causes of dyslexia remain unclear. Prognosis is unknown. Suggestions for management of the condition are given, including alleviating pressures on the child, remedial reading, sympathetic understanding of the problem by parents, and methods for teaching the child in spite of his handicap. The physician should be directly involved in the management.

203 Söderling, Bertil. "Studies on special disturbances within the reading and writing function in children ('dyslexia' 'word-blindness'). II. Contribution to the question of origin." <u>Acta Paediatr</u> 51(Suppl. 135): 219-24, June, 1962. (4 References).
The child otherwise capable of learning who cannot learn to read and/or spell during the first three years of school is dyslexic. He has a handicap and should be given special instruction as early as possible. A recovery rate of 100 percent is too much to hope for. It is necessary to determine how much of the improvement in a case that has been "cured" resulted from spontaneous healing through the natural maturation process and how much can be credited to the special tutoring. Unless this is known, effectiveness of the special teaching cannot be estimated. Children of superior intelligence are able to read before they start school, having learned by a kind of shortcut, homemade process. They show no difficulties with reading and writing in spite of lack of instruction. The dyslexic bright child is resistant and disinterested in letters and in forming words. It is impossible to prevent dyslexia. It is an error to blame it on faulty teaching methods in the early stages of instruction.

204 "Some Johnnies just can't." <u>Time</u> 87(19): 56, 61, May 13, 1966. (0 References).
Summarizes the symptoms of dyslexia, including both horizontal and vertical reversals; confusion of the sequence of sounds; and confusion of left and right. If diagnosed before emotional problems become severe because of frustration over his reading problem, the dyslexic child can readily be taught to read. Teaching methods to overcome the dyslexic's faulty

visual and auditory perception are described. Recent efforts to make
educators and medical experts aware of each other's efforts in the field
are related.

205 Spache, George D. "Diagnosis and remediation in 1980." In: Inter-
    national Reading Association. Conference proceedings: reading
    disability and perception. Vol. 13(Part 3). Edited by George D.
    Spache. Newark, Deleware: International Reading Association, 1969.
    135-51. (0 References).
In a satirical discussion, the article ridicules what are regarded as the
excesses and follies that have appeared in the treatment of reading disability. These are mostly the products of persons from other disciplines
who know nothing about teaching reading. A warning is sounded that if
reading experts are not more outspoken in their leadership, the field of
reading will be taken over by those regarded as charlatans. The wide use
of look-say methods with weak phonics instruction has contributed to the
increase of dyslexia in the schools.

206 Stanger, Margaret A. "They're going to learn to read." Parents Mag
    16(9): 22, 37-38, 91-92, September, 1941. (0 References).
Explains reversal tendency in terms of incomplete dominance of one cerebral hemisphere. A typical case history is presented to explain the
symptoms of reading disability. Early tests for children entering school
to find those with a high risk of developing dyslexia are described, including tests for directional orientation and eyedness. The look-and-say
method of teaching reading should not be used for children with poor
visual imagery. Phonics is a better method for the child with reversal
tendency. The left-handed child will not necessarily show a tendency to
reversal, but care should be taken to see that his paper is properly
placed when he learns to write. Interest in books and reading can be
encouraged by reading aloud to the child. Having children read orally
in the classroom is a good practice.

207 Thompson, Lloyd J. "Learning disabilities: an overview." Am J
    Psychiatry 130(4): 393-99, April, 1973. (27 References).
Finds that the literature is referring to the same child or condition
whether he is said to have "learning disabilities" or to suffer from "congenital word blindness," "specific reading disability," "developmental
dyslexia," or "MBD," among other terms. Inherent maturational lags
rather than brain damage or environmental influences are the fundamental
basis of dyslexia. The objections to the use of such terms as "MBD" or
"brain damage" which connote brain pathology are explained. The idea of
developmental lag is more accurate and constructive.

208 ————. Reading disability: developmental dyslexia. Springfield,
    Illinois: Thomas, 1966. 201p. (Bibliography p. 171-93).
This book summarizes current knowledge about specific language disabilities. After reviewing the early literature on dyslexia, including detailed discussion of the work of Samuel Orton, the author examines psychoanalytic literature on the emotional and environmental factors in reading
disability. Freud's work is discussed. The work of various neurologists
and what is known about causes of reading disability is considered. Cerebral dominance, possible biochemical origins, and brain damage are assessed. The book contains numerous case histories. The viewpoint presented
is that innate or constitutional factors, as seen in developmental lag,
are more frequent and important causes of reading disability than are
brain damage, emotional, or environmental influences.

209 ───────. "Reading disability in armed services." <u>Milit Med</u>
    135(5): 411-12, May, 1970. (0 References).
About 10 percent of all children, mostly boys, have some degree of reading disability. Many young men rejected by draft boards because of seem-
ing illiteracy or mental retardation are in fact dyslexics. Many military
men have shown residual signs of childhood dyslexia. It appears to be
caused by an innate maturational lag, not by environmental influences or
brain damage. Greater recognition of the handicap and better management
of it are necessary.

210 Tien, H. C. "Hyperlexia, hypolexia, or dyslexia." <u>J Spec Educ</u>
    5(3): 257-59, Fall, 1971. (7 References).
Differentiates the three terms listed. "Hyperlexia" is defined as ability to read material that the reader cannot comprehend. "Hypolexia" is
reading ability below general level of intelligence. "Dyslexia" is difficulty in learning to read because of a neurological deficit. All three
are useful terms, it is asserted.

211 Tomkins, Calvin. "The last skill acquired." <u>New Yorker</u> 39: 127-
    57, September 14, 1963. (0 References).
Introduces the field of reading disability. The article traces the development of thought and current developments and identifies and explores
the work of both pioneers and modern leaders in the field. Many causes
exist for reading failure in school. The one that has received least
attention is specific dyslexia, the usual term for reading failure that
results from a constitutional language disability. Some authorities say
there is no such thing; medical doctors have studied it for a century
without reaching clear agreement on a cause. Many neurologists and psychiatrists do agree on manifestations of specific dyslexia: reading
ability markedly inferior to nonverbal IQ and performance in other areas
of learning. The method by which most dyslexics can learn to read is
painstaking phonic analysis. Short attention spans characterize these
children, and need for physical activity interspersed with work on phonics
seems to be needed.

About 100 years ago Paul Broca, a French surgeon and anthropologist,
arrived at the theory that language is controlled by the hemisphere of
the brain opposite the most skilled hand. It was observed that a wound
to the nondominant side of the brain did not affect language. James
Hinshelwood, a Glasgow ophthalmologist, early in the twentieth century
investigated the notion that a family history of language area difficulties lies behind many cases of dyslexia. Hinshelwood used the term
"congenital word blindness." He supposed word blindness to be the result
of a congenital defect in the visual centers of the brain. His ideas
dominated thought in the field until late in the 1920s.

The work of Dr. Samuel Torrey Orton, an American neuropsychiatrist at
the State University of Iowa and later at Columbia University, is evaluated. Orton believed dyslexia resulted from the incomplete dominance
of one cerebral hemisphere over the other with resulting competition
manifested as reading problems. The origin of language disorders may be
far more complex than Orton suspected, it is now thought.

The work of Mrs. Katrina De Hirsch of Columbia-Presbyterian Pediatric
Language Disorder Clinic in New York City is described. With her col-
leagues, Dr. William S. Langford, director of children's psychiatric
service at Columbia-Presbyterian Babies Hospital, and Jeannette Jansky,
De Hirsch hopes to perfect a basic series of tests, perhaps as many as

twelve, to predict reading, writing, and spelling problems in very young children. These would be simple enough for any kindergarten teacher to give. In this way problems could be caught before the emotional problems of failure overtake the child. Langford and De Hirsch believe there is need for flexibility in the teaching of reading. Mrs. De Hirsch was among the persons interviewed in the preparation of the article.

212 Trauttmansdorff, Antonia. "They do not see as we see." Times Educ
     Suppl 2823: 2106, June 27, 1969. (0 References).
In an interview, Dr. R. M. Crosby of Baltimore defines dyslexia as a disability in reading of neurological origin. It can be accurately diagnosed by age seven. Ideally, Crosby says, he would put severely dyslexic children until age twelve in a special school where all instruction would be done aurally. When neurologically mature enough, the children could be taught to read and write in a year. British neurologists estimate that 25 percent of the English school population is dyslexic. The proportion in the United States is believed to be 10 to 15 percent.

213 "Turning a blind eye to dyslexia." Times Educ Suppl 2958: 8,
     January 28, 1972. (0 References).
Dyslexia is not recognized as a specific disability requiring special remedial teaching, according to Dr. A. White Franklin, director of the Word Blind Centre in London (now closed). There are indications that pressure for recognition is growing. Dyslexia is not a simple syndrome. It is marked by unevenness in the development of skills in spite of normal intelligence. Many more boys than girls are affected.

214 Turvey, S. E. C. "Dyslexia." Bull Vancouver Med Assoc 26(1):
     15-18, 1949. (0 References).
Dyslexia means difficulty in reading. It should be broadly used to include any difficulty in interpreting or understanding language whether speech, reading, writing, or spelling. Under twelve years of age, 15 to 25 percent of children have dyslexia. The male/female ratio is four to one. Few or no known facts and no theories exist as to the cause of dyslexia. It is necessary to deal in hypotheses. Several causes are suggested, including heredity, central nervous system lesions, psychosomatic disorders, and mixed types. Although some dyslexic children may need special teachers, ordinary cases usually do well in the regular classroom. The article cites six case histories.

215 U. S. National Advisory Committee on Dyslexia and Related Reading
     Disorders. "Advisory committee on dyslexia." Elem Engl 46(5):
     679-80, May, 1969. (0 References).
The National Advisory Committee on Dyslexia and Related Reading Disorders was formed in August, 1968 to learn more about the problem of dyslexia, and its prevention and treatment. Plans of the committee and names and addresses of its members are given.

216 U. S. Secretary's (HEW) National Advisory Committee on Dyslexia and
     Related Reading Disorders. Reading disorders in the United States;
     report of the Secretary's (HEW) National Advisory Committee on
     Dyslexia and Related Reading Disorders. Bethesda, Maryland: Department of Health, Education, and Welfare, 1969. 90p.
This document is the final report of a committee which was asked to examine the areas of research, diagnosis, teacher preparation, and corrective education in regard to dyslexia and other reading disorders, and to make recommendations. The committee found that a sizable minority of

otherwise able students were not able to profit from reading instruction
adequate for most children. The reasons are complex. No clear-cut definition of dyslexia exists, and there is wide disagreement among professions as to its meaning. The committee believes that using the term
"dyslexia" serves no useful purpose. No systematic effort has been made
to implement a sound national reading program. Principles and procedures
for identifying, preventing, and treating reading disorders have not been
satisfactorily determined, although much relevant information exists.
The differences in definitions of terms and research methods have hindered
the development of a systematic body of knowledge.

The committee recommends the creation of an office on reading disorders
within HEW with an advisory council to include reading specialists, a
layman, and liaison representatives from other government agencies. The
committee outlines the duties and functions of this office and its advisory council. Setting up centers for research in reading is recommended
to foster more research and to develop programs for identifying, preventing, and treating reading disorders. Seventeen specific recommendations
for action by HEW are listed. There is little evidence that current
programs of instruction and remediation are effective. This document is
available from ERIC, order number ED 037 317. (For a related study see
Item No. 38.)

217 Vernon, Magdalen Dorothea. Backward readers. London: College of
     Special Education, 1968. 16p. (Guide Lines for Teachers, No. 4).
The particular difficulties of backward readers are very similar, but the
causes can be very different. Children may need various forms of prereading training before formal reading instruction begins. Environmental
factors may produce reading problems. Intelligence and emotional state
may also influence reading ability. Two types of dyslexia are distinguished: defects in visual perception and impaired language ability.
The latter includes children with poor auditory discrimination and speech
disorders. Severely dyslexic children cannot be greatly helped in the
regular classroom, but require individual instruction.

218 ————. "Specific dyslexia." Slow Learn Child 12(2): 71-75,
     1965. (18 References).
Much doubt and disagreement center on whether specific dyslexia really
exists, or whether backwardness in reading is caused by environmental
and emotional factors. If it does exist, the nature of the disability
and its causes are sources of controversy. Cases of reading backwardness
caused by emotional stress, low intelligence, and physical problems should
be excluded from the category of dyslexia. Specific dyslexia may occur
in children with minor brain damage, or with familial tendency to the
problem. Such children have poor visual perception of complex forms in
addition to the reading problem. Three main types of constitutional
dyslexia are described: those with (1) speech and language disorders;
(2) impairment of visual perception; and (3) defects primarily in conceptual reasoning processes. It would probably be desirable to classify
as specifically dyslexic only those children with brain injury or an
inherited disability. In practice the category is extended to cover all
retarded readers for whose backwardness there is not an obvious cause.
Much overlap exists in the three classes suggested.

219 Wagner, Rudolph F. "Bilingualism, multiple dyslexia, and polyglot
     aphasia." Acad Ther 12(1): 91-97, Fall, 1976. (12 References).

Discusses the handicaps said to be experienced by the bilingual person
even though potentially he is able to learn the second language and become absorbed in its culture. In general, when a bilingual child is dyslexic in one language, he is so in the other. When the person with two
languages has aphasic difficulties following illness or injury, it appears
that the way the languages were acquired (e.g., in home or school or both)
is of primary importance in language loss. It is suggested that remediation in one language would not affect the other language in cases of
aphasia. One language may be lost while the other remains intact. Remediation in multiple dyslexia provides a chance to treat the deficits
in both languages because the dyslexic has trouble with both languages
and shows similar error characteristics in both.

220 Waites, Lucius. "Definition of dyslexia." Can Med Assoc J 99(1):
     37, July 6, 1968. (0 References).
Letter to editor. Gives the definitions of "specific developmental dys-
lexia" and of "dyslexia" approved by the Research Group on Developmental
Dyslexia and World Illiteracy of the World Federation of Neurology.

221 Walbridge, A. "A view of dyslexia by an educational psychologist."
     AEP Newsl, No. 4, Autumn, 1965.

222 Wallin, J. E. Wallace. "Congenital word blindness--some analyses
     of cases." Train Sch Bull 17: 76-84, 93-99, September-October,
     1920. (9 References).
Published in two parts, this report details findings from St. Louis
schools on the examination of ninety-five cases of word blindness discovered among children who had been referred for examination because they
were thought to be mentally defective. "Word blindness" is the term used
as the generic concept. "Visual aphasia" applies to the more severe
degrees, and "dyslexia" is the term used for the lighter degrees of word
blindness. The children were found to be intellectually normal or
slightly retarded. Brain lesions of congenital or hereditary origin or
caused by birth injury are assumed to cause congenital word blindness.
A differential diagnosis cannot be safely arrived at until frank mental
defectiveness and physical factors can be ruled out, and the child has
had adequate opportunity to learn to read. If the child recognizes and
names objects and pictures and can spell the names orally, but cannot
recognize the corresponding names when shown print or script, word blindness is assumed. More boys than girls are affected, but there are no
facts to even begin to explain this sex difference. The Binet test did
not reveal any peculiar defects in auditory or visual imagery in this
group of children, except a possible defect in visual word imagery. At
least 85 percent of these children were subnormal in intelligence, but
it is not justified to assume this much subnormality in an unselected
group of word-blind children. There is no qualitative difference between
word blindness in a retarded and in a normal child. The differences are
like those found in general intelligence. They are differences in degree
and not in kind. Word blindness varies from a state of profound visual
aphasia to a slight degree of dyslexia. Word-blind children who are not
feebleminded should be assigned to special reading disability classes.
Different methods of teaching reading will reach different children.
Oral instruction should be given if necessary.

223 Watts, W. J. "Dyslexia and the pressure of social conscience."
     Int J Soc Psychiatry 20(3-4): 287-91, Autumn-Winter, 1974. (0
     References).

Traces briefly the legislative history establishing public education in
England. Pertinent sections are quoted of the report of a subcommittee
set up by the Advisory Committee on Handicapped Children, "Children with
Specific Reading Difficulties," published in February, 1972 and known as
the Green Paper on Dyslexia. This report is criticized as explaining
away dyslexia while providing nothing for the aid of dyslexic children
and their parents. Watts comments critically on the British legal position on dyslexia. A plea is made for persistence in waging the battle
for support.

224   Weeks, Arland D.   "A strange ailment." Education 56(6): 355-58,
       February, 1936. (0 References).
Reports the nightmare of a retired schoolteacher who looks into the future
almost forty years and sees a strange universal alexia settling over mankind in the year 1975: suddenly nobody can read anything at all. The
words on all the pages have become meaningless marks. University campuses
fall into disuse, and the buildings lie in ruins. Libraries are of value
only as fuel for primitive cooking fires. Banks close, law offices are
deserted, and newsstand shelves stand vacant. Congress is in permanent
recess, caused in part by the lapse of the Congressional Record and
franking privileges. Orators tour the country, and nobody knows whether
they lie because no written record is possible. City dwellers retreat
to farms because no one can read addresses. The post office is out of
business. Universal illiteracy leaves mankind reduced in numbers; people
become ignorant, quarrelsome vagrants in a decayed environment. The
strange and appalling alexia passes, and someone begins the long process
of retrieving the alphabet. But it will take thousands of years to get
back the world of 1975 as it was before universal alexia struck.

225   Wheeler, Lester R., and Wheeler, Viola D. "Dyslexaphoria: symptoms
       and remedial suggestions." Elem Engl 32(5): 305-11, May, 1955.
       (19 References).
"Dyslexaphoria" is defined as "the tendency toward linguistic associative
difficulties." A long list of symptoms is given, including poor auditory
and/or visual memory, reversal errors, and poor comprehension. The condition may be caused by pathological or congenital conditions or by low
intelligence, but the most common cause is faulty training and experience.
Remedial measures are suggested.

226   "When 'film' is 'flim.'" Newsweek 70: 48, July 31, 1967. (0
       References).
Describes symptoms and treatment for dyslexia. Reversals of letters in
words; difficulty in keeping ideas in their proper order; confusion between left and right; and awkwardness characterize dyslexic children.
Doctors and educators are unsure of the causes. Neurological problems,
familial tendency, and faulty development in some areas of the brain may
be among the causes. The look-say method of teaching reading and peculiarities of English spelling may contribute to the problem. Treatment
methods include exercises for motor retraining and tracing the shapes of
letters with fingers before writing them.

227   Wiener, Morton, and Cromer, Ward. "Reading and reading difficulty:
       a conceptual analysis." Harv Educ Rev 37(4): 620-34, Fall, 1967.
       (43 References).
The current confusion about reading arises from different ideas about the
reading process, and the many definitions of reading and variety of explanations of reading disability. Four issues are discussed in an effort

to clarify some of the ambiguity: (1) identification versus comprehension; (2) acquisition versus accomplished reading; (3) relative versus absolute criteria; and (4) reading versus language skills. Reading difficulty is analyzed in terms of the following assumptions which have been made by various investigators: (1) that reading difficulty is attributable to defect or malfunction; (2) that it is attributable to deficiency, the absence of some function; (3) that it occurs because of disruption, or something interfering with the reading process; or (4) an assumption of difference, i.e., the teaching method is not suited to the individual's behavior patterns. The implications for reading difficulty when reading is considered as identification or as comprehension are discussed.

228 Williams, Jessie, Lady Francis-Williams. Children with specific
     learning difficulties; the effect of neurodevelopmental learning
     disorders on children of normal intelligence. 2nd ed. Oxford,
     New York: Pergamon Press, 1970. 229p. (Bibliography p. 212-22).
Developmental dyslexia is one of a number of conditions described in this book which are believed to underlie the lack of school achievement of some children. Dyslexia is a familial or inherited disability unrelated to visual, auditory, or visuo-spatial defects. How children suffering from dyslexia and other specific learning disorders may be identified at the preschool level, and how to help such children both before and after starting formal schooling are discussed. The situation regarding the study and treatment of dyslexia in Britain is described as "confused." It is asserted that the Scandinavian countries have made the most comprehensive studies of the condition. The book's primary concern is the role of the psychologist in helping children with specific learning disabilities.

229 Witty, Paul. "Fiction and fact about retarded readers." Natl Parent
     Teach 42(7): 10-12, March, 1948. (0 References).
Articles in popular magazines have spread misconceptions about poor reading. It is not true that one-third of all high school students are nonverbal or that continuing reading instruction harms dyslexics. Simple panaceas fail to help poor readers because of the complexity of factors involved in each case. Most poor readers lack interest in reading. Suggestions for helping disabled readers are given, including individual study of each child, patience, and using materials close to the child's interest.

230 Wolfe, Lillian S. Experiments on reading disability in nine-year-
     old school children. Unpublished Ph.D. thesis. Yale University,
     1935.

231 Wolkomir, Richard. "They call it dyslexia: it's the reason why
     some children can't read." PTA Mag 68(8): 20-23, April, 1974.
     (0 References).
Explains the symptoms of dyslexia and discusses the problems of identification and remediation. Various methods of treatment are presented. The theories of Orton and the therapy method of Doman-Delacato are explained. Reasons for the neglect of dyslexics include public indifference, inadequately trained teachers, and lack of research on the problem.

232 Wollner, Mary H. B. "Some European research in reading disabilities."
     Education 78: 555-60, May, 1958. (12 References).

Study of educational centers in Austria, Germany, and France led to the conclusion that European specialists are well aware of reading disabilities and of the complex of causes of the condition. European observations on reading disability overlap those in the United States. Medical-neurological, psycho-pedagogical, and sociological viewpoints are found. Specialists agree that classroom teachers are often mistaken in their assessments of dyslexic children and need more material on it. A wide variety of remedial measures is being used.

233   Woodward, Kenneth L. "When your child can't read." McCalls 100(5): 48, 50, 52, 57, 109, February, 1973. (0 References).
Describes the symptoms of specific learning disability (SLD) which are used to identify all children with the perceptual handicaps sometimes termed "word-blind," "dyslexic," "strephosymbolic," or "minimally brain-damaged." Information is received by eyes and ears, but somewhere along the neurological line it becomes confused for SLD children. Four times as many boys as girls suffer from it. Perceptual impairment may be caused by birth injury, or it may be inherited. Causes are not known. Most teachers are not trained to recognize its symptoms, much less treat it. The case history of the author's own SLD child and his progress in tutoring him are reviewed. A system of training mothers as volunteer tutors of reading-disabled children is advocated.

234   "The word-blind and the mirror-writers." Lit Dig 96(1): 59, January 7, 1928. (0 References).
A connection appears to have been established between mirror writing and word-blindness which up until this time were not thought to be related. Educational psychologists investigating the two conditions suggest that congenital factors may not exist and that inhibiting habits, however acquired, may be at the bottom of the inability to read. Illness or absence from school between the ages of six and eight may result in failure to learn to read at the usual time. The child is pushed on, and nobody in the upper grades feels it is his business to teach the child to read. He becomes effectively word-blind. Usually, however, other intellectual shortcomings are discovered which limit his learning.

235   "Word blindness in children." Lit Dig 93(7): 65-67, May 14, 1927. (0 References).
Quotes part of an address by Walter F. Dearborn which was published in The Optometric Weekly. The emphasis in schools on verbal or linguistic knowledge results in handicaps to those who have not learned to read or who read poorly. A plea is made for the early discovery of persons of good ability who have not learned to read in order to forestall their scholastic failure and to preserve their morale and prevent the development of psychopathic or even delinquent personality traits. Disability in reading has a number of causes. Word blindness is commonly held to be the result of a congenital defect in certain areas of the brain. Some of these defects may produce no difficulties, but conspire to produce faulty habits, as in the left-handed child who begins at the center of his body and moves out to the left in writing. He has been told to watch his teacher and do as she does. The right-handed teacher begins at the center of her body and moves out to the right. The child must at the outset disregard his kinesthetic stimuli and imagery.

236   Worthington, Calvin R. "My father's hands." Read Dig 108(649): 169-72, May, 1976. (0 References).

Recounts a son's story of his illiterate father's struggle to earn a living. A skilled pipefitter, he followed blueprints without difficulty
but could not read or write words even after repeated attempts to do so.
Maybe because of a learning handicap such as dyslexia, this man of apparently better than average intelligence was never able to learn to read
and write. He died of a heart seizure while struggling to open the child-
proof cap on a bottle of nitroglycerin pills. He could not read the
directions for opening the bottle and reaching the medicine that might
have saved his life.

237 Young, R. A. <u>A study of reading disability cases.</u> Unpublished Ed.
      D. thesis. Harvard University, 1935.

238 Young, Warren R. "The enduring mystery of dyslexia." <u>Read Dig</u>
      108: 21-28, Februrary, 1976. (0 References).
Describes the symptoms of dyslexia. The struggles of Nelson Rockefeller,
Gen. George Patton, and other famous dyslexics are recounted. Possible
causes are discussed including Orton's theories.

239 Yule, W. "Dyslexia." <u>Psychol Med</u> 6(2): 165-67, May, 1976. (15
      References).
Discusses the controversies that have given rise to the heated arguments
over what dyslexia is, and if it really exists. Definition of the term
is needed. Underachievement is the core concept underlying most writing
on dyslexia. This seems simple, but it is filled with statistical pitfalls in application. The Isle of Wight studies of Rutter and Yule are
described in this connection. The idea of constitutional origin of dyslexia is an open matter. Disentangling genetic factors from socially
transmitted factors is difficult. "Dyslexia" as a label has served its
function in drawing attention to these children.

240 Zuercher, Evelyn L. "My son myself." <u>Acad Ther</u> 7(1): 37-39,
      Fall, 1971. (0 References).
A mother describes her own childhood struggles with reading. Her eyes
jumped and skipped from one line to another until the meaning was lost
in the physical effort of reading. Her daughter had no difficulty with
reading, but her son appeared unable to learn to read. He could not discriminate the direction of the letters. It is suggested that the child
needs to be convinced that learning to read is worth the effort no matter
how difficult, and that reading disability does not indicate lack of
intelligence. Reading about dyslexia was for the mother like understanding herself for the first time.

IV
Broadly Based Research

241 Benton, Arthur L., and Kemble, Joan D. "Right-left orientation and
     reading disability." Psychiatr Neurol 139(1-2): 49-60, January-
     February, 1960. (10 References).
Investigates the relationship of right-left orientation and reading disability in children. Two groups of children seven to ten years of age,
one group normal readers, the other severely retarded in reading, were
used in this study. There were no significant differences in age or sex.
A battery of tests to ascertain right-left discrimination was given. The
two groups did not differ significantly in respect to basic confusion in
right-left orientation, although reading-disabled children showed a
slightly higher tendency toward confusion. It is concluded that reading-
disabled children do not show basic disturbance in directional orientation or body schema. An effort is made to explain the conflicting findings and impressions on this question in terms of an inadequate sample.

242 Blakeslee, Sandra. "Scientists assay dyslexia clues." NY Times
     118(40,570): 26, February 20, 1969. (0 References).
Cites five recent studies of dyslexia reported by Dr. Charles A. Ullman,
George Washington University professor, and executive director of the
National Advisory Committee on Dyslexia and Related Reading Disabilities.
The studies estimated the number of dyslexic children in the schools of
the United States at between 11 and 27 percent. The advisory committee
is charged with the task of developing a continuing national policy on
dyslexia and to devise methods to tackle the problem. After six months
of discussion, the experts have not been able to agree on a definition
of dyslexia. Each professional speciality views it differently. They
do agree that it is not a pathological disease condition; and that it
does not imply emotional disturbance, inferior education, or that the
child necessarily has a learning problem. Causes of dyslexia are obscure.

243 Camp, Bonnie W., and Dahlem, Nancy W. "Paired-associate and serial
     learning in retarded readers." J Educ Psychol 67(3): 385-90,
     June, 1975. (18 References).
Reports the results of two experiments using retarded readers ages nine
to thirteen as subjects. IQs in the first group were above 75 with an

average of 91.1; the average was 90 for the second group. The paired-associate experiment used ten pairs of pictures which had no obvious association, e.g., fish-chair, clock-hat. The serial learning task used ten pictures presented in order. The pictures had no obvious association among them. In the first experiment each child was shown the pairs of pictures and instructed to try to remember which pictures went together (anticipation method). He was then shown one picture alone. Trials continued until two perfect responses were achieved. In the serial learning test, the child was asked to name each picture as it was presented. When he had seen them all, he was asked to name them in order (study-test method). Trials continued until two perfect responses were achieved. In the second experiment the paired-associate task was the same. The serial learning task was the same except that the child was instructed before any trials to try to remember the order of the pictures (anticipation method).

Correlations among the measures of paired-associate learning were highly significant in the first test, but correlations between measures of the two tasks were not significant. In the second experiment correlations between paired-associate and two serial learning measures were significant. It is not clear why the study-test method was more difficult for retarded readers than the anticipation method. It is suggested that the reason may lie in the retarded reader's need for external support for rehearsal, since spontaneous rehearsal is limited in retarded readers. Differences may also lie in the extent to which the task was perceived as difficult or boring.

244 Clark, Margaret M. "Severe reading difficulty: a community study."
     Br J Educ Psychol 41(1): 14-18, February, 1971. (1 Reference).
A series of tests carried out on all elementary-school children in a county in Scotland over a period of several years determined that severe reading difficulty in children of average intelligence in that county is not a problem of the magnitude that had been thought. In the children of average intelligence who did have reading and spelling difficulties, however, it was found that the problem did not improve with time, but rather grew worse. No severely backward readers of high intelligence were found. The study of this complete community was planned in an effort to determine the extent to which certain variables said to be significant in dyslexia are related to the reading progress of normal children. Ability to differentiate left and right; motor coordination; and left-handedness were tested. Reading ability and vocabulary were also determined individually for all 1,544 children taking part in the test. This number included 791 boys and 753 girls all born between April 1 and August 31, 1959. At the time of the study they were attending seventy schools in Dunbartonshire in west Scotland. In this way community figures for these characteristics were obtained. It is pointed out that because certain variables were found to be associated with lack of progress in reading, it does not necessarily follow that these factors were the cause of failure.

245 Cockburn, June M. "Annual surveys of reading disability in a
     Scottish county." Br J Educ Psychol 43(Part 2): 188-91, June,
     1973. (4 References).
Annual surveys of reading attainment of all seven-year-olds have been carried out by the Child Guidance Service in Angus, Scotland. In 1969 a follow-up survey of children between ten and eleven years old showed that more than half the children seriously backward in reading at ages seven

to eight were still seriously backward at ages ten to eleven. The size of the group of disabled readers seven to eight years old has increased continuously from 1967 to 1970.

246 Conners, C. Keith. Untitled letter to editor. Psychophysiology
     9(4): 473, July, 1972. (0 References).
Answers criticism of an article published by Conners concerning EEG findings in a family of dyslexics (Item No. 759). The criticism was by Kenneth A. Kooi, Psychophysiology 9:154, 1972, not included in this bibliography.

247 Copp, Barrie R. "Reading as viewed by our eastern European col-
     leagues." J Read 13(6): 441-46, March, 1970. (0 References).
Reports on the status of reading instruction and the manner of dealing with dyslexia or other reading disabilities in Czechoslovakia, Hungary, Romania, and Moscow. A report on the Second World Congress on Reading held in Denmark is also included. Information about the treatment of severe reading problems in Denmark was obtained from a reading specialist. This information is contained in the report.

248 Corwin, Betty Jane. "The relationship between reading achievement
     and performance on individual ability tests." J Sch Psychol 5(2):
     156-57, Winter, 1967. (0 References).
Compares WISC subtest patterns and scores on the Peabody Picture Vocabulary Test for groups of good and poor readers in the fourth and fifth grades of a public-school system. The groups were identified by their teachers, and were matched on age, grade, and scores on a nonverbal IQ test. Results suggest some relationship between WISC subtest scores and reading achievement. The groups differed only on Coding in performance subtests, with good readers scoring significantly higher. In verbal subtests, good readers were significantly higher in Information, Arithmetic, and Digit Span. They were somewhat higher on Similarities and Vocabulary.

249 Creak, Mildred. "Reading difficulties in children." Arch Dis Child
     11: 143-56, June, 1936. (18 References).
Reports on a study of fifty children all retarded two years or more in reading age below mental age. The chief interest was in seeing how far these cases of reading disability could be compared with other forms of aphasia. The difficulty that deaf children have in learning to speak, read, and write is noted, and some of the literature in the area is reviewed. Tests which did not use letters were given to assess the capacities needed for reading. These included recognizing and matching a simple geometric pattern, copying a pattern, listening to and reproducing a rhythm tapped on the desk, and discovering whether the children could identify by touch letters known to them by sight. IQs ranged from 70 to 110, with one case over 110. Thirty-three of the children had IQs of 90 or below. More boys than girls were affected. Results of the various tests are discussed. Orton's and Monroe's theories are discussed in connection with findings. It is suggested that reading disability cannot be explained on a neurotic basis alone. If the group had an emotional difficulty in common, it was an aversion to effort: an habitual evasion of the difficulty with reading which expressed itself in distractibility, restlessness, and lack of interest in books.

250 Cromer, Ward, and Wiener, Morton. Do reading tests measure 'read-
     ing'? Final report. 1974. 26p. (ED 094 362).

Groups of good and poor seventh-grade readers were given questions taken from a standard reading test under four conditions: (1) graphic form/ story and questions; (2) graphic form/questions only; (3) auditory form/ story and questions; and (4) auditory form/questions only. The hypothesis to be tested was that under the question-only form and the stories-and-questions condition, good readers would score better than poor readers on these modes of presentation. It was also hypothesized that while poor readers might score better on the auditory presentation than on the graphic, their performance would still be lower than that of the good readers. Results showed that in general the good and poor readers differed as predicted, but good readers scored lowest on the graphic form/ questions-only condition. Implications of these findings are discussed. The study was done pursuant to a finding that good and poor readers may have different patterns of response to reading tasks.

251 Davis, Sarah Elizabeth. "The effects of peripheral graphic stimulus complexity on the word recognition thresholds of normal and re-tarded readers." For a summary see: <u>Diss Abstr</u> 26(10): 6156, April, 1966.

252 Denney, Douglas R. "Relationship of three cognitive style dimensions to elementary reading abilities." <u>J Educ Psychol</u> 66(5): 702-9, October, 1974. (15 References).
In tests comparing good and poor readers from grades two to five, three "cognitive style dimensions" were investigated. They were: (1) Con-ceptual style preferences which used the Conceptual Styles Test--Form A in which the child was asked to select two pictures from a group of three that were alike or went together in some way. The child's response to each of the fifteen items of this test was classified as analytic, re-lational, or inferential. (2) Cognitive tempo using the Matching Familiar Figures Test which assessed reflection or impulsivity. (3) At-tentional style using the Fruit Distraction Test which assessed constricted or flexible attentional styles. A reading test was given, and the Peabody Picture Vocabulary Test was given as a measure of intelligence. The experimental and control groups were matched for age. Ten from each group were drawn from each grade for a total of eighty subjects. Attentional style best distinguished good and poor readers. Other tests were found to be better related to reading, however. These were tests of children's ability to transpose information from visual to verbal channels.

253 Dossetor, D. R., and Papaioannou, J. "Dyslexia and eye movements." <u>Lang Speech</u> 18(4): 312-17, October-December, 1975. (9 References).
Examines eye movements as a physiological measure associated with reading in order to determine possible eye-movement differences between dyslexic and normal children. Groups of normal and dyslexic children ages six to fifteen years were matched for age and sex. A group of normal adults was also tested. Electrooculograms were made to determine saccadic eye move-ments and to measure optokinetic nystagmus (rapid eye movements induced by following a moving object). Subjects were asked to fixate on a centrally located light until a second light appeared, then shift to the second light as quickly as possible. Saccadic reaction time of the dys-lexics was significantly longer than that of the other two groups. Dys-lexics had a shorter saccadic reaction time when they were asked to look to the right than toward the left. The reverse was true for the other two groups. No differences were observed among groups in optokinetically-evoked nystagmus.

254 Fernald, Grace M. "A study of specific traits in cases of alexia."
     Psychol Bull 36(7): 509, July, 1939. (0 References).
In a study of sixty cases of alexia in persons nine to twenty-two years
old, emotional instability was characteristic. In all but four cases
the instability began after or about the same time as the failure to learn
to read. Emotional stability was restored in all cases by development of
reading skill without treating the emotional disorder as such. In all
cases the learning rate was normal when the technique for teaching reading was adapted to the individual. Persons with alexia learned to read
braille slightly better than the control group. Intelligence and other
tests showed specific ways in which the alexia cases differed from normal
readers.

255 Frith, Uta. "Internal schemata for letters in good and bad readers."
     Br J Psychol 65(2): 233-41, May, 1974. (17 References).
Tries to show the distinction between perceptual difficulties and the use
of internal schemata (internal diagrammatic presentation) as a useful
notion for studying reading difficulties. Groups of children ages seven
to twelve that included both good and poor readers, and a group of adults
participated in two experiments. Ten upper-case letters of the alphabet
were used. Subjects were to copy them. In other trials they were to copy
them, reversing them. Ten letter-like forms were used in the same way,
subjects being asked either to copy or reverse them. It is concluded
that perception of single letters is relatively unimportant in reading
skill. Schemata (internal representations of the letters) appeared weak
in young children, strong in older children. Familiarity of appearance
had no effect on performance in older children and adults, but familiarity
of movement did. At age twelve, bad readers were more affected by familiarity of movement than were good readers. The opposite result was obtained in younger groups (seven and seven and one-half years of age).
This is seen as indicating that in poor readers appropriate balance between use of external information and internal schemata was lacking.
Various hypotheses were drawn from these results. It is noted that there
are implications for remedial teaching. Poor readers in this study are
not seen as necessarily dyslexic, but typical of poor readers found in
ordinary schools.

256 Gascon, G., and Goodglass, H. "Reading retardation and the informa-
     tion content of stimuli in paired associate learning." Cortex
     6(4): 417-29, December, 1970. (14 References).
Reports on a study of groups of retarded readers and normal readers matched
for age and IQ. All were in third grade. Average age was eight years,
four months, and average IQs for the groups were 114.4 and 113.6 for poor
and good readers respectively. Lists of nonsense syllables not resembling
English words (auditorily poor) and lists resembling English words (auditorily rich) were made up and paired with ink scrawls in letter-like
forms (visually poor stimuli) and with three-dimensional clay models in
letter-like forms painted in two colors (visually rich stimuli). Normal
readers did better under all four conditions used in the testing. The
visually rich stimuli (object-like forms) were recognized by name far
better than the visually poor stimuli (letter-like forms), an effect more
marked in retarded readers than in normals. Auditorily enriched syllables
did not produce significant increases in learning efficiency, although
the data leaned that way. The hypothesis that reading retardation might
be caused by impairment in forming associations between stimuli of low
informational content, whether visual or auditory, is supported strongly.
The significance of this finding for understanding dyslexic performances

of young subjects, age eight or younger, is discussed. Some practical applications of the findings for teaching reading retardates are suggested.

257 Giebink, John W., and Goodsell, Linda L. "Reading ability and as-
     sociative learning for children with a visuomotor deficit." Am
     Educ Res J 5(3): 412-20, May, 1968. (11 References).
Groups of good and poor readers in the first three grades matched for
age, sex, intelligence, and visuomotor skill were found to differ significantly in their ability to perform paired-associate learning. The
paired-associate tasks used: (1) five common geometric forms to be paired
with four-letter verbs commonly found in primary readers; and (2) five
simplified Japanese characters also paired with four-letter verbs. There
was a significant difference in the number of trials needed to learn the
two tasks. The geometric forms task proved more difficult than the
derivatives of Japanese characters. However, the type of paired-associate
task had no relationship to reading ability. Good readers needed significantly fewer trials than poor readers to learn the lists of paired
associates. Fewer trials were needed for learning as grade level increased. Results suggest that there is an apparent strength and perma-
nence in the relationship between paired-associate learning and reading
ability since third-grade poor readers still had more difficulty with
the tasks than did good readers in first grade.

258 Goodacre, Elizabeth J. Reading research 1968-1970 and reading re-
     search 1971. 1972. 27p. (ED 079 690).
Two booklets cover research in reading from 1968 through 1971. The first
covers the years 1960-1970 and includes summaries of general trends in
reading.. Among topics considered are research on specific dyslexia, the
initial teaching alphabet, and the early stages of beginning to learn to
read. The first booklet also contains a bibliography of fifty-four
articles and thirty-five books, the latter annotated, published from 1968
to 1970 in areas of research which have drawn active interest from teachers and researchers. The second booklet discusses research articles
dealing with dyslexia, remedial help available, and teaching approaches,
among other topics. Thirteen books in various areas of reading which
were published in 1971 are listed and annotated.

259 ────────. Reading research 1972. 1972. 19p. (ED 076 969).
Details British research developments in the field of reading in 1972.
Reading standards, dyslexia, provision made for remedial help, length of
schooling, language and reading, and materials and medium are all covered.
An annotated bibliography of articles and books in the area of reading
and its teaching, including items on dyslexia, is given.

260 Goyen, Judith D., and Lyle, J. G. "Effect of incentives upon re-
     tarded and normal readers on a visual-associate learning task."
     J Exp Child Psychol 11(2): 274-80, April, 1971. (11 References).
Groups of twenty-eight good readers and twenty-eight retarded readers
six and seven years old were tested on their ability to learn correctly
which two geometric shapes went together in an associate-learning task.
Eleven pairs of shapes, including such items as square, star, cone, and
half-moon, were devised. The shapes were drawn on white cards. Two were
shown together, and the child was told that they went together. He was
asked to respond from a multiple-choice response system. Part of each
group, retarded and normal, was given an incentive, one half-penny for
each correct response. Incentives were found to have positive reinforcement value. Normal children who received the incentive learned fastest

of all. Retarded readers who received the incentive performed second
best. Retarded readers who did not receive the incentive were third.
Lowest of all were normal readers who did not receive the half-pennies.
It appears that retarded readers do not have special difficulty in learning to associate shapes. It is pointed out that this is not the same
thing as the task of learning to read.

261   Graubard, Paul S. "Psycholinguistic correlates of reading disabil-
      ity in disturbed delinquent children." J Spec Educ 1(4): 363-
      68, Summer, 1967. (20 References).
Lower-class, disturbed, delinquency-prone children have great difficulty
in learning how to read. In an attempt to understand why this is so,
this experiment studied thirty-five children ages eight to ten who had
been placed in residential treatment by the court because of antisocial
behavior. For purposes of the experiment, reading was viewed not only as
a skill, but also as part of the communication process. The children
were given the ITPA and other tests to reveal auditory closure, right-
left discrimination, and eye-hand coordination. The most significant
finding was that these children did deviate from normal communication
processes. They showed significantly more directional confusion and mixed dominance than normal children. There were deficits in visual-motor
association; at the integrational level in auditory-vocal automatic; and
in visual-motor sequencing. These children's developmental levels were
more comparable to six-year-old than to ten-year-old children. Standard
English seemed almost a foreign language to them. They failed to distinguish past, present, and future. They could not delay gratification,
had poor impulse control, and had a distorted sense of time. It is suggested that the whole-word method of reading instruction is the worst
means for teaching these children. Phonics would appear to be the method
of choice since their auditory channel was open and they were not deficient in synthesizing sounds.

262   Gray, William S. "Problems of reading disabilities requiring scien-
      tific study." Elem Engl Rev 12(4): 96-100, April, 1935. (0
      References).
A chief cause of reading difficulty is mental deficiency. Other causes
include visual problems, congenital word blindness, psychological factors,
and emotional instability. It is urged that various groups of investigators concentrate on one type of reading deficiency until all of the major
issues have been reasonably well solved. The views of Hinshelwood on the
causes of word blindness, or dyslexia, are given. The case of a sixteen-
year-old boy who suffered a head injury and afterward was unable to read
anything he himself had not written is recounted. We need a broad program
of research to identify different types of nonreaders, to discover basic
causes and symptoms, and to develop appropriate treatment.

263   Hansen, Erik. "Reading and writing difficulties in children with
      cerebral palsy." Little Club Clin Dev Med 10: 58-61, 1963. (4
      References).
In a study of English and Danish cerebral-palsied children, reading and
writing difficulties were frequently found to be associated with other
signs of parietal lobe dysfunction, more often than in children with
specific dylsexia. Many were found to have a complicated dyslexia which
could probably be considered a part of a more general disturbance of
space, direction, and sequence perception. A future research project for
the study of specific dyslexia in mentally defective and feebleminded
children is described.

264 Hartlage, Lawrence C., and Hartlage, Patricia L. "Comparison of
     hyperlexic and dyslexic children." Neurology 23(4): 436-37,
     April, 1973. (0 References).
Compares the diagnostic profiles of groups of dyslexic and hyperlexic
children. Great similarity of psychometric and social factors was found
in hyperlexic children, independent of age and intellectual level. All
had highest abilities in both auditory and visual sequencing, with lowest
abilities in spatial integration. Reverse patterns were found in dyslexics whose patterns of strengths and weaknesses also had internally consistent similarities and were almost mirror images of the hyperlexics.
Hyperlexia appeared to be strongly correlated with environmental factors.
Dyslexia showed stronger hereditary factors. It is suggested that the
causes are different in spite of the inverse symmetry and apparently related underlying origins.

265 Holt-Hansen, Kristian. "A perceptual-psychological approach to dys-
     lexia." Slow Learn Child 16(3): 162-71, 1969. (8 References).
Reports the results of psychological investigations on how the components
of letters are perceived. Letters are made up of several components, including straight lines, circles, ellipses, curves, and parts of all of
these. The Hering Illusion, a figure of straight lines radiating from a
center with two parallel vertical lines superimposed, was used with
stroboscopic light to demonstrate reversals in letters by dyslexics. Persons who were not dyslexic did not perceive the letters as reversing themselves as the vertical lines (with "d's" and "b's" substituted for part
of the lines) appeared to move in and out. An explanation of the problems of perception requires an understanding of the way the optic system
and the brain function in actual situations. Thus an electronic working
model of a neural correlate to experience is described in an attempt to
give an electronic explanation of perception.

266 Katz, Leonard, and Wicklund, David A. "Letter scanning rate for
     good and poor readers in grades two and six." J Educ Psychol
     63(4): 363-67, August, 1972. (6 References).
Second and sixth graders who were good and poor readers were asked to
scan rows of one, two, or four letters in search of a predetermined key
letter. Scan rate and response time were both slower for second graders
than for sixth graders. No differences were found because of reader
ability, a finding that agrees with previous conclusions that scan rate
for words does not differ between good and poor readers. Previous findings that good and poor readers differed in efficiency of response is
questioned in light of this study.

267 Kavruck, Samuel. "A study of the relation of retardation in reading
     to test performance on the revised Stanford-Binet (Form L)." J
     Educ Res 36(3): 221-23, November, 1942. (0 References).
Two groups of boys ages thirteen to sixteen, all of whom were in a training school for delinquents, were subjects in this study. They were
matched for age and IQ. One group was made up of normal readers; the
other of retarded readers. On the Stanford-Binet (Form L), retarded
readers were inferior to normal readers in vocabulary, in defining abstract words, in Minkus completion, and in assembling dissected sentences.
They excelled in memory for designs, in sentence memory, and in constructing a bead chain from memory. The only significant differences in favor
of retarded readers were in tasks involving memory. There were no differences between the groups in arithmetic reasoning.

268 Kelly, George A. "Some common factors in reading and speech dis-
    abilities." Psychol Monogr 43(1, Whole No. 194): 175-201, 1932.
    (20 References). (University of Iowa Studies in Psychology, No.
    15).

In studies on college freshmen involving reading, visual imagery, auditory
and visual aphasia tests, silent reasoning, and other tests performed
while a polygraph recorded the subjects' breathing, pulse, and laryngeal
movements, it was found that persons with reading disabilities did not
show the same breathing irregularities as stutterers during silent reading.
It is concluded that there is a common element of a transient nature in
speech and reading defects, inasmuch as a connection was found between
reading disability and defective speech rhythm independent of general
intelligence. The connection of lack of cerebral dominance to both
speech rhythm defects, such as stuttering, and reading disabilities independent of intelligence is seen as indicating a common neurological condition underlying both. Transient visual aphasia was found linked to
reading disability, and transient auditory aphasia was linked to stuttering. Neural blocking resulting from lack of cerebral dominance results
in a transient sensory aphasia. The tests for aphasia are described.
It is concluded that speech and reading defects have, independent of low
intelligence, a common element.

269 Kender, Joseph P. "Is there really a WISC profile for poor readers?"
    J Learn Disabil 5(7): 397-400, August, 1972. (8 References).

Reviews some of the studies aimed at finding out whether a typical WISC
profile for poor readers exists. No generalizations can be drawn from
these studies because of variations in criteria for selecting poor
readers, and varying statistical treatment. To report that poor readers
as a group make higher or lower scores on a subtest is misleading. It
would be more helpful if attempts were made to understand the relationship of WISC subtests to the reading process itself. Identifying tasks
on the WISC similar to tasks involved in reading is needed.

270 Klees, Marianne, and Lebrun, Ariane. "Analysis of the figurative
    and operative processes of thought of 40 dyslexic children." J
    Learn Disabil 5(7): 389-96, August/September, 1972. (12 Refer-
    ences).

In a group of forty dyslexic children seven to ten years old, 80 percent
were found to have delays in the development of the "figurative" aspects
of intelligence. Tests to explore what is termed the figurative aspect
of thought, or intelligence, included, for example, the Assembly, Coding,
and Kohs blocks subtests from the performance scale of the WISC. Delays
were also observed in their modes of approach to problems. Their thought
processes lagged behind the level at which practical intellectual problems could be solved.

271 Kolers, Paul A., and Perkins, David N. "Spatial and ordinal com-
    ponents of form perception and literacy." Cognitive Psychol
    7(2): 228-67, April, 1975. (50 References).

Tested a theory that the visual nervous system compensates for variations
in the appearance of one object, enabling the viewer to continue to
recognize the object even though its physical appearance may change. It
was theorized that a "dialogue" goes on between the problem-solving
processes and the object being recognized. It is suggested that the
visual nervous system possesses compensatory rectifying mechanisms by
means of which it achieves "constancy" of visual recognition despite
variation in physical appearance of the stimulus object. Subjects were

fifty-six male college freshmen and sophomores who were right-dominant
for hand, eye, and foot. They were given training sessions in reading
typewritten pages where some of the pages were typed in mirror image or
upside down, or transformed in various other ways. Time spent reading
a test page varied with training received. This and other aspects of
the results are explained. The question for which an answer was sought
was: When a reader solves the pattern recognition problem posed by one
of the transformations, what has he actually done? Various answers to
this question are given, and a "components theory" is explained. Certain
aspects of the theory are applied to reading disability. It is suggested,
on this theory, that misreadings come when the reader loses track of the
transformation he is reading, or when he makes mistakes because the
orientation of the reading material is not thoroughly learned. On a
basis of the analysis put forward in this study, the three types of error
most common among dyslexics--order errors, reversals, and rotations--
are motivated by substantially different mechanisms.

272 Kopel, David, and Geerdes, Harold. "A survey of clinical procedures
     in the diagnosis and treatment of poor reading." J Educ Psychol
     35(1): 1-16, January, 1944. (Bibliographic Footnotes).
Reports data on methods, materials used, and estimates of effectiveness
in treating reading difficulties gathered in a 1940 survey of the facilities and practices of fifty-eight psychological reading clinics in many
parts of the country. In general, the better clinics followed some type
of case-study method in collecting pertinent information from the child,
his parents, physician, or others involved. Vision, hearing, emotional
adjustment, and reading ability were tested in general. More than three-
fourths of the clinics reported that none or few reading disability cases
were free from additional problems. About a fifth of the clinics provided only diagnosis and recommendations. The remainder provided some
degree of treatment, very often in the form of psychiatric help. Many
clinics estimated substantial success in 50 to 90 percent of their cases.
Some clinics were making studies of reading problems. A list of areas
needing more research is suggested.

273 ————. "A survey of clinical services for poor readers." J
     Educ Psychol 33(3): 209-20, March, 1942. (0 References).
In response to a questionnaire survey it was discovered that much service
is available to poor readers in various kinds of psychological and psychiatric clinics. Clinical personnel appear to have excellent professional qualifications, and public acceptance of the clinics is good.
The clinics report seeing more reading disability cases from primary
grades than from any other level, and that somewhat more cases of poor
reading were seen in 1938-39 than in 1937-38.

274 Krise, Morley. "An experimental investigation of theories of re-
     versals in reading." J Educ Psychol 43(7): 408-22, November,
     1952. (25 References).
Using adults who read at college level, with one exception, as subjects,
this study required subjects to learn unfamiliar, reversible symbols for
letters commonly reversed. These symbols were substituted in words in
such a fashion that even a misreading still produced a familiar word,
e.g., "dot" and "pot." The theory tested was that all subjects would
commit reversals in reading these unfamiliar symbols and continue to do
so with diminishing frequency until no more reversals were made. The
theory was proved. This result is discussed in light of various theories
as to why children who are beginning readers make reversals. The theory

that reversals are the result of visual immaturity which the child out-
grows would seem to be undermined by this finding. It would seem to
have implications for remedial work.

275 Lyle, J. G., and Goyen, Judith D. "Performance of retarded and
     normal readers on a visual-auditory learning task with and without
     reinforcers." Percept Mot Skills 38(1): 199-204, February, 1974.
     (19 References).
Groups of normal and retarded readers seven and eight years old from
London schools were given a learning task similar to learning the alphabet. Letter-like shapes were shown each child and he was told the letter-
like name to be associated with the shape. When tested for learning of
this material, some of the children were given reinforcement. They were
told when they were correct, and given a half-penny for each right response. Others were given no indication of the correctness of their
responses. In the group which received no reinforcement, retarded
readers had superior performance. Normal readers improved with reinforcement. Differences between the reinforced and unreinforced treatment
was not significant overall. It is concluded that simple learning of
letter labels is not an important problem in reading retardation.

276 Lytton, Hugh; Croxen, Mary E.; Pysh, Fred. "Regression to the mean
     misunderstood: a reply to Vockell and Asher." Dev Psychol 8(1):
     3-5, January, 1973. (7 References).
Presents a defense and reply to the criticism of research done by Croxen
and Lytton on reading disability and difficulties in finger localization
and right-left discrimination. (See Item No. 862). The criticism is by
Vockell and Asher. (See Item No. 296). Regression to the mean refers to
the tendency of extreme scores on a test to move toward the mean of the
population at retesting.

277 McLeod, John. "Some psycholinguistic correlates of reading dis-
     ability in young children." Read Res Q 2(3): 5-31, Spring, 1967.
     (33 References).
Three experiments with second graders revealed that the reading-disabled
group was consistently inferior to the normal control group in reproducing visually presented letter sequences. They were also inferior in
reproducing vocally words presented auditorily. Isolated monosyllabic
words were reproduced orally by both groups without significant difference. The reading-disabled children were inferior in discriminating between two monosyllabic words which differed in only one phoneme. Visual
test material consisted of tachistoscopically presented sequences of
letters. In order for the reading-disabled group to be successful 50
percent of the time in reproducing the orally presented words, it was
necessary to use a higher sound intensity. There was a tendency for
their performance to be better when the stimulus words were preceded by
context which more closely approximated spoken English. Much louder
presentation was necessary for disabled readers to achieve results comparable to that of normal readers in discriminating the monosyllabic
words.

278 Maxwell, A. E.; Fenwick, P. B. C.; Fenton, G. W.; et al. "Reading
     ability and brain function: a simple statistical model." Psychol
     Med 4(3): 274-80, August, 1974. (8 References).
Intelligence test results for two groups of children, good and poor
readers, are analyzed. It is concluded that poor readers use more of the
basic components of the brain on tests of verbal ability than do good

readers, but to less effect.   That is, there is more neural activity in
their brains.   Good readers age five and one-half have already developed
a facility for identifying and classifying verbal material.   To test the
idea suggested by this finding, that the EEG spectrum for poor readers
would be consistently higher than that for good readers, EEG tests were
performed on fourteen-year-old children divided into groups of good and
poor readers.   These expected amplitude differences were found between
the groups when eyes were open but not when eyes were closed.   This was
seen as the expected result.   In those subjects who comprehended poorly,
a difficult cognitive task would involve the total neuron pool; but only
a fraction of the brain elements of those who comprehended well was involved.   When eyes were closed it was to be expected that less information was being processed, more brain elements were freed, and differences
in neural activity between the two groups tended to disappear.

279   Mellone, Margaret A.   "An investigation into the relationship be-
      tween reading ability and I.Q. as measured by a verbal group in-
      telligence test."   Br J Educ Psychol 12(2): 128-35, June, 1942.
      (9 References).
Investigates whether lack of reading ability prevents children who are
poor readers from obtaining accurate IQ scores on verbal intelligence
tests.   Four groups of children ages eight, nine, ten, and eleven were
tested.   The influence of reading was no greater on the verbal IQ scores
of a group of backward readers at age eight than at age eleven.   In
eight-year-olds the mean verbal IQ was significantly lower than the mean
nonverbal IQ, but this was not true for children nine and older.   It is
concluded that lack of reading ability tends to interfere with the verbal
scores of the eight-year-olds, and that the tests do not measure the true
IQ until age nine and one-half years.

280   Noland, Eunice C., and Schuldt, W. John.   "Sustained attention and
      reading retardation."   J Exp Educ 40(2): 73-76, Winter, 1971.
      (11 References).
Two groups of fourth graders, one poor readers, the other normal readers,
matched for age, grade, sex, and IQ, were asked to press a switch in
response to the flash of a light.   Response time was measured in thou-
sandths of a second.   Presentations of the light on a prescribed schedule
lasted thirty minutes.   Results show that vigilance requiring sustained
visual attention did divide the groups.   Retarded readers detected significantly fewer visual stimuli than normal readers.   They also took
longer to respond.   Number of correct detections fell and time required
for response increased for both groups as the testing progressed.   Differences in response latencies (time required to respond) were not
statistically significant between the groups.

281   Olson, Madelyn E.   "Laterality differences in tachistoscopic word
      recognition in normal and delayed readers in elementary school."
      Neuropsychologia 11(3): 343-50, July, 1973. (21 References).
Normal readers ages seven to eleven showed a right visual field preference for word recognition as do adults.   It was not correlated with
handedness or lateral awareness.   Studies of poor readers the same age
also showed a right visual field preference.   Poor readers ages eight
and nine showed no field superiority.   It is suggested that the findings
support the theory that hemispheric specialization for language processing develops as the nervous system matures.   Subjects were seated in a
dimly lighted room.   They were asked to focus their eyes on a point on a
screen.   Three-letter or four-letter nouns were presented on the screen

for varying lengths of time and to the right or left visual field or to
both fields at the same time.

282 Otto, Wayne; Koenke, Karl; Cooper, Carin. "Good and poor readers'
     learning of verbal and pictorial paired-associate lists." Psychon
     Sci 11(10): 347-48, August 5, 1968. (8 References).
Groups of good and poor readers of average intelligence in grades two and
five were individually shown eight pairs of cards containing common objects represented either as line drawings (pictorially) or as words
(verbally). The cards were shown one pair at a time for five seconds.
The task was to tell the examiner what picture or word was on the other
card after one card was shown again. The prediction that poor readers
would make more errors when the verbal pairs were shown, but that there
would be no difference when the pictures were shown, was not supported.
Poor readers made more errors than good readers in both methods of
presentation. Both groups made fewer errors with pictures than with
verbal presentation.

283 Perot, Suzanne Baird. "Problems in cross-national analyses of read-
     ing failure." Read Teach 27(4): 375-78, January, 1974. (7 Ref-
     erences).
Deals with the problems of comparing reading failure between two countries,
which include the problems of assessing the degree of regularity and
grapheme-phoneme correspondence of a language and the amount of difficulty
children experience in learning to read it. The difficulty lies not so
much in analyzing the language as in comparing findings of a study done
in one nation with findings in another nation. The first group of problems include those concerned with the differences in writing systems,
e.g., the alphabetic systems of most Western languages as compared with
the ideographic characters employed by Chinese and Japanese. Other
problems are the direction in which the language is read; the degree of
a regular correspondence between a written symbol and its sound; and the
assessment of cultural and educational influences on reading within
countries. Arriving at a definition of reading failure that can be applied to all countries and considering forms of a given language that
are not standard are other problems to be faced.

284 Pikulski, John J. "A comparison of figure drawings and WISC IQ's
     among disabled readers." J Learn Disabil 5(3): 156-59, March,
     1972. (10 References).
Scores on the Goodenough and the Goodenough-Harris tests of human figure
drawing which have been used to measure the intelligence of children for
many years were compared with the WISC scores of reading-diabled children. Significant correlations were obtained with the performance, but
not with the verbal, section of the WISC. It is suggested that in some
cases the figure drawing scores could very seriously underestimate a
child's intellectual ability.

285 Robeck, Mildred C. "Effects of prolonged reading disability: a
     preliminary study." Percept Mot Skills 19(1): 7-12, August,
     1964. (5 References).
Two groups of retarded readers attending a reading clinic were observed.
One group contained children in grades two and three, with an average age
of seven years. The other group was made up of children in grades six
through nine, with an average age of thirteen years. Primary and teen-
age groups both revealed more frustration than did children in middle
grades. Adolescents with severe reading problems scored significantly

lower than the young children on WISC Information, Arithmetic, and Vocabulary subtests. Both groups scored significantly below the WISC population
samples in Information, Arithmetic, Digit Span, and Coding. Some characteristics of young children had disappeared in older cases, e.g., hyperactivity, distractibility, and confused laterality. It is suggested that
thorough investigation of the causes of reading difficulty must begin
early.

286 ————. "Subtest patterning of problem readers on WISC." Calif
      J Educ Res 11(3): 110-15, May, 1960. (6 References).
Studied the performance of problem readers on WISC subtests. Subjects
were four girls and thirty-two boys enrolled in a university reading
clinic. Ages ranged from six to thirteen years. Full scale IQs ranged
from 85 to 136 with average verbal IQ of 106.75 and average performance
IQ of 111.75. This group of reading-disabled children scored significantly higher than Weschler's population sample on six subtests: Comprehension, Block Design, Comparison, Picture Completion, Vocabulary,
and Object Assembly. They showed relative weakness which was statistically significant in four subtests: Digit Span, Arithmetic, Information,
and Coding.

287 Rowell, Charles Glennon. "Change in attitude toward reading and its
      relationship to certain variables among children with reading dif-
      ficulties." For a summary see: Diss Abstr 28A(5): 1630-31,
      November, 1967.

288 Rutter, Michael; Graham, Philip; Birch, Herbert G. "Interrelations
      between the choreiform syndrome, reading disability and psychiatric
      disorder in children of 8 to 11 years." Dev Med Child Neurol
      8(2): 149-59, April, 1966. (10 References).
In large samples of children ages seven to eleven and including some
mentally subnormal, some backward in reading, and some normal readers
who were used as controls, the movements termed "choreiform syndrome"
were found most often in boys, younger children, and those of subnormal
intelligence. No significant association was found between the movements and reading disability, psychiatric disorder, neurological abnormality, or the conditions of the mother's pregnancy. The question is
raised as to whether the movements are of any clinical significance.
"Choreiform syndrome" is the term used to describe the slight jerky movements of short duration which occur suddenly and irregularly and without
rhythm in different muscles.

289 Sawyer, Diane J. "The diagnostic mystique--a point of view." Read
      Teach 27(6): 555-61, March, 1974. (13 References).
It is time to look beyond the very latest diagnostic tools available for
focusing on the child and his relationship with the content of reading,
and to view the child as a fine precision mechanism programmed to process
information and to learn. The skill approach to reading has led us to
believe that if the child can master specific skills that he lacks, success in reading will follow. This may be true for mildly disabled
readers, but it has not been the norm for more severely disabled ones.
Research reports point to the variables in cognitive factors (those
relating to thought processes) and to variables in affective factors
(emotional responses). Such research makes a strong case for viewing
the disabled reader as a problem solver interacting with his environment,
not simply a child deficient in some crucial reading skill. Research
efforts related to materials and methods during the past fifty years have

not helped show why some children do not learn to read. Future efforts should focus on the learner and how to teach him more effective learning styles. We must abandon our too-simple approach to the learning process and to chronic learning problems.

290 Silver, Archie A., and Hagin, Rosa A. "Specific reading disability: follow-up studies." Am J Orthopsychiatry 34(1): 95-102, January, 1964. (22 References).

Individuals treated for specific reading disability as children were given the same tests as young adults ten to twelve years later. The perceptual and laterality problems were found to persist, but in less severe form. Those who had neurological signs as children showed less improvement than individuals who had no such signs in childhood.

291 Stanley, Gordon. "The processing of digits by children with specific reading disability (dyslexia)." Br J Educ Psychol 46(Part 1): 81-84, February, 1976. (9 References).

Two groups of dyslexics and a control group of normal readers ages eight to nine and nine to twelve were individually tested using the ten digits 0 to 9 presented visually. The child was instructed to press a response button labeled with the same digit to indicate which digit was displayed. A mask of dots covering the digits was presented at varying intervals between digits. Reaction time was measured. Dyslexics performed better than controls on digit identifications. Dyslexics made similar errors, making more errors with digits having curved features. Normal readers did not show this error profile. Dyslexics processed single digits at the same rate as controls. Difficulties with larger sets of digits, as in digit span tasks, presumably are caused by limited capacity.

292 Stanley, Gordon, and Hall, Rodney. "Short-term visual information processing in dyslexics." Child Dev 44(4): 841-44, December, 1973. (8 References).

Two groups of children eight to twelve years old who were normal physically and emotionally were divided on the basis of reading ability. Letters and geometric shapes were presented visually. Presentations were twenty msec. apart at first. The interval was increased until the child no longer reported the display as consisting of a composite figure. In a second experiment letters of the alphabet were visually presented interspersed with a pattern of dots which covered the area, masking the letter. The child's task was to identify the letter before it was covered. Results indicate that dyslexics have slower visual information processing time than normal readers. The implication is that the scan and retrieval process takes longer for dyslexics than for normal readers.

293 Stanley, Gordon, and Molloy, M. "Retinal painting and visual information storage." Acta Psychol 39(4): 283-88, August, 1975. (11 References).

It is assumed that in processing and storing information seen (visual information store), there is a literal persistence of information after the physical cessation of the stimulus that allows the observer to process the content of what he has seen. This persistence is literal, but of limited duration. If a narrow slit oscillates in front of a stationary drawing of some object, allowing only a segment to be seen at one time, the eye will perceive the object as a whole if the oscillation is at the appropriate speed. It has been suggested that the successive slices of the form are "painted out" across the retina. Two experiments were set up to examine the retinal painting task in relation to the assumption that it is a measure of visual information store. Adults and nine-year-old children were subjects in one test. Adults perceived pictures of animals at a slower sweep rate than children, which was interpreted to mean that adult visual persistence is greater than that of children. Groups of normal and dyslexic eight- to twelve-year-old children were subjects in the second experiment. No difference was found between the groups. This is seen as supporting the claim that retinal painting differs from other measures of visual information store.

294 Steinheiser, Rick, and Guthrie, John T. "Scanning times through prose and word strings for various targets by normal and disabled readers." Percept Mot Skills 39(2): 931-38, October, 1974. (9 References).
Three groups of twelve subjects each were used: disabled readers; a group matched with them for age; and a group matched for reading level. All were given a simple five-sentence passage to read, and instructed to find words of a given category, the letter "o" and the phomeme /ae/. All groups found the words first, the letter second, and the phoneme last. Disabled readers were superior to reading-level matched subjects in the search for the letter, but the disabled readers were extremely slow in searching for the phoneme. Results were interpreted to mean that words were encoded as "gestalts," the word being the unit of analysis.

295 Stewart, Mary Lou. "Slow developing normal boys as disabled readers: a speculative pilot study." Read Horizons 12(3): 117-28, 1972.

296 Vockell, Edward L., and Asher, William. "Methodological inaccuracies in Croxen & Lytton's 'reading disability and difficulties in finger localization and right-left discrimination.'" Dev Psychol 8(1): 1-2, January, 1973. (7 References).
See Item No. 862 for the Croxen and Lytton article criticized. This criticism of the research design and interpretation of the article charges that the results of the study are difficult to evaluate and to interpret. Suggestions for improvement are made.

297 Vogel, Susan A., and McGrady, Harold J. "Recognition of melody pattern in good and poor readers." Elem Engl 52(3): 414-18, March, 1975. (21 References).
Ability to identify different intonation patterns, e.g., whether a sentence is a statement or a question, was tested in good and poor readers by reading to them nonsense words arranged to imitate the melody pattern of a real English sentence. Subjects were second-grade boys seven and eight years of age. Good readers were superior to poor readers in their ability to identify melody patterns. Auditory memory was not a factor in performance on the test of recognition of melody patterns. The test did discriminate between good and poor readers better than eight other syntactic measures. It is suggested that much remains to be learned about the relationship between intonation and perception of syntactic patterns in the reading process.

298 Wallbrown, Fred H.; Blaha, John; Counts, Dorotha H.; et al. "The hierarchical factor structure of the WISC and revised ITPA for reading disabled children." J Psychol 88(1): 65-76, September, 1974. (28 References).
The WISC and ITPA often are used together to assess the abilities of learning-disabled children. Both have been studied for factor analysis. This study was undertaken to examine the factoral composition of the two

tests by obtaining an hierarchical factor solution on intercorrelations among the subtests comprising the two tests. Intercorrelations were obtained on 110 disabled readers ages eight through ten with IQs of 75 to 125. Statistical analysis of findings for the various subtests are explained. The two tests appear to be about equally effective for measuring general intelligence. The most effective single assessor from the WISC and the ITPA is the ITPA Auditory Association subtest. Vernon's hierarchical paradigm appears to be a useful framework for interpreting results on the two tests with reading-disabled children.

299 Wallbrown, Fred H.; Blaha, John; Huelsman, Charles B., Jr.; et al. "A further test of Myklebust's cognitive structure hypotheses for reading disabled children." Psychol Sch 12(2): 176-81, April, 1975. (16 References).
Tested three hypotheses: (1) The ability structure of severely reading-disabled children is distinguishable from that of normal readers by a different overall ability arrangement as indicated by WISC subtests. (2) The ability structure of severely reading-disabled children is distinguishable from that of normal readers by less effective ability integration as indicated by a smaller proportion of the variance on WISC subtests that can be attributed to general intelligence. (3) The ability structure of severely reading-disabled children is distinguishable from that of normal readers by less ability organization as reflected in WISC subtests. Data on WISC subtest intercorrelations was obtained for normal children from Wechsler's data for children ages seven and one-half, ten and one-half, and thirteen and one-half years. Subtest intercorrelations for 240 severely reading-disabled children were obtained from other studies. These data were subjected to appropriate statistical procedures to obtain hierarchical factor solutions on WISC subtest intercorrelations for the normal and reading-disabled children. The first two hypotheses were supported. The third was not. The method of statistical analysis used is seen as an effective research tool for this type of problem. It is suggested that test performance of the reading-disabled child cannot be interpreted in terms of the factor structure obtained for normals.

300 Wallbrown, Fred H.; Blaha, John; Wherry, Robert J., Sr.; et al. "An empirical test of Myklebust's cognitive structure hypotheses for 70 reading-disabled children." J Consult Clin Psychol 42(2): 211-18, April, 1974. (18 References).
Subtest intercorrelations on the WISC were obtained for seventy reading-disabled children ages seven to thirteen years. Full scale WISC IQs ranged from 89 to 120. Children with physical impairments or emotional disturbance were eliminated. The subtest intercorrelations for this group were compared statistically with intercorrelations for normal children given by Weschler to investigate Myklebust's hypotheses that learning-disabled children display less effective ability integration, less ability organization, and a different overall arrangement of abilities as indicated by the hierarchical factor structure of WISC subtests. Comparison of hierarchical factor structure obtained from normal and reading-disabled children tends to support the ability integration hypothesis. The hypothesis concerning ability organization was not supported. The ability structure of reading-disabled subjects appears to be distinguishable from that of normal readers by a different overall ability arrangement. These results may be accepted, subject to certain theoretical assumptions and operational procedures, which are described.

301 Wirtenberg, Thelma J., and Faw, Terry T. "The development of learning sets in adequate and retarded readers." J Learn Disabil 8(5):
304-7, May, 1975. (2 References).
Boys ages seven to nine years were divided into two groups, one group
good and one group poor readers. Older boys ten to twelve years were also
divided into groups of good and poor readers. The boys were shown pairs
of nonsense syllables presented in various colors, sizes, writing styles,
and positions. The task was to ignore all variables except the same
nonsense syllable on each trial. The purpose of the study was to determine whether retarded readers were deficient in ability to generalize
learning among many problems of a single kind. This ability to generalize
from the solution of one problem to the solution of a similar problem
presented at a different time is referred to as a "learning set," or
learning to learn. It was found that retarded readers needed more problems to reach the criterion set for success in learning than did adequate
readers. Younger children required more problems to reach criterion
than did older children.

302 Zedler, Empress Y. Research conference on the problem of dyslexia
and related disorders in public schools of the United States.
Final report. 1967. 96p. (ED 015 834).
This is the final report of a closed conference held at Southwest Texas
State College, San Marcos, Texas, May 15-16, 1967. Twenty-five participants from interested professions and interest groups and ten observers
representing federal agencies took part. Areas of research, diagnosis,
teacher preparation, and corrective education relevant to dyslexia and
other related learning disabilities were addressed. The reports of the
four working groups were endorsed and recommendation was made that a
commission be appointed to examine the problems, make recommendations
for a national program to deal with the problem, and develop guidelines.

V

Causes and Frequently Observed Accompanying Factors

A. CEREBRAL DOMINANCE ANOMALIES; MIXED LATERALITY

303 Anthony, George A. "Cerebral dominance as an etiological factor in dyslexia (severe reading disability)." For a summary see: Diss Abstr Int 30A(4): 1425-26, October, 1969.

304 Balow, Irving H. "Lateral dominance characteristics and reading achievement in the first grade." J Psychol 55(2): 323-28, 1963. (5 References).
No combination of hand and eye dominance, strength of dominance, lack of dominance, or knowledge of left and right was found to be significantly associated with reading achievement among 320 first-grade children.

305 Bannatyne, Alex. "Mirror-images and reversals." Acad Ther 8(1): 87-92, Fall, 1972. (0 References).
The distinction is made between the mirror images of letters and reversing words. It is explained that language functions are largely controlled in the left cerebral hemisphere of the brain. Mirror-image language problems are explained in terms of incomplete suppression of the right hemisphere during language activities. Maturational lag in older children may be responsible for mirror imaging. Speculation on causes and suggestions for treatment are offered.

306 Beck, Harry Sterling. "An experimental investigation of the relationship of hand-eye dominance and reversals in reading among second grade children." For a summary see: Diss Abstr 21(8): 2375-76, February, 1961.

307 Belmont, Lillian, and Birch, Herbert G. "Lateral dominance, lateral awareness, and reading disability." Child Dev 36(1): 57-71, March, 1965. (12 References).

No differences were found between groups of good and poor readers in Aberdeen, Scotland, in lateralization of preferential hand and eye usage. Significant differences were found in the level of right-left orientation. Subjects were 150 retarded readers and fifty normal readers, all nine- and ten-year-old boys. The lowest scores on sequential reading were associated with left-right confusion of the child's own body parts.

308 Benson, D. Frank, and Geschwind, Norman. "Cerebral dominance and
        its disturbances." Pediatr Clin North Am 15(3): 759-69, August,
        1968. (28 References).
A review of information available about cerebral dominance is presented together with a brief discussion of some of the conditions thought to be related to disorders of dominance. It appears to remain unclear whether delayed or mixed dominance is important as a cause of dyslexia.

309 Benton, Curtis D., and McCann, James W., Jr. "Dyslexia and domi-
        nance: some second thoughts." J Pediatr Ophthalmol 6(4): 220-
        22, November, 1969. (9 References).
Contrary to research conclusions previously published by these authors, they now believe crossed or mixed dominance is not a diagnostic or specific characteristic of dyslexia, and that eye dominance is not an important measure in evaluating dyslexia. Because research findings by several other investigators did not duplicate findings in previous studies by Benton, Benton reanalyzed his studies and reached different conclusions. A lack of homolaterality is still found more frequently in dyslexics than in good readers. But since many excellent readers also display mixed dominance, it cannot be said that crossed or mixed dominance is a diagnostic or specific characteristic of dyslexia. Almost all observers agree that the eyes are implicated in dyslexia. More than half the dyslexics tested in this research performed poorly on tests of eye-motor coordination, spatial relations, form constancy, figure-ground discrimination, and position in space. The significance of these findings is not fully understood, and it is now believed that eye dominance is not an important measure for evaluting dyslexia.

310 Benton, Curtis D.; McCann, James W., Jr.; Larsen, Marguerite. "Dys-
        lexia and dominance." J Pediatr Ophthalmol 2(3): 53-57, July,
        1965. (8 References).
In a group of 250 children with reading disabilities, all were found to have either crossed eye-hand dominance or more than normal retinal rivalry. The latter is believed to be an indication of improper eye dominance. Treatment was aimed at developing smooth cooperation between the patient's eyes, overcoming binocular conflict, and establishing hand and eye unilaterality. It is reported that 87 percent of the 150 patients followed up showed improvement.

311 Bergquam, Hazel H. "Neural confusion and academic failure."
        Education 82(6): 362-65, February, 1962. (0 References).
Neural confusion is caused by mixed dominance between the two cerebral hemispheres of the brain. It results in reversals, confusion of letters, mirror writing, and hesitant speech or stuttering. It affects boys more often than girls. It may be a family trait. The classroom teacher should be aware of the true nature of reading handicaps.

312 Bø, Ola O. "The extent of the connection between cerebral dominance
        of speech functions (auditory and vocal), hand dominance, and dys-
        lexia." Scand J Educ Res 16(2-3): 61-88, 1972. (76 References).

Presents a review of the literature and summary of studies investigating
the relationship between hand and cerebral dominance for language functions. It has long been assumed that some sort of relationship exists
among hand dominance, the cerebral hemisphere dominant for language, and
dyslexia. In right-handed persons the left hemisphere seems to be dominant for language functions, although the extent of some right-side representation is not clear. For left-handers results are not so clear.
In left-handed persons left dominance is probably more common than right,
but the lateralization seems not to be pronounced. A large number of
studies of the connection between dyslexia and hand dominance have been
carried out. As early as 1939, half of thirty such studies reported a
connection. Conclusions range from categorical statements that there is
a connection, to those suggesting that a connection may be possible.
The best viewpoint may be that there is a possibility that those having
reading difficulty have not established as complete a degree of dominance
as others. In reality, the problem of a connection between dyslexia and
hand dominance is unresolved. This is true partly because the terms are
not precisely defined.

313 Brod, Nathan, and Hamilton, David. "Monocular-binocular coordina-
     tion vs. hand-eye dominance as a factor in reading performance."
     Am J Optom 48(2): 123-29, February, 1971. (21 References).
A sample of 162 fifth graders was divided into three groups: good, average, and poor readers. They were asked to read three different passages
orally under three conditions: (1) with plano (flat) lenses on both
eyes; (2) with a plano lens on left eye and an aniseikonic lens on the
other eye; and (3) the reverse of the second condition. The aniseikonic
lens was used to disturb binocular vision without significantly affecting
monocular vision. A significantly larger number of children with mixed
hand-eye dominance were found among poor readers than among good readers.
There was no significant difference in distribution of hand dominance
among the three groups. Results supported the hypothesis that any relationship between hand-eye dominance and reading performance is very
likely a function of the dominant eye, rather than combined hand and eye
preference. It was also concluded that integration of monocular and
binocular functions is an important factor in reading performance.

314 Brown, Carl Fraser. "Lateral dominance and reading in the elementary
     school." In: George Peabody College for Teachers. Abstracts of
     dissertations. Nashville, Tennessee, 1946. 1-10.

315 Bryden, M. P. "Laterality effects in dichotic listening: relations
     with handedness and reading ability in children." Neuropsychologia
     8(4): 443-50, November, 1970. (21 References).
Children in grades two, four, and six were given dichotic listening tests.
This procedure involved presenting two different lists of numbers simultaneously, one to each ear. The children were scored, not on the number
of digits identified correctly, but on which ear they scored better. On
this basis, they were classified right-ear or left-ear dominant. Right-
ear dominance increased with age in right-handers, and decreased with age
in left-handers. Girls showed the adult pattern of ear dominance earlier
than boys. Boys who were poor readers were more likely to show crossed
ear-hand dominance than boys who were good readers. This effect was
found in girls only at the grade two level. It is suggested that in the
early grades dichotic listening tests might be of use in identifying
potential poor readers.

316 Capobianco, R. J. "Ocular-manual laterality and reading achieve-
     ment in children with special learning disabilities." Am Educ Res
     J 4(2): 133-37, March, 1967. (12 References).
The subjects in this study were forty-six children, mostly boys, with
learning disabilities and suggested cerebral dysfunction. The age range
was seven to sixteen years. The WISC and the WRAT were given to ascertain IQ and reading level. As a group, these children were about one
year retarded in reading achievement. No relationship was found between
laterality and reading performance. It is suggested that determination
of laterality preference as part of diagnostic procedure in cases of
reading disability is not of value.

317 Cassin, Barbara. "The eye and dyslexia." Am Orthopt J 19: 136-
     42, 1969. (3 References).
In tests for eye and hand dominance in 147 children in the third, fourth,
and fifth grades, 37 percent were found to be homolateral, or to have
the controlling eye and hand on the same side; 46 percent had incomplete
or mixed dominance; and 17 percent were cross-dominant, with the controlling eye on the opposite side from the controlling hand. Being homolateral almost insured development of at least average reading ability,
it is concluded. However, mixed or cross dominance did not necessarily
assure that the child would have reading problems. Most persons with
reading problems have normal visual acuity.

318 "The cause of 'wordblindness.'" Science (New Series) 80(2084):
     supplement 12, 14, December 7, 1934. (0 References).
Explains the theory attributed to Walter F. Dearborn that mixed cerebral
dominance or uncertain dominance, in which the person prefers neither
right nor left hand and eye, is the cause of word blindness or difficulties in reading. "Alexia" is the term used for absence of reading ability; "dyslexia" is used for lesser degrees of difficulty in learning to
read. This is a departure from the belief that reading disability is
caused by defects in the brain. Reading difficulties are best avoided
if the person is right-handed and right-eyed or prefers the left side
altogether. A report of a study with dyslexic schoolchildren indicates
a high proportion showed left-, cross-, or mixed-dominance. Dominance
problems are only one of several causes, however.

319 Cohen, Alice, and Glass, Gerald G. "Lateral dominance and reading
     ability." Read Teach 21(4): 343-48, January, 1968. (2 Refer-
     ences).
In this study first graders who were poor readers were found to be confused on knowledge of left and right, and to have mixed-hand dominance
more than good readers in first grade. IQ scores were not significantly
related to reading ability in first grade. Knowledge of left and right
and hand dominance were not related to reading ability in the fourth
grade children studied. IQ scores were significantly related to reading
ability in fourth grade.

320 Coleman, Richard I., and Deutsch, Cynthia P. "Lateral dominance and
     right-left discrimination: a comparison of normal and retarded
     readers." Percept Mot Skills 19(1): 43-50, August, 1964. (9
     References).
Tests revealed no differences between normal and retarded readers in
lateral dominance and right-left discrimination. It is suggested that
results indicate that laterality difficulties do not always accompany
reading disability in children ten years old or older. Subjects were

public-school children, mostly boys, ages nine to twelve and of lower
socioeconomic background. The Harris Test of Lateral Dominance and the
Benton Right-Left Discrimination Test were used. Both normal and retarded readers had difficulty with other-person items.

321 Craig, Lillian, with suggestions by Mrs. Samuel T. Orton. "The
     strephosymbolic can learn to read!" Va J Educ 38(6): 238, 247-
     48, February, 1945. (0 References).
Presents the plight of the bright child who attends school regularly, yet
cannot learn to read. Special schools are provided for the blind and
deaf, but the child who is strephosymbolic is often denied the education
he is capable of receiving. Dr. Samuel T. Orton's work in treating
strephosymbolics is described. This type of child can be identified by
his inability to recognize words no matter how often he is told, and by
the tendency to reverse letters, and to miscall small words. He may
have speech problems and write or spell poorly. He cannot learn by the
sight method. Phonics correctly taught is the method by which he can
learn to read.

322 Crider, Blake. "The lack of cerebral dominance as a cause of read-
     ing disabilities." Child Educ 10(5): 238-39, 270, February,
     1934. (9 References).
Describes Orton's theory that reading difficulties arise from one cerebral hemisphere having failed to become completely dominant. The theory
is not substantiated. Monroe's studies carried out under Orton's direction failed to support the Orton theory. Conclusions of Dearborn's
studies in the area must be accepted with reservation. Orton's theory
appears to be an oversimplification of the problem. It does not take
into consideration other causes of learning difficulties such as low intelligence, inadequate visual perception, and others. There is no proof
that eye preference is related to cerebral dominance or to handedness.
The opinions of Orton and Dearborn are hypotheses, not theories, and
even less facts.

323 Crosland, H. R. "Superior elementary-school readers contrasted with
     inferior readers in letter-position, 'range of attention,' scores."
     J Educ Res 32(6): 410-27, February, 1939. (0 References).
Thirty-one superior and thirty-four inferior readers, average age eleven
and one-half years, were compared. Superior readers surpassed defective
readers in the left visual field. Inferior readers surpassed superior
readers in the extreme right visual field. The majority of the defective
children were left-eyed, and a larger majority of superior readers were
right-eyed. Some relationship of left-eye dominance with defective reading is inferred, but it is believed that there are other causes of poor
reading skill.

324 Currier, Fred P. "Certain reading disabilities as related to
     speech." J Mich State Med Soc 37: 414-18, May, 1938. (6 Refer-
     ences).
Quotes from Orton's explanation of the three visual levels, the first
serving to give awareness of a visual sensation, the second that of objective memories, and the third the associative level. The first two
levels are criticized in terms of whether one can have visual impression
of an object without realizing meaning. The third level is criticized
because it is believed that the visual image impressed on the dominant
side of the brain is the same as that in the nondominant. There is no

more reason for symbols to be reversed than for reversal in visual memory
of objects. An explanation is attempted as to how a child could produce
a reversed visual image of something he has never seen before, considering only the "visual engram" of Orton. It is pointed out that reversals
are more common in left-handed, right-eyed children. The problem is considered principally a motor one. Whenever individuated motor patterns
are acquired by one side of the body, their mirror patterns are acquired
by the opposite half of the body, but with less accuracy. This is kinesthetic sensation or motor imagery, and it is involved in writing. If the
child is right-handed and left-eyed, or the reverse, this asymmetry adds
much to the confusion in the child's mind in acquiring the proper direction in writing. Mirror writing may be easier for a left-handed, right-
eyed child to read than normal writing because of this natural association with the motor imagery. The impressions in the brain (engrams) are
visuomotor, and the body movements of the whole left side form the dominant pattern. In some cases of aphasia, directional confusion may be
encountered. An illustrative case is given. The question is also considered as to why an adult who suffers a brain lesion, usually in the
dominant hemisphere, becomes paralyzed on the right side and loses all
power of speech, rather than retaining speech up to the five-year-old
level when handedness first began to function in reading, writing, and
spelling. The possibility of hereditary basis for handedness is considered. A seven-step program of practical action for the teacher is
outlined. It is noted that it is in substantial agreement with Orton.

325 Dearborn, Walter F. "The nature and causation of disabilities in
     reading." In: Conference on Reading, University of Chicago, 1939.
     Proceedings: recent trends in reading. Vol. 1. Compiled and
     edited by William S. Gray. Chicago, Illinois: University of
     Chicago, 1939. 103-10. (0 References). (Supplementary Educa-
     tional Monographs, No. 49).
In spite of findings by some researchers to the contrary, evidence continues to be found that left ocular or manual dominance is found more
often among disabled readers. It is reported that aniseikonia was
present in about 50 percent of the poor readers and in 23 percent of the
normal ones examined. A combination of causes is probably as characteristic of reading disability as any single cause.

326 ————. "Ocular and manual dominance in dyslexia." Psychol Bull
     28(9): 704, November, 1931. (0 References).
Finds that between a tenth and a fifth of cases of extreme difficulty in
learning to read may be described as congenital alexia or word blindness.
Causes of these conditions are better accounted for in terms of left-
eyedness, lack of ocular and manual dominance, and mixed conditions of
ocular and manual dominance than by the use of theories of cerebral localization or of cerebral dominance. Eye movements in our language must be
toward the right, and left-eyed children may tend to move in the other
direction. The three conditions described may produce uncertainty as to
sequence or the correct ordering of the words.

327 ————. "Structural factors which condition special disability
     in reading." Proc Am Assoc Ment Defic 57: 268-86, 1933. (8
     References).
Very little word blindness is caused by cerebral defects. Specific brain
defects, auditory difficulties, kinesthetic deficiencies, and neurotic
or psychopathic behavior may all be responsible for word blindness in
some cases. Some factors producing it may be inheritable. Left-eyedness

and crossed or mixed dominance must be considered more important causes of dyslexia. The condition may be prevented or corrected if found early enough by a few weeks of individual attention and training to help the child develop a sense of the direction in which reading proceeds. If the condition has persisted for years, eradication is difficult, but it can be done. The method is not so important as demonstrating to the child that he is not stupid, giving him some insight into why he is having difficulty, and offering assurance that the task can be accomplished.

328 Eames, Thomas Harrison. "The anatomical basis of lateral dominance anomalies." Am J Orthopsychiatry 4(4): 524-28, October, 1934. (5 References).
Lateral dominance problems do not occur much more often in poor readers than in normal ones. The brain locations controlling dominance are discussed. Reasons why reading difficulties may arise from lateral dominance problems are considered.

329 Evans, James R. "The relationship of unilateral usage and tactile sensitivity to right-left discrimination and spatial abilities." Cortex 5(2): 134-44, June, 1969. (13 References).
Two groups of white fourth-grade boys were tested for their knowledge of left and right discrimination in their own bodies and in a picture. They were also tested for degree of sensitivity to touch in both of their thumbs and both great toes. Eye, ear, hand, tongue, and foot preferences were tested. One group had average verbal IQs of 105; the other group 125.6. It was predicted that left-right discrimination and grasp of spatial relations would vary directly with the degree of unilateral skin sensitivity and unilateral usage of body parts. Only two correlations of significance were found supporting the hypothesis. Others were borderline but tending in that direction. In the high verbal group no significant correlations were found. Difficulties in right-left discrimination have been reported to be associated with reading disability.

330 Flax, Nathan. "The clinical significance of dominance." Am J Optom 43(9): 566-81, September, 1966. (58 References).
Finds only speculative evidence of any relationship between cerebral dominance and learning to read. Eye dominance in terms of controlling or predominance does not relate at all to reading disability. The reversal and perceptual problems of disabled readers are better explained by other aspects of visual function than by dominance.

331 Forness, Steven R., and Weil, Marvin C. "Laterality in retarded readers with brain dysfunction." Except Child 36(9): 684-85, May, 1970. (2 References).
Thirteen of seventeen boys of normal intelligence but retarded in reading were found to have minimal brain dysfunction in this study. There was much crossed dominance, but the children did not differ from normal children in hand dominance. The more severely disabled readers tended to be left-eyed.

332 Franklin, Henry L. "Reading difficulties." Southwest Med 22: 233-35, June, 1938. (11 References).
Excluding children who have reading problems because of poor lighting, refractive errors, mental dullness, or improper teaching methods, another group of children cannot learn to read because they suffer from what has been called word blindness, alexia, or aphasia. Mirror writing, left-handedness, and left-eyedness play parts in this phenomenon. The af-

fected individual is not able to interpret written or printed language.
Some cases show a familial incidence. There appears to be a specific
derangement or absence of visual perception. A particular brain center
fails to grasp the meaning of graphic symbols. Many word-blind children
are left-handed or use either hand indifferently. Whether dominance of
one cerebral hemisphere is a natural tendency or environmentally developed is a debated question. If a child does not grasp words through
vision, he will usually do so through the auditory apparatus. The ophthalmograph for photographing eye movements and the metronoscope for
developing better reading habits by preventing the eye from going back
over material already read are described.

333 Gates, Arthur Irving, and Bennett, Chester C. Reversal tendencies
     in reading; causes, diagnosis, prevention and correction. New
     York: Bureau of Publications, Teachers College, Columbia Univer-
     sity, 1933. 33p.
Describes a study on reversal tendencies in children's reading in which
reading data fail to confirm Orton's lack of cerebral dominance theory
of reading disability. Sex differences and mixed eye dominance do not
appear to be significant factors in reversals. Two groups of grade-
school children were compared. One group consisted of children making
the most reversal errors on a test of isolated words. The other group
was formed of children who made no reversal errors. Pupils were paired
for IQ and general reading ability. Theories of the causes of reversal
tendencies are discussed, including Orton's theory of cerebral dominance,
left-handedness, mixe eye-hand dominance, sex, and visual defects. A
method of remedial instruction for aiding children in learning to read
from left to right is included.

334 Gates, Arthur Irving, and Bond, Guy L. "Relation of handedness, eye-
     sighting and acuity dominance to reading." J Educ Psychol 27(6):
     450-56, September, 1936. (0 References).
Eye and hand dominance have little to do with reading difficulties on the
basis of data obtained on first-grade pupils, eight-year-old normal
readers, and eight-year-old reading problem cases. Eye dominance, single
eye superiority in acuity, hand dominance, and combinations of these were
studied in relation to achievement in reading, word pronunciation, reversal errors, and visual perception.

335 Greenbie, Marjorie Barstow. "It's hard to read." Atl Mon 160(4):
     477-80, October, 1937. (0 References).
Explains reading disability in terms of Orton's theory of the two cerebral hemispheres being mirrored reverses of each other. Incomplete dominance of one hemisphere produces the confusion in the direction of letters
and words because of conflicting memory patterns for words. Orton's
methods for diagnosis and remediation are briefly explained.

336 ————. "Some children can't read." Parents Mag 11(10): 30-31,
     88-91, October, 1936. (0 References).
Defines and explains specific reading disability as a condition which prevents a child of good intelligence from learning to read by ordinary
methods adapted to the majority of schoolchildren. It is differentiated
from the problems of children who can learn to read by usual methods but
do not for various obvious reasons. The theories of Samuel Orton that
reading disability is caused by incomplete cerebral dominance are explained. Afflicted children can record and recall language sounds correctly. It is the visual aspects of language encountered first in read-

ing which prove difficult. Building dependable visual images by sounding out one letter at a time and progressing from there is the teaching
method recommended. Sight-reading methods, while allowing most children
to make rapid progress in reading, only confuse those suffering from
specific reading disability.

337   Groff, Patrick J.   "A study of handedness and reading achievement."
      Read Teach 16(1):   31-34, September, 1962. (10 References).
Reading achievement of left-handed pupils was compared with reading
achievement of all pupils in grades four, five, and six in two California
school districts. Little relationship was found between reading achievement and hand preference.

338   Helveston, Eugene M.; Billips, William C.; Weber, Janet C.   "Con-
      trolling eye-dominant hemisphere relationship as factor in reading
      ability." Am J Ophthalmol 70(1): 96-100, July, 1970. (8 Refer-
      ences).
In studies of 310 third-, fourth-, and fifth-grade children, unselected
as to reading ability, and studies of sixty-seven reading-disabled children examined in a dyslexia clinic, no correlation was found between
laterality and reading ability. Determinations were made for all the
children of the controlling eye-dominant hemisphere relationship. It is
concluded that treatment of reading disability by attempting to change
laterality pattern is not justified. Laterality pattern is not a reliable predictor of reading ability.

339   Hildreth, Gertrude.   "The development and training of hand domi-
      nance: IV. Developmental problems associated with handedness."
      Pedagog Semin J Genet Psychol 76(First Half): 39-100, March,
      1950. (0 References).
Discusses laterality, handedness, and speech disturbances, and their relationship to stuttering. The relation of handedness to difficulties in
learning to read and write is discussed in terms of left-handedness and
mirror writing. Orton's theory of cerebral dominance is explained. Some
of the literature on the relationship of reading problems to cerebral
dominance is summarized. It is concluded that mixed cerebral dominance
alone does not cause reading disability. What mixed dominance often
signifies--shifted handedness--may be the complicating factor in both
reading and writing disability. Diagnostic techniques for appraising
handednedd and other aspects of lateral dominance are given. This article
is followed by Part V, "Training in handedness" (76: 101-44), which
does not concern dyslexia. At the end of Part V is a bibliography of
258 references which serves both parts.

340   ————.   "A school survey of eye-hand dominance." J Appl Psychol
      29(1): 83-88, February, 1945. (13 References).
Surveyed an elementary-school population ages six to eleven years in
kindergarten through grade six for evidence that children with mixed hand-
eye dominance (left-handed and right-eyed, or the reverse) are more likely
to suffer from reading disabilities than those whose eye and hand dominance are like-sided. All pupils were above average in general ability.
A somewhat larger proportion of children with mixed dominance had difficulty with reading than consistent dominant pupils. However, mixed
eye-hand dominance did not appear to be a major factor in these reading
disability cases.

341 Hogg, William F. "Reversal of eye preference at reading distance, associated with specific reading disability (dyslexia)." Can Psychiatr Assoc J 13(1): 85-86, February, 1968. (7 References).
Reports the case of an eleven-year-old boy with dyslexia and normal visual acuity who showed left-eye preference for near vision and preference for the right eye for distance. His WISC verbal score was 85; performance score 131. Full-scale IQ was 107, with grossly uneven development in subtest categories. His reversal of eye preference occurred at about eighteen inches. He was right-footed and -handed. The concepts of preference and dominance are distinguished. Dominance refers to organization of language function in one cerebral hemisphere or the other. Eye preference does exist, but cannot be linked to cerebral dominance. A technique for testing eye preference and determining the point of reversal (if reversal is present) is described.

342 Hosmer, Gladys E. "Has your child reading difficulty?" Hygeia 10(3): 255-57, March, 1932. (0 References).
Explains reading disability in terms of Orton's theory of cerebral dominance. Failure of the young child to settle on one hand to be used as the dominant hand underlies most reading difficulties. The theory that images stored in the nondominant hemisphere of the brain are reversed copies of those in the dominant hemisphere is explained. The case history of a boy of good intelligence who had difficulty in reading is included. It is suggested that the child was helped, not only by his own hard work and his teachers' patience, but also by his comprehension of the careful explanations given him of the causes of his problems.

343 Ihinger, Robert F. "Lateral dominance and reading achievement." Claremont Coll Read Conf Yearb 27: 126-29, 1963. (13 References).
Expresses surprise that the matter of lateral dominance and reading achievement should still intrigue researchers. After much research on the topic, it would appear that most studies have failed to find any relationship between dominance and reading. Reasons for the confusion in the area are discussed, and the opinion is expressed that it is unwise to prescribe remedial measures based on such tenuous evidence.

344 Jenkins, R. L.; Brown, Andrew W.; Elmendorf, Laura. "Mixed dominance and reading disability." Am J Orthopsychiatry 7: 72-81, January, 1937. (0 References).
Two case histories of twins are presented. In each pair there was a single placenta at birth. In each pair one child was consistent in laterality, the other inconsistent. There is a strong association between mixed dominance and confusion of left and right.

345 Jones, Mary M. Wilcox. "Relationship between reading deficiencies and left-handedness." Sch Soc 60(1554): 238-39, October 7, 1944. (0 References).
Among 569 right-handed and fifty-seven left-handed children who were tested for reading ability, no significant differences in reading ability were found between clearly left-handed and clearly right-handed children.

346 Kempkes, Elisabeth. "Handicaps in reading." Educ Adm Super 24(2): 127-34, February, 1938. (0 References).
Forcing children who are naturally left-handed to use their right hands causes them to lose their "definite brain dominance." They become uncertain and have greater than normal difficulty with reversals in reading and writing. Left-handedness and slow speech development may accompany

reading problems. Permitting left-handed children to develop in line with their natural dominance is recommended.

347 Kershner, John R. "Reading and laterality revisited." J Spec Educ
       9(3): 269-79, Fall, 1975. (45 References).
Defines crossed laterality and strephosymbolia, and describes the theories of Samuel Orton in regard to brain dominance. Body laterality is widely used as an index of neurological status, but confusion exists concerning the concept. Laterality is related to reading in a variety of ways. Some of the literature and research in the field is discussed. Confusion has been caused by the assumption that there is one "normal" laterality pattern (right hand-right eye), and by the unfortunate use of the term "dominant" which implies that one cerebral hemisphere commands thought and perceptual processes.

348 Koos, Eugenia M. "Manifestations of cerebral dominance and reading
       retardation in primary-grade children." J Genet Psychol 104(1):
       155-65, March, 1964. (13 References).
Hand and eye preferences were determined for 109 upper-middle-class children in primary grades of public school. IQ and reading achievement scores were obtained. The lack of a controlling eye in binocular vision was not found to be associated with lower reading ability. The theory that maturation lessens the effect of this factor was supported inasmuch as significantly lower reading scores were found in second graders lacking binocular control, rather than in third graders. No difference was found in the first-grade group. Therefore no conclusion could be drawn in the face of conflicting evidence. When children with mixed eye-hand preference and IQs under the group median of 125 were compared with children with unilateral preference in the same IQ range, a significant difference in reading achievement was found. No difference in reading ability was found in children with IQs above the median whether of mixed or unilateral eye-hand preference. This supports the hypothesis that the influence of dominance varies with IQ level. Some WISC subtest results were found related to reading ability. Results are seen as supporting the theory that cerebral dominance anomalies are associated with reading retardation.

349 LaGrone, Cyrus W., and Holland, B. F. "Accuracy of perception in
       peripheral vision in relation to dextrality, intelligence and read-
       ing ability." Am J Psychol 56(4): 592-98, October, 1943. (0
       References).
Children who were left-handed and left-eyed were found to prefer the right visual field. These factors were associated with low scores on tests for reading and intelligence. It is concluded that peripheral visual field preference is not acquired, but is symptomatic of conditions causing reading disability.

350 Leavell, Ullin W. "The problem of symbol reversals and confusions,
       their frequency and remediation." Peabody J Educ 32(3): 130-41,
       November, 1954. (12 Bibliographic Footnotes).
Discusses hand and eye preference and visual imagery and direction dominance as factors related to the language function. A therapeutic technique for remediation of mixed dominance is described.

351 Leavell, Ullin W., and Fults, Florence Chism. "Dominance and dis-
       placement of visual imagery in relation to reading achievement."
       Peabody J Educ 21(2): 103-8, September, 1943. (17 References).

The Keystone Ophthalmic Telebinocular was used for these studies with
elementary-school children. This instrument allows only the left half
of the visual field to be seen with the left eye, and the right half with
the right eye. The children were asked to draw what they saw when looking at slides through the machine. In binocular vision, the slides
fused, giving the impression of one picture. Monocular vision was tested
by occluding the slide for one eye or the other. Test results suggest
that regardless of the field in which a visual image is presented, the
child tended strongly to reproduce the figure in the field which corre-
sponded to his dominance pattern. Results also suggest that right dominance is more favorable to learning to read than is left dominance. Left
dominance is more favorable to acquiring reading skills than is mixed
dominance. Impartiality of dominance affects reading achievement very
little. Eye dominance, as well as hand and foot dominance, was found
to influence directional movement.

352   Liberman, Isabelle Y. "Basic research in speech and lateralization
      of language: some implications for reading disability." Status
      Rep Speech Res 25/26: 51-66, 1971.

353   Liberman, Isabelle Y.; Shankweiler, Donald; Orlando, Charles; et al.
      "Letter confusions and reversals of sequence in the beginning
      reader: implications for Orton's theory of developmental dyslexia."
      Status Rep Speech Res 24: 17-30, 1970.

354   ————. "Letter confusions and reversals of sequence in the be-
      ginning reader: implications for Orton's theory of developmental
      dyslexia." Cortex 7(2): 127-42, June, 1971. (27 References).
The reading ability of second-grade pupils was found to be more closely
related to sequence reversals of letters than to letter-orientation reversals. The two types of error were uncorrelated. Orton and his suc-
cessors assumed that both stemmed from the same underlying cause, a
failure to develop consistent left-to-right pattern of scan. Results,
when the two types of error are considered separately, do not support
Orton's theory. No support was found for assuming a common cause. Results suggest that problems of the beginning reader are more closely
related to word construction than to strategies for scanning text. The
children in this study ranged in age from seven to nine years and their
WISC scores ranged from 85 to 126 with a mean of 98.6. They were asked
individually to read a list of sixty words, were given a reading test,
and were asked to match a given letter to one of a list of five which
included four reversible letters (b, d, p, g). Almost all the reversal
errors were made by children in the lowest third of reading ability.
Even among the poorest readers, all kinds of reversal errors accounted
for only 10 to 15 percent of total errors.

355   Lockavitch, Joseph F. "Of course I'm not stupid...I just don't
      know my right from my left." Acad Ther 10(2): 159-65, Winter,
      1974-75. (4 References).
Relates some of the more common characteristics and difficulties observed
in nonreaders. Most common is a large degree of spatial confusion,
usually accompanied by a degree of difficulty in establishing laterality
and the notion of directionality. Laterality is defined as knowledge of
left and right sides of the body. Directionality is knowledge of left
and right in space. Lateral dominance refers to the preferred side of
the body. Laterality precedes and is independent of directionality.
Directionality is dependent upon laterality and laterality cannot be

taught in a sedentary situation. Reading-disabled children should be relieved of their feeling of stupidity by having the cause of their difficulties explained to them, by having their egos boosted, and by beginning training on the level where each child is operating.

356 Lyle, J. G. "Reading retardation and reversal tendency: a factorial study." Child Dev 40(3): 833-43, September, 1969. (30 References).

Two groups of normal and retarded readers, all boys ages six to twelve years from the same schools and of at least normal intelligence as measured by the WISC were given individual tests in reading and writing reversals, Memory-for-Designs test, spelling, arithmetic, finger agnosia, lateral dominance, and hand-eye dominance. All types of reversals were found to be associated with reading retardation. Not all types of reversals were associated with each other, and all tended to disappear with age. Mixed laterality, crossed hand-eye dominance, and finger agnosia were unrelated to reading retardation.

357 Marcel, Tony; Katz, Leonard; Smith, Marjorie. "Laterality and reading proficiency." Neuropsychologia 12(1): 131-39, January, 1974. (32 References).

In order to test the degree of cerebral hemisphere specialization, boys and girls who were good and poor readers ages seven and eight were shown familiar five-letter words. The words were exposed either to the left or to the right of a fixation point. Subjects were instructed to look at the fixation point and report any words or letters than they saw. Good readers showed greater right over left field superiority than poor readers. Poor readers were superior to good readers on presentations to the left field.

358 Mayer, Leo L. "Congenital reading disability--strephosymbolia: report of five cases of partial word blindness." JAMA 100(15): 1152-55, April 15, 1933. (43 References).

Reports five cases of word blindness where ocular dominance was the outstanding cause. Determining the dominant eye is important. The hope is expressed that by bringing this finding to the attention of ophthalmologists, word-blind children will be spared the stigma of being called "mental defectives." Some literature in the area is reviewed.

359 Mercure, Roland. "Right-left hemisphere dominance, short term memory, and reading in third grade children." For a summary see: Diss Abstr Int 36B(12): 6094, June, 1976.

360 Michaels, David D. "Ocular dominance." Surv Ophthalmol 17(3): 151-63, November-December, 1972. (60 References).

Proposes no new tests or theories of dominance, but examines some old and some more recent theories. Discussion centers on ocular dominance and tests for determining motor and sensory dominance, which are defined. Retinal rivalry tests and factors influencing it are described. Cerebral laterality does not appear to be a factor influencing retinal rivalry. Cross dominance has been implicated as a cause of reading disorders, but no scientific evidence supports the claims that the performance of dyslexic children can be improved by visual exercises or laterality training. Dyslexia and other school underachievement require a multidisciplinary approach, individualized for each child.

361 Neblett, Herbert C. "Mirror-writing and word blindness." South
     Med Surg 103(6): 340, June, 1941. (0 References).
Mirror writing and word blindness were not known to be intimately associated until publication of Orton's paper in 1925. The conditions result from failure to establish the physiological habit of working from
one cerebral hemisphere. Mirror writing is more common in men than in
women, in children of subnormal intelligence, deaf-mutes, and in otherwise normal absentminded persons. Maldevelopment of a part of the brain
may lead to a disability. It is found in about one in 2,500 children.

362 "A new theory of word-blindness." Lit Dig 98: 20, September 8,
     1928. (0 References).
Reports the theory of Samuel T. Orton that word blindness is caused by
a defect in the development of a small area of the temporal lobe of the
brain, and is not a form of feeblemindedness as had been previously supposed. The Lancet's report and comment on Orton's theory is quoted.

363 Orton, Samuel Torrey. "Certain failures in the acquisition of
     written language: their bearing on the problem of cerebral domi-
     nance." Arch Neurol Psychiatry 22(4): 841-50, October, 1929.
     (0 References).
Gives the symptoms of strephosymbolia, including: (1) confusion of reversible letters ("p" for "q"); (2) inability to associate a vowel with
its sound; (3) inconstancy in building associations between the visual
symbol and its sound; (4) mirror writing; (5) a tendency to omit parts
of words or reverse other parts; and (6) mixed cerebral dominance. Reading disability is not directly related to general intellectual capacity.
The theory of the persistence of records of material learned in the nondominant cerebral hemisphere is explained. It is pointed out that this
forms a physiologic rather than a pathologic hypothesis as to the problem some children have in learning to read. The disability should
therefore respond to training.

364 ————. "An impediment to learning to read--a neurological ex-
     planation of the reading disability." Sch Soc 28(715): 286-90,
     September 8, 1928. (0 References).
Children normal in intelligence and motivation who have difficulty in
learning to read are probably retarded because both cerebral hemispheres
are in use without clear dominance of one. The input (or engrams) from
the two cerebral hemispheres are probably antitropes (mirrored copies),
resulting in confusion in direction of reading and prompt recognition of
differences in words. With proper early training the condition can be
readily overcome.

365 ————. "Neurological explanation of the reading disability with
     some remarks as to the value of this explanation in treatment."
     Educ Rec 20(Suppl. No. 12): 58-68, January, 1939. (0 References).
Normal adults use only one side of the brain for reading. A combination
of hereditary and environmental factors determine which side for any individual. A little more than 10 percent of children experience difficulty in establishing one-sided predominance--the organic cause of their
reading disability. Disorders of speech, spelling, writing, and other
complications may be present. This theory of cause is an active aid to
treatment.

366 ————. "Neurological studies of some educational deviates from
     Iowa schools." J Iowa Med Soc 19(4): 155-58, April, 1929. (7
     Bibliographic Footnotes).

Reports studies of 125 reading-disabled children in Iowa. Symptoms of
the condition are described. They are ascribed to incomplete cerebral
dominance. The images of the letters and words are reversed in the nondominant hemisphere and cause confusion if not suppressed in learning to
read. The emotional problems suffered by the unrecognized reading-
disabled child are noted.

367   —————. "The relation of the special educational disabilities to
       feeblemindedness." Proc Am Assoc Study Feebleminded 53: 23-33,
       May, 1929. As reprinted in Orton, Samuel Torrey, "Word-blindness"
       in school children and other papers on strephosymbolia (specific
       language disability—dyslexia) 1925-1946. Compiled by June Lyday
       Orton. Pomfret, Connecticut: Orton Society, 1966. (0 References).
Otherwise intelligent children do not learn to read because exclusive
control from one hemisphere of the brain has not been established. Hinshelwood's view that a certain portion of the brain is destined for control of language function has now been replaced with the belief that
disturbances of associative processes, not loss of memories for words,
produce language problems. This is demonstrated by the nature of the
symptoms: the reversals of letters or whole words show that mirror images from the nondominant hemisphere are causing the difficulty. Since
special disabilities are caused by this poor physiological habit, retraining gives hope of improvement. We do not yet know very clearly the
anatomical basis for much mental defectiveness.

368   —————. "Some studies in the language function." Res Publ Assoc
       Res Nerv Ment Dis (1932 Proceedings) 13: 614-33, 1934. (0 Ref-
       erences).
Three levels of "cortical elaboration" can be distinguished. These levels
may be differentially impaired, producing anesthesia, agnosia, or aphasia.
Persons with strephosymbolia or reading, writing, or spelling disabilities suffer from a delay in the normal establishment of normal cerebral
dominance.

369   —————. "Some studies in the reading disability." In: Orton,
       June Lyday, ed. "Word-blindness" in school children and other
       papers on strephosymbolia (specific language disability—dyslexia)
       1925-1946. Pomfret, Connecticut: Orton Society, 1966. 269-274.
       (0 References). (Orton Society Monograph, No. 2). Address pre-
       sented at the Medical Convocation of the University of Pennsylvania,
       June 18, 1945, upon the occasion of receiving the honorary degree
       of Doctor of Science.
Observations of the similarity of the problems of schoolchildren who have
abnormal difficulty in learning to read and the symptoms observed in
adults who have lost the ability to read through disease or accident led
to Orton's thesis that interference from the nondominant hemisphere of
the brain prevents normal reading development. Handedness is not entirely
trustworthy as a guide to the native laterality of an individual.

370   —————. "Special disability in spelling." Bull Neurol Inst NY
       1(2): 159-92, June, 1931. (5 References).
Children with reading disability usually are disabled in spelling also.
Interference with the fixed associations needed for spelling probably
comes from inconsistent recall of visual, auditory, and kinesthetic images in the brain. The underlying reason is lack of complete unilateral
cerebral dominance, a disability often familial or associated with left-
handedness, reading, and speech disabilities. Tests of auditory and

visual acuity should be made. A knowledge of phonetics is necessary for
children with tendencies toward strephosymbolia (twisted symbols) confusions.

371 ————. "Specific reading disability--strephosymbolia." JAMA
     90: 1095-99, April 7, 1928. (15 References).
Offers the term "strephosymbolia"--twisted symbols--as a replacement for
"congenital word blindness." The classic symptoms of the condition are
described: (1) confusion of letters like "p" and "q" and of words like
"was" and "saw"; (2) a tendency to reverse letters or syllables; (3)
reading from right to left; and (4) mirror reading and writing. The condition is physiologic in origin, not pathologic. An explanation in terms
of cerebral organization is given. Visual records, or engrams, are recorded in both hemispheres of the brain, but in a mirrored pattern in
the nondominant side. If the "physiologic habit" of training the brain
to work only from the engrams from the dominant hemishere is not established, the mirror writing, reversals, and confusions in direction that
characterize reading disability appear. In right-handed people, the
left hemisphere of the brain is dominant and vice versa. It is suggested
that strephosymbolia is a physiologic variant, not a general mental defect.

372 ————. "Visual functions in strephosymbolia." Arch Ophthalmol
     30(6): 707-17, December, 1943. (0 References).
Strephosymbolia, or twisted symbols, expresses itself in the inability
to differentiate such letters as "b" and "d" and in a facility for mirror
reading and mirror writing. The cause is not a pathological factor, but
a physiologic deviation caused by the failure of one hemisphere of the
brain to become dominant. This physiologic theory is to be preferred
over the older term "congenital word blindness" because it is less misleading and offers a more favorable prognosis. The disorder is hereditary rather than congenital; and "developmental" is a better term for it
than either "hereditary" or "congenital." Left-eyedness is not the cause
of reading disability, but rather indicates a tendency in the person to
use the right hemisphere of the brain. While refractive errors may hinder
reading, corrective lenses do not enable the child with strephosymbolia
to read. It is suggested that children with this reading disability
represent intergrades between right-sided and left-sided family tendencies,
and the reading disability follows rather definite hereditary trends.

373 Orton, Samuel Torrey, and Gillingham, Anna. "Special disability in
     writing." Bull Neurol Inst NY 3(1-2): 1-32, June, 1933. (0
     References).
Cases of severe retardation in writing are described and methods of examination and training are discussed. Some phonic training, having the
child write the letter from its sound rather than its name, and in some
cases copying the letter are useful methods. In the absence of disease,
writing disability stems from the failure of one hemisphere of the brain
to achieve dominance without rivalry from the other nondominant hemisphere.

374 Piotrowski, Zygmunt. "The cerebral dominance theory of reading
     difficulties." Psychol Bull 31(9): 740-41, November, 1934. (0
     References).
Explains Orton's theory of incomplete cerebral dominance as a cause of
reading disability. It is pointed out that the difficulty does not appear to lie in associating a definite meaning with a printed word, but

rather in an unreliable perception since the confusion can be decreased
by strengthening the habit of uniform perception with kinesthetic and
phonetic training. The role of vacillating cerebral dominance in vision
is explained.

375 "Reading and spelling." Lancet 214(v. 1 for 1928): 1132-33, June
     2, 1928. (0 References).
Explains and criticizes Orton's theory of cerebral dominance as the cause
of word blindness. The theory is not convincing. It is difficult to
prove. His theories do not fit all the cases nor do they explain the
difficulties associated with word blindness. Orton includes cases which
do not even approximate word blindness.

376 Reinhold, Margaret. "The effect of laterality on reading and writ-
     ing." Proc R Soc Med 56(3): 203-6, March, 1963. (6 References).
Suggests that the concept that handedness and language are located or
represented in the dominant hemisphere of the brain is out of date. Handedness and writing may have occurred relatively late in the human development. Except for the development of the alphabet we would have no dyslexic children, since pre-alphabet writing depended on pictures, which
present no problem to congenital dyslexics. The development of writing,
reading, and laterality in the early history of humans is discussed. The
theory that culture and habit account for right-handedness and neither
cerebral hemisphere has any inherent functional difference is not entirely convincing. However, the question of whether handedness is caused
by a dominant cerebral hemisphere or is an acquired attribute is at
present unsolved. The connection between the origins of handedness and
reading and writing, particularly its relation to congenital dyslexia,
is considered. Right and left must be distinguished before even the
simplest reading and writing can be attained. Writing with the use of
the alphabet requires the ability to convert a sound or symbol into a
two-dimensional "visuomotor symbol." Orton's theory of mixed dominance
is explained. Orton's theory is seen as a suggestion that reading and
writing depend on handedness. Persons with congential dyslexia suffer
some degree of right-left confusion, and there is a defect in memory related to letters and words. It is suggested that lack of strong laterality, difficulties in reading and writing, and spatial orientation
represent several aspects of some as yet undetermined disturbance of cerebral function. The argument that weakness of laterality causes reading, writing, and spatial difficulties is less convincing.

377 "Research: what occurs when a left-handed child turns right."
     Newsweek 7(18): 40-41, May 2, 1936. (0 References).
Reports Samuel Orton's conclusions on the consequences of forcing naturally left-handed children to use their right hands. Orton believed this
change could produce grave psychological disturbances and disastrous
speech and sight effects. Alexia, or word blindness; word deafness in
which the victim cannot distinguish specific spoken words; and motor
agraphia in which the subject loses his ability to write, may occur. The
flash or whole-word method of teaching reading is ineffective for children with word blindness. Many cases of stuttering and stammering can
be traced to shifts in handedness.

378 Roode, C. D. "The relevance of audio-visual feedback mechanisms in
     the acquisition of reading skills." Can Psychol 9(2): 133-41,
     April, 1968. (0 References).

Brain damage is not usually responsible for the cases of congenital dyslexia which are encountered frequently in children. Rather, a developmental lag or neurological disorganization seems to be the cause in some
cases. It is being realized that cerebral laterality for speech and language skills is most important. Although almost nothing is done to
establish auditory dominance, it is extremely important in the acquisition and execution of language skills. When a subject's voice is picked
up by a microphone, delayed for two-tenths of a second, and then fed back
to the person in earphones, stuttering begins. It has been found that
the person's speech will be more impaired when this delayed feedback is
to the dominant ear rather than the nondominant ear. An assymetry of
the monitoring functions of the two ears is suggested. This finding, if
further investigated and validated, may have far-reaching consequences
in the remediation of language disorders.

379 Rosenberger, Peter B. "Visual matching and clinical findings among
       good and poor readers." <u>Am J Dis Child</u> 119(2): 103-10, February,
       1970. (20 References).
Children in grades one through six were given a WISC, a reading test, and
a battery of tests including drawing a picture, writing a sentence from
dictation, identifying colors, laterality preference (which hand, foot,
and eye were preferred for throwing, kicking, sighting), laterality awareness (e.g., did the child know which was his right thumb), mirror movements, and sample-matching. In this last test, the child was shown a
selection of three-letter words, or three-letter nonsense syllables, or
patterns of three shapes, and asked to point out the one that matched a
sample. Poor readers performed significantly worse than good readers on
laterality awareness of body parts (although not laterality preference).
Poor readers also performed worse than good readers on matching three-
letter words where the match involved only the order of letters within
the word. It is suggested that more study may reveal a more general
deficit of laterality awareness in significant numbers of poor readers
of normal intelligence. Good readers in this study were found to have
higher average IQs than poor readers.

380 Sabatino, David A., and Becker, John T. "Relationship between lat-
       eral preference and selected behavioral variables for children
       failing academically." <u>Child Dev</u> 42(6): 2055-60, December, 1971.
       (10 References).
A battery of tests designed to measure seventeen behaviors and three
areas of academic achievement was administered to a group of elementary-
school pupils who were failing in school and were retarded in reading.
They were tested individually for laterality. Results indicate that there
is little relationship between whether a child's preferences were uni-
laterally right, left, or were confused, and his achievement in language,
perceptual-motor development, and academic achievement.

381 Sadick, Tamah L. "Language laterality and handedness in relation
       to reading acquisition: a developmental study." For a summary
       see: <u>Diss Abstr Int</u> 36B(7): 3224, January, 1976.

382 Schonell, Fred J. "The relation of reading disability to handedness
       and certain ocular factors." <u>Br J Educ Psychol</u> 10(3): 227-37,
       November, 1940; 11(1): 20-27, February, 1941. (Bibliographic
       Footnotes).
From a study of 104 backward readers it is concluded that left-handedness
per se is not a cause of reading disability. While mixed dominance was

more common among reading-disabled children than among normal readers,
it only partly accounted for their difficulties. Emotional problems and
weakness in auditory discrimination were also found. After age nine,
confusions and reversals in both reading and writing diminished rapidly.

383   Sekuler, Robert, and Pierce, Scott. "Perception of stimulus direc-
        tion: hemispheric homology and laterality." Am J Psychol 86(4):
        679-95, December, 1973. (18 References).
Right-left orientation and mirror-image confusions in the orientation of
letters and words characterize dyslexic children. Research has provided
evidence that normal adults, normal children, and dyslexics all lie along
a continuum with respect to mirror-image confusions. Three experiments
were designed to show whether normal adults have a residual aspect of the
normal perceptual problems of very young children--problems resembling
dyslexia. Adult subjects were shown pairs of three-sided squares in
various relationships to each other. Response times, as a measure of
difficulty in discrimination, were longer for pairs of figures in a left-
right orientation to each other than in an up-and-down orientation. It
was also found that going from ipsilateral (affecting the same side) to
contralateral (affecting the opposite side) hemispheric projections did
not affect the ability to make left-right discriminations any more than
up-and-down discriminations. This finding is interpreted as eliminating
Orton's explanation of interhemispheric relationships as a cause for
left-right and mirror-image confusions.

384   Smith, Linda Cleora. "A study of laterality characteristics of re-
        tarded readers and reading achievers." For a summary see: Diss
        Abstr 14(10): 1625, 1954.

385   Sparrow, Sara Stelle. "Dyslexia and laterality: evidence for a
        developmental theory." Semin Psychiatry 1(3): 270-77, August,
        1969. (33 References).
Investigates how retarded readers differ from normal readers in the various ways laterality is manifested, and investigates the development of
laterality at various age levels. It has been observed that there is a
relationship between handedness and the hemisphere of the brain controlling speech. It was theorized that if laterality is a problem for dyslexics, these persons would exhibit deficits in language lateralization,
on the assumption that verbal skills represent the highest level of language differentiation and lateralization in humans. Subjects were two
groups of white boys ages nine through twelve: forty normal readers and
forty retarded readers. They were tested for ten signs of laterality.
The groups did not differ on the less complex measures of lateralization
such as manual preference, strength, and dexterity. Dyslexics did give
poorer performance than normal readers on all the higher level perceptual-
cognitive measures of lateralization, including facility in lateral
awareness, finger differentiation, and verbal intelligence. This is seen
as being consistent with a developmental theory of dyslexia. Some tasks
showed improvement with age. It appears that the left hemisphere is
implicated as the source of many symptoms seen in both acquired and developmental reading, writing, and spelling problems, form perception, and
verbal intelligence. It is hypothesized that a developmental lag in the
lateralization process in hearing, seeing, and touch frequently results
in deficits that interfere with learning to read.

386   ————. "Reading disability: a neuropsychological investigation."
        For a summary see: Diss Abstr Int 30B(1): 392, July, 1969.

387 Speech research: a report on the status and progress of studies on
     the nature of speech, instrumentation for its investigation, and
     practical applications. 1 October-30 December 1970. 1971. 184p.
     (ED 052 653).
Contains nine manuscripts and extended reports on a variety of topics related to the status and progress of studies on the nature of speech, aids
to its investigation, and practical implications. In addition to studies
on various aspects of speech perception, this title is included: "Letter
confusions and reversals of sequence in the beginning reader: implications for Orton's theory of developmental dyslexia."

388 Spitzer, Robert L.; Rabkin, Richard; Kramer, Yale. "The relation-
     ship between 'mixed dominance' and reading disabilities." J Pediatr
     54(1): 76-80, January, 1959. (22 References).
In view of the work of Orton and Dearborn, this study was done to investigate the possibility of a relationship between mixed eye-hand dominance
and reading disability. Among 103 retarded readers and 288 controls, no
significant difference was found in the incidence of mixed dominance between the two groups.

389 Stellingwere, Yvonne M. "Laterality in families with reading dis-
     ability." For a summary see: Diss Abstr Int 36A(5): 2952-53,
     November, 1975.

390 Stephens, Wyatt E.; Cunningham, Ernest S.; Stigler, B. J. "Reading
     readiness and eye hand preference patterns in first grade children."
     Except Child 33(7): 481-88, March, 1967. (21 References).
To test the assumption that learning problems are caused by a neurological
impairment that manifests itself as mixed dominance, first graders were
given a battery of appropriate tests. No significant differences were
found, except in one test in which the mixed dominance group scored better
than a unilateral group. It is observed that confusion is generated by
assuming that children who do poorly in reading have a neurological impairment, and then seeking evidence.

391 Stevenson, Lillian P., and Robinson, Helen M. "Eye-hand preference,
     reversals, and reading progress." In: Chicago. University. Read-
     ing Clinics. Clinical studies in reading. Vol. 2. Edited by
     Helen M. Robinson. Chicago, Illinois: University of Chicago Press,
     1953. 83-88. (10 References). (Supplementary Educational Mono-
     graphs, No. 77).
Progress of a group of pupils was followed from kindergarten through
second grade to determine whether those with mixed eye-hand preference
made slower progress or developed unique problems in learning to read.
Those with mixed eye-hand preference learned to read as well as those
with consistent right eye-hand preference. No unusual reversal tendencies
were noted in the children with mixed eye-hand preference.

392 Thomson, M. "Laterality and reading attainment." Br J Educ Psychol
     45(Part 3): 317-21, November, 1975. (19 References).
Sxity retarded readers and sixty normal readers, all eight years old,
were examined on various aspects of laterality. The relationship between
reading attainment and laterality was found to be more complex than previously thought. The individual nature of each person's laterality inconsistencies appears to be the significant factor. Being completely
unilateral was the best predictor of reading success. Being mixed-handed
with cross laterality (mixed-handed and eyedness) or left-eared gave the
best indication of reading failure.

393   Thomson, M. E. "A comparison of laterality effects in dyslexics
      and controls using verbal dichotic listening tasks." Neuropsycho-
      logia 14(2): 243-46, 1976. (15 References).
Groups of good and poor readers ages nine to twelve years matched individually for age, sex, socioeconomic status, and intelligence were given
dichotic listening tests. These involved hearing different material
simultaneously in each ear. Digits, words, or nonsense syllables were
used. Normal readers showed right-ear superiority for digits, words,
reversible, and similar words. The dyslexic group showed no difference
or a left-ear superiority for digits, words, reversible, and similar
words. They showed a right-ear effect for nonsense syllables, resulting
in no significant difference between groups for nonsense syllables. Results are seen as not inconsistent with the cerebral dominance theories
of the cause of dyslexia.

394   Tordrup, S. A. "Reversibility and its tendencies." Nord Psykol
      10: 117-28, 1958.

395   Trieschmann, Roberta Barbara. "The relationship of undifferentiated
      handedness and perceptual development in children with reading
      problems." For a summary see: Diss Abstr 27A(6): 1674-75,
      December, 1966.

396   ————. "Undifferentiated handedness and perceptual development
      in children with reading problems." Percept Mot Skills 27(3,
      Part 2): 1123-34, December, 1968. (21 References).
Groups of normal and problem readers, boys ages seven and eight who were
in second and third grades, were given a series of manual dexterity tasks
to establish hand proficiency. Tasks such as putting pegs or nails in
holes were included. The groups were also given a perceptual task. They
were shown a design and asked to select from memory the same design from
a variety of drawings. If the child was as fast with one hand as the
other on the dexterity tests, or if he was faster with one hand on some
tasks and faster with the other on other tasks, he was termed undifferentiated in handedness. Normal and problem readers showed no difference
in handedness vs. undifferentiated handedness in this test. The handedness factor was found to be unrelated to results on a perceptual test.
Problem readers made more perceptual errors than normal readers. Results are discussed in terms of evaluation and perceptual development and
its relation to differentiation of cerebral hemispheres.

397   Weber, C. O., "Strephosymbolia and reading disability." J Abnorm
      Soc Psychol 39(3): 356-61, July, 1944. (8 References).
The object of this work was to answer the question: To what extent do
inefficient readers manifest the symptoms implied by "strephosymbolia,"
or twisted symbols, a term used by Orton to describe various kinds of
reversals and confusions in writing, including reversals of letters which
have right-left symmetry, reversed words, and mirror writing. College
freshmen were used in this study. Results include the finding that
freshmen who fail to profit from remedial reading made more reversal
errors in proportion to other errors. They were also inferior to others
in spelling and in average college grades. No significant differences
were found between groups who profited from remedial reading and those
who did not in general intelligence scores or mirror-writing skills.

398   Weintraub, Samuel. "Eye-hand preference and reading." Read Teach
      21(4): 369, 371, 373, 401, January, 1968. (11 References).

The relationship of eye-hand preference to reading disability is confused. It appears that hand preference becomes better established as the child grows older. At present little evidence exists of relationship between laterality and reading achievement. Some patterns of eye-hand relationship may result from mild neurological impairment, but the neurological implications of laterality patterns are not clear.

399 Wile, Ira S. "Eye dominance: its nature and treatment." Arch Ophthalmol 28(5): 780-90, November, 1942. (0 References).
Considers the hypothesis that vision is more than seeing and that optical acuity is not the same thing as perception. The problem of dyslexia has been ignored by ophthalmologists because they fail to regard a deficiency in reading ability as a medical problem unless it is related to anatomic defects. Eye dominance is a significant element in efficient vision. It is important to diagnose eye dominance: the reasons are explored. Tests for eye dominance are described. A clinical study of fifty dyslexic children is described in which 62 percent were found to be left-eye dominant; 8 percent showed uncertain or mixed dominance; and 30 percent had right-eye dominance. Average age was eight years, and minimum IQ was 80. Of those who were right-eyed, 80 percent were right-handed by reason of conversion from left-handedness. The significance of left-eye dominance is demonstrated by the large percentage of dyslexic children who were found to be left-eye dominant. The problem of crossed dominance involves the total organization of the individual. General principles for therapy for dyslexia are given.

400 Wilson, Robert Frederick. Assessment of the cerebral dominance theory of dyslexia as measured by a visual-auditory integration task. Unpublished Ph.D. thesis. University of Victoria (Canada), 1971.
It was hypothesized in this study that normal readers would show right cerebral hemisphere dominance for nonverbal material and left hemisphere superiority for verbal material. Right-handed dyslexics were expected to show less dominance for verbal material and right hemisphere dominance for nonverbal material. It was also expected in the light of other investigations that normal readers would do better than dyslexics in tasks presented either to eye or to ear for translation into the other mode of learning, ear or eye. Materials used were both auditory and visual. They were presented in such a way that only one cerebral hemisphere was stimulated at a time, i.e., presentation was to the left visual field and left ear only or to the right visual field and right ear only. A second hypothesis predicted that dyslexics and normal readers would show similar left-visual field, left-ear dominance in integrating nonverbal material. Neither hypothesis was confirmed in studies done using twelve-year-old boys as subjects. Results suggest that normal and dyslexic readers have approximately the same amount of difficulty in dealing with material presented to the left or the right perceptual fields. Further research is suggested using modified procedures and more control studies. The nature of deficits in left-handed dyslexics is also an area suggested for further study. Results in this study suggest that the length of time the stimulus is presented may be important in examining hemispheric asymmetry. It was also found that it took significantly longer to process nonverbal material than to process verbal.

401 Witty, Paul A., and Kopel, David. "Sinistral and mixed manual-ocular behavior in reading disability." J Educ Psychol 27(2): 119-34, February, 1936. (49 References).

The data presented show "a lack of relationship" between handedness and degree of reading efficiency. Eyedness, mixed hand-eye dominance, and consistent hand-eye behavior were found to have no association with reading ability. It is not recommended, however, that study of laterality be discarded in diagnosing reading disability cases. Subjects were groups of eighty good readers and 100 poor readers of average intelligence from grades three to six of a public school system.

402 Wold, Robert M. "Dominance--fact or fantasy: its significance in learning disabilities." J Am Optom Assoc 39(10): 908-15, October, 1968. (35 References).
The relationship of cerebral dominance to reading problems remains cloudy. It is concluded that such a relationship may exist. The relationship is more apparent when the controlling eye for reading is used in testing instead of the sighting eye used in acuity tests which do not involve symbolic language (letters or words). Tests for eye dominance, for handedness, and for eyedness are given.

403 Wolf, I. J. "Strephosymbolia vs. congenital word blindness." Proc Am Assoc Ment Defic 59: 446-65, 1935. (11 References).
Discredits Orton's theory of mixed cerebral dominance as a cause of dyslexia. Lack of dominance is not a sufficient explanation for reading disability. Its causes lie in such factors as faulty perception, associative interference, and other related factors. Morgan and Hinshelwood late in the nineteenth century presented the idea of congenital word blindness, a defect dependent on a congenital anomaly of the word memory center, and comparable to acquired word blindness. The view of Orton (1925) that reading disability is caused by incomplete cerebral dominance is explained. Orton coined the term "strephosymbolia," meaning twisted symbols, to denote the disability. An analysis of the errors made in reading is presented. From this analysis of the reading errors of a normal person it is reasoned that they are not caused by interference from a nondominant hemisphere. Orton's theory of the cause of specific reading disability is not valid. It is concluded that reading disability may occur in either dominantly left-handed or right-handed children as well as in those of uncertain or disturbed laterality. Orton held to the contrary. Cases of reading disability may be observed which fit Hinshelwood's criteria of congenital word blindness. Six case histories are included.

404 Wolfe, Lillian S. "Differential factors in specific reading disability: I. Laterality of function." Pedagog Semin J Genet Psychol 58: 45-56, March, 1941. (14 References).
Two groups of nine-year-old boys, one normal, the other retarded in reading, were compared on eye and hand dominance and hand versus eye dominance. These factors were found not to be related in a primary way to reading disability of the severity suffered by the experimental group in this study.

405 Woody, Clifford, and Phillips, Albert J. "The effects of handedness on reversals in reading." J Educ Res 27(9): 651-62, May, 1934. (0 References).
Using 136 matched pairs of right-handed and left-handed children from the first three grades of a public school system as subjects, researchers found that handedness of itself had little or not influence on reading ability. Care was taken to obtain subjects displaying "pure" handedness. None of the children was a naturally left-handed pupil who had been

trained to be right-handed. Reading ability ranged from very good to
very poor in the pupils selected for study.

406 Wussler, Sister Marilyn, and Barclay, A. "Cerebral dominance, psy-
      cholinguistic skills and reading disability." Percept Mot Skills
      31(2): 419-25, October, 1970. (23 References).
Children with reading disabilities showed significant differences from
normal subjects in many areas of psycholinguistic functioning including
auditory vocal, visual motor, vocal encoding, and motor encoding activities. The subjects were nine to twelve years old, matched for age, sex,
race, IQ, socioeconomic status, number of children in family, and sibling
positions. They were each given the ITPA, and eye-hand dominance was
determined. Results suggest that inadequate cerebral dominance and the
accompanying perceptual-motor immaturity, as expressed through level of
psycholinguistic functioning, are integral parts of the dyslexic syndrome.

407 Wyckoff, Chauncey W. "Strephosymbolia: a pediatric and a pedagogic
      problem." J Pediatr 23(1): 95-100, July, 1943. (4 References).
Discusses reading disability from the standpoint of Orton's theory of
mixed laterality. Why the condition is of interest or importance to the
pediatrician is discussed. Suggestions for making the diagnosis are
given, including some of the tests that should be given. The sight method
of teaching reading is partly to blame for the increased incidence of
the problem.

408 Yeni-Komshian, Grace H.; Isenberg, David; Goldberg, Herman. "Cere-
      bral dominance and reading disability: left visual field deficit
      in poor readers." Neuropsychologia 13(1): 83-94, January, 1975.
      (33 References).
Good and poor readers from grades five to seven from Baltimore public
schools were individually tested for dichotic listening, visual half
field presentation of numerals, and visual half field presentation of
words. The listening test involved hearing a different sequence of
digits in each ear simultaneously. The numbers and words were presented
either to left or right of a central fixation point which the subject
was instructed to watch until the number or word appeared. As measured
by the visual half field tests, the poor readers were more lateralized.
Good and poor readers performed about equally on the tests of right
visual field. Poor readers did worse than good readers on tests of the
left visual half field. Both groups did worse with left than with right
ear in the listening test. Poor readers' scores were below those of good
readers for either ear. Not all of these results are statistically significant. Results appear to contradict the hypothesis that disabled
readers are not as well lateralized as normal readers. Nevertheless, it
is suggested that results indicate some kind of right hemisphere deficit
in reading disability.

409 Zeman, Samuel Steve. "A summary of research concerning laterality
      and reading." J Read Spec 6(3): 116-23, March, 1967. (0 Refer-
      ences).
Cites and summarizes fourteen studies that have been published concerning
the relationship of reading to various phases of laterality, including
identification of left and right, handedness, shifting handedness, eye and
hand dominance, and ear or foot preference. It is an area that has been
investigated for many years. In the majority of the investigations no
significant relationship is found to exist between reading disability and
laterality. In light of these findings it is suggested that the area has

been adequately researched, and further research time could be more ad-
vantageously used in studying other aspects of reading problems.

B. CONGENITAL WORD BLINDNESS

410 Alger, Ellice M. "Three cases of word-blindness." Trans Am
     Ophthalmol Soc 19: 322-34, 1921. (13 References).
Defines word blindness and gives one case history of an adult case of
acquired dyslexia. Congential word blindness implies a congenital defect
which prevents an otherwise normal child from learning to read. There
are very wide variations in the ability to store visual memories. In
congenital cases of word blindness the defects are more likely cortical
and due to lack of development rather than to destructive brain lesions.
Individual instruction and an understanding teacher are indispensable.
In childhood there is a possibility of the other hemisphere of the brain
taking up the function of the defective one. An occupation that depends
as little as possible on visual memories should be chosen. Case histories are included. In reported discussion following this paper, Dr. J. H.
Claiborne states that in 1906 he and Dr. A. Schapringer read papers on
word blindness before a section meeting of the New York Academy of Medicine. Schapringer's presentation came first, making him the first to
report on word blindness in the United States, according to Dr. Claiborne.
(See Items No. 2195 and No. 2240).

411 Carr, T. E. Ashdown. "Congential word blindness." Trans Ophthalmol
     Soc UK 57(Part 2, 1937 Session): 579-90, 1938. (0 References).
Visual memories are not stored in the brain haphazardly, but in neatly
arranged and distinct subcenters. These may be destroyed by cerebral
lesions. A congenital defect may also cause the visual memory center for
words and letters to be imperfectly developed. A typical case as presented to the oculist is described. Reading for afflicted persons is
slow, laborious, and tiring. It may help them to read or spell aloud or
move their lips. Auditory or glossokinesthetic brain centers can then be
used as aids. Case histories are given.

412 Chambers, E. R. "Congential word-blindness." Bristol Med Chir J
     51: 41-46, 1934. (9 References).
Reviews some literature, including Hinshelwood's view that reading consists of two stages. First, individual letters of the alphabet are stored
in memory. Second, words are gradually acquired and stored in visual
memory. In congenital word blindness, the visual memory for letters and
words is congenitally deficient. Fisher believed the problem was not
congenital, but probably caused by birth injury. Word-blind children
should be removed from the regular classroom and taught alone. After
adequate and considerate treatment, and if the cases are recognized early,
they are able to return to school and be educated like normal individuals.
Case histories are given.

413 Childs, Sally B. "Children who cannot read." Child Study 14(6):
     178-79, 188, March, 1937. (0 References).
Orton's theory of the neurological basis for reading disability is explained in nontechnical terms. Teachers should fully inform themselves
about reading disabilities and how to deal with them. Parents are not
to blame for the child's inability to learn to read. They should cooperate in remedial efforts. Schools should learn to recognize reading-
disabled children and plan adequate programs of instruction.

414 Hermann, Knud. Reading disability; a medical study of word-blindness
     and related handicaps. Translated by P. G. Aungle. Copenhagen,
     Denmark: Munksgaard, 1959. 183p. (Bibliography).
Views congenital word blindness, or dyslexia, as a clinical entity of
largely constitutional cause. Word blindness is a specific abnormality
characterized by: (1) its persistence into adult life; (2) the manifestation of characteristic errors; (3) its familial incidence; and (4) its
appearance in connection with other symbol defects (such as reading music)
rather than in isolation. Gerstmann's syndrome and gestalt psychology
are briefly commented on in the context of word blindness. The difficulties experienced by affected persons are described.

415 Holder, Vera. "Specific developmental dyslexia and word blindness."
     Acta Paedopsychiatr 39(7): 182-86, 1973. (11 References).
Explains and defines the very narrow entity of specific developmental
dyslexia, distinguishing it from poor reading resulting from low intelligence, poor school attendance, or cases in which emotional disturbance
is primary and not a reaction to the reading failure. Reversals, directional confusion, and left-right difficulties may result from haste,
nervousness, or emotional problems as well as from developmental dyslexia.
In word blindness the words are seen but not recognized. The child with
emotional difficulties or behavior problems may complain of not seeing
the words. A familial incidence of developmental dyslexia appears to
exist. The category of reading disability should be recognized, if for
no other reason than to alleviate the fear and sheer dread experienced
by these children as they face each school day. Some of the relevant
literature is reviewed.

416 Kerr, James. "Congenital aphasia." In: The fundamentals of school
     health. Chap. 32. New York: Macmillan, 1927. 611-23. (0 Refer-
     ences).
Word-blind or word-deaf cases need careful analysis. They are not as
simple as they look on paper or in final diagnosis. These children are
often highly intelligent and it requires weeks or months to work with
them in doing justice to their other capacities. Various aphasic defects
are discussed and some of the early literature is reviewed. Examples
are given of cases of word blindness. Congenital word deafness is described, including cases of children who hear well but remain mute, and
of cases deaf only for words and sentences. Others are unable to identify
some other sounds. Echolalia, and its use by some children as an aid to
a defective auditory word memory, is discussed. "Form blindness" is a
term that has been used for children who cannot reproduce a form, e.g.,
the Binet diamond. These various interferences with speech are blamed
on "failure in the lowest nervous mechanisms of auditory and visual
representation." It is noted that there are higher levels of association
about which little is known. It is speculated that intelligent mutes may
be in this category. It is useless to attempt to train nonexistent structures in the congenital aphasic. However, these children are plastic,
with great powers of compensation. Auditory aphasics do well in time,
and slighter cases of visual aphasia may end up only as bad spellers or
poor readers. Kerr cites his own article on school hygiene as the first
identification of congenital word blindness as a clinical group. (See
Item No. 2229).

417 Orton, Samuel Torrey. "'Word-blindness' in school children." Arch
     Neurol Psychiatry 14(5): 581-615, November, 1925. (20 References).

This is a statement of Orton's theory that word blindness results from
confused or incomplete cerebral dominance. It presents the case history
of a sixteen-year-old boy with an IQ of 71. Orton believed that he was
much more able than the score indicated. The boy suffered from severe
reading disability with symptoms fitting Hinshelwood's term "congenital
word blindness." Details of the case are given and it is compared with
other cases. Some of the literature on mirror writing and word blindness
is reviewed. Three areas in the brain are located and distinguished:
(1) "visual perceptive" where blindness results if the area is destroyed
in both hemispheres; (2) "visual recognitive" where the ability to recognize objects is destroyed only by bilateral destruction; and (3) "visual
associative" where destruction in the dominant hemisphere only results
in word blindness. This is the left hemisphere in right-handed persons
and vice versa. Because of the reversals seen in word blindness, it is
hypothesized that early impressions of letters and words are impressed
on both hemispheres in left and right orientations. To learn to read,
the person must suppress the reversed order and form from the nondominant hemisphere. It is suggested that the term "strephosymbolia"--
twisted symbols--be used to distinguish this difficulty in learning to
read from the acquired disorder seen in adults. Traditional phonics
methods of teaching reading are recommended over the look-and-say method
for the word-blind.

418 "Poor reading ability may be inherited." Sci Dig 39(1): 28,
       January, 1956. (0 References).
Reports the findings of Dr. Arthur L. Drew, as reported in the Univ Mich
Med Bull, that reading difficulties may be inherited, and may be genetically determined in some cases. Dr. Drew, a neurologist, believes a
series of three cases appears to imply strongly that some reading disturbances have organic backgrounds of a congenital nature. (See Item No.
545).

419 Schilder, Paul F. "Congenital alexia and its relation to optic
       perception." Pedagog Semin J Genet Psychol 65: 67-88, September,
       1944. (11 References).
Investigation of seven cases of congenital word blindness was made from
the point of view of its position in the system of aphasias and agnosias.
The conclusion is that the basic problem in congenital reading disability
is difficulty in breaking down the spoken word into its sounds and in
putting together the sounds of a word. In congenital word blindness we
are dealing with an isolated problem in "a gnostic-intellectual function."

420 Tamm, A. "Investigations regarding backward school children."
       Hygiea [Stockholm] 86: 673-706, October 15, 1924. (As abstracted
       in JAMA 83: 1806, November 29, 1924).
Among 736 children in a school for backward children in Stockholm, an unexpectedly large number suffered from word blindness. It was found to
be of three types: visual, auditory, and motor. The close resemblance
between congenital verbal blindness in children and alexia and agraphia
caused by disease in adults suggests the same localization in the brain.
Early recognition and treatment are emphasized.

421 Wallin, J. E. Wallace. "Congenital word-blindness." Lancet 1:
       890-92, April 23, 1921. (9 References).
Based on a study of word-blind children in St. Louis schools, this article
points out that word blindness has no characteristic, typical symptoms.
The vast majority of the eighty-five children studied were normal in sight

and hearing. The incidence of word blindness was greater than the combined incidence of epileptics, psychopaths, mongols, and cretins. Boys
outnumbered girls about four to one. IQs varied from 54 to 104 with 85
percent subnormal in general intelligence. "Word blindness" is defined
as a grave degree and "dyslexia" as a slight degree of reading disability.
Word-blind children who are not feebleminded should be assigned to special classes. The same teaching method does not work with all such children. They may have to be taught orally if all other methods fail. Reading disability is caused by word blindness where there is a defect in
brain centers concerned with imagery of words or in the connecting fibers
between secondary and primary visual centers.

C. CONSTITUTIONAL FACTORS;
FUNDAMENTAL MAKEUP

422   Abrams, Jules C. "Dyslexia--fact or fantasy?" In: Reading Confer-
      ence, Lehigh University, 22d, 1973. Highlights: teaching reading:
      the growing diversity. Edited by Joseph P. Kender. Danville,
      Illinois: Interstate Printers and Publishers, 1974. 79-88. (3
      References).
Dyslexia exists. It is a specific category of reading disability within
the broader range of reading problems. It is not caused by environmental
or cultural problems or by physical deficiencies. It may be acquired by
brain injury or it may be developmental (functional). Developmental dyslexia is probably of genetic origin. Children so afflicted have difficulty in forming associations involving "word-like objects."

423   Blau, Harold; Schwalb, Eugene; Zanger, Eugene; et al. "Developmental
      dyslexia and its remediation." Read Teach 22(7): 649-53, 669,
      April, 1969. (9 References).
Summarizes findings in twelve individual cases of dyslexia. To evaluate
dyslexics, visual perceptual screening tests, laterality tests, and oral
reading tests are recommended. Dyslexia appears to be caused by a specific organically determined cerebral defect. It occurs most often in
males. Evidence conflicts on the causal importance of mixed cerebral
dominance. No one training method can be recommended. The "modality
blocking" theory says that learning to read may be blocked or hindered
by presenting material visually and aurally at the same time. To avoid
this a nonvisual method should be used. One case history is given.

424   Critchley, Macdonald. "Developmental dyslexia: a constitutional
      disorder of symbolic perception." Res Publ Assoc Res Nerv Ment Dis
      48: 266-71, 1970. (0 References).
Describes the symptoms of specific developmental dyslexia and its negative
features. It is not of psychological origin or caused by inadequate
teaching methods, insufficient intelligence, or vision or hearing problems. The dyslexic child is not emotionally disturbed, although he may
become frustrated later. The nature of the language being learned is not
to blame. No obvious cerebral pathology exists. The dyslexic can identify ordinary signs and signals. By hard work and specialized help the
dyslexic gradually overcomes his problem. A dyslexic's writing is distinguished by overall untidiness of penmanship; rotation of letters; reversals of syllables or words; abnormal arrangement of the letters of a
word; and gross errors in spelling.

425 ————. "Developmental dyslexia as a specific cognitive disorder."
    In: Hellmuth, Jerome, ed. Cognitive studies: deficits in cogni-
    tion. Vol. 2. New York: Brunner/Mazel, 1971. 47-52. (0 Refer-
    ences).
Quotes the definition of "dyslexia" agreed upon by the Research Group of
the World Federation of Neurology on Dyslexia and World Illiteracy, and
defines "cognitive" in connection with the agreed definition of dyslexia
as indicating that the fault lies in an inherent disorder of mentation.
The fault causing dyslexia is independent of any environmental problems
which may coexist and possibly predispose the learner to emotional conflicts. The near-miracle of speech acquisition in the child ordinarily
occurs without formal instruction. Reading and writing skills require
a teacher. Failure to learn to read may stem from many causes. Within
this range of causes is a group of children with a specific and isolated
block in mastering written words. This is specific developmental dyslexia. No evidence suggests that this type of dyslexia is a manifestation of minimal brain damage. The disability is usually limited to difficulties in identifying verbal symbols, remembering their appearance,
and relating them to how they sound. Defective automatic recall of the
serial order of temporal items is one manifestation of cognitive disorder
in dyslexia. Gross specific defects and difficulty in consulting a dictionary or telephone directory result. Defective eye movements are the
product, not the cause, of difficulty in reading.

426 ————. The dyslexic child. 2nd ed. London: Heinemann Medical,
    1970. 137p. (Bibliography p. 122-35).
Seeks to trace the growth of knowledge about dyslexia and to describe conflicting ideas as to its nature and causes. The historic case reports on
dyslexia closed in 1917 with Hinshelwood's second monograph. This early
literature is reviewed. This period was followed by a period of analysis
and changing orientation. Doubts and confusion also existed about dyslexia. Dyslexics constitute a special group among the general community
of poor readers. Dyslexia is caused by an inborn defect, possibly genetic
in origin. It is independent of environment, lack of intelligence, eye
problems, or the peculiarities of English spelling. Immaturity of cerebral development, i.e., maturational lag, results in dyslexia and ambilaterality. Sequential disorders may point to the true nature of the
underlying defect. The literature on cerebral dominance as a factor in
dyslexia is reviewed. Disorders of spatial thought, spatial manipulation,
and inadequate temporal notions may appear. No cluster of neurological
defects exists which can be viewed as constituting a diagnostic formula,
however. Children who are brain-injured, victims of neurological disease,
disturbed or neurotic, or victims of unfavorable environments may be poor
readers. Children with defects in hearing or sight or with inconsistent
manual preference may also be poor readers. But all of these conditions
are irrelevant to the consideration of the hard core of cases of poor
reading in which the origins of the learning defect are inborn and independent of any intellectual or environmental shortcoming which may happen
to coexist. This hard core of cases constitutes the specific, or developmental, dyslexics. Any theory of minimal brain damage is not convincing.

The outlook for dyslexics is emphatically not hopeless. The dyslexic
child can be taught to read. Although teaching methods as such are not
discussed, the viewpoint is that skilled teaching, not psychotherapy, is
required. Psychiatric symptoms tend to disappear when the dyslexic gets
help. Not favored is the Delacato method. What is favored is a phonic
or analytic-synthetic system of instruction rather than the look-and-say

method for use with dyslexic children. The bibliography contains citations to materials in several languages.

427 ————. "Language acquisition in developmental dyslexics." In:
     Kirk, Samuel A., and McCarthy, Jeanne McRae, eds. Learning dis-
     abilities: selected ACLD papers. Boston, Massachusetts: Houghton
     Mifflin, 1975. 264-70. (2 References). (Reprinted from Associa-
     tion for Children with Learning Disabilities. Conference proceed-
     ings: the child with learning disabilities: his right to learn
     8. Chicago, Illinois, March 18-20, 1971, 3-9).
Developmental dyslexia is not caused by: (1) psychological factors; (2)
poor teaching; (3) intellectual insufficiency; (4) defective vision or
hearing; or (5) emotional disturbance. Specific developmental dyslexia
is an isolated entity. The agreed definition of the World Federation of
Neurology for developmental dyslexia is stated. This difficulty in learning to read is not aligned with any obvious cerebral pathology, and
"minimal brain damage" is an entity of dubious validity. Developmental
dyslexia is independent of the inherent structure of the language concerned. The child with developmental dyslexia can distinguish and identify commonplace signs and symbols, including traffic signs, dogs, birds,
postage stamps, automobiles, and airplanes. Only verbal symbols trouble
him. Usually dyslexics can identify numerals. They may or may not be
able to read musical notation. Difficulty in writing is a natural consequence of difficulty in reading. Spelling mistakes common in dyslexics
are listed. Confusion of serial order is a symptom. The words of Herbert
Spencer are quoted to the effect that there are three phases through
which human opinion passes: "the unanimity of the ignorant, the disagreement of the inquiring, and then the unanimity of the wise." It is suggested that we are passing through the second of these phases in the
matter of dyslexia at the time of this writing.

428 ————. "The problem of developmental dyslexia." Proc R Soc Med
     56(3): 209-12, March, 1963. (3 References).
Suggests that it is necessary for neurologists to restate their credo
concerning specific developmental dyslexia. Much confusion has arisen.
Many educators doubt whether such a condition even exists. Many--but not
all--educational psychologists have regarded the problem as a continuum
ranging from intellectual inadequacy to neurosis. Neurologists are prepared to agree that there is a spectrum of indifferent readers in which
the causes of the problem are quite diverse. They do not mean to include
in the congenitally word-blind group all persons who are illiterate, semiliterate, retarded readers, or bad spellers. The problem lies in a hard
core of cases. These children are of normal intelligence, are not neurotic, inattentive, or lazy, and have difficulty in learning printed or
written symbols and associating them with their appropriate sound. This
kind of dyslexia has nothing to do with orthography or teaching techniques.
Neurotic symptoms are reactionary, not causal. It is more common in the
male, and is genetically determined. Neurologists believe that dyslexia
can be considerably overcome with intensive, sympathetic, persevering
teaching. Other neurological concomitants may be observed. Some of these
are discussed. The notions that developmental dyslexia is a maturational
lag or that it is one aspect of inadequate achievement of the faculty of
language are discussed. The term "congenital aphasia" should be dropped.
Of the estimated 10 percent of poor readers in schools, perhaps 1 or 2
percent are dyslexics in the neurological sense.

429 De Hirsch, Katrina. "Reading and total language disability." In:
     International Reading Association. Conference proceedings: chang-
     ing concepts of reading instruction. Vol. 6. Edited by J. Allen
     Figurel. New York: Scholastic Magazines, 1961. 211-14. (0 Ref-
     erences).
Specific developmental language disability, seen as including dyslexia,
is defined as a condition in which the communicative intent is clearly
present in the child and the drive to learn is not impaired except when
it comes to handling verbal symbols. It does not include cases where
reading difficulty is part of a broader psychopathology. Nor does it include cases of nonspecific reading difficulty linked to emotional immaturity, defects in organization of the ego, or severe psychopathology.
The syndrome does involve a familial constitutional element. It includes
reading problems stemming from lack of language aptitude; the child with
no "gift" for dealing with linguistic entities. Individuals with language disorders often show subtle defects in other areas. Neurophysiological patterning must be carefully evaluated. It appears that a rather
marked degree of neurophysiological immaturity underlies various developmental language disorders. Dyslexic children have cluttered speech, show
defects in figure-ground organization, have short auditory memory spans,
and exhibit poor auditory discrimination.

430 Ettlinger, G., and Jackson, C. V. "Organic factors in developmental
     dyslexia." Proc R Soc Med 48: 998-1000, December, 1955. (11
     References).
Reports the results of studies of dyslexic children which tend to confirm
that developmental dyslexia is constitutional in origin. Neurological
examination was negative in all cases. Psychological examination gave
evidence of selective impairment on memory for designs and block tests.
It is concluded that in many dyslexics normal cerebral dominance is not
fully established in either hemisphere, a quality probably caused by some
hereditary factor. Crossed laterality and defects in spatial and temporal
perception point to a constitutional origin. Reading defects observed
in these cases could not be attributed to environmental or psychogenic
influences.

431 Hermann, Knud. "Specific reading disability; with special refer-
     ence to complicated word blindness." Dan Med Bull 11(1): 34-40,
     February, 1964. (13 References).
Reports several clinical observations of the word-blind supporting the
view that a specific anomaly underlies the condition. It is not merely
delayed reading maturity, as psychologists and educators generally believe. These observations include: (1) uniformity of symptomatology;
(2) a substantial number of word-blind persons in whom reading and writing difficulties persist into adult life; (3) familial occurrence pointing to a constitutional factor; and (4) studies of twins substantiating
the great significance of heredity in word blindness. Some relevant
literature is reviewed. Within the large group of genetically determined
dyslexics, subgroups can be distinguished displaying various groups of
symptoms. The identification of these subgroups is of value for the
prognosis and training of backward readers.

432 Hermann, Knud, and Voldby, H. "The morphology of handwriting in
     congenital word-blindness." Acta Psychiatr Neurol 21: 349-63,
     1946. (9 References).
Surveys the types of errors which appear to be most conspicuous and
characteristic of the handwriting of dyslexics, including confusion and

disfigurement of letters and mirror writing, among others. Written work
of dyslexics bears a striking likeness to the agraphia of Gerstmann's
syndrome. It is not believed that disturbances in a dyslexic's writing
can be explained by a failure in the cerebral area involved in Gerstmann's
syndrome. It is suggested that dyslexia is caused by partial failures
of several functions, and involves a diffuse rather than a localized disturbance of functions.

433 Lassen, T. J. "Reading disability--a case history and an essay."
     Va Med Mon 91(9): 421-23, September, 1964. (0 References).
In addition to the reading difficulties commonly seen in emotionally disturbed children and in juvenile delinquents, a primary type of reading
disability exists which is much more common than had been thought. A
case history of a twelve-year-old boy illustrating this type of reading
problem is given. Primary responsibility for recognition and treatment
of reading handicaps lies with the public school system. The psychiatrist should be cautious about invading the field of education, but should
be willing to help. It is noted that the primary type of reading disability is not diagnosed early enough or treated effectively. It is
emphasized that it should be. The causes of reading handicaps appear to
be multiplying.

434 Lovell, K.; Gray, E. A.; Oliver, D. E. "A further study of some
     cognitive and other disabilities in backward readers of average
     non-verbal reasoning scores." Br J Educ Psychol 34(Part 3): 275-
     79, November, 1964. (7 References).
Children who were retarded in reading were individually paired with children who were average to good readers. On a series of individual tests
it was found that boys backward in reading were greatly inferior to the
backward girls on tests of copying and dictation, but WISC Vocabulary
score for the backward boys was not below that of the girls. Reading
failure occurs among males at twice the rate of females even at ages
fourteen and fifteen. It is concluded that reading disability is often
one symptom of a larger syndrome affecting males more severely than
females.

435 Lovell, K.; Shapton, D.; Warren, N. S. "A study of some cognitive
     and other disabilities in backward readers of average intelligence
     as assessed by a non-verbal test." Br J Educ Psychol 34(1): 58-
     64, February, 1964. (13 References).
Children who were backward readers were matched and paired with average
to good readers. Poor readers showed no deficit on an oral test of language structure, but were poorer than good readers on tests of spatial
relationships and right-left discrimination. They also showed more rotations in a test involving the copying of abstract designs.

436 Miles, T. R. "More on dyslexia." Br J Educ Psychol 41(1): 1-5,
     February, 1971. (5 References).
Presents both sides of the argument for and against using the term "dyslexia." The chief reason not to use it is that it avoids assuming the
cause of the poor reading is constitutional. This is considered "in-
cautious." A child manifesting the general disabilities of the disabled
reader should be called "dyslexic" and the cause should be assumed to be
constitutional. Dyslexic children may be awkward and difficult as a consequence of the reading disability. Behavior problems tend to lessen
when the nature of the problem is explained to the child and his parents.
They virtually disappear if the child is able to make some progress and

bolster his self-confidence. A child should be diagnosed as dyslexic if
he manifests a number of the cluster of behaviors described. It should
be assumed that the behaviors are constitutional in origin. Those who
believe the cause of the disability to be poor teaching or emotional disturbance should think again.

437 Mongrain, M. R., and Butler, J. B. V. "Some aspects of reading
     problems in children." Trans Pac Coast Oto-Ophthalmol Soc 34:
     163-71, 1953. (14 References).
Discusses two types of specific reading difficulties: children with developmental aphasia who cannot learn by the flash method of reading instruction, and children with eye problems related to the neuromuscular or
fusional mechanism. It is estimated that about 80 percent of children
learn to read by the flash method. It is odd that so little has been
done for the remaining 20 percent, a substantial number. These should
have instruction in phonetics and kinesthetic methods. Developmental
aphasias are not uncommon. They have nothing to do with the child's intelligence, show a familial tendency, and predominate in males. Diagnosis of a child with a reading problem should include careful evaluation of eye muscle balance and fusion. Proper orthoptics can greatly
increase the ability to read comfortably.

438 Naidoo, Sandhya. "Specific developmental dyslexia." Br J Educ
     Psychol 41(1): 19-22, February, 1971. (32 References).
That reading disability is specific and that it stems from anomalies of
maturation or development are implicit concepts in discussing "specific
dyslexia." Four hypotheses are presented to account for the constitutional basis of "specific reading disabilities" which stem from developmental anomalies and delays: (1) genetic factors; (2) late or imperfect
establishment of cerebral dominance; (3) the theory that such delays
represent normal variations in the maturation of the brain; and (4) neurological disorders. These matters are discussed in terms of the treatment offered at the Word Blind Centre for Dyslexic Children in London.

439 Orton, Samuel Torrey. "Some disorders in the language development
     of children." Woods Sch Child Res Clin Proc, May, 1946. (As re-
     printed in Orton, Samuel Torrey. "Word-blindness" in school chil-
     dren and other papers on strephosymbolia (specific language dis-
     ability--dyslexia) 1925-1946. Compiled by June Lyday Orton.
     Pomfret, Connecticut: Orton Society, 1966. 263-68. (0 References).
Reading disability in children of normal intelligence often stems from
functional disorder in the reading centers of the brain. No organic
brain defect is present. Children may be word-blind, word-deaf, or abnormally clumsy. The only general process that appears to relate to all
three is sequence building. The child has trouble remembering the order
of the letters or sounds in a word, or the order in which motor activities are to be carried out.

440 Vellutino, Frank R.; Harding, Constance J.; Phillips, Forman; et al.
     "Differential transfer in poor and normal readers." J Genet Psychol
     126(First Half): 3-18, March, 1975. (43 References).
Groups of good and poor fourth-, fifth-, and sixth-grade readers were
shown pairs of geometric designs and nonsense words in a visual-verbal
association task which simulated reading: the task was to associate something they saw with something they heard. The children were also shown
sets of geometric designs in a visual-visual association task unlike
reading. As expected, poor readers performed significantly below good

readers on the visual-verbal task. Performance of the two groups was
comparable on the visual-visual task. It is concluded that the difficulties reading-disabled children experience in generalizing in early word
learning are most likely caused by difficulties in transferring what is
seen into its verbal equivalent (visual-verbal integration) and not by
a basic disorder or dysfunction in the ability to generalize or categorize.

D. CULTURAL BACKGROUND

441 Bell, D. Bruce; Lewis, Franklin D.; Anderson, Robert F. "Some per-
     sonality and motivational factors in reading retardation." J Educ
     Res 65(5): 229-33, January, 1972. (20 References).
One hundred junior-high-school boys, fifty Caucasians and fifty Negroes,
with no known neurological, emotional, or sensory problems were investigated for relationship of reading retardation to motivation, personality,
and other variables. Half of the boys in each group were retarded in
reading. Fifty-three variables submitted to factor analysis yielded fifteen factors. Five of these factors (or concepts) were related to reading. Results suggest that inadequate readers had verbal deficits and
came from low socioeconomic homes. They made one of three kinds of adjustment to their reading disability: aggressiveness, negativism, or
passivity. Some factors were more characteristic of one racial group or
the other.

442 Cavaney, June Gardner. "A study of socio-economic status, parental
     child-reading attitudes and marital adjustment as these factors
     relate to the rate of progress in special education for dyslexia
     in a given population of children." For a summary see: Diss Abstr
     Int 37A(4): 2424, October, 1976.

443 Davey, Elizabeth P. "Evaluating the needs of the culturally disad-
     vantaged reader in corrective and remedial classes." In: Confer-
     ence on Reading, University of Chicago, 1964. Proceedings: meet-
     ing individual differences in reading. Vol. 26. Compiled and
     edited by H. Alan Robinson. Chicago, Illinois: University of
     Chicago Press, 1964. 133-36. (1 Bibliographic Footnote). (Sup-
     plementary Educational Monographs, No. 94).
Each student in a reading clinic must be treated as an individual. To
help culturally disadvantaged students learn to read, it is necessary to
motivate them, build their confidence, and acquaint them with language
patterns that differ from their usual speech.

444 Dreikurs, Rudolf. "Emotional predispositions to reading difficul-
     ties." Arch Pediatr 71(11): 339-53, November, 1954. (8 Refer-
     ences).
Reading difficulties are expressions of emotional and social maladjustment in the child. In recent years emotional-sociological explanations
of reading failure have taken the place of the older mechanistic-
physiological explanations in which dyslexia was ascribed to physiological causes. Reading disabilities arise from: (1) the child's discouragement, lack of confidence, and lack of faith in himself; (2) poor work
habits; and (3) the child's antagonism toward school and learning. The
child has little motivation from within to work, and pressure from without is no longer effective. The teacher can no longer demand cooperation,

but can only stimulate it. The increase in reading difficulties reflects
cultural factors that influence the training of children.

445 Flaherty, Rose, and Anderson, Howard B. "Boys' difficulty in learn-
     ing to read." Elem Engl 43(5): 471-72, 503, May, 1966. (10
     References).
More boys than girls have difficulty in learning to read. Possible causes
for this are reviewed, including: (1) girls' earlier physiological maturity during the preschool period; (2) different cultural demands on the
sexes; (3) lack of objectivity in evaluating boys and girls; and (4) differences in motivation. Some researchers believe that school programs
are geared more to the needs and interests of girls than to those of
boys.

446 Huessy, Hans R. "The comparative epidemiology of reading disability
     in German and English speaking countries." Acta Paedopsychiatr
     34(9): 273-77, September, 1967. (25 References).
Reports that in German-speaking countries the incidence of reading disability is about half that in English-speaking countries. Children start
school in the German-speaking areas studied anywhere from six months to
a year or more later than in the United States. Reading disabilities
seem to disappear earlier in Germany than in America. The history of
reading disabilities is different in each language, but most children do
learn to read by age ten.

447 Lahaderne, Henriette M. "Feminized schools--unpromising myth to
     explain boys' reading problems." Read Teach 29(8): 776-86, May,
     1976. (25 References).
Expresses doubt of the validity of the belief that boys in elementary
schools have more reading problems than girls because there are more
women than men teachers, and that the women establish norms which discriminate in favor of girls. This notion is dismissed as a myth. A
number of studies comparing male and female elementary teachers' perceptions of pupils, the teachers' classroom behaviors, and pupil outcome
are summarized. Results of these researches, presented in tabular form,
indicate that male and female teachers did not differ significantly in
their perceptions and treatment of boys and girls. Any variation suggested that women discriminated less than men toward pupils on the basis
of sex and socioeconomic status. Attitudes in elementary schools appear
to mirror social forces that impinge on the school more than they do the
enforcement of female norms.

448 Lovell, K., and Woolsey, M. E. "Reading disability, non-verbal rea-
     soning, and social class." Educ Res 6(3): 226-29, 1964. (5
     References).
Reports the results of a reading test and a test of nonverbal reasoning administered to children in third-year junior school (British) and to pupils
fourteen and fifteen years old. In both groups about half the backward
readers had average or higher standardized nonverbal reasoning scores.
Father's occupation (or mother's where applicable) was obtained for these
children, and social class assigned by the use of a standard government
publication classifying occupations. While it is clear that children
from lower social classes tend to do less well in school generally, and
that social class does affect reading attainment when the whole range of
reading ability is considered, this may occur for many reasons. The
specific finding of this research is that whatever is responsible for
reading failure, it operates in all social classes. Low social class has

a "down-pulling" effect on school performance generally, but it does not
appear to cause severe reading backwardness.

449 Mingoia, Edwin M. "Possible causes of underachievement in reading."
    Elem Engl 39(3): 220-23, March, 1962. (0 References).
From the results of three surveys of elementary-school children two pictures of typical extreme underachievers were constructed. In one case,
the child is a boy from a home of cultural and economic deprivation.
He has had no language training and little experience with oral language.
He does not respond to group instruction. The other underachiever is a
boy from a middle-class background. He is bewildered and overpressured
by his mobile, overambitious parents. No common characteristics distinguish all underachievers, and attempts to establish direct cause-and-
effect relationships are not likely to be fruitful.

450 Peck, Bruce B., and Stackhouse, Thomas W. "Reading problems and
    family dynamics." J Learn Disabil 6(8): 506-11, October, 1973.
    (19 References).
A comparison of families with one child who is a problem reader with
normal families disclosed that the reading-problem families took longer
to make decisions and engaged in less discussion in reaching the decision.
In reading-problem families more time was spent in silence or in irrelevant exchanges, and less in exchanging explicit information, thus avoiding the confrontations necessary to make decisions. Rather than teaching
their children how to learn and make discoveries, they teach them instead the art of being stupid.

451 Roman, Melvin; Margolin, Joseph B.; Harari, Carmi. "Reading retarda-
    tion and delinquency." Natl Probat Parole Assoc J 1(1): 1-7,
    July, 1955. (0 References).
Presents the general considerations underlying the finding of a high relationship between reading disability and delinquency. Most of the children concerned came from homes of low socioeconomic status. Frequently
a pattern of reading retardation, truancy, and delinquency is followed.
Reading disability is the first signal of delinquency. The forces acting
on the child of low socioeconomic status are not conducive to learning
in a school system with middle-class orientation. He is deficient in
preschool readiness experience. His use of oral English is poor. Books
and materials geared to the middle-class child have little meaning for
him. Different materials are needed.

452 Werner, Emmy E.; Simonian, Ken; Smith, Ruth S. "Reading achievement,
    language functioning and perceptual-motor development of 10- and 11-
    year-olds." Percept Mot Skills 25(2): 409-20, October, 1967.
    (15 References).
The purpose of this study was to discover the relative effectiveness of
the Primary Mental Abilities (Elementary Form) of the Bender Gestalt tests
in identifying fifth-grade children with reading problems at different
levels of intelligence. Both are group tests. An entire school population in Hawaii was used. Results showed a dramatic increase in reading
difficulties as the socioeconomic status of the children declined. Only
4 percent of the children with reading problems obtained IQ scores above
the mean. It is concluded that the overwhelming majority of poor readers
need help in language skills and stimulation of interest in reading. Inadequacy in language function rather than lack of perceptual-motor skills
characterize most children with reading problems in the upper elementary
grades.

E. EMOTIONAL FACTORS

453 Axline, Virginia Mae. "Play therapy...a way of understanding and
       helping 'reading problems.'" Child Educ 26(4): 156-61, December,
       1949. (0 References).
Presents three case studies revealing emotional attitudes which are believed to underlie these children's reading problems. We can help the
child if we increase our understanding of his emotional life. The child
can and does help himself if given opportunity. Play therapy is one such
opportunity. Included in this description of problem readers is one
child who read "too much too soon," and used reading as an escape. Others
read "too little too late."

454 Bettelheim, Bruno. "Bringing up children; reading problems and
       dyslexia." Ladies Home J 90(1): 30, 32, 68, January, 1973. (0
       References).
A close connection exists between reading problems and emotional disturbance. The emotional factors cause the reading difficulty, although the
opposite may sometimes appear to be the case. Emotional disturbance may
not be obvious at early ages, and it is an elusive concept. The neurological bases blamed for reading disability tend to fade in and out of
fashion. The favorite term currently is "dyslexia," supposedly an inborn impairment. Misreadings and reversals have psychological causes.
What a child does, he does for good readons. It is our task to discover
these reasons and help the child function normally.

455 ----------. "The decision to fail." Sch Rev 69(4): 377-412, Winter,
       1961. (6 References).
Learning cannot take place if anxieties press too severely on the mind.
These emotional blocks to learning may be of three kinds: (1) those resulting from the influences of technology--reading now competes with
radio, movies, and TV; (2) those arising from the child's life history;
and (3) those caused by the learning situation itself. Motivation to learn
does not stem from some vague concept of society or pleasing parents and
teachers. The decision to learn arises from an inner conviction that
learning is personally useful. Education must be seen as more than a
tool; it must be seen as a source of personal growth and development.

456 Blanchard, Phyllis. "Psychogenic factors in some cases of reading
       disability." Am J Orthopsychiatry 5: 361-74, October, 1935. (0
       References).
Children whose emotional conflicts are preventing their learning to read
will not benefit from remedial teaching. When the conflicts are at least
partially resolved, children will learn to read without remedial teaching.

457 ----------. "Reading disabilities." Child Study 18: 11-13, 30,
       Fall, 1940. (0 References).
Describes various emotional problems underlying reading failure. Case
histories are given. It is not easy to give generalized advice to parents on reading disabilities. New problems in diagnosis and treatment
continue to present themselves. Parents are advised simply to seek the
best professional help available for the problem.

458 ----------. "Reading disabilities in relation to difficulties of per-
       sonality and emotional development." Ment Hyg 20(3): 384-413,
       July, 1936. (0 References).

The relationship of reading disabilities to emotional growth and development is explored. It is suggested that reading disability often stems from the same perplexities in emotional development that produce the personality and behavior problems or neurotic symptoms. Some children learn to read after psychotherapeutic treatment without other special instruction. Repressed feelings have been discharged and anxiety and guilt alleviated. Emotional factors are not the only cause of reading disability.

459 ————. "Reading disabilities in relation to maladjustment. Ment Hyg 12(4): 772-88, October, 1928. (0 References).
Reading disabilities, which are often unrecognized for years by parents and teachers, are intimately related to behavior. They often result in personality and behavior deviations. When corrected, the behavior problems usually disappear. Common causes of reading disability include vision defects, emotional problems, and poor teaching methods. Four case studies are included.

460 Bouise, Louise Metoyer. "Emotional and personality problems of a group of retarded readers." Elem Engl 32(8): 544-48, December, 1955. (8 References).
In a study of seventh graders it appeared that a majority of the retarded readers had either severe home problems or serious behavior problems. The good readers were not free from emotional disturbance, but it was not as frequent or as pronounced as in the poor readers. On the basis of the available data it could not be said whether the reading problems caused the emotional problems or vice versa. It is concluded that there is a definite link between emotional maladjustment and reading disability.

461 Carrithers, Lura M. "Beginning reading patterns and preschool emotional problems." Educ Horizons 44(1): 3-9, Fall, 1965. (5 Bibliographic Footnotes).
Investigated whether a child's reading patterns and success in the first years of school could be predicted from the child's emotional condition during preschool years. Among hypotheses posed were that: (1) a child with emotional difficulties during preschool years would have more difficulty learning to read; (2) his reading patterns and learning problems would be different from those of normal children; and (3) assessment of emotional classifications during the preschool years would provide clues to reading difficulties experienced later. Sixty-one children enrolled in the first three grades of a university campus elementary school were the subjects. Average IQs were 115-120. They were given a battery of reading tests, examined by a psychologist, and rated by their teachers. A social worker visited each mother in her home.

462 Catlin, Opal. "A school nurse studies non-readers." Ill Educ 38(2): 53, 69, 70, October, 1949. (0 References).
The difficulty of nonreaders in the early grades is emotional. One reason boys are much more likely to be disabled readers than girls is that they are not encouraged to vent their emotions with tears as girls are. Parents forget that boys need a sympathetic listening ear and demonstrations of love. Sometimes too much is expected of them in the home. The teacher can help by not embarrassing the child and by giving him extra help alone.

463 Causey, Oscar S., ed. "Emotional factors in reading improvement." In: Causey, Oscar S., ed. The reading teacher's reader. Part 5. New York: Ronald Press, 1958. 253-93.

This group of nine articles comprises one section of a book of general interest to teachers of reading. Most of the articles in this section are reprints, many of them from Elem Sch J. Included are articles on the emotional blocks and problems in reading and the diagnostic problems they present. Behaviors to watch for in preadolescent children which may suggest emotional maladjustment and psychotherapeutic principles as they apply to remedial reading are among the areas covered.

464 Centi, Paul. "College-level retarded readers with emotional problems." Cathol Educ Rev 56(5): 319-22, May, 1958. (0 References).
Emotional problems often accompany reading disabilities. They may cause the reading problem, or may be the result of the reading problem. Best results in remediation can be obtained when the reading specialist is trained both in reading and in psychological counseling techniques.

465 Connolly, Christopher. "The psychosocial adjustment of children with dyslexia." Except Child 36(2): 126-27, October, 1969. (0 References).
Administered the Rorschach Psychodiagnostic, Rosenzweig Picture-Frustration Study, and the Human Figure Drawing Test to forth children. Twenty were dyslexic boys and twenty were normal controls. Although certain personality traits were found commonly in dyslexics, these children did not seem to be characterized by emotional disturbance. Their reactions to their environments were not qualitatively different from children who were not dyslexic.

466 Dickenson, Irma C. "Emotional factors as contributing causes of reading disability." Va J Educ 31(6): 254-56, March, 1938. (0 References).
Children react to their emotional environment to such an extent that they may succeed or fail according to the amount of security and satisfaction they gain from it. Emotional blocking may prevent a child from using his innate ability. If a child fails to learn to read for no apparent physical or educational cause, then study the child himself. A series of questions that should be asked are suggested, including inquiry into his home background, school experiences, and methods the teacher can use to help the child progress in reading.

467 Earp, N. Wesley. "Challenge to schools: reading is overemphasized!" Read Teach 27(6): 562-65, March, 1974. (5 References).
Discusses the question that if the junior-high pupil has decided to fail, has no interest in learning to read, and has no really compelling need to do so if his goal is unskilled labor, why should society force it upon him? Recognize and accept the child's choice to fail, and do not hold the schools accountable for him any longer. The six-year-old is not mature enough to make such a decision. Possibly he has not matured enough to learn to read either. The pressure to be at a certain grade level, be in a certain group, know a standard vocabulary, etc., should be entirely eliminated. Relieved from pressure and freed to learn, the child may opt to learn to read. Reading is not overemphasized in terms of its importance to a full and satisfying life. It is overemphasized in respect to the emotional impact attached to reading difficulty and/or failure. The child may be forced to withdraw or to fail to protect himself from psychological damage. The teacher of the child who is doubtful of his capability in reading and/or unconvinced that he needs to learn to read is advised to cool down and reduce the pressure. A very low-key emotional climate gives the child a better opportunity to deal with his problems.

468 Ellis, Albert. "Results of a mental hygiene approach to reading
     disability problems." J Consult Psychol 13(1): 56-61, February,
     1949. (11 References).
One hundred reading disability cases were studied at a mental hygiene
clinic for one year. Significant coefficients of correlation existed
between reading gains and: (1) amount and quality of remedial reading
tutoring; (2) intelligence of the child: the higher the intelligence,
the greater the gain; (3) severity of emotional problems: the more disturbed the patient, the less reading gain; and (4) age: the older the
child when reading disability was diagnosed, the greater the tendency to
gain from tutoring. It is concluded that educational and emotional factors are both of vital importance as causes of reading disability.

469 "Emotional upsets may affect reading ability." Sci News Lett 55:
     397, June 18, 1949. (0 References).
Emotional upsets caused by family quarrels, sibling rivalry, or difficul-
ties in social relationships may result in specific reading disability.
Treatment should include psychotherapy as well as reading instruction.
Abnormal brain wave patterns were found in 75 percent of a group of emo-
tionally disturbed disabled readers between the ages of seven and twelve.

470 Ewers, Dorothea. "Reading difficulties in the primary grades."
     Ill Educ 46(4): 136-37, December, 1957. (0 References).
Third-grade pupils in a public school system who were having trouble with
reading were found to have transferred from another school and to have
psychological problems more often than normal readers. They also were
found to have had speech therapy more often. It is more important to
know what can be done for such a child than why he can't read. Grouping
by achievement in the regular classroom helps. Some reading problems
cannot be coped with in the regular classroom.

471 Gates, Arthur Irving. "The role of personality maladjustment in
     reading disability." Pedagog Semin J Genet Psychol 59: 77-83,
     September, 1941. (7 References).
No single personality pattern characterizes victims of reading failure
or disability. Personality maladjustment is a comparatively rare cause
of serious reading defect. However, personality maladjustment frequently
is found to coexist with reading disability.

472 Glick, Oren. "Some social-emotional consequences of early inadequate
     acquisitions of reading skills." J Educ Psychol 63(3): 253-57,
     June, 1972. (9 References).
It appears that early reading failure in school perpetuates and general-
izes the failure during subsequent years. Failure has negative consequences in such areas as self-concept, attitudes toward school, peer relations, and family relations. Academic success may be expected to have
positive consequences in these areas. These consequences may contribute
favorably or unfavorably to later academic performance. Data from the
areas expected to be affected by reading failure were obtained from two
groups of third-grade children, one group performing below and the other
at or above expected reading norms. Approximately 140 boys and 130 girls
took part. Areas assessed included general self-concept, academic self-
concept, attitudes toward teachers, school work, peers, and toward school
in general. Also assessed were parental behavior and classroom peer relations. The children were enrolled in all-white public schools serving
middle to lower-middle socioeconomic populations. In general poor male
readers suffered negative consequences in the areas assessed, while little

benefit in social-emotional status accrued to good male readers. Results among the girls were quite different. Benefits were gained by good female readers, but poor female readers did not incur negative consequences. It is concluded that early academic performance has social-emotional consequences that perpetuate and generalize patterns of success for females and of failure for males. It is suggested that the response to early reading performance by parents, teachers, and peers is different for males and females.

473 Glover, Clotile P. "Emotions can impede growth in reading; children respond to failure with aggression, withdrawal." Chic Sch J 44(4): 179-82, January, 1963. (3 Bibliographic Footnotes).
Continued failure in reading gives rise to emotional problems in children which work against subsequent success. Symptoms of emotional maladjustment are listed, including nervous tension and habits such as stuttering and nail-biting, aggressiveness, apathy and discouragement, withdrawal into daydreaming, self-consciousness, and destructive counterattack. Sometimes neither home nor school gives a child a sense of security about reading. The teacher's anxiety about a failing reader may add to the pressure on the child. If the reading problem can be solved it may ease the emotional problem.

474 Goldman, Margaret, and Barclay, Allan. "Influence of maternal attitudes on children with reading disabilities." Percept Mot Skills 38(1): 303-7, February, 1974. (16 References).
Concludes that attitudes of mothers appear to affect significantly the child's motivation to develop reading skills. Poor development of reading skill may be the child's resistance to his mother's pressure to achieve. The children in this study had superior verbal ability but had not learned to read adequately. They did not appear to retain material learned as well as persons of their intellectual ability should. Most of the children were boys who had been referred to a reading clinic because of reading disabilities. They ranged in age from nine to thirteen years.

475 Graham, E. Ellis. "The real bases of reading difficulties." Sch Soc 86(2129): 155-56, March 29, 1958. (0 References).
Suggests that reading disabilities are caused by such factors as the child's fear of assuming adult responsibility, resentments toward being told what to do, damaged self-concept, or personal anxieties.

476 ————. "Theories of the emotional bases for reading failure." J Colo Wyo Acad Sci 4(5): 49, December, 1953. (0 References).
Most theories concerning the emotional causes of reading failure include evidence of resistance. The resistance may be to the assumption of adult responsibilities and sexual roles. Unsuccessful readers perceive their fathers as extremely domineering.

477 Gregory, Robin E. "Unsettledness, maladjustment and reading failure: a village study." Br J Educ Psychol 35(1): 63-68, February, 1965. (21 References).
Tests in a West Berkshire village school revealed a significant connection between reading failure and restlessness and between reading failure and anxiety for the approval of other children among nine-, ten-, and eleven-year-olds.

478   Harris, Albert J. "Unsolved problems in reading." Elem Engl 31:
      416-18, November, 1954. (17 References).
Several different kinds of emotional blocking may interfere with progress
in learning to read. Failure to distinguish among the several types of
blocking that can be causally related to reading failure has handicapped
research on personality and reading disability. Various approaches could
be used to identify different kinds of emotional patterns, including individual analysis of the cases, or the identification of personality patterns or configuration thought to be found in a significant number of
reading disability cases. Once these distinctions are made, the way will
be open for successful attack on many reading problems.

479   Herman, Bernard. "An investigation to determine the relationship of
      anxiety and reading disability and to study the effects of group and
      individual counseling on reading improvement." For a summary see:
      Diss Abstr Int 33A(6): 2711-12, December, 1972.

480   Holmes, Donald J. "Disturbances of the preschool and very young
      school child." J Sch Health 45(4): 210-16, April, 1975. (8
      References).
Discusses the physical symptoms sometimes elicited by a child's inability
to read and of the emotional bases for reading disability. The author
concludes that: (1) All of us differ, some of us succeeding at one thing
while others succeed at something else. (2) Education is a privilege.
(3) Reading and writing are merely imitations of true conversation and
images of real experience. "Learning disability" is called an almost
meaningless generic term which is nearly always used to mean "reading
disability." Many illustrations from this doctor's practice with nonreaders are given.

481   Holmes, Jack A. "Emotional factors and reading disability." Read
      Teach 9(1): 11-17, 10, October, 1955. (22 References).
Considers the theoretical role of emotions in reading difficulties. The
nature and source of emotional influence on reading disability is difficult to pin down, but much clinical evidence gives weight to the idea
that a relationship exists. A summary of the opinions expressed in the
literature about this relationship is presented. Symptoms the teacher
should watch for (apathy, irritability, fatigue, restlessness, a short
attention span, among others), suggested causes, and remedial efforts
are discussed.

482   Jameson, Robert U., and Ketchum, E. Gillet. "Common sense about
      children's reading." Sat Evening Post 228(41): 23, 51, 55-56,
      April 7, 1956. (0 References).
About 10 percent of American children are poor readers. They need help,
but parents should not forget that 90 percent of our children have no
specific reading disability. Schools, in general, are doing a good job.
A large proportion of reading disability is caused by personality problems. Five types of emotional problems which produce poor readers are
identified.

483   Kaplan, Robert. "Reading disabilities." Am Orthopt J 7: 100-102,
      1957. (4 References).
Early recognition and treatment of reading disabilities is necessary.
The condition has numerous causes. Various physical and emotional causes
are discussed, including mental and emotional maturity and social adjustment. A combination of whole-word and phonic methods of teaching is

best. The first step in remediation is to reassure the child that reading disability is not a reflection on his intelligence. Alexia, or congenital word blindness, is very rare and possibly is a mythical concept.
It is not a useful diagnosis. Persons so diagnosed have been found to
respond satisfactorily to radical variations in psychological or educational techniques.

484 Kirkpatrick, Milton E. "Twenty-five non-readers." N Engl J Med
      220(26): 1064-67, June 29, 1939. (2 References).
Twenty-five nonreaders of normal intelligence from the first, second,
and third grades of one school were interviewed. Their parents were also
interviewed. Timidity, lack of interest in school, and indications of
early personality deviation were noted in many of the children. Seventeen were classified as immature. It appeared that the reading disability was a personality problem centering on emotional conflict and lack
of maturity.

485 Laurita, Raymond E. "Reversals: a response to frustrations?" Read
      Teach 25(1): 45-51, October, 1971. (7 References).
Persistent reversal errors in writing, long after the time they should
have been overcome, is a continuing problem for reading teachers. In
experiments it has been found that animals that are persistently frustrated developed abnormal fixations in which they continued their unsatisfactory behavior, even when alternate adaptive responses were possible. It is suggested that humans may fall victim to such fixated frustration in learning to read. Traditional methods of prolonged instruction may only worsen the problem. Procedures for breaking fixated responses are under study.

486 Leeds, Donald S. "Emotional factors and the reading process." J
      Read Spec 10(4): 246-59, May, 1971. (35 References).
Reviews studies on various concepts underlying the relationship between
reading and emotional factors. Ego functions, personality adjustment,
introversion, self-perception, dyslexia, bilingualism, and disruptive
classroom behavior are among the areas in which literature is reviewed.
The distinction is drawn between the problem child and the emotionally
disturbed child. Various techniques of diagnosis and classroom instruction of students with reading disabilities are discussed. Three underlying theories for the remediation of learning disabilities are presented:
(1) The psychogenic theory is based on the premise that reading disability
is caused by emotional or psychogenic factors. (2) The neurological
model is the premise that the child's problems are neurological or developmental in origin. (3) The neuropsychogenic theory sees an interaction between neurological and emotional factors creating a syndrome in
which both factors must be treated.

487 Louttit, C. M. "Emotional factors in reading disabilities: diag-
      nostic problems." Elem Sch J 56(2): 68-72, October, 1955. (0
      References).
The understanding of the individual child is necessary to identify the
emotional factors which may be pertinent to the child's reading disability.

488 Lund, Frederick H. "The dynamics of behavior and reading difficul-
      ties." Education 67(7): 416-21, March, 1947. (0 References).
The inner needs and inner life of the child are often given too little
attention. Under these conditions behavior and learning problems are

most apt to develop. The child's failure to learn is not caused by incapacity, but by a failure of desire and inclination. Adequate measures
of individual differences in these areas are needed to enable the teacher
to cope with the classroom problems that are related to personality differences, frustrations, and other variable sources of behavior and learning problems. The article lists reasons for reading failure and suggests
methods for helping the disabled reader.

489 McCarthy, Dorothea A. "Identifying and helping children with lan-
     guage disabilities." In: Syracuse University, School of Educa-
     tion, First Annual Conference on Elementary Education, 1954. Papers:
     frontiers of elementary education. Vol. 1. Compiled and edited
     by Vincent J. Glennon. Syracuse, New York: Syracuse University
     Press, 1954. 25-36. (28 References).
Cites the findings of studies indicating a link between emotional disturbance and reading disability and various speech defects. The qualities
of home life and general environment which seem related to these disabilities are discussed. Why some children from unhealthy emotional
backgrounds achieve at reading while others do not is not known. The
personality and competence of the remedial reading tutor are most important because properly handled remedial reading should be akin to real
psychotherapy. Suggestions are made for actions the school and community
can take to prevent or minimize the development of childhood language
disorders.

490 McLean, Terry Keith. "A comparison of the subtest performance of
     two groups of retarded readers with like groups of non-retarded
     readers on the Wechsler Intelligence Scale for Children." For a
     summary see: Diss Abstr 24(11): 4800-4801, May, 1964.

491 Natchez, Gladys. "Oral reading used as an indicator of reactions
     to frustration." J Educ Res 54(8): 308-11, April, 1961. (11
     References).
A study showed that children who were retarded readers exhibited more
signs of dependence, aggression, and withdrawal reactions in frustration
situations than did readers who were not retarded. Groups of retarded
and normal readers with an average age of ten years and matched for race,
school class, grade, sex, age, and intelligence were used as subjects
for this study.

492 —————. Personality patterns and oral reading; a study of overt
     behavior in the reading situation as it reveals reactions of de-
     pendence, aggression, and withdrawal in children. New York: New
     York University Press, 1959. 98p. (Bibliography).
Emotional disturbance may be the cause, effect, or result of frustration
in the oral reading situation. This study was carried out to determine
whether the retarded reader reacts to frustration in general in the same
way he reacts in the oral reading situation. Reactions in nonreading
situations were found to be highly correlated with reactions to oral
reading. Dependence, aggression, or withdrawal responses were very
similar for reading and nonreading situations for the retarded reader.

493 Odenwald, Robert P., and Shea, Joseph A. "Emotional problems of
     maladjustment in children with reading difficulties." Am J
     Psychiatry 107: 890-93, June, 1951. (4 References).
Emotional factors are frequently present in reading difficulties. Reading failure affects the emotional life of the child. It is important

for the child's teacher to help him with patience and love, and for both teachers and parents to understand the causes of reading difficulties. Reading disorders may arise from attempts to teach the child before he is ready. Strephosymbolia is rather like mirror reading. Professionals from several disciplines may need to work together to help the reading-disabled child.

494 Page, James D. "Emotional factors in reading disabilities." Educa-
     tion 72(9): 590-95, May, 1952. (0 References).
Emotional disturbances contribute to reading disabilities and vice versa. Any strong negative emotion (fear, anxiety, anger, resentment) impairs the individual's ability to function. Emotional disturbances in children could be much reduced if teachers and parents respected the child's needs for emotional security, personal worth, social acceptance, order and stability, and recreation and play. This does not mean he should be overprotected and coddled.

495 Patey, Henry C. "Reading problems of the emotionally disturbed."
     In: Handbook of private schools. 37th ed. Boston, Massachusetts:
     Porter Sargent, 1956. 91-96. (0 References).
Discusses the reading problems of bright children who have failed to learn to read for psychological reasons existing outside the classroom. Emo-tionally upset children fall into four groups in regard to reading: (1) those with physical problems or who are discouraged; (2) those who read well, and escape into reading; (3) those who read well, and gain in rich-ness and integration of personality through reading; and (4) those who escape from reading and are described as "blocked." Our culture demands that everyone be literate. In order to be challenged successfully to read, the rebel must often identify with an older person. Anxiety may prevent learning to read. Causes of anxiety must be found and treated. This may require residential therapy. Repressed resentment, fear of failure, guilt because of cultural demands, or rigidity (an ill-conceived approach to learning, a mental set) may all block learning to read. Teach-ing must take the child's personal idiosyncracies into account.

496 Reymert, Martin L. "Reading disabilities in the light of general
     child care and training." J Except Child 9(2): 35-39, 62,
     October, 1942. (0 References).
General maladjustment in the home or school situations or both frequently underlie reading problems. Reading research emphasizing factors such as eye movement records and brain potential recordings is not criticized. However, a broad general view of the problem is needed. Home, social, health, disciplinary, or personality problems may outweigh the more often investigated factors as causes underlying reading disability. Emotional personality factors are of primary importance. They are direct results of the particular child care and training procedures used. The attack on reading disabilities, like charity, begins at home.

497 Ridenour, Nina. "The troubled reader." Grade Teach 72: 8, April,
     1955. (0 References).
In the 1920s terms like "strephosymbolia" and "word blindness" were used to describe reading disability. These terms served to identify children who could not learn to read, but they did not explain the cause of read-ing disability nor tell us how to help such children. Reading disability is nearly always a symptom of emotional disturbance. The child's first experiences with reading, like all first experiences, is important. It may have much to do with whether he becomes a successful reader or not.

The sight method of teaching reading is best for most children, but it presents extraordinary difficulties for the disabled reader. The teacher can always help, usually a lot. She should give the child extra attention and encouragement. She should size up the situation as best she can, then work on the reading problem and/or try to get at the underlying emotional problem.

498   Robinson, Helen M. "Emotional problems and reading disability." In: Syracuse University, School of Education, First Annual Conference on Elementary Education, 1954. Papers: frontiers of elementary education. Vol. 1. Compiled and edited by Vincent J. Glennon. Syracuse: Syracuse University Press, 1954. 50-53. (1 Reference).
A definite relationship exists between emotional maladjustments and reading disability. The child may enter school with emotional problems which can cause reading failure. Or, his reading failure may produce pressure and emotional problems. Suggestions are made on how to appraise emotional problems and on teaching methods for use with the emotionally disturbed child. These include the use of small groups; creation of a warm atmosphere; changing the child's self-concept; wise choice of reading materials; and discussion with the child of material read.

499   Roswell, Florence G. "Are emotional problems a block to reading achievement?" In: International Reading Association. Conference proceedings: reading as an intellectual activity. Vol. 8. Edited by J. Allen Figurel. New York: Scholastic Magazines, 1963. 139-42. (0 References).
Although teaching the emotionally disturbed child is difficult, he can learn to read. In children suffering from maturational lag or other causes of reading problems, the reading failure may be causing the emotional disturbance. A method of instruction which avoids the children's weaknesses must be used. When learning begins and self-esteem increases, the emotional problems are helped. Emotionally disturbed children respond to order and structure in the classroom.

500   Russell, David H. "Reading disabilities and mental health: a review of research." Underst Child 16(1): 24-32, January, 1947. (34 References).
Summarizes the results of many research studies on the relationships between reading disabilities and personality maladjustments. The studies are considered either as large-group studies or as individual case studies. Typically the large-group studies correlate results from a group of children considered as a whole with various test scores such as personality tests or attitude scale ratings. Groups of good and retarded readers can be compared in this way. Examples of the various kinds of research and their findings are given. Implications for teachers are drawn with the opinion that further study is needed. The emotional effect of blame by parent or teacher may prevent the child from learning to read. Teachers should work to relieve this anxiety and tension. Experts believe reading disability has many causes. It may be a symptom of hidden motives. After working with the child for awhile, the teacher should reach a tentative conclusion as to whether emotional factors are the cause or the effect of reading disability.

501   Rutman, Hedy Rogan. "Neurological status, psychosocial development and reading disability." For a summary see: Diss Abstr Int 33B(12, Part 1): 6091-92, June, 1973.

502 Rutter, Michael. "Emotional disorder and educational underachieve-
     ment." <u>Arch Dis Child</u> 49(4): 249-56, April, 1974. (48 Refer-
     ences).
Defines and discusses underachievement and classifies different varieties
of underachievement. Emotional disturbance may lead to underachievement
by various mechanisms. Specific reading retardation has been studied
more than any other variety of underachievement. Emotional disorder does
not appear to be the cause of reading problems, although motivation may
be influential. Conduct disorders are associated with reading difficulties, but do not appear to lead to it. Evidence is lacking for the
existence of a single syndrome of dyslexia as it is usually defined.
Symptoms said to characterize dyslexia do not cluster as they should if
there were a single dyslexic syndrome. Psychological, social, and educational factors appear to interact with biological factors to produce specific reading retardation.

503 Schneider, Wilmot F. "Readiness and emotional problems associated
     with reading disabilities." <u>Am J Optom Arch Am Acad Optom</u> 26(10):
     413-26, October, 1949. (10 References).
For whatever reasons, reading problems are with us and will be as long
as human beings face the challenge of rearing children. Our efforts must
be directed toward early recognition of the problem and advancing techniques which can help the child rapidly adapt to his psychobiological
capacity, or lack of capacity. The eye doctor and the educator must work
closely together to prepare the child to read. Emotional problems may
arise from vision problems, from parents' failure to accept the child
with his own capacity or disabilities, or from other quarters. It is not
usually readily apparent that the behavior problems which bring the child
to the psychiatrist are the result of reading difficulties. It can never
be overlooked that the child is a total unit acted upon by the total
environment and reacting to it. It is often difficult for a parent to
realize that the reading disability is the basis of overt behavior. The
parent who demands 100 percent performance of the child and views the
problem emotionally rather than intellectually is probably not a good
remedial teacher for his own child. The role of the child psychiatrist
is rather like that of the traditional family doctor. He must see the
child as a whole and integrate the findings of other specialists. He
stands as a liaison officer to interpret parent and home to the school,
and to communicate what the school is attempting to do for the child.

504 Schubert, Delwyn G. "Understanding and handling reading-personality
     problems." <u>Elem Engl</u> 37(8): 537-39, 559, December, 1960. (0
     References).
Most researchers believe that a relationship exists between reading problems and personality maladjustment. In most cases the personality problem stems from the reading failure. In some cases maladjustment ante-
dates school entrance. It is important to discover the cause. A number
of symptoms are discussed, including unhappy home situations, tics, psychosomatic illness, apathy, and excitability, among others. The teacher
should attempt to make friends with the child. Suggestions are given for
helping the emotionally disturbed reader.

505 Shamsie, J. S. "Reading difficulties as a cause of behaviour prob-
     lems in adolescence." <u>Can Psychol</u> 9(2): 196-200, April, 1968.
     (6 References).
Whether reading problems cause socially deviant behavior or vice versa
is a difficult question to answer. It is not usually hard to decide in

an individual case. Among teen-agers of normal intelligence who present behavior problems, the majority have poor academic records, marked reading deficits, and poor motivation to learn. Treatment should be broadly based to help the teen-ager with emotional problems and defects and deficits in learning ability.

506   Sherman, Mandel. "Emotional disturbances and reading disability."
      In: Conference on Reading, University of Chicago, 1939. Proceed-
      ings: recent trends in reading. Vol. 1. Compiled and edited by
      William S. Gray. Chicago, Illinois: University of Chicago, 1939.
      126-34. (0 References). (Supplementary Educational Monographs,
      No. 49).
In working with those with reading disabilities it is important to recognize the interrelationship between emotional disturbances and reading
difficulties.

507   Smith, Nila Banton. "Research on reading and the emotions." Sch Soc
      81(2050): 8-10, January 8, 1955. (34 Bibliographic Footnotes).
Reviews some of the literature on the relationship of reading disability
to emotional disturbances. Included are studies that view reading failure
as the cause of emotional problems; studies that take the opposite view;
studies concluding that retardation in reading stems from multiple causes;
and studies using various kinds of therapy for the problem.

508   Soles, Edward M. "Emotional factors in reading disabilities."
      Hygeia 19(11): 940-43, November, 1941. (0 References).
Emotional factors may be either the cause or the effect of reading disabilities. The child may be conditioned against reading by his unpleasant
experiences with it. Some emotional factors associated with reading begin in the home. Parents who lack understanding of corrective methods
may handicap remedial work.

509   Stone, F. Beth, and Rowley, Vinton N. "Educational disability in
      emotionally disturbed children." Except Child 30(9): 423-26,
      May, 1964. (4 References).
A survey of 116 emotionally disturbed twelve-year-old children showed
disabilities in both reading and arithmetic. This was true when both
mental and chronological age were used in calculating the amount of disability. Mean IQ for the group was 96.52. Arithmetic scores were lower
than reading scores. Many more of the children were in grades below expectation for their chronological age than above. There was insufficient
evidence to draw conclusions about a causal relationship between emotional
problems and educational disability.

510   Towes, Anna. "Emotions and reading difficulties." Sch Community
      58(8): 35, April, 1972. (0 References).
Emotional factors involved in reading difficulties can be caused by: (1)
unfavorable home and school conditions; (2) inner conflicts or instability; (3) reading difficulties which lead to anxiety and further emotional
disturbances, hence increased reading problems and more pronounced emotional involvement. These are commented on briefly.

511   Tulchin, Simon H. "Emotional factors in reading disabilities in
      school children." J Educ Psychol 26(6): 443-54, September,
      1935. (14 References).
Emotional and personality factors came to be considered much later than
the physical aspects of reading disability. It is not always easy to

determine whether emotional factors are the primary cause of reading disability, or are themselves the result of the failure. An attempt should be made to analyze the causes as soon as the disability appears.

512 Vatcher, Joleen Meyers. "Reading disabilities and emotional prob-
      lems: a summary of research findings." N Engl Read Assoc J 5(2):
      16-21, Winter, 1970.

513 Wilf, Selma. "Observable student behaviors as indicators of emo-
      tional maladjustment and reading disability." For a summary see:
      Diss Abstr Int 33A(3): 911, September, 1972.

514 Wilking, S. Vincent. "Personality maladjustment as a causative
      factor in reading disability." Elem Sch J 42: 268-79, December,
      1941. (30 References).
The causes of reading disability are many and varied. Personality maladjustment is one of these causes. Literature that includes case studies
is reviewed with the recommendation that more research is necessary before definite conclusions can be drawn about the role of personality maladjustment in reading disability.

515 Wills, I. H., and Banas, Norma. "The fragile child." J Learn
      Disabil 4(6): 308-11, June-July, 1971. (0 References).
The fragile child, often a girl, has a delicate ego and makes enemies of
words. She is supersensitive, her emotional stability is poor, and she
can never afford to be wrong. She cannot accept a trial-and-error learning experience. She is seemingly placid and often answers, "I don't
know." She has difficulty with sequence in words, e.g., "shakemilk" for
"milkshake," and may make errors in recalling the right word. She has
good visual recall and learns to sight-read easily, but her thoughts are
disorganized and she is not able to use what she reads. Confusion and
misinterpretation of what is read hinder schoolwork. Suggestions for
helping this child are given.

516 Wittick, Mildred Letton. "The effects of social and emotional prob-
      lems on reading." Conference on Reading, University of Chicago,
      1964. Proceedings: meeting individual differences in reading.
      Vol. 26. Compiled and edited by H. Alan Robinson. Chicago,
      Illinois: University of Chicago Press, 1964. 75-82. (8 Refer-
      ences). (Supplementary Educational Monographs, No. 94).
Social and emotional pressures affect reading performance. Pressure for
academic excellence, material possessions, and togetherness; the emotional
problems arising from family disorganization; and developing an adequate
self-concept all influence reading ability. Schools should recognize
the importance of the preschool period and its relation to the child's
later development. Teachers should know more about the stresses on the
children they teach.

517 Wolf, Theta H. "The reading disability: a pediatric problem." J
      Lancet 65(5): 184-85, May, 1945. (0 References).
Reading disability may be highly significant in the physical and emotional
tensions found in schoolchildren. Beyond fourth, fifth, and sixth grades
school success depends on reading ability. If a child cannot compete, he
may try to compensate in various ways. Some of these are described.
Causes of reading problems include physical defects, poor or inadequate
instruction, emotional problems, and lack of cerebral dominance.

518   Young, Norman, and Gaier, Eugene L. "Implications in emotionally
      caused reading retardation." Elem Engl 28(5): 271-75, May, 1951.
      (13 References).
Reading retardation has many causes. Emotional factors play a pervasive
role as a basic cause of reading problems. Social and emotional maturity
are as necessary to reading ability as is intellectual ability. It is
suggested that boys have more reading problems than girls because the
reading materials do not interest them. There is need for more teacher
education in the area. Motivation plays a paramount role in a remedial
program. Areas for future research in the field are outlined.

519   Zolkos, Helena H. "What research says about emotional factors in
      retardation in reading." Elem Sch J 51(9): 512-18, May, 1951.
      (31 References).
Reading failure has been ascribed to emotional problems and vice versa.
Disagreement persists on the question of cause and effect. Factors affecting reading are discussed, including overprotection of the child,
environmental influences, and the emotional and personality problems resulting from failure. Literature on the subject is reviewed. Teachers
of retarded readers are urged to accept these children without emotional
reactions of their own, to help them change their undesirable behavior,
and to encourage them.

F. ENVIRONMENT

520   Alwitt, Linda F. "Attention in a visual task among non-readers and
      readers." Percept Mot Skills 23(2): 361-62, October, 1966. (6
      References).
Children with reading disability and matched controls were given a nonreading variation of the Stroop color-word test. Results suggest that
disabled readers are no more distracted by elements competing for attention than are normal readers.

521   "Backwardness in reading." Elem Sch J 28(7): 487-88, March, 1928.
      (0 References).
In a study of 130 backward readers drawn from a school population of about
10,000 children in London schools from good, intermediate, and poor neigh-
borhoods, 26 percent of the poor readers had IQs of over 100, 35 percent
between 85 and 100, and the rest below 85. In about half the cases,
causes of reading failure were extrinsic: poor school attendance, defects in vision and speech, etc. Intrinsic causes included defective
memory for verbal symbols and inability to discriminate forms. Substitution of similar words was characteristic of the emotionally unstable child.
Failure appeared to be caused by inefficient reading habits rather than
specific weaknesses.

522   Carrillo, Lawrence W. "The relation of certain environmental and
      developmental factors to reading ability in children." For a sum-
      mary see: Diss Abstr 17(6): 1251-52, 1957.

523   Chandler, Theodore A. "Reading disability and socio-economic
      status." J Read 10(1): 5-21, October, 1966. (33 References).
Reviews studies comparing reading ability and socioeconomic status. Greater ability was linked with high status in every case. Relationships have
been found between parents' income and children's reading achievement,

and between IQ scores of children and their fathers' occupational level. It is questioned whether socially disadvantaged children do poorly on standardized tests and whether such children have perceptual motor-visual differences that distinguish them from middle- and upper-class children. The level of intellectual stimulation in the home appears to produce differences in tests of intelligence and reading achievement.

524 Coleman, J. C.; Bornston, F. L.; Fox, J. "Parental attitudes as re-
      lated to reading disabilities in children." Psychol Rep 4: 47-
      51, March, 1958. (1 Reference).
Results of a study indicate that family background of a boy with reading disability may include a domineering mother and a father who is inadequate as a male role model.

525 Delacato, Carl. "The ontogeny of reading problems." Claremont Coll
      Read Conf Yearb 27: 119-25, 1963. (0 References).
Reception problems stem from faulty or incomplete neurological organization, and reading is a receptive process. Neurological organization, usually complete by about age six, is a "sequential continuum." It may be incomplete because of "genetic bias," some trauma, or lack of environmental opportunity. The last type is the most common. Since neurological organization develops sequentially, a process traced in this article, treatment for faulty development must follow the same sequence.

526 Denner, Bruce. "Representational and syntactic competence of prob-
      lem readers." Child Dev 41(3): 881-87, September, 1970. (3
      References).
Groups of average readers, problem readers, and Head Start children were asked to perform four tasks: (1) demonstrate their understanding of words by obeying commands to jump, walk, clap, etc.; (2) demonstrate that they knew the names of various objects presented in pictures; (3) associate the words from task 2 with abstract graphic forms (logographs); and (4) form a sentence by "reading" the logographs placed on a line to form a sentence. All children did well on task 1. All except Head Start children did well on task 2. Head Start children and problem readers required more assistance than others on task 3. Task 4, the synthesis task, separated the group best. The average readers did about as well on task 4 as on the other tests. Older (fifth-grade) problem readers did significantly poorer. First-grade problem readers and Head Start children demonstrated little syntactic competence. It is suggested that differences in the oral language of the children and formal, written language is so great that it inhibits reading.

527 DeVault, Spencer, and Stewart, Laurel G. "Differentiation of neuro-
      logical and social psychological etiology in reading retardation."
      Am J Orthopsychiatry 37(2): 380-81, March, 1967. (0 References).
Examines through the use of case histories the relationship between reading retardation and three possible influences: emotional disturbance, minimal brain dysfunction, and the environmental patterns found in culturally deprived homes. It is suggested that disabled readers who show signs of organic or language dysfunction on psychological testing may have no actual neurological involvement. These children are the victims of inadequate language and conceptual patterns associated with certain types of culturally deprived families of lower socioeconomic status.

528 Hardy, Miriam P.; Mellits, E. David; Willig, Sharon N. "Reading:
      a function of language usage." Johns Hopkins Med J 129(1): 43-
      53, July, 1971. (3 References).

Reports the results of three measures of reading achievement in a population of 300 children: (1) the relationship between oral language acquisition and reading ability; (2) growth of reading ability from age seven to
age eight; and (3) relationship between intelligence and reading achievement at age eight. Vocabulary increased greatly between age three and
age eight, but only half the children were close to expected vocabulary
at age eight. Reading achievement did not seem to be taking place between ages seven and eight. The child's ability to read appears to be
closely related to his automatic use of linguistic forms. Verbal IQ
scores on the WISC correlated highly with reading achievement. It is concluded that any specific reading disabilities among children in this group
were masked by the overriding effects of cultural deprivation.

529 Kerdel-Vegas, Oswaldo. "Strephosymbolia (incidence in the school
      sectors of Caracas)." Dis Nerv Syst 29(8): 548-49, August, 1968.
      (5 References).
In a study of children in second through sixth grade in Caracas, a much
higher incidence of strephosymbolia (or the tendency to reverse or invert
letters or digits) was found in children from lower socioeconomic backgrounds than in children from middle to high socioeconomic status. It
is concluded that external or secondary factors play an important role in
the incidence of strephosymbolia. The high level of premature births
and schizophrenia found in low socioeconomic areas is pointed out, as are
the numerous problems of families from these backgrounds.

530 McCleary, Elliott. "Rescuing the 'child failures.'" Todays Health
      38(10): 48-50, 71-75, October, 1960. (0 References).
Describes the work of the Dyslexia Memorial Institute, a nonprofit organization located on the Chicago campus of Northwestern University Medical
School. The institute achieves a 75 percent cure rate working with retarded readers of normal intelligence who have been labeled "hopeless" by
their teachers. The staff includes doctors, scientists, and educators.
Physical and psychiatric evaluating and speech therapy are included in
treatment. Weekly staff meetings bring together the various specialists
to diagnose new cases and continue work with the twenty-five or thirty
children undergoing treatment. Institute members believe the home, not
the school, is the chief source of a child's failure or success. Parents
are asked to follow a list of thirteen recommendations including setting
the right goals, freeing the child from the apron strings, and understanding the child's potential. Children will not outgrow learning difficulties, and it is important that something be done early to help them.
Physical ailments and loneliness should be spotted by the parent and overcome. The ideal parent is helpful, but not pushy. The institute believes
parents should present a unified stand. The staff also makes recommendations on work space, sleeping, and study habits.

531 McCrossan, John. The reading of the culturally disadvantaged. 1966.
      42p. (ED 010 755).
Surveyed aspects of reading related to cultural disadvantage. Socioeconomic status and children's reading achievement were found to be correlated. Lower-class persons tend to read less than those from higher
socioeconomic levels. Home environment of lower-class children was found
to contribute to reading retardation.

532 Morris, Joyce M. Reading in the primary school; an investigation
      into standards of reading and their association with primary school
      characteristics. n.p.: Newnes Educational Pub. Co., [1959].

179p. (Bibliography). (National Foundation for Educational Research in England and Wales, Publication No. 12).
The first of two reports on a large-scale study done in England aimed at discovering why some children do not learn to read. Reading attainments were examined in comparison to physical, socioeconomic, and educational characteristics of a selection of primary schools. Among the school characteristics studied were socioeconomic status of the school's area, size of school, size of classes, type of buildings, and whether teaching methods were formal or informal. High reading attainment was found to be associated with intelligence level, socioeconomic status, and large enrollment. The last, it is pointed out, is often associated with larger schools which have superior buildings. With warnings that interpretation of findings should be cautious, it is concluded that the phonics method is preferable for teaching beginning reading. Individual help for the child with reading difficulties is essential. Early diagnosis and treatment are important to prevent the problem from being firmly established. For the follow-up report of this study, see Item No. 533.

533 ————. Standards and progress in reading: studies of children's reading standards and progress in relation to their individual attributes, home circumstances and primary school conditions. Slough, England: National Foundation for Educational Research in England and Wales, 1966. 493p. (Research Reports: Second Series, No. 1).
This is the second report in a series of studies, begun in 1953, of Kent (England) schools. The first report was published in 1959. It reported the relationship between ability to read of 8,000 children ages seven to eleven and nine characteristics of the sixty primary schools the children attended. This report is more intensive and includes a longer period of observation. The design of the study is set forth. Reports on the reading attainment and nonverbal abilities of the children are given. While admitting to some statistical difficulties, the author expresses belief that phonic methods for teaching beginning reading appear to give better results than whole-word methods. Good and poor readers were compared on the basis of their individual attributes, home circumstances, and school conditions. A follow-up study of good readers was done. Full statistical information is provided. It is concluded that children who have not made any real progress in reading by age eight probably will continue to be poor readers all their lives. Basing selection of children for remedial treatment on the results of nonverbal ability tests alone was found to be a "doubtful procedure." Girls were better readers than boys at age eight, but the sex difference disappeared as the children grew older. No significant physical differences, including handedness, were found between good and poor readers. Speech defects were associated with reading problems. Home circumstances of poor readers were inferior to those of good readers. Intelligence as determined by nonverbal tests was significantly related to socioeconomic status. Reading attainment of children in larger schools and urban schools tended to be better than that in smaller schools and in rural schools. (See Item No. 532).

534 Mreschar, Renate I. "Influence of upbringing on the problems of dyslexic children." Read Teach 29(8): 838-39, 841, May, 1976. (0 References).
Reports the results of a study by Dr. Wilhelm Niemeyer of Bremen, Federal Republic of Germany, published under the title Legasthenie und Milieu (Hermann Schroedel Verlag, Hanover). In a 1970 survey of 1,927 primary-school children in Bremen, 159, or 8.3 percent, were diagnosed dyslexic. These were computer-matched for intelligence, background, age, and sex

with pupils who were not dyslexic. Questionnaires sent to pupils, parents, and teachers revealed social background to be less important than the environment in which the child is growing up. Most dyslexics in the study came from the lower classes, but forty-five of the 159 cases detected came from "better families." Most differences between dyslexics and the controls lay at the social and cultural level. Parents of dyslexics possessed fewer books and were less interested in cultural events. Dyslexics had fewer stories read to them and were less encouraged to talk at mealtime or to be independent. Dyslexics watched "a lot more television" than controls. Dyslexics' mothers obtained lower grades in the school-leaving examinations than the mothers of normal control children. Parents of dyslexic children appeared not to notice differences in their children as much as others. When they did react it was with particular severity and exaggerated expectations. Dyslexic children said they wanted understanding more than anything. They were distressed at having fewer friends than other children and at being laughingstocks. Improved personal relationships is one of the primary aims of the therapy Dr. Niemeyer suggests.

535 Park, George E. "Nurture and/or nature cause reading difficulties?"
     Arch Pediatr 69(11): 432-44, November, 1952. (0 References).
Discusses critically Bertil Hallgren's book Specific Dyslexia (Congenital Word-blindness), a Clinical and Genetic Study. (See Item No. 549). Hallgren's conclusion that dyslexia is hereditary and genetically transmitted is rejected, while at the same time the book is hailed as a significant contribution to the literature. It is suggested that heredity may occasionally provide circumstances that predispose to dyslexia. The condition may be nurtured, rather than being caused by nature. The latter cause would doom all treatment to failure, since child, parents, and teachers all would assume it was hopeless. A case study is included to illustrate the "disastrous" effect of presuming an hereditary cause for dyslexia.

536 Rutter, Michael; Yule, Bridget; Quinton, David; et al. "Attainment
     and adjustment in two geographical areas: III--some factors ac-
     counting for area differences." Br J Psychiatry 126: 520-33,
     June, 1975. (45 References).
Studies of ten-year-old children living in one inner London borough and of children the same age living in the Isle of Wight found that specific reading retardation, emotional disorders, and conduct disorders were all twice as common among the London group. Four sets of variables were found to be associated with problem children both in London and on the Isle of Wight: family discord, parental deviance (psychiatric disorders), social disadvantage, and certain school characteristics. This last variable included teacher turnover, pupil turnover, proportion of the children receiving free meals, and absenteeism, among other factors. All four variables occurred more commonly in London in almost all cases. It is suggested that the problems stemmed from living in the inner London borough. Further investigation is recommended to discover why life in a metropolitan area predisposes children to such problems.

537 Schubert, Delwyn G. "At home with the retarded reader." Elem Engl
     30(2): 94-95, February, 1953. (0 References).
The best way for the teacher to learn about a pupil's home is to visit it, preferably with the child and both parents present. A great number of factors in the home are linked to reading disability, including cultural level of the home, neighborhood conditions, language spoken in the

home, and parent-child and sibling relationships. The teacher should not
visit the home if she is not wanted. A suggested home environment checklist is included.

538 Tapia, Fernando. "Girls with conditions more commonly seen in boys.
     (A pilot study)." Dis Nerv Syst 29(5): 323-26, May, 1968. (8
     References).
It has been believed that psychiatric problems in children occur more
frequently in boys than in girls. The conditions apparently affecting
boys most often include, among others, tics, speech disorders, aggressive
behavior disorders, and reading disorders. This study of these four conditions used two groups of girls, a study and an control, average age
11.7 years. It was done with the thought that factors causing the problems might be more conspicuous in a series of girls. No clear-cut implications for particular organic causes were found. Overall, an association with lower socioeconomic status did exist. It appeared that there
was a slight lean to organic factors which was seen as at least suggesting an organic predisposition.

539 Tuckman, E. "The families of backward readers." Proc R Soc Med
     58(4): 234-36, April, 1965. (10 References).
Reports the results of interviews with the parents of groups of children
eight and nine years old. One group was made up of normal readers, the
other of backward readers with a discrepancy between nonverbal IQ score
and reading attainment scores. Findings show: (1) Socioeconomic backgrounds were similar. (2) Educational attainments of the parents were
similar. (3) Personality scores of the fathers were similar. (4) Families of backward readers were more maladjusted. (5) Mothers were more
neurotic. It is suggested that reading backwardness and its associated
emotional disturbance could be predicted by studying the mothers of preschool children. Literature is cited showing evidence for emotional instability in the homes of backward readers. It is suggested that if
neuroticism in the mother is an important cause of reading disability,
an effective treatment would be psychotherapy for the mothers. (A brief
report of this study appears in Practitioner 194(1160): 280, February,
1965. It is not included in this bibliography).

G. HEREDITY

540 Bakwin, Harry. "Reading disability in twins." Dev Med Child Neurol
     15(2): 184-87, April, 1973. (8 References).
Findings in this study support the theory that reading disability is
largely genetic in origin. Subjects were 676 twin children, all from
middle-income families. The incidence of reading disability was somewhat
higher than for the general population. Monozygotic twins shared the
disability in a significantly higher proportion of the cases than did
dizygotic twins. There was no difference in mean birth weights of readers and nonreaders.

541 Clark, Josephine E. "The relation of reading disability to left-
     handedness and speech defects in other members of the family."
     Smith Coll Stud Soc Work 4(1): 66-79, September, 1933. (12
     Bibliographic Footnotes).
Compared the family histories of a group of children who were reading
disability patients with similar histories of a group of normal readers

to test Orton's theory that left-handedness, speech defects, and possibly reading difficulties occur more frequently among relatives of reading-disabled children than in others. No relation between speech defects and left-handedness in the family history and reading disability in the patient was found. Reading difficulties were slightly more common in the families of children with reading disability than in those of other children.

542 Cole, Edwin M. "Disabilities in speaking and reading." Med Clin
     North Am 22(3): 607-16, May, 1938. (0 References).
Presents case histories illustrating the delay in speech development, unintelligible baby talk, stuttering, and reading disability. Heredity appears to play a large part in reading disability, displaying the same general characteristics as other disturbances of language function. Language function and speech are regulated entirely by the dominant cerebral hemisphere. Handedness is a convenient indicator of the dominant hemisphere. Reading disability, like other language problems, does not respond to sporadic attempts at training, but only to much carefully planned, repeated drilling until the skill is acquired.

543 Crawford, Charles, and Reeve, Antony W. "Reading difficulties and
     specific dyslexia." NZ Med J 65(411): 773-76, November, 1966.
     (14 References).
"Specific dyslexia" is the most common name for a condition usually affecting boys and at its worst from ages six to twelve. The child with specific dyslexia usually speaks fluently and has a large vocabulary. He appears to be of normal intelligence, but for some reason has trouble learning to read and write. He may confuse left and right and be a little clumsy. The cause is genetically determined, possibly by a failure of the two cerebral hemispheres to develop their usual asymmetrical function. This overlap or blurring of speech function, ordinarily limited to the dominant hemisphere, and spatial orientation, usually controlled in the minor hemisphere, produces deficiencies in both functions. The condition may improve spontaneously in adolescence. Specific dyslexia is not widely recognized in New Zealand. In diagnosing the condition, general mental deficiency, defective vision and hearing, brain damage, emotional disturbances, and lack of schooling should be eliminated as causes of poor reading. Specific dyslexia can be treated if recognized early, but a complete cure is not common. Look-say teaching methods should be discarded, and old-fashioned phonics used. Five case histories are given.

544 "Developmental dyslexia: a genetic survey." Med J Aust 2(21):
     766, November 23, 1974. (1 Reference).
There is no agreement as to the cause of developmental dyslexia. In a school survey of eight-year-olds in Sydney about 8 percent of boys and 2 percent of girls were found to suffer from specific dyslexia. Evidence strongly suggests that the difficulty may be inherited. In genetic terms, it appears that the gene involved is of the autosomal dominant variety, i.e., it may be transmitted by either parent, to 50 percent of the offspring on the average. The effect of the gene may be altered by education (environment).

545 Drew, Arthur L. "Familial reading disability." Univ Mich Med Bull
     21(8): 245-53, August, 1955. (24 References).
Offers a hypothesis to explain familial reading disabilities. The suggestion is that the disturbance is basically one of spatial relationship.

The suggested organic basis is delayed or incomplete maturation of function in the parietal or parietal-occipital areas. Further, it is suggested that the fundamental inherited defect in hereditary dyslexia is
best understood in terms of a disturbance in figure-ground or gestalt
formation. Three instances of reading disability in one family are given
as examples of familial reading disability. A father and his two sons
by different mothers all had extreme reading problems. The father was
forty-eight; the sons twenty-three and sixteen years old. The twenty-
three-year-old was barely literate; the father and the sixteen-year-old
were almost totally unable to read. The older son showed no abnormality
on a complete neurological examination; the father showed mild problems;
and the younger son was the most abnormal, showing symptoms of parietal
lobe difficulty. The father and youngest son appear to be true cases of
familial dyslexia. Some literature is reviewed with discussion of reasons for the confusion in terminology. It is indicated that the form of
dyslexia discussed in this paper is a highly selective disability without recognizable causes and one in which the dyslexia appears to be un-
associated with other aphasic or agnostic elements.

546 Eustis, Richard S. "Specific reading disability; a familial syn-
     drome associated with ambidexterity and speech defects and a fre-
     quent cause of problem behavior." N Engl J Med 237(8): 243-49,
     August 21, 1947. (15 References).
Specific reading disability is a definite entity usually associated with
ambidexterity and speech defects. The patient usually comes from a
family in which these symptoms are common. Ambidexterity, left-handedness, and speech defects are not causes of reading disability. They are
frequently associated findings. Crossed laterality does not occur more
often in reading-disabled children than in normal ones. Children of
average intelligence or above who have reading problems profit from treatment and do well in school and college. They should be taught by phonetic
and kinesthetic methods.

547 Finucci, Joan Martha. "Family patterns and genetic analysis of spe-
     cific reading disability." For a summary see: Diss Abstr Int
     35A(6): 3514, December, 1974.

548 Finucci, Joan Martha; Guthrie, John T.; Childs, Anne L.; et al.
     "The genetics of specific reading disability." Ann Hum Genet
     40(1): 1-23, July, 1976. (46 References).
Examined the immediate family members of twenty children with specific
reading disability to determine the prevalence of reading disability
within the families. Children selected for the study were fifteen boys
and five girls seven and eight years old, at least one and one-half years
retarded in reading, and with IQs of at least 100. Specific reading
disability is defined as that which cannot be explained by neurological
or sensory deficits; poor schooling or environment; emotional disturbance; or low intelligence. Eighty-one of the eighty-six parents and
siblings of these children were given reading and intelligence tests.
A comparison group of seventy-two adults who were said to read normally
was also tested. Forty-five percent of seventy-five first-degree relatives of the parents of retarded readers were affected. A significantly
larger number of males than females were affected. No single mode of
genetic transmission was evident. It is concluded that specific reading
disability tends to aggregate within families. It is suggested that it
is genetically heterogeneous and that subgroups of disabled readers
should be identified.

549 Hallgren, Bertil. "Specific dyslexia ('congenital word-blindness'):
     a clinical and genetic study." <u>Acta Psychiatr Neurol</u> (Suppl. 65).
     Translated from the Swedish by Erica Odelberg. Copenhagen, Denmark:
     Munksgaard, 1950. 287p. (Bibliography p. 273-287).
Concludes from a study of 116 cases of specific dyslexia (a term used
interchangeably with "congenital word blindness") and 160 cases of the
siblings and parents of the persons studied that there is a link between
speech defects and specific dyslexia, at least in boys. No link appeared
between specific dyslexia and left-handedness or mixed dominance. The
author examined each subject personally and visited most of the homes.
After briefly reviewing the literature concerning the role of heredity
in specific dyslexia and explaining the method used, he discusses the
factors studied. These include, among others, physical illnesses; neurological disorders; visual, auditory, and speech defects; cerebral dominance; intelligence; environmental factors; and birth order. Family
trees (pedigree charts) and case histories are included. For each factor studied, the findings of earlier investigations are presented briefly,
followed by findings on the point in the present study. Appendices
present the data in detail. Both child and adult dyslexics served as
subjects. (See Item No. 535).

550 Hansen, Erik. "Recent studies of dyslexia." <u>Dev Med Child Neurol</u>
     7(5): 574-75, October, 1965. (6 References).
It is important to distinguish children whose learning difficulty is delayed, not permanent, from those in whom learning difficulty is a permanent handicap. Poor results of psychotherapy in children with learning
disorders and uneven results from remedial classes make it clear that
these children must have a full assessment not only of psychological and
neurological factors, but also of sight, hearing, speech, and language.
Evidence suggests that dyslexia is more often genetically determined than
the result of minimum brain damage.

551 Hermann, Knud. "Congenital word blindness (poor readers in the
     light of Gerstmann's syndrome)." <u>Acta Psychiatr Neurol Scand</u>
     (Suppl. 108): 177-84, 1956. (7 References).
Concludes on the basis of a series of investigations that the fundamental
disturbance in Gerstmann's syndrome and in congenital word blindness is
the same. Congenital word blindness should not be considered an isolated
disorder with dyslexia and dysgraphia, but part of a more general disturbance in symbol functions. It is an underdevelopment in the function
controlling direction in space, and is transmitted by dominant genes.

552 Hermann, Knud, and Norrie, Edith. "Is congenital word-blindness a
     hereditary type of Gerstmann's syndrome?" <u>Psychiatr Neurol</u> 136:
     59-73, 1958. (20 References).
Explores the resemblance that may exist between dyslexia and the Gerstmann
syndrome. The four main symptoms of Gerstmann syndrome are confusion of
right and left; finger agnosia (inability to name fingers when asked to
do so); inability to do arithmetic; and inability to write. Some relevant
literature is discussed. Hermann cites an earlier study in which he carried out detailed analysis of dyslexic problems and several features
common to the word-blind and Gerstmann patients. On that basis it is
suggested that congenital word blindness might reasonably be caused by
an inherited disturbance in functions having to do with direction in
space, the same defect found in the Gerstmann syndrome. Many word-blind
patients resort to all kinds of roundabout methods to distinguish right
from left. In studies reported on elementary- and secondary-school

children nine to fifteen years of age and on word-blind adults it was
found that word-blind persons make mistakes in right-left discrimination
far more often than normal readers. The word-blind person's dysgraphia
also resembles the agraphia present in Gerstmann's syndrome. It is concluded that the close resemblance between symptoms of word blindness and
those of the Gerstmann syndrome justify the hypothesis that both conditions derive from the same basic disturbance.

553   Hof, J. Op't, and Güldenpfennig, W. M. "Dominant inheritance of
       specific reading disability." S Afr Med J 46(23): 737-38, June
       3, 1972. (9 References).
A family whose home language is Afrikaans was found in whom specific reading disability appeared to have been inherited as a dominant characteristic. Three males from a family of nine siblings were affected. One of
these became the father of two female normal readers and a reading-disabled male. This man in turn fathered four girls and one boy, all disabled readers. A sixth child, a boy, was too young to be examined. The
symptoms of specific reading disability, or developmental dyslexia, are
described. EEG analysis did not establish a cause. It was presumed to
be an underlying psychoneurological defect. The reading disability appeared to be associated with a visual-spatial integration problem.

554   McGlannan, Frances J. "Familial characteristics of genetic dys-
       lexia: preliminary report from a pilot study." J Learn Disabil
       1(3): 185-91, March, 1968. (18 References).
Gives an overview of Project Genotype, a study designed to gain knowledge
of sixty-five families containing one or more reading-disabled children
currently enrolled in a special school. Three generations of the research families were studied. Data were included only on persons in the
direct bloodlines. Twin births were found to be at a rate 284 percent
higher than that expected in the general United States population. Dia-
betic disorders were found in 75.6 percent of the families; significant
drug reactions in 76.9 percent; left-handedness in 70.7 percent; and red
hair in 51.4 percent. It is hypothesized that there is a "vulnerable
family" syndrome. Families with specific genetic characteristics are
more likely to produce a child with a learning disability. Genetic dyslexia is defined as one effect of a basic genetic anomaly manifested by
inconstancy of spatial and temporal relations. The result is inadequate
association and integration of symbols resulting in language difficulties. Typical symptoms include ambilaterality, directional confusion,
and maturational lags. All children in the sample population lacked
obvious organic or neurotic problems. The WISC and other tests of perceptual relations and reading ability were administered.

555   Matthews, Charles Edward. "An investigation of the syndrome of
       neurological disorientation found in a reading disability case and
       in his close relatives." For a summary see: Diss Abstr Int
       32A(5): 2312, November, 1971.

556   Orton, Samuel Torrey. "Familial occurrence of disorders in acqui-
       sition of language." Eugenics 3(4): 140-47, April, 1930. As
       reprinted in Orton, Samuel Torrey. "Word-blindness" in school
       children and other papers on strephosymbolia (specific language
       disability--dyslexia) 1925-1946. Compiled by June Lyday Orton.
       Pomfret, Connecticut: Orton Society, 1966. (0 References).
Children with no brain injury and normal intelligence sometimes have difficulty in learning to read and write. They reverse and confuse letters

or words and use mirror writing or mirror reading. The term "strepho-symbolia" (twisted symbols) is used to describe this condition, which is caused by incomplete dominance of one hemisphere of the brain. Case histories and charts of families showing the occurrence of left-handed persons, stutterers, and the reading-disabled are included. Hereditary patterns and training methods interact to produce the disabilities. If a child is clearly left-handed, he should not encounter much more difficulty than the clearly right-handed child.

557 Ravenette, A. T. "The concept of 'dyslexia': some observations.
      Acta Paedopsychiatr 38(4): 105-10, April, 1971. (0 References).
Expresses doubt of the theory that dyslexia is inherited. The condition may show familial links. Genetic transmission is transmission of physiological attributes, rather than psychological traits. An example is given of one family's need to maintain one child as the "stupid" member of the family. This would be the child with reading disability. It was a necessary part of a pathological family process that this be done. This is not the same as an assumed physiological disorder. A multidisciplinary approach or a wide range of ways to understand reading difficulties should be available to the investigator in diagnosing dyslexia.

558 Rossi, Albert O. "Genetics and learning disabilities." Behav
      Neuropsychiatry 4(4-5): 2-7, August, 1972. (24 References).
Reviews the underlying genetic principles that make each person unique. We are chemical factories. Learning processes are referred to as being largely neurological "dysfunctions" endowed by genes. Dyslexia, dysphasia, dysgraphia, and ataxia are interrelated. Their common denomination is cerebellar dysfunction caused by neurochemical lag. As psychogenic reading disabilities, autism, childhood schizophrenia, and similar conditions were recognized, a reconsideration of learning processes has been necessary. It can no longer be assumed that the child with normal hearing, vision, and mental capacity will learn without difficulty. It is predicted that in the years ahead chemical means of directing the action of the human brain will result in increased intelligence levels for many children, thus averting many behavior disorders. Some of the drugs effective for use with learning disabilities are listed and their action explained.

559 ————. "Genetics of higher level disorders." J Learn Disabil
      3(8): 386-90, August, 1970. (16 References).
Experience may modify a child's potential, but personality structure and the connected biochemical idiosyncracies are inherited. Most retarded children are the products of an intellectually limited parent, and are endowed with a fixed enzymatic dysfunction in the central nervous system. Dyslexic fathers have dyslexic sons. Educationally handicapped parents often produce slow-learning children. Discussed are: the genetics of dyslexia; developmental speech disorders and stammering; congenital inability to recognize sounds in the absence of hearing loss; and handedness and cerebral dominance. A small group of children among all retarded readers appears to suffer from a relatively pure reading disability caused either by a structural problem or delayed maturation without neurological defect. The frequency of dyslexia in the population is estimated between 0.5 and 25 percent, depending upon the criteria adopted. Problems raised in ascribing dyslexia to a genetic cause are explored.

560 Singer, Sandra Manes. "A behavior genetic approach to the study of
      certain types of reading disability." For a summary see: Diss
      Abstr Int 36B(5): 2061, November, 1975.

561 Symmes, Jean S., and Rapoport, Judith L. "Unexpected reading fail-
     ure." Am J Orthopsychiatry 42(1): 82-91, January, 1972. (19
     References).
When a population of children was screened for a number of characteristics
that might predispose them to reading difficulties, it was found that the
population produced by the screening contained only one girl and was generally superior in certain visual skills. Reasons for believing a genetic
cause underlies reading disabilities are presented. It is suggested
that a genetic link exists between spatial visualization and difficulty
in learning to read. High incidence of reading difficulties in immediate
families of the poor readers in this study and the absence of females
suggests the genetic explanation.

562 Vandenberg, S. G. "Possible hereditary factors in minimal brain
     dysfunction." In: De La Cruz, Felix; Fox, Bernard H.; Roberts,
     Richard H., eds. Minimal brain dysfunction. Ann NY Acad Sci
     205: 223-30, February 28, 1973. (29 References).
Considers dyslexia as one of several abnormal conditions of known genetic
origin which may lead to learning disabilities. The viewpoint expressed
is that it is plausible to regard dyslexia as a genetic entity, but this
is not firmly established.

563 Zahálková, M.; Vrzal, V.; Kloboukova, E. "Genetical investigations
     in dyslexia." J Med Genet 9(1): 48-52, March, 1972. (23 Refer-
     ences).
Sixty-five dyslexics (fifty-six boys and nine girls) were studied and
divided into three groups: (1) a hereditary group; (2) an encephalo-
pathic group in which the disorders could be traced to injuries and
problems in pregnancy and birth; and (3) a group in which both heredity
and early complications were present. It is concluded that the hereditary
form of dyslexia is inherited as an autosomal dominant influenced by sex.
Although both men and women may carry the trait without being affected
themselves, it is more common in women. No particular blood type was
found to be associated with dyslexia.

H. INTELLIGENCE

564 Ackerman, Peggy T., and Peters, John E. "Children with specific
     learning disabilities: WISC profiles." J Learn Disabil 4(3):
     150-66, March, 1971. (21 References).
A group of learning-disabled children and a control group of normal children were given the WISC. No characteristic WISC profiles were found
for the learning-disabled group. Serious reading deficiencies were
associated more with verbal deficiencies than with nonverbal deficits.
The higher the IQ, especially the verbal IQ, the lower the probability
of a reading problem. A child scoring in the low-average or dull-normal
range on either the verbal or performance scale was considered to be at
high risk of reading problems in middle-class urban schools.

565 Belmont, Lillian, and Birch, Herbert G. "The intellectual profile
     of retarded readers." Percept Mot Skills 22(3): 787-816, June,
     1966. (32 References).
Groups of 150 retarded and fifty normal readers, all boys nine and ten
years old, were matched for age and school class placement. A significantly higher number of retarded readers had higher performance than

verbal IQ scores on the WISC. Normal readers had significantly higher
verbal IQs. These differences persisted when parts of the groups were
eliminated in order to restrict IQs for all subjects to scores of 90 to
109. All WISC subtest scores except Coding were significantly higher
for normal readers than for the retarded readers. On the whole, retarded
readers were found to have significantly lower IQs than normal readers.

566 Black, F. William. "An investigation of intelligence as a causal
     factor in reading problems." J Learn Disabil 4(3): 139-42,
     March, 1971. (5 References).
Subjects in this study were children referred to the psychology department of a hospital because of moderate reading retardation. The average
full-scale WISC IQ of the group was 90.7, a marked downward skew from
normal IQ distribution. However, the difference between the average
reading quotients of high and low IQ groups was not statistically significant.

567 Bridger, Wagner H. "Cognitive factors in perceptual dysfunction."
     Res Publ Assoc Res Nerv Ment Dis 48: 255-65, 1970. (32 Refer-
     ences).
Presents evidence that retarded readers do not perform well on perceptual
tasks not because of perceptual deficits but because of a lack of ability
to apply abstract verbal labels. Human perception is most often mediated
by language and other symbolic functions and inseparable from them. Language skills play a crucial role in many perceptual motor tasks. Caution
should be used in assuming that a deficit in perception exists, at least
until the role of higher cognitive functions is ruled out. It is suggested that the difficulties dyslexic children experience in matching visual
light patterns with equivalent auditory sound patterns (cross-modal transfer) is a cognitive problem, not a perceptual deficit problem.

568 Burks, Harold F., and Bruce, Paul. "The characteristics of poor
     and good readers as disclosed by the Wechsler Intelligence Scale
     for Children." J Educ Psychol 46(8): 488-93, December, 1955.
     (6 References).
This study hypothesized that poor readers were weak in the parts of intelligence tests that are similar to the important characteristics of
written language. Groups of good and poor readers were given the WISC
and a reading test to see if a pattern of abilities existed. Poor readers were low on subtests of Information, Arithmetic, and Coding. They
were high on Picture Arrangement, Block Design, and Comprehension. Good
readers were high on the Similarities subtest. It is concluded that good
readers are better able to handle abstractions than poor readers who
approach learning problems in a concrete manner. Full-scale IQ of poor
readers was 101; good readers 117.

569 Dalton, Jack Cuthbert. "The relationship of the Wechsler Intelli-
     gence Scale for Children (classified according to selected struc-
     ture of intellect factors) and reading disability." For a summary
     see: Diss Abstr Int 36A(12, Part 1): 7849-50, June, 1976.

570 Ekwall, Eldon Edward. "The use of WISC subtest profiles in the
     diagnosis of reading difficulties." For a summary see: Diss Abstr
     27A(4): 950-51, October, 1966.

571 Feeler, Tilghman J. "A comparison of Wechsler Intelligence Scale
     for Children scores of specific learning disabled and reading

disabled students." For a summary see: <u>Diss Abstr Int</u> 36A(3):
1432-33, September, 1975.

572 Hill, Frances. "High IQ does not go with dyslexia." <u>Times Educ</u>
     <u>Suppl</u> 2871: 9, May 29, 1970. (0 References).
According to Margaret M. Clark's study of Scottish schoolchildren, few
children suffering from dyslexia are of high intelligence. Among a group
of 230 backward readers tested, very few were of average intelligence.
Most were below average. In a study of nine-year-olds only 1 percent of
1,544 children were two years or more below the reading norm and of average
intelligence. Margaret Clark is quoted as saying that misunderstanding
has arisen from different uses of the term "dyslexia." Individual attention can do wonders for backward readers, she stresses.

573 Keller, James F.; Croake, James W.; Riesenman, Carolyn. "Relation-
     ships among handedness, intelligence, sex and reading achievement
     of school age children." <u>Percept Mot Skills</u> 37(1): 159-62,
     August, 1973. (14 References).
A sample of 277 boys and girls in grades three through twelve in Tallahassee, Florida, was tested for IQ, reading achievement, and handedness.
Those of mixed laterality were deleted from the sample. When IQ, grade
level, handedness, and sex were controlled, no significant differences
were found in mean reading achievement. When sex, handedness, and grade
level were controlled, no significant differences in mean IQs were found.
Significant correlation was found between IQ and reading achievement.
The correlation between IQ and reading achievement was significantly
lower among left-handers than among right-handed children.

574 Lerand, Leslie W. "Intelligence and reading level of girls. (Re-
     search study no. 1)." For a summary see: <u>Diss Abstr</u> 27B(6):
     2137-38, December, 1966.

575 Lyle, J. G., and Goyen, Judith. "Performance of retarded readers
     on the WISC and educational tests." <u>J Abnorm Psychol</u> 74(1): 105-
     12, February, 1969. (14 References).
Results on the WISC were analyzed for groups of retarded and adequate
readers of average intelligence from the six primary school grades. Ages
ranged from six to twelve. This study is part of a wider study aimed
at discovering: (1) whether discrepancies between verbal and performance
WISC scores characterize retarded readers; (2) whether retarded readers
show any characteristic scatter on WISC subtests; and (3) whether reading
retardation is part of general school backwardness or a special educational problem. Results showed that retarded readers had greater verbal-
performance differences than controls in both directions. They also performed significantly poorer than controls on untimed tests of spelling
and arithmetic. No support was found for the hypothesis that certain
of the differences were effects of reading retardation rather than correlated symptoms. It is concluded that, in general, retarded readers
are retarded learners in all basic school subjects. The means of both
samples were at about the middle of the average range of intelligence,
with the control group having a mean full-scale IQ 5.68 points higher
than the group of poor readers. This difference proved statistically
significant.

576 McDonald, Arthur S. "Intellectual characteristics of disabled
     readers at the high school and college levels." <u>J Dev Read</u> 7(2):
     97-101, Winter, 1964. (3 References).

Poor readers at the high school and college level did well on subtests
of the Wechsler Adult Intelligence Scale measuring nonverbal tasks like
Block Design and Object Assembly and on subtests of Picture Completion.
They did most poorly on Arithmetic and Digit Span subtests which reflect
concentration and attention. Disabled readers also did poorly on Digit
Symbol exercises reflecting perceptual-motor performance and memory.
They also did poorly on the Information subtest. Children who are disabled readers are known to follow this same pattern on the analogous sub-
tests of the WISC.

577   Neville, Donald. "The intellectual characteristics of severely re-
      tarded readers and implications for teaching techniques." In:
      Hellmuth, Jerome, ed. Learning disorders. Vol. 2. Seattle,
      Washington: Bernie Straub and Jerome Hellmuth, 1966. 281-94.
      (41 References).
Poor readers tend to score lower on IQ tests than do good readers. The
correlation between silent reading and intelligence is usually between
0.5 and 0.7. Poor readers tend to do poorly on many tasks involving
verbal abilities, especially automatic-sequential tasks and short-term
memory skills. Not all poor readers share these characteristics, however. Much more information is needed on how to match teaching methods
to a child's deficiencies.

578   Quadfasel, F. A., and Goodglass, H. "Specific reading disability
      and other specific disabilities." J Learn Disabil 1(10): 590-
      600, October, 1968. (15 References).
Considers reading disability as a medical entity, and discusses the place
of language skills among other specific intellectual endowments and disabilities. Some retarded readers have brain injury, but most cases of
reading disability should be understood in the context of variations in
talent for acquiring special skills. Inferiority in ability to learn
specific skills reflects functional inefficiency in the brain structures
underlying those skills. One subgroup of retarded readers always displays distinctive errors in reading and spelling accompanied by perceptual
motor deficits. Effort should be made to identify such persons. Emotional factors are secondary to deficiencies in learning ability. A
classification system for types of reading disability is proposed.

579   Reed, James C. "The ability deficits of good and poor readers."
      J Learn Disabil 1(2): 134-39, February, 1968. (5 References).
Six-year-old first graders and ten-year-old sixth graders were given the
WISC, the Category Test (Reitan Children's Form), and the Tactual Performance Test. The children's reading ability was determined from two
Gates reading tests. Most of the tests in the complete battery were
found to discriminate between good and poor readers at both age levels.
The higher intellectual functions as measured by WISC subtests discriminated best between good and poor readers. The Tactual Performance Test
which measures psychomotor functions was next, and least discriminative
were tests which primarily measured motor functions. Results suggest
that pure motor abilities have little to do with reading skills. There
is little justification for training children in motor skills in the hope
of improving reading ability.

580   ————. "Reading achievement as related to differences between
      WISC verbal and performance IQ's." Child Dev 38(3): 835-40,
      September, 1967. (5 References).

The WISC and a reading test were administered to six-year-old first graders and to ten-year-old fifth graders. Three groups were formed at each
grade level: those with verbal IQ scores several points above performance IQ; those with performance above verbal IQ; and those with nearly
equal performance and verbal IQ scores. Significant differences in reading achievement were found among the groups at age ten, but not at age
six. The group of ten-year-olds with higher verbal IQ read well, or above
expectation from full-scale IQ. The inference that fluent reading may
lead to superior verbal skills was supported. But evidence did not support the idea that poor reading necessarily follows a pattern of higher
performance than verbal IQ. At the six-year-old level, differences between verbal and performance IQ may not be reliable. Findings suggest
that primary reading skill depends upon level of intelligence. Deficiencies in either verbal or performance skills do not appear to hamper
initial acquisition of reading skills.

581 Schneyer, J. Wesley. "Underlying mental abilities and reading."
     Read Teach 24(1): 55, 57, October, 1970. (8 References).
The results of a number of studies seem to indicate that abstract thinking or conceptualization are among the underlying mental abilities vital
to successful reading performance.

582 Smith, Susan Jeter. "The relationship of the Stanford-Binet Intelli-
     gence Scale (classified according to selected structure-of-intellect
     factors) and reading disability." For a summary see: Diss Abstr
     Int 35A(10): 6374, April, 1975.

583 Warrington, Elizabeth K. "The incidence of verbal disability asso-
     ciated with retardation reading." Neuropsychologia 5(2): 175-179,
     May, 1967. (5 References).
The WISC was administered to seventy-six children, seventy boys and six
girls ages seven to fifteen, who were more retarded in reading than expected. A greater-than-expected number of these retarded readers were
found to have a discrepancy of twenty or more points in performance over
verbal score on WISC subtests. This was seen as reinforcing the idea
that delayed development of language is associated with reading retardation. A significant association was found between delayed speech development and poor verbal skills as compared with nonverbal skills. Delayed
development of the spatial sense did not seem to be associated with reading retardation.

I. LANGUAGE DIFFERENCES

584 Makita, Kiyoshi. "The rarity of reading disability in Japanese
     children." Am J Orthopsychiatry 38(4): 599-614, July, 1968.
     (37 References).
Dyslexia among children in Japan appears to be only about one-tenth as
prevalent as in Western countries. It is proposed that specific characteristics of each language contribute to reading disability. It is concluded that reading disability is more a philological than a neuropsychiatric problem.

585 ————. "Reading disability and the writing system." In: World
     Congress on Reading, 5th, Vienna, 1974. Proceedings: new horizons
     in reading. Edited by John E. Merritt. Newark, Delaware: Inter-
     national Reading Association, 1976. 250-54. (12 References).

The incidence of reading disability in Japan is about one-tenth that reported in Western countries. Biological differences are rejected as an
explanation, and it is suggested that the reason lies in the fundamental
differences between the Japanese language and Western languages. The
Japanese writing system is explained briefly. Reading disability appears
to arise from cognitive confusion. The writing system is an important
variable in the process of learning to read. Differences in that system
may explain the lack of reading problems in Japan.

586 Newton, Margaret A., and Thomson, Michael E. "Dyslexia as a phenom-
       enon of written language." Paper presented at the International
       Federation of Learning Disabilities, Brussels, Belgium, January
       3-7, 1975. 1975. 12p. (ED 113 865).
Concludes that dyslexia is a primary difficulty brought about by an incompatibility between the system of written language and the built-in
developmental skills of the individual's perceptual-motor system. Dyslexia is defined and reviewed from the point of view of neurological and
educational processes and the nature of written language. A script system is studied with current linguistic and psycholinguistic studies in
mind.

587 Rabinovitch, M. Sam, and Strassberg, Rhona. "Syntax and retention
       in good and poor readers." Can Psychol 9(2): 142-53, April, 1968.
       (8 References).
Investigates whether syntactic structure of reading material facilitates
recall in good readers and whether this effect exists in children who are
poor readers. A paired-associate task tested two groups of fourth graders
--one group good readers, the other poor readers--on ability to associate
words. Four sentences were constructed using nonsense syllable stems
similar to English word stems. The syllables followed English ortho-
graphic rules and were pronounceable by native English speakers at the
fourth-grade level. Sentences used some real English pronouns and con-
nectives. The sentences were structured, i.e., they followed the framework of, syntactically correct English sentences. Four unstructured sentences were formed by randomly rearranging the order of the items in each
structured sentence. Each child was asked to learn four sentences, two
structured and two unstructured, by listening to them through earphones.
Each sentence was repeated until three correct oral repetitions were obtained. The good readers learned the structured sentences more rapidly
than the unstructured sentences. The poor readers learned both kinds of
sentences with equal facility. There was no difference between the good
and poor readers' ability to retain the unstructured material. Hence,
the real difference between the good and poor readers lay in their ability
to perceive and use syntactic structure. Average IQ for the good readers
was 118.4, and for the poor readers 103.9, a significant difference. This
was not believed to be important in this study since IQ is related to
reading ability, but is not highly correlated with paired-associate learning.

588 Stark, Joel. "Reading failure: a language-based problem." ASHA
       17(12): 832-34, December, 1975. (14 References).
Debating the existence of a syndrome is not as important as defining the
symptoms. Children who fail to learn to read present highly individual
patterns of performance. The usefulness of training in visual perceptual
abilities and psycholinguistic skills is questioned. It is suggested
that reading-disabled children need to learn the rules of spoken language,
to learn about syntax and the logic of the language system. Forcing the

child to match individual phonemes to their letter counterparts is not useful because it is not the way speech is perceived. Speech pathologists can assist teachers in understanding the nature of language and modifying teaching procedures to increase understanding of the role language development plays in reading.

589   Vellutino, Frank R. "Psychological factors in reading disability."
      Paper presented at American Educational Research Association,
      Chicago, Illinois, April, 1975. 1974. 28p. (ED 116 422).
Reviews three types of theories about causes of dyslexia. These are theories of visual perceptual deficit; difficulties with sensory integration; and verbal deficiencies. It is concluded that recent findings support the verbal or linguistic deficit theory. The perceptual deficit theories of Orton and others tend to be discredited by recent research, and the sensory integration theory of Birch appears to need further research. Practical implications of these findings for remedial reading instruction are discussed.

J. MATURATIONAL LAG; MENTAL AGE; IMMATURITY

590   Ames, Louise Bates. "A developmental approach to reading problems."
      Claremont Coll Read Conf Yearb 30: 78-94, 1966. (2 References).
Most reading failure could be prevented by waiting until the child is ready for reading instruction. Remedial reading might be essentially eliminated. To prevent reading failure, the use of a reading readiness test and an IQ test are recommended. Many children are pushed far beyond what their intelligence permits. The Rorschach test is helpful in evaluating perception. Chronological age is no guarantee of readiness to learn to read.

591   Bender, Lauretta. "Problems in conceptualization and communication
      in children with developmental alexia." In: Proceedings of the
      46th annual meeting of the American Psychopathological Association:
      psychopathology of communication, 1956. Edited by Paul H. Hoch,
      and Joseph Zubin. New York: Grune & Stratton, 1958. 155-76.
      (42 References).
Language lags appear to result from a wider range of maturation age in various functions controlled by unilateral cortical dominance than other maturation patterns. Slow maturation of language skills and neurological patterning and an uneven pattern of intellectual development characterize reading-disabled children. Reading disability may be predicted in preschool years. At that time, future dyslexics often show: (1) motor-speech delay; (2) delay in establishing cerebral dominance; (3) immature visual-motor functions; (4) primitive body image ideas; and (5) disturbances in figure-ground relationships. The dyslexic child's concept of time and space is immature. Ideas of right and left, up and down, yesterday and tomorrow may be confused. Developmental language lags and childhood schizophrenia may be compared since both involve maturational lags. Points of similarity are enumerated. There is evidence that both may be caused by genetic or familial factors.

592   Cohn, Robert. "A neurological study of delayed acquisition of read-
      ing and writing abilities in children." Trans Am Neurol Assoc
      85: 182-84, 1960. (0 References).

Attributes failure to acquire reading and writing ability in a group of
schoolchildren seven to ten years of age to a general disturbance in
neurological function. Most of the children showed aggressive antisocial
behavior. These children and a control group of normal children ages
six to twelve were tested in four major neurological categories: language; somatic receiving and expressive systems; personal and interpersonal spatial organization; and social adaptation. Deficiencies in the
normal group occurred, but they were not nearly so universal. To test
the hypothesis of general brain organization inadequacy, the rate of
maturation of the elements of language and the EEG were studied two years
later in the abnormal group and compared with rate of development of the
normal children. Retardation in development was found to be a very applicable term. At least a two-year delay in acquisition of the ability
to work with graphic symbols was observed in the abnormal children.

593 ————. "The role of immaturity in reading disabilities." J
     Learn Disabil 3(2): 73-74, February, 1970. (0 References).
Delayed language ability is often ascribed to immaturity, a very imprecise term. It is necessary to select a time to start education, and by
age six it is believed that all children will respond in some way to the
teacher-pupil couple. Some children need special attention at this age.
It is better to put the child into this challenge-response situation than
to detain him in a placid, undemanding atmosphere until he is eight or
nine years old.

594 Critchley, Macdonald. "Is developmental dyslexia the expression of
     minor cerebral damage?" Clin Proc Child Hosp DC 22(8): 213-22,
     September, 1966. (0 References).
Names have changed over the years, but the concept of a pure but circum-
scribed delay in achievement of language has been accepted by neurologists
as an entity. Various teaching methods and other nonmedical causes have
been suggested for dyslexia. These may aggravate, hinder, or delay, but
they do not provoke reading disability. Perinatal history of these
children is usually unremarkable. Various conditions that have been considered as causes are discussed, including birth problems, slow speech
development, cerebral dominance, clumsiness, spatial concepts and confusions, and others. The hypothesis that mild degrees of structural
brain damage underlie dyslexia is unconvincing. The theory of a maturational lag is the best explanation. Areas needing further research are
listed.

595 ————. "Is developmental dyslexia the expression of minor cere-
     bral damage?" Slow Learn Child 13(1): 9-19, 1966. (0 Refer-
     ences).
Concludes that developmental dyslexia is an entity, an organic problem
not typically caused by minor brain damage. It may be a specialized
instance of cerebral immaturity. It is doubtful whether any demonstrable
lesion will be found when pathological studies of dyslexia become available. But it is an organic entity; any theory of psychogenesis is strongly rejected. Brain-injured children, spastics, etc., who have trouble
learning to read should be regarded as "symptomatic dyslexics." The best
explanation so far advanced as a cause of dyslexia is that of maturational
lag. Minor neurological signs are evidences of cerebral immaturity. The
belief of educational psychologists that there is a spectrum or continuum
of late readers and inefficient readers is incorrect. Emotional and environmental causes, born of neurological ignorance, have been offered.
Delayed reading and poor spelling may appear in more than one member of

a family. Matters needing further study are enumerated, and the problem
of how to interpret the cause of dyslexia is discussed.

596 De Hirsch, Katrina. "The concept of plasticity and language dis-
       abilities." Speech Pathol Ther 8(1): April, 1965. As reprinted
       in Sapir, Selma G., and Nitzburg, Ann C., eds. Children with learn-
       ing problems: readings in a developmental-interaction approach.
       New York: Brunner/Mazel, 1973. 477-84. (15 References).
This is a study of three case histories of boys with good intelligence
who suffered from severe developmental language lags. Their problems
are seen in terms of plasticity, i.e., they were still so immature at
the ages of eight, ten, and fourteen, respectively, that all of their
behavior, including perception and motor activities, was unstable--
plastic--in ways characteristic of much younger children. When severe
language disability is viewed in terms of the plasticity of extreme immaturity, many of its characteristics can be better comprehended by
those attempting to help these children.

597 ————. "Potential educational risks." Child Educ 41(4): 178-
       83, December, 1964. (0 References).
Many young children of adequate intelligence display a variety of difficulties with reading and oral language. Many have family histories of
such problems. These children lag behind their peers in motor control,
visual perception, and recognition of spatial relationships. Since reading is a pattern laid out in space, they have trouble learning to read.
Problem readers often show maturational lags in several of these areas.
Maturation is promoted by training. Boys are one full year behind girls
in developmental age at chronological age six. Developmental differences
should be recognized when children enter first grade. How they learn
best--by visual, auditory, or kinesthetic means--should be explored and
used.

598 Fabian, A. A. "Vertical rotation in visual-motor performance--its
       relationship to reading reversals." J Educ Psychol 36(3): 129-
       54, March, 1945. (36 References).
When the normal child of preschool and beginning-school age copies hori-
zontally directed configurations, he tends to rotate the figures to the
vertical position. Physiological, psychophysical, and psychological
forces contribute to this tendency. Symbol and word reversals are related to this "verticalization." Verticalization is a developmental
phenomenon. If it persists, it may indicate either mental deficiency or
organic brain disease. In the general school population it is relatively
infrequent, and can be readily detected by the use of visual-motor tests.
Much more common are infantile behavior patterns caused by emotional or
environmental handicaps which inhibit learning and betray themselves in
primitive visual-motor tendencies such as verticalization. Exercises
to correct these tendencies should be started as soon as the problem is
discovered.

599 Ford, June Brooks. "Identification of a specific language disability
       (dyslexia)." For a summary see: Diss Abstr 26(3): 1827-28,
       September, 1965.

600 Frank, Helene. "A comparative study of children who are backward in
       reading and beginners in the infant school." Br J Educ Psychol
       5(1): 41-58, February, 1935. (16 Bibliographic Footnotes).

In this study, backward readers ages seven to eleven and one-half made the same mistakes as beginning readers ages four and five. This finding is attributed to the child's mode of perception: the older children's perception has remained at the same level as that of the beginners. It is suggested that the whole-word method of teaching is likely to be most successful. Backward readers should be taught by methods similar to those used with beginning readers.

601 Gellerman, Saul W. "Causal factors in the reading difficulties of
     elementary-school children." Elem Sch J 49(9-10): 523-30, May-
     June, 1949. (0 References).
On the basis of an analysis of sixty children referred to a university child-study clinic for educational difficulties it is concluded that most reading difficulties are unnecessary. They result from forcing the child to read beyond his ability, and from inadequate remedial techniques. Both the school and the home are to blame. The longer reading difficulties are allowed to persist, the more serious they become.

602 Goyen, Judith D., and Lyle, J. G. "Effect of incentives and age on
     the visual recognition of retarded readers." J Exp Child Psychol
     11(2): 266-73, April, 1971. (13 References).
Results of a tachistoscopic form-recognition task support the theory that developmental lag is a chief cause of reading retardation. Subjects were groups of normal and retarded readers divided within each group by age. Half of each group were seven and one-fourth to eight and one-fourth years old; and half were eight and one-half to nine and one-half years old. All the children were pupils in primary schools in London. Members of each age- and reading-level group were given verbal encouragement and one half-penny for correct responses. The task was to match the form shown on the screen with the same form from a multichoice response card. Incentives did not affect performance of either retarded or normal readers. Latency of response, practice effects, and reversal errors were not related to reading ability in this study.

603 Harris, Albert J. "Lateral dominance, directional confusion, and
     reading disability." J Psychol 44: 283-94, 1957. (11 References).
At age seven more children with reading disability showed confusion in identifying left and right and mixed hand dominance. At age nine reading-disabled children in this study still had a higher incidence of mixed-handedness than the normal readers. The ability to distinguish left and right and clear hand preference appear to develop more slowly in reading-disabled children than in normal readers. This is interpreted as indicating a slowness of maturation, possibly of neurological origin, in these groups. No significant findings were noted on eye or foot dominance. Subjects were 316 children with marked reading disability who had been tested at educational clinics and 245 unselected schoolchildren.

604 Ingram, T. T. S.; Mason, A. W.; Blackburn, I. "A retrospective
     study of 82 children with reading disability." Dev Med Child
     Neurol 12(3): 271-81, June, 1970. (41 References).
In a study of eighty-two previously selected children with reading and spelling difficulties who were of normal intelligence and had had normal educational training, sixty-two fulfilled the definition of specific dyslexia. That is, they were underachieving in reading or spelling without adverse home environment, interrupted schooling, inadequate teaching, or poor motivation. Unfavorable conditions not excluded were neurological dysfunction, slow speech development, or family histories of

reading or speech difficulties. It was found that the most severe degree
of reading disability existed with no evidence of brain damage. It is
suggested that the cause of dyslexia may lie in a developmental lag in
perceptual or motor function. When brain damage was present, the dyslexia was more often associated with backwardness in school subjects in
general. The children were seven to fifteen years old.

605 Kinsbourne, Marcel. "Minimal brain dysfunction as a neurodevelop-
     mental lag." In: De La Cruz, Felix; Fox, Bernard H.; Roberts,
     Richard H., eds. Minimal brain dysfunction. Ann NY Acad Sci 205:
     268-73, February 28, 1973. (8 References).
In contrast to children with gross brain damage, children diagnosed as
having minimal brain dysfunction would be considered normal if they were
younger. The symptoms indicate a delay in neurological maturation. No
way is known to speed this process of cerebral control of various activities. Motor development, development of attentiveness, and development
of intelligence (cognitive development) are discussed. Cognitive immaturities are almost never noticed unless they affect the child's ability to learn to read and write. Reading readiness implies that sufficient
visual memory, orientation, and sequence discrimination, among other
factors, are present for reading to be possible. The use of phonics
teaching lightens the load on visual memory, and is helpful to children
whose visual memory and associations are limited. However, phonics
teaching makes other cognitive demands: the child must be able to pronounce words and their components.

606 ————. "Prospects for the study of developmental reading back-
     wardness." Br J Disord Commun 2(2): 152-54, October, 1967. (6
     References).
Describes the characteristics of those backward readers whose problem is
not environmental or emotional, but is attributable to failure of maturation of relevant areas of the brain. The fault may be genetically or
otherwise determined. Difficulty in learning will occur if there is weakness in visual memory, verbal memory, or memory for visual-verbal associations. The nature of the child's errors may indicate which function is
disturbed. Investigation of the child's problem should go beyond the
cursory preliminaries that precede the attachment of some label such as
"congenital dyslexia."

607 Lachmann, Frank M. "Perceptual-motor development in children re-
     tarded in reading ability." J Consult Psychol 24(5): 427-31,
     October, 1960. (19 References).
This study hypothesized that if reading disability reflected a lag or
retardation in perceptual-motor development, retarded readers would perform less maturely on the Bender Gestalt test than either normal readers
or emotionally disturbed children who are normal readers. The groups
were tested on their ability to construct angles; rotation of figures;
responses in drawing circles or loops instead of dots; and other abilities. Children retarded in reading showed more distortion in perceptual-
motor development than normal children. The amount of distortion showed
by retarded readers fell just short of being a significantly higher
amount than that shown by emotionally disturbed but normal readers.
Younger children showed more distortion than older children.

608 Lyle, J. G., and Goyen, Judith. "Visual recognition, developmental
     lag, and strephosymbolia in reading retardation." J Abnorm Psychol
     73(1): 25-29, February, 1968. (9 References).

Retarded readers performed less well than normal readers on all tasks in a battery of tests designed to measure visual recognition of forms under immediate, delayed, or sequential conditions. The groups were matched for grade placement and were of normal intelligence. Differences in perceptual speed are offered as a reason for the results. This is seen as support for the developmental lag theory of dyslexia.

609 O'Neill, G., and Stanley, G. "Visual processing of straight lines in dyslexic and normal children." Br J Educ Psychol 46(Part 3): 323-27, November, 1976. (13 References).
Two groups of twelve-year-olds, one made up of normal readers, the other of dyslexics, were shown overlapping straight lines. The lines were presented using a tachistoscope. The children were to judge whether one or two lines were being presented. A second study was done using a variation in the stimulus and procedure. The chief concern was to discover whether separation and detection threshold differences existed between dyslexics and normals. Dyslexics required longer interstimulus intervals in the first experiment, and longer times to detect a target line in the second. These findings were interpreted as meaning that dyslexics require more time than normal readers for visual storage of the preceding line (stimulus) to fade. This was seen as supporting the theory of a developmental lag in dyslexic children.

610 Parker, Claudia, and Waterbury, Eveline A. "Reading disability." Educ Method 12(7): 411-19, April, 1933. (0 References).
Those responsible for reading programs should consider the need for kindergarten training in helping to prevent reading disabilities. Children should attain a stated mental age before reading instruction is begun. Disabled readers should be challenged and required to make reasonable progress in reading. Close cooperation among school administrators and teachers is necessary if reading disability is to be prevented. Case histories are given.

611 Paul, Samuel E. "Reading problems in children." Acad Ther 2(3): 139-44, Spring, 1967. (21 References).
Evaluates the relationship of reading to cerebral dominance and maturational lag. It is difficult to diagnose dyslexia early because of the variable of maturational lag. Some of the tests used on a population of schoolchildren in efforts to find factors which correlate with reading ability are described. The one common denominator in reading problems is the varying rates of individual development. The development within one individual is uneven. It is not possible to answer questions about reading disability because of the intermingling of many factors.

612 Poloni-de Levie, Aletta. "Cognitive and personality correlates of reading difficulty." For a summary see: Diss Abstr 27B(6): 2144, December, 1966.

613 Rawson, Margaret B. "Congenital word blindness or specific developmental dyslexia." Med J Aust 1(11): 600, March 15, 1969. (0 References).
Letter to editor. Points out that Orton found peripheral laterality problems and developmental language disability to be indicative of maturational delay or anomaly, and not causes of language learning problems. Attention is called to the Orton-Gillingham approach to the treatment of word blindness which has been used successfully with thousands of dyslexic students in the United States.

614   Satz, Paul; Rardin, Donald; Ross, John. "An evaluation of a theory
      of specific developmental dyslexia." Child Dev 42(6): 2009-21,
      December, 1971. (18 References).
Presents research supporting the theory that developmental dyslexia reflects a lag in the maturation of the central nervous system. This delays the acquiring of skills necessary for reading, including visual-
motor and auditory-visual integration which should be in developmental
ascendancy in younger children (ages seven and eight). The same lag
when present in older dyslexic children (ages eleven and twelve) delays
language and formal operations which should be in developmental ascendancy
at that time.

615   Satz, Paul, and Van Nostrand, Gary K.   Developmental dyslexia: an
      evaluation of a theory. 1971. 50p. (ED 059 557).
Evaluates a theory advanced by Satz and Sparrow (1970) which hypothesizes
that developmental dyslexia is not a unitary syndrome but is caused by a
maturational lag in the left hemisphere of the brain. This, in turn, delays various skills which are in primary ascendancy at different chronological ages. It is concluded that the nature of the child's handicap
will vary largely as a function of chronological age. This approach
should be pursued instead of determining whether the primary handicap in
dyslexics is perceptual, linguistic, or both.

616   Seremeta, John Michael. "Developmental changes in the natural clas-
      sification skills in normal and dyslexic boys." For a summary see:
      Diss Abstr Int 37A(2): 896, August, 1976.

617   Snyder, Robert T., and Freund, Sheldon L. "Reading readiness and
      its relation to maturational unreadiness as measured by the spiral
      aftereffect and other visual-perceptual techniques." Percept Mot
      Skills 25(3): 841-54, December, 1967. (17 References).
Suggests that many children of normal intelligence are not ready to begin reading in first grade. This study explores the relationship between
first-grade reading difficulties and perceptual immaturity as measured
by a battery of visual-motor-perceptual tests including the Spiral After-
effect (SAE), Necker Cube, Bender Gestalt, and the Schroeder Staircase.
These tests and procedures are explained. Subjects were 667 first-grade
children with IQs of 85 or above. From 25 to 80 percent of these children were unable to perceive perceptual phenomena seen by 100 percent of
normal ten-year-old children, depending upon the complexity of the task.
Norms and base rates for various SAE functions are given by age, sex,
socioeconomic level, reading readiness, and Bender Gestalt test groupings. The SAE is considered valuable as a diagnostic tool.

618   Thompson, Lloyd J. "Possibility of a third camp in child psychiatry."
      Am J Psychiatry 125(4): 576-77, October, 1968. (3 References).
Letter to editor. Suggests that autism may be a developmental lag, as
developmental dyslexia is believed to be. The so-called "soft neurological signs" may also be part of a developmental lag, and not brain
damage. The idea of maturational lag, where an ability may be unformed,
but capable of being formed, is more optimistic than a diagnosis of brain
damage.

619   Wolfe, Lillian S. "An experimental study of reversals in reading."
      Am J Psychol 52: 533-61, October, 1939. (0 References).
The reading of children inferior in reading ability was compared with
that of normal children in six experiments concerned with the frequency

and consistency of reversal errors. The assumptions that reversals result from right-to-left observation of words or from lack of attention
to word forms were not upheld. It is submitted that normal readers pass
more quickly through the immature stages of learning where reversals are
common, while inferior readers, for reasons which can only be conjectured,
remain abnormally long at this normal, but immature, stage in learning
to read.

K. MEMORY DEFICITS

620 Burns, Sandra Mader. "An investigation of the relationship between
     sequential memory and oral reading skills in normal and learning
     disabled children." For a summary see: Diss Abstr Int 36A(7):
     4395, January, 1976.

621 Carroll, James L. "Assessment of short-term visual memory and its
     educational implications." Percept Mot Skills 37(2): 383-88,
     October, 1973. (19 References).
Reviews the research literature concerning tests for short-term memory.
The Memory-for-Designs test and various other tests of memory for shapes
or colors to be recalled almost immediately have been used. In some
studies significant differences have been found in scores on short-term
memory tests between retarded and normal readers. It is uncertain whether
visual memory problems can be helped with remedial training.

622 Kastner, Sheldon B., and Rickards, Carol. "Mediated memory with
     novel and familiar stimuli in good and poor readers." J Genet
     Psychol 124(1): 105-13, March, 1974. (7 References).
Confirms the position that poor readers are deficient in their ability
to apply verbal labels to certain physical stimuli. Groups of good and
poor third-grade readers were asked to point to a series of blocks with
imprinted designs in the same order the examiner had pointed to them
after a lapse of fifteen seconds and with the blocks rearranged. Each
child was questioned about his methods for recalling the order. Good
and poor readers did equally well on stimuli involving familiar objects.
Good readers were significantly better than poor readers under novel
conditions. Good readers maintained a consistent verbal strategy (verbalizers) in recall. Poor readers proved to be nonverbalizers who
switched to a visual strategy during the novel presentations. They tried
to remember such things as the appearance of the spot the examiner had
touched.

623 Katz, Leonard, and Wicklund, David A. "Simple reaction time for
     good and poor readers in grades two and six." Percept Mot Skills
     32(1): 270, February, 1971. (2 References).
Good and poor readers in second grade and good and poor readers in sixth
grade were tested for reaction times. The child pressed a key in response to a light. No significant differences were found. In a previous
study no differences were found between good and poor fifth-grade readers
in scanning time. It is hypothesized that differences in reading ability
may lie in memory processes, since results of these studies do not appear
to show differences in perceptual or motor processes between good and
poor readers.

624   Mackworth, Jane F., and Mackworth, Norman H. "Spelling recognition
        and coding by poor readers." <u>Bull Psychon Soc</u> 3(1B); 59-60,
        January, 1974. (7 References).
Good and poor readers ages fifteen to seventeen were contrasted in this
study. The poor readers had prolonged reaction times; marked difficulty
in spelling recognition; and difficulty in deciding whether two printed
words sounded alike. The conclusion is that poor readers do not have
adequate visual models of words in long-term memory.

625   Noelker, Robert W., and Schumsky, Donald A. "Memory for sequence,
        form, and position as related to the identification of reading re-
        tardates." <u>J Educ Psychol</u> 64(1): 22-25, February, 1973. (9
        References).
Three memory tasks were administered to groups of normal and retarded
readers. All were nine-year-olds. Nonsense shapes printed on cards were
used for sequencing and memory-for-form tests. Cards with black or white
circles printed on them were used in a memory-for-position test. The
child was shown the shapes. The cards were removed. The child was asked
to count to ten. Then the cards were shown again. All three tasks revealed differences between the normal and retarded groups. The position
task was the best test for discriminating between the groups.

626   Rugel, Robert P. "The factor structure of the WISC in two popula-
        tions of disabled readers." <u>J Learn Disabil</u> 7(9): 581-85,
        November, 1974. (16 References).
WISC subtest scores from two groups of disabled readers were subjected
to factor analysis. Disabled readers had lower scores on WISC Digit
Span and Coding subtests. Results of this study suggest that auditory
and visual short-term memory processes involved in the Digit Span and
Coding subtests are independent. The lowered scores on these subtests
found in disabled readers cannot be accounted for by a single underlying
memory deficit. Other results are discussed. It is suggested that findings provide support for regrouping the WISC into Spatial, Conceptual,
and Sequential categories.

627   ————. "WISC subtest scores of disabled readers: a review with
        respect to Bannatyne's recategorization." <u>J Learn Disabil</u> 7(1):
        48-55, January, 1974. (46 References).
WISC subtests were reclassified into three categories: Spatial, Conceptual, and Sequential according to a classification suggested by Bannatyne.
Disabled readers were ranked in these three areas, using data from twenty-
five studies which had reported WISC subtest scores. Disabled readers
did best in the Spatial category, poorer in Conceptual, and poorest in
Sequential. It is concluded that disabled readers' deficits are in short-
term memory processes and attention.

628   Senf, Gerald M. "Development of immediate memory for bisensory
        stimuli in normal children and children with learning disorders."
        <u>Dev Psychol</u> 1(6, Part 2): 1-28, November, 1969. (37 References).
In tests using three pairs of items for free and directed recall, normal
readers ordered items in audiovisual pairs. Disabled readers preferred
the auditory modality. In directed recall, retarded readers were distinctly inferior and did not improve with age. Retarded readers mis-
ordered items more frequently. It was postulated that retarded readers stored information in a manner that makes combining it for recall
more difficult. Misordering is thought to be closely connected with reading retardation.

629 Senf, Gerald M., and Freundl, Pamela C. "Memory and attention fac-
     tors in specific learning disabilities." J Learn Disabil 4(2):
     94-106, February, 1971. (22 References).
Children with reading problems have been found in previous research to
have particular difficulty in recalling three visual items followed by
three auditory items when the items were presented as three audiovisual
pairs. However, disabled readers have been found as able as normal readers to recall the three item-pairs in their actual order of presentation.
These results were duplicated in the present study using normal and disabled readers in Iowa from a much different sociocultural background than
those used in the prior research. The children in the previous study
were in California. Children in the Iowa study were boys eight and nine
years old. Mean IQ of the reading-disabled group was 90.6; for the
normal controls mean IQ was 107.9. Each child was shown a series of three
digits and simultaneously he heard a series of three digits. A given
digit occurred only once per trial. Two other forms of presentation were
used alternating visual and auditory digits. Under one condition, children were asked to recall the digits in the order of their presentation.
Under the other recall condition, children were asked to recall all three
visual items before recalling the three series of digits presented by
auditory means. Under the second condition of recall disabled readers
performed much more poorly than normal readers. Various theories are
offered as to why this is so, including the theory that dyslexics are
peculiarly distracted or dominated by auditory signals.

630 Spellman, Charles Richard. "Short-term memory processing of read-
     ing disabled and normal children." For a summary see: Diss Abstr
     Int 33A(12, Part 1): 6758, June, 1973.

631 Spring, Carl. "Encoding speed and memory span in dyslexic children."
     J Spec Educ 10(1): 35-40, Spring, 1976. (8 References).
Examines the theory that memory-span impairment in dyslexic children is
caused by slow speech-motor encoding. Subjects were two groups of boys
ranging in age from six to twelve years; one group dyslexic, the other
normal readers. Tasks included naming fifty randomly sequenced digits
typed in a single row as fast as possible; naming color patches; and
naming pictures of common objects as fast as possible. Dyslexic children
were slower at all three tasks than normal children, but the discrepancy
was larger for digits than for the concrete stimuli of colors and pictures. It is believed, however, that another source of variation in
addition to encoding speed contributed to the impaired memory spans of
dyslexic children. More study is recommended.

632 Spring, Carl, and Capps, Carolyn. "Encoding speed, rehearsal, and
     probed recall of dyslexic boys." J Educ Psychol 66(5): 780-86,
     October, 1974. (10 References).
Poor readers named visually presented nonverbal stimuli (color patches
and pictures) more slowly than normal readers in an experiment using boys
ages seven to thirteen with IQs above 90. The normal readers more often
used a "cumulative rehearsal strategy" during the probed-recall task than
did the poor readers. The probed-recall task consisted of cards each
containing one digit which were presented in random order one at a time,
and turned face down in front of the subject. The boy was then shown one
digit and asked to point to the card with the matching digit. It is
noted that these results apply only to poor readers of normal intelligence. Results are seen as indicating that dyslexics have short-term
memory storage as good as that of normals. Long-term storage in dyslexics
appears to be impaired.

633 Vellutino, Frank R.; Steger, Joseph A.; DeSetto, Louis; et al.
     "Immediate and delayed recognition of visual stimuli in poor and
     normal readers." J Exp Child Psychol 19(2): 223-32, April, 1975.
     (33 References).
Groups of children ages seven to fourteen who were in the second, fourth,
and sixth grades were shown nine sets of randomly arranged Hebrew letters,
each set on a separate card. One group was made up of good readers familiar with Hebrew. The other two groups were unfamiliar with Hebrew:
one group good readers, the other poor readers. The children were asked
to identify from a list the symbols seen immediately after presentation,
twenty-four hours later, and six months later. Good and poor readers
unfamiliar with Hebrew retained equivalent amounts at each of the three
times. Performance of both was poorer than that of those familiar with
Hebrew on immediate and twenty-four hour recall. None of the three groups
differed on the sixth-month recall. It is concluded that inadequate
visual memory is not a likely source of specific reading disability (dyslexia). Other explanations of the disorder are considered.

634 Wakefield, Mary W. "Sequential memory responses of normal and clinic
     readers." Elem Engl 50(6): 939-40, September, 1973. (3 Refer-
     ences).
Compares results obtained from a group of normal readers with results
from a group of reading-disabled children on a battery of tests requiring
sequential responses. Ages ranged from six to thirteen years. The
sequence-response tests included WISC Digit Span and Picture Arrangement,
and ITPA Digits and Visual Motor Sequencing. Part of the groups also
received other tests. Normal readers scored significantly higher on the
WISC and ITPA subtests. Difficulty with short-term memory tasks requiring sequencing is often observed in reading-disabled children. It is
suggested that classroom practice in this area be provided.

L. MINIMAL BRAIN DYSFUNCTION (MBD)

635 Charlton, Maurice H. "Minimal brain dysfunction and the hyperki-
     netic child." NY State J Med 72(16): 2058-60, August 15, 1972.
     (0 References).
Most cases of dyslexia today are thought to be the result of a degree of
brain damage usually sustained at birth. "Minimal brain dysfunction" is
the preferred term. Such cases of learning disabilities stem from primarily organic causes, and exclude children whose problems arise from
environmental problems, retardation, or from purely psychogenic causes.
A thorough history of pregnancy and birth and a scrupulously performed
neurologic examination are necessary. Psychological testing is important, but interpretation of results by the physician and the psychologist may vary. Specific dyslexia of a genetic type may be easily diagnosed on the basis of a positive family history. Drugs may be used
profitably to control the hyperkinesia. Placement of the child in special reading classes may be of great value. Knowledge of prognosis is
poor, since interest in the child with minimal cerebral dysfunction is
so recent.

636 Irwin, Theodore. "Helping children overcome learning disabilities."
     Todays Health 47(5): 20-25, 70, May, 1969. (0 References).
Explains minimal brain dysfunction (MBD). It is a catchall term used to
describe widely differing problems. It refers to a child's learning

handicap caused by a subtle, slight irregularity of brain function. MBD is largely an inference: the cerebral impairment is assumed. About 100 symptoms have been identified. The subtle effects of the learning disability do not affect general intellectual capacity. Symptoms include such conditions as over- or underactivity; poor coordination; poor attention span; poor memory; poor writing, reading, and spelling; and developmental lag. Dyslexia often accompanies MBD, but an MBD child is not necessarily dyslexic. Problems in diagnosis and treatment are discussed.

637 Lyle, J. G. "Performance of retarded readers on the memory-for-designs test." Percept Mot Skills 26(3, Part 1): 851-54, June, 1968. (3 References).
Retarded readers and controls, both of normal intelligence, were compared on the memory-for-designs test using two different scoring methods. Both methods discriminated significantly between the two groups. The result was the same when IQ difference was adjusted. It is suggested that minimal cerebral dysfunction may account for reading retardation.

638 Peters, John E. "Minimal brain dysfunctions in children." Am Fam Physician 10(1): 115-23, July, 1974. (0 References).
Discusses various types of MBD. Terms such as "dyslexia," "word blindness," and "specific learning disability" came into use because of the language problems of MBD. Slowness in acquiring use of sentences is an early sign of MBD. Slowness in detecting and using different vowel sounds and blends of sounds is also a subtle sign of the syndrome. Disturbances in directionality appear in MBD, and impair reading. Suggestions for diagnosis and management of MBD children are given.

639 Schain, Richard J. "Minimal brain dysfunction in children: a neurological viewpoint." Bull Los Angeles Neurol Soc 33(3): 145-55, July, 1968. (34 References).
Reviews the concept of minimal brain dysfunction (MBD) and outlines an approach to it from a neurological point of view. Neurologists have attempted to avoid use of the term as a diagnostic expression in children, but that has proved a losing battle. Problems of definition have hindered classification of the syndrome. A list of equivalents of the term "minimal brain dysfunction" is given, including "specific dyslexia," "strephosymbolia," "developmental dyslexia," and "congenital word blindness." Symptoms of MBD are listed and discussed. The "soft" neurological signs are described. An important responsibility of the neurologist is to rule out unrecognized neurological disorders in diagnosing MBD. Brain tumors and other conditions that may produce symptoms similar to those of MBD are described. Various possible causes are considered. Cause is difficult to determine because the condition is not clearly defined. Treatment is discussed. Early recognition is the single most important factor in developing a successful program of therapy.

640 Statten, Taylor. "Behavior patterns, reading disabilities, and EEG findings." Am J Psychiatry 110(3): 205-6, September, 1953. (0 References).
In a study of children referred to the psychiatric outpatient department of a children's hospital, it was found that children who had histories of marked reading disability and behavior problems often had histories of brain damage and showed visuomotor disturbances as measured by the Goodenough test. Wechsler performance IQs were frequently lower than the verbal IQs. EEG findings all showed a similar type of disturbance in the occipital region. The question is raised whether this research

has identified a group of children with minimal brain damage dating from
the early years of life.

641 Tarnopol, Lester. "Introduction to neurogenic learning disorders."
     In: Tarnopol, Lester, ed. Learning disorders in children; diag-
     nosis, medication, education. Boston, Massachusetts: Little,
     Brown, 1971. 1-22. (14 References).
This overview of the problem indicates that "dyslexia" is one of thirty-
seven terms used to designate the condition labeled "learning disability."
Children suffering from it are not mentally retarded, but nevertheless
have difficulty in learning to read and write. It is an international
problem, referred to in the late nineteenth century as "congenital word
blindness." Various treatments that have been tried with such children
are outlined. Current programs to help them are presented.

M. MOTIVATION

642 Alm, Richard S. "Causes of reluctance." In: Conference on Reading,
     University of Chicago, 1962. Proceedings: the underachiever in
     reading. Vol. 24. Compiled and edited by H. Alan Robinson.
     Chicago, Illinois: University of Chicago Press, 1962. 101-9.
     (0 References). (Supplementary Educational Monographs, No. 92).
Some reading disability cases are a reluctance on the part of the pupil
to read because he or she does not know how or what to read; has little
opportunity to read; or sees no prestige in reading. These are among
eight causes of reluctance to read listed. Teachers of reading should
be aware of these problems and work toward solutions.

643 Granzow, Kent Rayburn. "A comparative study of underachievers,
     normal achievers, and overachievers in reading." For a summary
     see: Diss Abstr 14(4): 631-32, 1954.

644 Hansburg, Henry G. "A reformulation of the problem of reading dis-
     ability." J Child Psychiatry 3(2): 137-48, August, 1956. (12
     References).
Reviews some of the prominent literature in the field, pointing out that
there is general agreement that each child must be studied individually
and that reading-disabled children show disturbance in motivation. Reading disability is viewed as a symptom, not an illness. Each afflicted
child faces forces and circumstances which together prevent normal learning to read. Low tolerance of frustration and fatigue are the result.
A diagnostic approach based on these ideas is presented. It includes
analysis of the child's specific handicaps; evaluation of the factors
disturbing motivation; and the use of trial lessons to assess frustration tolerance and memory difficulties.

645 Lord, Elizabeth Evans; Carmichael, Leonard; and Dearborn, Walter F.
     "Special disabilities in learning to read and write." Harvard
     Monographs in Education, Series I. Studies in educational psy-
     chology and educational measurement. Vol. 2(1, Whole No. 6).
     Edited by Walter F. Dearborn. Cambridge, Massachusetts: The
     Graduate School of Education, Harvard University, 1925. 76p.
     (36 References in two lists).
Contains separate articles on the study and training of a word-blind
child (Lord); a study of a case of mirror writing (Carmichael); and an

article on the causes of congenital word blindness (Dearborn); all following an introduction by Dearborn. The introduction describes the particular problems of left-handed children in learning to read and write. The
case study of the word-blind child concerns a twelve-year-old boy who was
initially considered feebleminded, having scored successively 94 and 88
on the Stanford-Binet. The case conformed to Hinshelwood's classification of congenital word blindness in severity and purity of symptoms.
Various methods of instruction used in an effort to teach the boy to recognize words as ideograms were used, including spelling the words aloud,
writing them repeatedly, and drawing the shape of the words. Phonetics
drills were given. Weakness in auditory memory span for letters and numbers was found. The psychological analysis of the reading program is
presented. Five years later the boy was reading very adequately and was
doing quite well in a trade school. The mirror-reading case was that of
a nine-year-old boy. He was markedly left-handed. He could write either
normally or in mirror script. The literature on mirror writing is briefly reviewed. No proof is found for a hereditary base for mirror writing.
The theory is offered that the left-handed child integrates out of his
random actions, as he begins first to scribble and then to write, a mirror script rather than a normal one.

Dearborn reviews the literature on the causes of congenital word blindness. It is concluded that defects in specific centers of the brain
where visual memories are said to be stored account for only a small number of cases of word blindness. Central and peripheral auditory deficiencies and muscular and kinesthetic deficiencies and peculiarities must
be considered. Some cases appear to arise out of pure habit, especially
those with neurotic or psychopathic behavioral backgrounds. These factors may only complicate the first-named deficiencies. The perceptual
and motor deficiencies usually observed in reading-disabled children are
not usually sufficient to keep the child from learning to read. They are
sufficient to require a little extra application and motivation. It is
suggested that in the child who is lacking in discipline in the home,
this extra motivation is likely to be lacking. This type of child may
gain the necessary motivation as he becomes older and sees other children surpass him. Some of the factors responsible for word blindness do
appear to be inheritable, but motivation may also be a cause. Various
teaching methods appear to be equally successful.

646 Mary Aloise, Sister. "Johnny can't read because..." Cathol Educ
     Rev 54(4): 256-61, April, 1956. (0 References).
Johnny cannot read because he does not really care to learn to read,
write, or speak correctly. He can get a job he considers adequate without these skills. He is not convinced that the effort to read is worthwhile because his parents and other adults do not seem to think it important. Children of immigrants who cannot speak English frequently do
better than native-born Americans because they are more highly motivated.
Johnny will learn to read when he realizes it is a problem he himself
must actively work to solve with the help of parents and teachers.

647 Sibley, Sally Annette. "Reading rate and accuracy of retarded
     readers as a function of fixed-ratio schedules of conditioned re-
     inforcement." For a summary see: Diss Abstr 27B(11): 4134-35,
     May, 1967.

648 Walters, Richard H., and Kosowski, Irene. "Symbolic learning and
     reading retardation." J Consult Psychol 27(1): 75-82, February,
     1963. (9 References).

In order to test whether reading ability is related to the number of
trials required to learn symbolic learning tasks and to reaction times
related to visual and auditory symbols (response latencies), groups of
good, poor, and average readers were selected from boys in grades six,
seven, and eight. No boy under eleven was included. IQ range was 90
to 126. A multiple-choice box with four compartments was used. Each
compartment was paired with a colored light. The task was to locate a
small object placed in one of the compartments. The color of the light
illuminated was the key to location. Response time and choice of compartment were recorded. An auditory task was given in which the correct
compartment was associated with one of four tones heard in earphones.
A reward was promised for good performance. Test data were seen as suggesting that retarded readers need more incentive in difficult learning
situations than normal readers. Unless highly motivated, retarded readers tended to be less attentive to stimuli. It is suggested that this
lack of attention might be the cause of difficulties in symbolic learning. Retarded readers who were promised rewards did significantly better
on the auditory task than unrewarded retarded readers. Rewards did not
significantly affect performance by average or advanced readers.

N. MULTIPLE FACTORS

649 Abrams, Jules C. "Learning disabilities: a complex phenomenon."
     Read Teach 23(4): 299-303, 367, January, 1970. (3 References).
Learning disabilities have many causes. Brain damage, inadequate cognitive stimulation in early life, and neurotic factors may all be causes.
Dyslexia has not had a known cause, but there is now some evidence that
it is a genetically determined constitutional disorder. This would seem
to rule out environmental factors. In treating learning disabilities a
working diagnosis must be established. Ongoing evaluation of the child
is necessary.

650 Abramson, Phillip. "Learning difficulties." Med J Aust 2(11):
     452, September 13, 1975. (0 References).
Letter to editor. It appears that difficulty in learning to read results
more often from a multifaceted general condition which makes reading-
disabled children unresponsive to regular classroom instruction than from
a specific disability. The writer's conclusion is based on his experience
at a center for the treatment of reading-disabled children.

651 Anderson, Irving H. "An interpretation of reversal errors in read-
     ing." Univ Mich Sch Educ Bull 30: 1-5, October, 1958. (0 Ref-
     erences).
Reversal of letters in writing has long been associated with reading disabilities. Children who make this error are able to copy words correctly.
The problem is not one of vision, but of recognition and recall. Some
possible causes of reversal errors are reviewed including faulty cerebral
dominance, maturational lag, and the whole-word teaching method. Copying
and tracing as an aid in establishing left-to-right directional sense is
recommended.

652 Austin, Mary C. "Personal characteristics that retard progress in
     reading." In: Conference on Reading, University of Chicago, 1950.
     Proceedings: keeping reading programs abreast of the times. Vol.
     12. Compiled and edited by William S. Gray. Chicago, Illinois:

University of Chicago Press, 1950. 112-17. (9 References). (Supplementary Educational Monographs, No. 72).
Pupils seriously retarded in reading may show anomalies in many areas.
No single isolated cause of reading disability exists. Among the personal
characteristics that may retard reading progress are physical handicaps;
lack of educational opportunity or teacher's analysis of the pupils'
errors; lack of intelligence; environmental factors; and emotional problems.

653 ————. "Problem readers." In: Conference on Reading, Univer-
        sity of Chicago, 1966. Proceedings: reading: seventy-five years
        of progress. Vol. 28. Compiled and edited by H. Alan Robinson.
        Chicago, Illinois: University of Chicago Press, 1966. 152-61.
        (0 References). (Supplementary Educational Monographs, No. 96).
Successful remedial teaching of problem readers is much aided if the cause
of the child's reading disability is correctly diagnosed first. Rapid
and valid diagnosis is possible. Causes of reading disability are numerous. They can be grouped broadly into two categories: intrinsic factors
such as personality and intelligence; and extrinsic factors stemming from
home, school, and community.

654 Bakker, Dirk J., and Satz, Paul, eds. Specific reading disability:
        advances in theory and method. Rotterdam, Netherlands: Rotterdam
        University Press, 1970. 166p. (Bibliography p. 147-59).
This book of readings in the area of reading disorders concentrates on
methods and theoretical aspects and excludes consideration of treatment.
Intense examination of the specific deficits of dyslexia is the result.
The book begins with a "Review and Outlook" summary. Laterality, handedness, cerebral dominance, and temporal perception are among the factors
considered in relation to dyslexia. Visual information processing in
learning-disabled children and selective attention are also considered.
The papers were originally presented at an international symposium on
reading disorders held in conjunction with the sixteenth International
Congress of Applied Psychology in Amsterdam, August, 1968.

655 Bannatyne, A. D. "The aetiology of dyslexia." Slow Learn Child
        13(1): 20-34, 1966. (27 References).
Presents a classification of causes and types of dyslexia. "Reading disabilities" is defined as the universe of study. One of several genera
is the grouping of disabilities called "dyslexia." Four types of dyslexia
are defined and described: (1) "Emotional dyslexia" is reading disability
in which the primary cause has been poor communicative relationship between mother and child during infancy when language was developing. (2)
"Neurological dysfunction dyslexia" describes those children with an abnormal qualitative difference in the brain which disturbs the child's
linguistic development. (3) "Genetic dyslexia," or "specific developmental dyslexia," includes those children who have not inherited the
specific ability to acquire language functions easily. As the tone-deaf
person may practice music for years and make little headway, so the
genetic dyslexic has no facility for making much of a success of language.
This is the most difficult and most controversial category of dyslexics.
More boys than girls are affected. As a group, these dyslexics do well
in spatial tests which do not demand arranging items in a sequence. Auditory sequencing, auditory discrimination, and associating auditory symbols
with sequences of visual symbols are problem areas. The training program
for the child must be in careful listening for auditory sequence of sounds
with reading and spelling taught with phonics. (4) "Social, cultural, and

educational dyslexia" includes children who will learn to read when their
environmental conditions become conducive to reading, if they are not too
maladjusted. It is emphasized that these four types of dyslexia are not
mutually exclusive.

656 Barbe, Walter B. "Reading problems and their causes." Instructor
      65(9): 8-9, May, 1956. (0 References).
Causes of reading difficulty are interrelated. The basic causes are lack
of readiness for school, poor physical condition, and poor or inadequate
instruction. The child's impatience to learn may also contribute to the
problem. Remedial programs are valuable, but should not replace a general
improvement in reading instruction.

657 Beckey, Ruth E. "Handicapped children: can your child read well?"
      Hygeia 20(6): 458-60, June, 1942. (0 References).
Children should not be urged to read until they are sufficiently mature
mentally and physically, usually at age six or seven. Reading disabilities have many causes. The cause must be found before the child can be
helped. Ways in which the parent can help develop the child's reading
skills and prevent difficulties are given.

658 Bell, Anne E., and Aftanas, M. S. "Some correlates of reading re-
      tardation." Percept Mot Skills 35(2): 659-67, October, 1972.
      (28 References).
Results on a battery of perceptual, visual-motor, and intellectual tests
administered to seventy-one boys and seventy-one girls just before they
entered first grade were compared with the children's first-grade reading
achievement. Reading retardation did not appear to be related to any
specific trait in isolation. Results did give some support to the presence of a large number of developmental deficiencies among the poor
readers. Good readers were found to have particular perceptual, visual-
motor, and, in some aspects, intellectual deficiencies. These deficiencies did not appear in constellations as they did in the poor readers.

659 Bennett, Chester Clarke. An inquiry into the genesis of poor read-
      ing. New York: Teachers College, Columbia University, 1938.
      139p. (Bibliography of 85 titles). (Contributions to Education,
      No. 755).
The purpose of this study was to inquire into the causes and beginnings
of reading retardation. Fifty second and third graders who were poor
readers were matched for sex, grade, chronological age, and mental age
with fifty good readers. The two groups were found to be very similar
in most respects, including home background, vision, personality, leisure
interests, and reading experience. Although caution is advised in accepting generalizations about the causes of poor reading, the data best support these inferences: (1) The eldest child in a family is more likely
to be a good reader. (2) Children with speech defects seem likely to
fail in reading. (3) Teachers regard poor readers as lacking in persistence and sustained attention. (4) Poor readers appear likely to be
less gregarious and physically vigorous than good readers. (5) Poor
readers tend to find school difficult and unpleasant. (6) Poor readers
tend to regard themselves as somewhat inadequate to face life's difficulties. (7) All reading instruction should be fitted to the individual
child's needs. Two areas of interest for further research are suggested:
the relationship of reading achievement to the child's personal and
social adjustments, and inquiry into the genetic approach.

660 Benton, A. L., and Sahs, A. L. "Aspects of developmental dyslexia."
     <u>J Iowa Med Soc</u> 58(4): 377-83, April, 1968. (12 References).
Lack of a reasonably precise definition of developmental dyslexia plagues
the field. Five distinctions are made. Dyslexia is not caused by: (1)
mental deficiency; (2) major visual defect; (3) auditory defect; (4) inadequate schooling; or (5) infantile neurosis. The child with developmental dyslexia is usually a boy free of the five limitations and with
normal motivation at the outset of schooling. This constitutes about the
same definition as that given by Hinshelwood, a pioneer in the field.
Possible mechanisms underlying dyslexia include mixed handedness and lack
of cerebral dominance; failure of integration between higher-level auditory and visual processes; and weakness in conceptualization, that is,
the capacity to perceive realistically lengths, times, heights, etc.
Dyslexics may be unable, for example, to name the months of the year.
Dyslexia may have hereditary causes.

661 Betts, Emmett Albert. "Factors in reading disabilities." <u>Education</u>
     72(9): 624-37, May, 1952. (14 References).
Reading disabilities may be classified in two major types: (1) "Language
deficiencies" describe the retarded reader whose mental age, hearing
comprehension level, or capacity is higher than his reading achievement
level. His achievement and capacity may not be equal. (2) "Experience
deficiencies" occur when the child fails in comprehension while still
able to "read," or parrot the words without understanding. Type of reading programs, symptoms of reading disability, and causes of reading failure are discussed. Questions to ask in attempting to define the type of
problem are suggested. No one cause is responsible for all reading disability cases.

662 ————. "Reading disability correlates." <u>Education</u> 56(1): 18-
     24, September, 1935. (0 References).
Presents a classification system of causes of reading disability which
summarizes factors that appear to contribute to reading disability. It
is concluded that reading difficulty is typically characterized by a
constellation of difficulties, and that no one remedial procedure is
likely to be the whole answer.

663 Botel, Morton. "Dyslexia: is there such a thing?" In: Inter-
     national Reading Association. <u>Conference proceedings: current
     issues in reading</u>. Vol. 13(Part 2). Edited by Nila Banton Smith.
     Newark, Delaware: International Reading Association, 1969. 357-
     71. (15 References).
Much ambiguity continues to exist about dyslexia; this has led to confusion among researchers attempting to explain their work. Two theories
about reading problems are given: (1) The theory of developmental dyslexia makes a case for a biological or anatomic defect underlying serious
reading disability. (2) The theory of developmental immaturity explains
reading disability as the result of a syndrome of deficits which interact to delay maturation. Without special educational techniques, individuals suffering from developmental immaturity become retarded in
reading. Continuing research is needed, especially studies aimed at
relating various causes of reading problems to the most desirable instructional method.

664 Bowers, Joan E. "Study of children with unusual difficulty in read-
     ing and arithmetic." <u>Can Educ Res Dig</u> 4(4): 273-78, December,
     1964. (0 References).

In a study of forty children making below average progress in first grade, school principals were asked how they accounted for the lack of progress. The study followed a school year in which an unusually large number of children failed to progress normally in reading, writing, and arithmetic. The reasons given most frequently were relative immaturity and unsatisfactory school conditions. Other reasons included emotional disturbance, unsatisfactory conditions in the home, and below-average intelligence.

665 Bryant, N. Dale. "Learning disabilities in reading." In: International Reading Association. Conference proceedings: reading as an intellectual activity. Vol. 8. Edited by J. Allen Figurel. New York: Scholastic Magazines, 1963. 142-46. (0 References).
Reading disability is not an entity. It is an extremely variable symptom. The term "disability" has meaning only when understood in terms of the material and teaching methods used. Confusion from missed or erroneous learning, emotional factors, or neurological dysfunctions may be involved. Teachers of children with reading disabilities should adhere closely to basic learning principles; use flexible methods that will not compound confusion; and establish a sound relationship with the child.

666 Carnvale, Elaine. The etiology of reading disability. Adelphia, Maryland: Community Projects Section, National Institute of Mental Health, 1961. 25 leaves. (Laboratory Paper, No. 2).

667 Cashell, G. T. Willoughby. "Congenital dyslexia." Proc R Soc Med 62(6): 562-63, June, 1969. (0 References).
Congenital dyslexia must be recognized as an organic entity. It has definite characteristics which are described. "Word blindness" is a bad term; the child is not blind but is unable to appreciate visual symbols. Features of congenital dyslexia include a familial incidence, mixed dominance, reversing letters or mirror writing, and bizarre spelling. Dyslexic children are often good at arithmetic. They cannot translate what they hear into written words and cannot translate the written word into speech. They have poor visual memories and become emotionally disturbed if the condition is not diagnosed. A general physical examination should be made. Often a diagnosis can be drawn from careful questioning of the child. The condition should be fully explained to the child and his parents. Two case histories are given.

668 Cole, Edwin M. "Specific reading disability; a problem in integration and adaptation." Am J Ophthalmol 34(2, Part 1): 226-32, February, 1951. (4 References).
The failure to learn to read by intelligent children is baffling to parents and teachers. The child with specific reading disability and his parents should have a careful explanation of the cause. Reading disabilities are not mysterious; explanations encourage the child. School curriculum should be adjusted to his needs. Physical, mental, and hereditary factors are discussed. Current reading instruction methods which use flash cards and emphasize visual memory are not suitable for the disabled reader.

669 Cornell, Ethel L. "Causes and treatment of extreme reading disabilities." Educ Method 9(1): 12-19, October, 1929. (0 References).
Failure to learn to read has far-reaching effects. It is extremely important that any helpful tactic be attempted. Causes of reading failure are: insufficient mental maturity; lack of drive on the child's part;

defects in vision and hearing; poor ability to discriminate among sounds; lack of ability to distinguish visual details; poor visual perceptual span; motor inadequacy; emotional instability; and various language handicaps. Types of confusions resulting from these causes and tests for them are described.

670 Dauzat, Sam V. "Good gosh! my child has dyslexia." Read Teach
    22(7): 630-33, April, 1969. (6 References).
"Dyslexia" is a general term so broad that it could be applied to 20 to 40 percent of the school population. It tells parents little; further explanation is necessary. Reading disability has many contributing causes, including eye problems, seizures, cultural deprivation, and possibly brain damage. Children of dull-normal intelligence will be disabled readers if instruction is not paced to meet their needs. Lack of readiness for reading and emotional factors may cause reading problems. No one method of treatment works for all disabled readers. Dyslexia should not be used as an excuse for all of a child's past and future shortcomings.

671 De Hirsch, Katrina. "Learning disabilities: an overview." Bull
    NY Acad Med 50(4): 459-79, April, 1974. (40 References).
No pure categories of learning disorders exist. Symptoms overlap. Four categories of disorders of learning are presented here with the stipulation that they are gross simplifications: (1) Psychogenic learning disorders include children who are psychotic, or who have impaired ego functions. They do not delight in learning new things; do not persevere; and do not take pride in achievement. (2) Neurogenic learning disorders include those with minimal brain dysfunction who show all degrees of irritability, hyperactivity, and perceptual deficits. (3) Children with disorders of printed or written language have no known neurological impairment, but display massive perceptual and visuomotor deficiencies. (4) Children whose learning disorders stem from environmental deprivation make up this category. Neurological deficits are prevalent. The children's environments may be changing. The emphasis is not on achievement.

672 De Hirsch, Katrina, and Jansky, Jeannette J. "The kindergarten
    protocols of high achievers, slow starters and failing readers."
    Am J Orthopsychiatry 37(2): 343-44, March, 1967. (0 References).
Three groups of kindergarten children were tested for behavioral control; motility patterning; fine manual coordination; human figure drawing; visuomotor organization; comprehension and use of oral language; and reading readiness. The findings were compared with achievement in reading, writing, and spelling at the end of second grade. The groups were designated high achievers, slow starters, and failing readers. A progression from diffuse, unstable, and primitive levels in the failing readers to highly integrated and sharply defined performances in the high achievers was observed. The slow starters were failing at the end of first grade but caught up a year later.

673 Devine, Thomas G. "Causes of reading difficulty." Clear House
    37(2): 83-86, October, 1962. (0 References).
Reading disabilities are blamed on many things: poor vision; congenital word blindness; crossed dominance; emotional blocks; and poor teaching methods. A basic cause appears to be too many teachers who are lacking in the training and personality traits necessary to teach the complex skill of reading.

674   Eames, Thomas H.   "Physical factors in reading."   Read Teach   15(6):
         427-32, May, 1962.   (12 References).
Early concepts of reading failure were neurological, since medicine could
offer only alexia as an explanation.   Faulty vision was blamed next.   But
partial blindness does not preclude learning to read.   Nearsightedness
(myopia) is rarely associated with poor reading.   Farsightedness, fusion
difficulties, astigmatism, and other eye problems may make reading un-
comfortable, but they are not generally associated with poor reading
ability.   Inadequate convergence may produce fatigue, causing the child
to lose his place and read poorly.   Whether crossed or confused lateral
dominance is a cause for poor reading is still uncertain; about half the
studies hold this view.   Certain brain areas are known to be related to
various kinds of memory.   Damage of the angular gyrus invariably results
in some reading disability.   "Brain damage" is a very broad term.   In
general, brain-damaged children are likely to give poor attention and be
distracted by nonessentials.   Motor activity, e.g., tracing, writing,
and drawing, helps keep these children from wandering from the task at
hand.   Endocrine gland defects sometimes interfere with reading.   Pituitary gland deficiencies, hypothyroid conditions, and uncontrolled diabetes may all disturb the ability to read in various ways.   There is no
single cause of reading failure.   Emotional, environmental, pedagogic,
and other factors all play variable roles in reading failure.

675   Early, Margaret J.   "What does research tell the classroom teacher
         about the basic causes of reading disability and retardation?"
         In: Jewett, Arno, ed.   Conference proceedings: improving reading
         in the junior high school.   Washington, D.C.:   United States Depart-
         ment of Health, Education, and Welfare, Office of Education, 1957.
         16-25.   (45 References).   (U.S. Office of Education Bulletin
         1957, No. 10).
Causes of reading failure are multiple: they can be physiological, mental, environmental, educational, and emotional.   Remediation, therefore,
must use many approaches.

676   Faigel, Harris C.   "The origins of primary dyslexia."   GP   36(3):
         124-32, September, 1967.   (0 References).
Eighty-eight dyslexic children (eleven girls and seventy-seven boys) were
divided into three groups: (1) In this group, forty-two boys were normal
physically and neurologically, but had family histories of specific language disability limited to males.   (2) Group two contained thirty-six
boys and girls with normal intelligence, vision, and hearing and no family
history of dyslexia.   They all showed abnormal neurologic signs.   (3)
This group of six boys and four girls did not fit either pattern.   Some
had family histories of dyslexia and abnormal physical examinations.
Others had neither.   Typical case histories are included.   It is concluded
that the cause is less important than diagnosis and treatment of each
child.   Remedial education should be combined with medication, limited-
goal psychotherapy, and perceptual training.   Reading problems can be
predicted and assistance given to susceptible preschool children.

677   Fargo, George.   "Framework for approaching reading problems."
         Claremont Coll Read Conf Yearb   29:   134-40, 1965.   (8 References).
Increasing emphasis on reading problems has produced three trends in approaching the subject: (1) Biological points of view see the child with
a reading problem as brain-damaged, hyperactive, perceptually handicapped,
etc.   (2) Ego approaches rely generally on Freudian psychoanalytic theory.
From this viewpoint the disabled reader is seen as emotionally disturbed

or socially maladjusted. Teachers need to remember that the educational process itself has therapeutic value. (3) Sociocultural approaches view the child as disadvantaged, disaffected, and economically, educationally, or culturally deprived.

678 Gates, Arthur Irving. "Causes of failure in reading." Psychol Bull
        33(9): 805, November, 1936. (0 References).
Presents an abstract of an address describing a remedial reading project in New York City manned by Works Progress Administration (WPA) workers. Twelve thousand pupils participated. Ten factors were studied for their relationship to reading disability. Greatest influence is found in low intelligence, unfortunate classroom conditions, and inadequate teaching material and techniques. Other factors are rated for importance.

679 ————. "Pedagogic concepts." Am J Orthopsychiatry 17: 391-93,
        July, 1947. (0 References).
Discusses probable causes and remedial needs for reading disability. Almost any deficiency can cause reading difficulty. Emotional problems; lack of motivation; faulty learning strategies used by the child in his attempts to read; poor teaching; and physical problems all may contribute to the disabled reader. The remedial program should be rich and broad. Often remedial instruction has been narrow and characterized by peculiar systems.

680 Gates, Arthur Irving, and Bond, Guy L. "Reading readiness: a study
        of factors determining success and failure in beginning reading."
        Teach Coll Rec 37(8): 679-85, May, 1936. (0 References).
As a result of studies done on first graders who began reading instruction soon after entering first grade, it is concluded that readiness for reading is something to develop rather than something for which to wait passively. Various tests were given at the beginning of school, in the middle, and at the end of the year. Mental age was found not to be a critical factor in reading achievement. Correlation with hearing loss was not high, but failing readers as a whole could not hear as well. There was no relation between reading ability and visual acuity. Hand and eye dominance, motor coordination, and speech defects were unrelated to reading progress. Home background did not seem to matter much, but previous instruction in reading at home or in kindergarten did make a difference. When teachers took failing readers "in hand" and adjusted instructions and material to their needs, they learned rapidly.

681 Gofman, H. "Etiologic factors in learning disorders of children."
        J Neurol Sci 2(3): 262-70, May-June, 1965. (5 References).
Learning difficulties in the lower grades, usually in reading, writing, and spelling, were until recently thought to stem largely from emotional causes. But many learning difficulties do not stem solely from emotional problems. The physician's differential diagnosis should consider specific reading disability, which may involve difficulty in dealing with visual, auditory, or kinesthetic symbols. The hyperkinetic syndrome which might be explained in terms of nervous system dysfunction should be considered. Learning difficulties may also be associated with dull-normal intelligence, hearing and visual problems, and various environmental and physical handicaps. The physician should use care in diagnosing one or several problems because a child's success or failure in school influences the remainder of his life.

682 Goldberg, Herman K. "What is reading?" Trans Pa Acad Ophthalmol
     Otolaryngol 19(1): 35-38, Spring, 1966. (0 References).
Early diagnosis and the diagnostic approach to reading problems are well
accepted now by teachers. Implementation of some other concepts lags
far behind. Some of these ideas are discussed. Perception is not the
same thing as vision. Seeing the letters on the Snellen chart is vision.
This initiates the learning process, but it has very little to do with
reading problems. Perception of what is seen leads to conception or
understanding. A "developmental reader" is a child learning to read
normally by whatever technique. A "corrective reader" is not dyslexic
but falls behind because of some deprivation. The "remedial reader" is
the child who reverses letters, writes backwards, and cannot seem to read
by any technique. The ophthalmologist should ascertain by IQ tests which
of these types of reader the patient is. He should have administered a
perception test by testing the child's ability to reproduce geometric
shapes. The whole child must be considered by an interdisciplinary approach that determines neurologic, educational, psychiatric, visual, and
auditory deficits. Educational and psychiatric factors which influence
reading are discussed. Three factors influence learning: psychological,
physiological, and anatomical.

683 Goldberg, Herman K., and Drash, Philip W. "The ophthalmologist and
     the disabled readers." In: Hellmuth, Jerome, ed. Learning dis-
     orders. Vol. 3. Seattle, Washington: Special Child Publications,
     1968. 453-79. (47 References).
Reading retardation is a complex problem requiring the cooperation of the
physician, parents, psychologist, and educator. Early identification is
important. The physician who knows little of reading problems may not
give other specialists the help they need. Some literature on causes of
reading problems is reviewed. Visual problems that can exist without eye
abnormalities are covered. Neurological, anatomical, psychiatric, and
educational aspects of reading retardation are discussed.

684 Goldberg, Herman K., and Schiffman, Gilbert R. Dyslexia: problems
     of reading disabilities. New York: Grune & Stratton, 1972. 194p.
     (Bibliography, 131 items).
Dr. Goldberg, an ophthalmologist, and Dr. Schiffman, an educator, attempt
to relate the discipline of medicine and education as they apply to children suffering from reading disabilities. Various educational and psychological tests which may be used in predicting reading disability are
discussed. Genetics, central nervous system problems, cerebral dominance,
vision, hearing, and perception problems, and the role of psychiatry in
treating reading disabilities are presented. Psychological evaluation,
education and remediation, and the chemistry of learning and drug therapy
are considered. The case history of a dyslexic boy is related and predictive studies are described.

685 Hardwick, Rose S. "Types of reading disability." Child Educ 8(8):
     423-27, April, 1932. (0 References).
Most cases of reading difficulty involve more than one cause. Lack of
motivation, short auditory memory span, emotional problems, and hearing
and eye problems are among the causes. Learning to read at all is something of a miracle. We should not grow callous at the wonder of it merely
because it is a common accomplishment.

686 Harris, Albert J. "Reading and other subject disabilities." In:
     Brower, Daniel, and Abt, Lawrence E., eds. Progress in clinical

psychology. Vol. 2. New York: Grune & Stratton, 1956. 146-60.
(155 References).
The causes of reading disabilities, diagnosis and testing, and remedial
reading instructional methods are among the topics covered in this article.
Physical causes, lateral dominance and reversals, and emotional difficulties are discussed as causes of reading disability. Findings of literature published in the area from 1952 to 1954 are included.

687 Hepworth, Thomas S. Dyslexia; the problem of reading retardation.
     Sydney, Australia: Angus and Robertson, 1971. 100p. (Bibliography
     p. 95-100).
Presents briefly various viewpoints on the causes of dyslexia. Some
methods for diagnosis and treatment are summarized. The viewpoint of
the book is that severe reading disability may stem from many different
causes, including social, cultural, and educational factors. These include: genetic factors, psychoanalytic factors arising from the subconscious, slow development, brain damage, and emotional problems. Some
case histories are included. The book is not presented as a manual for
treatment, but emphasizes the various viewpoints on the causes of reading problems.

688 Huessy, H. R. "Medical and epidemiological aspects of reading dis-
     ability." Claremont Coll Read Conf Yearb 37: 163-66, 1973. (7
     References).
This description of reading disability emphasizes that it is not necessary to know the cause in order to treat it. The cause need be understood only in order to prevent reading disability. Five points of epidemiological knowledge are listed including the observations that: (1) 15
percent of newborns are "difficult" babies; (2) 15 percent of all elementary-school children have some sort of learning or behavior problems; (3)
reading disability occurs in all written languages that require sound
blending; (4) the IQ distribution of affected children is normal; and (5)
the rate of reading disability grows higher as socioeconomic status grows
lower. Suggestions for prevention or remediation include one-to-one
activities; small group activities; providing the child with success experiences; and any sort of life enrichment.

689 Hume, G. "Disability in reading." Rep Annu Meet Br Assoc Adv Sci
     95th meeting: 372, 1927. (0 References).
Reading disability is a complex condition. Its many causes include emotional instability, inability to discriminate forms, and poor memory for
symbols.

690 Hunter, Edna J., and Johnson, Laverne C. "Developmental and psycho-
     logical differences between readers and nonreaders." J Learn
     Disabil 4(10): 572-77, December, 1971. (29 References).
Testing of matched groups of reading-disabled and normal male readers revealed that the normal readers had higher WISC verbal IQs. A number of
WISC subtest scores were higher. Mean Bender Gestalt scores were lower
for normal readers. Significant correlations were also found between
reading ability and attention and between reading ability and right-hand
dominance. Statistically significant differences between the reading-
disabled and control groups appeared in mixed laterality and reading
ability and in the earlier age at which normal readers crawled. It is
suggested that mixed laterality is not a cause of reading deficit but
that both are the result of some underlying deficit. The most apparent
characteristic of the disabled readers was their lack of attention, concentration, or immediate memory.

691   Ingram, T. T. S.   "Symposium on reading disability: 2. specific
        learning difficulties in childhood: a medical point of view." Br
        J Educ Psychol 41(1): 6-13, February, 1971. (45 References).
Reading and spelling difficulties are widespread and have many causes.
Some are: absence from school; parental indifference; relatively low
intelligence; family history of reading problems; and frank brain damage.
It is naive to assume that reading and spelling difficulties are caused
by a single disease entity. Specific dyslexia is not a disease entity,
but a syndrome resulting from many different factors. The precise causes
of the individual child's reading and spelling problems should be explored thoroughly before remedial measures are undertaken.

692   Jampolsky, Arthur. "The problem of the poor reader." Calif Med
        74(4): 230-32, April, 1951. (0 References).
A number of the characteristics of the complex problem of the poor reader
are presented, together with suggestions for treatment and prophylactic
measures. Physical impediments, emotional distress, or teaching methods
may be involved. The child with specific reading disability shows confusion in recognizing language symbols. The disability is usually associated with ambidexterity, clumsiness, persistence of tendencies to reverse letters and symbols, normal intelligence, and poor visual recall of
words. Teaching methods emphasizing visual associations can cause specific reading disability in children having deficiencies in that area.

693   Johnson, Doris J., and Myklebust, Helmer R. "Dyslexia in childhood."
        In: Hellmuth, Jerome, ed. Learning disorders. Vol. 1. Seattle,
        Washington: Bernie Straub and Jerome Hellmuth, 1965. 259-92.
        (33 References).
This presentation relates an analysis of sixty dyslexic children studied
in an effort to find the nature of the problem and how to treat it. Dyslexia is defined as a "dysfunction in the brain" and as a "basic language
and learning disability." Multiple causes seem probable. Remedial education should center on the child and his problem, not on one method of
treatment. Most dyslexics are well motivated. They want to learn to
read and most dyslexics do learn to read.

694   Johnson, Marjorie Seddon. "Factors related to disability in read-
        ing." J Exp Educ 26(1): 1-26, September, 1957. (179 References).
In this review of some of the studies related to reading failure in children of normal intelligence, it is observed that no single cause can
generally be identified. A group of factors is usually to blame. The
possibility for correction is good if the causes are identified and the
remedial program adjusted to the causes.

695   Kasdon, Lawrence M. "Causes of reading difficulties." In: Parents
        and reading. Compiled and edited by Carl B. Smith. Newark,
        Delaware: International Reading Association, 1971. 23-36. (31
        References). (Perspectives in Reading, No. 14).
Reviews some of the literature concerning etiologies of reading problems.
The many causes of reading difficulty interact with each other making it
extremely difficult to isolate causes and to separate cause from effect.
It is pointed out that researchers from many disciplines have given varying and often conflicting explanations of the sources of reading difficulties. The problem is confounded by the extreme confusion in terminology as experts from many specialities write about reading. A child
is called "dyslexic," or "perceptually handicapped," or "minimally brain-
damaged," or "suffering from a language disorder," etc., depending on

the term the child's school uses. We must be careful about pinning
labels to children. Such labels may become self-fulfilling prophecies.
Carefully designed longitudinal studies are needed before we can speak
with certainty about causes of reading failure. Physical, intellectual,
emotional, and educational factors all enter the picture.

696 Ketchum, E. Gillet. "Reading disorders." <u>Pediatr Clin North Am:</u>
     <u>Symposium on handicaps and their prevention.</u> 697-700, August,
     1957. (0 References).
Six times more boys than girls suffer from reading disorders. Reading
disorders are not new. Factors such as good general health and intelligence, adequate social and environmental background, adequate vision, and
personality adjustment must be present in addition to skilled teaching
before children can learn to read. Many causes for reading disorders
exist, and together constitute a syndrome. Personality problems and emotional difficulties, rather than secondary reactions, should be viewed
as primary causes of reading failure.

697 Klein, Joseph V. "Speech and reading problems in childhood." <u>Can</u>
     <u>J Public Health</u> 55(7): 303-9, July, 1964. (4 References).
Reading disability is one of several disorders of communication considered. The reasons for and effects of articulation defects and delayed
speech development are evaluated. Stammering, hearing loss, and cleft
palate are discussed. Reasons given and discussed for reading disorders
include delayed maturation, perceptual deficits of neurological origin,
psychological factors, and "specific language disorder" which appears in
the absence of these other factors. "Specific dyslexia" is defined as
a reading disability of neurological origin. Childhood aphasia is also
considered.

698 Kline, Carl L., and Lee, Norma. "A transcultural study of dyslexia:
     analysis of reading disabilities in 425 Chinese children simulta-
     neously learning to read and write in English and Chinese." <u>Am J</u>
     <u>Orthopsychiatry</u> 40(2): 313-14, March, 1970. (0 References).
Studies the causes of reading disability. The 425 Chinese children were
in grades one, two, and three of a public school in Vancouver, British
Columbia, which was predominantly Chinese. They were of similar sociocultural background. All also attended Chinese language school for two
hours each day. A battery of tests revealed that 9 percent of the children were having trouble learning to read English and 13 percent were
having trouble with Chinese. The percent of children having trouble with
both languages was 4.4. Disability appears to be related to the difficulty of the language and to the patterns of association needed for learning it. Factors found not to be related to learning to read were sociocultural factors, visual perception, body image, emotional problems, and
intelligence above a base line. Teaching method appears basically important to learning to read. Functional neurological factors may play a
role in some cases.

699 Krippner, Stanley. "Etiological factors in reading disability of
     the academically talented in comparison to pupils of average and
     slow-learning ability." <u>J Educ Res</u> 61(6): 275-79, February,
     1968. (19 References).
Children with reading disabilities were divided into three groups: high,
average, and low intelligence as derived from their WISC scores. Diagnostic tests were given to determine the cause of reading problems.
Etiological factors were divided into functional and organic categories.

Organic factors included poor vision, hearing, or speech; directional
confusions; neurological organization problems; and endocrine abnormalities. Functional factors included social immaturity; poor educational
and cultural experiences; and neurotic or psychotic tendencies. The
reading disabilities of the high-intelligence group were found to be more
often functional rather than organic in origin than were the difficulties
of the other two groups.

700 Leland, Bernice. "Case study approach to difficulty in reading."
     Child Educ 13(8): 374-78, April, 1937. (0 References).
As a result of the study of many reading disability cases, four points
of emphasis have emerged: (1) Nonconforming behavior and delinquency
are more intimately related to reading disability than has been recognized. (2) Reading disability has many causes. (3) No one cure works
in all cases. (4) It is very important to detect reading disability
cases early since they are problems of degree as well as of kind. Some
case histories are given.

701 McCallister, James M. "Character and causes of retardation in read-
     ing among pupils of the seventh and eighth grades." Elem Sch J
     31(1): 35-43, September, 1930. (0 References).
Reports on a survey of seventh- and eighth-grade pupils who were seriously
retarded in reading. The reading problems of pupils in this age group
can be best handled by individual study and diagnosis. Individually
planned remedial reading instruction is best. A battery of tests was used
to uncover all types of reading deficiencies in the group, including comprehension, interpretation, rate of reading, and deficient fundamental
reading habits. They appeared chiefly as retarded development.

702 MacMillan, D. P. "Important factors in reading disabilities." J
     Am Inst Homeopath 33(3): 137-43, March, 1940. (0 References).
Points out the great importance of reading in our society, the interest
in reading and reading disabilities that has been generated, and the
array of factors considered responsible for reading difficulties. It has
seemed natural for investigators to attack one factor at a time of this
large problem. But confusion and much controversy have resulted when
the findings of the various studies have conflicted. Physical, mental,
and social aspects have been studied with much earnestness. Reading is
a complex of activities; normally represents the functioning of the whole
person in a definite direction; and is an acquired social art facilitated
by teaching. It has seemed natural, however, for investigators to point
out indicators of the part of the process they analyzed in the belief
that such information would provide useful procedures in correcting reading disabilities. The study of reading handicaps in any individual should
measure the reader's capabilities as they relate to his person as a whole,
the situation as a whole, and to his learning in every aspect. The first
stages of a child's instruction are the most important in mastering reading. The child should be measured in every aspect: biologic and mental
endowment, environment, complete life history, and his ways of learning.
Two lines of approach in investigations of reading disability are broadly
discernible: emphasis on fitness or condition of the reader, and methods
of learning and teaching.

703 McMurray, J. G. "Some correlates of reading difficulty in satis-
     factory and disabled readers: a preliminary study in grade 3."
     Ont J Educ Res 5(2): 149-57, 1963. (11 Bibliographic Footnotes).

Presents a list of sensory, intellectual, emotional, and environmental
factors believed to be associated with reading failure and examines the
incidence and nature of reading errors considered by teachers to be most
likely to occur in disabled readers in grade three. Two checklists were
distributed to third-grade teachers. The first contained thirty-five
items which have been found by other investigators to be significantly
associated with reading performance. It was completed by the teachers
on all their pupils. The second checklist contained twenty-nine items
considered representative of the kinds of reading errors made by third-
graders. This was completed by the teachers on those pupils who were
significantly poor readers in terms of expected academic performance.
Age range of the children was seven to eleven years. From a total of
742 children, 102 were considered by their teachers to be in the latter
group. Twenty percent of these 102 pupils had IQ scores below 89. The
complete checklists are reproduced. From the first checklist eight factors were isolated which differentiated good readers from poor ones.
They were grade repetition, lack of energy, short attention span, the
child who is compared unfavorably with others, does not assume responsibility, daydreams more than average, is seldom relaxed, and seldom completes assignments. The second checklist listed reading speed, omission
of words or letters, auditory spelling skills, confusion of initial letters, incorrect letter sequence, and others. The teachers' opinion of
why the pupils could not read listed, in order: lack of acceptable
phonic and other word-attack skills most frequently followed by lack of
effort, immaturity, home problems, poor class adjustment, and lack of confidence.

704 Malmquist, Eve. Factors related to reading disabilities in the first
     grade of the elementary school. Stockholm, Sweden: Almqvist and
     Wiksell, 1958. 428p. (Bibliography p. 414-28). (Stockholm
     Studies in Educational Psychology 2).
Investigates the relationship between intelligence, home background, and
personality traits of good, medium, and poor first-grade readers. Historically, congenital word blindness had been considered a medical problem caused by a cerebral defect. Environmental conditions were known to
influence reading achievement, but such factors were considered secondary
or nonspecific. The viewpoint of this book is that, while not impossible,
a diagnosis of congenital word blindness rests on a very insecure basis.
Reading disabilities should be regarded, rather, from the viewpoint of
educational psychology, only as phenomena which fall within the framework
of normal variation. A great number of factors can influence human personality development and affect reading progress: some were selected
for study.

No standardized tests of reading, spelling, visual perception, or rating
scales for assessing personality traits were available for this age group
in Sweden. Tests were constructed and standardized in investigations
carried out in Malmö between 1946 and 1949. The main investigations were
done in Kristianstad in 1951 and in Linköping in 1952, using 399 first-
grade children. Further standardization of the tests was done in 1954.
A total of 2,439 children took group tests and 241 first graders were
given individual tests. In addition to oral and silent reading tests and
tests of visual perception, the children were rated on self-confidence,
social attitudes (making contact with others), persistence, ability to
concentrate, intelligence, dominance-submissiveness, and emotional stability. Birth and developmental histories were obtained. Home background
factors included parents' taxable income, parents' educational level,

number of books in the home, size of house, number of children and parents' social status.

A wide range of both intelligence and mental age was found. The distribution of intelligence for poor readers in the sample did not correspond to distribution of intelligence in the general population. The mean IQ of poor readers was 96.62; for good readers 107.9, a significant difference. Parents' educational and social level for good readers was higher than for poor readers and the relation between number of books in the home and reading level was highly significant statistically. The relationship between birth injuries and poor reading achievement was not verified, but more poor readers were born prematurely and weighed less at birth. Boys outnumbered girls among poor readers. The analysis of oral reading errors showed no types of errors especially characteristic of poor readers. Children with "special reading disabilities" deviated markedly from the total population investigated in several variables other than reading ability. It is suggested that reading disabilities at first-grade level are never isolated defects.

The most important conclusion is that the attempt to find a single factor which will entirely explain the occurrence of reading errors is almost always a vain undertaking. Usually several factors, often closely interrelated, appear in constellation. There appears to be an interplay between the development of the child's reading ability and his general physical, intellectual, emotional, and social development. It is pointed out that the study was made using a normal school population rather than one drawn from clinics or special classes. The study indicates relationships between factors and reading disabilities rather than giving information as to causes of the occurrence of reading disabilities in first grade. Suggestions for further research are made.

705 Nicholls, John V. V. "Congenital dyslexia: a problem in etiology."
     Can Med Assoc J 82(11): 575-79, March 12, 1960. (30 References).
Discusses ocular, emotional, neurological, and educational factors contributing to dyslexia. About three out of four children learn to read with ease, probably by any teaching method. Of those who do not, three out of four will learn to read well with modified teaching methods if they are given enough time and protected from emotional stress. Eye defects may contribute to, but do not cause reading failure. Early recognition is important. Varied and flexible educational methods are necessary.

706 O'Sullivan, Mary Ann, and Pryles, Charles V. "Reading disability
     in children." J Pediatr 60(3): 369-75, March, 1962. (22 References).
Lists and describes causes of reading disability including emotional or developmental lag, teaching method, brain lesions, hearing and vision problems, disturbances in cerebral dominance, and emotional causes based on disorders in ego function. The typical child with reading disability is described as male, anxious, hyperactive, a daydreamer, without pre-primary training, and from parents who are themselves disinterested or disturbed. Suggestions are made for diagnosis and treatment.

707 "Other problems may cause reading troubles." Sci News Lett 70(20):
     313, November 17, 1956. (0 References).
Lists four main causes for reading failure: (1) brain damage from injury or disease; (2) inability to learn that certain marks on paper (symbols) represent given ideas; (3) slow development of the nervous

system (developmental lag); and (4) lack of motivation or poor instruction. Most children have more than one problem; these other problems may cause reading failure. The general goal of research in clinical psychology should be to improve diagnostic techniques and prevent reading difficulties at age seven or eight.

708   Park, George E.   "Clinical approach to reading difficulties in
      normally intelligent children."   J Am Inst Homeopath   56(3-4):
      219-27, March-April, 1963. (5 References).
Defines functional dyslexia as a group of symptoms characterized by an inability to read properly even though the person is of normal intelligence. Atypical factors associated with this type of dyslexia are functional, preventable, and correctable in most cases. This differentiates functional dyslexia from other similar conditions caused by organic lesions or lack of intelligence. Reading is a complex achievement. Attention should be paid to every symptom evident; the collaboration of several disciplines is helpful. It is important that the various disciplines find and use terminology intelligible to the others. Researchers need to find the causes of abberations in the learning process (causality). To do this, they musst understand the concept of the relationship between the individual and his internal balance (homeostasis). Functional dyslexia and its causes are discussed from this viewpoint. Reciprocal responses, free will, moral and social standards, physical (clinical) factors, relationships with other persons, and family climate are among factors considered.

709   —————.   "Medical aspects of reading failures in intelligent chil-
      dren."   Arch Pediatr   76(10): 401-9, October, 1959. (0 References).
Dyslexia cannot be considered as a simple reading disability. Its ramifications extend into the physical, psychological, and social fields. In about 85 percent of cases the abnormal factors associated with dyslexia are functional and correctable. It is distinguished in this way from alexia which is caused by brain injury or lack of intelligence. Medical factors are examined including endocrine function, reaction to stimuli, and variations in the EEGs, bone maturation, and blood picture of dyslexics. Emotional factors, auditory, speech, and visual functions are discussed.

710   —————.   "Medical aspects of reading failures in intelligent chil-
      dren."   Sight Sav Rev   29(4): 213-18, Winter, 1959. (0 References).
Factors associated with dyslexia include various developmental considerations including personality and emotional maturation, hereditary traits, and the child's environment.

711   Park, George E., and Linden, James D.   "The etiology of reading
      disabilities: an historical perspective."   J Learn Disabil   1(5):
      318-30, May, 1968. (0 References).
Considers the multiple causes of dyslexia under the three major theoretical views of reading disability: neurological, emotional and social, and functional. Included under functional considerations are visual and speech problems, memory problems, and problems in learning to form associations between previous experience and printed symbols. It is concluded that the many causes of reading disorders support speculation that a multidisciplinary approach, geared to the individual, seems most feasible. Suggestions for treatment are given.

712 Pitman, Sir James. "Let's clear the clutter." Educ Horizons 51(1):
      13-19, Fall, 1972. (6 References).
It is necessary to want change very badly before anything can be done in
a new way. In teaching reading, writing, and language we need to think
anew and burn the old books in which a false mythology of reading failure
has been put forward. Nine factors usually associated with reading failure or success are exploded as myths. Because a correlation can be shown
between reading failure and some factor does not necessarily mean the two
are causally related. The spurious factors falsely given in the past as
responsible for reading failure are: (1) IQ is the determining factor
in the child's ability to learn to read; (2) socioeconomic level determines how well a child reads; (3) culture of the home; (4) the example
of parents reading silently to themselves; (5) emotional stability; (6)
deprivation of the child; (7) physical amenities of the home; (8) maturity
of the learner; and (9) a teacher is absolutely essential and the best
teachers obtain success in teaching all children to read. None of these
factors is necessarily related to reading success. The reasons are explained. The author, the inventor of the Initial Teaching Alphabet (ITA),
recommends changes in English spelling.

713 Quinn, Lester H. "Reading problems: their causes and effects."
      Tex State J Med 37(6): 428-433, October, 1941. (18 References).
Many causes for reading difficulty exist. Several causes may be present
in one case. Orton's theory of lack of cerebral dominance, speech defects, poor muscular coordination in the eyes, environmental and emotional
problems, poor teaching methods, and attempts to teach reading before the
child is ready to learn are among the causes of reading disability. Some
literature regarding the relation of vision to reading is reviewed and
case histories are included. Reading difficulties produce tremendous
emotional effects in the child. The results of reading failure are so
serious that each case should be thoroughly reviewed.

714 Ravenette, Arthur Thomas. Dimensions of reading difficulties.
      Oxford, New York: Pergamon Press, 1968. 102p. (Bibliography).
      (The Commonwealth and International Library. Problems and Progress
      in Development).
The viewpoint of this book is that the child may be observed in a number
of different dimensions. Rather than looking for causes of reading disability which are fixed and may become ends in themselves, we should look
for dimensions which are provisional. Dimensions so viewed open up areas
for exploration and suggest courses of action. Learning to read involves
the intersection of many dimensions: the child, his family, the culture
pattern, the school, the child's teacher and peers, the subject matter
to be learned, and the resources available to the child for learning.
Dyslexia is defined as "the neurological dimension." Some literature on
the subject is reviewed. Reading ability, or disability, probably must
be viewed in relation to age and intelligence level.

715 "Reading failure. New York City Division of Instructional Research."
      Educ Dig 8(3): 12-14, November, 1942. (0 References).
The search for the causes of reading failure has been long and painstaking. Physical origins were studied early and extensively. The early
theory of "word blindness" caused by lack of development in the brain has
long been rejected. More recently emphasis is being placed on teaching
methods and materials. Currently the most widely accepted view is that
a constellation of causes produces reading failure. It is necessary to
find out which factors carry the most weight. Certain factors seem to
recur to form causal patterns.

716 Robinson, Helen Mansfield. "Causes of reading failure." <u>Education</u>
     67(7): 422-26, March, 1947. (0 References).
It is so important and so difficult to identify cause and effect in reading failure. More refined research techniques are urgently needed. Attempts at identifying and evaluating causes of severe reading retardation
are described in which consideration of the child as a whole was attempted. The results substantiate earlier findings that causes appear in constellations rather than separately. Included among causes are maladjusted homes; emotional maladjustments; visual difficulties including binocular incoordinations; inappropriate teaching methods; alexia or some
structural or functional deficiency of the brain; hypothyroidism; and
hearing loss. Dominance tests were indeterminant. A follow-up study
aimed at discovering the abilities and disabilities of children first
entering school is planned.

717 ———. "Special difficulties in word perception as revealed in
     clinical studies." In: Conference on Reading, University of
     Chicago, 1948. <u>Proceedings: basic instruction in reading in ele-
     mentary and high schools</u>. Vol. 10. Compiled and edited by William
     S. Gray. Chicago, Illinois: University of Chicago Press, 1948.
     122-26. (0 References). (Supplementary Educational Monographs,
     No. 65).
Six general types of difficulties in word perception have been identified
at the University of Chicago Reading Clinics. They include: (1) lack
of visual efficiency and faulty visual perception; (2) faulty auditory
perception; (3) pupils who do not apply themselves; (4) pupils with meager
language backgrounds; (5) associative learning disability (inability to
remember words learned from one day to the next); and (6) pupils who
mature more slowly than average.

718 ———. "Types of deficient readers and methods of treatment."
     In: Conference on Reading, University of Chicago, 1939. <u>Proceed-
     ings: recent trends in reading</u>. Vol. 1. Compiled and edited by
     William S. Gray. Chicago, Illinois: University of Chicago, 1939.
     159-69. (0 References).
While reading failure usually appears to have a constellation of causes,
one can usually be selected as the most predominant cause. Children
should be grouped according to the cause of their reading disability in
order to achieve maximum progress in remedial programs.

719 ———. "Why pupils fail in reading." In: Hunnicutt, Clarence
     William, and Iverson, William J., eds. <u>Research in the three R's</u>.
     New York: Harper, 1958. 248-54. (0 References).
No single cause for reading failure has been isolated. In this study,
thirty retarded readers ages six to fifteen years and with an IQ range
of 85 to 137 were individually examined by twelve specialists from medicine, psychology, and education. An intensive remedial program was
undertaken with twenty-two of the children to determine the importance
of each of many possible causes for reading failure. Maladjusted homes
or poor family relationships were found in 54.5 percent of the cases.
Visual anomalies were found in 73 percent. Emotional problems were present in 41 percent, inadequate teaching methods in 18 percent, and alexia
or some other neurological difficulty in 18 percent. Children who were
the most seriously retarded in reading exhibited the most anomalies.
Reading difficulty may be seen as part of general deviation from normal.
Or, this observation may be interpreted as the hampering action of many
defects that produce reading retardation. The study concludes in favor

of the first interpretation. Some of the factors, for example visual difficulties, which appeared to contribute to reading failure, may not do so. Certain types of anomalies were found to operate as causes more often than others.

720 ————. Why pupils fail in reading: a study of causes and remedial treatment. Chicago, Illinois: University of Chicago Press, 1946. 257p. (Bibliography).
This comprehensive diagnostic study reports the case histories of thirty retarded readers ranging in age from six years, nine months, to fifteen years, three months. Each was examined by a team of specialists including a psychiatrist, pediatrician, neurologist, ophthalmologist, speech correction specialist, otolaryngologist, endocrinologist, and social worker. Results were assembled and discussed in group conference. The greatest single cause for reading failure was diagnosed as "maladjusted home environments or poor intrafamily relationships," a major contributing factor in 54.5 percent of the cases. Visual problems were present in 50 percent of the cases, and emotional difficulties in 32 percent. Other factors in order of frequency of occurrence included endocrine, neurological, general physical, auditory, and school factors. A program of treatment was developed and carried out. The children most seriously retarded in reading deviated from normal expectancies in the largest number of areas, including some anomalies that appeared to be unrelated to reading.

721 Rosebrook, Wilda. "Factors in reading deficiency." Public Health Nurs 29(1): 29-31, January, 1937. (9 References).
Reading deficiency is an acute problem in education. Many theories have been formed and exploded. In individual cases these factors should be checked as contributing causes: intellectual ability, school history, home conditions, emotional factors, and physical factors. The school nurse should develop a sympathetic attitude toward reading problems; familiarize herself in a general way with administrative and educational aspects of the reading situation in her own school; and become a specialist in the study of physical factors and their relation to reading deficiency. The nurse makes her biggest contribution as a skilled go-between who has the vocabulary to speak to parents, teachers, doctors, and the child himself about the problem of reading disability.

722 Roswell, Florence. "Observations on causation and treatment of learning disabilities." Am J Orthopsychiatry 24(4): 784-88, October, 1954. (3 References).
Significant numbers of reading disability cases show evidence of weakness in visual-motor coordination, visual and auditory discrimination, and ability to blend sounds. Mixed cerebral dominance is common. Slow maturation or constitutional factors may also cause reading retardation. Prodding a child to read before he is ready may produce frustration, resistance, and other negative emotional reactions. The wide variety of IQ levels and reading abilities found in most classrooms complicates matters for even experienced teachers as well as for the child reading below grade expectancy. A combination of psychotherapy and remedial teaching is probably ideal but is not always feasible. Remedial teaching carried out by a qualified tutor with a psychological orientation can be therapeutically effective. The goal of any psychotherapy is to increase understanding and acceptance of himself by the pupil. Form of treatment should depend on the individual case.

723 Rucker, Helen Fouch. "Why can't you read, Johnny?" Instructor
        83(7): 14, March, 1974. (0 References).
The child does not know why he cannot read. But he gives his teacher all
the clues she needs to make a diagnosis by the things he tells her.
Quotations from the children are given which reflect neglect, hunger,
parental indifference, lack of motivation, poor self-concept, poor relationships with others, fear, teacher apathy, and other causes for reading
failure.

724 Rutherford, William L. "What is your DQ (dyslexia quotient)?" Read
        Teach 25(3): 262-66, December, 1971. (18 References).
Presents a questionnaire of seven questions requiring a total of seventeen responses concerning victims of dyslexia and some of its characteristic effects. The reader is asked to test his knowledge of dyslexia in
the light of current research findings as given in the test.

725 Schubert, Delwyn G. The doctor eyes the poor reader. Springfield,
        Illinois: Thomas, 1957. 101p. (Bibliography).
Discusses causes of reading disability: visual, hearing, and speech defects; physical, sexual, or neurological problems; lack of cerebral dominance; emotional disturbances; intelligence; and educational or home factors. The doctor's role in recognizing reading disability and diagnosing
the cause is analyzed. Material on the kinds of help available to retarded readers is included, as well as a section on how the doctor can
improve his own reading skills.

726 Shedd, Charles L. "Ptolemy rides again or dyslexia doesn't exist?"
        Ala J Med Sci 5(4): 481-503, October, 1968. (47 References).
Compares the lack of acceptance of objective evidence for dyslexia to
the conflict between the Church and Galileo when Galileo was condemned
for teaching that the earth revolved around the sun. In similar fashion
the fallacy of employing simple sovereign principles to understand complex phenomena plagues the understanding of dyslexia. Many diseases
have no unique identifying signs, but display a unique pattern of signs
that appear in contiguity. Dyslexia is one of these. Discrepancies in
perceptual-motor skills development and characteristics of social behavior in the dyslexic are discussed.

727 Shimota, Helen E. "Reading skills in emotionally disturbed, insti-
        tutionalized adolescents." J Educ Res 58(3): 106-11, November,
        1964. (20 References).
In this study of emotionally disturbed and hospitalized Caucasians ages
thirteen to fifteen years, neither brain damage, mixed dominance, emotional problems, nor physical handicaps proved to be important causes of
reading disability. Boys were more likely to be disabled readers than
girls. A statistically reliable discrepancy between performance and
verbal IQ appeared in disabled readers. Far more of the adequate readers
had histories of prenatal or birth problems than did the disabled readers.

728 Silver, Archie A.; Hagin, Rosa; Lubin, Harold. "Dyslexia unmasked:
        a multidisciplinary study of the causes of reading failure." Am
        J Orthopsychiatry 39(2): 271-72, March, 1969. (0 References).
The many causes of reading failure and the frequency of the causes are
presented in this paper. Of a group of fifty first and second graders
in New York City public schools referred by their teachers because of
dyslexia (difficulty in learning to read), 37 percent were diagnosed
after extensive investigation as suffering from specific (developmental)

reading disability. Another 37 percent had neurological defects in addition to perceptual problems. Thirteen percent showed a general slowness in maturation and of these 40 percent had birth histories of prematurity. Schizophrenia was the primary diagnosis in 8 percent of all the cases.

729   Spache, George D.   "Factors which produce defective reading." In: Conference on Reading, University of Chicago, 1953. Proceedings: corrective reading in classroom and clinic. Vol. 15. Compiled and edited by Helen M. Robinson. Chicago, Illinois: University of Chicago Press, 1953. 49-57. (19 References). (Supplementary Educational Monographs, No. 79).
Defective reading may be caused by physical factors, like poor vision. Laterality, eye-hand dominance, cerebral dominance, and reversals are no longer generally regarded as causes of reading disability. Poor motor coordination is no longer used to explain poor reading. Low intelligence is less likely to be blamed than formerly. Wide divergence of opinion still exists as to the role of emotional problems. What do appear to produce reading failures are some educational methods, including the sight methods for teaching reading, and social promotions. Home attitudes may also hinder a child's progress.

730   Stauffer, Russell G.   "Certain psychological manifestations of re-tarded readers." J Educ Res 41(6): 436-52, February, 1948. (38 References).
Identifies thirteen factors which may cause reading retardation. Great individual differences exist: almost never do two persons retarded in reading exhibit the same pattern of causative factors. Significant re-lationships were found between different associative learning test find-ings on retarded readers. Some persons appear unable to recall or asso-ciate meaning with visual symbols such as words. Any procedure used to analyze the difficulties of retarded readers should include tests of associative learning. Retarded readers made higher scores on material presented by both visual and auditory means than on material presented by visual-visual means. The diagnostician of reading disabilities should be alert to the numerous causes and their interrelatedness, rather than seeking to establish a single cause.

731   ————.   "Reading retardation and associative learning disabili-ties." Elem Engl 26(3): 150-57, March, 1949. (30 References).
Failure in an associative learning process like reading where symbols and experience must be associated has been attributed to three causes: (1) neuropsychological impediments to association, as in the dyslexias; (2) blocking of associations caused by emotional and social problems; and (3) verbalism, or reading and memorizing without understanding. Im-mature children need guidance and counseling; the dyslexics need a spe-cial remedial program; and the verbalizers need better teachers.

732   Street, Roy F.   "Educational cripples: a study of reading failures." J Mich State Med Soc 57(2): 242-46, 265, February, 1958.
Many children come to doctors' offices suffering from assorted aches and pains which appear to have no physical basis. These children may have developmental problems, emotional disturbances, or reading problems. The poor reader is an educational cripple, prone to develop the secondary physical symptoms that bring him to the doctor. In a study of 260 chil-dren, an effort was made to characterize the kind of child who is unable to learn to read and to indicate fundamental causes. Five categories were identified: (1) the left-eyed; (2) the left-handed; (3) those with

alexia used in a psychological rather than a neurological sense to mean
that letters, numbers, or words, or all three, do not seem to convey any
meaning to the child; (4) those with physical problems, usually visual;
and (5) those with emotional problems, including children who are fear-
ful of failure, have anxieties, or are allergic personalities very sensitive to all of life's stresses. Most problem readers are boys, although girls seem to have more visual problems which are sufficiently
upsetting to hinder learning to read. Treatment of reading failure can
be very difficult. Screening tests given to first graders are rather
reliable, but the danger is in how they are used. They tell what a child
can do but not why. Each child must be seen individually. About 14 percent of children will have trouble learning to read at age six and will
need extra help.

733 Stullken, Edw. H. "Retardation in reading and the problem boy in
     school." Elem Engl Rev 14(5): 179-82, May, 1937. (0 References).
Among boys enrolled in two Chicago schools for problem boys, three groups
were identified among the problem readers: those with personality problems, physiological handicaps, and low intelligence. The third group was
the largest. When remedial reading courses enabled the boys to overcome
their reading handicaps, they were often able to adjust in other ways to
the regular school situation.

734 Swartout, R. "A medical approach to reading difficulty." GP 6(3):
     49-52, September, 1952. (0 References).
Dyslexia as a syndrome is common, but it unfortunately is receiving little
attention in any branch of medicine. Five fundamental physical causes
of dyslexia are: low intelligence, bad hearing, poor vision, strephosymbolia (mixed symbols), and lesions below the cerebral cortex. Strephosymbolia, the most common cause, is explained in terms of cerebral dominance. Treatment should include: (1) correct diagnosis by the family
physician; (2) giving the child loving individual attention; and (3) less
emphasis on school and reading and more concentration on an area where
the child has skills.

735 Taft, Lawrence T., and Cohen, Herbert J. "Reading disability: a
     developmental neurological assessment." Bull NY Acad Med 44(4):
     478-87, April, 1968. (24 References).
Examines dyslexia from the standpoint of Bannatyne's four diagnostic
categories: (1) primary emotional disorders, or children who appear to
be unable to learn to read because of emotional inhibitions; (2) social,
cultural, or educational deprivation; (3) genetic dyslexia, or children,
mostly boys, from families where reading disability is common; and (4)
minimal neurological impairment. Various theories on the causes of dyslexia are discussed. Treatment must be aimed at symptoms because so
little is known about specific causes. The physician must advise parents
as to what kind of help the child needs.

736 Thompson, Alice C. "Reading deficit and its relation to social
     maturity." Claremont Coll Read Conf Yearb 32: 228-34, 1968. (0
     References).
Persons in the lower one-third of the normal distribution of general intelligence are not particularly handicapped by failure to attain much
skill in reading. Either emotional or constitutional factors are usually
given as causes why some persons of average intelligence, or above, do
not learn to read. Emotional causes may arise from unhappy family circumstances or from the child's failures in early attempts to learn to

read. Constitutional factors may be genetically determined. Dyslexia
may be more a problem of retaining what is learned than a problem in the
learning process itself. The deficit may be caused by disease or injury
or inherent weakness. Hyperactive children may have reading problems.
Reading deficits are frequently found among persons who lack adequate
self-direction and the sound judgment to order their lives successfully.

737 Tinker, Miles A. "Diagnostic and remedial reading." I. Elem Sch
    J 33(4): 293-306, December, 1932; II. Elem Sch J 33(5): 346-
    57, January, 1933. (180 References).
General intelligence is without doubt the leading determinant of reading
ability. However, in the absence of intellectual retardation and visual
and auditory defects, causes of reading difficulty include congenital
word blindness, heredity, problems of cerebral dominance, and unfortunate
reading habits, among others. Unhealthy emotional reactions may be
present. These tend to disappear as progress is made in reading. The
deficiencies causing reading disability tend to be specific, not general.
The most successful remedial treatment is designed to remedy these specific needs. Adequate diagnosis is usually possible. The bibliography
of 180 entries in the field of diagnostic and remedial reading is printed
with Part I of the article.

738 Vernon, Magdalen Dorothea. Backwardness in reading: a study of its
    nature and origin. Cambridge, England: Cambridge University
    Press, 1957. 228p. (Bibliography p. 208-17).
In addition to introductory and concluding chapters, this book contains
four chapters on the nature and causes of reading disability, one chapter
on therapy, and two on visual and auditory development. It is a survey
of the investigations of the factors related to reading disability. It
is believed that backwardness in reading is caused by the child's failure to learn one of the essential steps in the development of reading
rather than because of a visual, auditory memory, or imagery defect.
Such factors as innate cognitive inability, changing teachers, or a lapse
of interest, among others, are mentioned as reasons for reading failure.
No one method is effective in affecting a cure in all cases. In severe
cases of reading disability the prognosis is poor no matter what cures
are attempted.

739 ————. "The dyslexic syndrome and its basis." In: World Con-
    gress on Reading, 2d, Copenhagen, 1968. Proceedings: reading:
    a human right and a human problem. Vol. 2. Edited by Ralph C.
    Staiger, and Oliver Andresen. Newark, Delaware: International
    Reading Association, 1969. 167-71. (31 References).
This review of some of the literature on the causes of dyslexia points
out that there is a characteristic pattern of symptoms, though all are
not found in any one case. Three principal types of dyslexia are identified: (1) persons who appear to be weak in language functions; (2)
those who are defective in their ability to analyze complex visual shapes;
and (3) dyslexia possibly of hereditary origin.

740 ————. "Review of recent research on backwardness in reading."
    In: International Reading Symposium, 2d, College of St. Mark and
    St. John, 1965. Edited by John Downing, and Amy L. Brown. London:
    Cassell, 1967. 217-29. (45 References).
Environmental factors and inadequate teaching do not explain reading disability entirely. Disabilities arising within the child himself include
subnormal intelligence, inadequate visual perception, some hearing loss,

emotional disturbance, slow or uneven maturation of the brain of various kinds, or a weakness in lateralization. Although there is little general agreement on the best way to teach remedial reading, some phonic method is usually advocated. The nature of each child's disability must be determined if he is to be helped. Grouping all backward readers together for teaching is usually unsuccessful.

741 Westman, Jack C.; Arthur, Bettie; Scheidler, Edward P. "Reading retardation: an overview." Am J Dis Child 109(4): 359-69, April, 1965. (83 References).
The pediatrician is in a key position to detect and evaluate the retarded reader. A selection of the literature about reading disabilities is reviewed. It is divided into four categories: studies centered on physical factors, the child, the family, and the school. It is concluded that learning to read successfully depends on personality, family, and a sufficiently mature central nervous system.

742 White, Carol S.; Dwyer, William O.; Lintz, Elizabeth. "Dyslexia: is the term of value?" Acta Symb 4(2): 6-28, Fall, 1973. (98 References).
Considers the term "dyslexia" from two points of view in order to assess its usefulness. For purposes of treatment, the term is not useful. The important consideration is not labeling it, but relieving the reading handicap. Effort should be directed at the child's specific behaviors. For purposes of research, the term has value. It is crucial to discover the causes of dyslexia. If the condition can be diagnosed before the child enters school, the advantage to the child is great and the need for remediation prevented. Causes of dyslexia are considered, including educational deprivation, emotional and behavior problems, neurological trauma, minimal brain dysfunction, inherited neurological deficits, and cerebral dominance.

743 Wolfe, Lillian S. "Differential factors in specific reading disability: II. Audition, vision, verbal association, and adjustment." Pedagog Semin J Genet Psychol 58: 57-70, March, 1941. (20 References).
In two groups of nine-year-old boys, one normal, the other retarded in reading, tests of auditory acuity, discrimination, and memory span did not discriminate at a statistically significant level between the groups, but the experimental group was consistently lower than the control group. Most of the other perception tests showed the same general result. The experimental group was significantly inferior to the control group in emotional adjustment, as determined by teachers and observations of the examiner. Factors of attention and motivation appeared to be of great importance in differentiating the groups.

744 Young, Robert A. "Case studies in reading disability." Am J Orthopsychiatry 8(1): 230-54, April, 1938. (15 References).
Forty-one case studies of children with reading disabilities are reported in an effort to determine the effect of the reading problem on the later lives of these individuals. The roles of lateral dominance, visual problems, and emotional attitudes as factors in reading disability were also investigated. Results suggest that a child who has a reading disability never completely overcomes it. Poor spelling and incomplete lateral dominance were found to be associated with poor reading. Suggestions for remediation are offered.

O. NEUROLOGICAL FACTORS

745 Abrams, Jules C. "Dyslexia--single or plural." Paper presented at
      National Reading Conference, Los Angeles, December 5-7, 1968. 14p.
      (ED 028 048).
Identifies three types of severe reading disability: (1) The brain-
damaged, ego-disturbed child has a defect in the central nervous system.
This child is almost always hyperactive and has difficulty with the
basic skills of perception, concept formation, and language. (2) Specific brain-injury cases, also called "organic remedial," have actual
lesions in the occipital-parietal areas of their brains which cause language impairment. (3) Children called "functional remedial" are without
definite brain damage. They have a disturbed pattern of neurologic
organization. Verbal IQs are significantly higher than performance IQs
in the ego-disturbed child. The reverse is true for the other two types.

746 Ayers, Floyd W., and Torres, Fernando. "The incidence of EEG ab-
      normalities in a dyslexic and a control group." J Clin Psychol
      23(3): 334-36, July, 1967. (11 References).
Groups of reading-disabled third graders were found to have significantly
more abnormal EEGs than a randomly selected group from the same population.

747 Balow, Bruce; Rubin, Rosalyn; Rosen, Martha J. "Perinatal events
      as precursors of reading disability." Read Res Q 11(1): 36-71,
      1975-76. (82 References).
Reviews literature on the relation between reading disability and complications of pregnancy and birth. Procedures and results, research
design, test use, and statistical methods are examined in the major
studies. A statistically significant correlation does exist between
reading disability and perinatal events although the relationship is of
a low order. Neonatal neurological damage is suggested as an area where
further research is needed.

748 Baro, W. Z. "Is there an EEG abnormality in reading difficulties?"
      Electroencephalogr Clin Neurophysiol 24(4): 393-94, April, 1968.
      (0 References).
Describes a technique for obtaining EEG abnormalities in cases of reading disability. A case report is given in which the child's EEG was
normal except when he read aloud. Drug therapy was begun and improvement in school was noted. The WISC, repeated two years later, showed
an increase in IQ.

749 Bean, William James. "The isolation of some psychometric indices
      of severe reading disability." For a summary see: Diss Abstr
      28A(8): 3012-13, February, 1968.

750 Benton, Arthur L. "Right-left discrimination." Pediatr Clin North
      Am 15(3): 747-58, August, 1968. (21 References).
Right-left discrimination is a complex concept that is mastered slowly
by children. Its impairment may be associated with brain damage. However, contrary to the impression of many clinical observers, when the
variable of intelligence level is controlled, systematic study shows no
important relationship between right-left discrimination and reading
ability. Clinicians seeing the two deficits together may believe dyslexia to be typically determined by more pervasive perceptual disturbances, but this is an unwarranted generalization.

751 Benton, Arthur L., and Bird, Joseph W. "The EEG and reading dis-
     ability." Am J Orthopsychiatry 33(3): 529-31, April, 1963. (9
     References).
In a review of the literature it was found that dyslexic children showed
a higher-than-expected incidence of EEG abnormalities. No specific association between EEG and reading disability has been unequivocally demonstrated, however.

752 Black, F. William. "EEG and birth abnormalities in high- and low-
     perceiving reading-retarded children." J Genet Psychol 121(2):
     327-28, December, 1972. (0 References).
Electroencephalograms and birth histories for three groups of thirty
children each who were matched for age, school grade, and IQ were evaluated and classified as normal or abnormal. One group was made up of
normal readers. The two groups of retarded readers were divided into
groups having adequate and inadequate visual perception on the basis of
the Frostig test. In the normal reader sample only two cases of birth
abnormalities were found. Eight were found in the high-perceiving group,
and sixteen in the low-perceiving group of retarded readers. Similar
incidence of EEG abnormalities was found. The differences were significant. Results are seen as supporting an organic cause for some cases
of reading disability.

753 —————. "Neurological dysfunction and reading disorders." J
     Learn Disabil 6(5): 313-16, May, 1973. (11 References).
Describes a study of two groups of reading-disabled children. All members of one group showed positive signs of neurological dysfunction.
Members of the other group did not. Except for performance on tests of
visual perception, the children with neurological problems did not differ appreciably from the other group whose reading problems were not
associated with neurological dysfunction. It is suggested that demonstrating neurological dysfunction is not particularly useful when cognitive functioning or academic achievement is the primary concern.

754 Bowley, Agatha. "Reading difficulty with minor neurological dys-
     function. A study of children in junior schools." Dev Med Child
     Neurol 11(4): 493-503, August, 1969. (11 References).
Poor readers who were also restless and clumsy were subjected to neurological testing. Disordered language, memory, motor, or visual-motor
function were found. These problems appeared to be caused by immaturity
and/or neurological disorder. Remedial instruction brought great improvement in reading and in general behavior.

755 Bryant, N. Dale. "Reading disability: part of a syndrome of neuro-
     logical dysfunctioning." International Reading Association. Con-
     ference proceedings: challenge and experiment in reading. Vol. 7.
     (Part 3). Edited by J. Allen Figurel. New York: Scholastic
     Magazines, 1962. 139-43. (7 References).
Reading disability can result from numerous causes. However, the pattern
is consistent enough in most cases to be explained as an aspect of neurological dysfunction. Because of the many elements of neuropsychological
functioning involved in word recognition, individual cases may vary widely. Emotional problems may also be present. Reading specialists should
not consider these cases hopeless. A model of how words are recognized
and learned is presented. It is believed that this type of model will
help specialists identify the difficulty and select appropriate and successful remedial techniques.

756 Chesher, Earl C. "Reading disability from a neurologic point of
     view." Arch Ophthalmol (New Series) 24(2): 420, August, 1940.
     (0 References).
The child whose loss of reading ability results from cerebral pathological
lesions is compared to the child of good intelligence who fails to learn
to read. It is assumed that the latter is caused by a developmental defect analogous to the acquired form.

757 Cohn, Robert. "Delayed acquisition of reading and writing abilities
     in children. A neurological study." Arch Neurol 4(2): 153-64,
     February, 1961. (5 References).
Forty-six public-school children ages seven to ten years who had failed
to learn to read and write and who were considered to show "specific"
reading and writing difficulties were given neurological investigation,
including EEG examination. Nearly all these children also had behavior
problems. Two groups of children served as controls. One of the control
groups contained children ages six to twelve years. They were in normal
classrooms and showed no major problems. The second group of controls
was made up of children ages seven and one-half to fourteen. They were
experiencing some difficulty with reading but were in normal classrooms
and were neurologically indistinguishable from the normal learners. On
the basis of the neurological data it is concluded that the delays in
acquisition of reading and writing were an expression of general disturbance in neurological function. It is postulated that behavior problems
are not so much expressions of reaction to misunderstanding by peers and
elders as they are an externalized disorganization of motor patterns because the child fails to form concepts from the stimuli that bombard him
from the environment.

758 Condon, William S. "Multiple response to sound in dysfunctional
     children." J Autism Child Schizophr 5(1): 37-56, March, 1975.
     (11 References).
Describes basic methods and findings in the discipline of kinesics, or
the study of body motion, on nonverbal behavior, and in linguistics-
kinesics, or the study of the interaction of speech and body motion, in
normal behavior. The same methods of frame-by-frame analysis of sound
film have been used to study pathological behavior in conditions like
autism, epilepsy, stuttering, and schizophrenia. It is hypothesized that
among the pathological responses of such children is responding more than
once to the same sound. Their bodies move later with the pattern of sound
that has occurred earlier. The response may occur many times as if the
sound were reverberating. They appear to be controlled by the sound.
The children would tend to move more, and be more tired than normal children. It is suggested that a continuum exists for children with autism
at one end and learning disabilities with difficulty in reading and doing
arithmetic at the milder end. Neurological involvement may be etiological
in these cases.

759 Conners, C. Keith. "Cortical visual evoked response in children
     with learning disorders." Psychophysiology 7(3): 418-28, Novem-
     ber, 1970. (23 References).
EEG tracings for three groups of poor readers showed significant relationships between verbal skills and the late components of the visual
evoked response. One group of subjects were all members of one family
of dyslexics. For the EEG examination all subjects were seated and instructed to press a telegraph key in response to a bright flash of light.
Dim flashes were interspersed in a random pattern. Subjects kept their

eyes closed during the entire test. The family of poor readers showed
weakening of the visual evoked response in the left parietal area, an
assymetry which suggests that the known language disorder might possibly
be of genetic origin.

760 Critchley, Macdonald. "Inborn reading disorders of central origin."
     Trans Ophthalmol Soc UK 81: 459-80, 1961. (0 References).
In this Doyne Memorial Lecture for 1961, some early literature in the
field is reviewed. The fundamental nature of developmental dyslexia is
discussed from the viewpoint that the condition is organic and not psychogenic. It is genetic and not situational. Why this condition occurs is
not clear, but it appears to be related to a lack of cerebral maturation.
The neurologist sees it as a parieto-occipital dysfunction. The studies
from the standpoint of gestalt psychology emphasize how but not why and
are not helpful. Pedagogic considerations, maternal and natal factors
in causes, clinical symptoms, ophthalmological aspects, cerebral dominance, minor neurological signs, and genetic factors are all discussed.

761 Crosby, Robert MacGonigle Nelson with Robert A. Liston. Reading
     and the dyslexic child. London: Souvenir Press, 1969. 241p.
     (Bibliographic Notes, p. 227-36).
Originally published under the title The Waysiders (New York: Delacorte
Press, 1968), this book was written by a pediatric neurologist and a
professional writer. Intended for a wide audience of parents, teachers,
physicians, and laity, the book discusses dyslexia as a specific disease
entity of neurological origin. It can be diagnosed but cannot be medically cured. Treatment of dyslexia lies with teachers through the development of educational programs that will help dyslexic children. Case histories illustrate various forms of dyslexia. Suggestions for treatment
of reading disabilities are made. An appeal is issued to teachers for
acceptance of the existence of dyslexia as a genuine cause of reading
disorders.

762 Currier, Fred P., Jr., and Dewar, Murray. "Word blindness: diffi-
     culty in reading in school children." J Mich State Med Soc 26:
     300-304, May, 1927. (0 References).
Reviews some of the literature on word blindness with particular reference to Orton's views. A case history is presented of a fourteen-year-
old girl whose right visual field is impaired in her right eye. She is
left-handed and has had difficulty in learning to read. She tends to
mirror write. The difficulties are ascribed to organic brain lesions.
The child experienced head injury in birth. The value of the case is
seen as being a demonstration of the importance of taking visual fields
in such children. It is also suggested that neurological diagnosis is
not yet advanced enough to discern a cerebral lesion which might produce
a tendency toward mirror writing and left-handedness. The case also suggests the possibility of a localized area in the visual cortex for the
nasal half of one retina and another for the temporal half, a condition
believed to be not yet proved.

763 Davis, Walter D. "Possible organic basis for a syndrome: reading
     disability, hyperactivity, and behavior problem in boys." Del
     State Med J 26(8): 199-201, August, 1954. (0 References).
Observes that reading disability, hyperactive behavior, and altered elec-
trocortical activity occur together with sufficient frequenty to appear
to constitute a syndrome and to be worth further research and clinical
observation. The children studied were between ages seven and fourteen.

Most were boys of average intelligence, although some might have been
labeled "stupid" in an earlier day. At home they were reported to be
restless, irresponsible, overactive, thoughtless, but not mean. Many
came from poor home environments, but they had siblings not similarly
affected. Many were reported overactive from the time they could walk.
Neurological examinations were negative, but EEGs were consistently abnormal in a diffuse--not localized--way. About half could not read, and
none of them had much interest in learning to read. WISC performance
scores were above verbal scores. Psychiatric findings were normal. Some
of the children responded well to suppressive medication like dilantin
or phenobarbital. The hypothesis presented to explain the syndrome is
that these children have sustained minimal brain damage either prenatally
or in infancy which has resulted in a lowered capacity to sustain psychic
tension. An alternate suggestion is that there is a congenital deficiency
in capacity to sustain attention. The clinical picture would be of a
restless child made even more so by parental attempts at restraint. In
school, reading requires the child to sit still and concentrate, that is,
sustain tension. Some sort of organic deficit in the central nervous
system appears to exist, although no claim is made for scientific validation of these hypotheses.

764 Delacato, Carl H. The treatment and prevention of reading problems:
     the neuropsychological approach. Springfield, Illinois: Thomas,
     1959. 122p. (Bibliography p. 111-17).
The relation of reading disorder to neurological organization, sleep,
brain injuries, handedness and footedness, and vision is explored. Neurological development and organization provide the basis for all language
and reading development. Reading difficulties will not be overcome by
any remedial measure until the child's hemispheric dominance has been
established. Reading problems can be prevented. The responsibility for
prevention rests with parents and teachers.

765 Denckla, Martha Bridge. "Color-naming defects in dyslexic boys."
     Cortex 8(2): 164-76, June, 1972. (15 References).
Five boys, ages seven to ten years, were found to suffer from very severe
dyslexia and inability to name colors although they could name objects
and pictures and were not color-blind. It is suggested that: (1) the
boys' defect is comparable to the aphasic type of color anomia occurring
in adults with acquired lesions; (2) cerebral language areas are highly
specific in differentiating functions which may account for the various
subtypes of dyslexia; (3) the boys suffered from a remarkably severe and
pure dyslexia coupled with the color-naming defect; and (4) they represented a rare subgroup of dyslexia.

766 Drew, Arthur L. "A neurological appraisal of familial congenital
     word-blindness." Brain 79(Part 3): 440-60, September, 1956.
     (102 References).
A review of the literature reveals that the familial form of word blindness must be inherited, but little has been written about the neurological
basis of the condition. It is observed that the inherited condition seems
similar to cases of acquired word blindness that involve the parietal
lobes. The defect may be viewed as a disturbance in gestalt function
which is inherited as a dominant trait. Delayed development of the
parietal lobes may be the underlying anatomical cause for the condition.

767 Early experience and visual information processing in perceptual and
     reading disorders. Proceedings of a conference held October 27-30,

1968, at Lake Mohonk, New York, in association with the Committee
on Brain Sciences, National Research Council. Edited by Francis
A. Young, and Donald B. Lindsley. Washington, D.C.: National
Academy of Sciences, 1970. 533p. (Bibliography).
This conference focused on possible causes of reading disabilities through
a study of the structure and mechanisms of the eye and brain and their
roles in perception. The goal was to integrate knowledge in the fields
of eye and brain. Participants included educators looking for better
ways to teach reading; psychologists and others experimenting in the
fields of vision, hearing, and other cognitive functions; and practitioners from various medical specialities, including ophthalmology, neurology,
and pediatrics. Articles in this collection contain reports on the
structure and function of the entire visual system; mechanisms of attention and perception, and the effects of the experiences of very early
infancy on later development. Also included is material describing the
meaning of dyslexia, and how the condition came to be recognized historically. Visual perception and management are considered. A glossary
of terms in this field is included.

768   Ellert, JoAnn C. "The Gerstmann syndrome--a caveat regarding its
      classroom use by the reading teacher." J Read Spec 8(2): 73-75,
      78-80, December, 1968. (20 References).
The Gerstmann syndrome found in adults may appear in children on a developmental basis and hinder the acquisition of reading and other educational
skills. The Gerstmann syndrome includes the inability to recognize one's
own fingers or to name them, or to point to an individual finger when
asked to do so. It includes difficulties in writing, arithmetic, and
right-left orientation. It has been considered an important indication
of dysfunction in the dominant parietal lobe. Gerstmann first described
it in 1924. Although by the 1960s neurologists were skeptical of its
existence, it is suggested that testing in the classroom for the four
classic components of the Gerstmann syndrome provides a useful means of
identifying backward readers who may have a developmental cerebral defect. Some researchers have found difficulty in finger identification
three times more common in dyslexic than in normal children.

769   Faure, J. M. A.; Rozier, J.; Bensch, C.; et al. "Association po-
      tentials evoked by combined auditory and visual stimulation in
      amblyopic and dyslexic children." Electroencephalogr Clin Neuro-
      physiol 25(6): 586, December, 1968. (0 References).
Results of EEG examinations performed on ten dyslexic children ages seven
to fourteen years and on ten strabismic amblyopic children ages eight to
sixteen are seen as indicating that in children with normal vision and
hearing, the cause of the perceptual difficulties should be sought as
much in the subcortical mechanisms of attention as in a particular function of parts of the occipital lobe (the part of the brain concerned
with vision). Level of alertness is an important condition of perceptual
activity. Strabismic amblyopia is suppression of vision in one eye by
the patient to avoid diplopia, or double vision.

770   Fenelon, B. "Expectancy waves and other complex cerebral events
      in dyslexic and normal subjects." Psychon Sci 13(5): 253-54,
      December 15, 1968. (3 References).
Investigates the nature of the cortical response to semantic stimuli, and
the course of habituation of the contingent negative variation (CNV) or
expectancy waves (E-waves). Subjects were four adults and four children.
Two children were dyslexic and two were normal readers. EEG recordings

were made for all subjects. They listened to tones, saw light flashes, and were shown on a screen three letters at a time forming consonant-vowel-consonant trigrams. Subjects were asked to find word associations as quickly as possible. No real words were included in the trigrams. A peculiarity in the brain response under conditions of uncertainty was noted. Cerebral responses by dyslexics to semantic stimuli differed from those of normal subjects. It is suggested that age levels need to be taken into account in evaluating cortical responses of dyslexics. Further study of varying levels of arousal in E-waves, and investigation of the effects of mental set are proposed in an effort to improve remediation of dyslexia by a better understanding of the dyslexic's actual cerebral response to learning situations.

771   Fenelon, B.; Holland, J. T.; Johnson, C. "Spatial distribution of
       the EEG of dyslexic children." Electroencephalogr Clin Neurophysiol
       34(7): 737, 1973. (0 References).
Reports findings in an experiment in which educational and psychological tests and EEGs were administered to three groups of children: dyslexics, children with behavior problems, and normal children. Change in spatial organization of the EEG was measured at eight-week intervals on three occasions. The two clinical groups were given either the active drug nitrazepam or a placebo during one of the eight-week intervals. Normals received placebos throughout. In dyslexics, but not in the other groups, significant changes in S-indices of both hemispheres took place following administration or withdrawal of the nitrazepam. Improvement in scholastic achievement and general behavior was reported in more than half the dyslexics while on the drug, and EEG abnormalities decreased significantly. Results are seen as supporting the theory of attention-distraction factors in dyslexic children.

772   Frank, Jan, and Levinson, Harold. "Dysmetric dyslexia and dyspraxia:
       hypothesis and study." J Am Acad Child Psychiatry 12(4): 690-701,
       October, 1973. (13 References).
In neurological and psychiatric screening of 115 dyslexic children ages six and one-half to fourteen, 112 (97 percent) showed cerebellar-vestibular dysfunction. This was manifested by difficulty in tandem walking, articulatory speech disorders, various disturbances during finger-to-nose or heel-to-toe pointing, and other abnormalities. Seventeen of these children were randomly selected for neurological examinations, and thirty for ear, nose, throat, audiographic, and electronystagmography (recording of eye movements) examinations. All seventeen cases were found to have a cerebellar deficit. Twenty-six of the thirty cases showed eye movement abnormalities. On the basis of these findings, it was hypothesized that cerebellar-vestibular circuits may play an important role in causing "dysmetric dyslexia," a term referring to the dysmetric, steering, and spatial orientation disturbances noted in the writing and drawing of such children. It was hypothesized that cerebellar-vestibular circuits provide a harmonious, stable motor background for visual perception which is nothing more than the subliminal, automatic, integrated motor activity of the eye muscles, head, and neck so that ocular fixation and sequential scanning of letters and words can take place. In the presence of this dysfunction, scanning is disordered and scrambling of words results. This scrambling leads to the deficits of dyslexia. Treatment with drugs is suggested.

773   Gardner, Howard. "Developmental dyslexia: the forgotten lesson of
       Monsieur C." Psychol Today 7(3): 62-65, 67, August, 1973. (0
       References).

Reviews the nineteenth-century work of Joseph Déjérine, the French neurologist, and the case history of Déjérine's patient, Monsieur C, who was unable to read following a stroke. The works of Paul Broca and Hinshelwood are discussed. Today's ideas about treating dyslexia as a condition caused by slow maturation or deficiencies in the anatomical connections in the brain necessary to learn in the usual way are discussed. The works of Orton, Bernard Sklar, Norman Geschwind, and Paul Rozin are described. Rozin's theory that the dyslexic's problem is chiefly blending a sequence of letters into an English word is approved.

774 Gehring, Kathryn B. Dyslexia--reading disability with neurological involvement. 1966. 27p. (ED 015 085).
Discusses the symptoms and treatment of dyslexia. Visual perception, auditory perception, speech, and neurological abnormalities are considered. Treatment depends upon diagnosis and must be constantly evaluated. Although some treatment programs are available, the outlook for dyslexics is not favorable. Diagnosis and special methods of instruction are almost never begun early enough to avoid emotional problems.

775 Gerdine, Marjorie Wells. "Reading process errors and organic brain damage in dyslexia." For a summary see: Diss Abstr 28B(5): 2135-36, November, 1967.

776 Goldberg, Herman Krieger; Marshall, Curtis; Sims, Edith. "The role of brain damage in congenital dyslexia." Am J Ophthalmol 50(4): 586-90, October, 1960. (7 References).
In studies of groups of normal and retarded readers who were public school pupils, evidence of subclinical brain damage was suggested by the results of electroencephalographic and psychological tests involving perception. EEG abnormalities were predominantly in the parietal-occipital area. They were characterized by asymmetry, much slow activity, and occasional sharp waves, but no seizure discharges. This agrees with other research in the area. All the children were of normal or superior intelligence. The anatomical basis for reading and its problems is explored. It is important for educators to be aware of this group of subclinically brain-damaged children so that remedial training can be started early. Educational, psychiatric, and subclinical brain damage factors are all proven causes of congenital dyslexia.

777 Gooddy, William, and Reinhold, Margaret. "Congenital dyslexia and asymmetry of cerebral function." Brain 84(2): 231-42, June, 1961. (5 References).
Theorizes that congenital dyslexia may result from an abnormality of cerebral function which results in inability to coordinate sensory information. This deficiency or lack of coordination of sensory information may render the victim unable to translate aural symbols into written symbols. The reverse may be true, and right-left confusion may also be present. It is suggested that such a cerebral defect may be caused by a lack of asymmetrical function of the two hemispheres, that it, to a too-close similarity of function. The condition may possibly be inherited. It is not caused so far as is known by organic brain disturbance or by metabolic disturbance in nerve tissue. The symptoms of congenital dyslexia are described. Treatment includes an explanation of the problem to the child and his family and phonetic teaching methods, among others.

778 Hughes, J.; Leander, R.; Ketchum, G. "Electroencephalographic study of specific reading disabilities." Electroencephalogr Clin Neurophysiol 1(3): 377-78, August, 1949. (0 References).

Abnormal EEGs were found in 75 percent of a group of 125 patients with specific reading disability. Unstable rhythms, abnormally high voltage, slow waves, and high-voltage sharp waves were observed. Spike and wave formations associated with clinical petit or grand mal seizures were seen in eight patients. Many of these patients showed clinical evidence of crossed dominance, but there were no related EEG changes. None of these patients, although all were more than eight years old, showed stable cortical rhythms.

779 Hughes, J. R., and Park, G. E. "Electro-clinical correlations in
      dyslexic children." Electroencephalogr Clin Neurophysiol 26(1):
      119, January, 1969. (0 References).
Abnormal EEGs were found in 36 percent of 157 children of normal intelligence who had reading disabilities. The abnormal cases were divided into four groups: (1) Those with positive spikes had highest IQs and the greatest difference between potential and actual reading ability. (2) The occipital slow group included the poorest readers with the least difference between actual and potential ability. (3) The fronto-temporal group was similar to the second, but showed some evidence of ocular deficiency. (4) The epileptiform discharge group showed some evidence of organic problems.

780 Isom, John B. "Neurological research relevant to reading." In:
      International Reading Association. Conference proceedings: per-
      ception and reading. Vol. 12(Part 4). Edited by Helen K. Smith.
      Newark, Delaware: International Reading Association, 1968. 67-72.
      (23 References).
Vast variation exists in rate and degree of development of a child's neurological functions. Oversimplification of the concept of cerebral dominance should be guarded against in light of research showing that cerebral organization is not as clear-cut as once thought. Cerebral organization is less predictable in left-handed and ambidextrous persons. Continued development of our understanding of cerebral dominance and of "sequencing," that is, the concurrent organization of language in space and time, should aid our understanding of reading disability.

781 Kennard, Margaret A.; Rabinovitch, Ralph; Wexler, Donald. "The ab-
      normal electroencephalogram as related to reading disability in
      children with disorders of behaviour." Can Med Assoc J 67(4):
      330-33, October, 1952. (9 References).
In a study of forty-seven children ages eight through thirteen who were admitted to a children's psychiatric ward and were shown to have sufficient intelligence to learn to read, a positive correlation was found between mixed dominance and reading ability. No correlation occurred between reading disability and type of EEG. It is concluded that no relationship exists between the disorders producing EEG abnormalities and the disorders producing reading difficulties in children with behavior disorders. Both may indicate irregularities in developmental patterns. Evidence exists that reading difficulties may be divided into two categories: reading retardation with anxiety and negativism being important; and reading disability which results from uneven or retarded development.

782 Ketchum, E. Gillet. "Neurological and psychological trends in read-
      ing diagnosis." Read Teach 17(8): 589-93, May, 1964. (13 Ref-
      erences).
Researchers of reading deficiency agree in general that a retardation in learning to read that is inconsistent with the child's general intelli-

gence and educational experience constitutes reading deficiency. Beyond
that point, discord arises as to the causes. Differential diagnosis is
essential. Direct function-to-location relationship in the brain and
mixed-dominance theories seem no longer tenable. Casual attitudes toward
diagnosis and treatment of reading disorders are unfortunate. Careful
interdisciplinary work is necessary. Three general causes of reading
disorders are now recognized: psychologic; those associated with brain
damage; and those of constitutional or congenital origin.

783 Kinsbourne, Marcel, and Warrington, Elizabeth K. "Developmental
     factors in reading and writing backwardness." Br J Psychol 54(2):
     145-56, May, 1963. (47 References).
Two groups of patients backward in reading and writing were identified:
(1) One group suffered from a developmental cerebral deficit based on
difficulties in sequential ordering. (2) The other group exhibited a
syndrome concerned with the language sphere. Each condition gave rise
to a characteristic type of delay in learning to read and write. Children with these cerebral cortical deficits are probably a minority among
retarded readers and writers.

784 —————. "The relevance of delayed acquisition of finger sense to
     backwardness in reading and writing." Little Club Clin Dev Med
     10: 62-64, 1963. (6 References).
A disorder of cortical function, the Gerstmann syndrome, appears to be
analogous to congenital dyslexia. It involves the inability to identify
one's fingers in order on the basis of their relative positions in sequence on the hand. It also involves right-left disorientation. In this
study, tests found among poor readers a minority of children who showed
all the features of Gerstmann's syndrome in a developmental setting.
These children are late in developing the ability to retain and reproduce
order in space. It is not to be implied, however, that the syndrome has
the same anatomical implications in childhood as it does in adulthood.
As a practical matter, teachers of retarded readers should keep in mind
the relevance of delayed acquisition of "finger sense" in understanding
some cases of reading and writing backwardness.

785 —————. "A survey of finger sense among retarded readers." Little
     Club Clin Dev Med 10: 65-66, 1963. (0 References).
Groups of retarded readers from middle-class and working-class backgrounds
and a group of delinquents were tested for their development of finger
differentiation and order. The delayed acquisition of finger sense,
which has been shown to be associated with delayed acquisition of reading and writing skills in some cases, varied widely between different
groups of backward readers depending on their backgrounds. Among children from a higher income group, neurological problems were more prominent
than among the delinquents where emotional disorder was more frequent.
Among lower-income groups, educational deprivation and somewhat lower intelligence appeared to be more important factors in reading problems
than neurological problems. Caution is suggested in too-ready acceptance
of unsupported statements as to the incidence and importance of neurological factors in reading disability. Only carefully controlled large-
scale studies can do justice to this problem.

786 Knott, J. R.; Muehl, S.; Benton, A. L. "Electroencephalograms in
     children with reading disabilities." Electroencephalogr Clin
     Neurophysiol 18(5): 513, April, 1965. (0 References).

Fifty retarded readers were given EEGs. Average age was eleven years,
three months; average IQ was 102. Sleep EEGs were made in thirty-seven
of the children. Abnormal EEGs were recorded in thirty-one. It is concluded that reading disability appears to be associated with abnormal
EEGs. The abnormalities found are summarized.

787 Krippner, Stanley. "Space, time, and dyslexia: central nervous
       system factors in reading disability." Paper presented at a work-
       shop on learning disabilities, Coney Island Hospital, Brooklyn,
       New York, December, 1969. 1969. 57p. (ED 042 569).
Reading disabilities are discussed as central nervous system dysfunction.
Dyslexia may be developmental or the result of injury or disease. The
importance of an interdisciplinary approach to diagnosis is stressed.
Diagnostic techniques are given, including twelve tests. Sixteen remedial approaches are presented. Whether neurological organization can be
changed to help language problems is still a controversial issue.

788 ————. "Time, space and dyslexia: central nervous system fac-
       tors in reading disability." J Read Spec 10(3): 128-48, March,
       1971. (56 References).
Dyslexia is seen as a type of reading disability resulting either from
brain dysfunction brought about by physical injury or disease (posttrau-
matic) or by genetic or maturational factors (developmental). An understanding of the concepts of time and space is essential to the understanding of language disabilities. Identification of central nervous system
factors in reading disability is a medical procedure. Unfortunately, it
is neglected by parents, teachers, and physicians in dealing with the
reading-disabled child. Dyslexic children typically exhibit spatial confusion in identifying letters. They have difficulty in associating the
sound with the written symbol of a letter. The condition is often mis-
takenly diagnosed as emotional disturbance. Or, if diagnosed, remediation may consist only in repeating classroom procedures. Space and time
are discussed from a theoretical standpoint. Prompt and accurate diagnosis is viewed as the first step in remediation and should be interdisciplinary in nature. Fourteen psychological tests which show promise in
the diagnosis and treatment of dyslexia are described as well as a number of remediation methods and facilities for dyslexics.

789 Kris, E. C. "Synchronized high-voltage 5-7 c/sec EEG and EOG acti-
       vation during open-eyed gaze in dyslexic children." Electroenceph-
       alogr Clin Neurophysiol 33(3): 353, September, 1972. (0 Refer-
       ences).
Learning-disabled children were asked to read aloud graded paragraphs of
increasing difficulty while EEGs (electroencephalograms), EOGs (electrooculograms), and ECGs (electrocardiograms) were simultaneously recorded.
It was observed that when many of these children were given new and too-
difficulty reading material, EEG manifestations were akin to the first
stage of sleep, when their eyes were open. To prevent such drift from
control of attentiveness and intentional responsiveness, the difficulty
and amount of the work load was assessed in selecting suitable reading
material. Observed eye movements and the location of the EEG activity
are discussed.

790 Lovell, K., and Gorton, A. "A study of some differences between
       backward and normal readers of average intelligence." Br J Educ
       Psychol 3(Part 3): 240-48, November, 1968. (22 References).

A battery of tests was administered to groups of normal and backward readers ages nine and ten. Factor analysis showed that the patterns for the two groups were different. Reading age was clearly linked to the poor readers' test performance suggesting the possibility of neurological impairment. It is believed that administering a single test rather than a battery has caused confusion in the literature since it was the clustering of the scores in this study that shed light on the causes of reading disability.

791 MacKinnon, F. A. "Neurological factors in reading disability." Can Med Assoc J 91(2): 73-76, July 11, 1964. (29 References).
Reviews the literature on reading disability in which neurological defect is seen as a cause or correlate. Brain injury, maturational lag, neurological defect of congenital nature, and metabolic disorders such as biochemical imbalance inhibiting synaptic transmission are considered. It is concluded that if reading disability cannot be ascribed to the usual environmental, intellectual, or observable physiological causes, a neurological basis for it should be considered.

792 Mehegan, Charles C., and Dreifuss, F. E. "A neurological study of reading disability." Va Med Mon 94(8): 453-59, August, 1967. (18 References).
Reemphasizes the presence of organic disease of the nervous system as a factor in the genesis of dyslexia. Findings are reported on neurological examination of a group of dyslexic children ages six to twelve. Complications of pregnancy, left-handedness or mixed hand preference, hyperactivity, and poor attention span were among the problems commonly noted. Only one child showed a completely sound neurological examination. No familial influences were found. It is suggested that unilateral or bilateral hemisphere disease is present in some dyslexics. Literature is reviewed.

793 Muehl, Siegmar; Knott, John R.; Benton, Arthur L. "EEG abnormality and psychological test performance in reading disability." Cortex 1(4): 434-40, December, 1965. (6 References).
Fifty-nine reading-retarded children ages seven to fifteen were administered the WISC and an EEG. Drowsy and sleep recordings were included when possible. Sixty-three percent had abnormal EEG records, the most common anomaly being positive spike patterns occurring much more often than in normal children. WISC scores ranged from 79 to 125 with an average of 101.5. EEG records were divided into three classifications: normal for age; abnormal with 14 and 6/sec positive spike patterns; and other abnormalities. It was suggested that EEG abnormality is associated with reading disability when the disability is uncomplicated by behavior disorders. No rational relationship appeared between EEG abnormality and degree of reading retardation. Analysis of WISC verbal and performance IQs failed to provide a psychological measure for differentiating children with and without abnormal EEG records. Results suggested that whatever neurological deviations may be revealed by the EEGs, these are not solely responsible for the reading retardation.

794 Murdoch, B. D. "Changes in the electro-encephalogram in minimal cerebral dysfunction. A controlled study over 8 months." S Afr Med J 48(14): 606-10, March 23, 1974. (21 References).
EEGs were recorded on two groups of children matched for age and sex. One group was made up of children diagnosed as having minimal cerebral dysfunction. Many were poor readers. The other group was composed of

normal readers. For eight months the abnormal group received remedial instruction. Then another EEG was made on each child. The second set of EEGs showed that differences between the two groups were reduced. This suggests that the minimal cerebral dysfunction group was becoming more normal. EEG abnormalities of a slow wave type previously noted in other studies of minimal cerebral dysfunction children were significantly more frequent than in the normal children. Another difference found was that right posterior EEG dysfunction appeared to be specifically related to reading disability.

795 Newton, Margaret A. "A neuro-psychological investigation into dys-
     lexia." Paper presented at International Federation of Learning
     Disabilities, Brussels, Belgium, January 3-7, 1975. 9p. (ED 113
     866).
Findings of electroencephalographic studies on twenty-five dyslexic and twenty-five normal readers ages eight and thirteen years suggest the presence of unresolved dominance problems in the dyslexic children and established lateral dominance and cortical organization in the control group of normal readers. Dyslexic children showed more alpha activity on the dominant side or no difference at all. Normal readers showed more alpha activity on the nondominant side. Among the dyslexic children, 35 percent were thought to have dyslexia genetically determined, and another 40 percent were believed to be possibly neurologically impaired.

796 Oettinger, Leon, Jr.; Nekonishi, Harold; Gill, Ian G. "Cerebral
     dysrhythmia induced by reading (subclinical reading epilepsy)."
     Dev Med Child Neurol 9(2): 191-201, April, 1967. (11 References).
Five of nineteen dyslexic children who were given EEGs had definite ab-
normalities. They were given standard EEGs, then asked to gaze about the room, look at pictures, and read both silently and aloud. Abnormali-
ties suggested an induced dysrhythmia while reading. One child developed an autonomic seizure while reading and another later developed a grand mal seizure while watching television. Reading was the activating procedure in these five cases. The causes and mechanism of the action are not clear.

797 Olson, Norinne H.; Olson, Arthur V.; Duncan, Patricia H. "Neuro-
     logical dysfunction and reading disability." Read Teach 22(2):
     157-62, November, 1968. (11 References).
Reports research on neurological dysfunction associated with reading dis-
ability and on the parts of the brain involved in the reading process. Alexia, dyslexia, mixed dominance, and strephosymbolia are all regarded as disabilities involving neurological dysfunction. These conditions often exist in conjunction with more broadly classified neurological categories. It is concluded that neurological symptoms should be considered together with other related elements in making a diagnosis of reading disability.

798 Orton, Samuel Torrey. "Developmental disorders of the language
     faculty and their psychiatric import." Ment Hyg 20(3): 512-14,
     July, 1936. (0 References).
Abstracts Orton's presentation at the fourth annual Thomas W. Salmon Memorial Lecture. Whether a left-handed child should be shifted to the use of his right hand is a question that must be answered on an individual basis. If the child has a distinct preference it seems logical to allow him to develop it. As well as handedness, there is eyedness and legged-
ness. The brain centers controlling language are not open to training

as are those controlling handedness. Word blindness or word deafness may
be so severe that such children would be considered dull or feeble-minded.
Word blindness is explained as a mental short circuit blocking the ordinary recognition of words. It appears to be familial in origin. It often
goes with stuttering. Word deafness; motor agraphia, or difficulty in
writing; and motor aphasia, or speech difficulty are all explained.

799 ————. "The neurologic basis of elementary education." Arch
       Neurol Psychiatry 21(3): 641-46, March, 1929. (1 Reference).
Neurologic background has been overlooked in planning teaching methods.
It should be invaluable in selecting children who deviate from the norm
and need special methods in education. Interaction between auditory and
visual spheres is necessary to the neurological process of learning to
read. Reversals and errors in pronunciation are common in disabled
readers. Simultaneous tracing and sounding of a letter as a teaching
method is recommended.

800 ————. Reading, writing and speech problems in children: a
       presentation of certain types of disorders in the development of
       the language faculty. New York: Norton, 1937. 215p. (Thomas
       W. Salmon Memorial Lectures, New York Academy of Medicine).
The study of language losses in adults could be the key to understanding
developmental language disorders in children, that is, those that are
incidental to growth, including both hereditary and congenital influences
and those of environment. From this viewpoint word blindness, word deafness, inability to write (motor agraphia) or speak (motor aphasia) in the
absence of paralysis, and apraxia (inability to carry out skilled acts,
for example, typing) are analyzed. These disabilities are considered
in their developmental form, that is, as they appear in the child who,
unlike the adult, has never had the skill and lost it. Laterality is
discussed as our only guide to which hemisphere of the brain is dominant
in an individual. It is believed that childhood language disorders may
stem from failure to establish unilateral brain superiority in individual
areas of the brain. Individuals suffering from these conditions can be
helped with specific training methods. A glossary is included.

801 ————. "The three levels of cortical elaboration in relation to
       certain psychiatric symptoms." Am J Psychiatry 85(4): 647-59,
       January, 1929. (0 References).
After reviewing in general terms the pyramidal functioning of the central
nervous system in which partially autonomous structures, each with its
own functions, are more or less under the guidance of superior structures,
Orton separates the sensory functions of the cortex into three levels.
In the visual area they are: (1) cortical blindness in which there is
no vision but the lower reflexes of the eye remain; (2) mind blindness
in which the person or animal avoids collisions but does not recognize
the meaning of objects seen; and (3) word blindness or alexia in which
pictures are recognized and used adequately but language associations
are defective. The third level of function is the concern in strephosymbolia or reading disability. This condition rests on a physiological
basis and is not the result of either general or focal defects of development. Discussion of the part of the brain involved in each of the three
levels of cerebral elaboration is included.

802 Paradowski, William, and Ginzburg, Mejer. "Mirror writing and
       hemiplegia." Percept Mot Skills 32(2): 617-18, April, 1971.
       (6 References).

Frank mirror writing was found in only one of forty-one hemiplegics in a
rehabilitation service. This man had a pre-stroke history of difficulty
with reading and fit the picture of developmental dyslexia. The case
provides support for Macdonald Critchley's original hypothesis concerning the association between mirror writing and dyslexia.

803 Park, George E. "Electro-encephalogram and ocular function." Am J
      Ophthalmol 36(12): 1705-8, December, 1953. (2 References).
Fifty dyslexic children with IQs above 85 and no history of brain injury
did not show significant correlations between abnormalities of the electroencephalogram and fusion ability, ocular dominance, muscular imbalances,
or ductions. Weak fusion amplitude, especially weak recovery from diplopia (double vision) is associated with dyslexia, with or without abnormalities in the electroencephalogram.

804 Penn, Julia M. "Reading disability: a neurological deficit?"
      Except Child 33(4): 243-48, December, 1966. (55 References).
Reviews and discusses medical studies and other theories on the causes
of reading disabilities. Attention is drawn to studies which support
the theory that most dyslexics have abnormal EEG readings implicating
neurological injury as the leading cause of reading disability, rather
than multiple causes. Evidence supports neurological impairment or neurological maturational delay as the cause in almost 75 percent of reading
disability cases. Implications of this conclusion are considered.

805 Preston, Malcolm S.; Guthrie, John T.; Childs, Barton. "Visual
      evoked responses (VERs) in normal and disabled readers." Psycho-
      physiology 11(4): 452-57, July, 1974. (8 References).
Less response to flashes of light was obtained from reading-disabled
children than from normal children as measured by an electrode placed in
the region of the left angular gyrus. Both normal and reading-disabled
children showed less response to words than to light flashes. Results
of this test are seen as suggesting a neurological origin for reading
disability.

806 Preston, Ralph C., and Schneyer, J. Wesley. "The neurological back-
      ground of nine severely retarded readers." J Educ Res 49: 455-59,
      February, 1956. (17 References).
Full neurological examination of nine severe dyslexics ages eight to
eighteen years produced case histories that raised questions in all cases
about possible brain damage which could have produced the alexia. Although the causes and even the name of the condition are uncertain, a
call is issued for a broadening of research, including work by neurologists and psychiatrists.

807 Reed, James C. "Lateralized finger agnosia and reading achievement
      at ages 6 and 10." Child Dev 38(1): 213-20, March, 1967. (9
      References).
Finger localization errors were not related to primary reading skills at
age six. At age ten there was association. Those ten-year-old children
who made more right-hand errors did not read as well as the group with a
majority of left-hand errors. Acquisition of primary reading skills was
unrelated to inability to differentiate among the fingers on the basis
of touch alone. It was found to be associated with limitations in development of the reading skills of older children. It is suggested that the
finger localization errors may be related to some disturbance in the
left cerebral hemisphere.

808 Robb, P. "Neurological aspects of reading disabilities." In: In-
     ternational Reading Association. Conference proceedings: reading
     for effective living. Vol. 3. Edited by J. Allen Figurel. New
     York: Scholastic Magazines, 1958. 116-19. (0 References).
After a brief review of the literature of neurology as it relates to the
development of our knowledge of where speech and reading abilities are
localized in the brain, the author presents several case histories of
adults who have suffered speech and reading problems following surgery.
Childhood reading disabilities are discussed. Evidence is presented that
reading disability is linked to abnormal EEG results, which tends to suggest that minimal organic brain disease in the occipital region can be a
cause of reading disabilities.

809 Robbins, Melvyn P. "A study of the validity of Delacato's theory
     of neurological organization." Except Child 32(8): 517-23, April,
     1966. (7 References).
Results of this investigation do not support Delacato's theories of a
relationship between neurological organization and reading. Further, no
support is found for the usefulness of Delacato's program in improving
either reading or lateral development of the second-grade children used
as subjects. Warning is given against measuring neurological organization by behavioral tasks. Neither can reading be used as an index of
the quality of neurological organization.

810 Sellers, Charles W., and Sellers, Donald A. "Dyslexia: a neuro-
     logic dysfunction." Mich Med 66(24): 1556-59, December, 1967.
     (27 References).
Dyslexia is an impairment in communication between the eye and the brain,
between vision and perception, between looking with the eye and seeing
with the brain. Most children with reading difficulty are not stupid,
although they may appear to be. Dyslexic children may have mirror images
of letters and words. Many are ambidextrous with no clear hand preference and an imperfect directional sense. Such a child may have trouble
identifying the same letter or word if it is written in script or printing or in another size or color. Most dyslexic children are emotionally
unstable, disturbed, and immature. They should be sent to special reading classes. Dyslexia is a continuing problem. Treating it presents
barriers but they are not insurmountable. A good teacher, understanding
parents, early diagnosis, and one or two years of intensive study will
prepare some dyslexics for reentry into regular classrooms.

811 Shelton, Margaret M. K. "Specific language disability." Med Rec
     Ann 56(Suppl.): 13-14, 19, December, 1963. (16 References).
Describes the symptoms of specific language disability. Among poor readers are some children of normal intelligence who have difficulty associating a written symbol with its sound or meaning. The name of the disorder
varies with geographic location. "Specific language disability," "strephosymbolia," or "developmental dyslexia" is an organic condition, not psychogenic. It is genetic, not situational. There is an error in visual
perception; the condition may be considered a parieto-occipital dysfunction. Ideally it should be discovered when the child begins school. The
child's medical history is of great value in diagnosing the condition.
Most students respond to proper remedial instruction.

812 Silver, Archie A., and Hagin, Rosa. "Specific reading disability:
     delineation of the syndrome and relationship to cerebral dominance."
     Compr Psychiatry 1: 126-34, April, 1960. (39 References).

Describes the results of study of 150 children with reading disability who were between the ages of eight and fourteen years when first seen at a hospital mental hygiene clinic. Each child was studied neurologically and perceptually, including, among other evaluations, tests of right-left discrimination, handedness, eyedness, footedness, and EEG. Perceptual-integrative evaluations consisted of visual-motor tests, including the Bender Gestalt; auditory tests, including Gates tests for word discrimination, auditory blending, and sound matching; tactile ability tests such as finger gnosis and tactile-figure-ground; and the Goodenough drawing test. Results of these tests and others are reported. No increase in mixed laterality was found in disabled readers over controls. All but 8 percent of children with reading problems were found to have defects in visual perception. Half the children had little or no auditory perceptual defects. As measured by the Draw-A-Person test, 80 percent of the reading-disabled children showed problems with body-image schema. Various signs of neurological immaturity are reported as typical of children with specific reading disability.

813   Sklar, Bernard. "A computer classification of normal and dyslexic children using spectral estimates of their electroencephalograms." For a summary see: <u>Diss Abstr Int</u> 32B(10): 5760-61, April, 1972.

814   Sklar, Bernard; Hanley, John; Simmons, William W. "A computer analysis of EEG spectral signatures from normal and dyslexic children." <u>IEEE Trans Biomed Eng</u> BM20(1): 20-26, 1973. (25 References).
This study proved that it is possible to differentiate between normal readers and dyslexics on the basis of their electroencephalograms. Subjects were mostly boys ranging in age from nine to eighteen years with IQs from 90 to 110. The groups were matched for sex and age. The most prominent differences in EEG appeared in the parieto-occipital region during the resting, eyes-closed phase. During the reading tasks, normal readers showed more energy in some bands than poor readers. This energy level was reversed during the rest phase. During reading tasks dyslexics showed higher coherence between regions in the same hemisphere than normals.

815   Smith, Donald E. P. "A new theory of the physiological basis of reading disability." In: International Reading Association. <u>Conference proceedings: reading for effective living</u>. Vol. 3. Edited by J. Allen Figurel. New York: Scholastic Magazines, 1958. 119-21. (0 References).
Based on a study of forty cases of reading disability, it is suggested that the condition is caused by borderline abnormalities in endocrine functioning. The abnormalities are concerned with synaptic transmission and memory. Reading-disabled children differ in their level of activity. The reasoning is that the placid child is "bound," or fixed on one stimulus too long, by a low level of cholinesterase, an enzyme which controls the duration of transmissions within the nervous system. This allows another transmitter agent, acetylcholine, to keep attention fixed in one place for too long. The hyperactive child, on the other hand, has too much cholinesterase, and his attention shifts too fast. The normally active child who is alexic may have balanced amounts of the necessary enzymes for retention and transmission, but at low levels of concentration. Superior readers appear to have balanced amounts of both enzymes in high concentration.

816 Stockwell, Charles W.; Sherard, Earl S.; Schuler, Jean V. "Electro-
        nystagmographic findings in dyslexic children." Trans Am Acad
        Ophthalmol Otolaryngol 82(2): 239-43, March-April, 1976. (9
        References).
To test whether dyslexic children suffer from abnormal eye performance
as measured by the standard clinical electronystagmographic examination,
a group of dyslexic children ages seven to seventeen and a group of their
siblings who were normal readers and ages nine to sixteen were given a
battery of tests for eye-movement control and the caloric test in which
each ear was irrigated with warm water. Results suggested defective eye-
movement control in some dyslexic children. None of the children showed
significant evidence of vestibular dysfunction in their ears. The hypothesis that cerebellar-vestibular dysfunction is a primary cause of
dyslexia was not supported. Electronystagmography is an electronic means
of recording eye movements that provides objective documentation of induced and spontaneous eye movements (nystagmus).

817 Tait, James Fulton. The role of mild neurological impairment in
        reading disability, an experimental study. Unpublished Ph.D.
        thesis. University of Southern California, 1958.

818 Torres, F., and Ayers, F. W. "Evaluation of the electroencephalo-
        gram of dyslexic children." Electroencephalogr Clin Neurophysiol
        24(3): 287, March, 1968. (0 References).
Waking and spontaneous sleep EEGs were obtained on three groups of third-
grade children. EEGs were repeated fifteen to thirty months later. Group
I subjects had minimal neurological abnormalities and reading problems.
Group II subjects were all in remedial reading classes. The third group
was a normal control. Group I had 49 percent abnormal EEGs, Group II
55 percent, and the control group 29 percent. The experimental groups
were statistically alike, but both were different from the control group,
in which 56 percent of the abnormal EEGs occurred in the bottom quartile.

819 Tuller, Dorothy, and Eames, Thomas H. "Electroencephalograms of
        children who fail in reading." Except Child 32(9): 637, May,
        1966. (3 References).
Six children who were failing reading showed electroencephalogram tracings unlike those of normal children. Differences were observed in the
parietal-post temporal region, but no single deviation was characteristic.

820 Walker, Marjorie. "Perceptual, coding, visuomotor and spatial dif-
        ficulties and their neurological correlates: a progress note."
        Dev Med Child Neurol 7(5): 543-48, October, 1965. (8 References).
From a group of thirty-three primary-school children, a "neurological"
group was formed on the bases of the children: (1) having failed a finger
gnosia test; (2) fallen below a certain level on an associated movements
test (moving one or more fingers at a time); (3) having deficits in motor
ability; and (4) exhibiting choreiform movements. Where the neurological
disabilities were marked, there were always associated reading and spelling problems. Boys were the most severely affected. Perceptual, coding,
visuomotor, and spatial difficulties were found scattered throughout the
entire group of thirty-three children. No particular difficulty was
found to be consistently associated with the deficits found in the neurological group. However, children with many of the specific difficulties
had marked neurological disabilities. No direct relationship between
the physiological and neurological problems and general intelligence
appeared to exist.

821   Yaeger, Mariam. <u>A comparative study of the reading disability in</u>
      <u>neurologically organized and neurologically disorganized fifth</u>
      <u>grade children</u>. Unpublished Ph.D. thesis. Loyola University of
      Chicago, 1965.

822   Zangwill, O. L. "Developmental dyslexia." <u>Bull Br Psychol Soc</u>
      No. 35: A25-A26, May, 1958. (0 References).
Although in recent years it has been popular to ascribe reading backwardness to emotional or environmental causes, some cases appear to have a
more fundamental defect. This defect appears to be linked to lateral
preference and directional orientation. It seems to reflect faulty neurological maturation. It is important to recognize this kind of reading
disability and to develop remedial teaching methods.

823   Zigmond, Naomi Kershman. "Intrasensory and intersensory processes
      in normal and dyslexic children." For a summary see: <u>Diss Abstr</u>
      27A(10): 3534, April, 1967.

P. NEUROPHYSIOLOGICAL FACTORS

824   Crider, Blake. "Certain visual functions in relation to reading
      disabilities." <u>Elem Sch J</u> 35(4): 295-97, December, 1934. (7
      Bibliographic Footnotes).
Theorizes that eye-muscle imbalance, alternating vision, lack of fusion,
and eye dominance are all probably dependent on some common phenomenon.
All of these are thought to be connected in some way to hemispheric dominance in the brain. Photographs of eye movements can give clues to the
problems of reading disabilities.

825   De Hirsch, Katrina. "Psychological correlates of the reading pro-
      cess." In: International Reading Association. <u>Conference proceed-</u>
      <u>ings: challenge and experiment in reading</u>. Vol. 7. Edited by
      J. Allen Figurel. New York: Scholastic Magazines, 1962. 218-26.
      (0 References).
Discusses reading processes in light of gestalt psychology. Reading is
not just perceiving letters and words; it is an intellectual act. Dyslexic children see letters but do not grasp their symbolic significance.
Gestalt psychology teaches that humans have a tendency to respond to a
constellation of stimuli as a whole. We see and hear separate forms or
tones as whole configurations, as, for example, whole words or tunes.
Fluent readers are global readers, seeing words in an organized way. Beginning readers cannot take in so much at one time. Separate letters
also stand out as separate gestalts. Reading readiness, perception, spatial organization, and temporal organization are among the aspects of
language development discussed in the light of gestalt concepts. Implications for teaching reading are discussed.

826   Douglass, Malcolm P., ed. "About reading disorders." In: <u>Reading</u>
      <u>in education: a broader view</u>. Columbus, Ohio: Merrill, 1973.
      359-420.
This section forms part of a collection of papers selected from the proceedings of the Claremont College Reading Conferences from 1963 through
1971. It includes articles by Alice C. Thompson on the relation of reading deficit to social maturity (Item No. 736); by Elena Boder on a diagnostic screening procedure for identifying types of developmental dyslexia

in children (Item No. 1274); by Robert E. Carrel on the neurophysiological
aspects of learning; by John B. Isom on neuropsychological findings in
reading-disabled children (Item No. 851); by C. Keith Conners on neurophysiological studies of learning disorders (Item No. 1505); by Clara Lee
Edgar on perceptual-motor training as an aid to development of reading
ability; and by Leon Oettinger, Jr. on the physical concomitants of reading. Each article has a bibliography.

827 Eames, Thomas H. "Comparison of children of premature and full term
    birth who fail in reading." J Educ Res 38(7): 506-8, March, 1945.
    (0 References).
In two groups of school-age children, one group full-term and one group
premature at birth, those who were born prematurely showed more cases of
neurological lesions, defective vision, slow recognition speed, and some
lateral dominance variations. Fifteen percent of the severe cases of
reading disabilities investigated were children born prematurely.

828 Eustis, Richard S. "The primary etiology of the specific language
    disabilities." J Pediatr 31(4): 448-55, 1947. (14 References).
Study of four generations of one family leads to the conclusion that left-
handedness, ambidexterity, bodily clumsiness, and specific language disabilities are of a familial nature. It is believed that all these conditions stem from slow neuromuscular maturation. This slow tempo probably
indicates equally slow myelination of motor and association nerve tracts.

829 Frank, Jan, and Levinson, Harold N. "Compensatory mechanisms in c-v
    dysfunction, dysmetric dyslexia, and dyspraxia." Acad Ther 12(1):
    5-27, Fall, 1976. (9 References).
Explores the interaction of neurophysiological and neuropsychological
processes used to compensate "silently" in dysmetric dyslexia and dyspraxia in an attempt to neutralize the underlying disturbances. The
"blurring speed" method for diagnosing this type of dyslexia is discussed.
Dysmetric dyslexia and dyspraxia are said to be caused by cerebellar-
vestibular problems. The prognosis for such children is good, provided
psychological and educational "scarring" do not occur. The cerebellar-
vestibular symptoms appear to diminish with age. Reading, writing, spelling, and drawing orientation, and coordination and balance all improve
with age and puberty. It is believed that a subclinical nystagmus exists
in dysmetric dyslexia and dyspraxia. A number of hypothetical formulations are set forth. It is suggested that some of the assumptions concerning primary dyslexia (of unknown origin) are fallacious.

830 ————. "Dysmetric dyslexia and dyspraxia: synopsis of a con-
    tinuing research project." Acad Ther 11(2): 133-43, Winter,
    1975-76. (8 References).
Defines and reports on a condition called dysmetric dyslexia and dyspraxia
observed in many children usually diagnosed as having specific, primary,
or developmental dyslexia. Children diagnosed as having dysmetric dyslexia and dyspraxia were found to have definite evidence of cerebellar-
vestibular dysfunction, that is, dysmetric sensory-motor functioning.
In these children the cerebellar-vestibular circuits do not provide the
spatial and temporal harmony of the material brought in by the senses.
It is analogous to vertical and horizontal television stabilizers. The
resulting scramble makes perception difficult. This type should be distinguished from conceptual or agnostic dyslexia in which, by analogy,
the television picture is clear, but the viewer does not comprehend it.
The "blurring speed" method used in diagnosis is explained. It is sug-

gested that causes of this type of dyslexia include delayed maturation,
ear infections, and/or antibiotics used for treatment which may damage
the labyrinthine-vestibular-cerebellar circuits. Emotional and cultural
deprivation may also delay the development of these circuits. Suggestions for treatment are given.

831 Gallistel, Elizabeth Ransom. "The effect of differing capacities
      for extinction on cognitive processes: their relation to motor
      inhibition and to reading disability." For a summary see: Diss
      Abstr 28A(6): 2091, December, 1967.

832 Hanley, John, and Sklar, Bernard. "Electroencephalographic corre-
      lates of developmental reading dyslexias: computer analysis of
      recordings from normal and dyslexic children." In: Leisman,
      Gerald. Basic visual processes and learning disability. Spring-
      field, Illinois: Thomas, 1976. 217-43. (86 References).
Over the years researchers have found that in general, EEGs or recordings
of electroencephalograms (brain wave patterns) in dyslexic children are
not different from those of normal children. Exceptions exist, however,
but the abnormalities have never shown a consistent pattern common to
dyslexia. In this study groups of dyslexic and normal children matched
for sex and age were asked to perform various reading and nonreading
tasks while EEG recordings were made. No obvious basic differences appeared between the groups. Some segments of the EEGs were submitted to
computer analysis. According to the computer program, the most consistent
discriminating feature between normal and dyslexic EEG patterns was in
left parieto-occipital activity. Normal children had greater shared activity between cerebral hemispheres at symmetrical locations. Dyslexics
showed more activity within the same hemisphere. Dyslexics showed poor
development of the alpha rhythm. There is no speculation on why this is
so. It is pointed out that it is the left parieto-occipital area which
appears important in discriminating dyslexic and normal readers. This
may be partly responsible for the dyslexic's inability to read.

833 Hunter, Edna J.; Johnson, Laverne, C.; Keefe, F. Barry. "Electro-
      dermal and cardiovascular responses in nonreaders." J Learn Disabil
      5(4): 187-97, April, 1972. (20 References).
Analyses of various autonomic physiological response patterns, including
heart rate, finger pulse, skin conductance levels, and electrodermal responses, showed that male nonreaders ranging in age from seven years,
eleven months to eleven years, four months were unable to maintain a constant level of attention. They showed deficient or fluctuating attention
as compared with normal readers in a control group the same age and sex.
Nonreaders also showed significantly longer motor reaction times. Findings suggest that dyslexics were physiologically less mature than matched
controls.

834 Jensen, Milton B. "Reading deficiency as related to cerebral injury
      and to neurotic behavior." J Appl Psychol 27(6): 535-45, December,
      1943. (16 References).
Defines "reading disability" as reading deficiency whose primary cause is
organic. "Reading inability" is the term used to describe cases depending
on emotional and intellectual factors. A wide variety of symptoms of
both these conditions was observed in twenty-two cases of reading disability. Case histories are included.

835 McClurg, William H. "The neurophysiological basis of reading dis-
      abilities." <u>Read Teach</u> 22(7): 615-21, 633, April, 1969. (14
      References).
Reading disabilities appear to stem from malfunctioning or developmental
lags in the integration of the visual, auditory, sensory, and motor areas
of perception. The base of reading difficulty is in the neurophysiological fields. Psychological, sociological, and educational factors are
secondary causes. The child will not outgrow it. Reading problems may
go undetected until the child has trouble with symbolization and abstraction.

836 McFie, J. "Cerebral dominance in cases of reading disability." <u>J
      Neurol Neurosurg Psychiatry</u> 15(3): 194-99, 1952. (26 References).
Twelve persons suffering from specific reading disability were given tests
to establish cerebral dominance. Results in general agreed with subjects'
handedness. Results of the testing do not support Orton's theory that
dyslexia results from confused cerebral dominance. It is suggested that
reading disability results from neurophysiological organization corresponding to dominance not being normally established in either hemisphere.

837 Martinius, Joest W., and Hoovey, Zeecam B. "Bilateral synchrony of
      occipital alpha waves, oculomotor activity and 'attention' in chil-
      dren." <u>Electroencephalogr Clin Neurophysiol</u> 32(4): 349-56, April,
      1972. (22 References).
Reports on a study of the behavior of bilateral synchrony of occipital
alpha waves and of oculomotor activity while the subjects were resting
and while they were listening to a series of tones. The sequence and
quality of tones were to be reported on later. Subjects were three
groups of ten- and eleven-year-olds: controls, attention problem children, and dyslexics. It was found that the alpha background rhythms reacted to the experimental activation in two distinct ways: (1) quanti-
tative increase of alpha waves over both occipital areas; and (2) improvement of synchrony between alpha pairs. It is concluded that the alpha
wave increase was an expression of a more general activation process,
whereas the improvement of interoccipital alpha synchrony was clearly
related to the partial function of attention tested. The EEG results
reliably distinguished between normal controls and clinical groups. Neurophysiological implications of these findings are discussed.

838 Paine, Richmond S. "Syndromes of 'minimal cerebral damage.'"
      <u>Pediatr Clin North Am</u> 15(3): 779-801, August, 1968. (38 Refer-
      ences).
Outlines the characteristics of minimal cerebral dysfunction; the incidence of the syndrome; and the evaluation, treatment, and prognosis of
the child suspected of suffering from the condition. The particular relationships observed between dyslexia and minimal cerebral damage are
considered.

839 Rosenthal, Joseph H. "Recent advances in the neurophysiology of
      some specific cognitive functions." <u>Acad Ther</u> 8(4): 423-28,
      Summer, 1973. (14 References).
Reviews physiological and psychological research related to reading difficulties, localization of brain functions, and hemisphere specialization.
Primary developmental dyslexia, often of genetic origin, is defined and
distinguished from reading incompetence stemming from lack of motivation
or opportunity. Subgroups within the primary developmental type are described in terms of cerebral hemisphere development. Results of electro-

encephalograhic (EEG) studies of dyslexics are discussed, including familial aspects of the condition. Research findings that EEG alpha waves
tend to increase in the resting hemisphere and decrease when a specific
task is being processed are discussed in relation to reading difficulties.

840 Ross, John J.; Childers, Donald G.; Harwood, Frank C. "Visual evoked
        potential spatiotemporal characteristics in childhood developmental
        dyslexia." Neurology 23(4): 442-43, April, 1973. (0 References).
Reports studies of boys ranging in age from eight to fourteen years who
were diagnosed as having developmental dyslexia, and a group of matched
controls. The scalp-monitored spatiotemporal potential field patterns
evoked when the boys were shown displays of colored lights and other visual stimuli indicate that the dyslexic children showed less coupling of
interhemispheric activity. This and other results suggest that boys with
developmental dyslexia process cerebral information differently from
normal readers.

841 Smith, Donald E. P. "The neurophysiology of reading disability."
        In: National Reading Conference for Colleges and Adults. Yearbook:
        significant elements in college and adult reading improvement.
        Vol. 7. Edited by Oscar S. Causey. Fort Worth, Texas: Texas
        Christian University Press, 1958. 54-59. (6 References).
Concludes that reading disability is a functional and not a structural
problem. It has a physical base and is not caused by poor instructional
methods. It is a medical problem caused by abnormal synaptic transmission
which, like neural functioning generally, is greatly influenced by endocrine functioning. Therapy should be aimed at correcting glandular function.

842 ————. "A synaptic transmission theory of severe reading dis-
        ability." Univ Mich Sch Educ Bull 29(2): 25-28, November, 1957.
        (Bibliographic Footnotes).
The perceptual symptoms noted in the severely reading-disabled child,
whether he is placid, normally active, or hyperactive, may be accounted
for by a theory based upon the functioning of the brain rather than upon
its structure. "Brain-damaged" behavior may result from too much or too
little of the ingredients necessary for normal brain function. The chemical theory of neural transmission is explained. The placid child appears
to be "stimulus-bound," having too much of the transmitter agent acetylcholine (ACh). This child is unable to move attention ahead fast enough
to blend letters or sounds. The hyperactive child is termed cholinesterase (ChE) dominant. ChE is an enzyme which inactivates ACh. The result
is a brief memory. The normally active child who is a poor reader may
have a normal balance of these substances, but at a low level of concentration. Superior readers appear to have a balance of ACh and ChE at a
high concentration level. The relationship of endocrine level to reading
and other problems warrants continuing study.

843 Thompson, Lloyd J. "Reading disorders in children." JAMA 207(2):
        369-70, January 13, 1969. (0 References).
Letter to editor. Developmental dyslexia is caused by an innate neurophysiological developmental lag. It is therefore organic but is different from brain damage. It is a mistake to believe that developmental
dyslexia is either organic or environmental in origin. It is constitutional, very often genetically determined, and is not caused by damage
to the brain even in a minor degree. Most dyslexic children can be helped
through special remedial reading techniques.

844   Witty, Paul A., and Kopel, David.   "Factors associated with the
        etiology of reading disability."   J Educ Res   29:   449-59, February,
        1936.   (18 References).
Concludes that the cause of reading disability lies in no single visual
(or other noumenal) factor.   Visual defects, including slow fusion, no
fusion, lateral muscle imbalance, deficient acuity, and ametropia appear
to contribute little to reading disability.

Q. NEUROPSYCHOLOGICAL FACTORS

845   Benton, Arthur L.   "Language disorders in children."   Can Psychol
        7a(4, Institute Supplement):   298-312, 1966.   (9 References).
After discussing language as communication in general terms, the author
reviews four language problems in more detail: acquired aphasia; developmental aphasia; developmental dyslexia; and acquired brain damage and developmental dyslexia.   The neuropsychological aspects of the problem are
considered: handedness and cerebral dominance, heredity as a cause; the
slight evidence for endocrine involvement, and cerebral maturation. Other
cases may arise from brain damage acquired by the child before reading
instruction begins.

846   Corkin, Suzanne.   "Serial-ordering deficits in inferior readers."
        Neuropsychologia   12(3):   347-54, July, 1974.   (9 References).
Preschool boys four and five years old and groups of schoolboys ages six
to eleven who were average or inferior readers were given tests of serial
ordering.   The visual tests involved cubes in which the examiner tapped
the cubes in various orders, and the child was asked to repeat the tapping.
The auditory tests used strings of digits.   The child was asked to repeat the digits.   Efficiency in all groups increased markedly with age.
Results suggest that reading disorders in children may arise from a general deficit in serial organization ability.   Not being right-handed and
crossed hand-eye dominance were as common in poor as in average readers.

847   De Hirsch, Katrina.   "Gestalt psychology as applied to language
        disturbances."   J Nerv Ment Dis   120(3-4):   257-61, September-
        October, 1954.   (20 References).
It has been observed that children ages three, four, and five years who
have trouble learning to speak intelligibly, later at ages nine or ten
have difficulty learning to read, even though in the intervening years
their oral language background has become good and their speech patterns
thoroughly acceptable.   Intelligence in these children is normal, yet
they are dyslexics: failing in reading.   It is suggested that the reason is that speech-delayed, dyslalic, and dyslexic children have trouble
at every level of integration.   The theory is stated that they have difficulty with structuralization and organization of gestalten.   Gestalt
psychology defines the gestalt function as the ability of the organism
to respond to a given constellation of stimuli as to a whole: as a
figure, a series of musical tones, a pattern of pencil strokes (seeing
a pattern as a square, for example, even when presented at a different
angle).   It is suggested that the ability to experience and respond in
terms of gestalten is one basic condition of successful handling of language.   Many dyslexic youngsters of good intelligence do relatively poorly in abstract performance; have difficulty in fine muscular control;
and are late in establishing laterality.   It is believed that maturational
delay is a significant factor in language disorders.

848 Doehring, Donald Gene. Patterns of impairment in specific reading
      disability; a neuropsychological investigation. Bloomington,
      Indiana: Indiana University Press, 1968. 193p. (Bibliography
      p. 186-90). (Indiana University Science Series, No. 23).
Describes research done with the explicit theoretical consideration of
the possibility that retarded readers might display a pattern of disability resembling that of adults with lesions of the left cerebral hemisphere.
Thirty-nine boys with severe specific reading problems between the ages
of ten and fourteen years and IQs above 90 with normal vision and without
environmental deprivation were selected as subjects for the study. Groups
of thirty-nine boys and thirty-nine girls designated as normal readers
were matched with the retarded readers for age and performance IQ. The
entire set of tests given yielded 109 measures for use in statistical
comparison of the groups. Most were from the Indiana Neuropsychology
Battery and the Minnesota Aphasia Test. Details of the procedure, scoring methods of analysis, and test-by-test comparison of the groups of
children are given. Neurological status, developmental and birth history,
and family history findings are included. Statistical methods and results and methods used in the individual analysis of the children are
shown in detail.

The test-by-test comparison of the groups does not markedly resemble the
patterns of impairment which result from cerebral lesions in adults. What
these comparisons do reveal is that reading disability in this group of
children was accompanied by impairment of a wide variety of skills which
do not require reading. This appeared most consistently in a small set
of visual and verbal tasks which required that related material be dealt
with in a particular order (sequential processing). Other visual and
verbal tasks were done at normal levels. This finding is interpreted in
relation to several psychological theories which are explained. No direct
evidence of neurological disturbance was found, but findings of interest
are discussed. The idea of "otherwise normal intelligence" in retarded
readers is seriously questioned. Retarded readers were found to be significantly deficient on all WISC verbal subtests and on one of the five
performance subtests. Suggestions are made for redefining reading disability in terms of a comprehensive and detailed list of abilities.

849 Eisenberg, Leon. "Reading retardation: I. Psychiatric and socio-
      logic aspects." Pediatrics 37(2): 352-65, February, 1966. (45
      References).
Presents statistics on the prevalence of illiteracy and reading retardation. Sources of reading retardation are described, including defects
in teaching and deficiencies in the child's environment and motivation.
Psychophysiological sources of reading retardation are discussed under
five categories: general poor health; defects of vision and other senses;
intellectual defects; brain injury; and specific reading injury for which
there is no known cause. Suggestions for treatment are given.

850 Greenhill, Neil Jon. "The relationship between language, categoriza-
      tion, and primary dyslexia." For a summary see: Diss Abstr Int
      34A(4): 1699, October, 1973.

851 Isom, John B. "Some neuropsychological findings in children with
      reading problems." Claremont Coll Read Conf Yearb 32: 188-98,
      1968. (10 References).
Poor readers ages seven to sixteen years who had been referred to a medical facility for evaluation of reading disability were given tests to

establish IQ and laterality. IQs ranged from 80 to 130 with most scores
between 90 and 120. Comparisons were made with normal and superior
readers. Results show: (1) The three groups were equal in amount of
left-handedness. (2) Left eyedness was about equal in normal and superior groups, but the difference in reading ability between the two groups
was enormous. (3) Crossed eye-hand laterality occurred less often in
advanced than in poor readers, but more often in advanced than in average readers. (4) The superior readers were not equated for IQ with other
groups, the superior readers' scores ranging from 125 to 170. It is
concluded that poor readers differ from average or superior readers in
their ability to process information presented in sequence. Normal readers learn to associate the auditory and visual symbol and learn the meaning of either or both simultaneously. Strongly right- or left-handed
individuals tend to be more advanced than those without well-defined handedness.

852 Knights, Robert M., and Bakker, Dirk J., eds. The neuropsychology
     of learning disorders: theoretical approaches. Baltimore, Mary-
     land: University Park Press, 1976. 532p. (Bibliography p. 469-
     521).
The frequency of occurrence and the relationship to learning disabilities
and to reading disability of physiological, biochemical, genetic, and
maturational factors are considered. Cerebral dominance and perceptual
factors are discussed. The use of drugs in cases of learning disability
is evaluated. It is pointed out that study of reading problems has been
hindered by lack of agreement as to what constitutes reading difficulty.
It is suggested that children who are disabled readers are unable to integrate information from ears and eyes as efficiently as normal readers.
It appears that one important condition underlying reading retardation
is the inability to perform well visual and verbal tasks that require
sequential ordering. Reading-disabled children do not appear to share
the pattern of disabilities of adults with left-hemisphere lesions. The
viewpoint in general of this collection of articles is that topics like
developmental lag, hemispheric asymmetry, cognitive and perceptual deficits, attention, and arousal are genuine topics for discussion under the
general heading of "human neuropsychology."

853 McProuty, Vivian Helen. "Piaget's theory as the basis for the
     assessment of reading disability and suggested remediation through
     an adapted science curriculum." For a summary see: Diss Abstr
     Int 32A(5): 2488, November, 1971.

854 Mattis, Steven; French, Joseph H.; Rapin, Isabelle. "Dyslexia in
     children and young adults: three independent neuropsychological
     syndromes." Dev Med Child Neurol 17(2): 150-63, April, 1975.
     (44 References).
In an attempt to isolate the causes of dyslexia, researchers divided 113
children and young adults eight to eighteen years old into three groups:
(1) those with brain damage who could read; (2) those with brain damage
who were dyslexic; and (3) those without brain damage who were dyslexic.
A battery of neuropsychological tests was administered. No significant
differences were found between the two dyslexic groups. Three syndromes
were found among most of the children with dyslexia: language disorder;
articulation and graphomotor incoordination; and visuoperceptual disorder. The results suggest that dyslexia is caused by multiple independent defects in higher cortical functioning rather than a single cause.
Each syndrome is described. The desirability of including brain-damaged

readers as a control group in any future study on causal factors in dyslexia is stressed.

855 Mosley, James L., and Knights, Robert M. "Neuropsychological test
       results of dyslexic, non-dyslexic and normal children." Can Psychol
       9(2): 285-86, April, 1968. (0 References).
Reports a study investigating the results of a battery of motor, sensory,
verbal, and reasoning ability tests given to groups of children classified as dyslexic, "non-dyslexic," and normal. The intent of the study
was to investigate the pattern of abilities of the children. Results
suggest that developmental dyslexia was not different from mild forms of
brain damage.

856 Myklebust, Helmer R., and Boshes, Benjamin. "Psychoneurological
       learning disorders in children." Arch Pediatr 77: 247-56, June,
       1960. (25 References).
Psychoneurological learning disorders are those which have their origins
in neurological disorders. The term includes only psychological and behavioral disorders which stem from neurological sources no matter what
the cause or age of onset. Among these, apraxia, expressive aphasia,
congenital agnosia, receptive aphasia, dyslexia, and dyscalculia are defined. Some case histories are cited.

857 Rabinovitch, Ralph D., and Ingram, Winifred. "Neuropsychiatric con-
       siderations in reading retardation." Read Teach 15(6): 433-38,
       May, 1962. (8 References).
Distinguishes between children with primary reading retardation of biologic nature and those with secondary difficulties caused by emotional
disturbance or limited educational opportunity. The focus is mostly on
those with the first disorder. Three major diagnostic groupings are
identified. The broad term "reading retardation" is used to describe all
cases in which there is a significant discrepancy between mental age on
performance tests and level of reading achievement. These groups are:
(1) Primary reading retardation which is biologic or endogenous in origin.
It appears to reflect a basic disturbed pattern of neurological organization. The child has impaired capacity to learn without evidence of definite brain damage. The defect is in ability to deal with letters or words
as symbols and hence derive meaning from written material. (2) Brain
injury with resultant reading retardation. In these cases capacity to
learn to read is impaired by frank brain damage. They appear similar to
the adult dyslexia described in early medical literature. (3) Secondary
reading retardation where the causes are exogenous or external. The child
has the capacity to learn to read but it is not utilized sufficiently for
the child to achieve a reading level appropriate to his mental age. Im-
pairing factors include negativism, anxiety, depression, emotional blocking, psychosis, limited schooling opportunity, or other external influences. Everyone working with children with severe reading problems
realizes the need for more precise diagnostic criteria. The researchers
working from the standpoint of these three groups are approaching the
problem in two ways: longitudinal study of reading progress of public-
school children using a large battery of tests; and attempts to refine
diagnostic criteria by detailed analysis of test data.

858 Vellutino, Frank R.; Steger, Joseph A.; Harding, Constance J.; et al.
       "Verbal vs non-verbal paired-associates learning in poor and normal
       readers." Neuropsychologia 13(1): 75-82, January, 1975. (23
       References).

Groups of poor and normal readers were selected from grades four, five, and six in a suburban school system. Tasks included asking the children to learn to give an oral response to the presentation of each of five simple designs (the visual and auditory nonverbal pairs); and learning to associate verious nonsense visual and verbal pairs of drawings and letters or letter-like figures. Poor readers did as well as good readers on nonverbal tasks, but were inferior on verbal tasks. Results were interpreted and analyzed in terms of possible select language disorder (intrahemispheric) in poor readers, or a dysfunction in visual-verbal interhemispheric integration.

R. PERCEPTUAL PROBLEMS

1. GENERAL DISCUSSION OF PERCEPTUAL DEFICIT

859   Bakker, Dirk J.   Temporal order in disturbed reading: developmental and neuropsychological aspects in normal and reading-retarded children.   Rotterdam, Netherlands: Rotterdam University Press, 1972. 100p.
Reviews the literature, and presents a series of studies concerning the relationship of a number of variables including age, sex, and reading ability as they relate to temporal order perception (the perception of things or events in their order in time).   There is speculation on the implications of these research findings.   The relation of temporal order perception (TOP) and reading does not appear to be the same under all conditions, although it always distinguished normal and reading-disturbed children in the tests reported in this study.   TOP defined reading ability in girls at an earlier age than boys.   At an older age, TOP correlated with reading ability in boys, but not with that of girls.

860   Catterall, Calvin D., and Weise, Philip.   "A perceptual approach to early reading difficulties."   Calif J Educ Res   10(5):   212-19, 225, November, 1959.   (33 References).
Defines "perception" as the integration of current sensory input--all that the person takes in through eyes, ears, and other senses--in the light of past experiences.   Reading difficulties are discussed from the viewpoint that perception so defined plays a vital role in the beginning processes of reading.   It is pointed out that this view does not necessarily contradict the theories that reading problems are caused largely by poor teaching methods or by emotional problems.   Some literature in the field is discussed from this standpoint.   Several experimental studies are described.   It is concluded that the most successful approach to beginning reading will take into account the overall maturational growth of the child.   Emotional disturbance is more often secondary to the reading problem.   Current thinking is directed to the idea that reading-disabled children have disturbances in perceptual-developmental growth, rather than definite trauma to brain cells as the term "brain-injured" implies.   It is hoped the approaches outlined will bring about developmental and screening processes that will help circumvent early reading problems.

861   Crawford, John Edmund.   Children with subtle perceptual-motor difficulties.   Pittsburgh, Pennsylvania: Stanwix House, 1966.   264p.
Although the main focus of this book is on "invisibly handicapped" children who are slow about learning for many neurological or perceptual

reasons, the book also discusses reading disability and dyslexia. Reading problems often appear in children with the other classic signs of classroom trouble: distractibility, motor problems, figure-background disturbances, and various distortions in perception. Some reading disability is caused by the use of sight methods of teaching reading rather than the use of phonetic methods. Dyslexia is not commonly caused by slight head injuries or ordinary infections alone. Interhemisphere confusion rather than left-hemisphere dominance in the brain may be a cause.

862   Croxen, Mary E., and Lytton, Hugh. "Reading disability and diffi-
       culties in finger localization and right-left discrimination."
       Dev Psychol 5(2): 256-62, September, 1971. (10 References).
The results of tests for finger localization and right-left discrimination in English children nine and ten years old who were reading at a
level below expectation show that these children had significantly greater
difficulty with both the localization and discrimination than normally
reading controls. The conclusion is that some reading disability is
associated with general perceptual deficit. This defect in ordering in
space is possibly of neurological origin. It manifests itself in deficient body schema and praxis. (See Items No. 276 and 296 for a criticism
of this research and a reply).

863   De Hirsch, Katrina. "Concepts related to normal reading processes
       and their application to reading pathology." J Genet Psychol
       102(2): 277-87, June, 1963. (34 References).
Some aspects of the normal reading process shed helpful light on the
problems of dyslexics. Reading requires integration of the letters and
sounds into a whole, and differentiation of these visual and auditory
patterns from each other. Dyslexic children lag in both of these abilities. Any remedial approach must take into account the dyslexic child's
difficulties with basic configurations. Phonetic teaching is useful for
this approach. The views expressed are stated in terms of gestalt psychology.

864   Hamilton, Gladys. "Handicaps in perception." Monday Morning 4(4):
       28-29, 1970.

865   Ingram, T. T. S. "Perceptual disorders causing dyslexia and dys-
       graphia in cerebral palsy." Little Club Clin Dev Med 2: 97-104,
       1960. (1 Reference).
Describes symptoms of dyslexia and dysgraphia in normal children and discusses some of the reasons they are more severe in children with cerebral
palsy. A child who has had normal educational opportunities and is two
or more years behind his mental age in reading and writing may be arbi-
trarily considered to have dyslexia and dysgraphia. Difficulties may be
classified into three categories: visuospatial, correlating difficulties,
and speech-sound. Beyond difficulties of hearing and vision, emotional
problems, or damage to dominant brain hemisphere early in life lie more
subtle causes for these problems. In some families slow speech development and/or developmental dyslexia are common, especially in males.
These reading and writing difficulties may be similar to those in children with cerebral palsy. Very often all one can say is that the cause
is unknown.

866   Leppmann, Peter K. "Reading disability and perceptual flexibility."
       For a summary see: Diss Abstr 29B(10): 3943-44, April, 1969.

867   Potter, Muriel Catherine. <u>Perception of symbol orientation and</u>
       <u>early reading success</u>. New York: Bureau of Publications, Teachers
       College, Columbia University, 1949. 69p. (Teachers College,
       Columbia University Contributions to Education, No. 939).
Six hundred first-grade children were individually presented with a drawing or a group of letters. This figure was then covered, and the child
was asked to pick the one like it from a group of four similar forms or
letters. Scores on this perceptual discrimination test did not seem to
improve with retesting. The shape-matching, two-letter matching, and a
mirror-error test were found to have the highest relationships to reading achievement. No significant sex differences were found.

868   Snyder, Audrey Ethel. "An investigation into the nature of reading
       disability." For a summary see: <u>Diss Abstr</u> 12(3): 336-37, 1952.

869   Walters, Richard H., and Doan, Helen. "Perceptual and cognitive
       functioning of retarded readers." <u>J Consult Psychol</u> 26(4): 355-
       61, August, 1962. (8 References).
Boys in seventh and eighth grades with IQs between 90 and 120 were divided
into three groups: retarded, average, and advanced readers. They were
given a battery of tests to measure perceptual and cognitive abilities,
especially symbolic learning. Tests included: (1) perceptual closure
using the Steer-Beatty Closure-Threshold Test; (2) a test of perceptual
differentiation in which the child was asked to select from a group of
designs the design that matched a standard design; (3) reaction times as
measured by his response to a multiple-choice test; and (4) a test of
symbolic learning ability in which the task was to learn to associate a
colored light with the appropriate compartment in a box. In general,
advanced and average readers performed better than retarded readers.
Some of the tasks were rewarded with a prize of a small toy. The reward
did not influence performance consistently, but in most cases improved
the performance of both advanced and retarded readers. Reward had little
effect on average readers. Retarded readers had trouble with decision-
making; in associating a symbol with an object; and in perceptual discrimination. It is suggested that retarded readers' difficulties are
both cognitive and perceptual. They may also lack motivation.

870   Whipple, Clifford I., and Kodman, Frank, Jr. "A study of discrimina-
       tion and perceptual learning with retarded readers." <u>J Educ Psychol</u>
       160(1): 1-5, February, 1969. (23 References).
In experiments where retarded readers were given items to be learned both
simultaneously and successively, the retarded readers differed significantly from normal readers in both tasks. They also differed from normal
readers in perceptual learning tasks. Subjects were fourth- and fifth-
grade boys and girls.

2. VISUAL PERCEPTION

871   Alexander, Duane, and Money, John. "Reading ability, object con-
       stancy, and Turner's syndrome." <u>Percept Mot Skills</u> 20(3, Part 1):
       981-84, June, 1965. (7 References).
In learning to read it is necessary for the child to recognize that a
slight change in form alters the meaning of a letter. Results of a test
using victims of Turner's syndrome as subjects showed, it is believed,
that reading deficits must be specific to the language function and are
not connected with the space-form blindness and directional disorientation said to be characteristic of Turner's syndrome. The patients used

in this study were not deficient in reading. Thus, in spite of difficulties in space-form perception and directional orientation, they had learned to read adequately. Subjects ranged in age from ten to twenty-four
years. Turner's syndrome is a genetic disorder characterized by retarded
growth and sexual development and various physical deformities.

872 —————. "Reading disability and the problem of direction sense."
    Read Teach 20(5): 404-9, February, 1967. (7 References).
The young child is accustomed to finding objects such as tables and chairs
called by the same name no matter in what direction they are rotated in
space. This is not true of letters of the alphabet which modify their
identity by being rotated or reversed in some fashion. It is not true of
words where changing the order of the letters changes the meaning of the
word. Defective direction sense and defective space-form perception do
not of themselves cause reading retardation. If they do so, it must be
assumed that it is because they are related in the brain to areas and
neural circuits mediating the language function. Direction sense and
territoriality may be more complex and liable to failure in boys than in
girls, causing the greater number of dyslexic boys.

873 Ball, Thomas S., and Owens, Earl P. "Reading disability, perceptual
    continuity, and phi thresholds." Percept Mot Skills 26(2): 483-
    89, April, 1968. (18 References).
In laboratory tests using a display of alternating lights in a darkened
room, the phi phenomenon was used to obtain data supporting the idea that
visual perceptual discrimination is intact among disabled readers as
claimed by Birch. Results do not support the claim that disabled readers
tend to rely exclusively on details of a form, rather than reacting to
the entire stimulus. It is suggested that a more fruitful line of investigation would be one attacking reading disability directly in the
reading process itself rather than through investigation of various perceptual and cognitive measures. Results are interpreted as not supporting Kephart's view that disabled readers suffer from a qualitatively inferior perceptual process.

874 Ball, Thomas Strand. "Form perception and reading retardation."
    For a summary see: Diss Abstr 21(7): 1998, January, 1961.

875 Black, F. William. "Neurogenic findings in reading-retarded chil-
    dren as a function of visual perceptual ability." Percept Mot
    Skills 36(2): 359-62, April, 1973. (8 References).
Two groups of reading-retarded children were studied. One group had no
visual perceptual problems. The other group was significantly higher in
visual perceptual dysfunction. The latter group had significantly more
incidence of EEG abnormalities, birth abnormalities, motor clumsiness,
hyperactivity and/or distractibility than the other group. When the
groups were matched for age, school grade, and intelligence the reading
achievement of children with low visual perception was significantly
better than reading achievement of children with adequate visual perception. No explanation for this is offered. It is concluded that factors
not controlled in this test operated in these children. The use of tests
of visual perception performance such as the Frostig test for purposes
of academic placement and remediation is not supported by these findings.

876 Blackmon, Thomas Oliver. "Reading disability and right-left dis-
    crimination." For a summary see: Diss Abstr 27B(9): 3302,
    March, 1967.

877 Blank, Marion; Higgins, Thomas J.; Bridger, Wagner H. "Stimulus
     complexity and intramodal reaction time in retarded readers." J
     Educ Psychol 62(2): 117-22, April, 1971. (13 References).
Third graders retarded in reading were found to have significantly longer
reaction time than normal third-grade readers. The children were asked
to raise a finger as quickly as they could when either a white light or
a multicolored, lighted cartoon picture appeared. The more complex stimulus, the cartoon, required a longer reaction time for both groups, and
led to difficulty in responding to the next stimulus. The light and picture were presented in a random sequence. It is suggested that poor performance on cross-modal tests (for example, seeing something and lifting
the finger) may result from physical differences in the stimuli (in this
case the light and the cartoon) and not from perceptual deficiencies
alone. The question has practical importance since impairments in perceptual functioning have been blamed for reading retardation. IQ differences between normal and retarded readers were not assessed in this study.

878 Blank, Marion; Weider, Serena; and Bridger, Wagner H. "Verbal de-
     ficiencies in abstract thinking in early reading retardation." Am
     J Orthopsychiatry 38(5): 823-34, October, 1968. (12 References).
In laboratory tests involving the selection of a printed visual-spatial
dot pattern that was equivalent to a sequence of flashes of lights, first
graders who were retarded in reading and first graders who were normal
in reading were compared. The children were matched for IQ. It had been
previously determined that fourth-grade retarded readers had difficulty
with the sort of task that required the child to establish equivalences
among physically different stimuli. The overall results suggest that
such deficiencies are present at the outset in reading retardation and
may be responsible for, rather than a result of, reading difficulties.

879 Clifton-Everest, I. M. "The immediate recognition of tachistoscopi-
     cally presented visual patterns by backward readers." Genet Psychol
     Monogr 89(2): 221-39, May, 1974. (13 References).
Groups of backward and normal readers ages eight and eleven years, matched
for intelligence and age, were shown meaningless line patterns presented
for time periods either greater than or less than a single fixation in
reading. The patterns were such that they had to be stored visually in
the memory. Immediate memory was tested by recognition of the patterns.
Recognition performance by both groups was so low that it is suggested
that this kind of visual memory has little relation to efficient reading.
There was little difference between the groups.

880 Coleman, James C. "Perceptual retardation in reading disability."
     Percept Mot Skills 9(2): 117, June, 1959. (0 References).
As interpreted from results on the Primary Mental Abilities Test, it appears that marked retardation in visual perceptual development characterizes reading disability cases as a group. Subjects were twenty boys
ranging in age from seven to eleven years and with a mean IQ of 115. They
were retarded from two to five years in reading. It is speculated that
the perceptual retardation existed before the reading disability and contributed to it. Perhaps there is a circular relationship in which poor
reading and poor perceptual development contribute to each other. The
test used in this study measures ability to visually discriminate fine
details.

881 ─────. "Perceptual retardation in reading disability cases."
     J Educ Psychol 44(8): 497-503, December, 1953. (7 References).

Studies the relationship between perceptual retardation and reading disability. Of thirty-three children under thirteen years of age who showed
reading disability, twenty-seven were found to be perceptually retarded.
It is concluded that perceptual retardation is a significant factor in
reading disability. The children were tested by the use of the nonverbal
part of the Alpha Test of the Otis Quick-Scoring tests. Each of 100 items
consists of three pictures with one aspect in common and a fourth picture
which is different. Perceptual discrimination is tested by identifying
the different picture.

882   Davis, Louise Farwell. "Visual difficulties and reading disabili-
      ties." In: Conference on Reading, University of Chicago, 1939.
      Proceedings: recent trends in reading. Vol. 1. Compiled and
      edited by William S. Gray. Chicago, Illinois: University of
      Chicago, 1939. 135-43. (0 References). (Supplementary Educational
      Monographs, No. 49).
Deals with visual anomalies and functional disturbances. Conditions include suppressing vision in each eye alternately and physical fatigue
from reading; lack of visual memory; and confusion in spelling. Both
functional and organic eye problems may produce reading disability.

883   Elkind, David; Larson, Margaret; Van Doorninck, William. "Percep-
      tual decentration learning and performance in slow and average
      readers." J Educ Psychol 56(1): 50-56, February, 1965. (12
      References).
Groups of children who were slow and average readers were tested before
and after training to detect hidden figures in sets of ambiguous pictures.
Poor readers made significantly lower scores on all tests. The children
were elementary-school pupils in grades three through six. They were
matched for age, sex, and intelligence as obtained from a nonverbal intelligence test. The background rationale of the investigation and the
results are interpreted in the light of Piaget's decentration theory of
perception as it applies to reading, the hypothesis being that reading
involves the ability to decenter perception: the more decentered a
child's perception, the better his reading ability. Piaget held that the
young child's perception is centered on the dominant aspects of his visual field. As he get older and develops higher orders of perceptual
organization, his perception is decentered progressively by being freed
from field effects. These field effects include principles of good form,
continuity, closure, etc.

884   Feild, Claire T., and Feild, Hubert S. "Performance of subjects
      with reading disabilities on a series of perceptual closure tasks."
      Percept Mot Skills 38(3, Part 1): 812-14, June, 1974. (3 Refer-
      ences).
To test previous research indicating that disabled readers have difficulty
in perceiving and organizing abstract or ambiguous material, researchers
designed a series of perceptual closure tests. Disabled readers gave
significantly fewer correct responses on the tasks. However, normal and
disabled readers took about the same amount of time to perform the tasks.
Material used for the testing consisted of nineteen simple four-letter
words embedded in confused backgrounds. The subjects' ability to perceive and organize visually ambiguous stimuli was measured from their
ability to read the words. The number correctly read and length of time
for reading were used as measures. Subjects were normal and disabled
readers. All were eighth-grade boys matched for mental and chronological
age, with IQs between 90 and 125.

885 Flax, Nathan. "Problems in relating visual function to reading dis-
     order." Am J Optom 47(5): 366-72, May, 1970. (16 References).
No very conclusive relationship appears to exist between vision and reading. Visual deficiencies that might interfere with learning to read are
found by investigation of the development of vision and visual-motor function with emphasis on intactness of form perception ability and the interrelation of vision with other sensory-motor systems. Visual form perception and inappropriate integration of vision with other senses characterize the individuals who suffer from severe, early reading difficulty and
inability to learn word-recognition skills.

886 ————. "Visual function in dyslexia." Am J Optom 45(9): 574-
     87, September, 1968. (61 References).
Attempts to analyze the role of visual function in dyslexia. The obvious
visual problems, such as acuity and refractive errors, do not seem to be
related to the problem. Visual perception factors do form an important
factor in dyslexia. Most investigators agree that visual perception and
visual motor skills are part of the syndrome of dyslexia. The role of
visual factors in dyslexia is largely a function of the definition of
vision used. A comprehensive definition of vision, including structuring
and interpreting eye signals, would assist therapeutic approaches by development of more stable perception of direction and form in dyslexics
and improvement in integration between their senses.

887 Frank, Helene. "'Word blindness' in school children: the predomi-
     nant causal rôle of delayed development of perceptual functions."
     Trans Ophthalmol Soc UK 56: 231-38, 1936. (0 References).
The mistakes of the backward reader are the same as those of the young
child. In the very young, predominance of the general shape, and unim-
portance of position in space are features of perception. Details are
overlooked. The backward reader is a child with delayed development of
perceptional functions who has remained at a relatively immature stage
of perception. Remedial teaching should be started early.

888 Frostig, Marianne. "Visual modality, research and practice." In:
     International Reading Association. Conference proceedings: per-
     ception and reading. Vol. 12(Part 4). Edited by Helen K. Smith.
     Newark, Delaware: International Reading Association, 1968. 25-33.
     (55 References).
Deficiency in visual perception is one of the most common of the multiple
causes of reading difficulties. Certain aspects of motor development
influence reading skills, especially ocular-motor functions, laterality,
and general motor coordination. Poor association between auditory and
visual processes and poor memory for visual sequences also contribute to
reading difficulties.

889 Fuller, Gerald B. "Perceptual considerations in children with a
     reading disability." Psychol Sch 1(3): 314-17, July, 1964. (7
     References).
This study considers reading disability as an impairment of directional
orientation in visual perception. Four categories of good and retarded
readers ranging in age from eight to fifteen years were tested for perceptual stability by measuring the number of degrees from the original
axis they perceived figures to have been rotated. The four groups were:
(1) normal readers (normal children with no behavioral or psychiatric
problems; average IQ 107.21); (2) primary reading disability (forty-nine
children of impaired reading ability without evidence of brain damage,

but who were unable to work with letters and words as symbols; average age
eleven, mean IQ 96.3); (3) secondary reading disability (sixty-three children with intact reading capacity who were not achieving at a level appropriate to intelligence; average age eleven, mean IQ 101.2); and (4)
organic readers (seventy-three children whose reading capacity was impaired by obvious brain damage; age ten, mean IQ 90.7). Each child was
shown six cards one at a time. Each card contained one figure. The instruction was to copy the figure. Care was taken to allow no rotation
of the card or the sheet of paper. Average degrees of rotation were:
good readers, 12.62 degrees; primary disability, 15.12 degrees; secondary
disability, 45.10 degrees; and organic readers, 72.10 degrees. The difference in visual orientation between good readers and secondary and
organic readers was significant. No significant difference appeared between good readers and primary readers.

890 ————. "Three categories of visual-motor performance of children
     with a reading disability and their theoretical implications."
     Psychol Sch 10(1): 19-23, January, 1973. (11 References).
Describes several types of reading retardation in relation to the children's performance on the Minnesota Percepto-Diagnostic Test (MPD), a
test in which reproduced designs are scored for the degrees of rotation
that each figure deviates from its original axis. The child is shown
the design and asked to reproduce what he sees. A population of good and
poor readers was used in the study. Poor readers were divided into three
groups: (1) Primary reading disability is defined as one where the problem is associative rather than perceptual: the child perceives the letters or words but does not grasp their symbolic significance. (2) Secondary reading disability is defined as one caused by emotional disturbance.
(3) The third group was made up of children retarded in reading because
of organic brain damage. The MPD differentiated the secondary and organic
types of reading problems from the primary type because disturbances in
visual perception and orientation are related to these two types, but not
to the primary.

891 Fuller, Gerald B., and Shaw, Charles R. "Visual orientation in read-
     ing disability: diagnostic considerations." J Am Acad Child
     Psychiatry 2(3): 484-94, July, 1963. (13 References).
Reading difficulties in children who are not brain-damaged appeared to be
related to difficulties in symbol association rather than to perception,
according to interpretation of findings in this study. Subjects were
ninety children ages eight to fifteen years who had been referred to a
clinic for psychiatric evaluation or for remedial reading. WISC scores
were average or above. A group of ninety normal schoolchildren served
as controls. There were 166 boys and fourteen girls in the two groups.
Each child was asked individually to copy three figures reproduced on
white cards. Figures were from a set of thirty reproduced from various
presentations of five of the standard Bender figures. The degrees of
rotation of the child's copy from the orientation of the figure on the
card presented were determined. Good readers and those with primary
reading disability (no brain damage but an inability to deal with letters
and words as symbols) showed virtually no rotation. Those with organic
brain damage showed much rotation. Children with secondary reading disability (causative factor exogenous, that is, from emotional blocking,
limited school opportunity or other external influence) fell in an intermediate range. Diagnosis of primary or secondary reading disability and
the presence of organic brain damage was made according to the criteria
of Rabinovitch.

892   Gordon, Stanley, and Hall, Rodney. "Short-term visual information
        processing in dyslexics." <u>Child Dev</u> 44(4): 841-44, December,
        1973. (8 References).
In experiments for measuring the visual information processing of dyslexic and normal children, it was found that the dyslexics needed more
time to identify letters and to separate the parts of a stimulus exposed
sequentially than did normal children. Subjects were groups of normal
and dyslexic readers eight to twelve years of age. A little more than
half the control group was male; about two-thirds of the dyslexic group
was male. In the first experiment the children were shown on a screen
three pairs of figures, an "N" and an "O," two halves of a square, and a
square and a cross. The figures were displayed at an interval so short
that each pair was at first perceived as a composite. The interval between showings was increased until each half was perceived and identified separately. Dyslexics took longer to separate the figures and to
identify them than did normal readers. In a second experiment various
letters of the alphabet shown on a screen were masked by a pattern of
dots, with the interval between the showing of the letter and the masker
being gradually increased. Dyslexics needed more time for this test also.
The implication of the tests is that dyslexics have longer scan and retrieval times than normal readers and slower processing times for visual
information.

893   Goyen, Judith D., and Lyle, J. G. "Short-term memory and visual
        discrimination in retarded readers." <u>Percept Mot Skills</u> 36(2):
        403-8, April, 1973. (9 References).
Groups of retarded and normal readers were asked to judge whether pairs
of geometric shapes were the same or different. There was a delay between presentation of the first and second shape. Retarded readers made
more errors under all testing conditions. Retarded readers characteris-
tically made errors of equivalence. They failed to notice critical differences which distinguished the figures. Errors of nonequivalence were
made equally by both groups and were related to the length of delay between presentation of the two figures.

894   Graubard, Paul Stuart. "Psycholinguistic correlates of reading dis-
        ability in disturbed children." For a summary see: <u>Diss Abstr</u>
        26(6): 3172-73, December, 1965.

895   Greenlee, William Edwards. "A matched-pair design comparison of
        cognitive integrative functions between specific developmental
        dyslexics and adequate readers." For a summary see: <u>Diss Abstr
        Int</u> 34A(5): 2422-23, November, 1973.

896   Guthrie, John T., and Goldberg, Herman K. "Visual sequential memory
        in reading disability." <u>J Learn Disabil</u> 5(1): 41-46, January,
        1972. (5 References).
Investigated the relationship between visual sequential memory and reading ability. Groups of normal and disabled readers ages eight to ten
years were tested by such methods as presentation of a series of geometric forms with the requirement that the form be remembered after it was
removed. The Knox Cube Test and subtests of visual memory from the ITPA
were also used. Reading tests revealed correlations between visual
sequential memory and paragraph comprehension, oral reading, and word
recognition. Test results suggest that reading disability may result
from lack of coordination, interaction, and simultaneity of the various
visual memory abilities required for reading.

897   Harris, Albert J.   "Visual sensation and perception of disabled
        readers." J Dev Read 4(4):   246-53, Summer, 1961. (13 Refer-
        ences).
Eye defects which can be corrected with lenses are of little significance
in reading disability. Binocular coordination is more important, but
clear perception for reading occurs in the brain, not the eyes. Young
children tend to see things as wholes. They appear to receive a total
impression of an alphabet letter rather than the details of its exact
shape. Such perceptual skill is achieved slowly. Whether there is directional confusion or not is of more importance than which hand or eye
is preferred. The visual perception of poor readers can be much improved
through specific, individual training.

898   Jaffe, Brian. "Improving perception of word and letter configura-
        tion." Acad Ther 5(2): 115-17, Winter, 1969-1970. (0 References).
Presents examples of the faulty ways in which dyslexic children deal with
visual stimuli. Audio techniques suitable for classroom use are described.

899   Johnston, Philip William.   The relation of certain anomalies of vi-
        sion and lateral dominance to reading disability. Washington, D.C.:
        Society for Research in Child Development, National Research Council,
        1942. 154p. (Monographs of the Society for Research in Child De-
        velopment. Vol. 7[2]: Serial No. 32).
In tests using public-school children in Reading, Massachusetts, as subjects, no relationship was found to exist between reading ability and
visual acuity or muscle imbalance. A small but significant association
was found between hyperopic defects (farsightedness) and reading ability.
No association was found between lateral dominance and reading ability.

900   ————.   The relation of certain anomalies of vision and lateral
        dominance to reading disability. Unpublished Ph.D. thesis. Harvard
        University, 1942.

901   Krise, E. Morley. "Reversals in reading: a problem in space per-
        ception?" Elem Sch J 49(5): 278-84, January, 1949. (12 Refer-
        ences).
In otherwise normal children, the tendency to reverse and confuse symbols
in reading is believed to be one of the main causes of reading failure.
It is hypothesized that the confusion is caused by lack of familiarity
with the relationship of symbols and their background. A test of this
hypothesis led to the conclusion that reversals are not produced by
"backward vision," left-handedness, mixed lateral dominance, or other
such factors. Reversals and confusion of symbols are caused by lack of
familiarity with the symbol the reader is attempting to read.

902   Leton, Donald A. "Visual-motor capacities and ocular efficiency in
        reading." Percept Mot Skills 15(2): 407-32, October, 1962.
        (74 References).
Three groups of boys from the intermediate grades were selected as subjects for this study: (1) a control group of normal readers; (2) poor
readers whose problem appeared to be caused by perceptual factors; and
(3) poor readers who appeared to be emotionally troubled. On a group
intelligence test the control group showed higher average scores than
the groups of disabled readers. Electrooculogram recordings were made
under three conditions: (1) reading of paragraphs; (2) with the child
viewing rotating stripes; and (3) with the child's head inside the opto-

kinetic drum. Three visual-motor tests were given. Correlations between the electrooculogram tracings and reading ability and correlations between visual-motor tests and reading ability were in the expected direction but did not reach significance, with the reading-disabled children less able to perform the tasks than normal readers.

903   Lyle, J. G. "Errors of retarded readers on block designs." Percept
      Mot Skills 26(3, Part 2): 1222, June, 1968. (2 References).
Retarded readers performed significantly less well than normal readers on the Memory-for-Design subtest of the WISC. Subjects were nine years old. Errors made by the poor readers were similar to errors of brain-injured subjects. An analysis of errors on the Block Design subtest is also given. Average IQ of disabled readers was 100.85; for the normal controls, 106.53.

904   Lyle, J. G., and Goyen, Judith D. "Effect of speed of exposure and
      difficulty of discrimination on visual recognition of retarded
      readers." J Abnorm Psychol 84(6): 673-76, December, 1975. (14
      References).
Two groups of readers, one normal, the other retarded, were given a recognition test. The children were six years, five months to seven years, five months in age. Cards containing twenty rectangular shapes were shown tachistoscopically, one shape at a time. The task was to identify the standard shape from a multiple-choice response card shown after each presentation. Some response cards were easy, some were difficult. Speed of exposure, not difficulty of response cards, differentiated between retarded and normal readers. It is concluded that the perceptual deficit manifested by retarded readers at this age arises not from short-term memory deficits or difficulty in discriminating between alternatives, but through incomplete analysis of the stimulus shape so that distinctive features are not taken into account.

905   McDaniel, Ernest. "Ten motion picture tests on perceptual abili-
      ties." Percept Mot Skills 36(3, Part 1): 755-59, June, 1973.
      (9 References).
Reports on ten tests developed to measure various perceptual abilities including spatial orientation of objects, form identification, and temporal memory span. These tests grew out of examinations originally developed by the Army Air Force to select pilots and other personnel. The tests were given to groups of normal and dyslexic children of normal intelligence. Results suggest that ability to recognize visual patterns accurately, hold them in memory, and find these patterns again among distracting elements are some of the more important perceptual factors related to severe reading disability.

906   Miles, T. R. "In defense of the concept of dyslexia." In: Inter-
      national Reading Symposium, 2d, College of St. Mark and St. John,
      1965. Papers on past and present practices in the teaching of
      reading, research and theory in reading, new approaches to begin-
      ning reading, and retardation in reading. Edited by John Downing,
      and Amy L. Brown. London: Cassell, 1967. 242-60. (16 References).
Much of the disagreement about the existence of the concept of dyslexia may come from misunderstanding and argument at cross-purposes. If one takes dyslexia seriously, it is necessary to make clear what sort of child should be labeled "dyslexic." The viewpoint of this article is that generally, low intelligence and emotional problems are not included in the category of dyslexics. The main characteristics are: (1) confu-

sion over direction, especially letter reversals; and (2) an inability
to make sense of written language, which can result in bizarre spelling.
In the absence of these two signs, there should be hesitation to diagnose
dyslexia.

907 Olson, Arthur V. "School achievement, reading ability, and specific
     visual perception skills in the third grade." Read Teach 19(7):
     490-92, April, 1966. (0 References).
Hypothesizes that if Frostig's theories (that visual perception difficulties are the most important source of learning difficulties) are sound,
then there should be a direct relationship between her tests and the
skills necessary for reading. Third graders were used as subjects. They
were given Frostig's Developmental Test of Visual Perception, the California Achievement Test, and four reading skills tests. The Frostig DTVP
was a fair predictor of school achievement and specific reading skill
ability and proved to predict better for girls than for boys. However,
results of this study do not support Frostig's theories concerning the
relationship between her tests and specific reading difficulties.

908 Robbins, Herbert. "Field articulation: its relationship to reading
     disability and social class." For a summary see: Diss Abstr
     27B(12, Part 1): 4566, June, 1967.

909 Rudisill, Mabel. "Flashed digit and phrase recognition and rate of
     oral and concrete responses: a study of advanced and retarded
     readers in the third grade." J Psychol 42(Second Half): 317-28,
     July, 1956. (0 References).
Two groups of third-grade children, forty-three of the most advanced readers, and forty-eight of the most retarded readers, were given a battery
of tests to determine digit recognition and phrase recognition and the
rate for responding. Material was presented by tachistoscope. It was
determined by previous testing that all words in the phrases were known
to all the children. A highly significant relationship was found to exist
between reading accomplishment and span and accuracy of flashed digit
recognition and phrase recognition.

910 Seifert, Joan G. "The relationship between visual motor perception
     and the speed of eye movements by selected boys." For a summary
     see: Diss Abstr 28A(11): 4493-94, May, 1968.

911 Seigler, Hazel Gantt. "Visual perceptual patterns and their rela-
     tion to reading: a study of one hundred first grade children."
     For a summary see: Diss Abstr 21(7): 2018, January, 1961.

912 Shepherd, Clyde W., Jr. "Childhood chronic illness and visual motor
     perceptual development." Except Child 36(1): 39-42, September,
     1969. (8 References).
Members of a group of second graders who had suffered chronic illness
severe enough to confine them to bed for at least three consecutive months
between the ages of one and six years were found to perform significantly
below expected levels on visual motor perceptual tasks even though they
appeared to have normal intelligence. It is suggested that if visual
motor perceptual ability is related to reading, training in that area as
soon as possible after the illness might prevent these developmental
deficits.

913 Shumard, C. H. "Reading and visual perception." Ohio Sch 46: 23-
     24, October, 1968.

914 Simpson, Dorothy M. <u>Learning to learn</u>. Columbus, Ohio: Charles
      E. Merrill, 1968. 86p. (The Slow Learner Series). (ED 028 556).
Considers the close relationship of difficulties with numbers, copying,
and tracing to reading disability. Also discussed are the importance of
visual perception, eye motility, the child's early development, and physical activities aimed at developing coordination and laterality. Teaching methods and materials are explained. The results of an experiment
with twenty-four first-grade children in perceptual training are included.

915 Spring, Carl. "Perceptual speed in poor readers." <u>J Educ Psychol</u>
      62(6): 492-500, December, 1971. (17 References).
In tests designed to discover whether poor readers took more time than
good readers to decide whether two letters presented simultaneously were
alike or different and press switches to indicate their choice, it was
found that the poor readers were slower than good readers only in the
last half of the testing session. It is concluded that central processing speed for dyslexic readers deteriorated significantly during a testing period of ten minutes. It is pointed out that the observed shift
from normal to long perceptual latency is not a cause of reading disability, but must be regarded as a correlate: one factor among several associated with the disability.

916 Spring, Carlton James, Jr. "Same-different reaction time for letters
      in dyslexic and normal children." For a summary see: <u>Diss Abstr</u>
      <u>Int</u> 31A(8): 3974-75, February, 1971.

917 Stanley, Gordon. "Two-part stimulus integration and specific read-
      ing disability." <u>Percept Mot Skills</u> 41(3): 873-74, December,
      1975. (2 References).
Groups of dyslexic and normal readers ages eight to twelve years were
shown two halves of a black cross. The time between display of the first
and second halves varied: it was gradually increased in five- and then
in one-millisecond steps. The test was presented under both separate
eye and binocular (both eyes) conditions. Dyslexics showed separation
thresholds at greater intervals than controls. Results are seen as supporting the idea that dyslexics have longer visual persistence than controls.

918 Stanley, Gordon, and Hall, R. "A comparison of dyslexics and nor-
      mals in recalling letter arrays after brief presentation." <u>Br J</u>
      <u>Educ Psychol</u> 43(Part 3): 301-4, November, 1973. (7 References).
Groups of normal and dyslexic children ages eight and twelve years were
shown four different displays of six consonants, one display at a time,
at varying exposure times. The children were tested individually. Results show significant differences in the level of performance rather
than differences in kind of visual information processing and support
the idea of a developmental lag in visual memory.

919 Storch, Herbert R. "Retinal rivalry: its relation to reading dis-
      ability, eye movements in reading, ocular dominance, and visual
      acuity." For a summary see: <u>Diss Abstr</u> 19(3): 578-79, September,
      1958.

920 Tien, H. C. "Use of the Organic Integrity Test (OIT) with children
      who cannot read." <u>Am J Psychiatry</u> 122(10): 1165-71, April, 1966.
      (11 References).

The Organic Integrity Test (OIT) is based on the theory that brain damage or dysfunction means the loss of the brain's capacity for form perception or pattern recognition. Since reading is a type of form perception, the OIT was given to children who were nonreaders, good readers,
poor readers, and a control group. The nonreaders scored significantly
lower than the controls. Children who were poor readers were not significantly different from the control group, and appeared not to suffer
from any loss of form perception. It is suggested that poor readers cannot read for reasons other than mental deficiency, brain damage, or organic brain dysfunction. Nonreaders scored significantly lower both on
the OIT and in IQ. This is seen as an explanation of reading disability
and as a unifying concept: brain damage, schizophrenia, mental deficiency, and other neuropsychiatric disorders are all problems of decreased ability to perceive form.

921 Tinker, Miles A. "Remedial methods for nonreaders." Sch Soc 40:
     524-26, October 20, 1934. (4 References).
Remedial methods for word-blind persons should be aimed at helping them
maintain the proper direction of perceptual sequences from left to right
in reading, an area where almost all nonreaders have difficulty. It is
believed that motivation is more important than any other factor. With
sufficient motivation any of several remedial methods will be successful.
Diagnostic signs are described.

922 "Tracing letters helps failures in reading." Sci News Lett 67(13):
     200, March 26, 1955. (0 References).
Reports on a study in which persons who were reading failures were found
to be significantly inferior to normal readers in visual perception. The
reading failures were helped by tracing words with a finger in addition
to looking at them. Findings are seen as supporting the theories of
Grace Fernald who believes that most children who are reading failures
are deficient in visual perception and are primarily kinesthetic learners.
It is suggested that schools should incorporate finger tracing for children who learn better that way.

923 Vellutino, Frank R.; Pruzek, Robert M.; Steger, Joseph A.; et al.
     "Immediate visual recall in poor and normal readers as a function
     of orthographic-linguistic familiarity." Cortex 9(4): 370-86,
     December, 1973. (55 References).
In this assessment of the comparative visual-perceptual skills of poor
and normal readers, researchers employed a visual recall task using Hebrew
characters. Results suggest that visual-spatial deficit does not commonly cause reading disability. The experiment also provides indirect support for the opinion that reading disability is caused by a dysfunction
in visual-verbal integration. Subjects were one group each of poor and
normal readers unfamiliar with Hebrew, and one group of normal readers
who were learning to speak, read, and write Hebrew. All were in grades
four, five, and six and were ten to thirteen years old. The children
were shown groups of Hebrew consonants (called "designs" by the examiner),
and asked to copy them from memory immediately after seeing them. Poor
and normal readers who were unfamiliar with Hebrew did not differ significantly in proportion of correct responses or in types of errors. It is
concluded that poor readers have no organic deficiency in dealing with
visual-spatial problems. Differences between the groups familiar and unfamiliar with Hebrew are seen as stemming chiefly from the children's
knowledge of the language and not from visual-spatial differences. It
is concluded that the visual-perceptual skills of poor and good readers

are comparable. Visual-spatial deficit is an unlikely cause of reading
disability. A more likely cause is dysfunction in visual-verbal integration.

924 Vellutino, Frank R.; Smith, Harry; Steger, Joseph A.; et al. "Reading disability: age differences and the perceptual-deficit hypothesis." Child Dev 46(2): 487-93, June, 1975. (22 References).
Supports the view that specific reading disability is not attributable
to visual-spatial disorder. Good and poor readers from second grade and
sixth grade were asked to copy geometric designs presented briefly on a
screen. They were also asked to describe orally what they saw in another
group of designs and words similarly presented. In the case of words
they were asked to pronounce the word first and then spell it. Poor
readers did as well as normals in immediate visual recall of designs.
Poor readers' performance approximated that of good readers in letter reproduction and naming. They were inferior to normal readers in word
identification and spelling. They made different types of errors than
normals. Findings are interpreted to mean that poor readers' mistakes
in orientation ("was" for "saw," for example) result from a malfunction
in verbal identification rather than optical distortion.

925 Vellutino, Frank R.; Steger, Joseph A.; Kaman, Mitchell; et al.
"Visual form perception in deficient and normal readers as a function of age and orthographic-linguistic familiarity." Cortex
11(1): 22-30, March, 1975. (20 References).
Groups of good and poor readers from the second and sixth grade were compared with normal readers learning Hebrew on their ability to produce
Hebrew words of varying length presented visually and copied from memory.
Both good and poor readers in the group that did not read Hebrew scored
comparably. Both groups were inferior in performance to the normal readers learning Hebrew. Results were interpreted to mean that visual perceptual disorder is not a likely cause of reading disability. The primary purpose of this study was to contrast perceptual skills of poor and
normal readers at earlier and later stages of development.

926 Vellutino, Frank R.; Steger, Joseph A.; Kandel, Gillray. "Reading
disability: an investigation of the perceptual deficit hypothesis."
Cortex 8(1): 106-18, March, 1972. (31 References).
This experiment tested the idea that poor readers assimilate mentally
what they see as well as normal readers do, but poor readers cannot integrate and/or retrieve information as well verbally. The popular view
of reading disability is that it is a visual perceptual deficit. Test
results do not support the hypothesis. The conclusion is that reading
disability should be viewed as a cognitive rather than a perceptual disorder. It is suggested that the perceptual errors observed are a manifestation and not a basic cause of reading disability.

927 Waites, Lucius. "Dyslexia, a form of visual imperception in children." Tex J Med 59(3): 196-98, March, 1963. (10 References).
Dyslexia is a common neurological problem in normal children, the most
common of the disorders of perception. Early reports of its occurrence
are mentioned. Incidence, causes, and symptoms are discussed. Suggestions are made for diagnosing and treating it. Dyslexia may not be correctable, but patients can be trained to overcome the condition so that
only slight difficulties are left.

928   Wechsler, David, and Hagin, Rosa A. "The problem of axial rotation
       in reading disability." Percept Mot Skills 19(1): 319-26, August,
       1964. (13 References).
Tests revealed a significant relationship between rotational errors and
reading readiness and reading achievement in first- and third-grade children. No more errors were observed among left-handed children than among
right-handed ones. Results suggest that all types of axial rotations--
vertical, horizontal, and depth axes--and not only left-right rotations,
should be considered in diagnosing reading disability. The Lamb Chop
Test was used to study the problem of axial rotations. It is described.

929   Wieder, Serena. "Conceptual deficiencies in handling temporal pat-
       terns in first grade readers." Grad Res Educ Rel Discip 3(2):
       89-105, 1967. (19 References).
Groups of good and poor readers in the first grade who were matched for
age and sex were tested for their ability to tell which pattern of light
flashes presented was the same as a pattern of dots, that is, convert a
temporal pattern of flashes into a spatial pattern of dots. Four versions of this test were carried out. Two other tests were also included.
One tested the ability to match dot patterns and the other tested ability
to describe, that is, interpret, accurately patterns of lights shown.
Findings support the hypothesis that these good and poor readers would
differ in their ability to convert the temporal patterns of light flashes
into equivalent spatial patterns of dots. With one exception, good readers did better on all complex temporal tasks. Findings are seen as suggesting that a conceptual deficiency exists in the ability to order what
is seen or heard in a time sequence in some cases of reading disability.
It is noted that before the child can read, he must have the ability to
mediate stimuli symbolically, that is, to form connecting links between
the material seen and heard.

930   Zangwill, O. L., and Blakemore, Colin. "Dyslexia: reversal of eye
       movements during reading." Neuropsychologia 10(3): 371-73,
       September, 1972. (5 References).
Eye movements of a twenty-three-year-old dyslexic were recorded. He
showed frequent fixation pauses, many regressive movements, and a strong
tendency to scan from right to left rather than in the correct direction.
It is suggested that this confusion may explain the errors in the order
of words and syllables. He showed mixed laterality, and two members of
his family were also partly left-handed. He read isolated words, letters,
and digits with normal speed and accuracy. It is suggested that some
dyslexics may be helped by simple training in scanning from left to right.

3. AUDITORY PERCEPTION

931   Barr, David F. "Comment on 'auditory processing factors in language
       disorders.'" J Speech Hear Disord 39(2): 227-28, May, 1974.
       (24 References).
Letter to editor. Literature in the field does not support the view put
forward by Norman S. Rees that failure in auditory processing is not a
factor in dyslexia and specific learning disability. On the contrary,
many researchers have found an important relationship between auditory
perceptual problems and dyslexia. Lack of cerebral dominance and increased theta activity have been found among dyslexics.

932   Blank, Marion. "Cognitive processes in auditory discrimination in
       normal and retarded readers." Child Dev 39(4): 1091-1101,
       December, 1968. (11 References).

Auditory discrimination as a cause of reading failure was studied in
groups of good and poor Israeli readers in the first grade. Israelis
were chosen because Hebrew is highly inflected. Poor readers performed
worse than normal readers on two tests: one where pairs of words were
identified as the same or different; and the other where the words were
to be imitated. A third test presented only one word at a time for imi-
tation. Poor readers did as well as good readers. It is suggested that
other factors besides how the word was presented were at work.

933 Bruininks, Robert H.; Lucker, William G.; Gropper, Robert L. "Psy-
     cholinguistic abilities of good and poor reading disadvantaged
     first-graders." Elem Sch J 70(7): 378-86, April, 1970. (26
     References).
Reports the results of a study of slum-area first graders. The children
were divided into two groups. One was taught to read using the Initial
Teaching Alphabet (ITA), the other using traditional orthography. At the
end of the school year, sample groups of good and poor readers were identified from each teaching method by their scores on subtests from the
Metropolitan Achievement Test (MAT). These children all had IQs between
90 and 110. The samples had the same proportion of boys and girls and
were equivalent in chronological age. Good readers taught by either
method were significantly superior in overall reading achievement to poor
readers taught by either method. It had been predicted that poor readers
would be significantly inferior to good readers in psycholinguistic abilities. This was only partially supported. All the children were given
the ITPA at the end of the first grade. In the groups taught by the ITA
poor readers were inferior to good readers on four subtests. Good readers taught by traditional orthography exceeded the poor readers in their
sample only in two subtests: Auditory-Vocal Association and Visual-Motor
Association. Results suggest the need for auditory perception and vocal-
expressive language training in reading readiness programs for disadvantaged first graders with auditory deficits.

934 Chall, Jeanne; Roswell, Florence G.; Blumenthal, Susan Hahn. "Audi-
     tory blending ability: a factor in success in beginning reading."
     Read Teach 17(2): 113-18, November, 1963. (9 References).
In tests using Negro children in two first-grade classes in New York City
public schools it was found that auditory blending (the ability to reproduce a word by synthesizing its component sounds) was a significant
factor in beginning reading, especially in word recognition and analysis.
Auditory blending ability and IQ in grade one were not significantly correlated. The test used did not require visual recognition. But silent
reading ability in grade three was substantially related to intelligence
level in grade one. However, within a stated IQ range silent reading
ability in grade three depended to an equal extent on auditory blending
ability in grade one.

935 Christine, Dorothy, and Christine, Charles. "The relationship of
     auditory discrimination to articulatory defects and reading retarda-
     tion." Elem Sch J 65(2): 97-100, November, 1964. (8 References).
Three groups of children from grades one, two, and three were studied to
test whether there is a difference in auditory discrimination ability
between: (1) normal and retarded readers; (2) retarded readers and children with functional speech problems in articulation; and (3) children
with such speech defects and those free of articulation problems. It
was found that there is a difference in auditory discrimination between
retarded and normal readers. No difference was found to exist in audi-

tory discrimination between children retarded in reading and those with
speech defects. Differences did exist in auditory discrimination ability
between children with functional speech defects and those without the
defects. Auditory discrimination appears to be a factor in reading retardation and in functional faulty articulation.

936 Deutsch, Cynthia P. "Auditory discrimination and learning: social
       factors." Merrill-Palmer Q 10(3): 277-96, July, 1964. (17 Ref-
       erences).
Hypothesizes that auditory discrimination and other basic psychological
processes are subject to environmental influences. It is also hypothesized that minimal levels of auditory discrimination must be present before reading can be learned. The paper is concerned only with audition,
not with hearing; it presupposes a normal sensory apparatus. It is concerned with the discrimination of one sound from another and with the
recognition of sounds. It is suggested that research using mostly middle-
class children as subjects would not discover auditory discrimination
problems as frequently as research using culturally deprived children.
Early in their lives, middle-class children experience more speech and
less noise and crowding than do lower-class children. The discrepancy
of incidence of reading retardation between the classes is very large.
Possibly part of the cause is difficulty in distinguishing and discriminating sounds. Even if the child's auditory skills mature later, he may
have fallen too far behind to catch up. This would mean that early auditory discrimination training is very important. Statistical data are
presented showing the relationship of the Wepman Auditory Discrimination
Test to other measures for first and fifth graders. Data are also presented on the relationship of reaction time, a serial learning task, and
digit span to reading ability using good and poor readers in the elementary grades as subjects.

937 Doehring, D. G., and Libman, Ruth A. "Signal detection analysis of
       auditory sequence discrimination by children." Percept Mot Skills
       38(1): 163-69, February, 1974. (15 References).
Tests on normal readers and on persons with reading problems were aimed
at discovering ability to match a sound to a sound given, or to pick out
the odd sound from those given. Age span for the groups was seven to
twenty-five for normals, and eight to sixteen for those with reading
problems. Few subjects picked the sound most remote in position from the
sample being matched. Normal subjects and those with reading problems
showed no difference in the position of the sounds selected. Patterns
of sequential responding were almost identical for normal and disabled
readers. Results support the hypothesis that only processing of verbal
sequences is impaired in disabled readers.

938 Firestone, Barbara A. "Auditory reaction time of reading disabled
       children on three processing tasks." For a summary see: Diss
       Abstr Int 36A(11): 7337, May, 1976.

939 Flynn, P. T., and Byrne, Margaret C. "Relationship between reading
       and selected auditory abilities of third-grade children." J Speech
       Hear Res 13(4): 731-40, December, 1970. (8 References).
Auditory abilities of advanced and retarded third-grade readers were compared. Tests which distinguished the groups significantly were those
requiring blending of phonemes and syllables, and discriminating between
pairs of words, nonsense syllables, and musical pitches. These tests
which differentiated the groups required the addition of acoustical tran-

sitions between phonemes or for making judgments in sounds. Socioeconomic
level did not influence auditory ability. One very significant difference
between the groups was IQ level. Advanced readers were more than one
standard deviation above retarded readers regardless of socioeconomic
level.

940 Friedlander, Bernard Z., and De Lara, Hans Cohen. "Receptive lan-
     guage anomaly and language reading dysfunction in 'normal' primary-
     grade school children." Psychol Sch 10(1): 12-18, January, 1973.
     (17 References).
Reports on a study which found a relationship between children's ability
to select between a natural sound track and a distorted sound track and
the child's reading and language performance. Subjects were forty-four
children ages five to eight years. Each child was allowed to select by
the use of a switch among videotapes consisting of Muppet dialogue sequences from Sesame Street television program in which the sound track
was: (1) natural; (2) somewhat degraded; and (3) unintelligible. The
sequence used was the same in each case. All children were given the
listening and reading subtests of the Cooperative Primary Tests. Every
"nonselective" listener proved to have recognized patterns of reading and
language dysfunction. Results appear to confirm the general belief of
authorities that effective organization of what is heard is a prerequisite for the growth of language functions.

941 Holroyd, R. G., and Riess, R. L. "Central auditory disturbances in
     dyslexic school children." J Spec Educ 2(2): 209-15, Winter,
     1968. (24 References).
Identifies two forms of dyslexia: (1) visual-perceptual form which is
accompanied by minor neurological signs; and (2) an auditory form characterized by defects in speech, language, and verbal memory. Auditory dyslexia is associated with defects in verbal memory; with difficulty in
association of sounds with visual symbols; and in general recognition and
interpretation of sounds in the presence of normal hearing. The auditory
form appears to be more subtle and elusive than the visual-perceptual
form. Children with visual-perceptual dyslexia have difficulty perceiving and remembering shapes (visual forms) and are said to manifest clumsiness, hyperactivity, right-left confusion, and "soft" neurological signs.
Techniques for diagnosing auditory dyslexia are given. Findings in the
field of central auditory research are reviewed. While most of these
studies have concerned diagnosis of diseases of the spinal cord and brain
in adults, they are promising avenues for the exploration of central
hearing disorders in children.

942 Kennedy, Helen. "A study of children's hearing as it relates to
     reading." J Exp Educ 10(4): 238-51, June, 1942. (0 References).
Tests for hearing acuity and sound discrimination, and reading tests were
administered to 433 children in grades one, two, three, five, seven, and
ten. No clear-cut relationship between hearing and reading ability could
be obtained. Some of the literature on hearing as a factor related to
reading disability is reviewed.

943 Koehler, Warren B. "Word-deaf children." Elem Sch J 43(5): 273-
     81, January, 1943. (2 References).
Intelligence is misjudged in every age group because of poor auditory
memory. Much can be done to help the child with this problem. Symptoms
of word deafness are discussed. A child with poor auditory memory has
no problem with hearing sounds. He often does not like to be read to.

He has trouble in most school subjects. He confuses oral instructions, and makes a poor errand boy. Unless proper treatment takes place, his intellectual life will be increasingly restricted and actual mental development will be retarded. He may sometimes recognize all the phonetic units in a word and yet be unable to blend them into a word he knows. Suggestions for diagnosis and remedial teaching are made.

944 Lingren, Ronald H. "Performance of disabled and normal readers on the Bender-Gestalt, auditory discrimination test, and visual-motor matching." Percept Mot Skills 29(1): 152-54, August, 1969. (12 References).

Groups of disabled and normal readers ten years old were compared on the Bender Visual Gestalt Test, the Wepman Auditory Discrimination Test, and on a visual-motor matching and speed test. The latter involved matching the faces painted on sets of blocks. Significant differences were found only on the auditory discrimination test on which normal readers were superior to the disabled. Lack of development of the ability to discriminate sounds may be a major cause of reading problems. Early identification and treatment of such deficits would facilitate normal reading progress.

945 Poling, Dorothy L. "Auditory deficiencies in poor reading." In: Robinson, Helen M., ed. Clinical studies in reading II. Chicago, Illinois: University of Chicago Press, 1953. 107-11. (0 References). (Supplementary Educational Monographs, No. 77).

Reports the study of auditory problems of disabled readers of normal intelligence ages eight through thirteen in an attempt to discover whether these problems are related to specific errors in word discrimination. Auditory skills studied included acuity, the ability to hear sounds; discrimination, the ability to distinguish between similar speech sounds; and memory span, the ability to remember sounds. The children included fifty-eight boys and twenty girls mostly from middle- or upper-class homes. The retarded readers in this study appeared to have adequate acuity and discrimination in the majority of cases. They did not show adequate auditory memory. It is suggested that the inadequate auditory memory span accounts for some of the failure to learn to read.

946 Price, Landon Dewey. "The trouble with 'poor auditory discrimination.'" Acad Ther 8(3): 331-38, Spring, 1973. (4 References).

Auditory discrimination is not the problem: it is a symptom of deeper trouble. These underlying causes each require a different remedial teaching approach in reading. They are not fully understood. Three possible interpretations are given: (1) The assumption that normal and retarded readers differ in underlying perceptual capacity. A child with this disorder cannot differentiate speech sounds. (2) The assumption that good and poor readers differ in their familiarity with speech sounds and experience with the English language. The poor reader is linguistically impoverished in general and does not lack inherent perceptual ability. This explanation is offered for social class differences in reading ability. (3) Inattentiveness, or inability to pay attention to the reading material may result in poor reading habits and poor auditory discrimination.

947 Rees, Norma S. "Auditory processing factors in language disorders: the view from Procrustes' bed." J Speech Hear Disord 38(3): 304-15, August, 1973. (45 References).

Challenges the widely accepted claim that a major or contributing cause
of language learning disorders in children and adults, including defective
articulation, aphasia, dyslexia, and specific learning disability, is a
failure in auditory processing. No strong evidence exists concerning the
nature of the basic auditory skills necessary in order for a child to
speak or read. Nor is there solid evidence that any particular auditory
factor underlies language or learning disorders. Experimental efforts
to find such a factor have used procedures and drawn conclusions that are
inconsistent with recent research findings in speech perception. The
implications for traditional educational, diagnostic, and therapeutic
procedures involving basic auditory skills (for example, speech-sound
discrimination) are discussed.

948   Robert, Nan B. "Discrimination of auditory durations in normal and
      dyslexic subjects." For a summary see: Diss Abstr Int   34A(6):
      3193-94, December, 1973.

949   Roberts, C. J.; Simon, A.; Thomas, G. "A study of audio-vocal re-
      action time responses in schoolchildren with conductive hearing
      loss." Audiology 11(3-4):   194-98, May, 1972. (0 References).
Two groups of children eight to fourteen years old were matched for age,
sex, general intelligence, and socioeconomic status. One group had normal hearing, the other group had conductive hearing loss. In hearing
tests it was found that sound was perceived faster by both groups at
thirty decibels above auditory threshold. The thirty-decibel rise in
the sound significantly shortened the auditory-vocal reaction time for
the group with hearing loss, and almost eliminated any difference in
auditory-vocal reaction time between the groups. Findings suggest a reciprocal relationship between intensity of a sound and speed of its perception. It is suggested that children with even moderate degrees of
conductive hearing loss may perceive the loudest units of speech before
the quietest ones, producing an auditory dyslexia possibly analogous to
the visual-spatial inversions suffered by children with specific reading
disability.

950   Rose, Florence C. "The occurrence of short auditory memory span
      among school children referred for diagnosis of reading difficul-
      ties." J Educ Res   51(6):   459-64, February, 1958. (3 References).
Severely retarded readers were found to fail the auditory memory span
test on the Stanford-Binet Form L more frequently than any other subtest.
Readers scoring above the median mental age did not show this difference.
The range of scatter on the Stanford-Binet showed retarded readers to be
unevenly developed, with auditory memory span lagging several years behind achievement in other tests on the Stanford-Binet.

951   Tomatis, Alfred.   Dyslexia.   Translated by Agatha Sidlauskas.
      Ottawa, Canada: University of Ottawa Press, 1969. 102p. (ED 033
      522).
Dyslexia is a disorder of auditory origin. The medical and educational
aspects of dyslexia are considered in an effort to alert teachers to the
necessity of emphasizing hearing in education rather than sight only.
The roles of teacher, doctor, and psychologist are discussed. It is
concluded that better listening leads to better reading.

4. KINESTHETIC PERCEPTION

952   French, Edward L. "Kinesthetic recognition in retarded readers."
      Educ Psychol Meas   13(4):   636-54, Winter, 1953. (35 References).

Examines the hypothesis that children retarded in oral reading not attributable to known causes will be significantly inferior to normal readers in kinesthetic recognition. Kinesthetic recognition is defined as the ability to identify previously experienced hand and arm movement patterns when they are encountered again. The hypothesis was sustained. Subjects were white gentile boys eight to ten years of age in grades three, four, and five. They were of normal intelligence and matched for mental and chronological age and for IQ. Only right-handed boys were included. The boys were blindfolded and asked to trace with a stylus a design cut in a masonite block. One hundred designs were used. The child was asked to trace an original, then choose a matching design from two choices immediately presented. Retarded readers were found inferior to normal readers at a statistically significant level.

5. AUDITORY AND VISUAL PERCEPTION

953 Alworth, Robert M. "Audiovisual equivalence of stimuli in acquisition of associations at two reading levels." Percept Mot Skills 38(3, Part 2): 1271-74, June, 1974. (8 References).
An investigation of the difficulty retarded readers have in forming associations between auditory and visual information showed that the below-average readers were inferior to normal readers in all areas tested. Subjects were first and second graders who were either above or below average readers.

954 Blank, Marion; Berenzweig, Susan S.; Bridger, Wagner H. "The effects of stimulus complexity and sensory modality on reaction time in normal and retarded readers." Child Dev 46(1): 133-40, March, 1975. (12 References).
Groups of normal and retarded readers who were third graders were presented with three stimuli: a cartoon picture, a light, and a buzzer. Each of these was presented an equal number of times and each stimulus was preceded by the other two an equal number of times. There were 165 trials in all. Reaction time was measured. For all three stimuli the retarded readers took more time. Both groups responded more slowly to the picture. The light was faster, and the sound fastest of all. When the same stimulus was repeated (intramodal shifting), reaction time was faster than when a different stimulus was presented (crossmodal shifting). Results were interpreted to suggest that the demands of a complex visual stimulus, rather than the demands of crossmodal shifting, were related to reading ability.

955 Burg, Leslie Anne. "An analysis of factors related to reading disability as evidenced in three specifically identified groups." For a summary see: Diss Abstr Int 33A(4): 1311-12, October, 1972.

956 Erickson, Marlowe Oscar. "Orientational skills of children with reading problems." For a summary see: Diss Abstr 25(6): 3686, December, 1964.

957 Heckerl, John Raymond. "Integration and ordering of bisensory stimuli in dyslexic children." For a summary see: Diss Abstr Int 32A(7): 3788, January, 1972.

958 Hincks, Elizabeth Mary. "Disability in reading and its relation to personality." Harvard Monographs in Education, Series I. Studies

in educational psychology and educational measurement   2(2, Whole
No. 7). Edited by Walter F. Dearborn. Cambridge, Massachusetts:
Harvard University Press, 1926. 92p. (33 References).
Eleven case studies of children with reading disability are presented.
On the basis of these findings it is not believed that there are separate,
unrelated abilities to perceive forms of "a certain general character in
a certain general way." The children studied had limited peripheral
vision and had difficulty in distinguishing phonetic sounds. About one-
third of the group were left-handed.

959 Jaranko, Arreta. "Danger points in reading instruction." Read
       Teach 22(6): 507-9, March, 1969. (0 References).
Two danger points in reading instruction are first grade and third grade.
The usual method of presenting first-grade reading is visually. The
child who fails first grade often lacks the ability to make visual discriminations. The configuration of the words may not remain stable for
him and he cannot master a sight vocabulary. He falls behind and loses
confidence. Or, a child may pass first and second grade only to fail
third grade. He probably lacks auditory discrimination. As the pace of
instruction quickens, he cannot keep up with visual learning alone, and
his power to hear and discriminate among sounds is too limited to aid
him. Without help, children in both of these categories are doomed to
failure. The most important side effect of reading failure is damaged
self-concept.

960 Jones, Bill. "Cross-modal matching by retarded and normal readers."
       Bull Psychon Soc 3(3A): 163-65, March, 1974. (13 References).
Normal and retarded readers seven and eight years old were given tests
of visual-auditory matching ability. A pattern of lights flashing and
of tones heard through earphones was presented. One pattern consisted
of some combination of four lights and/or tones, each of the four "events"
occurring separately. A second pattern was presented immediately. The
task was to say whether the second pattern was the same or different
from the first. It was found that retarded readers did poorer than normal readers on the visual-auditory matching tests only when the auditory
pattern was presented first. Retarded readers appeared less able than
normal readers to retain an auditory pattern in short-term memory. There
was no difference in retention of a visual pattern.

961 Katz, Phyllis A., and Deutsch, Martin. "The relation of auditory-
       visual shifting to reading achievement." Percept Mot Skills
       17(2): 327-32, October, 1963. (12 References).
In this study forty-eight Negro males from first-, third-, and fifth-
grade classes were used as subjects. On the basis of a reading test they
were divided into high and low readers. They were tested for reaction
time to flashing lights and to sounds. Retarded readers were found to
have more difficulty, that is, a longer reaction time, than normal readers in responding to the sound when it followed the light, or vice versa.
When light followed light or sound followed sound, reaction times were
faster for both groups than when the stimuli were crossmodal, that is,
sound followed light or the reverse. The groups differed in IQ scores,
but the correlation between IQ score and reaction time was not statistically significant. Results suggest that the ability to shift attention
may be basic to reading performance.

962 McKeever, Walter F., and VanDeventer, Allen D. "Dyslexic adoles-
       cents: evidence of impaired visual and auditory language process-

ing associated with normal lateralization and visual responsivity."
    Cortex 11(4): 361-78, December, 1975. (29 References).
Teen-age dyslexic, right-handed males ages eleven to eighteen and a similar control group were given tachistoscopic tests for word recognition.
Both visual half fields and full visual field were tested. Tests were
repeated a year later with modifications and the addition of some other
tests. The dyslexics were found to have left hemisphere language specialization. They showed normal interhemispheric processing delays for
single letters. They appeared to be impaired in the efficiency of visual
and auditory processing of language stimuli and to have auditory memory
deficits. They may possibly have deficits in left hemisphere visual
association function.

963 Rossky, Ellen Susan. "Visual-auditory paired-associate learning in
     reading-disabled children." For a summary see: Diss Abstr Int
     37B(2): 986, August, 1976.

964 Sandstedt, Barbara. "Relationship between memory span and intelli-
     gence of severely retarded readers." Read Teach 17(4): 246-50,
     January, 1964. (18 References).
A group of retarded readers of average intelligence, ages eight to thirteen, was given the WISC and the memory-span test battery from the Detroit
Tests of Learning Aptitude. No significant difference was found between
verbal and performance IQs. The memory-span tests appeared to measure
the same abilities as a test of general ability. The retarded readers
were more successful on visual tests of unrelated objects than on auditory tests of unrelated words. Total visual memory-span test scores
tended to be higher than total auditory memory-span scores. The conclusion is that this might indicate aural difficulty with verbal materials
rather than deficient auditory memory. Such a memory-span battery would
have diagnostic value for use with disabled readers.

965 Shipley, T., and Jones, R. Wayne. "Initial observations on sensory
     interaction and the theory of dyslexia." J Commun Disord 2(4):
     295-311, December, 1969. (21 References).
Describes two experiments which tested the theory that dyslexia is a disorder of intersensory matching and discrimination. In the first experiment, twenty normal and twenty dyslexic eleven-year-old children were
shown a series of geometric designs. Dyslexics made simple figure-ground
distinctions as well as normal readers. For the experiment in this study,
the child was shown a figure, then asked to pick it out from memory from
four choices on one card, one correct, after a ten-second interval. Each
child was tested under four conditions: no noise, noise during initial
exposure, noise during rest delay, or noise during recall card. Dyslexics made more errors than normals under all four conditions. Irrelevant noise during the initial exposure for intake of the form to be
remembered was significantly more distracting for dyslexic than for normal children. A second experiment using evoked brain potential techniques studied the electroencephalograms of dyslexic boys eight to fourteen years old during simultaneously presented visual and auditory stimulation using a light and a series of clicks presented to both ears. It
was predicted that brain wave amplitudes would be enhanced in normal
children and unchanged, or even slightly inhibited in dyslexic children
because dyslexics appear unable to process simultaneously distracting
inputs from two sensory sources. While some reservations are expressed
about the findings, the theory is confirmed in general that dyslexia is
a disorder involving intersensory matching and discrimination.

966 Stanley, Gordon; Kaplan, Ida; Poole, Charles. "Cognitive and non-
     verbal perceptual processing in dyslexics." J Gen Psychol 93(1):
     67-72, July, 1975. (8 References).
Groups of dyslexic and normal readers, the latter used as controls, ages
eight to twelve years were tested on four tasks involving perception:
(1) In the visual matching with spatial transformation (VMST) task, the
children were shown photographs of three wooden blocks rotated at different angles. Two were alike. The child was asked to identify the different form. (2) In the tactual serial matching (TSM) task, the child was
asked to tell whether the differently shaped block was presented first,
second, or last. Wooden replicas of the forms from the first task were
used. The other two tasks were the (3) Auditory Sequential Memory (ASM)
and (4) Visual Sequential Memory (VSM) subtests from the ITPA. Contrary
to expectation, dyslexics and controls performed at the same level on the
VMST. No significant difference was found on the TSM. Dyslexics were
inferior to controls on VSM and ASM. It is concluded that dyslexics do
not suffer impaired visual spatial transformation ability as such.

967 Steger, Joseph A.; Vellutino, Frank R.; Meshoulam, Uriel. "Visual-
     tactile and tactile-tactile paired-associate learning by normal
     and poor readers." Percept Mot Skills 35(1): 263-66, August,
     1972. (9 References).
The hypothesis that poor readers suffer from a general perceptual deficit
was not borne out by this study. It is suggested, however, that possibly
poor readers have a specific integration problem in auditory-visual pairing. Subjects ranged in age from eight to twelve years. Groups of normal and poor readers were studied.

968 Straus, Erwin W.; Aug, Robert G.; Ables, Billie S. "A phenomenolog-
     ical approach to dyslexia." J Phenomenol Psychol 1(2): 225-35,
     Spring, 1971. (0 References).
Discusses the progressive development of speech into reading and writing,
investigating the complex task of this transformation. Implications for
the problems of the dyslexic are drawn. Speech is analyzed in terms of
its ability to command the attention of a hearer, even a hearer who does
not see the speaker. The temporal sequence qualities of sound are discussed: it fades and dies in the moment of hearing. In translating
speech to the printed page, direct contact between speaker and listener
is lost. Artificial shifts in attention must be learned, for example,
sentence structure, and symbols that stand for sound rather than meaning.
The reader has two basic tasks: (1) He must leave the concrete, immediate,
personal relationship of spoken conversation, and face the silent written
page. (2) He cannot rely any longer on temporal cues of speech and sound
as guides to comprehension. It is these tasks which bewilder the dyslexic. His problems with telling time, reading a calendar or a map, and
sequencing the syllables of a word are rooted in these two basic problems. Distinguishing tenses on the basis of very slight differences and
reading words without substantive meaning are difficulties to be expected
if these two basic problems for the dyslexic are accurate. The dyslexic
fails in reading because of his close attachment to concrete situations.

969 Vande Voort, Lewis, and Senf, Gerald M. "Audiovisual integration
     in retarded readers." J Learn Disabil 6(3): 170-79, March, 1973.
     (15 References).
Groups of retarded readers and normal controls were given a variety of
audiovisual tasks to test the idea that disabled readers have difficulty
in integrating information presented to eyes and ears. Tasks involving

visual-spatial and auditory-temporal integration distinguished the two groups. Visual-temporal and auditory-temporal/visual-spatial tasks did not. Results conflict with the theories of Birch and Belmont who held that auditory-visual integration was the critical skill missing among disabled readers.

970 Zurif, E. B., and Carson, G. "Dyslexia in relation to cerebral dominance and temporal analysis." Neuropsychologia 8(3): 351-61, July, 1970. (26 References).
This study compared fourteen poor readers and fourteen normal readers who were equal in arithmetical ability. The subjects were fourth-grade boys of average intelligence. Each child was tested individually for hand preference and manual dexterity; auditory and visual-temporal processing; and dichotic listening. In the auditory tests, subjects were asked whether one pattern of "beeps" was the same or different from a second pattern. The visual test used two patterns of light flashes in the same way. In the dichotic listening task, stereophonic headphones were used to deliver one number to one ear while another number was heard simultaneously in the other ear. Dyslexics were inferior to normal readers in the auditory and visual-temporal tests, in manual dexterity, and in their efficiency in assimilating auditory-verbal input as measured in dichotic listening. Normal readers showed right-ear superiority; dyslexics were better at reporting material delivered to the left ear. The skills tests were found to be related to reading skill in a correlation analysis. Results are discussed in relation to cerebral dominance and more general language disturbances.

6. AUDITORY, VISUAL, AND KINESTHETIC PERCEPTION

971 Camp, Bonnie W. "Psychometric tests and learning in severely disabled readers." J Learn Disabil 6(7): 512-17, October, 1973. (30 References).
Describes a study aimed at determining whether scores on psychometric tests (tests of visual-motor functioning, auditory perception, auditory-visual integration, and the like) are related to learning rate in dyslexic children being tutored in reading. If learning rate varies as a function of perceptual or sensory integrating ability, a high correlation should exist between the psychometric tests and tests of learning rate in response to remedial instruction. In this study the psychometric tests used were found to be quite reliable, correlating highly with each other. But no relationship was found between these tests of visual-motor ability and visual-spatial perception, and other similar measures, and learning rate or achievement in the tutoring program. Subjects were sixty-nine children ages nine to thirteen years, all severely dyslexic. Findings are seen as supporting the idea that the presence of perceptual handicaps does not predict response to learning in a remedial program. It is concluded that perceptual deficiencies may be more frequent in disabled readers, but learning rate and achievement are not related to the degree of perceptual deficiency.

972 Hurley, Oliver L. "Perceptual integration and reading problems." Except Child 35(3): 207-15, November, 1968. (36 References).
A battery of tests was administered to matched pairs of second- and third-grade normal and retarded readers from two different communities to test the hypothesis that good or poor readers could be distinguished on a basis of visual-tactual-kinesthetic integration since reading is thought to involve a process of continuous integrations among the senses.

No support was found for this hypothesis. In spite of matching, there was evidence that problem readers from town A were different from those selected from town B. Sampling appears not to be from similar populations in the two communities. Significant differences in the data resulted.

973   Nachtman, Robert Martin. "A comparison of reading disabled, reading non-disabled, and visually impaired junior high school students on selected intrasensory and intersensory haptic, auditory, and visual processing tasks." For a summary see: Diss Abstr Int   35B(8): 4149, February, 1975.

974   Otto, Wayne. "Ability of poor readers to discriminate paired associates under differing conditions of confirmation." J Educ Res 56(8):   428-31, April, 1963. (3 References).
Poor readers in grades four to seven were tested on their ability to associate a familiar geometric form with a nonsense syllable (paired associates). It is concluded that differences in the number of trials needed for learning are not associated with lack of ability to distinguish the figures or with the additional task of learning to pronounce the nonsense syllable (trigram).

975   Rudel, Rita G.; Denckla, Martha B.; Spalten, Elinor. "Paired associate learning of Morse Code and Braille letter names by dyslexic and normal children." Cortex   12(1):   61-70, March, 1976. (22 References).
Twenty normal and twenty dyslexic ten-year-olds matched for age, sex, average IQ, with normal vision and hearing were asked to: (1) learn to identify letters in braille by touch; (2) identify braille letters by sight; and (3) learn letters in Morse code by hearing them only. Dyslexics learned fewer letters than normal children by all three methods. For both groups braille learned by vision was easier. Results suggest that the deficits of the dyslexics were caused by general encoding and retrieval difficulties and not by lack of function in one area, whether visual, auditory, or tactual. It is noted that some dyslexic children may be helped by multisensory teaching techniques, but the substitution of one modality for another would not appear to be useful.

976   Sidman, Murray, and Kirk, Barbara. "Letter reversals in naming, writing, and matching to sample." Child Dev   45(3):   616-25, September, 1974. (28 References).
Fifteen children, fourteen boys and one girl, between the ages of seven and fourteen years, who had been referred by their schools to a reading clinic, were tested on a battery of tests for reversal errors in oral letter naming, in writing the letter, and in matching it to a sample presented orally, visually, or tactually. Some of the tests for letter-matching were simultaneous; some were delayed. Details of the testing procedures are given. These children, who had reading problems beyond the age when letter reversals usually disappear, showed a consistent tendency to reversals in several types of testing. Findings suggest that these children were able to distinguish the letters from each other. Since the children were able to copy letters accurately no matter how the letters were oriented in the particular presentation, inability to make left-right discriminations was ruled out as a cause of reversals. Most of the reversals occurred in matching a letter with a sample. Motor problems and any differences in the way the task was interpreted by children and tester were ruled out. The children's performance in some of

the tests improved with continued testing. Letter reversals persisted
in the tests involving matching to sample. It is suggested that a relation does exist between letter reversals and reading difficulty. But the
problems with matching to sample were unexpected and remain unexplained.

977 Wiener, Judith; Barnsley, Roger H.; Rabinovitch, M. Sam. "Serial
     order ability in good and poor readers." Can J Behav Sci 2(2):
     116-23, April, 1970. (19 References).
In tests on poor and good fourth-grade readers nine years old, no differences were found between groups on ability to sequence material in the
auditory, visual, and tactual modes. In the visual sequencing test, each
child was shown two patterns of lights and asked to tell which light had
changed position in the second pattern. In the visual nonserial test the
two patterns of lights were presented simultaneously instead of one after
the other in sequence. The auditory sequencing test asked the child to
say which tone in a pattern of tones had changed position when the pattern was repeated. For the tactual sequencing test, the child's back
was tapped in several places. When the tapping was repeated, the position of one tap was changed, and the child was asked to identify which
one. Nonserial tests were also given in the auditory and tactual modes.
The relationship between sequencing ability and reading ability was found
not to be significant. It is suggested that, while the ability to order
serially is not an important variable in older children, the concept of
order develops gradually between ages three and six. Serial ordering
may be important in the initial steps of learning to read. Girls performed better than boys on the auditory tasks and good readers were superior to poor readers on tactual tasks. The results are discussed in perceptual rather than linguistic terms.

7. VISUAL AND KINESTHETIC PERCEPTION

978 Bakker, Dirk. "Sensory dominance in normal and backward readers."
     Percept Mot Skills 23(3, Part 2): 1055-58, December, 1966. (6
     References).
Birch has hypothesized that the failure of the visual system to dominate
creates reading problems. Studies with groups of normal and dyslexic
readers ages nine to fourteen years support the theory. Dyslexics appear
to have lower visual sensitivity than normals, rather than greater kinesthetic sensitivity. The smaller visual dominance may produce more
kinesthetic interference in reading. Kinesthetic difference thresholds
were determined by asking the subjects to judge while blindfolded whether
a variably-sized instrument felt larger than another instrument of a
constant size. Visual difference thresholds were measured by showing
the subjects pairs of circles, one of a constant size and the other varying.

979 Binkley, M. Edward; Maggart, William; Vandever, Thomas R. "Reading
     retardation and Bender Gestalt performance." Psychol Sch 11(4):
     400-402, October, 1974. (10 References).
Poor readers who also had perceptual problems were found to be more
severely retarded in reading than poor readers without perceptual problems. Both groups were measured by the Bender Visual Motor Gestalt Test.
Subjects were seventh-grade pupils retarded in reading and enrolled in
corrective reading classes. A second test given several months after
the first confirmed the results of the first. In this study adequate
performance on the Bender test was associated with mild reading retardation. Inadequate Bender performance was related to more severe reading

problems. It is suggested that the conflicting results in previous studies of the relationship of reading problems to Bender performance were
obtained because the severity of the reading problem was not considered.
Poor readers with perceptual problems were not more maladjusted than
those without perceptual problems, but results tended in that direction.

980 Erickson, Richard C. "Visual-haptic aptitude: effect on student
       achievement in reading." J Learn Disabil 2(5): 256-60, May,
       1969. (9 References).
Defines the person who has a preference for optical experiences and visual imagery over tactile, kinesthetic, or other sensory experiences as
a "visual." The person who relies mostly on nonvisual sensory perception
and imagery is called "haptic." "Indefinites" are persons with little
or no preference in these areas. In a study using seventh-grade boys
as subjects it was found that visuals were the best readers, the indefinites next, and the haptic, or nonvisuals, the poorest readers. This
visual-haptic aptitude is seen as a significant factor in development of
reading skill. It is hypothesized that the phenomenon is related in
some manner to failure in the early development of perceptual skills.

981 Kendall, Barbara S. "A note on the relation of retardation in read-
       ing to performance on a memory-for-designs test." J Educ Psychol
       39(6): 370-73, October, 1948. (5 References).
It did not appear in this study that there was significant relationship
between retardation in reading and the child's visual-motor integration
as measured by difficulty in remembering drawings or in a tendency to
reverse the designs. The memory-for-designs test is made up of fifteen
straight-line figures, each on a separate card. Subjects were asked to
reproduce each design from memory after seeing it for five seconds.
Subjects were six to sixteen years old.

982 Lawton, M. Shaune, and Seim, Robert D. "Developmental investigation
       of tactual-visual integration and reading achievement." Percept
       Mot Skills 36(2): 375-82, April, 1973. (18 References).
An equal number of boys from grades two, four, and six took part in this
study; average ages were seven, ten, and eleven. All were given a mental
abilities test and a reading test. They were asked to feel a raised geometric shape made of balsa wood mounted on cardboard without seeing it.
They were then asked to select the matching shape by vision alone from
four possible choices (tactual-vision). In a second task, the presentation order was reversed, the cards being shown before the tactual exploration of the test form (visual-tactual). It had been hypothesized that
both tactual-visual and visual-tactual performance would be related to
reading performance. Tactual-visual integration was not significantly
related to reading in grades two and four, but was related to comprehension in grade six. Visual-tactual integration was not significant for
any grade considered separately, but was found to be related to reading
ability if data from all three grades were combined. The observed correlations between integration and reading were attributed to the relationship between intelligence and integration and reading.

983 Nielsen, Helle H., and Ringe, Kirsten. "Visuo-perceptive and visuo-
       motor performance of children with reading disabilities." Scand J
       Psychol 10(4): 225-31, 1969. (13 References).
A group of reading-disabled nine- and ten-year-old children and a similar
group of normal children were compared on a battery of tests. Results
showed more similarities than differences in performance. Only the

Bender Visual Motor Gestalt Test discriminated significantly. Frostig Test of Visual Perception and Goodenough Draw-a-Person Test did not. The conclusion is that impaired visual perception and visuomotor dysfunction are not related significantly to reading disability.

984   Richardson, Graham. "The Cartesian frame of reference: a structure unifying the description of dyslexia." J Psycholinguist Res 3(1): 15-63, January, 1974. (87 References).
Attributes six characteristics of dyslexia to the lack of a "visual, Cartesian frame of reference." The characteristics are: (1) reading errors caused by reversals and rotations; (2) form recognition independent of the form's orientation to the viewer; (3) defects in ability to scan in sequence resulting in confused letter and word order; (4) poor physical body balance; (5) failure to grasp time relationships not related to space, as time of day and tenses; and (6) a WISC performance IQ higher than the verbal IQ.

985   Roberts, Richard W., and Coleman, James C. "An investigation of the role of visual and kinesthetic factors in reading failure." J Educ Res 51(6): 445-51, February, 1958. (1 Reference).
An experimental group of children suffering from reading failure was found to benefit from the addition of kinesthetic elements (tracing with a finger) used in addition to visual presentation of nonsense syllables. A control group of normal readers did not benefit. It was found that reading failure cases were significantly inferior to normal readers on a test of visual perception.

986   Robinson, Marion E., and Schwartz, Lindi B. "Visuo-motor skills and reading ability: a longitudinal study." Dev Med Child Neurol 15(3): 281-86, June, 1973. (21 References).
In a study of the relationship between perceptual problems and reading ability in the early school years, a high-risk group of preschool children was identified. They scored below the mean on tests of visual perception and/or visuomotor coordination. After three years of school, testing showed the high-risk children still had perceptual problems and lower IQs than the control group, but their reading scores were not significantly lower than scores of the control group. The children whose reading scores were lower than the control did not have significantly lower visuoperceptual or visuomotor skills, but both their full-scale and verbal IQs were lower. Results support the conclusion that reading difficulty results from a number of deficiencies rather than any one deficit. Findings do not support the belief that perceptual training will improve reading ability.

8. AUDITORY-VISUAL INTEGRATION

987   Beery, Judith Williams. "Matching of auditory and visual stimuli by average and retarded readers." Child Dev 38(3): 827-33, September, 1967. (3 References).
Children of normal intelligence who suffered from specific reading disability were matched with a control group for IQ, sex, and age. All were given three tests of auditory-visual integration. The dyslexics were inferior to the controls on all three tests.

988   Blank, Marion, and Bridger, Wagner H. "Perceptual abilities and conceptual deficiencies in retarded readers." In: American Psychopathological Association. Proceedings: psychopathology of mental

development. Vol. 56. Edited by Joseph Zubin, and George A. Jervis. New York: Grune & Stratton, 1967. 401-12. (13 References).
In two tests using nine-year-old matched retarded and normal readers it was found that the retarded readers had more difficulty than normal readers in reporting how many lights they had seen or the pauses between lights in a series of flashes. The difficulty appeared in labeling temporal patterns, not with analogous spatial patterns. The second experiment was devised to test whether this problem was caused by inability to "absorb" the temporal flashes and hence label them correctly. In the second test, no difference was found in perceptual task performance. The retarded readers, however, had more difficulty than normals in using words to label abstract concepts. The groups were equal in the ability to label concrete objects. It is suggested that the retarded reader's problem is in the structuring of a conceptual task, and not in the perceptual requirements of such tasks.

989 Boder, Elena. "Developmental dyslexia: prevailing diagnostic concepts and a new diagnostic approach." In: Myklebust, Helmer R., ed. *Progress in learning disabilities*. Vol. 2. New York: Grune & Stratton, 1971. 293-321. (72 References).
Developmental dyslexia may be diagnosed either directly by frequency and persistence of particular errors or indirectly by the presence of neurological and psychometric factors. Dyslexic children show one of three distinctive patterns of reading and spelling which are not found among normal readers and spellers. They are dysphonetic (deficit in sound-symbol integration); dyseidetic (deficit in perceiving whole letters and words as configurations, or visual gestalts); and mixed (deficits in both the other areas).

990 Brewer, William Francis, Jr. "Paired-associate learning of dyslexic children." For a summary see: *Diss Abstr* 28B(8): 3467, February, 1968.

991 Evans, James R. "Auditory and auditory-visual integration skills as they relate to reading." *Read Teach* 22(7): 625-29, April, 1969. (15 References).
Some of the research on the relationship of auditory acuity (ability to hear sounds) and skill in auditory perception (ability to distinguish sounds) is discussed. Auditory acuity seems almost unrelated to reading retardation, and auditory discrimination only slightly related. Auditory-visual integration (the ability to relate the meaning of sounds heard to their written form) appears moderately correlated with reading achievement. Poor readers seem to be significantly impaired in this area. Auditory-visual integration skills should receive attention in remedial reading and readiness classes.

992 MacKinnon, G. E., and McCarthy, Nancy A. "Verbal labelling, auditory-visual integration, and reading ability." *Can J Behav Sci* 5(2): 124-32, April, 1973. (16 References).
Good readers performed better than poor readers on verbal labeling in this study. No difference between good and poor readers was observed in auditory-visual integration. This is seen as supporting the idea that poor readers have difficulty generally in linking symbols with objects or actions. Subjects were boys in grade two. The verbal labeling task used in this study was the matching of nonsense sounds with various letter-like forms. It was essentially a paired-associate learning task. The auditory-visual integration task required the child to select, from

three visual patterns of dots, the one he thought to be the same as a pattern of dots presented auditorily.

993 Mohan, Philip J. "Acoustic encoding in normal and retarded readers."
     Child Dev 46(2): 593-97, June, 1975. (14 References).
Reports the results of a study in which groups of boys who were good and poor readers were asked to scan groups of four to six letters of the alphabet presented as slides on a screen, then repeat them. The same children were also asked to listen to groups of other letters spoken on a tape and repeat them. Two age groups were included in each sample of readers: seven-year-olds and eleven-year-olds. Some of the groups of letters were similar visually or acoustically; other groups were formed of letters which did not look alike or sound alike. It was predicted that poor readers would substitute more erroneous letters on the sequences that looked alike and make relatively fewer incorrect substitutions in the letter groups that sounded alike. This did not prove to be true. The prediction that the type of substitution error made on letter sequences that sounded alike and on groups of letters that looked alike would differentiate the groups proved untrue. The hypothesis was based on the idea that the problems retarded readers have in integrating what they see and hear is caused by inadequate acoustic encoding. Test results do not support the hypothesis. It is suggested that the experimental task used in this study lacked sufficient range and sensitivity to detect differences in problem-solving strategies that may have been used by good and poor readers.

994 Senf, Gerald M., and Feshbach, Seymour. "Development of bisensory
     memory in culturally deprived, dyslexic, and normal readers." J
     Educ Psychol 61(6): 461-70, December, 1970. (19 References).
Findings in this study suggest that the learning disabilities of poor readers who are culturally deprived and the learning disabilities of poor readers who are learning-disabled are functionally different. In free and directed recall of digits in various tests of memory and attention, normal readers and culturally deprived poor readers, all elementary and junior-high children, gave results more similar than those obtained from learning-disabled readers. Culturally deprived and normal readers on the whole were not significantly different. They were unlike the learning-disabled readers who were unable to organize the audiovisual stimuli into pairs.

995 Siller, Harry. "The relationship of auditory-visual integration
     to reading disability in adolescents." For a summary see: Diss
     Abstr Int 30B(1): 392, July, 1969.

996 Vande Voort, Lewis; Senf, Gerald M.; Benton, Arthur L. "Development of audiovisual integration in normal and retarded readers."
     Child Dev 43(4): 1260-72, December, 1972. (19 References).
Groups of retarded and normal readers matched for age, sex, and IQ were asked to tell whether patterns of dots they were shown were the same or different from a pattern of auditory signals played while the visual stimulus was shown. As measured in this way, auditory-visual integration was found to develop with age and to be deficient in children who were poor readers. Retarded readers also performed worse on tests for matching within one mode, as auditory-auditory and visual-visual. However, results do not support the hypothesis that integration between these two senses is the sole or even primary developmental skill which accounts for better performance with increasing age. The idea that

retarded readers fail to develop integration skills among the various senses is not supported. Poor attention or inability to assimilate the stimuli accurately are probably causes for poor performance.

997 Vellutino, Frank R.; Steger, Joseph A.; Pruzek, Robert M. "Inter- vs intrasensory deficit in paired associate learning in poor and normal readers." Can J Behav Sci 5(2): 111-23, April, 1973. (40 References).

Conflicting with earlier studies, this study did not find support for the belief that reading disability may be caused by deficiencies in the ability to integrate information coming in by way of two different senses (crossmodal transfer). The conclusion is that, while such deficiencies do not characterize the disabled readers studied (who were ages nine to twelve years), it may be a feature of the disabilities of younger chil- dren. Tests involved learning to associate pairs of written symbols which did not resemble letters, learning to associate a written symbol with a sound, and association of a sound with another sound. Poor read- ers performed as well as normal readers in learning to associate both intermodal (sight with sound) and intramodal (sound with sound or sight with sight) symbols.

998 Vernon, M. D. "Specific dyslexia." Br J Educ Psychol 32(Part 2): 143-50, June, 1962. (16 References).

Reading disabilities are not all of one type; backward readers must be considered as individuals. There appears to exist a severe type of read- ing disability, specific dyslexia, which can be differentiated from other types. It is hypothesized that in addition to specific dyslexia, two other types of reading disability exist: that caused by environment, and that coming from emotional maladjustment. Dyslexics appear unable to perceive and identify sequences of letter sounds and they cannot read words as entities. The cause may be in the organization and coordination of visual and auditory perceptions. Other possible causes are reviewed. The value of remedial training is unclear.

S. PERSONALITY CHARACTERISTICS

999 Bazemore, Judith S., and Gwaltney, Wayne K. "Personality and read- ing achievement: the use of certain personality factors as dis- criminatory." Calif J Educ Res 24(3): 114-19, May, 1973. (16 References).

Reports a study which found that two specific personality factors dis- criminated between normal and disabled readers. Normal readers scored significantly higher on factors labeled "expedient-conscientious" and "tough-minded/tender-minded." Subjects were sixty-eight children ages eight to twelve years enrolled in a summer school. They had just com- pleted third, fourth, fifth, or sixth grade. All children were given a test of mental maturity, a reading test, and the Children's Personality Questionnaire. It is concluded that the normal reader is more conscien- tious, more staid, and more rule-bound than the disabled reader. The normal reader was also found to be more tender-minded, dependent, and more sensitive than the disabled reader. It is speculated that perhaps the sensitive, dependent person--in this case the good reader--was more easily influenced by traditional teaching methods.

1000 Challman, Robert C. "Personality maladjustments and remedial read-
      ing." J Except Child 6(1): 7-11, 35, October, 1939. (0 Refer-
      ences).
Most children with reading disabilities have personality maladjustments
of varying degrees of seriousness. The emotional factors may produce
the maladjustment which interferes with reading skill. Or, nonemotional
factors may produce reading disability which in turn causes maladjustment. Or, emotional factors may cause maladjustment, while an independent complex of nonemotional factors produces the reading disability.
Remedial work in reading must be pleasurable for the child and bring a
feeling of success. Plenty of time is needed. Remedial sessions should
be scheduled at a time when no activities the child particularly enjoys
are taking place. The child should not be embarrassed. Books marked for
certain ages or grades must be avoided since the child may respond negatively if they are below his own.

1001 Gann, Edith. Reading difficulty and personality organization.
      New York: King's Crown Press, 1945. 149p. (Bibliography).
In a statistical comparison of retarded, average, and good readers, Rorschach tests revealed the poor readers to be less well-adjusted than the
others. Retarded readers show less interest in reading. Their teachers
are in a highly favorable position to help them toward security and
growth. The retarded reader is a functioning personality organized in
ways detrimental to efficiency in learning. The children were in grades
three through six in several schools in four cities. Average, good, and
poor readers were matched in "triads" for chronological age, IQ, mental
age, sex, and school experience. The hypothesis to be tested was that
dynamic processes in personality organization which determine its means
or types of adaptation are related to and influential in the reading
experience. These processes may be responsible for, or are associated
with, the reading difficulties. The Rorschach analysis of personality
organization is explained. On the basis of test findings, poor readers
gave much more attention to small, unimportant detail. Normal readers
stressed normal detail and this group contained many personalities labeled Practical. Superior readers stressed whole responses. Both superior
and poor reader groups contained more Abstract Type than the group of
normal readers. Poor readers showed less adequate personality adjustment
than either of the other groups. Normal readers were well-adjusted, the
least abstract and most practical, accepting tasks and dealing with them
without too much anxiety. Superior readers' Rorschach responses reflected an abstract mode of thinking. Intellectual curiosity and a variety
of interests were shown. Superior readers' emotional adjustment was between poor readers' inferior adjustment and average readers' superior
adjustment.

1002 Holmes, Jack A. "Personality characteristics of the disabled
      reader." J Dev Read 4(2): 111-22, Winter, 1961. (22 References).
Extensive research has resulted in little agreement on the relationship
of personality and reading difficulties. Most of the literature still
confirms, as Gates did in 1941, that no single personality pattern is
characteristic of reading failure. An attempt is made to put the problem in perspective, and to that end some of the literature in the area
is reviewed. It is suggested that discrepancies between attitudes of
parents toward their children and the attitudes of the children toward
themselves may be a more important factor in school success than the
children's attitudes toward themselves alone. The idea is explored that
if the value a person himself places on the achievement of success or

failure in some area of learning does indeed affect that success or failure, then it is realistic to speak of personality characteristics in terms
of the value the person places on an activity, for example, spelling or
reading. A "mobilizer" as a dimension of personality is defined as a
deep-seated value system, a deeply ingrained stabilizer of behavior. When
the child's self-fulfilling behavior is in conflict with what his parents and others in authority believe he should be doing, trouble can be
expected.

1003   Kagan, Jerome. "Reflection-impulsivity and reading ability in
        primary grade children." Child Dev 36(3):   609-28, September,
        1965. (4 References).
Children in this study were tested in grade one and again at the end of
grade two on visual-matching problems which involved matching a design
or picture with one in a group of similar designs or pictures. They were
also given a reading test. Those with fast response times and high
error scores (impulsive children) made more errors in reading English
words than reflective children with long decision times and low error
scores on the visual-matching tests. It is suggested that poor scores
on the Bender Gestalt test may not be the result of the child's poor
perception, but is a result of his impulsivity. Remedial reading programs should take into account this disposition in some children who
have trouble learning to read.

1004   Murray, Michael Edmond. "A study of personality, prolonged read-
        ing failure, and early success in initial remedial language train-
        ing in children with specific reading disabilities." For a summary
        see: Diss Abstr Int 34A(11): 7077-78, May, 1974.

1005   Riggs, Sheldon Kenneth. "Manifestations of impulse, ego, and
        superego in boys identified for remedial reading instruction in a
        public school system." For a summary see: Diss Abstr 28A(11):
        4492-93, May, 1968.

1006   Russell, David H. "Research on reading difficulties and personality
        adjustment." In: American Educational Research Association.
        Official report: improving educational research, 1948. Washington,
        D.C.: American Educational Research Association, 1948. 10-13.
        (0 References).
Traces the development of the experimental approach to problems of personality and learning. This approach came into use about 1920. By 1948
much research interest was centered on the interrelationships of reading
ability and personality. To that date approximately 100 studies in the
general field of reading disabilities and personality maladjustments had
been published. Seven hypotheses concerning reading disability and personality are stated which may be confirmed or denied in the coming years.
These include, among others: (1) the idea that no single personality
pattern is characteristic of reading failure; (2) the idea that personality maladjustments do not always lead to reading maladjustment; (3)
the shift in emphasis from one cause of reading difficulty to a group of
causes; and (4) the shift from reliance on one remedial technique to
reliance on a variety of activities. It is pointed out that there is
urgent need for research on the positive aspects of the relationship between reading achievement and personality adjustment. Some studies have
suggested a relationship between reading interests and intelligence,
sex, and general maturity. The relationship of reading interests to personality remain largely unknown.

1007   Solomon, Ruth H.   "Personality adjustment to reading success and
       failure."   In: Robinson, Helen M., ed.   Clinical studies in read-
       ing   II.   Chicago, Illinois: University of Chicago Press, 1953.
       64-82.   (Bibliographic Footnotes).   (Supplementary Educational
       Monographs, No. 77).
The Rorschach test was given to a group of children in first grade and
repeated when the group was in third grade in order to study the relation
of personality adjustment to reading achievement.   Mean IQs for both successful and unsuccessful children were above-average, but IQs of successful readers were higher.   Rorschach patterns revealed personality patterns unique to each group.   The successful readers tended to be more
impulsive and less mature than unsuccessful readers.   Unsuccessful readers gave more attention to minute, unimportant detail than normal readers
did, with overemphasis on the abstract at the expense of the practical
and concrete.   Personality patterns showed change accompanying failure
in reading revealing more immature, impulsive, emotional reactions.   Poor
readers retained their capacity for mature interpersonal relations. These
groups had superior intelligence; marked differences in intellectual
capacity did not distinguish the groups as much as the manner in which
the children approached their problems.   It is suggested that classroom
teaching should be aimed at improvement of perception.

1008   Stauffer, Russell G.   "A clinical approach to personality and the
       disabled reader."   Education   67(7):   427-35, March, 1947.   (14
       References).
The child's attitude and emotional reaction to reading are clues to personality.   Important are the child's acceptance of himself and his reaction to his acceptance by others.   The more fully the clinician understands the disabled reader's areas of conflict, the more systematically
the treatment can proceed.   It is necessary to begin at the learner's
level.   Three case histories are cited.   A number of definitions of personality are presented.

1009   Walraven, Maurice Peter.   "Perceptual relationships: personality-
       reading."   For a summary see: Diss Abstr   27A(11):   3742, May,
       1967.

1010   Zirbes, Laura.   "Some character and personality problems of reme-
       dial cases in reading."   Child Educ   5(4):   171-76, December, 1928.
       (0 References).
Presents case histories illustrating that reading deficiency is often
related to personality problems.   This fact must be reckoned with in
planning remedial reading work.   Often the personality difficulties are
the basic problem and the reading problem is a complication or effect
rather than a first cause.   Remedial work that classifies all poor readers by some single rating is very likely to fall short of its intended
mark.

T. PHYSICAL FACTORS

1011   Berner, George E., and Berner, Dorothy E.   "Reading difficulties
       in children."   Arch Ophthalmol   20(5):   829-38, November, 1938.
       (0 References).
Use of the sentence method of teaching tests the child's powers of attention and concentration to the limit.   Because a high degree of visual

attention is required, minor defects of less importance under old teaching methods now have become significant. These include visual immaturity
and deficient fusion (or deficient fusional convergence, that is, suppressing the vision in one eye which sees only sporadically, producing
confusion). Manifestations of visual immaturity in a first grader may
include poor resolution, or lack of experience in resolving and interpreting the meaning of a symbol. Reversals and slight farsightedness
may be considered as other signs of visual immaturity at age six. Children of normal intelligence who still cannot learn to read after taking
account of these factors probably have emotional difficulties and should
be referred to a psychiatrist.

1012 "Can they really train kids to see better?" Changing Times 23(1):
      45-47, January, 1969. (0 References).
Dyslexia is defined as a symptom, not a disease or ailment, caused by one
or more very slight neurological impairments. Some of its manifestations
and probable sources are discussed. Dyslexia, strabismus (cross-eye),
amblyopia ("lazy eye"), and myopia (nearsightedness) are all evaluated
as sources of reading problems.

1013 Cinotti, Alfonse A., and Rados, Walter T. "Ocular aspects of read-
      ing disabilities." J Med Soc NJ 64(10): 551-53, October, 1967.
      (8 References).
The problem of dyslexia and related learning disorders is of paramount
interest to the physician, the psychologist, and the educator, among
others, because the person who cannot read is seriously handicapped. The
role of uncorrected refractive errors (farsightedness, nearsightedness,
astigmatism) and problems of muscle balance and fusion in relation to
reading disability are considered. Some studies have found large numbers
of visual problems of these kinds among reading-disabled children of normal intelligence. Other studies found fusional problems not to be real
factors. True dyslexia is inability or decreased ability to acquire the
necessary skills and comprehension required in the learning process. It
must be distinguished from disorders which cause difficulty in maintaining the ocular efforts required in reading. All the ocular problems mentioned above fall into the latter category and have no bearing on actual
dyslexia. If they coexist with dyslexia they will aggravate an already
severe problem. Much of the therapy proposed is at best controversial,
and, at worst, sheer nonsense. Reading disabilities are best treated
by a team effort including neurologist, psychiatrist, ophthalmologist,
and other specialists. Therapy must be designed for each pupil depending
on findings of the members of the team.

1014 Clark, Brant. "The importance of the correction of ocular defects
      in a remedial reading program. Results of recent research." Am J
      Optom 12(5): 169-75, 1935. (14 References).
Summarizes current literature on the relation of eye defects to reading
disability. Differences in refractive errors between normal and disabled
readers appear not to be great. Disabled readers show many more eye
problems of other kinds, for example, eye muscle balance problems, low
fusion convergence, and eye movement problems.

1015 Cravioto, Joaquin; Gaona, Carlos Espinosa; Birch, Herbert G. "Early
      malnutrition and auditory-visual integration in school-age chil-
      dren." J Spec Educ 2(1): 75-82, Fall, 1967. (12 References).
Explores the effect of nutrition in childhood on the ability to determine when a sound is equivalent to a visual stimulus (crossmodal integra-

tion). Children ages seven through twelve enrolled in primary school in
a rural village in southwestern Mexico were weighed and measured by a
pediatrician. Two groups, the upper 25 percent and the lower 25 percent
in height for each sex, were identified. The total was 296 boys and
girls. Height was taken as a measure of exposure to nutritional risk.
Sounds were tapped out and each child was asked to identify a corresponding visual pattern of dots from a multiple choice card. Ability to integrate auditory and visual information improved with age in general.
But the mean performance of the tall group was higher than that of the
short group at each age level. Since judgments of auditory-visual equivalence underlie reading readiness, it is suggested that early malnutri-
tion may be the starting point for school failure.

1016 Eames, Thomas Harrison. "A comparison of the ocular characteris-
      tics of unselected and reading disability groups." J Educ Res
      25(3): 211-15, March, 1932. (0 References).
The principal finding of this study is that in reading disability the
eyes tended to be exophoric (deviate outward), and that there was more
hypermetropia (farsightedness) than in unselected schoolchildren. Subjects were 114 children suffering from reading disability, and 143 unselected schoolchildren. Visual acuity, refractive errors, and visual
coordination were among the visual characteristics studied. The various
ophthalic terms used are explained.

1017 ————. "A frequency study of physical handicaps in reading dis-
      ability and unselected groups." J Educ Res 29(1): 1-5, September,
      1935. (13 Bibliographic Footnotes).
The causes of reading disability are two: psychological-educational
causes, and physical causes. Of the latter, incoordination of the eyes
is the most frequently encountered factor in reading disability.

1018 ————. "Incidence of diseases among reading failures and non-
      failures." J Pediatr 33(5): 614-17, November, 1948. (4 Refer-
      ences).
To aid understanding of the part physical factors play in reading failure, 875 children failing in reading and 486 successful readers were examined for various diseases and defects. The children ranged in age from
nine to eleven years. Children failing in reading exhibited 21.1 percent
more diseases of various types than did successful readers. Diseases of
the mouth, nose, throat, and eyes (exclusive of dental problems) showed
the greatest difference.

1019 ————. "The ocular conditions of 350 poor readers." J Educ
      Res 32(1): 10-16, September, 1938. (9 Bibliographic Footnotes).
Refractive errors were very common in the vision of a group of poor readers. More than the average number of various other visual defects were
also found. About one-fourth of the children were left-eyed and right-
handed. Ages of the 350 children ranged from eight to eleven years;
grade level from second to fifth. Eighty percent were boys, with about
half of the IQs between 90 and 110, and a little more than one-fourth
below 90.

1020 Eberl, Marguerite T. "Summarization, criticism and explanation of
      data pertaining to the relation of visual disorders to reading dis-
      abilities." Am J Optom Arch Am Acad Optom 18(12): 537-49, 1941.
      (35 References).

Reviews literature reporting investigations of the relationship between
visual problems and reading disabilities. Many studies have been done
with seemingly contradictory conclusions. It does appear well-established
that reading disabilities are usually the result of a group of factors,
each of which must be investigated. Much study has centered on visual
acuity (refractive errors, muscle imbalances, functional disturbances,
eye movements, and dominance). Lack of visual acuity appears to have
little effect on reading ability. A number of these studies are described and discussed. Authorities are divided on whether such problems as
low fusion, suspension, stereopsis, etc., are related to reading disability. The reason some investigators have been unable to prove statistically that visual difficulties are associated with reading disability is
seen as the incompleteness of the examinations, making it impossible to
analyze the visual disability. Confusion has also resulted from a mis-
conception concerning the significance of findings: symptoms have been
seen as causes. Many optometrists do not regard myopia, phorias, etc.,
as causes but as measurements of varying significance. Optometry believes sight to be a learning act in which focus, or accommodation, and
convergence must occur. This philosophy of vision is explained and elaborated. It is concluded that all the school visual investigations reviewed were incomplete and valueless. No valid conclusion can be drawn
about the relation of vision to reading disability until a complete visual analysis is made.

1021 Frisk, M.; Wegelius, E.; Tenhunen, T.; et al. "The problem of dys-
      lexia in teenage." Acta Paediatr Scand 56(4): 333-43, July,
      1967. (10 References).
The causes of dyslexia in teen-agers, when persons of low general intelligence and defective sight and hearing are excluded, appear to be from
brain lesions or heredity, or a combination. Dyslexia is found to appear
sometimes in connection with general neurological immaturity and delayed
bone age. Misunderstanding by parents and teachers complicates the problems of these individuals. Subjects in this study were eighty-one boys
and forty-one girls divided into groups ages ten to thirteen, fourteen
to sixteen, and over seventeen. Findings are reported in two groups:
the teen-agers with known dyslexic heredity and those without such heredity. Abnormal EEG findings, various speech disturbances, marked difference between verbal and performance IQ, and disturbed emotional balance
were among the findings. Results suggest a causal relationship between
dyslexia and functional disturbance of the central nervous system, and
point to the hypothesis that dyslexia has a physical origin.

1022 Goldberg, Herman K., and Arnott, William. "Ocular motility in
      learning disabilities." J Learn Disabil 3(3): 160-62, March,
      1970. (0 References).
Examines the theory that improving eye movements will assist children
with learning disabilities. The eye movements of twenty-five dyslexic
children and a number of controls were examined with an electronystagmo-
graph (apparatus for indicating on a graph movements of the eyeball in
any direction) while reading materials either too easy or too hard for
them to comprehend. Poorly coordinated movements were found in children
with reading problems, but results do not support the theory that learning difficulties were due to lack of binocular coordination. It is suggested that the extent to which the child comprehended what he read
governed the type of eye movement, rather than the reverse, that is, the
ocular motility producing the degree of comprehension. Learning is done
in the brain, and not in the eye.

1023 Kauner, Richard S., and Byne, Robert. "A survey of relationship
      between visual analytical findings and reading difficulty." Am J
      Optom Arch Am Acad Optom 49(11): 965, November, 1972. (0 Refer-
      ences).
In a study of 150 cases of reading difficulty where asthenopia (weakness
or easy fatigue of the eyes) was present, five factors of the vergence
sequence proved to have statistical significance. (Vergence is the
tendency of the eyes to move in opposite directions.)

1024 Martin, Harold P. "Vision and its role in reading disability and
      dyslexia." J Sch Health 41(9): 468-72, November, 1971. (14
      References).
Poor eye coordination or convergence, discrepancies in dominance, and
other similar problems appear not to be significantly related to reading
disability. The ophthalmologist can do little to help the child who
reads poorly. The causes of reading disability may be numerous and poorly understood. The child's central nervous system may be functionally
immature or impaired. But such problems in the disabled reader are not
localized in the ocular apparatus. This same article appears in Sight
Sav Rev 41(4): 185-90, Winter, 1971, not included in this bibliography.

1025 Nicholls, John V. V. "Children with reading difficulties." Am J
      Ophthalmol 60(5): 935-37, November, 1965. (10 References).
Reading disabilities fall into one of three categories: (1) Congenital
dyslexia, a familial problem much more common in the male. It is probably caused by a physiologic disturbance or delayed maturation of a part
of the brain. (2) The slow reader whose disability is caused by low intelligence, faulty vision or hearing, emotional disturbances, or a combination. (3) The mixed type that includes the first two types. The
ophthalmologist is frequently the first physician consulted. He should
not expect to find more eye defects in dyslexic children than in normal
children. When found, they should be managed in exactly the same way.
The ophthalmologist should protect dyslexic patients and their parents
from charlatans who find a fertile field among panicky parents in an area
where much is still uncertain. The ophthalmologist's role includes co-
ordinating diagnostic studies made by several specialists.

1026 ————. "Reading disabilities in the young: the ophthalmolo-
      gist's role." Can J Ophthalmol 4(3): 223-30, July, 1969. (24
      References).
Divides reading problems into three groups: (1) dyslexia, a specific
reading disability in children of normal intelligence probably caused by
a disturbance in function of the parietotemporal lobe of the dominant
hemisphere; (2) the slow reader whose problems are caused by low intelligence, physical, emotional, or environmental problems; and (3) a combination of the first two types. Characteristics of the dyslexic child are
listed. Some literature linking refractive errors and other eye problems
to dyslexia is discussed. Crossed dominance is discussed. Crossed dominance is more common in dyslexics than in normal children, but it is only
an associated disturbance with no predictive value. The ocular mechanism
may simulate dyslexia in two ways: (1) the child may find it impossible
to obtain a clear and/or unitary visual image and maintain it for a significant period of time; and (2) to obtain such an image may require so
much effort that fatigue results, discouraging reading.

1027 Norn, M. S. "Testing of dyslectic children by Jampolski's prism
      test." Acta Ophthalmol 47(5-6): 1116-23, 1969. (4 References).

Tested eighty-four dyslexic children ages nine to fourteen years with
Jampolski's prism test. Only 1 percent reacted pathologically and 2 percent showed an uncertain reaction. It was concluded that suppression of
one eye or jerkiness was no higher among dyslexics than is to be expected
in a group of normal readers. The Jampolski test was devised in 1964 to
disclose quickly a possible suppression of one eye. How the test is administered and how it works are explained. The reaction will be pathological in cases of strabismic amblyopia, or if one eye is suppressed
for other reasons. Strabismic amblyopia is suppression of vision in one
eye by the patient to avoid diplopia, or double vision.

1028   Norn, M. S.; Rindziunski, Eva; Skydsgaard, H.   "Ophthalmologic and
       orthoptic examinations of dyslectics."   Acta Ophthalmol   47(1):
       147-60, 1969.   (16 References).
In a study of 117 word-blind children ages nine to thirteen and a control
group matched for age, sex, grade in school, and intelligence, it is concluded that dyslexia is not caused by refractive errors, impaired vision,
or orthoptic disorders. No preponderance of crossed eye-hand dominance
was found. No causal relation exists between specific dyslexia and
visual defects in the widest sense. Primary reading retardation, called
also "congenital word blindness" or "constitutional specific dyslexia,"
is defined and distinguished from secondary reading difficulties. There
is evidence that the primary form, perhaps inherited, may be associated
with a brain lesion in the parieto-occipital lobe. Difficulty lies in
interpreting rather than in just seeing the symbols. The secondary form
is associated with many exogenous factors including emotional, physical,
and environmental problems.

1029   Park, George E.   "Ophthalmological aspects of learning disabili-
       ties."   J Learn Disabil   2(4):   189-98, April, 1969.   (12 Refer-
       ences).
Recommends a multidisciplinary approach to reading disabilities. Visual
functions have a wide range of adjustment and only very limited influence
on dyslexia. Mirror and reversed vision seem to be psychological in
origin. About one-third of dyslexics have abnormal EEG changes associated
with the syndrome.

1030   Park, George E., and Appleman, James H.   "Dyslexia from the physi-
       cal viewpoint."   Ill Med J   97(1):   30-35, January, 1950.   (0 Ref-
       ences).   Correction 97(2):   81, February, 1950.
Distinguishes dyslexia, a functional condition which is correctable and
preventable, from alexia. Correction is best attained after full physical, emotional, and pedagogic examination of the child. Anything that
influences a child's life affects his learning ability. Among the physical problems observed in a group of dyslexic children of normal intelligence were disturbed nutrition, endocrine imbalances, sluggish or exaggerated reflexes, compulsive types of personality, and nasal obstructions.
Loss of hearing of twenty decibels in all or certain frequencies was
found in 23 percent of the cases. Speech problems and visual refractive
errors were also noted. Ocular dominance, eyedness, or handedness seemed
to have no correlation to the occurrence of dyslexia. Mirror reading may
be self-imposed by the child as an escape or to get attention. Treatment
depends on diagnosis and the ingenuity of the persons working with the
case. Stereotyped methods are impractical.

1031   Park, George E., and Burri, Clara.   "The relationship of various
       eye conditions and reading achievement."   J Educ Psychol   34(5):
       290-99, May, 1943.   (0 References).

Two hundred twenty-five students from first through eighth grade were given complete ophthalmological examinations without knowledge by the tester of reading ability. The lower the child's reading scores the more likely it was that the child had peripheral ocular dysfunction. It is concluded that a definite relationship existed between the kinds of eye conditions tested for in this study and reading skill. The relationship seemed to remain constant through all grade levels.

1032 Park, George E., and Schneider, Kenneth A. "Thyroid-function in relation to dyslexia (reading failures)." J Read Behav 7(2): 197-99, Summer, 1975. (2 References).
Serum total thyroxine was measured in a group of dyslexic children and a group of normal children matched for age and sex. The age range was seven to fifteen years. Thyroxine content of serum was markedly elevated in the dyslexics over levels found in normal children. None of the dyslexic children showed overt clinical evidence of hyperthyrodism. It is pointed out that the increased thyroxine may be due to increased thyroid binding globulin levels, but results indicate an association of dyslexia with a systemic change in metabolism.

1033 Park, George E., and Tarsitano, Rosemary. "Granulocytopoiesis concomitant to functional dyslexia." Chic Med 70(21): 773-78, October 14, 1967. (23 References).
In blood studies done on groups of dyslexics and normal readers it was found that dyslexics are not losing blood cells faster than normal readers. The process by which neutrophils are naturally removed from the blood of a normal person is explained. Dyslexics showed a lower number of white blood cells than normal readers. It is suggested that since increased destruction is not the cause, the reason must be decreased production in the bone marrow. Erythrocytes were not affected.

1034 Romaine, Hunter. "Reading difficulties and eye defects." Sight Sav Rev 19(2): 96-99, Summer, 1949. (0 References).
Ocular factors are only a small part of the entire picture of reading difficulties. They are usually found as one among many causes. Visual acuity, refractive errors, and fusion problems should be corrected if possible; a small defect may not trouble one reader but completely block another. The physician and educator must work together to eliminate reading problems. Since reading disorders are often seen in persons with high IQs, there must be some underlying factor that can be corrected.

1035 Romano, Paul E. "Pediatric ophthalmic mythology." Postgrad Med 58(4): 146-50, October, 1975. (2 References).
Explains the facts and dispels the myths surrounding several eye problems of young children. Among facts presented are: (1) Headaches in children are almost never caused by eye problems. (2) Even babies can be fitted with glasses. (3) Cross-eye (strabismus) almost never disappears without treatment, and the earlier it is treated the better. (4) Dyslexia is not the result of eye problems and is not helped by eye exercises. (5) Using drops to dilate the eyes of young children is not hazardous.

1036 Rosborough, Pearl M., and Wilder, Marion Howe. "Postural alignments as applied to problems in reading." Acad Ther 5(1): 27-31, Fall, 1969. (29 References).
Discusses the possible relationship between the posture of a child and his reading performance. A report is given on twenty children retarded

in reading who were found upon osteopathic examination to have "tight heads" (limitation of normal mobility of cranial articulations within the membranes of the skull). Thirty percent had postural problems from the area of the "widow's hump," and 10 percent had flat backs. These children were also found to have muscular weaknesses and were unable to do frontal "sit-ups." Dyslexia is defined as a symptom, not a specific disease, and is distinguished from word blindness. Posture involves the whole organism. Postural problems may begin in the prenatal period. Clinically, how the child stands, sits, and walks should be observed. When total alignment of the body is improved, the child's entire academic performance is improved.

1037 Schubert, Delwyn G. "Why the confusion in visual-reading relation-
      ships?" Calif J Second Educ 29(1): 16-17, January, 1954. (7
      Bibliographic Footnotes).
Reviews some of the literature concerning visual problems as a cause of
reading disability. The wide disparity in findings in the area is ascribed to the many different kinds of specialists working in the field.
Each sees the problem through his own little window of specialization.

1038 Velzeboer, C. M. J.; de Wit, J.; Hagedoorn, J. M. "Reading dis-
      orders." Ophthalmologica 160(5): 319-20, 1970. (0 References).
The typical mistakes, clear hereditary pattern, persistence into adult
life, and frequent association with other symbol defects suggest that
developmental dyslexia is a specific clinical entity. There is less
agreement about other defects that may be associated with it, including
form perception, cerebral dominance, and speech disorders. A study done
in the Netherlands is reported in which no relation was found between
strabismus and other vision problems, and reading problems. The best
way to treat dyslexia is educationally through the cooperation of doctor,
psychologist, and teacher.

1039 Witty, Paul A., and Kopel, David. "Heterophoria and reading dis-
      ability." J Educ Psychol 27(3): 222-30, March, 1936. (15 Ref-
      erences).
The visual defects examined in this study, including fusion difficulties
and lateral imbalance, appear to play a relatively negligible role in the
attainment of good and poor readers. However, it should be recognized
that visual problems may impede the reading progress of both good and
poor readers. All children should have eye tests at intervals. Subjects
in this study were groups of eighty good and 100 poor readers, all of
average intelligence, selected from grades three through six of a public-
school system.

1040 ————. "Studies of eye-muscle imbalance and poor fusion in
      reading disability: an evaluation." J Educ Psychol 27(9): 663-
      71, December, 1936. (16 References).
Reaffirms the earlier conclusion that there is no relation between reading
disability and other visual problems such as slow or no fusion, lateral
muscle imbalance, deficient acuity, and ametropia. (See Item No. 1039).

U. PHYSIOLOGICAL FACTORS

1041 Anapolle, Louis. "Vision problems in developmental dyslexia." J
      Learn Disabil 4(2): 77-83, February, 1971. (8 References).

In studies aimed at discovering the relation of developmental dyslexia
to binocular vision, it was found that although good vision is not essential to learning to read, binocular eye coordination appeared to be a
major problem for dyslexic persons.

1042 ————. Visual skills survey of dyslexic students." J Am Optom
       Assoc 38(10): 853-59, 1967. (10 References).
Examines the status of binocular vision skills in relation to developmental dyslexia. A total of 207 dyslexics ages eight to eighteen years
who were enrolled in a summer remedial reading program were given a battery of visual skills tests to investigate any manifestations of stress
in the visual performance of the reading task. Tested were: visual
acuity, simultaneous binocular perception, visual efficiency (the ability
of the brain to utilize the maximum potential acuity of each eye under
binocular conditions), eye dominance, lateral and vertical imbalance,
fusion, stereopsis, oculomotor control, suppression, and saccadic movements. Results of these tests are analyzed.

1043 Betts, Emmett Albert. "A physiological approach to the analysis
       of reading disabilities." Educ Res Bull 13(6): 135-40, September
       19, 1934; 13(7): 163-74, October 17, 1934. (0 References).
Lists various factors believed to be related to reading disabilities, including slow maturation; difficulties in vision and hearing; kinesthetic
irregularities (speech and eye coordination defects, handwriting difficulties, and problems with spatial orientation); language problems; emotional factors; sex differences; and external factors such as irregular
school attendance. Maturation is considered to be of great importance.
There should be a physiological readiness to read. Various eye tests are
described.

1044 "Biochemistry on the horizon." J Read Disabil 8(1): 56-57,
       January, 1975. (0 References).
Reports a lecture by Dr. Macdonald Critchley. Speaking at the twenty-
fifth annual meeting of the Orton Society in November, 1974, Dr. Critchley
held out hope for our eventually gaining better understanding of dyslexia.
Myelination of a child's pyramidal tract does not occur until somewhere
between the ages of one and two years. More complex brain structures may
not myelinate until later, perhaps at ages three to six years. Since
myelination is a histochemical process, it seems reasonable to suppose
that its delay could be genetically determined and that it could be stimulated by artificial means. It is pointed out that five neurohumoral
transmitter substances are already known. The loss of one of these,
dopamine, in Parkinson's disease, can be replaced with L-dopa. Someday
perhaps an analogous pharmacological treatment for dyslexia will be possible, and the key to the mystery of delayed cerebral maturation will be
unlocked.

1045 Bogacz, J.; De Mendilaharsu, S. A.; Mendilaharsu, C. "Electro-
       oculographic abnormalities during pursuit in developmental dys-
       lexia." Electroencephalogr Clin Neurophysiol 34(7): 795, 1973.
       (0 References).
Concludes that the abnormal saccadic pursuit movements observed in electrooculograms recorded in thirty-five persons suffering from developmental
dyslexia could be basic to the disorganized visual sensorimotor structure
seen in developmental dyslexia. The abnormalities observed are described.
It is suggested that the abnormal saccadic movements may be responsible
for the building of an inadequate visual code in these persons. An

electrooculogram is a brain wave tracing made while the subject is moving
his eyes between two fixation points.

1046 Bogacz, J.; Mendilaharsu, C.; De Mendilaharsu, S. A. "Electro-
     oculographic abnormalities during pursuit movements in develop-
     mental dyslexia." Electroencephalogr Clin Neurophysiol 36(6):
     651-56, June, 1974. (26 References).
In a study and comparison of the electrooculograms of normal and dyslexic
persons ages six to twenty-three years, it was found that good and poor
readers showed similar eye movements when the movements were made on
command. Random saccadic pursuit movements (short, rapid jerks) following eye movements occurred in only four out of twenty-four good readers,
but was common in dyslexics. It is concluded that in developmental dyslexia saccadic movements as a dysfunction of the ocular pursuit system
could influence and limit the amount taken in visually and hinder reading.

1047 Carrigan, Patricia M. "Broader implications of a chemical theory
     of reading disability." J Dev Read 5(1): 15-26, Autumn, 1961.
     (16 References).
Two enzymes, acetylcholine (ACh) and cholinesterase (ChE), are believed
to be the "circuit-maker" and "circuit-breaker" respectively in the transmission of impulses across the synapses of the human nervous system.
This chemical theory of the transmission of nerve impulses has application to reading disability. An imbalance of these chemicals may produce
individuals who are quiet or immature or hyperactive or flighty or slow,
depending upon the chemical balance, with various abnormal reading behaviors associated with the imbalances. Treatment and prevention of such
problems should be emphasized rather than modification of the environment.

1048 Cline, Carolyn Joan. "An investigation of cerebral interhemispheric
     transfer in normal and dyslexic children." For a summary see: Diss
     Abstr Int 31B(7): 4357, January, 1971.

1049 Drake, Charles. "Reading, 'riting and rhythm." Read Teach 18(3):
     202-5, December, 1964. (0 References).
Dyslexics of normal intelligence, strong motivation, and no emotional
problem have been observed to have very little sense of rhythm. Rhythm
pertains to fine motor and patterned motor skills. Coordination denotes
gross motor skills. Musical talent among dyslexics appears to be almost
entirely missing. Children who had trouble in reproducing hand-clapping
patterns were found to have difficulty with language symbols. Attempts
to teach rhythm proved difficult. When combined with remedial reading,
there was some carry-over of rhythm into reading.

1050 Eames, Thomas Harrison. "Amblyopia in cases of reading failure."
     Am J Ophthalmol 27(12): 1374-75, December, 1944. (0 References).
Children referred to a physician for failure to learn to read were found
to suffer more often from amblyopia (dimness of vision) in one or both
eyes unimproved by lenses and without demonstrable lesion than were normal readers. A group of 100 poor readers was compared with 100 normal
readers referred to a physician for ocular complaints. The age range
for both groups was six to nineteen years. The poor readers showed on
the average more amblyopia in the left eye only.

1051 ──────. "Association pathways in language disabilities." J Educ
     Psychol 47(1): 8-10, January, 1956. (2 References).
Reading disability may possibly result from physiological problems in
the brain. Pathways connecting language and association areas may impair
language function. Reading, hearing, speech, writing, and vision are
controlled from centers which are interdependent. The remedial teacher
is taking advantage of this interdependence when she uses many sensory
channels to teach reading. If pathways between hemispheres of the brain
are hindered, lateral dominance may be influenced.

1052 ──────. "The blood picture in reading failure." J Educ Psychol
     44(6): 372-75, October, 1953. (4 References).
Some slight abnormalities in hemoglobin and red and white cell counts in
the blood of persons failing in reading were noted; 20 percent of the
cases showed some abnormal cell forms. These changes were not frequent
enough to be statistically significant, but they merit attention as possible contributing causes of reading disability.

1053 ──────. "Low fusion convergence as a factor in reading disabil-
     ity." Am J Ophthalmol 17(8): 709-10, August, 1934. (5 Refer-
     ences).
This study compared eighty-eight reading disability cases with fifty-two
normal readers. All the children were from grades two, three, and four
in a public school. Ages of the groups were approximately the same.
Fusion convergence was lower in the nonreaders. The smaller the type to
be read, the lower the amplitude of fusion convergence for both groups,
but the percentage of reading disability cases falling below the median
of the control group increased as the size of the letters grew smaller.
The idea tested is that in normal binocular vision three images are
formed: one arising from each eye, and a third resulting from the fusion
of the other two. If the images from each eye do not fall on exactly
the same point on the cerebral cortex, fusion will be imperfect and
letter-like or unfamiliar combinations of characters will result, confusing the child.

1054 Festinger, Leon, et al. Eye movement disorders in dyslexia. Final
     report. 1972. 19p. (ED 074 691).
Evaluated eye movements in eighteen male and seven female dyslexic children to determine whether disorders of eye movement were linked to symptoms of dyslexia. The children's eye movements were studied as they
moved their eyes from one fixation point to another in a nonreading situation. Vertical eye movement errors were significantly different for
normal and dyslexic children. Large vertical eye movement errors were
found in children whose reading errors involved skipping or repeating
lines and losing the place. It is concluded that eye movement problems
are probably the cause of reading disorders in one subgroup of dyslexic
children.

1055 Friedman, Nathan. "Is reading disability a fusional dysfunction?"
     J Am Optom Assoc 45(5): 619-22, May, 1974. (0 References).
Tragic confusion and bewilderment confront the educator who tries to
understand the causes of reading disability. "Dyslexia" is a term typifying this utter confusion. Several authorities in the field are quoted.
Both critical and supporting viewpoints on dyslexia are presented to reveal the confusion that the term creates. Reading difficulties are attributed to the physiological problem of fusional-eye-movement stress.
These children cannot write words in proper alignment or in sequence

primarily because the words blur and go out of focus as the child breaks
focus to find relief from fusional pain. Poor readers see the words in
confusion and reproduce the confusion they see. After fusional-eye training such children write with balance, control, and even understanding.
The block to learning is physiologic, not neurologic. The lack of experimental or clinical evidence makes the concept of dyslexia suspect as a
nonexistent entity. The 100-year search for causes of dyslexia in neurological dysfunction has led to a wasteland of futility.

1056 Griffin, Donald C.; Walton, Howard N.; Ives, Vera. "Saccades as
     related to reading disorders." J Learn Disabil 7(5): 310-16,
     May, 1974. (17 References).
The little jumps the eyes make in reading (saccadic movement) possibly
are a contributing cause of reading problems rather than a result of
reading experiences. In studies of groups of adequate and inadequate
readers, the inadequate group showed more fixations per line, more regressions, fewer forward fixations, and more time on all cards. When
nonlanguage materials were used, inadequate readers showed less efficient eye movements. Some moved their eyes too rapidly, skipping material. Others moved too slowly.

1057 Grosvenor, Theodore. "The neglected hyperope." Am J Optom 48(5):
     376-82, May, 1971. (21 References).
Studies relating the refractive state of the eye to intelligence have
reported increasing IQ as myopia (nearsightedness) increased. IQ decreased with increasing hyperopia (farsightedness). Hyperopes tend to
avoid reading. Therefore a relationship between hyperopia and difficulty
in learning to read would seem reasonable. Such evidence is hard to
find and we are not now in a position to answer the question of whether
hyperopia contributes to reading disability. Myopia has received much
more attention in the literature than hyperopia. The time has come to
give more attention to the problems of hyperopes.

1058 Hunter, Edna Josephine. "Habituation of electrodermal responses
     in children with specific reading disability." For a summary see:
     Diss Abstr Int 31B(5): 2988, November, 1970.

1059 Kopel, David. Physiological factors associated with the etiology
     of reading disability. Unpublished Ph.D. thesis. Northwestern
     University, 1935.
In tests of visual perception, oculomotor and perceptual habits, and
laterality ("sidedness") given to publicschool children in grades three
through six, reading disability appeared to have no significant visual
cause. All visual defects tested seemed to play only a small role in
reading attainment. No phase of laterality seemed related to reading
achievement. Subjects were tested for IQ and consisted of a group of
readers and a control group of normal readers.

1060 Kučera, Otakar; Matejček, Zdenek; Langmeier, Josef. "Some obser-
     vations on dyslexia in children in Czechoslovakia." Am J Ortho-
     psychiatry 33(3): 448-56, April, 1963. (19 References).
In a study in Prague, four types of dyslexics were identified: cere-
brally impaired, hereditary, cerebral impairment in the hereditarily pre-
disposed, and neurotic. Characteristics of each type are described. The
conclusion is that the basic mechanisms underlying the dyslexias are the
result of disturbances in physiological processes.

1061 Lewis, Franklin D.; Bell, D. Bruce; Anderson, Robert P. "Relation-
      ship of motor proficiency and reading retardation." Percept Mot
      Skills 31(2): 395-401, October, 1970. (15 References).
This experiment measured the relationship of motor development to reading
proficiency. Four groups of junior-high-school boys ages twelve to sixteen with WISC scores of at least 80 were given a battery of tests to
measure school achievement. They were given also the Lincoln-Oseretsky
Motor Development Scale which includes thirty-six tasks measuring finger
dexterity, eye-hand coordination, and fine and gross motor movements,
among others. Fifty of the boys were Negro and fifty were Caucasian.
Half were adequate readers and half were poor readers. The motor proficiency test significantly differentiated the good readers from poor
readers. It did not show differences between the races. Retarded readers had greater difficulty with tests measuring locomotion, bilateral
movements, synchrony, and sequence of movements. Although tentative, it
is believed that findings are better accounted for by the explanations
of Kephart and Harmon than by those of Bender and Delacato.

1062 Mateer, Florence. "A first study of pituitary dysfunction in cases
      of reading difficulty." Psychol Bull 32(9): 736, November, 1935.
      (0 References).
Analysis of 100 cases of children with pituitary deficiency who were old
enough to have had reading experiences revealed that no matter how high
the intelligence, the child was relatively poor in reading. Such cases
tend to show a familial tendency. These cases yield more rapidly to
medication than to corrective education. When the two are combined, recovery is most rapid. Not all reading disabilities are caused by pituitary dysfunction, but 90 percent of pituitary deficiency cases show
reading defects.

1063 Orton, Samuel Torrey. "A physiological theory of reading disability
      and stuttering in children." N Engl J Med 199(21): 1046-52,
      November 22, 1928. (8 References).
In a series of experiments designed as a follow-up to his preliminary
report in 1925, Orton finds support for his earlier idea that reading
disability is a fairly clear-cut clinical entity. It can be diagnosed
by the frequency of occurrence of certain types of errors. In connection
with the work on reading disability, studies were conducted with stutterers, and that work is also reported here.

1064 Park, George E. "Functional dyslexia (reading failure) vs. normal
      reading. Comparative study of ocular functions." Eye Ear Nose
      Throat Mon 45(3): 74-80, March, 1966. (6 References).
Compares various ocular functions in failing and normal readers. Functional dyslexia is defined as the inability to learn to read normally
even though intelligence is normal. Factors causing the syndrome are
different from reading failures associated with organic brain lesions or
lack of intelligence. Duction amplitude, the number and degree of
phorias, the incidence of refraction errors, and the incidence of fusion
and stereopsis were all found not to be significantly different in dyslexic and in normal children. Reversals and mirror reading and writing
are most likely psychological techniques used as attention-getting or
escape techniques. Multidisciplinary cooperation among teachers, physicians, speech therapists, social workers, and psychologists is important.

1065 ————. "Reading difficulty (dyslexia) from the ophthalmic point
      of view." Am J Ophthalmol 31(1): 28-34, January, 1948. (9 Ref-
      erences).
Discusses some of the physical, psychological, and physiological aspects
of dyslexia and analyzes the ophthalmic findings in 133 cases of dyslexia.
It is concluded that dyslexia is an entity and that it occurs often enough
to warrant attention. Ametropia, lack of stereopsis, and other ocular
defects were frequently found in these cases. Fusion did not seem to be
an important factor. Eighty percent of the cases showed no preference
for eye dominance. Peripheral ocular mechanisms and visual acuity should
not be taken as measures of perception. Nor, conversely, should cerebral
processes be taken as measures of ocular functions.

1066 Park, George E.; Bimmerle, John F.; Schmieding, Alfred; et al.
      "Biological changes associated with dyslexia." Arch Pediatr 72(3):
      71-84, March, 1955. (20 References).
Reports on a study of 198 dyslexics ages seven to twenty-two, with an
average age of ten years, ten and one-half months. Various blood tests
and basal metabolic rate were studied. WISC and psychological tests were
administered . Dyslexia is defined as being caused by functional factors,
usually correctable. The study was undertaken because of the observation
that almost all dyslexics live under conditions of stress or in tension
states, and stress is believed to alter the blood and many body tissues.
It was expected that changes would be found in the white blood cell picture. This was confirmed in a majority of the dyslexics in this study.
Stress produces complex physiological manifestations; it would be unrealistic to expect to find the same physiological changes in all dyslexics.

1067 Rubino, Carl A., and Minden, Harold A. "Visual-field restrictions
      in cases of reading disability." Percept Mot Skills 33(3, Part 2):
      1215-17, December, 1971. (3 References).
A group of twenty-three children with reading disability was tested for
both visual-field limits and central visual-field deficiencies. Almost
all had visual fields within normal limits. The same results were obtained with a second test on children selected randomly from the group.
The children had an average age of eleven years. None wore corrective
lenses.

1068 Sinclair, A. H. H. "Developmental aphasia; also known as congenital
      word-blindness and sometimes referred to as alexia or dyslexia."
      Br J Ophthalmol 32(9): 522-31, September, 1948. (11 References).
About 5 percent of schoolchildren need special treatment in order to learn
to read. Insufficiently developed cerebral dominance accounts for some
of the symptoms. Word memory failure is more serious and may be related
to delayed myelination of cortical neurons. Such localized delay or failure in the development of myelination of certain nerve fibers in the
cerebrum is the most probable cause of failure to learn to read. Developmental aphasia is an isolated disability. Diagnosis is uncertain in
mentally defective children, but clearly recognizable in those of normal
general intelligence.

1069 Sinclair, William Andrew. "The effect of motor skill learning up-
      on specific dyslexia." For a summary see: Diss Abstr Int 31A(11):
      5830, May, 1971.

1070   Smith, Donald E. P. "Etiology of reading disability: the neuro-
       chemical theory." In: International Reading Association. Confer-
       ence proceedings: new frontiers in reading. Vol. 5. Edited by
       J. Allen Figurel. New York: Scholastic Magazines, 1960. 63-66.
       (0 References).
The first-grade child must learn to read to adapt to society. Described
in the chemical terms of the theory put forward here, adaptability in
the fast-maturing child is achieved by the presence in his nervous system
of a balance of acetylcholine, a circuit maker in neural transmissions,
and cholinesterase, a circuit breaker, both at high levels of secretion.
According to the theory, low but balanced levels of both would produce
children delayed in maturation with minimum ability to adapt. Imbalances
in either chemical would produce the specific syndromes of reading disability. Overproduction of one with accompanying underproduction of the
other should result in psychotic behavior. Case histories are cited.
It is suggested that reading errors are a perceptual manifestation of a
physiological event.

1071   Smith, Donald E. P., and Carrigan, Patricia M. The nature of read-
       ing disability. New York: Harcourt, Brace, 1959. 149p. (Bibli-
       ographical Footnotes).
A case is made for the chemical theory of neural transmission, which is
explained. Reading disability is thought to be caused by abnormal synaptic transmission. Imbalances between acetylcholine, the supposed
transmitter agent, and cholinesterase, the enzyme thought to end transmission, appear to cause the problem. Glandular therapy to restore proper
endocrine functioning is recommended. Physical factors, not poor instruction, cause reading disability. It is a medical problem. A psychological test battery and norm tables are included.

1072   Smith, Richard J. "The physiology of reading." J Educ Res 67(9):
       397-402, May-June, 1974. (27 References).
Forty-one years of research have produced more questions and hypotheses
than conclusions concerning a physiological basis for reading disability.
The suspicion lingers that persons who are dyslexic or learning-disabled
have a physiological problems. The idea is appealing to various medical
specialists who see a select clientele. Unfortunately, continuing research in the area still has produced no definitive answers. Some literature in the field is reviewed.

1073   Solan, Harold A. "Some physiological correlates of dyslexia." Am
       J Optom Arch Am Acad Optom 43(1): 3-9, January, 1966. (16 Ref-
       erences).
Discusses the causes of dyslexia including ill-defined laterality; problems of pregnancy and birth; incomplete neurological organization; perceptual deficiencies; glandular deficiencies; and visual deficiencies.
Those treating dyslexia are warned against considering each symptom as a
separate problem. Rather, all symptoms should be seen together as constituting the syndrome of dyslexia.

1074   Spache, G. "The role of visual defects in spelling and reading
       disabilities." Am J Orthopsychiatry 10(2): 229-38, April, 1940.
       (50 References).
A review of the literature reveals that visual defects appear to be the
cause of reading and spelling disabilities in some cases, although there
are research reports to the contrary. Nearsightedness is not associated
with poor reading. Astigmatism may be. Eye-muscle imbalance, the chang-

ing distance between the pupils of the eyes as the child's head grows, and losses in peripheral vision resulting in a smaller visual span all may be associated with reading disability.

1075   Thomas, Evan Welling.   "The problem of dyslexia."   In: Brain-injured children; with special reference to Doman-Delacato methods of treatment.   Chap. 8.   Springfield, Illinois: Thomas, 1969.   61-71.   (0 References).
Defines dyslexia as a reading disorder caused by some kind of neurological "dysorganization."   It is a term with many meanings.   It may be genetic or acquired either before or after birth.   The viewpoints on dyslexia of Critchley, Orton, and Delacato are examined.   Literature reviewing dyslexia as caused by acquired brain damage is cited.

1076   Wagenheim, Lillian.   "Learning problems associated with childhood diseases contracted at age two."   Am J Orthopsychiatry   29(1):   102-9, January, 1959.   (6 References).
Studies on approximately 1,600 children revealed a relationship between retardation in reading and contraction of measles and other similar diseases before the age of three years in boys.   This relationship did not exist in girls.   No relationship was found to exist between early contraction of these diseases and intelligence.

1077   Walton, Howard N.   "Saccades as related to reading disorders."   Am J Optom   50(9):   746, September, 1973.   (0 References).
Considers saccadic eye movements of adequate and inadequate readers.

V. PREGNANCY AND PERINATAL DIFFICULTIES

1078   Jordan, Thomas E.   "Early developmental adversity and classroom learning: a prospective inquiry."   Am J Ment Defic   69(3):   360-71, November, 1964.   (41 References).
Two groups of twelve-year-old children, control and experimental, who were all born in the same hospital in the same year, were studied.   All members of the experimental group had experienced some adverse perinatal history.   These factors were studied in relation to four aspects of their classroom performance.   In general, children with abnormal perinatal history avoided damage in three of the four areas: communications skills, for example, speech problems; physical factors such as height or neuromotor difficulties; and behavior problems.   In the fourth area, intellectual functioning, significant differences were found, including a significantly higher proportion of mental retardation.   Reading difficulties were outstanding among the learning problems found.

1079   Kawi, Ali A., and Pasamanick, Benjamin.   "Association of factors of pregnancy with reading disorders in childhood."   JAMA   166(12):   1420-23, March 22, 1958.   (13 References).
Hospital records for 205 white boys with reading disorders disclosed a higher incidence of complications in pregnancy and delivery than were present in 205 normal controls.   The maternal disorders most often associated with reading disorders were preeclampsia, hypertensive disease, and bleeding during pregnancy.   All of these are likely to lead to fetal anoxia.   It is suggested that a relationship exists between certain abnormalities of birth and the later development of reading disorders.   The theory is offered that there exists a continuum running from still-

birth at one end to behavior disorders at the other with reading disability included. Full hospital records were available on 205 of the 372
cases which comprised the original study group.

1080 ————. Prenatal and paranatal factors in the development of
      childhood reading disorders. Lafayette, Indiana: Child Develop-
      ment Publications of the Society for Research in Child Development,
      1959. 80p. (Monographs of the Society for Research in Child De-
      velopment, Vol. 24[2, Serial No. 73]).
In a study involving 372 matched pairs of white male children, a relationship was found between reading disorders and various abnormal conditions, including premature birth, toxemias of pregnancy, and bleeding
during pregnancy. It is hypothesized that childhood reading disorders
are one part of a continuum of reproductive problems ranging from spontaneous abortion and stillbirth through cerebral palsy, epilepsy, mental
deficiency, and behavior disorders.

1081 Lyle, J. G. "Certain antenatal, perinatal, and developmental vari-
      ables and reading retardation in middle-class boys." Child Dev
      41(2): 481-91, June, 1970. (18 References).
Normal and retarded readers were contrasted on several variable factors
concerned with their birth and development. Early speech difficulties
best predicted all factors of reading retardation studied. Toxemia of
pregnancy and low birth weight were not related to factors studied. Possible brain injury at birth was the best predictor among the birth variables.

1082 Pasamanick, Benjamin, and Knobloch, Hilda. "Race, complications of
      pregnancy, and neuropsychiatric disorder." Soc Probl 5(3): 267-
      78, Winter, 1957-58. (24 References).
Reports on a series of studies relating biological and psychological
function to socioeconomic variables. Seven neuropsychiatric disorders
of childhood, including reading disability, were studied. Significant
differences between controls (a patient not known to have a neuropsychiatric disability), and a case (a person having one of the disease
conditions being investigated) were found in the incidence of complications of pregnancy, prematurity, and twinning. These complications were
found to be related to socioeconomic differences, not only between
whites and nonwhites, but within the white group. It is concluded that
differences in sociocultural milieu rather than genetic endowment make
one individual behaviorally different from another. Subjects were selected from a large population of children in Baltimore.

1083 Tjossem, Theodore D.; Hansen, Thomas J.; Ripley, Herbert S. "An
      investigation of reading difficulty in young children." Am J
      Psychiatry 118(12): 1104-13, June, 1962. (21 References).
Twenty-four children with reading problems were studied using medical
history as a diagnostic tool. The majority of reading-disabled children
in this study showed a family history of reading problems and/or laterality problems. Others had histories of difficulties before or during
birth. It is suggested that subtle central nervous system dysfunction
may be a factor in reading performance. Visual perception skills seemed
more closely related to reading success than intelligence. Shifting a
child from his congenital laterality to environmentally determined laterality may be a factor in early reading problems. Two different methods
of reading instruction are assessed.

W. PSYCHIATRIC FACTORS

1084 Arajärvi, Terttu; Mälkönen, Kristiina; Repo, Inkeri; et al. "Specific reading and writing difficulties in preadolescents who have
received treatment at a child psychiatric hospital." Acta Paediatr
Scand (Suppl) 256: 60, 1975. (0 References). (Proceedings of
the First International Symposium on Adolescent Medicine. Helsinki,
August 4-8, 1974).
Among 151 children eleven to fifteen years of age who had severe psychic
disorders, seventy-five had reading and writing difficulties. Sixty-one
percent had auditory, visual, and motor-specific difficulties and 36 percent were diagnosed as showing the MBD syndrome. Those with reading and
writing difficulties often had neurological symptoms including clumsiness, incoordination, cross dominance, and speech disturbances. Parents
appeared to discriminate frequently against the dyslexia-dysgraphia child.
Psychiatric tests showed more immaturity of personality than neurosis.
Intelligence tests requiring the most abstract differentiation were the
best predictors of dyslexia-dysgraphia symptoms.

1085 Downes, Mildred Gignoux, and Schuman, Rita S. "Pathogenesis of
reading disability." N Engl J Med 252(6): 217-21, February 10,
1955. (11 References).
Describes the symptoms of reading disability including reversals, misreadings, and malapropisms. Emotional, physical, and psychiatric symptoms of reading-disabled children are examined. Disabled readers appear
to live in a world filled with a terrifying kind of discord. They feel
inadequate, inferior, and alarmed. There is underlying hostility. Causes
for these feelings are many and varied. Reasons that boys are more often
unable to learn to read than girls are given.

1086 Jacobson, J. Robert, and Pratt, Helen Gay. "Psychobiologic dysfunction in children." J Nerv Ment Dis 109(4): 330-46, April,
1949. (2 References).
Two groups of children ages six through thirteen, one retarded in reading, the other normal, were examined psychobiologically for carelessness,
impulsive, and uncritical tendencies. The two groups differed significantly. Findings for both groups of children were compared to similar
psychobiologic dysfunctions in the mentally ill. It is suggested that
qualities like immaturity and irresponsibility in young children are
pathologic entities which will respond to treatment. Stimulating supervision which includes standards and aims at acceptance of responsibility
provide the child with the support he needs. When the child is very impulsive, he exhibits a stumbling, fumbling response with numerous errors.
Immaturity, negativism, and confusion are discussed as manifestations
of psychobiologic dysfunction. Findings are seen as useful in diagnosis
and treatment.

1087 Jarvis, Vivian. "Clinical observations on the visual problem in
reading disability." Psychoanal Study Child 13: 451-70, 1958.
(13 References).
Although poor readers show a variety of emotional adjustment patterns,
it is suggested that a certain uniformity characterizes the underlying
unconscious factors in reading. The two most frequent causes of reading
disability--unfavorable family conditions and visual defects--are related. The visual problem in reading is one of looking (scopophilia)
rather than a physical vision problem. Not the reading content, but the

active part of looking creates the difficulty for the retarded reader.
The child's fantasies, the denial of voyeurism and compensating exhibi-
tionistic activities have implications for reading therapy. The method
of teaching reading should be modified depending upon whether the reading disability is caused by neurotic mechanisms or factors such as prolonged absence from school.

1088 Krippner, Stanley. "Sociopathic tendencies and reading retarda-
      tion in children." Except Child 29(6): 258-66, February, 1963.
      (16 References).
Sociopathic persons are also referred to as suffering from "psychopathic
states" or "character disorders." Sociopaths are difficult to treat.
It is the most destructive of all forms of abnormal behavior. It is
characterized by antisocial behavior, lying, incapacity to love, lack of
responsibility and personal insight, and failure to learn from experience, among other symptoms. Learning is difficult for afflicted children because they will not work for long-range goals or in close personal
relationships. Four case histories are given. The four boys had lower
WISC verbal than performance scores and had not received adequate parental
affection and discipline in early years. Remedial reading is most successful when combined with psychotherapy since the teacher and school
often become targets for the sociopath's resentment.

1089 Marks, Alexander, and Saunders, John C. "Strephosymbolia in chil-
      dren with neuropsychiatric disorders." Am J Psychiatry 119(11):
      1087-88, May, 1963. (10 References).
Reports on a study carried out to investigate whether a relationship
exists between strephosymbolia (specific reading disability) and emotional disorders. Nineteen childhood schizophrenics and twenty children
with primary behavior disorders (six girls and thirty-three boys ages six
to thirteen) were asked to perform various writing tasks, including writing words from dictation and procedures aimed at discovering tendencies
to mirror writing, an indication of latent strephosymbolia. Results indicate a probable relationship between primary behavior disorders and
strephosymbolia. It is pointed out that the schizophrenic child has a
slower rate of maturation than the normal child, which may explain the
continuation of strephosymbolia beyond the age when such confusions
usually disappear in children. Psychoanalytic theories of the causes of
strephosymbolia are explained.

1090 Missildine, W. H. "The emotional background of thirty children
      with reading disabilities with emphasis on its coercive elements."
      Nerv Child 5(3): 263-72, July, 1946. (22 References).
In a group of reading-disabled children, one-third had overly hostile
mothers and one-third had tense, coercive, criticizing mothers. Almost
all the children were insecure and restless. Their reading disabilities
formed only a small part of their maladjustment. Almost without exception the children suffered from an emotional disturbance in connection
with some member of their families. Psychiatric examination is recommended for reading-disabled children who do not respond promptly to specific remedial techniques.

1091 Nichtern, Sol. "Reading disability and the child psychiatrist."
      Bull NY Acad Med 44(4): 488-93, April, 1968. (0 References).
One approach to reading disability is seeing it as based on school refusal rather than on an inability to read. Seven types of school refusal,
in which the child refuses to function in school, are identified: (1)

fear of school; (2) an inhibition or unwillingness to learn; (3) an inability to learn because of genetic constitutional impairment; (4) an
acute school phobia where school performance is unrelated to the child's
capacities; (5) withdrawals from function where the child drops out of
school entirely; (6) destruction of function where antisocial and delinquent behavior appear; and (7) destruction of self where progressive
withdrawal, depression, and self-destructive behavior appear. No one
method of teaching is suitable for all children. Mass education with
big classes will result in some failures.

1092 Pond, Desmond. "Communication disorders in brain-damaged children."
      Proc R Soc Med 60(4): 343-48, April, 1967. (30 References).
Deals with specific disturbances in speech, writing, and reading function which are regarded as related to specific disorders in particular
parts of the cerebral cortex. These are not seen as evidence for cerebral lesions but as localizations of function. Global mental deficiency
is not included. Central psychological processes which may be related
to disturbances in the central nervous system are the main concern. In
spite of reports of familial incidence of reading difficulties, the case
for specific inheritance of specific psychological functions is more
dubious. Leading literature in the field is reviewed. A general theory
of the cause of specific disturbances in speech and reading is suggested
in these terms: the main learning process consists, not in making new
pathways, but in cutting out or inhibiting irrelevant responses at the
psychological as well as the physiological level. These specific disabilities are similar in origin to adult neurotic syndromes. The child
with congenital dyslexia cannot read, not because of neurological lesion
or immaturity, but because of an emotional block.

1093 Pugh, Derek S. "A note on the Vorhaus configurations of 'reading
      disability.'" J Proj Tech Pers Assess 18(4): 478-80, December,
      1954. (6 References).
Points out that 78 percent of a group of normal boys eleven years old
with superior ability in English showed Rorschach configurations associated with reading disability by Pauline Vorhaus, and described by her
in journal articles. It is concluded that much more research should be
done before this association can be considered proved. (See Items No.
1101 and 1102).

1094 Rapoport, Jack. "The psychopathology of learning difficulties."
      NY State J Med 57(21): 3471-76, November 1, 1957. (9 References).
Defines "reading disability," "strephosymbolia," and "alexia" as some
of the clinical terms used to designate learning difficulties. These
difficulties are not clinical entities; they are symptoms of a larger
problem. Primary and secondary behavior problems are distinguished and
the latter discussed. Learning difficulty and behavior problems are related. Distractibility is the factor producing learning difficulty.
Treatment should be aimed at the total clinical picture, modifying behavior and aiding the learning problem. A case report is included and
the use of drugs in behavior modification is discussed.

1095 Silverman, Jerome S.; Fite, Margaretta W.; Mosher, Margaret M.
      "Clinical findings in reading disability children--special cases
      of intellectual inhibition." Am J Orthopsychiatry 29: 298-314,
      April, 1959. (23 References).
Reading disability is a symptom of a more basic disturbance in a child's
emotional life. It is a symptom of an inhibition of learning and in-

telligence, a disorder in ego function. Inhibition is usually an expression of a restriction arising from the need to avoid conflict with
certain urges somehow regarded as dangerous if consciously considered
or acted upon. A typical case history is given. Reading disability may
be one sign of serious unconscious conflicts.

1096 Singer, Erwin, and Pittman, Marion E. "A Sullivanian approach to
      the problem of reading disability: theoretical considerations and
      empirical data." J Proj Tech Pers Assess 29(3): 369-76, Septem-
      ber, 1965. (18 References).
Tests the idea that reading disabilities have much in common with the
operationally hysterical disorders and that some of H. S. Sullivan's
conceptions about hysteria are applicable in understanding the symptom
of reading disability. Full citations to Sullivan's work are found in
the bibliography appended to this article. Sullivan discussed the hys-
teric as a self-absorbed person who unfortunately encountered hostility
at crucial times in his life expressed through disrespect and disinterest. It is pointed out that the reading-disabled child, like the hys-
teric, spreads discomfort by acts of omission. His inability to learn
and the implied disinterest in what the world has to say to him through
the written word makes him the center of busy efforts by the responsible
adults around him. His proud claim may be that absolutely nobody can
teach him to read. He perceives the interest around him as being essential disinterest hypocritically disguised as interest, and responds in
contemptuous disdain. The reading-disabled child expresses detached,
noncommunicative self-absorption and derogatory selective attention to
the contemptible aspects of his surroundings.

To test these ideas, a study was devised to measure and assess the degree
to which children are selectively attentive to hypocritical, insincere,
or silly aspects of the world around him, and/or their readiness to accept its sincere aspects. Subjects were a group of reading-disabled
children and a matched control group of normal readers. Findings confirmed the assumptions. Disabled readers did better on Verbal Absurdi-
ties items and normal readers performed better on Proverbs items of the
Stanford-Binet test.

1097 Solomon, Marilyn. The relation of reading achievement to one
      aspect of 'realism' among 7- to 12-year-old boys. n.d. 60p.
      (ED 010 251).
The relationship between reading achievement and moral realism was studied in boys ages seven through twelve. Children retarded in reading
achievement were found to be also somewhat retarded in development of
moral concepts as measured in Piaget's terms. Evidence was found of a
lag in moral realism in retarded readers compared with normal readers.

1098 Spache, George D. "Personality characteristics of retarded read-
      ers as measured by the Picture-Frustration Study." Educ Psychol
      Meas 14(1): 186-92, Spring, 1954. (14 References).
Retarded readers were found to be more aggressive and cocky and to be
significantly less insightful, and less likely to acknowledge blame or
admit they were at fault than normal readers as measured by the Rosenzweig Picture-Frustration Study. It is not necessary to try to prove
whether emotional maladjustments cause reading failure or whether emotional problems result from repeated failure. It is necessary to evaluate personality characteristics of retarded readers before attempting
the usual methods for treating reading failure with remedial work or

tutoring. The average retarded reader has made a relatively poor social
adjustment toward both adults and other children. Some psychotherapeutic
approach should be used with the average retarded reader.

1099 Strang, Ruth. "Reading and personality formation." Personality
      1: 131-40, 1951. (11 References).
The relation of retardation in reading to the healthy personality is
circular. The limits set by heredity and the child's early relationships with family and school determine his initial response to school
and reading instruction. If he fails in reading because of premature
or poor instruction, his failure may be viewed with alarm by his parents.
Success in learning to read has prestige value. The very pressures which
were unfavorable at first may be increased. The inability to learn to
read may affect his relationships with family and friends as he grows
older. The child may feel hopeless, submissive, and inadequate at the
same time he is being pressured to achieve in increasingly difficult
reading tasks. The result is a vicious circle. The child is caught.
He becomes progressively more maladjusted and less able to achieve. Remedial procedures are described.

1100 Vorhaus, Pauline G. "Non-reading as an expression of resistance."
      Rorschach Res Exch 10(2): 60-69, June, 1946. (8 References). .
Explains reading disability as an expression of resistance. The group
of disabled readers studied were ages seven to nineteen. All were of
normal intelligence, not psychotic, and at first appeared to work hard
and to be eager to learn. All were nonreaders. The nonreading appears
to arise as a result of interplay between the child and his environment:
if either had been different, the resulting picture would have been different. Growing up becomes synonymous in the minds of these children
with fitting into a straitjacket: all extraneous needs and interests
must be repressed. Repression leads to listlessness and apathy. One
cannot have zest for stifling much of oneself. Effort is directed toward
"being good," not in the task for its own sake. Factors such as mental
retardation, physical defects, and frequent school absence are seen as
contributory, not primary, factors. Results of Rorschach evaluations are
given.

1101 ————. "A reply to Pugh's 'note on the Vorhaus configurations
      of reading disability.'" J Proj Tech Pers Assess 18(4): 480-81,
      December, 1954. (2 References).
In this article, Vorhaus replies to a criticism of her work in which she
asserts that four Rorschach configurations were found to be associated
with severe reading disability in children who were under environmental
pressure. Her critic, Derek S. Pugh, states that 78 percent of his normal subjects performed in the same manner. Vorhaus notes possible differences in cultural factors between her subjects and Pugh's that may
account for the differences in findings. (See Items No. 1093 and 1102).

1102 ————. "Rorschach configurations associated with reading dis-
      ability." J Proj Tech Pers Assess 16(1): 3-19, March, 1952.
      (18 References).
Considers the hypothesis that marked reading disability appearing in persons of normal intelligence indicates resistance, often unconscious, to
environmental pressure. Four Rorschach configurations are examined. It
is believed that these four figures characterize nonreaders who were
studied and indicate ways in which these children adapted to the pressure.
It is suggested that reading disability should be treated not as an entity
but as part of a deeper problem. (See Items No. 1093 and 1101).

1103   Wagenheim, Lillian. "First memories of 'accidents' and reading
       difficulties." <u>Am J Orthopsychiatry</u> 30(1): 191-95, January, 1960.
       (0 References).
When fifth- and sixth-grade boys and girls were asked, "What is the first
thing you can remember?" replies were classified as to whether they were
of real accidents and body aggression (such as hitting) or of other in-
cidents. Chronological age, reading comprehension, and IQ scores were
used to test the hypothesis that poor readers frequently recalled accidents as first memories. Boys whose IQ expectancy deviated most from
reading ability were found to have first memories of accidents and physical aggression. This relationship was not true for girls, although
girls recalled accident memories as freely as boys. Boys with low IQs
had similar first memories. Among the best readers, most of the memories
were pleasant. It is suggested that memories are projections of physical
inadequacy and conflict over aggressive and destructive impulses.

1104   —————. "First memories of 'accidents' and reading failure."
       <u>Claremont Coll Read Conf Yearb</u> 24: 52, 1959. (0 References).
Fifth- and sixth-grade boys whose reading skills were most inconsistent
with IQ expectancy or who had low IQs differed markedly from other boys
in first memories. Boys in these two groups remembered accidents to
themselves with no named aggressor such as falling or tripping, and physical aggression toward others with guilt. Other boys tended to recall
pleasant experiences.

1105   Walters, Richard H.; Van Loan, Malle; Crofts, Irene. "A study of
       reading disability." <u>J Consult Psychol</u> 25(4): 277-83, 1961. (11
       References).
Reading disability has been attributed by psychoanalysts to three factors: (1) fear and avoidance of looking; (2) hostility, primarily toward
the same-sex parent; and (3) failure to identify with the same-sex parent.
This psychoanalytic theory of reading disability was tested in this study.
It was hypothesized that retarded readers would show more hesitation in
looking at a sexual object than would normal readers. Subjects were
fifty-eight boys of average intelligence in grades three through six.
They were divided into three groups: retarded, average, and advanced
readers. Two tests of visual perception were given each child of kinds
that appeared to require "active looking" in the psychoanalytic sense.
"Fear of looking" was tested with the use of a multiple-choice apparatus
in which the task was to locate a doll behind one of four doors. A nude
male doll and two conventional clothed dolls, one male and one female,
were used. A parent-preference test and a test in which the child told
what he thought the people were doing in a series of pictures were given.
Retarded readers performed more poorly than the other groups on the visual
perception tests. Retarded readers were also slower in searching for the
male nude doll than were the other groups and chose their fathers less
often on the parent-preference test. Some data failed to support the
"fear of looking" or hostility hypothesis. Results were seen as yielding
less support for the psychoanalytic theory than for explanation in terms
of parental conditioning of exploratory and sexual responses.

1106   Wilderson, Frank B., Jr. "An exploratory study of reading skill
       deficiencies and psychiatric symptoms in emotionally disturbed
       children." <u>Read Res Q</u> 2(3): 47-73, Spring, 1967. (11 References).
Investigates the nature of the relationship between reading disability
and emotional disturbances in children. Subjects were children ages nine
to fourteen who had been referred to a psychiatric hospital because of

emotional disorders. Evidence is presented for the hypothesis that specific reading disabilities are expressions of more central emotional disorders. Reading disability is one of a number of behavioral-emotional
symptoms characteristic of this group of children. Each child was given
psychological and psychiatric evaluation and diagnostic reading tests.
Parents were interviewed. Data were coded and analyzed. These procedures
yielded four psychiatric and seven reading deficiency factors. Within
the limitations of this study it is concluded that problem readers can
be classified by means of a restricted number of psychiatric syndromes
and/or of reading deficiency clusters. Considerable overlap exists between psychiatric and reading skill realms.

1107 Yule, William, and Rutter, Michael. "Educational aspects of child-
      hood maladjustment: some epidemiological findings." Br J Educ
      Psychol 38(1): 7-9, February, 1968. (7 References).
In studying a population of schoolchildren, those with some clinically
important psychiatric disorder were designated maladjusted. The largest
diagnostic groups among the maladjusted children were those with neurotic
disorders and those with antisocial disorders. A strong association was
found between antisocial disorders and severe reading retardation. Reading retardation was only slightly more common among neurotic children
than in the general population. It appears that either the reading disability is the primary handicap which leads to the behavior problems, or
that both psychiatric and educational difficulties stem from other factors in the child and his family.

X. PSYCHOLOGICAL FACTORS

1108 Abrams, Jules C. "Parental dynamics: their role in learning dis-
      abilities." Read Teach 23(8): 751-55, 760, May, 1970. (3 Ref-
      erences).
Concludes that parents play a most important role in helping or hindering
the reading-disabled child. They should be informed of the nature of the
child's difficulty and the emotional consequences that flow from it. The
learning-disabled child must be considered within the context of family
relationships. Two illustrative case histories are given. The case of
a nine-year-old boy with an overprotective mother illustrates the notion
that parents of brain-damaged children feel guilt. They erect defenses
in the form of overprotection against their feelings of anger and hostility. In another illustration it is demonstrated that parents of dyslexic
children often find it difficult to accept the fact that the child has a
problem. In both cases the child develops severe feelings of inadequacy.

1109 Abrams, Jules C., and Smolen, Wendy O. "On stress, failure and
      reading disability." J Read 16(6): 462-66, March, 1973. (6
      References).
Much deviant behavior is a reaction of the organism under stress. No
matter what the basic cause of reading disability, the disability can be
sustained by the stress reaction long after the original causes have lost
their significance. The child who experiences reading failure for whatever reason ultimately comes under emotional stress. This does not happen
abruptly. But finally the child's emotional reserves are depleted and
he can no longer even force himself to concentrate. The more a situation
resembles reading, the greater the aversion and stress. After one or more
years of severe reading failure, the primary cause has probably been re-

moved or much relieved. It is his reaction to stress that perpetuates the problem.

1110 Alexander, J. Estill. "Relationship between personality and reading disability." Coll Stud J 5(3): 121-28, November-December, 1971. (32 References).
Reviews studies indicating that reading problems and personality maladjustments do not have a cause-and-effect relationship. Good readers display the same personality traits as poor readers. Improving reading achievement may relieve emotional difficulties. The three popular positions taken by reading specialists are that: (1) reading disability is caused by personality maladjustment; (2) personality maladjustment is caused by reading disability; or (3) both occur together as part of a larger constellation of personal difficulties. The studies described attempted to determine if any of these relationships existed, and if one could be predictive of the other.

1111 Ball, Thomas S., and Deich, Ruth F. "Reading disability and hypothesis-formation: an application of the Postman and Bruner theory." Percept Mot Skills 34(2): 383-86, April, 1972. (8 References).
Postman and Bruner's theory holds that the individual under stress tends to form premature perceptual hypotheses that interfere with correct perception, that is, under stress he becomes reckless. The result is lowered accuracy in the task. This study was carried out to test whether the phenomenon observed by Postman and Bruner might apply to reading disability. Groups of fifth- and sixth-grade normal and disabled readers were presented with three-word sentences exposed tachistoscopically for very short times. All the words were in the children's reading vocabulary. Errors were analyzed in terms of guessing, perseverance, or omission. The hypothesis was not supported. Disabled readers did not make more premature, interfering guesses than normal readers.

1112 Barber, Lucille Knecht. "Immature ego development as a factor in retarded ability." For a summary see: Diss Abstr 12(4): 503, 1952.

1113 Black, F. William. "Self-concept as related to achievement and age in learning-disabled children." Child Dev 45(4): 1137-40, December, 1974. (15 References).
Groups of eleven-year-old children who were normal or disabled readers were given the WISC, the WRAT, and a self-concept test. Normal readers had mean full-scale WISC scores of 103.24. Disabled readers' mean full-scale WISC scores were 99.12. The self-concept scores of retarded readers were significantly lower than those of normal readers. Older learning-disabled children tended to view themselves more negatively than did similar younger children. Findings imply that children who do not achieve in school tend to have a more negative view of self than do similar children who are normal readers.

1114 Blanchard, Phyllis. "Psychoanalytic contributions to the problem of reading disabilities." Psychoanal Study Child 2: 163-87, 1946. (41 References).
Probably only about 20 percent of reading problems are caused by personality maladjustments. This article is chiefly concerned with these. Careful differential diagnosis must be employed to distinguish other reading disabilities from the reading disorder which appears as one of a

child's neurotic symptoms. Some literature is reviewed and case histories illustrating the problem of neurotic reading disability are presented. It is pointed out that no single situation or personality maladjustment can be isolated as a cause of this type of dyslexia. The cause of
reading disability in one child may provide strong motivation to learn
to read in another individual.

1115 Boyd, Robert Dean. "Reading retardation as related to personality
      factors of children and their parents." For a summary see: Diss
      Abstr 13(5): 872, 1953.

1116 "Difficulty in reading may be due to individualism." Sci News Lett
      65(19): 292, May 8, 1954. (0 References).
In tests of schoolchildren nine and ten years old who were beginning work
in remedial reading, 89 percent were found to look at the white space in
the background of the Rorschach (ink blot) figures rather than trying to
see pictures in the black ink daubs. The tendency was interpreted as a
sign of negativism or unconscious resistance toward fitting into required
behavior patterns. Although this finding in kindergarten children did
not identify those who would later have trouble with reading, it did distinguish the poor readers after reading instruction had begun.

1117 Fabian, Abraham A. "Reading disability: an index of pathology."
      Am J Orthopsychiatry 25(2): 319-29, April, 1955. (29 References).
Organic problems or poor teaching methods are not as important as causes
of reading disability as are psychological factors, especially family
influences during preschool years which shape the child's psychological
reactions. Reading disability is an ego disability, a secondary symptom
caused by some primary neurotic conflict. It serves as an index of the
pathology in an individual or a group.

1118 Filipelli, John James. "Personality factors in reading disability."
      For a summary see: Diss Abstr 25(9): 4918-19, March, 1965.

1119 Graham, E. Ellis. "Wechsler-Bellevue and WISC scattergrams of un-
      successful readers." J Consult Psychol 16(4): 268-71, August,
      1952. (6 References).
The test profiles of ninety-six unsuccessful readers between eight and
sixteen years of age who had been given Wechsler-Bellevue Form I or Form
II or the WISC IQ tests and had achieved either a verbal or performance
scale IQ of 90 or above were studied. The child had attended school the
expected number of years and had fallen 25 percent or more below mean
reading grade level on the Wide Range Achievement Test (WRAT). Performance scale scores were higher than verbal scale scores in most cases.
A 1949 study revealed that the test profile for reading-disabled adolescents is very similar to that of the adolescent psychopath. Findings in
this study replicate the similarities, although these subjects were not
in trouble with the law. Subtests in which these subjects scored above
and below the mean are listed. Their greatest successes appeared to be
in tests most distant from the classroom situation. Results are seen in
terms of an unconscious resistance to the emotional climate at home or
school.

1120 Günzburg, H. C. "The unsuccessful reader." Ment Health 8: 34-
      37, November, 1948. (4 References).
Many persons who do not learn to read when young arrive at age fifteen
or sixteen and realize the importance of reading. Most of the reading

material available for beginning readers is intended for much younger children. The regret and disappointment probably strengthens the asocial tendencies of these young people. Much work has been expended in studying the significance of such features of reading disability as reversals, omissions, substitutions, or repetitions of sounds. But these are not by themselves characteristic of a particular reading disability. Nor does some sensory or combination of psychological and physical handicaps explain the existence of reading disability. The child is probably insecure and anxious, with a weak and immature personality and a lack of drive. In one class of teen-age unsuccessful readers the boys were unstable, immature, anxious, and weak. As long as these attitudes remain, the non-reader or poor reader will remain unsuccessful in reading.

1121   Henderson, Edmund H.; Long, Barbara H.; and Ziller, Robert C.
        "Self-social constructs of achieving and nonachieving readers."
        Read Teach 19(2): 114-18, November, 1965. (5 References).
Reports on a study of three components of self-concept in reading-disabled children: (1) differentiation, or the degree to which the self is distinguished in the social field; (2) esteem, the general way in which the person compares himself with others; and (3) individualism, or the perception of self as being in a position separate from a group rather than within it. The disabled reader's perception of himself is thought to be damaged by years of failure. It is concluded that disabled readers are characterized by a relatively high degree of dependency.

1122   Hobbs, Howard E. An affective-perception psychology of adolescent
        reading failure. Ph.D. thesis, Walden University. 1974. 193p.
        (ED 112 305).
Subjects for this study were 180 seventh- through tenth-grade black male pupils who were evaluated through personal interviews, questionnaires, and observation over an eighty-week period. The intent of the study was to develop an interpersonal theory concerning adolescent reading failures. The theory hypothesizes that reading failure in such persons results from and is maintained by the adolescent's conscious choice of perceptual preferences. It is concluded that reading failure in a group such as this is characterized by retreat into one of three kinds of perception preferences: (1) unsocialized aggression, with hostility, quarrelsomeness, vengefulness, and destructiveness; (2) social approval anxiety with unrealistic fears, immaturity, self-consciousness, and inhibition; or (3) unsocialized withdrawal reflecting detachment, shyness, and lack of desire to form close personal relationships.

1123   Jackson, Joseph. "A survey of psychological, social, and environmental differences between advanced and retarded readers." Pedagog Semin J Genet Psychol 65(1): 113-31, September, 1944. (1 Reference).
From a comparative study of 300 advanced and 300 retarded readers, it is concluded that reading disability is not necessarily confined to pupils with poor grades. The causes of reading ability or disability are many and intertwined. They include fears, worries, failures, and lack of interest. A formal remedial program of reading beginning at a primary level is recommended.

1124   Jensen, Milton B. "Some psychological aspects of extreme reading disability." Psychol Bull 35(8): 517-18, October, 1938. (0 References).

A child of normal health and vision who learns well in other fields and
has had adequate opportunity, but who reads poorly, may be assumed to
have had faulty methods of instruction, at least so far as he is concerned. A reading-disabled child may develop emotional problems. He should
be shown how and why he does not read well and given training in emotional control.

1125 Kass, Corrine Evelyn. "Psycholinguistic disabilities of children
      with reading problems." Except Child 32(8): 533-39, April, 1966.
      (15 References).
Children of normal intelligence and educational opportunity with reading
disability were found not to be deficient in either auditory or visual
motor tests at the representational level. They were found deficient in
this study in tests like visual sequencing, sound blending, mazes, memory
for designs, and perceptual speed. It is concluded that methods for
training the integrational processes in such children are needed.

1126 ————. "Some psychological correlates of severe reading dis-
      ability (dyslexia)." For a summary see: Diss Abstr 23(7):
      2421-22, January, 1963.

1127 Krugman, M. "Reading failure and mental health." Natl Assoc
      Women Deans Couns J 20: 10-12, October, 1956.

1128 Lantz, Beatrice, and Liebes, Genevieve B. "A follow-up study of
      non-readers." J Educ Res 36(8): 604-26, April, 1943. (10 Ref-
      erences).
Thirty-three boys living in a cottage-plan orphanage were systematically
followed up. The difficulty in learning to read appeared to be just one
expression of the boys' difficulty in educational adjustment. Emotional
maladjustments were present in 85 percent of the cases. Personality
characteristics of these boys, when grown, remained consistent: the
aggressor, the daydreamer, and the nervous hyperactive all remained true
to their earlier classification, with behavior patterns tempered to make
them more socially acceptable. The average IQ of the group was 100.3.
Age and grade when nonreading was detected and intelligence appeared to
be unrelated to the number of remedial reading lessons necessary to overcome the defect. Nor did these factors appear to be related to the number or type of obstacles to be overcome in learning to read. On the
basis of this study it cannot be assumed that nonreaders who have their
reading difficulties corrected will then progress through an educational
career without further marked difficulty.

1129 Leslie, Lauren. "Susceptibility to interference effects in short-
      term memory of normal and retarded readers." Percept Mot Skills
      40(3): 791-94, June, 1975. (6 References).
Concludes that short-term memory capacity of normal and retarded readers
is similar, but the short-term memory of retarded readers is more susceptible to interference. Members of two groups of third- and fourth-grade
pupils matched for IQ were shown individually a series of six pictures
one at a time. The pictures were scrambled and given to the child who
was asked to reconstruct the sequence. The same pictures were used in
different orders for six trials. A new set of pictures was used on a
seventh trial. Performance on the first trial was similar for both
groups. Performance of retarded readers deteriorated more rapidly than
that of normal readers. Both groups improved on the seventh trial.

1130 Lytton, H. "Some psychological and sociological characteristics
      of 'good' and 'poor achievers' (boys) in remedial reading groups:
      clinical case studies." Hum Dev 11(4): 260-76, 1968. (27 Ref-
      erences).
Two groups of eight-year-old children matched for sex, age, and mean nonverbal IQ were used as subjects in this study. The group of good readers
was reading close to age norm after remedial training. The poor readers
still were not achieving in reading after an exceptionally long period
in the remedial group. The children were given the WISC, the Rorschach,
and other psychological tests. Home environment was assessed. Results
were consistent with findings of other researchers. Considerable evidence not exists that physical factors, symptoms of emotional maladjustment, and severe reading difficulties are related. Poor achievers had
considerably lower drive level in reading tasks and family histories of
reading failure in addition to the combination of other adverse factors
which differentiated them from children whose reading disabilities responded to remedial treatment.

1131 Mann, Helene Powner. "Some hypotheses on perceptual and learning
      processes with their applications to the process of reading: a
      preliminary note." J Genet Psychol 90(2): 167-202, June, 1957.
      (23 References).
Reports the results of a series of reading improvement classes made available to college students, most of them freshmen, who scored in the lowest
percentiles on a reading test. Marked increase in self-confidence or
courage was noted in students who made reading gains. Reading problems
provided a kind of cross section of the student's general behavior. His
reading seemed to reflect his approach to life in general. It is not new
to suggest the roles of identification, immature ego development, vision,
and fear in reading problems. But in order to devise appropriate remedial measures, it is necessary to develop a theory of learning based on
an appropriate concept of emotion. Various conclusions and hypotheses
are drawn from this concept of reading as an example of perceptual and
learning processes. Among these are that reading is a perceptual process
first and a learning process next. It is therefore interfered with by
fear. Reading problems are symptoms whose real causes are embedded in
the individual's early life experiences. The degree to which fear can
be reduced partly determines the amount of reading improvement. If these
hypotheses concerning the effect of fear on reading are true, then fear-
producing stimuli may be expected to influence other areas involving perception and learning. The general hypothesis is that fear inhibits many
physiological and psychological processes. Courage-producing stimuli
may be expected to have opposite results and should have increased emphasis in our culture.

1132 Manney, Agnes Ann. "The temporal orientation of the retarded
      reader." For a summary see: Diss Abstr 17(8): 1708, August,
      1957.

1133 Mutimer, Dorothy; Loughlin, Leo; Powell, Marvin. "Some differences
      in the family relationships of achieving and underachieving read-
      ers." J Genet Psychol 109(1): 67-74, September, 1966. (2 Ref-
      erences).
Using the "Two Houses Technique," researchers tested groups of achieving
and underachieving readers individually on their family relationships.
Significant differences were found between the groups of children.
Achieving girls identify with their mothers and reject some siblings more

than underachieving girls do. Achieving boys identify with their fathers and interact with some siblings more than underachieving boys do.

1134 Otto, Wayne. "Inhibitory potential related to the reading achievement of Negro children." Psychol Sch 3(2): 161-63, April, 1966. (6 References).
Black children in grades four, five, and six with IQs from 90 to 115 were asked to copy from a chalkboard inverted digits 1 to 10 as written by the experimenter. They were given a group of trials, a rest, and another group of trials. The children were identified and grouped as good readers and poor readers by reading test scores and teacher judgment. The experiment was designed to test the idea that the poor readers would make greater gains on the task after a rest (that is, show greater reminiscence) than good readers because of a more rapid dissipation of reactive inhibition. It had been assumed in earlier tests that the difference reflected more rapid accumulation of reactive inhibition by poor readers. It was found that good and poor readers did not differ in initial trials or in trials after the rest period. They did differ significantly in favor of the good readers in the last trial before rest. Results are seen as implying that poor readers dissipated more reactive inhibition than good readers. Thus the earlier finding that good readers accumulate less reactive inhibition in a given period than do poor readers was confirmed. Results are seen as confirming a general finding for white as well as Negro pupils.

1135 Park, George E. "Mirror and reversed reading." J Pediatr 42(1): 120-28, January, 1953. (0 References).
Mirror vision and reversals are symptoms, not causes, of dyslexia. These devices may be used by the child to express dissatisfaction, escape from reality, or to gain greater protection and attention. The process is psychologic and without organic basis. The abnormal factors responsible for dyslexia are functional, preventable, and correctable.

1136 Parker, Isabel. "Personality problems and reading disability." Natl Elem Princ 19(6): 603-11, July, 1940. (20 References).
Emotional and environmental factors which may contribute to reading disability include emotional immaturity caused by overprotection at home or emotional conflict because of insecurity at home. Personality problems may also appear as a result of reading difficulties. Case histories and suggestions of ways the teacher can help the maladjusted child are included.

1137 Rosenthal, Joseph H. "Self-esteem in dyslexic children." Acad Ther 9(1): 27-39, Fall, 1973. (6 References).
Reports the results of a study of self-esteem in three groups of white boys ages eight to fourteen years: dyslexic, normal, and asthmatic. Half the dyslexics and their parents were given information on the causes, symptoms, and possible consequences of dyslexia. The other half were told nothing. The dyslexics who had information about the condition had higher self-esteem than those who were ignorant of it. No significant correlation appeared between self-esteem ratings and behavior ratings among the three groups. The self-esteem inventory and the behavior rating form used are included. Major factors contributing to self-esteem are discussed.

1138 Santostefano, Sebastiano; Rutledge, Louis; Randall, David. "Cognitive styles and reading disability." Psychol Sch 2(1): 57-62, January, 1965. (33 References).

Tests the idea that the reader is not a passive perceiver but that an individual's cognition is active in selecting, sorting, and organizing information according to principles influenced by motivation and personality factors. Groups of boys who were normal or retarded readers and matched for age, IQ, and grade placement were given tests aimed at measuring their manner of dealing with material to be learned. Ages ranged from eight to thirteen years; IQ range was 65 to 116 for retarded readers and 80 to 126 for normal readers. The three cognitive styles explored were: (1) Focusing-Scanning which concerns how the individual distributes attention among objects he is comparing. (2) Leveling-Sharpening which concerns how the individual deals with ongoing, changing information. (3) Constricted-Flexible which concerns how the individual deals with distracting or contradictory material. Only the third seemed to be implicated in reading disability. Findings suggest that the one cognitive mechanism crucial to reading is concerned with distractions and with the individual's ability to withhold attention selectively from irrelevant and intrusive information.

1139 Siegel, Max. "The personality structure of children with reading disabilities as compared with children presenting other clinical problems." Microfilm Abstr 11(4): 1100-1101, 1951.

1140 ————. "The personality structure of children with reading disabilities as compared with children presenting other clinical problems." Nerv Child 10(3-4): 409-14, 1954. (25 References).
Explores the personality structures of reading-disabled children. Results suggest that these children should not be regarded as educational problems as such, but as emotionally disturbed children in need of therapy. No personality pattern was found to be characteristic of reading failure. Patterns found were consistent with the range of personality variables that might be found in any group of emotionally disturbed persons. Findings emphasize the importance of home and family relationships to the educational adjustment of the child. School and parents should cooperate. The individual personality of the child should be understood by the teacher.

1141 Spache, George. "Personality patterns of retarded readers." J Educ Res 50(6): 461-69, February, 1957. (5 References).
Finds five major personality patterns among retarded readers: (1) an aggressive or hostile group in conflict with those in authority; (2) an adjustive group whose members seek to be inoffensive; (3) a defensive group of people who are sensitive and resentful; (4) a peace-making group; and (5) a group whose members withdraw in an autistic or blocked manner.

1142 Tabarlet, B. E. "Poor readers and mental health." Elem Engl 35(8): 522-25, December, 1958. (0 References).
The results of a study of groups of normal and retarded fifth-grade pupils suggest that retarded readers are not as mature in behavior as children reading up to grade level. The retarded readers also: (1) were deficient in skills in personal relations; (2) took less part in social affairs; (3) had fewer satisfying hobbies; and (4) were less sought after by their classmates than normal readers. Findings suggest a relationship between poor mental health and reading retardation.

1143 Thomas, Hugh B. G. "Genetic and psychodynamic aspects of developmental dyslexia: a cybernetic approach." J Learn Disabil 6(1): 30-40, January, 1973. (22 References).

Discusses the causes of dyslexia in terms of brain damage, heredity, and family environment. The results are reported of examination of thirty-three families attending a dyslexia clinic as to the extent to which these individuals set themselves standards of inference, either lax or stringent. Disorders of inference or inferential justment--that is, of "common sense"--in judging the meaning of language were found more often in dyslexic children than in their parents. It is suggested that these disorders give rise to a wide range of educational and behavioral problems.

1144   Upson, P. G. "The psychodynamics of reading disability--a pilot study." Br J Proj Psychol Pers Study 13(2): 15-21, 1968.

1145   Veltfort, Helene Rank. "Some personality correlates of reading disability." For a summary see: Diss Abstr 16(10): 1947-48, 1956.

1146   Vernon, Magdalen Dorothea. Reading and its difficulties; a psychological study. Cambridge, England: University Press, 1971. 211p. (Bibliography p. 181-201).
Visual perception, auditory factors, and the relation of reasoning, intelligence, motivation, and emotional factors to learning to read are assessed in this book. Defective functioning in any of these areas gives rise to reading difficulties. About one-fourth of the book is devoted to a discussion of specific developmental dyslexia. Neurological impairment, maturational lag, and hereditary factors are considered as causes. The difficulty appears to lie in grasping temporal or spatial sequential relationships of the sounds or letters of words. Little is known of the precise nature of the disability; it is difficulty to differentiate dyslexic children from retarded readers who are not dyslexic. Remedial teaching, especially with individual attention, may help the retarded reader improve, but the severely dyslexic child remains difficult to help.

1147   Wattenberg, William W., and Clifford, Clare. "Relation of self-concepts to beginning achievement in reading." Child Dev 35(2): 461-67, June, 1964. (7 References).
Tests for self-concept and mental ability were administered to kindergarten children. Reading progress and self-concept were measured for the same group two and one-half years later. The self-concept measure taken in kindergarten was significantly related to reading progress. Self-concept test scores were not found to be related to intelligence test scores.

1148   Witty, Paul A., and Kopel, David. "Causes of poor reading and remedial technique." Ill Teach 24(1): 21-31, September, 1935. (14 References).
In spite of improved methods of reading instruction, the number of extremely poor readers has not decreased. It is regrettable that we have not realized that reading is a thinking enterprise demanding the use of creative intelligence in situations associated with the growing child's total development. Physiological factors have been blamed for reading failure. Some physiological problems obviously accompany reading disability, but there is a general lack of relationship between reading disability and physiological factors. Low intelligence is a factor, but many poor readers are of adequate intelligence. The errors made by a group of poor readers ages fourteen to sixteen years are analyzed. Eleven

contributing factors to poor reading are identified. The four most frequent are lack of interest, meager background of experience, incorrect
placement in school in terms of reading skills, and inability to sustain
attention for a desired end. Individual psychological diagnosis is recommended in cases of poor reading. Suggestions for a remedial reading
program suitable for a moderate-size school system are made.

1149 Zamm, Michael. "Reading disabilities: a theory of cognitive in-
     tegration." J Learn Disabil 6(2): 95-101, February, 1973. (10
     References).
Traces the cause for the reading difficulties of black and Puerto Rican
children in poverty areas to cognitive disintegration, that is, difficulty in comprehension generally and in responding to words. The underlying cause for this is the child's lack of experiences in his orientation in space and lack of emotional experiences at crucial stages of development. Without such experiences the child is not able to grow biologically and psychologically in a way that allows him to grasp the
spatial concepts implicit in language. Possible remedies are suggested.

Y. RESEARCH

1150 "Backwardness in reading: some causes revealed." Times Educ Suppl
     650: 460, October 15, 1927. (0 References).
Reports on Miss G. Hume's investigation in London schools of the causes
of reading disability. About half the cases were ascribed to extrinsic
factors such as irregular school attendance, low culture at home, physical defects, emotional disturbances, and improper teaching methods. The
other half were caused intrinsically. Weak specific ability for reading
which manifested itself as defective memory for verbal symbols or inability to discriminate between word and letter forms was one intrinsic cause.
Another was innate emotional instability characterized by substitution of
similar words. Faulty teaching methods led to substitution, repetition,
and insertion of letters, syllables, or words. Remedial methods have
been largely developed in America.

1151 Barnard, Maryline. Reading disability and levels of perceptual
     efficiency: an experimental study. Unpublished Ph.D. thesis.
     University of Southern California, 1958.

1152 Birch, Robert William. "Attention span, distractibility and in-
     hibitory potential of good and poor readers." For a summary see:
     Diss Abstr 28B(11): 4742-43, May, 1968.

1153 Busby, Walter A.; Fillmer, H. T.; Smittle, Pat. "Interrelationship
     between self-concept, visual perception, and reading disabilities."
     J Exp Educ 42(3): 1-6, Spring, 1974. (31 References).
Groups of randomly selected seventh- and ninth-grade students were given
tests measuring self-concept, visual perception, reading ability, and intelligence. Twenty-four variables from this data were submitted to factor
analysis and multiple correlation. The hypothesis that self-concept and
visual perception are related to reading disabilities was not clearly supported. There was some support for the conclusion that three-dimensional
visual perception is made up partly of intellectual ability.

1154   Camp, Bonnie W.   "Learning rate and retention in retarded readers."
       <u>J Learn Disabil</u> 6(2): 65-71, February, 1973. (15 References).
Since differences in retention are known to be a function of degree of
learning, the results of this study of the relationship between rate of
learning and long-term retention suggests that learning rate is an indication of the degree of original learning. Subjects were reading-disabled
children ages eight to eighteen who were being tutored in reading. Individual learning curves accelerated initially, followed by gradual slow-
ing--much the same kind of learning curves shown by normal children.
Correlations between learning rate and retention were significant. It
had been expected that the learning curves of reading-disabled children
might be very different from those of normal children since reading-
disabled children's problems might tend to alter the ways they perceive
the learning problem. This was not the case. This implies that a study
of the way normal children learn can be applied to most disabled readers.
The further implication is drawn that the general pattern of initial ac-
celeration followed by gradual slowing may represent a standard of
"normalcy" in each child. It is expected that most reading-disabled
children exhibit this learning pattern even though classed as suffering
from "pathological" learning disability. The general conclusion is that
individual differences in learning rate may account for most individual
differences in reading achievement even among severely retarded readers.
What procedures can be used to modify learning rates remains to be seen.
Drill and repetition may offer much gain in learning, in spite of the
present disfavor into which they have fallen.

1155   Critchley, E. M. R.   "Reading retardation, dyslexia and delin-
       quency." <u>Br J Psychiatry</u> 114(517): 1537-47, December, 1968.
       (27 References).
While the theory is still unproved that young people progress from dyslexia to truancy or delinquency, this study revealed that 60 percent of
the children in a London facility for delinquents were retarded in reading. Fifty percent were retarded by more than three years; many of these
were dyslexic. However, retarded readers were not truant more than normal readers of similar full-scale intelligence. Some of the children
had family histories indicative of dyslexia. Few had medical problems
that would cause reading problems. The opinion is expressed that these
findings support the "immaturity" theory of dyslexia.

1156   Denckla, Martha Bridge, and Rudel, Rita G.   "Naming of object-
       drawings by dyslexic and other learning disabled children." <u>Brain
       Lang</u> 3(1): 1-15, January, 1976. (40 References).
Children eight to ten years old who were diagnosed as suffering from minimal neurological impairment (minimal brain dysfunction or MBD) but were
not dyslexic; another group diagnosed as dyslexic MBD; and a group of
normal controls were all given the Oldfield-Wingfield Picture-Naming
Test. This test made use of a set of thirty-six simple black-on-white
drawings of objects whose names occurred across a broad range of frequency on a word-frequency count test. The children were asked to name
the object as quickly as possible. A stopwatch was used to time responses. Dyslexics named fewer pictures correctly, performing more slowly than MBD children who were not dyslexic or the normal controls. The
distribution of errors was similar for dyslexics and normal children.
This was seen as evidence that there is no perceptual impairment underlying dyslexics' low scores. The MBD group produced a high percentage
of wrong names, suggesting that they mistook the picture for some other
visually similar object. It is concluded that dyslexic MBD children

resemble adult dysphasics in that they have language retrieval problems. Nondyslexic MBD children are verbally competent, but fail because of faulty perception of the pictures.

1157   deQuirós, J. B.   "Dysphasia and dyslexia in school children." Folia Phoniatr 16(3): 201-22, 1964. (54 References).
Describes dysphasia as a condition characterized chiefly by delay in learning, generally in reading and writing. Infantile dysphasia is related to a series of conditions of the developmental age in children concerning language. Dyslexia is usually used to describe a similar syndrome characterized by difficulties in learning to read. The various problems are all subsumed under the heading "infantile speech and language organization impairments" (ISLOI). Results of a study of 1,278 schoolchildren, most in first or second grade when first seen and followed up periodically, are reported. The children were from three schools in Rosario, Argentina, and from upper, middle, and lower socio-economic levels. They were examined for hereditary and family factors; environment; motor, linguistic, and toilet control development; attention and visual and auditory memory; and other physical points. No severe cases were included—only children who were considered normal by their parents and who attended regular schools. Six percent of the children showed neurological and psychomotor immaturities in relation to chronological age. Difficulties in learning to read and write were seen in 18.66 percent; 12 percent of these were dyslexic, with 2 percent of them showing severe dyslexia. It is noted that the dyslexic child shows perceptual disturbances, especially in the ability to visualize and auditorize, and sometimes in tactual perception. They exhibit instability in attention and memory. Eye and vision problems are ruled out as having any relationship to dyslexia. Statistical data are presented.

1158   Eakin, Suzanne, and Douglas, Virginia I.   "Automatization and oral reading problems in children." J Learn Disabil 4(1): 26-33, January, 1971. (23 References).
Concerns the child who shows marked impairment in performing oral reading, but appears able to comprehend satisfactorily. Automatized behaviors are those which are so highly practiced that they require a minimum of conscious effort, for example, walking, talking, reading, writing. It seems logical to expect the poor oral reader to have poor "automatic" skills. Some research supporting this idea is reviewed. Groups of good and poor readers were selected. They were boys from grades four and five with average IQs of 114. Automatized tasks given the boys included the speed of naming repeated objects, speed of naming repeated color hues, and word-color interference. Tasks not automatized included the WAIS Block Design test, Porteus Mazes, and the Children's Embedded Figures Test. Poor readers' performance on automatized tasks was significantly worse than that of good readers. No significant differences were seen in two of the tasks which were not automatized, and poor readers did significantly better than good readers on the third test, the Mazes Test. Results support the idea that poor oral readers have impaired ability in automatized tasks.

1159   Fabian, Abraham A.   "Clinical and experimental studies of school children who are retarded in reading." Q J Child Behav 3(1): 15-27, January, 1951. (34 References).
Describes a study of twenty retarded readers (nineteen boys, one girl) eight to nine years old who had completed second grade, were of normal intelligence, and had had adequate school experience. They were drawn

from a class of 210 children on the basis of reading and IQ tests. They
were given physical and neurological examinations. Physical factors,
handedness, eyedness, and confusion in dominance did not contribute much
to the reading problem. It is concluded that reading retardation is a
symptom of underlying individual, and often familial, psychopathology.
These children were ego-disabled, emotionally retarded, infantile, and
dependent. They retained infantile habits of perception and visual-
motor maturational lags which produced reversals and other perceptual
distortions. Psychiatric implications are discussed and recommendations
made for prevention.

1160   Gold, Lawrence, and Huebner, Dale M. "An investigation of the in-
        cidence of developmental dyslexia and selected factors associated
        with the condition: results of a two year study." Paper presented
        at the International Reading Association Conference, Anaheim,
        California, May 6-9, 1970. 1970. 10p. (ED 040 828).
Reports an analysis of factors associated with developmental dyslexia in
children attending a learning disability center during a two-year period.
Of the approximately 400 pupils involved, the average age was about ten
and one-half years, average IQ about 98, and the ratio of boys to girls
seven to one. A battery of reading and diagnostic tests was given the
children. They were about two years below actual grade placement in
reading on the average. Most pupils showed general immaturity and emotional problems. Family pathology was third in importance.

1161   Harris, A. J. "Causes of reading retardation; and evaluation."
        Conference on Reading. University of Pittsburgh. Report   1960.
        21-30.

1162   Hunter, Edna J. "Autonomic responses to aircraft noise in dyslexic
        children." Psychol Sch 8(4): 362-67, October, 1971. (11 Refer-
        ences).
Noise from low-flying aircraft distracted dyslexic children more than it
distracted normal readers, as measured by autonomic patterns (heart rate,
skin conductance level, and various other physiological tests). This
was true only when the children were engaged in some task. Almost identical response patterns were observed in the two groups while the children were resting between tasks. It is concluded that the results support the hypothesis that defective inhibitory mechanisms (inability to
block out external or irrelevant stimuli), not defective arousal levels,
underlie the nonreader's inability to pay attention to his task. Subjects were boys ages seven to eleven years. Dyslexics and a control
group of normal readers were matched for sex, grade, race, IQ, and socioeconomic status.

1163   Karlsen, Björn. "A comparison of some educational and psychological
        characteristics of successful and unsuccessful readers at the ele-
        mentary school level." For a summary see: Diss Abstr 15(3):
        456-57, 1955.

1164   Kline, Carl L., and Lee, Norma. "A transcultural study of dys-
        lexia: analysis of language disabilities in 277 Chinese children
        simultaneously learning to read and write in English and Chinese."
        J Spec Educ 6(1): 9-26, Spring, 1972. (34 References).
Studied the incidence of dyslexia in Chinese children in grades one, two,
and three in learning Chinese and the incidence of dyslexia in these same
children in learning English. The study was done in Vancouver, British

Columbia, which has a large Chinese population. The children attended
English-teaching public school all day. They then attended a private
Chinese language school for two additional hours. All were learning to
read and write English and Chinese simultaneously. It is explained that
English is 86 percent phonetic and is best learned by a sound-sight association system. Chinese is nonphonetic and must be learned by rote
memorization. Details of the method of testing are given. Males experiencing difficulty outnumbered girls with reading problems three to
one. Those having trouble in both languages was 6 percent, in Chinese
only 13 percent, and in English only 9 percent. The incidence of disability in each language dropped off rapidly. At the end of grade three,
3 percent had trouble with English, 5 percent with Chinese, and 2 percent with both. It is speculated that these are the "hard-core" dyslexics. This pattern of rapid decrease with age is not typical of most
studies done in English. Problems of auditory discrimination or crossed
dominance do not seem to be causes of reading difficulties. The WISC,
Bender Gestalt, and Draw-a-Person tests do not appear to be reliable
predictors or indicators of reading problems. Bilingualism in the home
created no problems. Indeed, findings support the notion that preschool
years are the ideal time to teach a second language.

1165 Kolers, Paul A. "Pattern-analyzing disability in poor readers."
      Dev Psychol 11(3): 282-90, May, 1975. (12 References).
Two groups of schoolchildren ages ten to fourteen years, one group above
average in reading ability, the other below average, were asked to read
fifty-six sentences taken from stories in a grade three reader. Some of
the sentences were typed in the normal way. Some were in reversed ty-
pography, reading from left to right, but will all letters reversed.
Reading the sentences took substantially longer for poor readers than for
good readers. Both groups required more time to read reversed sentences
than normal ones. Poor readers made more errors in reading. Contrary
to expectations, good readers were more sensitive to features of typog-
raphy than were poor readers. Poor readers differed from good readers
in their pattern-analyzing ability, that is, in correlating the graphemic
(pictorial) part of the sentences with the semantic (linguistic) part.
It is suggested that the problem is not so much perceptual, concerned
with dealing with words as visual objects, as it is cognitive, dealing
with words as linguistic marks to be analyzed and interpreted.

1166 Levine, Maureen, and Fuller, Gerald. "Psychological, neuropsycho-
      logical, and educational correlates of reading deficit." J Learn
      Disabil 5(9): 563-71, November, 1972. (18 References).
Concludes that poor readers do better when presented with material to be
received through only one sense at a time, especially vision. They tend
to be able to deal more adequately with visual stimuli. They are less
proficient with auditory material. They do poorly when confronted with
material coming to eyes and ears together, suggesting problems in integration of sensory material. Reading-disabled eleven-year-old children of
normal intelligence were subjects for this study. They were given the
WRAT and the WISC to determine reading deficit. These and other tests
made up a battery of fifty-nine tests and subtests given the children.
Results support the idea that reading deficits are associated with deficiencies measured by some of the WISC subtests and by the Minnesota
Percepto-Diagnostic Test. Statistical data are given comparing disabled
readers at ages nine, ten, eleven, twelve, and thirteen with a normal
population of the same ages on a selection of the tests.

1167 Lewis, Franklin D.; Bell, D. Bruce; Anderson, Robert P. "Reading
      retardation: a bi-racial comparison." J Read 13(6): 433-36,
      474-78, March, 1970. (27 References).
Describes a study of 100 junior high school boys. Adequate and inadequate
readers were compared within each of two racial groups, Caucasian and
Negro. There were twenty-five in each group. All the black pupils came
from one junior high school; all white students came from another school.
No child with a WISC IQ below 80, from a bilingual home, or with a neurological, emotional, or sensory difficulty was included. The factor of
educational opportunity was held constant. Twenty-six variables were investigated including, among others, the role of intelligence, socioeconomic status, family situation, and motor proficiency as factors in reading difficulties. The two reading groups differed significantly on twenty
variables: the racial groups on twelve. The WISC Comprehension subtest
results showed black adequate readers scoring higher than white adequate
readers, while the opposite was true for inadequate readers. Inadequate
readers were significantly less intelligent than adequate readers as measured by the WISC. Black readers made lower scores on three WISC subtests, Picture Completion, Object Assembly, and Coding, and on the entire
performance IQ than did white readers.

1168 McIlroy, Elsie. "Why does Johnny have a reading problem?" Ariz
      Teach 53: 8-10, March, 1965. (0 References).
Reports the results of a study set up by a first-grade teacher to find
out why first-grade children have reading problems. The fifteen children
studied ranged from percentile one to percentile fifty-eight on the
Metropolitan Reading Readiness test. Many did not perform according to
prediction, with some from the lowest percentiles reading at top level by
the end of first grade. Every child who performed below average on the
context clue subtest of the Ginn primer test was a poor reader. The five
best readers all did well on the Ginn context clue subtest, were above-
average IQ, and had the ability to appraise realistically the task of
learning to read. Poor readers appeared to be unwilling to make the
extra intellectual effort to extract meaning from what was read. Low
socioeconomic status of itself could not be considered a consistent factor contributing to reading problems.

1169 Malmquist, E. J. T. "Some studies on reading disabilities in
      various countries." Conference on Reading. University of
      Pittsburgh. Report 24: 7-24, 1968.

1170 Matejcek, Z. "The care of children with reading disability in
      Czechoslovakia." Slow Learn Child 11(2): 67-74, 1964. (12 Ref-
      erences).
Describes the program of research and treatment of dyslexic children in
Czechoslovakia. Systematic care for them did not develop until after
World War II. Three stages of research are described. The first was
directed toward finding causes. Two major groups of etiological factors
were isolated: genetic factors and milder forms of organic brain damage
denoted collectively "mild encephalopathy of childhood" (MEC). About
45 percent of the children studied showed signs of MEC. The second stage
of research involved a study of Prague schoolchildren to obtain some idea
of the incidence of mild forms of reading disorders. In the third stage
a classification of dyslexics was made based on dyslexic and writing disturbances. It is suggested that the mild forms are more influenced by
the character of the language and teaching methods. Because Czech has
consistent phonetic spelling and English does not, it is believed that

comparative studies of dyslexia in the two languages can make a large
contribution to understanding the nature of the common basis of the disorder and how much can be attributed to the particular characteristics
of the language being taught.

1171 Naidoo, Sandhya. Specific dyslexia; the research report of the
      ICAA Word Blind Centre of Dyslexic Children. London: Pitman Pub-
      lishing, 1972. 165p. (Bibliography p. 153-60).
In 1962 the Invalid Children's Aid Association (ICAA), London, began to
concern itself with the problem of intelligent children with learning
difficulties. It set up the Word Blind Centre for Dyslexic Children.
The center has now closed, and this book is the research report on the
project carried out at the center. It is written by the educational psychologist who served as research director beginning in September, 1966.
The workers at the center began with the view that if specific dyslexia
is a reality, then it should be possible to produce evidence of the
characteristics by which it may be recognized. Accurate diagnosis should
be possible. This report is an investigation into the existence, nature,
and causes of specific dyslexia.

A control group of normal readers of similar characteristics and a group
of ninety-eight boys between the ages of eight and twelve years who had
severe reading and spelling difficulties were examined medically and
psychologically. The WISC IQs were at least 90 with a verbal score of
at least 85. They were without gross physical, neurological, or emotional
problems and had experienced no major absence from school. Parents were
interviewed. Extensive information is given in the report on the home
and school backgrounds of the boys. Testing procedures are described,
together with details of the results of the psychological and neurological
examinations and the boys' developmental history. The reading, spelling,
speech difficulties, and handedness of other family members were investigated. The majority of both groups were from the two upper socioeconomic
classes.

Among the conclusions are these: The results of this investigation support the concept that some reading and spelling disorders are constitu-
tionally determined. The evidence does not support the existence of
clearly defined subtypes of dyslexia. Only multiple causes would account
for the observations in many of these boys, but these patterns of disability are insufficiently distinct to allow a clear-cut identification
of subtypes. Family histories of reading and spelling difficulty are
significantly more common in dyslexics than in the controls. No greater
frequency of mother/child separations, behavior problems, early illness,
birth hazards, nor difference in birth weight or birth order are found
in the dyslexics than in the controls. Some striking differences between
groups suggests the existence of one type of genetic dyslexia characterized by speech and language delays and disorders. Another group displayed atypical patterns of laterality. Difficulty in blending sounds
was commonly found among dyslexics. Dyslexic children need specialized
teaching; teachers should be familiar with a wide range of methods. The
record forms used in the study are reproduced. A history of the concept
of specific dyslexia is included, and current concepts are summarized.

1172 Reid, Jessie F. "Dyslexia: a problem of communication." Educ
      Res 10(2): 126-33, February, 1968. (30 References).
Presents the arguments made by those who believe that dyslexia is environmentally caused and those who maintain that a more fundamental constitutional condition is responsible. Some of the recent literature is re-

viewed. The controversies and conflicting opinions that exist in the study and definition of dyslexia are reviewed. An attempt is made to clarify these issues. It is concluded that there is an overwhelming need for rigorous study in the area. Three types of possible research are suggested.

1173 Samuels, S. Jay. "Success and failure in learning to read: a critique of the research." Read Res Q 8(2): 200-39, Winter, 1973. (143 References).
Reviews the literature, including critical analysis of research methods used to study reading problems. Suggestions for improving research methods are given. Some popular explanations of causes of reading difficulty are criticized. Labels such as "dyslexia" and "learning disability" delude the person doing the labeling into believing that he has found a cause for reading failure when he applies a label. Actually, labels provide no useful information as to why a pupil is failing. Diagnostic problems, testing irrelevant variables, the piecemeal approach of much research, inadequate matched group designs in research, and other shortcomings are discussed. It is concluded that most research in reading retardation does not amount to much. Research investigating factors seen as relevant to reading, such as attentional processes, visual and auditory memory, and auditory discrimination, are summarized and criticized. Suggestions for overcoming specific criticisms are made.

1174 Shearer, E. "Physical skills and reading backwardness." Educ Res 10(3): 197-206, June, 1968. (55 References).
Reports a study aimed at establishing norms for right-left discrimination, lack of strong hand preference, and evidences of body schema disturbance thought to be related to reading disability. Unselected groups of English schoolchildren ages seven to ten were tested for handedness, right-left discrimination, and finger localization in order to establish norms. All children attending remedial reading classes, ages eight to twelve, in the local schools were also tested. Right-left discrimination was defined as the child's ability to identify right and left parts of his own body. Mean IQs for all age levels were lower for retarded readers than for normals. It is concluded that discrepancies between the groups in the areas tested would probably still have existed, even if they had been matched for IQ. Retarded readers performed considerably worse on all tests at all ages than normal readers. Ability in right-left discrimination and finger localization increased with chronological age. The skills tested were positively correlated with both chronological age and IQ. There did appear to be a group of retarded readers who showed complete inability to distinguish left and right, and who had difficulty with crossed movements and finger localization. Findings do not clarify whether this group can be referred to as "specific dyslexics" even though they presented very acute forms of some of the symptoms of dyslexics.

1175 Valtin, Renate. Report on research on dyslexia in children. 1973. 12p. (ED 079 713).
Summarizes several research studies which were designed to test some of the German theories on dyslexia. As defined in Germany and used in this study, the dyslexic child is one of normal intelligence who has reading and writing disabilities. Groups of children were matched for IQ, sex, age, grade level, and occupation of father. The groups were compared in visual perception, dominance factors, and spatial orientation, theories especially considered in this study. Grammatical structure of oral language and concept formation did not differ in the groups. Dyslexics were

inferior to normal readers in articulation, auditory discrimination, and vocabulary. It is suggested that conditions in the home and early parent-child relationships are relevant to reading and writing problems. It was found helpful to consider specific personality traits of dyslexia in remedial education. Nondirective play therapy was one technique found to be successful.

1176   Vogel, Susan Ann. Syntactic abilities in normal and dyslexic children. Baltimore, Maryland: University Park Press, 1975. 118p. (Bibliography p. 85-95).
Compares the oral syntactic abilities of good and poor readers. Dyslexic children made up the group of poor readers. Dyslexia is defined as inability to learn to read in the expected manner and at the expected age because of central nervous system dysfunction. Only twenty children, all boys, met the criteria for this group among all the children in the fourteen elementary schools of a large school district. Sex, socio-economic differences, and language differences were eliminated as variables to preclude their causing differences in syntax in the children. Twenty normal readers were chosen as controls. Four areas of behavior were assessed: (1) syntactic abilities; (2) receptive vocabulary (the ability to understand the meaning of individual words); (3) auditory memory for both digits and words; and (4) reading ability. Full data on and results of the tests used in these investigations are given. In three of the five aspects of syntactic ability measured, dyslexics were found to differ from normals. These aspects were recognition of melody pattern, sentence repetition, and syntax and morphology in expressive language. In the other two aspects, recognition of grammaticalness and comprehension of syntax, there were no significant differences. It is recommended that assessment of syntactic ability be included in evaluation and diagnostic procedures. The child having trouble with reading comprehension may have syntactic deficiencies.

1177   Wagner, Rudolph F. "Form symbolization in normal readers and dyslexics based on a modified pattern recognition theory." Int J Symb 1(3): 51-56, 1970. (8 References).
If reading is a process of form and pattern recognition, then it is worthwhile to assess these abilities in poor readers. In four studies using the Kahn Test of Symbol Arrangement, poor readers were found to possess less form-pattern awareness than good readers. The Kahn Test of Symbol Arrangement is a structured personality test which makes use of plastic objects (for example, a heart) arranged on a felt strip. The subject is asked to abstract symbolism from these objects. He is scored by his ability to interpret the objects on the basis of form, quality, or pattern. Form-pattern symbolization may explain the success of some perceptual training methods. It should be possible to enhance perception by perceptual training and experience.

Z. SEX DIFFERENCES

1178   Harper, Clive B. J. "Preventing reading difficulties." In: World Congress on Reading, 4th, Buenos Aires, 1972. Proceedings: reading for all. Robert Karlin, editor. Newark, Delaware: International Reading Association, 1973. 207-15. (42 References).
Reading disability is a major scholastic problem. It is proposed that current learning theory suggests new ways of overcoming some of the major

obstacles to literacy. This point of view is explained by reference to
two problem areas: sex differences in reading achievement and disadvantaged children's reading performances. Many more boys than girls have
difficulty in learning to read. Although research shows that boys and
girls begin school with about the same vocabulary capabilities, girls
seem to be able to perceive more readily the desires and expectations of
their teachers and peers. It is suggested that cultural definition of
male and female roles may be a potent factor in the child's adjustment
to his new environment at school. Difficulties of disadvantaged groups
of children may stem from some of the same sources as the troubles experienced by boys. These groups tend to value masculinity, and early
reading materials are invariably not masculine. The use of programming
techniques is also discussed.

1179   Peterson, Joe. "Effects of sex of E and sex of S in first and
          fifth grade children's paired-associate learning." J Educ Res
          66(2): 81-84, September, 1972. (13 References).
This study was designed to test the hypothesis that the higher incidence
of reading disability among boys (Subjects or "S") is linked to the large
number of female elementary-school teachers (Experimenters or "E"). It
is concluded that the sex of the teacher is not a major influence in the
higher incidence of reading disability among boys.

1180   Thompson, G. Brian. "Sex differences in reading attainments."
          Educ Res 18(1): 16-23, November, 1975. (55 References).
Among English-speaking children, boys appear to lag behind girls in reading attainment up to age ten. After that no sex differences are apparent.
Teachers and parents should be aware of this developmental trend. However, sex differences in reading attainment are less than many differences between individuals of either sex. Because a boy lags behind in
the first three or four years of schooling does not imply any pathology
such as dyslexia. Various hypotheses as to the cause for this sex difference are considered.

AA. SPEECH DISORDERS

1181   Artley, A. Sterl. "A study of certain factors presumed to be asso-
          ciated with reading and speech difficulties." J Speech Hear Disord
          13(4): 351-60, December, 1948. (22 References).
Surveys the literature on the relationship between speech and reading
defects. The conclusion is that there is a relationship but its extent
is uncertain. Speech problems appear to be either the cause or the result of reading problems. The two may coexist as the result of a common
cause. Silent reading may be affected by speech problems. Reduced auditory acuity, lack of auditory discrimination, or short auditory memory
may cause reading retardation, although these problems do not seem to be
related to speech defects.

1182   Cabrini, Sister M. "Auditory memory span and functional articula-
          tory disorders in relation to reading in grade two." J Dev Read
          7(1): 24-28, Autumn, 1963. (4 References).
In studies of 182 second graders it was concluded that reading ability
does not necessarily depend upon speech ability, but children with more
normal speech had greater reading ability. Shortness of auditory memory
span may be a factor which impedes learning to read, but it is not a determining factor in functional disorders of articulation.

1183   Cole, Edwin M., and Walker, Louise. "Reading and speech problems
       as expressions of specific language disability." <u>Res Publ Assoc</u>
       <u>Res Nerv Ment Dis</u> 42(Section 2): 171-89, 1964. (97 References).
Reviews some of the literature on specific language disability. The work
of Samuel Orton is seen as the most adequate frame of reference from
which to view later concepts in the field. Orton's method of treatment
forms much of the basis for present methods of treatment. Stuttering is
discussed as part of an overall language problem. The late talker and/or
the child who persists in baby talk is likely to have a reading disability or even be a stutterer. It appears that a genetic relationship
exists as part of the cause of reading and speech disabilities.

1184   Eames, Thomas H. "The relationship of reading and speech diffi-
       culties." <u>J Educ Psychol</u> 41(1): 51-55, January, 1950. (24 Ref-
       erences).
A review of the literature reveals no general agreement about the relationship between reading and speech failures. Broadly speaking, it may
be concluded that they appear to be connected and are very likely to
stem from the same basic defect. The observations are made that: (1)
neurological lesions in the language centers may impair both speech and
reading; (2) speech defects occur in some persons who fail at reading;
and (3) emotional reaction from speech difficulties may impair reading.
The problem is "neurophysiological with psychological overtones."

1185   Gaines, Frances Perlowski. "Interrelations of speech and reading
       disabilities." <u>Elem Sch J</u> 41(8): 605-13, April, 1941. (13 Ref-
       erences).
A survey of thirteen studies examining the relationship between speech
defects and reading disability reveals a lack of standardization that
renders any conclusions almost useless. A table summarizing and classifying the thirteen studies is included.

1186   ————. "Interrelations of speech and reading disabilities."
       <u>Q J Speech</u> 27(1): 104-10, February, 1941. (12 Bibliographic
       Footnotes).
Reviews relevant literature in an attempt to discover the relationship,
if any, between speech deviations and reading disabilities. Research
results suggest that there is a link. Nonstandardization in the terms
and inexact control in the studies make it necessary to qualify conclusions so much as to make them of little use. Further study is recommended.

1187   Hildreth, Gertrude H. "Speech defects and reading disability."
       <u>Elem Sch J</u> 46(6): 326-32, February, 1946. (17 References).
A large proportion of children with speech problems tend to be retarded
in reading. Speech defects can be important secondary causes of reading
disability although they may not be the only cause. Some literature in
the area is reviewed. Suggestions for the prevention and treatment of
speech defects related to reading problems are given.

1188   Kelly, Edward James. "A measurement of the extent of the relation-
       ship between articulatory defects and reading disability." For a
       summary see: <u>Diss Abstr</u> 27A(2): 546-47, August, 1966.

1189   Mason, Anne W. "Specific (developmental) dyslexia." <u>Dev Med</u>
       <u>Child Neurol</u> 9(2): 183-90, April, 1967. (35 References).

Distinguishes specific (developmental) dyslexia from other reading difficulties. Children of normal intelligence who are diagnosed as specific
dyslexics who have histories of speech retardation tend to do poorly on
draw-a-man tests. They do better on verbal tasks than on performance
tasks which is seen as evidence of minimal cerebral dysfunction. The
phonic approach to the teaching of reading appears to be best for such
children. The I.T.A. does not appear helpful in general, although in
some cases it may be used profitably.

1190 Mussafia, M. "Various aspects of cluttering." Folia Phoniatr
      22(4/5): 337-46, 1970. (7 References).
The common characteristics of cluttering, including the lack of articulation and repetition of syllables, the unconsciousness of the disorder,
and the tense personality are noted. Cluttering often occurs with dys-
lalia, dyslexia, and dysorthographia (speech, reading, and writing or
spelling problems, respectively). Case histories are given.

1191 Van Riper, C. "The speech pathologist looks at reading." Read
      Teach 17(7): 505-10, April, 1964. (0 References).
Points out that children with speech defects must learn to identify sounds
before they can use them. A parallel exists in reading disabilities.
Analogies are drawn between reading problems and the speaker who lisps
or fails to move his tongue independently of his jaw (the laller), and
the clutterer. Reading and speech both have motor and phonetic features.

1192 Vent, Faythe. "Speech and language characteristics of children
      with developmental dyslexia." For a summary see: Diss Abstr Int
      31B(11): 6975-76, May, 1971.

1193 Yedinack, Jeanette G. "A study of the linguistic functioning of
      children with articulation and reading disabilities." Pedagog
      Semin J Genet Psychol 74(First Half): 23-59, March, 1949. (40
      References).
A study of second-grade children revealed that those with functional
articulation defects were significantly inferior in both oral and silent
reading to children with normal speaking ability. Children with reading
disability were found to have more articulation defects than normal
readers. It is suggested that greater emphasis be placed on training
children in speech, vocabulary, and oral language usage before reading
instruction begins.

BB. TEACHING METHODS

1194 Allais, Edith. "Our children can't read!" Horn Book Mag 20:
      88-93, March-April, 1944. (0 References).
Criticizes the whole-word method of teaching reading. This method makes
reading laborious and dull for children because they misread so many
words. Without phonics training from the start, schools will continue
to turn out poor and unenthusiastic readers.

1195 Allington, Richard L. "Sticks and stones...but, will names never
      hurt them?" Read Teach 28(4): 364-69, January, 1975. (17 Ref-
      erences).
Focuses on the negative aspects of labeling pupils with reading deficits
"hyperactive," "brain damaged," "learning disabled," "maturational lag,"

"dyslexic," "perceptually handicapped," "minimal brain dysfunction," and others. These labels are often misleading or in error and shift the burden of failure to the child. The cause of reading disability is very difficult to discover and does not matter anyway. The real solution is to modify instructional methods and provide better teaching.

1196 Barbe, Walter B. "Instructional causes of poor reading." Education 77(9): 534-40, May, 1957. (0 References).
No single cause of reading disability exists. Physical and emotional problems are to blame in some cases. However, many children fail at reading because of inadequate or improper instruction. Teachers do not like to admit that the form of instruction may be the cause because it threatens the teacher. Lack of skilled instruction, inflexible programs, changing teachers frequently, and lack of systematic reading programs may all produce reading failure. Adequate diagnosis of the child's problem must be made before the child can be helped.

1197 Bond, Guy Loraine. The auditory and speech characteristics of poor readers. New York: Teachers College, Columbia University, 1935. 48p. (21 References). (Contributions to Education, No. 657).
A group of poor readers and a control group of good readers matched for age, schooling, sex, and intelligence were selected from the second and third grades of four public schools in New York City. No child with an IQ below 85 was used as a subject. Some of the children were being instructed in reading by the look-say method and some by an oral-phonetic method. Sixty-three percent of the poor readers being taught by the phonetics method were found to have some hearing loss. Only one good reader from this group had hearing loss. No significant differences in auditory acuity were found between the two groups in those children taught by the look-say method. The blending (fusion) tests showed significant differences between all classes of good and poor readers. Significant differences were found between the total groups in auditory discrimination, auditory perception, and memory for digits. No difference was found in the occurrence of speech defects. However, because of other differences distinguishing the groups by method of instruction, it is concluded that auditory ability is important in relation to reading disability if the pupil has oral-phonetic type instruction. Auditory factors are less important in look-say methods. Some relationship exists between method of instruction and the extent to which auditory abilities are factors in reading disability. (For a companion study assessing the visual attributes of the same population, see Item No. 1206).

1198 Camp, Bonnie W. "Research with the SMART reading program." In: Learing disability/minimal brain dysfunction syndrome: research perspectives and applications. Edited by Robert P. Anderson, and Charles G. Halcomb. Springfield, Illinois: Thomas, 1976. 204-16. (21 References).
In an investigation using the Staats Motivation Activation Reading Therapy (SMART) tutorial program, it was concluded that in severely retarded readers in upper elementary and junior high school the learning process was intact in most cases. The rate of learning varied widely. It was believed to be more profitable to continue to pursue methods for modifying learning rates through altered teaching procedures rather than to seek a pathological or neurological basis for reading problems.

1199   Carner, Richard L. "Psycho-ecology and reading failure." J Read
       16(7): 556-59, April, 1973. (0 References).
Ecological systems exist on many different levels and they are interdependent. In the ecology of the classroom, children depend upon the
teacher and upon each other. A proper balance of success and challenge,
capacity, and individual interests must be maintained. Overcrowded and
chaotic classrooms are a prime example of environmental decay. The
teacher has no time to teach, but must devote too much energy to maintaining law and order. Sometimes teachers are not aware of the diagnostic procedures available for helping the child read. Poor reading instruction also can lead to failure because it ignores the real reasons
that the child is not making progress.

1200   Caukins, Sivan Eugene. Why Johnny can't learn to read; or, sex
       differences in education. [San Gabriel ? California: 1970.] 140
       leaves. (Bibliography leaves 130-40). (Ph.D. thesis, San Gabriel
       University).
Maintains that boys make stronger use of proprioceptor stimulation (stimulation of sensory receptors excited by stimuli arising within the
organism) than do girls. In American education our approach to boys and
girls has been the same. It is hypothesized that the difficulties normal students experience in learning to read and spell are based on sex
differences in learning, males being more muscular and kinesthetic in
learning pattern, while girls are more visual-auditory. The failures of
males in the classroom are the result of the culture and teaching methods
where reading is viewed as a symbolic thought process presented through
visual symbols of auditory and mental processes. Emotional and physical
damage can result from these mistaken educational methods. Homosexuality
and emotional illness may be one outcome of feminizing men.

1201   Collette-Harris, Martha, and Minke, Karl A. "A behavioral experi-
       mental analysis of dyslexia." Paper presented at International
       Federation of Learning Disabilities, Brussels, Belgium, January
       3-7, 1975. 1975. 26p. (ED 112 621).
This study supports the view that dyslexia is a function of past deficient
learning. Subjects were two groups of six children ages nine and ten
years who were given either traditional remedial reading treatment or
Staats motivated action reading technique, a behavioral therapy. This
method uses positive reinforcement for correct responses. The behavioral
intervention groups of both dyslexic and normal subjects showed about
the same degree of improvement in reading achievement. Dyslexics also
improved in some measures of perception and attention.

1202   Crews, Ruthellen. "More myths on the teaching of reading." J Read
       15(6): 411-14, March, 1972. (6 References).
Discusses myths held by classroom teachers about nonreaders. It is
claimed that all would be well if elementary teachers would drill pupils
on a list of sight words, would quit teaching everything but reading, or
would get some mechanical device to teach speed reading. The faults of
these myths and other ideas commonly held about reading problems are
discussed.

1203   Crisp, William H. "The psychology of the poor reader." Trans Am
       Ophthalmol Soc 47: 158-76, 1949. (7 References).
Refractive errors play a relatively small part in the problems of poor
readers. Learning to read well is the most important goal in the first
two or three years of school. Steps should be taken to correct reading

problems promptly. Probably the greatest mistake made in education has
been the departure from old more or less mechanical methods of teaching
word structure and recognition. John Dewey and the whole-word, flash-
card teaching methods are criticized. This article appears also in Am J
Ophthalmol 33(2): 235-42, February, 1950, and, without the references,
in Rocky Mt Med J 46: 833-36, October, 1949, neither of which appears
in this bibliography.

1204   Emery, Donald. "The need to read." Sch Libr 21(1): 25-30, Fall,
       1971. (0 References).
It is critical that everyone learn to read. American business and in-
dustry is finding it must retrain workers in reading and mathematics, an
expensive procedure we thought we paid for when we paid our school taxes.
One reason we have reading problems is that compulsory education deals
with an extremely broad spectrum of pupils with a wide range of reading
readiness and potential. We have added new subjects to the three R's,
as though we had unlimited ability to absorb them, without lengthening
the school day or the school year. A well-educated teacher equipped with
diverse reading materials is the best answer to the reading problem. No
single method of teaching reading is best. Individualized teaching is
a major aid to most children.

1205   Evvard, Evelyn. "A comparative study of two groups of children
       with reading disability." For a summary see: Diss Abstr 25(11):
       6429-30, May, 1965.

1206   Fendrick, Paul. Visual characteristics of poor readers. New York:
       Teachers College, Columbia University, 1935. 54p. (34 References).
       (Contributions to Education, No. 656).
Using a public school population of second and third graders, some of
whom were being instructed in reading by the phonetic method and some by
look-and-say method, Fendrick attempted to ascertain whether there is a
relationship between some ocular factors and reading disability. The
children were divided into matched groups of good and poor readers. None
had an IQ below 85. Findings indicated that good readers had better than
normal visual acuity for distant vision in the right eye. This difference was much less marked for children taught by phonetic methods than
for the look-and-say groups where the difference was striking between
good and poor readers. Predominance of the left eye did not characterize
the poor readers. Differences favored good readers on all perception
tests. It is concluded that sensory differences should be heeded in
choosing teaching methods. Visual characteristics seemed to exert a more
profound influence on reading disability in schools using look-and-say
techniques than in those using phonetic methods. (For a companion study
assessing auditory and speech characteristics of the same population,
see Item No. 1197).

1207   Gates, Arthur I. "The psychological basis of remedial reading."
       Educ Rec 17(Suppl. 10): 109-23, October, 1936. (0 References).
Reading failure is as serious to a child as financial or material failure
is to an adult. The curriculum of American schools is primarily a reading program, and reading failure is relatively frequent. Low intelligence, eye and ear deficiencies, emotional stress, and motor incoordination are among the constitutional handicaps to reading. Factors like
mixed dominance have been exaggerated. It is misleading to say reading
failure is caused by a particular constitutional deficiency. The cause
of reading failure is always failure to adjust materials and instruction

methods to the needs of the particular child. Remedial instruction at
its best consists of adapting methods to the child's need. The idea that
word blindness or lack of cerebral dominance makes learning to read impossible is a residual from earlier decades before more modern methods
were developed.

1208   Gates, Arthur I., and Bond, Guy L. "Prevention of disabilities in
       reading." Natl Educ Assoc J 25(9): 289-90, December, 1936. (0
       References).
It is important to prevent reading disability and save the child frustrating failure. To do this the cause must be known. Many causes of
reading failure have been advanced. One general cause is failure to
adapt instruction methods and materials to the child's need. Individual
reading handicaps are subtle, and require special techniques. Most books
for the beginning reader introduce too many new words too quickly. Easy
reading material is essential in remedial work.

1209   Haring, Norris G., and Hauck, Mary Ann. "Improved learning condi-
       tions in the establishment of reading skills with disabled readers."
       Except Child 35(5): 341-52, January, 1969. (19 References).
When learning conditions were individually tailored for each child in a
group setting as to arrangement of reading material and systematic presentation, the progress of the students was much faster. The conclusion
is that when a child is reading-disabled we should not look for biological
or constitutional causes but, instead, refine our teaching methods.

1210   Hester, Kathleen B. "A study of phonetic difficulties in reading."
       Elem Sch J 43(3): 171-73, November, 1942. (0 References).
A group of children admitted to a university reading clinic because of
reading difficulties was tested for vocabulary, word recognition, and
word analysis. Fifty-eight percent scored below third-grade level on
these tests. The children were given a phonetic inventory test and were
found to lack the knowledge of phonics essential for independent word
attack. An analysis of the letters, sounds, and blends that caused the
most difficulties is reported. It is pointed out that without a concept
of letter sounds the child is unable to attack new words when other
methods fail.

1211   Holt, John. "How children fail." In: Reading Conference, Lehigh
       University, 14th-15th, 1965-1966. Proceedings: the wide world of
       reading instruction. Vol. 5. Edited by Albert J. Mazurkiewicz.
       Bethlehem, Pennsylvania: The Bureau of Educational Services,
       School of Education, Lehigh University, 1965, 1966. 25-28. (0
       References).
Children fail to learn to read because we try to teach them. If we would
put beginners in the room with older children who are already reading,
the younger ones would want to imitate them. A supply of suitable reading material will help each child learn to read in his own time and way.
Adults should be available to help, but not to teach reading in the
usual understanding of that process.

1212   Hoover, Floyd W. "Reasons why pupils fail in reading." Elem Sch
       J 46(7): 381-83, March, 1946. (0 References).
Poor teaching methods are a common cause of reading failure. Eager
teachers push children into reading instruction before the children have
developed reading readiness. Too much stress is sometimes placed on
mechanics while meaning is ignored. Often a teacher appears unsympathetic
because he fails to recognize the significance of the child's mental age.

1213 Kline, Carl L. "Cognition conflict." Am J Orthopsychiatry 43(3):
      495-96, April, 1973. (0 References).
Letter to editor. Criticizes Alfred Lucco's article, "Cognitive development after age five," on the grounds that reading failure almost always
is the result of poor teaching methods. A phonics program using a multisensory approach is advocated. Lucco replies that the causes of reading
failure are not that simple: he defends early intervention programs
which aim to stimulate cognitive development after age five rather than
focus primarily on skill acquisition.

1214 Linksz, Arthur. On writing, reading, and dyslexia. New York:
      Grune & Stratton, 1973. 256p. (Bibliography).
Dyslexia is defined broadly as any kind of inability to read, a learning
problem that can be overcome by teaching. An ophthalmologist, Dr. Linksz
presents his system of spelling comprehension. Hungarian by birth, he
defends English spelling and points out the beauty, "refined logic," and
subtleties in the structure of English spelling. Phonics is presented
and it is pointed out that many English words of more than one syllable
are of Latin and Greek origin. Monosyllables are usually of Anglo-Saxon
origin. Poor teaching, particularly the absence of phonics instruction
and kinesthetic training, is blamed for reversals and word confusion in
dyslexics. Bilingualism is seen as a blessing, not a handicap, because
another language provides a second tool for use in clarifying the bases
of English spelling. Materials on left-handedness and the reasons the
optic nerves cross is included.

1215 Mosse, Hilde L. "Reading disorders in the United States." Read
      Teach 16(2): 90-94, 101, November, 1962. (5 References).
In the United States reading disabilities have reached massive proportions. It is a gigantic breakdown in education. Although English
orthography is difficult, the real cause of the trouble is teaching
methods. Children must pass "reading readiness" tests which have nothing
to do with reading. Children treated thus develop strong feelings of
inferiority. The chief villain in reading disorders is the whole-word,
or sight-word, method of teaching. Children and their parents often reject the nonsense of memorizing a squiggle which is supposed to represent
a word without ever having been taught how a word comes to be. Unless
a child has been taught to read and write the alphabet at home he probably will not learn to read readily by the whole-word method. Many
teachers have realized all along that the whole-word method is a failure.
Some have taught phonics secretly. A storm still rages about the method
because educators have invested too much financially and psychologically
to give it up. Reading disorders on a mass scale have social causes.
This article was published in all West German teachers' journals.

1216 Mosse, Hilde L., and Daniels, Clesbie R. "Linear dyslexia. A new
      form of reading disorder." Am J Psychother 13(4): 826-41,
      October, 1959. (30 References).
Linear dyslexia is a form of reading disorder in which the performance
of linear reading and the automatic return sweep to the beginning of the
next line are impaired. Case histories are presented. Causes are thought
to be too much comic-book reading and certain teaching techniques. A
thorough grounding in phonics is advised to prevent the development of
linear dyslexia.

1217 Oakan, Robert; Wiener, Morton; Cromer, Ward. "Identification,
      organization, and reading comprehension for good and poor readers."
      J Educ Psychol 62(1): 71-78, February, 1971. (10 References).

In tests using fifth-grade pupils, results suggest that many poor readers' comprehension troubles stem from the way material is organized as
it is being read. Drilling poor readers on unknown words in a passage
before it was read did little to help their comprehension. Good readers'
comprehension was found to be markedly hindered by presenting reading
passages in poorly organized form. It is suggested that "preorganized"
reading materials would be helpful to beginning readers.

1218 Orton, Samuel Torrey. "The 'sight reading' method of teaching
      reading, as a source of reading disability." J Educ Psychol
      20(2): 135-43, February, 1929. (7 References).
Where there exists no clear-cut, unilateral brain habit of using only
images perceived by the dominant cerebral hemisphere, this physiological
deviation produces varying degrees of reading disability. The sight-
reading method of teaching reading may give greater average progress for
a group of students, but it may prove a serious obstacle to children
with reading disability. The sight reading method may even produce reading retardation in some children. Every effort should be made to correct
the condition since it impedes personality development.

1219 Pearson, Viola. "Is Johnny dumb?" Tex Outlook 35: 13, May,
      1951. (0 References).
Teachers are to blame eight times out of ten if a first-grade child does
not learn to read. In defense, the teacher gives him an IQ test which
proves, the teacher and the child both believe, that he is stupid. The
test almost certainly depends on silent reading skill. From 60 to 80
percent of retarded readers have normal or superior intelligence. If a
teacher promotes a child without correcting his difficulty she has done
him an injustice. Simple tests for reading skill and for classifying
the problem reader's difficulty are suggested.

1220 Rosebrook, Wilda. "Preventing reading deficiency." Elem Sch J
      36(4): 276-80, December, 1935. (0 References).
The main causes of reading failure are: (1) following one teaching method
to the exclusion of all others; (2) inflexible grouping of children; and
(3) immaturity on the part of pupils. No child should be expected to
learn to read until he has attained a mental age of six and one-half to
seven years. It is suggested that academic success may have been overemphasized as a criterion for promotion from grade one or two.

1221 Sorenson, Harold. "Johnny's real need." Mont Educ 27(3): 10,
      November, 1950. (0 References).
This is a teacher's plea for help for the elementary-school children who,
for some reason, pass through several grades without learning to read.
Now is the time to rescue these children. Educators will have failed if
these children are not taught to read. Many primary- and elementary-
school teachers have not been instructed in how to teach remedial reading.

CC. TESTING METHODS

1222 Reed, James C. "The deficits of retarded readers—fact or arti-
      fact?" Read Teach 23(4): 347-52, 393, January, 1970. (9 Refer-
      ences).

Problems of method occur when the researcher attempts to measure a child's deficiencies on the basis of tests that measure what may be expected. In deficient readers the pattern of deficits and the amount of retardation depend on which reading expectancy formula is used. The number of persons found to be retarded in reading in a given population varies according to the index used as a measure. Teachers and reading specialists should be skeptical of any statement concerning the intellectual, cognitive, or perceptual deficiencies of a retarded reader. A child's reading potential is probably more related to teaching methods and materials than to arbitrary indexes of expectancy.

1223 Ullmann, Charles A. "Prevalence of reading disability as a function of the measure used." J Learn Disabil 2(11): 556-58, November, 1969. (6 References).
When reading disability is defined by the number of years below grade formula commonly used, the results obtained are difficult to distinguish from normal human variation. This method also makes it appear that the number of cases of reading disability increases as years of schooling increase. The years below normal grade for age formula is of doubtful utility. When other measures are used, much less reading disability is found.

1224 Vernon, Magdalen D. "The investigation of reading problems today." Br J Educ Psychol 30(Part 2): 146-54, June, 1960. (17 References).
In spite of much research, reading problems are imperfectly understood. Part of the reason may lie in the experimental methods used. It appears that some failure of reasoning in reading-disabled children prevents the analysis of printed words and the association of sounds with letters. Studies carried out for longer periods of time with better controls are needed.

DD. OTHER ASPECTS

1225 Alwitt, Linda F. "Decay of immediate memory for visually presented digits among nonreaders and readers." J Educ Psychol 54(3): 144-48, June, 1963. (12 References).
To test the rate of decay of immediate memory traces, groups of good and poor readers were given visual digit-span tests. There was no significant difference in the groups. The reasons for poor readers' lowered digit-span memory must be sought elsewhere. Possible causes are: poor attention; a smaller limit on the amount of material poor readers are capable of holding in immediate memory; or the necessity of a longer response time allowing immediate memory traces to disappear. Normal readers showed a greater rate of increase in digit span with increases in chronological age than did poor readers.

1226 Barbe, Walter B.; Gannaway, Virginia; Williams, Thelma. "Factors contributing to reading difficulties." Sch Soc 85(2117): 285-86, October 12, 1957. (0 References).
Children under treatment in a reading clinic were found to come from all economic levels. No birth-order position seemed to produce more reading problems than another. The children had trouble with other academic subjects; many were retained in second grade after "social promotion" from first grade. The children displayed a large amount of mixed cerebral dominance. Parental attitudes were good.

1227 Black, Francis L., and Davis, Dorothy E. M. "Measles and readiness
for reading and learning. II. New Haven study." Am J Epidemiol
88(3): 337-44, November, 1968. (7 References).
Using the method described in Black, et al., researchers studied 556
first-grade children in eleven New Haven, Connecticut, schools. Subjects
were mostly nonwhite and from widely differing socioeconomic and cultural
backgrounds. Both the incidence of measles and scores on the Monroe
Primary Aptitude Test varied significantly with age, race, and environmental factors. Children who had had unmodified measles made significantly lower test scores than children who had escaped or been protected
against the disease. A similar but smaller difference was found for
those who had had mumps. For other parts of this study see Items No.
1228, 1242, 1243, and 1250.

1228 Black, Francis L.; Fox, John P.; Elveback, Lila; et al. "Measles
and readiness for reading and learning. I. Background, purpose
and general methodology." Am J Epidemiol 88(3): 333-36, November,
1968. (15 References).
This study hypothesizes that measles without the complication of enceph-
alitis may result in minor changes in mental ability and behavior which
up until now have escaped notice. A method for testing this hypothesis
on first-grade children is described. For other parts of this study see
Items No. 1227, 1242, 1243, and 1250.

1229 Bogle, Marion Warner. "Relationship between deviant behavior and
reading disability: a retrospective study of the role of the
nurse." J Sch Health 43(5): 312-15, May, 1973. (6 References).
Reports findings in a study of the relationship between behavior problems and inability to read in schoolchildren, and the role of a community
health nurse as a part of the multidisciplinary team needed to diagnose
and treat nonreading children. Data were from a sixth-grade inner-city
population. Findings support the hypothesis that behavior differences
exist between disabled readers and children without reading problems.
A high-risk population can be identified by first grade, and the child
thus identified can be helped. The importance of the nurse's role in
visiting families of disabled readers; impressing upon them their contribution to the child's education; and getting prenatal history are
stressed.

1230 Boyd, John E. "Why children fail--reasons or rationalizations?"
Acad Ther 11(2): 233-34, Winter, 1975-76. (1 Reference).
Complains that classroom teachers, when asked why a child is failing in
reading, recite a litany of causes about which the reading specialist
can do nothing. The specialist's job is to diagnose and treat students
with reading problems. If the teacher can give no information on factors like sight vocabulary, word recognition, etc., then the better answer to the reading specialist's request for information is, "I don't
know. Please find out."

1231 Braun, Jean S. "Relation between concept formation ability and
reading achievement at three developmental levels." Child Dev
34(3): 675-82, September, 1963. (6 References).
Test results confirmed that children with average or better general ability but poor concept formation ability were more likely to be retarded
readers. Subjects were third-, fifth-, and seventh-grade boys who were
public-school pupils. They formed two groups: those who achieved beyond expectations and underachievers. IQ scores were determined. Means

were slightly higher for the group of high achievers in reading than for
the underachievers. The concept formation test consisted of groups of
words typed on three-by-five cards. One word on each card had something
in common with one word on each of the other cards. Each boy had each
card read to him. He was asked what concept had appeared on every card.
It is suggested that concept formation ability is probably a cognitive
process relatively independent of intelligence.

1232   Burns, Alan R. "Overcoming difficulties in learning to read."
       Elem Engl 50(6): 911-20, September, 1973. (31 Bibliographic
       Footnotes).
American children experience reading problems because of the lack of
isomorphic correspondence between phonemes and graphemes. A language
with little correspondence between sounds and symbols is difficult to
learn to read: in English one sound may be spelled in several ways and
one written symbols may have several sounds. Details of these differences are analyzed. A suggested solution is the use of a single sound-
symbol system called English-Unifon. Details of this system are explained.

1233   Copple, Lee Biggerstaff. "Motor development and self-concept as
       correlates of reading achievement." For a summary see: Diss Abstr
       22(4): 1241, October, 1961.

1234   Cromer, Ward. "The difference model: a new explanation for some
       reading difficulties." J Educ Psychol 61(6): 471-83, December,
       1970. (8 References).
Four models are described to account for reading difficulty: (1) defect,
or a sensory impairment; (2) deficit, or the absence of some function or
ability which must be learned before reading can be done, as, for example,
phonic skills; (3) disruption, or the presence of a neurotic or other
atypical factor which prevents learning to read; and (4) difference, or
a mismatch between the child's accustomed mode of responding and the expected mode. An example of the last would be the case of a child's verbal language patterns not matching the language patterns in his books.
Difference group readers are assumed to read word-by-word, thus losing
the meaning. Results of studies using college freshmen and sophomores
suggest that inability to organize the material as it is read is a source
of comprehension difficulty.

1235   Davis, Frances. "And after all that schooling he can't read."
       South Atl Q 53(1): 50-60, January, 1954. (0 References).
The automobile, movies, and television have replaced the family story
hour and reading in the lives of children. The fact that children cannot read is not the school's fault. Yet it is the school which must
solve the problem of the nonreader, for the very survival of the school
depends upon the written word and the ability to read it. Schools have
done more for the nonreader in this century than in any other. In earlier
periods of history the nonreaders faded away and became successful in a
world less tied to the printed page than ours. It is concluded that
homes where books are read and discussed will not produce total nonreaders.

1236   Denckla, Martha Bridge. "Performance on color tasks in kindergar-
       ten children." Cortex 8(2): 177-90, June, 1972. (12 References).
A group of kindergarten children was found to be highly competent in
identifying colors by several methods. Only 6 percent of the children

who were not color-blind and who were familiar with color names were
hesitant and inconsistent in color-naming. The investigation was made
after the discovery of a number of dyslexic school-age boys with persistent color-naming difficulties.

1237 "Developmental dyslexia: the visual component." Med J Aust 1(26):
      799-800, June 28, 1975. (1 Reference).
Calls attention to journal articles explaining the characteristics of
dyslexia and expounding a theory of its cause in terms of a defect in
visual discrimination. The more widely accurate information on dyslexia
is distributed, especially to the medical community, the better it will
be for all concerned.

1238 Douglas, J. W. B. "Early hospital admissions and later distur-
      bances of behaviour and learning." Dev Med Child Neurol 17(4):
      456-80, August, 1975. (32 References).
A study of almost all the children born in Great Britain during one week
in March, 1946 reveals strong and unexpected evidence that children admitted to hospitals before age five (particularly between ages six months
and four years) have an increased risk of behavior disturbance and poor
reading in adolescence. In follow-up reports over the succeeding twenty-
six years it appeared that persons with a record of preschool hospital
admissions showed more delinquency and less stable job patterns. The
high proportion of poor readers is partly attributable to poor application to work in the classroom. These children cause more trouble out of
class with more difficult social behavior. However, nervous, shy, or
withdrawn behavior in adolescence is not more frequently reported among
children who have had early hospital admission. The most vulnerable
children seem to be those who are highly dependent on their mothers or
who were already under stress at time of admission. Neither the physical
problems sometimes carried into later life nor initial selection of the
children for hospital explains the association of troublesome behavior
and poor reading with early admission. Some children appear to benefit
from a stay in the hospital.

1239 Downing, John. "Cognitive factors in dyslexia." Child Psychiatry
      Hum Dev 4(2): 115-20, Winter, 1973. (15 References).
Considers dyslexia from the standpoint of the child's cognitive confusion
concerning language. The reading-disabled child appears to be confused
and uncertain as to why certain printed letters should correspond to certain sounds in words. This child does not seem to understand why written
language is what it is. His visual and auditory discrimination may be
satisfactory. His problem appears to be not so much inability to hear
the sounds or see the letters as it is inability to grasp the concept of
phonemes and graphemes and to understand their relationships. One of
the beginning reader's problems is that he cannot see exactly what a
reader is doing. This creates mental confusion. Learning to read would
seem to be a movement from confusion to knowledge (cognition) to cognitive clarity. Some literature in the area is reviewed.

1240 Eames, Thomas Harrison. "Comparison of eye conditions among 1,000
      reading failures, 500 ophthalmic patients, and 150 unselected
      children." Am J Ophthalmol 31(6): 713-17, June, 1948. (4 Ref-
      erences).
Certain eye defects, retarded speed of word recognition measured tachistoscopically, and lower IQs occurred more frequently in poor readers than
in unselected children or in children who were ophthalmic patients. The

median amount of defectiveness was not appreciably greater in any of the
groups.

1241 ————. "The physical condition of reading disability cases."
    Arch Pediatr 54(8): 489-95, August, 1937. (14 References).
Reviews the medical histories of twenty-five children with reading disability. Children from the first six grades were included and all were
below senior high school level. Birth and early development histories
were not remarkable. All began talking near the upper limit of the normal age range. Left-eyed, right-handed mixed dominance was the most common, occurring in 16 percent of the cases. Average IQ was 91. Muscular
imbalance in the eyes was much more common that in an unselected group
of children.

1242 Fox, John P.; Black, Francis L.; Elveback, Lila; et al. "Measles
    and readiness for reading and learning. III. Wappingers Central
    School District study." Am J Epidemiol 88(3): 345-50, November,
    1968. (5 References).
Using the method described in Black, et al., 587 first-grade children
in a school district about seventy-five miles north of New York City were
studied. The children were mostly white and from upper-middle-class
backgrounds. Age, birth order, number of siblings, and father's occupation were all related to the incidence of measles and to scores on the
Metropolitan Readiness Test. Children who had unmodified measles made
lower scores than those who had been protected from the disease. Children who had had mumps made higher reading readiness scores than those
who had not. It is suggested that the statistical methods used did not
take full account of environmental factors that influenced test scores.
For other parts of this study see Items No. 1227, 1228, 1243, and 1250.

1243 Fox, John P.; Black, Francis L.; Kogon, Alfred. "Measles and readi-
    ness for reading and learning. V. Evaluative comparison of the
    studies and overall conclusions." Am J Epidemiol 88(3): 359-67,
    November, 1968. (19 References).
In evaluating the series of studies described in Am J Epidemiol 88:
333-358, it is suggested that results obtained in Seattle, where no significant relationship was found between incidence of unmodified measles
and reading readiness test scores, are the most valid. Environmental
influences were most fully accounted for in the Seattle study. This does
not rule out the possibility that other unaccounted-for factors were
operating in the studies. For other parts of this study see Items No.
1227, 1228, 1242, and 1250.

1244 Gordon, Neil. "Reading retardation." Dev Med Child Neurol 14(4):
    520-23, August, 1972. (8 References).
Discusses reading disability as a condition caused by a variety of factors. Reading failure may be part of a general retardation in development. The role that function plays in determining and maintaining inter-
cerebral connections is considered: how much do structural connections
alter as a result of learning? Maturational lag and whether there is a
developmental schedule in higher cerebral functions is examined. In a
small number of children who appear to have a specific reading and spelling difficulty there is no evidence of visual-motor disability or disorder of language development. Failure to make links between certain
parts of the brain appears to be present and is probably best explained
on an anatomical basis. The relation of reading retardation to delinquency may have to do with a failure of the cerebral integration which

underlies maturation and learning. "Dyslexia" and "word blindness" are terms that seem to cause more confusion than they resolve. But "dyslexia" may serve to identify a group of children who are in great need of special help.

1245 Heiman, Julia R., and Ross, Alan O. "Saccadic eye movements and reading difficulties." J Abnorm Child Psychol 2(1): 53-61, March, 1974. (14 References).
Two groups of children ages seven to twelve, one containing normal readers and one children with reading difficulties, were compared for saccadic eye movements. Problem readers' rate of eye movement was markedly lower than that of normal readers. Problem readers were given individual tutoring for seven months. Testing after training showed that the eye-movement rate of the problem readers equaled and surpassed that of the normal readers. It is suggested that eye movement is a response which can be modified through learning. It has an information-gathering function which varies with the material being looked at. Eye movements do not seem to provide a true measure of attention unrelated to the subject the person is studying. Until more is known, routine study of eye movements contributes no information helpful to the reading teacher.

1246 Kaschube, Dorothea V. "Dyslexia: a language disorder." Anthropol Linguist 14(9): 339-56, December, 1972. (56 References).
Reviews the history of research on dyslexia and discusses its characteristics, symptoms, and possible causes. The relationship to bioanthropological research is considered. It is pointed out that dyslexia is sometimes confused with psychiatric and behavioral disturbances. The gap between the dyslexic child's competence and his performance may result from a defect in his biological rhythm. Dyslexia may be of genetic origin and thus have demographic implications.

1247 Kerr, J. "Crime and dyslexia." Criminologist 8(29): 29-32, 1973. (0 References).
One cause of illiteracy is dyslexia. The semiliterate individual of average intelligence who leaves school unable to read well enough to function in a literate society wants to prove he is clever and winds up in trouble. It is estimated that a high percentage of children who appear in juvenile court are dyslexic. It would be better to spend more money early in a child's life to educate him than to let him fall into delinquency and become a burden on the taxpayer. The dyslexic, unable to compete in the classroom, becomes frustrated and angry, then rebellious. He may be placed in a residential school for the maladjusted. His future is bleak. Research has shown that many delinquent adolescents changed their entire outlook and personality after being taught to read. Dyslexic persons are extremely ashamed and aggressive about not being able to read.

1248 Kinsbourne, Marcel. "Mechanism of reversals in reading and writing." Pediatr Res 6(4): 333/73, April, 1972. (0 References).
Inquires why beginning readers and older dyslexics frequently reverse letters. To determine the source of the orientation difficulty, kindergarteners were asked to identify one of two mirror-image shapes in two ways: the alternatives were presented together; or, the shapes were presented one at a time in succession. Children learned faster under successive presentation. It is concluded that reversals occur because the child's attention is drawn to other aspects of the task and orientation is ignored. It is believed that if memory were involved, learning would have been faster with simultaneous presentation.

1249   Klapper, Zelda S. "Reading retardation: II. Psychoeducational
       aspects of reading disabilities." Pediatrics 37(2): 366-76,
       February, 1966. (38 References).
Views dyslexia as a major disturbance in adaptive behavior. It results
from deficient mechanisms for processing sensory information. Vision and
hearing are the two sensory mechanisms necessary to reading. The dyslexic's problems arise when he is confronted with stimuli (words) which
are distributed in space or time as they are seen or heard. Impaired
ability to integrate what is heard and seen and problems of right-left
orientation are symptoms of disturbed functioning, not sources of defective reading. Procedures for diagnosis and remedial techniques are
suggested. The essential ingredient in remedial programs is an individual training program outside the classroom conducted by a well-trained,
confident teacher. Alphabets and writing systems are discussed.

1250   Kogon, Alfred; Hall, Carrie E.; Cooney, Marion K.; et al. "Measles
       and readiness for reading and learning. IV. Shoreline School
       District study." Am J Epidemiol 88(3): 351-58, November, 1968.
       (6 References).
Using the method described in Black, et al., researchers studied 696
first-grade children in a school district in suburban Seattle. Occurrence
of measles was related to age, number of siblings, and birth order, but
not to level of parents' education. The children were all white, from
a relatively homogeneous middle-class district. No relation was found
between measles status and scores on the Metropolitan Readiness Test.
Among children who had had unmodified measles, a marginally significant
correlation was found between test score and length of time since measles.
No overall measles effect was demonstrated. No relationship was found
between mumps and test performance. For other parts of this study see
Items No. 1227, 1228, 1242, 1243.

1251   McCready, E. Bosworth. "The aphasias of childhood: congenital
       word-blindness and word-deafness as causes of mental retardation
       and deviation." South Med J 18(9): 635-46, September, 1925.
       (26 References).
Isolated defects and disabilities in language frequently interfere with
education and may lead to serious and undesirable temperament, character,
and behavior difficulties. Normal or superior intelligence is not in-
compatible with marked language difficulties. Knowledge of the occurrence and prevalence of aphasic conditions should be extensive in those
working with children in the early school years so that aphasics can be
distinguished from mental defectives and proper remedial measures applied.
Considered are: articulate speech and the conveying of meaning by symbols as the exclusive property of humans; the use of language by animals;
and the idea that language is much more than speech.

1252   McKillop, Anne. "Why many children and youth are retarded in read-
       ing." In: International Reading Association. Conference proceed-
       ings: better readers for our times. Vol. 1. Edited by William
       S. Gray, and Nancy Larrick. New York: Scholastic Magazines, 1956.
       120-24. (0 References).
Children are retarded in reading for as many reasons as there are children. Because of the uncertainty of definition of retardation it seems
unwise to set up an arbitrary criterion for retardation. The answer to
why so many children have difficulty in learning to read should be sought,
not in environmental and personal characteristics, but in an analysis of
the nature of the reading process. Reading is a complex perceptual task.

It is abstract and learned. It is the most personal and least structured of the forms of communication that depend on printed symbols.

1253 Miller, Wilma H., and Windhauser, Eileen. "Reading disability: tendency toward delinquency?" Clear House 46(3): 183-87, November, 1971. (14 References).
At secondary-school level, reading-disabled students and delinquents have many similar personality characteristics. Emotional maladjustment, hostility, suspicion, negative self-concept, and low tolerance to frustration characterize both groups. Improved reading ability can result in better emotional adjustment in delinquent students. The school has great responsibility for these students by preventing reading failure in elementary school. Good developmental teaching of reading is always preferable to later remedial reading instruction.

1254 Naiden, Norma. "Ratio of boys to girls among disabled readers." Read Teach 29(5): 439-42, February, 1976. (5 References).
A study of fourth-, fifth-, and eighth-grade populations in Seattle public schools showed a ratio of three boys to two girls who were disabled readers. Various reasons are advanced. Boys outnumber girls about four to one in learning disability classes in the Seattle public schools. Most research literature on reading disability is in rough agreement with this ratio.

1255 Parker, D. H. H. "Musical perception and backwardness in reading." Educ Res 12(3): 244-46, June, 1970. (12 References).
Concludes that musical perception in terms of pitch discrimination and memory for tunes and rhythms is not related to reading ability. Groups of twelve-year-old children, one group backward readers, the other group normal readers, were matched for nonverbal IQ, sex, chronological age, and sociological background. A large difference existed in the reading ability of the two groups, but the means of the two groups on the Bentley Test of Musical Abilities showed little difference. There was some indication that lack of adequate rhythmic perception can slow reading progress.

1256 Potts, Albert M. "Reading disorders in children." JAMA 206(3): 638-39, October 14, 1968. (5 Bibliographic Footnotes).
Physicians, having seen normal adults lose reading ability completely after a cerebral lesion, tend to feel that all severe childhood reading difficulty has an organic basis. The educator, having worked with children and knowing that reading function can be improved greatly, may insist that there is no such concept as developmental dyslexia. Educators' vocabulary of terms concerning reading disabilities tends to repel physicians. From all the children with reading problems some groups may be extracted: (1) some who appear equivalent to the adult alexic; (2) some with neurological signs or general retardation; and (3) a third group whose maturation is delayed. Books stating the educators' view are recommended. It is considered significant that much of the progressive writing on the subject has come from outside the United States.

1257 Reed, James C., and Pepper, Roger S. "The interrelationship of vocabulary, comprehension and rate among disabled readers." J Exp Educ 25(4): 331-37, June, 1957. (12 References).
The question raised in this study is how the factors of reading speed or rate, vocabulary, and comprehension interact in persons with reading disabilities. Do these factors operate in the same way for reading-

disabled persons as for normal readers? A large group of college freshmen was given a diagnostic reading test. Speed of reading was compared
with comprehension in one study and with vocabulary in a second study.
A third study compared vocabulary and comprehension scores. Vocabulary
was affected by rate. Comprehension appeared to be related only to
vocabulary. Speed of reading is a function of both vocabulary and comprehension. It is suggested that rate of reading should be studied not
in terms of perception, but in terms of rate of concept formation, organizational ability, and general word knowledge. The three variables studied appear to operate in reading deviates in the same way they do in
normal readers.

1258 Rubino, C. A., and Minden, H. A. "An analysis of eye-movement in
      children with a reading disability." Cortex 9(2): 217-20, June,
      1973. (7 References).
Eye movements were recorded and studied in a group of children with learning disabilities and in a normal control group. None wore corrective
lenses. All members of the control were at or above expectations in
reading. All members of the experimental group were below expectation
in reading. The normal readers had significantly fewer fixations and
regressions, the span of recognition (number of word parts taken in each
time the eye stops) was longer, and they read more words per minute.
There was no difference between the groups in comprehension. It is suggested that this may mean eye movements are related to reading skills,
but the question of cause and effect remains unanswered.

1259 Shankman, Albert L. "Are poor reading skills a symptom or disease?"
      Acad Ther 10(1): 83-91, Fall, 1974. (9 References).
Poor reading ability is not a specific disease. It is a symptom of "dysrelatia," a word coined from the Greek "dys," difficult, and the Latin
noun "relatia," relationships, and defined as difficulty in forming relationships. If the child has not made himself seek higher levels of
making relationships (thinking), he will adopt behavior characteristics
for use as substitutes for doing his own thinking. Twelve different behavior responses of such children are listed. Among them, for example,
are "the guesser" who keeps guessing until you say, "That's right," or
"the devious child" who avoids committing himself with any positive answer, or the "I can't do it" child who knows if he says it often enough
no one will force him to do it. Methods for dealing with reading-disabled
children are suggested, including several using physical activities.
When the dysrelatia is remedied, children learn to read regardless of
the reading instruction method used.

1260 Silberberg, Norman E., and Silberberg, Margaret C. "Hyperlexia:
      the other end of the continuum." J Spec Educ 5(3): 233-42, Fall,
      1971. (18 References).
An evaluation of hyperlexic children (those reading above their general
ability level in which the reading is often word-calling with little
comprehension) led to the hypothesis that reading ability is a normal
physiological variant correlated with, but relatively independent of,
general verbal functioning. Thus both dyslexia and hyperlexia could be
viewed as expected individual variations and not dysfunctions or disorders. Physiological variant means that learning to read is a brain-
related phenomenon relatively independent of the child's environment--
as long as reading instruction of some kind is given.

1261 Wagner, Rudolph F. "Specific reading disabilities: the incompat-
        ibility of two systems." J Learn Disabil 4(5): 260-63, May,
        1971. (6 References).
The learner and the task are two separate systems that may be more, or
less, compatible. Learning disabilities are viewed as the partial or total
incompatibility of the parts in this dual system. However, analysis of
the dual system is limited to reading. It is suggested that this system
is modified by environment. Its advantage lies in giving opportunity for
parallel assessment of learner and task.

1262 Wechsler, David, and Pignatelli, Myrtle L. "Reversal errors in
        reading: phenomena of axial rotation." J Educ Psychol 28(3):
        215-21, March, 1937. (0 References).
The problem of children's reversal errors in reading is much more complicated than it appears at first. Reversals include not only turning
over a letter, but also its rotation in several planes: vertical, horizontal, in depth, or rotated around two axes. Reversed sequences of
letters or of words are parts of the problem. Up-and-down reversals are
more frequent than left-right reversals. Errors may occur through fixating on only one part of the letter or by disregarding the orientation
of the letter on the paper, that is, ignoring the background and fixating
strongly on only the letter.

1263 "Why many 'Johnnys' still can't read." US News World Rep 62(24):
        72-74, June 12, 1967. (0 References).
Disturbing evidence mounts that millions of youngsters graduate from
high school with minimal reading ability. Literacy may become obsolete.
Prospective employers and the Job Corps both report reading problems
among applicants. Various philosophies of how reading should be taught
are described. Remedial reading methods employed in Denver and Prince
Edward County, Virginia, are described. Educators see fear, frustration,
and, finally, hostility underlying the awesome reading problems in big-
city schools.

VI
Diagnosis

A. OVERALL EVALUATION

1264 Alford, T. Dale. "Dyslexia." J Arkansas Med Soc 73(4): 187-88,
      1976. (7 References).
The retarded reader should be distinguished clearly from the retarded
child. The retarded reader belongs to the ophthalmologist-orthoptist
team first. The pediatrician-child guidance team has first responsibility
for the retarded child. Dyslexia is confined to children who are otherwise normal physically. Dyslexia is a true entity and the dyslexic child
with no other problems can be helped. From the viewpoint of the ophthalmologist there appears to be gross lack of standardization in the definition, classification, and causes of dyslexia. The same lack appears in
determination of the relation of emotions and behavior to dyslexia; the
neurological implications; and the proper role of the ophthalmologist and
orthoptist in the care of children with reading problems. Examination of
the dyslexic child should include physical and ophthalmological evaluation, auditory tests, tests for speech defects, and psychological tests.

1265 Anderson, Ursula M. "Reading disability--what should the school
      physician look for in determining its causation." J Sch Health
      35(4): 145-53, April, 1965. (19 References).
Children with reading disabilities should be screened for defects in
vision and hearing, and for defects in cortical function, mixed dominance,
and visual and auditory agnosia (failure to identify and recognize what
is seen or heard). Emotional adjustment and intellectual capacity should
also be assessed. If untreated, such disabilities can have devastating
effects on the child and his family.

1266 Arajärvi, Terttu; Louhivuori, Kerttu; Hagman, Harriet; et al. "The
      role of specific reading and writing difficulties in various school
      problems." Ann Paediatr Fenn 11(3): 138-47, 1965. (29 References).
Neurological, psychological, and social studies were made of thirty-three
children, three girls and thirty boys, who were under treatment for reading and writing disabilities. Six had abnormal births. Thirteen had

speech defects. IQs ranged from 80 to 124. Auditory disturbances led to
mixing of letters and misreading of sounds. Fifteen had bed-wetting and
nineteen school difficulties. Eight were considered mentally healthy;
eight had psychic reactions secondary to dyslexia; and seventeen had been
mentally ill before school age. Five of the homes were emotionally stable;
several homes had severe emotional conflicts. Parents' attitudes toward
the child had an effect on the child's psychic reaction. The most important treatment was individual special training in reading and writing.
In follow-up examinations it was found that the reading and writing impairment improved in twenty-three children.

1267 Aten, Eugene L. "Children with reading problems." Tex State J Med
        43(8): 526-30, December, 1947. (6 References).
Physical, intellectual, and emotional factors should be ruled out before
a diagnosis of pure reading disability is made. If the child has a reading problem, it is necessary to determine whether it is caused by extrinsic
factors or by lack of development of cerebral dominance. The child's
difficulty should be explained to him in terms he can understand and his
cooperation and interest elicited. Tutoring is necessary. Excellence
in academic performance should not be expected of the child with a severe
reading problem. Rather, his other assets, such as mechanical ability,
should be developed. Fernald's method of teaching reading by sight, hearing, and touch is very necessary in reading disability cases. The sight
method only increases reading problems.

1268 Baker, Harry J., and Leland, Bernice. In behalf of non-reading.
        Bloomington, Illinois: Public-school Publishing Company, 1934.
        40p.
A statement of the problem of reading disability is presented together
with case histories illustrating the symptoms, sources, and diagnosis of
the problem. A detailed diagram illustrating the relationships of the
many sources of what is termed "educational disability in reading" is a
feature of the book. Care should be taken to aim remedies at the source
of the child's difficulties, not toward symptoms. A warning is given of
a connection between juvenile delinquency and reading failure.

1269 Bannatyne, Alex. "Diagnostic and remedial techniques for use with
        dyslexic children." Acad Ther 3(4): 213-24, Summer, 1968. (18
        References).
Considers the differential diagnoses of the different types of dyslexia
and some of the basic theories which appear to underlie their various
causes. A classification scheme is presented of the causes and types of
dyslexia. These types are discussed and methods for aiding differential
diagnosis are given. The main types of dyslexia are: (1) primary emotional communicative, (2) minimal neurological dysfunction, and (3)
genetic. Various remedial techniques for these dyslexic types are proposed as guidelines. Many teachers make the mistake of applying one
remedial method to all types of children. Each child must be treated
individually. One type of impairment requires very different treatment
from another. In general, thoroughly train the child where he is deficient and reinforce that training through intact areas.

1270 Barbe, W. "Informal diagnosis of reading difficulties." In: Con-
        ference on Reading. University of Pittsburgh. Report, 1955.
        119-23.

1271 Benton, Curtis D., Jr. "Dyslexia and the private practitioner."
      J Fla Med Assoc 55(10): 898-902, October, 1968. (0 References).
The ophthalmologist should know enough about dyslexia to guide his patients
into getting the necessary help from other disciplines. Otherwise he has
not done the child much of a service. Studies of dyslexic children who
were ophthalmological patients are described. More boys than girls were
affected. About half the dyslexics had behavior problems. More left-
handedness, ambidexterity, and convergence insufficiency were apparent
than in normal children used as controls. More had crossed dominance and
a rapid retinal rivalry. Dyslexia is very rare in monocular amblyopia;
binocularity is almost a prerequisite for having dyslexia. Another method
in addition to the controlling eye concept is described for determining
eye dominance. Frequent characteristics of dyslexics include a high
familial incidence, birth or early life traumas, common behavior problems,
much hyperactivity, mixed laterality, poor body muscle control, poor
auditory and/or visual memory, and various neurological defects. Treatment is directed first at establishing proper laterality and second toward
counseling and recommending help for weaknesses outside the ophthalmologist's speciality.

1272 Betts, Emmett Albert. "Signs of reading difficulties." Education
      77(9): 566-71, May, 1957. (13 References).
Dislike for reading, signs of tension (high-pitched voice in oral reading,
tics, scowling, etc.), reversing letters and words, inability to sound
out words, and low comprehension are among the danger signs of reading
problems that parents and teachers should note.

1273 Block, Walter M. "Cerebral dysfunctions: clarification, delinea-
      tion, classification." Behav Neuropsychiatry 5(7-12): 13-17,
      October, 1973-1974. (7 References).
Enters a plea for a return to simplicity as a way out of the jungle of
terminology now existing in the area of cerebral dysfunction. On the
basis of a multidisciplinary study of 365 children, it is proposed to
separate these disorders into five groups: (1) organic brain damage
(encephalopathy); (2) hyperkinetic brain syndrome; (3) specific learning
disabilities, including dyslexia; (4) maturational lag; and (5) vague
cerebral dysfunction. The purpose of this type of classification would
be to make it possible for professionals from various disciplines to communicate with each other, to focus sharply on the patient's main problem,
and to secure prompt and adequate treatment for his difficulties. The
term "minimal brain damage" should be abolished.

1274 Boder, Elena. "Developmental dyslexia: a diagnostic screening
      procedure based on three characteristic patterns of reading and
      spelling; a preliminary report." Claremont Coll Read Conf Yearb
      32: 173-87, 1968. (20 References).
Developmental dyslexia, a common cause of school failure, is frequently
unrecognized. It is a multidisciplinary problem and should be diagnosed
early and treated by teachers, psychologists, or physicians. Three patterns of dyslexia useful in diagnosis are identified: (1) The child who
reads known whole words by sight, but is unable to sound out and decipher
new words by ear. (2) The child who reads as if each word were entirely
new to him. He spells phonetically--by ear--as a rule. (3) The child
who combines both problems. This is the hard-core nonreader. He is
neither "visual" nor "audile." Dyslexia and secondary reading retardation are distinguished. The diagnostic, prognostic, and therapeutic implications of the dyslexic child are discussed.

1275 ————. "Developmental dyslexia: a new diagnostic approach based
     on the identification of three subtypes." J Sch Health 40(6):
     289-90, June, 1970. (5 References).
Describes three distinctive, atypical patterns of reading and spelling
observed among dyslexic children which fulfill standard diagnostic criteria for developmental dyslexia. None of the described patterns has
been found among normal readers. These patterns remain stable in the
dyslexic child even when his reading achievement level has risen significantly. The first group makes numerous nonphonetic misspellings which
are unintelligible. The second group makes intelligible misspellings
which are phonetic. The third group does both, being deficient in both
phonetic skills and in perceiving whole words as gestalts. The first
group is by far the largest. These children may also make semantic substitutions in reading, for example, "chicken" for "duck."

1276 ————. "School failure--evaluation and treatment." Pediatrics
     58(3): 394-403, September, 1976. (2 References).
Recommends a multidisciplinary effort involving neurological, psychological, and educational factors combined to accomplish a comprehensive
diagnostic evaluation. Office procedures for a neuropediatric evaluation
are described. A diagnostic screening test for developmental dyslexia
which identifies three atypical reading-spelling patterns is explained.
Various approaches to treatment are presented. Children failing in school
are a heterogeneous group, but the child referred to the pediatrician
for school failure is a child in crisis. The challenge to the pediatrician is to help the child and his parents as promptly as possible.

1277 Carmichael, Miriam W. "Medical aspects of learning disabilities."
     In: Conference on Children with Learning Disabilities, Williams-
     burg, Virginia, 1969. Proceedings. [Richmond, Virginia: Virginia
     Council on Health and Medical Care. 1970?]. 116p. (29 References).
A general presentation of the causes of learning disabilities is followed
by discriptions of two specific syndromes, minimal brain dysfunction (MBD)
and dyslexia. A long, outlined list of "preliminary categories and signs
and symptoms" of MBD is included. Four groups of dyslexics are identified:
(1) dyslexia associated with childhood aphasia; (2) dyslexia caused by
brain damage; (3) "specific reading disability" of undetermined cause;
and (4) dyslexia caused by exogenous factors including maturational lag
and emotional factors. Suggestions for medical management are made.
"MBD" and "dyslexia" are considered labels for the condition, not diagnostic labels.

1278 Cornford, H. W. "Dyslexia and allied disorders." Curr Med Drugs
     5: 17-25, November, 1964. (21 References).
"Dyslexia" means difficulty in reading. As a diagnosis it is no more
helpful than describing lower back pain as "lumbago." "Specific developmental dyslexia," "congenital dyslexia," or "word blindness" are terms
describing the condition in which children of normal intelligence and
physical makeup have undue difficulty in learning to read. The condition
is one of difficulty in interpreting symbols. The word can be seen, but
ability to interpret it is lacking. Specific developmental dyslexia is a
clearly recognizable syndrome although there is controversy about its
exact definition, causes, and incidence. Specific developmental dyslexia
is usually not recognized until age seven or eight. Emotional problems
may be present. The child may become tense and anxious when asked to
read. Reversing small words and mirror-image letters, and slowness at
arithmetic and in learning to tell time, are common. Victims often come
from mixed-handed families. Examinations for diagnosis are described.

1279 Crabb, Ned. "Dr. Satz is a wise guy: he looks for trouble before
      it starts." PTA Mag 69(3): 28-30, November, 1974. (0 References).
Describes the theories and testing procedures of Dr. Paul Satz, clinical
psychologist at the University of Florida who believes that reading disabilities can be prevented. He believes that his series of tests can
predict by about age five and one-half whether severe reading difficulties
will develop when the child starts school. Intervention and treatment
can begin while the child's nervous system is still plastic and before
the child knows he has a problem and has been given a negative classification. Tests include finger localization (the ability of the child to
know where his fingers are in relation to the rest of his body), visual
perception, and auditory discrimination, among others.

1280 Crider, Blake. "Diagnosing special disabilities in reading." Educ
      Method 15(6): 308-10, March, 1936. (0 References).
Distinguishes diagnosis of reading problems from the collection of data
necessary to make the diagnosis. Symptoms like reversals, omissions,
etc. are not causes, but only signposts pointing to the basic cause.
Various causes are listed. The diagnosis must explain how the disability
was brought about by a particular cause. Some experimental evidence must
be shown to justify the diagnosis, and other possible causes must be ruled
out. Intelligence tests, reading, personality, and psychological tests,
and an inventory of errors should be used. The term "inability" would
seem more accurate than "disability" when applied to reading.

1281 ————. "The psychological approach to reading disabilities."
      Ohio State Med J 32: 434-36, 1936. (0 References).
Describes diagnostic and treatment procedures in a reading clinic. Before
the child can be properly called a reading disability case, the relationship between his intelligence and his reading level must be known. For
example, if he is eight years old but is found to have a mental age of
six years, it is not surprising if he has not learned to read. Besides
intelligence, tests of visual perception, physical condition, and eye
and hand dominance are used. Eye movements may be photographed. Limited
social and economic background may hinder reading. Treatment is aimed at
removing the causes of the symptoms. Ways of motivating children to read
are given.

1282 Davis, D. Russell, and Cashdan, Asher. "Specific dyslexia." Br J
      Educ Psychol 33(Part 1): 80-82, February, 1963. (5 References).
Little is known about the causes of any kind of reading backwardness.
Nor are we able to say why remedial training helps some children while
others show no improvement. There are two ways that advancement in the
field could be made: by clinical investigation, or by examining one at a
time any relevant factor whether it relates to cause, symptoms, or prognosis. It is legitimate to call one class of backwardness in reading
"specific developmental dyslexia" as a hypothesis for research purposes.
But until some evidence is found, we cannot know whether a class of backward readers exists. So far no evidence has been shown.

1283 Dechant, Emerald V. Diagnosis and remediation of reading disability.
      West Nyack, New York: Parker, 1968. 296p. (Bibliography).
This book is about equally divided between methods for identifying reading
disability and diagnosing its cause, and discussion of remedial methods.
Causes of reading disability are examined and the characteristic symptoms
are listed. The viewpoint of the book is that remedial methods are not
special, but rather an intense and personal application of methods that

work well in the regular classroom. A number of these are discussed, such as the I.T.A., the Diacritical Marking System, and Programmed Learning, among others. Individualized remedial methods for various types of disabled readers, including dyslexics, the emotionally disturbed, and the disadvantaged are given. Lists of materials for teaching reading and lists of various types of reading tests are found in the volume.

1284 De Hirsch, Katrina. "Diagnosis of developmental language disorders." Logos 4: 3-9, April, 1961. (53 References).
Developmental language disability is viewed as a clinical syndrome, and the diagnostic approach to it outlined is strictly clinical. After years of experience it has become possible to recognize clinically that children between three and six years referred to a language disorder clinic for delayed speech and children between seven and twelve referred for severe reading, spelling, and writing disabilities fall into a distinct pattern. This pattern is described and diagnostic considerations are listed and explained. It is assumed that developmental disability has a familial constitutional element. Diagnostic procedures include taking a careful neonatal, natal, and postnatal history of the child and a family history of speech, reading, writing, or spelling disabilities. Overall motility and motor patterning are evaluated. Often these children are hyperkinetic and display immaturity of the central nervous system. Finer manual control and handedness are observed. Results on the Bender Gestalt test often reveal immature visual-motor patterning and spatial organization. Dyslexic children often have very short memory spans for what is heard. Their oral language is often monotonous, cluttered, and dysrhythmic. They are disoriented in time, space, weight, and size concepts. Even at age fourteen or older, children with histories of language disabilities still give evidence of physiological immaturity. This type of child has to be helped early to structure motor, perceptual, and behavior patterns. He must be protected against overwhelming anxiety. He needs help with the repercussions in his environment which stem from his original disabilities.

1285 ————. "Prediction of future reading disabilities in children with oral language disorders." Folia Phoniatr 7: 235-50, 1955. (27 References).
Presents a series of tests which enable the prediction of future reading disabilities in five- to six-year-old children who have oral language disorders. Many of these children have difficulty with the structure of motor, perceptual, visual-motor, and language configurations. Children are tested on hopping on one foot; drawing a figure of a person; imitating the examiner's movements when sitting beside him before a mirror; and repeating a series of nonsense syllables, among other tests. It is important to discover these children before they run into difficulty in first grade and suffer adverse emotional experiences.

1286 ————. "Tests designed to discover potential reading difficulties at the six-year-old level." Am J Orthopsychiatry 27(3): 566-76, July, 1957. (18 References).
The best time for testing to predict future reading disability is at the end of the kindergarten year. Tests like those described in this article are aimed at determining the child's level of maturation: is he able to classify and categorize, give definitions, and pattern his speech properly? Tests should indicate areas where the child lags and what remedial techniques would be helpful.

1287 Deich, Ruth F. "Reading time and error rates for normal and re-
      tarded readers." Percept Mot Skills 32(3): 689-90, June, 1971.
      (4 References).
Groups of sixth-grade children who were retarded readers were matched on
the basis of WRAT scores with normal second graders. In oral reading
tests no differences appeared between the retarded readers and younger
normals reading at the same level except that the older retarded readers
made more errors.

1288 Dolch, E. W. "Diagnosis and remediation of disability in oral
      reading." In: Conference on Reading, University of Chicago, 1955.
      Proceedings: oral aspects of reading. Vol. 17. Compiled and
      edited by Helen M. Robinson. Chicago, Illinois: University of
      Chicago Press, 1955. 91-95. (0 References). (Supplementary
      Education Monographs, No. 82).
Diagnosis and remediation mean finding out where the child is in his reading and helping him to grow from that point. Four questions should be
asked in making the diagnosis: (1) How does the child feel? (2) Where
does he read and how well? (3) How does he attack words? (4) How much
does he think about his reading?

1289 Duguid, K. "Congenital word-blindness and reading disability."
      Guys Hosp Rep 85(Series 4, Vol. 15): 76-93, January, 1935. (12
      References).
Word blindness is difficult to diagnose because the picture is often complicated by other factors. Three distinct groups may be identified: (1)
word blindness; (2) visual imperception caused by confusion in learning
similar letters and the tendency to reverse them; and (3) problems of
ocular dominance described by Orton. The last two are similar but the
cause appears to be different. Six case histories are given, two illustrating each of the three types of reading disability. The role of heredity is a difficult factor to assess in reading difficulties. Because
various factors cause reading disability, various methods of treatment
must be used. Building the child's confidence, individual coaching, and
the look-and-say method are recommended.

1290 Eisenberg, Leon. "Office evaluation of specific reading disability
      in children." Pediatrics 23(4): 997-1003, April, 1959. (15
      References).
Learning to read is very important in a literate society. Only infre-
quently do the parents presenting the child at the pediatrician's office
mention difficulty in reading as their specific concern. Many symptoms
are mentioned, frequently behavior disorders. A screening test for reading ability should be administered. A multiplicity of terms are used to
describe reading disorders and many causes are mentioned, but there is
no general agreement on cause. Successful treatment is much more likely
if the problem is recognized and treated early. Symptoms of reading
disorder are detailed. It is suggested that the antisocial behavior of
delinquents may have its origin in the frustrations accompanying reading
failure.

1291 Erickson, Marilyn T. "The z-score discrepancy method for identify-
      ing reading disabled children." J Learn Disabil 8(5): 308-12,
      May, 1975. (6 References).
The z-score method which reflects the relative standing of a child within
a group was used to compare the scores of third graders on the Slosson
Intelligence Test and the Slosson Oral Reading Test. More than other

methods, the z-score identified children with intelligence scores above the mean and reading scores below the mean. The z-score unit is found by subtracting the group mean from each child's test score and dividing the result by the standard deviation of the test.

1292 Erickson, Ruth Rogers, and Erickson, Edsel L. How to diagnose and correct your child's reading problem. Holmes Beach, Florida: Teaching and Learning Publications, 1975. 171p.

1293 Faglioni, P.; Gatti, B.; Paganoni, A. M.; et al. "A psychometric evaluation of developmental dyslexia in Italian children." Cortex 5(1): 15-26, March, 1969. (26 References).
Describes a method for selecting poor readers from a wide sample of schoolchildren. Children between eight and ten years of age who scored lower than 95 percent of the population on reading and spelling tests were diagnosed dyslexic. The scores were corrected for age and intelligence by the use of a culture-free intelligence test. This psychometric method ruled out the influence of intelligence on reading performance, providing what was believed to be an objective criterion for identifying dyslexic children. The test was administered to 969 children and is the first attempt at a study of developmental dyslexia in Italy carried out on a wide sample.

1294 Fish, Nicholas, and Hutchins, Wayne W. "Are certain learning disturbances a definite disease?" J Maine Med Assoc 63(4): 68-74, April, 1972. (8 References).
An entity called dyslexia which divides learners from those who do not learn to read but are of adequate intelligence appears to exist on the basis of studies made at a residential treatment home for emotionally disturbed children. Dyslexic and normal controls were grouped according to sex and IQ. Five major signs of dyslexia, called defects, are identified: series (difficulty in learning to count, learning days of the week, etc.); temporal; speech; spatial; and place defects. Emotional deprivation and some psychiatric diagnostic entities appear to have little relation to a child's learning ability.

1295 Fitzgerald, James A. "Diagnosing reading deficiencies." Cathol Sch J 56: 12-14, 46-48, January-February, 1956. (34 Bibliographic Footnotes).
Defines the retarded reader as one whose attainments do not equal his ability to learn. Many causes are listed. Diagnosis concerns two appraisal problems: identifying the individual pupils who are retarded in reading, and discovering causes for the deficiencies and difficulties in each child. Identification may be done through testing. To find the causes, a list of questions to be asked about each retarded reader is provided. Diagnosis should be continuous; difficulties should be considered as they arise, not later. Factors which should be diagnosed include mental, physical, educational, reading, interest, experience, activity, personality, and environmental. Each is assessed as it pertains to a program of diagnostic testing. The interests and strong points of the child should be utilized in remedial instruction.

1296 Franklin, Alfred White. "The delayed reader and the paediatrician." London Clin Med J 5(2): 27-35, July, 1964. (6 References).
Lists criteria for diagnosing dyslexia. Many causes of delayed reading exist. One is specific developmental dyslexia, probably with an organic basis. It is, however, a defect of organization rather than of primary

perception. Direction and orientation in space are often if not always
involved. Dyslexia is a "fringe handicap," an important one. It needs
to be recognized and studied sympathetically. Only recently has attention shifted from the gross handicaps to those like dyslexia. Psychiatrists may blame emotional problems for the child's failure without considering that he has something wrong with him when tests reveal a visual-
spatial problem. Many educational psychologists are uneasy at the interest in dyslexia by medical persons, especially pediatricians. Reasons
are given.

1297 Fuller, Gerald B. "Three diagnostic patterns of reading disabili-
      ties." Acad Ther 10(2): 219-31, Winter, 1974-75. (18 Refer-
      ences).
Explores the concept that not all retarded readers are alike; that at
least three subgroups exist. Three groups of ten-year-old retarded
readers were established on the basis of scores on the Minnesota Percepto-
Diagnostic Test (MPD). Groupings were those of Rabinovitch: (1) primary
reading retardation; (2) secondary reading retardation; and (3) organic,
or reading retardation associated with brain damage. All children were
given a battery of five intelligence, reading, and achievement tests.
Results clearly support the idea that the three subgroups have unique
behavioral characteristics. The need to study and treat retarded readers
according to the above groupings is pointed out.

1298 Gallagher, J. Roswell. "Specific language disability: a cause of
      scholastic failure." N Engl J Med 242(12): 436-40, March 23,
      1950. (10 References).
Describes the symptoms and method of diagnosis of specific language disability. Failure in school is likely to be related to emotional adjustment, interest, or intelligence. In addition, about 10 percent of schoolchildren fail because of specific language disability. Old-fashioned drill
on letters, syllables, and words with the child seeing, hearing, saying,
and writing is recommended for teaching such children. Early treatment
is most desirable. A case history is cited.

1299 Gates, Arthur Irving. "Diagnosis and treatment of extreme cases
      of reading disability." Natl Soc Study Educ Yearb 1937(Part 1):
      391-416. (15 References).
A discussion of the causes of extreme disability ranging from low intelligence to personality problems is followed by consideration of diagnostic
methods. The same factors causing extreme reading disability also cause
milder defects. It is impossible to say how many children are affected,
since severe disability gradually shades into lesser problems which
finally blend with those of normal readers. In place of the older terms
"word blindness" and "congenital alexia" which are not considered helpful, the terms "extreme reading difficulty" or "extreme reading disability" are used. Among many causes of extreme reading disability are constitutional and educational immaturity, physical problems, and eye and
ear defects. Some specialized intellectual defect such as weakness in
imagery, memory, perception, or reasoning was once blamed for reading
failure. More recent studies make it appear that disability can rarely
be blamed on this cause. The role of hand, eye, and brain dominance is
discussed. Unfortunate management of the child may cause reading problems.
Observation of the child's approach to reading, psychological and educational testing, and analysis of the child's motivation and mental adjustments are considered in their relation to diagnosis of reading problems.
Remedial materials and methods are analyzed in terms of adjustment of the
reading program to fit individual needs.

1300   Girardin, N. B. "The diagnosis of developmental dyslexia." Can
       Psychol 9(2): 279, April, 1968. (0 References).
Examines the relationship of various psychological variables to the assessment and diagnosis of dyslexic children. It was found that dyslexics had
significantly lower scores than normal children on some WISC subtests and
on tests of right-left orientation, rhymes, and ability to reproduce designs.

1301   Gold, Lawrence. "Approaches to diagnosis and treatment of pupils
       with developmental dyslexia." Paper presented at Annual Conference
       of School Psychologists of Upper New York State, Binghamton, New
       York, October 10, 1968. 1968. 19p. (ED 031 012).
Provides a history of the growing interest and knowledge about dyslexia.
Diagnostic criteria and techniques, instruction, evaluative techniques,
staff roles, and methods and materials for the instructional program are
included in the report.

1302   Graubard, Paul S. "Assessment of reading disability." Elem Engl
       44(3): 228-30, March, 1967. (6 References).
Many diagnostic tests and measures are available to aid the classroom
teacher in identifying reading-disabled children and referring them more
quickly to the proper specialist. Nine variables in assessing the child
are listed, including auditory and visual perception and acuity, level of
physical energy, signs of emotional disturbance, and speech.

1303   Gregory, Warren C. "Medical evaluation for reading disability--
       last time around." Pediatrics 51(1): 152-53, January, 1973. (1
       Reference).
Letter to editor with reply. Replying to Kenny, Clemmens, et al., Gregory
suggests that early medical evaluation of school failures is most important. The pediatrician sees LD children complaining of psychosomatic,
physical, or emotional ailments. The physician should know about learning disabilities and work with the school and parents to meet the special
education needs of the child. Preschoolers should have hearing tests.
The history, neurologic examination, and electroencephalogram have little
to do with evaluating dyslexia. In a reply published with this letter,
Kenny and Clemmens agree with Dr. Gregory, particularly in the matter of
the need for pediatricians to learn about learning difficulties. (See
Item No. 1323).

1304   Guthrie, D. I., and Bermingham, I. H. "A clinic for children with
       reading problems: the rehabilitation centre, Broken Hill District
       Hospital." Med J Aust 1(4): 149-58, January 22, 1972. (15 Ref-
       erences).
Reports on the establishment of a clinic in New South Wales, Australia,
for diagnosis and treatment of children with reading disabilities. The
approach is multidisciplinary with full medical and neurological examinations. School histories, personality and emotional factors, the family
background, and an assessment of reading level are all considered. An
attempt is made to classify the children according to the cause of difficulty. The problems faced by the clinic and future plans are outlined.
Primary remedial responsibility must rest with the schools, but some
supplementary remedial help for the children is planned.

1305   Hackman, Roy B. "The interview as a technique in the analysis of
       reading problems." Education 67(8): 482-87, April, 1947. (0
       References).

Whether clinical expert or classroom teacher, no one interested in reading can hope to function adequately without skill in interviewing. Individual diagnosis and treatment are the cornerstones of the clinical approach to reading problems. Objective and reliable testing methods for
analyzing causes of reading disability exist; in a way these are standardized interviews. The interview with parents and child at a reading
clinic is described. It is an integral part of the clinical procedure.
The way to learn to interview is by practice in interviewing. The classroom teacher should learn the technique of writing complete and accurate
records of interviews.

1306 Harris, A. J. "Diagnosis of reading disabilities." In: Confer-
      ence on Reading. University of Pittsburgh. Report, 1960. 31-37.

1307 Hartlage, Lawrence C. "Diagnostic profiles of 4 types of learning
      disabled children." J Clin Psychol 29(4): 458-63, October, 1973.
      (4 References).
A group of 134 children with an average age of nine years, seven months
was evaluated by a diagnostic team as representing mutually exclusive
cases of: (1) emotional disturbance; (2) minimal neurological dysfunction; (3) intellectual subnormality; or (4) specific dyslexia. The children in the dull-normal group had average WISC IQs of 84. The IQ average
of the other groups was 99. In an attempt to develop differential diagnostic profiles, the study compared the children on sixty-eight variables.
Analysis of variance among groups identified more than twenty variables
that were of differential diagnostic utility. Behavioral profiles were
found to be especially useful. Behavioral, social, academic performance,
and personal characteristics typifying each group are given.

1308 ————. "Differential diagnosis of dyslexia, minimal brain damage
      and emotional disturbance in children." Psychol Sch 7(4): 403-6,
      October, 1970. (0 References).
Eighty-one children were classified by a team of professionals into three
groups: those with dyslexia, minimal brain damage, or severe emotional
problems. WISC, Bender Gestalt, and WRAT results were considered. IQs
ranged from 85 to 133. The WISC was found not to differentiate among
children suffering from dyslexia, minimal brain damage, or emotional disorder. The Bender Gestalt administered to the same group resulted in
erroneous diagnoses of the dyslexics as brain-damaged in nineteen of
thirty-one cases. The WRAT revealed differences among the groups most
satisfactorily. Caution is advised for several reasons, among them the
lack of any clearly established criteria for the exact specifications of
dyslexia.

1309 Hartlage, Lawrence C., and Lucas, David G. "Group screening for
      reading disability in first grade children." J Learn Disabil 6(5):
      317-21, May, 1973. (16 References).
Explains a group screening procedure for detecting reading disability in
first graders. On the basis of the tests, 1,132 children beginning first
grade were taught reading either by a phonetic special alphabet, or by
the look-say method. Retesting at the end of first grade found significant relationships between the predictions from the screening and actual
reading skills, and between certain screening predictors and the various
teaching methods. The screening test had five sections: auditory sequencing, visual motor skills, auditory spatial skills, visual sequencing,
and combined auditory and visual spatial skills. These variables have
been demonstrated to be involved in reading.

1310 Hearns, Rudolph S. "Dyslexia and handwriting." J Learn Disabil
     2(1): 37-42, January, 1969. (15 References).
Reviews the symptoms and causes of dyslexia. Work being done in Europe
with dyslexics is described. A variety of tests can be used to detect
dyslexia, among them handwriting analysis. Further research in the field
of handwriting can be valuable in this area.

1311 Herrick, Virgil E. "The challenge of poor readers in wartime and
     basic principles underlying their identification." In: Conference
     on Reading, University of Chicago, 1943. Proceedings: adapting
     reading programs to wartime needs. Vol. 5. Compiled and edited
     by William S. Gray. Chicago, Illinois: University of Chicago,
     1943. 224-28. (0 References). (Supplementary Educational Mono-
     graphs, No. 57).
Poor readers are usually identified by comparison of an individual's performance with a test norm. A child's reading accomplishment should be
evaluated in relation to his overall developmental pattern. Individual
differences should be noted. Too much dependence on a single index is
dangerous.

1312 Hewett, Frank M. "Reading difficulties in children. II." Int
     Ophthalmol Clin 3(4): 1009-21, December, 1963. (0 References).
The cause of reading retardation is not easy to find. In the first two
grades it is often hoped that the child who does not learn to read will
mature and catch up. By third grade, both teacher and parent become
alarmed, and the child is referred for evaluation. The physician should
undertake medical evaluations. Psychological assessment should include
measures of intelligence, perceptual-motor functioning, and personality
structure. Educational evaluation should include measures of reading
readiness, reading vocabulary, and reading comprehension. A list of
questions of concern in assessing the child's oral reading are given.

1313 Hollingsworth, Paul M. "Diagnosis and prognosis: an interdisci-
     plinary approach." Paper presented at the International Reading
     Association Conference, Anaheim, California, May 6-9, 1970. 1970.
     8p. (ED 042 582).
In spite of support for a theory held for many years that reading disability has many causes, there has been lack of interdisciplinary approach
to the diagnosis and treatment of reading disability. Diagnosis must be
specific if appropriate instruction and remediation are to be carried out.
Six levels of diagnosis are suggested and examples are given for effective
use of specialists from related fields.

1314 Hornsby, Bevé. "Dyslexia as cause of psychiatric disorder." Br
     Med J 1(5851): 487, February 24, 1973. (0 References).
Letter to editor. In responding to a prior publication, the writer in-
sists that the distinction between dyslexic patients and persons illiterate for other reasons should be more carefully drawn, and agrees that
dyslexia could cause psychiatric disorder.

1315 Hrastnik, Marjory. "Making detailed clinical studies of unusually
     handicapped readers." In: Conference on Reading, University of
     Chicago, 1950. Proceedings: keeping reading programs abreast of
     of the times. Vol. 12. Compiled and edited by William S. Gray.
     Chicago, Illinois: University of Chicago Press, 1950. 143-47.
     (0 References). (Supplementary Educational Monographs, No. 72).

A reading laboratory's goals are to find the cause of a reading problem and ways to resolve it. The definition of a reading problem is discussed. Diagnostic methods used at a reading laboratory are considered. Children with learning problems usually fall into one of two types: (1) the hostile, "mad" child who gains attention in every way possible regardless of whether results are good or bad; and (2) the frightened, withdrawn child who functions at such a low level that he appears feebleminded. Problem readers in the clinic described are dealt with by every teaching device that comes to the attention of the staff. Each child is observed for emotional reaction. The staff seeks to establish rapport with the child on a skilled, professional basis.

1316   Ingram, T. T. S. "Paediatric aspects of specific developmental
       dysphasia, dyslexia and dysgraphia." Cereb Palsy Bull 2(4): 254-
       77, 1960. (62 References).
Dysphasia, the inability to speak in spite of normal articulatory apparatus, normal hearing and intelligence; and dyslexia and dysgraphia, the inability, respectively, to read or write in spite of normal intelligence, are all disturbances of articular language functions. Dyslexia and dysgraphia in particular are likely to be regarded as discrete clinical entities, and the fact that they are disorders of language ignored. Rational treatment requires that the fundamental nature of the disorders be understood. Considerations in the differential diagnosis of each of these conditions are discussed, including distinguishing whether the conditions are acquired or developmental. Classifications of terms used by various workers and classification of symptoms in specific developmental dysphasia, dyslexia, and dysgraphia are given. All three affect boys more severely than girls. Strong evidence suggests that the developmental form is genetically determined. In specific developmental dyslexia and dysgraphia there may be no history of retarded speech development.

1317   Jansky, Jeannette Jefferson, and De Hirsch, Katrina. Preventing
       reading failure; prediction, diagnosis, intervention. New York:
       Harper & Row, 1972. 207p. (Bibliography, p. 175-95).
To prevent reading failure it is necessary to have: (1) preschool identification of children likely to fail; (2) diagnostic assessment of the children; and (3) correct intervention. An overview of prevention is given, including discussion of the factors commonly thought to contribute to reading failure. Such factors as perceptual problems, emotional problems, and quality of teaching are considered. Ways in which failure can be predicted are discussed, and tests for prediction listed with comments. Tests have two purposes: (1) wide screening to identify children likely to fail; and (2).a second round of testing of the children identified to diagnose the underlying area of incompetence which will probably lead to reading failure. One chapter covers how and when to intervene, perhaps as early as age two. Sample screening and diagnostic tests are included. The effort to identify children who are potential reading failures led to the discovery of complex relationships among sex, race, sociocultural status, and achievement. In the population tested, 16 percent of the white girls, 23 percent of the white boys, 41 percent of the black girls, and 63 percent of the black boys were failing at the end of the second grade.

1318   Jay, Edith. "Evaluation of materials for diagnosing intellectual
       aspects of reading." Elem Sch J 56(2): 64-67, October, 1955.
       (0 References).

Three steps are involved in helping a child become an adequate reader:
(1) identify the child with a reading disability; (2) identify the problem area; and (3) select remediation methods. Observations are included
on how testing should be done. Local norms are probably better than
published norms which compare the child to some unknown population rather
than to his classmates.

1319 Kaiser, Robert A. "Diagnosis: by whom and for whom?" Paper pre-
      sented at the International Reading Association Conference, Anaheim,
      California, May 6-9, 1970. 1970. 15p. (ED 042 576).
Stresses the importance of diagnosis in reading instruction. The responsibilities of teacher and clinician are compared. It is pointed out that
the most immediate concern is to find and treat the estimated eight million children (15 percent of otherwise able pupils) who are having reading problems. Individuals must be trained to gather and apply the data
that will make treatment possible.

1320 Kallos, George L.; Grabow, John M.; Guarino, Eugene A. "The WISC
      profile of disabled readers." Pers Guid J 39(6): 476-78, February,
      1961. (4 References).
Concludes that WISC subtest patterns may predict reading disability. Interpretations of these patterns are set forth. A low Coding score seems
to be characteristic. Low Arithmetic or Information scores or a high
Block Design score would help confirm the diagnosis of reading disability.

1321 Kass, Corrine Evelyn. "The psycholinguistic abilities of retarded
      readers." Kans Univ Stud Educ 18(1): 35-47, April, 1968. (21
      Bibliographic Footnotes).
Equates reading problems with learning or language disorders. The discussion is based on the ITPA. The test is described. It assesses the
child's ability in certain aspects of language at two levels: representational and at the integrate level. The six subtests of the first and the
eight subtests of the latter level are described, and the aspect of language they are believed to test is indicated. In a study of disabled
readers ages seven to nine using the ITPA, disabled readers were found
to have psycholinguistic disabilities, especially at the integrate level.
It is suggested that disabled readers of normal intelligence compensate
by gathering information from pictures. They have difficulty predicting
a whole from its parts. The integrate level of the communication process
appears to be more clearly related to acquisition of reading skill than
is the representational level. Theoretical and practical implications
are pointed out. Psycholinguistics is a new science of language which is
attempting to understand the psychosocial implications of the use of language. Disabilities in psycholinguistic functions may interfere with
general learning development.

1322 Keeney, Arthur H. "Medical diagnostics and counseling in dyslexia."
      Med Clin North Am 53(5): 1123-29, September, 1969. (0 References).
Specific developmental dyslexia is defined as a defect in the development
of the ability to interpret visual symbols, especially letters and words.
It appears to be a male sex-linked dominant trait. It may occur in successive generations. Soft neurologic signs may be concomitant. Secondary,
or symptomatic, dyslexias are also defined. Diagnostic steps are outlined, including such factors as medical history of the pregnancy and
infancy; cerebral dominance; and the child's success at drawing such items
as a person, a bicycle, and the face of a clock. Various medical specialists should work together in diagnosing a case of dyslexia. Treatment is
largely in the hands of educators and educational psychologists.

1323   Kenny, Thomas J.; Clemmens, Raymond L.; Cicci, Regina; et al. "The
        medical evaluation of children with reading problems (dyslexia)."
        Pediatrics 49(3): 438-42, March, 1972. (5 References).
This report attempts to assess the efficiency of diagnostic procedures
recommended for children with reading problems. The children studied had
been referred to a clinic for a medical evaluation because of reading
problems. All were between the ages of six and twelve years and had IQs
above 80. Since no statistical relationships were established in this
study to suggest a diagnostic pattern in a group of children with reading
problems, it is believed the evaluation and treatment of dyslexia is
primarily an educational problem. Medical evaluation plays only a minor
role in diagnosis or treatment.

1324   Ketchum, E. Gillet. "Reading disorders." Postgrad Med 22(3):
        299-301, September, 1957. (0 References).
Learning to read is not a simple task. Causes of reading retardation are
the subject of much controversy. If perceptual confusions, e.g., letter
and syllable reversals, persist after the early learning stages the
errors indicate a need for inquiry. Seven diagnostic criteria are listed:
(1) good general health; (2) adequate background of social and environmental experience; (3) average or better intelligence; (4) adequate
vision; (5) a cerebral cortex that efficiently perceives letters and words
and associates their phonetic values; (6) adequate personality adjustment;
and (7) skilled teaching. Reading disability should be accepted as a
syndrome. Many authorities should share responsibility for treatment.
Five personality patterns typical of reading failure are listed.

1325   Kirk, Samuel A., and Kirk, Winifred D. Psycholinguistic learning
        disabilities; diagnosis and remediation. Urbana, Illinois: Uni-
        versity of Illinois Press, 1971. 198p. (Bibliography).
This book was written to assist those using the Illinois Test of Psycholinguistic Abilities (ITPA) to interpret test results and to organize
remedial programs. Specific learning disabilities, including dyslexia,
are defined. How the ITPA was developed, research findings on the use of
the ITPA as a diagnostic tool, and how to interpret ITPA scores are explained. Suggestions for making a full assessment of a child's learning
problems are offered. General guidelines for remediation are suggested
and separate chapters on the treatment of each of a number of specific
deficits are given including auditory reception, auditory association,
verbal expression, grammatical and auditory closure (sound blending),
auditory sequential memory, visual reception, visual association, visual
sequential memory, and others.

1326   Kress, Roy A. "Implementing the changing concepts in diagnosis."
        In: International Reading Association. Conference proceedings:
        changing concepts of reading instruction. Vol. 6. Edited by J.
        Allen Figurel. New York: Scholastic Magazines, 1961. 64-67. (3
        Bibliographic Footnotes).
The role of the diagnostician in reading failure cases has shifted somewhat toward prevention of reading problems rather than toward correction
or remediation. Success for the diagnostician is measured in terms of
the child's success in the program recommended for him. Remediation is
viewed as an extension of the diagnostic procedure. There are no short-
cuts in a thorough diagnostic procedure. Implementation of the diagnosis
is discussed at three levels: clinic, classroom, and community. The goal
is that all reading problems should be identified and treated so early
that the child never has to leave the regular classroom.

1327 Krippner, Stanley. "Perceptual training and reading remediation for children with learning disabilities." In: Pope, Lillie, ed. Issues in urban education and mental health. Brooklyn, New York: Book-Lab, 1971. 61-93.

1328 Lichtenstein, Arthur. "An investigation of reading retardation." Pedagog Semin J Genet Psychol 52(2): 407-23, June, 1938. (6 References).
A group of retarded readers (average age twelve years, three months) was given a battery of reading and intelligence tests. Individual recommendations were made on the basis of findings. Evidence was found that individual analysis of children with marked reading defects does much to improve their status. In those cases where follow-up was done, the difficulties seem to have been diagnosed correctly.

1329 Lillywhite, Herold. "Can reading problems be predicted?" Claremont Coll Read Conf Yearb 37: 181-89, 1973. (15 References).
If a "high-risk register," or a list of factors that contribute to, or are associated with, reading disabilities could be developed, it would be of great benefit to those working with young children. Such potential reading problems can be predicted now, but there are pitfalls. Included is a list of twelve symptoms which may be useful in predicting some communication disorders in four-, five-, and six-year-old children. Pinpointing reading disorders specifically is more difficult.

1330 McLeod, John A. Handbook for dyslexia schedule and school entrance checklist. St. Lucia, Queensland, Australia: University of Queensland Press, 1969. 28p. (49 References).
Describes the construction of the Dyslexia Schedule, a questionnaire developed over a number of years. It is an attempt to collect systematically social information that has been found relevant about children who have been referred to a specialist for treatment of reading disability. The full Dyslexia Schedule is not reprinted in this book. The much shorter School Entrance Check List (SECL), a questionnaire of eighteen items, is included. It is pointed out that all eighteen items are pertinent questions which discriminate significantly between normal and disabled readers and have been extracted from the full Dyslexia Schedule. The SECL is for use as a screening device to be answered by the parents of all children entering school as a predictor of dyslexia. If a child is referred to a remedial clinic or to a psychologist, use of the full Dyslexia Schedule is recommended. The items may appear heterogeneous in our present state of psychological knowledge, yet they predict dyslexia reliably. It would therefore seem reasonable to regard the items as valid. The concept of dyslexia should be regarded as a condition which really exists, a "hard core" of children within the total group of those suffering from reading problems. However, all hopes that a set of symptoms that can be enumerated and which will uniquely define dyslexia are doomed. The clinical picture is vague. If six or more adverse answers are obtained on the SECL it suggests the real possibility of a communication disorder, possibly dyslexia. A statistical item analysis of the SECL provides evidence for the validity of the individual items of the schedule. McLeod's full Dyslexia Schedule is presented in his article, "Prediction of childhood dyslexia." (See Item No. 1331).

1331 ————. "Prediction of childhood dyslexia." Slow Learn Child 12(3): 143-54, 1966. (49 References).

The Dyslexia Schedule, an instrument for predicting childhood dyslexia, is reproduced in full in this article. Because of the many contradictions and the continuing controversy over dyslexia, including the idea that it may not even exist, some researchers have thought prediction an impossible task. The problem of predicting development of childhood dyslexia was approached from the viewpoint of assessing the child's "aptitude" for dyslexia. Test items may appear heterogeneous in nature, but they may be regarded as valid if they have predictive validity. The history of the development of the Dyslexia Schedule is given. Originally it contained ninety items which formed the nucleus of an interview between the social worker and parents of children referred for remedial help. The testing was initiated in Brisbane, Queensland, Australia, where the rate of reading retardation was very low at the time. Several validation experiments were carried out using second graders in Brisbane. The twenty-three-item School Commencement Check List which evolved is reprinted. Questions include information about the child's vision, hearing, hospitalizations in his first three years of life, activity level, speech development, and other family members who had trouble learning to read and/or spell.

1332   Menkes, John H.   "The clinical evaluation of school difficulties." *Neuropaediatrie* 5(3): 217-23, August, 1974. (16 References).
Proposes that, as part of his evaluation of the reading-disabled child, the neurologist should determine what part of school the child finds difficult--the social aspect or the learning process. IQ tests, information from parents and teachers on behavior and motivation, and tests of auditory-visual integration will single out children of normal cognitive function and intelligence who lag in school achievement. Birch and Belmont's auditory-visual integration test, Benton's right-left discrimination test, Bender Gestalt test, and other tests are described.

1333   Miles, T. R.   "Experiences with dyslexic children. 1. Diagnostic criteria. 2. Teaching-methods." *Int J Soc Psychiatry* 21(4): 259-61, Winter, 1975. (9 References).
Sets forth thirteen criteria by which dyslexia in children may be diagnosed based on the assessment of 222 children. It is believed that children counted as dyslexic by these criteria are similar to children described by Orton, Hermann, Critchley, Naidoo, and MacMeeken. These signs appear to be clear-cut diagnostic criteria, and it is not understood why some researchers insist that such criteria do not exist. Criteria given include, among others: (1) discrepancy between intellectual level and performance in spelling and reading; (2) reversals beyond normal limits; (3) left-right confusion; (4) bizarre spelling; and (5) similar difficulties in other family members. Teaching methods geared to the special needs of the dyslexic and not to remedial readers in general are presented. The basic assumption is that the child is compensating for a disability. Pupils and their parents are encouraged to raise morale. Because the amount of material the child can handle is limited, it is broken up into small units. Much of the work is phonic. Training skilled teachers is a need at present.

1334   Morgan, R. A., and Fernandes, E. A. S.   "What can we do for dyslexics?" *Can J Ophthalmol* 9(1): 37-41, January, 1974. (7 References).
The ophthalmologist should be concerned with learning disorders because the dyslexic child is often brought to him first: somebody thinks the child may have an eye problem. If the ophthalmologist does not diagnose

dyslexia it is likely that nobody else will until too late. The ophthalmologist can help make the diagnosis, refer the child to an educational
specialist, or to a pediatrician, and reassure the mother and provide her
with explanatory literature. Suggestions for ophthalmologists on how to
make the diagnosis are given.

1335   Neville, Donald. "A comparison of the WISC patterns of male re-
       tarded and non-retarded readers." J Educ Res 54(5): 195-97,
       January, 1961. (8 References).
In a study using thirty-five matched pairs, retarded readers scored lower
in Information, Arithmetic, and Digit Span subtests than normal readers.
The poor readers scored high in Picture Arrangement and Block Design,
tasks seen as being somewhat removed from formal types of learning. Their
low scores were related to scholastic types of tasks.

1336   Nicholls, John V. V. "Children with reading difficulties." Sight
       Sav Rev 36(1): 27-30, Spring, 1966. (0 References).
Points out three categories of reading disabilities: congenital dyslexia,
the slow reader, and a mixture of the first two types. Vision is by no
means the only element in this complex problem. Congenital dyslexia
expresses itself in many ways in the individual: through visual and
auditory perception and integration problems, or in psychiatric problems.
These children should have complete ophthalmologic examinations. Eye
problems should be treated exactly as in any other child. Crossed dominance is not a serious problem. The ophthalmologist's most important
role is probably coordinating all the necessary diagnostic studies before remedial care can be undertaken.

1337   Oak, Marilyn. "Symbolic language disorders of childhood." Provo
       Pap 11: 56-69, Summer, 1967. (13 References).
Focuses on the problems of children with various kinds of abnormal language development. "Aphasia" or "dysphasia" refers to problems of spoken
language. The "expressive aphasic" child is one who understands what is
said, but cannot reproduce sounds except in a garbled manner if at all.
In "receptive aphasia," the child may be thought deaf because he does not
respond to speech. Some of these children can talk, but the speech is
often random with little meaning. In "alexia" or "dyslexia" the child is
unable to receive, understand, or associate meaning with written words.
"Agraphia" or "dysgraphia" describes the inability of the child to express himself in writing. Agraphia and dyslexia are highly interrelated.
Characteristics of all these conditions are described as an aid to teachers and speech clinicians in diagnosing the problems.

1338   Obrzut, John E.; Taylor, Henry D.; Thweatt, Roger C. "Re-examina-
       tion of Koppitz' Developmental Bender Scoring System." Percept
       Mot Skills 34(1): 279-82, February, 1972. (16 References).
The Koppitz Developmental Scoring System for the Bender Gestalt test was
reexamined using children from grades one, three, and six. Total Koppitz
scores did correlate with reading achievement, but no items differentiated
all grades. There was an inconsistency among the Koppitz items as dis-
criminators of good and poor reading scores. It is suggested that the
Koppitz test should not be used as the sole indicator of reading problems.
Some children in this study had good scores but demonstrated poor reading
ability.

1339   Ottoson, William E. "Specific dyslexia." Tex Outlook 50: 36-37,
       55, October, 1966. (0 References).

Uses the case history of a ten-year-old dyslexic boy to illustrate Orton's theories of mixed laterality as a cause of dyslexia. Symptoms of dyslexia are discussed: confusion of appearance and sounds of the letters, reversals, mixed dominance, speech difficulties, and low scores on motor development and coordination tests. Stable association of the sound and the recognition of words are difficult for dyslexics. Remedial work should not consist of repeating regular classroom procedures. A trained tutor is preferable, but the Gillingham-Stillman materials may be used to good advantage by any interested teacher.

1340 Park, George E. "Causes and symptoms of dyslexia (reading diffi-
        culties)." Arch Pediatr 66(7): 289-300, July, 1949. (2 Refer-
        ences).
Defines dyslexia as inability to read in spite of adequate intelligence, and ascribes the cause to all the abnormal factors to which the child has been exposed which interfere with learning to read. Various proce- dures for diagnosing dyslexia are explored, including psychological, psychiatric, physical, and educational methods. No two cases can be treated alike. Treatment depends on the diagnosis and the ingenuity of the persons treating the child.

1341 Patterson, Natalie E., compiler. Multi-sensory approach to read-
        ing disabilities. 1968. 25p. (ED 037 841).
Reports methods and materials used to screen children for reading disabili- ties. In a group of 750 children, 15 percent had these difficulties. A highly structured language arts program was used for treatment. Chil- dren remained in their usual homerooms while motor training, rhythm, and patterning programs took place. Academic gains and reading age increases were noted.

1342 Rabinovitch, Ralph D.; Drew, Arthur L.; DeJong, Russell N.; et al.
        "A research approach to reading retardation." Res Publ Assoc Res
        Nerv Ment Dis 34: 363-96, 1954. (69 References).
"Reading disability" is a generic term used for a wide variety of clinical entities of differing causes with different treatment needs. Three major groups appear to be valid designations: (1) those children with organic brain damage who cannot read because of gross neurological deficits; (2) primary reading retardation where no neurological defect is known, but there appears to be a basic, biologic incapacity to integrate written materials and associate concepts with symbols; and (3) secondary reading retardation in which a child has normal potential for reading, but out- side factors such as emotional blocks, lack of opportunity for proper education, or personality problems have hindered learning. Standards for differentiating primary and secondary reading retardation are presented from five viewpoints: (1) psychometric testing with an analysis of WISC scores; (2) achievement testing and the use of reading tests; (3) psy- chiatric evaluation; (4) neurological assessment; and (5) response to remedial reading treatment. Findings in primary retardation suggest a developmental problem rather than brain injury. Early preventive programs are aided by a clear understanding of the differentiating diagnostic standards set forth.

1343 Rayner, F. W. "Reading retardation in children." S Afr Med J
        40(38): 943-44, October 22, 1966. (3 References).
Gives seven signs and symptoms of reading retardation where the child's abilities are otherwise unimpaired. If the child's capacity to learn to read is intact, he may have a general failure in all school subjects

because of emotional trauma, inadequate teaching, or ill health. If his capacity to learn to read is impaired, only his reading ability is affected; other school subjects are not involved. This may occur either in connection with brain damage or without it. Ways to recognize and distinguish these groups of children are suggested. Treatments recommended include remedial reading, psychotherapy, and medication.

1344 "Reading tests; clinics work to uncover and cure troubles of re-
        tarded readers." Life 21(10): 115-16, 118, 121, September 2,
        1946. (0 References).
Shows the work of New York University's Reading Clinic. The reading problems of a twelve-year-old boy who is right-handed and left-eyed are
ascribed to a conflict between the left and right sides of his brain.
Tests for eye movement and eye balance are demonstrated. Metronomic
readers which set a pace for reading, and the recording of a child's oral
reading are among the teaching methods shown to aid disabled readers.

1345 "Reading troubles seen." Sci News Lett 88(10): 147, September
        4, 1965. (0 References).
Reports warnings that teachers should be on the lookout for children in
the lower grades who are not making expected progress in learning to read
and write. Some children who cannot tell the difference between words
or who reverse letters may suffer from dyslexia or dysgraphia (difficulty
in writing). Word blindness, mental retardation, family problems, and
brain damage also may cause reading problems.

1346 Rizzo, Nicholas D. "Dyslexia and delinquency: a new dyslexia
        screening test." Int J Offender Ther Comp Criminol 19(2): 164-77,
        1975. (14 References).
Describes a quick screening test for dyslexia suitable for administration
to children between the ages of eight and eighteen years. It is a preliminary examination when dyslexia is suspected or when a special learning difficulty exists. It consists of asking the subject to write his
full name, address, and the date; three partial sentences to complete; a
ten-word spelling test; and fourteen simple arithmetic computations. The
test has proved effective in detecting cases of reading disability in
court clinics. A relationship appears to exist between dyslexia and
delinquency. At least three out of four juvenile delinquents have learning problems. Perception and its role in learning and some causes of
dyslexia are considered. Instruction in phonetics is recommended as a
treatment method.

1347 Robinson, H. Alan. "Trends in identifying and diagnosing retarded
        readers." In: International Reading Association. Conference
        proceedings: challenge and experiment in reading. Vol. 7 (Part 2).
        Edited by J. Allen Figurel. New York: Scholastic Magazines, 1962.
        61-65. (34 References).
Children who need, and can profit from, treatment for reading disabilities
are being identified in several ways. Group intelligence tests with deep
and careful analysis of test results are widely used. Minimal brain
damage is very difficult to diagnose, but some investigators consider
neurological examination of disabled readers very important. WISC subtest profiles have been used. Findings show more agreement in weak areas
than in strong. Tests for visual and auditory perception, sound blending,
and ocular-motor skills are also used.

1348   Robinson, Helen Mansfield. "The challenge to schools in identify-
       ing and providing for retarded readers." In: Conference on Reading,
       University of Chicago, 1949. Proceedings: classroom techniques in
       improving reading. Vol. 11. Compiled and edited by William S.
       Gray. Chicago, Illinois: University of Chicago Press, 1949. 143-
       47. (0 References). (Supplementary Educational Monographs, No.
       69).
Reading problems are fairly universal but problem readers can be taught
to read. Schools have an obligation to evaluate and diagnose reading
failure in pupils and make remedial instruction available.

1349   ————. "Clinical procedures in diagnosing seriously retarded
       readers." In: International Reading Association. Conference
       proceedings: better readers for our times. Vol. 1. Edited by
       William S. Gray, and Nancy Larrick. New York: Scholastic Magazines,
       1956. 152-56. (0 References).
Outlines several steps that should be taken to diagnose severely retarded
readers. They include as full a case history as possible, as accurate
a measure of reading capacity and achievement as possible, an analysis
of the reading problem, discovery of any inhibiting factors, interpretation of the accumulated data, and recommendations for remediation. Diagnosis must be continuous during the period of remedial instruction.

1350   Rogers, C. D. "Diagnosing reading needs through the tell-tale
       error." Read Improv 11(3): 48-49, Winter, 1974. (0 References).
The mistakes a child makes in pronouncing words are clues to his mental
routes. Analyzing the errors can tell the teacher whether the child has
a visual perceptual difficulty, or needs phonic skills, or has a comprehension problem. Remedial or corrective reading needs can be diagnosed
by analysis of errors.

1351   Rusch, Reuben R. "Note on the validity of the claim that final
       closure is related to reading achievement." Percept Mot Skills
       32(2): 394, April, 1971. (3 References).
Authors of the Higgins-Wertman Test of Visual Closure have said that the
test was developed to shed light on intellectual functioning, especially
reading readiness and reading disability. In a study of groups of first
graders who were good and poor readers, the Higgins-Wertman test did
identify good and poor readers at a significant level.

1352   Satz, Paul, and Friel, Janette. "Some predictive antecedents of
       specific reading disability: a preliminary two-year follow-up."
       J Learn Disabil 7(7): 437-44, August-September, 1974. (18 Refer-
       ences).
Reports on the predictive accuracy of a battery of developmental and neuropsychological tests designed to identify the beginnings of developmental
dyslexia. The tests were given to white male kindergartners, who were
retested at the end of first grade. An evaluation of the predictive
accuracy of the tests was made. Over 90 percent of both high-risk and
low-risk children were correctly identified. It is hoped that these
tests will be of predictive value. The theory of cause for reading disability used for this testing was that of a lag in brain maturation.

1353   Schiffman, Gilbert B. Multi-disciplinary diagnosis. 1967. 20p.
       (ED 038 260).
Interdisciplinary concerns in the diagnosis of severely retarded pupils
are discussed. The severe reading disability syndrome is described in

the terms used by several disciplines. Neurological, physical, intellectual, psychosocial, and pedagogical factors are all considered. A diagnostic team should include at least the services of an educator, a psychologist, a language consultant, a visiting teacher or social worker,
and a pediatrician. Other specialists may also be needed.

1354 Schmieding, Alfred. "How Dyslexia Memorial Institute helps the
      non-reader." Except Child 13(2): 36-40, 60, November, 1946. (0
      References).
Dyslexia Memorial Institute, an independent, nonprofit organization in
Chicago, helps persons having IQs of 85 or above who for some reason
have not learned to read satisfactorily. This article describes the work
of the professional staff of the Dyslexia Memorial Institute. It is not
primarily engaged in research, but the importance of a thorough diagnosis
is pointed out.

1355 Shedd, Charles L. "Some characteristics of a specific perceptual-
      motor disability--dyslexia." J Med Assoc State Ala 37(2): 150-
      62, 1967. (54 References).
Lists and discusses the chief symptoms and indicators of dyslexia. Diagnosis must depend on clinical appraisal of a whole set or configuration
of symptoms; a syndrome must be present. Modern educational practices
concerning reading disabilities and a wide variation in procedures and
terminology have resulted in general misunderstanding. Much of the disagreement results from terminology rather than actual differences. The
collaboration of many specialists is necessary in treating dyslexia. One
of the most urgent needs is the collecting, organizing, and disseminating
of existing knowledge on dyslexia. There is no unique identifying sign
of dyslexia, but rather a pattern of signs which appear in contiguity.
Test performances characteristic of dyslexia are analyzed. Impairment of
concept formation and perception are discussed in terms of lack of left-
right discrimination and dominance. Included in the discussion are:
specific neurological indicators; speech and motor function disorders;
aspects of academic achievement and adjustment; social behavior; and disorders of attention and concentration indicative of dyslexia.

1356 Silver, Archie A., and Hagin, Rosa A. "Specific reading disability:
      an approach to diagnosis and treatment." J Spec Educ 1(2): 109-
      18, Winter, 1967. (32 References).
Defines specific reading disability as retardation in reading in spite
of adequate intelligence and sensory ability, adequate opportunities to
learn, and adequate motivation. The term "specific reading disability"
is preferred to other terms because it implies an intrinsic defect specific to language without assumptions as to its cause. Diagnosis of the
syndrome must take into consideration the child's reading and intellectual
levels, educational opportunities, and neurological status. Perceptual
defects, cerebral dominance, and minimal brain damage are among topics
evaluated. While lack of cerebral dominance may not be the cause of
specific reading disability, it is suggested that lack of cerebral dominance is an important part of the syndrome. Remediation should be aimed
at enhancing cerebral maturation to the point where the child is physiologically capable of learning to read. Remediation aimed at training
areas of greatest perceptual strength is not helpful.

1357 Silver, Archie A.; Hagin, Rosa A.; DeVito, Estelle; et al. "A
      search battery for scanning kindergarten children for potential
      learning disability." J Am Acad Child Psychiatry 15(2): 224-39,
      Spring, 1976. (15 References).

All children in first grade at a New York City public school were studied over two successive years. A test battery called SEARCH was devised and used to identify five- and six-year-olds vulnerable to learning failure. It was designed to study visual, auditory, and body-image perception thought to be basic to learning to read. The test was found to be effective in predicting reading achievement at the end of first grade. It also proved useful in identifying psychiatric and neurological problems. Five case studies are included.

1358 Sleisenger, Lenore. "Diagnostic and remedial procedures at the Teachers College Reading Center." Acad Ther 2(1): 13-17, 58, Fall, 1966. (11 References).
Reports on the diagnostic and treatment methods used at the Reading Center at Teachers College, Columbia University. The child's parents are interviewed, and the child is assigned to a graduate student who makes the reading diagnosis. Diagnosis usually takes six one-hour sessions over a period of six weeks. The reading tests used and tests used to diagnose various problems and the resulting deviant behavior are detailed. Emotional problems are considered. Recommended tutoring procedures are carried out once diagnosis is complete.

1359 Snyder, Russell D. "How much medical evaluation for reading disability?" Pediatrics 50(2): 338-40, August, 1972.
Letter to editor with replies. Snyder comments on an article by Kenny, Clemmens, et al. (See Item No. 1323). Children with reading problems do not have previously unrecognized physical or neurological problems. What has been overlooked is the physician's very important role as the child's advocate to prevent halting of the child's education because of his reading problem, to prevent overtreatment, and to encourage alternatives to reading. Part of the viewpoint of Kenny, et al. is questioned. Another response to Kenny, et al. by Harris C. Faigel (with two references appended) points out the pediatrician's role in providing support and counseling for the child and his family. It is fruitless to lump all children with school problems together. Labeling the child "dyslexic" has advantages. These are real and important, though more psychological and social than medical. A comment from Kenny and Clemmens agrees with the idea that the physician should be the child's advocate and defender against questionable school practices. Dr. Faigel's letter is answered in detail.

1360 Spache, George D. Diagnosing and correcting reading disabilities. Boston, Massachusetts: Allyn and Bacon, 1976. 397p. (Bibliography).
This book was written as a companion volume to the author's Investigating the Issues of Reading Disabilities. The first book reviewed research in the area. This book implements the implications and conclusions to be drawn from the research. It discusses the practices of diagnosis and remediation of reading disabilities. Designed for use as a classroom text, each chapter begins with a preview of material to be covered, and ends with suggested activities called "learning projects." Part one introduces and defines terms. Part two discusses diagnosis as it relates to vision and the problems of visual perception, auditory perception, the integration of the senses of vision and hearing, and the interpretation of WISC test results. Pupil-teacher relationships and assessing the child's personality are also considered. Part three discusses the analysis and interpretation of various reading skills. Detailed analysis of how to interpret results of thirteen individual diagnostic reading tests is

given. The last two parts of the book are devoted to strategies of remediation, how to improve reading through various kinds of mechanical
training, and how to organize a remedial reading center.

1361 ————. "Diagnosis of reading problems in the classroom." Read
    Teach 14: 14-18, September, 1960. (11 References).
The severely retarded reader is defined as a child retarded in a number
of reading skills by one year or more in primary grades, and by two years
or more if older. This assumes he has had normal opportunities for
schooling and is still functioning below his capacity in spite of months
of corrective efforts. This definition is aimed at eliminating wasted
time in diagnosis and remediation on pupils having trouble with only one
skill or who are functioning near estimated capacity. Group reading and
intelligence tests should be given. The intelligence test should involve
little reading.

1362 Sprung, Evelyn. "Dyslexia: many definitions, few answers." Nurs
    Care 9(1): 8, January, 1976. (0 References).
Reviews some of the definitions and symptoms of dyslexia offered by various researchers in the field. The psychiatrist or psychologist sees the
dyslexic child's emotional problems, the pediatrician sees his motor and
neurologic features, and the teacher his learning process. The nurse may
put all these factors together. She may hear complaints from parents and
teachers that point to dyslexia. She should listen carefully.

1363 Staiger, Ralph C. "Remedial procedures for severely retarded
    readers." In: International Reading Association. Conference
    proceedings: better readers for our times. Vol. 1. Edited by
    William S. Gray, and Nancy Larrick. New York: Scholastic Magazines,
    1956. 159-63. (8 References).
The most prominant characteristic of the dyslexic is his inability to
learn words by sight and to attack new words. The chief aim of diagnosis
is to ascertain the retarded reader's present status and to discover past
influences on his development with a view toward planning future activities. An effective teacher-student relationship is essential. Teaching
techniques are subordinate to his relationship and to the analysis of the
difficulty. Look-say, phonics, or the kinesthetic method may each be
used, depending upon the needs of the student.

1364 Stolarz, Theodore John. "An analysis of procedures used in repre-
    sentative reading clinics to diagnose reading problems." For a
    summary see: Diss Abstr 15(10): 1791, 1955.

1365 Svoboda, William B. "Reading disabilities, continued." Pediatrics
    50(6): 969-71, December, 1972. (2 References).
Letter to editor. A reply to Kenny, Clemmens, et al. (See Item No. 1323).
Although primary treatment for reading disabilities should be educational,
the diagnosis and monitoring of the child's response to treatment is the
responsibility of all concerned disciplines: medical, psychological, and
educational. Specific steps to achieve this approach in diagnosis and
treatment are outlined. A reply to the letter by Kenny and Clemmens
charges that the central issue is the dearth of relevant, useful information obtained from medical evaluation of children with reading problems.

1366 Thompson, Lloyd J. "Mental retardation and dyslexia." Acad Ther
    6(4): 405-6, Summer, 1971. (0 References).

Criticizes the definitions of dyslexia which automatically exclude exceptional children from consideration. Mentally retarded children also suffer from dyslexia. Some of the literature implies that normal or above-average intelligence is a requisite for diagnosing dyslexia. It is reasonable to assume that if 10 percent of all children have some degree of dyslexia, that an equal proportion of blind, deaf, or spastic children, or children with IQs below 75 also show signs of the dyslexic syndrome.

1367   Thurstone, Thelma G. "Co-ordinating classroom and clinical efforts in dealing with retarded readers." In: Conference on Reading, University of Chicago, 1949. Proceedings: classroom techniques in improving reading. Vol. 11. Compiled and edited by William S. Gray. Chicago, Illinois: University of Chicago Press, 1949. 147-52. (2 References). (Supplementary Educational Monographs, No. 69).

The author, director of the Division of Child Study for the Chicago public schools, describes the work of the diagnostic reading clinic maintained by the Division.

1368   Vernon, M. D. "Specific dyslexia: a reply to Dr. Russell Davis and Mr. Asher Cashdon." Br J Educ Psychol 33(Part 1): 83, February, 1963. (0 References).

Defends the hypothesis presented in an earlier article that dyslexia is characterized by several symptoms and behaviors that appear with more than chance frequency. Causal factors are very obscure. It is not unusual for a disease to have no unique identifying signs, but rather a unique pattern of signs appearing in contiguity.

1369   Vogel, Susan A. "Syntactic abilities in normal and dyslexic children." J Learn Disabil 7(2): 103-9, February, 1974. (24 References).

Assessed the abilities of two groups of seven- and eight-year-old boys, one group normal and the other dyslexic, in oral syntax. Nine measures were used, for example, recognition of melody pattern; recognition of whether a sentence heard is grammatically correct; and repeating sentences read aloud. None of the tests required reading or writing. Dyslexic children were found to differ from normal children on seven of the nine tests. Dyslexics were found to be deficient in oral syntax. Normal children performed better at a high level of statistical significance.

1370   Ward, Jane. "Clinical testing of children for reading disability." Am Orthopt J 20: 81-86, 1970. (1 Reference).

Much misunderstanding exists concerning dyslexia. It may be broadly divided into primary or specific developmental dyslexia, a genetic neurological dysfunction; and secondary reading retardation caused by other problems such as immaturity, perceptual and auditory impairments, and environmental influences, among other factors. Techniques for estimating a child's reading ability, as an addition to standard orthoptic procedure, are described. Early diagnosis is important. Orthoptists should be alert to possible symptoms of reading disability.

1371   Weinschenk, C. "The significance of diagnosis and treatment of congenital dyslexia and dysgraphia in prevention of juvenile delinquency." World Med J 14(2): 54-56, March-April, 1967. (0 References).

Defines congenital legasthenia, or congenital defect in reading and writing, as a congenital difficulty of various degrees in learning to read

and write in spite of adequate intelligence, satisfactory sensory function, and apparently normal neurological function. Very little corrective work has been undertaken, and many adults write poorly because of
congenital legasthenia. Primary symptoms of congenital legasthenia are
those which appear in all persons with this defect under similar circumstances. Secondary symptoms are induced by extraneous individual situations. Where the legasthenia is not recognized and correctly treated,
it may lead to discouragement, school anxiety, truancy, and often antisocial behavior which may end in demoralization and criminality. If the
condition is diagnosed early and correctly treated, and these children
learn to read and write, there need be no serious deviant behavior. Investigation revealed that more than 20 percent of the inmates in a German
institution for juvenile delinquents and about 30 percent of those in a
German prison were congenital legasthenics. Diagnosis can be made by
testing reading and writing to dictation (not copying) in addition to an
intelligence test. Diagnosis can be made with certainty only at the beginning of the second year of school. All children with congenital
legasthenia can learn to read, and, with some reservations, to write,
after suitable remedial treatment. Discouragement must be combated with
psychotherapy. Inmates of reformatories and prisons should be examined
for congenital legasthenia, and the time in institutions used to combat
its results. Otherwise the disability may lead to further criminal acts
when the persons are released.

1372   Wolf, Clifton W. "A statistical study of specific dyslexia--char-
       acteristics and syndrome patterns." For a summary see: <u>Diss Abstr</u>
       29B(7): 2643, January, 1969.

1373   Wright, Helen C. "Identification and diagnosis of the able re-
       tarded reader." In: Strang, Ruth, ed. <u>Understanding and helping</u>
       <u>the retarded reader</u>. Tucson, Arizona: University of Arizona Press,
       1965. 14-18. (10 References).
Intelligence tests and a diagnostic reading test are central in diagnosing
the retarded reader. Directional confusion and letter reversals may be
indicative of reading disability. The child's medical history and the
history of his reading problem are also important.

B. EDUCATIONAL EVALUATION;
READING READINESS

1374   Adelman, Howard S., and Feshbach, Seymour. "Predicting reading
       failure: beyond the readiness model." <u>Except Child</u> 37(5): 349-
       54, January, 1971. (31 References).
The lack of success in predicting reading failure is attributed to the
reliance on measurements of reading readiness and on procedures which do
not take into account the many factors which determine a child's success
or failure. Discussed is a method for predicting reading failure which
uses the interaction between the child's abilities and his specific classroom environment.

1375   Ahnsjö, Sven. "Tests for children with special difficulties in
       reading and writing." <u>Acta Paediatr (Suppl)</u> 44(Suppl. 103): 130-
       32, July, 1955. (0 References).
Describes efforts to find suitable reading and writing tests for use with
children of normal intelligence, vision, and hearing who have difficulty
with reading and writing. A "mutilated words" test has proved very useful, and is suggested as a basic group test for use by teachers.

1376   Altus, Grace T.   "A WISC profile for retarded readers."   J Consult
       Psychol   20(2):   155-56, April, 1956.   (2 References).
Describes what is thought to be a "reasonably characteristic" WISC pattern of subtest scores for children with severe reading disability.   Subjects were twenty-five elementary-school children.   Full-scale WISC average scores was 98.6.   Coding and Arithmetic subtest scores were found to
be significantly lower than Vocabulary, Digit Span, Picture Completion,
Object Assembly, and Picture Arrangement subtests.   Information subtest
was significantly lower than Picture Completion, Vocabulary, and Digit
Span.

1377   Askov, Warren; Otto, Wayne; Smith, Richard.   "Assessment of the
       de Hirsch predictive index tests of reading failure."   In: Some
       persistent questions on beginning reading.   Edited by Robert C.
       Aukerman.   Newark, Delaware: International Reading Association,
       1972.   33-42.   (3 References).
Because the De Hirsch Predictive Index Tests of Reading Failure are being
cited in the professional literature and used, it seemed appropriate to
test their validity and general usefulness on a more general kindergarten
population than the one used in developing the test.   It was found that
the De Hirsch tests given in kindergarten are useful in predicting reading achievement in second grade two years later.   The question is raised
whether the time and expense of administration is worthwhile for all children.   It is suggested that the tests be used on kindergarten children
whose ability to learn to read appears marginal.

1378   Austin, Mary C.   "Identifying readers who need corrective instruc-
       tion."   In: Conference on Reading, University of Chicago, 1953.
       Proceedings: corrective reading in classroom and clinic.   Vol. 15.
       Compiled and edited by Helen M. Robinson.   Chicago, Illinois:
       University of Chicago Press, 1953.   19-25.   (11 References).   (Sup-
       plementary Educational Monographs, No. 79).
No generally accepted definition of the retarded reader exists.   Pupils
may be selected for special reading instruction by: (1) discrepancies
between mental age and reading age; (2) the Monroe reading index; (3) the
informal reading inventory; (4) Olson and Hughes' "split-growth" analysis;
and (5) the case-study technique.   These methods are described.

1379   Berger, Michael; Yule, William; Rutter, Michael.   "Attainment and
       adjustment in two geographical areas.   II--The prevalence of spe-
       cific reading retardation."   Br J Psychiatry   126:   510-19, June,
       1975.   (20 References).
In studies of ten-year-old children living in one inner London borough
and children the same age living on the Isle of Wight, specific reading
retardation was found to occur in 9.9 percent of the London children and
in 3.9 percent of the Isle of Wight children.   General reading backwardness was also more common in the London children (19.0 percent vs. 8.3
percent).   The same methods of study were used for both groups.   Retarded
readers from both locations showed similar psychological characteristics.
It is concluded that a real difference exists in prevalence of reading
retardation and reading backwardness between London and the Isle of Wight.

1380   Betts, Emmett Albert.   "Corrective and remedial cases: analysis
       and follow-up."   Elem Engl   24(3):   137-50, March, 1947.   (10 Ref-
       erences).
Classification of reading problems is one step toward a reading program
differentiated to meet the varying needs of the problem readers involved.

"Developmental reading" is the term used for the kind of instruction most normal readers need. "Corrective reading" programs are aimed at nonreaders and retarded readers who have no associative learning disabilities. "Remedial reading" programs are needed for those children with associative learning disabilities, including the dyslexias. Information is given on how to analyze reading problems.

1381 ————. "Teacher analysis of reading disabilities." Elem Engl
    Rev 11(4): 99-102, April, 1934. (0 References).
Describes a series of tests developed to aid the teacher in recognizing and analyzing the causes of reading disability. In the past, symptoms of reading disabilities were recognized, but the causes remained unidentified. Six major factors contribute to reading success: maturation, vision, hearing, kinesthetic imagery, language, and emotional reactions. The battery of tests used to measure each of these factors is described. The factor of maturation, that is, immaturity, may be the reason more boys than girls suffer from reading disabilities.

1382 Boder, Elena. "Developmental dyslexia: a review of prevailing
    diagnostic criteria." Claremont Coll Read Conf Yearb 36: 114-25,
    1972. (27 References).
Diagnosis of dyslexia is made in two ways: (1) indirectly, on the basis of neurological or psychometric factors; or (2) directly, on the basis of the types of errors in reading and spelling. A new diagnostic approach to dyslexia is proposed. On the basis of this approach dyslexic children would be divided into three groups: (1) "dysphonetic," or those who respond to whole-word configurations but are unable to decipher phonetically unknown words because they recognize only words from their sight vocabularies; (2) "dyseidetic," or those who have deficits in their ability to see words as wholes and tend to spell all words, known and unknown, phonetically; and (3) a group with both phonetic word analysis and whole-word perception deficits.

1383 Case, L. "Dyslexia and reading difficulties." High Points 3-6,
    Spring, 1968.

1384 Castner, B. M. "Prediction of reading disability prior to first
    grade entrance." Am J Orthopsychiatry 5(4): 375-87, October,
    1935. (0 References).
Observation of the presence or absence of certain behavior and personality traits brought out in the routine examination of preschool children can be used as a clinical method to predict reading failure. These factors include, among others, inconsistency on successive examinations; reversal tendencies; a history of sinistrality or reading disability in the family; atypical speech development; unstable or excitable personality; and specific weakness on drawing tests.

1385 Cillizza, Joseph, and Devine, John M. Modular sequence: teaching
    reading to bilingual learners. TTP 002.04; reading readiness.
    Teacher corps bilingual project. 1974. 13p. (ED 106 241).
A teaching module about reading readiness. When participants have completed the module, they should be able to: (1) assess readiness needs; (2) know what items make up readiness; (3) develop a program of readiness for individual pupils; and (4) be able to determine the special needs of the dyslexic child in regard to readiness.

1386 Cleland, Donald L. "Clinical materials for appraising disabilities
      in reading." Read Teach 17(6): 428-34, 440, March, 1964. (31
      References).
Although scores on standardized reading tests such as the Durrell-Sullivan
Reading Capacity Test, Reading Survey Test or Stanford Achievement Test:
Reading, are of great value in assessing a child's progress, there is no
substitute for a qualified clinician who can observe the child's reaction
to testing. Much behavior cannot be measured by tests and standardized
testing instruments have limitations.

1387 Cotterell, Gill. Diagnosis in the classroom; including checklist
      of basic sounds. Reading, England: Centre for the Teaching of
      Reading, University of Reading, 1974. 26p.

1388 Critchley, Macdonald. "Dysgraphia and other anomalies of written
      speech." Pediatr Clin North Am 15(3): 639-50, August, 1968. (0
      References).
"Dysgraphia," or a disorder in writing, typically refers to the breakdown of a mature, learned skill. It is incorrect to use the term to
refer to the imperfect writing of a young child or of one who is the
victim of developmental dyslexia. Dysgraphia is discussed from the standpoint of neurological disease or injury and psychiatric disorders. The
handwriting of children with developmental dyslexia contains spelling
errors with features so specific that sometimes a dyslexic can be diagnosed on the basis of handwriting. Throughout life a dyslexic who has
mastered many of his difficulties may continue to betray his former
handicap by the way he writes and spells.

1389 Dockrell, W. B. "The use of Wechsler Intelligence Scale for Chil-
      dren in the diagnosis of retarded readers." Alta J Educ Res 6:
      86-91, 1960.

1390 Durrell, Donald D. "Tests and corrective procedures for reading
      disabilities." Elem Engl Rev 12(4): 91-95, April, 1935. (0
      References).
While some progress has been made in developing methods for analyzing the
causes of reading disabilities, much remains to be done. Means for appraising the effectiveness of corrective procedures are nonexistent. A
method needs to be established for discovering quickly whether a remedial
method is working or not.

1391 Edinger, Dennis Lloyd. "A free operant analysis of programmed in-
      struction performance with reading disabled children." For a
      summary see: Diss Abstr Int 31A(5): 2215, November, 1970.

1392 Edwards, Thomas J. "Lexic-dyslexic diagnostic instruction." Paper
      presented at International Reading Association Conference, Boston,
      Massachusetts, April 24-27, 1968. 1968. 12p. (ED 028 019).
Reading ability should be considered as a continuum ranging from lexia to
dyslexia. Instead of concern about the cause and labeling the child with
a reading problem a failure, the teacher should be responsible for diagnosing individual differences in learning styles. Teaching techniques
currently used should be judged on the basis of their effectiveness. It
is suggested that all students be provided with a rich language experience in order to allow identification of quick perceptual learners. Individualized approaches could then be used with the slower learners.

1393 Faigel, Harris C. "Language disability. Survey of an elementary
      school for dependent children of military personnel." Am J Dis
      Child 110: 258-64, September, 1965. (23 References).
To determine the incidence of language disabilities at the elementary
school serving children living on Andrews Air Force Base in Maryland,
256 children in grades two through six and those repeating grade one
were given a battery of tests. Handwriting and spelling were analyzed.
Results show: (1) thirty-three children were found to be word-blind;
(2) one child in eight had some degree of language disability; (3) boys
affected outnumbered girls four to one; and (4) all children were of
normal intelligence. Manifestations of word blindness are discussed,
including bizarre spelling, slow oral reading, and the emotional problems appearing in adolescence. Teaching methods are considered.

1394 Farrar, J. E., and Leigh, J. "Factors associated with reading
      failure. A predictive Tasmanian survey." Soc Sci Med 6(2):
      241-51, April, 1972. (11 References).
On the basis of a simple screening procedure, reading success was predicted correctly 89.5 percent of the time. Such early detection methods
are urged. Questions on the screening test included, among other things,
sex, size of family, and father's occupation. A physical assessment of
the child was made, including speech, hearing, and laterality. Subjects
were 1,198 children in Tasmania entering school for the first time.

1395 Ferraro, Pamela. "Identifying the clinically retarded reader."
      In: Burkowsky, Mitchell R., ed. Orientation to language and
      learning disorders. St. Louis, Missouri: Warren H. Green, 1973.
      101-23. (36 References).
Because of the multiplicity of symptoms and disagreement among experts
in the field as to which are most important, the only behavior shared by
all children labeled "dyslexic" or some similar label, is that they cannot read and are hampered in academic learning and/or personal and social
adjustment. Therefore, the chief concern of the reading clinician is
not cause of the problem, identifying symptoms, or applying labels, but
the reading deficiency itself. The immediate goal of the reading clinician is to confirm and identify the nature of the difficulty. Ultimately
the goal is discovering strengths as well as weaknesses in order to treat
the child. Recommending instructional approaches is the reading clinician's chief task. Areas and strategies of clinical investigation to
achieve accurate diagnosis and realistic recommendations for treatment
are given. A case history illustrating the methods recommended is documented.

1396 Gaskins, A. Irene West. "Characteristics that differentiate dys-
      lexics from nondyslexic poor readers." For a summary see: Diss
      Abstr Int 31A(7): 3336, January, 1971.

1397 Gates, Arthur Irving. The improvement of reading: a program of
      diagnostic and remedial methods. 3rd ed. New York: Macmillan,
      1947. 657p. (Bibliography).
This book presents a background for understanding the numerous causes of
reading difficulties. Case studies of reading disability and directions
for the use of the author's diagnostic and achievement tests are included.
Better teaching and highly individualized instruction are needed to overcome reading problems. Most reading difficulties need not have developed
if proper instruction had been available at the right time. Detailed instructions are given for diagnosing and treating reading problems, and

for the diagnosis and improvement of comprehension. Directions for instructing extremely disabled readers and other handicapped pupils are
given.

1398 Guthrie, John T. "Models of reading and reading disability: Kennedy
      Institute Phonics Test." J Educ Psychol 65(1): 9-18, August,
      1973. (18 References).
Groups of normal and disabled readers ages seven to nine years were given
IQ tests and reading tests, including the Kennedy Institute Phonics Test
(KIPT). Subtests of the test are described. The KIPT is a criterion-
referenced test, that is, one which describes specific behaviors the child
can produce rather than relative ability compared with other children.
Reading subskills were found to be highly intercorrelated in normal
readers. Such correlations were insignificant among the disabled readers.
It is concluded that such interrelation among subskills is necessary for
normal reading. Lack of integration and interrelation among subskills
appears to be one source of reading disability. Subskills tested include
nonsense-word production, and production of long vowels, short vowels,
consonant clusters, and single letters; and the recognition of nonsense
words, consonant clusters, and initial letters.

1399 ————. "Reading comprehension and syntactic responses in good
      and poor readers." J Educ Psychol 65(3): 294-99, December, 1973.
      (10 References).
A group of disabled readers and two groups of normal readers were used in
this study. Disabled readers were inferior to both control groups in
sentence comprehension even though the children possessed adequate sight
vocabulary. Both normal and disabled readers used syntactic cues more
for comprehension of verbs and function words than for nouns and modifiers.
The comprehension of nouns and modifiers appears to rely on semantic cues.
Although poor readers were inferior in total reading comprehension, the
types of errors made by disabled readers were not different from errors
made by the normal control groups. It is suggested that specific remediation in comprehension may be necessary as well as instruction in
decoding.

1400 Halitsky, Sylvia. "Cognitive style variables as related to compen-
      sated and uncompensated dyslexia in emotionally disturbed adoles-
      cents." For a summary see: Diss Abstr Int 37A(3): 1488,
      September, 1976.

1401 Harris, Albert J. "A comparison of formulas for measuring degree
      of reading disability." In: International Reading Association.
      Conference papers: diagnostic viewpoints in reading. Vol. 15.
      Edited by Robert E. Leibert. Newark, Delaware: International
      Reading Association, 1971. 113-20. (10 References).
A generally accepted formula for expressing the degree of reading disability in numerical terms would be very helpful, especially in making
surveys, selecting persons in need of treatment, and conducting research.
Several formulas are in use, including Bond and Tinker, Monroe, Johnson
and Myklebust, and the WISC used as a reading expectancy predictor, among
others. Which test is used makes a great difference in the resulting
score. These and other procedures for arriving at a child's true reading
level are discussed.

1402 Harris, Albert J., and Roswell, Florence G. "Clinical diagnosis of
      reading disability." J Psychol 36(Second Half): 323-40, October,
      1953. (39 References).

Reading disabilities constitute much of child guidance clinic practice.
Causes are difficult to trace, and testing and diagnosis are time-consuming. Medical and neurological factors must be considered in diagnosis.
Because of the variety of causes of reading disability, conventional tests
of mental level and IQ may not give accurate indications of the ability
to learn to read. Details of the authors' diagnostic procedures are
given. Intelligence tests, personality evaluation, and tests designed to
test specific skills are used. An experimental reading lesson using
various approaches depending upon the child's skills is a valuable diagnostic tool.

1403 Herrick, Virgil E. "Selecting the child in need of special read-
      ing instruction." Elem Sch J 40(6): 424-34, February, 1940. (0
      References).
Selecting children who will profit from special reading instruction is
the concern of every teacher. Selection should be based on comparison
of the child's reading development with his development in other areas.
Any valid comparison should be based on a cross-sectional inventory of
important developmental areas at any given time. First, the child's
reading ability should be compared to some external standard. This is
widely done, as, for example, the use of a reading test to compare him
to others in his class. The second group of procedures is based on the
assumption that the only criterion of reading success is the child's
growth and maturation. Is his reading ability significantly lower than
his ability in other areas? By this standard, he may be the poorest
reader in his class, and still not be a reading problem.

1404 Hill, Walter. "Conditions related to specific reading disability."
      In: Bateman, Barbara D., ed. Reading performance and how to
      achieve it. Seattle, Washington: Bernie Straub Publishing Co.,
      and Special Child Publications, 1973. (16 References). (Reprinted
      from New frontiers in special education, selected convention papers,
      43rd annual Council for Exceptional Children Convention, Washington,
      D.C., 1965. 196-205).
Examines the use by schools of underachievement as the criterion for measuring reading disability. The pitfalls of using a single approach in
working toward solutions to reading problems are outlined. Factors associated with general reading disability and extreme reading disability
are listed. Recommendations for a school program to deal with reading
problems are presented.

1405 Hobson, Cloy S., and Parke, Wallace E. "Using a group test to
      identify types of reading difficulty." Elem Sch J 32(9): 666-75,
      May, 1932. (0 References).
Reports an attempt to determine whether a child's reading problems are
caused by mechanics alone, by comprehension alone, or by a combination
of both. Form 1 of the Monroe Standardized Silent Reading Test, Revised,
was given according to directions supplied with the test. In Form 2
pupils were allowed all the time they needed to complete the test. Form
3 was read aloud to the pupils while they looked at their copy of the
test. The test was found to be of low reliability, but it was concluded
tentatively that the testing was helpful in identifying causes of reading difficulty, and that there are two types of comprehension: interpretation of the written symbol, and interpretation of the spoken symbol.

1406 House, Ralph Woodard. The diagnosis, remedy, and prevention of
      reading difficulties. New York: Silver Burdett, 1938. 27p.

Presents several individual tests for reading readiness for first graders, and suggestions for making a reading survey in later grades. Other topics included are: home background; physical factors, including auditory and visual problems and laterality; and emotional factors as influences on reading performance.

1407 Houston, Camille, and Otto, Wayne. "Poor readers' functioning on the WISC, Slossen Intelligence Test and Quick Test." J Educ Res 62(4): 157-59, December, 1968. (7 References).

Examines the usefulness of the Slossen Intelligence Test (SIT) and the Quick Test (QT) with poor readers. The relative validity of these two short, easily administered intelligence tests was compared with the longer, more comprehensive WISC. Subjects were fifty-six pupils ages seven to fourteen years enrolled in a summer remedial reading program. They were of average or better intelligence. All had marked gaps between capacity and achievement in reading. Scores from both brief tests correlated significantly with the WISC. However, the SIT was significantly more closely related to the WISC full-scale scores than was the QT. It was concluded that both short tests are appropriate for a rough measure of intelligence of students with reading disabilities. The SIT is recommended over the QT because of its superior reliability in relation to WISC scores.

1408 Kapelis, Lia. "Early identification of reading failure: a comparison of two screening tests and teacher forecasts." J Learn Disabil 8(10): 638-41, December, 1975. (6 References).

The Meeting Street School Screening Test and Slingerland's Pre-reading Screening Procedures were administered to 110 first-grade children two weeks after the beginning of school. Teachers were asked six weeks after the beginning of school to predict the reading level at the end of first grade for each child. The purposes of the study were: (1) to determine the predictive validity of the tests; (2) to compare it with the accuracy of teacher judgment; and (3) to obtain the most powerful combination of predictors and examine its usefulness in predicting first-grade reading success. Each of the three devices significantly predicted reading success. However, test results on individual children can be misleading, and users are warned against permanent placement of children on the basis of screening test results alone.

1409 Kirk, Samuel A., and McCarthy, James J. "The Illinois Test of Psycholinguistic Abilities—an approach to differential diagnosis." Am J Ment Defic 66(3): 399-412, November, 1961. (10 References).

The authors of the Illinois Test of Psycholinguistic Abilities (ITPA) introduce and describe their test. It is submitted as a diagnostic tool for the appraisal of acquired or developmental defects in young children in the psycholinguistic field. Its purpose is assessment of the child's status leading to remediation of developmental defects. The nine subtests are described. Six are tests at the representational level, that is, the meaning level where activities or responses are made requiring that meaning or significance be attached to what is seen or heard (auditory or vocal symbols). Three tests are at the automatic-sequential level where responses to what is seen and heard incorporate a memory and imitative factor, but no meaning has been established, as in the case of a baby who imitates sounds. Problems in development of the test are described. Four case histories are presented as examples of its use. The ITPA makes no assumptions as to neurological status, but attempts to assess the behavior manifestations of psycholinguistic problems. The aim is diagnosis of deficits leading to remediation.

1410 Langner, Helen P. "Medical and psychiatric problems in reading
      disabilities." <u>NY Soc Exper Study Educ Yearb</u> 1963: 148-50.
      (0 References).
Enumerates some of the complications in diagnosing and treating learning
disabilities. Developing reading skills in late readers or in those with
special learning disabilities brings with it more motivation for further
learning and a more optimistic attitude about themselves on the part of
pupils. It also brings improved acceptance of discipline. Often the
best therapy is teaching even seriously disturbed children on the level
of their greatest retardation. It is important to include in the child's
social and medical history information about the family's place in the
community and the family's attitudes toward education and health. Psychological and psychiatric examinations are needed for these children.
A particular concern is nonreading children chronologically of high
school age and of average or better intelligence. It is believed that
recent refinements in diagnostic techniques will make it possible to discover and help nonreading children earlier than was formerly possible.

1411 Long, Donna Janet. "An analysis of the reading difficulties of re-
      tarded readers in second, fourth, and sixth grades." For a summary
      see: <u>Diss Abstr</u> 20(3): 924-25, September, 1959.

1412 McLeod, John A. <u>Dyslexia in young children. A factorial study
      with special reference to the Illinois Test of Psycholinguistic
      Abilities</u>. IREC Papers, Vol. 2. Urbana, Illinois: University of
      Illinois, Institute for Research on Exceptional Children, 1967.
      33 leaves. (23 References).
The performance of twenty-three dyslexic children seven years old on
several psychological and psycholinguistic tests was compared with test
performance of a similar number of controls. The WISC Information and
Digit Span subtests discriminated significantly in favor of the control
group. The ITPA discriminated between the dyslexic and control groups
even more significantly than the WISC in the sense that the ITPA still
showed significant difference after adjustment had been made for differences in IQ. The dyslexics were consistently inferior in reproducing
visual letter sequences. They were also inferior in vocal reproduction
of words that had been orally presented in context. The detailed statistical analysis carried out on the data and the author's Dyslexia Schedule
are included with the text.

1413 ———. "Reading expectancy from disabled learners." <u>J Learn
      Disabil</u> 1(2): 97-105, February, 1968. (16 References).
In order to decide which children will profit from remedial reading training and to decide when a child is no longer a disabled reader, it is
necessary to identify the skills that are relevant to the child's learning deficiency and to analyze them in terms of behavior—what the child
can and cannot do. The IQ test, although simple and widely used to determine what reading level to expect of an individual child, may not be
the best way to arrive at a child's reading potential. Long-range fore-
casting of a disabled reader's progress in a remedial program is hazardous.
Diagnosis must be continuous. Expectancies must be short-term. The
answer to what to expect from disabled readers is not as simple and
straightforward as a numerical index obtained from an IQ test.

1414 ———. "The search for measurable intellectual causes of read-
      ing disability." <u>Slow Learn Child</u> 11(2): 80-93, 1964. (0 Refer-
      ences).

Points out the limitations of the usual IQ test, which is a test of global
intelligence, as an instrument for diagnosing reading retardation. Intelligence tests have reflected three approaches to the measurement of intelligence: (1) tests based on empirical validity, such as the WISC; (2)
tests based on the results of factor analysis, such as Thurstone; and (3)
tests based on some theoretical model of behavior, such as the ITPA. The
ITPA is described and discussed. It is seen as a most promising instrument for the precise assessment of the handicapped child's total language
processes. An assessment of the total process is seen as a necessary
prerequisite to planning remedial programs. Relating diagnosis and remedial treatment more closely will bring great benefit, and the ITPA
appears to make that possible. Too often the usual IQ test does not provide a direct indication of specific remedial needs. Results of some of
the research in the area are reported.

1415   Malmquist, Eve. "Studies on reading disabilities in the elementary
       school." In: International Reading Association. Conference
       proceedings: forging ahead in reading. Vol. 12(Part 1). Edited
       by J. Allen Figurel. Newark, Delaware: International Reading
       Association, 1968. 504-13. (6 References).
The poor readers studied did not all fall into a specific, sharply defined group. A smooth gradation existed from the poorest to the best
readers. The same kind of errors were made by all in oral reading. The
poor readers made many more errors than normal readers, however. The
hypothesis tested in this six-year study was that reading disability
could largely be prevented if the child's reading readiness and general
readiness for school were diagnosed, and if teaching methods for continuing diagnosis and help were established in accord with the findings.
It was found that reading readiness tests were better predictors of success than school maturity tests. Eighty-three percent of potential reading disability cases were prevented by this method, but it proved impossible to entirely eliminate the problem by remedial procedures.

1416   Marcus, Albert. "Diagnosis and accountability." Elem Engl 51(5):
       731-35, May, 1974. (5 References).
Believes the standardized silent reading tests currently used in urban
schools are not appropriate for measuring reading disabilities of many
retarded readers. As students fall farther below the established norms,
the tests become less pertinent as measures of individual reading ability.
What the test scores do indicate is the failure of schools to teach reading adequately. Ultimately individual diagnostic reading tests will have
to be given to a large proportion of urban schoolchildren if they are to
be taught to read successfully. If teachers are to be held accountable
for teaching reading skills, diagnostic testing periods will probably be
necessary at six- to eight-week intervals during the school year. In
urban schools with high proportions of retarded readers, the school should
provide for explicit ongoing diagnosis of the pupil's basic reading
abilities. Reading abilities actually measured by the diagnostic tests
are discussed. It is unrealistic to think a classroom teacher could
maintain a high level of individual diagnostic testing. It is suggested
that programs could be developed where paraprofessionals and college
students could administer the tests.

1417   Mary Alodia, Sister. "Identifying and diagnosing the underachiever."
       In: Conference on Reading, University of Chicago, 1962. Proceedings:
       the underachiever in reading. Vol. 24. Compiled and edited by
       H. Alan Robinson. Chicago, Illinois: University of Chicago Press,

1962. 137-41. (11 Bibliographic Footnotes). (Supplementary
Educational Monographs, No. 92).
Intelligence and achievement tests should be administered to poor readers.
If reading age is considerably lower than mental age, the "analytical
diagnosis stage" should be pursued to discover the child's relative reading strengths and weaknesses. Beyond that, case-study diagnosis should
be done for particularly severe problems. In this type of diagnosis all
pertinent facts concerning the whole child should be assembled. The
accumulated information should serve as a blueprint for planning a program of treatment.

1418   Monroe, Marion. "Methods for diagnosis and treatment of cases of
       reading disability." Genet Psychol Monogr 4(4-5): 335-456,
       October-November, 1928. (0 References).
The purposes of this study were to assess the significance of the kinds
of reading errors made by normal and disabled readers, and on the basis
of this comparison to formulate a series of reading tests for use in
diagnosing reading disability. By the use of these tests it was hoped
that one individual's performance could be analyzed as a guide for remedial training for that person and that progress could be measured.
Toward these goals the reading performances of 120 normal and 175 retarded readers were compared. The retarded readers were consistently
distinguished from normal readers by greater numbers of reversals, repetitions, and greater number of total errors. Retarded readers showed a
greater facility for mirror reading and mirror writing. A larger number
of retarded than normal readers named a row of pictures from right to
left. The children ranged from grades one through nine and from inferior
to superior intelligence. The criteria for classifying readers "normal"
or "retarded" for this study are given. On the basis of differences
found in the groups a series of analytic tests were constructed as diagnostic measures of specific reading disability. An analysis of errors
made by an individual and the types of errors in which he exceeds normal
children of his reading grade can be determined. Some errors gave higher
negative correlation coefficients with reading grade than others. These
included total errors, reversals, faulty vowels, faulty consonants, and
addition of sounds. Some of the retarded readers were given remedial
help by methods directed toward overcoming the child's worst errors as
determined by the diagnostic test. Children trained by this method made
rapid reading progress. A foreword by Samuel T. Orton is included.

1419   "The nature of the reading problem." In: Newman, Harold, ed.
       Reading disabilities; selections on identification and treatment.
       n.p.: Odyssey Press, 1969. 17-21. (0 References). (Reprinted
       from New York City Board of Education, Bureau of Reference, Research,
       and Statistics. Educ Res Bull No. 3, March, 1942. 5-10).
The reading problem as the teacher confronts it is made up of phonic difficulties, difficulties in visual retention, poor word identification,
guessing, and poor attitude. The last includes the child's sense of
failure, lack of confidence, and inability to concentrate. The composite
picture of reading problems in the first year of school is of a child
immature physically, intellectually, or emotionally.

1420   Newell, Peter Randall. "The function of clinical and non-clinical
       judgments in the diagnosis of reading disability." For a summary
       see: Diss Abstr Int 30A(2): 590, August, 1969.

1421 Nolan, Esther Grace. "Reading difficulty versus low mentality."
      Calif J Second Educ 17(1): 34-39, January, 1942. (0 References).
Placing pupils with severe reading disabilities in classes for the mentally retarded has devastating results on their personality development.
This error is often the result of placing children according to group intelligence tests that require reading. Tests that measure both language
and nonlanguage mental maturity should be used to screen children with
reading difficulties. Suggestions are given for suitable tests. Three
case histories illustrate this problem.

1422 Norfleet, Mary Ann. "The Bender Gestalt as a group screening in-
      strument for first grade reading potential." J Learn Disabil
      6(6): 383-88, June, 1973. (22 References).
The group Bender Gestalt test was administered to 311 first graders at
the beginning of the school year to predict good, average, and poor reading potential. Results correlated with those of a reading test given to
the same children at the end of their first grade year. The Bender
Gestalt was especially useful in predicting good reading performance.
Teacher judgment of the child's ability and the Bender Gestalt were significantly associated, but there were indications that other measures
should be used as supplements in making predictions, especially for
potentially poor readers. Many sex differences appeared, generally favor-
ing girls, which have important implications for screening programs.

1423 Robinson, Helen M, and Solomon, Ruth H. "Individual reading prob-
      lems." Grade Teach 72: 43, May, 1955. (0 References).
Suggests ways for teachers to analyze reading problems without the use of
any special diagnostic material. The kinds of errors the child makes on
a standardized test of reading achievement, his approach to oral reading,
whether he gives attention to specific details and loses interest in the
main idea, signs of visual or auditory problems, and his home environment
should all be considered in evaluating reading problems.

1424 ————. "Who are the retarded readers?" Grade Teach 72: 31,
      October, 1954. (0 References).
Retarded readers are the pupils who show a marked discrepancy between
capacity to progress in reading and their level of reading achievement.
This discrepancy must be determined in the light of a variety of situations. What is the general level of achievement and expectation in the
child's particular school? How does he perform in oral reading situations? Intelligence tests should not require reading, which would measure reading ability rather than intellectual capacity. Vision and hearing must also be considered.

1425 Rönne, Henning. "Clinical testing of school childrens reading
      abilities." Acta Ophthalmol 14: 39-56, 1936. (0 References).
Describes four reading tests designed to diagnose word blindness. Most
good readers are found to have "intelligence age" and "age of life"
(chronological age) close to "mean reading ability." In most poor readers
the intelligence age and reading age are close together, and are both
below chronological age. But in a few poor readers intelligence age is
found to be above chronological age, and thus far above their reading
age. These are the word-blind. A method for plotting the data on graphs
is described giving a graphic representation of the child's ages in these
areas. Correct diagnosis of word blindness is important both to the
home and the school. The physician is the correct arbitrator between
them.

1426 Rutherford, William L. "From diagnosis to treatment of reading
      disabilities." Acad Ther 8(1): 51-55, Fall, 1972. (6 Refer-
      ences).
Four diagnostic levels are discussed to answer the questions, "What should
I do to improve the child's reading performance?" They are: (1) General
causes, a method which classifies reading problems in broad categories.
These are useful, but give the teacher inadequate guidance. (2) Terminology, that is, selecting an appropriate term and applying it to a child's
reading problem. This may only add complexity, as, for example, in the
use of the term "dyslexia" whose meaning is unclear. (3) Overt behavior
which may form a basis for describing reading difficulties. (4) Prescription, used when the teacher explains the child's reading problem in terms
of reading skills he does and does not have, and reading activities he
can and cannot perform. This is the desired diagnostic level.

1427 Savage, R. D., and O'Connor, D. J. "The assessment of reading and
      arithmetic retardation in the school." Br J Educ Psychol 36(3):
      317-18, November, 1966. (5 References).
Describes a method for assessing and predicting reading and arithmetic
levels to be expected for a given IQ. The IQ test used was a group nonverbal test. Two reading tests and two arithmetic tests were also administered. Children in the study were 419 Northumberland (England)
schoolchildren with an average age of seven and one-half years. It is
suggested that the information obtained by this method is valuable in
screening for early diagnosis of backwardness in reading or arithmetic.

1428 Sawyer, Rita I. "Does the Wechsler Intelligence Scale for Children
      discriminate between mildly disabled and severely disabled readers?"
      Elem Sch J 66(2): 97-103, November, 1965. (13 References).
Presents evidence that it is possible to discriminate between severely
disabled readers and mildly disabled readers on the basis of either eleven
subtests or seven subtests of the WISC. Discrimination appears to be
more effective at younger age levels. Subjects in the study were 140
boys and forty girls ages eight to fifteen years with IQs of 90 to 119.
Ninety were mildly disabled and ninety were severely disabled readers.
It is concluded that the severely disabled reader can be distinguished
from the mildly disabled reader. Schools need to identify reading-
disabled children early and to present them with a different kind of instruction since severely disabled readers do not progress in schools using current teaching methods. Different subtests played different parts
when boys only were considered. For the entire group the discriminating
tests in order of influence were Arithmetic, Digit Span, Comprehension,
Object Assembly, Picture Completion, and Vocabulary.

1429 Schiffman, Gilbert. "Early identification of reading disabilities."
      Trans Pa Acad Ophthalmol Otolaryngol 18: 25-27, Spring, 1965.
      (0 References).
In evaluating remedial reading programs, a major concern of educators is
the early identification of reading disabilities. Pupils whose reading
disabilities are identified by the time they are in second grade have
more than ten times the chance for being successfully treated in a comparable period of time as does a ninth-grade child with a similar disability. The nonreader's problems multiply as he moves up through the
primary grades. The child is bewildered, and failure by parents and
teachers to recognize the problem will have devastating results. Retarded
readers in secondary school may be so lacking in self-worth and proper
values that they cannot use or maintain reading skills. The answer is
early identification and proper correction.

1430 Silberberg, Norman E.; Iversen, Iver A.; Silberberg, Margaret C.
      "A model for classifying children according to reading level." J
      Learn Disabil 2(12): 634-43, December, 1969. (12 References).
Reviews the problems of definition that lead to failure to classify children properly as to reading level. Definitions of reading level have
been so vague as to be of doubtful validity. Reasons may include: (1)
the fact that a child scores differently on two different reading tests;
(2) the difficulties of assessing accurately a child's level of word
recognition and comprehension; and (3) the problems surrounding the composition of the group used as a norm in developing any test. Using a
random sample of ninety-seven third-grade, middle-class children, researchers found intercorrelations of the WRAT and the Gilmore Accuracy
reading tests. These scores were averaged and plotted as a scattergram
to show their relationship to the WISC scores for these children. A
method for using such data and a technique to plot children's reading
level from the data are described. Limitations of the technique are also
noted.

1431 Slingerland, Beth H. "Early identification of preschool children
      who might fail." Acad Ther 4(4): 245-52, Spring, 1969. (26
      References).
Need for delay in beginning reading instruction may occur regardless of
intelligence. Each child's introduction to reading should take into
consideration his individual strengths and weaknesses. Reading disabilities may be perpetuated by teachers or the school system because alternate teaching methods to meet the needs of reading-disabled children are
not available. The earlier the condition is diagnosed the better. Suggestions for carrying out a screening program are given.

1432 Smith, Louis M., and Fillmore, Arline R. "The Ammons FRPV test and
      the WISC for remedial reading cases." J Consult Psychol 18(5):
      332, October, 1954. (1 Reference).
Scores from two forms of the Ammons Full Range Picture Vocabulary Test
were combined and correlated with the full scale of the WISC. The correlation was .82 when administered to a group of reading disability cases
in a clinic. The conclusion is that the Ammons is a useful test for
screening the intelligence of children with reading handicaps.

1433 Smith, Zelda Brooks. "Early identification of remedial reading
      problems." For a summary see: Diss Abstr 28A(3): 884, September,
      1967.

1434 Stake, Robert E., and Mehrens, William A. "Reading retardation and
      group intelligence test performance." Except Child 26(9): 497-
      501, May, 1960. (5 References).
Group intelligence tests have been thought to be biased against retarded
readers because such tests are verbal in nature. This idea was tested
by administering the WISC (an individual intelligence test) and the
California Test of Mental Maturity (a group test) to groups of sixth
graders. The groups included retarded, normal, and accelerated readers.
Scores were compared statistically. The retarded readers were not handicapped by the group test requiring reading. Their abilities were not
underestimated. The group intelligence test underestimated the predicted
verbal ability of normal readers. Predicted nonverbal scores for the
accelerated groups were found to be much underestimated by the group test.

1435 Stauffer, Russell G. "An analysis of reading problems." <u>Optom</u>
<u>Wkly</u> 41(24): 897-900, 907-8, June 15, 1950. (34 References).
Considers a procedure for analyzing reading problems. Effective diagnosis and treatment require that factors contributing to the reading failure must be determined. Current diagnostic procedures attempt to determine the difference between the child's reading achievement and the level
of reading expected of him. Personality development of the child as it
relates to reading achievement and changing concepts of reading brought
about by cultural changes are evaluated. Assessing the difference between capacity and achievement is not a simple process. The validity and
reliability of tests used to measure both qualities largely determine
the accuracy of the diagnosis. Analysis procedures for use in cases of
reading retardation are discussed, including case-history taking and
capacity and achievement tests.

1436 Strang, Ruth May. <u>Diagnostic teaching of reading</u>. New York: McGraw-
Hill, 1964. 314p. (Bibliography).
Detailed information concerning both group and individual methods for
diagnosing children's reading problems are given. Oral reading, the
child's own appraisal of his reading, and physical factors bearing on
reading are all considered from the diagnostic viewpoint. Reading tests
are seen as aids to teaching: if the test does not help a teacher teach
better, why administer it? Interview techniques and protective methods
(those aimed at revealing personality problems that may influence reading ability) are detailed. How to interpret information is explained.

1437 Teegarden, Lorene. "Tests for the tendency to reversal in reading."
<u>J Educ Res</u> 27(2): 81-97, October, 1933. (16 References).
This research found that the strength of the reversal tendency had a positive relation to reading achievement at the end of the first year of
school. The study was done to measure the strength of the tendency to
reverse and confuse symbols in first-grade children and to measure the
relationship, if any, between the strength of the tendency to reverse
symbols and the actual reading progress. The correlation between scores
on reversal tests and reading achievement was lower for kindergarten-
trained children than for children without such training.

1438 Thissen, Mollie Jackie. "An investigation of the predictive relationship of certain measurements obtained on first grade boys to
reading disability in grade two." For a summary see: <u>Diss Abstr</u>
18(3): 933-34, March, 1958.

1439 Torrant, Katherine E. "Classroom techniques of identifying and
diagnosing the needs of retarded readers in elementary school."
In: International Reading Association. <u>Conference proceedings:</u>
<u>better readers for our times</u>. Vol. 1. Edited by William S. Gray,
and Nancy Larrick. New York: Scholastic Magazines, 1956. 124-26.
(0 References).
Presents several methods by which teachers can obtain help in identifying
and working with retarded readers. Included are faculty meetings, demonstrations and workshops, reading laboratories for the children, and case
studies.

1440 Veatch, Jeannette. "The materials and diagnosis of reading problems." <u>Read Teach</u> 14(1): 19-25, September, 1960. (0 References).
Urges individualized instruction in reading problems. Reading distress
may occur at any stage in development. The teacher should take the

learner back to the stage where reading ability broke down, and proceed
from there. New material should be used for repeating a stage of instruction. Stages of reading development are outlined. Classroom materials can be selected by the children themselves.

1441 Vogel, Susan Ann. "An investigation of syntactic abilities in
      normal and dyslexic children." For a summary see: <u>Diss Abstr Int</u>
      33A(6): 2795-96, December, 1972.

1442 Watkins, Mary. "A comparison of the reading proficiencies of
      normal-progress and reading disability cases of the same I.Q. and
      reading level." For a summary see: <u>Diss Abstr</u> 14(4): 644, 1954.

1443 Waugh, Kenneth W., and Bush, Wilma Jo. <u>Diagnosing learning dis-</u>
      <u>orders</u>. Columbus, Ohio: Charles E. Merrill, 1971. 182p. (Bib-
      liography). (The Slow Learner Series).
Identifies "learning disorder" as a general term which includes "dyslexia," "specific language disability," "word blindness," "strephosymbolia," and eight other terms. These are defined and explained, and
symptoms are listed. A number of the more widely accepted diagnostic
tests are described. How to interpret test data is considered. The difficulties of using test patterns alone for diagnosis and the need to rely
on the significance of erratic scatter are noted. Case studies grouped
according to grade levels are included, with reproductions of score
sheets from the ITPA and the WISC. The case studies identify various
types of learning handicaps. The book is designed to: (1) help the
special education consultant in identifying major learning disorders in
terms of behaviors; (2) show how to use data in diagnosis; (3) improve
communication between teacher and consultant; and (4) show by the use of
case studies how to translate diagnostic information into effective parts
of the teaching-learning process. A glossary of terms is included.

1444 Wilson, Margaret T. "Detection of reading difficulties in a rural
      public school." <u>Train Sch Bull</u> 39: 41-46, May, 1942. (0 Refer-
      ences).
Two groups of children, one from fourth and fifth grades and one from
sixth and seventh grades in a rural public school, were given the Otis
Self-Administering Test of Mental Ability. Teachers were asked to refer
for study children who were difficult to teach, did not progress, or who
had behavior problems. Seven children, ages nine to fourteen, were referred. They were given a battery of intelligence and reading tests.
Results contrasted with the Otis test, which requires that the testee
read it and write answers himself. It is concluded that reading disability was the cause for school failure in these cases. A reading rehabilitation program was recommended. Individual conferences with the teacher
to enable the pupil to realize his disabilities and take advantage of the
treatment were offered.

1445 Wilson, Robert M. <u>Diagnostic and remedial reading for classroom</u>
      <u>and clinic</u>. 3rd ed. Columbus, Ohio: Merrill, 1977. 287p.
      (Bibliography).
This book was designed as a text in diagnostic teaching. It is intended
for use by reading teachers already familiar with the problems of children having difficulty learning to read. Characteristics of problem
readers; classroom and clinical diagnostic procedures; and intellectual,
physical, and emotional diagnosis are among areas covered. A team effort
is recommended for using all of the school's resources to assist disabled

readers. Chapters are included on remedial activities to aid in reading readiness skills, word recognition, and word meaning and comprehension. The roles of parents and of the professional reading specialist in helping the child are detailed.

1446 Wurtz, Robert E. "Reading retardation and verbal aptitudes." Pers
      Guid J 38(6): 508, February, 1960. (0 References).
Letter to editor. Children do differ in verbal aptitude. Low scores on both a reading test and a verbal intelligence test may result from lack of verbal facility. This letter is a reply to the article abstracted in Item No. 1454.

1447 Yule, W. "Differential prognosis of reading backwardness and spe-
      cific reading retardation." Br J Educ Psychol 43(Part 3): 244-
      48, November, 1973. (13 References).
This preliminary report on a five-year follow-up study of poor readers ages nine to eleven years on the Isle of Wight, confirms that children with severe reading problems at age ten will probably continue to be handicapped in reading for all of their school days. Children with specific reading retardation have a poorer outlook than do backward readers. "Reading retardation" in this study is defined as including those children reading two years, four months or more below the level predicted on the basis of age and WISC IQ, that is, the underachievers. "Reading backwardness" is the term applied to children whose reading level is two years, four months or more below chronological age. It is concluded that the distinction between backwardness and retardation is of prognostic importance.

1448 Yule, W.; Rutter, M.; Berger, M.; et al. "Over-achievement and
      under-achievement in reading--distribution in general population."
      Br J Educ Psychol 44(Part 1): 1-12, February, 1974. (29 Refer-
      ences).
Studied populations of schoolchildren ages nine to fourteen years from the Isle of Wight and from London. Statistical methods applied to the results of reading and IQ tests revealed that reading achievement does not exactly parallel IQ at all levels of intelligence. Thus, the achievement ratio (a child's reading age divided by mental age multiplied by 100) and other similar measures of the reading level to be expected from a child are seen as inappropriate measures of reading expectation. Other results of this study include the discovery of wide departure from normality at the extreme lower end of the reading achievement curve for the group. Gross underachievement in reading occurred with higher frequency than expected. It is concluded that there exists a group of children with specific reading retardation whose performance cannot be explained simply in terms of the bottom of a continuum.

1. MEASURING INTELLIGENCE IN DYSLEXICS

1449 Frauenheim, John Gilbert. "A follow-up study of adult males who
      were clinically diagnosed as dyslexic in childhood." For a summary
      see: Diss Abstr Int 36A(5): 2741, November, 1975.

1450 Hirst, Lynne Schellberg. "The usefulness of a two-way analysis of
      WISC sub-tests in the diagnosis of remedial reading problems." J
      Exp Educ 29(2): 153-60, December, 1960. (6 References).
The WISC was administered to groups of mildly retarded and severely retarded readers. Subjects ranged in age from eight to thirteen and one-

half years and were of normal intelligence. Half the mildly retarded group scored above the means on Picture Completion and Picture Arrangement subtests. Twenty-eight percent scored significantly below the means on Coding and Arithmetic. Among severely retarded readers, 42 percent scored significantly above means on Picture Completion, Object Assembly, and Picture Arrangement. Half of this group was significantly below the mean on Arithmetic and Coding subtests. Substantial numbers were below the mean in Digit Span, Vocabulary, and Similarities. It is suggested that further research is needed to determine the meaning of the subtest scoring patterns that emerged.

1451   Huelsman, Charles B., Jr. "The WISC subtest syndrome for disabled readers." Percept Mot Skills 30(2): 535-50, April, 1970. (26 References).
WISC subtest patterns for groups of fourth graders from ten states, including both good and poor readers, were compared with the results of twenty previous studies. A pattern of low scores on Information, Arithmetic, and Coding subtests appeared to characterize groups of disabled readers. About 20 percent of the underachievers had high performance IQs. It is suggested that, in the light of these results, in considering the individual child it appears better not to search for a WISC subtest pattern, but to analyze low subtest scores for significance in that child's individual instructional program.

1452   Muzyczka, Marjorie J. "WISC characteristics and Devereux behavior scale ratings for third grade reading disabled children identified by the years below, Bond and Tinker, and Erickson z-score methods." For a summary see: Diss Abstr Int 35B(8): 4226, February, 1975.

1453   Pikulski, John J. "The validity of three brief measures of intelligence for disabled readers." J Educ Res 67(2): 67-68, 80, October, 1973. (5 References).
Results on the Slosson Intelligence Test, Quick Test, and Peabody Picture Vocabulary Test (PPVT) were all found to be correlated with the WISC when administered to a group of reading-disabled children ages seven to fourteen years. Factors to consider in choosing a brief measure of intelligence are discussed. For a rough, global measure of intelligence the PPVT appears better for reading-disabled children who may tend either to guess wildly or to be more rigid than normal readers. Wide variability may occur in one individual case on any intelligence test.

1454   Plattor, Emma E.; Plattor, Stanton D.; Sherwood, Clarence; et al. "Relationship between reading retardation and the measurement of intelligence." Pers Guid J 38(1): 49-51, September, 1959. (0 References).
Scores on verbal intelligence tests do not measure accurately the intelligence of pupils with reading disabilities. Low scores may reflect reading disability rather than inability to learn. In a study of scores on verbal and nonverbal tests given to retarded readers, it is concluded that both verbal and nonlanguage tests should be administered in elementary school. The discrepancy between the scores should be considered in planning remedial programs.

1455   Ravenette, A. T. "An empirical approach to the assessment of reading retardation: vocabulary level and reading attainment." Br J Educ Psychol 31(1): 96-103, February, 1961. (10 References).

Reports on a study aimed at showing the relationship between reading
ability and intelligence, and examining discrepancies between reading
ability observed and reading ability predicted. The purpose was to aid
in selection of children for remedial teaching. Schoolchildren seven to
ten years of age were given an IQ test, the Crichton Vocabulary Scale,
and the Schonell Graded Word Reading Test. Children with vocabulary
scores equivalent to an approximate IQ of 80 were generally not considered for remedial classes, since most rapid improvement was thought to
occur with brighter children. Children with discrepancy scores of twenty
(two years of reading age) or more between expected and observed reading
scores were highly recommended for remedial teaching. Theoretical implications of the detailed findings in the testing are discussed.

1456 Silberberg, Norman E., and Feldt, Leonard S. "Intellectual and
      perceptual correlates of reading disabilities." J Sch Psychol
      6(4): 237-45, Summer, 1968. (15 References).
Investigated the test-score patterns on the WISC and the Bender Gestalt
test of pupils in grades one, two, and three who had reading problems.
Contrary to findings in other research on older children, these younger
retarded readers did not consistently show higher WISC performance than
verbal IQs. The Koppitz norms, a scoring system devised for use with
the Bender Gestalt in diagnosing learning problems, did not appear useful
for isolation of types of reading disorders with this group of children.
No evidence appeared for a typical WISC subtest profile for retarded
readers in children this young. IQ alone does not seem to be sufficient
for accurate prediction of school success, unless the individual's reading skills are considered. It is concluded that WISC score patterns are
not very useful in analyzing the reading problems of very young retarded
readers.

C. LATERALITY AND RELATED FACTORS

1457 Bettman, Jerome W., Jr.; Stern, Earl L.; Whitsell, Leon J.; et al.
      "Cerebral dominance in developmental dyslexia." Arch Ophthalmol
      78(6): 722-29, December, 1967. (53 References).
The role of cerebral dominance as a cause of developmental dyslexia is
poorly understood. The ophthalmologist often sees the child with reading problems first because eye problems are suspected. The ophthalmologist should be prepared to diagnose the condition and recommend treatment.
In a study of forty-seven dyslexic children and a control group ages
seven through fourteen years, a statistically reliable number of mothers
had had difficulty in pregnancy and delivery. A statistically reliable
number of dyslexics were found to have poor readers in the family, and
to suffer from foveal suppression detected on ophthalmologic examination.
More dyslexic children than controls showed mixed dominance, but the difference was not statistically significant. It is suggested that dyslexia
is not caused by incomplete cerebral dominance, but is a symptom resulting from cerebral dysfunction. It may be congenital or perinatal (associated with birth) in origin.

1458 Delacato, Carl H. "Neuro-psychological factors as causes of read-
      ing disabilities." In: International Reading Association. Con-
      ference proceedings: new frontiers in reading. Vol. 5. Edited
      by J. Allen Figurel. New York: Scholastic Magazines, 1960. 60-
      63. (0 References).

A lack of neurological organization is the most significant common trait exhibited by poor readers. Twenty-eight traits which were not found significantly related to poor reading are listed. Human neurological organization progresses vertically from the low spinal cord area to the cortex. The basic difference neurologically between humans and the lower animals is the human achievement of hemispheric dominance at the cortical level. Children who do not fit this developmental pattern of dominance have language and/or reading problems. Diagnosis by the Delacato system proceeds from the cortical level down to ascertain the dominant hand, eye, and foot. Dominance at lower levels is also determined. The preremedial program of treatment is based on these findings. Children so treated become able to profit from remedial reading instruction whereas they had not made progress in remedial work before treatment.

1459   Drews, Elizabeth Monroe. "The significance of the reversal error in reading." For a summary see: Diss Abstr 14(7): 1044-45, 1954.

1460   Furness, Edna Lue. "Perspective on reversal tendencies." Elem Engl 33(1): 38-41, January, 1956. (16 References).
"Strephosymbolia," or twisted symbols, is the term given the tendency of some persons to reverse letters or words or to experience directional confusion. Some research in the field that is reviewed briefly includes that of Morgan, Hinshelwood, and Orton, and the more recent work of Fildes, Nila Banton Smith, and Hildreth. It is observed that the condition has been associated in the past with heresy, imbecility, cerebral imbalance, and now with normality.

1461   Ginsburg, G. P., and Hartwick, Ann. "Directional confusion as a sign of dyslexia." Percept Mot Skills 32(2): 535-43, April, 1971. (19 References).
As the result of testing of 429 second graders, confusion of left and right was linked to dyslexia. Crossed hand-eye dominance was not. Severe reading errors of three types--sound-symbol association errors, confusion of similar-appearing words, and reversals--appear to be made unusually often by the dyslexic child. Thus, numerous severe reading errors and directional confusion appear to be intertwined as components of dyslexia. Mixed hand-eye dominance probably is not related to dyslexia. It is suggested that a test of right-left orientation would be a good screening test for early detection of dyslexia. Descriptions of tests used are included.

1462   Leland, Bernice. "Symptoms of directional confusion among children who cannot read." Child Educ 14(9): 406-10, May, 1938. (0 References).
Many children who have difficulty in learning to read show tendencies to proceed from right to left or to be confused about which direction is correct. Symptoms of this problem reveal themselves in a number of ways. It is important to discover the problem early and correct it as soon as possible. Case histories are given.

1463   Teegarden, Lorene. "Clinical identification of the prospective non-reader." Child Dev 3(4): 346-58, December, 1932. (13 References).
First-grade children were tested for intelligence and for tendency to reverse symbols. Both factors proved to be of importance in learning to read. Both factors are independent variables. When other factors are

constant, the more intelligent child makes better reading progress. Reversal tendency itself is not abnormal. It is not possible to predict
reading progress from results of the reversal tests alone. Intelligence
tests used with tests for lateral dominance and reversal provide a fair
degree of accuracy in predicting reading progress.

1464 Totten, Eileen. "Aston index a way to pick out dyslexia in the
      early stages." Times Educ Suppl 3079: 10, May 31, 1974. (0
      References).
Margaret Newton, a professor of psychology at Aston University, Birming-
ham, England, has devised an index for diagnosing dyslexia called the
Aston Index. The three-part test attempts to: (1) assess the child's
underlying ability; (2) inquire into his family history, especially in
regard to laterality and birth history; and (3) assess the child's performance on a variety of factors including reading, writing, tests for
laterality, tests for visual and auditory sequential memory, and for
sound blending and discrimination. Mrs. Newton believes the index will
facilitate early diagnosis of dyslexia. Many dyslexic children suffer
left-right confusion which results in inconsistent perception.

D. MATURATIONAL LAG

1465 De Hirsch, Katrina. "Clinical spectrum of reading disabilities:
      diagnosis and treatment." Bull NY Acad Med 44(4): 470-77, April,
      1968. (0 References).
Discusses a variety of reasons children cannot grasp and assimilate the
numerous processes that make up learning to read. Excluded from the
definition of specific reading disability used in this article are those
children with limited intelligence, gross sensory defects, or extraneous
factors such as anxiety or environmental deprivation. Reading-disabled
children who read below their intellectual level and do well in other
subjects appear to suffer from subtle integrational deficits on many
levels of central nervous system organization. Their central nervous
systems appear immature. Visual and auditory perception are impaired.
Afflicted children have difficulty with auditory and visual sequencing:
the order in which sounds and letters occur in a word. Words and letters
appear to shift, to move on the page. Some of these maturational lags
are so severe as to constitute a type of cerebral dysfunction. Diagnosis
requires obtaining familial history and assessing neurological, sensory,
and academic histories and status. Treatment should be centered on the
child, not the method. No one type of remediation works for all. The
earlier diagnosis is made the better.

1466 De Hirsch, Katrina; Jansky, Jeannette J.; Langford, William S. Pre-
      dicting reading failure: a preliminary study of reading, writing,
      and spelling disabilities in preschool children. New York: Harper
      & Row, 1966. 144p. (Bibliography p. 115-36).
Children who lag severely in overall maturation can be predicted to fail
academically. A battery of predictive tests was constructed and given to
children before they entered first grade. Eleven of the tests outranked
IQ in predicting the degree of reading skill acquired two and one-half
years later. No single item clearly distinguished the future reading
failure, but rather a cluster of traits characterized kindergarten per-

formance of children who later failed to learn to read by the end of
second grade. Comparing learning patterns of prematurely born children
with those carried to full term suggests a relationship between prematurity and relatively poor future performance. Maturation depends on
such factors as inherited patterns, biological growth, and emotional,
cultural, and educational experiences, and varies among children. Recommendations include the use of small transition classes for children showing a pattern of maturational lag. Structured teaching of skills like
motor patterning, visual and auditory perception, orientation in time and
space, and language training in specific areas of deficit should be included. Evidence is cited that basic perceptual-motor functions which
underlie reading failure may be harder to train as a child grows older.
Eventually these deficits may become irreversible. Findings suggest
that it is possible to predict reading level at the end of second grade
from kindergarten performance.

E. PERCEPTUAL FACTORS

1467   Brodlie, Jerome F., and Burke, John. "Perceptual learning disabili-
       ties in blind children." Percept Mot Skills 32(1): 313-14,
       February, 1971. (4 References).
About 15 percent of groups of totally blind and legally blind children
showed the same error patterns in learning to read braille as sighted
children. Some of the legally blind children had been taught reading by
traditional visual methods before learning braille. Those diagnosed as
having perceptual problems in learning by sighted methods showed the same
pattern of reversals and confusion in letter placement when learning
braille.

1468   Goldberg, Herman Krieger. "Neurological aspects of reading prob-
       lems." Trans Pa Acad Ophthalmol Otolaryngol 18: 5-8, Spring,
       1965. (0 References).
Distinguishes three types of readers: (1) the developmental reader who
shows little difference between mental age and reading achievement; (2)
the corrective reader who is retarded, but shows no associative learning
problems; and (3) the remedial reader with whom this paper is concerned.
Remedial readers comprise about 2 to 5 percent of the school population.
The earlier this type of child is discovered, the better the chances of
helping him. Because of brain damage, educational factors, or emotional
stress these children are not able to learn to read by the whole-word,
or sight, method. Perception is explained in terms of the journey made
by the image from the retina through the brain to the frontal lobe where
the image takes on meaning. Dejerine's work in demonstrating this process of perception in 1880 is described. The EEG examination of 100
children disclosed that those who were poor in drawing a square, triangle,
or a flag frequently had abnormal EEGs. Reading is perceptual, and eye
muscle balance has little to do with it. Psychological reading problems
are considered. Children have many facets of disability. Diagnosis
should be made by several professionals, not by the ophthalmologist alone.

1469   Koppitz, Elizabeth Munsterberg. "Brain damage, reading disability
       and the Bender Gestalt test." J Learn Disabil 3(9): 429-33,
       September, 1970. (17 References).
Although the Bender Gestalt test is a good screening test for school beginners, it diagnoses reading problems only if they are caused in part

by visual-motor perception difficulties. Language disabilities or specific memory deficits must be diagnosed by other means. Brain damage should be assessed by the Bender Gestalt test only in connection with other tests and information.

1470 McLeod, John A. "Some perceptual factors related to childhood dyslexia." Slow Learn Child 14(1): 5-12, 1967. (10 References).
Discusses the term "perception" as it applies in the field of reading. It is something more than mere sensation, although the physical stimulus must be present, and less than a cognitive process. Perceptual behavior involves a learned response which is a function of frequency and/or contiguity with the stimulus. Semantic interpretation is not involved in perceptual behavior. It involves, rather, something almost inevitable or automatic. Attempts to assess this sort of perceptual behavior have been made by means of the automatic-sequential level subtests of the ITPA. In a study of a group of reading-disabled second graders in Brisbane, Australia, schools, the WISC, the ITPA, and several tests of auditory and visual discrimination were given. McLeod's Dyslexia Schedule was also administered. A normal control group matched for sex from the same class of school was also tested. A factor analysis was performed and four factors were found to identify severely reading-disabled children significantly. Two of these were of an integrative or perceptual nature. The Dyslexia Schedule was found to be significantly related to the two predominant factors. Cautious optimism is expressed that the test can be used to predict reading disability before the disability manifests itself.

1471 Sapir, Selma G., and Wilson, Bernice M. "Patterns of developmental deficits." Percept Mot Skills 24(3, Part 2): 1291-93, June, 1967. (6 References).
Fifty-four children of kindergarten age were given the Sapir Developmental Scale as part of a pilot study. The assumption on which the testers were working was that children with problems in perceptual-motor, bodily schema, or language development can be identified by kindergarten age and then trained in the areas of deficit. Two hypotheses were confirmed: (1) that immaturity of development is reflected as impairment in a variety of functions; and (2) that patterns of deficits differ widely in each child. It is suggested that the wide variation in developmental deficiencies creates vast difficulties for educators in designing programs for such children. More research on the training in specific developmental deficiencies is needed.

1472 Spearman, Leonard Hall O'Connell. "A profile analysis technique for diagnosing reading disability." For a summary see: Diss Abstr 21(8): 2198-99, February, 1961.

1473 Tansley, A. E. Reading and remedial reading. London: Routledge & Kegan Paul, 1967. 176p. (Bibliography).
General considerations on reading readiness and detailed discussion of how to train a child in perceptual abilities are followed by a discussion of phonics teaching and the teaching of spelling. The same principles are applicable to normal and perceptually handicapped children. The latter part of the book discusses reading failure and its causes, including intelligence, home conditions, and neurological problems. It deals at some length with diagnostic techniques and related remedial treatment techniques for severe reading disability.

1. AUDITORY DISCRIMINATION

1474 Flower, Richard M. "The evaluation of auditory abilities in the appraisal of children with reading problems." In: International Reading Association. Conference proceedings: perception and reading. Vol. 12(Part 4). Edited by Helen K. Smith. Newark, Delaware: International Reading Association, 1968. 21-24. (2 References).
Learning to read depends heavily on auditory processes including: (1) perceiving the sounds of the words accurately; (2) responding to them discretely; (3) retaining the sounds in accurate sequence; and (4) organizing them into words. Because of this, the child's auditory skills and processes should be carefully evaluated if he/she is having difficulty in learning to read. Five levels for evaluating auditory processing that appear helpful in planning the child's education are outlined.

1475 Gillespie, Patricia Hall. "A study of the performance of dyslexic and normal readers on the Slosson intelligence test for children and adults." For a summary see: Diss Abstr Int 31A(5): 2003, November, 1970.

1476 Harris, Robert. "A comparison of central auditory integration in children with and without reading disability." For a summary see: Diss Abstr 23(4): 1274, October, 1962.

1477 Mangrum, Charles Thomas, II. "A comparison of the performance of normal and dyslexic readers on the auditory test of dichotic stimuli and the visual test of dichoptic stimuli." For a summary see: Diss Abstr 29A(6): 1826, December, 1968.

2. VISUAL DISCRIMINATION

1478 Bindler, Stephen Bruce. "Patterns of conceptual functioning in children with 'reading disability.'" For a summary see: Diss Abstr Int 33B(1): 435, July, 1972.

1479 Black, F. William. "Reversal and rotation errors by normal and retarded readers." Percept Mot Skills 36(3, Part 1): 895-98, June, 1973. (7 References).
No significant differences in the frequency with which reversal and rotation errors occurred were found in two matched groups of 100 normal and 100 retarded readers. The results do not support the idea that written reversal and rotation errors are higher in retarded than in normal readers. The practice of using such errors as an index for predicting future reading retardation is not warranted.

1480 Clarke, Bryan R., and Leslie, Perry T. "Visual-motor skills and reading ability of deaf children." Percept Mot Skills 33(1): 263-68, August, 1971. (22 References).
A battery of tests, including the Bender Gestalt, the Graham and Kendall Memory-for-Designs, and various subtests from the WISC, was administered to a group of deaf children, some of whom were retarded readers. The deaf children's performance on visual-motor tasks, without regard to reading ability, was found to be well below the level regarded as normal for their hearing peers. It is suggested that the tests did not discriminate between good and poor readers because of the generally lower reading achievement of all of these subjects.

1481 Dunlop, Donald B.; Dunlop, Patricia; Fenelon, Bernard. "Vision-
      laterality analysis in children with reading disability: the re-
      sults of new techniques of examination." Cortex 9(2): 227-36,
      June, 1973. (21 References).
Studied the incidence of visual defects and crossed laterality in a group
of children suffering severe reading handicap of a dyslexic nature, in
comparison with a group of children free of reading problems. Included
in the study was consideration of the significance of crossed control in
binocular functioning in reading-disabled children. Groups of normal
and reading-disabled public-school children ages seven to eleven years
were given intelligence, language and reading tests, and psychological
testing. WISC full-scale IQs of the normal readers averaged 123.1; that
of disabled readers averaged 101.4. Detailed orthoptic examination was
carried out. It revealed that the incidence of certain specific ocular
defects was much greater in the dyslexic group than in the normal readers.
A combination of the measures of stereopsis, crossed control, and eso-
phoria achieved almost total separation of dyslexics from the normal
group. While ocular measures distinguished reading-disabled from normal
children, they were less successful as predictors of the degree of reading disability. Results are seen as indicating strong justification for
including orthoptic procedures in diagnostic procedures used on suspected
cases of reading disability.

1482 Frostig, Marianne, and Orpet, Russell E. "Four approaches to the
      diagnosis of perceptual disturbances in reading disability." Br J
      Disord Commun 4(1): 41-45, April, 1969. (20 References).
Visual perceptual handicaps can be discovered by tests, but their cause
and their effects on the child's total development can be found only by
further diagnostic procedures. Four points of view from which disabilities in perception can be approached and understood are: (1) psychosocial, or the influence of feelings, attitudes, and emotions on perceptual
functions; (2) neuropsychological, or the relation of structure and function of the brain and nervous system to behavior; (3) developmental, or
appraising the child's level of development and using teaching methods
focusing on the child's developmental status; and (4) functional, or
evaluating the child's level of functioning in the specific abilities involved in discriminating and recognizing stimuli. Examples of types of
the fourth category are given. It is suggested that a combination of
these approaches is necessary for best treatment of an individual case.

1483 Jordan, Brian T., and Jordan, Susan G. "Jordan left-right reversal
      test: a study of visual reversals in children." Child Psychiatry
      Hum Dev 4(3): 178-87, Spring, 1974. (15 References).
Describes a test constructed to standardize measurement of reversals of
letters and numbers by children ages six through ten years. Testing of
2,500 schoolchildren established age-sex norms for symbol reversals. When
the test was administered to a group of children with minimal brain dysfunction, results suggested that the test had adequate ability to diagnose the condition. Results also suggested that reversals are a symptom
of minimal brain dysfunction.

1484 Levinson, Betty Shiela. "Color-form preference in dyslexic chil-
      dren." For a summary see: Diss Abstr Int 34B(11): 5530, May,
      1974.

1485 Lombard, Avima, and Stern, Carolyn. An instrument to measure visual
      discrimination of young children. 1967. 23p. (ED 015 510).

Reports on the University of California at Los Angeles Discrimination
Inventory (VDI), a test of visual discrimination ability which eliminates
the testing of motor skills and eye-hand coordination, often confusing
elements in such tests. Responses are made by selection rather than by
drawing. Figure-ground, form constancy, closure, and position in space
are tested with the use of four subtests totaling fifty-two items. The
hope is expressed that the test will identify children with a variety of
learning disorders, particularly dyslexia.

1486   McDaniel, Ernest. "New film tests of visual perception." Paper
       presented at American Education Research Association annual meet-
       ing, New York, New York, February, 1971. 1971. 9p. (ED 054 201).
Examines a series of motion-picture tests of perceptual abilities in
young children. The rationale and development are considered and preliminary data on the reliability and validity of the tests are presented.

1487   Pontius, A. A. "Dyslexia and specifically distorted drawings of
       the face--a new subgroup with prosopagnosia-like signs." Experientia
       32(11): 1432-35, 1976. (26 References).
Explains the identification of a subgroup of dyslexics identified by the
method which these children used to indicate the forehead, nose, and eyes
in their drawings of the human face. Drawings were considered normal if
the bridge of the nose was depicted as narrowed or indented, the nose began at or below eye level, and there was no direct emerging of the nose
out of the forehead. Abnormal drawings by the dyslexics showed a "neo-
lithic" direct continuation of the forehead into the nose without indenta-
tion, the whole being "flattened out." Such a configuration was seen as
analogous to those visually experienced in prosopagnosia, a form of inability to recognize what is seen, characterized by inability to recognize
the faces of other people or even one's own face. The syndrome may occur
in adults following stroke or brain injury. This is interpreted as the
result of specific early ways of processing what is seen--letters, words,
or facial features--as if they were concrete entities and not abstract
parts. Thus "d," taken as an entity, may be equated with "b," or "N"
with "Z."

1488   Sabatino, David A., and Ysseldyke, James E. "Effect of extraneous
       'background' on visual-perceptual performance of readers and non-
       readers." Percept Mot Skills 35(1): 323-28, August, 1972. (13
       References).
Two groups, readers and nonreaders, were selected from children who had
demonstrated learning disabilities and had been referred for psychological
evaluation. The Bender Visual-motor Gestalt Test was administered in
four different ways to the children. In one of these tests, a meaningless background design was added. The child was asked to disregard the
background and draw only the design in the middle of the card. There
were no differences between the groups on the standard Bender copy or on
the Bender memory test. When the extraneous background pattern was added,
nonreaders' performance decreased significantly.

1489   Shedd, Charles L. "The diagnosis and treatment of symbolic confu-
       sion." In: International Reading Association. Conference proceed-
       ings: changing concepts of reading instruction. Vol. 6. Edited
       by J. Allen Figurel. New York: Scholastic Magazines, 1961. 97-
       102. (8 References).
Unfortunately, research in perceptual difficulties has proceeded along
such specialized lines that data from one area are often ignored by other

researchers. We need to realize that: (1) reading problems come from a
number of causes all leading to a similar state; (2) some are highly correlated with performance in other areas; and (3) reading problems from
varying causes require specific treatment. One such symptom syndrome is
termed "symbolic confusion." This term is to be preferred to others applied to the same general pattern such as "specific language disability,"
"word blindness," "primary retardation," or "dyslexia." It is emphasized
that in symbolic confusion more interest is centered on the interrelation
of variables which constitute a syndrome rather than in specific expression in reading level. The syndrome includes: confusion in right-left
discrimination, field-dependent perception, disturbance in the visual-
motor gestalt function, nonspecific awkwardness, dysrhythmia, dysgraphia,
and spelling difficulties. Tests to determine the child's performance
in each of these fields are described. When remedial techniques are aimed
at specific dysfunctions, a condition is created in which learning can
take place. Realizing that specific symptom syndromes can be related to
specific remedial treatments is one of the most important steps in eliminating reading difficulties.

1490 Swanson, William L. "Strephosymbolia--what can we do about it?"
      J Am Optom Assoc 38(8): 646-53, August, 1967. (9 References).
Lists and explains tests used in the diagnosis of "strephosymbolia," a
term used synonymously with "dyslexia" and other related terms. Tests
for fusion, stereopsis, duction, suppression, visual acuity, dominance,
and visual imagery are explained and their relationship to dyslexia noted.
Reading tests, tests of perceptual forms, vocabulary tests, and tests of
hand-eye coordination are described and their use with dyslexia explained.

1491 Thompson, M. "A pilot instrument of dyslexic-type language diffi-
      culties: the Aston index." Paper presented at International
      Federation of Learning Disabilities, Brussels, Belgium, January
      3-7, 1975. 1975. 7p. (ED 113 873).
The Aston index, an instrument intended for screening young children for
dyslexic-type difficulties, is described. Three forms are available for
testing children at three stages of development. Specific items on the
index which cover different aspects of the problem are evaluated, such
as copying geometrical designs for testing underlying ability; laterality
as an aspect of family history; and visual sequential memory as a test
of performance.

1492 Wilhelm, Rowena. "Evaluating score differences on a visual acuity
      test." Percept Mot Skills 27(2): 419-23, October, 1968. (3
      References).
As a part of diagnostic evaluation of severely disabled readers ages seven
to twenty-one at a university reading clinic, a visual acuity test was
administered under both an unaided (standard) condition, and with an aid
to fixation. The aid to fixation was a pencil held by the examiner next
to the figure being viewed until the subject had identified the figure.
A considerable increase in accuracy was found between the two trials.
This was attributed to a practice effect. However, the aid to fixation
appeared to have even greater effect on the scores than habituation.
Clinical observations reveal that stress impairs the normal ability to
fixate. Results indicate the need for perceptual training for disabled
readers.

3. AUDITORY AND VISUAL DISCRIMINATION

1493 Boder, Elena. "Developmental dyslexia: a diagnostic approach based
      on three atypical reading-spelling patterns." Dev Med Child Neurol
      15(5): 663-87, October, 1973. (42 References).
Identifies three atypical patterns of reading and spelling found in dyslexic children. These patterns are labeled "dysphonetic" (unable to integrate
symbols with their sounds); "dyseidetic" (unable to perceive letters and
whole words as configurations or gestalts); and a combination of both. One
of these patterns is found in all severely retarded readers diagnosed as
having developmental dyslexia. The reading and spelling patterns of these
children remain consistent even after great progress has been made in
reading level. This suggests that the three patterns are diagnostic in
themselves. Each has its own prognosis, and therapy differs for each type.

1494 ————. "Developmental dyslexia: a diagnostic screening pro-
      cedure based on reading and spelling patterns." Acad Ther 4(4):
      285-87, Summer, 1969. (0 References).
Details a diagnostic screening procedure for dyslexia which reveals three
distinct patterns among dyslexic children. Group I includes those who
read globally, that is, seeing words as whole gestalts. Since these children are without phonetic skills they cannot decipher unknown words. They
have auditory deficits which make it difficult for them to associate a
sound with the written symbol. Group II children have visual deficits.
Their spelling errors are phonetic and therefore intelligible, unlike
Group I whose spelling errors are bizarre. Group III has deficits both in
whole-word (gestalt) perception and in phonetic skills. Developmental
dyslexia is seen as a neurodevelopmental disorder.

1495 Bryden, M. P. "Auditory-visual and sequential-spatial matching in
      relation to reading ability." Child Dev 43(3): 824-32, September,
      1972. (10 References).
Sixth-grade students matched for age and IQ were divided into groups of
good and poor readers on the basis of a reading test. Patterns of dots
were presented auditorially and visually. The patterns were paired. Some
pairs were the same, others different. Children were tested individually
and were asked if the dot patterns were the same or different on each
trial. The patterns were presented in three ways: auditory sequences,
visual sequences using flashes of light, and visual-spatial using dot patterns printed on cards. Various combinations of stimuli were presented.
Overall matching-test performance was correlated with reading ability. It
differentiated good from poor readers. Within the group of good readers,
neither IQ nor reading ability was found to be correlated with matching-
test performance. Within the group of poor readers, both IQ and reading
ability were highly correlated with ability to perform the matching tasks.
Matching tasks were found to differ significantly in difficulty.

1496 Golden, Nancy E., and Steiner, Sharon R. "Auditory and visual
      functions in good and poor readers." J Learn Disabil 2(9): 476-
      81, September, 1969. (15 References).
Investigated the relationship between auditory and visual functions and
reading performance. All subjects were in the second grade. Twenty children were divided into ten matched pairs of one good and one poor reader,
each on the basis of mental age, IQ, and chronological age. All IQs were
between 90 and 110 and all the children showed a deviation of approximately one year above or below mental age reading expectancy. Six tests of
auditory and visual ability from the ITPA and the Monroe Visualization
Test were given the children. These tests, five from the ITPA and one

from Monroe, are described. Findings suggest that poor readers were deficient in auditory ability rather than visual. Good readers were significantly superior to poor readers in sound blending, auditory sequential memory, auditory closure, and on the Monroe test. Good readers were
not significantly higher than poor readers in visual sequential memory
and visual closure.

1497 Kris, C. "Simultaneous measurement of binocular EOG and bilateral
        EEG activation patterns in dyslexic children." Electroencephalogr
        Clin Neurophysiol 29(4): 413, October, 1970. (0 References).
Reports on the use of an electrooculograph-encephalograph to measure eye
calibration, eye scanning, and brain-wave activation patterns in children with perceptual and reading difficulties. Results were compared
with findings from matched controls. Results were helpful in determining whether visual, auditory, or a combined method of reading practice
helped to improve the child's work efficiency and performance.

1498 McLeod, John A. "Psychological and psycholinguistic aspects of
        severe reading disability in children: some experimental studies."
        In: Kirk, Samuel A., and McCarthy, Jeanne McRae, eds. Learning
        disabilities: selected ACLD papers. Boston, Massachusetts:
        Houghton Mifflin, 1975. 286-303. (19 References). (Reprinted
        from Association for Children with Learning Disabilities. Confer-
        ence proceedings: an international approach to learning disabili-
        ties of children and youth. Vol. 3. Tulsa, Oklahoma, March 3-5,
        1966. 186-205).
Reports on experiments carried out mostly in Brisbane, Australia, schools
involving twenty-three retarded readers six and one-half to seven years
of age in grade two (grade one, United States equivalent). They were
matched with twenty-three normal readers of the same age, sex, and school.
Normals reproduced letter sequences better than dyslexics, but each group
did progressively better the more nearly the letter groups resembled
English words. A series of tests was carried out to determine characteristics which separated dyslexics from normal readers by measuring various
skills used in reading. Numerous researchers have described a "characteristic pattern" for severe reading disability. In an attempt to evaluate these alleged symptoms, workers at the Remedial Centre in Brisbane
constructed a test called the Dyslexia Schedule. With further refinements, it is hoped that the test can be used to help identify children
who will become dyslexics.

1499 Olson, Arthur V. "The Frostig Developmental Test of Visual Percep-
        tion as a predictor of specific reading abilities with second-grade
        children." Elem Engl 43(8): 869-72, December, 1966. (5 Refer-
        ences).
In a study carried out with second-grade children to determine if the
Frostig Test of Visual Perception predicted specific reading difficulties,
it was found that the test was of little value in predicting the specific
reading abilities tested. These abilities included word recognition,
hearing sounds in words, and visual memory, among others.

1500 Spraings, Violet E. "The dyslexias--a psycho-educational and phys-
        iological approach." In: Tarnopol, Lester, ed. Learning dis-
        abilities: introduction to educational and medical management.
        Springfield, Illinois: Thomas, 1969. 238-55. (31 References).
In our present state of knowledge, unanswered questions about dyslexia
predominate. Terminology is imprecise. Tests included in Spraings'

"Visual perceptual analysis battery" are described. Ways to assess how
a child learns should be considered apart from what he learns. Common
symptoms of the dyslexia syndrome are listed. Types of dyslexia identified are visual, auditory, and a mixture of both. It remains uncertain
whether a fourth type, familial dyslexia, exists.

4. AUDITORY, VISUAL, AND KINESTHETIC DISCRIMINATION

1501 Meehan, Trinita. "An informal modality inventory." <u>Elem Engl</u>
      51(6): 901-4, September, 1974. (0 References).
Children at the fourth-grade level who are having reading problems can
be helped by the Informal Modality Inventory (IMI) which tests visual,
auditory, and other modes of learning. If the child tested does not
score 90 percent in a mode, he or she may have insufficient skill in that
mode to do well in ordinary educational tasks delivered through that mode.

1502 Oliphant, Genevieve Griebel. "A study of factors involved in early
      identification of specific language disability (dyslexia)." For a
      summary see: <u>Diss Abstr Int</u> 31A(1): 305-6, July, 1970.

1503 Richardson, Sylvia O. "Language disorders in children." <u>J Lancet</u>
      85: 516-18, November, 1965. (4 References).
Disorders of language include: (1) dysphasia, the inability to receive
or express spoken symbols; (2) dyslexia, a problem in reception of written symbols; and (3) dysgraphia, a problem in the expression of written
symbols. The process of symbolization is impaired in each. There is a
tendency to regard them as discrete clinical entities and to disregard
the fact that they are all disorders of language. Problems in distinguishing and diagnosing the three conditions are explored. Brain lesions
and gross psychiatric disorders are rare in children. The influence of
environmental factors in producing clinical manifestations is often
ignored. The most urgent need is for early recognition of language disorders in children.

F. PHYSIOLOGICAL CONSIDERATONS

1504 Bahill, A. Terry, and Stark, Lawrence. "Overlapping saccades and
      glissades are produced by fatigue in the saccadic eye movement
      system." <u>Exp Neurol</u> 48(1): 95-106, July, 1975. (33 References).
The short eye movements used in such activities as reading (saccades)
change significantly as the human fatigues and are a sensitive indicator
of fatigue. This study concerns the unusual eye movements of fatigued
persons and seeks to provide insight into variations in accompanying
neuronal firing pattern. Various research uses for eye movements as
measures of general physiological state are suggested. Among these is
discriminating among dyslexic children by their level of resistance to
fatigue for various sized eye movements.

1505 Conners, C. Keith. "Neuro-physiological studies of learning dis-
      orders." <u>Claremont Coll Read Conf Yearb</u> 35: 99-108, 1971. (2
      References).
Test evidence is reported suggesting that in some types--not all--of reading disorder there may be direct involvement of neural structures which
is detectable by the evoked response method. In studies aimed at finding
specific brain dysfunction associated with reading failure and in develop-

ing an orderly classification system of learning disorders, cortical evoked responses (for example, flashes of light or clicks which produce changes in the EEG) and various stimulant drugs were used. While conclusions are tentative, it appears that learning disorders are heterogeneous in origin and arise from various environmental, maturational, and genetic influences. They can be classified in a limited way on the basis of psychological and/or physiological procedures. Some learning disorders respond dramatically to stimulation with drugs and concomitant changes in brain function can be measured directly. Different children respond in different ways to the drugs, however.

1506 Reitan, Ralph M. "Relationships between neurological and psychological variables and their implications for reading instruction." In: Conference on Reading, University of Chicago, 1964. Proceedings: meeting individual differences in reading. Vol. 26. Compiled and edited by H. Alan Robinson. Chicago, Illinois: University of Chicago Press, 1964. 100-110. (0 References). (Supplementary Educational Monographs, No. 94).
Adults with cerebral lesions were given various tests in an effort to obtain information as to whether dyslexia exists independently or is closely related to other aspects of aphasia. The relationship of dyslexia to any group of aphasic symptoms was also investigated. The loss of ability to receive and express the significance of language symbols was found to be usually associated with a lesion of the left cerebral hemisphere, regardless of handedness. The implications of these findings for childhood dyslexia are discussed. The situation is very different for the child with developmental dyslexia who has not once had the language function and then lost it. The causal factors for the child are more complex. Additionally, the deficits in the child may result in maladjustment during formative years. A case history is included of a child who made great gains in reading ability after instruction with a visuospatial training program. The child appeared to have definite brain dysfunction. It appears that detailed diagnosis of the specific disabilities underlying reading retardation is of great importance.

1507 Rønne, Henning. "Congenital word blindness in school children." Trans Ophthalmol Soc UK 56: 311-33, 1936. (0 References).
Children with normal eyes who cannot read may suffer from a weakness in the cerebral center which directs reading. Congenital dyslexia is often unrecognized and undiagnosed. For word-blind children longer words present more difficulties than short ones. The child attempts to guess at words. The mother's reading all school exercises aloud to the child is so typical as to be a symptom in support of the diagnosis. It is not necessary to isolate these children from the regular classroom, but certain special rules should be observed. These are listed. A test to permit comparing the child's reading ability with that of the normal child his age is presented as an aid in diagnosis of dyslexia.

1508 Schain, Richard J. Neurology of childhood learning disorders. Baltimore, Maryland: Williams & Wilkins, 1972. 144p. (Bibliography).
Explores a spectrum of learning disorders, including hyperactivity, minimal brain dysfunction, cerebral palsy, ocular and auditory disorders, and others in addition to developmental dyslexia. Childhood learning disorders are viewed as complex functional disturbances deriving from faulty neurologic organization. A distinction is drawn between these and reactive disturbances in the child brought about by poor rearing or

faulty educational methods. Developmental dyslexia is believed to be caused by genetic factors rather than acquired brain damage. Both older and more current views of the condition are reviewed. It is concluded that most victims of dyslexia can be taught to read and spell adequately under favorable conditions. "Learning disability" is an alternate term for dyslexia. It is acknowledged that the category is controversial. The general management of children with learning disorders is considered. A classification which divides the various learning disorders into diagnostic categories is given. Bibliographies are included with each chapter.

1509   Shelburne, Samuel A., Jr. "Visual evoked responses to language
        stimuli in normal children." Electroencephalogr Clin Neurophysiol
        34(2): 135-43, February, 1973. (6 References).
Twenty normal children ages eight to twelve were presented with groups of three letters—two consonants with a vowel in the middle. The subject's task was to decide whether the letters formed a word. The groups of letters were presented visually one letter at a time. EEG recordings were made during the testing. The evoked response differences appeared to be related to the subject's decision-making after viewing the third letter in each group. Studies using this method, correlating reading ability with objective neurophysiological measurements, are currently being carried out.

1510   Smith, J. Lawton. "Dyslexia and the neuro-ophthalmologist." J
        Fla Med Assoc 55(10): 906-9, October, 1968. (0 References).
Dyslexia must be considered an organic disease until proven otherwise. Poor home environment or a hard life are not related to dyslexia. About 90 percent of the time it is organic. It is related to disease involving the posterior midcerebrum of the dominant hemisphere well over 90 percent of the time. Four areas for examination in diagnosing dyslexia are described. They are: (1) History: (a) take a thorough family and obstetric history; (b) check developmental landmarks; (c) determine if the child has had seizures; and (d) determine handedness. (2) General examination: (a) induce a smile in the child and look for a slight central paralysis, a relative weakness on one side; (b) compare the size of thumbnails (one smaller than the other may indicate a slight one-sided paralysis); (c) spin the child if he is quite young to observe movement of the eyes and other responses; and (d) measure the head circumference. (3) Eye examination: (a) look for optokinetic nystagmus (rapid movement of the eyes induced by looking at a moving object); (b) play the "E" game up through age ten or twelve; (c) check for spasticity of conjugate gaze; and (d) take an external photograph to enable more leisurely inspection of the face. (4) Four helpful tests: (a) an EEG; (b) skull films; (c) physical examination; and (d) a test for syphilis on the mother. The most important test on a child with dyslexia is the one for optokinetic nystagmus. A tape can be moved so that the child watches a parade of pictures while his eye movements are monitored. Movements to look for are described. Examination of these four areas will lead to the discovery of much neurologic disease in dyslexics.

G. PSYCHOLOGICAL EVALUATION

1511   Abrams, Jules C. "A study of certain personality characteristics
        of non-readers and achieving readers." For a summary see: Diss
        Abstr 16(2): 377-78, 1956.

1512   Berman, Bernice Ullman. "Dependency in the preschooler as a pre-
       dictive factor in reading disability." For a summary see: <u>Diss</u>
       <u>Abstr Int</u> 36A(11): 7180, May, 1976.

1513   Connolly, Christopher George. "The psychosocial adjustment of
       children with dyslexia." For a summary see: <u>Diss Abstr</u> 29A(10):
       3456-57, April, 1969.

1514   Flanary, Woodrow. "A study of the possible use of the Wechsler-
       Bellevue scale in diagnosis of reading difficulties of adolescent
       youth." For a summary see: <u>Diss Abstr</u> 14(7): 1045, 1954.

1515   Gordon, Myron H. "A clinical study of personality patterns in
       children with reading disability." For a summary see: <u>Diss Abstr</u>
       13(1): 68-69, 1953.

1516   Griffin, Donald Cassatt. "Constricted-flexible control of attention
       in pupils with and without reading disability." For a summary see:
       <u>Diss Abstr</u> 29A(11): 3873, May, 1969.

1517   Griffiths, Anita N. "Self-concepts of dyslexic children." <u>Acad</u>
       <u>Ther</u> 11(1): 83-90, Fall, 1975. (0 References).
A number of dyslexic children ages six to fourteen years were asked to
rate themselves on a self-concept scale. The thirty-five items of the
scale were read aloud to them. Results showed the children had a desirable self-concept, although considering the home background and intelligence level of the children it was believed that it should have been
better. They liked their names, liked to try new things, and liked to
work with others. The children thought they had plenty of energy and
liked their physical characteristics. Three strong negative traits were
that they believed they were not intelligent, did poorly in school, and
were poor readers. The self-concept scale is reproduced in the article.

1518   Harborth, Martin. "Psycho-linguistics and reading failure." In:
       International Reading Symposium, 3d, Southampton, England, 1967.
       <u>Today's child and learning to read: papers on the modification</u>
       <u>of the school curriculum as a result of recent changes in school</u>
       <u>and home environment</u>. Edited by John Downing, and Amy L. Brown.
       London: Cassell, 1968. 146-63. (0 References).
Describes the use of a psycholinguistic test, the Illinois Test of Psycholinguistic Abilities (ITPA), as a method of diagnosing the strengths and
weaknesses of a child who is failing in reading. "Linguistics" is defined as a language in all its aspects. "Psycholinguistics" is defined
as the study of the psychological development of language at two main
levels: (1) that of interpretation, or meaning; and (2) the level where
habits are formed and retained automatically. A brief outline of the
various subtests on the ITPA is given. Kass' use of this test in diagnosing reading difficulties is discussed.

1519   Lipton, Aaron. "Relating remedial strategies to diagnostic con-
       siderations." <u>Read Teach</u> 23(4): 353-59, January, 1970. (3
       References).
Treatment of reading disabilities depends on how one views the process
of reading. Diagnosis is not once-for-all, but ongoing. Diagnosis of
reading disability and its remediation must consider the whole child in
his position in his family and in his attitudes toward himself, toward
adults, and toward his surroundings. Two case histories of boys whose

reading disabilities appeared to be affected by tensions in their home situations are related.

1520   Macione, Joseph R.   "Psychological correlates of reading disability as defined by the Illinois Test of Psycholinguistic Abilities." For a summary see: <u>Diss Abstr Int</u> 30A(9): 3817-18, March, 1970.

1521   Meyer, George.   "Some relationships between Rorschach scores in kindergarten and reading in the primary grades." <u>J Proj Tech Pers Assess</u> 17(4): 414-25, December, 1953. (4 References).
Presents evidence that Rorschach records may be used to assess first-grade reading readiness and to predict reading achievement in primary grades. Eight Rorschach variables were found to distinguish achieving from retarded readers. These are listed.

1522   Money, John.   "Psychological aspects of reading disability." <u>Trans Pa Acad Ophthalmol Otolaryngol</u> 18: 16-24, Spring, 1965. (0 References).
Discusses the role of psychological testing in specific dyslexia. Testing can be used in two ways: (1) the traditional assessment of personality to discover problems that may have produced symptoms like school failure; and (2) assessment of the dyslexic child's developmental level and impairment or intactness of neuropsychological functions. Tests like the WISC do both. Projective tests like the Rorschach and the Thematic Apperception Test (TAT) assess personality and are useful in uncovering emotional factors that may be powerful influences in the person's life. The difficulties of dyslexics with directional sense and visual memory are considered. Examples are given.

1523   Osburn, Worth J.   "Emotional blocks in reading." <u>Elem Sch J</u> 52(1): 23-30, September, 1951. (0 References).
Emotional blocks in reading arise from interruptions or frustrations. Original or primary factors include lack of adequate auditory discrimination, lack of reading readiness, lack of visual discrimination, previous illness, adverse home conditions, and speech defects. To grant a non-reader a social promotion to the next grade, under the mistaken notion that membership in a fixed social group is all-important, is the cruelest segregation of all. He is <u>in</u> his group but not <u>of</u> it, denied participation. Secondary factors in reading blocks stem from the upset in the home in response to the child's reading failure, arising out of the primary causes. Tertiary factors involve the child's reaction to the unhappy situation in which he finds himself. Techniques of diagnosis and treatment used at the University of Washington clinical services are described. Three methods of treatment used are labeled "encasement," "catharsis," and "psychodrama." Until the problem is diagnosed and treated, it is impossible to teach the child.

1524   Shultis, George Walker.   "Cognitive and personality differences in 'orality' between successful and disabled readers." For a summary see: <u>Diss Abstr</u> 19(8): 2152, February, 1959.

1525   Stavrianos, Bertha K.   "Can projective test measures aid in the detection and differential diagnosis of reading deficit?" <u>J Pers Assess</u> 35(1): 80-91, February, 1971. (20 References).
Comparison of Bender Gestalt, House-Tree-Person, and Rorschach test scores of good and poor readers differentiated between emotional and specific deficits and between organic and nonorganic deficits in poor readers in

most cases in this study. Subjects were 325 socioeconomically advantaged boys ages six to eleven and one-half years.

1526 ————————. "Emotional and organic characteristics in drawings of deficient readers." J Learn Disabil 3(10): 488-501, October, 1970. (11 References).
An attempt was made in this study to identify the emotional patterns typical of children with various specific reading deficits. House-Tree-Person drawings were compared for: (1) normal, good readers; (2) deficient readers with emotional problems; and (3) two groups of poor readers (those with perceptual-motor difficulties with and without neurological signs). Deficit readers produced drawings showing more withdrawn, dependent patterns than good readers. Younger boys of average intelligence with neurological involvement showed the greatest deviation from normal patterns.

H. RESEARCH

1527 Arthur, Grace. "An attempt to sort children with specific reading disability from other non-readers." J Appl Psychol 11(4): 251-63, 1927. (0 References).
A method is needed to separate children who do not learn to read because of emotional factors from those who do not learn in spite of eagerness to learn and normal intelligence. The first group learns readily when adequately motivated. The other group needs teaching suited to specific difficulties. Characteristic of nonreaders in this study was a difference between performance and verbal IQ scores on the Binet scale. In generally dull children this difference did not appear. Nonreaders found abstract words much more difficult to learn than concrete words. Readers did not show this difference. Word lists were compiled containing words of various emotional connotations, for example, colors, physical activities, tastes, geometric shapes, tools, etc. By using these word lists, readers were sorted accurately from true nonreaders. It is suggested that with a larger sample, these tests could be used to distinguish more completely true nonreaders from other children.

1528 Bennett, Annette. "An analysis of errors in word recognition made by retarded readers." J Educ Psychol 33(1): 25-38, January, 1942. (0 References).
The beginnings and endings of words were found to be most frequently used cues in word recognition, with the beginning the dominant cue. Errors in median vowels, i.e., the failure to observe the middles of words, were most common. Word reversals were the next most common error. Subjects were elementary school pupils who were retarded in word recognition. Errors were not haphazard, but appeared to be governed by the context in which the incorrectly identified word appeared, and by bad learning habits of the pupils. One distinct tendency of these pupils was to respond before seeing clearly all parts of the word--beginning, middle, and ending.

1529 Bruininks, Robert H.; Glaman, Gertrude M.; Clark, Charlotte R. "Issues in determining prevalence of reading retardation." Read Teach 27(2): 177-85, November, 1973. (20 References).
Focuses on studies to determine prevalence of reading-retarded children: (1) factors that influence estimates of the proportion of children with reading problems; and (2) approaches to and findings of these studies.

Divergent results have created a confusing picture of the amount of reading retardation in general school populations. Recommendations for improving future studies include suggestions that they employ: (1) more
precise definitions of reading retardation; (2) better techniques for
identifying the population the researcher wishes to study; and (3) improved statistical procedures to avoid skewing the sample or the results.

1530 Calavrezo, C.; Gheorghiţă, N.; Fradis, A. "The detection by error-
     frequency and reading-time analysis of children having reading
     difficulties." Rev Roum Neurol 8(5): 339-44, 1971. (6 Refer-
     ences).
Analyzed the reading errors of eighty first graders and 112 second graders.
Eighteen principal kinds of errors were found when individual reading
tests were given. The most frequent for both classes was on the level
of words. Half as many errors occurred at the level of syntactical unit
composed of one or more words, or a phrase as part of a sentence. The
fewest errors were found on the phoneme level, the phoneme being the
smallest unit of speech used to distinguish sounds, often a single letter
of the alphabet. The most frequent error was substitution of words. A
significant correlation was established between the number of word substitutions and the time it took the child to read the text. Children
were identified as having reading difficulties if they appeared in both
groups: those with the greatest error-frequency and those with the highest reading time.

1531 Denckla, Martha Bridge, and Rudel, Rita G. "Rapid 'automatized'
     naming (R.A.N.): dyslexia differentiated from other learning dis-
     abilities." Neuropsychologia 14(4): 471-79, 1976. (33 Refer-
     ences).
Describes tests which differentiated dyslexic children not only from
normal controls but also from learning-disabled children who were not
dyslexic. Subjects were four groups of normal children ages seven, eight,
nine, and ten years, and four groups of learning-disabled children the
same ages. IQs were above 90. The children were divided into dyslexic
and nondyslexic groups post hoc by determining the difference between
reading age and mental age. The children were asked to read rapidly and
repetitively charts containing colors, numerals, letters, or pictures of
commonly used objects. Errors were rare, and analysis of data was done
on the basis of differences in speed of naming the materials presented.
Letters and numbers were easier for all of the children to name than
were colors. Objects were named slowest of all. A deficit in automatization of verbal responses to visual stimuli, not restricted to numbers
and letters, correlated specifically with dyslexia. On all four types of
stimuli dyslexics were slowest, learning-disabled children who were not
dyslexic were in the middle, and normal children responded fastest. It
is not believed that this result reflects a general slowing of reaction
time.

1532 Elenbogen, Elaine, and Simmons, Benita. "Diagnosis and remediation
     of potential reading failure: a modality approach." Ill Sch Res
     9(2): 46-50, 1972.

1533 Feshbach, Seymour; Adelman, Howard; Fuller, Williamson W. "Early
     identification of children with high risk of reading failure." J
     Learn Disabil 7(10): 639-44, December, 1974. (6 References).
Compares two methods of predicting reading failure in kindergarten-age
children. One method emphasizes psychometric testing to assess linguistic

and perceptual-motor skills related to reading. The other method is
based on the kindergarten teacher's evaluation of the child's skills and
behavior. In a study of more than 800 kindergarteners, the WPPSI, the
Otis-Lennon group intelligence test, and the De Hirsch Predictive Index
of Reading Failure were compared with teacher ratings of the same group
of children using an instrument called the Student Rating Scale. Preliminary results indicated that the rating scale was at least as efficient as the psychometric battery in early identification of reading
failure.

1534 Fradis, A., and Gheorghiță, Natalia. "Complex investigation for
      differentiation of primary from secondary dyslexia in children."
      Rev Roum Med 12(6): 387-92, 1974. (10 References).
Reports an attempt to differentiate primary from secondary dyslexia as
defined by Rabinovitch on the basis of medical and psychological data.
Thirty dyslexic children in second through fourth parallel classes in
elementary school were given oral reading tests and the types of errors
noted. All were given a medical examination, including an EEG, and the
WISC Pedagogical Questionnaires were filled out by the children's teachers. Parents were asked for cooperation in filling out a questionnaire
concerning the child's family relations and behavior outside of school.
Left-handedness in a child or in a member of his family was noted in
only three cases. It was concluded that on the basis of these data, primary and secondary dyslexia could be distinguised. Sixteen of the children were diagnosed as having the primary form which reflects a neurological dysfunction in the absence of cerebral lesions. The remaining
fourteen appeared to have secondary dyslexia caused by the existence of
psychological problems, reduced level of intelligence, adverse family
conditions, lack of motivation, etc.

1535 Fuller, Gerald B. "Perceptual-motor characteristics of dyslexia
      and their theoretical implications." Proc Am Psychol Assoc 76,
      3: 587-88, 1968. (7 References).
Considers the theoretical implications of the research finding that the
Minnesota Percepto-Diagnostic (MPD) Test differentiates good readers from
those with two types of reading retardation (secondary and organic) but
does not differentiate good readers from those with primary reading retardation. Division of poor readers according to cause into primary,
secondary, and organic classifications follows the classification method
used by Rabinovitch, et al. The MPD Test measures perceptual stability
by measuring the child's perception of the number of degrees the figures
are rotated from their original axes. It is pointed out that in the
child with primary reading retardation the problems are associative rather
than perceptual. The word or letter form is perceived but the symbolic
significance is not grasped. He sees the words or letters correctly in
their spatial orientation, but cannot deal with them as symbols. The
result is lowered ability to associate them in a way that will furnish
meaning to a sentence. This type of child will not profit from reading
instruction that emphasizes perceptual training from reading instruction
that emphasizes perceptual training stressing figure-ground relationship
and spatial orientation. Secondary reading retardation is diagnosed where
a child's capacity to read is intact, but he does not achieve because of
a basic disturbance in emotional life. He appears to be less aware of
surrounding stimuli. He is affected by figure-ground combinations and
the number and kind of cues available. He perceives considerable rotation on the MPD Test. The child with organic brain damage perceives the
most rotation. Since too many peripheral cues are taken in, it is almost

impossible for him to distinguish the relevant cues. It is suggested
that the organically poor reader needs help in learning to distinguish
figure from ground by emphasizing the important figure.

1536 Hartlage, Patricia L., and Hartlage, Lawrence C. "A comparison of
      the pediatric history and pediatric neurological examination in the
      differential diagnosis of learning disabilities." Pediatr Res
      7(4): 295, April, 1973. (0 References).
Investigates the absolute and relative amounts contributed by the pediatric history and the pediatric neurologic examination in making the differential diagnosis of common types of learning disabilities. One hundred children were studied: forty-three with minimal cerebral dysfunction
(MCD), twenty with dyslexia, eleven of dull normal intelligence, and
seventeen with emotional disturbance. In 70 percent of the MCD children
there were abnormalities in the history; 88 percent showed abnormalities
in the neurological examination. Dyslexics showed no abnormal pediatric
history. Nearly 60 percent showed soft neurological signs, but these
were right-left confusions rather than motor system abnormalities. The
dull-normals were free of neurological problems, but developmental histories were significant in most cases. Neither source contributed in
diagnosing emotional disturbances. False negatives in both history and
neurological examination were most likely to occur in dyslexics and emotionally disturbed children.

1537 Holt-Hansen, Kristian. "A new method of investigating symptoms of
      dyslexia." Int Rev Appl Psychol 17(1): 33-49, 1968. (24 Refer-
      ences).
Demonstrated how symptoms of dyslexia can be produced regularly in dyslexic subjects. This study was part of a larger project aimed at finding
new ways of diagnosing dyslexia. The Hering illusion, a figure made up
of lines radiating from a center intersected by two parallel vertical
lines, was used. For purposes of this study, a circular area was cut
from the center of the Hering illusion figure and vertical rows of "b's"
and "d's" were inserted in one figure. In another figure similar rows
of "og's" and "go's" were inserted. These letters were in the place of
the central portions of the two vertical parallel lines. Subjects were
seated in an optical box. Stroboscopic light flashes were used. The
forty-five subjects were both male and female adults as well as children.
Some were dyslexic, some were normal readers. Intelligence levels were
approximately the same. Subjects usually experience movement in the
figure, with the two vertical lines swinging toward and away from each
other, like two strings. Dyslexic subjects experienced reversal of the
letters "b" and "d" as the lines oscillated. Normal readers observed
the letters appearing to move with the lines, but experienced no reversals.
A similar result was obtained with "og" and "go"; dyslexics experiencing
inversion as the letters changed place during the swinging movement of
the lines. Also described are a number of variations of these experiments. Results are discussed in terms of psychological investigations
of perception. It is concluded that a particular determining feature of
the function of the brain must exist in dyslexics. The difficulties
arise where remedial reading classes include children suffering from reading problems from many causes in addition to constitutional dyslexia.

1538 Jack, W. H., and Hebert, Barbara Hatch. "Delayed auditory feedback
      with dyslexics." J Educ Res 68(9): 338-40, May-June, 1975. (8
      References).

Tested the hypothesis that the differences in performance between direct auditory feedback and delayed auditory feedback (DAF) would be greater for ten normal college students than for five dyslexic college students. Results did not support the theory. The normal and dyslexic readers were given the Minnesota Test for Differential Diagnosis of Aphasia. All were asked to read a paragraph under direct auditory feedback conditions, and then to read the same paragraph under DAF conditions. Earphones were used and the delay used was 120 msec. The average difference in performance between direct and delayed auditory feedback was 9.0 errors for dyslexics and only 2.2 errors for normals. DAF is seen as a good test for the diagnosis of dyslexia, inasmuch as the effect of DAF was to magnify differences in performance between dyslexics and normals.

1539 "The learned ape." Newsweek 78(17): 78, October 25, 1971. (0 References).
Describes experiments with apes in which the animals demonstrated that they were capable of cross modal integration. They were able to look at objects, or photographs of objects, and identify the same object by touch. It is suggested that the technique used with apes will prove useful in the early diagnosis of dyslexic children if dyslexia is caused, as some researchers believe, by the child's inability to link information obtained by different senses, that is, to achieve cross modal integration. Studies in the area are planned.

1540 McAllister, James Maurice. "An analytical study of reading deficiencies of junior high school pupils." University of Chicago Abstracts of Theses, Humanistic Series 7: 117-24, 1930.

1541 McLeod, J. "A comparison of WISC sub-test scores of pre-adolescent successful and unsuccessful readers." Aust J Psychol 17(3): 220-28, December, 1965. (15 References).
Compares the scores on eleven WISC subtests for 177 successful and 116 backward readers, average age twelve and one-half years. When adjustments were made for differences in performance IQ, the retarded readers scored significantly lower than the successful readers on all verbal subtests. When differences were adjusted in verbal IQ or full-scale IQ the retarded group scored significantly lower than successful readers on Information, Vocabulary, Arithmetic, Digit Span, and Coding subtests. Retarded readers scored significantly higher than good readers on the Picture Completion subtest. Findings seem to support the hypothesis that successful readers can be differentiated from retarded readers by subtests which are essentially verbal in nature.

1542 Maxwell, A. E. "The WPPSI: a marked discrepancy in the correlations of the subtests for good and poor readers." Br J Math Stat Psychol 25(2): 283-91, November, 1972. (7 References).
This attempt to explain the difference in correlations between subtests of the Wechsler Pre-School and Primary Scale of Intelligence (WPPSI) concludes that the test is a predictor of reading ability. It was discovered by chance in the course of other research that WPPSI subtest scores for a group of children, average age five years, five months, showed a marked and consistent correlation with a test of reading ability given when the children were about seven years of age. Mean scores for the ten subtests for good readers consistently exceeded mean subtest scores for poor readers, while standard deviations for the two were comparable. Good readers, in the light of this finding, are seen as "brighter" than poor readers. But the most interesting point is the marked discrepancy between the two

correlation matrices. The whole WPPSI is seen as a good predictor of
reading ability, but it is suggested that subtest scores be used as well.

1543 Muehl, Siegmar, and Forell, Elizabeth R. "A followup study of dis-
      abled readers: variables related to high school reading perfor-
      mance." Read Res Q 9(1): 110-23, 1973/1974. (22 References).
A follow-up report for forty-three disabled readers revealed that if they
were poor readers in elementary and junior high school they continued to
be poor readers five years or more after diagnosis. EEG classification
at diagnosis and high school reading skill were not related. Early diagnosis was associated with improved reading performance, regardless of
the amount of remedial help given.

1544 Ramig, Christopher J. "The Reading Miscue Inventory. A promising
      approach to diagnosis of the reading-disabled." Clin Pediatr
      14(4): 326-34, April, 1975. (6 References).
Analyzes the reading process in terms of what are called (1) graphic cues,
or the writing system; (2) syntactic cues, or language-based cues; and
(3) semantic cues, or word meaning. Reading requires competency in using
these cue systems. The Reading Miscue Inventory is helpful in diagnosing
reading problems. The student reads orally. The examiner notes his
errors, or "miscues." Not all miscues are considered equal. The variety
and quality of errors as shown by the reader's use of the three kinds of
cues are determined. From this the reader's strengths and weaknesses in
reading are determined. Questions used to analyze the miscues are included.

1545 Robeck, Mildred C. "Identifying and preventing reading disabili-
      ties." In: Wilson, John A. R., ed. Diagnosis of learning dif-
      ficulties. New York: McGraw-Hill, 1971. 157-88. (0 References).
Covers three topics: (1) the intellectual characteristics of failing
readers; (2) a procedure for using WISC subtests for individual diagnosis
of reading problems; and (3) some problems faced in developing a program
for preventing reading difficulty. In general, pupils who were in a
reading clinic because of difficulty in learning to read made low scores
on Information, Arithmetic, Digit Span, and Coding WISC subtests. Since
WISC subtest scores must be considered in relation to general intellectual
ability, the factor of general intelligence must be eliminated, that is,
compensated for, before the subtest pattern of an individual child can
be used to diagnose his reading disability. Results are presented of
studies on groups of disabled readers in a clinic population. WISC subtest patterns for children with decoding problems but no emotional problem and patterns for children in whom the chief cause of reading disability appeared to be tension were found to be very similar. The pattern
of strengths and weaknesses was also found to be similar in disabled
readers at ages seven and one-half and at thirteen and one-half to seventeen years. Children with high IQs (121 to 145) who were disabled readers also showed subtest patterns similar to poor readers of average intelligence when the difference in general intelligence had been accounted
for. Implications of the findings are evaluated. Preventing reading
difficulties and critical abilities for learning to read are considered.

1546 ————. "Readers who lacked word analysis skills: a group diag-
      nosis." J Educ Res 56(8): 432-34, April, 1963. (3 References).
Chief contributing causes suspected for the reading problems of children
enrolled in a reading clinic because of difficulty in word-attack skill
(ability to "sound out" a familiar word) were found to be minimum entrance
age and poor auditory and visual memories.

1547   Rutter, Michael, and Yule, William. "The concept of specific read-
       ing retardation." J Child Psychol Psychiatry 16(3): 181-97,
       July, 1975. (41 References).
Much of the chaos and confusion in the terminology referring to reading
difficulties stems, not alone from vagueness and loose use of words, but
from fundamental disputes about the nature of reading problems. The controversy continues as to whether dyslexia really exists. To test whether
a distinction can be drawn between general reading backwardness (reading
below average for age, regardless of IQ), and specific reading retardation (a disability in reading relative to the child's age and general
intellectual level--underachievement), data on intelligence and reading
ability for large numbers of nine- to eleven-year-old children were
analyzed. Children identified as those with specific reading retardation
were systematically compared with children showing general reading backwardness alone. WISC scores for those with reading backwardness averaged
80; for those with specific retardation the average was 102.5. This was
expected from the definition. It is concluded that the traditional distinction between these two groups is valid. Specific reading retardation
is more than just the lower end of a normal distribution. Its frequency
exceeds that predicted on statistical grounds. Reading retardation is
shown to differ significantly from reading backwardness in terms of sex
ratio, neurological disorder, pattern of neurodevelopmental deficits, and
educational prognosis. Evidence is discussed which shows that these findings do not support the view of a genetically distinct syndrome of dyslexia.

1548   Satz, Paul, et al. Some predictive antecedents of specific read-
       ing disability: a two-, three-, and four-year follow-up. Hyman
       Blumberg Symposium on Research in Early Childhood Education, Johns
       Hopkins University, 1974. 1974. 54p. (ED 101 298).
Focuses on the degree to which a developmental-neuropsychological test
battery predicted future reading achievement while children are in kindergarten. An unselected group of white kindergarten boys was given the
test. Their reading progress was assessed at the end of grades one, two,
and three. The test battery was found to be highly predictive of the
child's reading progress, especially for those children who became either
superior or severely disabled readers. Findings support the validity and
utility of early detection of reading problems, economically, before the
child begins formal reading instruction. The purposes of the project were
to: (1) test a theory which was said to identify antecedents which predicted developmental dyslexia several years before the disorder is
clinically evident; and (2) evaluate the factors thought to underlie the
disorder and influence changes in it as it develops.

1549   Sklar, B.; Hanley, J.; Simmons, W. W. "An EEG experiment aimed
       toward identifying dyslexic children." Nature 240(5381): 414-16,
       December 15, 1972. (4 References).
Electroencephalograms were made on twelve Caucasian dyslexic children and
on normal controls matched for age and sex. The age range was seven to
eighteen years. All but two of each group were boys. The purposes were
to: (1) search for features identifying dyslexic children; (2) demonstrate the statistical significance of any such features; and (3) begin
the compilation of data which could ultimately result in a reliable way
to detect reading disabilities early. Results suggest that EEG spectra
for dyslexic children have some prominent differences from those of normal
children. The most recurring of these is higher theta-band activity and,
during mental tasks, higher coherence between regions in the same hemi-

sphere. EEGs were monitored during eyes-closed rest, eyes-open attention, performing mental arithmetic, reading word lists, and reading text.

1550   Stank, Peggy L., and Hayes, Robert B. An investigation of the ef-
       fects of a diagnostic prescriptive kindergarten program on the
       predicted reading levels of children identified as potential read-
       ing failures. Final report. 1972. 100p. (ED 069 435).
Evaluates the effect of a diagnostic structured kindergarten program on predicted reading levels of children from low-income areas. Results were compared with a traditional kindergarten program. The Jansky Predictive Index of Reading Performance and the ITPA were used in establishing criteria and in diagnosis. Results indicate that the diagnostic program was superior to the traditional program.

1551   Wagner, Rudolph F. "Symbolization deficits in dyslexic conditions."
       Acad Ther 6(4): 359-65, Summer, 1971. (3 References).
Defines symbolization as the ability to abstract meaningful information from concrete situations, not necessarily semantically, but at higher cognitive levels. The level of symbolization is one aspect of reading and distinguishes the dyslexic from the normal reader. To test the role of symbolization in reading, four groups were formed: normal and dyslexic children ages eight to twelve years, and normal and dyslexic adolescents ages fourteen to eighteen years. The groups were compared on the basis of performance on the Kahn Test of Symbol Arrangement. Responses of dys-lexics were generally more concrete symbolizations than those of normal subjects. The scoring categories of the Kahn test are given. The Kahn test is suggested as a useful adjunct tool for diagnosis.

1552   Ward, Byron J. "Two measures of reading readiness and first grade
       reading achievement." Read Teach 23(7): 637-39, April, 1970.
       (1 Reference).
Compares kindergarten pupils' scores on the Coding subtest of the WISC and their total scores on the Murphy-Durrell Reading Readiness Test to their achievement in reading at the end of the first grade as measured by the Stanford Achievement Test. Both the Coding subtest and the Murphy-Durrell Test are reading readiness measures. It was reasoned that if the Coding subtest proved to be a better predictor of reading failure than the Murphy-Durrell, further studies could be undertaken to investigate the feasibility of using the single Coding score as a predictor of first-grade reading achievement to help identify probable reading failures prior to grade one. The two tests were given to 500 kindergarten pupils in a public school. The Stanford test was given at the end of their first grade year to those still attending school in the same system. Com-plete data were obtained on 278 children. It was found that the total Murphy-Durrell Test score had a significantly higher degree of relation-ship to the Stanford results than did the WISC Coding subtest score. It is concluded that using the Coding subtest alone would not be preferable to using the Murphy-Durrell for predicting first-grade reading achievement.

VII
Treatment

A. COMPREHENSIVE CONSIDERATIONS

1553   Allen, James E., Jr. "The right to read--challenge for local leader-
      ship." Paper presented at the annual civic dinner of the Citizens
      Schools Committee, Chicago, Illinois, October 3, 1969. 1969. 11p.
      (ED 034 665).
One of the priorities for our schools should be to help the estimated ten
million American children who have reading difficulties. Teachers should
strive for more results and should be goal-conscious. They should be less
secretive about their program results. To be a success, the right-to-
read effort must come from the grass roots.

1554   ————. "The right to read: the role of the volunteer." Paper
      presented at the conference, The Right to Read: the Role of the
      Volunteer, Washington Technical Institute, Washington, D.C., March
      30, 1970. 1970. 10p. (ED 039 113).
Volunteers are needed in the effort to eliminate reading failure in the
United States. They can provide the person-to-person help that means
success for the right-to-read program.

1555   Anderson, Robert P. The child with learning disabilities and guid-
      ance. Boston, Massachusetts: Houghton Mifflin, 1970. 83p.
      (Bibliography). (Guidance Monograph Series. Series 5: Guidance
      and the Exceptional Student).
Uses "dyslexia" interchangeably with "learning disability" and numerous
other terms to describe the child of normal intelligence and adequate
educational opportunity who does not learn normally in school. A general
overview of the problem is given with consideration of medical, emotional,
and neurological aspects. Ways to diagnose and evaluate the condition
and the role of the school counselor in dealing with LD children are discussed. Remedial programs and vocational planning for dyslexic individuals are presented.

1556   Artley, A. Sterl, and Hardin, Veralee B. "A current dilemma: read-
       ing disability or learning disability?" <u>Read Teach</u> 29(4): 361-
       66, January, 1976. (19 References).
Concern for the reading-handicapped child was underway in the 1930s. In
the 1930s and 1940s no distinction was made between learning and reading
disabilities. In the 1960s researchers began to make the distinction.
To do so is very difficult. Definitions of each are given. The plea is
made for those working in the field to drop the labels, forget their
vested interests in one program or another, and see that the child with
an educational problem receives treatment. The teacher to whom the child
is referred should be able to diagnose and treat the difficulty no matter
what the child's learning needs.

1557   Askew, Jewell. "The fellow with reading difficulties really needs
       a friend." <u>Tex Outlook</u> 35(11): 20-21, November, 1951. (0 Ref-
       erences).
Describes the work of the Houston (Texas) Reading Clinic. The Fernald
method of tracing words is used in some cases. Children with reading
difficulties deeply feel the stigma placed on them and need help in overcoming their reading problems and the accompanying frustrations.

1558   Balow, Bruce. "The long-term effect of remedial reading instruc-
       tion." <u>Read Teach</u> 18(7): 581-86, April, 1965. (5 References).
This study reports that under remedial instruction, groups of disabled
readers who had been progressing at half the normal class rate were able
to increase their progress to many times the normal class rate. After
intensive remedial instruction ceased, those who had no further help did
not lose their new skills, but they did not continue to progress. With
some additional supportive assistance the other subjects continued at a
pace faster than their rate before remedial treatment--about 75 percent
of normal growth. The conclusion is that severe reading disability is a
chronic condition requiring long-term remediation.

1559   Bannatyne, Alex D. "The slow developer." <u>Acad Ther</u> 5(4): 255-57,
       Summer, 1970. (12 References).
The slow developer will almost never catch up by himself. Early detection and treatment of dyslexia is most important. Screening during kindergarten or early in first grade is ideal. If no specialist is available, the teacher faced with a dyslexic pupil should inform herself on
remedial methods and their application. Various possible deficits of
dyslexia are mentioned.

1560   Barsch, Ray H., and Bryant, N. Dale. <u>A symposium on the education
       of children with learning disabilities</u>. Rutgers, the State Uni-
       versity, April 29, 1966. [Title supplied]. 1966. 33p. (ED 014
       176).
Surveys the problem of classifying children in educational programs for
special learning disabilities, and discusses the major areas of knowledge
necessary for the diagnosis and treatment of learning disorders. The
dyslexic child is used as an example of learning disability. Principles
that should be followed in treating the dyslexic include starting with
the most basic element with which the child has trouble and making learning steps small enough to avoid confusion and negative learning.

1561   Benton, Curtis D., Jr. "Ophthalmologists recommend less emphasis
       on the eyes in learning disorders." <u>J Learn Disabil</u> 3(10): 536-
       38, October, 1970. (0 References).

Speaking for a group of ophthalmologists, Benton states that remediation
of dyslexia is primarily a task for educators. The value of perceptual
motor training for dyslexia is unproved. An interdisciplinary approach
is recommended and eye care should not be treated in isolation in dyslexics. Eye dominance has nothing to do with dyslexia. More educational
research is needed in the area. Children with reading disabilities should
be removed from the regular teaching methods and given special instruction. It has been found that almost any type of program for dyslexic
children results in improvement because increased work output results
from almost any type of environmental change. This is known as the
Hawthorne effect.

1562 Betts, Emmett Albert. "Reappraisal with reference to analysis of
      reading disabilities." Educ Method 15(6): 305-7, March, 1936.
      (0 References).
One important area of change in educational methods has been in dealing
with the disabled reader. Large numbers of researchers have been at work
on the problem and a great range of problems associated with reading has
been studied. Speculative issues such as eye dominance, eidetic imagery,
and others have not been resolved. But valuable techniques for research
and analysis of the problem have been developed. Certain corrective measures have been established.

1563 ————. "Remedial and corrective reading: content area approach."
      Education 68(10): 579-96, June, 1948. (34 References).
Intensive research during the last generation has increased our knowledge
of reading problems, though much is still to be learned. We now know
more of the reasons boys have more difficulty with reading than girls.
We also know that nonreaders or retarded readers are likely to be of
normal or superior intelligence. We know more about the sequence of development of language. Adequate teaching materials and teaching techniques are available. To rid our schools of nonreaders and retarded
readers we need only "the perseverance, ceaseless toil, vision, and the
will to do it."

1564 Birch, J. "Specific reading disabilities; their diagnosis and
      correction." In: Conference on Reading. University of Pittsburgh.
      Report 1960. 67-74.

1565 Bond, George W. "Meeting the needs of children with reading dis-
      abilities." Educ Adm Super 38(1): 33-41, January, 1952. (7
      Bibliographic Footnotes).
Recommends methods for preventing reading disability. Conclusions are
based on findings in a follow-up study of children who had been back in
the regular classroom for one to four years after receiving a series of
individual remedial lessons under the guidance of a teacher in a university reading clinic. Three approaches to preventive measures are recommended: school administration, the classroom, and several cooperating
social agencies. Early detection, visual screening, and frequent instruction are recommended; children receiving remedial help three or more
times a week made better gains. Children with speech defects did not
make significant gains in reading in this study. Help with speech correction should be available. Ways to cope with various problems encountered
in retarded readers are explained.

1566 Boutillier, Jessie W. "Some fallacies in remedial reading programs."
      Engl J 30(7): 581-84, September, 1941. (0 References).

Four fallacies may hinder remedial reading programs: (1) that overcoming visual handicaps will overcome a dislike for reading; (2) that poor school work indicates a reading disability; (3) that poor reading ability indicates low intelligence; and (4) that teaching a child to read will make him a good student.

1567 Bryant, N. Dale. "The child who doesn't fit--the clinical referral."
      In: Reading Conference, Syracuse University. Proceedings: read-
      ing: practice and perspective. 7th-8th, 1965-1966. Edited by
      Frank P. Greene; E. Coston Frederick; Robert A. Palmatier. Syracuse,
      New York: The Division of the Summer Sessions, Syracuse University,
      1967. 27-32. (0 References).
Whether the child's problems are emotional or neurological, referral to
a reading clinic should be used to gain an understanding of what the
child can and cannot do. It is then necessary for the teacher to work
with both the child and the clinic to enlarge that understanding and to
apply findings to the child. Clinical referral should never be used
simply to get rid of the child.

1568 Carter, Homer L. J., and McGinnis, Dorothy J. Diagnosis and treat-
      ment of the disabled reader. New York: Macmillan, 1970. 370p.
      (Bibliography).
The purpose of the book is to aid teachers in identifying disabled readers
who can be helped in the regular classroom; those who need temporary
therapy; and those who must have clinical study. Ways to make these
judgments are explained. Two approaches to reading problems are explored:
clinical, in which the whole individual is studied in a search for causes
underlying the reading failure; and corrective, in which the problem of
reading needs alone is attacked. Diagnosis and treatment of various
problems are covered, including orientation and vocabulary problems, and
difficulties in reading for meaning. How to appraise the success of
remediation and how to prevent reading problems are considered. A glossary is included.

1569 Cebulash, Mel. "The right to read--an editor's point of view."
      Paper presented at the International Reading Association Conference,
      Anaheim, California, May 6-9, 1970. 1970. 4p. (ED 043 455).
Junior high and high school students who read below the fourth-grade
level must be identified and treated. Their reading disabilities must
be corrected through motivation and skill-building. Scholastic Magazine's
ninety-day multimedia program for reading-disabled students is described.

1570 Černý, Luděk. "Experience in the reeducation of children with dys-
      lexia in Czechoslovakia." Int J Ment Health 4(4): 113-22, Winter,
      1975/76. (3 References).
Describes the program in Czechoslovakia for teaching dyslexic children.
True systematic care began in 1952 when a program was initiated at a
children's psychiatric hospital. A four-level program is used to deal
with dyslexia: (1) In the least serious cases the teacher works directly
with the parents. (2) In more serious cases an outpatient program from
child psychiatric services and counseling centers directs practical
exercises and instructs the parents. These centers also diagnose dyslexia. (3) In cases so serious that the child cannot keep up in regular
school, he attends special classes. (4) In the most serious cases the
child may be admitted to a children's psychiatric hospital specially
equipped to handle dyslexia cases. Results are given of a fifteen-year
follow-up study of dyslexic children.

1571 Chilton, Thomas H. "Dyslexia." Science 173(3993): 190, July 16, 1971. (0 References).
Letter to editor. Comments on a suggestion that the syllable might be a suitable means with which to introduce reading. It is pointed out that Noah Webster used nothing but syllables in the first few reading lessons in his Blue-Backed Speller nearly 150 years ago. Only later did he combine them into words.

1572 Clarke, Louise. Can't read, can't write, can't takl too good either; how to recognize and overcome dyslexia in your child. New York: Walker, 1973. 280p.
This book is a mother's story of the reading of her severely dyslexic son. The book spans an eighteen-year period. Her highly personal account tells how she shrugged off the little boy's jargon speech, sure he would outgrow it. She recounts his struggles to learn and his fight for acceptance by his peers and teachers in elementary school, high school, and college. Described are many teaching and remedial techniques which the author encountered in exploring various avenues of help for her son. Several schools and specialists in the field of learning disability in the New York City area who dealt with the boy are mentioned by name, and the work of a number of special-education groups is described. Suggestions are offered for parents. The hope is expressed that help for dyslexics will become increasingly available.

1573 Clowes, Helen Coe. "Measures which can be used in kindergartens to prevent reading disability cases." Child Educ 6(10): 452-57, June, 1930. (0 References).
Describes the methods and procedures used in a reading clinic to prevent the development of reading disabilities. If unified programs of prevention were carried out from kindergarten through primary school many problems in reading would be avoided. Thorough physical examinations and checks of vision should be made. Reliable mental tests should make sure the child is mentally mature enough to discriminate among letter shapes. The child must have an adequate verbal vocabulary before beginning reading instruction. Other characteristics of reading-disabled children are a dislike of books; ignoring the printed story in books altogether; and a lack of belief in their own ability to learn. Suggestions for combating these are given.

1574 ─────. "The reading clinic." Elem Engl Rev 7(4): 98-100, 111, April, 1930. (0 References). Same, Educ Res Bull 9(10): 261-68, May 14, 1930.
Details the methods employed at the reading clinic of the School of Education of Western Reserve University at the time of its establishment in 1929. All the children were given physical and eye examinations. A social worker visited homes in order to discover social and personality maladjustments. Diagnostic reading tests were given. The all-sided view of reading problems obtained by the college students working with the children who were clinic patients produced teachers able to cope with many reading problems as they occur in the classroom.

1575 Cohen, S. Alan. "Cause vs. treatment in reading achievement." J Learn Disabil 3(3): 163-66, March, 1970. (18 References).
Written in rebuttal of earlier criticism, this paper reiterates the belief that in most cases diagnostic efforts aimed at finding the cause of a reading disability are useless and unnecessary. A better approach is to begin intensive instruction, taking the child's behavior as it is. Great

effort to rebuild basic concepts of spatial perception (schemata) is not necessary.

1576 ─────. "Minimal brain dysfunction and practical matters such as teaching kids to read." Ann NY Acad Sci 205: 251-61, February 28, 1973. (23 References).
Clinical labels such as "minimal brain dysfunction" and "dyslexia" and other perceptual or neurological designations are useless. The difference between a learning-disabled child and a normal one is his learning behavior, not his neurology. The cause of the child's learning problem is usually irrelevant to teaching him to read. Certain laws of learning dealing with stimulus control and reinforcement are more effective than theories of development. The major conclusions of research in child development rarely have practical implications for remediation of learning disabilities. Since classroom teachers and remediation specialists cannot bear to face their own failures, they look elsewhere for explanations. If strong teaching methods were used, most learning-disabled children would be reading and writing adequately. We have not used existing pedagogical knowledge. Why resort to drugs and perceptual motor training before we have exhausted pedagogical remedies?

1577 "The controversy about dyslexia." Educ Dig 34(1): 51-53, September, 1968. (0 References).
"Dyslexia" is the most difficult and controversial word in reading today. It is proclaimed by its proponents as a physiological impairment rather than a simple intellectual failure to learn. The work of Orton is explained, and the viewpoint of his critics set forth. The Doman-Delacato theories concerning development of the central nervous system are explained and their skeptics' views given. Those who refuse to accept the theory of dyslexia are nevertheless concerned about nonreaders, and their techniques differ little from those used in dyslexia clinics. The article asks whether it really matters if the dyslexia theory is validated. The important concern is that these children get help.

1578 Crump, C. Wiegal. "Dyslexia." Ann Ophthalmol 5(8): 839-40, August, 1973. (0 References).
Learning disability and dyslexia demand a multidisciplinary approach. The importance of the problem has generated a large number of diagnostic and remedial procedures. In spite of this groping, important research has been done, but different disciplines are working in isolation. Dyslexic children have no more eye problems than do normal children. A neurological basis for dyslexia has not been proved. Ophthalmic therapy has no value in the treatment of dyslexics beyond correcting ocular defects. Remedial education remains the province of trained learning-disability therapists.

1579 Cutts, Warren G. A model program for remedial reading. n.d. 22p. (ED 001 724).
Provides general guidelines for a remedial reading program. The distinction is made between corrective reading instruction given in the regular classroom, and remedial reading instruction given by a special instructor outside the classroom. A model reading center is described.

1580 Deadman, Ronald. "Backward readers." New Statesman 72(1868): 962-63, December 30, 1966. (0 References).
Most children who do not learn to read satisfactorily suffer from poor teaching. Only a small percentage of backward readers have neurological

disorders; dyslexia or word blindness is only an excuse in most cases. The most important thing a beginning reader needs is a willing listener. A mother or a sympathetic teacher is needed to help the beginner over the hurdles. How children learn to read is a mystery; nobody can define the psychological process. Nobody can remember just how the accident of learning to read happened to him. Perhaps the ITA works as well as it does as a teaching aid for reading because it drives teachers back over long-hidden paths through a new learning process which makes them more patient with the children.

1581   Dechant, Emerald V., ed.   Detection and correction of reading difficulties; readings with commentary.   New York: Appleton-Century-Crofts, 1971. 411p. (Bibliographical References).
A collection of forty-two articles reprinted from various sources, this book presents guidelines, procedures, and techniques for preventing, diagnosing, and remediating reading disabilities. A program for the teacher of retarded readers is outlined. Various approaches to the diagnosis and remediation of reading problems are represented in the material to form a survey of the field. Each section and chapter is introduced with text by the editor presenting the point of view of the author or authors whose work follows. Ways to identify reading difficulties, diagnostic testing, discussions of the various causes of reading disability, and corrective and remedial teaching all form major sections of the book. A group of articles on the special concerns of the remedial teacher, such as junior and senior high school reading problems, training reading specialists, and materials for the teaching of reading is at the end of the volume.

1582   "Developmental dyslexia: the Australian scene." Med J Aust 2(8): 399-400, August 19, 1972. (4 References).
The field of medicine is concerning itself with areas formerly considered peripheral or irrelevant. Cooperation is growing between medicine and ancillary disciplines. These facts are demonstrated in the work done in the field of developmental dyslexia. Specific learning disabilities are defined. The work of the Specific Learning Difficulties Association (SPELD) in remediation is described. The immediate needs are for an adequate number of properly trained remedial teachers and adequate facilities to cope with the important problem of dyslexia.

1583   "Divided over dyslexia." Times Educ Suppl 3002: 10, December 8, 1972. (0 References).
Determining whether a child is or is not dyslexic was the problem voiced at a one-day conference on "The Dyslexic Child" held at Sussex University. Government interest in treatment should be on a scale similar to that for spastics or thalidomide children. Instead, the government has removed the need for special services by denying the existence of dyslexia, and by lumping all reading difficulties in one general sphere. There was agreement at the conference, however, that there is a group of children who display a unique cluster of symptoms. The extent of the problem is unknown and cannot be accurately surveyed until the condition is recognized and defined.

1584   Dozier, Paul. "Specific reading disability." J Lancet 60(5): 202-4, May, 1940. (11 References). (As reprinted in Bull Orton Soc 11: 33-36, May, 1961).
Specific reading disability has many causes. If a child of normal intelligence is consistently a year or more behind his class in reading skills,

he will usually be found to have a specific disability. Treatment should include reeducation beginning with elementary phonics. Auditory and kinesthetic reinforcement help. Much repetition is required with this type of pupil. Some environmental adjustment, such as a change in curriculum, is helpful. Persons who deal with the reading-disabled child should learn to regard him without prejudice or anxiety. Many factors must be considered in treatment including the age of the child when the condition is identified, his intelligence, the degree of the disability, and his attitude toward it.

1585   Dungworth, David. "Special training on dyslexia." Times Educ Suppl 3141: 7, August 15, 1975. (0 References).
Examines West German efforts in the special training of teachers to deal with dyslexia. Emphasis is toward early detection. Hamburg is said to be the most progressive of the federal states in this respect. Every primary and secondary school has at least one specialist teacher who can diagnose dyslexia. The city maintains remedial reading centers. Bavaria has granted dyslexia legal status. Dyslexics are given special consideration in the first two years of school. It is proposed that colleges should offer short courses for dyslexics. It is suggested that the only long-term solution would be a grading system which recognized that performance in German language is less important as a reflection of general ability than performance in most other subjects.

1586   Dunlap, Edward A. "The role of strabismus in reading problems." Am Orthopt J 16: 44-49, 1966. (7 References).
While some children with eye-muscle imbalance have reading problems, others do not. We do not know why. Treatment of dyslexia should be aimed at early detection and early examination and diagnosis of probable cause. The ophthalmologist is responsible for: (1) establishing the status of the eyes in general; (2) cooperating with educators and psychologists in the study of reading disabilities; and (3) guiding the patient and his parents away from quacks. By ignoring their responsibilities in this field, ophthalmologists contributed to the existing confusion. Characteristics of dyslexia are listed and a classification of types is given. Factors to consider in diagnosis are listed.

1587   "Dyslexia 'more than a spelling and reading problem.'" Times Educ Suppl 3153: 12, November 7, 1975. (0 References).
Dyslexia is more than a spelling and reading problem: it should be regarded as a language handicap. Early detection is important but difficult, since there are no outward physical signs. Schools are not tailored to dyslexic children who do not fit into groups for either slow learners or bright learners. More training for teachers is needed in how to distinguish the slow learner from the dyslexic. Parents can help by reading to their children from an early age.

1588   Early, George H. "Low-level functional deficits in learning-disabled children." Acad Ther 8(2): 231-34, Winter, 1972-1973. (5 References).
Suggests that the problem of many poor readers is that they must spend their conscious, cognitive efforts on decoding and processing the words. This should be automatic, with conscious effort focused on the message of the printed page. Such readers suffer from "cognitive overload." It is suggested that remedial efforts should be aimed at these lower-level functions where many basic deficits lie. Too much remediation is aimed at the higher, cognitive levels; it offers intellectual approaches to the

problem of reading disability. We need instead to upgrade the low-level functional deficits.

1589   "The eye and learning disabilities." <u>Pediatrics</u> 49(3): 454-55, March, 1972. (15 References).
Presents the conclusions of a committee formed from several professional bodies of pediatricians and ophthalmologists concerning the relationship between the eye and visual training and the treatment of dyslexia. Conclusions are: (1) Learning disability and dyslexia require a multidisciplinary approach in treatment. Eye care should never be instituted in isolation. (2) No peripheral eye defects cause dyslexia. (3) No known scientific evidence supports claims for improving school performance of dyslexics through visual training or neurological organizational training. (4) With the exception of correctable ocular defects, glasses have no value in treating dyslexia. (5) Teaching dyslexic children is an educational problem. No one approach is applicable to all children.

1590   Fiddler, Jerry B. "Who says the boy's no angel?" <u>Read Teach</u>
        26(2): 145-48, November, 1972. (0 References).
Charges that those working with disabled readers--"angels"--sometimes label their clients "dyslexic" rather than admit their ignorance and/or inability to help the problem reader. The labeling should stop at "poor reader." This is not to say that sincere attempts should not be made to identify specific strengths and weaknesses, and, in severe cases, to use multiple diagnostic and remedial approaches through the coordinated team efforts of medical, educational, psychological, and sociological experts. The fallacious labeling system should not survive. It is so much easier to label children "dyslexic" as if it were a terminal illness than it is to identify and remediate the problem.

1591   Fletcher, Mary C. "Biostatistical approach to learning disabilities." <u>Am Orthopt J</u> 17: 73-77, 1967. (10 References).
A child has six major areas of development: sensory, motor, language, intellectual, emotional, and social. A lag in any of these may result in learning difficulties. The physician should take an interest in all of these areas, including language. The physician has a responsibility in the diagnosis and treatment of language disabilities. No cause for dyslexia has yet been generally accepted. Nine different specialists are listed who may be involved in diagnosing dyslexia, including physicians, psychologists, speech pathologists, and educators. Some current methods of treatment and expected results are considered.

1592   Forell, Elizabeth Rossing. "No easy cure for reading disabilities."
        <u>Todays Educ</u> 65(2): 34-36, March-April, 1976. (0 References).
Discounts glowing reports of startling gains made by nonreaders in remedial programs. Only rarely does a child make more than a year's progress in a year. In a follow-up study of young people who had been referred as children to a university reading clinic for evaluation, it appeared that the reading disability was likely to stay with a student throughout his school career. In addition to the persistence of reading disability, there is the implication that early identification of reading problems is important. Reading teachers should not be discouraged if progress is very slow with some children in spite of the very best teaching. A plea is entered for other teachers to adjust their instruction to the limitations of problem readers.

1593 Franklin, Alfred White, and Naidoo, Sandhya, eds. <u>Assessment and</u>
      <u>teaching of dyslexic children: lectures given as a training course</u>
      <u>organised by the I.C.A.A. Word Blind Centre for Dyslexic Children,</u>
      <u>London, 1969</u>. London: Invalid Children's Aid Association, 1970.
      124p.

1594 Frierson, Edward C. "Clinical education procedures in the treat-
      ment of learning disabilities." <u>Am Orthopt J</u> 17: 78-87, 1967.
      (0 References).
Analyzes clinical education procedures, describes some of these procedures,
and makes suggestions for increasing the effectiveness of clinical education programs. "Clinical education" is a term meaning educational procedures based on thorough clinical evaluation of the child. The effectiveness of clinical education depends on thorough diagnosis; good selection
of teaching procedures; and objective measurement of success. Twelve
methods of teaching reading are described, including, among others, the
use of basal readers, language experience, kinesthetic, alphabetic, phonics, linguistics, words in color, and the rebus approach.

1595 Frostig, Marianne. "Disabilities and remediation in reading."
      <u>Acad Ther</u> 7(4): 373-91, Summer, 1972. (34 References).
Presents in chart form: (1) the various symptoms of reading disability
observed in the classroom; (2) the possible underlying deficits producing
the problem; (3) methods of evaluating the deficits; (4) suggested training methods; and (5) suggested reading-instruction methods for coping
with each problem. The material is intended to alert the teacher to the
possible relationships among the child's reading difficulties, possible
causes, and methods designed to improve reading. Suggestions for classroom use are made.

1596 ————. "The needs of teachers for specialized information on
      reading." In: Cruickshank, William M., ed. <u>The teacher of brain-</u>
      <u>injured children</u>. Chap. 6. Syracuse, New York: Syracuse Univer-
      sity Press, 1966. 89-109. (49 References).
Advocates a perscriptive approach to the teaching of reading in which the
methods used are varied depending on the symptoms displayed by the child.
Specific, highly developed skills should be applied as needed. The teacher in special education who is teaching reading must be skilled in diagnosis and remediation. The aim is not only to improve the reading process but also to improve the underlying abilities which are necessary for
reading skill to progress. Reading is a complicated process. Teachers
of children with reading difficulties should be aware of the necessary
abilities, of the development of psychological functions during childhood, and have in mind the concept of "readiness." Visuomotor skills and
eye movements, which are the basis of later perceptual development, are
established during the first two years of life. Among the visual-perceptual abilities involved in reading are form perception, figure-ground
perception, perception of position in space, and perception of spatial
relationships. Causes of reading failure may be many; those dealt with
here occur chiefly because of deficits in the central nervous system.
Emotionally based reading problems are not discussed. Difficulties in
sensorimotor skills; visual-perceptual skills; auditory skills; association of sight with sound; and difficulties in higher thought processes
(for example, how to keep a thought in mind); or in associating symbols
with meaning should be dealt with as they arise.

1597   Gates, Arthur Irving.   "Diagnosis and remediation in reading."
       Elem Engl Rev 19(8):   286-90, December, 1942.   (10 Bibliographic
       Footnotes).
It is becoming evident that a number of tendencies are appearing in the
treatment of reading disabilities which will develop into trends in the
field.   Nine are mentioned, including: (1) recognition of the importance
of early diagnosis; (2) that teachers can be crucial in preventing or
correcting reading disabilities; (3) that both social maladjustment and
psysiological factors are important; and (5) that reading machines and
drills are not superior to free library reading.

1598   Geis, Robley.   A preventive summer program for kindergarten chil-
       dren likely to fail in first grade reading.   Final report.   1968.
       42p.   (ED 030 495).
Describes a six-week summer enrichment program for twenty-three middle-
class kindergarten children who made low scores on tests of cognitive
development.   Parents of these children were given advice on ways to help
the children.   The parents were invited to visit and observe the program.
A control group of twenty-three children who also made low scores received
no help.   In August, 1967 after the training, the experimental group
scored close to the score of normal children in a reading readiness test.
In September, 1967 the experimental group did not score significantly
higher than the control group on another form of the readiness test.   In
May, 1968, after the children had completed first grade, the experimental
group of children scored significantly higher than the control group on
an achievement test, but significantly below the score of the entire
first-grade population.   Findings support the prediction that the readiness test used would correctly predict first-grade achievement and that
the summer program did aid the children who participated.

1599   Gilliland, Hap.   A practical guide to remedial reading.   Columbus,
       Ohio: Charles E. Merrill, 1974.   324p.
This book is intended as a practical guide for teachers of children with
various types of reading problems.   Theoretical background and experimental research in the teaching of reading are not emphasized.   Numerous
instructional guides for use with particular remedial reading problems
are included.   The symptoms, possible causes, and recommendations for
treatment of many reading problems are given in tabular form in the guides.
Such areas as problems in sight word recognition; sound blending; comprehension; time, space, and directional orientation; visual-motor coordination; and many others are covered.   It is pointed out that the majority
of slow readers are simply low in ability.   The remaining one-fourth to
one-half, however, have the ability to achieve more, and remedial reading
is worthwhile for them.   Material is included on how to discover, diagnose, and alleviate the causes of reading problems.   Motivation, word
recognition, comprehension, learning disabilities, and the special problems of the culturally different child are discussed.   A list of tests
for reading and/or diagnosis is included.

1600   Gold, Lawrence.   Preparing classroom teachers to work with severely
       underachieving pupils through an internship in a regional learning
       disability center.   1970.   18p.   (ED 040 829).
Over a period of almost two years, a total of twenty-three classroom
teachers served internships at a regional learning disabilities center.
At the end of their training, most of them became reading specialists in
the school district sponsoring the program.   Each training session lasted
eleven weeks and included working with children individually and in small

groups, as well as practice in diagnostic testing, and attending case conferences, seminars, and other related meetings.

1601 Goldberg, Herman Krieger. "Reading difficulties in children. I." Int Ophthalmol Clin 3(4): 997-1007, December, 1963. (24 References).
Developmental readers are normal children progressing in regular classroom work. Corrective readers are those not working up to their potential. These children can be helped to attain their normal grade level by an experienced classroom teacher with proper methods and identification of their problems. Remedial readers are described by many terms, including "dyslexia," "strephosymbolia," "specific language disability," "word blindness," and "visual agnosia." Afflicted children are usually male, of normal intelligence, often of mixed cerebral dominance, and may have emotional problems. They are not the same as slow readers (children reading below grade level), but are at a level consistent with their intelligence. It is important to diagnose dyslexic children early. Therapy should be with the use of an immediate phonetic approach combining structural, phonetic, auditory, visual, and kinesthetic methods. The roles in the treatment of dyslexic children played by the educator, ophthalmologist, neurologist, and psychiatrist are discussed.

1602 Gray, William S. "Reading clinics." Elem Sch J 44(9): 500-501, May, 1944. (0 References).
Reports the rapid growth of reading clinics. The work of two new clinics in Kansas City, Missouri, one in Tulsa, Oklahoma, and one in Fort Valley, Georgia, is pointed out. Their programs are described and commented on.

1603 "H. E. W. releases reading disorder report." J Learn Disabil 3(2): 119-20, February, 1970. (0 References).
The National Advisory Committee on Dyslexia and Related Reading Disorders of the U.S. Department of Health, Education, and Welfare reports that 15 percent of otherwise able children in the United States are having difficulty learning to read. This is a much higher figure than reported elsewhere. A suggested program of action is outlined.

1604 Hartman, Nancy C., and Hartman, Robert K. "Perceptual handicap or reading disability?" Read Teach 26(7): 684-95, April, 1973. (80 References).
Reviews the literature on the effectiveness of different methods of dealing with reading problems. The reading teacher and the learning disabilities specialist often see the same symptoms within the same child from different viewpoints. A false dichotomy has resulted from different terminology, diagnostic approaches, and remedial techniques. Research does not support perceptual training approaches. It does support the task-oriented approach. Communication and acceptance of ideas are needed between reading specialists and learning disability specialists.

1605 Heckerl, John R. "Teaching reading skills: a problem in task analysis." Acad Ther 5(1): 11-14, Fall, 1969. (3 Bibliographic Footnotes).
Outlines a step-by-step approach to teaching reading skills, particularly to severely retarded readers of average or better IQ. Fourteen teaching steps, ranging from simple to complex, are detailed. Materials needed and what the teacher should say are given. It is pointed out that the level of difficulty can often be lowered if the teacher will sequence the learning into simple steps that progress toward the more difficult.

1606 "Helping Johnny to read." Sight Sav Rev 26(2): 103, Summer, 1956.
      (0 References).
Describes the work of the Dyslexia Memorial Institute at Northwestern
University Medical Center in Chicago. The president of the institute is
Dr. George E. Park, an ophthalmologist, who believes that dyslexia can
be prevented and corrected.

1607 Hoffman, Mary. "Mixed-handed have reading problems." Times Educ
      Suppl 3135: 4, July 4, 1975. (0 References).
Reports on a conference on children with reading and spelling difficulties
held in London. Michael Rutter, Margaret Newton, Alex Bannatyne, and
Jack Tizard were all conference speakers. Points made are that: (1)
dyslexia has nothing to do with IQ; (2) "mixed-handed" children rather
than those who are clearly left-handed or right-handed are most likely
to have reading and spelling problems; and (3) the term "dyslexia" might
be useful as a rallying point for action. Bannatyne's remedial training
in spatial awareness, motor control, and memory was demonstrated.

1608 Ingram, Philippa. "For 'dyslexia' read srd." Times Educ Suppl
      2960: 5, February 11, 1972. (0 References).
The report of a government advisory committee chaired by Prof. Jack Tizard
draws attention to the confusion surrounding the term "dyslexia." The
members of the committee suggest using instead "specific reading difficulties" (SRD). They do not fully accept the idea of a specific syndrome
of developmental dyslexia. The cause of SRD is not important to the educators who recommend skilled remedial teaching as the best solution for
backward readers. They also recommend early screening for all children
to detect reading problems.

1609 "Is dyslexia a disease?" JAMA 212(9): 1515-16, June 1, 1970.
      (2 References).
Children suffering from developmental dyslexia do not appear to constitute
a significant proportion of poor readers. The syndrome cannot be ignored,
even though it accounts for only a small number of the total number of
children suffering from the related complaint, poor reading ability. The
doctor's role remains consultative, since the practical aspects of the
problem are educational. Measures the doctor may suggest are given.

1610 Johnson, Marjorie Seddon. Reading disabilities in the classroom
      and clinic; a summary. Philadelphia, Pennsylvania: Temple Univer-
      sity, 1957. 13p.

1611 Jones, H. Lee, Jr., and Harvey, Ann. Perceptual development center
      for children with dyslexia and related disorders. Final project
      report. (Natchez Municipal Separate School District, Mississippi).
      1970. 148p. (ED 060 166).
To explore the nature, diagnostic techniques, and remediation of dyslexia
was the purpose of the Dyslexia Association established by school offi-
cials, teachers, and parents of the school district. Concerns of the
association included the shortening of treatment time by the use of programs which could be incorporated into the school operation and be economically feasible. Procedures were developed for the use of persons
working as instructors who were not fully trained teachers. The point of
view was that specific developmental dyslexia was a neurological dysfunction, probably hereditary. It was also believed that other related disorders were probably not hereditary but resembled dyslexia. An alphabetic,
phonetic, structural linguistic approach to teaching reading was adopted.

1612   Kaluger, George, and Kolson, Clifford J.   Reading and learning dis-
       abilities. Columbus, Ohio: Charles E. Merrill, 1969. 447p.
       (Bibliography). (The Slow Learner Series).
Dyslexia is one of several severe learning disorders described in some
detail, including symptoms and characteristics of dyslexic children. The
book is designed for those concerned with teaching the disabled reader
effectively. The viewpoint is that children in need of remedial reading
instruction differ widely in the reasons for their reading problems, and
that these diverse reasons require particular methods of teaching reading.
The child learns only through his perception and conception of things.
It is important to know more about the sensory and neurological processes
that underlie perception in order to teach him efficiently. Comments are
made on the nature of reading, symptoms of disabilities and how to diagnose them, and specific suggestions for remedial teaching of reading.
Phonics, word recognition skills, comprehension, and vocabulary building
are also considered. The book contains a glossary of terms used in the
field of reading.

1613   Karlin, Robert. "Disabled readers, are they getting the right
       help?" Child Study 35(1): 59-60, Winter, 1957-1958. (0 Refer-
       ences).
Cautions against permitting the treatment of reading-disabled children by
persons without adequate training for the task. Clinics, centers, or
individuals offering such instruction may do so without meeting any standard of training or preparation.

1614   Keeney, Arthur H. "Vision and learning disabilities." Sight Sav
       Rev 39(2): 73-78, Summer, 1969. (3 References).
Learning is acquired through six possible routes. Beyond doubt the visual
route is the most important. Preschool vision screening has long been
recognized as important. The ways in which youngsters attempt to compensate for uncorrected refractive errors and measures that may be taken
to help the visually handicapped child are examined. Prematurity, birth
injuries, congenital defects, and heredity are all factors in visual problems and in reading difficulty. Prematurity and various brain injuries
may contribute to specific dyslexia, but in its pure form it appears to
be difficulty in interpreting symbols in an otherwise healthy child (usually male) of good intelligence. A family history of reading difficulty
is often present and should be uncovered with courteous but thorough
questioning. Better results are achieved when the condition is discovered
early. These healthy children usually respond and improve distinctly when
reinforcement drills are used by the teacher. These drills involve
visual, auditory, tactile, and kinesthetic practice with emphasis on
visual or auditory, depending on the way the child responds.

1615   Kline, Lloyd W. "Follow the yellow brick road or lost in the forest
       of professional educational argument." J Spec Educ 9(2): 167-77,
       Summer, 1975. (19 References).
Points out logical and stylistic inconsistencies in J. W. Lerner's analysis of the fields of remedial reading and learning disabilities. (See
Item No. 1618). The paper is criticized for drawing superficial distinctions between the two fields; the tendency to make sweeping generalizations; and the tendency to quote out of context. The lack of a clear-cut
conceptualization of reading is noted and examined in relation to the
problem of defining various reading problems such as dyslexia. Everyone
in education professes to be ultimately interested in the welfare of the
individual learner. The major problem obviously lies in the failure to

act on the individual learner's needs. If those concerned honestly cared about this learner's welfare, they would argue not as learning disability partisans or as remedial reading specialists, but would set aside differences and concentrate on the child.

1616 Knipp, H. B. "Helping the disabled reader." In: Conference on Reading. University of Pittsburgh. Report 1959. 169-75.

1617 Knox, Gerald M. "Your child can't read: how can you help?" Better Homes Gard 50: 34, 38-41, October, 1972. (0 References).
Describes ways parents can help children become good readers. If your child's school has no diagnostic program, this article explains how you can create one at home. This is necessary because large numbers of American children have reading problems, and neither they, their parents, nor their teachers realize it. Tips to parents include: (1) maintaining a good reading climate in the home by talking to the preschooler; (2) reading aloud to children; (3) having good books available; and (4) using word games, the public library, and storytelling. If your child still fails to make progress in overcoming reading deficiencies, consult a diagnostic reading center where reading specialists can provide help. Suggestions are given on how to evaluate your child's school reading program.

1618 Lerner, Janet W. "Remedial reading and learning disabilities: are they the same or different?" J Spec Educ 9(2): 119-31, Summer, 1975. (43 References).
Analyzes the controversy concerning reading-disabled children from two perspectives--the field of reading and the field of learning disabilities. Reading and learning disabilities are disciplines representing contrasting issues, theories, approaches, and points of view. Each has a full course of study in universities. Four areas of difference are discussed: (1) mental processing vs. the developmental skills approach; (2) remedial reading vs. psychoeducational treatment; (3) dyslexia or reading disability; and (4) views of task analysis. The hope is expressed that these contrasting approaches may become cooperative, not competitive and collaborate rather than dispute with each other. Several recommendations are made to integrate these two approaches to reading problems into a perspective that would accommodate both fields of study. For a reply to this article see Item No. 1615.

1619 Lieben, Beatrice. "Attitudes, platitudes, and conferences in teacher-parent relations involving the child with a reading problem." Elem Sch J 58(5): 279-86, February, 1958. (0 References).
The teacher should take a positive attitude toward parents of poor readers. Rather than dismissing the parents as having caused the problem in the first place, teachers should approach the parent-teacher conference with the idea that teacher and parent both want to work together to the / best of their abilities to help the reading-disabled child.

1620 Logue, G. D. "Dyslexia." S Afr Med J 49(27): 1101-3, June 28, 1975. (17 References).
Reviews some of the early literature on dyslexia. It is suggested that only about 10 percent of reading disability cases are truly dyslexic. This group resists the best efforts of remedial teachers. The other 90 percent of pupils can be completely rehabilitated. In the past too much attention has been given cortical processes underlying integration of audiovisual perception and spatial orientation, and not enough to the

attentional skills underlying these processes. More emphasis should be put on attentional skills in general, and on reticular function in particular. Medication should be more extensively used and at higher doses than usually prescribed.

1621 Lorentz, Richard J. "Dyslexia." J Rehabil 37(5): 25-27, 13, September-October, 1971. (15 References).
Discusses the causes of dyslexia, including such contributing factors as heredity, environment, postnatal complications, and emotional problems. "Primary" or "developmental dyslexia" where the cause is unknown, and the symptoms constitute the basic impairment, is distinguished from "secondary dyslexia" which is defined as one manifestation of another primary condition which has been proved present in the individual. Most dyslexics below the age of twelve must be considered primary dyslexics because we are not able to detect the underlying pathology. Methods of diagnosis and treatment are presented. Because adequate diagnosis and treatment require the cooperation of professionals from several fields, little has been done in many communities, thus leaving the door open for charlatans. Examples of good community action are given.

1622 MacMillan, Daniel P. "Dyslexia (reading difficulty)." Libr J 71(12): 890-95, June 15, 1946. (0 References).
Describes the approach to treatment of dyslexic children and the work of the Dyslexia Memorial Institute in Chicago, an independent, nonprofit organization. Any child or youth with an IQ over 85 who is having difficulty with school work or life adjustment, especially if reading disability is involved, can be accepted by the Institute. The child's home life, physical state and history, and intellectual, social, and emotional states are examined. Teaching methods to which the child has been exposed are evaluated. Donors have been so generous that cost of treatment can be kept low.

1623 McNeilly, R. B. "Developmental dyslexia: Australian scene." Med J Aust 2(12): 688, September 16, 1972. (0 References).
Letter to editor. It is a shame to treat everyone who has trouble learning to read as if he suffered from primary (neurological) dyslexia. Most are probably victims of secondary dyslexia caused by deprivation or distortion of early language experience. We should accept a simple and orderly method of teaching English. A book describing one method is recommended.

1624 Mann, Philip H. "Dyslexia. An educator's view." J Fla Med Assoc 56(1): 24-27, January, 1969. (5 References).
Attempts to define dyslexia and relate to each other the contributions medicine and education can make by working together. Physicians were initially interested in the area of learning disabilities called dyslexia and aphasia. But it is the educators who must begin where the child is functioning and treat him. Medicine and many other disciplines all have contributions to make to treating the dyslexic. Definitions of dyslexia vary reflecting the philosophy of the group putting forward the definition. Some of these differing views are given. Dyslexia is seen as part of a larger category called learning disabilities. The learning-disabled child is described as one whose behavior indicates faulty, inadequate, or inappropriate learning which may or may not be caused by brain injury. The teacher can learn to use the contributions of many disciplines, including medicine. Emphasis is shifting from diagnosis and classification to treatment of dyslexia.

1625 Maryland. Governor's Commission on Dyslexia. <u>Report to the gover-
      nor and general assembly of Maryland.</u> [Cockeysville, Maryland]:
      1972. 62p.
Pursuant to a resolution passed by the Maryland House of Delegates, the
governor appointed a committee of medical and educational experts to
study dyslexia in Maryland and make recommendations for coping with it.
This publication is the report of that committee. It is estimated that
some 130,000 children in Maryland are affected. Recommendations include:
(1) a state-wide screening program to identify and diagnose the problems
of dyslexic children; (2) new programs for adequate training of teachers
in alternate methods of teaching reading; and (3) involvement of parents
in the program. Specific suggestions on the organization and funding of
the reading program are given. Various model programs already in operation in the state are described.

1626 "Mirror reading." <u>Hygeia</u> 18(1): 71, January, 1940. (0 Refer-
      ences).
Suggests methods for training children who mirror-read and show reversal
tendencies. Recommended are: (1) using a pointer by the teacher and/or
the child; (2) tracing or copying words from models; (3) using a word-
picture dictionary; and (4) establishing dominance in one hand.

1627 Misner, Paul J. "Administrative steps in providing for retarded
      readers." In: International Reading Association. <u>Conference
      proceedings: better readers for our times.</u> Vol. 1. Edited by
      William S. Gray, and Nancy Larrick. New York: Scholastic Magazines,
      1956. 165-67. (1 Reference).
Draws five general conclusions about a remedial reading program within a
school system. Points include: (1) the effectiveness of a reading program cannot be judged on the basis of mass achievement results; (2) definition of "retarded reader" should be broad; (3) retarded readers should
be recognized as early as possible; (4) the reading consultant's duties
and responsibilities should be clearly defined at the outset; and (5) the
importance of continuing to improve the reading program of the entire
school system should not be minimized.

1628 Morsink, Catherine. "LRNG to read: a simulation for teacher train-
      ing." <u>J Learn Disabil</u> 6(8): 479-85, October, 1973. (4 Refer-
      ences).
Using a weather code for pilots, this simulation "teaches" a small group
from an audience as if they are students learning to read. The purpose
of the demonstration is to simulate for teachers the learning experience
of the disabled reader. The entire audience follows silently, with discussion later. It is hoped that through failure, empathy and insights
into helping the disabled reader will develop. Flash cards are prepared
using the abbreviations and symbols from a weather code as "sight words."
Procedure for "teaching" these is given.

1629 Myklebust, Helmer R., ed. <u>Progress in learning disabilities.</u> Vol.
      3. New York: Grune & Stratton, 1975. 226p. (Bibliography).
Although this book concerns learning disabilities in general, reading
problems are so much a part of learning disability that much material on
reading disability is included. Interdisciplinary approaches to treatment
are emphasized. Articles address themselves to when and how parents,
teachers, and remedial specialists should intervene to help the child.
Intervention programs in the schools, by parents, and through psychological and educational means are considered. Articles on the role of seizures

in reading disabilities and on the relationship of cerebral dominance to
learning are also included.

1630 Nicholls, John V. V. "The office management of patients with read-
        ing difficulties." Can Med Assoc J 81(5): 356-60, September 1,
        1959. (2 References).
Reviews knowledge about incidence and causes of reading defects. Many
more boys than girls are affected. Eye defects and crossed dominance appear to be only slightly related to reading disability. Early diagnosis
is important. The status of the child's IQ, sight, and hearing should
be examined. The great majority of these children improve if given phonics training. This type of training can often be reinforced at home by
the parents. Word games and word-building games are effective. Remedial
classes should be maintained as a part of the school system.

1631 Orbell, G. B. "Congenital word blindness. (A review of some of
        the literature and a report on four cases.)" Trans Ophthalmol Soc
        NZ 13(Suppl.): 60-67, 1961. (5 References).
When a word-blind child is brought to an ophthalmologist because it is
assumed there is something wrong with his vision, it can have a disastrous
effect on the child's life if the ophthalmologist fails to recognize the
condition. The ophthalmologist does not treat word blindness, but he
should know the course parents and teachers should take in order that the
child may receive treatment as early as possible. Some literature is
reviewed, including Hinshelwood's recommendations for teaching word-blind
children. This includes the use of the ABC method (phonics) rather than
the look-and-say method of teaching reading. Four case histories are
given, including that of a thirty-two-year-old word-blind man who decided
to learn to read at the age of twenty-nine. Word-blind children and their
teachers are advised that it is very hard to learn to read, but it can be
done. Word-blind children should never stop working on reading or they
will forget the words they have learned.

1632 Park, George E. "This, they would choose to do; challenge and a
        plea." Arch Pediatr 68(11): 533-39, November, 1951. (0 Refer-
        ences).
Dyslexia is caused by one of many abnormal factors or a combination of
factors, including physical or emotional problems, poor teaching, or
others. The causes are functional, observable, preventable, and correctable and distinguish "dyslexia" from "alexia" which is an inability to
read because of a brain disease or lack of intelligence. Dyslexia has
many ramifications. Personality and emotional status and environment,
both at home and at school, as well as physical factors, must be considered. The economic burden imposed on society by the failures of dyslexic
children is very large. They have had little attention, and funds for
their care are almost nonexistent.

1633 "Programs for disabled readers." Read Teach 21(8): 706, May,
        1968. (0 References).
Trying to get all children to read "up to grade level" is vain. Many
children in remedial programs are already reading up to their capacity.
More should be done to diagnose reading disabilities and correct these
difficulties. Programs for disabled readers should not be allowed to
take precedence over programs for normal children. Early identification
and treatment of children who are potential reading disability cases is
a better approach.

1634 Rains, Sylvester; Eichenwald, Heinz; Helton, William B. "Is this
       child dyslexic?" Tex Outlook 51: 18-19, 43, April, 1967. (0
       References).
Presents and discusses five guidelines to use in answering the question,
"Is this child dyslexic?" They include: (1) Require a definition of
terms. The term "dyslexia" has been bandied about until it can mean almost anything. (2) Be sure there really is a reading problem. (3) Remember that reading disability is an educational problem which deserves
the attention of a reading specialist. (4) Multidisciplinary diagnostic
procedures are often needed. (5) Custom-tailored therapy is required.
Each child's case is unique. Some typical questions by parents include
those concerning the incidence of dyslexia; claims of successful treatment by various doctrinists; mixed-dominance theories; and emotional
problems related to reading difficulties.

1635 Reading Institute, Temple University, 25th, 1968. Proceedings:
       reading difficulties: classroom and clinic. Vol. 7. Edited by
       Marjorie Seddon Johnson, and Roy A. Kress. Philadelphia, Pennsyl-
       vania: Temple University, 1970. 132p.

1636 Robbins, Edward L. Tutors handbook. 1973. 78p. (ED 075 778).
Developed at the National Reading Center, Washington, D.C., this handbook
details what the trained tutor must know in order to help a reading-
disabled child. Characteristics of children with reading problems are
explained; general principles of successful tutoring are given; and major
areas of reading skills and a reading skills checklist are provided.
Sixty sample lessons aimed at developing various reading skills are included.

1637 Robbins, Richard C., et al. A model exemplary clinic for learning
       disabilities; a project of Title III, ESEA. 1967. 83p. (ED 030
       997).
Six teachers, working in teams of two, taught seven remedial classes with
a maximum of twelve students in a class. Basic reading skills were taught
to functional nonreaders in grades three through six and, with a different
emphasis in instruction, reading skills were taught to elementary and
secondary classes. The purpose of the two ten-week teacher-training
courses was to demonstrate theory and creative methods and materials for
remediation of severe learning disabilities. All classes but one made
significant progress in all areas of reading and spelling. The report
includes an outline of the methods and materials used.

1638 Robinson, Helen M. "Fundamental principles for helping retarded
       readers." Education 72: 596-99, May, 1952. (0 References).
Three principles necessary in helping disabled readers are: (1) providing a climate and interpersonal relations that will encourage reading;
(2) identifying and employing proper techniques, methods, and materials;
and (3) keeping communication free among all the persons helping one
pupil.

1639 Rosner, Jerome. Helping children overcome learning difficulties:
       a step-by-step guide for parents and teachers. New York: Walker,
       1975. 326p.
Outlines a plan of action for helping children who are not progressing
satisfactorily in school. Testing to determine what actions should be
taken to help the child should be done only when it will provide information necessary for decision-making. Teaching the child is considered

next. Finally, material is offered on prevention of educational difficulties. Testing for and teaching visual perceptual skills, auditory
perceptual skills, and general motor skills are discussed. How to teach
the learning-disabled child reading, arithmetic, spelling, and writing is
covered, with each subject considered separately. Measures to prevent
learning disability are explored in terms of what characterizes the high-
risk child, and what to do about him. Descriptions of activities in
visual and auditory perceptual skills and general motor skills for the
preschool child are included. "Dyslexia" is given as one example of a
word which originally referred to a specific kind of brain injury, but
now is a term with no precise meaning, used as a synonym for a reading
problem, regardless of the cause or severity of the problem. Dyslexia
is one among many terms used to refer to learning disabilities.

1640 Rosner, Stanley L. "Dyslexia: a problem definition." <u>Am Orthopt</u>
      <u>J</u> 18: 94-97, 1968. (0 References).
"Dyslexia" is a term almost impossible to define to everyone's satisfaction. The problem of definition is complicated by two factors: (1)
reading disability has been viewed in a wide variety of ways by persons
from various disciplines; and (2) use of the term has become widely diffused: it is used to describe a wide variety of reading disabilities
from mild to severe. Dyslexia is first and foremost an educational problem. Symptom collection is interesting, but reading is the central concern, and treatment of dyslexia should be our first interest. This requires the help of well-trained teachers.

1641 ————. "Ophthalmology, optometry, and learning difficulties."
      <u>J Learn Disabil</u> 1(8): 451-55, August, 1968. (9 References).
Examines assumptions and approaches of ophthalmologists and optometrists
to the problem of learning disabilities. The vast majority of children
with reading and learning problems do not have serious eye problems.
Once he rules out eye problems, the ophthalmologist is inclined to place
further diagnosis and treatment in the hands of other specialists, including the psychologist or neurologist. The optometrist distinguishes
vision and sight. The skill of comprehending information and learning
involves four major performance areas termed the anti-gravity process,
the centering process, the identification process, and the speech-auditory
process. These are defined. Vision emerges from all four processes.
The ophthalmologist sees the visual motor concept as vague and not striking the heart of the problem, which is to recognize visual symbols in
terms of auditory or phonetic equivalents and thus arrive at meaning.
The optometrist sees the visual motor system as complex, and hand-eye
coordination exercises as valuable in treating dyslexia.

1642 Roswell, Florence G., and Chall, Jeanne S. "Helping poor readers
      with word recognition skills." <u>Read Teach</u> 10: 200-204, April,
      1957. (10 Bibliographic Footnotes).
Word recognition is the major difficulty in most reading disability cases.
A simplified table of word analysis skills is given, and suggestions for
testing to determine a child's specific needs in word recognition are
offered. Standardized silent reading tests are not adequate for this
purpose. To help poor readers, teachers should know clearly what sequence
of reading skills they will follow. Suggestions for teaching are given.
Children who still have extreme difficulty in word recognition even with
adequate instruction and effort are usually found to lack the ability to
blend sounds. Suggestions for coping with this problem are offered.

1643 Roth, Lois H., et al. Reading problems--diagnosis and instruction, design for developing Colorado reading programs. Invitational Reading Work Conference (Denver, February 20-23, 1966). 1966. 32p. (ED 011 500).
Presents the results of a conference held to develop guidelines for planning and implementing diagnostic reading programs.

1644 Roy, F. Hampton; Fraunfelder, Frederick T.; Peters, John E. "The poor reader." J Arkansas Med Soc 68(6): 191-94, November, 1971. (16 References).
Defines dyslexia as various degrees of inability to read or understand printed symbols in persons of otherwise normal intelligence. It is widespread. A child so affected should have complete medical and ocular evaluation and sometimes consultations with other specialists. Eye exercises, coordination exercises, special bifocal glasses, and mixed-dominance therapy should be strongly discouraged. Physicians should be alert to their responsibility to help dyslexic children learn to read and should not shirk it. The greatest help for a dyslexic is a full evaluation and attempts to get local school districts to provide special curricula and other special help for poor readers. Various types of dyslexia are described. Information on diagnosis and treatment is also given.

1645 Ruchlis, Hyman. Guidelines to education of non-readers. Brooklyn, New York: Book-Lab, 1973. 159p.

1646 Rychener, Ralph O. "Ophthalmic aspects of reading disabilities." Sight Sav Rev 24(3): 150-53, Fall, 1954. (0 References).
Reproduces a letter sent by the author, an ophthalmologist, to parents of reading-disabled children after examining them. Often parents of such children consult an ophthalmologist hoping glasses will help a condition which is congenital and often associated with left-handedness and mirror reading and/or writing. The letter gives the results of the ophthalmic examination. It gives general suggestions, including embarrassing the child as little as possible about his reading. When phonics training is indicated (to teach sound recognition) the parents can help the child with slow, careful pronunciation of words to be learned. They should help him pronounce by syllables or by words as a whole, enlist the child's interest and enthusiasm, and check his comprehension of material read silently. Sympathetic understanding should be the dominant factor.

1647 Samuels, S. Jay. "Reading disability?" Read Teach 24(3): 267, 271, 283, December, 1970. (4 References).
"Reading difficulty" describes the problem of the student who has trouble learning to read for any reason. "Reading disability" defines the situation of a cooperative child of normal intelligence, vision, and hearing with adequate instruction who fails to learn to read. The first is easy to identify; the second difficult to identify. How can we be certain that instruction has been adequate? Use of a system of task analysis of reading skills would improve reading instruction.

1648 Schell, Leo M., and Burns, Paul C., eds. Remedial reading; classroom and clinic. 2nd ed. Boston, Massachusetts: Allyn and Bacon, 1972. 587p. (Bibliography).
This volume is a collection of fifty-five articles, some written for this book, others reprinted from other sources, on many aspects of remedial reading. The treatment of reading disorders is viewed from several

angles: (1) why children have difficulty learning to read; (2) what can be done to diagnose the problems; and (3) how the reading-disabled child can best be helped. Ways to treat some specific reading problems, for example, comprehension, and ways for dealing with the special needs of the culturally deprived child are suggested. The roles played in treatment by teachers, parents, and experts from other professions are considered. Some of the reprinted articles are abstracted elsewhere in this bibliography, cited from their original sources.

1649   Schiffman, Gilbert B. "The administrative problems involved in executing clinical recommendations for the treatment of severe reading disorders within an ongoing educational system." Paper presented at International Reading Association, Atlantic City, New Jersey, April 19-23, 1971. 1971. 12p. (ED 053 866).
Four major problems plague a program for treatment of dyslexic children: (1) definition of the reading disability; (2) administrative and educational inertia; (3) getting the program organized; and (4) the need for evaluation and research. Much disagreement exists concerning definitions of reading disabilities. But a good program of treatment must be based on a clear understanding of what reading disability is. School administrators do not always have sufficient understanding of reading problems to support such a program. The most difficult problem can be organization. Much research and evaluation of dyslexics and of educational programs for them are needed.

1650   ————. "Educator speaks on dyslexia." J Rehabil 37(5): 28-29, September-October, 1971. (0 References).
Transcript of an interview discussing dyslexia as it is understood and handled by teachers. Early treatment offers hope. Various treatment techniques are discussed including Fernald and Gillingham methods. The confusion in terminology is a continuing problem for everyone involved with dyslexia. Parents and teachers can be misled by so-called experts in the field. No effective differential diagnosis exists at this time. If one treatment approach does not work, the teacher must change to another. There is no panacea for all dyslexic children.

1651   Shedd, Charles L. "Some exploratory studies on the clinical management of dyslexia." Paper presented at Association for Children with Learning Disabilities Conference, Fort Worth, Texas, March 6-8, 1969. 1969. 27p. (ED 031 366).
Describes problems concerning dyslexia and suggests ways for working with them. The necessary items for clinical management of dyslexics are one-to-one instruction, a multisensory approach, and highly structured material. A highly trained tutor is not necessary, and there is no need for special machines and games. What should be emphasized is decoding skills including skills like reading from left to right, learning letter-sound correspondence, and correct sound discrimination and blending. No one method is always best. A variety of situations should be used and modified as necessary.

1652   Stephenson, Harold H. "Reading difficulties." Calif Teach Assoc J 47: 16, March, 1951. (0 References).
Remedial reading will remain a necessary part of the school program as long as there is no one best way to teach reading. Remedial reading has been taught largely at the elementary level in the past. It should be a part of adult educational programs in public schools. The teacher of remedial reading needs special training. Suggestions are given on develop-

ing such skills. Reading difficulties have many causes. They appear in constellations rather than in isolation. Emotional problems, inappropriate teaching methods, and various physiological conditions are among the causes of reading problems.

1653   Stevens, D. "Dyslexia." Br Med J 1(5641): 428, February 15, 1969. (0 References).
Letter to editor. Describes the work of the Bath Association for the Study of Dyslexia. It teaches both children and adults, trains remedial teachers, and does research on dyslexia. It is noted that most educational authorities appear disinterested in dyslexia. An appended note from the editor gives the name and address of the Word Blind Centre for Dyslexic Children and comments on remedial methods.

1654   Stolarz, T. "Methods of correcting specific reading difficulties." In: Conference on Reading. University of Pittsburgh. Report 1955. 124-36.

1655   Swarts, M. "Problems to be considered in correcting reading disabilities." In: Conference on Reading. University of Pittsburgh. Report 1960. 105-19.

1656   Tufvander, Ellis A., and Zintz, Miles V. "A follow-up study of pupils with reading difficulties." Elem Sch J 58(3): 152-56, December, 1957. (0 References).
Children ranging in age from eight to seventeen years who had been treated at a reading clinic for severe reading retardation were recalled to determine the extent to which they had been helped by the clinic. IQs ranged from 80 to 134. It was found that the clinic's services were valuable to the children and to their parents. More reading growth takes place when parents receive and follow recommendations from the clinic. Most parents believed that help for their children in lower grades would have helped prevent reading problems.

1657   Ventura, M., and Ferrara, J. "Children with reading problems: implications for the school-nurse teacher." J NY State Sch Nurse Teach Assoc 6(3): 25-29, Spring, 1975.

1658   Wagner, Rudolph F. Helping the wordblind: effective intervention techniques for overcoming reading problems in older students. West Nyack, New York: Center for Applied Research in Education, 1976. 240p. (Bibliography).
Focuses specifically on the problems of the poor reader in adolescence or early adulthood, especially middle and senior high school students. The particular concern of the book is the older disabled reader who has the potential and the motivation to become an average or nearly average reader if given proper remedial treatment. It is not concerned with the unmotivated student or the person whose general mental ability is borderline or below and who could not be expected to read at grade level. The volume is intended for secondary school reading teachers or specialists or reading clinic teachers specializing in dyslexia. Most aids for diagnosis and treatment of reading problems are intended for use with elementary school children. Many reading exercises and games for the older child or young adult are given. Material is included on how to: (1) assess a reading problem; (2) establish a good tutor-pupil relationship; (3) select specific remedial techniques; and (4) plan and organize remedial programs. Suggestions in the areas of behavior modification, vocational counseling, and juvenile delinquency are offered.

1659 Waites, Lucius, and Cox, Aylett R. Developmental language disabil-
      ity...basic training...remedial language training. Rev. and enl.
      ed. Cambridge, Massachusetts: Educators Publishing Service, 1969.
      93p. (Part 1 originally published as Specific developmental dys-
      lexia, 1966, by Texas Scottish Rite Hospital for Crippled Children.)

1660 White, Jeffrey, and White, Margaret. Dyslexia; an introduction to
      causes and treatment with special reference to management in the
      secondary school. Perth, Australia: Alpha Print, 1971. 28p.

1661 White, Margaret; Lefroy, Robert; Weston, Deidre. Treating reading
      disabilities. San Rafael, California: Academic Therapy Publica-
      tions, 1975. 80p.

1662 Whitsell, Leon J. "A clinic team approach to reading problems:
      role of the neurologist." In: International Reading Association.
      Conference proceedings: perception and reading. Vol. 12(Part 4).
      Edited by Helen K. Smith. Newark, Delaware: International Read-
      ing Association, 1968. 72-77. (39 References).
Reviews literature on reading disability, and points out that the neurologist should assist the educator and pediatrician, or other primary physician, in developing an individualized program of treatment for the
child with reading disability. This program can include psychotherapy,
drugs, and physical and occupational therapy, as well as remedial teaching. A neurological profile should be used to discover the child's
strongest sensory, motor, or perceptual capacity. This strongest channel
should be used in teaching.

1663 Williams, Robert F. "Removing reading disabilities." Va J Educ
      38(7): 272-73, March, 1945. (0 References).
The chief reason children fail to be promoted to the next grade is reading disability. Diagnostic tests should be used to compare general
ability with accomplishment. Most retarded pupils who are capable are unaware of their ability. The remedial method used will not be so important
in motivating the child as will his awareness that he is not a numskull
and can improve. Poor readers usually come from homes where there is
little interest in reading. Phonics is particularly important in dealing
with remedial reading cases.

1664 Winsberg, Bertrand G. "Programed learning, teaching machines, and
      dyslexia." Am J Orthopsychiatry 39(3): 418-27, April, 1969.
      (40 References).
Argues that although teaching machines and programmed learning methods
are being used more and more, there is an alarming lack of scientific
evaluation of these procedures. Some methods have not been sufficiently
evaluated in controlled studies. It is suggested that students are being
subjected to unproved procedures. Teaching machines and programmed instruction have too much potential to be lost by default. However, if
these techniques can do no better than to continue the mediocrity of our
present educational system, the situation is very serious. A complete
renovation of the educational system is needed. It is well to be aware
of the deficiencies of our efforts in assessing and attempting to help
the dyslexic child.

1665 Witty, Paul A., and Kopel, David. "Preventing reading disability:
      the reading readiness factor." Educ Adm Super 22(6): 401-18,
      September, 1936. (93 References).

Reviews the literature and asserts that teaching of reading should be delayed until children are eight or nine years old. By then maturation
will have progressed to the point where reversals will be infrequent and
the child's background of experience and mental growth will make word
perception possible. Reading tasks will then have meaning for him.

1666 Woestehoff, Ellsworth S. Students with reading disabilities and
      guidance. Boston, Massachusetts: Houghton Mifflin, 1970. 62p.
      (Bibliography). (Guidance Monograph Series. Series 5: Guidance
      and the Exceptional Student).
The purpose of this book is to inform guidance counselors, who are not
necessarily reading specialists, of the nature of reading disabilities
in order that the counselor can be better able to help reading-disabled
students. It discusses diagnosis and treatment of reading disabilities.
In the case of young children the counselor's role may be in advising
parents. The counselor's role in dealing with older children is explained.
Lists of intelligence tests and reading tests are included.

1667 Yasuna, Elton. "Reading disability and the ophthalmologist." Eye
      Ear Nose Throat Mon 47(12): 630-33, December, 1968. (13 Refer-
      ences).
Outlines the characteristics of the dyslexic child and indicates the
professionals who should be available to help correct the defect, including the pediatrician or family doctor, audiologist, psychologist, neurologist, and psychiatrist. The look-say method of teaching reading is
criticized as producing more reading disability than any other method.
If an ophthalmologist sees the child first, he would be doing a great
service if he considered or established the diagnosis of reading disability. Ophthalmic problems almost never exist in such cases, but the
earlier they are discovered and treated the better.

1668 Zedler, Empress Y. Report of the Southwest Texas State College
      research conference on the problem of dyslexia and related dis-
      orders in public schools of the United States. Report of the Work-
      ing Group on Teacher Preparation. 1968. 5p. (ED 017 431).
Offers guidelines and recommendations for improving the education of
teachers in order to meet the needs of learning-disabled children. Training should include the study of dyslexia. Recommendations include: (1)
material should be prepared for various kinds of training for teachers
while they are in active teaching; (2) national conference should be held
to consider research needs; and (3) grants should be awarded to further
study and specialized training.

1669 Zink, Lydia Pearl. Helps for identifying and teaching the problem
      reader. Hicksville, New York: Exposition Press, 1975. 240p.
      (Bibliography). (An Exposition-university Book).

B. COPING WITH THE DYSLEXIC
IN THE REGULAR CLASSROOM

1. RESEARCH; GENERAL ASPECTS OF
MANAGEMENT; IMPROVING INSTRUCTION

1670 Ablewhite, Ronald Clifford. The slow reader: a problem in two
      parts. London: Heinemann, 1967. 95p. (Bibliography).
The child whose reading problem is neglected turns into a social misfit.
It is most important to begin remedial work early to avoid turning loose

on society those whose reading disabilities will result in lives of destructiveness. Most backward readers respond to a program of systematic
coaching. For those who do not, various teaching techniques aimed at
helping the child develop auditory or visual discrimination and hand-eye
coordination are presented. The development of the slow-reading child's
image of himself as a failure is outlined. It must be realized that most
children who fail in reading make low intelligence test scores. However,
this book is aimed at "the main problem": how to cope with the nonreading child in the classroom.

1671   Alden, Clara L.; Sullivan, Helen B.; Durrell, Donald D. "The fre-
       quency of special reading disabilities." Education 62(1): 32-36,
       September, 1941. (0 References).
In a study of the frequency of reading disabilities, it was found that
twice as many boys as girls were affected in grades two through six, and
that there were too many such children to be cared for in occasional remedial reading classes. Severe cases can be so treated, but most retarded readers need special reading programs in the regular classroom.

1672   Arnold, Richard D., and Sherry, Natalie. "A comparison of the
       reading levels of disabled readers with assigned textbooks." Read
       Improve 12(4): 207-11, Winter, 1975. (6 References).
The reading levels of individual disabled readers nine to eleven years
of age who were in fourth, fifth, and sixth grades were compared with the
reading levels of each pupil's assigned reader, his assigned social
studies text, and his assigned English text. Statistically significant
differences were found. In general the students in this study were being
assigned reading materials too difficult for them. This is seen as in-
defensible educational practice. It is concluded that very little is
being done in the regular classroom to accommodate disabled readers.

1673   Bennett, H. K. "Dearborn trains teachers to catch problem readers
       young." Sch Exec 72: 50-51, May, 1953. (0 References).
Describes the remedial reading program of the Dearborn, Michigan, school
system. A reading center was established to train classroom teachers to
detect problem readers early and to apply techniques designed to prevent
the development of reading problems. The center deals directly with slow
readers only as they are needed as subjects with whom trainees can work.
Training lasts for six weeks. The goal is to eliminate disabled readers
from the schools by equipping teachers to develop individualized programs
for them.

1674   Betts, Emmett Albert. "Prevention and correction of reading dis-
       abilities." Elem Engl Rev 12(2): 25-32, 48, February, 1935.
       (76 References).
Most reading disabilities can be prevented or remedied. Severely handicapped readers and nonreaders require individual instruction, and teachers
should have available the tools for analysis of reading problems. No one
type of corrective material can be equally effective for all children.
Problems which are not pedagogical should be referred to a specialist.
Teachers should work with psychologists, physicians, and other specialists
to identify these aspects of reading problems. Larger type is helpful
for corrective reading materials. Awareness of success is helpful to the
disabled reader.

1675   Bishop, Julia M. "Encouraging the discouraged." Grade Teach
       77(3): 138-41, November, 1959. (0 References).

Emotional problems, school absences, and physical ailments are among the causes of reading disability. Beginning in second grade, retarded readers should have an additional training period in reading each day. The work should be planned to create interest in reading and to build self-confidence. Parent-teacher conferences; variety in methods and materials; and frequent testing are three basic approaches necessary to build a strong remedial reading program.

1676   Bloom, Sophie. "Helping the retarded reader; in kindergarten through grade three." In: Conference on Reading, University of Chicago, 1966. Proceedings: seventy-five years of progress. Vol. 28. Compiled and edited by H. Alan Robinson. Chicago, Illinois: University of Chicago Press, 1966. 162-66. (0 References). (Supplementary Educational Monographs, No. 96).

Because of the large numbers of retarded readers from disadvantaged backgrounds who are now in some schools, it is not possible to teach them outside the regular classroom. The classroom teacher must handle the problem. Retarded readers can be taught in the classroom and can learn to read. Suggestions for diagnosing the problem and selecting suitable materials are offered.

1677   Boney, C. DeWitt. "The disposition of a group of slow first-grade readers." Elem Sch J 37(3): 203-8, November, 1936. (0 References).

Describes a plan for dealing with slow readers in the regular classroom. Under this plan a child in grades one, two, or three was promoted to grade four if it was believed that he could fit into an average fourth-grade group. "Average group" was defined as a two-year spread around grade norm. Instruction was largely on an individual basis using varied methods. Basal readers were not used in grades two and three. As the children who learned to read quickly became independent, the teacher could devote more time to the slow readers. Good readers could select reading materials under the teacher's guidance, reading independently of the group. Causes of fluctuations in the rate at which children progress in beginning reading are unknown; probably they are a part of normal growth. If slow readers are kept together, and instructed at their own levels, most will be able to go into an average fourth-grade group at the end of grade three. Backwardness in reading is not believed to be a great deterrent to progress in the subjects taught in the primary grades.

1678   Boyd, John E. "Teaching children with reading problems." In: Hamill, Donald D., and Bartel, Nettie R., eds. Teaching children with learning and behavior problems. Boston, Massachusetts: Allyn and Bacon, 1975. 15-59. (0 References).

Types of reading problems and their assessment are discussed. Tests for diagnosing reading problems are listed and explained, including such instruments as the San Diego Quick Assessment, Queens College Educational Clinic Sample Word List, and tests which the teacher can prepare. Various approaches to the teaching of reading are explained. These include basal approaches using a reading text and other materials, individualized reading, the language experience approach, programmed reading, the Peabody Rebus program, the Initial Teaching Alphabet (ITA), Words in Color, Distar, and the Stern Structual Reading Series. Special techniques including the Fernald visual-auditory approach, the Gillingham phonics approach, and other methods are explored. Some are designed for group use; others are better suited to individualized instruction.

1679   Brooks, Charlotte. "Reclaiming the alienated reader." <u>Instructor</u>
       81(9): 49-50, May, 1972. (0 References).
Youngsters who are convinced they will fail at reading and who have been
turned against reading by faulty teaching and the wrong materials can be
recaptured by the use of reading materials that say to such a pupil, "I
know you." Teachers should find books that reflect the pupils' lives,
have many photographs, and are colorful and attractive. Paperbacks, music,
short poems, records, tapes, and books of myths and fairy tales can all
be useful.

1680   Chall, Jeanne Sternlicht. <u>Learning to read: the great debate; an
       inquiry into the science, art, and ideology of old and new methods
       of teaching children to read, 1910-1965</u>. New York: McGraw-Hill,
       1967. 372p. (Bibliography p. 315-30).
Acknowledging that there has been a long-standing debate among authorities
on how to teach beginning reading, this book sets forth what is believed
to be the relevant facts in this debate. Some of the classic clinical
reports on why children fail to learn to read are reviewed, although these
studies do not prove that any one method used in the beginning stages of
reading produces more failures than another. Only one chapter is directly
concerned with reading failure. What is termed the "code-emphasis" method
rather than "meaning-emphasis" programs is strongly recommended. The
code-emphasis methods in general tend toward a heavier use of phonics in
the initial stages of reading instruction. Very little of the material
in this book deals with the dyslexic viewed as a child with an inherent
problem. The book focuses on a review of methods in the teaching of reading as they relate to failure by rank-and-file pupils.

1681   ————. "Reading disability and the role of the teacher." <u>Elem
       Engl</u> 35(5): 297-98, May, 1958. (0 References).
Teachers wonder whether they should teach the child to read, or attempt
to get at the basic cause of the reading difficulty, often a difficult,
time-consuming task. Because of the complexity of the causes of reading
disability, teachers are advised to be the most understanding, competent
teachers possible, but to teach the child to read by the best techniques
without delving into his deeper problems.

1682   Clark, Margaret Macdonald. <u>Reading difficulties in schools: a
       community study of specific reading difficulties, carried out with
       a grant from the Scottish Education Department</u>. Harmondsworth,
       England; Baltimore, Maryland: Penguin Books, 1970. 144p. (Bib-
       liography p. 138-42).
Reports on a study to determine the incidence of dyslexia among children
who had had two years of school. All of the children in the county of
Dunbartonshire near Glasgow who were born between April 1 and August 31,
1959, were tested after they had completed two years of school. The
total was 1,544 children. They were tested again after three years of
school. The research was planned so that the incidence of the various
characteristics of dyslexia could be determined, indicating the pattern
of such disabilities. About 15 percent of the children had no real reading ability after two years of school. Poor motor coordination and left-
right confusion was common in the seven-year-olds. Left-handedness and/or
left-eyedness did not predict reading level. Absence rate from school
and changing schools were both high. Some of the seven-year-olds who were
backward in reading were of average intelligence, but most were of low
general intelligence. Girls of average intelligence seemed unlikely to
be backward readers. Those who were poor readers were duller in general

than the reading-disabled boys. By the time retesting was done when the
children were nine years of age, about 1 percent, or nineteen children,
who had average intelligence were found to be severely reading-disabled
from all causes. Of the nineteen, fifteen were boys. Only one of the
nineteen had all three WISC IQ scores over 100. Speech defects, poor
auditory discrimination, and poor visuomotor coordination were common.
A diversity of disabilities was observed without any underlying pattern
common to all the children. Implications for changes in teaching approaches are discussed. Brief histories of most of the nineteen most
severely disabled readers are included.

1683 Conference on Reading, University of Chicago, 1953. Proceedings:
      corrective reading in classroom and clinic. Vol. 15. Compiled and
      edited by Helen M. Robinson. Chicago, Illinois: University of
      Chicago Press, 1953. 256p. (Supplementary Educational Monographs,
      No. 79).
After general statements of the problem of reading retardation and its
remediation, articles deal with how to diagnose reading retardation, including specific kinds of problems. Word recognition, increased comprehension, and the selection of materials for disabled readers are other
areas covered. All ages are considered from kindergarten through college.
The particular problems of diagnosing reading disability in a clinic are
examined.

1684 Conference on Reading, University of Chicago, 1962. Proceedings:
      the underachiever in reading. Vol. 24. Compiled and edited by H.
      Alan Robinson. Chicago, Illinois: University of Chicago Press,
      1962. 198p. (Supplementary Educational Monographs, No. 92).
Describes the underachiever in reading. Methods for locating and diagnosing disabled readers, and ways to test and teach them are considered.
Methods for stimulating children and suggestions for administering reading programs are also included. The various aspects of reading problems
covered in the book are discussed from the points of view of different
grade levels.

1685 Cox, Margaret, compiler and ed. The challenge of reading failure.
      Slough, England: National Foundation for Educational Research in
      England and Wales, 1968. 45p.
Presents the findings of an intensive study of more than 8,000 schoolchildren in England. It compares the reading standards of children ages
seven to eleven in Kent with children of the same age in the country as
a whole. Bigger schools in better-class urban areas were found to have
generally higher reading standards. The most able readers were produced
in schools using a formal, systematic approach to reading. Phonic methods
produced better results with five-year-olds, especially those of average
or just below average ability. Early diagnosis is important since a long-
term follow-up study showed that a child's reading level at age eight was
predictive of his entire future. The poorest teachers came from the most
unfavorable home and school conditions. It is urged that teachers of
English-system junior grades as well as primary grades should be well-
trained in techniques of teaching reading and in remedial reading methods.
(For full details of this study see Item No. 532.)

1686 Davis, Joanna S., and Edgington, Ruth. "Classroom teaching sugges-
      tions for language-learning problems." Acad Ther 5(1): 67-74,
      Fall, 1959. (0 References).

Offers suggestions for teachers of children with language-learning problems. Material is presented in tabular form with columns for identification of the underlying problem, the observable classroom behavior, and
teaching suggestions for groups or individual pupils. Among the problems
covered are difficulties in understanding what is seen or heard, difficulties in organizing material, in writing and spelling, and in coping
with the child who is impatient and easily distracted by outside stimuli.

1687   Davis, Marianne K. "The problem reader in the classroom." Can
      Psychol 9(2): 162-73, April, 1968. (0 References).
Slow starters are not always slow learners. Some children develop reading problems because their development is slower than that of most children. If formal reading instruction is begun too soon or they are pushed
too fast, problems develop. Teachers should gear the program to the
child's rate of learning. Difficulties in middle and upper grades stem
from incomplete mastery of early reading skills. Children should be
taught good work habits very early in order to learn how to learn. They
should receive encouragement both at home and at school.

1688   Doerr, Andrea. "Help for the rural LD child." Am Educ 10(5):
      26-29, June, 1974. (0 References).
Beginning with almost nothing in 1970, a part-time speech therapist in
central Nebraska pioneered in helping learning-disabled (LD) children, including bright children who could not read. The project has now become
the Regional Assessment Center, one of the activities of Education Service
Unit No. 9, a political subdivision of the Nebraska state government.
Federal funding was also obtained. Dr. James C. Chalfant gave initial
help at an all-day workshop attended by 600 teachers. The center now
sends trained teachers throughout a 3,000-square-mile area. Using formal
testing methods, these teachers evaluate and work with LD children individually or in small groups. Classroom teachers are learning to allow children to work at their own pace within each individual's own learning style.

1689   Dolch, E. W. "What to do with reading deficiencies in the elemen-
      tary school." Educ Outlook 16: 56-61, January, 1972. (0 Ref-
      erences).
Gives whole-classroom, small-group, and individual methods for helping
the poor reader. Whole-room methods include: (1) a daily individual
reading period when each child reads as much as he can from the book he
has selected; (2) individual practice in sounding; and (3) developing
thought reactions by asking the child questions about his reading. The
slower readers can be helped as a small group with the use of easier books
and work on sight vocabulary. Individual help must be given the child
with severe reading deficiencies. The first task is to secure his confidence. Then secure effort on his part, give him an oral reading test,
and finally, ascertain whether the child realizes he is reading for meaning.

1690   Durrell, D. D. Reading disability in the intermediate grades. Un-
      published Ed.D. thesis. Harvard University, 1930.

1691   Edwin, Sister Mary. "Helping the retarded reader; in grades four
      through eight." In: Conference on Reading, University of Chicago,
      1966. Proceedings: seventy-five years of progress. Vol. 28.
      Compiled and edited by H. Alan Robinson. Chicago, Illinois: Uni-
      versity of Chicago Press, 1966. 166-69. (0 References). (Supple-
      mentary Educational Monographs, No. 96).

Grouping of retarded readers should be made on a school-wide basis. Each teacher of the same grade could be given a group of normal readers and a group of retarded readers all of whom are reading at about the same level below grade. This aids selection of materials. Suggestions are included for planning adequately for both groups. The teacher must assess each child's strengths and weaknesses.

1692   Erickson, Allen G. Handbook for teachers of disabled readers.
       Iowa City, Iowa: Sernoll, 1966. 80p.
Suggestions are given for successful teaching of the disabled reader, including ways to find the child's reading level, and discovering weakness in auditory discrimination. Case studies, word lists suitable for various reading levels, and book lists for children are included.

1693   Faigel, Harris C. "When children can't read: the dyslexic in the
       classroom." Clin Pediatr 8(1): 11-15, January, 1969. (6 References).
Dyslexia is defined as the inability to learn to read well by usual teaching methods in spite of normal intelligence, vision and hearing, and normal achievement in oral or nonverbal school work. The classroom teacher must recognize the condition and build up the child's self-esteem by making him feel he can do the tasks she asks, and learn in spite of his handicap. The earlier it is diagnosed, the easier dyslexia is to treat and the less handicapped the individual. The classroom teacher is in the front line of recognition and treatment of dyslexia.

1694   Font, Marion McKenzie. "Orientation in clinical approach through
       remedial reading instruction." Am J Orthopsychiatry 12(2): 324-
       34, April, 1942. (12 References).
This description of a course in remedial reading instruction for teachers at Tulane University includes case reports. Teachers previously inexperienced in remedial methods were able to help reading-disabled children more successfully and to work more successfully with clinics and social agencies after completing this course of study.

1695   Frostig, Marianne, and Maslow, Phyllis. Learning problems in the
       classroom: prevention and remediation. New York: Grune & Stratton,
       1973. 353p. (Bibliography).
Theoretical considerations and educational procedures, including practical teaching methods for the classroom, aimed at the prevention and remediation of many kinds of learning difficulties are the concern of this book. The viewpoint is that the child's abilities and deficits should be analyzed. Teaching methods must then be adjusted to achieve the best results in educating that child. The book is directed primarily toward teachers. The extent to which a child's learning problems are the result of environment and heredity are not the province of this book. Medical diagnosis is not extensively discussed. The focus is on what the teacher can do in the classroom to diagnose the child's needs and take the best possible approach for the prevention or remediation of that problem. This is termed the "psychoeducational approach." Only one chapter is directly concerned with problems in teaching reading. It discusses some of the skills necessary for reading, including sound-blending, auditory and visual perception, motivation, and memory. Other chapters cover ways to teach visual and auditory perception and ways to develop language abilities.

1696 Gagermeier, Louis. "An experimental approach to the problem of
        poor readers." Mont Educ 42(4): 8-9, November, 1965. (0 Refer-
        ences).
Five poor readers of normal intelligence and physical characteristics were
assigned to one classroom and seated together. In order to avoid any
stigma, the class was told that these five had been selected for a special
experiment. The poor readers listened to tape recordings of all silent
reading assignments, following in their books during the reading. The
rest of the class read silently in the usual way. All five began to make
average grades whereas they had been failing before. They were tested in
the same fashion as the rest of the children. The tape players did not
disrupt the classroom, and the teacher had more time to spend in normal
discussion. The mental attitudes of the children and their parents improved considerably.

1697 Gerstmyer, Eva E. "Diagnosing serious reading difficulties in the
        primary grades." Natl Elem Princ 17(7): 397-402, July, 1938.
        (0 References).
Describes methods used in the Baltimore school system to help retarded
readers. If the pupil does not show improvement after one semester in a
remedial reading group, he is referred to a clinician for detailed diagnosis. An individual program is planned for the child in consultation
with his classroom teacher and others. Findings in this program indicate
that extreme nonreaders usually suffer either from physical defects or
from poor teaching methods and not from innate deficiencies. A case
history is documented.

1698 Glasser, William. "An approach to the solution of reading diffi-
        culties." Claremont Coll Read Conf Yearb 34: 47-53, 1970. (0
        References).
Four basic changes need to be made in our schools: (1) teachers must
stop failing children; (2) ability grouping in the teaching of reading
must be abandoned; (3) reading material must be made interesting to children; and (4) teachers must become more involved with pupils.

1699 Great Britain. Advisory Committee on Handicapped Children. Chil-
        dren with specific reading difficulties; report on the Advisory
        Committee on Handicapped Children. London: H. M. Stationery Office,
        1972. 8p. (0 References).
The Advisory Committee (Prof. J. Tizard, chairman) was asked whether local
education authorities needed guidance on the education of children suffering from dyslexia. Conclusions in this report indicate that the committee
prefers not to use the term "dyslexia" at all since it has been so loosely
employed. They prefer "specific reading difficulties." They believe that
all such children need to be screened early in their careers, with continued checking. Remedial reading courses should be given, with special
centers set up for those who cannot be helped adequately in regular classrooms. These centers should work with the regular schools. Full use
should be made of oral learning methods for these children.

1700 Griffiths, Anita H.; Gillen, Joseph F.; Dankel, Roberta. "Leave
        dyslexics in the classroom." Acad Ther 8(1): 57-65, Fall, 1972.
        (6 References).
Teachers selected a number of children with diagnoses of dyslexia from
regular classrooms and for twelve weeks gave them a program of individualized instruction within the classroom. Improvement was significant,
which strongly suggests that dyslexics can make satisfactory progress in
the regular classroom with some individual help.

1701 Harris, Albert Josiah, and Sipay, Edward R. How to increase read-
     ing ability: a guide to developmental and remedial methods. 6th
     ed. New York: McKay, 1975. 713p. (Bibliography p. 576-629).
This general text on reading covers in some detail such areas as reading
readiness; how to meet the child's individual needs in the teaching of
reading; and how to teach reading to groups. All these topics are intended for use by teachers of normally developing readers. In addition,
material is included on reading difficulties and on remedial reading.
Six chapters are devoted to diagnosis of reading problems. The multiplicity and confusion of terms used to describe reading deficiencies are
pointed out. An attempt is made at clarifying definitions. Methods for
assessing the reading level to be expected from a child and for assessing
reading performance are given. Various tests are discussed including the
informal reading inventory and silent and oral reading tests. Causes of
reading disability are considered. The favored viewpoint is multiple
causes. Cognitive factors, including intelligence, and specific factors
such as visual and auditory perception, physical and physiological factors, and cultural problems are evaluated as causes. Basic remedial
reading techniques and specific methods and goals are explained. Remedial
procedures for teaching word identification and improving reading comprehension are covered. A bibliography of more than 1,100 items is included.
An annotated list of educational tests of all kinds, a graded list of
books for remedial reading, and a list of publishers and their addresses
are found in appendices.

1702 Hartman, Nancy C. "Response: low tolerance for frustration: target
     group for reading disabilities." Read Teach 27(7): 675, April,
     1974. (0 References).
In response to Orlow (Item No. 1724) it is contended that low frustration
tolerance may result from reading failure, rather than the reverse. Suggestions for avoiding this difficulty are presented.

1703 Hedley, Carolyn. "Reading and language difficulties." In: Wilson,
     John A. R., ed. Diagnosis of learning difficulties. New York:
     McGraw-Hill, 1971. 135-56. (0 References).
No definition of reading disability is generally accepted. Reading disability may be assessed in terms of the child's chronological age or his
mental age. Causes of reading disability are examined including readiness, visual and auditory problems, perceptual problems, subvocalizing,
and environmental, emotional, and sex factors. Little time should be
spent waiting for readiness to develop. The child should be exposed to
symbolic activity and given practice in the skills he needs. Suggestions
are made for meeting various teaching problems. Factors such as grouping
children for reading instruction; the youngsters' emotional development
and home environment; and the role anxiety plays in reading problems are
considered. It is believed that little new information has been advanced
about reading disabilities in the past forty years. However, much new
experimental material is currently being published in the field. There
is great concern about reading instruction. It is suggested that we are
really doing much better than we imagine in the teaching of reading.

1704 Hirsch, Bianca Zwang, and Smith, Grace White. "Activating a pro-
     gram for the dyslexic child within the framework of the public
     school." For a summary see: Diss Abstr Int 32A(3): 1381, Sep-
     tember, 1971.

1705 Hocker, Mary Elsa. "A case-study approach to reading problems."
      Read Teach 21(6): 541-43, March, 1968. (0 References).
Details an approach to reading problems using a case study group consisting of a child psychiatrist, clinical psychologist, reading consultant,
school nurse, counselors, principal, and teachers. The group described
serves 3,000 children in four elementary schools and one junior high.
Correctional behavior counseling is emphasized. A danger in this method
is that participants are played against each other. This must be avoided
as this approach has been very successful in alleviating reading problems.
Adequate communication among all parties is essential. The team must
present a unified front to the parents, just as parents must present a
unified front to the children. Education will not cure all ills, but
much can be done through good communication among those concerned with
the child.

1706 Johnson, Marjorie Seddon, and Kress, Roy A., eds. Corrective read-
      ing in the elementary classroom. Neward, Delaware: International
      Reading Association, 1967. 142p. (Perspectives in Reading, No. 7).
This collection of eleven conference papers defines "corrective reading"
as those procedures designed to help the dyslexic child in the regular
classroom. "Remedial reading" procedures are those carried out by a
special teacher. Attention is given to various possible methods of identifying the problem reader, and to discovering the characteristics of
that individual child in order to help him overcome his weaknesses and
capitalize upon his strengths as a reader. The viewpoint is toward doing
these things within the regular classroom. The aim is not merely diagnostic, but instructional, that is, to help the child overcome his problems. Among areas considered are: (1) characteristics of typical children with reading problems which can be treated in the regular classroom
(corrective reading disabilities); (2) the pathology and prediction of
reading problems such as those in word recognition and comprehension; and
(3) the place of corrective reading in the total school program. Psychological and psychophysiological factors are discussed.

1707 Jordan, Dale R. Dyslexia in the classroom. Columbus, Ohio: Charles
      E. Merrill, 1972. 194p.
Provides detailed descriptions of visual dyslexia, auditory dyslexia, and
the dysgraphia syndrome. The causes of dyslexia are not dealt with extensively. Instead, the book provides detailed directions for teachers,
including methods for correcting each syndrome in the "here-and-now"
classroom situation. Checklists for screening for these various reading
disabilities and checklists for distinguishing dyslexia from aphasia,
hyperkinesis, and some other aberrant childhood behaviors are included.
It is the viewpoint of the book that an essential factor in correcting
dyslexia is mercy, and that dyslexics must begin with a structured experience. Bibliographies and a glossary are included.

1708 Kress, Roy A. "When is remedial reading remedial?" Education
      80(9): 540, 542-44, May, 1960. (10 References).
Much confusion of terms exists in the literature on reading problems.
Clarification of terms is necessary in order for professional workers in
the field to communicate with each other. "Corrective" reading problems
are defined as those which involve basic neurological or psychological
learning difficulty. The child with a "remedial" reading problem may,
like the corrective reader, be below grade level in reading, but part of
the cause lies in some associative learning problem with a neurological
or psychological base.

1709   Lichtenstein, Jack. "In search of 'the impossible dream.'" <u>Elem</u>
       <u>Engl</u> 47(2): 262-64, February, 1970. (0 References).
Reports the systematic search by a task force of public school educators
for a teaching method to minimize reading failure. After a year of research, three methods were selected for testing: Words in Color; Initial
Teaching Alphabet (ITA); and the Lippincott Basic Reading Program supple-
mented by other basic readers. No method showed clear superiority. The
hope of finding a magic, universally successful method is admittedly
"the impossible dream." A teacher equipped with good methods who is
sensitive to the needs of individual pupils is the best magic available
in teaching reading.

1710   Lloyd, Bruce A. "Helping the disabled reader at the elementary
       level." In: International Reading Association. <u>Conference pro-</u>
       <u>ceedings: reading and realism</u>. Vol. 13(Part 1). Edited by J.
       Allen Figurel. Newark, Delaware: International Reading Associa-
       tion, 1969. 171-76. (0 References).
The teacher's first task is to identify the disabled reader--the pupil
who is not reading at a level commensurate with his ability. Diagnosing
the causes of the disability is complex. Overlapping deficiencies or
impairments; the pupil's background and experience; and his perception of
his world all influence reading ability. After diagnosis, an individualized reading program should be worked out for each pupil. Specific teaching suggestions are offered.

1711   McClurg, William M. "Dyslexia: early identification and treatment
       in the schools." <u>J Learn Disabil</u> 3(7): 372-77, July, 1970. (18
       References).
Early diagnosis and treatment of dyslexia requires teamwork on the part
of elementary school staffs, but it should be done. Major responsibility
falls on the teacher for detecting reading disabilities. Symptoms of
dyslexia and diagnostic tests are outlined. Nine helpful instructional
methods are listed including flexible grouping, Fernald's kinesthetic
method, phonics, and medication in some cases.

1712   McGuire, Marion L. "Dyslexia: a reading specialist's opinion."
       <u>J Learn Disabil</u> 3(4): 232-33, April, 1970. (0 References).
Dyslexics can learn to read when methods are adjusted to their learning
styles. Early diagnosis is important. Because of behavior problems a
dyslexic child may have to be placed in a special class. However, most
dyslexics can and should be taught in the regular classroom using the
method that works best for the individual child.

1713   Mariam, O. P., Sister. "Using special modes of learning to improve
       reading instruction: in kindergarten through grade three." In:
       Conference on Reading, University of Chicago, 1964. <u>Proceedings:</u>
       <u>meeting individual differences in reading</u>. Vol. 26. Compiled and
       edited by H. Alan Robinson. Chicago, Illinois: University of
       Chicago Press, 1964. 34-36. (0 References). (Supplementary Educa-
       tional Monographs, No. 94).
Different techniques must be used to enable each child to achieve maximum
learning. The child's mental and language ability and his neurological
development must be assessed. Some children learn to read better by the
visual approach, others by the auditory. Children with difficulties in
cerebral dominance, directionality, and spatial orientation probably need
special assistance.

1714 Mary Julitta, Sister. "Classroom methods in correcting reading
      deficiencies in elementary school." In: International Reading
      Association. Conference proceedings: better readers for our
      times. Vol. 1. Edited by William S. Gray, and Nancy Larrick. New
      York: Scholastic Magazines, 1956. 134-38. (3 References).
Outlines methods for helping the retarded reader through differentiated
instruction. To meet the needs of individuals within the regular classroom, grouping is necessary. Grouping according to general instructional
level is probably the most basic of these. For pupils requiring more
work in certain ideas, special skills groups can be formed. Each group
can study one aspect of reading, for example, word analysis, oral reading, etc. Team groups and interest groups may also be formed. The entire class should also meet together. Suggestions for helping retarded
readers are given.

1715 Mazow, Malcolm L. "Dyslexia and the open concept school." J
      Pediatr Ophthalmol 13(4): 232-33, July/August, 1976. (0 Refer-
      ences).
The open concept school is one where all grades of elementary education
are conducted in one large room and each child can proceed at his own
pace in any subject of study. More individual attention is available to
each child. There is opportunity to develop better learning habits and
self-discipline. This type of education will certainly benefit the child
with a learning disability.

1716 Miller, Wilma H. Identifying and correcting reading difficulties
      in children. New York: Center for Applied Research in Education,
      1971. 237p. (Bibliography).
This book is intended to help the elementary classroom teacher diagnose
and correct the problems of moderately disabled readers before the difficulties become so complex that special help in a reading clinic becomes
necessary. The reading process is explained. The major causes of reading disability are discussed. Discussed are: (1) ways to tell the disabled reader from a slow-learning child or a reluctant reader; (2) ways
to construct, give, and score the individual reading inventory; and (3)
the details of various remedial reading methods. Material on how to gain
the parents' cooperation is included. Lists of reading tests and book
publishers, and generalizations about phonetics are given.

1717 Mingoia, Edwin M. "A program for immature readers." Elem Engl
      41(6): 616-21, October, 1964. (0 References).
As many as 20 percent of the total number of children in some underprivi-
leged classrooms may show delays in maturity. A program is outlined for
helping immature children learn to read. A delay of several years before
formal instruction begins is advised. By third grade these children are
generally able to read first readers and to begin to master word-attack
skills.

1718 Mitchell, Joanne R. "Getting poor readers ready to read." Teach
      Except Child 6(2): 103-10, Winter, 1974. (0 References).
Describes a method used to instruct first graders who were not learning
to read with usual methods. The children were highly motivated to learn
their own names. Each child learned to read his name followed by "is,"
and one of the words, "sad," "glad," or "mad," followed by a face showing
the appropriate emotion. Other simple sentences followed, the strategy
being to cue each sentence heavily with a picture and gradually compare
similar sentences while reducing the strength of the picture cue. Teach-

ing was largely by sight repetition and the use of context cues, rather than the linguistic technique of emphasizing letter-sound correspondence and blending.

1719   Monroe, Marion, and Backus, Bertie. Remedial reading; a monograph
       in character education. Boston, Massachusetts: Houghton Mifflin,
       1937. 171p.
Many reading failures are unnecessary and could be avoided if adequate remedial reading programs were available. The large number of children needing such programs; the hindrance to later school progress; and the relation between reading disabilities, personality, and character all justify remedial reading programs in the public schools. It is believed that a connection exists between development of character and the ability to read. Causes and symptoms of reading disability are listed, and general principles of remedial instruction are set forth. Methods used and results obtained in public schools in Washington, D.C. are given. About 20 percent of the children in the remedial program made gains that brought their reading scores up to their grade levels. Improvements in personality were observed in some of the children, with favorable changes in attitude.

1720   Moseley, David. Children with special problems. Milton Keynes,
       Buckinghamshire: Open University Press, 1973. 52p. (Reading
       Development, Unit 14).
This book is one of the texts for the course in Reading Development offered by Harper and Row's Open University. Problems faced by backward readers, a description of dyslexia, and the diagnostic significance of various reading errors are discussed. Ways to help the problem reader are suggested. This book is intended for use in connection with other readings which are listed.

1721   Murphy, M. Leonore. "The children we fail." Slow Learn Child
       14(1): 30-36, 1967. (3 References).
Praises and explains Caleb Gattegno's Words in Colour method of teaching reading. It has been most effective in bringing slow learners up to grade level as well as enlivening the entire second-grade classroom in the situation described. The scope of Words of Colour and how it works are explained.

1722   Nemeth, Joseph. "How the classroom teacher can help the corrective
       reader." In: Reading Conference, Lehigh University, 13th, 1964.
       Proceedings: reading and child development. Vol. 4. Edited by
       Albert J. Mazurkiewicz. Bethlehem, Pennsylvania: The Bureau of
       Educational Services, Department of Education, Lehigh University,
       1964. 40-45. (7 References).
Defines the "corrective reader" as one who can be helped in the regular classroom, and the "remedial reader" as one who requires help by a specially trained teacher outside the classroom. To help the disabled reader in the classroom, the teacher must: (1) identify him; (2) diagnose his reading deficiencies; (3) know corrective teaching techniques; and (4) evaluate their effectiveness. It is imperative to begin at the child's level. Methods of diagnosis, corrective procedures, and ways to evaluate progress are outlined.

1723   Newton, Margaret, and Thomson, Michael. Dyslexia; a guide for
       teachers and parents. London: University of London Press, 1975.
       56p. (Bibliography).

A guide to the teaching of dyslexics, this book considers the nature of written English as a skill to be learned. Ways to diagnose the pupil's problem and present written language by a method as compatible as possible with the child's pattern of learning are explained. Specific teaching techniques are given. Dyslexic symptoms are described with advice on coping with them.

1724 Orlow, Maria. "Low tolerance for frustration: target group for reading disabilities." Read Teach 27(7): 669-74, April, 1974. (14 References).
A large number of children enter school psychologically ill prepared to succeed in beginning reading because they cannot tolerate frustration. These children often become acute reading disability cases. A kindergarten program to prevent the development of reading disability is suggested. It would combine overlearning of reading readiness skills with deliberately structured emotional support. Some of these children may also require skilled individual tutoring.

1725 Ort, Lorene Love. "Reading difficulties--a contributing factor to underachievement and failure in school." Except Child 28(9): 489-92, May, 1962. (0 References).
Reading failure in a child is equivalent to bankruptcy in an adult. Both result in frustration and failure in the view of one's peers. Several factors that would help avert reading failure are listed: avoiding droning monotony, use of appealing literature, excellent teachers, reading research, and more emphasis on sound practices to prevent reading failure. It is believed that too much emphasis is placed on the age at which the child begins to read.

1726 Peterson, Miriam E. "Helping the slow reader." Libr J 81(22): 2977-79, December 15, 1956. (6 References).
Focuses on how the elementary school library can aid retarded readers. The librarian and the classroom teacher must cooperate and must know something about the background and characteristics of the disabled reader and the nature of his individual problem. Suggestions are made for selecting and organizing library materials and publicizing them. Special projects and activities to help retarded readers are suggested.

1727 Plessas, Gus P., and Petty, Walter T. "Spelling plight of the poor reader." Elem Engl 39(5): 463-65, May, 1962. (7 References).
Children with reading difficulties have little success in spelling instruction unless their individual reading disabilities are treated. It is better for such children to learn to spell a few selected words than to struggle with a longer list. More attention should be devoted to reading (if necessary), even if spelling lessons must be slighted.

1728 Preston, Mary I. "The school looks at the nonreader." Elem Sch J 40(6): 450-58, February, 1940. (0 References).
Reports on the results obtained by the use of all methods applicable in teaching forty nonreaders to read. It is emphasized that teachers of beginning reading should be trained in the art of teaching reading no matter what the individual differences in the learning processes of the pupils.

1729 Rieger, Arlene A. "Improving self-concepts for reading underachievers." Elem Engl 52(3): 364-66, March, 1975. (0 References).

Describes a two-fold plan for eleven-year-old fifth-grade reading underachievers focused on two areas: building reading skills and building
self-concept. It is suggested that there must be concentrated, organized
effort to prove to slow readers that they can do grade-level work. The
children described worked in pairs, helping each other. Drill was given
in study techniques, including study "tricks" such as skimming material
for key words, numbers, and special print. Races were held to find specific words in a section of a book. It is suggested that some pressure
to push slower students is a means for building self-concept and improving morale because in reality life is a balance of competition with oneself and comparison with one's peers.

1730   Roberts, Geoffrey R. "A study of motivation in remedial reading."
       Br J Educ Psychol 30(Part 2): 176-79, June, 1960. (0 References).
Three forms of motivation, each combined with a suitable method of learning to read, were compared under normal classroom conditions. Ten-year-
old retarded readers from low cultural backgrounds were the subjects.
Method A allowed the children to write their own stories using Fernald's
tracing-vocalization-writing method for teaching new words. Curiosity
and creative drive were the basis of motivation. Method B used gregarious-
ness as a basis for motivation. Competition was eliminated, cooperative
reading in pairs was used, and the children's work was never compared.
The basis of the method was that advocated by A. E. Gates and Schonell.
Method C used competition for motivation. A system of awards and prizes
was used. A phonetic teaching method based on work by Marion Monroe was
used. Method A proved to be superior. The advantages and disadvantages
of the methods are discussed. Inability to learn new words appears to
be a major cause of retardation.

1731   Robinson, Helen M. "Prevention and correction of reading diffi-
       culties." Education 77(9): 541-45, May, 1957. (7 References).
Almost all reading difficulties can be corrected or prevented, usually
without the services of a reading specialist. The individual child's
needs must be assessed and books interesting to him that he is able to
read must be found.

1732   Saunders, Roger E., and Malin, David H. "Prevention and remedia-
       tion of dyslexia: a classroom approach." Am J Orthopsychiatry
       41(2): 323-24, March, 1971. (0 References).
Summarizes a study of ways the classroom teacher can identify, prevent,
or remediate dyslexia. Specific screening procedures selected first-,
second-, and third-grade children who had symptoms of dyslexia.

1733   Schiffman, Gilbert. "Dyslexia--the administrator's dilemma." J
       Learn Disabil 2(11): 566-67, November, 1969. (0 References).
The reason most school systems do not have effective programs for the prevention and treatment of dyslexia is that school administrators fail to
understand the problem. If a child does not learn by the traditional
teaching methods, then he is a problem. Local administrators must be
educated and involved in the planning and carrying out of any program for
the treatment of dyslexia.

1734   Schleich, Miriam. "The disabled reader in the regular class." In:
       Reading Conference, Syracuse University. Proceedings: reading:
       practice and perspective, 7th-8th, 1965-1966. Edited by Frank P.
       Greene; E. Coston Frederick; Robert A. Palmatier. Syracuse, New
       York: The Division of the Summer Sessions, Syracuse University,
       1967. 33-38. (2 References).

After listing four criteria by which the disabled reader can be identified, the author describes the kinds of reading disability in terms of
their severity. To treat disabled readers in the regular classroom, several plans are suggested, including grouping the children by reading
level; pairing a good reader with a poor one; or organizing the classroom
for maximum individualized instruction. The classroom teacher with
neither the time nor the training to deal with a seriously disabled reader should encourage him in learning by making maximum use of learning by
means other than reading.

1735   Schoeller, Arthur W. "Reading: emerging role of the 'RRT.'"
      Instructor 82(1): 69-70, August-September, 1972. (0 References).
The reading resource teacher (RRT) works with teachers instead of working with pupils in remedial reading work. By helping each teacher improve his teaching skills, the reading program becomes more effective
thus preventing reading failure. An RRT should be a thoroughly trained
reading specialist who works easily with others and who has sufficient
training and experience to help classroom teachers. Such a person can
be more helpful as more diagnostic information becomes available about
each pupil. He can help the teacher in doing more diagnostic-prescriptive
instruction.

1736   Schubert, Delwyn G., and Torgerson, Theodore L. Improving the
      reading program. 3rd ed. Dubuque, Iowa: W. C. Brown, 1972. 379p.
      (Bibliography).
Suggests many approaches to improvement in a school's reading program.
Of particular interest to students of dyslexia are the following: Chapter
two describes the educational factors which may cause reading failure.
Group instruction where no effort is made to meet the needs of individual
pupils is particularly criticized. Chapter three discusses the many
other causes of reading disability including problems of dominance, neurological impairment, abnormal neural transmission, emotional, and environmental factors. Chapter six emphasizes the importance of accurate
diagnosis of reading disability. Ways of doing this are suggested. The
first two editions of this book were published under slightly varying
titles.

1737   Smith, Nila Banton. "Classroom teacher's responsibility to re-
      tarded readers." Education 77(9): 546-50, May, 1957. (0 Refer-
      ences).
The school is often blamed for the child's reading failure. Teachers
should be concerned about and sensitive to the symptoms of reading disability. Teachers should explain the causes of reading disability to
parents and not use lack of reading readiness as a catchall. Teachers
should improve their attitudes toward retarded readers and improve instruction.

1738   Stocker, Dolores Sandoval. "Responses to the language experience
      approach to reading by black, culturally different, inner-city
      students, experiencing reading disability in grades five and
      eleven." For a summary see: Diss Abstr Int 32A(1): 291, July,
      1971.

1739   Tally, Dorothy S. "Teaching the hard to reach." Engl J 61(7):
      1054-56, October, 1972. (0 References).
A junior high school teacher found herself suddenly with classes of slow
or nonreaders as a result of busing within the school system. She dis-

carded traditional language arts instruction. Her first plan to capture interest, for example, was to give points for students who brought their books to class and read them for the first fifteen minutes. The students were surprised to find they were given the grades promised for cooperation. Interest grew. She also read aloud to them and gave points for written summaries of the readings turned in every other day with no penalties for spelling, punctuation, or sentence structure. The students learned to like the methods, it is reported.

1740 Wagner, Guy W., and Frahm, Izetta. "Just who is the retarded reader, anyhow?" Midland Sch 68: 18-19, 40-41, April, 1954. (0 References).
The retarded reader is any child who, no matter what his intellectual level, is reading below his mental capacity. Causes of retarded reading are numerous and range from poor social and emotional adjustment and physical problems, through poor teaching techniques, to malfunctions of the nervous system which require specialized diagnosis and treatment. Corrective procedures recommended include: (1) making reading an experience of success; (2) using materials suited to the individual child's present ability; (3) using teacher techniques corresponding to each child's needs; and (4) using attractive books. The developmental reading program should be adjusted to the individual's needs, talents, and personal interests.

1741 Walby, Grace. "Classroom techniques for the identification of retarded readers." In: World Congress on Reading, 2d, Copenhagen, 1968. Proceedings: reading: a human right and a human problem. Vol. 2. Edited by Ralph C. Staiger, and Oliver Andresen. Newark, Delaware: International Reading Association, 1969. 180-83. (3 References).
Four questions should be asked in planning remedial reading instruction: (1) How difficult a book can the child read? (2) What skills have not yet been developed? (3) What are the inhibiting factors? (4) What interests has the child upon which to build? Most children can be helped in the classroom if time is taken to find answers to these questions.

1742 Zintz, Miles V. Corrective reading. 2nd ed. Dubuque, Iowa: W. C. Brown, 1972. 449p. (Bibliography). (ED 080 941).
Designed primarily for the teacher, this book discusses specific methods for use in corrective reading. Areas covered include: (1) how to appraise reading problems in the regular classroom; (2) causes of reading failure; (3) evaluating oral and silent reading; (4) the cloze procedure; (5) reversals; (6) organizing corrective reading instruction by the unit method; (7) the language problems of black children; (8) information needed to diagnose reading problems; (9) the teacher's attitude toward failing readers; and (10) a discussion of psychoneurological problems.

2. KINESTHETIC APPROACH

1743 Catterall, Calvin D., and Weise, Phillip. "A perceptual approach to reading disability." Education 80(5): 275-78, January, 1960. (0 References).
Relates the case history of Peter, a second grader, who was not learning to read. He was helped to make a start by understanding cooperation between his parents and the teacher and by the use of a revised teaching method which allowed him to write or trace the word as he attempted to learn it.

1744   Cronin, Bob. "A new technique using braille to teach print read-
       ing to dyslexic children." New Outlook Blind 66(3): 71-74, 1972.
       (0 References).
The use of braille in teaching dyslexic children is recommended only for
the severest cases and when other methods have failed. By utilizing a
mode of perception that is not impaired, the braille method may help
these children learn to read. Since the dyslexic's eyesight is usually
unimpaired, it is hoped that the child will transfer what he learns by
tactile perception of the letters to information visually presented. The
case of a dyslexic boy who was repeating first grade is given as an example. He used the same reading book his peers used but with the braille
embossed on transparent sheets superimposed over the print. Transition
from tactile to visual reading began to occur very shortly. Using braille
to treat dyslexia is new. It is hoped that more books will be published
in print and braille. There are definite advantages to using braille as
a temporary mode of reading for children with severe reading disabilities.

1745   Gentry, Larry. "A clinical method in classroom success--kinesthetic
       teaching." Read Teach 28(3): 298-300, December, 1974. (8 Ref-
       erences).
Busy teachers can find time to capitalize on the economy and efficiency
of the kinesthetic method described by Grace Fernald to help nonreaders.
This method helps children who have difficulty learning to read by the
usual auditory and visual methods. Only paper to write the words on is
needed. Other activities can be used in connection with this method to
increase motivation. The visual-auditory-kinesthetic-tactile (VAKT)
technique of Fernald lends itself well to use by parents, aids, and
tutors because it requires no professional knowledge of phonics. Its
use is described.

1746   Shea, Dorothea P. "The case for the kinesthetic method." Grade
       Teach 74: 60, 108, 110, October, 1956. (1 Reference).
Kinesthetic teaching and learning are very old, having been used in Roman
schools. The method is erroneously criticized today as being too time-
consuming. The method has not been thoroughly investigated. If it were,
it would be found that kinesthetic training can complement academic
learning. Some children learn better through eye and ear. Others need
kinesthetic training for a limited period. A third group of children
will always need concrete learning and kinesthetic devices and will perform best in these activities. The method is described and suggestions
are made for its use not only in primary grades but also in intermediate
and upper grades.

3. SENSORY PERCEPTION TRAINING

1747   Sheppard, Marlene J. "An experiment in predicting and averting
       reading failure." In: Anderson, J., ed. Learning disabilities:
       diagnosis and treatment. Armidale, N.S.W., Australia: University
       of New England, 1971. 93-100. (14 References).
In an attempt to put into classroom practice some of the findings of modern research, this study tested children entering kindergarten in kinesthetic, visual, auditory, and tactile abilities. Training was given in
areas where scores were low. The training was integrated into the
school's regular curriculum. Reading ages in first grade averaged 1.4
years higher than those of corresponding classes the year before the
program began.

4. PHONETIC APPROACH

1748 Filbin, Robert L. "Prescription for the Johnny who can't read."
     Elem Engl 34(8): 559-61, December, 1957. (0 References).
Current techniques of teaching reading by the sight method do not work
with all children. Large groups of children suffering from specific
reading disability need a phonetic method such as that developed by Anna
Gillingham. With its use they learn to read normally. With usual classroom methods these children would probably be classified as "slow learners" or "dumb."

C. REMEDIAL TEACHING

1. COMPREHENSIVE VIEWS

1749 Abrams, Jules C., and Belmont, Herman S. "Different approaches to
     the remediation of severe reading disability in children." J Learn
     Disabil 2(3): 136-41, March, 1969. (13 References).
Compared the effects of full-time specialized reading instruction with
typical public school instruction. Much disagreement among investigators
has occurred over whether social and emotional maladjustment is a cause
or a result of reading disability. Research from other disciplines has
made it appear that there is a type of reading retardation that reflects
some kind of basic disturbance in neurological organization. In this
study sixteen Caucasian boys ages eight to twelve years, with IQs over 90
as measured by the WISC, and with severe reading problems were divided
into one of four experimental groups. Over a period of two years, one
group received full-time specialized reading instruction at a university
reading clinic and individual psychotherapy. The second group received
full-time specialized reading instruction and group psychotherapy. The
third group had no special educational help but had individual psychotherapy. The fourth group had no special educational help but had group
psychotherapy.
Results show that both groups receiving educational help made significantly greater improvements than either of the groups who received no
educational help. No differences were found in reading test results or
beneficial effects between those in individual therapy and those in group
therapy. Findings support the idea that full-time specialized reading
instruction is superior to the reading instruction offered by representative public schools in remediating severe reading disability. The boys
receiving no special reading instruction were public school pupils matched
with the others for age, IQ, and school experience. It is concluded that
full-time specialized reading instruction is the most vital step in remediation. There appears to be no difference in the effect of individual
or group psychotherapy in relieving severe reading disability.

1750 Arena, John I., ed. Building handwriting skills in dyslexic chil-
     dren. San Rafael, California: Academic Therapy Publications,
     1970. 117p. (Bibliography).
This collection of articles largely reprinted from the Fall, 1968, issue
of Academic Therapy, offers a range of suggestions for dealing with problems in teaching handwriting. These include: the kinesthetic technique;
how to teach cursive writing to children with learning problems; ways to
reduce stress in teaching handwriting; and many other aspects.

1751 Ashlock, Patrick; Grzynkowicz, Wineva Montooth; Dervin, Richard L.
      Teaching reading to individuals with learning difficulties. Spring-
      field, Illinois: Thomas, 1969. 195p. (Bibliography p. 163-74).
After describing the nature of reading and learning difficulties in general, this book traces the history and development in the United States
of reading instruction and of instruction for children with learning difficulties. Educational therapy (the application of educational and psychological principles of learning) in conjunction with special educational
techniques for instructing the reading-disabled is discussed. Various
approaches in the treatment of reading difficulties are explained, including visual, auditory, tactile, kinesthetic, and combinations of these
methods. Various individualized approaches to reading instruction for
the disabled reader are suggested. How to organize and administer a remedial reading program is explained. Lists of books for the reading-
disabled child, a bibliography of professional materials for teachers,
and a list of publishers' addresses are included in the volume.

1752 Bechtel, Leland P. The detection and remediation of learning dis-
      abilities. Progress report. 1973. 118p. (ED 079 878).
Details a one-year program for preschool children and a summer program
for ten-year-olds. All were perceptually handicapped children. The preschoolers took a battery of eight tests, and received daily remediation
in fine and gross motor training and in applied skills. Gains as measured by tests were highly significant. Early identification and intervention can help these children. The elementary-school children took a
battery of seven tests and received daily remediation in reading, English
composition, and mathematics. They also received perceptual and gross
motor training. Significant gains were achieved. The program was carried out in a model cities area, and was reported by the Androscoggin
County Task Force on Social Welfare, Inc., Lewiston, Maine.

1753 Betts, Emmett Albert, and Donnelly, Helen E. "Systematic instruc-
      tion for retarded readers." J Except Child 3(3): 66-74, 89;
      Part II, 3(4): 118-25, February - April, 1937. (8 References).
This is the second annual report on summer session remedial reading cases
at the Oswego, New York, State Normal School Reading Clinic. More boys
than girls were found to be poor readers. Most reading problems occurred
in the first four grades. The cause was, in some cases, attempts to
teach reading when the child's mental age fell far behind his chronological age and the reading material was much too difficult for the child.
The testing program for the analysis of the children's reading difficulties is given. Children in the clinic ranged in age from six to sixteen
years. They had IQs from 60 to 139 with most falling in the 90-109
normal range. Results of the testing are analyzed. Part II deals with
corrective procedures and outcomes.

1754 Bluestein, Venus W. "Long-term effectiveness of remediation."
      J Sch Psychol 6(2): 130-35, Winter, 1968. (7 References).
This study was undertaken to help determine whether gains made by pupils
in remedial reading programs were permanent, and whether such late readers ever catch up with their peers and become normal readers. Children
from the Cincinnati public schools who were alumni of the school system's
remedial reading centers were examined four times: (1) at time of placement; (2) when released; (3) one year later; and (4) three years after
remediation. Wide individual differences were seen, but the evidence
suggests that as a group these children made considerable gains in reading during remediation. The gains appeared to be persistent at least

three years later, and the children were catching up with their grade peers.

1755   Camp, Bonnie W. "Remedial reading in a pediatric clinic." <u>Clin</u>
       <u>Pediatr</u> 10(1): 36-42, January, 1971. (7 References).
Describes a remedial reading program conducted in a pediatric clinic operating in a socially and economically depressed area. Tutors were from
the neighborhood initially and received some training in the technique
used in helping the children. Eventually pediatricians, nurses, and
others who became interested learned the technique and began to work with
the children. Admission requirements for the child were that his reading
problem be severe enough to fall within the range of lessons available
and that he have transportation. If he could read eighty out of 100
words from a vocabulary from the lessons or if his IQ was below 70 he was
not accepted. If it was then found that he had severe short-term memory
problems or had trouble generalizing from one part of the lesson to
another, further arrangements were made for the child. Qualifications
for tutors are given. Case histories are included. Research is being
done on matching diagnosis to remediation.

1756   Chapman, Carita A. "Helping the retarded reader; in corrective
       and remedial classes." In: Conference on Reading, University of
       Chicago, 1966. <u>Proceedings: seventy-five years of progress</u>. Vol.
       28. Compiled and edited by H. Alan Robinson. Chicago, Illinois:
       University of Chicago Press, 1966. 174-77. (0 References).
       (Supplementary Educational Monographs, No. 96).
Describes how one teacher diagnosed and instructed problem readers referred to a reading clinic.

1757   Chicago. University. Reading Clinics. <u>Clinical studies in read-</u>
       <u>ing</u>. Vol. 1. By the staff of the Reading Clinics of the University
       of Chicago. Chicago, Illinois: University of Chicago Press, 1949.
       173p. (Supplementary Educational Monographs, No. 68).
This book about the services, research, and dissemination of information
carried out during one year at the University of Chicago Reading Clinics
describes how poor readers were diagnosed and selected for admission to
the clinics. The clinicians believe that their methods proved sufficiently effective for recommendation to others concerned with genuinely
retarded readers. Comments are made on the treatment of emotional difficulties as they relate to reading disability. A list of diagnostic tests
is included.

1758   Cohn, Stella M., and Cohn, Jack. <u>Teaching the retarded reader; a</u>
       <u>guide for teachers, reading specialists, and supervisors</u>. New York:
       Odyssey Press, 1967. 174p. (Bibliography p. 132-36).
Defines the retarded reader as one who has marked difficulty even though
of sufficient chronological age and general intelligence so that learning
to read should be possible. The main thrust of the book is the reading
clinic. The details of the diagnostic considerations involved; what a
reading clinic should do; and how it should be organized are all described
thoroughly. Qualifications for the remedial reading teacher and reading
consultant are given.

1759   Detraz, Julia. "Reading methods for clinical cases." <u>Educ Res</u>
       <u>Bull</u> 9(10): 269-72, May 14, 1930. (0 References).
Describes the problems encountered with reading clinic pupils, including:
(1) lack of interest in reading; (2) lack of comprehension of the forms

of the words and letters; (3) poor eye movements; (4) lack of ability to
use phonetic aids; and (5) lack of comprehension of content. Methods for
meeting each of these difficulties is considered.

1760   Dolch, Edward William. A manual for remedial reading. 2nd ed.
       Champaign, Illinois: Garrard, 1945. 464p.
Covers a wide range of material on remedial reading. Ways in which children respond to the sense of failure that reading problems bring and the
child's physical condition are discussed. A five-step program for remedial reading is outlined. Beginning at the child's level and building
a sight vocabulary is advocated. However, it is pointed out that some
children learn better by beginning very early with phonics because they
learn best by "sounding" rather than by "sight." For the child who learns
neither by sight nor by sounding, slow training in sounding is advised.
Fernald's tracing method is recommended for some problem readers who
have difficulty in observing words carefully. Discussed are: (1) classroom and individual remedial methods; (2) ways to deal with inattention,
reversals, and spelling difficulties; (3) remedial reading for middle and
upper grades and in high school; (4) the parents' role in helping the
problem readers; (5) testing; and (6) prevention of reading problems.
The assumption is that all children can be taught to read.

1761   Edwards, Cliff. "Adults learn to deal with word blindness." Times
       Educ Suppl 2870: 4, May 22, 1970. (0 References).
Adult victims of word blindness (dyslexia) ranging in age from seventeen
to fifty-three years with IQs from about 50 to 110 are being taught to
read at Cambridge University Settlement in Camberwell, South London.
Teachers are volunteers, and psychologists do not seem to be needed.
Adult dyslexics are making great strides in learning to read under this
program.

1762   Ekwall, Eldon E. Locating and correcting reading difficulties.
       Columbus, Ohio: Charles E. Merrill, 1970. 140p. (Bibliography).
This book for teachers lists and defines twenty-seven reading difficulties. A sample form for use as a reading diagnosis sheet lists the
twenty-seven items. It is noted that the checklist does not indicate
which difficulties are more severe, but the user should be aware that
the reading difficulties listed do vary in their seriousness. Each of
the twenty-seven items is then discussed separately. How to recognize
each, a brief discussion of possible causes, and a list of recommended
methods for dealing with the problem are given. Word-by-word reading,
omissions, repetitions, reversals, unknown sounds, lack of comprehension,
and poor organization of response are among the difficulties considered.

1763   Elder, Vera. "The library and the retarded reader." Wilson Libr
       Bull 21(9): 661-65, May, 1947. (47 References).
Discusses the results of a questionnaire sent to 145 school librarians
concerning the role of the librarian in working with retarded readers in
remedial reading programs. It is generally agreed that the library should
not take the lead, but should cooperate in all classroom efforts. The
librarian should provide suitable reading materials and encourage and
stimulate pupils to read. One problem is the librarian's difficulty in
knowing who needs help. This is especially difficult in a big school
system where library attendance is voluntary and no direct contact between librarians and teachers is possible. Cooperation must emanate
from both classroom and library. The child with a reading disability who
is proud of being a nonreader and antagonistic toward school is an ex-

asperating problem for the librarian. He will not read and distracts
others from doing so. Some general principles for selecting books for
retarded readers are given.

1764 Ellingson, Careth, and Cass, James. "Teaching the dyslexic child:
      new hope for non-readers." Sat Rev 49: 82-85, 101, April 16,
      1966. (0 References).
Acknowledges that the cause of specific language disability (dyslexia) is
not known and describes the symptoms: imperfect directional sense,
reversals, up-and-down confusion. The dyslexic child is also likely to
be attracted by details and be unable to see a word as a whole, or to
distinguish the figure or word from its background. He will also probably have trouble distinguishing gradations of sound and telling one word
from another when he hears them. The dyslexic usually appears perfectly
normal until he goes to school. His family history may reveal relatives
who had difficulty in learning to read. His family becomes involved in
the child's failure and emotional problems are common. The work of the
McGlannan School in Miami is described. The school's purpose is to develop methods that can be used by large public schools for screening
dyslexic children. Three requirements are necessary to teach the dyslexic: (1) a teacher with adequate preparation, patience, and ingenuity;
(2) parents who understand the problem; and (3) early identification of
the problem.

1765 Gilliland, Cleburne Hap. Materials for remedial reading and their
      use. Billings, Montana: Reading Clinic, Education Division Eastern
      Montana College, 1965. 201p.

1766 Guthrie, D. I. "A clinic for children with reading problems."
      Med J Aust 1(7): 335, February 12, 1972. (0 References).
Letter to editor. Reports the progress of a reading clinic in New South
Wales, Australia. Almost all children treated had improved. The age of
the group treated has been gradually falling. Despite continuing loss
of professional personnel, the program continues to fourish.

1767 Hester, Kathleen B. "Dade County meets the reading problems."
      Elem Sch J 47(3): 148-56, November, 1946. (0 References).
Appropriate testing in the schools of Dade County (Miami), Florida, revealed 1,274 reading disability cases out of 3,907 children tested. Of
these, 382 completed a nine-week reading laboratory summer-school program.
Only sixteen of these failed to show improvement when retested. Behavior
problems and a negative attitude toward school appeared at the beginning
of the program. Methods are described.

1768 Kottmeyer, William. "Must we have remedial reading?" Natl Educ
      Assoc J 39(9): 677-78, December, 1950. (0 References).
Describes what is meant by the child eligible for remedial reading because he reads below grade level. How the gap widens between good and
poor readers as a heterogeneous group when they are moved together through
the grades is explained. The numbers of these poor readers who cannot
learn from their textbooks can be greatly reduced. Suggested are: (1)
prereading programs; (2) examinations for physical and sensory defects
at the prereading level; (3) ungraded primary schools; and (4) most important, teachers who will consciously work to develop basic reading
skills in these handicapped children--skills which bright, alert children
develop through uncontrolled experience with books. The problem is one
for the teachers. All will benefit by lowering the number of remedial
readers.

1769 Laurita, Raymond E. "Does remedial-reading therapy help?" Acad
      Ther 6(3): 279-86, Spring, 1971. (3 References).
Laymen often question whether remedial instruction is necessary or effective. Why shouldn't reading instruction have been accomplished in the
classroom, they ask. Proving the value of this type of teaching can be
difficult. However, a properly run remedial program can result in great
reading gains for problem readers. Such a program and the methods used
in it are described.

1770 McCollum, Mary E., and Shapiro, Mary J. "An approach to the reme-
      diation of severe reading disabilities." Education 67(8): 488-
      93, April, 1947. (0 References).
Explains the operation of the Baltimore Reading Clinic during its initial
year of operation after its organization in September, 1945. Children
with reading disabilities were screened. Those who were found to be
severely retarded readers were given reading analysis. Special instruction was provided for the 27 percent classified as clinical problems.
Teachers interested in clinical work received training while in service.
Detailed results of the reading analyses are given.

1771 McCullough, Constance M. "Relationship between intelligence and
      gains in reading ability." J Educ Psychol 30(9): 688-92, Decem-
      ber, 1939. (0 References).
As a result of a study of ninth-grade pupils with IQs ranging from 80 to
157, it is concluded that intelligence should not be the determining
factor in admission to a remedial reading program. No relationship appeared between intelligence and comprehension improvement in a ten-week
remedial reading course. The success of the program for an individual
appeared to depend on other factors. The success of the reading program
depends on the extent to which these other factors can be identified and
controlled.

1772 McGlothin, Melba. "Remedial teaching." Tex Outlook 23(9): 31-32,
      September, 1939. (0 References).
Argues the case for remedial reading as an important and necessary educational procedure. Its use avoids reading failure by means of early diagnosis and adequate treatment of children with reading difficulties. The
reading gains are reported of a group of children who were given special
remedial instruction as a supplement to their regular reading program.

1773 McMenemy, Richard A. "The effect of I.Q. on progress in remedial
      reading." Acad Ther 4(3): 191-94, Spring, 1969. (0 References).
In a study of large numbers of children in grades four through eight it
was found that children with higher IQs showed most gain as a result of
remedial reading instruction. All of the children began the program
with severe reading and learning problems. Sixth, seventh, and eighth
graders made more gains than fourth and fifth graders. Teaching methods
applicable to children with dyslexia, cultural disadvantages, emotional
disturbances, perceptual-motor difficulties, and other problems are described.

1774 Miller, Wallace D. "An experimental study of the effect of i.t.a.
      on reading achievement of disabled readers in grades seven and
      eight." In: International Reading Association. Conference pro-
      ceedings: forging ahead in reading. Vol. 12(Part 1). Edited by
      J. Allen Figurel. Newark, Delaware: International Reading Associa-
      tion, 1968. 546-50. (12 References).

In a study of disabled readers in the seventh and eighth grades the
Initial Teaching Alphabet (ITA) proved to be the best method for increasing speed of comprehension. However, no one method of instruction proved
superior in improving all the skills measured in this study. These included (besides speed of comprehension) comprehension skill, knowledge
of word meanings, and ability to identify words. Care is advised in
selecting the medium that will produce the best results for the skill
being taught.

1775 Model programs: childhood education. Perceptual development
      centre program. 1970. 19p. (ED 045 329).
Describes a federally funded (ESEA Title III) program of diagnostic and
remedial services concentrating on dyslexic children of elementary-school
age. The program allows approximately fifty children to attend the
center for a full school day. They remain in the center until achievement is sufficient to allow them to return to the regular classroom.
Regular school subjects are taught in addition to special reading instruction. A demonstration center, training for area teachers, community
education, and a diagnostic program for the children are all part of the
project. The center's goal is to train teachers to deal more ably with
reading difficulties in the classroom.

1776 Monroe, Marion. "Diagnosis and treatment of reading disabilities."
      Natl Soc Study Educ Yearb 34: 201-28, 1935. (2 References).
Cites estimates that 12 percent of schoolchildren suffer from reading retardation. Diagnostic procedure must follow two steps: (1) evaluation
of teaching methods and outcomes; and (2) analysis of the individual
child's difficulties in learning to read. Causes of reading difficulty
are discussed. A wide variety of factors that must be considered in
diagnosing a case of reading disability are set forth. These include the
child's medical and social history, results of a psychological examination, his intelligence, and auditory and visual discrimination. General
considerations for remedial work are pointed out. Time of day and length
of session should be planned to avoid fatigue. Individual remedial work
is best, but small groups may be taught together if the children have
similar types of difficulty. Suggested methods for instructing children
with specific difficulties are given. Remedial methods should be flexible
and adapted to the individual's needs. If diagnosis has been correct,
consistent remedial work is usually highly successful. Remedial work
should not stop too soon.

1777 Moorehead, Caroline. "Sandhya Naidoo: about to test her theories
      on dyslexia; interview." Times Educ Suppl 3100: 12, October 25,
      1974. (0 References).
Sandhya Naidoo, the daughter of parents from East Bengal who was reared
in Scotland, wears saris and speaks with a Glasgow accent. She is now
in her fifties. Trained as a teacher, she was always interested in reading and its difficulties. She has studied the relation between handedness
and reading difficulties. She became director of the Word Blind Centre
and wrote a book, Specific Dyslexia, an account of the Centre's work.
She is now headmistress for the Invalid Children's Aid Association's Dawn
House, a boarding school for children with dyslexia and other language
problems. It is located outside Nottingham and opened in October, 1974.
The school's plan is to concentrate on the child's language problem until
he is about nine, and then get back to his general education. He would
rejoin the normal educational system at age thirteen. Mrs. Naidoo thinks
children should be educated in their strengths, not to the level of their

disabilities. It is better if the remedial program can control the
child's whole environment, she believes.

1778   Newton, Margaret, and Thomson, Michael. Dyslexia--a guide to teach-
       ing. Birmingham, England: University of Aston in Birmingham, 1974.
       40p.

1779   O'Neal, Eldra, and Zylstra, Helen. Independent creative ideas for
       use with specific language disability children. 2 Vols. Cambridge,
       Massachusetts: Educators Publishing Service, 1972.

1780   Redmount, Robert S. "Description and evaluation of a corrective
       program for reading disability." J Educ Psychol 39(6): 347-58,
       October, 1948. (0 References).
Twenty-four children retarded in reading lived as a group in a fraternity
house for six weeks. They were on a twenty-four-hour schedule including
study aimed at improving their reading in as natural a setting as possible. Rorschach tests were given before and at the end of the six-week
period. Thirty-nine percent showed personality improvement. Twenty-six
percent appeared to have been adversely affected, having withdrawn further and become more rigid in their thinking. Reading test scores showed
corresponding trends in 70 percent of the cases: 48 percent improved, 12
percent showed lower scores. Ages ranged from eight to eighteen. The
older children's reading improved most, but these were also the most
maladjusted and least improved in personality. Children assigned to the
more maladjusted teachers showed the least improvement.

1781   Ridenour, Nina. "The treatment of reading disability." Ment Hyg
       19(3): 387-97, July, 1935. (0 References).
Building motivation and frequent lessons are two important points in successful remedial reading instruction. Any method that works should be
used freely. Reading materials selected should be easy for the child.
Anyone who has good rapport with the child can tutor him. Common sense
and ingenuity are more important than teaching experience.

1782   Robinson, Helen M. "The study of disabilities in reading." Elem
       Sch J 38(1): 15-28, September, 1937. (0 References).
Describes methods used in investigating reading difficulty at the Orthogenic School of the University of Chicago. It is concluded that the
diagnosis and treatment of children with severe reading difficulties is
in the experimental stage. More data are needed before final conclusions
can be reached. Treatment must be planned on the basis of findings in
each case. Efforts are being made to link specific defects to special
difficulties in reading in order to attack the problem more directly.
Diagnostic methods, causes of reading difficulties, and methods of treatment are discussed.

1783   Rowe, Cecil Ann. "Techniques for teaching dyslexic children: using
       the tape recorder." Acad Ther 3(3): 171, Spring, 1968. (0 Ref-
       erences).
Describes a method for using a tape recorder to aid development of the
dyslexic child's recall and retrieval systems. It is suggested that the
method also helps develop fine auditory discrimination.

1784   Russell, Sheldon N. "A crucial problem facing secondary education."
       J Read 17(8): 600-603, May, 1974. (3 References).

Secondary teachers have difficulty in teaching severely disabled readers at the high school level because of the teachers' preparation, orientation to content teaching, and personal commitment. Many teachers have spent years of rigorous study preparing to teach the content of their various disciplines. Their dilemma is very real when faced with the severely disabled reader who reads at an elementary level so low that reading is still a decoding process. He can be taught reading and content, but not simultaneously. Suggestions are offered for meeting this problem in terms of the school's commitment to helping a nonreading student through a secondary reading specialist and development of a competent reading staff. Suggestions for developing a remedial reading program are given.

1785 Serio, Martha, and Anderson, Annetta. "Remedial procedures from the classroom: from theory to practice." Acad Ther 6(3): 321-25, Spring, 1971. (0 References).
Gives instructions for teaching learning-disabled children to read and write. Each child is unique and demands a different approach. One approach to learning to write is described in detail. Other suggestions are made, including: (1) listening to the child; (2) analyzing his mistakes; (3) teaching through the stronger sense; (4) using concrete, three-dimensional materials to start; (5) remembering that reading is not just a visual task; and (6) remembering the sequential steps in the development of learning.

1786 Slingerland, Beth H. "Meeting the needs of dyslexic children." Acad Ther 1(2): 66-72, 113, Winter, 1965-1966. (16 References).
Dyslexic children are now the objects of the study and research they deserve. Early identification and diagnosis are important steps in meeting the needs of dyslexics. Few teachers are trained to carry out successful programs, and teaching techniques for reaching these children are still inadequate. Screening tests to identify dyslexic children and teaching to prevent the development of reading problems are recommended.

1787 Spache, George D. "Integrating diagnosis with remediation in reading." Elem Sch J 56(1): 18-26, September, 1955. (36 References).
A lag exists in coordination of diagnosis and remedial techniques. Among suggestions for making remediation more relevant to diagnostic findings are: (1) that the reading teacher follow up referrals to vision and hearing specialists by seeing that visual and auditory training materials are used; and (2) that the teaching method best suited to each pupil's IQ level and performance is used. Each pupil should be taught how to read for differing levels of comprehension, depending upon the type of literature.

1788 Stahl, Ray. "Diagnose those reading problems early." Tenn Teach 39(7): 10-12, 1972. (0 References).
Describes the work of the East Tennessee State University reading clinic. The problems of children with reading difficulties can be treated most effectively if diagnosed early. Most children with reading problems have been forced into psychological, social, or emotional situations that hinder reading. The reading problem can be helped by removing the emotional or personal block. Some children develop reading troubles because they are forced to learn before they are ready. Although correcting a serious reading problem is slow and tedious, it can be done.

1789   Thompson, Christine. "The prevention of reading disabilities in
       Chicago Heights." In: Conference on Reading, University of Chicago,
       1943. Proceedings: adapting reading programs to wartime needs.
       Vol. 5. Compiled and edited by William S. Gray. Chicago, Illinois:
       University of Chicago, 1943. 233-38. (0 References). (Supple-
       mentary Educational Monographs, No. 57).
Describes a program of remedial reading aimed at the prevention of reading disabilities in the schools of Chicago Heights, a suburb of Chicago.
The counselor attempted to assess the child's ability and achievements,
interpret errors, discover causes of the reading problem, and suggest
remedial treatment. Counselors helped children only upon invitation
from regular teachers. Results were encouraging. Almost half the pupils
referred for remedial reading were below average intelligence, 14 percent
above average, and 38 percent average.

1790   Townsend, W. B. "A diagnostic and remedial program in reading."
       Instructor Part I, 45(4): 20, 82, February, 1936. (17 References).
       Part II, 45(5): 22, 77-78, March, 1936. (11 References).
Part I considers ways to discover the causes of a child's reading problem. Questionnaires on home background, physical and school history,
behavior, and reading ability should be filled out. Each child should
be given reading tests and interviewed individually about his reading
problems. Sample checklists are included. Part II recommends treatment
methods. To eliminate reading problems, poor readers should be put in a
special room and given full-time remedial work. Suggestions are given to
help the teacher who has not had special training in remedial reading.
Remedial classes must be made interesting.

2. INDIVIDUALIZED INSTRUCTION

1791   Abrams, Jules C. "Teaching reading to neurologically handicapped
       children." In: International Reading Association. Conference
       proceedings: reading for effective living. Vol. 3. Edited by
       J. Allen Figurel. New York: Scholastic Magazines, 1958. 126-29.
       (0 References).
The impaired learning ability and disturbed behavior of the brain-injured
(neurologically handicapped) child represent a defect in the structure
of the ego. In limited neurologic handicaps, such as word blindness,
there is less stress and therefore less marked deviate behavior. These
children can be taught to read but usual educational methods are of little
value. Keeping distractions to a minimum; presenting material in concrete forms; and using kinesthetic or tactile approaches are helpful.
Even more important is the emotional acceptance of the child, love and
acceptance combined with firm, clearheaded realism that strengthens the
child's weak ego.

1792   Alm, Richard S. "Individual help for retarded readers." Sch Rev
       59(4): 212-20, April, 1951. (0 References).
A group of experienced classroom teachers worked for five weeks on an individual basis with retarded readers. Each teacher diagnosed the one or
two cases assigned to him or her as extensively as possible, and planned
and carried out a series of lessons. Training proved very effective and
all pupils showed gains. Results demonstrated the effectiveness of individual instruction.

1793   Betts, Emmett Albert. "Developmental deficiencies and reading dis-
       abilities." Teach Coll J 12(2): 37-44, November, 1940. (15
       Bibliographic Footnotes).

Deplores the degree to which children are forced into undifferentiated
mass instruction which falsely assumes that all children in a given grade
are fundamentally alike and that their progress can be dictated by the
calendar. There is little basically wrong with dividing children into
grades. But providing for individual differences may become a challenge.
Reasons are listed and explained as to why unitary and unified school
reorganization leads to undesirable results. The systematic analysis of
a remedial reading case should include: (1) determination of the type
of services needed to help the child; (2) his general achievement level;
(3) his capacity; (4) his specific difficulties; and (5) determination
of the sequence of remedial activities. Neither adults nor children can
be regimented. Schools should be learner-centered, not dictated by
grades and calendars.

1794 ————. "Provisions for individuals with extreme reading dis-
       abilities." Sch Week Univ Pa Proc 1950: 51-59. (9 References).
Distinguishes between corrective and remedial reading problems. Corrective reading is used to indicate the kind of reading program required
for nonreaders and retarded readers who do not have associative learning
disabilities. These are the nonreaders whose language skill deficiency
leads to word-by-word reading, substitutions, regressions, etc. Or it
may manifest itself as mere rhythmic word-calling with lack of comprehension. Remedial reading is used to designate the type of program required by retarded readers with associative learning disabilities. These
children have unusual difficulty in establishing and retaining reading
skills, especially when a visual-auditory teaching approach is used. They
learn a word today and forget it tomorrow. These are the dyslexic or
word-blind children. How to select remedial reading groups is discussed.
The general nature and chief objectives of remedial reading instruction
are considered. Some goals include developing the ability to associate
personal experience with written language and the development of general
language ability. One extremely retarded reader of the dyslexic type is
found among 300 to 500 schoolchildren. Dyslexics are misunderstood,
rarely identified, and as a result often have emotional aberrations. The
approach should be through meaning, visual, auditory, kinesthetic, and
tactile associations. Daily instruction is profitable. Corrective reading groups may number from ten to twenty-five children; remedial groups
usually are small, no more than four.

1795 Bricklin, Patricia M. "Implementing the changing concepts in re-
       mediation." In: International Reading Association. Conference
       proceedings: changing concepts of reading instruction. Vol. 6.
       Edited by J. Allen Figurel. New York: Scholastic Magazines, 1961.
       67-71. (0 References).
Discusses changing ideas about remediation within the framework of two
major trends in the field of reading disabilities: (1) a more widely
accepted and more inclusive definition of reading disabilities; and (2)
a wider acceptance of reading disabilities as only one symptom of the
reasons for the child's poor functioning. The most direct result of the
first trend has been to bring much larger numbers of children under the
definition of reading-disabled. The clinic can help these moderately
disabled readers indirectly by training classroom teachers in techniques
for these children as well as in remedial and corrective techniques for
severely disabled readers. Such moderately impaired readers can also be
helped directly by cooperation between classroom and clinic teachers.
The second major trend—the view that reading disability is only one
symptom affecting the whole child—has rid the literature of the

"isolated defect" view of reading disabilities. Psychological, physiological, sociological, and pedagogical factors are all involved in the
problems of the severely disabled reader. Treatment must not be confined to each contributing factor; it requires a cooperative approach among
concerned specialists. In addition to the two trends already mentioned,
the reading clinic has two other functions in implementing changing concepts toward treatment: public relations and research.

1796   Brookes, Malcolm J. "Dyslexia." Science 173(3993):   190-91,
       July 16, 1971. (0 References).
Letter to editor. Comments on the study of Rozin, Poritsky, and Sotsky
in which American children who were retarded readers were successfully
taught Chinese characters. (See Item No. 1855). It is pointed out that
these children learned because of fresh motivation; they were already
discouraged with learning English orthography. While not degrading the
value of the study as a means for pointing out the poor quality of current teaching methods, Brookes notes that the study did little to teach
comprehension.

1797   Bryant, N. Dale. "Some principles of remedial instruction for dys-
       lexia." Read Teach 18(7):   567-72, April, 1965. (4 References).
Children with dyslexia, or specific, severe disability in word recognition, may remain virtual nonreaders in spite of years of remedial teaching. The condition is usually resistant to standard remedial procedures.
Dyslexics can learn to read only if the teacher uses procedures suited
to the nature and extent of the child's difficulties. Five principles
that form a partial framework on which to build effective remediation
are outlined: (1) Remediation should focus at first on the simplest,
most basic perceptual and associational elements in reading. Calling
attention to the details within a word is an important aspect of remedial
teaching. (2) The remedial teacher must present tasks which will cause
the child to develop automatic responses in the basic elements of reading one at a time. (3) The remedial teacher should modify the presentation of the task and material so that the child can have a high level of
success. (4) When two discriminations or associations interfere with
each other, the remedial teacher should teach first one and then the
other to an automatic level, reviewing the first. The two can then be
integrated. (5) Reviews of basic perceptual, associational, and blending skills should be frequent. These reviews should involve actual reading as quickly as possible.

1798   Campbell, Dorothy Drysdale. "Typewriter contrasted with handwrit-
       ing: a circumvention study of learning-disabled children." J Spec
       Educ 7(2):   155-68, Summer, 1973. (47 References).
Two groups of children with IQs over 80 who were having difficulty learning to read were selected. All showed lags in psychomotor functions as
measured by the Bender Gestalt test. One group used typewriters entirely
and never used pencils. The other group used handwriting, a complex
motor task. Typewriting using the "hunt-and-peck" system is a simpler
motor task. The same teaching materials were used in both groups. The
typewriter group made a greater gain statistically in reading-vocabulary
skills. It is concluded that developmental lag is not necessarily predictive of reading failure, but only of vulnerability. Reasons for this
difference are discussed.

1799   Carter, Homer L. J. "Disabilities in reading." Elem Sch J 31(2):
       120-31, October, 1930. (0 References).

Reports the case history of an eleven-year-old girl of good intelligence who was having difficulty in learning to read. Remedial measures used and the results are given. Results of similar remedial instruction applied to a group of children in grades four to six are given. Methods used and gains achieved are given.

1800 Clymer, Theodore. "A developmental study of a retarded reader."
      In: International Reading Association. Conference proceedings:
      reading for effective living. Vol. 3. Edited by J. Allen Figurel.
      New York: Scholastic Magazines, 1959. 129-33. (0 References).
This case history concerns a boy named Will whose full-scale IQ was 109 as measured by the WISC. He was seen over a period of four years at a university reading clinic. Entering sixth grade at the time of writing, Will's achievement continues to be well below his ability and he remains very immature for his age. He is the youngest of three children and is coddled by his parents, who continue to do his homework for him. His mother addresses him in baby talk. Will continues to postpone in any way possible learning to read. He appears happy and is unconcerned about his lack of progress in reading skills.

1801 Coe, Sister Mary Andrew. "Parental involvement in remedial-reading
      instruction." Acad Ther 6(4): 407-10, Summer, 1971. (2 Refer-
      ences).
Describes a remedial program for second graders in which eighteen mothers worked as reading aids in an after-school program. Each child in the program was tutored individually for thirty minutes daily for five months. Gains were very significant. The regular classroom teacher provided instructions for each session.

1802 Dole, Phyllis W. "Improving the language-arts skills of teenage
      disabled readers." Acad Ther 3(1): 9-12, Fall, 1967. (0 Refer-
      ences).
Teen-age students in a remedial program not only read, write, and spell poorly, but also have a sense of futility and a poor self-image. A successful method in which students are taught to read by learning to read the written text of their own taped speech is described. The words they learn to read and spell are those that interest them because it is their own material. After reading their own ideas, they learn to write them, tracing difficult words with a finger. They realize they can succeed.

1803 Edgington, Ruth. Helping children with reading disability. Rev.
      ed. Niles, Illinois: Developmental Learning Materials, 1968. 96p.
Intended for parents or others who work with reading-disabled children, this book gives specific teaching suggestions in phonics and ear training. Included are: (1) word games aimed at correcting directional confusions, improper word-attack methods, and other weaknesses; (2) activities for relaxing the child; (3) exercises for training muscles in writing skills. Lists of preprimers and readers are given.

1804 Ekwall, Eldon Edward. Diagnosis and remediation of the disabled
      reader. Boston, Massachusetts: Allyn and Bacon, 1976. 489p.
      (Bibliographical References).
After outlining the major causes of reading failure, this book presents material on the diagnosis and remediation of reading failure from various educational standpoints: letter knowledge, sight words, word analysis skills, and others. Remediation is also considered from psychological and sociological standpoints. Written primarily for teachers, the book

includes much material on specific teaching methods. Pointing out that
the term "dyslexia" does not appear to mean the same thing to different
people, it provides material on the prevalence, diagnosis, and remediation of dyslexia. It concludes that no one method of diagnosis or remediation is invariably helpful. The best diagnosis and remedy can be
achieved by the careful observation of the teacher and the use of diagnostic teaching.

1805 Farrell, Lyle H. "A remedial reading program." In: The handbook
      of private schools. 37th ed. Boston, Massachusetts: Porter
      Sargent, 1956. 81-83. (0 References).
Describes the remedial program at Proctor Academy. The most common cause
of language disability is confused or mixed dominance. Orton's explanation for this is set forth. The boy should be encouraged to use the
hand that is most natural for him. Confused or mixed dominance is not
the only cause of reading disability. Low intelligence, emotional blocks,
vision problems, and poor attitudes toward himself and others may hinder
the child's learning. The instructor should attack the reading problems
as hard and as fast as the boy can assimilate it. He must convince the
boy that he likes him and that he believes he can learn. To see a gleam
of hope in a boy's eyes after years of discouragement is a great reward.
Auditory perception is usually much better than visual. The teacher must
find some other activity the boy can do well and encourage him in that
area.

1806 Ferster, C. B. "Discussion of Dr. Cameron's paper on remedial
      reading." Br J Med Psychol 45(Part 3): 279-81, September, 1972.
      (0 References).
Describes the operation of the personalized classroom and the methods
used in the remedial teaching of reading viewed as a therapeutic intervention. The article suggests that personalized, programmed teaching
could succeed even better if used in the regular classroom and not in
the after-school class alone. Many aspects of the classroom described
are similar to psychotherapy. The teacher assumes responsibility for
the student's welfare without regard to the causes of the reading problem.

1807 Forer, Ruth K. "Catch a falling star: early prediction of reading
      failure." Claremont Coll Read Conf Yearb 39: 167-74, 1975. (9
      References).
Two large groups of kindergarten children were given two IQ tests and a
battery of tests designed to predict reading failure. Smaller groups of
children showing significant deficits on the tests but with average or
above-average intelligence were selected. These smaller groups were further divided into groups receiving various types of individualized instruction. The conclusion is that it is possible to identify youngsters
at high risk of future problems, but with a considerable number of errors.
No single intervention strategy could be recommended to correct the problems.

1808 Fradis, A.; Gheorghiţǎ, N.; Calavrezo, C. "Methods to retrain read-
      ing and writing in dyslexic children." Rev Roum Neurol 9(5):
      321-31, 1972. (8 References).
Presents a method for retraining first- and second-grade dyslexic children in reading and writing. The most frequent reading error was found
to be word substitution. The most frequent writing error was letter
omission. The method consisted of selecting a passage from a clear writer
at the child's grade level and which he had never read before. This

selection was broken into "syntagms" [sic] and read to the child. Then
the child read it back. The same material was to be read at home three
or four times a day between sessions. A "syntagm" is described as "a
stable syntactical unit" composed of one or more words or a phrase as
part of a sentence. [It is assumed that the term is derived from "syn-
tagma," a systematic collection or grouping, as of writings.] As he
progressed, the pupil was asked to divide the text into syntagms himself
and finally to read without the divisions. In correcting writing disability, a list of his errors was made and commented on with him. He
was asked to copy and then write to dictation material from a schoolbook.
The pupil had to find his errors himself under the teacher's guidance.
Errors were discussed with him. Improvement was noted. Pupils avoided
second examinations and repetition except in those cases where dyslexia
occurred in connection with lowered general intelligence.

1809 Gates, Arthur Irving, and Bond, Guy L. "Failure in reading and
      social maladjustment." Natl Educ Assoc J 25(7): 205-6, October,
      1936. (0 References).
If serious difficulty in reading disrupts a pupil's entire school career
--as it does--it may be expected to disturb his personal and social adjustment as well. Various emotional responses to reading failure are
listed. A city-wide project in New York City for detecting, diagnosing,
and treating serious cases of reading disability is described. Most of
the children helped were found to have IQs from 70 to 95, the dull-normal
range. Under individual remedial instruction most made very significant
gains in reading and were given a new lease on school life. Improvements
in emotional and social adjustment usually accompanied or followed improved scholastic ability.

1810 —————. "Reading disabilities." Natl Educ Assoc J 25(8): 243-
      44, November, 1936. (0 References).
Describes the program of instruction and the results of a city-wide remedial reading Works Progress Administration (WPA) project in New York
City. The clinic was established in the Speyer School (Public School
500). It is concluded that the majority of reading disability cases can
be substantially helped if taught individually by a competent teacher.
Only about 10 percent of reading disability cases are so complicated that
they require expert diagnosis and treatment. The success of remedial
work depends on the teachers' knowledge of modern diagnostic and remedial
techniques.

1811 Geschwind, Norman. "Dyslexia." Science 173(3993): 190, July 16,
      1971. (4 References).
Letter to editor. Comments on the study of Rozin, Poritsky, and Sotsky
in which American children who were retarded readers were taught Chinese
characters successfully. (See Item No. 1855). Their study appears to support the idea that the human nervous system handles differently complex
visual patterns of ideographs and the blending of smaller phonetic elements. It is pointed out that one early writer believed that dyslexic
children should be taught English words as if each whole word were a
symbol, as in Chinese.

1812 Gillingham, Anna. "Selective language disabilities." Prog Educ
      14(4): 256-59, April, 1937. (0 References).
No challenge is so insistent for the teacher as that of the nonreader.
Intelligent, sensible in other things, with rich real-life experiences,
this type of child has great difficulty in learning to read. The condi-

tion is not rare. Such a child develops personality problems. He should
be dealt with individually and he should not be considered cured when he
only learns to read after a fashion. Schools are becoming increasingly
aware of the importance of remedial training. Schools must recognize
the existence of specific reading disabilities and adapt school routine
to help these children.

1813 Girdon, Mary Bowers. "Helping the disabled reader." Elem Engl
      50(1): 103-5, January, 1973. (0 References).
Many seventh- and eighth-grade students are bored and frustrated because
they are reading at first- or second-grade level. Methods for helping
these disabled readers are described. Among the methods used was one in
which pictures were posted on the bulletin board. The children described
what was happening or suggested other captions which the teacher wrote
and posted. The children also dictated to the teacher stories which
they made up. These creative stories grew out of the bulletin board
stories. The stories reflected the children's experiences. Through use
of the stories, the teacher showed her acceptance of the pupils and aided
them in improving their self-concepts and reading skills.

1814 Goldberg, Herman Krieger. "The ophthalmologist looks at the read-
      ing problem." Am J Ophthalmol 47(1, Part 1): 67-74, January,
      1959. (36 References).
Reports that a review of 100 cases of reading retardation confirms
Rabinovitch's classification of problem readers into two categories: (1)
primary reading retardation or failure to learn because of frank brain
damage; and (2) secondary reading retardation in children of normal intelligence and basic learning capacity, caused by exogenous factors.
Eye problems have little to do with reading failure. There is no single
best method for teaching reading. Children who cannot learn by usual
methods can be identified at first-grade level. The problem should be
dealt with then before secondary emotional problems develop. A complete
analysis of the child and his needs is the most important part of a remedial reading program. The various professionals called in to examine
and help the child must work as a team.

1815 Greensill, R. "Coping with remedial reading as a programmed sub-
      ject." Slow Learn Child 13(3): 132-37, 1967. (0 References).
Reports on an experiment to utilize unpaid community volunteers as remedial reading tutors at a school in New Zealand. A twelve-week training
course was designed to train volunteers, many of them former teachers,
who responded to a newspaper advertisement. The course included instruction in the causes and symptoms of reading disability and accompanying
personality disorders, testing procedures, primary school reading and
remedial reading techniques, and lists of available reading materials.
Students were selected on the basis of psychological and diagnostic reading tests. No child was tutored in remedial reading without the parents'
permission. Before tutoring began, tutors received the full case histories of remedial pupils assigned to them. Results were very favorable.

1816 Griffiths, Anita N. "Dyslexia: symptoms and remediation results."
      Q J Fla Acad Sci 33(1): 1-17, March, 1970. (6 References).
Presents the results obtained from treatment of reading-disabled children
at a private clinic. Of thirty-two children who entered the program,
twenty-eight (twenty-one boys and seven girls) completed the three-month
period of individual remedial treatment. Ages ranged from six to fifteen
years with an average of nine years. WISC full-scale IQs ranged from 79

to 133, with an average of 108. Performance IQs had a lower average than
verbal IQs with a high variability among subtests. Correlations among
all subtests revealed that most verbal subtests correlated with each other
but rarely with any performance subtests, as contrasted with Wechsler's
findings with a normal population. Test results are tabulated and compared with Wechsler and Sabatino's study of learning-disabled children.
All the children were given the WISC, the Frostig Test of Developmental
Perception, and an oral reading test. Scores on the Frostig test were
well below those expected for the chronological age of the children.
Reading test scores were below those expected for the IQ levels. Seventy-
five percent showed mixed laterality and 85 percent were or had been
hyperactive. Treatment results suggest that the child with visual perceptual problems and reading difficulties can be helped in one-to-one
sessions. Improvement was obtained in reading ability, visual perception,
and IQ, but not in arithmetic. Major factors in rapidity of response to
treatment appear to be age at beginning of remediation, severity of
visual perceptual difficulties, and the state of the child's self-concept.

1817 ————. "Self-concept in remedial work with dyslexic children."
      Acad Ther 6(2): 125-33, Winter, 1970-1971. (3 References).
Recommends focusing on trust, positive attitudes, and empathy and the
use of individual sessions in remedial work with dyslexic children.
Situations and materials which have come to be associated with failure
should be avoided as much as possible. These were among the conclusions
presented as a result of remedial work with groups of dyslexics ranging
in age from six to fifteen years. The children were given the Frostig
Developmental Test of Visual Perception, the Gilmore Oral Reading Test,
the WISC, and a personality checklist both before and after remedial
work. Improvement in all areas was found, including improved behavior
both at home and at school. Attitudes of teachers, parents, and others
are discussed in relation to their effect on the child's self-concept.

1818 Hallenbeck, Phyllis N. "Remediating with comic strips." J Learn
      Disabil 9(1): 11-15, January, 1976. (11 References).
Suggests that comic strips are especially good for developing conceptual
or logical abilities, including sequencing, abstract thinking, reversibility of figure and ground, and noticing small details in order to see
why the strip is funny. Comics are excellent for dyslexic children to
teach left-to-right progression, discrimination of important details, and
to give practice in reading. It is suggested that guided work with
comics may help the child distinguish fantasy from reality. The child's
explaining why the strip is funny may encourage good verbal expression.
The learning-disabled child is further benefited in his comprehension of
social situations and the development of his sense of humor. Comic strips
have the added advantage of being universally available.

1819 Harris, Albert J. "Motivating the poor reader." Education 73(9):
      566-74, May, 1953. (7 Bibliographic Footnotes).
Expounds the thesis that remedial reading is fundamentally a problem of
arousing and sustaining motivation. Without the will to learn, the child
who is a poor reader rarely accomplishes much. The successful remedial
reading teacher conveys to poor readers the feeling that they are liked,
appreciated, and understood. For most poor readers, supplying motivation
is the teacher's problem. For the child with reading problems caused by
emotional maladjustment, remedial help in reading should not be replaced
with therapy aimed at the emotional problems. Reasons include the facts
that: (1) remedial teaching does help most poor readers; (2) improved

reading ability results in gains in self-confidence and adjustment; and
(3) facilities for psychotherapy are so limited that it is visionary to
think of using them for all poor readers.

1820 Heckelman, R. G. "A neurological-impress method of remedial-reading
      instruction." Acad Ther 4(4): 277-82, Summer, 1969. (0 Refer-
      ences).
In the neurological-impress method of reading instruction, pupil and
teacher hold the book jointly, and read aloud rapidly in unison. The
teacher directs her voice into the pupil's ear. She slides her finder
along the line following the words spoken. The history of the method is
given and its experimental use in selected schools in Merced County,
California, is described. A large percentage of pupils taught in this
way made remarkable progress. Gains made were statistically significant.
It is pointed out that in the days before formal schools, the family
patriarch probably taught the children to read by reading the Bible aloud
while they followed his pointing finger.

1821 ————. "The phonics bound child." Acad Ther 1(1): 12-13,
      Fall, 1965. (0 References).
Defines "phonics-bound" children as those of normal intelligence who progress in reading to about third-grade level, and do not get much further.
They are "word-callers" rather than readers, sounding out each word laboriously and reading very slowly with many errors. Most of these pupils
have had intensive phonics training early in school. It is suggested
that further phonics training is unproductive with children who have
difficulty in distinguishing or interpreting sounds. Other methods of
remedial reading which do not depend on distinguishing sounds should be
used.

1822 ————. "Using the neurological impress remedial technique."
      Acad Ther 1(4): 235-39, 250, Summer, 1966. (3 References).
The neurological-impress method is most effective in a one-to-one relationship where the teacher and pupil read aloud in unison while the teacher follows the line being read with her finger. It can be used in a group
with the teacher using a microphone and the pupils using earphones while
the material read is projected. Without earphones, students hear each
other's mistakes, become disorganized, and the effect is lost. In experimental use the method has been found to produce significant reading gains.
Ten to twenty pages of elementary reading material may be covered in one
session of ten minutes or so. Grade-level reading can be achieved with
about eight to twelve hours of instruction. It is not realistic to expect the method to raise the child above the reading expectancy level
warranted by his IQ and age.

1823 Hickerson, Pat. "Curing the con artist." J Read 13(7): 507-12,
      April, 1970. (0 References).
The middle-class child of average intelligence who is having learning
difficulties is in a worse position than the poverty-class child in some
ways. He has had little publicity and presumably has had "cultural advantages." Yet he is failing in school. What is his excuse? Such a
nonreader has given up on overcoming the obstacles--perceptual factors
or whatever--because the psychological rewards are not great enough. He
learned at an early age that more satisfying rewards could be gained by
not learning to read. This type of child is articulate and understands
and retains material gained aurally: he has to because he depends on
these skills for his minimum functioning in school. Below grade level in

reading, he sheds a few tears of self-pity when his peers shout, "Stupid!"
But it is a world he can manipulate. It is the world of a con artist,
nightmarish as it might seem to the average student. These cases require
extreme treatment. The remedial classroom may be structured to make success or failure a collective effort. The other approach, explored here,
is to remove all responsibility from the pupil, including the teacher's
affection, until the nonreader can cope with interaction with the teacher
and with his peers. The remedial classroom for the junior-high level
should be structured with a rather hospital-like cool, silent, efficient
atmosphere where any activity becomes a privilege. Nonreading children
dread being left out or isolated. They will fight for some privilege,
even if they have to learn to read and write to obtain it. The pupil
should know precisely what the structure is and where he stands within
it. Inwardly chaotic children are sicker than we realize and need a kind
of outer-space calm around them.

1824 Hodges, Kathleen M.; Pool, Lydia B.; Callaway, Byron; et al. "Edu-
      cational survey to determine reading disabilities." In: Inter-
      national Reading Association. Conference proceedings: reading
      and realism. Vol. 13(Part 1). Edited by J. Allen Figurel. Newark,
      Delaware: International Reading Association, 1969. (0 References).
A survey of 11,311 pupils in grades four through seven in twelve Georgia
rural school systems revealed that about two-thirds of the children were
disabled readers. One-fourth were more than a year and a half below
expected level. Results were determined by the use of a formula taken
from Bond and Tinker. An intensive remedial program was given to twenty-
six representative children. Gains averaged approximately twice the
progress made in all previous school years. Individual instruction and
motivation were emphasized.

1825 Hunter, Madeline C. "Reasons for reading difficulty are not excuses
      for reading disability." Claremont Coll Read Conf Yearb 33: 191-
      95, 1969. (4 References).
In the past we have used the reasons children did not learn to read as
excuses for the learning failure. Physical reasons--poor vision or hear-
ing--used to be the excuse. A low IQ was the next excuse offered. Emotional disorders were also blamed. Currently we excuse reading difficulties by blaming them on "perceptual problems." We need to use what is
known to practice prescriptive teaching where different pupils need to
do different things at different times and in different ways. Our focus
should be "Has he learned?" instead of on "Have I taught?"

1826 Jackson, M. S. "The visuo-thematic approach to the teaching of
      reading and language to backward readers." Slow Learn Child 16(3):
      172-82, 1969. (11 References).
Presents a method for teaching reading to children who lack ideas to think,
talk, or subsequently read about. The task is to generate ideas for these
children who appear unable to focus on any specific theme long enough to
sustain a sequence of ideas. This approach, called the visuo-thematic,
makes use of series of pictures appearing in a magazine on a weekly basis.
The child is presented with a sufficient number of ideas to generate discussion and eventually tell a story with a minimum of imagination required. The child is asked to think of six words in each of three categories for each picture: naming words, describing words, and action
words. A case history of a twelve-year-old boy using the visuo-thematic
approach is presented. The method includes at each session reading,
writing, thinking, and organizing around a central picture with a coherent

theme. The method is said to provide "conceptual focalization" so that the child can generate his own concepts, ideas, and sequences.

1827 Jameson, Augusta. "Methods and devices for remedial reading." In: Conference on Reading, University of Chicago, 1939. Proceedings: recent trends in reading. Vol. 1. Compiled and edited by William S. Gray. Chicago, Illinois: University of Chicago, 1939. 170-78. (0 References). (Supplementary Educational Monographs, No. 49).
Remedial reading treatment must begin with establishing rapport with the child. The child should be well-rested, motivated to learn, and find that he can succeed. Repeated practice on the materials to be mastered is necessary. Reading games are helpful and many are available.

1828 Jones, Joyce. "Dyslexia: identification and remediation in a public school setting." J Learn Disabil 2(10): 533-38, October, 1969. (3 References).
In a three-year experimental program conducted in Natchez, Mississippi, it was found that volunteer teachers using highly structured material who were tutoring disabled readers on a one-to-one basis were able to help the children improve their reading skills. The gain was retained or improved upon after the children were dismissed from the program. Average WISC IQ for children seven to ten years old in the program was 99. Average IQ was 96 for the children eleven to fifteen years old.

1829 Jones, Morris Val. "Programs for dyslexics." Rehabil Lit 26(8): 236-40, August, 1965. (17 References).
Describes a pilot program for children with a discrepancy between mental ability and reading level set up by the California State Department of Education at a school for cerebral-palsied children. Criteria for guidance in referring children to the program are listed. Neurological symptoms and medical history typical of the dyslexic child are recounted. The battery of diagnostic tests available and other facilities of the school are listed. Observations pertinent to the diagnosis of dyslexia are pointed out. Characteristics primary to dyslexia include: (1) difficulty in learning associations between letter symbols and word sounds; (2) use of insufficient cues in recognizing words, that is, concentrating on initial letter and general shape of the words while ignoring internal details; and (3) left-right confusion with reversals of letters.

1830 Karlin, Robert. "Programs for disabled readers." J Dev Read 6(4): 230-37, Summer, 1963. (0 References).
A good remedial program need cost no more than a poor one. To succeed, remedial reading programs must observe sound principles of learning. "Shotgun" approaches without regard for the pupil's specific weaknesses will not be successful.

1831 Kass, Corrine E. "Educational management of reading deficits." In: Irwin, John V., and Marge, Michael, eds. Principles of childhood language disabilities. New York: Appleton-Century-Crofts, 1972. 329-39. (23 References).
Presents what is termed "a theoretical philosophy" about the types of childhood reading deficits and outlines three steps in the educational management of such deficits. It is suggested that language consists of two systems. One is the "integrational" or "automatic-sequential" level which includes processes like closure, short-term memory, and speed of perception. The other level is "representational" and concerns comprehension, concept development, and abstraction. Teachers must understand the

child's reading disabilities in terms of these two systems if appropriate
educational remediation is to be carried out. The three educational
steps are to: (1) understand the child's deficit; (2) plan and carry out
remediation; and (3) transfer remediation efforts to improve overall reading performance.

1832 Kohl, Herbert R. "Approach to reading problems." Grade Teach
      88(8): 4, 6, 8, 10, April, 1971; 88(9): 93-96, May-June, 1971.
      (0 References).
Many problem readers panic when they make a mistake. They have no idea
how to deal with their reading problems and think reading a mysterious
process. They lack stamina and their skills tend to degenerate with
time. Students need to understand what reading is and what their problems are. Talking with pupils about reading and what it can do for them
is recommended.

1833 Krabbe, Maria J. "Word-blindness and image thinking; (treatment
      and didactics)." Acta Psychother Psychosom Orthopaedagog 2(1):
      52-64, 1954. (0 References).
Describes the symptoms and lists the intellectual strengths and weaknesses
of dyslexic children. Many dyslexics are "image thinkers," that is, the
words in a sentence are immediately forgotten, but evoke a vivid image.
A dyslexic child may see in his book the sentence, "The sky was blue,"
actually see the blue sky, and report that the sentence is, "It was a
fine day." The majority of persons are "notion thinkers," expressing
their thoughts in words, not visual images. Not all image thinkers are
word-blind, and not every bad writer is an image thinker. The use of
the "compensation-correction" method of teaching is recommended. Therapy
and didactics must go together. Create a new visibility, without words,
by means of diagrams.

1834 Lamberg, Lynne. "How one family copes with dyslexia." Todays
      Health 53(8): 26-29, 48-49, September, 1975. (0 References).
Relates the story of a family with four sons, three of whom have some
form of learning disability. Two of the boys who are dyslexic became
pupils at the John F. Kennedy Institute, a special hospital and educational facility for children with mental and physical handicaps, affil-
iated with Johns Hopkins University School of Medicine in Baltimore. The
diagnostic testing performed on the youngest son in order to determine
what remedial methods to use is described. The entire family was evaluated and the mother was found to share some of the boys' problems. A
comfortable parent-child relationship is maintained in the home. Some
of the work of the Kennedy school is described.

1835 Langford, Ken, and Johnson, Terry D. "Behavior modification and
      beginning reading." Acad Ther 10(1): 53-63, Fall, 1974. (12
      References).
Reports on a method for teaching reading to children with severe reading
problems. It is based on behavior modification. A one-to-one tutor-
pupil ratio is necessary. The child and the tutor sit side by side.
The child reads the text aloud. Each word correctly pronounced has a
dot placed over the top by the tutor. If a word is missed no dot is
given, even though the pupil corrects it. Praise may be given for the
correction, but no dot. The number of dots is totaled on each page and
points are given for the number of dots. These points may be exchanged
for some tangible reward, for example, candy, field trips, etc. Accuracy,
not reading rate, is stressed. A method is given for plotting progress

on a graph. Speed and accuracy are plotted in relationship to the child's preinstructional reading ability which is used as a baseline.

1836 Leland, Bernice. "An administrative plan for diagnostic and re-
        medial teaching of children who cannot read." Natl Elem Princ
        19(6): 631-38, July, 1940. (0 References).
Describes the plan in use in Detroit schools for helping children with
very high degrees of reading disability. The plan is concerned not with
symptoms or causes of reading disability, but with early detection and
analysis. Treatment by a specially trained teacher using diagnostic
and remedial teaching methods is carried out until the child can be returned to his regular classroom. Effective treatment must be intensive.
Careful records of analysis should be kept. The personality of the remedial teacher is of major importance. Attitude of the child and his
parents toward the program is largely determined by the attitude of the
school administration.

1837 Lopardo, Genevieve S. "LEA-cloze reading material for the dis-
        abled reader." Read Teach 29(1): 42-44, October, 1975. (2
        References).
Examines the language-experience approach (LEA) and the cloze procedure
in helping disabled readers. In LEA the child dictates or writes his
own story. In this way there is no mismatch between the child's own
oral language and his reading material. It also maximizes motivation.
In cloze procedure every fifth word of a passage may be deleted. Or,
if the child needs help with a particular class of words (for example,
articles or prepositions), these words may be selectively deleted. A
method for combining these two methods is described.

1838 Love, Harold D. Parents diagnose and correct reading problems:
        for parents of children with reading disabilities. Springfield,
        Illinois: Thomas, 1970. 112p.
That parents can diagnose and correct their children's reading problems
is the thesis of this book. That parents have been told not to try this
is deplored. Why, it is asked, should parents not diagnose and help such
children who need help as soon as possible? A warning is issued against
expecting instant results, with an explanation of how to start. An informal reading inventory for parents and reading-readiness tests are included with direction for their use. The more common causes ascribed
for reading disability are discussed. These include hearing and speech
problems, minimal brain damage, mixed dominance, and constitutional
factors. Word recognition and comprehension are discussed. Material on
learning disabilities is included where the terms "dyslexia," "learning
disabilities," and "communication disorders" are used synonymously.
Suggestions are given for helping the gifted child at home.

1839 McBroom, Maude. "Handling of reading disabilities." Nations Sch
        37(5): 29-30, May, 1946; 37(6): 47-48, June, 1946. (0 Refer-
        ences).
Describes the diagnostic and treatment work of the reading clinic at the
State University of Iowa.

1840 Malmquist, Eve. "Provisions made for children with reading dis-
        abilities in Sweden." In: World Congress on Reading, 1st, Paris,
        1966. Proceedings: reading instruction: an international forum.
        Vol. 1. Edited by Marion D. Jenkinson. Newark, Delaware: Inter-
        national Reading Association, 1967. 109-24. (5 References).

The number of remedial classes and reading clinics has greatly increased in Sweden since 1947. Small classes and a variety of teaching methods are emphasized. The use of only one method for teaching reading is disapproved.

1841 Mendelsohn, Fannie S., and Cowin, Pauline. The treatment of reading disabilities; an experience of 15 years at the New York Infirmary Reading Clinic. New York, 1963. 19p.
This book is a brief history of the reading clinic at the New York Infirmary which was begun in 1947. The specialists there attempt to make the child feel accepted and acceptable. Methods are devised--almost custom-made--which are suitable for each child's need. They are optimistic about the lasting effects of remedial help. Most children make rapid progress. Four case histories are given.

1842 Monroe, Marion. "Helping children who cannot read." Prog Educ 10(8): 456-60, December, 1933. (0 References).
Remedial instruction in reading is a valid therapeutic technique. Two steps should be followed in treating reading disabilities: (1) a thorough study and analysis of the child's difficulties; and (2) application of appropriate remedial measures in a suitable program of instruction. Various perceptual and motor difficulties are discussed. Remedial work should be flexible and should not be stopped too soon.

1843 Natchez, Gladys. "Are 'toughs' teachable?" Elem Sch J 65(4): 198-205, January, 1965. (11 References).
Presents methods used by a junior high school English teacher and a reading consultant to teach reading to failing pupils thirteen and fourteen years old. It is concluded that if both teacher and pupils discover that there is hope of learning even at such a late date, both will be motivated to work hard and try again.

1844 Parsky, Larry Melvin. "Biofeedback induced suppression of sub-vocalization in sixth grade reading disabled children; effects on reading comprehension and vocabulary." For a summary see: Diss Abstr Int 36A(10): 6603, April, 1976.

1845 Pollock, Joy. Dyslexia: the problem of reading. London: Helen Arkell Dyslexia Centre, 1976. 26p.

1846 ————. Dyslexia: the problem of spelling. Rev. ed. London: Helen Arkell Dyslexia Centre, 1976. 26p.

1847 Pope, Lillie. "Blueprint for a successful paraprofessional tutorial program." Paper presented at American Orthopsychiatric Association, San Francisco, California, March 25, 1970. 1970. 24p. (ED 043 463).
Paraprofessionals have made successful tutors for retarded readers. A program is described which made use of paraprofessionals from the neighborhood of the school, an extremely depressed urban community. Dyslexics, emotionally disturbed children, disruptive children, and those who had had inappropriate teaching were among those helped. Guidelines used for this program are described. The tutorial program involved cooperation between the local school district and a hospital mental-health facility.

1848 Project read. 1973. 58p. (ED 096 610).

Demonstrates an individualized continuous-progress reading program for
pupils educationally disadvantaged in reading. Teachers and aids assisted individual pupils as needed during a daily programmed individualized
reading period. The objective was to reduce the number of children who
were reading below grade level at their schools. Findings indicate that
the pupils in the project, especially kindergarten and grades one and
two, were for the most part meeting the performance objectives. Materials
and activities used are given. The project is reported from the Ingle-
wood, California, Unified School District.

1849   Rawson, Margaret B. "Prognosis in dyslexia." <u>Acad Ther</u>   1(3):
       164-73, Spring, 1966. (11 References).
Fifty-six boys enrolled in a private day school and taught by the Orton-
Gillingham method were followed up to discover whether dyslexic students
diagnosed between the ages of six and twelve have poorer prospects for
success in adult educational and vocational achievement than do children
who are not dyslexics. Socioeconomic backgrounds and general intelligence were similar for all the boys. Those in the group who needed remedial help received individual instruction. By the time the boys' ages
ranged from twenty-six to forty years, all had graduated from high school,
and all but one had some college work. Those with the lowest language
ability at ages six to twelve were found to have attained the most years
of college and graduate work. The lowest ranking twenty-five report
residual problems with spelling and slow reading. It is suggested that
it would have deprived society of the large contribution of these men if
the school and their families had given up hope of higher education for
them. Instead the boys were supported, encouraged, tutored, and given
the help they needed.

1850   Reich, Riva R. "More than remedial reading." <u>Elem Engl</u> 39(3):
       216-19, 236, March, 1962. (0 References).
Certain attitudes characterize almost all poor readers. These children
are usually discouraged, frustrated, and easily bored. It appears to
help the reading-disabled child to inform him of his diagnosis. An
accepting attitude of partnership by the teacher is most helpful in gaining the child's cooperation. The child should also be informed of his
progress. Suggestions for ways to do this are offered.

1851   Rich, Leslie. "Hartford's reading circus." <u>Am Educ</u> 8(4): 30-34,
       May, 1972. (0 References).
Four of Hartford, Connecticut, school system's twenty-four elementary
schools now have Intensive Reading Instruction Team (IRIT) centers.
Forty-five students attend each center in the mornings in ten-week cycles.
They return to their regular classrooms in the afternoon. A large variety
of books and machines is used. Methods to create competition encourage
students to read more books. Geared to third and fourth graders, selection criteria are described as simple. The child must be reading below
grade level, be able to profit from work in the intensive atmosphere,
and have a good attendance record. Results from this inner-city program
have been gratifying.

1852   Richards, T. W. "A case of reading disability due to deficient
       visual imagery." <u>Psychol Clin</u> 20(4): 120-24, June, 1931. (0
       References).
An intelligent boy, six years, ten months old, whose spelling and reading
were unsatisfactory was helped by special teaching using auditory and
kinesthetic methods. He had poor visual imagery. His auditory ability

was better, but insufficient as an aid in reading. The alphabet was
taught by the old-fashioned, mechanical method. Words were learned me-
chanically with constant drill. After thirteen weeks of remedial instruction using these methods, the boy had caught up with his second-
grade class by January and was able to do satisfactory schoolwork.

1853 Robinson, Helen M. "Provisions made for children in the United
      States who have difficulties in reading." In: World Congress on
      Reading, 1st, Paris, 1966. Proceedings: reading instruction: an
      international forum. Vol. 1. Edited by Marion D. Jenkinson.
      Newark, Delaware: International Reading Association, 1967. 125-
      33. (9 References).
Diagnosis of reading disability is achieved by the use of standardized
tests and the teacher's judgment. An attempt is made to determine the
cause of the trouble and to treat it specifically. Examples of three
reading programs are given: in a county, in Chicago, and in New York
City. An inadequate supply of trained teachers is among the current
problems faced.

1854 Rozin, Paul, and Gleitman, Lila. "Dyslexia." Science 173(3993):
      191, July 16, 1971. (2 References).
Letter to editor. Answers Brookes' letter of criticism concerning the
research reported by Rozin, Poritsky, and Sotsky in which dyslexic
American children were taught to read Chinese characters successfully.
(See Items No. 1796 and 1855). It is agreed that the novelty of the
reading materials may have contributed to the success. It is pointed
out that Chinese characters are translated directly into meaning in being
learned without having to be heard and pronounced. In English this
whole-word system of memorization eventually becomes unworkable. It is
therefore proposed in the original article that the syllable be the unit
for instructing children in turning symbols into sounds.

1855 Rozin, Paul; Poritsky, Susan; Sotsky, Raina. "American children
      with reading problems can easily learn to read English represented
      by Chinese characters." Science 171(3977): 1264-67, March 26,
      1971. (15 References and Notes).
Eight second-grade inner-city children with reading disability were taught
to read English material written as thirty different Chinese characters
in two and one-half to five and one-half hours of tutoring. Success was
attributed to the novelty of the Chinese characters and to the fact that
each character represented a word instead of a phoneme. It is proposed
that much reading disability is caused by the highly abstract quality of
phonemes. It is suggested that reading be introduced with syllables
rather than letters. Results are seen as eliminating visual-auditory
memory deficit as an explanation for dyslexia. (See Items No. 1796 and
1854).

1856 Rychener, Ralph O., and Robinson, Jean. "Reading disabilities and
      the ophthalmologist." Trans Am Acad Ophthalmol Otolaryngol 53:
      107-20, November-December, 1948. (13 References).
Reviews the personal experience of an ophthalmologist who dealt with 225
cases of reading disability. Examination with the ophthalmograph to measure fixations, regressions, and the child's reading span and speed was
found valuable in establishing a diagnosis. Remedial reading instruction
with a good teacher and understanding and sympathetic help from parents
produced good results. Teaching phonetics and the kinesthetic method for
spelling are the most important factors in remedial training next to

motivation to learn. A sample form letter to be sent by the ophthalmologist to the parents outlining therapy is found in the article.

1857 Scher, Zeke. "Room 230 makes the difference." <u>Am Educ</u> 10(2):
      17-23, March, 1974. (0 References).
Describes the remedial reading program at a junior high school in North-
glenn, Colorado, a community near Denver. The remedial reading room
serves seventh, eighth, and ninth graders. When pupils reach grade level
in reading they need not continue in the program. Much time is spent by
teachers in talking with students, building trust, and attempting to overcome reluctance to read. Lively techniques, interesting materials, and
novel methods characterize this approach to reading.

1858 Sidgwick, J. E. "The design of a remedial programme for dyslexia."
      <u>Langage Homme</u> 19: 23-30, 1972. (0 References).
Details a program of remedial teaching in a school where the pupils were
English-speaking children of business executives who moved a great deal.
A battery of thirteen tests was given each entering pupil. The tests
were spread over one week. Pupils were divided into three groups: new
arrivals, suspected dyslexics, and normal children. Difficulties typical
of dyslexia are described. Children six to nine years old who needed
remedial treatment spent their entire day in small remedial classes of
twelve to fifteen pupils. Children ten to twelve years old were members
of a normal classroom, but attended small remedial classes for ten lessons a week in groups of seven to ten children. The weaknesses in reading, language, spelling, and arithmetic are presented in tabular form for
twelve cases, revealing the "clusters" of weaknesses. The transient
nature of the school population made retest results impossible. Two consequences of the constant moving about of these children were that they
had been exposed to two or more languages since birth, and that they exhibited insecurity which created emotional problems.

1859 Silberberg, Norman E., and Silberberg, Margaret C. "The bookless
      curriculum: an educational alternative." <u>J Learn Disabil</u> 2(6):
      302-7, June, 1969. (17 References).
In order to be educated, the child in an American school must learn to
read. Historically this made sense because until the twentieth century
there was no alternative to the written word for communicating information. This has caused increasing problems in schools because education
is no longer reserved for the intellectual and/or social elite. The
lower half of the IQ range now appears at more grade levels and many
children of higher intelligence experience learning difficulties which
impede progress in school. There is no agreement among professional
educators on how to define a reading problem, but estimates run to as
many as 20 percent of children of normal intelligence who experience
reading difficulties. We now have alternatives to the printed word. It
is suggested that a school curriculum using no books but tape recorders,
films, art, music, field trips, and any other means of conveying information without books be developed. A problem reader could be reevaluated
every year and returned to the regular book curriculum at any point.
Remedial reading instruction would be used to teach the mechanics of
reading. Other information would be imparted to these children by the
bookless mode.

1860 Singer, Harry, and Beasley, Sherrel. "Motivating a disabled
      reader." <u>Claremont Coll Read Conf Yearb</u> 34: 141-60, 1970. (14
      References).

This is a case study of Eddie, a fifth grader of normal intelligence, and a severely disabled reader. Both the boy and his parents were highly anxious about his academic retardation. Remedial efforts were aimed at motivating Eddie by using graphic displays to show him the cause and effect between effort and progress. Instructors also capitalized on his competitive spirit (he did well in athletic activities) to get him to compete against himself successfully. He was encouraged to select his own reading goals and attain them. In sixth grade, private tutoring was continued and Eddie served as a tutor himself for second graders, thus practicing his own skills.

1861   Smith, Carl Bernard, in cooperation with Barbara Carter and Gloria Dapper. Treating reading difficulties; the role of the principal, teacher, specialist, and administrator. Washington, D.C.: U.S. Department of Health, Education, and Welfare, Office of Education, National Center for Educational Communication, 1970. 132p. (Superintendent of Documents Catalog No. HE 5.230: 30026).
States the problem of disabled readers and describes what several cities are doing to cope with the problem in their public schools. Influences of the home on a child's ability to read are considered and suggestions made for overcoming environmental handicaps. Directions for establishing a reading clinic are given. Suggestions for coping with reading problems within the school are outlined, including the ways reading specialists can help. The chapters of this book have been published separately by HEW as PREP reports (Putting Research into Educational Practice).

1862   Smith, Carl Bernard; Carter, Barbara; Dapper, Gloria. Establishing central reading clinics: the administrator's role. Washington, D.C.: U.S. Department of Health, Education, and Welfare, Office of Education, National Center for Educational Communication, 1972. 32p. (DHEW Publication No. (OE)72-9; Superintendent of Documents Catalog No. HE 5.212: 12063).
After a brief outline of the characteristics of severely disabled readers for whom reading clinics are intended, several clinics are described. Floor-plan drawings are included. Directions for setting up a clinic are given, including suggestions on cost, policy considerations, and staffing.

1863   ————. Treating reading disabilities: the specialist's role. Washington, D.C.: U.S. Department of Health, Education, and Welfare, Office of Education, National Center for Educational Communication, 1972. 41p. (DHEW Publication No. (OE)72-9; Superintendent of Documents Catalog No. HE 5.212: 12065).
This general discussion of diagnosing and treating reading problems suggests several methods for management of reading disability within a school, including the use of a reading coordinator (a teacher specializing in remedial reading), special tutoring, and small-group remedial work. Procedures for establishing a remedial reading program are given, together with a list of common mistakes to be avoided. Sample exercises for developing visual perception, word identification, and comprehension skills are given.

1864   Staples, Joan. "Using special modes of learning to improve reading instruction: in corrective and remedial classes." In: Conference on Reading, University of Chicago, 1964. Proceedings: meeting individual differences in reading. Vol. 26. Compiled and edited by H. Alan Robinson. Chicago, Illinois: University of Chicago

Press, 1964. 45-48. (0 References). (Supplementary Educational
   Monographs, No. 94).
Each pupil is a unique learner. If the individual appears to learn better
through one sense modality, either vision or hearing, than another, new
material should be introduced through the stronger modality. Other activities should be planned to strengthen the weaker modalities.

1865 Stevenson, Nancy. The natural way to reading; a how-to method for
   parents of slow learners, dyslexics, and learning disabled children.
   Boston, Massachusetts: Little, Brown, 1974. 239p.
Using a question-and-answer format, this book gives information on many
phases of the teaching of reading. Points covered include: (1) why
children have trouble with short words; (2) why the sight method replaced
phonics; (3) why the study of phonics is necessary if the child is to
learn to spell; and (4) why phonics is a better method for teaching reading than the sight method, especially with disabled readers. A system
of teaching reading called the Integral Phonics Reading Program (IPRP) is
presented. Although IPRP is designed especially for parents' use in
tutoring their own dyslexic children, it can also be used in the regular
classroom. The major portion of the book is made up of the daily lessons.
Long vowels and some consonants are introduced first so that simple sentences can be formed early in instruction. It is pointed out that dyslexics need individual attention. Instruction at home in another method
quite different from his regular school reading instruction will not confuse him. If he is not succeeding, he cannot be worse off, and the supplementary instruction using this phonics method will bring improvement
in his schoolwork. How to deal with personality clashes with a discouraged, disabled reader; problems of long-term and short-term memory; and
how to reward a child for success without bribing him are among other
topics detailed.

1866 Summers, Lillian A., and Walden, Adele C. "Adjusting disabled
   readers." Chic Sch J 30(5-6): 145-50, January, 1949. (43 References).
Describes a program of remedial reading instruction in which disabled
readers were placed in a special classroom with a teacher able and willing to give individual help. Far from feeling set apart from their
regular classrooms, the children were thrilled with the special attention.
Materials and methods used are described. Teachers working in the special program are referred to as "adjustment teachers."

1867 Svagr, Virginia. "Teaching upper elementary students with severe
   learning disabilities." (Oakland Unified School District, California), 1968. 60p. (ED 027 167).
Outlines a remedial program for fourth-, fifth-, and sixth-grade children
who: (1) have already been unsuccessful in the regular classroom; (2)
have had special help with reading; (3) have normal intelligence; and (4)
do not fit the criteria for any special education program. Objectives,
skills taught, and teaching methods are recounted.

1868 "Volunteer on-the-job training pays off." Natl Elem Princ 50(3):
   55-56, January, 1971. (0 References).
Reports the results of using volunteers as remedial reading teachers in
an elementary school in Montgomery County, Maryland. The program began
as the result of a series of lectures on dyslexia. Most of the volunteers
have college degrees; some are former teachers. Many have children with
reading problems. None works in her own child's school. The volunteers

are highly motivated and take a very professional approach to the work. The reading specialist at the school prepares materials and the volunteers work with each child individually. Most volunteers give one to five hours twice a week. Some give an hour five days a week. The program was not an overnight success. But as it is perfected, teachers and pupils alike are enthusiastic.

1869 Waller, Elisabeth. Dyslexia: the problem of handwriting. Rev.
      ed. London: Helen Arkell Dyslexia Centre, 1978. 21p.
Considers some of the reasons behind the dyslexic's poor handwriting. Examples are reproduced of the sort of writing produced as a result of poor motor control, malformed letters, tension, haste, hesitations, and numerous corrections. Many children are never taught to write or shown how to form the letters correctly. To improve a pupil's writing, he should be dealt with on an individual basis. The advantages of good writing should be discussed with him. Examples of poor writing can be used to point out various faults. The pupil should practice the six basic shapes from which all of our letters are formed. Cursive (connected) writing is often easier for the dyslexic than printing. Its use often brings considerable improvement in both writing and spelling in a relatively short time. In connected writing, each letter begins on the base line and ends in a tail. Examples are given of how to progress with the child from practice with one letter to groups of letters and to breaking words into syllables.

1870 Waugh, Lynne, and Waugh, John. "Subduing the dragons of reading."
      Am Educ 8(1): 13-15, January, 1972. (0 References).
Describes the remedial reading program of the Pojoaque Valley School system in northern New Mexico. The remedial reading room is equipped with a tachistoscope, an audio-flash card system, and other instruments for teaching reading. The keystone of the system is that reading must be fun. Few children in the program have failed to improve, and the entire school system has benefited. Each child's reading level is pinpointed and the cause of trouble determined.

1871 Weinberg, Warren A.; Penick, Elizabeth C.; Hammerman, Marc; et al.
      "An evaluation of a summer remedial reading program--a preliminary
      report on the development of reading." Am J Dis Child 122(6):
      494-98, December, 1971. (12 References).
Under a government grant ninety-six boys of normal intelligence in fourth, fifth, and sixth grades who had reading disabilities were divided into three groups: a summer remedial program, a recreational program, and an untreated control group. No group showed significant gains in reading proficiency at the end of the summer. At the end of one year all showed gains, with wide variations in gains by individuals within the groups. Groups were matched for age, grade, intelligence, and socioeconomic background. It is suggested that although much money has been spent, government reading programs are not well-organized. The small-group, individualized method of instruction has not yet been demonstrated to improve children's reading abilities. There is little justification for indiscriminately referring disabled readers to summer instructional programs for older children.

1872 Wendon, Lyn. "Hairy hatman to the rescue." Spec Educ Forward
      Trends 1(2): 11-12, June, 1974. (0 References).
Outlines the use of pictograms (letters of the alphabet drawn with heads, hands, feet, and other animations) as a method for helping children with

various perceptual disorders learn to read. In spite of otherwise normal
intelligence, these children are retarded in reading because of disorders
in receiving and processing symbol information: they see or hear a letter
or word, but cannot relate it to anything nor derive any meaning from it.
Letters are depicted moving from left to right, for example, the "h" hopping to the right, the "r" running to the right. Writing is encouraged
by such devices as a "d" animated into a duck which is to be stroked
down his back first, up under his tummy, and then all the way up his long
neck. The children can identify the letters, and identify with them.
It is warned that some slow learners may fasten on to the imagery and be
unable to transfer to the underlying structure of language. Individual
assessment of children must be made.

1873 Whitsell, Alice J., and Whitsell, Leon J. "Remedial reading in a
      medical center." Read Teach 21(8): 707-11, May, 1968. (1 Ref-
      erence).
Discusses the operating procedure in a remedial reading clinic within the
framework of a major medical center based on experience at the University
of California Medical Center in San Francisco. How this kind of clinic
differs from a private clinic or public school clinic; who is in charge;
and the special advantages of a hospital clinic are described. Several
teachers work with children individually or in groups of not more than
five. Medical students, interns, residents, and fellows aid in diagnosis. Clinical teachers, the child, and the community all benefit from
the presence of the facility. The greatest advantage is that all members
of the remedial team share a unique opportunity for mutual education and
personal professional growth.

1874 Willis, Jerry W.; Morris, Betty; Crowder, Jeane. "A remedial read-
      ing technique for disabled readers that employs students as behav-
      ioral engineers." Psychol Sch 9(1): 67-70, January, 1972. (3
      References).
Reports the effects of immediate rewards on remedial reading progress.
Subjects were fourth-grade pupils ages nine to eleven years. IQs ranged
from 71 to 91. Interesting reading material was available. Retarded
readers worked with a bright eighth-grade student, called a behavioral
engineer (BE), who provided a green plastic chip and praise for each sentence of five words or more read correctly. Red chips were given for
errors. Chips were counted and recorded at the end of daily thirty-
minute sessions. For the last thirty days inexpensive toys were given
each Friday as prizes in exchange for accumulated chips. The BEs were
also systematically praised and rewarded. An average reading gain of
one and two-tenths was achieved by the students in seventy-five days of
treatment. All students exceeded their predicted rates of progress.

1875 Willson, Margaret F. "Clinical teaching and dyslexia." Read Teach
      21(8): 730-33, May, 1968. (9 References).
Three groups of eight- to ten-year-old dyslexic boys were studied to
determine if the success of various approaches to the teaching of reading
was related to the cause of the difficulty. Children whose reading difficulty appeared to be caused primarily by psychological factors as evidenced by emotional disorders responded best to a "linguistic approach"
where phoneme-grapheme relationships are taught first. Children with
evidence of organic neurological disorders responded best to an "experience approach," or "gestalt method" in which the learner associates meaning with the word as a whole. It was hypothesized that cases with educational causes (poor teaching, etc.) would respond best to a traditional

basal reader approach, but no such children were in the groups and no
conclusion could be drawn.

1876 Zabawski, Irene. "Survival kit for non-reading boys." Grade Teach
      86(9): 56-57, 112-13, May-June, 1969. (0 References).
Boys who are disabled readers are not interested in reading the usual
nice little stories in grammar school. They need reading approaches that
capitalize on their "maleness." Road signs, want ads, maps, instructions
for making model planes, and TV listings are among the reading materials
used in the remedial reading classes described. Reading-disabled boys
also need help in learning to arrange items in sequential order.

1877 Zedler, Empress Y. "Better teacher-training--the solution for
      children's reading problems." J Learn Disabil 3(2): 106-12,
      February, 1970. (11 References).
Points out that if dyslexic children are not taught from the outset by
teachers with special training in how to teach children who cannot learn
to read by conventional methods of instruction, they are very likely to
become educational casualties. The general principles of conventional
reading instruction are outlined. It is also pointed out that the literature contains little relative to preparing special teachers, but abounds
with descriptions of methods purported to be effective with children who
do not learn by usual methods. Already successful teachers are being
recruited and given brief training in remedial procedures to meet the
demand for teachers of reading-disabled children. This is seen as an inadequate solution. A preferable plan suggested is to begin the training
of teachers at the undergraduate level and proceed at least through a
fifth year of training. The goal should be the prevention rather than
remediation of reading problems. Children taught beginning reading by
prepared teachers are much less likely to develop frustration and depression from failure.

1878 ————. "Language therapy for scholastic underachievers." Paper
      presented at the International Reading Association Conference,
      Boston, Massachusetts, April 24-27, 1968. 1968. 18p. (ED 020
      096).
Reports on a two-year study which concludes that neurologically handicapped children of normal intelligence can improve their academic performance if helped with language therapy. Greater gains were achieved
when underachieving children were kept in the regular classroom with individual language therapy after school hours. Therapy was aimed at helping the children understand what they heard, to express themselves orally,
to read, and to write. It is suggested that reading confusion is often
the result of the format of the books and the difficulty of the language.

3. LINGUISTIC APPROACH

1879 Murphy, Sister Mary Leonore. Douglas can't read. Reading, England:
      Educational Explorers, 1968. 52p.
This is the case study of a nonreading ten-year-old named Douglas. Using
the Words in Colour method of Dr. Caleb Gattegno, it was possible to
teach Douglas to read. In the Words in Colour method one color represents
one, and only one, sound regardless of spelling.

1880 Wilson, Rosemary G., and Lindsay, Helen G. "Applying linguistics
      to remedial reading." Read Teach 16(6): 452-55, May, 1963. (0
      References).

Linguistic methods for teaching inner-city, reading-disabled seventh
graders are described. The alphabet was taught, then three-letter words
containing short vowels. Charts displaying the words and their rhyming
patterns were shown. Pupils used their individual flash cards to construct sentences.

4. PERCEPTUAL METHODS; VISUAL, AUDITORY, KINESTHETIC, AND/OR TACTILE METHODS; VAKT

1881   Arnold, Richard D. "Four methods of teaching word recognition to
       disabled readers." Elem Sch J   68(5):   269-74, February, 1968.
       (7 References).
The visual, auditory, and kinesthetic methods and a combination of these
were each used in an attempt to improve word recognition among disabled
readers who were delinquents. Results obtained with each of the four
methods were inconclusive.

1882   Banas, Norma, and Wills, I. H. "The vulnerable child and cursive
       handwriting." Acad Ther   4(1):   53-55, Fall, 1968. (0 References).
The "vulnerable child," also called dyslexic, is one who appears either
to attend to everything or to tune out everything completely. He has
perceptual confusion and an uneven learning pattern. He has difficulty
with cursive writing. The teaching technique of kina-writing may be an
aid. It involves printing each word on a card, drawing a pictogram on
the back of the card to illustrate the word's meaning, connecting each
letter to make the word appear cursive, and tracing the word three times
with a crayon. The child keeps a file of his words. The use of colors
may aid children with figure-ground problems.

1883   Cohen, Martin E., with Davidson, Barbara. Bets wishs doc. New
       York: Arthur Fields, 1974. 305p.
Presents through the medium of breezy, informal case histories descriptions of the disabilities that prevent children from learning to read.
The teaching strategies employed at the author's school for learning-
disabled children are described. The book examines typical symptoms and
defines terms often used in the reading disabilities and learning disabilities contexts. Diagnostic tests and the author's system of perceptual and visual training are detailed. In addition to perceptual
training, a program of hard work in the classroom designed to let the
child win victories and develop pride in himself and a no-nonsense approach to discipline are described and the successful results recounted.
The "tough fatherly-type friend" approach has been applied with success
in many of these cases. In a study conducted in the school, intensified
perceptual training produced greater gains in reading and mathematics
than the school's usual perceptual training program. Results confirm
the view that a close relationship exists between perceptual training
and academic improvement, especially reading. Apparently no one method
works with all LD children. Constant innovation is recommended to discover what aids can be combined with a structuring of the children's
lives to enable them to get down to work. Suggestions are offered for
parents on how to manage an LD child.

1884   Cohen, S. Alan. "Studies in visual perception and reading in dis-
       advantaged children." J Learn Disabil   2(10):   498-503, October,
       1969. (12 References).

Disadvantaged populations show severe visual-perceptual deficits. Studies have found Puerto Rican and black first graders making much lower scores on the Frostig Developmental Test of Visual Perception than did white and Chinese first graders. All were pupils in public schools on New York City's lower east side. Tests should not be substituted for measures of reading readiness and are of doubtful value if the primary goal is teaching reading. Letters and words are the important subjects to teach, not dominance, laterality, or spatial orientation.

1885 Cotterell, Gill C. "Non reader at 14--what action?" Spec Educ
      61(3): 14, September, 1972. (0 References).
Daily individual help with writing was the approach suggested in the attempt to help a fourteen-year-old boy who appeared to suffer from a disability approaching perceptual deafness. The boy had great difficulty in remembering sounds, in distinguishing similar sounds, and in blending sounds. The Fernald kinesthetic method was recommended. Long vowel sounds should be introduced first and similar sounds kept apart to avoid confusion in the child's mind.

1886 Dearborn, Walter F. "Teaching reading to non-readers." Elem Sch
      J 30(4): 266-69, December, 1929. (5 Bibliographic Footnotes).
Two methods of training or retraining nonreaders who have difficulty learning to read by usual classroom methods have found favor. They are the kinesthetic method, or tracing the form of written words, and the alphabet method of oral spelling out of the words letter by letter. Steps must be taken in remedial work to establish the nonreader's confidence in himself.

1887 Fernald, Grace M. "Certain points concerning remedial reading as
      it is taught at the University of California." Education 67(7)
      442-58, March, 1947. (0 References).
Describes and explains the teaching of reading at the reading clinic of the University of California at Los Angeles. The first task is to discover the best method by which an individual can learn. Often writing is a good place to start because he is already extremely discouraged with reading. Too much attention has been paid to visual methods of teaching reading at the expense of the kinesthetic. Both should develop together. The most direct expression of the word in terms of the learner's own movement is to write it.

1888 ————. Remedial techniques in basic school subjects. New York:
      McGraw-Hill, 1943. 349p. (Bibliography p. 331-41).
Giving primary emphasis to Fernald's kinesthetic method of teaching reading, this book is mainly a summary of the author's remedial work. The viewpoint is that no child of normal intelligence need be educationally handicapped because of word blindness. After explaining the emotional aspects of reading failure and the various traditional methods of teaching reading, the book explains the kinesthetic method of teaching reading. The child selects any word he wants to learn. The word is written for him in blackboard-size script or print. He then traces it with his finger, saying each part of the word as he traces it. This is repeated until the word is learned. He also writes it. The pupil makes a word file, placing each new word he has learned in alphabetical order, an aid to learning the alphabet. He also makes up a story using the words he has learned which is typed so that he can see it in print. Details of the Fernald method and its use as a remedial technique with various age groups are explained. Ways to overcome failures in spelling and arith-

metic and the application of remedial techniques to mental defectives are
explained. Case studies are cited in the volume.

1889 Fernald, Grace M., and Keller, Helen. "The effect of kinaesthetic
      factors in the development of word recognition in the case of non-
      readers." J Educ Res 4(5): 355-77, December, 1921. (0 Refer-
      ences).
Most of the children having difficulty learning to read who were treated
by the authors either learned easily by ordinary methods when given individual instruction and proper motivation, or else proved to be mentally
deficient. The few true nonreaders remaining were taught by a kinesthetic
method. This involves having the child trace the word while he says the
syllables to himself. Six case histories are given. It is theorized
that lip and hand kinesthetic elements appear to be essential links between the visual cue and the associations that give the word meaning.
Children trained by this method surpass other children in the same grades
in their ability to look at new words, pronounce them, and write them.

1890 ————. "Kinaesthetic methods for helping nonreaders." In:
      Hunnicutt, C. W., and Iverson, William J., eds. Research in the
      three R's. New York: Harper and Bros., 1958. 241-47. (0 Refer-
      ences).
Many children who are nonreaders learn by ordinary methods if given individual instruction and proper motivation; others are mentally deficient.
Most nonreaders fall into one of these two groups. The method used for
instructing the few remaining who have been found to be nonreaders with
IQs of at least 100 is described. A word the child wished to learn was
written in large script on blackboard or cardboard. The child said it
over to himself and traced it. Tracing was always done with two fingers
resting on the copy. It was never done in the air or with a pencil. He
was never allowed to copy the word. Tracing and saying the word were
repeated until he could write it correctly without the copy before him.
Usually the child asked to trace sentences after a few days. When he
could read simple sentences he was allowed to select a book at the library. Progress seems to take place in four distinct phases: (1) learning to write words; (2) associating the written with the printed words;
(3) ability to write a new word from memory; and (4) ability to pronounce
new words. It seems necessary for the child to develop a kinesthetic
background before he can appreciate the visual sensations of the printed
word. The study cites one case history.

1891 Forrest, Elliott B. "The visual auditory-verbal program." J Learn
      Disabil 5(3): 136-44, March, 1972. (11 References).
Presents a program designed specifically to help the severely reading-
disabled child who has good visual memory for words, but cannot translate
written words (visual-sound symbols) back into sound. The program includes four stages: (1) ideographic drawing in which the child is asked
to "draw a story;" (2) pictographic writing in which words form part of
a message-sentence; (3) syllabic writing in which picture symbols are
used to represent individual or syllable sounds; and (4) alphabetic coding in which the child is helped to make the transition from his own pic-
ture-symbols to the generally accepted alphabetic symbols.

1892 Frostig, Marianne. "Corrective reading in the classroom." Read
      Teach 18(7): 573-80, April, 1965. (5 References).
Distinguishes three major approaches to the teaching of reading: (1) the
"basic approach" in which teachers use basic readers and the children

are grouped according to reading achievement; (2) the "individualized reading approach" in which children make their own selection of reading material; and (3) the "language experience approach" in which much of the reading material is written by the children themselves. All are useful, but in teaching children with various developmental language disorders it is necessary to modify the approaches. Several modifications are explored. They include: (1) labeling, or associating a word with the picture of the object or activity; (2) the highly controlled vocabulary, which intensifies the usual repetition of words in preprimers and primers; (3) the child's own book, in which a book is constructed based on the child's experiences; (4) phonics, which help the child associate the sound with the printed word or symbol; (5) color cues, or printing each distinct sound in a word in a different color; (6) kinesthetic methods accomplished by tracing the words--useful where the child has disturbances in visual perception; and (7) blind writing in which the child traces with chalk over a word written on the chalkboard with his eyes closed while the teacher guides his hand. These corrective methods can be used with all children in the regular classroom.

1893   Herman, Barbara. "Teacher training in a multisensory technique for use with dyslexic children." Acad Ther 3(4): 275-77, Summer, 1968. (3 References).
Describes the program at a summer school for training teachers and for helping children with specific learning disability. The multisensory teaching techniques worked out by Samuel Orton and Anna Gillingham are used.

1894   Isgur, Jay. "Establishing letter-sound associations by an object-imaging-projection method." J Learn Disabil 8(6): 349-53, June-July, 1975. (7 References).
Explains an object-imaging-projection method (OIP) for teaching a disabled reader to associate the sound of a letter of the alphabet with the appearance of that letter. Subjects in this study were ten disabled readers. Nine were ages five to ten; one subject was twenty-nine. They varied in race, sex, and intelligence. At the beginning of the study seven knew no letter-sound associations, and three knew less than half the twenty-six letter-sound associations. Common household objects were used, one for each initial sound, and not pictures of the objects. They had the general shape of the letter, for example, key for "k," and pan for "p." The object was placed on a table beside the book used for reading. The object was named, and the initial sound said. Similarities in shape between the object and the letter it began with were pointed out (identification). The object was traced (object). It was traced again in space (imaging). The printed letter was traced (projection). Five to ten minutes per letter were required by these subjects to learn each letter by this method. It is suggested that the OIP method may also be useful in teaching brain-damaged persons to read again.

1895   McAndrew, William. "Is it a reading miracle?" Sch Soc 44(1145): 748, December 5, 1936. (0 References).
Word-tracing has been used with spectacular success to teach some children to read who appeared immune to all other methods. Word-tracing is used regularly in the early stages of reading instruction. But teachers with thirty or forty children to be taught five or six subjects do not have time to continue to use it to teach one child who is different. Parents have more time with children than do teachers. Let them use word-tracing and teach their own children to read. It is a great opportunity.

1896 Madison, Betty D. "A framework for reading." In: Arena, John I.,
      ed. Teaching educationally handicapped children. San Rafael,
      California: Academic Therapy Publications, 1967. 49-54. (25
      References).
Children suffering from specific language disability may be helped by
starting with individual parts of the learning process, and building toward a meaningful whole, or gestalt. Auditory, visual, and kinesthetic
associations built concurrently with sensory-motor development programs
planned in sequence brings these pupils a sense of achievement. The
various skills and the order of presentation recommended are outlined.

1897 Maes, Josephine P. Children who can't read--and how to help them.
      New York: Vantage Press, 1972. 137p.
After a general discussion of reading disability, its symptoms and causes,
the Position And Sound Symbols (PASS) method for teaching reading is explained. It combines elements of the sight method and phonics. Diagnostic tests and lessons emphasizing by turns visual, auditory, and word-
pattern perception are presented.

1898 Morsink, Catherine Voelker. "Teaching early elementary children
      with reading disability." Read Teach 24(6): 550-55, 559-60,
      March, 1971. (19 References).
A remedial program using small groups and careful diagnostic teaching
with much reevaluation is described. The results suggest that early recognition and treatment of reading disability is most important if emotional problems are to be avoided. Features of the teaching methods of
Cruickshank, Johnson and Myklebust, Gillingham, and Fernald were used.
A warning is issued against ceasing remedial programs too soon and
against placing reading-disabled children in regular groups using sight
or unstructured phonics methods.

1899 Neifert, James T., and Gayton, William F. "Prerequisite skills
      for use of a multi-sensory method." Acad Ther 6(4): 381-83,
      Summer, 1971. (2 References).
Reports on the multisensory method for teaching reading to severely
reading-disabled children. The child is taught to trace and say a word
simultaneously. Often it is necessary to develop visual and kinesthetic
awareness before multisensory teaching can be undertaken. If the method
fails it may be because the child is not getting helpful information from
one or both of the visual or kinesthetic modalities. An illustrative
case history is included.

1900 Ofman, William, and Shaevitz, Morton. "The kinesthetic method in
      remedial reading." J Exp Educ 31(3): 317-20, March, 1963. (9
      References).
Thirty retarded readers were given remedial reading training using the
Fernald method. This method employs the tracing of letters and words
with a finger to aid students in using tactual-kinesthetic cues in learning to read when the usual visual and auditory methods fail. These
subjects learned nonsense syllables by eye-tracing, finger-tracing, or
simply by reading the word after the examiner had pronounced it. No
differences in results were found in the two tracing methods. Both were
superior to simple reading. It is theorized that attention is the variable at work in teaching retarded readers of this type rather than any
tactual-kinesthetic function. The success of the kinesthetic method may
be its ability to hold the pupil's attention.

1901 Preston, Ralph C. "Case study: an eight-year study of a severely
      retarded reader." In: International Reading Association. Con-
      ference proceedings: reading in action. Vol. 2. Edited by Nancy
      Larrick. New York: Scholastic Magazines, 1957. 160-67. (0
      References).
Relates the case history of Fred, a child who seemed well-adjusted in
spite of constant bickering between his parents. He exhibited typical
alexic symptoms of poor visual memory, visual discrimination, and auditory discrimination, and a lack of phonic sense. At age ten he could
not read in spite of four years of usual schooling and a Binet IQ of
121. He learned to read by the use of Fernald's four-step VAKT method
but progress was slow.

1902 Richards, T. W. "A clinical study of a severe case of reading dis-
      ability in a left-handed child who was taught to read by a combined
      grapho-motor and voco-motor method." Psychol Clin 19(9): 285-90,
      February, 1931. (0 References).
An intelligent seven-year-old girl who had difficulty with word recognition because of a tendency to read from right to left was taught to read
by emphasizing kinesthetic factors. She was instructed by first seeing
the word printed and written, then copying it in writing, then writing
it several times without looking at the original. Phonic analysis was
introduced by teaching that each letter is made in a certain fashion and
placed in the word for a certain reason.

1903 Robinson, Tony. "Teaching dyslexics." Times Educ Suppl 2919: 25,
      April 30, 1971. (0 References).
Reports on the program of teacher training and of teaching of dyslexic
children at a language training laboratory in Dallas, Texas. It is part
of the pediatric neurology unit of a children's hospital. About ninety
children are trained during a school year. They are referred from other
medical sources and must have WISC scores of at least 90. The child's
training is based on a multisensory approach with visual, auditory, and
kinesthetic training. Sensory-motor training in the gymnasium is given
those children with problems in coordination. The teacher's basic course
lasts six weeks and consists of lectures on teaching materials and techniques, the neurological and psychological aspects of dyslexia, and testing procedures. To fully complete the course, teachers in training must
return for more advanced work over the next eighteen months. They also
observe and participate in the teaching. Whether the organization and
teaching methods employed would work in England is discussed. The hope
is expressed that British authorities can soon cooperate in organizing
facilities for the special education of dyslexic children.

1904 Schiffman, Gilbert, and Clemmens, Raymond L. "Observations on
      children with severe reading problems." In: Hellmuth, Jerome,
      ed. Learning disorders. Vol. 2. Seattle, Washington: Bernie
      Straub and Jerome Hellmuth, 1966. 295-310. (5 References).
Careful individual testing reveals that children with reading problems
often have normal intelligence or higher. Group tests are not adequate
for reading-disabled children. Early and accurate diagnosis of the
causes of reading problems is important if appropriate educational methods
are to be used. Special teaching methods are necessary. In this study
of 240 severely retarded readers, children instructed in the regular
classroom using developmental (normal) or corrective reading methods were
not helped. Remedial reading in a clinical program using multisensory
programs including tactile and kinesthetic techniques did make progress.

1905 Schmidt, Bernardine G. "Teaching the auditory learner to read."
      Chic Sch J 19: 208-11, May, 1938. (0 References).
Examines the results of six tests given to a group of 306 children referred for various individual problems. The tests were designed to measure associative preferences in the process of learning to read. Six
associative situations in reading had been previously identified, including such skills as: (1) ability to associate pictures or diagrams
with other pictures or diagrams; (2) ability to associate a picture with
a word or phrase; or (3) ability to associate a picture with a word or
phrase presented orally. Of the 306 children tested, 133, or 43 percent,
showed auditory preferences. Adaptations in reading instruction that
take this into consideration are described. Learning habits of auditory
learners were observed and are listed. The auditory learner depends less
on manual activities than the normal child, and is slow to respond to
approaching words independently. He is not able to use blendings very
well.

1906 Schmitt, Clara. "Developmental alexia: congenital word-blindness,
      or inability to learn to read." Elem Sch J 18(9): 680-700;
      18(10): 757-69, May, June, 1918. (0 References).
Reviews the literature on word blindness beginning with Kerr in 1896.
The physical and mental examinations of thirteen children diagnosed as
suffering from word blindness are described. The children were found
in a school population of 42,900 in fifty schools. Word blindness was
not diagnosed in failing readers who had attended school irregularly,
were in poor health, had poor vision, were of inferior mental ability,
or were the victims of other interfering factors such as foreign language
in the home or dislike of school. The thirteen case histories are documented. Some of the children were retained in regular classrooms; others
received special instruction from a specially trained reading teacher.
The method used reading materials full of action where the child could
act out what he read before attempting to read it orally. Words such as
"run," "fly," "come," and "jump" were presented on cards and the blackboard in print and script simultaneously. A child was asked to do what
the word said. Thus a complex of associations was built in the child's
mind with which to connect the new material. Children taught in the
special room gained in phonics mastery and made about a normal gain in
six months. They had previously made no progress in school. These children were seven to ten years old. Their progress was credited to the
teaching method. Those who did not receive special teaching were ages
eight to thirteen and had not made much progress in reading. It is suggested that in light of the progress made by those specially trained,
the theory of a specialized brain-center lesion must be doubted. That a
brain center biologically set aside for storing word images has undergone development of some sort resulting in the improved reading is considered untenable. Other causes for reading disability are speculated
on. Building a background of logical association by the method described
is recommended for treatment.

1907 Schwalb, Eugene; Blau, Harold; Zanger, Eugene. "Developmental dys-
      lexia: diagnosis and remediation by modality blocking." NY State
      J Med 68(14): 1931-36, July 15, 1968. (17 References).
Distinguishes "developmental dyslexia," a specific, organically determined cerebral defect, from "symptomatic dyslexia," often caused by a
visual perceptual lag. The prime difficulty in symptomatic dyslexia is
the inability to sort and screen out various stimuli. In accordance
with the modality blocking theory, it is suggested that learning,

especially learning to read, may be interfered with by what is seen.
The use of a nonvisual auditory-kinesthetic-tactile method for teaching
reading is suggested. In this method the eyes are covered with a blindfold. The word to be learned may be lightly traced on the child's back
while he traces it with his finger, and it is spoken. Two case histories
are given.

1908 Slack, Georgia. "Dade County's first-grade dropout fighters." Am
      Educ 9(8): 4-8, October, 1973. (0 References).
Describes the Dade County (Miami), Florida, program for diagnosis and
treatment of a child's deficits in the abilities he needs to begin to
learn to read. It is called Early Childhood Preventive Curriculum (ECPC).
Prereading skills are divided into four categories: auditory, visual,
perceptual-motor, and sequencing and memory. Examples of test items for
these skills are explained. Children are grouped in classrooms according to their needs as assessed by the ECPC testing. Groupings are not
permanent and depend on the kind of activity being carried out. Funding
and cost of the program are described. The pupils' interest in ECPC
teaching and response to the program have been high.

1909 Small, Mary Walsh. "Just what is dyslexia?" Instructor 77(1):
      54-57, August-September, 1967. (5 References).
Lists symptoms and causes of dyslexia and describes tests of motor activities that reveal perceptual motor disabilities. These include tests for
cerebral dominance, coordination, body image, and ability to manipulate
objects. Methods of treating dyslexic children at the Perceptual Educational Research Center in Massachusetts are detailed. Frostig worksheets
and methods similar to Montessori were used.

1910 Stothers, C. E. "Some effects of the mirror reading technique in
      individual programs of remedial reading." Can Educ Res Dig 3(1):
      17-27, March, 1963. (8 References).
For children suffering from reading disability ascribed to mixed cerebral
dominance, a system of teaching reading using a mirror-reading technique
was developed. It was used in connection with the kinesthetic methods
of Fernald and Gillingham. A case history is cited.

1911 Stuart, Marion Fenwick. Neurophysiological insights into teach-
      ing; a report on reading, writing, and spelling disabilities and
      discussion of the interrelated use of the sensory-motor avenues--
      an integrated approach to teaching. Palo Alto, California: Pacific
      Books, 1963. 125p.
"Neurophysiological approach" means using eyes, ears, speech, touch, and
motion together to establish ideas of words and their parts. The book
covers ways to teach reading-disabled children and the necessity for
using special methods. Some of the literature is reviewed and the
Gillingham, Fernald, and Montessori methods are described. Reading disability as impaired gestalt function is considered. Specific teaching
methods for use with reading-disabled children are given. It is noted
that the same methods are useful with normal children.

1912 Talmadge, Max; Davids, Anthony; Laufer, Maurice W. "A study of
      experimental methods for teaching emotionally disturbed, brain
      damaged, retarded readers." J Educ Res 56(6): 311-16, February,
      1963. (8 References).
Emotionally disturbed children with signs of central nervous system involvement (hyperactivity, short attention span, poor ability to abstract

and generalize, etc.) were taught reading with the use of three-dimensional block letters, vowels in color, tracing, and other kinesthetic and
auditory aids. Children taught by the method gained more than a year in
reading skill in three months.

1913 "The tummy tickler." Mosaic 6(1): 10-15, January-February, 1975.
      (0 References).
Describes a tactile approach to the teaching of reading to word-blind
children of normal intelligence who fail to learn by usual methods of
reading instruction. The machine used for teaching employs a computerized typewriter keyboard. It has two matrices each about three and one-
half inches square. The child holds one of these against his abdomen.
When activated, blunt rods snap out of the matrix one by one, gently
tracing the forms of letters across the child's abdomen in the same direction he would see them on a blackboard. The device was built to the
specifications of Helen Schevill, an educational psychologist. The first
children who used it called it the "tummy tickler." It seems to work
very well in helping dyslexic children discern the form and direction
of letters. In the experimental trials, it appeared that within six
weeks both normal and dyslexic children could recognize the letters the
machine traced on their abdomens. As the letters are traced the children
can also watch the letter being traced in lights on a visual console.
The uses of the machine in instructing both dyslexic and normal children
are described.

1914 "Use mirrors to teach children to read." Sci News Lett 67(11):
      169, March 12, 1955. (0 References).
Reports success in teaching children with severe reading disabilities to
read with the use of a mirror. Reading disability is ascribed to mixed
dominance, with the result that these children see letters as most persons would see them in a mirror. In a study of seventy children using
the mirror method all improved, usually gaining two years of reading
progress in six months.

1915 Waites, Lucius. Specific developmental dyslexia and related lan-
      guage disabilities; an interdisciplinary approach utilizing multi-
      sensory techniques for remedial language training. Dallas, Texas:
      Texas Scottish Rite Hospital for Crippled Children, 1966. 62p.

1916 Wallin, J. E. W. "Suggestions for applying the kinesthetic method
      of overcoming reading difficulties." Train Sch Bull 42: 185-86,
      January, 1946. (0 References).
Reviews the essentials of the Fernald kinesthetic technique for overcoming reading problems. In this method the teacher writes the word. The
child traces the word with the tip of his finger, never with a stylus.
The child repeats the tracing until he can write the word without looking at the copy. The word is used in a story (a sentence on the child's
level) to teach recognition of typescript. The child files the new word
in his alphabetical word file.

1917 "When primers fail." Natl Bus Woman 36(6): 2-3, 10, June, 1957.
      (0 References).
Explains the work of one teacher, Diana King, with reading-disabled children. The causes of dyslexia are presented in terms of Orton's theories
of lack of cerebral dominance. Reading-disabled children appear to have
a weak linkage among auditory, visual, and kinesthetic responses. It is
difficult for them to connect a visual symbol--the printed letter--with

what they hear. The object of treatment is strengthening the linkage by repeating the letter again and again to the child while he forms it with his hand. Mrs. King recounts parts of various case histories to illustrate points.

5. PHONETIC APPROACH

1918 Bannatyne, Alexander. <u>Reading: an auditory vocal process</u>. San Rafael, California: Academic Therapy Publications, 1973. 96p. (Bibliography).

1919 Cole, Edwin M. "The correction of speech and reading difficulties." <u>RI Med J</u> 28(2): 94-97, 131-32, February, 1945. (0 References).
Discusses failure or delay in acquiring speech in childhood, stuttering, and loss of speech or reading ability in adults and children. The confusion of letter and word patterns by children who have difficulty in learning to read is described. A phonic method of reading instruction for such children is recommended. Postponement in attempts to teach reading may be helpful. Reading and speech problems appear to be increasing, probably because we are not teaching adequately.

1920 Gillingham, Anna. "Pedagogical implications of specific language disability." <u>Indep Sch Bull</u> Series of 1951-52(2): 6-10, January, 1952. (6 References).
The idea that the area of a child's handicap may become his area of strength and greatest contribution as an adult cannot be ignored in remedial teaching. Children who have trouble learning to read often manifest great interest in linguistics and want to know where words come from. Writing has progressed through three levels in human history: (1) picture writing, representations of animals or things; (2) word-writing as in Chinese where each word is represented by a conventional sign; and (3) alphabetic writing in which a single symbol represents a unit of speech-sound. The method of teaching reading that has been used in American schools during the last 100 years almost assumes that our system of writing is word-writing. Children who cannot learn by this sight-word method become remedial readers. Orton's theory of cerebral dominance as it applies to the language function is explained. A system of phonics instruction suitable for instructing the 10 to 15 percent of children who learn to read poorly or not at all by the whole-word method of instruction is explained. Letters with which to begin instruction are selected because they do not lend themselves to reversal or substitution. Each letter is taught using all senses: it is seen, copied, and sounded aloud. After the concept of alphabetic language is established, non-phonetic words can be taught. Suggestions for doing so are given. The child benefits from a complete explanation of the defect in his language mechanism which causes the reading difficulty. Evasive euphemisms are not comforting, but create vague foreboding.

1921 Gillingham, Anna, and Stillman, Bessie M. <u>Remedial training for children with specific disability in reading, spelling, and penmanship</u>. 8th ed. Cambridge, Massachusetts: Educators Publishing Service, 1970. 344p.
Miss Gillingham was a research associate with Dr. Samuel T. Orton whose theory of incomplete cerebral dominance as a cause of dyslexia has had wide influence in the field of reading disabilities. After leaving that association, she and Miss Stillman taught at the Ethical Culture School, New York City, and its uptown branch, Fieldston Lower School. This book

is their basic manual for teaching reading-disabled children. It evolved through several editions and over years of teaching dyslexic children. Its aim is the successful instruction of the nonreader of average or superior intelligence who tries very hard to learn to read but has little success. Sympathetic understanding of the problem on the part of parents and teachers and honestly facing the problem with the pupil are part of the authors' remedial technique. It is based on the belief that children with specific reading difficulties cannot learn to read successfully by "sight-word" methods. Basically a phonics method, the instruction is based on associating all of these: how a letter or word looks, how it sounds, and how it feels when saying it or writing it.

The teaching method begins with an explanation to the child of the history of the alphabet. Some history of the English language is also presented. It is pointed out that if a child does not know the letters from which words are formed, each whole word becomes to him an ideogram and very difficult to remember. By using what is termed the "alphabetic method," the child has the alphabet explained to him. Then words are formed, with new letters and words gradually added. The close association of the visual, auditory, and kinesthetic elements is maintained at all times. The book gives detailed instructions for teachers for introducing new letters or new words and new spelling rules. Also included are: extensive word lists illustrating various letters and sounds; a chapter on dealing with handwriting disability and how to retrain pupils suffering from it; and a chapter on how to use the dictionary. Beginning with the sixth edition, material on remedial methods for older pupils was added.

1922 Heller, Theodore M. "The challenge of dyslexia: experiences of a pediatrician as teacher of a class of dyslectic children." Clin Pediatr 8(8): 442-46, August, 1969. (11 References).
A pediatrician was permitted by Tucson, Arizona, public-school authorities to teach remedial reading to a class of seven children. Pupils selected were normal in intelligence, vision, and hearing and ranged in age from nine to twelve years. The class met for one hour each day for about four months. A phonic teaching method was used with favorable results.

1923 Hillman, H. H., and Snowdon, R. L. "Part-time classes for young backward readers." Br J Educ Psychol 30(Part 2): 168-72, June, 1960. (5 References).
Small groups of reading-retarded children ages eight to eleven received remedial teaching using a phonics method. Teachers were experienced in elementary-school teaching but had no special instruction in remedial methods. Results were compared with similar backward children not receiving remedial instruction. Improvement of the remedial groups was highly significant statistically.

1924 Hornsby, Bevé, and Shear, Frula. Alpha to omega: the A-Z of teaching reading, writing and spelling. London: Heinemann Educational Books, 1975. 283p.
Presents a highly structured program of phonetic and linguistic instruction designed specifically for dyslexics. It is said to be useful for either adults or children with reading problems, and also for persons learning English as a second language. "Phonetics" is defined as the scientific study of speech sounds, and "linguistics" as the scientific study of language. Spelling patterns and sound patterns of English are presented with exercises and word lists. Materials for the guidance of

the teacher are included. The alphabet is presented first. Short vowels, long vowels, hard and soft sounds, vowel digraphs, and rules for suffixes follow. Syllable division, homonyms, silent letters, and finally, a group of odd words are presented. The authors acknowledge their debt to Gillingham and Stillman for these methods. They say, however, that the book grew from their own clinical observation of the areas dyslexics find especially difficult. The opinion is expressed that dyslexics, aphasics, and autistics all learn much better through the use of a highly structured phonetic program than through a random approach.

1925 Kline, Carl L.; Kline, Carolyn L.; Ashbrenner, Marjorie; et al. "The treatment of specific dyslexia in a community mental health centre." J Learn Disabil 1(8): 456-66, August, 1968. (13 References).

Describes a major program for diagnosis and treatment of specific dyslexia in a community mental health center. The Dyslexia Quotient, a method for expressing the degree of reading disability, is described. The method for calculating the Dyslexia Quotient is given. The results obtained with the first fifty patients who completed the program of dyslexia therapy are analyzed. Ages ranged from six to seventeen years. Lay therapists were used successfully with a minimum of training. A multisensory approach, based on a good basic phonics program is considered essential.

1926 Kottmeyer, William. Teacher's guide for remedial reading. New York: McGraw-Hill, 1959. 264p. (Bibliography).

Furnishes background information for elementary-school teachers on the causes, diagnosis, and treatment of reading disability. The remedial reader is defined as a child who cannot participate profitably in the regular classroom in activities in which textbooks are used. The essential difference between teaching remedially and in the regular classroom is the use of single-letter phonics, a teaching system which is explained, and is said to be profitable in remedial teaching of reading. This type of teaching removes poor readers from the regular classroom and isolates and telescopes basic reading skills so they can be taught more quickly. The system requires that the pupil become familiar with both consonant and vowel sounds immediately. Causes of reading disability include health, vision, hearing, speech defects, intelligence, laterality (which is discounted as a cause), and emotional disturbance. Whatever the cause, almost all disabled readers have in common varying degrees of inability to use basic word-perception techniques. Suggestions are made and sample forms included for keeping background records on remedial pupils. The book explains: (1) physical and sensory tests and the use of standardized IQ tests; (2) how to summarize and analyze the disability diagnosis; (3) details of how to teach a remedial reader; (4) how to build some sight vocabulary--the first goal in remedial training; (5) word-perception skills, spelling, and oral reading; and (6) how to correct bad reading habits. Information on the operation of a reading clinic is provided.

1927 Lane, Alaine. "Severe reading disability and the initial teaching alphabet." J Learn Disabil 7(8): 479-83, October, 1974. (12 References).

In a pilot study the Initial Teaching Alphabet (ITA) was used for 100 days in an intensive training program with sixth-grade children who were reading at or below second-grade level. Reading levels improved significantly.

1928 "Learning to read." Newsweek 54(15): 110, October 12, 1959. (0
      References).
Explains Anna Gillingham's theories about the cause of dyslexia and describes her method of teaching reading. The basis of reading difficulty
is neurological, caused by a lack of complete cerebral dominance. The
problem is inherited. The Gillingham method teaches children to build
words from the sounds of letters, not from the sounds of syllables as
most phonetic systems do. The Gillingham method's strength lies in being
rigorously scientific and resting on physiological, not psychological,
grounds.

1929 Lovitt, Thomas C., and Hurlburt, Mary. "Using behavior-analysis
      techniques to assess the relationship between phonics instruction
      and oral reading." J Spec Educ 8(1): 57-72, Spring, 1974. (15
      References).
Summarizes the results of two experiments regarding the relationship between phonics instruction and oral reading. The first study assessed
the effects of phonics instruction on the child's ability to read orally
from a Ginn or from a Lippincott reader. The Lippincott emphasizes
phonics more than the Ginn. The subject was a ten-year-old fourth-grade
boy labeled "dyslexic." The exact elements of the phonics instruction
used are described. They were based on the Slingerland procedures. Records were kept of number of correct answers, number of errors, the time
of session, correct rate, and error rate per minute. The remedial sessions were conducted in the teacher's home. The boy improved in all five
of the phonics areas and in oral reading from both readers. It is concluded that systematic phonics instruction can improve a pupil's performance on selected phonics tasks. The second experiment investigated
the effects of two types of phonics instruction on oral reading from the
Palo Alto reading series, a phonics-based text. The two types of instruction were the Slingerland and the type recommended in the Palo Alto
reading series. Subjects were four nine-year-old boys, two dyslexics
and two slow learners. The dyslexics received Slingerland instruction;
the slow learners the Palo Alto method. Both phonics methods proved
effective. Average correct rates and average percentage of correct
scores improved across conditions. General conclusions are that when
phonics skills are defined and systematic teaching procedures followed,
the skills can be taught in a short time. Oral reading improved as
phonics skills developed.

1930 Miles, Thomas Richard. On helping the dyslexic child. London:
      Methuen Educational, 1970. 70p. (Bibliography).
The causes and symptoms of dyslexia are presented in terms of helping
the dyslexic child and his parents with day-to-day problems. Suggestions
for teaching methods are given. The "phonetic cues" method, a modified
phonic method, is described. It involves having the child build his own
dictionary of words by saying the words and following rules for their
construction. Word lists and exercises are included in the book.

1931 Monroe, Marion. Children who cannot read; the analysis of reading
      disabilities and the use of diagnostic tests in the instruction of
      retarded readers. Chicago, Illinois: University of Chicago Press,
      1932. 205p. (Bibliography p. 178-81).
Detailed study and statistical analysis of data collected on a large number of children with reading disabilities and a control group reveal that
a "reading index" obtained from comparison of a composite reading grade
with chronological, mental, and arithmetic grades discriminated well be-

tween normal readers and those with reading defects. The effectiveness
of remedial instruction was found to depend on the child's age, intelligence, personality difficulties, and the duration and intensity of training, as well as on the severity of the reading difficulty. Causes of
reading disability are discussed. The various methods of remedial instruction used in the studies are described and results are presented.
The remedial methods are outlined according to the type of error the
method was designed to correct. Drill on vowel sounds and association
between letters and their sounds was emphasized. Tracing the handwritten
word while speaking its sound and other phonetic methods were used successfully. Case histories are included.

1932 Norrie, Edith. "Wordblindness in Denmark: its neurological and
      educational aspects." Indep Sch Bull Ser. 59-60(3): 8-12, April,
      1960. (9 References).
Acquired word blindness, or alexia, is a pathological condition in which
the person has difficulties in reading and writing. It has been recognized for about 100 years. The congenital form of reading and writing
disorder, called word blindness, dyslexia, or reading disability, was
formerly thought to be a manifestation of mental retardation in children.
In 1896 two English writers described these types of reading and writing
difficulties in children of normal intelligence. Congenital word blindness produces similar symptoms no matter what language the child is learning to read and write. They all seem to have disturbances in the sense
of direction. Confusion in the form and sequence of letters results in
mistakes which make the word-blind child unable to grasp the meaning of
what he is reading. All beginning readers experience these problems at
first. However, the normal child overcomes them in the first year of
school. The dyslexic may never overcome them, especially in writing.
Norrie's "composition box" and its use are explained. The letters are on
blocks arranged phonetically. Vowels are printed in red, voiced consonants in green, and unvoiced letters in black. The child forms words
and sentences from the letter blocks. It is valuable to let him find
his own mistakes. Only after all mistakes are corrected can the sentence be copied into his book. The work must be varied, but it is important to advance slowly. Words should be practiced in sentences, not
in isolation. In reading, if the child finds a word he does not know,
he is often helped by constructing it from the box. The processes of
reading and writing are very hard for word-blind children. Working with
the composition box helps relieve monotony. Children who use it are
never in danger of practicing mistakes.

1933 Perlo, Vincent P., and Rak, Elsie T. "Developmental dyslexia in
      adults." Neurology 21(12): 1231-35, December, 1971. (6 Refer-
      ences).
When severe developmental dyslexia is not completely treated in childhood, afflicted persons grow to adulthood with reading disabilities remaining. The most effective treatment of adults with dyslexia is prevention by early diagnosis and intensive remedial language therapy in
the early grades. Since 1963, fifty dyslexic adults have been evaluated
and treated at the Language Clinic at Massachusetts General Hospital
using Orton-Gillingham techniques with repetitive visual, auditory, and
kinesthetic reinforcement. This approach produced satisfactory results.
The cause of developmental dyslexia appears to be a developmental disorder with a strong hereditary basis.

1934 Pollock, Joy. Signposts to spelling. London: Helen Arkell Dys-
      lexia Centre, 1978. 64p.
This book is intended as a handbook for teachers of poor spellers, dyslexics, and persons learning English as a foreign language. A brief
history of the English language is given. It is designed to give children some idea of how present English spelling came about. Poor spellers
may despair at what seems the illogicality of English spelling. The
intent of this book is to mitigate such feelings by describing the country
of origin of many English words and the reasons we now spell them as we
do, showing that English spelling is not as illogical as it appears at
first. The approach is a study of phonics: short vowels are presented
first, then long vowels. Consonants follow. Spelling rules are introduced between introduction of various letters and letter groups. Suffixes, how to form plurals, and other material on how to spell English
words are included.

1935 Revelle, Dorothy M. "Aiding children with specific language dis-
      ability." Acad Ther 6(4): 391-95, Summer, 1971. (0 References).
Ideas and thoughts cannot be formulated in any child's mind unless there
is input of information and concepts. Children suffering from specific
language disability do not learn through conventional teaching methods.
In order to teach these children, certain instructional principles for
teaching phonemic-graphemic associations must be observed. These principles are presented in five steps: (1) begin at the simplest, and work
up to the complex; (2) break down concepts into smallest units; (3) provide ample practice and overlearning; (4) create environmental structure
and requirements so that the child experiences daily success; and (5)
keep performance highly structured. These five concepts are based on the
work of Samuel T. Orton and Anna Gillingham.

1936 Richardson, Ellis, and Collier, Lucy. "Programmed tutoring of de-
      coding skills with third and fifth grade non-readers." J Exp Educ
      39(3): 57-64, Spring, 1971. (18 References).
Reports a study in which twelve reading-disabled subjects, who scored
below average on various psychomotor tests, were given four and one-half
hours of tutoring distributed across forty-three sessions. It is concluded that children labeled "dyslexic" can be taught basic reading
skills. The use of a highly structured, programmed approach was credited
with the success of the tutored children as compared with a group of
twelve untutored controls.

1937 Robbins, Samuel D. "The cause of reading disabilities and their
      remedy." J Speech Disord 2(2): 77-83, June, 1937. (0 References).
Explores the relation between reading disabilities and speech defects.
Nonreaders are sometimes referred to a speech pathologist for treatment.
Defective speech and reading disabilities may have the same cause. Eleven
causes of reading disability are discussed, including mental deficiency,
overemotionalism, carelessness, blindness, lack of visual imagery with
normal vision, short auditory memory span or poor sound discrimination,
fusion problems, and lack of unilateral cerebral dominance. Suggestions
for diagnosis are given. Most nonreaders cannot learn to read by the
flash system but must be taught phonics. A method for doing this is described.

1938 Schweizer, Ilva T. "Orton revisited: learning disabilities."
      Read Teach 28(3): 295-97, December, 1974. (8 References).

Reviews Samuel Orton's work in teaching children with reading, writing, and speech disabilities. The effect of his theories on present-day teaching is examined. The approach of Anna Gillingham, who worked with Orton, is briefly summarized.

1939   Stanger, Margaret A., and Donohue, Ellen K.   Prediction and pre-
       vention of reading difficulties. New York: Oxford University
       Press, 1937. 191p.
Intended for parents or teachers of reading-disabled children, this book describes a series of tests to determine handedness, eyedness, and whether the child sees images correctly. Although confusion in sight or motor control is a likely source of trouble in learning to read, it can be overcome. The book includes drills and procedures for teaching nonreaders to read. The viewpoint of the book is that reading difficulties have a neurological basis resulting in confused cerebral dominance. The authors worked with Anna Gillingham for many years.

1940   Vail, Esther. Tools of teaching; techniques for stubborn cases of
       reading, spelling, and behavior. Springfield, Illinois: Thomas,
       1967. 163p. (Bibliography).
Observing that no technique works if the teacher cannot control the children, the author begins with a discussion of methods for maintaining discipline in special classrooms for reading-disabled children who are behavior problems. A phonics method of teaching reading is presented. Five points of difficulty are discussed, each followed by practical exercises, study guides, and reading games. The areas are: consonant sounds, short vowel sounds, consonant blends, long vowels, and "teams" or letter combinations. Sections are also included on the teaching of unusual consonants and prefixes and suffixes. Speed, comprehension, and organization in reading are also considered.

6. IN SMALL GROUPS

1941   Delacato, Janice F., and Delacato, Carl H. "A group approach to
       remedial reading." Elem Engl Part I, 29(3): 142-49, March, 1952;
       Part II, 30(1): 31-33, January, 1953. (0 References).
Reports the method and results of a six-week summer remedial reading program for a group of boys ranging in age from eight to thirteen years. They were in grades three to eight, and were of normal intelligence. All were considered educational problems and had been referred for treatment after diagnosis by a reading clinic. The group met from 8:30 to 3:30 five days a week. The boys made their own daily activity plans. They were free to talk and move about in a permissive group environment. A social studies hour was included as a cathartic. The group swam together each day. Other sports were also selected by the boys. Reading gains averaged one and two-tenths academic year for the group, higher than expected. Results are seen as indicating need for further investigation of the value of group remedial instruction as it relates to personality adjustment and the causes of reading disability. A similar program carried out the following summer produced almost identical results.

1942   Edelstein, Ruth R. "Use of group processes in teaching retarded
       readers." Read Teach 23(4): 318-24, 393, January, 1970. (6
       References).
Severely retarded readers in the fourth grade met in groups of four or five for twice-weekly reading classes. Those who did not progress were assigned to a clinical team including the teacher and a psychiatrist,

among others. Combining the reading instruction group with the therapy groups is discouraged on the basis that it adds uncertainty of status and confusion of purpose to the child's problems. Two distinct, separate settings should be provided for the permissive atmosphere and for the structured program for teaching specific material. If this is impossible, it might be best for the group to adhere exclusively to one approach or the other.

1943 French, Lillian A. "A study of the progress made by twenty-four retarded readers in an improvement program." For a summary see: Diss Abstr 16(8): 1413, 1956.

1944 Johnson, M. Jane. "A reading center for disabled readers." In: International Reading Association. Conference proceedings: reading and realism. Vol. 13(Part 1). Edited by J. Allen Figurel. Newark, Delaware: International Reading Association, 1969. 358-63. (0 References).
The reading center in White Plains, New York, is described. Daily programs for very severely disabled readers and less intensive programs in corrective and remedial reading for children with less severe problems are provided as well as training for teachers. Methods for selecting pupils, organization of the center, and the instructional program are outlined. The Fernald and Gillingham approaches are used at the center.

1945 Morsink, Catherine. "Using a bookmobile as a resource room." Except Child 39(3): 235-38, November, 1972. (8 References).
Reports on the use of a bookmobile permanently parked near an elementary school as a classroom for reading-disabled children. Problems with electrical supply and heating and cooling had to be met, but on the whole it was satisfactory. It provided a quiet, private place for the children and their teacher to work. Improvement in reading was approximately two months for each month a child spent in the program.

1946 Rawson, Margaret B. "Teaching children with language disabilities in small groups." J Learn Disabil 4(1): 17-25, January, 1971. (36 References).
The kinds of reading disabilities likely to respond to small-group therapy are described. Methods of approach are given, including both clinical and classroom situations. The skill and flexibility of the teacher are emphasized. The distinctive features of the various methods of approach are outlined, and some of the materials available for use in teaching are given.

1947 Reid, Hale C.; Beltramo, Louise; Muehl, Siegmar. "Teaching reading to the low group in the first grade--extended into second grade." Read Teach 20(8): 716-19, May, 1967. (0 References).
Three different methods were used in teaching reading to groups of low readers in first and second grade. Low readers are defined as children with IQs over 80 and low scores on a reading test. Objectives of the study were to measure: (1) the influence of training on the performance of teachers working with poor readers; (2) the influence of special lessons designed for the low-reading children in second grade; and (3) the influence of small-group instruction for these children in addition to regular classroom instruction. Results show that it was beneficial to use a different series of basal readers to instruct the low readers, and that a positive attitude both toward and from children in the low-reading group can be fostered by training for teachers. A positive

attitude toward doing the best possible teaching job with these children can be encouraged.

1948 Riddick, Ruth M., and Estacio, Ceferina. "The use of the repetitive
      8mm loop with underachievers in reading." Audiov Instr 10(4):
      308, April, 1965. (1 Reference).
Reports on the use of reading films by a traveling language laboratory
housed in a van. Two methods of viewing were used: large-screen projection and small-table screen viewing. The van was used by underachieving fourth graders. Grades one, two, and three used the small screens
in another pilot study in classrooms. The methods employed slow letter
intake, controlled sentence structure, graded vocabulary building, and
visual display of sentences. Good results are reported with the methods.

1949 Schab, Fred. "Motivation in remedial reading." Read Teach 20(7):
      626-27, 631, April, 1967. (0 References).
How to motivate retarded readers remains a problem. It was found that
some military experience of fathers or other relatives and some television shows were common to the interest of a group of fifth graders who
were retarded in reading. Their instructor became the senior officer in
command, and each child a company commander under him. In order to plan
and carry out activities from basic training through the imaginary inva-
sion of a Pacific island, it was necessary to look up much information.
The pupils wrote letters home and censored each other's letters. Interest in reading and gains in reading skill were good.

1950 Schiffman, Gilbert. "Helping the disabled reader." In: Reading
      Conference, Lehigh University, 10th, 1961. Proceedings: contro-
      versial issues in reading. Vol. 1. Edited by Albert J. Mazurkie-
      wicz. Bethlehem, Pennsylvania: Lehigh University, 1961. 45-49.
      (0 References).
In the Baltimore County schools three types of reading classes are available: (1) regular classroom instruction (also called the developmental
reading program); (2) special instruction in small groups (called the
corrective reading program for pupils who learn to read only after much
more work than the typical child); and (3) the remedial reading clinic
for retarded readers who cannot profit from the other two approaches.
The program is for pupils of normal or higher intelligence. Mentally retarded children or those with discipline problems from other causes
should not be referred. The work of this clinic is described.

1951 Shankman, Florence V. Successful practices in remedial reading.
      New York: Teachers Practical Press, 1963. 63p.
Distinguishes remedial reading from a developmental reading program. Remedial reading isolates basic skills and reteaches them to pupils who
have not mastered them in the usual classroom program. Characteristics
of retarded readers are given. Techniques include ruling out physical
problems first, then building an interest in reading; developing spatial
relations; visual and auditory skills; and vocabulary. The children should
be grouped according to the skills they have mastered. Other methods of
grouping are detailed. The initial interview between teacher and pupil
and how the teacher should make a reading appraisal are outlined. Methods
for teaching word recognition and work attack and a sample lesson sequence
are included. Practical activities and exercises for young disabled
readers are considered. These include activities for developing a knowledge of patterns, spatial relations, and motor skills. Details of ways
to give phonics instruction are included. Study skills must be developed;
a program of exercises is suggested.

1952   Shedd, Charles L. "Dyslexia and its clinical management." J Learn
       Disabil 1(3): 171-84, March, 1968. (24 References).
Focuses on dyslexia and existing methods for its clinical management. A
summer remedial program for dyslexics is described. Carried out on a
college campus, the program used instructors who were college or upper-
level high-school students without previous experience in remedial teaching. Small-group and individual instruction in an alphabetic, phonetic,
structural, linguistic approach was used. Average gain in oral reading
ability in the eight-week session was one and one-half years. A similar
program at a university is also detailed. It is believed that these
programs deal with many of the problems of the clinical management of
dyslexia.

1953   Strang, Ruth. "Why special classes for seriously retarded readers?"
       Education 68(10): 604-9, June, 1948. (0 References).
Special reading classes must be formed in the regular classroom to meet
the needs of nonreaders, pupils with emotional disturbances, and those
of whom regular texts are too difficult. This has become necessary because pupils have been pushed along through school without achieving
grade standards. If all primary teachers individualized their instruction this way, and had adequate materials, special reading groups outside
the classroom would not be necessary.

1954   Tyson, M. C. "Helping slow readers." Trends Educ No. 32; 26-29,
       October, 1973. (0 References).
Calls attention to the remedial program in the schools of the London
borough of Hounslow. A team of more than thirty peripatetic remedial
teachers instruct children who are retarded readers in groups of not
more than six at a time for periods of thirty to forty-five minutes daily.
If the child's problem is too severe for the remedial teachers to cope
with, a more intensive level of remedial help somewhat like that used at
the Word Blind Centre in London is given. Initial screening is done by
the school using standard reading tests. More detailed screening, not
using any set group of tests, may be done if necessary. Teacher-training
programs and research aimed at predicting reading failure are described.

1955   Wells, Edward Bradner. "Reading disability and antisocial behavior
       in early adolescents." For a summary see: Diss Abstr 22(10):
       3503-4, April, 1961.

7. SURVEY OF METHODS

1956   Arena, John I., ed. Building number-skills in dyslexic children.
       San Rafael, California: Academic Therapy Publications, 1972. 108p.
Although described by many different labels, a very common problem for
dyslexic children is understanding numbers. Techniques for helping these
children are reported in this collection of articles. The collection is
based on the Fall, 1970, issue of Academic Therapy Quarterly which is devoted to building number skills in learning-disabled children. Auditory
approaches to learning number skills are presented. The lack of ability
for abstract thinking and for deductive reasoning and ways to aid students with these deficits are considered. Included are: (1) use of
money and the calendar for learning concepts of mathematics; (2) games
for teaching arithmetic; and (3) material on how to deal with lags in
perception and sequential skills.

1957   Arena, John I., ed. Assisted by Bonnie Harrington. Building
       spelling skills in dyslexic children. San Rafael, California:
       Academic Therapy Publications, 1968. 99p.
This is a collection of thirty-one articles on various strategies for
teaching spelling to dyslexic children. Some are reprinted from the
Fall, 1967, issue of Academic Therapy Quarterly; others are new. The aim
is to present a wide variety of approaches, adaptable to many teaching
situations. It is intended to provide creative approaches for remedial
teachers who are looking for new methods for reaching intellectually able
children who cannot learn to spell by conventional teaching methods.
Methods for developing and reinforcing the underlying perceptual and
academic skills necessary for good spelling are given. Directions for
spelling games for use either with the individual child or as a class
activity are included. Among topics covered are: aids to memory; the
use of colors in teaching spelling; diagnostic clues; information on the
ITA; and ways to administer spelling tests.

1958   Banas, Norma, and Wills, I. H. "The vulnerable child and prescrip-
       tive teaching." Acad Ther 4(3): 215-19, Spring, 1969. (3 Ref-
       erences).
The vulnerable child, or dyslexic, has perceptual disability that may go
undetected and misunderstood for years. Differential diagnosis that considers the whole child is essential. Three prescriptive teaching guides
are presented in table form listing the items tested on the WISC, the
Detroit Tests of Learning Aptitude, and the ITPA. Teaching methods for
use in strengthening each area are given.

1959   Cleland, Donald L. "The seriously retarded reader." High Sch J
       39(4): 239-42, January, 1956. (0 References).
Careful diagnosis should precede any attempt at remediation. Principles
for a remedial program are given. Various remedial techniques are described including the visual-motor, the kinesthetic or tracing method,
and the phonic.

1960   Fletcher, Lillian G. "Methods and materials for teaching word
       perception: in corrective and remedial classes." In: Conference
       on Reading, University of Chicago, 1960. Proceedings: sequential
       development of reading abilities. Vol. 22. Compiled and edited
       by Helen M. Robinson. Chicago, Illinois: University of Chicago
       Press, 1960. 46-50. (1 Reference). (Supplementary Educational
       Monographs, No. 90).
Sight method, kinesthetic method, and the phonetic approach to the teaching of reading are described.

1961   Gearheart, B. R. Learning disabilities: educational strategies.
       St. Louis, Missouri: C. V. Mosby, 1973. 233p. (Bibliography).
Designed primarily for college use in an introductory course in learning
disabilities, this book provides information on the major educational
approaches for use with children with learning disabilities. It defines
learning-disability children as always manifesting these three characteristics: average or above-average intelligence; adequate sensory acuity;
and achievement considerably less than IQ, age, and educational opportunity would predict. LD children may also display many other characteristics, for example, hyperactivity; visual, auditory, tactual, or kinesthetic perceptual disorders; and memory disorders, either auditory or
visual. Practices described include perceptual-motor systems (Kephart,
Getman, Barsch, Cratty); the Delacato system; the ITPA; the Marianne

Frostig Center of Educational Therapy; multisensory systems (Fernald); language-development systems (Myklebust, McGinnis); the work of Orton and Gillingham; and the environmental control systems of Strauss and Lehtinen and of Cruickshank. This last is designed primarily for use with brain-injured children. The use of drugs and other medical approaches to children's learning problems are discussed. The facilities for special education in four actual school systems are described. This is intended as a guide for selecting an educational strategy for a specific school setting. Seven model programs in as many states funded by an agency of the United States government are presented. The role of the computer in planning instructional activities for children, especially in special education, is discussed.

1962   Johnson, Marjorie Seddon. "A study of diagnostic and remedial procedures in a reading clinic laboratory school." J Educ Res 48: 565-78, April, 1955. (0 References).
An intensive study of thirty-four children suffering from severe reading disability and enrolled in a remedial program was made in order to analyze the program and make recommendations for improvement. Recommendations include: (1) keeping better case histories, including information on the child's ability to make associations between visually presented material and written symbols; (2) devising better means of assessing the pupil's emotional adjustment; and (3) obtaining further physical examinations when indicated. Numerous other suggestions are offered for the use of classroom teachers, parents, and remedial instructors.

1963   Kimbrell, Harrison W., and Karnes, Lucia R., eds. Dyslexia: a common sense guide to the diagnosis and treatment of specific language disability. Monograph 1. 1975. 18p. (ED 110 977).
Defines dyslexia as a specific language disability that involves a communication breakdown in either spoken or written language. Guidelines for evaluating schools and other facilities and services for dyslexic children (including private educational facilities) are discussed in terms of motive, general community reputation, educational philosophy, quality of administration, curricula, funding, and other related matters.

1964   Money, John, ed. The disabled reader; education of the dyslexic child. Gilbert Schiffman, advisory ed. Baltimore, Maryland: Johns Hopkins Press, 1966. 421p. (Bibliography p. 389-403).
The twenty-one articles in this book cover most types of reading disabilities and present various teaching methods that may be of use in relieving reading disability. The book is designed to give those who work with disabled readers specific techniques and tools. It includes a glossary. No material is included on the whole-word or look-and-say method of teaching reading since the viewpoint is that, although widely used, the look-and-say method is useless with disabled readers. The Gillingham-Orton phonics method, kinesthetic tracing methods, the ITA, and the Gattegno words in color are among teaching techniques presented.

1965   Myers, Patricia I., and Hammill, Donald D. Methods for learning disorders. New York: Wiley, 1969. 313p. (Bibliography).
Although intended for use in the general educational management of children with many kinds of learning disabilities, this book includes much material on language development. The rationale and procedures for the educational evaluation of LD children and systems of instruction are explained. Each chapter ends with a list of references; there is much reference to literature in the field throughout. The book explains:

(1) the perceptual-motor instructional methods and techniques devised by Newell C. Kephart, Elizabeth Friedus, Gerald N. Getman, and Ray Barsch; (2) the multisensory systems of Laura Lehtinen, William M. Cruichshank, and Grace Fernald; (3) the language development systems of Helmer R. Myklebust, Hortense Barry, and Mildred A. McGinnis; (4) the phonic instruction systems of Samuel T. Orton, Anna Gillingham, and Romalda Bishop Spalding; (5) the structured system devised by Edith Fitzgerald; and (6) the Marianne Frostig program of visual perception training. The intent of the book is to: (1) present a theoretical framework for viewing learning disorders in children; (2) provide a general textbook in teaching methods applicable to such children; and (3) give an overview and descriptive orientation for assessing and treating learning disorders.

1966 Newell, Nancy. "For non-readers in distress." Elem Sch J 32(3): 183-95, November, 1931. (0 References).
Various manifestations of reading disability are examined. Remedial instruction early in a child's school career is recommended. Caution is urged in the use of drill without the child's understanding why it is being done.

1967 Pitkanen, Allan M. "Diagnostic instruction in remedial reading classes." Clear House 32(8): 487-91, April, 1958. (0 References).
Enumerates methods of teaching remedial reading. Small-group instruction, reading games, relating reading material to the child's daily life, and kinesthetic approaches are among the methods presented. Diagnosis of causes of the reading problem and instruction must go together.

1968 Robinson, Helen M. "Appraisal of methods of teaching nonreaders and pupils who make slow progress in learning to read in the primary grades." In: Conference on Reading, University of Chicago, 1945. Proceedings: the appraisal of current practices in reading. Vol. 7. Compiled and edited by William S. Gray. Chicago, Illinois: University of Chicago Press, 1945. 130-36. (7 References). (Supplementary Educational Monographs, No. 61).
Explanations are given of four methods for teaching reading: The Dolch see-and-say method using his basic sight vocabulary; Monroe's phonetic method; the Fernald and Keller kinesthetic method; and the short-exposure method.

1969 Sherwood, Mildred E. "Nature of the adjustments in teaching to meet the needs of nonreaders and the socially and emotionally handicapped. A.--The nonreader." In: Conference on Reading, University of Chicago, 1941. Proceedings: adjusting reading programs to individuals. Vol. 3. Compiled and edited by William S. Gray. Chicago, Illinois: University of Chicago, 1941. 300-306. (10 References). (Supplementary Educational Monographs, No. 52).
The nonreader is the child of normal intelligence who has not learned to read after some amount of teaching. Various remedial methods for teaching reading are reviewed, including those of Fernald and Keller; Gales and Bennett; Stanger and Donohue; Monroe; Dolch; and Hinshelwood. Little progress can be made in remedial reading without adequate motivation. Such teaching must be on an individual basis.

D. REMEDIAL TRAINING

1. COMPREHENSIVE APPROACHES

1970   Belmont, Ira; Flegenheimer, Hannah; and Birch, Herbert G.   "Compari-
       son of perceptual training and remedial instruction for poor begin-
       ning readers."   J Learn Disabil 6(4):   230-35, April, 1973.   (19
       References).
Two matched groups of poor beginning readers were given supplementary
training, one group in perceptual training, the other in remedial reading
instruction using letters and words.   In seven months both groups had made
equivalent advances, indicating that neither program is superior to the
other.

1971   "Dyslexia; clinical gadgets amuse children while curing reading dif-
       ficulties."   Life 16(15):   79-82, April 10, 1944.   (0 References).
Defines dyslexia as "the medical term for reading difficulties."   It has
many causes.   The diagnostic and treatment work done at the Dyslexia
Institute in Wesley Memorial Hospital, Chicago, is described.

1972   Silver, Archie A.; Hagin, Rosa A.; Hersh, Marilyn F.   "Reading dis-
       ability: teaching through stimulation of deficit perceptual areas."
       Am J Orthopsychiatry 37(4):   744-52, July, 1967.   (29 References).
This experiment was devised to test whether perception can be modified by
training and whether improved reading achievement reflects improvement in
accuracy of perception.   Subjects were boys ages seven to eleven years.
One group had individual tutoring for six months using conventional teaching techniques.   This was followed by six months of perceptual stimulation
activities which were directed toward improvement in accuracy of perception of visual, auditory, tactile, and kinesthetic stimuli and improvement
of the child's awareness of his body's orientation in space.   Treatment
was reversed for the second group, which received perceptual training
first.   Results suggest that training aimed at the child's perceptual
deficit areas gives reading instruction a better chance.   Generally improved perception was seen and gains were made in reading which were not
achieved by usual tutoring methods alone.

1973   Stank, Peggy L.   The effects of a diagnostic structured kindergarten
       program on the predicted reading levels of children identified as
       potential reading failures.   Ed.D. dissertation, Pennsylvania State
       University, 1973.   131p.   (ED 091 652).
Evaluated the effect of a structured kindergarten diagnostic program on
the predicted reading levels of disadvantaged urban children.   Results
were compared with the effect of a traditional kindergarten curriculum.
Members of eight kindergarten classes totaling 196 children were subjects.
Of these, 70 percent were from low socioeconomic homes, and more than 60
percent were predicted to be reading failures.   The experimental group
devoted one hour of each three-hour kindergarten session to structured
learning activities planned to develop specific cognitive and conceptual
skills related to reading.   The control group used this hour for free
play and other activities of their choice.   Testing before and after indicated that the diagnostic structured program raised test scores significantly for children who were predicted reading failures.

1974   White, Margaret.   "Congenital word blindness or specific develop-
       mental dyslexia."   Med J Aust 1(25):   1104-5, June 22, 1968.   (0
       References).

Letter to editor. Comments on an article by T. D. Hagger. (See Item
No. 121). It is believed that diagnosis of congenital word blindness is
less difficult than Hagger has proposed, and that it can readily be diagnosed even at the preschool level. Hagger's method of treatment, stressing repetition in learning to read and write, is also questioned.

2. AUDITORY TRAINING

1975 Durrell, Donald D., and Murphy, Helen A. "The auditory discrimina-
      tion factor in reading readiness and reading disability." Education
      73(9): 556-60, May, 1953. (11 References).
Reports favorable results from ear-training exercises as an aid to reading progress. For children with normal hearing who are extremely deficient in identifying the separate sounds in spoken words, exercises used
with the deaf are necessary. These exercises bring about a marked increase in rate of learning to read. Different methods of ear-training
are evaluated, and several studies are reported. Children severely handicapped in their ability to discriminate sounds in words almost never
achieve primer level in reading. More boys than girls have difficulty
in learning to read, but when boys are given help in auditory and visual
discrimination, this difference disappears.

1976 Feldmann, Shirley C.; Schmidt, Dorothy E.; Deutsch, Cynthia P.
      "Effect of auditory training on reading skills of retarded readers."
      Percept Mot Skills 26(2): 467-80, April, 1968. (20 References).
In studies aimed at discovering any relationship between auditory skills
and reading achievement in third-grade children from socially disadvantaged backgrounds, it was found that a program aimed at developing auditory skills did not facilitate reading achievement. It is suggested that
third-grade children are past the optimum age for being helped by this
type of training. Perhaps earlier training in discriminating sounds
would have produced better results. The children were divided into three
treatment groups and a control group. Reading instruction or auditory
training were given. Auditory and reading tests were administered before
and after training. No improvement was found in any of the groups in the
areas tested.

1977 Hamilton-Fairley, Daphne. Dyslexia: speech therapy and the dys-
      lexic. London: Helen Arkell Dyslexia Centre, 1976. 26p.

3. KINESTHETIC APPROACH

1978 Betts, Emmett Albert. "Remedial reading procedures." Vis Dig
      9(4): 39-44, 1946. (4 References).
Depending on the severity of the dyslexia, the Temple University Reading
Clinic employed a kinesthetic technique, or, for the most severe cases,
the Fernald tracing method in aiding disabled readers. Both techniques
are described. In the kinesthetic technique the child pronounces the unknown word, then writes it without copy after studying it by syllables.
In the Fernald technique, the teacher writes the word, and the child
traces it with his finger, not with a stylus or chalk. When he can trace
it without looking at the copy, then he begins to write the word without
copy. These techniques are valid for use with children who are word-
blind. They are not recommended for all children.

1979 Dragsten, Susan Sommer. "The importance of kinesthetic cues for the
      learning and retention of graphic forms: a comparison between good

and poor readers." For a summary see: <u>Diss Abstr Int</u>   36B(9): 4683-84, March, 1976.

1980   Early, Frances. "Developing perceptual-motor skills: new uses
       for the old template." <u>Acad Ther</u> 4(4): 295-97, Summer, 1969.
       (2 Bibliographic Footnotes).
Describes a method of perceptual-motor training using a template containing various geometric forms. The child is blindfolded and asked to lie
down. The therapist guides the child's fingers around the figure. The
aim of the exercise is to aid the child in differentiating limbs from
early generalized or mass movement. After some progress is made in differentiation, the blindfold is taken off and a patch big enough for the
eye to follow is applied to the dominant hand. The child's eye follows
the movement of his hand as he traces the template figures. This aids
hand-eye training.

1981   Early, George H. "Developing perceptual-motor skills: overbur-
       dened cognitive processes." <u>Acad Ther</u> 5(1): 59-62, Fall, 1969.
       (3 Bibliographic Footnotes).
Discusses the problem of the child who must use conscious thought (deal
cognitively) to perform tasks which should be done automatically without
specific recall and planning for each movement. The example is given of
a ten-year-old boy who wrote his name laboriously by memorizing all the
necessary movements, thus overburdening his cognitive processes. Suggestions are made for helping this type of child.

1982   Fernald, Grace Maxwell. <u>On certain language disabilities; their</u>
       <u>nature and treatment</u>. Baltimore, Maryland: Williams & Wilkins,
       1936. 121p. (Bibliography p. 113-21). (Mental Measurement Mono-
       graphs, No. 11).
Fernald describes her work with children and adults suffering from total,
or nearly total, reading disability. Only individuals of normal intelligence who had received regular schooling, had no emotional instability,
and had normal vision and hearing were included. The stages of Fernald's
tracing method for teaching reading to dyslexics are delineated in detail. Results are reported and case histories included. Partial disability was found to respond to the same kinesthetic methods. The reversals, omissions, and other errors typical of the dyslexic disappeared
as adequate motor expression developed. All but one of the cases appeared to lack visual imagery during the initial stages of training. The
necessity for logical organization of material in order to learn is
pointed out. Most of the cases were male. Handedness did not seem of
importance and findings on eye dominance were inconclusive.

1983   Fogerty, Elsie. "Notes on some cases of word blindness." <u>J Speech</u>
       <u>Disord</u> 3(2): 113-16, June, 1938. (0 References).
Presents five case histories of word blindness. A treatment regimen is
described in which the child is blindfolded and asked to feel wooden
block letters, describing the shape of each letter. He is then asked to
name the letter by sight. If he cannot, he returns to the blindfolded
feeling of the letter shapes. This exercise in feeling is not given up,
even after the child has progressed to drawing the letters and to reading words under pictures. This is seen as an intensification of one
stage of the normal child's approach to learning to read. It is suggested that some cases of word blindness are not caused by a cerebral
defect, but are functional.

1984 Hamilton, Andrew. "They think with their hands." <u>Rotarian</u> 74(4):
     32-34, April, 1949. (0 References).
Explains Fernald's system of treating word blindness by having pupils
trace words, learning them by kinesthetic means.

1985 Kirshner, A. J. "A cause of poor reading is poor reading." <u>Spec
     Educ Can</u> 47(3): 13-19, 22-25, 1973.

1986 Lanham, Joan Haines. "The effect of braille on the decoding pro-
     cesses of a group of reading disabled students with sight." For a
     summary see: <u>Diss Abstr Int</u> 35A(9): 5783, March, 1975.

1987 O'Bruba, William S. "Kinesthetic activities for primary children
     with reading difficulties." <u>Read Improve</u> 11(1): 17-18, Spring,
     1974. (0 References).
Gives methods for involving the primary school child's tactile sense and
body movement. Although they are useful for all children, these methods
are especially important for the reading-disabled child. They are focused
in three areas: word recognition, left-to-right progression, and coordination and visual discrimination. Procedures include tracing words
on index cards; writing in sand or salt; use of flannel board or chalkboard to promote left-to-right progression; and duplication of patterns
drawn on paper.

1988 "Treatment of strange reading disability." <u>Sch Soc</u> 96(2308): 277,
     317, Summer, 1968. (0 References).
Depicts specific dyslexia as a neurological disorder of unknown cause.
Symptoms are listed as difficulty in distinguishing words and letters,
clumsiness, short attention span, and restlessness. The condition responds well to treatment. The work of one clinic treating dyslexia by
kinesthetic methods is described.

1989 Wiggam, Albert Edward. "Touch, and lo! learning the kinesthetic
     way." <u>Read Dig</u> 29(175): 91-94, November, 1936. (0 References).
Relates the story of how Dr. Grace Fernald happened by chance to discover
the kinesthetic method of teaching disabled readers. She and her assistant, Mrs. Helen Bass Keller, have used the method successfully with many
persons. It is asserted that everyone can be taught to read easily and
well. The kinesthetic method, which involves having the teacher write
the word and the learner trace over the word with his finger until he
learns to write it and recognize it unaided, is explained. Case histories are given.

4. NEUROLOGICAL TRAINING

1990 Barger, William Calvin. "Late reading in children: a review of
     its origins, with discussion of a correcting device for the aphasic
     type." <u>Cereb Palsy Bull</u> 1(7): 20-26, 1959. (18 References).
When the beginning reader suffers from strephosymbolia (twisted symbols)
and mixed lateral dominance, it has been found helpful to teach the child
to read well in a mirror first. Mixed lateral dominance does not always
result in reading problems. The late reader is the child who has not
been able to adjust internally to his directional confusion. The "mirror-
reading board" technique for teaching reading is detailed.

1991 Campbell, Sister St. Francis. "Neurological approach to reading
     problems." <u>Cathol Educ Rev</u> 63(1): 28-34, January, 1965. (5
     Bibliographic Footnotes).

Presents an explanation of Delacato's theory of neurological organization and urges the use of his training program not only with the brain-
injured and reading-disabled, but also with normal children. The viewpoint is that with his method, good readers and speakers can be made even
better. The reasons for establishing clear dominance of one cerebral
hemisphere or the other are explained.

1992 Cohen, Herbert J.; Birch, Herbert G.; Taft, Lawrence T. "Some con-
        siderations for evaluating the Doman-Delacato 'patterning' method."
        Pediatrics 45(2): 302-14, February, 1970. (48 References).
Analyzes evidence which evaluates the Doman-Delacato treatment of children with various neuromuscular, behavior, and learning disorders. Called
"patterning," the treatment is said to help brain-damaged children, and
those with visual, speech, and reading disabilities. General concepts
of the progressive changes in the human nervous system that underlie patterning and how these concepts are translated into treatment are explained
with details of the treatment. The terms used by Doman and Delacato--
"homolateral crawling," "cross-pattern creeping," "crude walking," and
"cross-pattern walking"--are explained. Questions that must be faced are:
(1) whether evidence supports the conclusion that use of the method brings
improvement; (2) whether more improvement is seen with this method than
with alternative therapies; and (3) whether negative consequences of the
method exist. Some of Doman and Delacato's reports are compared with
clinical findings using other methods of therapy. Although children did
about as well under one method as another, it is emphasized that data
are presented not so much to refute the Doman-Delacato reports as to
emphasize the need for comparable data from an appropriately selected
control group. What are seen as the shortcomings of some of the Doman-
Delacato data are considered. It is concluded that data thus far advanced do not justify the conclusions about the system.

1993 Covey, Mr. and Mrs. James V., and Covey, Dan. "Dan and dyslexia:
        two points of view." Acad Ther 4(2): 129-36, Winter, 1968-1969.
        (0 References).
Recounts the experiences of parents and their son, an undiagnosed dyslexic. During grade school Dan was labeled "immature." He repeated
second grade without profit. Although he had private tutoring, phonics
lessons, and psychotherapy, he showed very little improvement. The
methods of Delacato and Doman finally came to the family's attention when
Dan was in high school. The boy improved rapidly under instruction designed to increase cerebral dominance. He attended the Academy at the
University of Plano (Texas) where these methods are used.

1994 Delacato, Carl H. The diagnosis and treatment of speech and read-
        ing problems. Springfield, Illinois: Thomas, 1963. 188p.
        (Bibliography).
Delacato explains his basic premise that the development of neurological
organization in humans progresses from lower to higher levels. Each
progression must become dominant as it supersedes lower levels. To do
so, adequate development on all lower levels must be present. The two
cerebral hemispheres have different functions. Trauma to the dominant
hemisphere results in loss of language skills. Man must follow this plan
of organization or problems of communications or movement result. If
some part of the neurological organization is missing, the deficits are
overcome by passively imposing the movement upon the nervous system or
teaching the missing functions to those with speech or reading problems.
Various language problems are presented in relationship to this develop-

mental theory. Some of the literature in the field is reviewed, and the biological history of man's neurological development is traced. Diagnostic and treatment procedures in accord with Delacato's theories of neurological development (cross-pattern creeping and walking) are described.

1995 ————. Neurological organization and reading. Springfield,
     Illinois: Thomas, 1966. 189p. (Bibliographical Footnotes).
Delacato presents evidence to support his theory that neurological organization is responsible for the reading problems observed in some children. Delacato's theory of neurological organization is explained: If any part of the individual's neurological organization is not complete, all aspects of development that follow the incomplete aspect will be adversely affected. Children with reading disorders suffer from incomplete neurological organization because of trauma or a deprived environment. To treat the problem, the state of neurological organization must be evaluated and opportunity provided for its complete development. About one-third of the book explains the author's theory. The rest of the book is devoted to ten studies by various authors who have tested his theory. Bibliographic material has been largely deleted from these studies.

1996 ————. A new start for the child with reading problems; a
     manual for parents. New York: McKay, 1970. 176p.
A manual for parents for using the Delacato system of therapy for reading problems at home with their own child. Included is the story of the author's association with Dr. Temple Fay, Dr. Glenn Doman, and Dr. Robert Doman, and others over a period of seventeen years during which they developed their system for solving reading problems in children. This system teaches the child and his parents to return to the lowest stage at which the child failed a developmental test and to work through a program of daily therapy with the child under the supervision of his parents. The complete program as used at the Institutes for the Achievement of Human Potential is outlined. Full and open discussion of the treatment and the child's willing cooperation are essential. Questionnaires for determining the child's medical background and developmental history are given. Tests for checking a child's developmental level applicable to children ages six to sixteen years are given, with directions for evaluating the child's development. How to apply the therapy at home is explained. One-sided crawling, cross-pattern creeping and walking (extending the left foot while pointing to it with the right hand and the reverse), visual practice, and hearing practice are delineated. Ways to help a child become completely one-sided, that is, consistently right-handed, footed, eared, and eyed, or consistently left-sided, are presented. Suggestions on coping with negative attitudes toward reading and how to deal with problems that persist after training are offered.

1997 Glass, Gene V., and Robbins, Melvyn P. "A critique of experiments
     on the role of neurological organization in reading performance."
     Read Res Q 3(1): 5-51, Fall, 1967. (48 References).
Critically reviews fifteen empirical research studies used as evidence of the effect of neurological organization therapy to improve reading performance. The results of twelve experiments are examined. The shortcomings of their statistical analyses and their lack of controls are evaluated. In these studies, used by Delacato as scientific appraisals of his theory of neurological organization, quite different implications

are drawn from the data than the implications drawn by Delacato. These
studies are all found to be of uncertain value.

1998 Hoopes, Amy T. Splash down to reading. 1973. 13p. (ED 077 171).
Suggests that the kind of physical activity and coordination involved in
swimming might be helpful in preventing dyslexia in some cases and in
improving academic performance in many learning-disabled children. The
mastery of neurological activities demanded by swimming may provide patterning experiences similar to those recommended by Delacato and Doman.
Children who do not develop bilateralness during the creeping stage may
later develop reading problems. Academic improvement has been observed
to accompany improved swimming skills. It is suggested that swimming
pools should be constructed in all elementary schools for instructional
purposes.

1999 Hudspeth, William J. "The neurobehavioral implausibility of the
      Delacato theory." Claremont Coll Read Conf Yearb 28: 126-31,
      1964. (13 References).
States that Delacato's theory on the causes and treatment of reading disability is based on inadequate or inaccurate reasoning, research, and
statements. Delacato's theory, it is believed, assumes that reading
problems are caused by a lack of cerebral lateral dominance, a theory
not borne out because the concept of lateral dominance does not distinguish good from poor readers. Additionally, reading is suspected to be
more a perceptual than a motor problem.

2000 Joseph Cecilia, Sister. "The Doman-Delacato approach to the teach-
      ing of reading." Mont Educ 42(9): 17-22, February, 1966. (22
      References).
Recounts the history of the development of the neurological approach to
the teaching of reading as set forth in the methods of Doman and Delacato.
The theories underlying this program of neurological training and methods
of training brain-injured children are detailed. Lists of those characteristics common to poor readers; those fairly common; and those not considered common are included. The Doman-Delacato theories and the pattern
of neurological development are explained.

2001 M. Vivian, Sister. "The neurological approach to the prevention
      of reading problems." Acad Ther 7(4): 421-31, Summer, 1972. (8
      References).
Describes a daily program aimed at neurological development to prevent
reading problems. The program included sleep positioning, crawling,
cross-patterning, creeping, and walking, and visual pursuit exercises.
All techniques were aimed at developing sidedness or dominance in one
hemisphere of the brain. Subjects were forty-five children assigned at
random to one section of first grade. A control group matched for age,
sex, IQ, and reading readiness was formed from other first-grade sections at the same school. No attempt was made to choose a select group
for the experimental group. The program lasted from October until May.
Results were very favorable. Follow-up studies of the same children in
grades two through five showed that good results were persistent. Methods
used were from Delacato's neurological approach to the prevention of
reading problems. It is suggested that many children's reading difficulties have been misdiagnosed, and their true intellectual ability unrecognized.

2002 "'Patterning' under attack." <u>Time</u> 91(22): 50–51, May 31, 1968.
      (0 References).
Reports that the Doman-Delacato method of patterning in which children
with brain damage, mental retardation, or reading disabilities are given
rigid physical therapy, is under attack from ten major medical and health
organizations as lacking merit. The medical groups criticize Doman and
Delacato for claiming cures without documentation. The method is described. Its faults as given in an article in <u>JAMA</u> are summarized.
(See Item No. 2005).

2003 Perkins, F. Theodore. "Problems arising from assertions or assump-
      tions of Delacato." <u>Claremont Coll Read Conf Yearb</u> 28: 119–23.
      1964. (16 References).
Emphases in language and reading appear to undergo cyclic changes, and
Delacato seems to have revived Orton's theory of cerebral dominance as
an explanation for reading problems. Eleven areas in Delacato's work are
questioned. It is believed that these areas need further research before they can be accepted as guides. Among others mentioned are
Delacato's assumptions on: (1) critical periods in the child's motor
development; (2) the existence of a hierarchy of levels of organization
in the central nervous system; (3) motivation; and (4) the nature of perception.

2004 "Potential for what?" <u>Newsweek</u> 70(20): 98–99, November 13, 1967.
      (0 References).
Reports the attack on the Doman-Delacato theory by <u>JAMA</u>. (See Item No.
2005). The methods of patterning and crawling, creeping, and walking to
improve neurological organization used at Doman and Delacato's Institutes
for the Achievement of Human Potential in Philadelphia are described.
The exercises are prescribed for brain-injured children and those with
reading difficulties. Doman and Delacato believe their training to be
beneficial to normal persons to help them attain maximum neurological
organization. Criticisms of Delacato's method point out that the regimen
may disrupt normal family relations and that the reading therapy does
not work.

2005 Robbins, Melvyn P. "Test of the Doman-Delacato rationale with re-
      tarded readers." <u>JAMA</u> 202(5): 389–93, October 30, 1967. (15
      References).
A study was devised to test the Doman-Delacato rationale that human neurological organization is measured along a continuum from neurological disorganization to complete organization. According to this theory, speech
and reading skills are at the top of the organization, and improved
sensory-motor function can be achieved by a series of exercises designed
to improve neurological organization. Retarded readers were divided
into three groups. One group continued its normal activities; one performed the Delacato program of creeping; and one performed a nonspecific
program of activities not known to be correlated to reading ability.
Findings show that reading achievement was not related to creeping, to
laterality, or to any of the nonspecific (placebo) activities. The
central concept of Delacato's theory that a relationship exists between
reading and neurological organization was not supported and the entire
theory is suspect.

2006 Rosborough, Pearl M. <u>Physical fitness and the child's reading prob-
      lem; the report on a technical study of twenty 'problem readers,'
      their physical handicaps and therapy</u>. New York: Exposition Press,
      1963. 80p.

Reports the results of the study of and remediation of twenty problem
readers ages five to seventeen. Fourteen were boys; six were girls. All
had extreme reading problems. A battery of tests confirmed reading and
spelling levels. A test of physical fitness was also administered. At
the outset of treatment none of the children could do frontal sit-ups.
It is noted that all of them "had lesions in areas interrelated to the
eyes and/or lesions in other areas that were remedial." These children
were believed to have adequate intelligence but improperly functioning
bodies. They were hindered by poor posture and an underlying movement
pattern which was upset. Eighty-five percent of the children were found
to have "abnormally low cerebrospinal fluid fluctuations." Therapy which
increased relaxation and which enabled them to do sit-ups, skip rope, do
balance-board work, and improve hand coordination was carried out. Reading, schoolwork, and personalities improved. Cranial osteopathy is
recommended.

2007 Ross, Eli T. "Can potentially poor readers be detected during pre-
      school years?" J Dev Read 6(4): 270-72, Summer, 1963. (0 Ref-
      erences).
Applauds and explains Delacato's theory that reading disabilities stem
from improper neurological development. Disoriented sleep positions may
provide a clue to the presence of the condition. Training to promote
complete cerebral dominance is recommended.

2008 Ryback, David. "Cognitive behavior modification: increasing
      achievement using filial therapy in the absence of supervision."
      Can J Behav Sci 3(1): 77-87, January, 1971. (33 References).
Studied the effectiveness of administration of the Staats Motivation-
Activating Reading Technique (SMART) by a parent rather than by a professional psychologist. The subject was a thirteen-year-old mentally retarded boy with dyslexia. His mother was given four hours of training
in the use of SMART materials and some professional supervision for the
first two weeks. The method used tokens assigned various values redeem-
able in cash paid by the parent. The child was allowed to use the money
he earned by making correct reading responses in any way he pleased.
Over a seven-and-one-half month period the child's reading ability improved significantly. In an additional two-and-one-half month period
(which fell during the normal summer school holiday), parent and child
continued to spend time in reading training. That the child was willing
to do this in the summer vacation time was seen as confirmation that the
SMART program does motivate children.

2009 Taylor, Raymond G., Jr., and Nolde, S. Van L. "Correlative study
      between reading, laterality, mobility, and binocularity." Except
      Child 35(8): 627-31, April, 1969. (2 References).
Children admitted to a reading clinic using Delacato's program were tested
for reading ability, laterality, mobility, and binocularity. No relationship was found between reading and the other variables. By the third
visit to the clinic (an average of 4.6 months later) reading scores and
changes in laterality and mobility showed a positive correlation. Binocularity did not show such a correlation. It is concluded that the
Delacato program and the improved reading were connected.

5. VISUAL TRAINING

2010 Atkinson, Joan K. "Programmes of visual perception, phonics and
      language." In: Anderson, J., ed. Learning disabilities: diag-

nosis and treatment. Armidale, New South Wales, Australia: University of New England, 1971. 81-91. (11 References).
Reading requires the combination of many skills. Remedial reading programs must include treatment of several areas including the five identified by Frostig: visual-motor coordination, figure-ground perception,
perceptual constancy, position in space, and spatial relationships. Evidences of each deficit are described and activities to improve performance in each area are given. Phonic programs and general language development programs are discussed.

2011 Barger, William Calvin. "An experimental approach to aphasic and
      to nonreading children." Am J Orthopsychiatry 23(1): 158-70,
      January, 1953. (43 References).
Reports on studies of two groups of children. One group was composed of
children with some degree of inability to speak (speech or verbal aphasia).
The other group was suffering from reading aphasia (nonreaders). Children in the latter group were observed not only to reverse letters but
also to make pencil strokes from bottom up rather than from top down.
They confused both horizontal axis (reversals) and vertical axis (inversions). These children were helped with the use of mirror images where
the vertical axis as well as the horizontal axis were inverted. Children
in this study transcribed the upside-down and backward words correctly
in the usual left-to-right fashion. Speech aphasia was treated through
all avenues of approach, including visual, kinesthetic, auditory, and
tactile. There is a high incidence of mixed cerebral dominance in such
children. Boys outnumber girls eight to one as victims.

2012 Barger, William Calvin; Lavin, Ruth; Speight, Frederick E. "Con-
      stitutional aspects in psychiatry of poor readers." Dis Nerv Syst
      18(8): 289-94, August, 1957. (30 References).
Recommends the use of a mirror-reading technique for helping reading-
disabled children. Children who had previously made little progress in
reading under intensive remedial instruction by numerous other methods
progressed very well with its use. Mixed cerebral dominance is seen as
the chief cause of reading disability. It is suggested that reading disability is of neurophysiological, rather than organic or emotional origin.
Handedness and laterality may be of genetic origin. The mirror-reading
technique should be employed only in situations where trained persons,
including a neuropsychiatrist, are available.

2013 Benton, Curtis D., Jr. "Comment: the eye and learning disabili-
      ties." J Learn Disabil 6(5): 334-36, May, 1973. (7 References).
Replies to Nathan Flax' challenge to the position statement issued
jointly by several pediatric and ophthalmological professional groups in
criticism of the use of vision training in the treatment of dyslexia.
(See Item No. 2017). Optometrists and ophthalmologists have some very
real differences of opinion about the eye and learning disabilities.
Dyslexic children have been found to improve in reading whether the
dominance factor was ignored or was central to treatment. Various points
made by the organizational statement are explained. Seven steps the eye
specialist, whether optometrist or ophthalmologist, should take whan a
learning-disabled child is referred to him are suggested. It is concluded that eye exercises, training in vision and visual perception, and
similar methods are a waste of time and money.

2014 Bieger, Elaine. "Effectiveness of visual perceptual training on
      reading skills of non-readers, an experimental study." Percept Mot
      Skills 38(3, Part 2): 1147-53, June, 1974. (21 References).

Second- and third-grade nonreaders were all given remedial reading instruction. Half also received the Frostig Visual Perception Training
Program. Only children of normal intelligence and without vision problems were included. All the children had been estimated at the outset
to have visual perceptual deficiencies. Results revealed that while
visual perception training did improve the visual perception of second-
and third-grade nonreaders, it did not influence the achievement of
reading skills for this group.

2015   Carbonell de Grompone, María A. "Children who spell better than
        they read." Translated from the Spanish by John Downing. <u>Acad</u>
        <u>Ther</u> 9(5): 281–88, Spring, 1974. (4 References).
Reading and writing are not the same. They use different receptive channels, vision and hearing respectively. Reading would seem to be easier
than writing, but some children can spell and write better than they can
read. In a study of Spanish-speaking Uruguayan third graders, those who
spelled better than they could read appeared to have problems in visual
perception. Each language must be analyzed separately for teaching
literacy. In Spanish, good auditory perception is of little help in
developing the necessary visual skills. For treating reading problems,
training in visual perception seems more important than auditory teaching.

2016   Dearborn, W. F. "Remedial reading: case histories and recent ex-
        perimentation." In: Conference on Reading, University of Chicago,
        1939. <u>Proceedings: recent trends in reading</u>. Vol. 1. Compiled
        and edited by William S. Gray. Chicago, Illinois: University of
        Chicago, 1939. 110–18. (0 References). (Supplementary Educational
        Monographs, No. 49).
Some disabled readers overcome the condition; others never completely do
so. Methods of remedial instruction are discussed and training eye movements is defended. Providing fresh motivation for the retarded reader
is as important as the methods used.

2017   Flax, Nathan. "The eye and learning disabilities." <u>J Am Optom</u>
        <u>Assoc</u> 43(6): 612–17, June, 1972. (15 References).
Challenges the viewpoint that vision training and glasses are ineffective
in the treatment of dyslexia and learning disabilities. The position
statement prepared and published jointly by several pediatric and ophthalmological professional groups condemning vision training in the treatment of dyslexia is challenged on the basis that there are "gross distortions and inaccuracies" in the use of supporting documentation cited
by the joint statement. It is charged that the statement was directed
at a licensed profession, optometry. The full text of the joint organizational statement is reprinted with this refutation. This article was
reprinted in <u>J Learn Disabil</u> 6(5): 328, 1973, together with a reply
by Curtis D. Benton, Jr. (See Item No. 2013).

2018   ————. "The eye and learning disabilities." <u>J Sch Health</u>
        44(2): 83–85, February, 1974. (17 References).
Replies to a joint organizational statement published by several pediatric
and ophthalmological groups critical of vision training in the treatment
of dyslexia. Although the statement contains strong criticism aimed
specifically at optometry, it charges that the documentation offered in
support of conclusions is distorted and inappropriately used. References
used in the organizational statement are reviewed. Inappropriate or distorted inferences are pointed out. Methods used are called "unscholarly

and unscientific." See Item No. 104 for an abstract of the joint organizational statement.

2019 Friedman, Nathan. "Fixation stress: a cause of retarded reading."
     J Am Optom Assoc 38(6): 463-72, 1967. (11 References).
Identifies fixation stresses of the eyes as a major block to reading
achievement in a group of boys who were poor readers. An experimental
study is described in which groups of lower-school and upper-school
(seventh grade) boys who were poor readers received training in: (1)
binocular object fixation (teaching both eyes to fixate targets); (2)
binocular space fixation (ability of eyes to fixate an imaginary point
in space binocularly); and (3) moving fixation (following rhythmically
changing lights with steadiness). Criteria for diagnosing stress in
these areas are given. The boys in the study were of adequate intelligence. They saw more clearly and read more easily as the visual training eased the fixation stresses. Their classroom behavior and attention
were better. The visual training was carried out five days a week for
eight weeks. Treatment methods are described.

2020 Gardiner, Peter. "The eye and learning disability." Dev Med Child
     Neurol 16(1): 95-96, February, 1974. (3 References).
Many children learn well with imperfect eyes. It cannot be argued from
that fact that children with some eye defects will not benefit from
visual training. Many infants appear to see little or nothing, but
eventually have normal vision. Such visual maturation may take ten
years. The problems of dyslexia and interpretation of symbols in reading may be subject to a similar kind of maturation and spontaneous process where the dyslexic suddenly seems to understand what reading is.
The improvement may not have been the result of some sort of concurrent
eye training.

2021 Hammerberg, Else, and Norn, M. S. "Defective dissociation of ac-
     comodation and convergence in dyslectic children." Acta Ophthalmol
     50(5): 651-54, 1972. (7 References).
Visual accommodation was measured in seventy-eight children who were
pupils in a school for dyslexic children. Of these, twenty-one showed
signs of abnormal or subnormal accommodation. A thorough orthoptic investigation showed only eight of the twenty-one had a normal near point
of convergence. Defective dissociation of accommodation and convergence
seemed to be the main problem. Of the thirteen who completed therapy for
the problem, eleven showed normal accommodation after treatment. The
position is taken that there is not a connection between dyslexia and
defective dissociation of accommodation and convergence and that orthoptic
training did not cure the dyslexia. It is suggested that it is important
to remove all obstacles to clear vision.

2022 Helveston, Eugene M. "Dyslexia and the eye." Claremont Coll Read
     Conf Yearb 37: 200-204, 1973. (3 References).
Visual acuity, refractive errors, eye muscle imbalance, color vision,
fusion ability, accommodation of the eyes, eye dominance, and pursuit
movements of the eyes are all unrelated to reading ability. Dyslexia
may be a form of imperception or misperception, but it occurs in the
central brain and has nothing to do with eye function. Eye-hand coordination exercises are useless in reading disability cases.

2023 Kaplan, Max. "Advances in pediatric ophthalmology." Adv Pediatr
     16: 391-431, 1969. (73 References).

Considers many of the problems that beset children's eyes and the advances in treatment in recent years. One brief section discusses learning disabilities and dyslexia. The need for controlled objective research is pointed out. It is suggested that in general, eye exercises and similar programs are useless. The relationship between eye problems and dyslexia is not convincing up to this point.

2024   Kraskin, Robert A. "Dyslexia?" J Am Optom Assoc 39(10): 916-19, 1968. (13 References).
"Dyslexia" is an old term which was revived because of the innate desire for a label. Now that the public has a label, it is looking for solutions to the problem. The field of medicine would have us believe that dyslexia is a disease. No evidence exists that it is a neurological lesion. Such terms as "word blindness" and "dyslexia" are unfortunate because they imply an etiology. It is better to use a term such as "reading disability" which does not imply a cause. Once a cause is implied, hope of teaching nonreading children to read is abandoned. The literature is filled with coined terms to describe various groups afflicted with reading disability and various remedial approaches. Awareness, significance, and identification of reading problems has increased in the last generation. The contributions of optometry in this area cannot be ignored. Vision is the fundamental physiological process upon which learning is built. The optometric approach to visual training and to the visual process builds a sounder physiological foundation of the visual process. Coining of a term such as "dyslexia" was done by persons having no knowledge of vision as a process. From the optometrist's viewpoint, "dyslexia" is an educational term describing a syndrome which the optometrist views as a visual problem and deals with as such.

2025   Krippner, Stanley. "On research in visual training and reading disability." J Learn Disabil 4(2): 65-76, February, 1971. (47 References).
Fifteen factors which may cause or contribute to reading disability are listed. Some of the studies done on causes of the disorder, especially studies relating to the relationship between visual training and reading performance, are reviewed. It is believed that few controlled studies of visual training as it relates to correcting reading disability have appeared in the literature. Many semantic problems obscure the issue. Little basic research has been done on the validity of visual training. Ophthalmologists and optometrists often disagree on the advisability of visual training, refusing to admit that each speciality has something to offer disabled readers. Those who favor visual training should define their terms, communicate with each other, and do more research.

2026   Lancaster, J. E. "Function of orthoptics in reading disabilities." Optom Wkly 39: 278, February 19, 1948.

2027   Miles, Thomas Richard, and Miles, Elaine. More help for dyslexic children. London: Methuen Educational, 1975. 74p.
This book is intended as a supplement to T. R. Miles' earlier book, On helping the dyslexic child. (See Item No. 1930). Special attention is given to the needs of children ages eight to eleven. Methods for improving reading, writing, spelling, and arithmetic are included. One chapter on word endings and beginnings suggests ways to help the child after he has completed the word lists and exercises in the first book. Additional word lists arranged by similarity of spelling are given in this book. Methods for building the morale of dyslexics and their parents are suggested.

2028   Mullins, June B. "A rationale for visual training." J Am Optom
       Assoc 40(2): 139-43, February, 1969. (18 References).
Addresses the role the optometrist plays in helping the child with learning disabilities. Such children have been variously labeled "minimal
brain-damaged," "dyslexic," or "learning-disabled." The optometrist
stands in a central position among the various professions attempting to
help LD children and their parents. He can help meet the need for a
specialist who can communicate with the various professionals involved
with the troubled child. Visual training attacks the typical problems--
inefficient reading and writing--of the child who does not achieve.

2029   Pollock, Joy, and Waller, Elisabeth. Dyslexia: the problems of
       sequencing and orientation. London: Helen Arkell Dyslexia Centre,
       1975. 26p.
Dyslexics' problems are not confined to difficulty in reading. Handwriting, directional confusion, and poor sequencing and orientation are among
other problems. "Sequencing" is used to mean either doing things or
putting things in their correct order. "Orientation" is used to mean
bringing into clearly understood relationships with particular reference
to space and direction. Chapters on each of these problems are included,
together with suggestions for dealing with these difficulties. The usefulness of the WISC in diagnosing sequencing ability is explained. Given
also are games and exercises for teaching the ideas of left and right,
time, relative size of numbers, distance, shapes, sizes, and directions
on a compass or map.

2030   Savage, Elizabeth V. "Suggested approaches to overcoming reversals
       in reading." Acad Ther 1(1): 33-35, Fall, 1965. (5 References).
Explains the difficulty some children have in reversing the direction of
letters and words, and defines laterality. Also considered are various
readers and other teaching methods that have been used successfully to
aid the child in establishing the proper left-to-right direction in reading and writing.

2031   Sherk, John Kreider, Jr. "A study of the effects of a program of
       visual perceptual training on the progress of retarded readers."
       For a summary see: Diss Abstr 28A(11): 4392, May, 1968.

2032   Smith, William. "The visual system in reading and learning dis-
       abilities." J Sch Health 39(2): 144-50, February, 1969. (3
       References).
Examines the problem of dyslexia (reading disability) as an optometrist
concerned with the role of visual, motor, and perceptual performances in
reading and learning and the correction of their defects. Thirty-six
children with reading and learning disabilities were subjects in this
study. All were found to have unsuspected and obscure deficiencies in
vision, although the visual system as a factor in the child's learning
disability had been discounted. Two months of orthoptic treatment resulted in reading improvement. It is concluded that not all reading and
learning disabilities can be blamed on the visual system. However, even
in the presence of other causes the visual system may be indirectly involved. There is no agreement on cause and effect, but remedial reading
treatment without removing the cause is a waste of time. Since the educator's approach often fails, the orthoptic methods should be tried. It
has given good results in the cases described.

2033   Stinchfield-Hawk, S. "Dyslexia or reading disability." <u>Vis Dig</u>
       2: 8-12, 1938.

2034   Swanson, William L. "Optometric vision therapy--how successful is
       it in the treatment of learning disorders?" <u>J Learn Disabil</u> 5(5):
       285-90, May, 1972. (13 References).
Reports on the records of 100 consecutive cases treated by an optometrist
with optometric vision therapy. Forty-nine of the children were seven
to ten years old, and ninety-five of the 100 cases were nineteen or
younger. Dyslexia was present in 73 percent and various other reading
and learning problems were present in almost all cases. In several months
of individual office therapy sessions, the therapy was successful in 93
percent who reflected improved learning ability. All patients had normal,
healthy eyes. Some wore lenses for correction of refractive errors.

2035   Wold, Robert M., ed. <u>Visual and perceptual aspects for the achiev-</u>
       <u>ing and underachieving child.</u> Seattle, Washington: Special Child
       Publications, 1969. 492p. (Bibliography).
Deals with vision training as it relates to learning disabilities in children from the viewpoint of the optometrist. This collection of twenty-
five original articles is divided into three parts. The first deals with
the theory underlying the notion of "vision" as distinguished from
"sight," visual performance, and the experimental and theoretical bases
for vision development and training programs. Whether dyslexia really
exists and the role of cerebral dominance in learning disorders are the
subjects of separate articles. The second part of the book deals with
coordination and cooperation among the various professional persons who
deal with children with learning problems. The rivalry between optometrists and ophthalmologists and the role of optometrists in aiding learning-disabled children through vision training programs and in other ways
are examined. Testing and remediation are covered in the last section
of the book. Evaluated are: hand-eye coordination; visual memory; perception and laterality and their relation to directionality development;
and perceptual motor training. The use of drugs to treat minimal brain
dysfunction and the role of the optometrist in treating strephosymbolia
are considered. A glossary of terms used in the field of learning disabilities is found on pages 457-492.

6. PERCEPTUAL-MOTOR TRAINING

2036   Balow, Bruce. "Perceptual-motor activities in the treatment of
       severe reading disability." <u>Read Teach</u> 24(6): 513-25, 542,
       March, 1971. (49 References).
There is too little evidence to state definitely the role of perceptual-
motor activities in overcoming reading disability. Where perceptual-
motor activities have been reported successful, it would appear that the
success was because of some factor common to all the programs rather than
to some particular characteristic of a program. It is suggested that
perceptual-motor training be given to all primary-grade pupils and to
students of any age who are deficient in school skills.

2037   Bechtel, Leland P. <u>The detection and remediation of learning dis-</u>
       <u>abilities. Child welfare research and demonstration project.</u>
       <u>Final report.</u> (Androscoggin County Task Force on Social Welfare,
       Inc., Lewiston, Maine.) 1975. 314p. (ED 116 417).
Reports on the final two years of a program planned to identify and treat
sixty potentially dyslexic preschool children and forty-five dyslexic

elementary-school children. The preschool program stressed development of perceptual-motor skills, applied skills, gross motor skills, and free play. The experimental group made forty-four positive gains, out of fifty possible, over the control group. Twenty-seven of these were statistically significant. The program for elementary-grade dyslexics is explained. Reading, perceptual-motor skills, gross motor skills, English composition, methematics, and weekly field trips were included in the remediation. Pupils in the program gained significantly over the control group.

2038 Early, George H. "Developing perceptual-motor skills: integrating the perceptual modalities." Acad Ther 5(2): 133-36, Winter, 1969-1970. (1 Bibliographic Footnote).
Notes the significant difference that often appears in the efficiency of the different perceptual modalities in the learning-disabled child. Perceptual modality is defined as one of the avenues or channels through which a child receives information from his environment, processes and organizes it, and responds to it. Visual, auditory, tactual-kinesthetic, motor, and combinations of these channels are the perceptual modalities. Several techniques for developing integration of perceptual modalities are described, including Kephart's method using poker chips in two colors representing long and short sounds.

2039 "8 + 1 = 1 : 1." Read Newsrep 5(7): 42-44, 1971.

2040 Frostig, Marianne, and Horne, David in association with Maslow, Phyllis. Frostig program for the development of visual perception; teacher's guide. Rev. ed. Chicago, Illinois: Follett, 1973. 144p. (Bibliography).
Frostig identifies five areas of visual perception: visual-motor coordination, figure-ground perception, perceptual constancy, position in space, and spatial relationships. This book is divided about equally between directions for giving children the physical training exercises in each of the five areas of visual perception and directions for teachers in the use of the worksheets for written work in the same five areas.

2041 Greenblatt, Augusta. "Hidden handicaps to learning." Parents Mag 45(10): 53-55, 77, October, 1970. (0 References).
Details the symptoms of reading disability. These include difficulty in telling up from down, right from left, awkwardness, and abnormally short attention span, lack of interest in books and difficulty in learning tasks like how to tie a shoelace. While reading disability was formerly thought to be rare, it is now realized that a great many children suffer from varying degrees of it. "Specific reading disability," "dyslexia," and "strephosymbolia" are among the names by which the disorder is known. There is an increasing awareness that something can be done about these problems. The methods of an "extended readiness" class for kindergartners who do not appear ready for first grade are recounted. The goal of the methods is to help these children develop the perceptual skills necessary to learn to read. They trace each other's outlines on large sheets of paper, and play tic-tac-toe using themselves as the X's and O's to develop an appreciation for detail and direction. As the child performs a series of actions he describes what he is doing out loud. Thus he reinforces himself and retains what he has just learned.

2042 Greenspan, Steven B. "Effectiveness of therapy for children's reversal confusions." Acad Ther 11(2): 169-78, Winter, 1975-1976. (12 References).

Reports the results of a comparison of perceptual-motor training and orthoptic visual training as treatment for reversal confusions in reading and writing in a group of fifty-two children. The children tested were eight years old and were carefully matched on a wide range of variables. There were twenty-six children in each group. The experimental group who had perceptual-motor training was significantly superior to the group which had only orthoptic visual training, as measured by three tests, in the behaviors being studied, and in expressing reversal confusion tendencies. It is concluded that therapy in perceptual-motor training is effective, especially for younger children.

2043 Hirsch, Steven M., and Anderson, Robert P. "The effects of perceptual motor training on reading achievement." In: Learning disability/minimal brain dysfunction syndrome: research perspectives and applications. Edited by Robert P. Anderson, and Charles G. Halcomb. Springfield, Illinois: Thomas, 1976. 162-81. (55 References).

An evaluation of experimental literature on the effect of perceptual-motor training on academic achievement, particularly reading achievement, this article reports numerous errors in the experimental designs of these studies. It is concluded that positive gains in reading ability attributed to perceptual-motor training are invalid and can be accounted for in other ways. It is believed that it has not been demonstrated that positive change in reading ability is brought about by perceptual-motor training because such training does not effect any changes in cognitive ability. More adequate test designs are necessary before the merits of perceptual-motor training can be assessed.

2044 Hoyle, Dorothy Beatrice. A study of five children with dyslexia in an experimental program of physical education activities. Unpublished Ph.D. thesis. Texas Woman's University, 1966.

Reports on a program of physical education training planned especially for a group of dyslexic boys. Among other reasons for carrying out the program were the desires to gain understanding of such children and to test some of Kephart's theories on the motor training of dyslexic children. After three months of training some improvement in reading skills and physical coordination was noted, but improvement was more obvious at the end of the school year.

2045 McCormick, Clarence C.; Schnobrich, Janice Nelson; Footlik, S. Willard; et al. "Improvement in reading achievement through perceptual-motor training." Res Q Am Assoc Health Phys Educ Recreat 39(3): 627-33, October, 1968. (22 References).

Forty-two first graders retarded in reading and matched for age, IQ, sex, and scores on reading-grade-level tests were divided into three groups at random. One group received perceptual-motor training in such areas as cross-lateral crawling, walking, balancing, and rope-jumping. The second group received exercises from the regular physical education program, and the third group was a control. The perceptual-motor training group had made statistically significant gains in reading when retested after seven weeks of training. The other groups did not register gains.

2046 Marks, Herman B. "Evaluation of visual perceptual training for reading disabilities." RI Med J 53(3): 150-51, 162, 167, March, 1970. (9 References).

Concludes that visual perceptual exercises of the sort recommended by optometrists are not worthwhile. Reading is a complex process calling for many skills, including visual perception. Perceptual development and perceptual training cannot be resolved by simplistic theories. Physical, sensory-motor, and perceptual development in children proceed at different rates in different children. Perceptual lags may appear for a variety of reasons. The treatment of emotional, neurological, or psychological poor development is educational and is best left in the hands of the educators. Children suffering from equivocal signs in any of these areas should be identified early and provided with the educational services they need.

2047 Meredith, Patrick. Dyslexia and the individual. London: Elm Tree
      Books, 1972. 190p. (Bibliography).
Believes that dyslexia has been ignored by educators unwilling to change their methods and by psychologists busy arguing among themselves. Both groups are criticized as part of an outmoded establishment. The approach to dyslexia is that a letter is "a structure in space." Remedial efforts should be aimed at developing the child's identification and control of his perception of the position of things in space and direction, and the order of things in time. We can identify only recognizable objects; the amount the brain can handle at one time is limited. Successful teachers anticipate the child's inevitable confusion.

2048 Sullivan, Joanna. "The effects of Kephart's perceptual motor-
      training on a reading clinic sample." J Learn Disabil 5(9):
      545-51, November, 1972. (15 References).
Children in grades four to twelve who were poor readers and enrolled in a reading clinic were divided into groups matched for age, grade, IQ, and reading performance. All received two hours of reading instruction daily. Half the children (the experimental group) received three types of perceptual-motor training for thirty minutes daily for six weeks. The exercises included: (1) chalkboard training to establish a sense of direction (directionality) and orientation in space; (2) ocular pursuit training requiring fixation on a moving object; and (3) sensory-motor training to improve balance, laterality, and directionality. The training did not improve reading comprehension. However, the improvement in oral reading was almost statistically significant. The exercise did not improve the reading of children with binocular fusion difficulties.

2049 Tischer, Selma. "Psycho-motor re-education for children with read-
      ing difficulties." Can Psychol 9(2): 187-95, April, 1968. (0
      References).
Psychomotor reeducation is defined as a specialized treatment based on movement to allow the child to understand his psychomotor development, body image, spatial organization, and corporal expression. Learning disability caused by psychomotor disharmony is improved by this type of training. Constant reference to concrete learning experience is also maintained by this method. Ways in which these exercises are particularly applicable to dyslexia are pointed out.

2050 Wagner, Rudolph F. Dyslexia and your child: a guide for parents
      and teachers. New York: Harper & Row, 1971. 148p. (Bibliography).
Focuses on how to aid dyslexic youngsters when specialized help is not available. Ways for parents to assess and treat their child's problem are given. Characteristic signs of reading disability and of specific learning disabilities are listed. Many exercises for strengthening perception and specific remedial techniques are included. A typical case history is presented.

2051 Weisman, Eva A. "A multidiscipline approach to the development of
      reading skills." Child Welfare 52(5): 305-12, May, 1973. (1
      Reference).
Describes an experimental program devised for use in an inner-city public
school system to help inner-city children who often achieve poorly in
communication skills. Called a "concentrated, sequential instruction
program," it includes: (1) the regular instructional program of the
school; (2) physical education oriented to perceptual-motor development;
(3) a social-work program to deal with children's physical problems and
home-school, parent-child relations; and (4) a testing program. The program began the second semester of kindergarten and ran through grade
one. A control class of children received the regular classroom instruction. By the end of grade one, the experimental group had moved up two
levels, the control group one level. Verbal achievement was also higher.
Parental attitudes were better in the experimental group. The plan is
now operative in several schools.

E. PSYCHOLOGICAL THERAPY

2052 Abrams, Jules C. "Minimal brain dysfunction and dyslexia." Read
      World 14(3): 219-27, March, 1975. (4 References).
Uses the terms "minimal brain dysfunction" (MBD) and "specific reading
disability" interchangeably. Brain damage before, during, or after birth
may damage the primary ego apparatuses which are concerned with such
basic skills as perception, concept formation, motility, and language
development. The symptoms of dyslexia are described and methods of treating MBD children are suggested. The strongest factor in success or failure of treatment is the interpersonal relationship--how contact with the
child is maintained. Impersonal, insincere, or patronizing approaches
can only add to the child's pain.

2053 Ackerman, Adrienne. Dyslexia: the importance of motivation. Rev.
      ed. London: Helen Arkell Dyslexia Centre, 1979. 22p.
Outlines activities that motivate different children and describes teaching techniques. Methods described include: (1) typing his own story,
which gives the child reinforcement of the letters as he searches the
keyboard for them; (2) making up stories using the same group of letters
repeatedly; and (3) reading poems with simple words and easy rhythm.

2054 Akins, Keith. "A psychotherapeutic approach to reading retarda-
      tion." Can Psychiatr Assoc J 12(5): 497-503, October, 1967.
      (20 References).
Reading retardation must be adequately diagnosed by a multidisciplinary
team. The majority of children with reading retardation suffer from
emotional problems as a reaction to their reading problems. Only a
minority cannot learn to read because of emotional difficulties. Remedial reading is central to the successful treatment of this majority
in combination with supportive psychotherapy. Three categories of reading retardation are distinguished: (1) For children whose reading problems are caused by underlying emotional upset, traditional psychotherapy
and remedial reading in combination are suggested. (2) For retarded
readers deficient in autonomous language skills, remedial reading and a
corrective emotional experience provided by the teacher may be effective.
(3) For children whose reading problems stem from unconscious conflicts
on the part of parents or child, more intensive psychotherapy is needed.

2055 Arcieri, Libero, and Margolis, Muriel. "A clinical approach to
the understanding and treatment of reading disabilities." Pathways
Child Guid 8:1 ff, February, 1966. As reprinted in Natchez,
Gladys, ed. Children with reading problems. New York: Basic
Books, 1968. 418-26. (0 References).
Educators must consider three groupings in assessing reading needs of a
student population: (1) the broad developmental reading program for most
pupils; (2) the corrective reading program for slower pupils, or for
those who require modified reading programs because of lack of early
learning experiences; and (3) a remedial program for pupils who are unable to learn by usual methods of instruction or within the regular
classroom group. Theories as to the basic causes of reading disabilities
range from psychoanalytic formulations to neurophysiological explanations.
In addition, socioeconomic disparities in family, school, and community
institutions create a gulf between what the present educational programs
can offer and what the socially disadvantaged pupil must have in order
to derive meaning and motivation from the program. It is essential to
understand the factors contributing to the child's learning difficulty
in order to determine the nature and extent of treatment approaches.
Suggested approaches include: (1) attempts to involve parents more
actively in their children's schoom problems; (2) attempts to approach
both the emotional and learning parts of the reading problem; and (3)
treatment in which the remedial teacher and a therapist work together.

2056 Axline, Virginia Mae. "Nondirective therapy for poor readers."
J Consult Psychol 11(2): 61-69, March-April, 1947. (0 References).
Using a variety of techniques aimed at aiding personal adjustment and
acceptance of help with their problem was helpful to a group of second-
grade retarded readers. They achieved better-than-average improvement
in reading.

2057 Beecher, Marguerite, and Beecher, Willard. "Remedial reading."
Individ Psychol Bull 7: 99-118, 1949.

2058 Berkowitz, Pearl, and Rothman, Esther. "Remedial reading for the
disturbed child." Clear House 30(3): 165-68, November, 1955.
(0 References).
The majority of emotionally disturbed children are retarded in reading.
Children who were patients in a psychiatric hospital were encouraged to
express their fantasies in drawings, then tell their teachers the meanings. These stories were typed by the teacher and the children learned
to read the words of their own choosing. Action songs were used in the
same way with accompanying movement. A battery-operated quiz game using
reading cards and a red light which indicated a correct response also
was helpful.

2059 Bills, Robert E. "Nondirective play therapy with retarded readers."
J Consult Psychol 14(2): 140-49, April, 1950. (10 References).
Slow-learning third graders retarded in reading were observed to make
significant gains in reading after six weeks of individual nondirective
play therapy. It is concluded that the child with a reading difficulty
is having difficulty with personal adjustment. Personal changes appeared
after as few as six individual and three group-play therapy sessions.
No personality maladjustment common to all members of the group was observed.

2060 ————. "Play therapy with well-adjusted retarded readers." J
  Consult Psychol 14(4): 246-49, August, 1950. (3 References).
Third graders retarded in reading but well-adjusted in their group were
found to make no significant gains in reading after six weeks of nondirective play therapy. It is concluded that gains in reading ability
are directly proportional to the amount of emotional maladjustment present in the child.

2061 Cameron, John L.; Borst, C. A.; Fifer, W. P.; et al. "Remedial
  reading: psychoanalytic and operant approach." Br J Med Psychol
  45(3): 273-78, September, 1972. (4 References).
Presents the use of programmed materials in a remedial reading program
using the Bell and Howell Language Master. A psychoanalytic approach was
employed. Special cards designed for use with the Language Master are
described. The goal was to complete one year's school work in six to
seven weeks with three remedial sessions a week, and return the child to
his regular classroom. Each session was carefully monitored using
closed-circuit videotaping. In no case was the child told he was wrong.
Attempts were made to structure the environment in such a way that it
would cause as little conflict for the child as possible. Before the
child read his text he worked with a programmed series of tasks designed
to insure success when he finally did try to read. The human and interpersonal contact was kept to a minimum, but was controlled to be always
positive and reinforcing.

2062 Dahlberg, Charles C.; Roswell, Florence; Chall, Jeanne. "Psychotherapeutic principles as applied to remedial reading." Elem Sch J
  53(4): 211-17, December, 1952. (0 References).
Most children with severe reading disabilities have emotional problems.
Whether the disabilities cause the emotional difficulty or the reverse is
not known. Intensive psychotherapy and remedial reading training should
be separated. However, the remediation can be more constructive if it:
(1) follows psychotherapeutic principles in establishing rapport; (2)
establishes a framework for the sessions; (3) sets up consistently kept
rules; and (4) accepts the child exactly as he is.

2063 Dolan, G. Keith. "Counseling as an aid for delayed readers." J
  Read 8(2): 129-35, November, 1964. (9 References).
Seventh-grade students retarded in reading made better gains in reading
if the remedial program also included personal counseling sessions. It
is concluded that the learning process can be limited by attitudes toward
the learning. These attitudes can be changed favorably by effective
counseling.

2064 ————. "Effects of individual counseling on selected test scores
  for delayed readers." Pers Guid J 42(9): 914-19, May, 1964. (13
  References).
Whether poor personality traits cause reading disabilities or are a result of them is uncertain. It is certain that the individual's emotional
state influences learning. In a study of delayed and normal seventh-grade
readers it was found that individual counseling made significant differences in reading achievement scores. Attitudes toward learning can be
altered favorably through effective counseling.

2065 Fisher, Bernard. "Group therapy with retarded readers." J Educ
  Psychol 44(6): 354-60, October, 1953. (22 References).

Reports findings of a study of reading-disabled delinquent boys ages ten
to twelve years whose reading ages ranged from six to eight years. All
were residents of an institution for delinquents; had the same classroom
teacher; and had three hours of remedial reading instruction each week
from the same remedial reading teacher. The group that met for group
psychotherapy with a therapist once a week for one hour for six months
made greater gains in correcting reading difficulties than a control
group. This is seen as an important factor in the correcting of reading
disabilities in this group.

2066   ————. "An investigation of the effectiveness of group therapy
    for the remediation of reading disabilities." For a summary see:
    Diss Abstr   13(4):   590-91, 1953.

2067 Font, Marion McKenzie. "What happens to children who cannot read?"
    J Except Child 13(3): 70-72, 96, December, 1946. (7 References).
The case history of a disabled reader who developed paranoid schizophrenia
as an adult is recounted. Both reading disability and this psychosis are
characterized by fearfulness and feelings of inadequacy. Poor teaching
is poor mental hygiene. What is needed to prevent reading failures from
becoming mentally ill is a happy school experience adapted to individual
needs.

2068 Gardner, James, and Ransom, Grayce. "Academic reorientation: a
    counseling approach to remedial readers." Read Teach 21(6):   529-
    36, 540, March, 1968. (11 References).
Reports the initial findings of a pilot project termed "academic reorientation." Its general goal is to change the attitude and behavior of remedial readers toward school. Subjects were male pupils in a university
reading school. The technique is highly verbal, with the counselor im-
parting much specific information about school to the boy. The technique
is not recommended for children under nine years of age because of this
verbal aspect. Eight points are made with each child. It seems necessary
to repeat them many times before it can be assumed that he understands.
These include: (1) an adequate rationale for the boy's learning problem;
(2) helping the child to learn when and under what circumstances he tends
to behave in certain ways; (3) teaching him the immediate adverse consequences of continuing to avoid the reading task at hand. (An example of
this is missing words and falling behind because of the bad habit of daydreaming.) Results of the counseling were encouraging. Fourteen of the
sixteen children manifested marked changes in attitude toward school.
It is pointed out that the personality of the counselor is a factor.
Academic reorientation counseling is not a substitute for more intensive
counseling procedures that may be necessary. The program can, however,
be quickly mastered and used by school counselors and reading teachers.

2069 Goodman, Elizabeth; O'Connor, Eileen; Shugerman, Estelle E. "Train-
    ing in remedial reading and psychotherapy." Am J Psychother 1(2):
    161-82, April, 1947. (10 References).
Reports a study of children enrolled in a program which combined remedial
reading instruction and psychotherapy. "Reading disability" is defined
as reading disorders caused by a brain lesion. "Reading inability" is
used to describe all other types of reading disorder. Results are seen
as confirming the belief that all reading-disabled children of adequate
intelligence can be taught to read. Remedial reading for children with
neurotic symptoms should be taught outside the school in a place where
psychotherapy is also available. Many of these children do not progress
in school without both the remedial reading class and the therapy.

2070 Harrison, Betty Farrel Dodge. "Conditions of reward and patterns
      of dominance as factors in the learning rate and retention of
      second grade students with developmental dyslexia." For a summary
      see: Diss Abstr 26(3): 1481, September, 1965.

2071 Hirst, Lois T. Reading for children with problems in social ad-
      justment. 1974. 11p. (ED 089 241).
Suggests that before a child can achieve on a normal level academically
he must have remediation of his reading difficulties and relief of severe
behavior problems. Daily success should be provided in a reading program
for children with deviant behaviors. Continuing reinforcement from the
teacher enables the child to achieve more self-reinforcement. Reading
materials should be provided which offer challenge without frustration.
The pupil has more opportunity to overcome reading deficiencies and make
a better social adjustment to the classroom if he has a minimum exposure
to failure; if each achievement is reinforced; and if he is given full
support for all progress.

2072 Illovsky, Joseph. "An experience with group hypnosis in reading
      disability in primary behavior disorders." J Genet Psychol 102(1):
      61-67, March, 1963. (4 References).
Five boys fifteen and sixteen years old who were hypnotized as a group
before classes and given the suggestion that they increase their "retentive power towards the reading material" made much faster progress than
a similar control group who were not hypnotized, even though those who
were hypnotized were slightly weaker intellectually than the control
group. Those who considered hypnosis a kind of magic requiring no effort
on their part ceased to make gains when the sessions were over. The
others, more self-reliant, continued to improve even after the suggestions
ceased.

2073 Ingram, Philippa. "Non-professionals help backward readers." Times
      Educ Suppl 2988: 7, August 25, 1972. (0 References).
Denis Lawrence of the Somerset, England, schools psychological service,
has found that a once-a-week chat with a sympathetic adult from outside
school can improve the backward reader's self-image and general adjustment and attitude. In studies of the method, significant rises in reading attainment were noted. No special training in counseling is necessary. Any adult with the right temperament will do. Absolute privacy
for the sessions is necessary for the child to get his troubles off his
chest successfully.

2074 Lawrence, Denis. "Counseling of retarded readers by non-profession-
      als." Educ Res 15(1): 48-51, November, 1972. (3 References).
Groups of poor readers who were pupils in four different schools were
matched on sex, mental age, chronological age, and reading age. One
group received counseling. The other group did not and served as a control. Lay counselors, women from the area selected because they were
judged to be sympathetic, intelligent, and interested in children, saw
the retarded readers for an individual interview once a week for two
terms. The counselors met with the psychologist three times before and
three times during the experiment. A typical interview is included. The
counseled group showed a significant rise in reading attainment at the
end of the two terms.

2075 Lissak, David. "Reading difficulty--a psycho-educational analysis
      of a cognitive dysfunction." Can Psychol 9(2): 121-32, April,
      1968. (13 References).

Discusses the increasing concern of educators with the growing number of children who have reading difficulties. The wide existence of reading disabilities seems paradoxical because reading is considered an easy learning task which can be acquired at any age past four or five years. Reading and reading problems are discussed in terms of the history of language, the many methods devised to teach reading, and the complete confusion in the area of treating reading difficulty. In analyzing the confusion it appears that the nature of the reading process has never been thoroughly analyzed and that we do not have a systematic approach to its understanding. It is concluded that reading difficulty and its treatment are not purely educational problems, but are of concern to both education and psychology, that is, psychoeducational. To meet this need, the "thematic-experiential" program for treating reading has been developed at Douglas Hospital, Montreal. It has resulted from the cooperation of teachers, psychologists, and psychiatrists. The theoretical basis for the program is explained.

2076 McCollum, Paul S., and Anderson, Robert P. "Group counseling with reading disabled children." J Couns Psychol 21(2): 150-55, March, 1974. (25 References).
Group counseling was found not to have a generalized effect on reading achievement. Two groups of children, all diagnosed as having minimal brain dysfunction and/or a learning disability, were selected for study. The age range was ten to fourteen years, IQs ranged from 80 to 131, and all were attending classes for children with minimal brain dysfunction. Most were boys. The experimental group received ten group counseling sessions over a two-and-one-half-month period. The control group received no counseling. Those in the treatment group demonstrated significant increases in oral and reading vocabulary after counseling. Comprehension of sentences did not improve. The control group made about half the progress in oral and reading vocabulary during the same period as did the experimental group.

2077 McCord, Hallack. "A note on the use of the psychogalvanometer as an aid in the diagnosis of certain persons with reading difficulties." J Dev Read 5(2): 137-38, Winter, 1962. (0 References).
A psychogalvanometer, an instrument designed to measure emotional changes by recording changes in sweat-gland activity, was attached to remedial reading students. They were then asked to respond by free association to stimulus words concerned with reading. The method seemed to bring to light much diagnostic material and shows promise as a means for assessing the personality problems of persons needing remedial reading help.

2078 McGann, Mary. "Dramatic dialogues for simultaneous treatment of reading and personality problems." J Ed Psychol 38(2): 96-104, February, 1947. (9 Bibliographic Footnotes).
Dramatic dialogues are of outstanding value in the treatment of disabled readers, simultaneously treating their personality needs and the reading disability. Conversation, self-forgetfulness, social stimulation, oral reading, rapport, and learning favorable attitudes toward reading are some of the advantages of this method in remedial reading.

2079 Margolin, Joseph B.; Roman, Melvin; Harari, Carmi. "Reading disability in the delinquent child: a microcosm of psychosocial pathology." Am J Orthopsychiatry 25(1): 25-35, January, 1955. (0 References).

A large proportion of delinquent children appearing in the courts and coming from low socioeconomic environments manifest reading retardation. These children are basically different from middle-class children to whom schools are geared. They do not learn in the same way or from the same curriculum. In three forms of group reading therapy, the best progress in reading was made by using a tutorial group-therapy method where the delinquents were encouraged to discover for themselves why they could not read and to discuss their problems with reading.

2080 Mehus, Hilda. "Learning and therapy." Am J Orthopsychiatry 23: 416-21, April, 1953. (0 References).
Children with reading disabilities are typically anxious, discouraged, and passive about learning. Emotional drive, control, and motivation to read are lacking. The purpose of therapy is not to help the child until he is reading up to his ability but only to prepare him emotionally until he is able to profit from instruction. Four therapeutic approaches are presented.

2081 Mulligan, William. "A study of dyslexia and delinquency." Acad Ther 4(3): 177-87, Spring, 1969. (0 References).
Outlines the origin and characteristics of dyslexia and the concomitant emotional problems in connection with a study of sixty delinquent children ages thirteen to seventeen who were under the supervision of a county probation department. Although some of these read normally, a large percentage read below grade level. In treating the delinquent child it is important for the probation worker to understand dyslexia and the frustrations it brings to the child. The child's total problem, both emotional and physiological, must be faced in order to institute an effective therapeutic program. It is suggested that delinquency can be prevented if dyslexia is discovered and treated early. Some possible causes and some of the symptoms of dyslexia are explained.

2082 Peck, Harris B.; Zwerling, Israel; Rabban, Meyer; et al. "Reading disability and community psychiatry." Am J Orthopsychiatry 36(3): 420-33, April, 1966. (4 References).
Examines methods for predicting reading disability and suggests various strategies for intervention, including a family questionnaire, the school's reading-readiness test, and group consultations and counseling for teachers and parents. Reading problems frequently arise from emotional difficulties in the child and from pathology in the family.

2083 Robinson, Helen M. "Treatment of severe cases of reading disability." J Educ Res 32(7): 531-35, March, 1939. (0 References).
Outlines methods used in diagnosis and treatment of reading disability at the Orthogenic School of the University of Chicago. About one-fourth of the children who come to the Orthogenic School come because of reading disability. The disability has resulted in personality changes in every child. Each case must be handled individually, but among the general principles set forth are that: (1) training must be aimed at remediating the cause of the difficulty, whether physical, emotional, or educational; (2) the complete cooperation of the child is necessary; (3) the child may have to be separated from his parents and thus the pressures and tensions that have developed around his failure to read; and (4) the methods used are, in general, those of good early teaching, including the kinesthetic method.

2084   Russell, Milton. "Effect of group counseling with mothers on their
        attitudes toward children and on their sons' reading disability:
        an educational-therapeutic approach to parent attitudes and reading
        disability in a clinic situation." For a summary see: <u>Diss Abstr</u>
        20(2): 764, August, 1959.

2085   Schechter, Marshall D. "Psychiatric aspects of learning disabili-
        ties." <u>Child Psychiatry Hum Dev</u> 5(2): 67-77, Winter, 1974. (0
        References).
Presents case histories of three boys. One was diagnosed as suffering
from an anxiety neurosis, one from a reaction to insufficient parental
discipline, and one from a specific learning disability (minimal cerebral
dysfunction). All had learning difficulties. Treatment is aimed at relieving distressing symptoms by thorough diagnostic evaluation. The
general problems of LD children, including difficulty in learning to
read, are described and discussed. The use of drugs is considered.

2086   Seeman, Julius, and Edwards, Benner. "A therapeutic approach to
        reading difficulties." <u>J Consult Psychol</u> 18(6): 451-53, December,
        1954. (11 References).
Hypothesizes that there is a relationship between personality disturbance
and reading performance. In a study designed to test whether a therapeutic approach to teaching modifies personality and intellectual performance, it was found that a teacher-therapist using therapeutic principles in daily sessions was able to bring about significant reading
gains by students, but no significant personality changes. Subjects
were fifth- and sixth-grade pupils in a large city.

2087   Strang, Ruth. "Interrelations of guidance and reading problems."
        <u>Education</u> 75(7): 456-61, March, 1955. (0 References).
Emotional disturbances accompany most serious reading difficulties. Some
of the relationships between guidance problems and reading problems are
considered. In some cases emotional disturbance may be alleviated by
reading instruction. Guidance and personnel departments sometimes have
reading specialists on their staffs. The two departments should always
work closely together.

2088   Wagner, Rudolph F. "Secondary emotional reactions in children
        with learning disabilities." <u>Ment Hyg</u> 54(4): 577-79, October,
        1970. (0 References).
Emotional problems are secondary to the primary learning disabilities of
a dyslexic child. Four categories of emotional reactions can be identified. They are: (1) defense and avoidance mechanisms; (2) compensatory
mechanisms such as bragging and clowning; (3) aggressiveness; and (4)
anxiety and withdrawal. Six methods of remediation and therapy for the
emotional reactions to dyslexia are suggested: (1) tutorial relationships involving small classes; (2) supportive counseling; (3) psychotherapy; (4) medication; (5) behavior modification; and (6) curriculum
modification where the dyslexic child remains in the regular classroom
for the teaching of nonacademic courses such as shop and physical education, and is taught academic subjects by special teachers.

2089   Wheeler, Lester R. "Dealing with emotional reading problems in
        the classroom." <u>Education</u> 74(9): 566-71, May, 1954. (31 Ref-
        erences).
Feelings and emotions are present in some degree in all learning. Emotional problems may be grouped according to cause: physical, mental,

social, or educational. A checklist of symptoms of emotions in reading
and a list of remedial suggestions for emotional problems in reading are
included.

2090 Wiedis, Donald Louis. "Creative role playing therapy as an adjunct
      to remedial reading in the modification of reading disability and
      psycho-social maladjustment: an experimental investigation of the
      contribution of creative role playing therapy to the remediation
      of reading disability and the psycho-social adjustment to aggres-
      sive and dependency needs of elementary school boys." For a sum-
      mary see: <u>Diss Abstr</u> 25(10): 6069, April, 1965.

F. ROLE OF PARENTS

2091 Barclay, Dorothy. "Help for the retarded reader." <u>NY Times Mag</u>
      102(34,826): 40, May 31, 1953.
Parents can do little about their child's reading problem themselves.
The problem should be discussed with the child's teacher. Some of the
helpful things parents can do include maintaining a relaxed attitude
while seeking professional help and reading aloud to the child for fun
rather than as a teaching exercise.

2092 DeGenaro, Jennie Jennings. "What do you say when a parent asks,
      'how can I help my child?'" <u>J Learn Disabil</u> 6(2): 102-5,
      February, 1973. (0 References).
Gives suggestions to parents on ways to help a learning-disabled child
develop skills. Included are ways to: (1) increase visual discrimination and a left-to-right progression across the page; (2) increase visual
memory; (3) improve eye-hand coordination; (4) encourage interest; (5)
build awareness of phonetics; and (6) develop visual imagery. Old magazines, empty egg cartons, and a stenographer's pad are the sorts of
materials needed for these reading activities.

2093 Gates, Arthur I. "What we know and can do about the poor reader."
      <u>Education</u> 77(9): 528-33, May, 1957. (2 References).
Learning to read is one of life's most critical and difficult tasks.
There is no satisfactory substitute for learning to read to help the
child save face. No panacea is available, but parents can help prepare
the child to read by talking to the preschool child, taking him to new
places, and answering his questions.

2094 Hendryson, Irvin E. "Questions parents ask." Paper presented at
      the International Reading Association Conference, Kansas City,
      Missouri, April 30-May 3, 1969. 1969. 9p. (ED 033 009).
Discusses the teaching of reading, dyslexia, speed reading, and other
related issues from the layman's viewpoint. Parent-teacher cooperation
is emphasized. The questionable effects of the mass media on parental
attitudes toward the teaching of reading are considered.

2095 Kline, Carl L., and Kline, Carolyn Lacey. "Severe reading dis-
      abilities--the family's dilemmas: analysis based on study of 600
      consecutive patients." <u>Am J Orthopsychiatry</u> 43(2): 241-42,
      March, 1973. (0 References).
A high incidence of family problems was found to be associated with the
cases of 600 children diagnosed as having specific reading disability.

Three problems were especially difficult: (1) finding adequate diagnostic and treatment facilities; (2) the hostility, defensiveness, and ignorance of teachers and principals; and (3) cruelty by a teacher toward learning-disabled children in the classroom.

2096 Laffey, James L. "Some bright children can't read." PTA Mag
      65(2): 9-11, 36, October, 1970. (0 References).
Factors that interfere with learning to read fall into three broad classes: physical, psychological, and educational. Hearing loss, hypothyroidism, or minor brain damage may hinder learning to read. Personal, social, or emotional maladjustment hinders reading progress. The first educational reason children do not learn to read is the teacher. If reading is not taught effectively, some of the blame must fall on the school of education the teacher attended. Various ways to improve primary-grade reading programs are discussed, including developing the ungraded school; consulting the reading specialist; and the many actions parents can take to prepare children to learn to read. Dyslexia is defined as "impairment of the ability to read."

2097 Morrison, Joan. "If your child can't read." McCalls 80: 14, 16,
      October, 1952. (0 References).
Thousands of children are failing in school because they cannot read. If your child is one of them, it is up to you to find out why. Prompt treatment is important not only for school success but for the child's personality and future. Frequently it is up to the parent to recognize the problem and see that something is done about it because reading programs and trained teachers are scarce. Facts and suggestions to help parents are given. Reading difficulty, in the absence of eye defects, may be caused by an emotional upset such as divorce or death. IQ tests may cause confusion of reading difficulties with low intelligence, and overworked teachers may ignore serious reading defects. If a child seems bright but hates reading he may have a problem. Parents can take such a child to a university reading clinic for help. They can read to him regularly, talk with him about what he reads, and provide books that are easy but not too young. Various reading games for parents to use are included. If the reading clinic is too far away, pay one visit for advice and diagnosis and do the rest of the work yourself. Parents working with their own child sympathetically and consistently will be amazed at results.

2098 Orton, June Lyday. "Parents as participants in the team approach
      to their dyslexic children." J Learn Disabil 4(10): 586-88,
      December, 1971. (1 Reference).
Parents can usually supply the information needed to make a tentative diagnosis in dyslexia. Parents can also supply an account of the child's personality development and his environment. The wise consultant encourages parents to give their opinions and to tell what efforts have been made at home to help the child. The consultant should prepare parents to participate effectively in the child's treatment. Parents can help in innumerable ways.

2099 Peck, Bruce B. "Reading disorders: have we overlooked something?"
      J Sch Psychol 9(2): 182-90, 1971. (45 References).
Families in which a child has a reading problem have upset relationships within the family. Those outside the family attempting to help and members of the family frequently reach an impasse as each side attempts to outmaneuver the other. Suggestions for working with problem families

from the school's point of view are presented. The power struggle between the helper and the helped is described. Parents and child may
unite to "dump" the reading specialist. The child learns the art of
being stupid. His reading may improve, in order to get rid of the reading teacher, while concurrently he develops another problem. Thus he
can maintain his status as the family problem.

2100 Preston, Mary I. "The reaction of parents to reading failures."
      Child Dev 10(3): 173-79, September, 1939. (0 References).
One hundred children in grades two through ten, physically and mentally
normal, who were reading failures, and a control group of good readers
were interviewed. Their parents were also interviewed. Parents of children who were reading failures were found to be generally intolerant of
the difficulty. They tended to blame the child, describing their attitudes toward the failure in terms such as despair, anger, or mortifica-
tion. Failure in arithmetic was accepted more matter-of-factly with an
excuse that the child had no talent for figures. With reading failure,
however, the child was set apart as being not quite normal. Case histories are given. It is suggested that beginning reading should be
taught by a specialist with experience and training.

2101 Ryback, David, and Staats, Arthur W. "Parents as behavior therapy-
      technicians in treating reading deficits (dyslexia)." J Behav
      Ther Exp Psychiatry 1(2): 109-19, June, 1970. (30 References).
Parents were enlisted to aid in instructing their own children who had
reading problems. Children in the study ranged from eight to thirteen
years of age. Parents were given a four-hour training period. Therapy-
technicians and parents worked together to help the children for thirty-
five to sixty-five hours of training. Significant improvements were reported. It is suggested that it is feasible for parents to assist in
providing complex behavior therapy for their children if given standard
procedures to follow and some supervision. The number of new words
learned by the children ranged from 458 to 1,040. About half the words
were retained on a long-term retention test given ten to fifteen days
later.

2102 Samuels, Arline Frances. "The effect of intensive group discus-
      sion on certain attitudes of mothers toward children with reading
      disabilities and the relationship of changed attitudes on the read-
      ing growth of their sons." For a summary see: Diss Abstr 18(6):
      2216, June, 1958.

2103 Shatter, Florence. "An investigation of the effectiveness of a
      group therapy program, including the child and his mother, for the
      remediation of reading disabilities." For a summary see: Diss
      Abstr 17(5): 1032, 1957.

2104 Snyder, Russell D., and Worden, Don K. "Failure of parental tutor-
      ing in childhood dyslexia." Clin Pediatr 8(8): 436, August, 1969.
      (0 References).
Cause and prognosis for dyslexic children are difficult to categorize.
It is also difficult to plan effective therapy and to evaluate the results. One form of therapy, tutoring by parents, has been found to be
almost totally unsuccessful and possibly harmful. It becomes a very unpleasant and unsuccessful experience for both parents and child. In
cases in which there has been any success at all, parental tutoring appears to be better tolerated by girls than boys and by younger children
rather than older ones.

2105   Studholme, Janice MacDonald. "Group guidance with mothers of re-
          tarded readers." Read Teach 17(7): 528-30, April, 1964. (0
          References).
Mothers of retarded readers met for group guidance sessions while their
sons were attending remedial reading classes. The sessions helped parents
overcome feelings of isolation and shame. They afforded opportunity for
ventilation of feelings toward their sons and the reading problems. This
provided some relief in tension which probably helped relax the mothers'
attitude toward the sons.

2106   Sundstrom, Dale Alvin. "The influence of parental attitudes and
          child-parent interaction upon remedial reading progress: a re-
          examination." For a summary see: Diss Abstr 28A(7): 2571-72,
          January, 1968.

2107   Wagner, Rudolph F. "Games dyslexics play." Acad Ther 9(1): 23-
          26, Fall, 1973. (2 References).
All members of the dyslexic's family usually demonstrate emotional reactions to the child's situation. Many families with dyslexic children
exhibit a common thread in their behavior patterns. Six "games" dyslexics and their families play are described. One is "The Merry-Go-
Round," where parents play a frantic hopscotch searching for a diagnosis
and cure, treating dyslexia as if it were a "bug"--an organic disease.
Another game is "The Great Fetish," where "dyslexia" becomes a convenient
diagnosis and status symbol. Family members of a dyslexic child must
share the problem and search for a solution together. They should give
each other emotional support. The whole family should be informed about
dyslexia by the professional worker. As the dyslexic child's emotional
adjustment improves, so will his reading problem.

2108   Wollner, Mary H. B. "Should parents coddle their retarded readers?"
          Education 80(7): 430-32, March, 1960. (0 References).
Parents of children in remedial reading clinics should not attempt to
help the child with his reading at home. They should relax the pressure
on this sore point. They should establish and maintain firm, consistent
general discipline in the home.

2109   ————. "What parents should know about the retarded reader."
          Education 78(1): 14-21, September, 1957. (0 References).
Parents should realize that failure to learn to read is specific, not
caused by lack of intelligence. Failure in reading is linked to failure
to mature. It is a problem for experts; parents cannot help at home.
Quality of teaching influences reading disability. Each child must be
considered individually. Wise parents of the reading-disabled child will
seek professional advice. More boys than girls fail at reading.

2110   Worden, Don K., and Snyder, Russell D. "Parental tutoring in child-
          hood dyslexia." J Learn Disabil 2(9): 482, September, 1969. (0
          References).
Symptoms of dyslexia are recounted. As with many diseases of unknown
origin, effective therapy is difficult to plan. Although not conclusive,
findings would seem to suggest that dyslexic girls tolerate parental
tutoring better than boys and that tutoring is more likely to succed in
younger children than in older ones. It fails to produce improvement in
reading in most cases. Parental tutoring of dyslexics appears to have a
negligible place in the therapy of childhood dyslexia. It becomes both
an unpleasant and unsuccessful experience for parent and child.

G. ROLE OF PHYSICIAN

2111 Bannon, Robert E. "The role of the eye specialist in cases of
      reading difficulties." Sight Sav Rev 20(4): 216-24, Winter,
      1950. (24 References).
The eye specialist is often consulted in cases of reading difficulties.
Often such patients who have no eye problems are unsympathetically
treated and are not referred for help to a remedial reading clinic or
psychiatrist. On other occasions unneeded treatment is given or glasses
prescribed as a placebo. In some cases there is an underlying cause of
an ocular nature. Reading is a complex skill. Ideally a group of specialists should be consulted. The eye specialist should not consider
his duty done until he has made sure other possible causes have been considered and treated. Possible eye problems that may cause reading problems are discussed.

2112 Clemmens, Raymond L. "Pediatric aspects of learning disabilities."
      NC Med J 29(11): 451-55, November, 1968. (7 References).
Learning disability is defined as one or more defects in essential learning processes which must be corrected by special educational techniques.
The physician's role is to: (1) detect any disease process; (2) coordinate the necessary consultations; (3) interpret findings to parents;
and (4) periodically reevaluate the child's developmental status. Developmental learning disorders are also called "minimal brain dysfunction," "dyslexia," "congenital word blindness," "strephosymbolia," and
other terms. Some possible causes are considered.

2113 Helveston, Eugene M. "Dyslexia." Sight Sav Rev 38(4): 203-8,
      Winter, 1968. (0 References).
Currently there is renewed interest in reading problems among ophthalmologists. Education is an essential stepping stone. There has been
parental pressure to help Johnny learn to read. Another reason is the
entrance into diagnosis and treatment of reading disorders by many nonmedical specialists who recommend eye exercises and similar measures.
The ophthalmologist has been forced to assume a stand on his role and on
the role of eyes in reading disorders. That role is discussed under
three headings: examination of the patient, treatment, and research.
The approach to the problem of dyslexia at the Indiana University Medical
Center Dyslexia Clinic is described. Most ocular functions are not very
significant to reading disability, but research continues because of the
many unanswered questions. This article was reprinted in Nebr State Med
J 55(6): 357-60, June, 1970.

2114 ————. "The ophthalmologist's role in dyslexia. Arch Ophthalmol
      83(2): 132-33, February, 1970. (4 References).
States that the eyes have little to do with reading disorders. Dyslexia
is divided into three categories: (1) Primary specific developmental
dyslexia is a severe inability to read in persons of normal intelligence.
It is thought by some to be genetically determined and is not common.
It must be treated with special educational techniques. (2) Secondary
endogenous dyslexia is a true dyslexia caused by mental retardation,
overt brain damage, or minimal brain damage. It requires special teaching techniques. (3) Exogenous reading disability is caused by any of a
large number of environmental factors. Treatment consists of altering
the environment and using appropriate standard teaching methods. The
ophthalmologist has no role whatever in the diagnosis of reading dis-

ability. It is diagnosed by teachers. But dyslexia does exist, and ophthalmologists frequently are asked to examine the eyes of children with reading problems. The ophthalmologist should counsel parents against useless and expensive forms of treatment and encourage them to find effective treatment. He should meet his responsibility in the care of the eyes and encourage and cooperate with the interdisciplinary team treating the child.

2115 Hopkins, Guy H. "Reading defects in school children." Rocky Mt
      Med J 35(3): 218-22, March, 1938. (6 References).
Physicians should consider reading problems more thoroughly when such cases present themselves. Learning to read may be aided or impeded by a variety of conditions. Adequate perceptional and motor organization must have developed in the child before reading is possible. The perception and interpretation of visual patterns such as words require more than that. Orton's theory of lack of cerebral dominance and Monroe's experiments with hand and eye preference are described. No attempt should be made to change handedness in a child. Parents should be encouraged to give children having difficulty with handedness or reading special training when needed.

2116 Keith, Charles. "The pediatrician and treatment of learning dis-
      abilities." NC Med J 29(11): 455-58, November, 1968. (0 Refer-
      ences).
Gives observations and experience gathered in the practice of child psychiatry in association with a special school for children with learning problems. The pediatrician's role as mediator between parents and teachers is discussed. Treatment must be in small groups by a teacher who will observe each child's special style of learning. Remedial education usually will be in the home community. The pediatrician must serve as an emotional backstop in periods of impatience and discouragement.

2117 Kenny, Thomas J., and Clemmens, Raymond L. "Reading problems."
      Am Fam Physician 6(6): 77-80, December, 1972. (0 References).
Describes the role of the family physician in the management of reading problems. He can rule out disease as a cause; recommend proper psychological and educational diagnostic evaluations; prescribe psychoactive drugs as indicated; and serve as the child's advocate and protector from needless or unproved remedial programs and evaluations. Reading problems should be considered pedagogic problems and treated by psychoeducational rather than medical techniques.

2118 ————. "Reading problems." Sight Sav Rev 43(2): 103-6,
      Summer, 1973. (0 References).
Discusses the role of the physician in diagnosis and management of reading disabilities in children. Remedial instruction, changes in curriculum, parent counseling, psychotherapy, and prescribing psychoactive medication are included in the physician's contribution to treatment. Other responsibilities of the physician to these children are outlined. EEG and neurologic examinations were found to produce little of significance. Testing of the children with reading problems in this study revealed that the majority were below normal in intelligence, and a low IQ is an important cause of reading problems. The physician should be the child's advocate, protecting him from unproved remedial techniques offered to distressed parents.

2119   Lawson, Lawrence J., Jr. "Reading and learning problems: ophthal-
       mological management." Ill Med J 137(6): 623-26, June, 1970.
       (0 References).
The ophthalmologist, pediatrician, and psychologist each have valuable
contributions to make in assessing the child's visual and physical status.
However, the treatment of dyslexia remains primarily educational. It is
from the remedial teacher that the child ultimately receives treatment.
Findings of other disciplines must be coordinated with those of the educator.

2120   Montgomery, John L., Jr. "Reading retardation: the physician's
       role." J Tenn Med Assoc 62(12): 1138-41, December, 1969. (0
       References).
Defines and emphasizes the problem of reading retardation which affects
20 to 30 percent of public-school children. Reading retardation is classified into two main categories: primary developmental dyslexia caused
by a brain lesion which may be genetically determined and constitutional;
and secondary reading retardations. The latter stem from poor instruction, slow maturing by the child ("late bloomer"), poor motivation, low
intelligence, emotional problems, organic brain damage, or poor health.
The physician's responsibility in dealing with the child with a reading
disorder is to make an initial complete medical examination, including
hearing and eye examinations. The physician should refer the child to
the proper consultants, guarding against quacks and charlatans. He should
have a knowledge of the community and know what resources are available
in the way of reading clinics and psychological and psychiatric help.
Physicians should be outspoken advocates of better facilities in their
communities for diagnosis and treatment of reading problems.

2121   Nicholls, John V. V. "Reading difficulties in children." Int
       Ophthalmol Clin 5(2): 423-41, June, 1965. (31 References).
Classifies reading difficulties in three categories: (1) congenital dyslexia in which the child probably has a physiological disturbance in his
brain; (2) the slow reader whose problem is related to low intelligence,
faulty vision or hearing, and/or to emotional problems; and (3) a combination of these two. Some of the literature on the relationship of eye
problems to dyslexia is reviewed. The roles of auditory, neurological,
emotional, and educational factors in congenital dyslexia are discussed.
Three out of four dyslexics will learn to read well if the teaching
method is modified. The remedy is largely educational. It cannot be
rigid and may require great ingenuity. It is most important to discover
reading difficulties early. The ophthalmologist is often the first person consulted. Complete vision and hearing examinations should be made.
Intelligence should be assessed. Psychiatric assessment is important.
The ophthalmologist should be prepared to act as coordinator for all of
this, serving as liaison between parents and the remedial reading teacher.
He should warn parents against charlatans. The ophthalmologist has an
inescapable duty to insure that intellectual honesty and good sense are
brought to bear on the problem.

2122   "The ophthalmologist's role in dyslexia--position statements."
       Sight Sav Rev 39(3): 144, Fall, 1969. (0 References).
A reprint from the report of an international dyslexia seminar sponsored
by the Institute for Development of Educational Activities, Inc. (IDEA).
Its eleven points include the opinions that: (1) the value of perceptual-
motor training is still unproved; (2) the ophthalmologist's role should
be an interdisciplinary approach; (3) eye dominance is not the cause of

reading disability; (4) more educational research is needed; (5) teaching dyslexics is an educational problem; and (6) the number of dyslexics has been overestimated.

2123 Weisbach, Philip T. "The ophthalmologist's role in the management of dyslexia." Am J Ophthalmol 59(2): 265-71, February, 1965. (10 References).
Great confusion in the literature exists on the causes of dyslexia. Dyslexia, like glaucoma, consists of a number of different diseases all with one common symptom. Reading difficulty is the common factor in dyslexia. Causes include: minimal brain damage, heredity, refraction errors, visual immaturity, general physical condition, hearing loss, emotional disturbances, emotional or social immaturity, poor teaching methods, and indefinite cerebral dominance. Most cases of dyslexia have no demonstrable pathologic brain lesion. Symptoms, and suggestions for diagnosis and treatment are given. The hope of improvement is good if the dyslexic is of average or above-average intelligence.

2124 Wolf, C. W. "Dyslexic children. The physician's role in the identification of specific dyslexia." J Kans Med Soc 71(3): 101-3, March, 1970.

H. DRUGS

2125 Calvert, James J., and Cromes, George F., Jr. "Oculomotor spasms in handicapped readers." Read Teach 20(3): 231-36, 241, December, 1966. (3 References).
Very fine eye tremors, referred to as oculomotor spasms, were found in more than 90 percent of the reading-disabled children studied who were not helped by training in reading. This study was set up to test whether primedone medication might reduce the spasms and improve reading ability. Results were favorable. The drug was used in conjunction with further reading training.

2126 Fenelon, Bernard; Holland, John Terence; Johnson, Christine. "Spatial organization of the EEG in children with reading disabilities: a study using Nitrazepam." Cortex 8(4): 444-64, December, 1972. (15 References).
In this study Nitrazepam or a placebo was administered for eight weeks to three groups of children: reading-disabled, behavior-problem, and normal children. The reading-disabled group responded well with a number of improvements in the EEG. These effects appeared only in the group of reading-disabled children. It is believed that this nonstimulant drug holds promise for treating the neuropsychological bases of severe reading problems.

2127 Fenelon, Bernard, and Wortley, Sandra. "Effect of auxiliary acoustic stimulation on two-flash fusion thresholds of reading disabled children: a study using nitrazepam." Percept Mot Skills 36(2): 443-50, April, 1973. (28 References).
In an attempt to find ways of reducing the perceptual difficulties of dyslexic children, three groups of nine-year-olds were tested on their ability to respond to flashes of light by pressing a switch. The groups were: dyslexics taking the drug Nitrazepam, dyslexics taking a placebo, and normal readers taking a placebo. Greater visual acuity was found in

the active drug group than in the dyslexics on placebos. Basic thresholds for the three groups did not differ significantly, but normal readers performed best. Response of dyslexics on Nitrazepam was much closer to that of the normal readers than to the untreated dyslexics. The action of the drug appears to close the gap in perceptual discrimination between normal and reading-disabled children.

2128   Freed, Herbert; Abrams, Jules; Peifer, Charles. "Reading disability: a new therapeutic approach and its implications." J Clin Exp Psychopathol Psychother 20(3): 251-59, September, 1959. (20 References).
In a controlled study, reading instruction combined with the use of ataractic drugs in cases of reading disability was found to give results superior to those obtained in cases of reading disability in which either a drug or reading instruction was used alone. Sixty boys who were public-school pupils ages eight to thirteen with IQs of 90 or more who were three years or more below grade level in reading were divided into four matched groups: (1) group A received placebo; (2) group B received placebo and ten weeks of reading instruction; (3) group C received chlorpromazine; and (4) group D received chlorpromazine and ten weeks of reading instruction. It is tentatively observed that important factors in the many causes of reading disability include damping the fight-flight response; decreasing anxiety and increasing the attention span; and increasing use of the identification mechanism. Results indicate that the use of ataractics such as chlorpromazine or prochlorperazine is worth trying.

2129   Nichamin, Samuel J. "Reading disorders in children." JAMA 207(13): 2438-39, March 31, 1969. (2 References).
Letter to editor. It is preferable for reading disorders to be seen as a concept of constitutionality (geneogenous), associated with faulty neurological integration. Ubiquitous references to reading disability or dyslexia as if they were unique entities tend to confuse the issue. The physician can orient his long-term approach during infancy and childhood if he construes dyslexia as an inherent part of a perceptual syndrome, genetically determined. Incipient maturational disorders can then be apprehended earlier in the preschool years. This is an opportune time for intervention with remedial programs including drug therapy. The role of drugs in the management of perceptual disorders, including dyslexia, needs clarification and implementation. Persons with these disorders have benefited strikingly from the use of drugs.

2130   Spring, Carl; Greenberg, Lawrence; Scott, Jimmy; et al. "Reaction time and effect of Ritalin on children with learning problems." Percept Mot Skills 36(1): 75-82, February, 1973. (11 References).
Groups of poor and normal readers were asked to press one of two buttons, depending on whether visually presented pairs of letters were the same or different. Poor readers were slower than normal readers and their performance deteriorated faster than normal readers as testing progressed. Groups of hyperactive boys, some of whom were on medication and some off it, were tested for reaction time. The on- and off-medication groups performed about the same at first. Both were slower than a group of normal boys. As testing progressed, reaction time for normal boys and those on medication remained stable, while times for hyperactives off medication declined. Implications for reading problems are discussed.

I. RESEARCH

2131   Anderson, William F., and Stern, David.   "The relative effect of the
       Frostig program, corrective reading instruction, and attention upon
       the reading skills of corrective readers with visual perceptual de-
       ficiencies." J Sch Psychol 10(4): 387-95, December, 1972.   (13 Ref-
       erences).
The results of this study indicate that there is little or no reason to
use the Frostig program or any corrective reading program for children who
appear to have a visual-motor problem. Subjects were thirty-three children
from six to eight years of age in the second grade of a public school.
They were divided into three treatment groups of eleven children each.
Three teachers were assigned to work with the groups for sixteen weeks.
One group received Frostig visual-perception training and one group corrective reading instruction. The third group participated in supervised
games and contests as a placebo. The performance of the placebo group was
such that it appears logical to suppose the observed reading improvements
were more a function of the personal attention given the child than any
unique remedial powers of the other two treatments.

2132   Berman, Arthur.   "The influence of the kinaesthetic factor in the
       perception of symbols in partial reading disability."   J Educ
       Psychol 30(3): 187-98, March, 1939. (0 References).
A manual-tracing technique (tracing over the word with a finger) appeared
to aid the learning of nonsense syllables and geometrical figures by subjects with partial reading disability. Retention twenty-four hours later
did not seem to be aided by the technique. Subjects ranged in age from
eight years to seventeen years with an average age of nine years, nine
months. All were of normal intelligence and had reading difficulties.
It is suggested that all sensory channels should be utilized in teaching
reading. The kinesthetic is often neglected. It should be added to instruction in order to facilitate learning.

2133   Berres, Frances B.   "The effects of varying amounts of motoric in-
       volvement on the learning of nonsense dissyllables by male cultur-
       ally disadvantaged retarded readers." For a summary see: Diss
       Abstr 28A(7): 2547, January, 1968.

2134   Berson, Minnie Perrin.   "Changes in achievement and personality in
       children functioning below school reading norms in a remedial reading
       program." For a summary see: Diss Abstr 28A(9): 3496, March, 1968.

2135   Botel, Morton.   "Methods and systems for teaching dyslexic pupils."
       Paper presented at the National Conference on Dyslexia, Philadelphia,
       Pennsylvania, November 19, 1966. 1966. 24p. (ED 011 493).
Analyzes the reading and spelling performance of a group of 722 children
enrolled in grades two through six who were attending a reading program
to determine which methods were superior for use with dyslexics in clinical and classroom situations and which were best for dyslexics and for
normal pupils with minor reading problems. Subjects had an average IQ of
106 and were from a white, semirural, middle-class area. It is suggested
that dyslexia can be anticipated and minimized with a good developmental
reading program.

2136   Brown, Clair George, Jr.   "A longitudinal study of the psychological
       test results of severely retarded readers." For a summary see:
       Diss Abstr 27A(4): 945, October, 1966.

2137   Buerger, Theodore A. "Elementary school pupils who received re-
        medial reading instruction: a follow-up study of the educational
        progress and attitudes of remedial and non-remedial groups." For
        a summary see: <u>Diss Abstr</u> 27A(10): 3300-3301, April, 1967.

2138   ————. "A follow-up of remedial reading instruction." <u>Read
        Teach</u> 21(4): 329-34, January, 1968. (0 References).
Reports findings of a study undertaken to discover the long-term effects
of remedial reading instruction on the educational progress and attitudes
of pupils after the remedial program has been completed. Children were
studied from less than a year to more than five years after remedial
treatment. Those studied were seventy-two third- through seventh-grade
pupils who received fifty or more hours of remedial instruction and
seventy-two underachievers who did not receive instruction. Remedial
pupils made significant reading gains in every case immediately after
the remedial period. But remedial reading assistance during grades three
to seven did not appear to have a long-term significant effect on mental
ability, vocabulary and reading comprehension, or English and social
studies achievement. However, there was overall long-term educational
progress. Eighty-seven percent of the remedial subjects reported that
remedial assistance had been of value to them.

2139   Burgett, Russell Edward, and Dodge, Roger W. "Is there a differ-
        ence between learning disability and reading personnel?" <u>J Read</u>
        19(7): 540-44, April, 1976. (5 References).
Enumerates and discusses the differences between persons hired by schools
as reading-disability and as learning-disability specialists. They differ in training and in their philosophical approach to educating children
with these different disabilities. Results are given of a questionnaire
answered by a random sample of Wisconsin school districts investigating
thirty-nine position responsibilities of reading and learning disability
personnel. No significant differences were found between the two groups
in salary or in professional experience and job classification at the
master's degree level. Significant differences were found in these two
areas at the bachelor's level. At this level more reading personnel had
higher salaries and more years of experience.

2140   Carver, Clifford. <u>Motivation versus cognitive methods in remedial
        reading</u>. 1971. 9p. (ED 050 921).
Reading improvement in an experimental group of elementary-school children
appeared to be generated, not by any single remedial method used, but by
the atmosphere of approval and the success experienced by the children.
Thirty-two of the most severely retarded readers in a large elementary
school were selected and placed at random in eight groups of four children each. For seven months the groups were given one of four separate
teaching methods. Testing was done in January, May, and June. About
thirty months of reading progress was made by all the groups, total reading improvement being similar under any of the teaching methods. The
thirty next poorest readers from the same classes who did not have special treatment made about ten months' reading progress in the same time.

2141   Dailey, John T. <u>Evaluation of the contribution of special programs
        in the Washington, D.C., schools to the prediction and prevention
        of delinquency</u>. 1966. 73p. (ED 010 431).
Using a sample of 1,634 youths seventeen years of age to study the effect
of various school programs aimed at lowering delinquency, it was found
that school reading level, years of education of adult population, and

proportion of adult population with income above $2,000 were the school
and community factors most predictive of delinquency rate. It was found
that the best means of delinquency prevention for the schools was the
pursuit of their regular academic programs, and that the best way to
lower delinquency was to teach children to read adequately in elementary
school. The success of a school was found to be proportional to the
types of families it served, almost regardless of such factors as school
size, age of building, expenditure per pupil, overcrowding, or class
size. Where the families served were attempting to make their children
a part of modern organized society, whether white or black, performance
in school was good and juvenile crime was minimal.

2142 Damerau, Ruth. "Influence of treatment on the reading ability and
      behavior disorders of reading disability cases." Smith Coll Stud
      Soc Work 5(2): 160-83, December, 1934. (0 References).
Studies the effects of treatment on the personality and behavior problems
of children with reading disability. The children, mostly boys, ranged
in age from six to thirteen years and had IQs over 80. All had a reading disability and behavior problems. All had been referred to a behavior clinic devoted to the study of problem children. There was considerable variation in the amount and kind of treatment the children received
for behavior difficulties and considerable variation in quantity of
tutoring in reading. Improvements in reading and in behavior appear to
be related to each other. It was concluded that they were independent
variables: reading handicap may sometimes cause behavior problems, but
removing that disability by tutoring did not in itself improve the child's
behavior.

2143 Daniels, J. C. "Children with reading difficulties." Slow Learn
      Child 13(3): 138-44, 1967.
Details experiments done with kindergarten children three and one-half
to four years of age who were given training in left-right orientation.
Two years later none of these children showed orientation difficulty.
Almost 20 percent of the control group had difficulties. Seven-year-
olds benefited similarly from proper training. Also described are experiments in "aural readiness" to learn to read. While visual deficiencies
do exist, many more children lack auditory discrimination skills. It
was found well worth the investment of time to give beginning readers
aural analysis exercises. There are no critical ages for learning the
various skills needed for reading, but certainly there are optimal ages.
Clear and detailed diagnostic information about specific deficiencies in
children is important. The practice of labeling backward readers "dyslexics" should be approached with caution.

2144 de Lacy, Elizabeth. "Clinical reading cases--some speculations
      concerning sequence in words in colour and look-and-say." Slow
      Learn Child 20(3): 160-63, November, 1973. (4 References).
In a study of sequencing, one of the many skills underlying reading, two
groups of third-grade girls were taught by two different methods of reading instruction, whole-word (look-and-say) and Words in Colour. The
whole-word method is a gestalt approach and does not require the child
to build the word from its separate symbols. Words in Colour does require building words from symbols, but adds the extra cue of color. It
is concluded that Words in Colour facilitates vocabulary use and visual
sequential skills more than look-and-say. It is suggested that the dyslexic child with sequencing weaknesses would be under stress when taught
with Words in Colour. Its use with dyslexics is not recommended.

2145   Downing, John. "The effectiveness of i.t.a. (initial teaching
       alphabet) in the prevention and treatment of dyslexia and dys-
       graphia." Paper presented at World Mental Health Assembly,
       Washington, D.C., November 17-21, 1969. 1969. 19p. (ED 098 498).
Explains that the Initial Teaching Alphabet (ITA) was devised by Sir
James Pitman for use by beginning readers who later switch to traditional
orthography (t.o.). The ITA consists of forty-four characters and a set
of rules for standard spelling of English words using these characters.
The British Schools Council published a review of the use of ITA in 1969
which reports that after nine years of research and experimenting it is
believed that the exclusive use of t.o. actually slowed the progress of
average and above-average children in the first years of school and increased reading and writing problems. The use of ITA, on the other hand,
was thought to provide a very effective preventive measure against such
difficulties. The ITA seems most effective for remedial use when pupils
use it during most of their school day.

2146   Dunham, J. "The effects of remedial education on young children's
       reading ability and attitude in reading." Br J Educ Psychol
       30(2): 173-75, June, 1960. (0 References).
In a study aimed at obtaining experimental evidence on the effectiveness
of remedial education, a group of severely retarded readers nine years
old was paired with a control group. The children were of about average
intelligence. As carried out in this investigation, remedial education
was useful in improving reading ability and in improving attitudes toward
reading as measured by an attitude scale. Reading gains appeared to be
associated as closely with improvements in attitude toward reading as
with IQ. Evidence suggested that the retarded readers' general level of
verbal ability was lower than their general mental ability level.

2147   Eames, Thomas H. "The speed of picture recognition and the speed
       of word recognition in cases of reading difficulty." Am J Ophthalmol
       21(12): 1370-75, December, 1938. (7 References).
In a study of groups of children who were good and poor readers, the poor
readers tended to be slower in recognition of both pictures and words.
Good readers who had eye difficulties tended to be slower in recognition
time than good readers without eye troubles.

2148   Gilmore, Doug; Lukens, Jean E.; Martin, Clessen, J. "Auditory-
       vocal encoding of 'telegraphic' versus 'traditional' Durrell
       Analysis of Reading Difficulty paragraphs by children with learn-
       ing disabilities." Cereb Palsy J 29(2): 9-10, March-April,
       1968. (4 References).
Sixty-four learning-disabled children were matched for sex and chronological age with sixty-four normal children. Ages ranged from six to thirteen years. Two paragraphs at fifth-grade level from the Durrell Analysis
of Reading Difficulty were read aloud to subjects individually. One
paragraph had been put in "telegraphic" form, that is, summarized and
shortened about 50 percent. The other paragraph was in its original
("traditional") form. It was hoped that the shorter form would prove
easier for children with reading difficulties to comprehend. No significant differences in comprehension were observed in either group for the
telegraphic versus the traditional form. A significant difference in
comprehension scores was found between the disabled and the normal groups.

2149   Gold, Lawrence. Evaluation of the learning center by the cooper-
       ating school districts. 1968. 34p. (ED 033 834).

Reports the evaluation of a federally funded project under which a learning center was set up to develop a diagnostic and tutorial program for
severe underachievers, especially those children thought to suffer from
developmental dyslexia. Thirteen public and one private school district
in New York state which took part in the center's program during one
year completed a rating scale and questionnaire. Those responding indicated that no areas of emphasis should be decreased and made twenty-
six suggestions for increased emphasis. The majority of the districts
appeared to view the general program and its objectives favorably.

2150 Gottesman, Ruth; Belmont, Ira; Kaminer, Ruth. "Admission and
      follow-up status of reading disabled children referred to a medical
      clinic." J Learn Disabil 8(10): 642-50, December, 1975. (20
      References).
Reports on fifty-eight reading-disabled children who were admitted to a
medical clinic for developmentally disabled children. They were examined
for reading achievement with the WRAT upon admission and again three to
five years later after special educational treatment. Their ages ranged
from seven to fifteen years at time of admission. Mean IQs ranged from
82.5 to 91.6. Upon reexamination the group remained very poor readers.
About one-third of them, mostly the older ones, had achieved a minimal
degree of functional reading. Many were diagnosed as having neurologic
and/or psychiatric disorders unrelated to the reading failure. It is
suggested that such children are not representative of poor readers and
will require the use of special educational methods throughout their
schooling. Findings emphasize the limited effects of educational intervention for reading-diabled children.

2151 Griffiths, Anita N. "Academic achievement of dyslexic children
      during the first twelve months after intensive remediation." Fla
      Sci 36(1): 78-84, Winter, 1973. (3 References).
In a follow-up of reading-disabled children who had undergone twelve
weeks of remedial instruction, sixteen of these children were tested six
months and twelve months after completing the original remediation period.
Three reading tests and an arithmetic test were given. Seven of the sixteen children had received additional remediation which appeared helpful.
Oral reading ability and comprehension were much more improved than silent
reading and comprehension. Results suggest that the twelve weeks of remediation brought significant improvement but that additional remediation
would be helpful for most children. It appears that periodic or continual
remediation is essential for most dyslexic children if they are to achieve
their apparent capability.

2152 Groff, Patrick. "'Sight' words and the disabled reader." Acad
      Ther 10(1): 101-8, Fall, 1974. (28 References).
This article is a review of the research on teaching disabled readers by
"sight" first, that is, without analysis of the letters. It is concluded
that research results prove this commonly given advice to be wrong. Children who are beginning readers do not recognize words by configuration,
but in other ways. Understanding this fact is especially important for
the teachers of disabled readers.

2153 Halliwell, Joseph W., and Solan, Harold A. "The effects of a sup-
      plemental perceptual training program on reading achievement."
      Except Child 38(8): 613-21, April, 1972. (46 References).
At the beginning of first grade, 105 entering first graders were divided
into three groups of thirty-five each, trios matched on the basis of sex

and scores on the Metropolitan Readiness Test (MAT) which indicated that all 105 were likely to develop reading problems. Members of the control group of thirty-five were distributed through the school system and received no supplementary instruction beyond the regular reading program. The first group received supplementary perceptual training which is described. The second group received special reading assistance. Both experimental groups had regular reading instruction provided to all first graders. The MAT was given again at the end of the school year. Results show: (1) the group receiving perceptual training read best; (2) the group receiving conventional remedial help read better than the control group; (3) girls from the control group read better than the girls who had had conventional help; and (4) perceptual training was more effective with boys than with girls.

2154   Hargis, Charles H.; Gickling, Edward E.; Mahmoud, Cathy Crossland. "The effectiveness of TV in teaching sight words to students with learning disabilities." J Learn Disabil 8(1): 37-39, January, 1975. (4 References).

Eight children--five boys and three girls--ages seven to nine years and with IQs ranging from 93 to 132 who comprised a class for the learning-disabled were allowed to watch the television show "The Electric Company" for thirty-two consecutive school days. This show attempts to teach reading skills, including the intermittent introduction of sight words. Four weeks after viewing the program the children were individually shown ninety sight words, one at a time. Each word was printed on a separate five-by-eight card. Half these sight words had been seen on the television show. Half had not been seen on the show; if encountered by the child it would have been incidentally. Scoring was on the number correctly pronounced. Results indicate that the words seen on the television show were no more likely to be recognized than were words that had had no presentation. It is suggested that the difficulties LD children have with visual and auditory discrimination and memory tasks may have accounted for the results.

2155   Herjanic, Barbara M., and Penick, Elizabeth C. "Adult outcome of disabled child readers." J Spec Educ 6(4): 397-410, Winter, 1972. (41 References).

Reviews and summarizes the findings of nine long-term studies of disabled child readers. It is believed that little can be concluded from these studies. They are criticized for lack of adequate control groups, highly atypical samples, and limited information. It is a common assumption that the adult outcome of childhood reading problems is poor. Very often this assumption has been the result of a mistake in logic. Adult prognosis is poor for deviant groups who have associated reading problems, including young offenders, school dropouts, and the psychiatrically ill. However, it is a mistake to confuse the consequences of deviancy with the long-term consequences of reading disability. Investigations attempting to follow disabled child readers into adulthood have resulted in contradictory findings. Long-term studies are needed to assess the lasting effects of remedial teaching; current studies offer no information about the effect of treatment for reading disability on adult lives.

2156   Hunter, Edna J., and Lewis, Hadley M. "The dyslexic child--two years later." J Psychol 83(1): 163-70, January, 1973. (5 References).

In a follow-up study of groups of male dyslexics and a group of matched normal controls made two years after the initial study, it was discovered that the retarded readers had not overcome their reading problems in spite of remedial training. They still had more adjustment problems than normal readers. As predictors of success in learning to read, it was found that lower WISC full-scale IQ scores were associated with large reading deficits two years later. High WISC Arithmetic and Coding subtest scores were associated with large gains in reading skill. At the time of initial testing, dyslexics and controls had all been judged free of emotional and school adjustment problems. Two years later the dyslexics were found to have significantly lower achievement levels and significantly more adjustment problems. At the time of follow-up the boys ranged in age from nine to thirteen years. Results are seen as indicating that the emotional cost of not learning to read is high for dyslexics and that the return on the investment in remedial treatment is very low.

2157 Kauffman, James M.; Weaver, S. Joseph; Weaver, Ann. "Family Relations Test responses of retarded readers: reliability and comparative data." J Pers Assess 36(4): 353-60, August, 1972. (24 References).
The Family Relations Test was administered to a group of retarded readers of normal intelligence enrolled in a remedial reading program and ranging in age from about eight and one-half to sixteen years. The test was re-administered three weeks later. Scores on the retest were very similar to original scores. Responses of retarded readers were similar to those obtained from other clinics and from normal readers. Results were markedly different from those obtained from institutionalized emotionally disturbed children. The Family Relations Test is intended to reveal the child's subjective perception of his relationships with other family members. Suggestions for further research are made.

2158 Krippner, Stanley. "The relationship of reading improvement to scores on the Holtzman inkblot technique." J Clin Psychol 23(1): 114-15, January, 1967. (5 References).
Twenty-four elementary school children attending a reading clinic were administered the Holtzman inkblot test (HIT) before the five-week clinic and the California reading test both before and after the clinic. Reading improvement scores were correlated with all twenty-two variables on the Holtzman test. Four variables were found to be significantly related to reading improvement: location, shading, pathognomic verbalization, and hostility. The Holtzman inkblot technique consists of alternate parallel forms of forty-five inkblots each. Provision is made for a single response to each inkblot.

2159 Levin, Joel R. "Inducing comprehension in poor readers: a test of a recent model." J Educ Psychol 65(1): 19-24, August, 1973. (12 References).
Researches the premise that reading comprehension is based on complex organizational strategies on the part of the reader. Fourth graders were divided into groups of good and poor readers. The poor readers were divided into two groups, "deficit" and "difference" poor readers, on the basis of vocabulary scores. A deficit poor reader is defined as one who comprehends poorly because he lacks necessary prerequisite skills such as decoding or vocabulary. A difference poor reader has the prerequisite skills, but still has comprehension problems because his reading habits differ from those of good readers. Children with emotional disorders were excluded. Booklets were assembled telling a story in one of two ways: in twelve sentences or in twelve cartoon drawings with one picture

corresponding to each sentence of the printed version of the story. Each
child was shown one of the versions and told he would be asked some questions about it. Half the children receiving the printed text were given
suggestions for visual imagery: thinking up a picture for each sentence.
The best scores on the questions were obtained by good readers reading
with imagery suggestion. The visual imagery instructions benefited only
pupils with adequate basic reading skills, but who needed organizational
strategy. Deficit poor readers were not helped by imagery instruction.
Their best scores were from the use of pictures alone. Difference poor
readers improved their reading comprehension performance greatly with
the use of reading with imagery. It is suggested that visual imagery may
not be a suitable strategy for helping all poor readers. Overall the
pictorial treatment did not significantly facilitate comprehension for
these groups of children. Some literature in the area is discussed.

2160 Lewis, Edward R. Initial teaching alphabet (i.t.a.) for instruc-
      tion of reading disability classes. n.d. 22p. (ED 003 854).
Reports findings of an investigation of experimental British usage of
the ITA to determine if this method could be used in a San Jose, California, reading clinic. It is concluded that with slight modification
the available materials could be used.

2161 Lipton, Aaron. "Relationship of teacher rigidity to progress of
      retarded readers: a study of the relationship between teachers'
      cognitive and social rigidity patterns and the reading achieve-
      ment gains of their retarded readers." For a summary see: Diss
      Abstr 27A(12): 4170, June, 1967.

2162 Maginnis, George H. "Reading disability and remedial gain." J
      Learn Disabil 4(6): 322-24, June, 1971. (2 References).
To test the theory that students who are reading furthest below expectancy
levels (greatest reading disability) will gain the most in a remedial
program, twenty disabled readers ages eight through fourteen were individually tutored during a fifteen-week period. Findings do not support
the theory. It is pointed out that different methods of computing gain
show different results. It is questioned whether extent of disability
should be used as a device for selecting pupils for remedial programs if
extent of disability is not an indicator of potential gain.

2163 Meikle, Stewart, and Kilpatrick, Doreen L. "Changes in perceptual,
      motor and reading test scores in a remedial reading group." Can
      Psychol 12(2): 254-69, April, 1971. (32 References).
Two groups of ten-year-old children, all poor readers, were matched for
age, sex, and IQ. All were compared on a battery of perceptual, motor,
and reading tests. Tests of visual retention, auditory discrimination,
tactual perception, handgrip strength, and the WRAT Reading subtest were
among the measures used. One group was given remedial help with emphasis
on phonics, and indirect methods such as word games. The teacher was
experienced, with a firm, supportive attitude. Upon retest, the remedial
group had not only made gains in reading, but also in some of the perceptual and motor areas. No similar improvement was seen in the untreated
control group. Not all perceptual tests showed parallel improvement.
None of the auditory or visual perception test scores showed improvement
between testings for the remedial group in spite of improved reading
scores.

2164   Moorehead, Caroline. "Treatment for word blindness." <u>Times Educ</u>
       <u>Suppl</u> 2899: 4, December 11, 1970. (0 References).
The Word Blind Centre, set up six years ago by the Invalid Children's
Aid Association, has been housed in temporary quarters in Coram's Fields
in Bloomsbury, London. In addition to research, it continues to treat
fifty dyslexic children who come twice a week for two fifty-minute sessions. Over the past six years about 1,000 children have visited the
center, about 200 of them as pupils for periods of up to two years. The
ICAA is considering the future of the Word Blind Centre since the private
funding supporting the project ended six months ago.

2165   Newman, Anabel P. "Later achievement study of pupils underachiev-
       ing in reading in first grade." <u>Read Res Q</u> 7(3): 477-508,
       Spring, 1972. (25 References).
Reports the findings of a follow-up study of children from the Cedar
Rapids, Iowa, reading research project. The children were all in the low-
reading group in first grade when the first study was done. Four major
methods of teaching reading were designed and used in the belief that if
the low-group child could be taught with appropriate methods and materials in the earliest stages of reading, much frustration could be prevented
in later grades. The follow-up study, done when these same children were
in sixth grade, revealed no significant differences in sixth-grade reading achievement based on the kind of reading treatment used in first
grade. First-grade reading achievement was found to be a strong predictor
of sixth-grade reading achievement, and more reliable than first-grade
readiness measures. The hypothesis that the relationships of achievement-
related variables would not change significantly over the intervening
years was found to be either accepted or rejected, depending upon statistical interpretation. Implications of all of these findings are discussed.

2166   O'Donnell, Patrick A., and Eisenson, Jon. "Delacato training for
       reading achievement and visual-motor integration." <u>J Learn Disabil</u>
       2(9): 441-47, September, 1969. (18 References).
Studied the usefulness of the Delacato neurophysiological training program
as an adjunct to the teaching of disabled readers. Delacato's theory of
the relationship between reading failure and lack of adequate neurological
organization is explained. Three questions were posed for this study:
would the Delacato training or modifications of it make substantial differences in reading ability as measured by (1) the Gray Oral Reading
Test, (2) the Stanford Diagnostic Reading Test, and (3) the Developmental
Test of Visual-Motor Integration? Subjects were 678 second through
fourth graders ages seven to ten years enrolled in a California public
school district. All were poor readers. A battery of reading and lateral
dominance tests was given to each of the children individually. The
children were randomly divided into three groups. One of the groups received the recommended Delacato training, and the second group received
limited Delacato training for thirty minutes daily for twenty weeks. The
third group engaged in selected physical education activity for the entire training period. Results showed no significant difference in the
gains in reading ability measured by the Gray test for any of the groups.
The same was true for all seven subtests of the Stanford test, and for
the Visual-Motor Integration Test. It is noted that the younger pupils
(seven and eight years old) improved more in oral reading but less in
visual-motor integration during training. The reverse was true for pupils
nine and ten years old.

2167 O'Malley, John E., and Conners, C. Keith. "The effect of unilateral
      alpha training on visual evoked response in a dyslexic adolescent."
      Psychophysiology 9(4): 467-70, July, 1972. (8 References).
A fourteen-year-old Caucasian dyslexic boy with a WISC verbal score of
123 and a performance IQ of 89 was used as a subject to investigate the
possibility of training a person to increase alpha production, as recorded on his EEG, in one hemisphere, and thereby increase his visual
evoked response (VER) amplitude in the same hemisphere. Other investigators have reported a relationship between visual evoked response and
alpha waves. Attenuated VER in one hemisphere has been described in a
study as occurring in children with learning disorders. To correct such
attenuation seemed feasible. The method of training is described. During a five-day period alpha time on the left hemisphere significantly
increased.

2168 Parker, W. S. "Dyslexia--dysgraphia." Lancet 1(7487): 444,
      February 25, 1967. (0 References).
Letter to editor. A dyslexic boy seventeen years of age was found to
have a raised serum-uric-acid (s.u.a.) level. His father has the same
defect. Another son who is normal does not have the raised s.u.a. level.
Six months of treatment aimed at lowering the s.u.a. level led to great
improvement in the boy's reading and writing ability. Uncertainty is
expressed as to whether this result is fortuitous or specific. Further
study by others in the field is requested.

2169 Rubin, Melvin L. "Dyslexia and the research ophthalmologist." J
      Fla Med Assoc 55(10): 903-6, October, 1968. (0 References).
Describes a study in progress concerning the effect of cerebral dominance
and the controlling eye on reading progress. Subjects were 180 third,
fourth, and fifth graders in a university laboratory school. Reading
performance, IQ, handedness, and footedness were determined. An eye examination was made including determination of the sighting eye (the one
chosen for monocular tasks such as looking through a keyhole), and the
controlling eye. The controlling eye is the one more used when both eyes
are open and engaged in the same task such as reading. It is the one
with "more to say" to the cortex. The other eye is used, but the brain
ignores its information to some extent. Initial results indicate that
if a child is homolateral (eye and hand dominant on the same side) he
has an excellent chance of being a good reader. As mixed dominance (no
definite preference) increases, reading skill diminishes. Cross-dominance
(eye dominant on one side, hand on the other) does not seem correlated
with reading skill. Based on these results, the hypothesis is formed
that a child's becoming homolateral might increase his reading ability.
To test this hypothesis, the eye which was not wanted in the controlling
status was patched in this group of poor readers. The experiment was
double blind and results are not in, but early impressions are that the
method is working to improve reading skill. The problem of dyslexia is
receiving much attention all over the country. So many therapeutic
methods--some of them bizarre- have been offered that one is at a loss
to evaluate them.

2170 ————. "Research in reading disorders and their remedy." Invest
      Ophthalmol 13(3): 160-64, March, 1974. (4 References).
Reading disorders are a most important area for study, but good scientific
studies are rare. Facts known are that: (1) dyslexia affects at least
15 percent of schoolchildren; (2) children with reading problems are average or above in intelligence; and (3) affected children do not profit from

repeating a grade unless the cause of the disability is determined and treated. The schools have been blamed, but biological, educational, psychological, cultural, and socioeconomic factors interlock to create confusion. There is great need for a well-designed longitudinal study. Therapy as well as diagnosis are confused. Perceptual-motor training is not warranted for dyslexic children. There is urgent need for early detection and critical evaluation of therapy.

2171   Safer, Daniel J., and Allen, Richard P. "Factors associated with
       improvement in severe reading disability." Psychol Sch 10(1):
       110-18, January, 1973. (43 References).
Examines the relative significance of several factors commonly assumed to relate to reading improvement. Children studied were ages eight through thirteen, were reading at least 20 percent below expected level, and had been screened for a remedial reading program in a suburban public school system. Median IQ for the group was 102. Of twenty-six factors studied, only seven were related significantly to reading improvement: total IQ, verbal IQ, auditory attention span for unrelated words, percent below reading level at referral, behavior before referral, age at referral which was negatively correlated, and history of a speech impediment. The single best predictor of reading improvement was IQ and the significant aspect of IQ in this respect was verbal IQ. The factors were interrelated to some degree. Most of the factors commonly found in cases of reading impairment were found not to relate to reading improvement in this study, for example, reversals, a positive family history, emotional problems, and behavior problems, among others. Emotional disability and changes in behavior showed no relation to reading improvement. Literature in the area is reviewed. In general, long-term follow-up studies of severely reading-disabled children reflect optimism for improvement and a favorable outcome.

2172   Sklar, B., and Hanley, J. "A multi-fontal alphabet for dyslexic
       children." J Learn Disabil 5(3): 160-64, March, 1972. (17 Ref-
       erences).
Suggests presenting the alphabet in several different fonts of printing type to dyslexic children. The hypothesis, as yet untested, is that this would emphasize pattern differences without using new symbols. The hope is expressed that research will be undertaken to test the hypothesis. Other techniques for use with dyslexics are discussed.

2173   Stauffer, Russell G. "Research on reading retardation: its class-
       room implications." Education 68(10): 610-15, June, 1948. (10
       References).
Reports on a study of fifty-one boys nine to eleven years of age, of normal intelligence, who were extremely retarded in reading. Findings are discussed in terms of associative learning (how children learn words), and memory-span tests (the kind and amount of material that can be grasped at one presentation and accurately reproduced). Implications for the classroom teacher are explained.

2174   Walker, Kenneth P. "Follow-up study of two methods of treating
       retarded readers." Teach Coll J 38(3): 84-85, 121, 122,
       December, 1966. (22 References).
Compares the effectiveness of treatment of children who were diagnosed reading-disabled by a reading clinic when: (1) the clinic recommended follow-up by the school and parents; or (2) the clinic followed up with its own program of remedial instruction. The University of Iowa Reading

Clinic saw the children between 1954 and 1962. They must have been in
or above third grade at the time of initial contact. The children were
divided into groups by IQ range, age, seriousness of reading retardation,
and sex. Both groups—those treated by school and parents, and those
treated at the clinic—were found to have made average yearly gains of
one year, evidently more than their preclinic progress. Reading gains
appeared to be independent of the type of treatment followed. Statistical
analysis reveals no difference in reading progress when amount of retardation, age, or sex were compared. A significant difference existed in
progress between the low-IQ (89 to 102) and high-IQ (103-123) groups,
with a positive relation existing between IQ and reading gain.

2175 Work Training Program, Inc. Study of reading disorders in relation
      to poverty and crime; final report. Principal contributor, Ida
      Cordero and others. Prepared by Work Training Program, Inc.
      Santa Barbara, California, 1972. 101p. (ED 064 702).
Reports on a follow-up study made to discover whether eighty-three dyslexic job trainees were still benefiting three years later from remedial
training in reading and writing or whether they had regressed. Dyslexics
are defined as those unable to learn by conventional teaching techniques.
Before training 69 percent were on welfare. Three years after training,
45 percent were holding full-time jobs and 25 percent were on welfare.
The effect of reading remediation on two other groups is also reported
in this study: students in a city college and students in a high school
for delinquent boys. Social attitudes and self-esteem were much improved
by reading training.

2176 Zahálková, Milada; Vrzal, V.; Klobouková, Eliška; et al. "Dyslexia
      and serum-uric-acid." Lancet 2(7621): 651, September 20, 1969.
      (0 References).
Letter to editor. In a study of forty-four dyslexic and thirty-one normal
children, no significant differences in serum-uric-acid levels in the
groups were found. (See Item No. 2168).

2177 Zedler, Empress Y. "Educational programming for pupils with neuro-
      logically based language disorders." J Learn Disabil 3(12): 618-
      28, December, 1970. (28 References).
Fifty matched pairs of otherwise normal, underachieving pupils with neurologically based language-learning disorders were used in this study. All
had WISC scores above 80 and had normal vision, hearing, and normal use
of their bodies for regular classroom activities. All had been enrolled
in public school for at least one year and no more than eight years. The
experimental group remained in the regular classroom and received clinical
teaching after school. The controls were enrolled in special-education
classes and received no after-school clinical teaching. Half of each
group was taking anticonvulsive drugs prescribed by physicians. In both
academic achievement and mental functioning the experimental group (those
in the regular classroom) made significantly greater gains. Medication
did not make a difference and does not appear to contribute to scholastic
achievement. It is suggested that it is much better to leave the children
in the stimulating atmosphere of the regular classroom.

VIII
Historical Works

In the nineteenth century and the early decades of the twentieth a body
of literature grew up concerning word blindness, as it was then called,
in adults. Having once been able to read and write in a normal fashion,
these persons lost the ability as a result of disease or head injury.
Mixed into this literature are some writings concerning children who could
not learn to read. This bibliography's primary concern is with the latter
group: developmental dyslexia, the inability of the child who has never
known how to read to master the skill.

Because both categories of these historical materials are often cited in
modern literature on dyslexia, it was thought valuable to cite them here
and to provide full and, hopefully, accurate bibliographic citations to
a selection of the older books and articles. The serious student of reading disabilities is sure to encounter references to them in the literature.

The material included in this section is representative and not exhaustive.
Numerous old case reports, particularly of acquired word blindness, have
been omitted. Those included were selected because they contained material which appeared to bear on some of the same factors as those noted
in the modern studies of developmental dyslexia. The terminology of the
original authors is preserved. Case histories of this era are presented
here rather than in Section IX where newer case studies are collected.
With the exception of Wallin's reminiscences, no entry in this section is
more recent than 1922, and the majority are much older. Bastian, Hinshelwood, Kussmaul, and Morgan are among the pioneers in this field whose work
is mentioned.

Obviously adults still suffer the misfortune of acquired dyslexia, and
their cases are still reported in neurological literature. However, these
modern cases are not included in this bibliography because they are no
longer cited in modern works on dyslexia.

2178 "Aphasia from word-blindness, functional and otherwise." Physician
      Surg 2: 100, 1900-1901.

2179   Ball, A. B.   "A contribution to the study of aphasia, with special
         reference to 'word-deafness' and 'word-blindness.'"   Arch Med   5:
         136-61, 1881.   (0 References).
Documents the case history, with the report of the autopsy, of a fifty-
two-year-old New York doctor who died following a long series of paralytic
attacks which produced various results.   The most notable was a form of
aphasia.   His general intelligence was pretty well preserved and he understood much of what was said to him.   But he was markedly deficient in
verbal expression.   Occasionally he was able to carry on a normal conversation, but usually not.   He reacquired his ability to count quite perfectly, but was never able to relearn the spelling of any except very
simple words.   He could not write at first, but was finally able to relearn to write simple sentences.   He often could not comprehend what he
heard, but knew the words if he saw them.   He was unable to read after
the aphasic attack, but relearned well enough to gather something, though
imperfectly, from newspapers.   He retained knowledge of spatial relations.
His judgment remained good.

The psysiological basis for word blindness and word deafness are discussed.   The latter is very rare, but in this case was more pronounced
than the former.   Details of the autopsy are presented.   The case is
reported to confirm the view that, Broca to the contrary, there is no
single function of the brain which is strictly "a faculty of language."
No isolated cerebral part is exclusively a "speech centre."   The cerebral
lesion in this case was not the location of Broca's speech center.   This
case demonstrates the importance of faulty interpretation of word symbols
as an element of aphasia.   In this case, all auditory relations of language were imparied.   A lecture or sermon was unintelligible; music could
be enjoyed.   Aphasia can be explained by a lesion of the parietal or
sphenoidal lobes.   Word blindness and word deafness are explainable by
lesions in the sensory or perceptive regions of the cortex.   It is indirect in these cases: not caused by a break in sound-forming impulses,
but by a break in the other, receptive side of the circuit.

2180   Ball, M. V.   "A case of alexia in a boy of fifteen."   Ann Ophthalmol
         16(2):   247-48, April, 1907.   (0 References).
Presents the case history of an intelligent fifteen-year-old boy who has
never been able to read.   At age six before starting school he experienced
eight epileptiform convulsions but has had no recurrence.   It is uncertain
whether these contributed to the alexia.   The boy is disgusted with school.
His teacher has been advised to emphasize subjects in which he is good:
mathematics, manual and technical training, music, and drawing.

2181   Bastian, Henry Charlton.   "Some problems in connexion with aphasia
         and other speech defects."   Lancet   1(3840):   933-42, April 3,
         1897.   (52 Bibliographic Footnotes).
The first of the Lumleian lectures sets forth the first principles of the
physiology underlying reading, writing, and speech.   The various kinds of
word memory, the localization of the different word centers, the different
modes of exciting the word centers, and the reason for their functional
predominance in the left hemisphere are discussed.   Three distinct kinds
of memory are considered: auditory, visual, and kinesthetic.   The last
may be divided into two kinds: memory of the sensory impressions resulting from articulating different words ("glosso-kinaesthetic"), and memory
of different sensory impressions emanating from muscles, joints, and skin
during the act of writing individual letters and words ("cheiro-kinaes-
thetic").   The organic seats of these four different kinds of word memory

appear to be closely connected so that memory of a word in one of them must simultaneously revive activity in one or two of the other word centers. Disbelief is expressed in complete topographical distinctness of the sensory centers in the cerebral hemisphere, but it appears clear that there must be sets of cell and fiber mechanisms whose activity is associated with one or another of the sensory endowments. These nervous networks are diffuse but functionally unified and may be very different from a neatly defined center. It is convenient, however, to refer to such networks as "centers."

The four diffused centers for the four reading and writing activities are located and explained. Two views have been put forward: that words are recalled as "motor processes," that is, faint excitations of the processes occurring in motor centers during articulation of words; or, that they are recalled in ordinary thought as auditory ideas or images. It is suggested, however, that in the majority of persons revival of words during thought takes place by a subconscious process in the auditory center, followed by motor activities. There are persons in whom the memory of words is revived first in the visual centers, a notion which is explored. The complex process of reviving in memory words for use in speech is discussed. The routes by which the four different word centers are connected are diagrammed. The reason for the greater development of the left hemisphere is ascribed to the greater use of the right hand which brings greater functional activity upon the left cerebral hemisphere. Writings of those for and against the idea of existence of a separate center for "conception" and "naming" are cited and discussed. The idea is rejected and reasons given for the conclusion.

2182 ————. "Some problems in connexion with aphasia and other
        speech defects." Lancet 1(3841): 1005-17, April 10, 1897. (51
        Bibliographic Footnotes).
The second Lumleian lecture examines aspects of speech defects. Defects dependent upon brain lesions beneath the cortex (neither anarthria nor aphemia) are considered. Lesions of the commissures between the different word centers are not included except incidentally. After presenting twelve cases of persons teen-age or older who suffered from various sorts of aphasia and/or agraphia, the lecture concludes that there appears to be no actual proof as yet that there is a topographically distinct center for writing movements. The occurrence of inability to write (agraphic) as an isolated symptom is extremely rare. In the absence of cases where agraphia occurred alone, cases are cited where aphasia and agraphia are associated. The supposition is that complete or partial agraphia will be produced by lesions in the left hemisphere in right-handed persons and in the right hemisphere in left-handed persons. It is noted that following a publication of Wernicke's in 1874 it has continued to be fashionable to speak of "sensory aphasia" to mean defects in speech produced by lesions in the auditory and visual word centers, and "motor aphasia" to describe problems produced by damage in Broca's region. This is rejected since one of these portions of the brain is as much sensory as the other. Concerning the symptoms of what is called "sensory aphasia," it is observed that Kussmaul broke up the group of symptoms into two sets which he called "word deafness" and "word blindness." The former results from destruction of the hinder extremities of the upper temporal convolutions. Word blindness is related to destruction of the angular and parts of the supra-marginal gyri. Seven common combinations of symptoms arising from defects in the visual and auditory word centers are listed. The first of these, defects resulting from abnormal conditions of the left auditory word center, is discussed in detail. Twenty-one case histories are cited.

2183 ————. "Some problems in connexion with aphasia and other speech
      defects." Lancet 1(3843): 1131-37, April 24, 1897. (45 Biblio-
      graphic Footnotes).
The third Lumleian lecture continues the detailed discussion begun in the
second lecture of various common combinations of symptoms produced by defects resulting from damage or destruction to the auditory and visual
word centers in the brain. Considered in particular in this lecture are:
(1) effects produced by destruction of the left auditory word center;
(2) defects resulting from lesions of the auditory word center in each
hemisphere; (3) defects resulting from destruction of the auditory and
visual word centers in each hemisphere; and (4) defects resulting from
isolation of the left auditory word center. When the left auditory word
center is destroyed, a complete word deafness is produced so that the
patient can no longer comprehend spoken language. Word blindness (alexia)
is also an occasional consequence of such a lesion, although not a necessary accompaniment, Wernicke and Déjerine to the contrary notwithstanding.
The clinical condition produced by isolation of the left auditory word
center (cutting it off from all its afferent fibers) was first described
by Lichtheim in 1884, who referred to it as "isolated speech deafness."
Wernicke called it "subcortical word deafness," and Déjerine called it
"pure word deafness." Such a patient can hear ordinary sounds, talk and
write correctly, read aloud, and understand what he reads. His disabilities are three: inability to comprehend spoken words, from which follow
the other two: inability to repeat words or to write from dictation.
Several explanations given in the literature of the pathology of this
condition are given. These are rejected in the main and another explanation offered. Ten case histories are included.

2184 ————. "Some problems in connexion with aphasia and other
      speech defects." Lancet 1(3844): 1187-93, May 1, 1897. (29
      Bibliographic Footnotes).
The concluding part of the third Lumleian lecture continues the detailed
description begun earlier of various combinations of symptoms commonly
observed in cases where there has been damage or destruction of the auditory and visual word centers in the brain. Discussed are defects resulting from abnormal conditions of the left visual word center. In this
case, the variety of defects is less than in cases affecting the auditory
word center. It is suggested that this is true because in most persons
the recall of words occurs primarily in the auditory word center. The
visual word center is called into activity by stronger stimuli. Word
blindness is often associated with right-sided homonymous hemianopia
(loss of right visual fields). Agraphia may or may not be a symptom
present in cases of word blindness. Defects resulting from isolation of
the left visual word center, which results in pure word blindness and is
a comparatively rare condition, are discussed in detail. Twelve case
histories are presented in the lecture.

2185 ————. A treatise on aphasia and other speech defects. London:
      H. K. Lewis, 1898. 366p.

2186 Bluemel, C. S. "A case of congenital word-blindness." Colo Med
      17(5): 113-17, May, 1920. (0 References).
Presents the case report of a ten-year-old boy of about average intelligence described as congenitally word-blind. He did addition and subtrac-
tion of sums correctly and without difficulty, but his reading was limited
to a few words and his written spelling was highly inaccurate. He could
copy in script from typing accurately. The boy had suffered an apparent

concussion of the brain when he was five years old, the result of an automobile accident. However, the word blindness was thought not related to
the injury but to his mother's positive Wassermann reaction. It is suggested that congenital syphilis may be the cause of congenital word blindness.

2187 Bramwell, Byrom. "'Crossed' aphasia; mirror writing." Edinburgh
      Med J 20: 220-26, April, 1918. (0 References).
In right-handed persons, the left hemisphere is the "leading" or "driving" side, and vice versa for left-handed persons. With rare exceptions
the speech centers are in the leading hemisphere. Exceptions to this
rule occur. "Crossed aphasia" is the term used when destruction through
disease of the speech centers in the left hemisphere produces right-sided
hemiplegia and persistent aphasia (motor aphasia, word deafness, and word
blindness and agraphia) in a naturally left-handed person who had been
taught to write with his right hand. It is theorized that in such a person, forced use of the right hand tends to make the left hemisphere
develop into the leading side so far as speech functions are concerned.
In these cases the speech defect is temporary and evanescent. This is
explained on the theory that the nondriving hemisphere has some sort of
speech function which is carried on in conjunction with the function of
the speech centers on the driving side. Case histories are given, including a case of mirror reading and mirror writing.

2188 Broadbent, William Henry. "Cerebral mechanism of speech and
      thought." Med Chir Trans R Med Chir Soc London 55(Series 2, Vol.
      37): 145-94, 1872. (0 References).
Finds a close functional relationship between articulate speech and that
part of the upper edge of the fissure of Sylvius which forms the posterior
end of the third frontal convolution of the left hemisphere. Ten case
histories of adults are presented to corroborate this view. This part of
the hemisphere is not to be taken as the seat of a "faculty of language,"
but simply as part of the nervous or cell and fiber mechanism by means of
which speech is accomplished. Bastian's hypothesis as to the mechanism
of thought is recounted and modified with the notion that the several
"sense centers" at the base of the brain and in the medulla are connected
in a definite way each with its own set of cells in the cortical substance
of the hemisphere. An explanation of what is believed to be the intellectual elaboration of impressions is given. Words, considered as intellectual symbols, are remembered sounds, probably represented by cell
groups at the summit of the receptive side of the nervous system. It
appears that this is located in the marginal convolutions of the hemisphere. A degree of persistence is necessary both for formation of motor
cell groups for utterance or for use of remembered sounds as symbols.
Such persistence results from frequent repetition of the impression. It
is pointed out that this line of reasoning concerning speech can be
readily applied to reading and writing. When words have reached the cell
groups at the summit of the receptive side, impressions conveying to the
mind various properties of the objects the words stand for will be transmitted to other parts of the brain where the impressions will be associated and the word employed as the symbol for the resulting idea of the
object. At almost the same time motor cells in the corpus striatum are
grouped for production of articulate speech. The mechanism of these
processes is spelled out in some detail and a final point is made explaining alternate routes by which speech can be recovered following injury or
disease.

2189 ————. "Note on Dr. Hinshelwood's communication on word-
    blindness and visual memory." <u>Lancet</u> 1: 18, January 4, 1896.
    (0 References).
Points out an earlier reference to the condition of inability to read
printed or written words than Kussmaul's reference to it in 1877 which
is commonly referred to as the first. Hinshelwood is criticized for using the term "word blindness" with the observation that "the employment
of this term has been misleading and unfortunate." There is a reminder
that the case described by Broadbent in 1872 to which Hinshelwood referred
was a part of a much larger defect. The patient in that case was unable
to name an object on sight. (See Items No. 2188 and 2230).

2190 ————. "On a case of amnesia with post-mortem examination."
    <u>Med Chir Trans R Med Chir Soc London</u> 61(Series 2, Vol. 43): 147-
    58, 1878. (0 References).
Considers the brain cell and fiber apparatus concerned in intellectual
operations. A case is presented of a sixty-year-old man who responded
to questions or requests with entirely unintelligible strings of speech,
delivered with appropriate intonation and gestures and every indication
that the patient thought he was making himself understood. He apparently
was unable to read. It is believed that the case confirms the idea that
there is a distinction between words considered intellectual symbols--
the elaborated product of sensory impressions--and words considered motor
processes. The third left frontal gyrus has been considered the "way out"
for words. In this case, it appears to have been the "way in." Apparently the left hemisphere is employed predominantly, if not exclusively, at
other stages in the complex process by which language becomes the vehicle
of thought. Broca and Moxon are mentioned as having hypothesized that
this preeminence is a secondary consequence of right-handedness: right-
handedness implies sinistral preeminence of the brain. A marked functional difference exists between the two hemispheres. Whether the right
hemisphere has some less conspicuous superiority cannot yet be known.
Since 1872 considerable progress has been made in identifying and localiz-
ing "perceptive centers" for vision, hearing, smell, taste, and touch
through experiments by Ferrier and Hitzig using monkeys.

2191 Bruner, William Evans. "Congenital word blindness." <u>Ohio State</u>
    <u>Med J</u> 1: 74-78, 1905. (11 References).
Alexia or word blindness is a partial form of mind blindness, the latter
being the inability to name objects after merely looking at them. The
location of cerebral lesions which might produce this and other forms of
visual aphasia is discussed. As of 1905 twenty-one cases of congenital
word blindness had been reported in the literature. A child thus afflicted will have marked difficulty in learning the alphabet and in learning
to read. Not all persons who have trouble learning to read are word-
blind. There may be a general failure of mental development. In marked
contrast, word-blind children often have unusually retentive memories and
by this means their inability to read escapes detection at first. Often
their auditory memories are excellent. They may appeal to auditory memory
by spelling out words letter by letter in attempting to read. Many more
boys than girls are affected. Nothing is known of the cause. In none of
the cases, as reported, has any familial tendency been noted. The earlier
the condition is recognized the better the hope of success. The child
should be taught alone, not in regular school classes. Progress is apt
to be extremely slow. Hinshelwood's ideas on treatment are given.

2192 Burnett, Swan M. "A case of alexia (dysanagnosia)." Arch
      Ophthalmol 19(1): 86-90, 1890. (2 Bibliographic Footnotes).
Documents the case history of an eighty-two-year-old man who became unable to read following a series of convulsions. After he failed to read
either large or small letters on an eye test, it became apparent that the
fault lay in his brain. He was able to write either originally or from
dictation but could not read his own writing. At his doctor's instructions, his wife began to teach him to read from a child's primer, but
little progress was made. His general mental faculties were unusually
good. It is suggested that this was a case of alexia, pure and simple.
It would seem to demonstrate the existence of a "reading center" separate
and distinct from other parts of the brain. It would seem that the lesion
in cases of alexia must lie on the left side in the region between Broca's
frontal convolution, the facial center, and the central convolutions.
"Dysanagnosia" is the better term both etymologically and scientifically
than either "alexia" or "dyslexia." The latter two are hybrids of Latin
and Greek and their use should not be encouraged.

2193 Chance, Burton. "Developmental alexia: two cases of congenital
      word blindness." NY Med J 97(14, Whole No. 1792): 697-99, April
      5, 1913. (0 References).
Reports two cases of boys who cannot learn to read in spite of years of
schooling and apparently normal intelligence. The look-and-say method
of learning words was suggested for one; word games and other means for
increasing visual memory were suggested for the other. It is noted that
much has been written on congenital word blindness, yet hardly fifty
cases have been documented in the literature since 1896 when it was first
recorded. The condition cannot be rare. It is a singular fact that the
condition should be studied almost solely by ophthalmologists rather than
by neurologists. "Word blindness" is an incongruous term; "developmental
alexia" is preferred. A great variety of such cases exists. Neurologists
must locate the lesion. Certainly something hinders the transmission of
impulses connecting the visual word memory center and the auditory vocal
memory center.

2194 ————. "Two cases of developmental alexia." Trans Coll Physi-
      cians Philadelphia 35(Third Series): 404, 1913. (0 References).
Describes two cases, a boy of ten years and a man of eighteen years, who
read only with the greatest difficulty. The man found it necessary to
spell out the word vocally and arrange it in syllables before he could
read it. Even after this, he could not read the same word if it were
shown to him. The boy also had to have even the smallest words spelled
letter by letter vocally. Neither showed defects in color perception or
visual fields. The eighteen-year-old could read figures readily and had
a remarkable amount of general learning.

2195 Claiborne, J. Herbert. "Concerning types of congenital symbol
      amblyopia." Paper presented at the meeting of the Ophthalmological
      Section of the New York Academy of Medicine, February 19, 1906.
      104-9. (0 References). (Unpublished abstract of meeting).
Word blindness caused by tardy development of word-memory cells should be
distinguished from word blindness caused by cerebral degeneration, brain
injuries, or brain tumors or lesions. Case histories are presented of a
ten-year-old boy and of a nine-year-old boy. Both children were bright,
alert, and normal in every way except for an ability to read or pronounce
letters in one case or words in the other. Both defects were attributed
to lesions, probably in the cerebral cortex in the region of the angular

gyrus on the left side. Both were right-handed and had normal vision.
The boy who could not recognize letters showed signs of motor aphasia.
It is suggested that there is strong temptation to dismiss the boy as a
fool, except for his obvious general intelligence. The second child
probably had a good prognosis since he was able to learn letters. To
teach him to read would require much repetition to make impressions on
the cerebral cells. The basis for instruction for such abnormal children
should be repetition. Until these children are recognized, classed together, and properly instructed we will fail to get the best results with
them. Memory is the basis of it all, as it is of every intellectual act.
[This is said to be the second paper presented on word blindness in the
United States. The first, by Schapringer, is abstracted in this bibliography. See Item No. 2240].

2196   ————. "Stuttering relieved by reversal of manual dexterity;
       with remarks on the subject of symbol amblyopia." NY Med J 105
       (13, Whole No. 2000): 577-81, March 31, 1917. (0 References).
Suggests that in children who are letter- or word-blind, the symbol amblyopia might be corrected by reversing dexterity, that is, training a
right-handed child who is having difficulty learning to read letters or
words to be left-handed, or the reverse. The rationale underlying this
idea is that the letter or word blindness is caused in a child of normal
intelligence by a lesion at the speech centers, through torpidity or ar-
rested development of the cells concerned. Since it is unlikely that both
sides of one individual's brain should be so affected, the condition may
be improved by cultivating the speech, symbol, and sound centers on the
right side of the brain to the exclusion of those on the left by changing
dexterity in a right-handed person to the use of his left hand. Case
histories are given of naturally left-handed children who began to stutter
when efforts were made to force use of the right hand. A case is also
reported of a stutterer with difficulty in reading who began to improve
both in speech and reading when he began to use his left hand instead of
his right.

2197   ————. "Types of congenital symbol amblyopia." JAMA 47(22):
       1813-16, December, 1906. (5 References).
In addition to the word blindness which results from acquired cerebral
lesion, there exists an incomplete word blindness which is congenital in
origin. This type should be called "word-amblyopia." No doubt there
exists an incomplete congenital figure-blindness which may be called
"figure-amblyopia." These two forms together may be called "symbol-
amblyopia." An incomplete congenital musical-note deafness which may be
called "music amblykusis" or "amblymusia" no doubt exists. Schools should
make careful diagnoses. Instruction should be by patient repetition.
These children can be taught to be left handed.

2198   Clemesha, John C. "Congenital word blindness, or inability to learn
       to read." J Ophthalmol Oto-Laryngol 9(1): 1-6, 1915. (13 Refer-
       ences).
Attributes word blindness to congenital defect or deficiency in the brain
or to some pathological process. Congenital word blindness in children
is caused by some congenital defect in the visual memory center for words
and letters. Learning to read is described as a process of two stages.
First the letters of the alphabet are stored in the visual memory center.
In the second stage words are stored in the visual memory center. A definite cerebral area exists where visual memories of words and letters are
registered. It is the angular and supramarginal gyri of the left side of

brain in right-handed individuals. Morgan's case report of congenital
word blindness is quoted at length (See Item No. 2235). Citing a study
in London which estimates that one child in 2,000 suffers from word
blindness, this article speculates that a similar proportion must be
found in other schools. Such children are misunderstood. Very little
of the available physiological or psychological knowledge has so far been
applied to the practical problems of education.

2199 Crippen, H. H., and Casseday, F. F. "Notes on word-blindness and
      its concomitants." J Ophthalmol Oto-Laryngol 5: 89-100, 1893.
      (0 References).
Discusses the general concept and symptoms of acquired word blindness in
adults. Déjerine is quoted, including one of his case reports. Cases
reported by Charcot and various other cases of verbal blindness are presented. The opinions of several authorities on the pathology of word
blindness are included.

2200 Elder, W. "The clinical varieties of visual aphasia." Edinburgh
      Med J 7(New Series): 433-54, 1900. (0 References).
Details the symptoms of two varieties of word blindness. (1) Pictorial
word blindness, cortical alexia, or pictorial visual aphasia in which
the patient cannot read and cannot write either spontaneously or to dictation. He copies writing as if it were a drawing. He sees objects quite
well. (2) Infrapictorial word blindness, subcortical alexia, or cécité
verbale pure, in which the patient cannot read but is able to write
spontaneously or to dictation. He cannot copy printed into written characters and copies writing as if it were a drawing. It is possible for a
person to be letter-blind, word-blind, or sentence-blind. If one were
taught to read by the word-sentence method, it would probably affect the
symptoms of word blindness in the event of a pathological brain lesion.
Some of the variations seen in visual aphasia are discussed and case histories presented. This discussion is entirely concerned with adults who
became word-blind as the result of brain lesions.

2201 Fildes, Lucy G. "A psychological inquiry into the nature of the
      condition known as congenital word-blindness." Brain 44(3): 286-
      307, November, 1921. (0 References).
Reports on an investigation aimed at discovering something of the psychological characteristics of congenital word blindness. Twenty-six children
ranging in age from nine to sixteen years with an IQ range of 50 to 111
were the subjects. They were attending regular elementary schools or
special schools for the mentally defective. All were at least four years
retarded in reading. The children were asked individually to identify
forms as being like or different from previously shown forms. Forms used
are pictured. Other tests were: (1) studying whether length of exposure
to a form aided memory; (2) experiments in learning visually presented
material; (3) tests of power to reproduce numbers presented visually; (4)
tests of auditory discrimination and retention; (5) an experiment testing
the power to make auditory-visual associations; and (6) learning the names
of eight Greek letters. In all, twelve experiments are described. It is
concluded that nonreaders are found with all levels of intelligence and
that degree of reading failure shows little correlation with a general
defect. The defect underlying inability to read is to some extent specific. No support is found for the existence of a visual-word center controlling ability to recognize words. The theory supported is that word blindness is one aspect of a more general--yet still specific--defect in either
visual or auditory regions or in both. All the nonreaders had difficulty

remembering visually presented forms; some showed corresponding defects in auditory memory. There is indication that failure to associate, as well as retain, sounds and forms lies somewhat in this primary disability of auditory or visual regions. It should be noted that in this study one child had an IQ of 111; the rest had IQ scores below 88.

2202   Fisher, J. Herbert. "Case of congenital word-blindness (inability to learn to read)." Ophthalmic Rev 20: 315-18, 1905. (0 References).
The case history of a six-year-old girl who was having great difficulty in learning to read is detailed. She "mixed the letters up." She was also poor in arithmetic. Her younger sister was being taught to read by the look-and-read method and was making good progress. Her uncle was said to have had extraordinary difficulty in reading and not to have learned until he was ten years old. The patient was otherwise bright and intelligent and learned to repeat poetry readily. It appeared that the child had a congenital defect in the centers for visual memory for figures and musical notes as well as for words and letters. This is seen as supporting Hinshelwood's view that allied visual memory centers are located in adjoining areas of the cerebral cortex. It is suggested that the look-and-read system may be the best way to teach word-blind children to read since words can be studied as a whole. Hinshelwood and Nettleship are both of the other opinion: that the visual memory should be developed by teaching individual letters. In this case, the girl got on quite well with the use of the look-and-read method.

2203   ————. "Congenital word-blindness (inability to learn to read)." Trans Ophthalmol Soc UK 30: 216-25, 1909-1910. (13 References).
Reports several case histories and reviews other case reports in English medical literature. Success in teaching word-blind children by the look-and-say method is reported. Two distinct groups of congenital word blindness may be identified. One is a group whose failure is in development of the visual memory center for words in the left angular and supramarginal gyri. This group may show evidence of inheritance or familial defect. The other is a group in which the same center may have been injured by a very limited meningeal hemorrhage at birth. An investigation is reported showing word-blind boys outnumber girls four to one. Suggestions for further study are made.

2204   Gordon, Alfred. "Pure aphasias a propos of a case of pure alexia." Med Rec 98: 1059-60, December 25, 1920. (0 References).
Reports the case of an adult who cannot read at all, but speaks and understands speech normally. He can write to dictation and spontaneously correctly. He recognizes an occasional word correctly only if he follows each letter with his finger. He can recognize figures and do arithmetic. The case is described as "pure word blindness," or "pure alexia." Its cause is probably a cerebral lesion in the nerve fibers connecting the center for general vision and the angular gyrus, the center of visual images of speech.

2205   Grossman. "A peculiar form of affection of vision [dyslexia]." Med Press Circ 43(New Series): 465, 1887.

2206   Hamilton, Allan McLane. "A case of word-blindness, with impairment of the faculty of space association." Med News 44(4): 92-95, January 26, 1884. (0 References).

Recounts the case history of a thirty-three-year-old printer who abruptly
began to make mistakes while setting type for a legal brief. As he advanced his confusion increased. He finally became unconscious. He had
difficulty in moving his right leg. He could not speak for a month after
the seizure, then began to talk. He still could not read. When he began
to read, he did so with great difficulty. He substituted words of similar
length and form, as "New Haven" for "New Hampshire." Other aspects of
his difficulties are discussed. He recovered, with a slight weakness on
his right side. He was able to correct the proof sheet of the type he
had been setting when stricken. The proof sheet is reproduced in the
case report.

2207 Heitmuller, G. H. "Cases of developmental alexia or congenital
      word blindness." Wash Med Ann 17: 124-29, March, 1918. (0 Ref-
      erences).
Defines developmental alexia or congenital word blindness as a developmental defect of the visual memory center for the graphic symbols of language. It is located in the angular gyrus of the left side of the brain
in right-handed persons, and on the right side in left-handed persons.
The problem is manifested by the inability of an otherwise bright child
to learn to read and spell in an ordinary length of time. Two kinds of
developmental alexia exist. In the severe grade, the child is both
letter- and word-blind. Much more common is the less severe grade, word
blindness only. Some workers in the field believe it is caused not only
by a defect in the angular gyrus, but also by defects in the communicating paths to speech and other centers. Case histories are included.

2208 Hinshelwood, James. "A case of congenital word-blindness." Br Med
      J 2(Part 2): 1303-4, November 12, 1904. (0 References).
This is the case history of a twelve-year-old boy of normal intelligence
and eyesight who was good at spelling from dictation and in arithmetic
but could rarely recognize by sight the words he had spelled. Hinshelwood
diagnosed the difficulty as one of word blindness because of visual memory
defect. Short, daily, individual teaching sessions for the boy were
recommended. Medical examination and diagnosis of all backward schoolchildren so that their individual instructional needs may be met are
advocated.

2209 ————. "A case of congenital word-blindness." Ophthalmoscope
      2(10): 399-405, October, 1904. (5 References).
Presents the case history of a twelve-year-old boy who was unable to
learn to read although he was strong in arithmetic and good in spelling
and other subjects. Hinshelwood prescribed short, frequent reading
lessons. The boy's teacher was advised not to require him to attempt
to read with other pupils present. This is the fifth case Hinshelwood
has recorded, and he believes the condition is not rare but unrecognized.
The difficulty is in visual memory. If allowed to spell the word aloud
the boy in this case could then identify the word by use of his auditory
memory. It is important for the ophthalmologist to be familiar with
word blindness because such patients are brought first to him for diagnosis of eye defects.

2210 ————. "A case of dyslexia: a peculiar form of word-blindness."
      Lancet 2: 1451-54, November 21, 1896. (11 Bibliographic Foot-
      notes).
Dr. Hinshelwood discusses the case of a tailor forty-five years old who
could read only four or five words before finding himself unable to

continue. The man suffered from so much mental confusion generally that
he lost his job as a tailor. Two other cases are cited, both adults who
had lost the power to read. One was an alcoholic who gradually improved
when alcohol was withheld. This Hinshelwood describes as a "dyslexia...
of toxic origin." He agrees with Broadbent that the term "word blind"
has been used loosely by writers who intend different meanings and that
it is therefore misleading. Hinshelwood defines word blindness as "a
condition in which with normal vision...an individual is no longer able
to interpret written or printed language." The inability to read, termed
"alexia," is distinguished from difficulty in interpreting written or
printed symbols which is called "dyslexia." All cases cited in this
article refer to adults who formerly could read, but who are suffering
from cerebral disorders developed in adult life.

2211 ————. "A case of 'word' without 'letter blindness.'" Lancet
      1: 422-25, February 12, 1898. (16 Bibliographic Footnotes).
Cites three case histories of adults ages fifty-three, eighty-two, and
fifty-six who afford examples of cases where the patient could read individual letters but could not read words composed of those letters. These
persons could read figures both individually and in combination, and they
could write spontaneously and to dictation. But they could not read what
they had written. All three had formerly had normal ability to read and
at the time of the loss of reading ability retained other normal mental
powers.

2212 ————. Congenital word-blindness. London: H. K. Lewis, 1917.
      112p.
This standard early work draws together the author's work on the subject
of congenital word blindness done over a period of some twenty years.
The publication of this book is considered by some writers in the field
as closing the early history of this condition. After citing the case
histories of adults who lost their ability to read (acquired word blindness), the discussion turns to congenital word blindness which is defined
as a congenital brain defect in children who have otherwise normal brains.
The difficulty in reading, it is believed, is caused by a pathological
condition. Such children cannot be taught to read by ordinary means.
The contrast in auditory and visual memory in word-blind children is
noted. The author's observations on diagnosis, prognosis, and treatment
are included. Confining himself to cases of "pure" word blindness,
Hinshelwood says that most victims can be taught to read. Personal instruction is advised. The phonic method of reading instruction is considered superior to "look and say" for word-blind children.

2213 ————. "Congenital wordblindness." Lancet 1: 1506-8, May 26,
      1900. (5 Bibliographic Footnotes).
Reports four cases of word blindness, in particular two who were Hinshelwood's own patients. The first case, a boy eleven years old, displayed
a marked contrast between visual memory for words and letters and auditory
memory. He recognized pictures, objects, and persons at once, but lacked
visual memory for words and letters. After years of practice he still
did not know the entire alphabet. Figures he learned more easily. The
second case, a ten-year-old boy, read imperfectly with great effort, but
had no difficulty with figures at all. It is concluded that this can
only be explained satisfactorily by anatomical independence: visual
memories of letters, words, and numbers are registered in different areas
of the cerebral cortex. The two cases are alike, differing in degree,
not kind. Incidence of the congenital form of word blindness is not as

rare as the absence of recorded cases would make it appear. Cases are simply not recognized. Parents and teachers should not treat victims harshly as imbeciles or incorrigibles. Attempts to overcome the difficulty should be by patient, persistent training.

2214 ————. "Congenital word-blindness, with reports of two cases." Ophthalmic Rev 21(246): 91-99, April, 1902. (0 References).
Word blindness is not rare, but occurs with such frequency that it is important for ophthalmologists to be familiar with it and to recognize it. Two case histories, a girl ten years old and a boy seven years old, are given. Special reading lessons for each child alone were recommended. Periods of instruction were to be short and frequent, several times a day, to refresh and strengthen visual impressions. In the case followed up, that of the boy, rapid progress was made. Not all reading failure is congenital word blindness. It may be caused by lack of good eyesight or general intellectual failure. Learning to read has two distinct stages: acquiring visual memory of letters and acquiring visual memory for words. In these two cases, the children learned numbers, a further proof that visual memories of letters, words, and figures are deposited in different areas of the cerebral cortex. Early diagnosis of word blindness is most important. Block letters should be used to aid visual memory with the sense of touch. Word-blind children should not be in the regular classroom but must be taught separately by special methods.

2215 ————. "Four cases of congenital word-blindness occurring in the same family." Br Med J 2(Part 2): 1229-32, November 2, 1907. (9 References).
Four boys, ages twelve, fourteen, sixteen, and eighteen, the four youngest in a family of eleven children, are reported to have all had severe difficulty in learning to read. The visual memory for words appeared to be faulty. The eighteen-year-old, who left school at fourteen, had taught himself to read reports of football matches with comparative success, but his sight recognition of words from an ordinary book was very limited. Hinshelwood states that the problem of the word-blind child is cerebral, not ocular, and that prescribing glasses is not the answer. The center in the brain for the visual memory for words is located in the left angular gyrus in right-handed people. Some defect in this area causes the difficulty in storing the visual images of words. In every case of congenital word blindness he has seen, the child has been taught to read. This assumes that the brain is otherwise healthy. All the centers for speech are on the same side of the brain, and if defective, the same area on the opposite side of the brain can be trained to take over the function. The invention of the term "word blindness" is ascribed to Kussmaul.

2216 ————. "Four cases of word-blindness." Lancet 1: 358-63, February 8, 1902. (14 Bibliographic Footnotes).
These four cases, it is believed, illustrate especially interesting details of word blindness and confirm the views expressed in the author's earlier publications. All cases are adults who lost the power to read after suffering stroke or a "giddy attack." The novel elements of these cases are discussed, including one case in which the patient lost his power to understand spoken French, his native language, but could understand spoken English.

2217 ————. "Four cases of word-blindness." Trans R Med Chir Soc Glasgow 4: 33-34, 1901-3, 1904. (0 References).

Presents four cases of adults who were word-blind following attacks of
aphasia or unconsciousness. One case in particular is seen by Hinshelwood
as confirming his previously published views that past visual impressions
are arranged in the visual memory center in the angular gyrus of the left
cerebral hemisphere in definite and ordered groups. Hence, a patient who
knows several languages may lose the visual memory of one or more and
others may remain intact. The degree and extent of word blindness will
depend upon whether the lesion affects the whole or only a part of the
visual memory center. It is suggested that the auditory word center also
contains word memories of different languages arranged in different
groups. In one case, at Hinshelwood's suggestion, the patient began to
learn the alphabet and to read again using a child's primer. Good success is reported, seen as an indication that in some cases reeducation of
visual memory for words and letters can be achieved.

2218 —————. "'Letter' without 'word' blindness." Lancet 1: 83-86,
       January 14, 1899. (11 Bibliographic Footnotes).
Five case histories are recounted in which one characteristic was the
ability to read words without being able to identify the letters when
individually presented. All of these cases were adults who had previously
read normally before the onset of the illness which led to the word-
and/or letter-blindness.

2219 —————. Letter-, word- and mind-blindness. London: H. K. Lewis,
       1900. 88p.
In the first of five chapters, Dr. Hinshelwood gives this rationale of
visual memory: We see with our brains as well as our eyes, a fact which
has received less attention than the visual processes of the eyes. By
observation and experience humans develop ideas of the relative size and
distance of objects. Permanent impressions of stimuli from the outside
world, called memory, are left on the brain by prolonged or frequent repetition. There are many local memories, such as memories of vision, of
hearing, of smell, and of muscular movements. Each memory occupies a
distinct area of the cerebral cortex. Two distinct centers for vision
appear to be present: a visual perceptive center where external visual
stimuli are perceived, but where such perception disappears when the
stimulus does; and a visual memory center where such perceptions are
stored. This theory is strongly confirmed by clinical experience although
no modification of cerebral cells made by memories can be observed. Any
sighted person has visual memory, but it is possessed in widely varying
degrees by different persons. Some persons in recalling a passage from
memory do so by visual memory and see the words. These are referred to
by Hinshelwood as "visuels." Other persons use auditory memory and hear
the words. These have been called "auditives." When we see something or
someone we recognize it by comparing it with our stored visual memory of
that object or person. We forget the intricate cerebral processes of
visual memory until disease disturbs them. By studying such diseases we
find that visual memories are arranged in groups within the visual memory
area. Some of the groups may disappear leaving others intact. In this
way, letter, word, and mind blindness are produced. They are disorders
of the visual memory produced by lesions in a definite area of the cerebral
cortex where past visual impressions are arranged in definite and ordered
groups.

The first chapter of this book is Dr. Hinshelwood's rationale of visual
memory. It is abstracted in the paragraph above. The other four chapters
comprising this book are all reprinted from Lancet. All are case histories

of adults who had previously been able to read and had lost the ability in some measure because of cerebral lesions. This material and additional case material reported by Hinshelwood will be found in this bibliography. (See Item Nos. 2210, 2211, 2213, 2216, 2218, 2222).

2220 ————. "The treatment of word-blindness, acquired and congenital." Br Med J 2(Part 2): 1033-35, October 19, 1912. (9 References).
Presents several case histories of persons who had lost their ability to read because of a lesion in the brain. It is necessary to study acquired word blindness before congenital word blindness can be understood. The case of a thirteen-year-old boy who had never been able to learn to read is presented. The boy could write, draw, and do arithmetic. His reading instruction had been by the look-and-say method which was not suitable for this child with his poor visual memory. His auditory memory was good. In cases where auditory memory is not good, the look-and-say method may produce the best results. Word-blind children should not be taught in the classroom with normal children. Each child should be taught alone using many short reading lessons rather than one long one. Block letters which add the tactile dimension to teaching are helpful.

2221 ————. "Two cases of hereditary congenital word-blindness." Br Med J 1: 608, March 18, 1911. (6 References).
Presents two case histories of siblings ten and twelve years old who suffer from congenital word blindness. They have four normal siblings. The children are the nephew and niece of four word-blind persons, their mother's siblings. The cases are presented as confirmation of the hereditary tendency of word blindness. The fault is probably not the result of disease or injury at birth, but of defective development of the controlling part of the cerebrum in the early stages of embryonic growth. Both children can be taught to read. Pure congenital word blindness is a local affection of a limited cerebral area. With perseverance and proper educational methods the problem can be overcome.

2222 ————. "Word blindness and visual memory." Lancet 2: 1564-70, December 21, 1895. (26 Bibliographic Footnotes).
Considers several cases of adults who have lost the power to read while retaining other mental faculties. Emphasized are the cases of a fifty-eight-year-old male teacher of French and German and of a thirty-eight-year-old woman. Pointing out the scarcity of references to the condition in English medical literature, Hinshelwood notes that the term "word blindness" and its French and German equivalents are "not sufficiently precise without further definition." The locations of the "visual centres" in the brain are discussed. It is in this article that Hinshelwood ascribes to Kussmaul the first reference to "word blindness" as an isolated clinical condition. Hinshelwood's assertion was later challenged by Broadbent (See Item Nos. 2189 and 2230).

2223 ————. "Word-blindness and visual memory." Lancet 1: 196, January 18, 1896. (1 Reference).
Letter to editor. Contends that Kussmaul was the first to point out that word blindness may be dealt with clinically as an isolated condition. The term "word blindness" and its French and German equivalents are not sufficiently precise without further definition. Some patients recognize the object, but cannot read the word. Some can read the word if the individual letters are spelled out. Others recognize the letters, but cannot combine them into words.

2224 Hinshelwood, James; Macphail, Alexander; Ferguson, Alexander R.
      "A case of word-blindness, with right-homonymous hemianopsia."
      Br Med J 2(Part 2): 1304-7, November 12, 1904. (4 References).
Cites the case history of a fifty-eight-year-old teacher of French and
German who suddenly found one morning that he could not read. In addition, he had loss of vision in the right half of each visual field, that
is, right lateral homonymous hemianopsia. In six months of work with a
child's primer, he relearned the alphabet, but never learned to read
words on sight again. He died ten years later and at autopsy an old
lesion was discovered "on the inferior aspect of the left occipital
lobe."

2225 Hoisholt, A. W. "A case of pure word blindness." Occident Med
      Times 7(9): 483-87, 1893. (0 References).
Presents the case history of a sixty-three-year-old musician who had become unable to read either words or music. He could spell orally and
write but was unable to read what he had written, even his own name. An
orchestra leader and violinist, he played with great skill from memory
but could not play the simplest music by note. His left visual field
became defective and eventually he became entirely blind. A kidney ailment caused his death shortly thereafter. Autopsy showed the entire
occipital lobe on the left side to be yellowish-green and somewhat shrunk-
en. The occipital lobe of the right hemisphere also showed abnormalities
and small hemorrhages. Some of the early researches aimed at discovering
the localization of function of parts of the surface of the brain are
reviewed.

2226 Holmes, Gordon. "A case of persistent visual aphasia." Proc R
      Soc Med (Neurological Section) 2: 105, 1909. (0 References).
The case of a forty-four-year-old man of adequate education is detailed.
The man had been unable to read or write since a large superficial tumor
was removed from his left angular gyrus five years before this report.
At the time of this writing he had learned a few words. He expressed
himself well and understood all that was said to him.

2227 Jackson, Edward. "Developmental alexia (congenital word blindness)."
      Am J Med Sci 131(5), New Series: 843-49, May, 1906. (0 Refer-
      ences).
Reports nineteen cases of developmental alexia. Two were observed at
first hand; the others are from the reports of Hinshelwood, Morgan, and
others. It is believed these nineteen are all that are on record to this
date. "Developmental alexia" is suggested as the term of choice. "Congenital word blindness" as used by Hinshelwood and others seems inappropriate for a condition where vision is normal. The term "alexia" carries
no implication of poor vision and is therefore preferred. It is caused
essentially by a failure of development, or delayed development, of a
"group of coordinations, a coordinating center" essential to the recognition of written or printed characters. The coordinations required for
comprehending and using language are very complex. Failure to connect
with the visual impressions at any point would explain developmental
alexia. If it is true that the condition arises from several kinds of
defects, then different methods of treatment are necessary. These include:
teaching the letters early; cutting them out of paper; modeling them in
clay; and giving the child special instruction outside regular classes.

2228 Kerr, James. "Four unusual cases of sensory aphasia." Lancet 1:
      1446, May 19, 1900. (0 References).

Describes the case of a nine-year-old very intelligent boy who could not
understand words. He had been taught to read, write, and speak, his word
memories being apparently entirely visual and motor. Also described is
the case of a nineteen-year-old boy who could not read. He could copy,
but wrote gibberish to dictation. The case of an eleven-year-old boy who
was word-blind and had speech difficulties but could copy literally is
detailed. His hearing is normal. A fifty-five-year-old man who had become word-blind is also described.

2229 ————. "School hygiene, in its mental, moral, and physical
      aspects." J R Stat Soc 60: 613-80, September, 1897. (0 Refer-
      ences).
Consists of a report by the medical superintendent of a school board of
conditions within the school. The article is the Howard Medal Prize
Essay and is cited in several places in the literature on reading disability as the first reference to developmental alexia, or word blindness. The reference on p. 668 points out that agraphia, word blindness,
and certain other deficits are seen in children who are not generally
dull but are "mentally exceptional." It is suggested that these children
can be cared for in the regular classroom if the teacher is aware of their
peculiarities.

2230 Kussmaul, Adolph. "Word-deafness.--Word blindness." In: Diseases
     of the nervous system, and disturbances of speech. Vol. 14 of
     Cyclopaedia of the practice of medicine. Edited by Hugh von
     Ziemssen; Albert H. Buck, editor of American edition. New York:
     William Wood, 1877. Chap. 27, pp. 770-78.
Kussmaul, a German physician, notes that the ability to read might be
lost although sight, intellect, and speech remained normal. He is commonly credited with being the first to use the term "word-blind." (But
compare Broadbent, Item No. 2189). In this article Kussmaul deals entirely with word blindness and word deafness as they occur in adults who
lose the ability to understand the words they hear or to read the written
words they see, while retaining adequate sight and hearing and the ability to speak. In the case histories given, the conditions occurred
following loss of consciousness or other symptoms of cerebral involvement.
The condition as a developmental disorder of childhood is not mentioned.
These abnormal losses of ability are termed "word deafness" and "word
blindness" in order, Kussmaul says, "to have the shortest possible names
at our disposition." Among other case histories is that of an actor who
could write from dictation but could not read what he had written. The
man found that he was able to read dictated words by passing his finger
over each letter of the written word as if he were writing it again and
read it while so doing. "He then made a sort of calculation, and counted
off the sum of the separate letters," it is noted. Also cited are cases
of patients who could copy drawings but could not produce them spontaneously. Apraxia is defined as a condition in which "the memory for the
uses of things is lost as well as the understanding for the signs by
which the things are expressed." Kussmaul cautions that "apraxia" must
not be confused with "aphasia," which deals only with the signs by which
the ideas are expressed. An example of apraxia is given in which a
patient confounded the spoon and the fork, trying to eat soup with the
latter. In cases of apraxia, the opinion is expressed that the intellect
is never perfectly preserved. [References to Kussmaul and his coining
of the term "word blindness" are to be found with some frequency in the
literature of dyslexia.]

2231 Love, John. "Aphasia with almost complete letter-blindness and
      only partial word-blindness, and without hemianopsia." Glasgow
      Med J 50: 373-75, 1898. (0 References).
Presents the case of a man about twenty years old who became paralyzed
on one side and unable to read the letters of the alphabet following an
attack of epidermic cerebro-spinal meningitis. He was able to read words,
even long ones, but could not identify any individual letter except "I."
He could read Arabic figures but no Roman numerals. He was not word-
deaf and intelligence was unimpaired. Letter blindness is defined as
inability to recognize or interpret the signs known as the alphabet,
although previously well known to the person. The "visual memory centre"
for right-handed persons is assumed almost certainly to include the
angular gyrus and supramarginal convolution on the left side. Very
probably it is highly complex, and the various modes of visual memory are
functionally independent: any one mode may be lost without affecting
the others. Thus there must be a somatic or anatomical independence of
these cortical "centres." The type of case described is rare, but not
unique.

2232 McCready, E. B. "Congenital word-blindness as a cause of backward-
      ness in school children; case associated with stuttering." Laryn-
      goscope 20(5): 559, May, 1910. (0 References).
Reports the case of a twenty-year-old man who had great difficulty in
learning to read. He began to stutter at the age of ten from fright.
He had enteritis as an infant and pneumonia with cerebral symptoms at the
age of four. Family history is negative in this case, but it is suggested that hereditary influence is present without doubt in some cases.
Congenital word blindness is much more common than the number of reported
cases would indicate.

2233 MacLeod, R. A. "Congenital word blindness." Med J Aust 1(26):
      593-96, 1920. (0 References).
Focuses on the case of a fourteen-year-old congenitally word-blind boy.
He is one of eight children. The first three are girls and normal. He
is the middle one of three boys next in age. The other two boys are
mentally defective. The two youngest children are normal. The word-
blind boy has an excellent auditory memory, quickly learning and repeating poetry or the class roll. He can write the numbers but cannot read
them. All three boys are word-, letter-, and number-blind, the difference being in degree, not kind. The boy's teacher did not consider him
feeble-minded, just different from other children, a paradox. The idea
of a cerebral speech center and its location is discussed. Treatment
suggested for congenital word blindness like this case is inspired by
Pavlov's conditioned reflex work. The child should be alone and the
reflex between the word and its sound developed without any distracting
sound intruding.

2234 Mills, Charles K., and Weisenburg, T. H. "Word-blindness, with the
      record of a case due to a lesion in the right cerebral hemisphere
      in a right-handed man; with some discussion of the treatment of
      visual aphasia." Medicine 11: 822-28, 1905. (9 Bibliographic
      Footnotes).
Describes and distinguishes "cortical word blindness," in which the patient
is unable to read or write because his memory of visual images has been
destroyed, and "pure (or precortical) word blindness" in which the patient
can write but is unable to read what he has written, or to read anything
else. In the latter case the cortical center for visual images of words

and letters is not destroyed. Usually the lesions causing these conditions are in the left cerebral hemisphere. Some of the literature on
word blindness is discussed and case histories are reported and analyzed
illustrating variations in the disabilities reported. "Crossed aphasia"
is the term for the rare condition in which cerebral lesions on the right
side result in aphasia and right-side paralysis in a person who is right-
handed, or in left-side symptoms from a left-side lesion in a person who
is left-handed. In children who have not learned to read and write it
is assumed that handedness is determined by heredity, congenital tendency,
and acquired habit, and that the leading speech center is on the left
side in Broca's convolution. The two methods in use for teaching children to read, whole-word and by syllables, are discussed in connection
with the treatment of word-blind adults.

2235 Morgan, W. Pringle. "A case of congenital word blindness." Br
      Med J 2: 1378, November 21, 1896. (0 References).
A bright intelligent boy of fourteen years, quick at games and the equal
of his peers, was unable to learn to read in spite of in-depth, persistent training. He learned the alphabet with the greatest difficulty.
The difficulty is believed to be caused by some congenital defect. The
boy read figures fluently, but could not read words and made numerous
bizarre errors in spelling when asked to write from dictation, writing,
for example, "scone" for "song" and "seuing" for "shilling." It is observed that the boy appeared to have no power for preserving and storing
the visual impression of words.

2236 Nettleship, E. "Cases of congenital word-blindness (inability to
      learn to read)." Ophthalmic Rev 20(233): 61-67, March, 1901.
      (0 References).
Reports Hinshelwood's description of four cases of word blindness, noting
that Hinshelwood ascribed the difficulty to "congenital want of visual
memory" caused by "organic deficiency" in the part of the brain where
visual impressions of letters and words are stored. Five other case
histories are presented. It is pointed out that eight of the nine cases
are males. It is suggested that treatment must be in methodical and
persevering instruction in reading begun at the earliest possible age.
The old plan of early education which consisted in teaching the child
his letters is probably better for the word-blind child than some of
the newer methods. If a child's condition is found incurable, the sooner
this is recognized the better. It may prove best to abandon attempts to
teach him to read and educate him along other lines. It is easier to
detect word blindness in the children of educated parents whose children
get individual attention. Special methods for educating backward or defective children are getting more attention than formerly. If children
whose only difficulty is inability to learn to read can be sifted from
all backward children, the result will be useful both to individuals and
to the community.

2237 Paterson, J. V. "Three cases of word blindness with remarks."
      Scott Med Surg J 17: 21-30, 1905. (0 References).
Discusses the close relationship of: (1) the cerebral graphic center
(brain center controlling the ability to write); (2) the visual word
center; (3) the auditory word center; and (4) Broca's center (concerned
with speech production). Most people use auditory word images in silent
thought, but some people are "visuals," and make use of visual word images.
These ideas are discussed. Three case histories are presented of adults
who became unable to read. They illustrate different types of word
blindness.

2238   Pritchard, Eric.   "Intermittent word-blindness (congenital)." <u>Proc</u>
        <u>R Soc Med</u> (Section for the Study of Disease in Children). 4: 51,
        1910-11. (0 References).
Presents the case history of an eight-and-one-half-year-old boy who is
intelligent and quick at mental arithmetic. He reads Arabic numerals
without difficulty. He recognizes short words when spelled aloud but
usually cannot recognize them when written. On some days he can read
simple sentences. At other times he cannot distinguish single letters.
His visual memory for words and letters is defective but his auditory
and kinesthetic memories are good. Since the word blindness is intermittent, it is suggested that the cause may be a psychosis rather than
an inherent fault in the visual word center.

2239   Rutherford, W. J.   "The aetiology of congenital word-blindness;
        with an example." <u>Br J Child Dis</u> 6(71): 484-88, November, 1909.
        (0 References).
Presents the case history of a ten-year-old girl who cannot read. In
school she was in a class with six-year-olds. The family history is
given. Her six-year-old sister reads fairly well for her age. Neither
child appears to be feebleminded. The child's family has many cases of
goiter, as well as instances of weak-mindedness, alcoholism, diabetes,
and much illegitimacy. The case is seen as an excellent example of the
effect of defective hereditary material in causing congenital dyslexia.

2240   Schapringer, A.   "Congenital word-blindness in pupils of the public
        schools." Paper presented at the meeting of the Ophthalmological
        Section of the New York Academy of Medicine, February 19, 1906.
        103-4. (0 References). (Unpublished abstract of meeting).
Describes a quick way for establishing the diagnosis of congenital word
blindness. If the child reads the letters from an ordinary Snellen chart
less promptly than he did numerals from another Snellen chart, the case
may be diagnosed as congenital word blindness. Credit is given to Morgan,
Hinshelwood, Nettleship, and Wernicke for making other doctors aware of
this defect. Pure word blindness cannot occur in China because Chinese
writing is ideographic, not alphabetic. Reformers in Japan who advocate
the abolition of ideographic writing in favor of a system using the
Latin alphabet may find a new disease, congenital word blindness, cropping
up where it was hitherto unknown. This is said to be the first report
of word blindness in the United States. (See Item No. 410).

2241   Shaw, E. A.   "The sensory side of aphasia." <u>Brain</u> 16(4): 492-514,
        1893. (0 References).
Presents ten case histories of adults who had lost their powers of speech,
reading, or writing, and/or their appreciation of some or all forms of
language. All cases include postmortem findings. Three of the cases
concern word blindness in particular. Some relevant literature is reviewed, including various theories to explain the route through the brain
from written or spoken word to comprehension and intelligent response.
The nomenclature of the subject is discussed.

2242   Stephenson, Sydney.   "Congenital word-blindness." <u>Lancet</u> 2: 827-
        28, September 17, 1904. (8 Bibliographic Footnotes).
Reviews the fourteen cases of word blindness reported by six authors
which, it is noted, make up the literature on the topic to date. Most
victims appear to seek specialized advice from an ophthalmologist first
rather than general medical advice. No doubt exists that there is a
congenital condition not necessarily associated with any other mental or

physical defect where the learning of written letters or words is difficult or impossible. Most cases are males. Considerable improvement may
be expected. The earlier treatment is begun, the better the results are
likely to be. Diagnosis should not be difficult once it is grasped that
there is such a disorder as congenital inability to read. Characteristics of the recorded cases are reviewed. Two additional case histories
are given.

2243   ————. "Congenital word-blindness in children." Rep Soc Study
        Dis Child 4: 165-73, 1904. (7 References).
After reviewing some of the cases of word blindness reported by Morgan,
Hinshelwood, Nettleship, Lechner, and Wernicke, the author adds two
other case reports. They are of a nine-year-old boy and of a ten-year-
old boy. It is agreed that earlier reports are correct in the assumption that many more cases exist than are recorded in the literature.
Without doubt a congenital condition exists in word blindness. Diagnosis
should not be difficult once it is firmly grasped that there is such a
disorder as congenital inability to read.

2244   ————. "Six cases of congenital word-blindness affecting three
        generations of one family." Ophthalmoscope 5(9): 482-84,
        September 1, 1907. (0 References).
Reports the case history of a fourteen-year-old girl who was one of six
cases of congenital word blindness in three generations of her family.
Her grandmother was affected. The girl's mother was unaffected, but
four of the mother's siblings showed symptoms of word blindness. The
patient's sixteen-year-old brother had no difficulty in learning to read.

2245   Thomas, C. J. "Congenital word-blindness and its treatment."
        Ophthalmoscope 3(8): 380-85, August 1, 1905. (5 References).
Most adults fall into one of three memory types--audile, visual, or motor.
Congenital word blindness occurs much more often in boys than in girls.
Frequently persons suffering from word blindness have excellent visual
memory for things other than words. The child may be a "visual," and
yet have no visual memory for ideographs. If general intelligence is
good, the child can become an adequate reader. Individual teaching is
necessary. The phonic method should be used at first. Large letters
printed on signs and large letters carved from wood are most helpful for
very young children.

2246   Thomson, W. H. "Case of word-blindness--classification of the
        forms of aphasia." Med Rec 31(11): 291-93, March 12, 1887.
        (0 References).
Details the development of word blindness in a sixty-year-old woman in
connection with persistent pain in the left side of her head. She recovered her ability to read and write in about three months. Other kinds
of aphasia are described, including sensory and motor aphasia, paraphasia
(the use of wrong words), and other disorders in which an entire class
of words, usually nouns, is lost. It is pointed out that such cases
throw great light on the cerebral mechanism of speech.

2247   Thorton, Pugin. "Word-blindness and visual memory." Lancet 1:
        131-32, January 11, 1896. (0 References).
Letter to editor. Comments on Hinshelwood's article in Lancet (2: 1564,
December 21, 1895) concerning word blindness and visual memory. Thornton,
who says he has written a book on phrenology, believes phrenology describes the same conditions that Hinshelwood mentions. He describes the

locations and formations on the skull which characterize the presence of extraordinary visual memory in an individual according to phrenological analysis.

2248   Wallin, J. E. Wallace. "Congenital wordblindness (dyslexia) in
       children." J Educ 151(1): 36-51, October, 1968. (81 References).
In these personal recollections the author traces his acquaintance with severe reading disability in children from his first contact with it in 1912 at a clinic at the University of Pittsburgh. He traces the early publications of Kerr, Hinshelwood, and others. Case-study procedures Wallin used while in special education work in St. Louis are outlined. The term he uses for the most severe cases of reading disability is "visual aphasia." In addition to the bibliography, this article has an appendix which summarizes the professional opinions of a number of physicians and "psychoeducators" concerning congenital word blindness.

2249   Weber, F. Parkes. "Congenital word- and letter-blindness--congeni-
       tal alexia, with agraphia, without aphasia." Br J Child Dis
       14(163-165): 183-88, July-September, 1917. (0 References).
Reviews several case histories and some of the literature on word and letter blindness. Word deafness is also described. Such defectiveness in speech and reading offer difficult problems. It is not known whether any special method of teaching is possible in especially difficult cases, except for oral instruction for the word blind. Among the case histories presented is that of a ten-year-old word-blind boy, apparently normal physically and in intelligence. He can read and write his own name, but makes mistakes in copying words and copies them without understanding the meaning. He has a brother who reads and writes normally. The mother and both boys have positive Wassermann reactions. It is suggested that any relationship between congenital syphilis and conditions surrounding congenital word blindness is doubtful. This article was also published in Proc R Soc Med, Section for the Study of Disease in Children 10: 122-24, 1917. It is not included in this bibliography.

2250   Wernicke, O. "Congenital word-blindness." Ophthalmic Rev 23:
       19-22, 1904. (0 References).
This is a review of Wernicke's book, Congenital Word Blindness. The review is signed W.B.S., assumed to be William George Sym, then editor of the Ophthalmic Rev. Wernicke, of Buenos Aires, reports that the literature on congenital word blindness is very limited and confined entirely to English. He reviews and describes two additional cases of the condition which Wernicke had seen in his practice. Little or nothing is known of the causes of word blindness. Almost all the patients are boys, and treatment must be educational with much repetition and vocal training. Wernicke agrees with Nettleship and Hinshelwood that the condition may not be so very rare, but the cases seldom come to light.

2251   Whipham, T. R. "Case of congenital word- and letter-blindness--
       alexia congenita." Proc R Soc Med (Section for the Study of
       Disease in Children) 9: 8-12, 1916. (0 References).
Presents the case history of an eight-year-old word-blind girl. She is physically well-developed. Her writing seems to consist of a limited number of ideograms which may not be correctly performed. She transposes letters. She is not word-deaf and can memorize. Sight is good. The Wassermann is positive. An alternative title is suggested for this case: "alexia congenita." If the left cerebral centers are impaired, the question is raised as to why the other hemisphere does not assume

the function in so young a child. Cases of word-blindness are probably
not rare. This article was published under the title "Alexia congenita"
in Br J Child Dis 13: 33-37, February, 1916.

2252 ————. "Congenital word- and letter-blindness." Ophthalmoscope
       14(1): 11-14, January 1, 1916. (0 References).
Cases of congenital word- and letter-blindness (alexia congenita) are
probably more common than would appear from the number reported in the
literature. Only sixty-four cases have been reported. These are not in
the same category as an inability to read because of feeblemindedness.
More boys than girls are affected and several cases may be found in one
family. Causes of the condition are obscure. One writer suggests
atavism. In a case report included in this article, syphilis is suggested
as a possible cause because of a positive Wassermann reaction in an eight-
year-old word-blind girl. It is puzzling why, if word blindness arises
from impairment in language centers of the left cerebral hemisphere in
a right-handed person, the right side does not take over the function.
In children this might be expected to occur. Why it does not is difficult to explain.

2253 Wilgus, Sidney D. "Alexia (cortical word blindness) with agraphia
       in a child." Ill Med J 42(4): 291-95, October, 1922. (0 Ref-
       erences).
Presents the case history of a twelve-year-old boy who could not learn
to read. He had an excellent memory, but was found to have a mental age
of ten years on the Binet test. He had sustained a childhood injury in
the occipital region at the hands of his alcoholic father. He had failed
to thrive in the first year of life. It is suggested that some mental
defect appears in almost all cases of true aphasia, and that pure word
blindness (pure alexia) does not occur clinically. The findings and
opinions of Wernicke and Déjerine are reviewed from a neurological point
of view. It was suggested that this boy might be helped by learning
braille although his vision was normal. He learned the braille alphabet
readily but appeared unable to form words and sentences. After eighteen
months of instruction his writing was full of reversals, elisions, and
omissions. It is concluded that the trial was worthwhile although only
partially successful. It is believed that the boy had a brain lesion as
the result of injury. Attempting to substitute the sense of touch for
the sense of sight failed to establish clearly that the new associations
could replace those associations affected by the subcortical insult in
the region of the angular gyrus.

2254 Witmer, Lightner. "A case of chronic bad spelling--amnesia visualis
       verbalis, due to arrest of post-natal development." Psychol Clin
       1(2): 53-64, April 15, 1907. (0 References).
Details the case of a seventeen-year-old boy who took eleven years to do
the work of eight years of schooling. He was a little above average
intelligence, able to express his thoughts adequately orally, had good
memory for sounds, and good visual memory for color and simple geometric
figures. He had no visual memory for words and could not read. His
spelling was very limited. Only after training to improve visual memory
was begun did the boy admit that he had double vision when attempting to
read. He evidently supposed it to be a natural condition. The double
vision appeared to be caused by eye muscle imbalance. This was corrected
as well as possible with glasses. Reading lessons were undertaken and
the method used is described. He learned to read and to spell. It is
suggested that the best way available to discover and treat such cases is

a rigid insistence upon the requirements for promotion. If such children are held back until they perform the work required for a given grade,
teachers, parents, and superintendents will awaken to a recognition of
the problem confronting the schools. A clear visual image of the word
is essential before it can be stored. This boy did not have that clear
image until his formative years were past. The physical condition made
it impossible for the brain to pass through the various stages of normal
development. The brain must also be susceptible to training. Some children may lack the spelling eye as others lack the musical ear.

2255 "Word blindness." Sci Am 101(26): 486, December 25, 1909. (0
      References).
Describes the case of a word-blind fifteen-year-old German girl of otherwise good intelligence. Three of her relatives suffered from the same
defect. Called "word blindness" by the English, the problem appears to
be caused by a defect in one small part of the brain. In London one case
of word blindness was found in each 2,000 schoolchildren. Such children
are in danger of never reaching the higher classes in school. Proper
education should be possible if the child is otherwise intelligent. This
cannot be done by the school, but must be carried out by the parents or
by benevolent societies.

2256 Wray, Charles. "The treatment of word blindness." Lancet 2:
      885-86, September 23, 1905. (0 References).
True word deafness and word blindness exist when the words spoken to the
child or shown to him are in his vocabulary and he fails to recognize
them. Pseudo word blindness exists when the words are not in his vocabulary. He does not associate the printed word with a sound already
familiar to him, nor does he associate the word with the object it describes. Such children must be put into classes where they will hear a
maximum of talking, reading, and word-building. It is expedient to fill
their minds with intelligent speech before we attempt to teach them to
read in the usual way. True word blindness is very rare. Endless repetition is extremely important in teaching. Diagnostic methods and treatment are described.

IX
Case Studies

2257 Ables, Billie S.; Aug, Robert G.; Looff, David H. "Problems in the
       diagnosis of dyslexia: a case study." <u>J Learn Disabil</u> 4(8):
       409-17, October, 1971. (14 References).
To illustrate the problems, disagreements, inconsistencies, and contradictions in dealing with dyslexia, this article uses the case history of
an eight-year-old boy of normal intelligence with severe reading disability. The diagnostic findings on the child could support two different
interpretations as to the cause of the problem. That such contradiction
need not impair effective treatment is possible, it is believed.

2258 Ancevich, Singrida S., and Payne, R. W. "The investigation and
       treatment of a reading disability in a child of normal intelligence."
       <u>J Clin Psychol</u> 17(4): 416-20, October, 1961. (4 References).
A left-handed child retarded in reading and spelling was observed to be
writing in such a way that he covered the letters as he wrote. Retraining in a writing method that enabled him to see the whole words as they
were constructed resulted in much improvement in reading and spelling.
It is hypothesized that his difficulty was that he never formed visual
associations of sounds and letters since they were obscured by his hand
in writing.

2259 Atkinson, Joan K. "Reading improvement through psycholinguistic
       remediation." <u>Slow Learn Child</u> 14(2): 103-16, 1967. (0 Refer-
       ences).
Presents the case history of Jimmy B., a child of adequate intelligence
and without emotional or social disadvantages sufficient to cause difficulty. Nevertheless, he had difficulty in learning to read. He had
been hospitalized twice by the age of three and was slow to begin speaking. His WISC score at age eight and a half was 112, with little difference in verbal and performance IQ. Reading was nonexistent. Vision was
better than normal and hearing normal. The ITPA was used for diagnosis.
Some of the pictures used in teaching visual decoding, visual association,
and sequencing are reproduced. Descriptions of the activities used to
teach these skills are also included. No formal reading instruction was
attempted until he had had twenty lessons in reading skills. In five

terms (one and one-half years) at a reading center he made about three
years of progress.

2260   Balow, Bruce, and Blomquist, Marlys. "Young adults ten to fifteen
        years after severe reading disability." Elem Sch J 66(1): 44-48,
        October, 1965. (4 References).
A group of men twenty to twenty-seven years of age who had been enrolled
in a reading clinic sometime between the ages of seven and thirteen was
interviewed. Most had learned to read at or near average adult level.
Most had graduated from high school and an estimated 20 percent eventually
will graduate from college. As a group they have more schooling than
their fathers but are in less skilled occupations. Few give any credit
to teachers or institutions for help in overcoming reading problems.
They appear defeatist in attitude.

2261   Bender, Lauretta, and Schilder, Paul. "Graphic art as a special
        ability in children with a reading disability." J Clin Exp
        Psychopathol Psychother 12(2): 147-56, June, 1951. (13 Refer-
        ences).
Two case histories are presented, with other discussion to illustrate the
use of the victims' drawings in the rehabilitation of children with reading disabilities and the resulting personality problems. The drawings
of these two children were of high quality. Encouraging such a child to
draw should not be seen as an avenue of escape but as an aid to his self-
assurance. He may then be able to start the task of reading anew.

2262   Betts, Emmett Albert. "Are retarded readers 'dumb'?" Education
        76(9): 568-75, May, 1956. (11 References).
Sets forth case histories of children of normal intelligence who were
regarded as "dumb" because they were nonreaders. Underlying factors in
reading problems are considered.

2263   ————. "How a retarded reader feels." Elem Engl 34(1): 13-18,
        January, 1957. (7 References).
This case history of nine-year-old Tommy, who had failed to learn to read,
includes the boy's comments on how he felt about his failure and his desire to please his mother by learning to read. Failure appeared to be
caused by lack of individual attention and prolonged absences in the first
and second grades.

2264   Blaker, Charles W. "Sam and structure: a young man's odyssey."
        Acad Ther 4(2): 101-4, Winter, 1968-1969. (0 References).
One fourteen-year-old dyslexic boy with severe emotional problems is
studied. The method of treatment at a boarding school for learning-
disabled children is described. Tutorial treatment goes over and over
the same approach to the same problem until the neurological "rut" is
well-established and a goal can be reached easily. The environment is
equally structured. Aside from standard remedial techniques, structure
has been found to be the single most important weapon against learning
disability. Tutors must balance austere repetition and an attempt to
stretch the student's horizon. They must help the dyslexic understand
what is wrong. With discipline, confusion usually gives way to ordered
reality. An improved self-image takes the place of frustration.

2265   Bryant, Keith N. "Some clinical notes on reading disability. A
        case report." Bull Menninger Clin 28(6): 323-38, November, 1964.
        (14 References).

Details a case study of an emotionally disturbed twelve-year-old boy with serious reading and spelling disability. He first walked at sixteen months, spoke at age two, but did not use sentences until three and one-half or four years of age. At the time of referral he appeared handsome and dignified. He tried to bargain with the analyst and with his teachers for favors. His reading and spelling difficulties appeared to stem from an incapacity to associate and retain symbols from visual presentation and from uncertainty and inconsistency in associating sounds with phonic elements. Forming and remembering sounds was difficult for him. Psychoanalytic aspects of the case are discussed. The patient eventually learned to read well and comfortably. He attended college. Reading retardation is seen as a symptom with complex underlying factors. Without help the results are disastrous.

2266   Carner, Richard L.   "Dyslexia--two points of view."   Acad Ther
       1(3): 134-38, Spring, 1966. (0 References).
Presents through a case history the points of view of both the parents and child toward a severe reading disability. The school's role in recognizing and helping the dyslexic child is outlined. The school should be ready to adjust programs to the needs of the severely disabled reader. Dyslexia should be detected as early as possible.

2267   Carpenter, Robert L., and Willis, Diane J. "Case study of an audi-
       tory dyslexic." J Learn Disabil 5(3): 121-29, March, 1972. (10
       References).
This case report evaluates the function of auditory perception and its relation to reading. It is pointed out that disturbed auditory perception takes many forms.

2268   Cheyney, Arnold B. "Teaching the nonreader." Grade Teach 73:
       87-88, November, 1955. (0 References).
A fourth-grade boy was embarrassed and emotionally upset at having to use first-grade primers. Although progress was slow, he learned some spelling and reading from having stories read to him, then dictating his summary of the story to the teacher, and finally reading back the summary. The other children in his class cooperated with encouragement and help in reading to him and taking his dictation. He learned to enjoy school.

2269   Clements, Sam D.; Davis, Joanna S.; Edgington, Ruth; et al. "Two
       cases of learning disabilities." In: Tarnopol, Lester, ed. Learn-
       ing disorders in children; diagnosis, medication, education.
       Boston, Massachusetts: Little, Brown, 1971. 23-63. (0 References).
Case histories of an eight-year-old hyperactive boy and a dyslexic boy are presented. Family-social histories and psychological, educational, language, and neuropsychiatric evaluations were made.

2270   Clifford, Lawrence X., and Ward, William J. "The use of programmed
       instruction in a reading disability case with associated clinical
       implications." Ala J Med Sci 8(2): 238-41, April, 1971. (5
       References).
Details the case study of a thirteen-year-old caucasian girl who was extremely deficient in reading skills. Psychological evaluation was aimed at uncovering personality or emotional problems hindering learning. An educational evaluation was made. Experimental teaching was carried out. The girl gained rapidly in reading skill which generalized into improvement in other school subjects and in social skills.

2271   "Clinical reading cases involving personality problems and parents."
       Natl Assoc Women Deans Couns J 24: 104-7, January, 1961.

2272   Cohn, Maxine D. "Case study of a nonreader." Acad Ther 7(4):
       477-82, Summer, 1972. (3 References).
This twelve-year-old girl was a total nonreader with a full-scale WISC
score of 89. She received remedial reading instruction for two years
and achieved third- or fourth-grade level in all academic areas. She
worked slowly and needed much individual attention. It is concluded that
early diagnosis and testing are important. Finding the nonreader's individual interests and using unique approaches may aid in establishing
motivation to learn.

2273   Coombs, Caro Dallas. "Is he a strephosymbolic?" J Educ 121(9):
       295-97, December, 1938. (0 References).
Reports the case history of a child who scored 146 on the Binet test and
became a behavior problem because of his difficulties in reading and
spelling. Diagnosis and treatment were carried out according to Orton's
methods with good results.

2274   Cooper, J. Louis. "A procedure for teaching non-readers." Educa-
       tion 67(8): 494-99, April, 1947. (8 References).
Bobby, a twelve-year-old twin, was unable to read even the simplest material in spite of six years of formal schooling and an IQ of 110.
Fernald's method of tracing using visual, auditory, kinesthetic, and
tactual modes of learning was used in connection with auditory and visual
discrimination training. Tachistoscopic training was also used. Progress
was made.

2275   Cotterell, Gill. "How Robert made headway." Spec Educ Forward
       Trends 2(3): 17-19, September, 1975. (7 References).
Recounts the case of a shy, withdrawn boy whose early development was
very slow and whose speech was indistinct. He was, however, popular
with other children and a leader in organizing outdoor games. He was
found to have a hearing loss and was fitted with a hearing aid, but he
could not learn to read. Diagnosed at about age eight as having a mild
cerebral dysfunction with severe dyslexia, Robert was administered the
Fernald kinesthetic method for teaching reading. He remained in remedial treatment until age eleven and a half years, but problems of concentration and motor coordination remained. The boy at age seventeen
passed his school examinations and hopes to become a dentist.

2276   ————. "Jeremy learns how to read." Spec Educ 62(3): 26-29,
       September, 1973. (7 References).
Presents the case history of Jeremy, a hyperactive child from a family
of poor readers and spellers. Jeremy appeared to have above-average intelligence, but at age seven still could not read. A diagnostic assessment revealed superior nonverbal ability on the WISC but poor visual retention, poor auditory descrimination, extreme difficulty in sound-
blending, and that he was right-handed and left-eyed (cross-lateral).
Remedial lessons twice a week were carried out using the Edith Norrie
letter case to build words and sentences. Other remedial techniques
were also used. In one year he showed three years' progress on one test
and four and three-tenths years' progress on another. After the second
year of remedial teaching he was reading at age level and had become an
avid reader able to rejoin his regular class.

2277 D'Evelyn, Katherine. "Dick couldn't read." Prog Educ 20(7):
   325-27, 346-47, November, 1943. (0 References).
Describes a nonreader who was helped to overcome his confusion in orientation and emotional conflicts through the use of the kinesthetic method.
His classroom teacher gave him individual help during their lunch hour
each day. In twenty-two weeks he did about two years of work in reading.

2278 Deverell, A. F. "Specific dyslexia: nature and treatment." Can
   Educ Res Dig 4(4): 279-90, December, 1964. (21 References).
Presents the case history of an eight-year-old dyslexic boy. Considered
lazy by his teacher, he was found to have a full-scale WISC of 112 and
evidence of severe difficulties in perception of symbols. A remedial
program was carried out. Some of the literature defining specific dyslexia and its causes is reviewed. Most of the explanation is in terms
of cerebral dominance. The difficulties faced by the dyslexic are explained. Early treatment is recommended.

2279 Dolan, Mary C. "What made Tommy fight?" Pers Guid J 32(6): 357-
   58, February, 1954. (0 References).
This case study involves a third-grade boy who was a complete nonreader.
Through an individual reading program he was able to learn to read.

2280 Doongaji, D. R.; Sheth, Ashit; Seshia, S. S.; et al. "Childhood
   dyslexia: a neuropsychiatric study of nine children with reading
   disability." Neurol India 21(4): 175-86, December, 1973. (35
   References).
Evaluates nine case studies of children. They are divided into three
groups of three cases each: specific developmental dyslexia, dyslexia
secondary to brain damage, and a group with neurological signs and family
histories of poor spelling and left-handedness. Some of the literature
in the field is reviewed.

2281 Drake, William E. "Clinical and pathological findings in a child
   with a developmental learning disability." J Learn Disabil 1(9):
   486-502, September, 1968. (13 References).
Relates the case history of a twelve-year-old boy of average intelligence
who had experienced difficulty in elementary grades in learning to read,
and in completing his homework generally. He was troubled with behavior
problems at home but not at school. He complained of left frontal headaches. He died in his sleep unexpectedly at age twelve of a massive
brain hemorrhage. It is pointed out that this appears to be the first
case history offered in the literature concerning a child with developmental learning disabilities that also presents postmortem findings.

2282 Eames, Thomas Harrison, and Peabody, Robert Winthrop. "A nonreader reads." J Educ Res 28(6): 450-55, February, 1935. (0
   References).
Summarizes the case of Dick, an eight-year-old overindulged boy who suffered from very poor visual fusion. After correctional work for the eye
problem and enrollment in a school where no special consideration of his
conduct was allowed, he made rapid progress both in reading and in personality adjustment.

2283 "Experiences of a sufferer from word-blindness." Br J Ophthalmol
   20: 73-76, February, 1936. (0 References).
A dyslexic English woman writes this anonymous account of her experiences.
Her father and his brother were both stammerers. Her governesses labeled

her "slow," "dunce," and "lazy." Later, at school, when asked to read aloud, she made a "lamentable exhibition" of herself. She was rather good at arithmetic and geography and surpassed her sister in the former. As an adult, she can read to herself very slowly. It is a physical effort. There is a tendency to lose her place and her line in reading a book. Long words she must spell out in syllables. Reading words and music together as in hymn-singing is impossible. Her only child, a daughter born when she was forty, attends a university and is essentially a normal reader. This woman learned of word blindness only as an adult and rejoiced to hear about it.

2284 "Fighting dyslexia." Sci Dig 77(6): 14, June, 1975. (0 References).
Describes the case of Kathy Rice, a dyslexic earning a degree in civil engineering at Columbia University. Her textbooks are taped free for her by Recordings for the Blind.

2285 Font, Marion McKenzie. "'Dorothy'--case of reading disability." Del State Med J 5: 95-98, April, 1933. (0 References).
Presents the case of a pretty, doll-like little girl eight years, two months of age with a mental age of seven years and an IQ of 86. She had been in first grade for two years and now was failing second grade. She did not know her letters. Her idea of reading seemed to be to make up a story, since she could not recognize the words in her book. She was given remedial reading instruction for one hour once a week. By use of the sounding and tracing method recommended by Marion Monroe, the child was taught the alphabet with special drill on reversible letters. After twelve hours of training her reading was not much better, but her effort, interest, penmanship, and spelling were somewhat improved. Her parents and teacher reported decided improvement. It is noted that this case illustrates the handicap of reading-disabled children. Their problem is not widely understood and they are penalized. They should not be treated as behavior problems or as mental deficients.

2286 ————. "Thirty-nine cases of reading disability." Del State Med J 6: 119-22, May, 1934. (0 References).
Reports background and follow-up information on thirty-nine children who were diagnosed as suffering from reading disabilities. The children were examined over a period of about two and one-half years at a state mental hygiene clinic. Chronological ages ranged from seven to sixteen years, mental age from seven to thirteen years, and IQs from 70 to 120, with thirty-five of the children scoring from 70 to 100 on the Stanford Binet. In addition to poor reading, the children had been referred for behavior problems, suspected mental deficiency, or general scholastic retardation. Details of each of these categories is given. Some of these cases were followed over a period of time; this information is summarized. Only four children were given remedial help at the clinic. They all showed improvement. Four others were beginning remedial training at the time of writing.

2287 Ford, Charles A. "A case of congenital word-blindness showing its social implications." Psychol Clin 17(2-3): 73-84, May-June, 1928. (11 References).
This case history shows that more emphasis should be placed on congenital word blindness and dyslexia as elements in social maladjustment. The condition can cause severe school and social maladjustment. The case history is of a boy of elementary school age who was referred to a state

juvenile facility for lying, stealing, truancy, and bad behavior in
general. His mother died when he was quite young and part of his childhood was spent with his paternal grandparents. They appeared to be in-
dulgent with the boy, but have let him believe that he is dumb, backward,
or lazy. He has had trouble in school, especially in reading and spelling. After five years of schooling he is still unable to read. His
school failures were attributed to laziness and lack of attention. At
age five his IQ was found to be 97. He had behavior problems. At the
juvenile facility he was diagnosed as having congenital word blindness.
At the school he is not considered dull and is made to feel capable. He
has been in no trouble, has been reliable, and has not lied. This type
of child can be taught to read when the correct method is found.

2288 ————. "Methods and results of teaching a case of congenital
      word-blindness." Psychol Clin 17(8-9): 226-33, January-February,
      1929. (6 Bibliographic Footnotes).
Phonics and extensive drill were effective in treating Paul, a boy who
could identify a word if asked to do so, that is, could find "Rover" on
a page if asked to do so, but could not identify the same word in isolation a few minutes later. Tracing was also used.

2289 Foster, Gertrude Ella. "A short-term follow-up study of the aca-
      demic, social and vocational adjustment and achievement of children
      five to ten years following placement in a perceptual development
      program." For a summary see: Diss Abstr Int 35A(5): 2199,
      November, 1972.

2290 Freel, A. O. "Teaching non-readers to read." Natl Elem Princ
      27(3): 36-38, December, 1947. (0 References).
Calls attention to two case histories of children taught to read by
Fernald's techniques after years of failure.

2291 Fried, Y. "Dyslexia and organization of space." Acta Paedopsychiatr
      35(2-3): 79-85, February-March, 1968. (0 References).
A dyslexic boy thirteen years old was discovered to have the concepts of
space organization of a much younger child. The boy was examined using
Piaget's technique. The tests used are described. It is suggested that
the reading difficulty may be related to his lack of space organization
and that coaching to correct this may help his reading problem.

2292 Gray, William Scott. Remedial cases in reading: their diagnosis
      and treatment. Chicago, Illinois: University of Chicago Press,
      1922. 208p. (Supplementary Educational Monographs, No. 22).
The investigations reported were undertaken to develop information on
types of remedial reading cases; detailed descriptions of poor readers
to aid teachers in recognition and diagnosis of reading problems; information concerning appropriate instruction for remedial cases; and to
underscore the urgent need for trained teachers in the area of diagnostic
and remedial reading. Four distinct steps were carried out in pursuit
of the investigation: (1) a summary was prepared of remedial cases submitted by teachers and others; (2) plans were made for diagnosing individual cases and carrying out remedial instruction; (3) twenty-seven
pupils who encountered unusual difficulties in reading were studied at
or near the University of Chicago; and (4) a group of twenty-six retarded
readers in Toledo, Ohio, was studied to determine effective diagnostic
and remedial work in cities. These studies are detailed. Methods used
in the study of individual cases are described. Case studies are grouped

and presented according to the kind of difficulty in reading. Congenital
word blindness is one among fourteen possible causes of reading failure.
Other causes listed include defective vision, inadequate training in
phonetics, and lack of interest. The book covers a broad range of situations requiring remedial teaching.

2293 Green, Pat. "This bright child." J Learn Disabil 1(7): 423-28,
      July, 1968. (0 References).
Focuses on a case report of a dyslexic child. The nine-year-old had been
born three weeks early. Her mental maturity seemed to lag, even from
kindergarten days. She was written off at first as "slow." Later, with
professional help, she made good progress, although the battle continues.

2294 Greenblat, Helen J. "I hate reading!" Natl Probat Parole Assoc J
      1(1): 8-14, July, 1955. (7 Bibliographic Footnotes).
Three case histories are analyzed as examples of how assistance with reading problems may prove to be important therapy for delinquent boys. It is
concluded that if cases of reading difficulty and hatred of reading could
be helped earlier many children would have happier school experiences.

2295 Hardy, Madeline I. "Disabled readers: what happens to them after
      elementary school?" Can Educ Res Dig 8(4): 338-46, December,
      1968. (13 References).
Children referred to a reading clinic in London, Ontario, were followed
up from seven to eleven years after treatment. Gains were made in silent
and oral reading and in spelling during treatment. After help ended the
problem readers did not achieve on a par with their grade groups. Some
who had as much as five years of remedial training failed to overcome
learning problems. Instructors should be alert to the point at which
pupils cease to profit from remedial help. Early referral for help was
related to superior achievement. Children with certain visual, perceptual,
and motor deficiencies tended to retain them. Most of the subjects appeared better able to cope with life than they had as children.

2296 ————. "Follow-up of four who failed." J Read 12(5): 379-82,
      416-19, February, 1969. (0 References).
Case studies of four problem readers are detailed.

2297 Harris, Albert J., ed. Casebook on reading disability. New York:
      David McKay, 1970. 345p. (Bibliographical References).
Consisting of varied case histories of twelve to twenty-five pages each,
this book details the problems, diagnosis, and treatment of sixteen children who were referred to various types of clinics or schools for reading
disability. They were selected to provide a variety in location and
points of view. Each report was prepared by someone working in the field,
including, among others, Marianne Frostig, Gilbert B. Schiffman, Helen
K. Smith, and Archie A. Silver. The book is intended to be required or
supplementary reading for college or graduate courses in the diagnosis
and treatment of reading disability, or personal reading for reading
specialists, psychologists, teachers, parents, or others involved with
children who are reading-disabled. It was compiled to fill a need for
varied case reports presented in detail and at length. The cases are
grouped according to the type of facility dealing with the child: full-
time remedial schools, multidisciplinary clinics, remedial reading
clinics, and medical facilities. One case involving twins is presented.

2298 Hawkins, Thom. Benjamin: reading and beyond. 1972. 140p.
      (ED 070 073).

Compiles the lessons used in tutoring a nineteen-year-old with severe reading problems. In addition to the pedagogical aspects discussed, the friendship that developed between pupil and tutor forms a part of the journal.

2299 Heckerl, John R., and Sansbury, Russell J. "A study of severe read-
      ing retardation." Read Teach 21(8): 724-29, May, 1968. (8 Ref-
      erences).
Reports a study done with six boys eleven to fourteen years of age who had severe retardation in reading. They attended a remedial reading center daily for three years. Family histories revealed that high school had usually not been completed and some degree of learning difficulty was present in those interviewed. Meetings were held with parents periodi-cally. This combined with the remedial teaching resulted in much improve-ment in all the boys' reading at the end of the three years. All verbal IQs were in the dull-normal range with higher performance than verbal IQ scores. The discrepancy increased as the child grew older. Defects in auditory or visual acuity were rare. These children had difficulty in translating orientational concepts into symbols. For example, they knew which of two persons was taller, but they had difficulty in translating this into feet.

2300 Heller, Theodore M. "Word-blindness--a survey of the literature
      and a report of twenty-eight cases." Pediatrics 31(4): 669-91,
      April, 1963. (78 References).
Reviews the historical literature of word blindness, citing many nine-teenth-century reports. The criteria used in a program for screening schoolchildren for dyslexia are described. Points included are: (1) normal intelligence; (2) normal vision and hearing; (3) marked reduction in reading and spelling ability; (4) discrepancy between reading and other abilities; (5) inability to learn to read by the sight method; (6) ability to learn to read by auditory repetition; and (7) evidence of dis-sociation of visual word-image from acoustic word-image. The last item is considered most diagnostic. Twenty-eight word-blind children who met the diagnostic criteria were found in a screening of 6,000 children. Full personal background data, achievements, personality, and reading perfor-mance of the twenty-eight children are given in a series of tables. Word blindness is discussed in terms of developmental anomaly.

2301 Hess, Alexander. "Some aspects of dyslexia in the Hebrew language."
      Acta Paedopsychiatr 34(6): 153-62, June, 1967. (12 References).
Presents the case history of a nine-year-old Israeli boy whose symptoms of dyslexia and dysgraphia were about the same as those of children learn-ing to read European languages, even though Hebrew is written from right to left. The need for a cooperative approach from several disciplines--medicine, psychiatry, and education--is emphasized if an adequate diag-nosis is to be made. To treat a case suitably it is necessary to dis-tinguish between the original causes of reading retardation (the dys-lexia) and retardation caused by emotional, cultural, or pedagogic rea-sons.

2302 Hogan, Richard P. "The special child: secondary dyslexia." Acad
      Ther 7(1): 51-57, Fall, 1971. (2 References).
This case history of a ninth grader recounts how he was helped by having all classroom work presented orally by a tutor. His performance, motiva-tion, and attitude toward school improved with the use of this method.

2303 Hughes, C. Alston. "Congenital dyslexia." Trans Ophthalmol Soc
      UK 56: 307-11, 1936. (0 References).
Recounts the case history of a twenty-six-year-old man who could neither
read nor write although he had an elementary education. Although he
could write his name and recognize letters singly, he could not assemble
them into a word and say the word. It is suggested that the cause may be
one of defective development of congenital origin.

2304 Jackson, Merrill S. Reading disability; experiment, innovation and
      individual therapy. Sydney, Australia: Angus and Robertson, 1972.
      79p.
The five reports which make up this book include three case studies of
dyslexic children. A fourth is a description of the structured alphabet
kit, and the use of this equipment in instructing dyslexics. The fifth
report is a description of the problems of processing visual material,
that is to say, learning to read. There is a plea that children once
diagnosed dyslexic not be labeled this way for the rest of their lives,
or long after the problem has been overcome. Dyslexia is preventable
and remediable by the use of the techniques described in this book. The
therapeutic techniques also work well with normal children.

2305 Jansky, Jeannette. "A case of severe dyslexia with aphasic-like
      symptoms." Read Teach 15(2): 110-13, November, 1961. (0 Ref-
      erences).
Dick, a twelve-and-one-half-year-old boy, was first referred to a clinic
for help with reading at age seven. Both sides of his family had histories of language difficulties. Dick's dyslexia was severe. He had trouble
with naming--anomia--and time sequences. The passage of time meant little
to him. He could not generalize sufficiently to recognize a word in a
different place. He now enjoys reading, but still lacks self-confidence.

2306 Keeney, Arthur H. "Case studies in dyslexia." Doc Ophthalmol 26:
      601-8, 1969. (7 References).
Reviews some of the nineteenth-century literature on acquired dyslexia
in adults after stroke or injury. Case histories of children suffering
from developmental dyslexia are given. It is concluded that ophthalmologists have modest responsibilities for diagnostic studies and for counseling of dyslexic patients. Children with good performance IQs respond
well to visual, auditory, tactile, and kinesthetic sensory therapy from
affectionate and inspirational teachers.

2307 ————. "Case studies in dyslexia." Trans Am Ophthalmol Soc
      67: 68-77, 1969. (7 References).
The term "dyslexia" should be reserved for central difficulties in ability to interpret words or symbols in the presence of normal intelligence,
vision, and hearing. Used thus it should be designated "specific dyslexia." "Alexia" or "acquired dyslexia" should be used to describe the
loss of previously acquired ability to read. The ophthalmologist has
some responsibility for diagnostic studies and counseling of dyslexic
patients. Other specialists should be consulted as necessary. Often
found in these patients are minor ocular, oculomotor, or neuro-ophthalmic
disturbances that may not merit correction. Careful diagnosis should
precede educational remedies. Dyslexic children of good intelligence
respond to visual, auditory, tactile, and kinesthetic therapy from sympathetic teachers. Poor spelling and writing and slow reading may typify
individuals for life, but many dyslexics can achieve well enough educationally to sustain employment. The article documents some case histories.

2308 Kesten, Jacob. "Learning for spite." Psychoanalysis 4(1): 63–
      67, Fall, 1955. (0 References).
Recounts the case of a therapist who is successful in helping a ten-year-
old boy with his reading problem by challenging him to defeat the therapist by learning to read.

2309 Lee, King Y. "Alexia without agraphia." Am J Ophthalmol 62(6):
      1149, December, 1966. (10 References).
Alexia without agraphia is a neuro-ophthalmologic syndrome in which the
patient loses his ability to read while retaining his ability to write.
The condition usually follows stroke with involvement of the left posterior cerebral artery. The acquired alexia differs from congenital
alexia, or word blindness, because it is generally thought that no gross
or microscopic lesion of the brain exists in the congenital form. Heredity is regarded as the cause. The case report of a forty-year-old woman
suffering from alexia as the result of a head injury is reported. The
anatomy underlying the condition is discussed. Discussion of congenital
word blindness is included.

2310 Leland, Bernice. "Billy." Psychol Clin 17(1): 29–32, March,
      1928. (0 References).
Details a case history of a child with a persistent and severe reading
disability. In spite of the ingenuity and skill of his instructors,
Billy never learned to read. He forgot from one day to the next what he
had learned. He is classified "dull," yet does not look or act in any
way like the typical dull child. He is capable of sustained effort and
is pleasant and competent in situations not requiring much intellectual
effort. The child's nine siblings are similarly affected. It is suggested that the difficulty may be a congenital defect of attention, or
possibly "glandular difficulties," since he has been overweight from
birth.

2311 Lieben, Beatrice. "Reading disability and life style: a case."
      J Individ Psychol 23(2): 226–31, November, 1967. (3 References).
Presents a case report of an eleven-year-old boy who was reading at beginning second-grade level, four years below expectancy. He had attended
reading clinics for three summers and had repeated second grade. The
boy was cheerful, cooperative, avoided all challenges, and expected immediate help. His mother did not encourage his independence. He was
not allowed to make any decisions. He was using his genuine hinderance
to learning to elicit help and maintain his image as the helpless be-
loved, an incompetent from whom little could be expected. The therapist
made it clear that he was not fooling her; he was smart and could do the
work. There were tears and anger, but he improved. He was reading at
seventh-grade level when he entered high school and could now profit from
group remedial instruction.

2312 Loudon, Blanche, and Arthur, Grace. "An application of the Fernald
      method to an extreme case of reading disability." Elem Sch J
      40(8): 599–606, April, 1940. (0 References).
A thirteen-year-old boy's reading and writing were strikingly improved
by use of Fernald's kinesthetic or tracing method of teaching.

2313 Ludlam, William M.; Twaroski, Chester; Ludlam, Diana P. "Optometric
      visual training for reading disability--case report." Am J Optom
      Arch Am Acad Optom 50(1): 58–66, January, 1973. (0 References).

The case report of a fourteen-year-old boy with a history of chronic
reading problems is presented in detail as typical of one type of reading-
disabled patient who can be helped by visual training therapy. Fourteen
weeks of training resulted in improved reading ability and a more positive attitude toward study and school. No other therapy was used.

2314 McCoy, Lois E. "Braille: a language for severe dyslexics." J
      Learn Disabil 8(5): 288-93, May, 1975. (5 References).
Recounts the case history of a fifteen-year-old severely dyslexic girl
who was much helped by being taught to read in braille. Since braille
bypasses the auditory-visual route, it is suggested as an alternative
for the severely learning-disabled person.

2315 MacGillivray, Allister M. "Congenital word-blindness." Br Med J
      2: 1178-79, December 24, 1927. (0 References).
In congenital word blindness the visual memory for letters and words is
defective and great difficulty is experienced in recognizing printed
letters and words. Children who are diagnosed word-blind should be
carefully observed and given special individual teaching. A case history
is given of a fourteen-year-old boy whose word blindness was not diagnosed until he was at the point of leaving school to try to earn his own
living. He was kept in the infant classes for his entire school life.

2316 McKerracher, D. W. "Alleviation of reading difficulties by a
      simple operant conditioning technique." J Child Psychol Psychiatry
      8(1): 51-56, May, 1967. (9 References).
Details the case history of an eleven-year-old boy suffering from reading
disability, stammering, enuresis, and anxiety. He was not helped by
remedial teaching and therapy. While most of the other symptoms were
unchanged, the reading problem was much helped by the use of an operant
conditioning procedure. One light came on for every six words read
correctly. When all six lights were on together, the boy received a
sweet. The amount which had to be read correctly to activate a reward
light was gradually increased. When a word was mispronounced, a loud
buzzer sounded. The reward alone seemed to be as effective as the reward
and avoidance conditioning (buzzer) used together. Three months of remedial teaching and therapy without the reward conditioning had little
effect on the boy's reading progress. In six months of conditioning his
reading age increased by more than a year.

2317 McKnight, Roberta Vae. "A self-analysis of a case of reading,
      writing and speaking disability." Arch Speech 1: 18-47, 1936.
      (5 References).
This case study written in the first person analyzes and describes in
detail the kinds of reading errors made. A subjective analysis of why
the words appear as they do is made in terms of eye movements. Looking
at the word a second time often served to correct the error. Stopping
on a word and being unable to proceed in either direction or being unable
to recall the meaning of a familiar word ("blocking on it") are described.
Phonics and the kinesthetic method of tracing were necessary in order
to learn reading and writing. Stuttering and blocking of the whole
speech musculature were present. About four hours a day for almost two
years were devoted to remedial activities. The very severe stuttering
cleared up only to become extremely severe again later. Personality
tests indicated changes in maturity and degree of adjustment as the reading, writing, and speaking difficulties became better or worse. Progress
toward emotional adjustment came in adult life by changing from the study

of English and dramatics to psychology and by taking advantage of the
opportunity to direct some plays and give some lectures.

2318 Marshall, Wallace, and Ferguson, John H. "Hereditary word-blindness
      as a defect of selective association." J Nerv Ment Dis 89(1):
      164-73, January, 1939. (13 References).
Reports the case of a college student who had largely overcome a reading
disability of cerebral and apparently hereditary origin. It was necessary for him to hear the word to be sure what it was. Viewpoints on
speech functions are discussed, since, it is asserted, the word blind
are lacking in special skills of speech.

2319 Michal-Smith, Harold; Karp, Etta; Morgenstern, Murry. "Dyslexia
      in four siblings." Am J Orthopsychiatry 39(2): 272-73, March,
      1969. (0 References).
Dyslexia has some genetic origin, it is suggested. Its relation to the
child's environment is also discussed. The case of a family of four
children, all disabled readers, is presented. Both parents were professionals. The father's rigidity and lack of understanding of the problem
and the mother's siding with the children brought about severe conflicts
within the family and isolated them from outside contacts. Psychological
and educational therapy were undertaken.

2320 Michal-Smith, Harold; Morgenstern, Murry; Karp, Etta. "Dyslexia
      in four siblings." J Learn Disabil 3(4): 185-92, April, 1970.
      (0 References).
Four siblings from a middle-class background were all dyslexic. Background history suggests that a genetic factor may be the cause. Emotional problems are believed to be secondary to the major problem of dyslexia.

2321 Milano, Rachel. "Educational therapy in a case of reading dis-
      ability." Case Rep Clin Psychol 3(2): 75-82, 1953. (0 Refer-
      ences).
Reports the case history of a nine-year-old girl with reading difficulties
and poor scholastic progress. She was a moderately obese child who was
appraised clinically as extremely conforming and dependent. Her Stanford
Binet IQ was 102. The reading disability appeared to be caused by emotional factors. The mother was seen in the same clinic to which the
child was referred in an effort to improve mother-child relations.

2322 Miller, Julano. "What happened to those who got away?" Acad Ther
      9(1): 47-55, Fall, 1973. (0 References).
Presents four case histories of adults who were dyslexic as children, but
received either no help or the wrong methods in training.

2323 Miller, Marion Z. "Remediation by neurological impress." Acad
      Ther 4(4): 313-14, Summer, 1969. (4 References).
This article reports a case study of a nine-year-old third-grade boy with
an IQ of 90 who was failing in reading. After conventional reading
methods failed, the teacher used the neurological impress method. She
sat behind the boy while he held the book, and they pronounced the word
simultaneously as he pointed to each word. They worked together for
fifteen minutes a day before school began. After eight hours of instruction in this manner, his reading scores were considerably improved. The
exclusive contact with the teacher appears to have stimulated emotional
development.

2324   Minogue, Blanche M.   "Congenital word blindness, a case study."
       Psychiatr Q 1(2): 226-30, April, 1927. (2 References).
Presents the case history of a twelve-year-old girl who was in fifth
grade although unable to read. She had been considered a mental defective even though she did excellent work in arithmetic, a discrepancy considered significant. The parents and two siblings were of normal intelligence. Her scores on various psychological tests were superior. Her
score on the Healy Pictorial Completion Test II, a difficult test for a
true defective, was above-average for adults and very superior for a
twelve-year-old. She could not read at first-grade level. She appeared
to have almost no visual imagery. She could read and write the letters
of the alphabet. Special teaching methods were recommended. She learned
best through auditory channels. The prognosis was considered unusually
good because of her intelligence, understanding of her own problem,
determination to overcome it, and good environment.

2325   Monroe, Marion. "Reading disabilities--the importance of early
       diagnosis and prevention." Woods Sch Child Res Clin Proc 1:
       24-29, 1935. (0 References).
Focuses on eight case studies illustrating some of the factors which may
interfere with reading ability. It is possible for children with all
kinds of disabilities to learn to read. If these disabilities can be
discovered at an early age, later failure may be prevented. It may be
possible to make a specialized approach to the problem before the child
is nine or ten years old and has become a complex school problem. Diagnostic tests for use in the first grade are being devised. These take
into consideration five factors: visual, auditory, motor, articulation,
and language. Retesting at the end of the year will aid in adapting
teaching methods to the child's needs. Cases include children of both
high and dull-normal IQs who were good in arithmetic but not reading.
Some showed lack of motor control of eyes or in general. Others lacked
auditory discrimination ability in spite of normal hearing.

2326   Murphy, Mary Leonore. Barnaby; the struggle of a word-blind boy.
       Reading, England: Educational Explorers, 1968. 74p.

2327   Natchez, Gladys. Gideon, a boy who hates learning in school. New
       York: Basic Books, 1975. 185p.
This case study of a composite child, Gideon, is told in dialogue in a
fictionalized style. It describes the struggles of a reading-diabled
third-grade boy who profits from remedial treatment. The remedial procedures described are standard techniques. Appendices list books for
parents and for children with reading problems.

2328   Nattrass, F. J., and Caiger, H. "Inverted writing; inverted read-
       ing; mirror-writing, with illustrative case." Trans Ophthalmol
       Soc UK 52: 565-69, 1932. (1 Reference).
Documents case histories: (1) An eleven-year-old boy's method for writing was both inverted and reversed. He turned his paper upside-down and
began in the lower-right corner. When turned right-side-up, the writing
appeared quite normal. (2) An eleven-year-old boy who preferred to read
upside-down could also write upside-down. He could also read and write
in the ordinary way. He was otherwise a good student. He was left-
handed, as were three of his four siblings. Critchley is cited as suggesting that defective visual perception is probably the chief factor
in causing the condition. It is assumed that in such a case there is a
psychological failure to rectify the inverted images normally received

by the retina. (3) The case of a six-year-old right-handed girl who wrote mirror writing is detailed.

2329   Nelson, Louise. "A medical problem that became a psychological problem." <u>Ment Hyg</u> 15(2): 242-54, April, 1931. (0 References). This is a case history of Thomas, whose reading disability was not diagnosed until he was nineteen and failing in high school. His IQ was assessed at 94 or 97 on two tests and he had good general health. His birth was very difficult, following long labor. One retina was permanently damaged in delivery. The vision problem was not discovered until he was eleven years old. He showed above-average mechanical ability and superior ability to manipulate spatial relations. Remedial reading training was helpful but the outlook did not seem bright because of the boy's unwillingness to build on the foundation laid. It is believed that his emotional adjustment would have been better if the eye defect had been found earlier. Early and thorough examination of eyes and ears is advisable.

2330   Nolte, Karl F. "The case record of Jerry, a non-reader." <u>Elem Engl Rev</u> 21(2): 66-70, February, 1944. (9 Bibliographic Footnotes).
Details the case history of a little boy of mixed dominance and bright mind who overcame his reading handicaps and exceeded the norm in reading by the end of his fourth year of school with the help of a teacher trained in remedial techniques.

2331   Oberlin, Diana S. "The effects of treatment for reading disability: a case study." <u>Del State Med J</u> 11: 119-22, May, 1939. (0 References).
Summarizes the case history of a left-handed boy first seen at a mental hygiene clinic when he was seven years old. His IQ, as measured by the Stanford Binet, was 71. Seven years went by before he was seen again. He had managed to get to fifth grade. Test results found him to be of average intelligence with a marked reading disability, his reading and spelling being at second-grade level. Individual remedial reading instruction was given for one hour a week during the summer, beginning at a level below the point the boy had attained. Each letter was introduced singly; it was associated with its sound by writing and pronouncing. Small words were introduced by the old phonic method of families, that is, "cat," "mat," "bat," etc. He became enthusiastic and industrious and made progress when returned to the regular classroom in the fall. The assurance that he was not stupid was a great help to the child. This case is pointed to as typical of a large number of maladjusted schoolchildren. It is important to ascertain whether low IQ scores are influenced by reading disabilities.

2332   O'Brien, Frank J. "A child guidance approach to the treatment of a severe reading disability." <u>Underst Child</u> 7(1): 22-26, April, 1938. (0 References).
Reading disability rarely appears to be caused by a single factor. A "multiple-field" approach is necessary in treatment, just as a "multiple-sense" approach is used in tutoring. The case of Tony, a nine-year-old with an IQ of 120 and severe reading disability is given as an example of a full approach to a problem that did not respond to treatment of only one of its aspects. The boy needed help in social adjustment with his mother, in overcoming various perceptual difficulties, and in dealing with emotional problems generated by his school failure and his relationship with his mother.

2333   Park, George E.   "A case of simulated dyslexia."   Arch Pediatr
       68(4):   158-64, April, 1951.   (0 References).
Presents the case history of an eleven-year-old boy of superior intelligence who appeared to have simulated dyslexia in rebellion.   His mother
had exerted a great deal of pressure.   Both child and mother responded
well to suggestions of ways to lower the anxiety.   The child's school performance became very satisfactory.

2334   ————.   "Perplexing factors in reading retardation."   Arch Pediatr
       66(11):   500-511, November, 1949.   (6 References).
Offers a definition of dyslexia, pointing out that a child's learning
ability depends on his integrated capacities for evaluating and coordinating his experiences.   All abnormal factors may influence learning ability.
These factors are functional and treatable and may be corrected in con-
tradistinction to alexia.   A case history is offered to illustrate the
complexity of the factors which may cause dyslexia.

2335   Percival, A. S., and MacRae, Alex.   "Congenital tabes (?); congeni-
       tal word-blindness (?)."   Trans Ophthalmol Soc UK   47:   432-33,
       1927.   (0 References).
Although a sixteen-year-old girl displayed good general intelligence, she
was able to read only a few words.   Her reading ability appeared to depend partly on the size of the letters and partly on simplicity of the
words.   Her speech was normal; her eyes appeared to be normal except for
atrophic discs.   Knee and ankle jerks were absent which, with the atrophic
discs, suggests congenital tabes (progressive atrophy of the body or a
part of it).   The Wassermann test was negative.   It is suggested that she
suffered from congenital word blindness.

2336   Peterson, Adain.   "Dyslexia: a personal view."   Science   175(4025):
       946, March 3, 1972.   (0 References).
Letter to editor.   A father, who was a dyslexic child, reports his own
and his dyslexic son's approaches to their reading problems.   The grand-
father was also dyslexic.   The father memorized stories he heard being
read aloud, then compared the text with what he had memorized, thus
gradually learning to read.   The son learned with the aid of a tutor
using a reward system and a phonic approach.   It is concluded that dyslexia is a defect which seems lifelong.

2337   Phemister, Pippa.   "Dyslexia from the inside; with reply by Sandhya
       Naidoo."   Times Educ Suppl   3015:   4, March 9, 1973.   (0 References).
Recounts an adult's reminiscences of her childhood as a dyslexic.   She
was slow to walk and talk.   Vivid daydreams that turned any sort of pattern into people, trees, or mountains have persisted into adult life.
It is suggested that such daydreams are part of the "dyslexic temperament."   The letters of the alphabet—"shapes" as the dyslexic child
called them—all looked alike and all sounded alike.   Finally, in despera-
tion, at age twelve she learned to read print to find out what happened
in a serialized story.   Reading manuscript writing and learning to write
were frustrating because it appeared that the rules had been changed for
no reason: now all the "shapes" ran together.   Why was "m" one letter
and "in" two?   Her father's advice, "Never let the buggers get you down"
is the best advice a dyslexic can hear, she says.   She finally learned
to read, and became a writer.   In an appended reply titled, "Is she
typical?" Sandhya Naidoo of the Word Blind Centre points out that the
delays in walking and talking and speech problems are common concomitants
of dyslexia.   The fantasying and lack of envy of normal persons are not

typical. Today, reading and writing would be taught together and the
dyslexic child would be kept in the regular classroom, not allowed to
work alone as this child did. It is pointed out that in this case the
dyslexic child learned to read with exceptional speed when motivation
was sufficient. Educational opportunities should be geared to the height
of such a child's talents, rather than geared to the lowest point of
ability.

2338 Preston, Mary I. "Reading failure and the child's security." Am
      J Orthopsychiatry 10(2): 239-52, April, 1940. (0 References).
Matched groups of good and poor readers in the San Francisco area were
compared for their degree of security in home, social, and school situations. Case histories are given. Blighting insecurity caused by reading
failure was found in the poor readers' school and social worlds and sometimes at home. Some of the poor readers were taught to read by methods
suited to their individual needs, thus restoring security in all three
worlds.

2339 Preston, Ralph C., and Yarington, David J. "Status of fifty re-
      tarded readers eight years after reading clinic diagnosis." J Read
      11(2): 122-29, November, 1967. (16 References).
Fifty retarded readers who had been treated at the University of Pennsylvania reading clinic were followed up eight years later. Their achievements were found to roughly parallel those of their peers. However,
educational and vocational progress had come slowly. Most had repeated
grades in school and none had plans for professional or other graduate
study.

2340 Quinn, Margaret. "The abandoned child." Instructor 82(5): 16-17,
      January, 1973. (0 References).
Recounts a mother's story of her dyslexic son's struggles in school. The
boy wrote so slowly that he never finished an assignment. He could not
read fourth-grade arithmetic problems, and his spelling became a class
joke. He enjoyed being read to and his IQ was in the brilliant range.
After several school changes, the mother found a teacher who could cope
with a dyslexic child. A plea is made that no child be abandoned by
teachers and parents who misunderstand his problem.

2341 Rawson, Margaret B. Developmental language disability: adult ac-
      complishments of dyslexic boys. Baltimore, Maryland: Johns
      Hopkins, 1968. 127p. (Bibliography). (The Hood College Monograph
      Series, No. 2).
Presents a long-term study of fifty-six boys who attended a special school
for dyslexics. It is concluded that those boys diagnosed early as dyslexic have achieved educational and economical levels as high as those of
normal readers. Some find that their early reading problems are still a
hindrance, but that has not stopped their careers. It appears that some
may have been stimulated to greater achievement by their difficulties.
It is concluded that dyslexics aided by a special program can do as well
educationally and vocationally as the normal reader of the same intelligence and social class.

2342 Rench, Hazel S., and Moroney, Frances M. "A challenge: I can't
      read." Elem Engl 32(7): 455-58, November, 1955. (0 References).
This case history of Bob, a fifth grader, tells of the boy's progress
from overprotected withdrawal to normal relations with others. His resistance to learning to read gradually broke down as he gained confidence
in other areas.

2343 Risden, Gladys. "Nonreaders learned to read." Instructor 55(4):
      15, 71, February, 1946. (0 References).
Case histories are cited of three children who were upset emotionally by
their failure to learn to read. When given help with their problems they
learned to read quickly.

2344 Rockefeller, Nelson A. "Don't accept anyone's verdict that you are
      lazy, stupid or retarded." TV Guide 24(42): 12-14, October 16-22,
      1976. (0 References).
The former governor of New York and vice-president of the United States
recalls his difficulties as a dyslexic boy before there were special
schools and teachers for reading-disabled children. He learned to speak
three languages and credits his success to working harder than the students around him and never giving up.

2345 Rosen, Victor H. "Strephosymbolia: an intrasystemic disturbance
      of the synthetic function of the ego." Psychoanal Study Child
      10: 83-99, 1955. (56 References).
A twenty-one-year-old graduate student in mathematics sought psychoanalysis because of his inability to form any lasting relationships with women
and because of his disability in reading and spelling which threatened
to interfere with his academic ambitions. He was believed to suffer from
strephosymbolia. It is suggested that his writing errors arise from
alternate attempts to reproduce words in phonetic fashion without regard
to their visual appearance, or in ideographic fashion without regard to
the order of phonemes.

2346 Saunders, W. A. "Dyslexia versus illiteracy." Br Med J 2(5857):
      53, April 7, 1973. (0 References).
Letter to editor. Answers objections to an article by Saunders and Barker.
(See Item No. 2347). "Specific developmental dyslexia" and "dyslexia"
must be distinguished as they were by the research group on developmental
dyslexia of the World Federation of Neurology. The range of average intelligence on the WAIS is defended as being from 90 to 110.

2347 Saunders, W. A., and Barker, M. G. "Dyslexia as cause of psychi-
      atric disorder in adults." Br Med J 4(5843): 759-61, December
      30, 1972. (9 References).
Gives case histories of seven adult males who, in spite of conventional
schooling, were dyslexics, unable to read or write. They had hidden this
fact from business associates, friends, and children. Marital friction
was common. The men were often very sensitive about the disability. In
each case psychiatric disturbance appeared causally related to t.. dyslexia. A recognizable neurotic pattern was evident. Three patients
accepted individual reading help, but only one of these stayed in the
program and made impressive progress. The other refused help.

2348 Schwartzberg, Herbert. "The case of Andrew Miller: a retarded
      reader of above average intelligence." Elem Sch J 64(4): 200-
      204, January, 1964. (0 References).
It is necessary to treat the child's emotional difficulties before attempting to teach reading. This case study of an eleven-year-old sixth grader
shows the ways in which both parents and teachers failed to help the child
who could not read because of emotional factors.

2349 Scott, Ralph, and Pahre, Barbara. "The application of audio-tutorial
      techniques to remediation of learning disabilities: a case study."
      Psychol Sch 5(3): 277-80, July, 1968. (17 References).

Describes the case of a nine-year-old boy with a severe reading problem who was asked to listen to a story played on a tape, and then relate it orally. Results showed extensive oral language gains in this reticent child.

2350 Silberberg, Norman. "An open letter about a dyslexic man." <u>Minn Read Q</u> 15(1): 5-8, 38, October, 1970.

2351 Silver, Archie A., and Hagin, Rosa A. "Maturation of perceptual functions in children with specific reading disability." <u>Read Teach</u> 19(4): 253-59, January, 1966. (9 References).
Reading-disabled children seen in a hospital mental hygiene clinic from 1949 to 1951 were called back for study in 1962 when they were ages sixteen to twenty-four. As young adults, those with developmental reading disability (no clinical findings to suggest neurological disease) showed a greater degree of maturation in visual-motor functioning than did the young adults who as children had been classified as having organic neurological problems. Problems remained for the organic group in the perception of figure-background relationships, in orientation of figures in space, and in accurate perception of visual, auditory, and tactual stimuli. The developmental group had made striking progress in correcting perceptual deficits, but some problems of laterality persisted.

2352 Smith, Bert Kruger. <u>Dilemma of a dyslexic man</u>. Austin, Texas: The Hogg Foundation for Mental Health, University of Texas, 1969. 23p.

2353 ————. "Free to learn." <u>Am Educ</u> 8(5): 11-16, June, 1972. (0 References).
Recounts the childhood struggles of a young man named Murry Thompson in learning to read. In his twenties he discovered that he could learn by television. He is now attending college where he uses tape recordings to aid him in his academic work. He hopes to make a career of working with learning-disabled children. He developed ingenious ways to avoid revealing that he could not read or write. He finally found a doctor who diagnosed his problem as dyslexia. He was referred to teachers who specialized in teaching the reading-disabled. He has been helped by organizations that usually furnish recorded books to the physically blind. He is able to identify strongly with the reading-disabled youngsters to whom he teaches art.

2354 Stone, Clarence R. "A non-reader learns to read." <u>Elem Sch J</u> 30(2): 142-46, October, 1929. (0 References).
Documents a case study of a first-grade boy who had difficulty with reading probably because of mental immaturity and difficulty with remembering visual images of words. Under individual instruction he improved rapidly.

2355 Sylvester, Emmy, and Kunst, Mary S. "Psychodynamic aspects of the reading problem." <u>Am J Orthopsychiatry</u> 13(1): 69-76, January, 1943. (0 References).
Three case histories are presented, each illustrating one aspect of the problem of reading defects which have their origin in disturbances in psychobiological functions. The viewpoint is that disturbances in reading are disturbances in the child's exploratory function. The child must have the courage for active curiosity if he is to learn to read. Treatment by tutoring alone is not enough. When it succeeds, it is because the tutor has intuitively met some of the child's emotional requirements.

2356   Thompson, Lloyd J. "Language disabilities in men of eminence."
       J Learn Disabil 4(1): 34-45, January, 1971. (21 References).
As an encouragement to dyslexics and their teachers and parents, this
article lists some prominent men who, according to their biographies,
had difficulty learning to read and spell. Among those mentioned are
Thomas Edison, Albert Einstein, and General George S. Patton.

2357   VanWinkle, Edith. "Why first graders fail." Teach Coll J 14:
       7-8, 10, September, 1942. (0 References).
Brief case histories of sixteen children who were failing first graders
are presented. Most were thought to be too immature to learn to read.
Physical handicaps were common among the problem readers. Leaving these
children at home until they are older is not suggested as a solution
because the home environment is often unwholesome.

2358   Walsh, Maurice N. "Strephosymbolia reconsidered, a re-study of a
       specific inhibition of the use of visual and auditory verbal sym-
       bols." Int J Psychoanal 48(4): 584-95, 1967. (33 References).
This psychoanalytic case history analyses the twisting of symbols
(strephosymbolia) in terms of a retrogression in development rather than
as an initial failure to synthesize the phonetic and visual aspects of
words.

2359   Wightman, Jeannette K. "Teaching Becky to read." Acad Ther 10(3):
       369-71, Spring, 1975. (0 References).
Presents a case history of a first grader who was dropping behind in reading because she was being taught by the sight method. She learned to
read with tutoring by her mother in phonics. The method of beginning
with the short vowel, adding the final consonant, then adding the initial
consonant (for example, -a, -ad, mad) was her route to word-building and
sound-blending. It is pointed out that this method was used a century
ago when it was called the Syllabarium of the Alphabet Method of teaching
reading.

2360   Wollner, Mary H. B. "A case study of Bob." In: Conference on
       Reading, University of Chicago, 1960. Proceedings: sequential
       development of reading abilities. Vol. 22. Compiled and edited
       by Helen M. Robinson. Chicago, Illinois: University of Chicago
       Press, 1960. 205-9. (0 References). (Supplementary Educational
       Monographs, No. 90).
A twelve-year-old boy who worked very hard at his reading made progress
far below his apparent ability. He was found to have neurological involvement as a result of childhood chorea. His problem was complicated
by his lack of understanding of his problem and by his family's desperate
reaction to his problem. Because the child was a handsome, healthy-
looking youth, it was difficult to realize that he had specific handicaps.

2361   Word, Penny, and Rozynko, Vitali. "Behavior therapy of an eleven-
       year-old girl with reading problems." J Learn Disabil 7(9): 551-
       54, November, 1974. (4 References).
Through the use of desensitization techniques similar to those used to
alleviate specific fears, as of snakes or high places, an eleven-year-old
girl's fear of school punishment was reduced. Her reading problems were
reduced. The girl's extreme discomfort in situations where others were
reading appeared to stem from being punished in school. Relaxation training in which pleasant, relaxing feelings are associated with reading
situations was used. Such training engages the subject in behavior in-

compatible with anxiety. The association between the stimulus and the
resulting fear is broken in this way.

2362 Worster-Drought, C., and Allen, I. M. "Congential auditory imperception (congenital word-deafness): with report of a case." J Neurol
Psychopathol 9(35): 193-208, January, 1929. (14 References).
Describes the case of a twelve-year-old boy who was diagnosed as suffering
from "congenital auditory imperception," more exactly designated as word-
meaning-deafness. Slight word blindness, slight disabilities in writing,
and a pronounced speech defect were also present. The disorganization
of the speech mechanism was credited with causing the development of
idioglossia, an individual language of extremely mispronounced and ill-
expressed conventional language. The case illustrates the interdependence
of each part of the speech mechanism, especially of the dependence of
normal speech development upon the appreciation of variations in sounds.
The case is said to raise questions concerning the influence of "word-
deafness" on the development of idioglossia, on the development of general
intelligence, and on psychological reactions arising from such disability.

2362a ————. "Congenital auditory imperception (congenital word-deafness): investigation of a case by Head's Method." J Neurol
Psychopathol 9(36): 289-319, April, 1929. (6 References).
Describes a further investigation of the case of a twelve-year-old boy.
(See Item No. 2362). The method of study used was that of Henry Head.
(Head's tests consisted of a number of serial tests. These included the
naming and recognition of common objects, naming and recognition of
colors, tests using clock faces, and others. Originally devised for use
with men made aphasic by gunshot wounds in war, Head stressed the importance of maintaining the same order in which the tests follow each other.
Only then can the inconsistent responses typically produced by cerebral
lesions be successfully recorded. For a full description of Head's work
see Henry Head, "Aphasia and kindred disorders of speech." Brain 43
(Part 2): 87-165, July, 1920. (0 References). It is not included in
this bibliography.) The child had always had difficulty in speaking and
in appreciating the meaning of words. The studies included tests designed
to reveal spatial disorientations, the naming and recognition of common
objects, of colors, and other tests. The boy had developed idioglossia,
an individual language of his own in which he was fluent. On the receptive side he appeared to have a congenital inability to appreciate the
significance of words. On the executive side was his speech disturbance.
He could recognize letters, but some degree of word-meaning blindness
existed, and he applied his own idioglossic term in reading letters aloud.
He could copy written language perfectly. He used the same idioglossic
term consistently for naming common objects and colors, and attempted to
read conventional language by using idioglossic terms.

2363 Youmans, John S. "They call him 'dumb.'" Acad Ther 10(3): 363-
67, Spring, 1975. (2 References).
The case history of a reading-disabled boy who made up nine grade levels
of reading in two years of remedial training is related.

X
Bibliographies

2364 Becker, George J., and Trela, Thaddeus M. "Case studies in reading." <u>J Read</u> 15(6): 436-38, March, 1972. (0 References).
Lists ten books and journal articles which give case studies on reading
representative of diagnostic and instructional procedures. Grade levels
of the cases presented range from primary to adult.

2365 Betts, Emmett Albert. <u>Bibliography on the problems related to the</u>
  <u>analysis, prevention, and correction of reading difficulties</u>.
  Meadville, Pennsylvania: Keystone View Co., [1934]. 86p.
This mimeographed publication contains a total of 1,198 full bibliographic
entries. Except for a brief section of summaries of research, the entries
are unclassified and are arranged alphabetically by author. Most entries
are from the 1920s and 1930s. It is unannotated. Nearly all references
are to works in English. Included are many facets of remedial teaching,
speech, vision, hearing problems, handedness, mirror reading, intelligence
as a factor in IQ test performance, the psychology of reading, and other
areas.

2366 Betts, Emmett Albert, and Betts, Thelma Marshall. <u>An index to pro-</u>
  <u>fessional literature on reading and related topics (to January 1,</u>
  <u>1943)</u>. New York: American Book Co., 1945. 137p.
Gives full bibliographic entries for 1,278 references arranged alphabetically by author. Entries are unannotated. In addition to material
about normal readers, this book contains much material on remedial and
corrective reading, reversals in reading, word blindness, alexia, strephosymbolia, aphasia, causes of reading difficulties, and other phases of
reading disability. A subject index is provided.

2367 Brewer, William F. <u>Specific language disability: review of the</u>
  <u>literature and family study</u>. Honors thesis, Harvard College, 1963.
  6p.

2368 Chicorel, Marietta, series ed. <u>Chicorel abstracts to reading and</u>
  <u>learning disabilities</u>. Eileen Sargent and Muriel Vogel, coeds;

Mark Winwood, managing ed. New York: Chicorel Library Pub. Corp.,
1976. 384p. (Chicorel Index Series, Vol. 19).
This volume of the Chicorel series of bibliographies contains about 1,200
entries and is organized alphabetically by subject area. It provides
abstracts of journal articles in the areas indicated in the title published
during the preceding year. An author index is provided.

2369 ————————. Chicorel index to learning disorders--books. New York:
Chicorel Library Pub. Corp., 1975. 1027p. (Chicorel Index Series,
Vol. 18, pp. 1-528; Vol. 18A, pp. 529-1027).
Contains about 2,500 entries arranged by subject area. Entries in each
area are alphabetically listed by author. Materials included are English
language monographs (books) under such headings as hyperactivity, dyslexia, aphasia, auditory agnosia, minimally brain handicapped, neurologically handicapped, and many other subject headings. Entries are
annotated. Full bibliographic citations are given.

2370 ————————. Chicorel index to reading and learning disabilities:
an annotated guide: books. New York: Chicorel Library Pub. Corp.,
1976. 349p. (Chicorel Index Series, Vol. 14A).
Combines the fields of reading disabilities and learning disorders covered
in separate prior volumes in the Chicorel series. About 600 books are
entered and no duplicate entries from Vols. 14, 18, or 18A of this series,
all previously published, are included. Annotations are provided. This
book reverts to the format of Vol. 14 with all entries in one alphabetical
list with a separate subject index.

2371 ————————. Chicorel index of reading disabilities: an annotated
guide. New York: Chicorel Library Pub. Corp., 1974. 428p.
(Chicorel Index Series, Vol. 14).
This alphabetically arranged bibliography contains some 1,400 references
to English-language books and journal articles in the field of reading
disabilities. Evaluative annotations are included and a subject index
is provided.

2372 Dyslexia: a selective bibliography. Exceptional Child Bibliography
Series No. 652. 1975. 15p. (ED 104 063).
Contains about fifty abstracts on dyslexia which were published from 1966
to 1973 and taken from the files of the Council for Exceptional Children's
Information Services and ERIC. Most of the abstracts include bibliographic information, indication of subject matter, and a summary of contents. Various aspects of dyslexia are covered, including diagnostic
tests, remedial instruction, and causes.

2373 Dyslexia: Exceptional Child Bibliography Series. 1971. 20p.
(ED 054 579).
This bibliography of eight-four annotated references was selected from
Exceptional Child Education Abstracts. Material from journal articles,
texts, research reports, and teaching or program guides concerning dyslexia is included. Identification and educational diagnosis, laterality
and other neurological aspects, perception, reading difficulties and
skills, and treatment methods are among areas considered. Bibliographic
data and availability information are given.

2374 Edgington, Ruth, and Clements, Sam D. Indexed bibliography on the
educational management of children with learning disabilities
(minimal brain dysfunction). Chicago, Illinois: Argus Communications, 1967. 109p.

Consists of 370 entries covering nineteen subject areas which are keyed
to the bibliography entries. Among other areas covered are perception,
language disorders, and reading as a basic tool subject.

2375 Foxhall, G. J., compiler. Dyslexia: congenital word-blindness.
      Adelaide, Australia: State Library of South Australia, 1969. 22p.
      (Research Service Bibliographies Series 4, No. 122).
This bibliography includes 251 books and journal articles published from
1958 to 1969, inclusive. Most are in English but some French and German
materials are cited. It is not annotated. Arrangement is chronological.
The scope covers all relevant materials indexed in the Australian Educa-
tion Index; Education Index; Index Medicus; Library of Congress: Books:
Subjects; National Library of Medicine, Current Catalog; and Psychological
Abstracts. Dates searched vary with the publication.

2376 Gray, William Scott. Summary of investigations related to reading.
      Chicago, Illinois: University of Chicago, 1925. (Supplementary
      Educational Monographs, No. 28). 275p. Same. Supplement No. 1,
      a continuation of monograph No. 28. (July 1, 1924, to June 30,
      1925). Chicago, Illinois: Department of Education, University of
      Chicago, 1926. 46p. [Reprinted from Elem Sch J 26(6, 7, 8, 9),
      February, March, April, and May, 1926].
In a little more than 200 pages Gray summarizes most of the reports on
research in reading published in America and England prior to July, 1924.
To this is appended a bibliography of 436 items with brief annotations.
Most of the materials concern reading and methods of teaching it for
normal readers. However, one chapter on diagnosis of problems and remedial instruction is included, and the supporting researches are included
in the bibliography. The supplement carries the work forward through
June 30, 1925, with an annotated bibliography of seventy-three items and
a discussion of work similar to that presented in the main volume. This
appears to be the first comprehensive bibliography of research reports
on reading. For the following thirty-four years Gray presents an annual
summary of reading investigations in the Elem Sch J (1926-1932) and in
the J Educ Res. Helen M. Robinson continues his work with annual summaries of research in reading published in the Read Teach through 1965.
Beginning in 1966, the summary is published in Read Res Q under various
editorships. It is believed that more than 5,000 studies in reading
have been reported in these summaries. Individual citations are not given
to these annual summaries because the focus of these bibliographies is
all-inclusive and concerned chiefly with the needs of normal readers.

2377 Individual learning disabilities: a bibliography. 1968. 53p.
      (ED 034 340).
Contains 739 entries including books, journal articles, video and audio
tapes, films, testing materials, and catalogs, among other forms of information. The subject matter is mainly concerned with learning disabilities, but is not limited to that topic. Dates range from 1926 to 1968.

2378 Information Center for Hearing, Speech, and Disorders of Human
      Communication. Dyslexia; bibliography. Baltimore, Maryland:
      Information Center for Hearing, Speech, and Disorders of Human
      Communication. The Johns Hopkins Medical Institutions, 1973. 25p.
      Mimeographed. Numbered I-897.
Two hundred twenty items, most of them journal articles, are arranged
alphabetically by author under eleven subject headings. Most works cited
are in English, but some French and German references are included.

Bibliographies in the field, incidence of the condition, causes, medical
and psychological aspects, dyslexia as a learning disability, research
and testing, and rehabilitation are among the areas covered. The period
of the search is January, 1970 to December, 1972.

2379 ————. Language and learning disabilities; bibliography. 292
      references: 1962-1973. Period of search: January, 1969-May, 1973.
      Baltimore, Maryland: Information Center for Hearing, Speech, and
      Disorders of Human Communication, 1973. 26p.

2380 Kress, Roy A., and Johnson, Marjorie Seddon, compilers. Providing
      clinical services in reading; an annotated bibliography. Phila-
      delphia, Pennsylvania: Temple University, 1966. 9p.

2381 Learning disabilities; research studies and program considerations.
      Exceptional Children Bibliography Series. 1969. 32p. (ED 036 026).
Includes 139 entries in the area of learning disabilities. Diagnosis,
teaching methods, perceptual problems, physical problems, and treatment
are topics covered.

2382 Mangrum, Charles T., compiler. A citation bibliography of selected
      sources on dyslexia and learning disabilities. Bloomington, Indiana:
      Indiana University, ERIC Clearinghouse on Reading, 1968. 78p.
      (ED 020 865).
Contains approximately 1,400 citations from 1868 to 1967 relating to dyslexia and learning disabilities. The bibliography is a compilation of
lists submitted to ERIC/CRIER by investigators in the field. The arrangement is alphabetical by author. Cited are books, monographs, manuals,
and published and unpublished journal literature and papers.

2383 National Institute of Neurological Diseases and Stroke. Selected
      annotated bibliography on technical articles on dyslexia, 1960-
      1967 (267 references). Washington, D.C.: U. S. Department of
      Health, Education, and Welfare. [no date].

2384 National Library of Medicine. Dyslexia: diagnosis therapy, physio-
      pathology: Jan. 1967-Dec. 1969. 162 citations. Bethesda, Maryland,
      1970. 8p. (National Library of Medicine Literature Search, No.
      70-7).

2385 Rawson, Margaret B. A bibliography on the nature, recognition and
      treatment of language difficulties. Revised ed. Towson, Maryland:
      Orton Soceity, 1974. 152p.
First published in 1966, and revised in 1969 and 1974, and characterized
as a selected reading and reference list, this bibliography contains publications from 1887 to 1974. Materials are organized under the following
categories: (1) medicine, neurology, and psychology; (2) language and
semantics; (3) education; (4) various developmental and remedial approaches to language learning; (5) specific language disability; (6) psychological, achievement, and diagnostic tests; (7) manuals, workbooks, instructional materials, and texts for students; (8) journals--annual,
quarterly, and monthly; and (9) bibliographies. There is a section of
foreign publications. Almost all entries are in English and coverage is
a little broader than the field of dyslexia alone. Book entries provide
publisher and date, but generally do not cite place of publication or
pagination. Items are included if they were judged to be relevant to the
general interests and specific needs of persons concerned with language

and its disorders. Brief annotations are evaluative. Materials from the
Bulletin of the Orton Society are not included. The user is referred to
the cumulative indexes of that journal to be used in conjunction with
this bibliography.

2386 Reading diagnosis and remediation: a companion bibliography to
      Ruth Strang's monograph. ERIC/CRIER Reading Review Series, Bibliog-
      raphy 31. 1972. 276p. (ED 058 019).
Planned as a companion volume to Ruth Strang's monograph, Reading Diagnosis and Remediation (Item No. 28), this annotated bibliography contains complete citations to all literature cited in the Strang work in
addition to pertinent research literature which has appeared since the
original work was published. The same categories used in the monograph
are followed in the bibliography. Correlates and causes of reading disability and achievement, dyslexia, diagnosis and remediation of reading
disabilities, and future trends are all considered.

2387 Reading methods and problems: a selective bibliography. Excep-
      tional Child Bibliography Series, No. 613. 1972. 32p. (ED 072
      588).
This selected bibliography contains about 100 abstracts from the file of
abstracts held as of August, 1972, by the Council for Exceptional Children Information Center. Criteria for inclusion were availability of the
document to users, currency, information value, the author's reputation,
and classical content. Publication dates for documents included is from
1943 to 1971. The abstracts were originally published in Exceptional
Child Education Abstracts.

2388 Reading methods and problems: Exceptional Child Bibliography
      Series. 1971. 15p. (ED 051 594).
Fifty-seven entries with abstracts were selected from Exceptional Child
Education Abstracts including research reports, conference papers,
journal articles, texts, and program guides. Topics cover diagnosis and
remediation of reading problems, dyslexia, skill development, perceptual
handicaps, and instructional materials. The bibliography is one of a
series of more than fifty similar selected listings covering the education of the gifted or handicapped child. Bibliographic data and availability information are given.

2389 Reading methods and problems (handicapped children). Exceptional
      Children Bibliography Series. 1969. 13p. (ED 036 021).
Contains forty-one entries with abstracts on various aspects of reading
methods and problems. Dyslexia, sensory impairment, teaching techniques,
and physiological considerations are topics included. Information is
given on purchasing individual documents or the total collection.

2390 Recent research in reading. A bibliography 1966-1969. New York:
      CCM Information Corp., 1970. 300p.
Materials on all aspects of reading are covered. Subject and author
indexes are provided. Entry by ERIC document number is also given, with
the abstract for each entry. Coverage of dyslexia materials is not extensive.

2391 Shrigley, Roger M., compiler. "Dyslexia: a select bibliography."
      Educ Libr Bull No. 42: 24-28, Autumn, 1971.
A list of forty-nine entries in several languages comprises this bibliography. It is published as a supplement to the list produced by the

Invalid Children's Aid Association, London, and attempts to cover journal articles in particular. It is unannotated.

2392 Trela, Thaddeus M., and Becker, George J. <u>Case studies in reading: an annotated bibliography</u>. Newark, Delaware: International Reading Association, 1971. 15p.
This annotated bibliography lists approximately seventy-five titles of basic materials on reading disability and a few general works. The rest is divided into sections by the grade level with which the material is concerned.

2393 Vernon, Magdalen Dorothea. "Visual perception relating to reading --information sources." <u>Read Teach</u> 28(2): 184-86, November, 1974. (0 References).
Young children have difficulty in perceiving complex forms. This may hinder them in learning to read. This problem, although not common in older children, may persist in those who are backward in reading. Deficiencies may be especially apparent in visual memory, in verbal memory for sequential order, and in matching spatial with temporal sequences. Ten studies that have been done in this area are discussed.

2394 Vernon, Magdalen Dorothea, compiler. "Ten more important sources of information on visual perception in relation to reading." <u>Read Teach</u> 20(2): 134-35, November, 1966. (0 References).
This annotated bibliography of ten items includes references on the development of the ability to perceive forms accurately in normal children and on the visual-perceptual difficulties of backward readers. It is pointed out that perceptual difficulties do not appear to affect normal readers much, but backward readers display a variety of perceptual deficiencies.

XI
Directories, Dictionaries, Glossaries, and Serial Publications Devoted Entirely to Dyslexia

2395 Bulletin of the Orton Society. Towson, Maryland. Annual, Vol. 1, 1951-.
The Orton Society, a scientific and educational organization, was formed in 1949 in memory of Dr. Samuel T. Orton (1879-1948). The Bulletin of the society is published annually for the publication of selected papers presented at its annual meetings, together with original articles and reprints of articles from other sources. The outlook reflects that of Dr. Orton, a neurologist who coined the term "strephosymbolia," or twisted symbols, to describe the confusion in letter and word orientation and other symptoms manifested by some children of normal intelligence who have marked difficulty in learning to read. Such children, Dr. Orton believed, were the victims of delayed or incomplete establishment of one-sided motor preferences (unilateral cerebral dominance). Such children might be left-handed or ambidextrous and right-eyed, or the reverse. While showing no evidence of brain damage, such children often showed delays in development or defects in various language areas of the brain. They learned by the "sight" or "whole-word" teaching method only with difficulty and did much better with phonics instruction. They showed difficulty in remembering whole-word patterns. Anna Gillingham was associated with Dr. Orton for a time, and from this work grew the Gillingham-Stillman method of remedial reading instruction. Dr. Orton's interest in the reading, writing, and speech problems of children and his publications in the field extended from 1925 to 1946. Some issues of the Bulletin review and summarize his work. The bibliography of his publications is sometimes reprinted. Other papers published cover a variety of topics concerning specific reading disability. Articles include material on the background of the concept, description of the syndrome, diagnostic methods, treatment, and teaching problems and methods. Articles which are reprinted in the Bulletin of the Orton Society from other sources will be found abstracted in this bibliography with their original citations. No mention is made of reprint locations. Articles published originally in the Bulletin are not separately abstracted and do not appear individually in this bibliography. Early editions of the Bulletin were compiled and edited by June Lyday Orton, Dr. Orton's wife.

2396 Ellingson, Careth, and Cass, James. <u>Directory of facilities for the learning-disabled and handicapped.</u> New York: Harper & Row, 1972. 624p.
Arranged by state, this directory describes the facilities available for the treatment of dyslexia and a wide variety of other educational, speech, language, physical, and emotional handicaps in fifty states and in Canada. The diagnostic facilities of each organization are described. The remedial, developmental, and therapy programs available are reported, including ages accepted, cost, and qualifications of the staff.

2397 Gunderson, Doris V. "Reading problems: glossary of terminology." <u>Read Res Q</u> 4(4): 534-47, Summer, 1969. (0 References).
Presents the glossary of terms used in the area of reading problems compiled by the Interdisciplinary Committee on Reading Problems which grew out of a conference called by the Center for Applied Linguistics. Because reading is the concern of many disciplines, including, among others, psychology, education, sociology, linguistics, and several medical specialities, compiling a glossary was thought to be most appropriate. Different researchers from the various disciplines have used the same terminology to mean different things. Communication has been hampered. Terms are listed alphabetically. A key is used to identify the discipline or disciplines in which each term is used. A definition is given.

2398 "1967 directory of schools and clinics for the learning and reading disabled." <u>Acad Ther</u> 2(4): 236-38, Summer, 1967. (0 References).
Lists schools, clinics, and similar agencies in fourteen states which furnish supplementary and remedial programs for learning and reading-disabled persons.

2399 Pope, Lillie. <u>Learning disabilities glossary: a practical guide to the terminology used in learning disabilities, reading disabilities, and related areas.</u> Brooklyn, New York: Book-Lab, 1976. 60p.
Defines terminology encountered in the areas listed in a glossary for the layman. Medical, educational, and psychological terms are included. Some words of art that have come into special use in learning and reading disabilities are listed. For example, the terminology used in connection with the ITPA is explained. The introduction to the book contains a list of "labels" used in the areas covered by the glossary. They are included, it is reported, to expose and clarify some of the problems and confusion in the field. A bibliography (pp. 55-59) of recommended readings in learning and reading disabilities and related concepts and a selected list of professional and special-interest associations are other features of the book.

2400 Schubert, Delwyn G., in consultation with Theodore L. Torgerson. <u>A dictionary of terms and concepts in reading.</u> 2nd ed. Springfield, Illinois: Thomas, 1969. 376p.
This dictionary contains more than 1,900 terms used in the field of reading drawn from many related fields of knowledge: vision, speech, psychology, endocrinology, neurology, audiology, library science, and linguistics. Some of the clinical tests employed in reading by specialists, for example, the Bender Visual Motor Gestalt, are listed. All definitions are brief. Pronunciations of technical or unfamiliar words are given. Numerous terms used in connection with the teaching of normal children are included, together with terms used by those working with dyslexics.

2401 <u>Word blind bulletin</u>. London. Vol. 1, February, 1963-.
Published by the Word Blind Committee of the Invalid Children's Aid
Association, this periodical is devoted entirely to dyslexia and the
interests of dyslexics. Articles have appeared on various methods of
treatment, including the Fernald auditory-kinesthetic, the Stott programmed reading kit, and psychoeducational and physiological approaches. It
was in this publication that Alex D. Bannatyne published some of his
research proposals and his proposed classification system of the causes
of dyslexia. Alfred White Franklin, T. R. Miles, Macdonald Critchley,
and other writers in the field of dyslexia have contributed. Research
progress is covered. The parents' viewpoint and articles concerned with
the origins of dyslexia are included. Book reviews and case studies are
used. More emphasis is on treatment, however. The first number of
Volume 2 appeared in 1967.

Appendix A:
Basic Bibliographic Tools

1. Armed Forces Medical Library Catalog
2. Besterman, Theodore. A World Bibliography of Bibliographies
3. Bibliographic Index
4. British National Bibliography
5. Chicorel Index of Reading Disabilities, Vol. 14
6. Chicorel Index to Learning Disorders, Vol. 18 and Vol. 18A
7. Chicorel Index to Reading and Learning Disabilities, Vol. 14A
8. Child Development Abstracts
9. Cumulative Book Index
10. Current Index to Journals in Education (CIJE)
11. Current List of Medical Literature
12. Developmental Disabilities Abstracts
13. Dissertation Abstracts
14. Dissertation Abstracts International
15. Education Index
16. Exceptional Child Education Abstracts
17. Government Reports Annual Index
18. Index Catalogue of the Library of the Surgeon-General's Office
19. Index Medicus, all series
20. International Index to Periodicals
21. Language and Language Behavior Abstracts
22. Menninger Clinic Library Catalog
23. Monthly Catalog of U. S. Government Publications

24. National Library of Medicine Catalog
25. National Union Catalog
26. New York Academy of Medicine Subject Catalog of the Library
27. Perceptual Cognitive Development
28. Proceedings in Print
29. Psychological Abstracts
30. Readers' Guide to Periodical Literature
31. Recent Publications in the Social and Behavioral Sciences; the ABS Guide to Recent Publications in the Social and Behavioral Sciences
32. Research in Education (ERIC)
33. Research Relating to Children Bulletin
34. Resources in Education (ERIC)
35. Science Citation Index
36. Social Sciences Citation Index
37. Social Sciences and Humanities Index
38. Social Sciences Index
39. Sociological Abstracts
40. Sophia F. Palmer Memorial Library Catalog, American Journal of Nursing Company
41. Subject Guide to Books in Print
42. Subject Guide to Forthcoming Books
43. United States Catalog
44. United States Government Research Reports

Appendix B:
Some Definitions of Dyslexia

ARCHIE A. SIVER and ROSA A. HAGIN. "Dyslexia." Collier's Encyclopedia,
Vol. 8, 1975. pp. 462-63.

A condition in which an individual's reading ability is below expectation with respect to his intelligence and his opportunities for
education. It is a term used to designate a symptom, that of reading
retardation in a person of adequate intelligence who has had educational
opportunity equal to that of his peers. It does not represent a homogeneous group, but is a broad term including many categories of diverse
causes....
    The causes of reading retardation are many and varied. There are
environmental conditions, including educational, social, and cultural
factors; psychological problems of attitude, motivation, and attention;
and biological factors (genetic, physiological, and structural) that
interfere with the acquisition of those skills required for language....
    An important diagnostic subgroup is known as developmental dyslexia
or specific language disability. This diagnosis implies that vision and
hearing acuity is adequate, that there is no evidence of structural defect of the central nervous system, that there is sufficient motivation
to read, and that intelligence and educational exposure have been adequate. The child with developmental dyslexia has a basic disturbance
in spatial and temporal orientation, that is, in organizing symbols in
space and sounds in time....

ELOISE CALKINS. American Education 8(5): 16, June, 1972.

Contrary to widespread assumption, "dyslexia" does not have a
single, established definition that everyone accepts. Despite a good
deal of research--or perhaps because of it--the word has accumulated a

wide range of meanings, many of them contradictory. Thus a documented
list of definitions recently published in one of the professional journals
came to a total of 20, no two of them in agreement. Within the scientific and professional communities this wide variation of opinion extends
not only to a definition of the precise learning problem encompassed by
"dyslexia" but to what its causes and symptoms are.

Originally, the word was used to identify a form of brain damage
that deprives the patient of his ability to recall words, letters, and
symbols. By extension, it has come to refer simply to a disorder of
reading, without specific regard to what might lie behind that disorder
and how it should be treated.

Most authorities thus agree that pending the completion of considerable interdisciplinary communication and study aimed at eliminating
the confusion, the word should be used with great caution. As popularly
and loosely applied, it can unfairly label a child--and more important
deny him effective help by focusing on a problem he may not have.

RESEARCH GROUP OF THE WORLD FEDERATION OF NEUROLOGY ON DYSLEXIA AND
WORLD ILLITERACY, April, 1968, as quoted in Macdonald Critchley,
"Developmental dyslexia as a specific cognitive disorder." In: Jerome
Hellmuth, ed. Deficits in cognition. New York: Bruner/Mazel, 1971.
(Cognitive studies, Vol. 2). p. 47.

A disorder manifested by difficulty in learning to read despite
conventional instruction, adequate intelligence, and socio-cultural
opportunity. It is dependent upon fundamental cognitive disabilities
which are frequently of constitutional origin.

MACDONALD CRITCHLEY. The dyslexic child. 2d ed. London: William
Heinemann Medical Books, Ltd., 1970. p. 11.

The arguments in favour of the existence of a specific type of
developmental dyslexia occurring in the midst of but nosologically apart
from the olla podrida of bad readers, has been said to rest upon four
premises. These comprise: persistence into adulthood; the peculiar
and specific nature of the errors in reading and spelling; the familial
incidence of the defect; and the greater incidence in the male sex. To
these criteria may be added: the absence of signs of serious brain-
damage or of perceptual defects; the absence of significant psychogenesis;
the continued failure to read despite conventional techniques of instruction; and the association of normal if not high intelligence.

RICHARD B. ADAMS. "Dyslexia: a discussion of its definition." Journal
of Learning Disabilities 2(12): 616-33, December, 1969, at page 618.

If man is master of his own inventions then he is free to manage
the meaning of his words to suit his own conventions. But sometimes a
word gets born which, rather than live as servant to man, moves out in
life like a Frankenstein monster wreaking havoc in the discourse of
sensible men. Dyslexia is such a word. Its meaning is obscure and it
has divided the efforts of professional men when collaboration would have
been the better course....The definition problem has gotten so bad that
it must be made clear that the polyphony of semantics was not meant to
be carried on according to a private tune.

E. Y. ZEDLER. "Conference charge." Research Conference on the Problem
of Dyslexia and Related Disorders in Public Schools of the United States.

Final Report of U. S. Office of Education Project 7-8270, Southwest Texas
State College, San Marcos, Texas. As quoted by Richard B. Adams, Journal
of Learning Disabilities 2(12): 616-33, December, 1969, at pages 631-
32.

We should not permit semantics to dissipate our time and energies.
Many meetings and millions of words have not resolved the question of
What is dyslexia?... If you prefer some other term use it, with the
understanding that you are talking about the kind of child who cannot un-
scramble auditory and/or written symbols which reach the brain so that
they have the same order-pattern and meaning which they have for others.

S. ALAN COHEN. "Dyslexia." Encyclopedia Americana. Vol. 9, 1969. p.
516.

Dyslexia is regarded by some authorities as a definite neurological
or psychological disorder with characteristic symptoms and specifiable
causes. Most of these authorities include the combination of illegible
handwriting and poor spelling, together with average or above average
intelligence, among the symptoms of dyslexia. Some include general dyssymbolia, the inability to formulate thoughts into language, as a symptom
of dyslexia, and others limit dyslexic symptoms to problems of translating and combining symbols into concepts. Still others include as dyslexics poor readers who also have difficulties with hand-eye coordination. This poor coordination, they feel, accounts for the distorted
handwriting, poor spelling, and evidence of neurological disorders that
may be associated with dyslexia.
Among the causes suggested for dyslexia are brain damage and inherited neurological abnormalities not associated with brain damage.
Environmental factors, such as poor teaching, are also regarded as possible causes.

JOHN V. V. NICHOLLS. "Children with reading difficulties." American
Journal of Ophthalmology 60(5): 935-37, November, 1965, at p. 935.

It is a useful working basis to think of reading disabilities as
falling into one of three categories:
    1. Congenital dyslexia, which is a specific reading disability,
occurring in the presence of an average or above average intelligence.
It is much more common in the male. It often is familial, and is probably due to a physiologic disturbance or delayed maturation of the
parietotemporal lobe of the dominant cerebral hemisphere. Sometimes,
there is evidence of actual brain damage.
    2. The slow reader (who must be clearly distinguished from the
first type) is one in whom the disability is related to low intelligence,
faulty vision or hearing, to emotional disturbances, or to a combination
of these.
    3. The mixed type, a mixture of the first two types. A common
combination, particularly in a child who has gone a long time without
attention, is congenital dyslexia with emotional disturbance superimposed.

KNUD HERMANN. Reading disability: a medical study of word-blindness
and related handicaps. Copenhagen: Munksgaard, 1959, at pages 17, 18,
34.

The term is to be understood to signify a defective capacity for acquiring, at the normal time, a proficiency in reading and writing corresponding to average performance; the deficiency is dependent on constitutional factors (heredity), is often accompanied by difficulties with other symbols (numbers, musical notations, etc.), it exists in the absence of intellectual defect or of defects of the sense organs which might retard the normal accomplishment of these skills, and in the absence of past or present appreciable inhibitory influences in the internal and external environments....

This primary form of reading handicap is to be distinguished from several other, secondary, forms in which the development of reading ability is hampered by various factors in the internal and external environments. These latter cases of reading disability are not nearly so persistent nor so difficult to overcome as the primary form (word-blindness), provided the cause can be discovered and is such that it can be removed.

ARTHUR L. DREW. "Familial reading disability." University of Michigan Medical Bulletin 21(8): 245-53, August, 1955, at p. 247.

For [some]...purposes we may best define congenital dyslexia by exclusion. Thus there is said to exist a group of patients whose reading ability is grossly impaired and in whom no difficulty of basic visual or auditory receptive apparatus, amentia, dementia, neurological disease or injury, or serious psychiatric illness exists. These then are the "congenital dyslexic" patients. Whether they represent a clear-cut clinical entity is as yet uncertain.

RALPH D. RABINOVITCH; ARTHUR L. DREW; RUSSELL N. DeJONG; et al. "A research approach to reading retardation." Research Publications: Association for Research in Nervous and Mental Disease 34: 363-96, 1954, at page 364 and page 387.

Through the years the tendency has been to define the clinical entity in terms of its causation and there has been a wide diversity of opinion as to etiology with three major factors stressed: 1) A neurologic deficit akin to aphasia. 2) A developmental lag depending upon uneven growth in the child and compensated for in time. 3) An emotional disturbance to which the reading problem is secondary....

It seems valid and useful to recognize three major groups: (a) Those in whom the reading retardation is due to frank brain damage manifested by gross neurologic deficits, among which are aphasias of various types. (b) Those, with no history of gross clinical findings to suggest neurologic disease, who present a basic defect in capacity to integrate written material and to associate concepts with symbols. A neurologic deficit is suspected in these cases, and to describe them we have used the term primary reading retardation. (c) Those cases demonstrating reading retardation but with normal potential for learning to read; because the reading difficulty is the result of personality or educational neglect factors we have described these cases as secondary reading retardation....

In the primary group the defect appears to be part of a larger disturbance in integration. Our findings suggest that we are dealing with a developmental discrepancy rather than an acquired brain injury. The specific areas of difficulty manifested in the clinical examinations are those commonly associated with parietal and parietal-occipital dysfunction.

BERTIL HALLGREN. "Specific dyslexia ('congenital word-blindness'): a
clinical and genetic study." Acta Psychiatrica et Neurologica (Supplement) 65, 1950, at pages 1, 2, 4.

No clear and uniform definition of the disorder exists. Skydsgaard
(1942) summarized the view generally accepted in the medical literature
as follows: "Congenital dyslexia (a term which, on the whole, covers
the condition commonly named word-blindness) denotes in clinical medicine
primary constitutional reading difficulties which may occur electively
and which, in their pure form, differ distinctly from reading difficulties of other (endogenous or exogenous) origin."

From a clinical point of view, Skydsgaard drew the borderline between "constitutional dyslexia" and "physiological variants" at the
level where--taking into consideration the influence of exogenous factors
--normal reading ability could not be attained with the use of the
customary teaching methods. This borderline is, however, indefinite and
varies in the works of different authors....

More recently, the borderlines have become more elastic, so that
the term "congenital word-blindness" now includes milder reading and
writing disabilities as well....

It is customary to differentiate between primary and secondary
reading and writing disabilities. The primary disabilities occur when
there are disturbances in one or more of the partial functions necessary
for the processes of reading and writing. The secondary difficulties
are caused by factors not directly associated with these processes.
"Congenital word-blindness" is usually regarded as primary....

JAMES HINSHELWOOD. Congenital word-blindness. London: H. K. Lewis,
1917, at page 40.

By the term congenital word-blindness, we mean a congenital defect
occurring in children with otherwise normal and undamaged brains char-
acterised by a difficulty in learning to read so great that it is mani-
festly due to a pathological condition, and where the attempts to teach
the child by the ordinary methods have completely failed.

A Hierarchial Classification of the

Universe of Study   All Language and

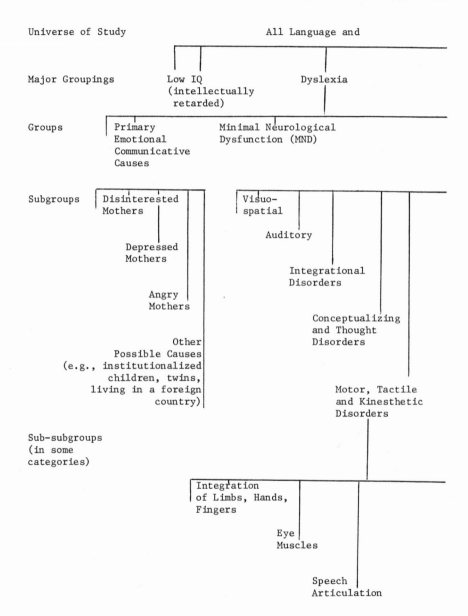

Major Groupings   Low IQ   Dyslexia
                       (intellectually
                       retarded)

Groups   Primary   Minimal Neurological
                  Emotional   Dysfunction (MND)
                  Communicative
                  Causes

Subgroups   Disinterested   Visuo-
              Mothers   spatial

                                              Auditory

                         Depressed
                         Mothers
                                              Integrational
                                              Disorders

                         Angry
                         Mothers
                                              Conceptualizing
                                              and Thought
                              Other   Disorders
                       Possible Causes
                  (e.g., institutionalized
                      children, twins,
                  living in a foreign
                          country)   Motor, Tactile
                                              and Kinesthetic
                                              Disorders

Sub-subgroups
(in some
categories)
                           Integration
                           of Limbs, Hands,
                           Fingers

                                   Eye
                                   Muscles

                                        Speech
                                        Articulation

Causes and Types of Dyslexia

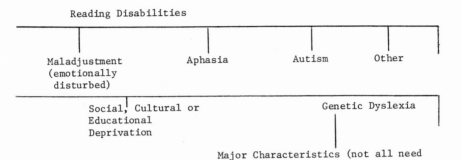

Reading Disabilities

Maladjustment (emotionally disturbed)   Aphasia   Autism   Other

Social, Cultural or Educational Deprivation   Genetic Dyslexia

Major Characteristics (not all need be present):

1. Often poor auditory discrimination of vowels.
2. Inadequate phoneme-grapheme sequencing memory (for matching).
3. Poor sound blending and auditory closure on experience.
4. Mildly deficient speech development and feedback which may persist.
5. Maturational lag in most language functions.
6. Reasonably efficient visuo-spatial ability.
7. Unlateralized gaze (when reading).
8. Mirror imaging and writing of letters (hemispheric in origin?)
9. Directional configuration inconstancy also causing mirror imaging of letters.
10. Difficulty in associating verbal labels to directional concepts but no visuo-spatial disorientation of any kind.
11. Residual spelling disability.
12. Poor self-concept

From Alexander Bannatyne. Language, reading and learning disabilities: psychology, neuropsychology, diagnosis and remediation, 1971. Courtesy of Charles C. Thomas, Publisher, Springfield, Illinois.

Appendix C:
Glossary

acalculia - Inability to do simple arithmetic. Inability to comprehend
the abstract concepts represented by numbers.

afferent nerve - Any nerve that transmits impulses toward the central
nervous system. A sensory nerve. See efferent nerve.

agnosia - Inability to recognize or interpret information gained from
one's senses, that is, what is seen, heard, felt, or tasted.
      finger agnosia - Loss of ability to identify one's own or
         another's fingers.

agraphia - Inability to write. Inability to remember how to write letters
of the alphabet; inability to relate the visual or mental images
of words to the movements necessary to write them.

alexia - Inability to read in the presence of normal vision and after
adequate opportunity to learn. See aphasia.

ambidextrous - Using the left and right hands with equal facility.

amblyopia - Dimness of vision not caused by refractive errors or by any
apparent change in the eye structures.
      strabismic amblyopia - Suppression of vision in one eye to
         avoid double vision.

anarthria - Speechlessness resulting from dysphasia (lack of coordination in speech).

angular gyrus - A cerebral convolution forming part of the back of the
parietal lobe of the human brain.

anomia - Inability to name objects although they may be clearly seen, or
to recognize names.

aphasia - Loss or impairment of the power to use words by speech, writing, or signs. Impairment or loss of the ability to comprehend spoken or written language.
> expressive aphasia - Inability to speak, even though one knows what he wants to say and is able to understand written and spoken words. Called also ataxic, Broca's, or motor aphasia.
> receptive aphasia - Inability to understand written, spoken, or tactile speech. Called also sensory aphasia.
> visual aphasia - Loss of ability to comprehend written language.

aphemia - Loss of the power of speech because of brain damage or disease.

apraxia - Loss or impairment of the ability to use objects correctly. Inability to perform a desired skilled act or series of movements.

astigmatism - A refractive error in which light is not properly focused on the retina but is spread over an area. It is caused by irregular curvature in the cornea or lens of the eye. See refractive error.

auditory dyslexia - Difficulty in writing what is heard or in associating a sound with the symbol for that sound. Difficulty in hearing speech sounds accurately in the presence of no organic ear problems.

auditory-visual integration - The ability to remember the printed letters standing for specific sounds in words, or the reverse.

Binet test - An intelligence test for children. Sometimes called the Binet-Simon test or the Stanford-Binet test.

body image - The picture or mental representation a person has of his own body. One's evaluation of his own body, a person's idea of how his body looks to others. Body image is derived from internal sensations, emotions, fantasies, and contact with others.

body schema - The characteristic way in which one is aware of his own body. The overall pattern of one's awareness of his own body.

boustrophedon writing - An ancient form of writing in which a line reading from left to right is followed by a line reading from right to left. So called because the direction of the writing is similar to the course followed by oxen plowing a field.

Broca's aphasia - Expressive aphasia. See aphasia.

Broca's center - The part of the cerebral cortex containing the speech center. So called for the nineteenth century French anthropologist and physician, Paul Broca.

central nervous system (CNS) - The brain and the spinal cord.

cerebral - Pertaining to the cerebrum.

cerebral cortex - The gray matter composing the external layer of the brain. See cerebrum.

cerebral dominance - The supremacy, or superior manifestation, of one cerebral hemisphere over the other in the case of some functions, especially speech and handedness. Right-handedness is thought usually to indicate that the left cerebral hemisphere is dominant.

cerebral hemisphere - One of the two symmetrical halves of the cerebrum. The brain is divided lengthwise by a deep valley (longitudinal fissure) extending from the brow to the back of the head forming the left and right cerebral hemispheres.

cerebrum - The largest and main portion of the brain. The outer coating of gray cells is called the cortex. The cortex is the part of the brain involved in thinking, reasoning, intellect, and direction of conscious movement. It receives information from the senses.

closure - The tendency to close or complete a situation in behavior or in a mental act. For example, if we see a drawing of an incomplete geometric figure the mind's tendency is to complete the drawing. Used in Gestalt psychology.

cluttering - Rapid, excited speech uttered in such a manner that it is indistinct, words are run together, and syllables may be dropped out. It may occur under emotional pressure.

CNS - See central nervous system.

cognition - Knowledge in its widest sense, including both awareness and judgment. Perception, memory, introspection, thinking, the process by which we become aware of objects of thought and perception, and the judgments based upon those perceptions are all included.

cognitive - See cognition.

cognitive style - The individual's characteristic approach to problem solving or other cognitive tasks.

concretism, concreteness - Used in the field of education to mean an approach to learning and behavior in which a person tends to regard each situation as unique. Inability to generalize from one situation to another, particularly in learning new things. Inability to see similarities between situations or things.

congenital - Refers to a condition present at birth which is assumed to result from faulty development, infection, injury, etc., in the uterus.

corpus callosum - The arched mass of white matter lying at the bottom of the longitudinal fissure of the brain. It is thick at each end, but thinner in its long central portion. The white transverse fibers connect the two cerebral hemispheres.

cortex - See cerebrum.

cross-modal integration - The ability to link information obtained by
     different senses. For example, to tell whether flashes of light
     are following the same pattern as sounds from a buzzer presented at
     or near the same time. Lack of cross-modal integration is the in-
     ability to coordinate sensory information, that is, learning ob-
     tained through one or more of the five senses: hearing, seeing,
     touch, taste, smell.

cursive writing - Writing with the letters joined together, as opposed
     to printing.

decoding - The process of translating unfamiliar material into a familiar
     form. Decoding skill is the term applied to the child's ability
     to read, i.e., to turn the unfamiliar written symbols into spoken
     words he knows. See encoding.

digraph - A group of two successive letters used to make one sound, for
     example, "ea" in bread. When the two letters are consonants, for
     example, "ch" in chip, the form may be referred to as a consonant
     digraph.

diplopia - Double vision.

dominant hemisphere - The side (hemisphere) of the brain which is more
     concerned than the other with the control and integration of many
     functions. Speech is thought to be represented and controlled by
     the dominant hemisphere.

double-blind experiment - A study in which neither the experimenter (ad-
     ministrator) nor the subject knows at the time the testing is done
     whether the substance being tested is active or inert.

duction - The movement of an eye by the external muscle of the eye
     under monocular conditions.

dyscalculia - Difficulty in learning to do arithmetic. Difficulty in
     comprehending the relationship between mathematical concepts and
     symbols.

dysgraphia - Impairment in the ability to write; difficulty in remember-
     ing how to form letters of the alphabet or mathematical symbols.

dysphasia - Lack of coordination in speech and failure to arrange words
     in proper order. Related to brain damage.

dysrhythmia - Used in reading disability literature to refer to a dis-
     turbance in rhythm observed in some children with speech disorders.
     In describing electroencephalographic tracings the term refers to
     irregularities or disturbances in the rhythm of the brain waves.

echolalia - Repetition by a person of what is said to him as if echoing.
     Often pathological.

EEG - See electroencephalogram.

efferent nerve - Any nerve that transmits impulses from the central
     nervous system outward. A motor nerve. See afferent nerve.

eidetic imagery - Voluntarily producible visual images of a peculiarly vivid type having almost photographic accuracy. Common in childhood.

electroencephalogram - A record or tracing of the electrical currents in the brain produced by a machine called an electroencephalograph. Called EEG.

electronystagmography - An electronic means of recording eye movements that provides objective documentation of induced and spontaneous eye movements (nystagmus).

emmetropia - The ideal optical condition; neither nearsighted nor farsighted, but with the rays of light entering the eye coming to a focus on the retina.

encoding - Used in the field of reading to mean the child's ability to write, especially to write to dictation, turning the spoken words into an acceptable written code. See decoding.

engram - A lasting mark or trace; a memory trace. Term used by Samuel Orton to describe the physiological records of words stored in both hemispheres of the brain. Orton believed engrams on the nondominant side to be mirror images of the engrams stored in the dominant hemisphere. Mixed laterality resulting in reversals and twisted symbols occurred when the mirror image engrams from the nondominant side were used.

etiology - The study of causes and origins, particularly of diseases or abnormal conditions.

exceptional child - A child who deviates from normal mental, physical, or social characteristics to such an extent that modified or special educational practices are necessary in order for him to develop to his maximum capacity.

Fernald method - A method of teaching reading perfected by Grace Fernald in which the child traces over the word to be learned with his finger, saying the word as he traces, until the word is learned. Called also the kinesthetic method.

field of vision - The entire area which can be seen without moving the eyes from the straight-ahead position; the visual field.

figure-ground discrimination - The process of detecting a difference between an object in the foreground and the background against which the object is seen. Any object with its background shows figure and ground, and the differences between figure and ground may be striking, depending upon the circumstances. The term has its origin in Gestalt psychology where it may refer to spatial, auditory, or temporal perception. As used in reading disability literature it refers most often to the pattern formed by the letters or words as seen against the background of the page upon which they are printed.

frontal lobe - The front portion of the brain. Concerned with motor activities and with volitional and emotional behavior.

genetic - Refers to a trait or condition assumed to be inherited not acquired; hereditary.

Gerstmann's syndrome - A disorder of cerebral function caused by a brain lesion in the area of the left angular gyrus and characterized by finger agnosia, right-left disorientation, acalculia, and agraphia.

gestalt (plural gestalten or gestalts) - A form or structure of physical, biological, or psychological phenomena which taken together constitute a unified whole with properties which cannot be derived from the parts. A whole perceptual configuration.

Gestalt psychology - The study of perception and behavior from the standpoint of the person's response to a whole perceptual configuration. Analysis of a percept or a response in terms of their being made up of many simple elements is rejected. Applied in reading by teaching the child to see a word as a whole rather than by breaking the word into its parts.

Gillingham method - A method of teaching reading perfected by Anna Gillingham, an associate of Dr. Samuel Orton. It is basically a phonic method.

grapheme - A letter of an alphabet. Also, all of the written letters or combinations of letters that represent one sound (phoneme) in a language. See phoneme.

haptic - Refers to the sense of touch. In reading literature often refers to tactile-kinesthetic response.

hemianopia, hemianopsia - Defective vision or blindness in half of the visual field. Caused by a brain lesion.
> homonymous hemianopia - Defective vision or blindness in the same half of each retina affecting either the right halves or the left halves of the visual fields of the two eyes.

hereditary - Refers to traits or conditions transmitted genetically, that is, from parents to offspring.

hyperactivity - Habitual nervous, fidgety behavior characterized by constant motion, excitability, distractibility, short attention span, and low tolerance for frustration. Although of normal intelligence, hyperactive children do not do well in school and are distracting in the classroom. Stimulant and antidepressant drugs paradoxically calm many such children, although drug therapy is regarded as controversial. Adolescence usually brings relief from the symptoms of hyperactivity.

hyperkinetic - Overactive. See hyperactivity.

idiopathic - Of unknown cause.

intersensory transfer - Term used in psychology and education to refer to the ability to transfer a stimulus from one sense to another. For example, the ability to write down as a series of dots, a series of taps being heard.

ITA - Initial Teaching Alphabet, a 44-letter alphabet in which each let-
    ter represents only one sound. Capital letters have the same shape
    as small letters. Designed by Sir James Pitman in England. Some-
    times written i.t.a.

ITPA - Illinois Test of Psycholinguistic Abilities. A test of language
    abilities for children. Development of this test brought with it
    its own technical terms. Representational level, decoding, encod-
    ing, association process, and automatic-sequential level are among
    the terms encountered in the literature of reading and its dis-
    orders which are used in a technical sense in this test.

kinesthesia - The sense by which position, weight, and movement are known.

kinesthetic - See kinesthesia.

kinesthetic method - A method of teaching reading by having the child
    trace the word to be learned with his finger saying it as he traces
    its outline. See Fernald method.

laterality - Sidedness. Used in referring to the hand, eye, or foot
    most preferred by an individual for writing, sighting, or kicking.

legasthenia - A condition characterized by inability to associate mean-
    ings with or to derive meanings from printed or written symbols.

lesion - A broad term referring to almost any kind of tissue damage.
    Used in the literature of dyslexia to refer to injury or disease
    of a part of the brain which damages or destroys the ability to
    read and/or write.

linguistics - The study of human speech. Includes the study of the
    units, nature, modification, origin, and structure of a language.

lobes of the brain - The four main divisions of the brain: frontal,
    parietal, temporal, and occipital.

logorrhea - Pathologically incoherent, repetitious speech; excessive or
    abnormal talkativeness.

look-and-say method - A method of teaching reading in which the child is
    taught to recognize and read a word as a whole configuration (its
    total visual appearance) rather than being taught to break the word
    into syllables or other phonetic units.

maturation - The process of becoming mature. The growth and development
    that results in maximum intellectual and emotional development with
    the emergence of personal and behavioral characteristics.

maturational lag - The uneven or irregular development and maturing of
    intellectual, emotional, and behavioral characteristics in a
    child.

MBD - See minimal brain dysfunction.

minimal brain damage - See minimal brain dysfunction.

minimal brain dysfunction – A term used to designate a syndrome affecting
    children, usually boys, which can be described, although the causes
    are still debated and no single symptom is sufficient for diagnosis.
    The MBD child is one with average or better intelligence with learn-
    ing and/or behavioral abnormalities ranging from mild to severe.
    Such children are usually hyperactive--restless, unable to sit
    still, always into everything, often clumsy. They have trouble in
    school, and may have particular difficulty with reading and writing,
    in addition to creating a distraction in the classroom.

mirror reading – Tendency to read words backwards, as "no" for "on."

mirror writing – Tendency to write from right to left. The words are
    reversed as if seen in a mirror.

mixed cerebral dominance – The condition in which an individual does not
    prefer the eye, hand, and foot all on one side of the body for
    skilled uses, as for example, the preference of the left hand for
    writing and the right foot for kicking in one person, or some other
    combination of mixed use. It has been thought to be an indication
    that one cerebral hemisphere does not consistently dominate the
    brain, leading to language problems, particularly in speech and
    reading.

mixed laterality – See mixed cerebral dominance.

multisensory – Using or appealing to more than one of the five senses at
    the same time. Sometimes used to refer to a method of teaching
    reading which appeals to sight, hearing, and touch all three or in
    some combination.

myelinization – Development of the soft material surrounding the nerve
    fibers.

myotactic – Pertaining to the ability of the muscles to give information
    concerning position and movement of the body through the action of
    the sensory nerve endings called proprioceptors.

neonatal – Refers to the first four weeks after birth.

neuropsychology – An area of study dealing with the relationship between
    behavior and the nervous system in normal organisms. Usually
    applied to experimental work with lower animals.

nystagmus – Rhythmic, involuntary movement of the eyes in any direction,
    vertical, horizontal, or rotary.
        optokinetic nystagmus – That induced by watching a moving
            object, for example, looking at a train passing by.

occipital lobe – One of the four main divisions of the brain. Located
    at the back of the brain; concerned chiefly with vision.

operant conditioning – Learning in which the learner performs a specific
    act, previously designated, because the act produces a reward or
    other desirable consequence. Called also instrumental conditioning.
        operant behavior – Behavior, usually initiated by the learn-
            er, whose rate or form is modified by the consequences.

ophthalmology - The branch of medicine dealing with the eyes, including
their anatomy, physiology, and diseases.

orthoptics - Treatment by the use of exercises for crossed eyes and other
forms of strabismus in order to develop complete binocular vision.

paired-associate learning - A procedure in which items to be learned are
presented in pairs. The first item of the pair is then presented
alone for a short time. The learner is asked to recall the other
item of that pair. The technique is used to study the ability to
learn and retain material.

parietal lobe - One of the four main divisions of the brain. The lobe
of a cerebral hemisphere which lies approximately above the ear
between the temple and the back of the head.

perception - The awareness of objects, relationships, or qualities.
Awareness of the elements of the environment. Conscious awareness
of sensory stimulation.

perception span, memory span - The number of discrete elements (for
example, digits) which can be remembered after hearing or seeing
them only once. Memory span tests sometimes form a part of intelligence tests.

perinatal - Refers to the period around the time of birth, from about
the eighth month of pregnancy until the child is from one to four
weeks of age.

phoneme - The smallest unit of speech that distinguishes one sound from
another in a language. The basic sound units of speech from which
words are built. See grapheme.

phonetics - The system of speech sounds of a language; the application
of such a system to language study. See phonics.

phonics - A method of teaching reading to beginners in which the sounds
in a language are studied and systematically classified. The letters, letter groups, and syllables are learned according to groups
and their phonetic value.

primary reading disability - Term sometimes used to describe a dyslexia
in which there is no evidence of gross neurological disease, but
a neurological deficit is suspected. A basic defect in capacity
to associate concepts with symbols which appears to be part of a
larger disturbance in integration. The source is usually considered to be developmental rather than the result of brain injury. Sometimes called primary reading retardation.

proprioceptor - Any of the nerve endings giving information on the movements and position of the body. Muscles, tendons, and the internal
ear are the chief sites of these sensory nerves.

psychoneurological learning disability - Abnormal behavior resulting from
a lack of function in the brain which produces some alteration in
the mental processes. Not a generalized inability to learn.

psychoneurology - Field of study in which the disorder observed is some aberration of behavior and the cause is neurological.

readability - A measure of the difficulty or complexity of any printed material.

refractive error - Any of these four conditions: nearsightedness (myopia), farsightedness (hyperopia), astigmatism, and presbyopia (lessening of the ability of the lens of the eye to accommodate for near vision). All of these defects in vision are caused by deviations from normal in the way an image is focused on the retina of the eye. In general, such errors can be corrected with eyeglasses.

reversals - The errors made by beginning readers in which single letters may be turned around (p for q, m for w) or the order of letters within words is reversed (yam for may, was for saw) or even whole phrases may be reversed in reading or writing. The tendency persists abnormally long in dyslexics.

rotation - Turning letters of the alphabet at incorrect angles so that they appear upside down or backwards (b for p, or d for p).

secondary reading retardation - Term sometimes used to refer to the condition in which a child of normal intelligence is unable to learn to read adequately evidently as a result of personality or emotional problems, physical problems, educational neglect, or some other external factor or factors.

sequencing ability - The ability to learn and remember a series of things (for example, letters in a word) in the order in which they were presented on a previous occasion.

sequential processing - Dealing with a series of items (for example, words or digits) in their proper sequence or serial order.

serial memory - See sequencing ability.

Snellen chart - A chart with letters or symbols printed on it in gradually decreasing sizes used to measure visual acuity.

"soft" neurological signs - Equivocal or borderline findings on standard clinical tests used by the physician in evaluating neurological soundness.

specific developmental dyslexia - A disorder in which the child, usually a boy, experiences unusual difficulty in learning to read in spite of adequate intelligence, conventional reading instruction, and adequate cultural and economic background. It may be of hereditary origin.

specific dyslexia - See specific developmental dyslexia.

specific language disability - See specific developmental dyslexia.

strabismus - Deviation from the normal position of an eye when both eyes are open and uncovered which the patient cannot control. Among the forms of strabismus are cross eye and squint.

strephosymbolia – A term coined from the Greek by Samuel T. Orton and meaning literally twisted symbols. Used by Orton and others to refer to symptoms such as reversals and left-right confusion which were thought to occur in children when complete unilateral cerebral dominance was not established. See mixed cerebral dominance.

synapse – The junction between two nerve cells; the point where a nerve impulse is transmitted from one nerve cell (neuron) and another. There is no direct contact between nerve cells. The transmission is chemical in nature.

syndrome – A group of symptoms or signs which, considered together, characterize a disease or other abnormal condition.

syntactic – Pertaining to the rules of syntax.

syntax – The way in which words are put together to construct phrases, clauses, or sentences.

tachistoscope – An instrument which gives a very brief timed exposure, which may be varied, of visual material such as pictures, digits, or letters.

tactile; tactual – Pertaining to touch.

temporal lobe – One of the four main parts of the brain. The inferior lateral area of the brain. Plays a role in hearing, listening, and in interpretation of sounds.

traditional orthography – Refers to the usual spelling of words using the traditional 26-letter alphabet. Used in contrast to some other systems for teaching writing which employ an alphabet or more or different characters, as, for example, the I.T.A. where a 44-letter alphabet is used in which each letter represents only one sound.

tropia – Any of the various forms of strabismus.

VAKT – Short way of referring to a multisensory teaching method involving visual, auditory, kinesthetic, and tactile senses. Sometimes used to refer to the Fernald kinesthetic method.

vergence – Tendency of the eyes to move in opposite directions.

visual aphasia – See aphasia.

visual dyslexia – Difficulty in interpreting printed or written symbols (words or letters) accurately in the presence of no organic eye problems. Letters or words may be perceived upside down, backward, or in some other unsatisfactory manner.

visual-motor integration – Refers to the efficiency with which hand or other motor movements are coordinated with the task the eye sees. The very young child is improving visual-motor integration when he develops the knack of putting the clothespin in the bottle.

WAIS - Wechsler Adult Intelligence Scale, an intelligence test for adults made up of a number of subtests and divided into two main parts, or scales. They are the verbal scale and the performance scale. The test score for the entire test is referred to as the full scale IQ. Originally prepared by David Wechsler, this test is sometimes referred to as the Bellevue intelligence test.

Wernicke's aphasia - Sensory aphasia. The inability to understand the meaning of written, spoken, or tactile speech symbols, due to disease of the auditory and visual word centers. Named for the nineteenth century German neurologist who discovered the region of the human brain concerned with comprehension of spoken or written language.

WISC - Wechsler Intelligence Scale for Children, an intelligence test for children made up of a number of subtests and divided into two main parts, the verbal test and the performance test. The test score for the entire test is referred to as the full scale IQ.

word-attack skills - A term applied to a reader's ability to analyze an unknown word by breaking it into syllables or other phonic elements in order to arrive at its pronounciation and possibly its meaning.

word blindness - A term for dyslexia more commonly used in the nineteenth and early twentieth centuries. It refers to the inability to learn to read by a person of normal intelligence with normal vision and hearing who has had adequate instruction in reading and has no particular emotional difficulties. Called also congenital word blindness.

Author Index

In the list below, the numbers after each name

refer to item numbers in the Bibliography

A

Ables, S., 968, 2257
Ablewhite, R. C., 1670
Abrams, J., 2128
Abrams, J. C., 422, 649, 745,
  1108, 1109, 1511, 1749, 1791,
  2052
Abramson, P., 650
Ackerman, A., 2053
Ackerman, P. T., 564
Adams, R. B., 59
Adelman, H., 1533
Adelman, H. S., 1374
Advisory Committee on Handicapped
  Children, See:
  Great Britain. Advisory
  Committee on Handicapped Children
Aftanas, M. S., 658
Ahnsjö, S., 1375
Akins, K., 2054
Alden, C. L., 1671
Alexander, D., 871, 872
Alexander, J. E., 1110
Alford, T. D., 1264
Alger, E. M., 410
Allais, E., 1194
Allen, I. M., 2362, 2362a
Allen, J. E., Jr., 1553, 1554
Allen, R. P., 2171
Allington, R. L., 1195
Allmond, B. W., Jr., 115

Alm, R. S., 642, 1792
Altus, G. T., 1376
Alwitt, L. F., 520, 1225
Alworth, R. M., 953
Ames, L. B., 590
Anapolle, L., 61, 1041, 1042
Ancevich, S. S., 2258
Anderson, A., 1785
Anderson, E., 62
Anderson, H. B., 445
Anderson, I. H., 651
Anderson, R. F., 441
Anderson, R. P., 1061, 1167,
  1555, 2043, 2076
Anderson, U. M., 1265
Anderson, W. F., 2131
Anthony, G. A., 303
Antonini, P., 11
Applebee, A. N., 1
Appleman, J. H., 1030
Arajärvi, T., 1084, 1266
Arcieri, L., 2055
Arena, J. I., 1750, 1956, 1957
Arkell, H., 63
Arnold, R. D., 1672, 1881
Arnott, W., 1022
Arthur, B., 741
Arthur, G., 1527, 2312
Artley, A. S., 1181, 1556
Ashbrenner, M., 1925
Asher, W., 296
Ashlock, P., 1751

Selective Key Word
Subject Index

In the list below, the numbers after each word

refer to item numbers in the Bibliography

1099, 1110, 1115, 1118, 1136,
1139, 1140, 1141, 1145, 1511,
1515, 1524, 2078, 2134, 2271
Phi Thresholds,   873
Phonetic,   1210
Phonics,   1398, 1821, 1929, 2010
Physical,   674, 1017, 1030, 1174,
1241, 2006, 2044, 2229
Physician, -s,   119, 183, 1265,
2120, 2124
Physiology, -ical,   141, 815, 1043,
1059, 1063, 1072, 1073, 1500
Piaget,   853
Picture-Frustration Study,   1098
Pituitary,   1062
Plasticity,   596
Play Therapy,   453, 2059, 2060
Postman and Bruner Theory,   1111
Post-mortem Examination,   2190
Poverty,   2175 See also:
Socioeconomic Status
Practitioner,   1271 See also:
Physician
Preadolescent, -s,   1084, 1541
Pregnancy,   1079, 1082
Prenatal,   1080 See also:
Antenatal; Paranatal; Perinatal
Preschool, -er,   461, 480, 1431,
1466, 1512, 2007
Prevention, -ing, -ive,   5, 333,
764, 1208, 1406, 1545, 1598,
1665, 1674, 1695, 1731, 1732,
1789, 1939, 2001, 2141, 2145,
2325, 2365
Primary Dyslexia,   676, 850, 1534
Primary Grade, -s,   348, 470, 940,
1003, 1521, 1697, 1968 See also:
Grade, and Individual Grade
Numbers, e.g., Grade Three
Primary School,   532, 533 See
also: Elementary School;
Infant School; School
Proceedings,   12, 13, 18, 164,
1635, 1683, 1684
Process, -es, -ing,   270, 291,
292, 767, 962, 966, 973
Prosopagnosia,   1487
Psychiatrist,   1091
Psychiatry, -ic,   288, 618, 798,
801, 849, 1084, 1106, 1314,
1410, 2012, 2082, 2085, 2347
Psychoanalytic,   1114, 2061
Psychobehavioral,   122
Psychobiologic,   1086
Psychodynamic, -s,   1143, 1144,
2355
Psychoecology,   1199

Psychoeducational,   16, 1249, 1500,
2075
Psychogenic,   456
Psycholinguistic, -s,   261, 277,
406, 894, 933, 1125, 1126,
1321, 1325, 1498, 1518, 2259
See also: Linguistic
Psychologist,   221
Psychology, -ical,   2, 14, 39,
57, 123, 141, 265, 527, 589,
690, 730, 782, 793, 825, 1122,
1123, 1124, 1130, 1146, 1163,
1166, 1203, 1207, 1281, 1498,
1506, 1520, 1522, 2136, 2201,
2329
Psychometric,   749, 971, 1293
Psychoneurological,   856 See
also: Neuropsychology
Psychopathology,   1094
Psychosocial,   465, 501, 1513,
2079, 2090
Psychotherapy, -eutic,   2054,
2062, 2069
Public School, -s,   302, 1005,
1444, 1668, 1704, 1828, 2240
See also: School
Pupil, -s,   699, 1212, 1301,
1600, 1656, 1968, 2135, 2165,
2177, 2240
Pursuit,   1045, 1046

Q

Quick Test,   1407

R

Race,   1082 See also: Black;
Negro
Rate,   647, 1257, 2070
Reaction Time,   623, 877, 916,
938, 949, 954, 2130
Readiness,   503, 1227, 1228,
1242, 1243, 1250, 1374 See
also: Reading Readiness
Reading Achievement,   248, 304,
316, 337, 343, 351, 452, 499,
573, 580, 807, 961, 982, 999,
1552, 1575, 1774, 2043, 2045,
2153, 2161, 2166 See also:
Achievement
Reading Epilepsy,   796
Reading Miscue Inventory,   1544
Reading Readiness,   390, 617,
680, 1552, 1665, 1975 See
also: Readiness
Regression to the Mean,   276

List of Journal Abbreviations

Abbreviation	Title
A	**A**
Acad Ther	Academic Therapy Quarterly
ACLD Proc	Association for Children with Learning Disabilities Conference Proceedings
Acta Ophthalmol	Acta Ophthalmologica
Acta Paediatr (Suppl)	Acta Paediatrica (Supplement) [Uppsala]
Acta Paediatr Scand	Acta Paediatrica Scandinavica
Acta Paediatr Scand (Suppl)	Acta Paediatrica Scandinavica (Supplement)
Acta Paedopsychiatr	Acta Paedopsychiatrica
Acta Psychiatr Neurol	Acta Psychiatrica et Neurologica
Acta Psychiatr Neurol (Suppl)	Acta Psychiatrica et Neurologica (Supplement)
Acta Psychiatr Neurol Scand (Suppl)	Acta Psychiatrica et Neurologica Scandinavica (Supplementum)
Acta Psychol	Acta Psychologica; European journal of psychonomics
Acta Psychother Psychosom Orthopaedagog	Acta Psychotherapeutica Psychosomatica et Orthopaedagogica
Acta Symb	Acta Symbolica
Adv Neurol	Advances in Neurology
Adv Pediatr	Advances in Pediatrics
AEP J	AEP (Association of Educational Psychologists) Journal
AEP J Newsl	AEP (Association of Educational Psychologists) Journal and Newsletter
AEP Newsl	AEP (Association of Educational Psychologists) Newsletter
Ala J Med Sci	Alabama Journal of Medical Sciences
Alta J Educ Res	Alberta Journal of Educational Research

Abbreviation	Title
Am Educ	American Education
Am Educ Res Assoc Off Rep	American Educational Research Association Official Report
Am Educ Res J	American Educational Research Journal
Am Fam Physician	American Family Physician
Am J Dis Child	American Journal of Diseases of Children
Am J Epidemiol	American Journal of Epidemiology
Am J Med Sci	American Journal of the Medical Sciences [Philadelphia]
Am J Ment Defic	American Journal of Mental Deficiency
Am J Neurol Psychiatry	American Journal of Neurology and Psychiatry
Am J Ophthalmol	American Journal of Ophthalmology
Am J Optom	American Journal of Optometry
Am J Optom Arch Am Acad Optom	American Journal of Optometry and Archives of the American Academy of Optometry
Am J Orthopsychiatry	American Journal of Orthopsychiatry
Am J Psychiatry	American Journal of Psychiatry
Am J Psychol	American Journal of Psychology
Am J Psychother	American Journal of Psychotherapy
Am Med Surg Bull	American Medico-Surgical Bulletin [New York]
Am Orthopt J	American Orthoptic Journal
Am Pract News	American Practitioner and News [Louisville]
Am Psychopathol Assoc Proc	American Psychopathological Association Proceedings
Ann Hum Genet	Annals of Human Genetics
Ann NY Acad Sci	Annals of the New York Academy of Sciences
Ann Ophthalmol	Annals of Ophthalmology
Ann Paediatr Fenn	Annales Paediatriae Fenniae
Anthropol Linguist	Anthropological Linguistics
Appl Ther	Applied Therapeutics
Arch Dis Child	Archives of Disease in Childhood
Arch Med	Archives of Medicine [New York]
Arch Neurol	Archives of Neurology
Arch Neurol Psychiatry	Archives of Neurology and Psychiatry [Chicago]
Arch Ophthalmol	Archives of Ophthalmology
Arch Otolaryngol	Archives of Otolaryngology
Arch Pediatr	Archives of Pediatrics
Arch Speech	Archives of Speech
Ariz Teach	Arizona Teacher
ASHA	ASHA: Journal of the American Speech and Hearing Association
Atl Mon	Atlantic Monthly
Audiology	Audiology: Journal of auditory communication
Audiov Instr	Audiovisual Instruction
Aust J Psychol	Australian Journal of Psychology

Abbreviation	Title
Aust Paediatr J	Australian Paediatric Journal

B	B
Behav Neuropsychiatry	Behavioral Neuropsychiatry
Better Homes Gard	Better Homes and Gardens
Br J Child Dis	British Journal of Children's Diseases
Br J Disord Commun	British Journal of Disorders of Communication
Br J Educ Psychol	British Journal of Educational Psychology
Br J Math Stat Psychol	British Journal of Mathematical and Statistical Psychology
Br J Med Psychol	British Journal of Medical Psychology
Br J Ophthalmol	British Journal of Ophthalmology
Br J Proj Psychol Pers Study	British Journal of Projective Psychology and Personality Study
Br J Psychiatry	British Journal of Psychiatry
Br J Psychol	British Journal of Psychology
Br Med J	British Medical Journal
Brain	Brain; a journal of neurology
Brain Lang	Brain and Language
Bristol Med Chir J	Bristol Medico-Chirurgical Journal
Bull Br Psychol Soc	Bulletin of the British Psychological Society
Bull Los Angeles Neurol Soc	Bulletin of the Los Angeles Neurological Societies
Bull Menninger Clin	Bulletin of the Menninger Clinic
Bull Neurol Inst NY	Bulletin of the Neurological Institute of New York
Bull NY Acad Med	Bulletin of the New York Academy of Medicine
Bull Orton Soc	Bulletin of the Orton Society
Bull Psychon Soc	Bulletin of the Psychonomic Society
Bull Vancouver Med Assoc	Bulletin of the Vancouver Medical Association

C	C
Calif J Educ Res	California Journal of Educational Research
Calif J Second Educ	California Journal of Secondary Education
Calif Med	California Medicine
Calif Teach Assoc J	California Teachers Association Journal
Can Educ Res Dig	Canadian Education and Research Digest
Can J Behav Sci	Canadian Journal of Behavioural Science/Revue Canadienne des Sciences du Comportement

Abbreviation	Title
Can J Ophthalmol	Canadian Journal of Ophthalmology
Can J Public Health	Canadian Journal of Public Health
Can Med Assoc J	Canadian Medical Association Journal
Can Psychiatr Assoc J	Canadian Psychiatric Association Journal
Can Psychol	Canadian Psychologist
Case Rep Clin Psychol	Case Reports in Clinical Psychology
Cathol Educ Rev	Catholic Educational Review
Cathol Sch J	Catholic School Journal
Cereb Palsy Bull	Cerebral Palsy Bulletin
Cereb Palsy J	Cerebral Palsy Journal
Changing Times	Changing Times; the Kiplinger magazine
Chic Med	Chicago Medicine
Chic Sch J	Chicago Schools Journal
Child Dev	Child Development
Child Educ	Childhood Education
Child Psychiatry Hum Dev	Child Psychiatry and Human Development
Child Study	Child Study
Child Welfare	Child Welfare
Claremont Coll Read Conf Yearb	Claremont College Reading Conference Yearbook
Clear House	Clearing House; a journal for modern junior and senior high schools
Clin Pediatr	Clinical Pediatrics
Clin Proc Child Hosp DC	Clinical Proceedings of Children's Hospital of the District of Columbia [Washington]
Cognitive Psychol	Cognitive Psychology
Coll Stud J	College Student Journal; a journal pertaining to college students
Colo Med	Colorado Medicine
Compr Psychiatry	Comprehensive Psychiatry
Conf Read Univ Chic Proc	Conference on Reading University of Chicago Proceedings
Conf Read Univ Pittsburgh Rep Annu Conf	Conference on Reading University of Pittsburgh Report of the Annual Conference
Cortex	Cortex; a journal devoted to the study of the nervous system and behavior
Criminologist	Criminologist
Curr Med Drugs	Current Medicine and Drugs
Curr Probl Pediatr	Current Problems in Pediatrics

D

Dan Med Bull	Danish Medical Bulletin
Del State Med J	Delaware State Medical Journal
Dev Med Child Neurol	Developmental Medicine and Child Neurology

Abbreviation	Title
Dev Psychol	Developmental Psychology
Dis Nerv Syst	Diseases of the Nervous System
Diss Abstr	Dissertation Abstracts
Diss Abstr Int	Dissertation Abstracts International
Doc Ophthalmol	Documenta Ophthalmologia
Drug Ther Bull	Drug and Therapeutics Bulletin

E

Edinburgh Med J	Edinburgh Medical Journal
Educ Adm Super	Educational Administration and Supervision
Educ Dig	Education Digest
Educ Horizons	Educational Horizons
Educ Libr Bull	Education Libraries Bulletin
Educ Method	Educational Method
Educ Outlook	Educational Outlook
Educ Psychol Meas	Educational and Psychological Measurement
Educ Rec	Educational Record
Educ Res	Educational Research
Educ Res Bull	Educational Research Bulletin
Education	Education [Boston]
Electroencephalogr Clin Neurophysiol	Electroencephalography and Clinical Neurophysiology
Elem Engl	Elementary English
Elem Engl Rev	Elementary English Review
Elem Sch J	Elementary School Journal
Engl J	English Journal
Eugenics	Eugenics
Except Child	Exceptional Children
Exp Neurol	Experimental Neurology
Experientia	Experientia; monthly journal of pure and applied science
Eye Ear Nose Throat Mon	Eye, Ear, Nose, and Throat Monthly

F

Fla Sci	Florida Scientist
Folia Phoniatr	Folia Phoniatrica

G

Genet Psychol Monogr	Genetic Psychology Monographs
Glasgow Med J	Glasgow Medical Journal
Good Housekeeping	Good Housekeeping
GP	GP
Grad Res Educ Rel Discip	Graduate Research in Education and Related Disciplines
Grade Teach	Grade Teacher
Guys Hosp Rep	Guy's Hospital Reports

Abbreviation	Title
H	H
Hahnemannian Mon	Hahnemannian Monthly
Handb Priv Sch	Handbook of Private Schools
Harv Educ Rev	Harvard Educational Review
Harv Monogr Educ	Harvard Monographs in Education
High Points	High Points in the Work of the High Schools of New York City
High Sch J	High School Journal
Horn Book Mag	Horn Book Magazine
Hum Dev	Human Development
Hygeia	Hygeia
Hygiea [Stockholm]	Hygiea [Stockholm]
I	I
IEEE Trans Biomed Eng	IEEE Transactions on Bio-medical Engineering
Ill Educ	Illinois Education
Ill Med J	Illinois Medical Journal
Ill Sch Res	Illinois School Research
Ill Teach	Illinois Teacher
Indep Sch Bull	Independent School Bulletin
Individ Psychol Bull	Individual Psychology Bulletin
Instructor	Instructor
Int J Ment Health	International Journal of Mental Health
Int J Offender Ther Comp Criminol	International Journal of Offender Therapy and Comparative Criminology
Int J Psychoanal	International Journal of Psycho-analysis
Int J Soc Psychiatry	International Journal of Social Psychiatry
Int J Symb	International Journal of Symbology
Int Ophthalmol Clin	International Ophthalmological Clinics
Int Read Assoc Proc	International Reading Association Proceedings
Int Read Symp Pap	International Reading Symposium Papers
Int Rev Appl Psychol	International Review of Applied Psychology
Int Rev Educ	International Review of Education
Invest Ophthalmol	Investigative Ophthalmology
J	J
J Abnorm Child Psychol	Journal of Abnormal Child Psychology
J Abnorm Psychol	Journal of Abnormal Psychology
J Abnorm Soc Psychol	Journal of Abnormal and Social Psychology
J Am Acad Child Psychiatry	Journal of the American Academy of Child Psychiatry

Abbreviation	Title
J Am Inst Homeopath	Journal of the American Institute of Homeopathy
J Am Med Wom Assoc	Journal of the American Medical Women's Association
J Am Optom Assoc	Journal of the American Optometric Association
J Appl Psychol	Journal of Applied Psychology
J Arkansas Med Soc	Journal of the Arkansas Medical Society
J Assoc Study Percept	Journal of the Association for the Study of Perception
J Autism Child Schizophr	Journal of Autism and Childhood Schizophrenia
J Behav Ther Exp Psychiatry	Journal of Behavior Therapy and Experimental Psychiatry
J Child Psychiatry	Journal of Child Psychiatry
J Child Psychol Psychiatry	Journal of Child Psychology and Psychiatry and Allied Disciplines
J Clin Exp Psychopathol Psychother	Journal of Clinical and Experimental Psychopathology and Psychotherapy
J Clin Psychol	Journal of Clinical Psychology
J Colo Wyo Acad Sci	Journal of the Colorado-Wyoming Academy of Science
J Commun Disord	Journal of Communication Disorders
J Consult Clin Psychol	Journal of Consulting and Clinical Psychology
J Consult Psychol	Journal of Consulting Psychology
J Couns Psychol	Journal of Counseling Psychology
J Dev Read	Journal of Developmental Reading
J Educ	Journal of Education [Boston]
J Educ Psychol	Journal of Educational Psychology
J Educ Res	Journal of Educational Research
J Except Child	Journal of Exceptional Children
J Exp Child Psychol	Journal of Experimental Child Psychology
J Exp Educ	Journal of Experimental Education
J Fla Med Assoc	Journal of the Florida Medical Association
J Gen Psychol	Journal of General Psychology
J Genet Psychol	Journal of Genetic Psychology
J Individ Psychol	Journal of Individual Psychology
J Iowa Med Soc	Journal of the Iowa Medical Society
J Kans Med Soc	Journal of the Kansas Medical Society
J Lancet	Journal-Lancet [Minneapolis]
J Learn Disabil	Journal of Learning Disabilities
J Maine Med Assoc	Journal of the Maine Medical Association
J Med Assoc State Ala	Journal of the Medical Association of the State of Alabama
J Med Genet	Journal of Medical Genetics
J Med Soc NJ	Journal of the Medical Society of New Jersey

Abbreviation	Title
J Mich State Med Soc	Journal of the Michigan State Medical Society
J Nerv Ment Dis	Journal of Nervous and Mental Disease
J Neurol Neurosurg Psychiatry	Journal of Neurology, Neurosurgery and Psychiatry
J Neurol Psychopathol	Journal of Neurology and Psychopathology
J Neurol Sci	Journal of the Neurological Sciences
J NY State Sch Nurse Teach Assoc	Journal of the New York State School Nurse Teachers Association
J Ophthalmol Oto-Laryngol	Journal of Ophthalmology and Oto-Laryngology
J Ophthalmol Otol Laryngol	Journal of Ophthalmology, Otology and Laryngology
J Pediatr	Journal of Pediatrics
J Pediatr Ophthalmol	Journal of Pediatric Ophthalmology
J Pers Assess	Journal of Personality Assessment
J Phenomenol Psychol	Journal of Phenomenological Psychology
J Proj Tech Pers Assess	Journal of Projective Techniques and Personality Assessment
J Psychol	Journal of Psychology
J Psycholinguist Res	Journal of Psycholinguistic Research
J R State Soc	Journal of the Royal Statistical Society
J Read	Journal of Reading
J Read Behav	Journal of Reading Behavior
J Read Spec	Journal of the Reading Specialist
J Rehabil	Journal of Rehabilitation
J SC Med Assoc	Journal of the South Carolina Medical Association
J Sch Health	Journal of School Health
J Sch Psychol	Journal of School Psychology
J Spec Educ	Journal of Special Education
J Speech Disord	Journal of Speech Disorders
J Speech Hear Disord	Journal of Speech and Hearing Disorders
J Speech Hear Res	Journal of Speech and Hearing Research
J State Med	Journal of State Medicine [London]
J Tenn Med Assoc	Journal of the Tennessee Medical Association
JAMA	Journal of the American Medical Association
Johns Hopkins Med J	Johns Hopkins Medical Journal

K

K

| Kans Univ Stud Educ | Kansas University Studies in Education |

Abbreviation	Title
L	**L**
Ladies Home J	Ladies Home Journal
Lancet	Lancet
Lang Speech	Language and Speech
Langage Homme	Le Langage et l'Homme
Laryngoscope	Laryngoscope
Libr J	Library Journal
Life	Life
Lit Dig	Literary Digest
Little Club Clin Dev Med	Little Club Clinics in Developmental Medicine
Liverpool Med Chir J	Liverpool Medico-Chirurgical Journal
Logos	Logos [New York]
London Clin Med J	London Clinic Medical Journal
M	**M**
McCalls	McCalls
Med Ann DC	Medical Annals of the District of Columbia
Med Chir Trans R Med Chir Soc London	Medico-Chirurgical Transactions of the Royal Medical and Chirurgical Society of London
Med Clin North Am	Medical Clinics of North America
Med J Aust	Medical Journal of Australia
Med News	Medical News [Philadelphia]
Med Press Circ	Medical Press and Circular
Med Rec	Medical Record [New York]
Med Rec Ann	Medical Record and Annals [Houston]
Medicine	Medicine
Ment Health	Mental Health
Ment Hyg	Mental Hygiene
Merrill-Palmer Q	Merrill-Palmer Quarterly
Mich Med	Michigan Medicine
Microfilm Abstr	Microfilm Abstracts
Midland Sch	Midland Schools
Milit Med	Military Medicine
Minn Read Q	Minnesota Reading Quarterly
Mod Teach	Modern Teaching
Monday Morning	Monday Morning; Canada's magazine for professional teachers
Mont Educ	Montana Education
Mosaic	Mosaic [Washington, D.C.]
N	**N**
N Engl J Med	New England Journal of Medicine
N Engl Read Assoc J	New England Reading Association Journal
Nations Sch	Nation's Schools
Natl Assoc Women Deans Couns J	National Association of Women Deans and Counselors Journal

Abbreviation	Title
Natl Bus Woman	National Business Woman
Natl Educ Assoc J	National Education Association Journal
Natl Elem Princ	National Elementary Principal
Natl Parent Teach	National Parent Teacher
Natl Probat Parole Assoc J	National Probation and Parole Association Journal
Natl Read Conf Coll Adults Yearb	National Reading Conference for Colleges and Adults Yearbook
Natl Soc Study Educ Yearb	National Society for the Study of Education Yearbook
Nature	Nature
NC Med J	North Carolina Medical Journal
NEA J	NEA (National Education Association) Journal
Nebr State Med J	Nebraska State Medical Journal
Nerv Child	Nervous Child
Neurol India	Neurology India
Neurology	Neurology
Neuropaediatrie	Neuropaediatrie; journal of pediatric neurobiology, neurology and neurosurgery
Neuropsychologia	Neuropsychologia; an international journal
New Era	New Era in Home and School; a monthly magazine for parents and teachers [London]
New Outlook Blind	New Outlook for the Blind
New Soc	New Society
New Statesman	New Statesman
New Yorker	New Yorker
Newsweek	Newsweek
Nord Psykol	Nordisk Psykologi
Northwest Med	Northwest Medicine
Nurs Care	Nursing Care
Nurs Times	Nursing Times
NY Med J	New York Medical Journal
NY Soc Exper Study Educ Yearb	New York Society for the Experimental Study of Education Yearbook
NY State J Med	New York State Journal of Medicine
NY Times	New York Times
NY Times Mag	New York Times Magazine
NYC Educ Res Bull	New York City Board of Education, Bureau of Reference, Research, and Statistics. Educational Research Bulletin
NZ Med J	New Zealand Medical Journal

O

O

Occident Med Times	Occidental Medical Times
Ohio Sch	Ohio Schools
Ohio State Med J	Ohio State Medical Journal
Ont J Educ Res	Ontario Journal of Educational Research

Abbreviation	Title
Ophthalmic Rev	Ophthalmic Review
Ophthalmologica	Ophthalmologica
Ophthalmoscope	Ophthalmoscope
Optom Wkly	Optometric Weekly
Orton Soc Monogr	Orton Society Monographs

P

Parents Mag	Parents Magazine
Pathways Child Guid	Pathways in Child Guidance
Peabody J Educ	Peabody Journal of Education
Pedagog Semin	Pedagogical Seminary
Pedagog Semin J Genet Psychol	Pedagogical Seminary and Journal of Genetic Psychology
Pediatr Clin North Am	Pediatric Clinics of North America
Pediatr Res	Pediatric Research
Pediatrics	Pediatrics
Percept Mot Skills	Perceptual and Motor Skills
Pers Guid J	Personnel and Guidance Journal
Personality	Personality; symposia on topical issues
Perspect Read	Perspectives in Reading
Physician Surg	Physician and Surgeon [London]
Postgrad Med	Postgraduate Medicine
Practitioner	Practitioner
Proc Am Assoc Ment Defic	Proceedings of the American Association on Mental Deficiency
Proc Am Assoc Study Feebleminded	Proceedings of the American Association for the Study of the Feebleminded
Proc Am Psychol Assoc	Proceedings of the American Psychological Association
Proc R Soc Med	Proceedings of the Royal Society of Medicine
Prog Educ	Progressive Education
Provo Pap	Provo Papers
Psychiatr Ann	Psychiatric Annals
Psychiatr Neurol	Psychiatria et Neurologia [Basel]
Psychiatr Q	Psychiatric Quarterly
Psychoanal Study Child	Psychoanalytic Study of the Child
Psychoanalysis	Psychoanalysis
Psychol Bull	Psychological Bulletin
Psychol Clin	The Psychological Clinic
Psychol Med	Psychological Medicine
Psychol Monogr	Psychological Monographs
Psychol Rep	Psychological Reports
Psychol Sch	Psychology in the Schools
Psychol Today	Psychology Today
Psychon Sci	Psychonomic Science
Psychophysiology	Psychophysiology
PTA Mag	PTA Magazine
Public Health	Public Health
Public Health Nurs	Public Health Nursing

Abbreviation	Title
Q	Q
Q J Child Behav	Quarterly Journal of Child Behavior
Q J Fla Acad Sci	Quarterly Journal of the Florida Academy of Sciences
Q J Speech	Quarterly Journal of Speech
R	R
Read Conf Lehigh Univ	Reading Conference Lehigh University
Read Dig	Reader's Digest
Read Horizons	Reading Horizons
Read Improve	Reading Improvement
Read Newsrep	Reading Newsreport
Read Res Q	Reading Research Quarterly
Read Teach	Reading Teacher
Read World	Reading World
Rehabil Lit	Rehabilitation Literature
Rep Annu Meet Br Assoc Adv Sci	Report of the Annual Meeting of the British Association for the Advancement of Science
Rep Soc Study Dis Child	Reports of the Society for the Study of Disease in Children
Res Educ	Research in Education [U.K.]
Res Publ Assoc Res Nerv Ment Dis	Research Publications: Association for Research in Nervous and Mental Disease
Res Q Am Assoc Health Phys Educ Recreat	Research Quarterly: American Association for Health, Physical Education and Recreation
Rev Educ Res	Review of Educational Research
Rev Neurol Psychiatry	Review of Neurology and Psychiatry
Rev Roum Med	Review Roumaine de Medecine
Rev Roum Neurol	Review Roumaine de Neurologie
RI Med J	Rhode Island Medical Journal
Rocky Mt Med J	Rocky Mountain Medical Journal
Rorschach Res Exch	Rorschach Research Exchange
Rotarian	Rotarian
S	S
S Afr Med J	South African Medical Journal
Sat Evening Post	Saturday Evening Post
Sat Rev	Saturday Review
Scand J Educ Res	Scandinavian Journal of Educational Research
Scand J Psychol	Scandinavian Journal of Psychology
Sch Community	School and Community
Sch Exec	School Executive
Sch Libr	School Libraries
Sch Rev	School Review
Sch Soc	School and Society

Abbreviation	Title
Sch Week Univ Pa Proc	Schoolmen's Week, University of Pennsylvania, Proceedings
Sci Am	Scientific American
Sci Dig	Science Digest
Sci Mon	Scientific Monthly
Sci News Lett	Science News Letter
Science	Science
Scott Med Surg J	Scottish Medical and Surgical Journal
Semin Psychiatry	Seminars in Psychiatry
Sight Sav Rev	Sight-Saving Review
Slow Learn Child	Slow Learning Child; the Australian journal on the education of backward children
Smith Coll Stud Soc Work	Smith College Studies in Social Work
Soc Probl	Social Problems
Soc Res Child Dev Monogr	Society for Research in Child Development Monographs
Soc Sci Med	Social Science and Medicine
South Atl Q	South Atlantic Quarterly
South Med J	Southern Medical Journal
South Med Surg	Southern Medicine and Surgery
Southwest Med	Southwestern Medicine
Spec Educ	Special Education [London]
Spec Educ Can	Special Education in Canada
Spec Educ Forward Trends	Special Education: Forward Trends
Speech Pathol Ther	Speech Pathology and Therapy
Status Rep Speech Res	Status Report on Speech Research
Suppl Educ Monogr	Supplementary Educational Monographs
Surv Ophthalmol	Survey of Ophthalmology

T

Abbreviation	Title
Teach Coll Columbia Univ Contrib Educ	Teachers College Columbia University Contributions to Education
Teach Coll J	Teachers College Journal
Teach Coll Rec	Teachers College Record
Teach Except Child	Teaching Exceptional Children
Tenn Teach	Tennessee Teacher
Tex J Med	Texas Journal of Medicine
Tex Outlook	Texas Outlook
Tex State J Med	Texas State Journal of Medicine
Time	Time; the weekly newsmagazine
Times Educ Suppl	Times Educational Supplement [London]
Todays Educ	Today's Education
Todays Health	Today's Health
Train Sch Bull	Training School Bulletin
Trans Am Acad Ophthalmol Otolaryngol	Transactions of the American Academy of Ophthalmology and Otolaryngology
Trans Am Neurol Assoc	Transactions of the American Neurological Society

Abbreviation	Title
Trans Am Ophthalmol Soc	Transactions of the American Ophthalmological Society
Trans Coll Physicians Philadelphia	Transactions of the College of Physicians of Philadelphia
Trans Med Chir Soc Edinburgh	Transactions of the Medico-Chirurgical Society of Edinburgh
Trans Ophthalmol Soc NZ	Transactions of the Ophthalmological Society of New Zealand
Trans Ophthalmol Soc UK	Transactions of the Ophthalmological Society of the United Kingdom
Trans Pa Acad Ophthalmol Otolaryngol	Transactions of the Pennsylvania Academy of Ophthalmology and Otolaryngology
Trans Pac Coast Oto-Ophthalmol Soc	Transactions of the Pacific Coast Oto-Ophthalmological Society
Trans R Med Chir Soc Glasgow	Transactions of the Royal Medico-Chirurgical Society of Glasgow
Trans R Med Chir Soc London	Transactions of the Royal Medical and Chirurgical Society, London
Trends Educ	Trends in Education
TV Guide	TV Guide

U

Underst Child	Understanding the Child
Univ Med Mag Pa	University Medical Magazine, Philadelphia
Univ Mich Med Bull	University of Michigan Medical Bulletin
Univ Mich Sch Educ Bull	University of Michigan School of Education Bulletin
US News World Rep	U.S. News and World Report

V

Va J Educ	Virginia Journal of Education
Va Med Mon	Virginia Medical Monthly
Vis Dig	Visual Digest

W

Wash Med Ann	Washington Medical Annals
Wilson Libr Bull	Wilson Library Bulletin
Woods Sch Child Res Clin Proc	Woods Schools (Langhorne, Pennsylvania) Child Research Clinic Proceedings
Word Blind Bull	Word Blind Bulletin [Invalid Children's Aid Association, London]
World Cong Read Proc	World Congress on Reading Proceedings
World Med J	World Medical Journal

ABOUT THE AUTHOR

MARTHA M. EVANS is a free-lance writer. She has an M.A. degree in Psychology and an M.S. degree in Library Science. Her publications include "A History of the Development of Classification K (Law) at the Library of Congress," *Law Library Journal*, February 1969.